The Practice of

BUSINESS STATISTICS

Using Statistics For Decision Making

The Practice of

BUSINESS STATISTICS

Using Statistics For Decision Making

Dr. Manish Sharma
Director General
RBMI Group of Institutions,
Bareilly and Greater Noida

Amit Gupta
Asst. Professor
Determent of CS & IT
Rakshpal Bahadur Management Institute,
Bareilly

KHANNA BOOK PUBLISHING CO. (P) LTD.
Publisher of Engineering and Computer Books
4C/4344, Ansari Road, Darya Ganj, New Delhi-110002
Phone : 011-23244447-48 **Mobile:** +91-9910909320
E-mail : contact@khannabooks.com
Website : www.khannabooks.com

Dear Readers,

To prevent the piracy, this book is secured with HIGH SECURITY HOLOGRAM on the front title cover. In case you don't find the hologram on the front cover title, please write us to at contact@khannabooks.com or whatsapp us at +91-99109 09320 and avail special gift voucher for yourself.

Specimen of Hologram on front Cover title:

Moreover, there is a SPECIAL DISCOUNT COUPON for you with EVERY HOLOGRAM.

How to avail this SPECIAL DISCOUNT:

Step 1: Scratch the hologram
Step 2: Under the scratch area, your "coupon code" is available
Step 3: Logon to www.khannabooks.com
Step 4: Use your "coupon code" in the shopping cart and get your copy at a special discount
Step 5: Enjoy your reading!

ISBN: 978-93-80016-51-1

The Practice of Business Statistics
by Manish Sharma & Amit Gupta

First Edition: 2010
Reprint Edition: 2026

To view complete list of books, Please scan the QR Code:

Published by:
Khanna Book Publishing Co. (P) Ltd.
CIN: U22110DL1998PTC095547

Visit us at: **www.khannabooks.com**
Write us at: **contact@khannabooks.com**

Printed in Bharat.

Dedicated

to

My **PARENTS** & Wife **SHILPI**

— Manish Sharma

Dedicated

to

My **PARENTS, WIFE**

& little daughter **ANYA**

Without their love and patience, I would never have had the time or strength to write.

— Amit Gupta

List of Reviewers

The authors and the publishers gratefully acknowledge all the reviewers for their praise as well as constructive analysis of the book. Here is a brief list.

Dr. R. P. Saxena	Punjab Technical University, Punjab
Dr. Manish Goel	ABS Management Institute, Bharuch
Vikas Gupta	Regional HR Head (North) GKB Lens Rx, New Delhi
Prasant Gupta	FIT, Meerut

Preface

It gives us great pleasure in presenting the first edition of the book "***The Practice of Business Statistics***" to our esteemed readers; it is a unique book valuable for beginners, intermediate and advance users.

Today's good decisions are driven by data. In all aspects of our lives, and more so in the business context, an amazing diversity of data is available for inspection and analytical insight. Business managers and professionals are increasingly required to justify decisions on the basis of data. They need statistical model-based decision support systems.

Statistical skills enable them to intelligently collect, analyze and interpret data relevant to their decision-making. Statistical concepts and statistical thinking enable them to:

- Solve problems in a diversity of contexts.
- Add substance to decisions.
- Reduce guesswork.

Business Statistics is a science assisting you to make business decisions under uncertainties based on some numerical and measurable scales. Decision making processes must be based on data, neither on personal opinion nor on belief.

This book has been written as a practical response to the needs of students who want to obtain a reasonable grasp of basic statistical techniques or methods in a limited time. The emphasis throughout the book is on understanding through practice. This will encourage students who lack confidence in their mathematical ability to understand statistical techniques.

An Invaluable and Ideal text for

Undergraduate and postgraduate students of Management at various levels as well as reference for professional students. Other than providing useful guidance to the students in various professional and competitive examinations, this book should serve as core textbook for the students of:

- MBA, PGDBM, M.Com., MA(Eco)
- CA, ICWA,AMIE
- MCA, BE, B-Tech. (CS & IT)
- BBA, BCA, B. Com

Distinguishing Features

Some of the most distinguishing features are:

- Each chapter provides a step-wise development of the subject matter under reference.
- **More than 800** solved examples. (With CD), on occasions, deliberately very simple examples are given to highlight the theoretical aspects of statistics so that the concepts do not get submerged in complicated numerical examples.
- Each chapters ends with "***List of Formulae***" which are useful for a quick review of the subject.
- Special emphasis has been given on the topics like ***Probability & Probability Distributions*** to make them as simple as possible to be within the understanding of the students.
- A detailed discussion of simple regression & correlation analysis. In simple regression (Chapter 11), we give concise explanations of the simple linear regression model, least squares, and confidence and prediction intervals.
- A simple and easy to understand example introducing sampling distributions.
- A step-by-step Hypothesis-Testing approach that is used in almost all hypothesis-testing examples in Chapter 16 (Hypothesis Testing). This approach consists of a five-step procedure that is designed to break hypothesis testing down into small, easy to understand steps and also to clearly show how to use the book's hypothesis-testing summary boxes.
- Confidence intervals for and hypothesis tests about a population mean presented by using the σ known versus s unknown approach. This approach simplifies the choice of *Z*- or *t*-based procedures.
- Apart from simple language and lucid presentation, the emphasis is also on making the subject interesting by including interesting examples from day to day life and work environment.

With these features in view, we are sure that the book will be found useful by the students and teachers as well for whom it is primarily written.

Inspite of all efforts, some errors might be there, we shall be grateful to our readers if the same are brought to our notice. Suggestions and comments for further improvement of the book will be gratefully acknowledged.

Manish Sharma
Amit Gupta

Acknowledgement

First and foremost, we would like to thank the Almighty God who gave us inspiration to take up this task.

We would like to acknowledge our deep sense of gratitude to ***Mrs. Veena Mathur***, Founder and Chairperson of Rakshpal Bahadur Group of Institutes, Bareilly & Gr. Noida and to ***Er. Naveen Mathur***, Managing Director of RBMI Group for their benevolent support, suggestions and guidance.

We would like to acknowledge our sincere thanks to our learned professors and authors of a number of excellent books on the subject, and inquisitive students who motivated us to understand the subject better and present it in an engaging manner.

Most important, we want to thank you, the reader, for considering the thoughts, tools, and techniques we lay out in these pages. We understand the importance of your business analyses, and appreciate that you are taking time to consider our ideas for using statistics to make better decisions on the potential, quality, and performance of your enterprise and your career. We hope this book, with its practical examples, will revolutionize your understanding of statistical analysis, without burdening you with the details that keep you from getting the business information you really need to know.

Mr. Punit Khanna and ***Mr. Mukul Seth***, the publisher of this book, deserve special appreciation for the pain they have taken in bringing out this book in such an excellent form.

Finally, thanks to everyone at Khanna Publication who has played a role in getting this book onto the shelves.

Authors

Acknowledgement

How This Book is Organized

Welcome to "The Practice of Business Statistics". This book Business Statistics is an outcome of long teaching experience of the subject. It includes the fundamental concepts, illustrative examples and application to various business problems. These illustrated examples have been selected carefully on each topic and sufficient numbers of unsolved questions are provided which aim at sharpening the skill of the students.

The chapters of the book could be classified to include conventional as well as unconventional statistical topics as follows:

- **Introduction-Meaning, Definition and Scope** (Chapter-01)
- **Collection of Data, Classification and Tabulation** (Chapter-02 and 03)
- **Presentation of Data: Diagrammatic & Graphic** (Chapter-04 and 05)
- **Measures of Central Tendency, Dispersion, Skewness, Moments & Kurtosis** (Chapter- 06, 07 and 08)
- **Index Numbers** (Chapter-09)
- **Correction & Regression Analysis** (Chapter-10 and 11)
- **Time Series Analysis & Forecasting** (Chapter-12)
- **Probability & Probability Distributions** (Chapter-13 and 14)
- **Sampling Distributions and Estimation** (Chapter-15)
- **Statistical Inference encompassing Confidence Intervals, Test of Hypothesis, Chi-Square, ANOVA** (Chapter-16, 17 and 18)
- **Association of Attributes** (Chapter-19)
- **Statistical Decision Theory** (Chapter-20)
- **Statistical Quality Control** (Chapter-21)

Appendix

Appendix A of the book provides the various tables.

Request to Readers

We request the readers to send their valuable suggestions for any modification or addition by way of text, examples. These would be gratefully acknowledged in the edition. The communication to authors could be mailed to **dr.manish@rbmionline.com** and **amitgupta@rbmionline.com** with subject "Suggestions of BS".

Manish Sharma
Amit Gupta

Contents

PART — 1

PART — 2

PART — 3

CHAPTER 1

Introduction — Meaning, Definition and Scope

1.1 INTRODUCTION

Statistics has become an important subject having useful applications in various walks of life. Statistics has gained importance in day to day working because our every day life is bounded up with ideas of numbers and measurements. Even though you may not have realized it, you probably have made some statistical statements in your everyday conversation or thinking. Statements like "I sleep for about eight hours per night on average" and "You are more likely to pass the exam if you start preparing earlier" are actually statistical in nature.

Statistics is a discipline which is concerned with:

- Designing experiments and other data collection,
- Summarizing information to aid understanding,
- Drawing conclusions from data, and
- Estimating the present or predicting the future.

The two statements at the beginning illustrate some of these points.

In making predictions, Statistics uses the companion subject of Probability, which models chance mathematically and enables calculations of chance in complicated cases.

Today, statistics has become an important tool in the work of many academic disciplines such as medicine, psychology, education, sociology, engineering and physics, just to name a few. Statistics is also important in many aspects of society such as business, industry and government. Because of the increasing use of statistics in so many areas of our lives, it has become very desirable to understand and practise statistical thinking. This is important even if you do not use statistical methods directly.

Statistical information is truly everywhere. You can't look at a newspaper without seeing statistics on virtually every page. You can't talk about the weather forecast without invoking statistics. Statistics obviously arises in business and social science but even enters the arts in analyzing manuscripts. And you'd better not go to a casino without understanding statistics.

"It's really harder to find somewhere where statistics *isn't* important than to find the places where it is," says ***Professor Starbird***.

1.2 WHAT IS STATISTICS?

The word ***'Statistics'*** is derived from the Italian word ***"STATISTA"*** or Latin word ***"STATUS"*** both meaning ***"political state"***. Originally the word statistics was applied to numerical statement of facts used by the state or country for official purpose. Clearly, statistics is closely linked with the administrative affairs of a state such as facts and figures regarding defence force, population, housing, food, financial resources etc.

The purpose of statistics is to develop and apply methodology for extracting useful knowledge from both experiments and data. In addition to its fundamental role in data analysis, statistical reasoning is also extremely useful in data collection (design of experiments and surveys) and also in guiding proper scientific inference (Fisher, 1990).

Major activities in statistics involve:

- design of experiments and surveys to test hypotheses
- exploration and visualization of sample data
- summary description of sample data
- stochastic modelling of uncertainty (e.g. flipped coin)
- forecasting based on suitable models
- hypothesis testing and statistical inference
- development of new statistical theory and methods

Statistics is concerned with scientific methods for collecting, organising, summarising, presenting and analysing data as well as deriving valid conclusions and making reasonable decisions on the basis of this analysis. Statistics is concerned with the systematic collection of numerical data and its interpretation.

The word 'Statistic' is used to refer to

1. Numerical facts, such as the number of people living in particular area.
2. The study of ways of collecting, analysing and interpreting the facts.

1.3 MEANING OF STATISTICS

The word statistics has several meanings. Commonly it is described in two senses namely "Plural" and "Singular".

In the first place, it is a ***plural noun*** which describes a collection of numerical data such as employment statistics, accident statistics, population statistics, birth and death, income and expenditure, of exports and imports etc. It is in this sense that the word 'statistics' is used by a layman or a newspaper.

DO YOU KNOW?

Statistics is a mathematical science pertaining to the collection, analysis, interpretation or explanation, and presentation of data. It also provides tools for prediction and forecasting based on data.

Secondly the word statistics as a ***singular noun*** is used to describe a branch of applied mathematics, whose purpose is to provide methods of dealing with collections of data and extracting information from them in compact form by tabulating, summarizing and analysing the numerical data or a set of observations.

The various methods used are termed as statistical methods and the person using them is known as a statistician. A statistician is concerned with the analysis and interpretation of the data and drawing valid worthwhile conclusions from the same.

Lastly the word statistics is used in a specialized sense. It describes various numerical items which are produced by using statistics (in the second sense) to statistics (in the first sense). Averages, standard deviation etc. are all statistics in this specialized third sense.

The word ***"Statistics"*** in the first sense is defined by Professor ***Secrit*** as follows:

"By Statistics we mean aggregate of facts affected to a marked extent by multiplicity of causes, numerically expressed, enumerated or estimated according to reasonable standard of accuracy, collected in a systematic manner for a predetermined purpose and placed in relation to each other."

This definition gives all the characteristics of statistics which are

- Aggregate of facts
- Affected by multiplicity of causes
- Numerically expressed
- Estimated according to reasonable standards of accuracy
- Collected in a systematic manner
- Collected for a predetermined purpose
- Placed in relation to each other.

Similarly according to ***Yule***, "Statistics are quantitative data affected to a marked extent by multiplicity of causes."

The word 'Statistics' in the second sense is defined by ***Croxton and Cowden*** as follows:-

"Statistics may be defined as the science of collection, presentation, analysis and interpretation of numerical data".

"Statistics is a way to get information from data"

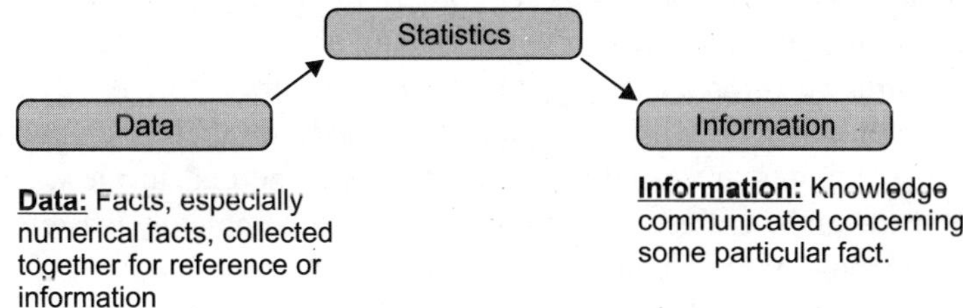

Fig. 1.1: Statistics is a *tool* for creating new understanding from a set of numbers.

This definition clearly points out four stages in a statistical investigation, namely:

- Collection of data
- Presentation of data
- Analysis of data
- Interpretation of data

NOTE: In addition to this, one more stage i.e. organization of data is suggested.

1.4 DEFINITIONS OF STATISTICS

The term statistics has been defined differently by different authors. None of these is exhaustive but few of these can be combined to explain the fundamental aspect of statistics. A number of such definitions are discussed:

Plural Sense

(i) Horace Secrist: Statistics means aggregate of facts affected to a marked extent by multiplicity of causes numerically expressed, enumerated or estimated according to reasonable standards of accuracy, collected in a systematic manner for a predetermined purpose and placed in relation to each other.

This definition makes it clear that statistics (as numerical data) should possess the following characteristics:

(a) ***They should be aggregates of facts;*** because single unconnected figures cannot be used to study the characteristics of the phenomenon.

(b) ***They should be affected to a marked extent by multiplicity of causes*** e.g. In social science the observations recorded is affected by a number of controllable and uncontrollable factors at the same time. In statistics, one study's the effect of these factors simultaneously as well as separately.

(c) ***They should be numerically expressed.*** Statistics cannot study qualitative information. Hence all the information should be capable of being expressed quantitatively directly or indirectly.

(d) ***They should be enumerated or estimated according to reasonable standards of accuracy.*** It is a fact observations can never be measured with cent percent accuracy. There is bound to be some magnitude of difference will depend upon the nature of the inquiry and the method of measurement e.g. in the measurement of height one may measure correct up to 1/10 of a cm.

(e) ***They should be collected in a systematic manner.*** If the observations are collected in a haphazard manner then one can never be sure about the degree of accuracy in the data.

(f) ***They should be collected for a predetermined purpose.*** It is obvious that if statistics data are not collected with some predetermined aim their usefulness would be almost negligible. Figures are usually collected with some end in view, as without it all the efforts made in the collection of figures would be completely wasteful and the figures so collected would not be in any way useful.

(g) ***They should be placed in relation to each other. Statistics are generally collected for the purpose of comparison.*** The figures recorded should be comparable otherwise these cannot be placed in relation to each other e.g. Height of a person has no relation with his colour.

Webster has also defined statistics in the same sense in which Secrist has defined it. Webster's definition of statistics is as follow:

(ii) Webster: Statistics are the classified facts representing the conditions of the people in a State and specially those facts which can be stated in numbers in tables of numbers or in any tabular or classified arrangement.

This definition tries to explain the classification and tabulation aspect of numerical data in statistics. This is inadequate because the word statistics is not applied only to state but is applicable to almost every phenomenon.

The definitions of Horace Secrist and Webster describe the data characteristic of statistics. In plural sense the definition of Horace Secrist is more exhaustive.

Singular Sense

(i) **Dr. A. L. Bowley:** Statistics are numerical statement of facts in any department of enquiry placed in relation to each other.

Statistics may be called the ***science of counting*** in one of the departments due to Bowley, obviously this is an incomplete definition as it takes into account only the aspect of collection and ignores other aspects such as analysis, presentation and interpretation.

Bowley gives another definition for statistics, which states 'statistics may be rightly called the scheme of averages'. This definition is also incomplete, as averages play an important role in understanding and comparing data and statistics provide more measures.

(ii) **Lovitt:** "Statistics is the science which deals with the collection, classification and tabulation of numerical facts as a basis for explanation, description and comparison of phenomena. This definition is quite comprehensive."

(iii) **Boddington:** He defined it as the science of estimates and probabilities. It gives expression to certain methods used for deriving conclusions.

(iv) **W. L. King:** The science of statistics is the method of judging collective, natural or social phenomena from the results obtained by the analysis of enumeration or collection of estimates.

Modern Definition

Statistics is the science of decision making in the face of uncertainty. This definition explains the fundamental role of statistics in our everyday life. The life has become so complex these days that one has to take some suitable decision from a number of alternative courses. Moreover the nature of the outcome of these alternatives is unpredictable. One cannot say what will happen tomorrow. In such situations one tries to get an idea about the outcome from past behaviour of the system.

This is the situation where statistics can be applied. So statistics inspire of being numerical statement of facts also helps in making decisions where there is uncertainty due to incompleteness or unsuitable nature of information.

Some Definitions "Statistics as Statistical Methods and Numerical Data"

1. "Statistics refers to the body of technique or methodology which has been developed for the collection, presentation and analysis of quantitative data and for the use of such data in decision." ***–Nester & Wasserman***
2. "Statistics is a body of methods for making wise decisions in the face of uncertainty" ***–W. A. Wallis & H. V. Robert***
3. "An aggregate of knowledge brought together for a practical end namely knowledge of a concrete state". ***–Wappaus***
4. Statistics is the science of counting. ***–A.L.Bowley***
5. Statistics may rightly be called the science of average. ***–A.L.Bowley***
6. "Statistics is a method of decision making in the face of uncertainty on the basis of numerical data and calculated risks." ***–Prof. Ya-Lun-Chou***
7. "The science and art of handling aggregate of facts-observing, enumeration, recording, classifying and otherwise systematically treating them." ***-Harlow***
8. "Statistics is the science which deals with methods of collecting, classifying, presenting, comparing and interpreting numerical data collected to throw some light on any sphere of enquiry." – ***Selligman***

Characteristic features of the Science of Statistics

From the various definition of statistics described in section 1.4 one can extract the following characteristics of statistics

- Statistics is concerned with reduction of data or obtaining correct facts from figures.
- Aggregate of facts.
- Statistics deals with variations
- The facts are numerically expressed
- Logic use in Statistical inferences is inductive
- Statistical inferences are uncertain
- The results may be fallacious

1.5 BRANCH OF STATISTICS

Theory of statistics can broadly be divided into two main branches-

- Statistical Methods
- Applied Statistics

1.5.1 Statistical Methods

Under the statistics methods are studied all, rules of procedure and general principle which are applicable to all kinds or groups of data. Thus, they include all the general principles and techniques which are commonly used in the collection, analysis and interpretation of data relating to any sphere of enquiry. Statistics methods are the tools in the hands of a statistics investigator.

These are derives for achieving the desired ends explained in theory. Since a method is always a means to an end, its accuracy and precision depends on the object which is desired to be achieved and this in turn is considerably affected by the peculiar features of the problem to which it is related. This is the reason why different statistics methods are used in different types of enquiries and no uniform standard of accuracy is desired to be achieved in different types of investigations.

The study of Statistics Methods can be observed in following areas:

1. **Collection of Data:** It is the first step and this is the foundation upon which the entire data set. Careful planning is essential before collecting the data. There are different methods of collection of data such as census, sampling, primary, secondary, etc., and the investigator should make use of correct method.

2. **Organization of Data:** Data collected from published sources are generally in organized form. However, large mass of figures that are collected from a survey frequently needs organisation. The first step in organizing a mass of data is editing. After the data have been edited the next step is to classify some common characteristics possessed by the items constituting.

3. **Presentation of Data:** The mass data collected should be presented in a suitable, concise form for further analysis. The collected data may be presented in the form of tabular or diagrammatic or graphic form.

4. **Analysis of Data:** The data presented should be carefully analysed for making inference from the presented data such as measures of central tendencies, dispersion, correlation, regression etc.

5. **Interpretation of Data:** The final step is drawing conclusion from the data collected. A valid conclusion must be drawn on the basis of analysis. A high degree of skill and experience is necessary for the interpretation.

On the basis of functional area the above ***Methods of Statistics*** can be divided-

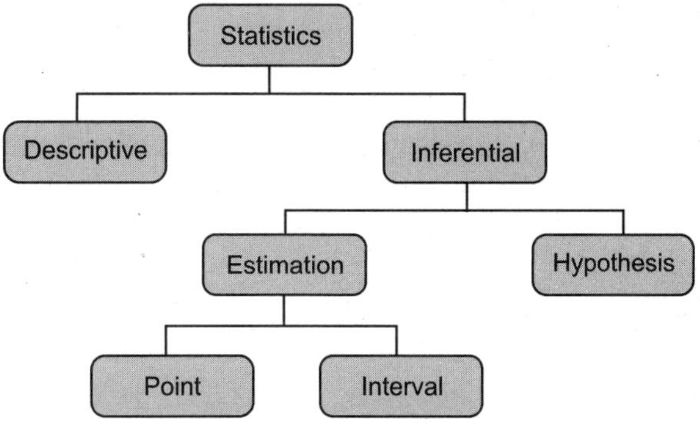

Fig. 1.2: Statistics Methods

Descriptive and Inferential Statistics

- ***Descriptive Statistics*** are used to reveal patterns through the analysis of numeric data.
- ***Inferential Statistics*** are used to draw conclusions and make predictions based on the analysis of numeric data.

(A) Descriptive Statistics

Descriptive Statistics is concerned with exploring, visualising, and summarizing data but without fitting the data to any models. This kind of analysis is used to explore the data in the initial stages of data analysis. Since no models are involved, it can not be used to test hypotheses or to make testable predictions. Nevertheless, it is a very important part of analysis that can reveal many interesting features in the data.

According to ***Ronald E. Walpole***, "Descriptive statistics comprises those methods concerned with collcting and describing a set of data so as to yield meaningful information."

On the whole, descriptive statistics is related to those methods, which are used in the treatment of numerical facts for the purpose of describing their original characteristics.

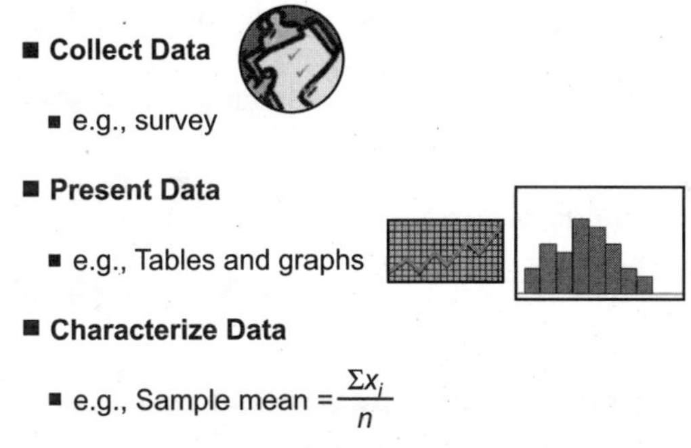

Fig. 1.3: Descriptive Statistics

Revealing Patterns Using Descriptive Statistics

Descriptive statistics, not surprisingly, "describe" data that have been collected. Commonly used descriptive statistics include frequency counts, ranges (high and low scores or values), means, modes, median scores, and standard deviations. Two concepts are essential for understanding descriptive statistics: ***variables*** and ***distributions***.

(B) Inferential Statistics

Inferential Statistics is the next stage in data analysis and involves the identification of a suitable model. The data is then fit to the model to obtain an optimal estimation of the model's parameters. The model then undergoes validation by testing either predictions or hypotheses of the model. Models based on a unique sample of data can be used to infer generalities about features of the whole population.

According to ***Ronald E. Walpole***, "Statistical inference comprises those methods which are concerned with the analysis of a sub-set of data leading to predictions or inferences about the entire set of data."

Inferential Statistics is defined as the branch of statistics that is used to make inferences about the characteristics of a populations based on sample data.

- The goal is to go beyond the data at hand and make inferences about population parameters.
- In order to use inferential statistics, it is assumed that either random selection or random assignment was carried out (i.e., some form of randomization is assumed).

Inferential Statistics are used to draw inferences about a population from a sample. Consider an experiment in which 10 subjects who performed a task after 24 hours of sleep deprivation scored 12 points lower than 10 subjects who performed after a normal night's sleep. Is the difference real or could it be due to chance? How much larger could the real difference be than the 12 points found in the sample? These are the types of questions answered by inferential statistics.

There are two main methods used in inferential statistics: ***estimation*** and ***hypothesis testing***. In estimation, the sample is used to estimate a parameter and a confidence interval about the estimate is constructed.

In the most common use of hypothesis testing, a "straw man" null hypothesis is put forward and it is determined whether the data are strong enough to reject it. For the sleep deprivation study, the null hypothesis would be that sleep deprivation has no effect on performance.

- **Estimation**
  - e.g., Estimate the population mean weight using the sample mean weight
- **Hypothesis testing**
  - e.g., Test the claim that the population mean weight is 120

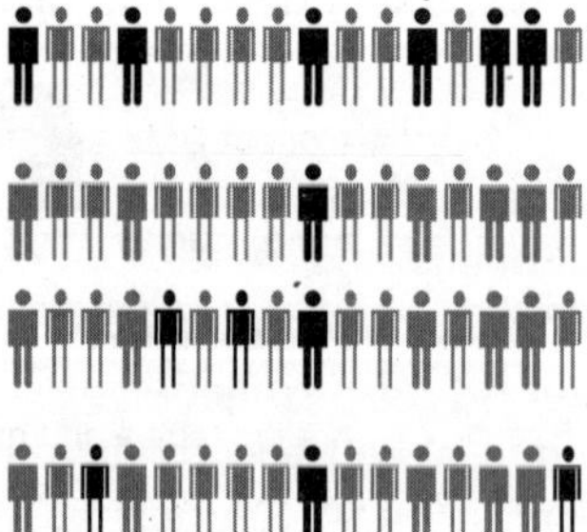

Drawing conclusions about a **population** based on **sample** results.

Fig. 1.4: Inferential Statistics

Making Predictions Using Inferential Statistics

Inferential statistics are used to draw conclusions and make predictions based on the descriptions of data.

Much of climate analysis is still at the descriptive stage, and this often misleads climate researchers into thinking that statistical results are not as testable or as useful as physical ideas. This is not the case and statistical thinking and inference could be exploited too much greater benefit to make sense of the complex climate system.

Comparison of Descriptive and Inferential Statistics

Both these aspects of statistics may be clarified with following examples:-

(i) If population statistics of a country are presented in the form of table after classifying on the basis of age, sex, rural/urban etc., and according to need, such statistics are presented with the help of percentage, ratio, measures of central tendency and correlation table, etc., they are called as descriptive statistics. On the other hand, estimation of population growth rate or age structure on the basis of some samples is inferential statistics.

(ii) The arithmetic mean of a sample of observations is a descriptive measure but if this mean is used to estimate the arithmetic mean of the population from which the sample has been drawn, inferential procedure is involved.

In brief, these two types of statistics may be compared as follows:-

(i) **Approach**- The use of descriptive statistics is very old and it has been an important aspect of traditional approach toward statistics, while inferential statistics is an important aspect of modern approach to the study of statistics.

(ii) **Methods**- The methods, which are used in descriptive statistics, are collection, arrangement, presentation and analysis of data, while in inferential statistics, probability and sampling techniques play an important role.

(iii) **Objective**- The main objective of descriptive statistics is to highlight the latent characteristics existing in the set of data, while inferential statistics deals with estimation, forecasting and generalisations on the results of data collected or samples drawn.

(iv) **Element of uncertainty**- There is no element of uncertainty in descriptive statistics. However, this element exists in statistical along with the element of risk on account of estimation of population parameters on the basis of sampling statistic.

EXAMPLE 1.1: Classify the following statements as belong to the area of descriptive statistics or inferential statistics.

1. As a result of recent poll, most of the Indian plants not in favour of building up additional nuclear power plants.
2. A doctor studies the relationship between cigarette smoking and heart disease.
3. An investigator records population growth within a particular area.
4. As a result of recent cutbacks by the oil-producing nations, we can expect that the price of petrol will increase by 80% during the next year.
5. A cricket club statistician wishes to determine the batting averages of the players of Indian cricket team in World Cup Tournament.

Solution: 1. Inferential 2. Descriptive 3. Descriptive 4. Inferential 5. Descriptive

1.5.2 Applied Statistics

Applied Statistics deals with the application of statistical methods to specific problems or concrete forms. If we have to estimate the national income of a country or its industrial or agricultural production then the special technique followed to achieve these ends the results obtained thereof would form part of applied statistics.

According to ***George Simpson*** and ***Fritz kafka***, "The applied statistician puts statistical methods into practice in a particular subject-matter.

As it is clear from the above explanation applied statistics can be further divided into two main groups. They may be either **descriptive** or **scientific**.

(i) Descriptive Applied Statistics deals with data which are known and which naturally relate either to the present or to the past. ***For example***, business statistics are descriptive applied statistics, as they deal with the analysis, measurement and presentation of business facts relating to past or present. On the basis of these facts decisions about various business problems are usually taken.

(ii) Scientific Applied Statistics deals with formulation of physical and psychological laws on the basis of quantitative data collected for descriptive purpose by the use of appropriate statistics methods. If, ***for example***, by the use of some business statistics we are in a position to derive certain conclusions, which we use for forecasting the future trend or tendency of that particular phenomenon, we are making use of scientific applied statistics. For purpose of business forecasting we have to make use of such statistics.

1.6 WHAT IS BUSINESS STATISTICS?

There is another part of applied statistics which is known as ***"Business Statistics"***. The main objective of business statistics is to make inferences (e.g., prediction, making decisions) about certain characteristics of a population based on information contained in a random sample from the entire population. The condition for randomness is essential to make sure the sample is representative of the population.

Statistics is a tool that enables us to impose order on the disorganized cacophony (Conflict) of the real world of modern society. The business world has grown both in size and competition. Corporate executive must take risk in business, hence the need for business statistics. Business Statistics has grown with the art of constructing charts and tables. It is a science of basing decisions on numerical data in the face of uncertainty. Business Statistics is the science of 'good' decision making in the face of uncertainty and is used in many disciplines, such as financial analysis, econometrics, auditing, production and operations, and marketing research. It provides knowledge and skills to interpret and use statistical techniques in a variety of business applications. Business Statistics is a scientific approach to decision making under risk. In practicing business statistics, we search for an insight, not the solution. Our search is for the one solution that meets all the business's needs with the lowest level of risk. Business Statistics can take a normal business situation, and with the proper data gathering, analysis, and re-search for a solution, turns it into an opportunity. While business statistics cannot replace the knowledge and experience of the decision maker, it is a valuable tool that the manager can employ to assist in the decision making process in order to reduce the inherent risk, measured by, e.g., the standard deviations.

Business Statistics is a science assisting you to make business decisions under uncertainties based on some numerical and measurable scales. Decision making processes must be based on data, neither on personal opinion nor on belief.

1.7 NATURE OF STATISTICS: SCIENCE OR ART

Statistics is both a science and an art. It is related to the study and application of the principles and methods applicable in the collection, presentation, analysis, and interpretation and forecasting of data or statistical facts influenced by several factors and related to any area of knowledge or research so that concrete and intelligent decisions may be taken in the phase of uncertainty.

DO YOU KNOW?

Statistics is neither really a science nor a branch of mathematics. It is perhaps best considered as a meta-science (or meta-language) for dealing with data collection, analysis, and interpretation.

It is both science and an art. It is a science in that its methods are basically systematic and have general application and an art in that their successful application depends to considerable degree on the skill and special experience of the statistician and on his knowledge of the field of application, e.g. economics. [***Tipett***]

1.8 IMPORTANCE AND SCOPE OF STATISTICS

Statistics is widely used in modern times. Initially it was employed by the state to collect information on public affairs. But gradually, its use was extended to all scientific experiments where observations were to be recorded and compared so that valid inferences could be drawn on important matters.

In short, statistics finds use wherever a mass of quantitative data needing simplification and analysis is involved, or where estimates have to be made in regard to certain unknown and uncertain events on the basis of past experience or on available information.

The human brain cannot compare and interpret a large number of numerical figures at the same time. Thus it becomes impossible to understand and analyse two or more groups of observations without proper simplification e.g. the day to day records of prices of different commodities in market cannot be compared directly. Statistical methods reduce these unwidely and haphazardly placed observations to numerical totals or averages which may be used like other numbers. Graphs and diagrams can be used to describe the general behaviour of a phenomena to laymen. In point wise statement we can say that statistics is gaining importance to the following facts:

- ***It simplifies the complexities:*** Classification, tabulation and various statistics measures make the complex data readily understandable.
- It helps in measuring and comparing the results about various aspects of a phenomenon.
- Studies relationship in various phenomenons.
- ***Enlarges human experience:*** it makes easier for man to understand, describe and measure the effects of his own actions or the actions of others.

Scope of Statistics

The scope of statistics is so vast and ever-increasing that not only it is difficult to define but also unwise to do so. The use of statistics has permeated almost every face of our lives.

Statistics is not a mere device for collecting numerical data, but as a means of developing sound techniques for their handling, analysing and drawing valid inferences from them. Statistics is applied in every sphere of human activity – social as well as physical – like Biology, Commerce, Education,

Planning, Business Management, Information Technology, etc. It is almost impossible to find a single department of human activity where statistics cannot be applied. Let us examine a few fields in which statistics is applied:

(A) Statistics in Economics

Statistics is of great asset in proper study of economic problems. Various economic phenomenons can be described, compared and correlated with the help of statistics e.g. Statistics of consumption informs about the relative desire of people; wealth of a nation can be studied by the statistics of production. The exchange statistics throws light on the commercial development of a nation. The statistics of distribution describes the economic conditions of various classes of people.

Statistical methods are useful in measuring numerical changes in complex groups and interpreting collective phenomenon. Now-a-days the uses of statistics are abundantly made in any economic study. Both in economic theory and practice, statistical methods play an important role.

Alfred Marshall said, "Statistics are the straw only which I like every other economist has to make the bricks".

It may also be noted that statistical data and techniques of statistical tools are immensely useful in solving many economic problems such as wages, prices, production, distribution of income and wealth and so on. Statistical tools like Index Numbers, Time Series Analysis, Estimation Theory, Testing Statistical Hypothesis are extensively used in economics.

(B) Statistics in Commerce

Statistics is an aid to business and commerce. These days the success in business mainly depends on the forecast. Economic barometers are the gift of statistics and are extensively used in solving and studying business problems. Producer estimates probable demand of goods, analyses effects of trade cycles etc. to decide about the quantity of production. In business, statistics can be used in

(i) Forecasting
(ii) Establishment relationship
(iii) Production planning
(iv) Laying down standards etc.

Various branches of commerce use statistics in different forms e.g. the promotion of new concerns cannot be done sound lines without the use of statistics. The concept of cost accounting is entirely statistical in outlook sampling methods are extensively used in auditing.

Statistics are lifeblood of successful commerce. Any businessman cannot afford to either by under stocking or having overstock of his goods. In the beginning he estimates the demand for his goods and then takes steps to adjust with his output or purchases. Thus statistics is indispensable in business and commerce.

(C) Statistics in Planning

Now-a-days the economic policies of an organisation are formulated for production of such goods and the provision of such services which are most urgently required. Thus proper planning is essential for the success of any activity. A good plan should be based on the correct analysis of complex statistics data. Planning cannot be imagined without statistics.

Statistics is indispensable in planning. In the modern world, which can be termed as the "world of planning", almost all the organisations in the government are seeking the help of planning for efficient working, for the formulation of policy decisions and execution of the same.

In order to achieve the above goals, the statistical data relating to production, consumption, demand, supply, prices, investments, income expenditure etc and various advanced statistical techniques for processing, analysing and interpreting such complex data are of importance. In India statistics play an important role in planning, commissioning both at the central and state government levels.

(D) To Bankers, Brokers and Insurance

A banker has to study business cycles statistically for forecasting probable boom or depression and variations in demand for money from its clients. These studies are also important from the view point of brokers, speculators etc. this success depends upon the accuracy of these forecasts. Similarly insurance companies cannot carry on their business without the study of life tables and premium rates. Insurance is an institution which cannot run without statistics.

(E) Statistics in Government

Every state has to formulate its policies to increase the welfare of its people. The problems in the field of poverty, famines unemployment, defence, economic planning, agriculture etc. requires proper analysis and interpretation of the situation with the help of necessary information. Before enforcing any policy every state has to examine its pros and cons e.g. national income figures are estimated to find the property of the inhabitants, demands estimates are required to formulate a suitable production schedule.

(F) Statistics in Research

A research is always conducted in the face of uncertainty. One does not know any thing about the nature of the outcome. Experiments about crop yield with different type of fertilizers and different type of soils are conducted in the field of agricultures select the best combinations. Similarly in medical science efficiency of new medicines and various methods of treatments are to be compared. All this require careful planning and analysis involving extensive use of statistics methods. As a matter of fact for a research worker in any field of inquiry involving numerical data a Statistical study is not useful but is necessary.

(G) Statistics and Agriculture

Analysis of Variance (ANOVA) is one of the statistical tools developed by Professor ***R.A. Fisher***, plays a prominent role in agriculture experiments. In tests of significance based on small samples, it can be shown that statistics is adequate to test the significant difference between two sample means. In analysis of variance, we are concerned with the testing of equality of several population means.

For an example, five fertilizers are applied to five plots each of wheat and the yield of wheat on each of the plots is given. In such a situation, we are interested in finding out whether the effect of these fertilizers on the yield is significantly different or not. In other words, whether the samples are drawn from the same normal population or not. The answer to this problem is provided by the technique of ANOVA and it is used to test the homogeneity of several population means.

(H) Statistics and Education

Statistics is widely used in education. Research has become a common feature in all branches of activities. Statistics is necessary for the formulation of policies to start new course, consideration of facilities available for new courses etc. There are many people engaged in research work to test the past knowledge and evolve new knowledge. These are possible only through statistics.

(I) Statistics and Medicine

In Medical sciences, statistical tools are widely used. In order to test the efficiency of a new drug or medicine, t-test is used or to compare the efficiency of two drugs or two medicines, t-test for the two samples is used. More and more applications of statistics are at present used in clinical investigation.

(J) Statistics and Modern Applications

Recent developments in the fields of computer technology and information technology have enabled statistics to integrate their models and thus make statistics a part of decision making procedures of many organisations. There are so many software packages available for solving design of experiments, forecasting simulation problems etc.

SYSTAT, a software package offers mere scientific and technical graphing options than any other desktop statistics package. SYSTAT supports all types of scientific and technical research in various diversified fields as follows

1. **Archaeology:** Evolution of skull dimensions
2. **Epidemiology:** Tuberculosis
3. **Statistics:** Theoretical distributions
4. **Manufacturing:** Quality improvement
5. **Medical research:** Clinical investigations.
6. **Geology:** Estimation of Uranium reserves from ground water

(K) Statistics and Industry

Statistics is widely used in many industries. In industries, control charts are widely used to maintain a certain quality level. In production engineering, to find whether the product is conforming to specifications or not, statistical tools, namely inspection plans, control charts, etc., are of extreme importance. In inspection plans we have to resort to some kind of sampling – a very important aspect of statistics.

1.9 FUNCTIONS OF STATISTICS

At this stage it would be worthwhile to examine and identify the functions of the science of statistics and the role which statisticians should play. The functions of the statistics are beautifully summed up by ***Robert W Burgess*** in the following words:

"The fundamental gospel of statistics is to push back the domain of ignorance, rule of thumb, arbitrary or premature decisions, tradition and dogmatism and to increase the domain in which decisions are made and principles are formulated on the basis of analytical quantitative facts."

If we analyse the above statement we would find that the main functions of the science of statistics are as given below.

- ***To collect and present facts in a systematic manner:*** One of the most important functions of statistics is to collect facts and figures in a systematic manner and to present them in such a form that they are intelligible and readily understood.
- ***To help in the formulation and testing of hypothesis:*** statistics methods are very useful in formulating and testing various types of hypothesis. In the field of social sciences the importance of hypothesis formulation and their testing is very important.
- ***To help in forecasting of certain types of events and thereby to help in the formulation of suitable strategies and policies:*** In most organisations, plans of development are prepared much in advance of the time when they have to be implemented. Even at the governmental level happen in future. Our five years plans are an example in this context.
- ***To enlarge human experience and to enable man to make rational decisions:*** The science of statistics enlarges human experience and knowledge by making it easier for man to understand, describe, and measure the effects of his action on the action of others. Many fields of knowledge would have ever remained closed to mankind but for the efficient and refined technique and sound methodology provided by the science of statistics. It has provided such master key to mankind that we can use it anywhere and can study any problem in its correct perspective and on right lines.
- ***To draw valid inferences:*** Statistics tests are devised to help in drawing valid inference in regard to the nature and characteristics of the universe on the basis of the study of the sample. It can also be the other way when the nature of the sample is judged on the basis of the parameters based on the study of the universe.
- ***To study relationships between different phenomena:*** Certain statistical measures such as coefficient of correlation, regression, etc. establish relationship between different types of data. ***For example***, it is possible to observe the relationship between income and expenditure, literacy and employment, etc, through statistical methods.

1.10 USES OF STATISTICS

1. ***To present the data in a concise and definite form:*** Statistics helps in classifying and tabulating raw data for processing and further tabulation for end users.
2. ***To make it easy to understand complex and large data:*** This is done by presenting the data in the form of tables, graphs, diagrams etc., or by condensing the data with the help of means, dispersion etc.
3. ***For comparison:*** Tables, measures of means and dispersion can help in comparing different sets of data.
4. ***In forming policies:*** It helps in forming policies like a production schedule, based on the relevant sales figures. It is used in forecasting future demands.
5. ***Enlarging individual experiences:*** Complex problems can be well understood by statistics, as the conclusions drawn by an individual are more definite and precise than mere statements on facts.
6. ***In measuring the magnitude of a phenomenon:*** Statistics has made it possible to count the population of a country, the industrial growth, and the agricultural growth.

1.11 DISTRUST OF STATISTICS

It is often said by people that, ***"Statistics can prove anything."*** There are three types of lies - lies, demand lies and statistics - wicked in the order of their naming.

A ***Paris banker*** said, "*Statistics is like a miniskirt, it covers up essentials but gives you the ideas.*"

Thus by ***"distrust of statistics"*** we mean lack of confidence in statistical statements and methods. The following reasons account for such views about statistics.

1. Figures are convincing and, therefore people easily believe them.
2. They can be manipulated in such a manner as to establish foregone conclusions.
3. The wrong representation of even correct figures can mislead a reader. ***For example***, Mr. X earned Rs. 4000 in 2003 - 2004 and Mr. Y earned Rs. 5000. Reading this one would form the opinion that Mr. Y is decidedly a better worker than Mr. X. However if we carefully examine the statement, we might reach a different conclusion as Mr. Y's earning period is unknown to us. Thus while working with statistics one should not only avoid outright falsehoods but be alert to detect possible distortion of the truth.

Statistics can be misused

In ***French Food factory*** which I know, workers were accusing the management for not providing them with proper working conditions. In support they quoted the number of accidents. When I considered the matter more seriously, I found that most of the staff was inexperienced and thus responsible for those accidents. Moreover many of the accidents were either minor or fake. I compared the working conditions of this factory to other factories and I found the conditions far better in this factory. Thus by merely noting the number of accidents and complaints of the workers, I would not dare to say that the working conditions were worse. On the other hand due to the proper statistical knowledge and careful observations I came to conclusion that the management was right.

Manish Sharma

Thus the usefulness of the statistics depends to a great extent upon its user. If used properly, by an efficient and unbiased statistician, it will prove to be an efficient tool.

Collection of facts and figures and deriving meaningful information from them is an important program.

As an example, suppose "**Mr. X**" has a shoe company. His company wants to establish their business in India, particularly in New Delhi. Let us see a few ways in which statistics will be useful to him.

1. He does not wish to manufacture equal quantities of shoes ranging from size 1 to 10. Mr. X would like to know which sizes are more in demand and which are in less demand. Knowing this they can devise the manufacturing strategy.
2. Now the company wants to advertise the 'Brand name' and thus their product in the market. To make the product popular the brand name must be attractive: Mr. X selects the name 'Strong foot'. The 'Strong foot' and its qualities have to be made to look appealing to the people in New Delhi and this requires publicity. Nothing is more appealing than what has been said in one's own mother-tongue. So Mr. X wants to print and distribute leaflets among people for this he needs to know the mother-tongues of various groups of people in New Delhi. This information is the most important factor for his business. In order to get this information, his company will have to appoint personnel who will go from door to door and find out the necessary information about the shoe market, people's choice, their mother tongue etc. This process is known as taking a survey. The objects under study are known as Individuals or Units and the collection of individuals is known as the population.

Often it is not possible or practical to record observations of all the individuals of the groups from different areas, which comprise the population. In such a case observations are recorded of only some of the individuals of the population, selected at random. This selection of some individuals which will be a subset of the individuals in the original group is called a Sample; i.e. instead of an entire population survey which would be time-consuming, the company will manage with a 'Sample survey' which can be completed in a shorter time.

Note that if a sample is representative of the whole population, any conclusion drawn from a statistical treatment of the sample would hold reasonably well for the population. This will of course, depend on the proper selection of the sample. One of the aims of statistics is to draw inferences about the population by a statistical treatment of samples.

Thus, choosing a random sample is a critical part of the statistical process and we will discuss this in more details in the chapter "Sampling."

We give below more illustrations regarding the miss-interpretation of statistical data.

1. The number of car accidents committed in a city in a particular year by women drivers is 10 while those committed by men drivers is 40. Hence women are safe drivers". The statement is obviously wrong since nothing is said about the total number of men and women drivers in the city in the given year. Some valid conclusions can be drawn if we are given the proportion of the accidents committed by male and female drivers.
2. A report: "The number of traffic accidents is lower in foggy weather than on clear weather days. Hence it is safer drive in fog."
   The statement again is obviously wrong. To arrive at any valid conclusions we must take into account the difference between the rushes of traffic under the two weather conditions and also the extra cautiousness observed when driving in bad weather.
3. "80% of the people who drink alcohol die before attaining the age of 60 years. Hence drinking is harmful for longevity of life." This statement is also fallacious since no information is given about the number of persons who do not drink alcohol and die before attaining the age of 60 years. In the absence of the information about the proportion of such persons we cannot draw any valid conclusions.

NOTE: Numerous such examples can be constructed to illustrate the misuse of statistics methods and this is all due to their injudicious applications and interpretations for which the science of statistics cannot be blamed.

1.12 LIMITATIONS OF STATISTICS

1. ***Statistics does not deal with individual measurements.*** Since statistics deals with aggregates of facts, it can not be used to study the changes that have taken place in individual cases. ***For example,*** the wages earned by a single industry worker at any time, taken by it is not a statistical datum*. But the wages of workers of that industry can be used statistically. Similarly the marks obtained by Swati of your class or the height of Anu (also of your class) are not the subject matter of statistical study. But the average marks or the average height of your class has statistical relevance.
   "Statistics is essentially totalization, because it is not connected with individual values, but only with classes."- ***Tipett***
   "Statistics from the very nature of the subject cannot and never will be able to take into account individual cases."- ***W. L. King***

* Plural of data.

2. ***Statistics cannot be used to study qualitative phenomenon*** like morality, intelligence, beauty etc. as these can not be quantified. However, it may be possible to analyse such problems statistically by expressing them numerically. ***For example*** we may study the intelligence of boys on the basis of the marks obtained by them in an examination.
3. ***Statistical results are true only on an average:*** The conclusions obtained statistically are not universal truths. They are true only under certain conditions. This is because statistics as a science is less exact as compared to the natural science.
4. ***Statistical data, being approximations, are mathematically incorrect.*** Therefore, they can be used only if mathematical accuracy is not needed.
5. ***Statistics, being dependent on figures,*** can be manipulated and therefore can be used only when the authenticity of the figures has been proved beyond doubt.
6. ***Statistical laws are not exact:*** It is well known that mathematical and physical sciences are exact. But statistical laws are not exact and statistical laws are only approximations. Statistical conclusions are not universally true. They are true only on an average.
7. ***Statistics table may be misused:*** Statistics must be used only by experts; otherwise, statistical methods are the most dangerous tools on the hands of the inexpert. The use of statistical tools by the inexperienced and untraced persons might lead to wrong conclusions. Statistics can be easily misused by quoting wrong figures of data. As ***King*** says, "Statistics are like clay of which one can make a God or Devil as one pleases".
8. ***Statistics is only, one of the methods of studying a problem:*** Statistical method does not provide complete solution of the problems because problems are to be studied taking the background of the countries culture, philosophy or religion into consideration. Thus the statistical study should be supplemented by other evidences.
9. ***Statistical laws are not exact:*** It is well known that mathematical and physical sciences are exact. But statistical laws are not exact and statistical laws are only approximations. Statistical conclusions are not universally true. They are true only on an average.

Common mistakes Committed in Interpretation of Statistics

- ***Bias:*** Bias means prejudice or preference of the investigator, which creeps in consciously and unconsciously in proving a particular point.
- ***Generalization:*** Some times on the basis of little data available one could jump to a conclusion, which leads to erroneous results.
- ***Wrong conclusion:*** The characteristics of a group if attached to an individual member of that group, may lead us to draw absurd conclusions.
- ***Incomplete classification:*** If we fail to give a complete classification, the influence of various factors may not be properly understood.
- There may be a wrong use of percentages.
- Technical mistakes may also occur.
  - — An inconsistency in definition can even exist.
  - — Wrong causal inferences may sometimes be drawn.
  - — There may also be a misuse of correlation.

1.13 STATISTICS OF SOFTWARE

The development of computer technology since the 1950s has led to the creation of many very useful statistical software packages for analysing data. Off-the-shelf statistical software now makes it possible to perform analyses on a personal computer that would have been completely impossible in the pre-computer era. For this reason, computational statistics is now a large and rapidly advancing branch of modern statistics. Many diverse statistical software packages are currently available that offer a wide variety of capabilities. They can be broadly classified into three main categories:

1. Powerful language-based packages

For example, ***Splus*** and ***SAS***, which are packages that allow the user to develop their own statistical macros and functions in addition to the comprehensive range of statistical routines available. These powerful language-based packages are used by many practising statisticians. They are not particularly user-friendly but once mastered can be extremely powerful tools.

2. Interactive packages

For example, ***MINITAB*** and ***SPSS***, which are packages that allow the user to perform many standard statistical operations at the click of a mouse. These are quick and easy to use and are useful for applying standard methods but not ideally suited for developing new functions. A big danger with such packages is that the user can easily perform operations that they do not understand. This can create a "black box" view of statistical methods that often leads to poor interpretations.

3. Packages with statistical libraries

For example, ***MATLAB*** and ***PV-Wave/IDL***, which are primarily data analysis and visualization programs/languages that also, include libraries including statistical functions. These packages can be useful in climate analysis since they can cope with the large girded data sets quite easily and can also be used to quickly visualise spatial data. A problem with these packages is that the libraries often contain only a subset of standard statistical functions, and do not benefit from input from professional statisticians. This is particularly the case with certain spreadsheet packages such as ***EXCEL*** that contain rather idiosyncratic and poorly developed statistical libraries.

SELF PRACTICE EXERCISES

I. CHOOSE THE BEST ANSWER

1. The origin of statistics can be traced to
   (a) State (b) Commerce
   (c) Economics (d) Industry.
2. 'Statistics may be called the science of counting' is the definition given by
   (a) Croxton (b) A.L.Bowley
   (c) Boddington (d) Webster.
3. The word "Statistics" is used as:
   (a) Singular (b) Plural
   (c) Singular as well as Plural (d) none of these

4. From the view of nature statistics is:
   (a) A science
   (b) an art
   (c) Science and Art both
   (d) neither science nor an art
5. Statistics is the science of analysing:
   (a) Qualitative data
   (b) Quantitative data
   (c) Any kind of data
   (d) Only very simple facts
6. What is the singular of Data?
   (a) Datum
   (b) Dat
   (c) Data
   (d) none
7. Who stated that "Statistics is a science of estimated and probabilities."
   (a) Webster
   (b) Bowley
   (c) Boddington
   (d) Seligman
8. Who stated that "Statistics is not a science, it is a scientific method."
   (a) Croxton and Cowden
   (b) Wallis and Roberts
   (c) Yule and Kendall
   (d) Johson and Jackson
9. Which of the following is not related with presentation of data:-
   (a) Editing of data
   (b) Statistical Tables
   (c) Diagram
   (d) Graphs
10. "Statistics may rightly be called the science of average" was defined by….
    (a) Bowley
    (b) Boddington
    (c) Secrist
    (d) Seligman
11. The word statistics implies:
    (a) Both data and statistical methods
    (b) Data only
    (c) Statistical Method
    (d) none of these
12. The father of statistics is:
    (a) Marshall
    (b) Gottfried Achenwall
    (c) Galton
    (d) Bowley

II. FILL IN THE BLANKS

1. In the olden days statistics was confined to only ....
2. Classification and .... are the two methods that are used to condense the data.
3. The analysis of time series and regression analysis plays an important role in ....
4. .... is one of the statistical tool plays prominent role in agricultural experiments.
5. The word statistics has been derived from the Latin word .... or the German word ....
6. The word statistics is used to convey different meanings in .... and .... sence.
7. Statistics is an .... and also a ....
8. .... defined statistics as 'numerical statement of facts'.
9. In plural sense, statistics means ....
10. Bowley A.L. defined statistics as .... country.
11. Statistics are of .... help in human welfare.
12. Prof. .... is the real giant in the development of the theory of statistics.

13. "Statistics are the .... out of which I, like every other economist, have to make ...." Alfred Marshall.
14. Two Indian statisticians who have made significant contribution in the development of statistics are .... and ....

III. SHORT ANSWER TYPE QUESTIONS

1. Write the definitions of statistics by A.L.Bowley.
2. What is the definition of statistics as given by Croxton and Cowden.
3. Explain the four stages in statistics as defined by Croxton and Cowden.
4. Write the definition of statistics given by Horace Secrist.
5. Describe the functions of statistics.
6. Explain the scope of statistics.
7. What are the limitations of statistics?
8. Explain any two functions of statistics.
9. Explain any two applications of statistics.
10. Describe any two limitations of statistics.

IV. LONG ANSWER TYPE QUESTIONS

1. Discuss in detail the importance of statistics with special reference to business and industry.
2. "Statistics affects everybody and touches life at many points. It is both a science and the art". Explain the above statement with suitable examples.
3. Comment on the following statements:
   (a) "Statistics is the science of counting."
   (b) "Statistics is the science of averages."
   (c) "Statistics is the science of estimates and probabilities."
4. What role does Business Statistics play in the management of a business enterprise? Explain its scope and limitations. **[MBA, Delhi University, 1998]**
5. How far can statistics be applied for business decision? Discuss briefly bringing out limitations, if any. **[MBA, Delhi University, 2001]**
6. Describe the main areas of business and industry where statistics are extensively used. **[MBA, Delhi University, 1997]**
7. "All statistics are numerical statements but all numerical statements are not statistics." Examine. **[CS (Foundation) Dec 2000]**
8. What do you understand by distrust of statistics? Is the science of statistics to be blamed for it?
9. Statistics methods are most dangerous tools in the hands of the inexpert." Discuss and explain the limitation of Statistics.
10. Give two definitions of statistics, one of which should be modern.
11. Write an essay on the importance and uses of statistics.
12. Give your opinion on the following:

    (a) "Figures do not lie, but liars figure".

    (b) There are three types of liars:

    (i) Liars, (ii) Damn Liars, and (iii) Statisticians

13. "Statistics should not be used as a blind man does a lamp-post for support instead of for illumination". Discuss.
14. With the help of a few examples explain the role of statistics as a managerial tool.
[MBA, Osmania University, 1996, Vikram Univ. 1999, UPTU, 2002]
15. Are statistics methods likely to be of any use to a business firm? Illustrate your answer with some typical business problems and the statistical techniques to be used there.
[MBA, Delhi University, 2002, HPU, 1996, Roorkee Univ, 2000]
16. "Sciences without statistics bear no fruit; statistics without science have no root." Explain this statement.
17. What is meant by "Descriptive Statistics" and "Inferential Statistics"? Discuss the methods of descriptive statistics?

ANSWERS

I. CHOOSE THE BEST ANSWER

1. (a)	2. (b)	3. (c)	4. (c)	5. (b)
6. (a)	7. (c)	8. (a)	9. (a)	10. (a)
11. (a)	12. (b)			

II. FILL IN THE BLANKS

1. state affairs	2. tabulation
3. forecasting	4. analysis of variance (or ANOVA)
5. status, statistik	6. singular, plural
7. art, science	8. A.L. Bowley
9. numerical sets of data	10. science of
11. great (immense)	12. R.A. Fisher
13. straws, bricks	14. P.C. Mahalanobis, C.R. Rao

CHAPTER 2

Collection of Data

2.1 INTRODUCTION

Everybody collects, interprets and uses information, much of it in numerical or statistical forms in day-to-day life. It is a common practice that people receive large quantities of information everyday through conversations, televisions, computers, radios, newspapers, posters, notices and instructions. It is just because there is so much information available that people need to be able to absorb, select and reject it. In everyday life, in business and industry, certain statistical information is necessary and it is independent to know where to find it how to collect it. As consequences, everybody has to compare prices and quality before making any decision about what goods to buy. As employees of any firm, people want to compare their salaries and working conditions, promotion opportunities and so on. In time the firms on their part want to control costs and expand their profits.

One of the main functions of statistics is to provide information which will help on making decisions. Statistics provides the type of information by providing a description of the present, a profile of the past and an estimate of the future. The following are some of the objectives of collecting statistical information.

1. To describe the methods of collecting primary statistical information.
2. To consider the status involved in carrying out a survey.
3. To analyse the process involved in observation and interpreting.
4. To define and describe sampling.
5. To analyse the basis of sampling.
6. To describe a variety of sampling methods.

Statistical investigation is a comprehensive and requires systematic collection of data about some group of people or objects, describing and organizing the data, analyzing the data with the help of different statistical method, summarizing the analysis and using these results for making judgements, decisions and predictions. The validity and accuracy of final judgement is most crucial and depends heavily on how well the data was collected in the first place. The quality of data will greatly affect the conditions and hence at most importance must be given to this process and every possible precaution should be taken to ensure accuracy while collecting the data.

2.2 NATURE OF DATA

It may be noted that different types of data can be collected for different purposes. The data can be collected in connection with time or geographical location or in connection with time and location. The following are the three types of data:

1. Time series data. 2. Spatial data 3. Spacio-temporal data.

1. Time Series Data

It is a collection of a set of numerical values, collected over a period of time. The data might have been collected either at regular intervals of time or irregular intervals of time.

Example: The following is the data for the three types of expenditures in rupees for a family for the four years 2001, 2002, 2003, 2004.

Year	Food	Education	Others	Total
2001	3000	2000	3000	8000
2002	3500	3000	4000	10500
2003	4000	3500	5000	12500
2004	5000	5000	6000	16000

2. Spatial Data

If the data collected is connected with that of a place, then it is termed as spatial data. ***For example***, the data may be

1. Number of runs scored by a batsman in different test matches in a test series at different places
2. District wise rainfall in Tamil Nadu
3. Prices of silver in four metropolitan cities

Example: The population of the southern states of India in 1991.

State	Population
Tamil Nadu	5,56,38,318
Andhra Pradesh	6,63,04,854
Karnataka	4,48,17,398
Kerala	2,90,11,237
Pondicherrry	7,89,416

3. Spacio Temporal Data

If the data collected is connected to the time as well as place then it is known as spacio temporal data.

Example:

State	Population	
	1981	1991
Tamil Nadu	4,82,97,456	5,56,38,318
Andhra Pradesh	5,34,03,619	6,63,04,854
Karnataka	3,70,43,451	4,48,17,398
Kerala	2,54,03,217	2,90,11,237
Pondicherry	6,04,136	7,89,416

2.3 TYPE OF DATA AND LEVELS OF MEASUREMENT

Information can be collected in statistics using qualitative or quantitative data. Qualitative data, such as eye colour of a group of individuals, is not computable by arithmetic relations. They are labels that advise in which category or class of an individual, object, or process fall. They are called categorical variables.

Quantitative data sets consist of measures that take numerical values for which descriptions such as means and standard deviations are meaningful. They can be put into an order and further divided into two groups:

- Discrete data are countable data and are collected by ***counting***, ***for example***, the number of defective items produced during a day's production.
- Continuous data are collected by ***measuring*** and are expressed on a continuous scale. ***For example***, measuring the height of a person.

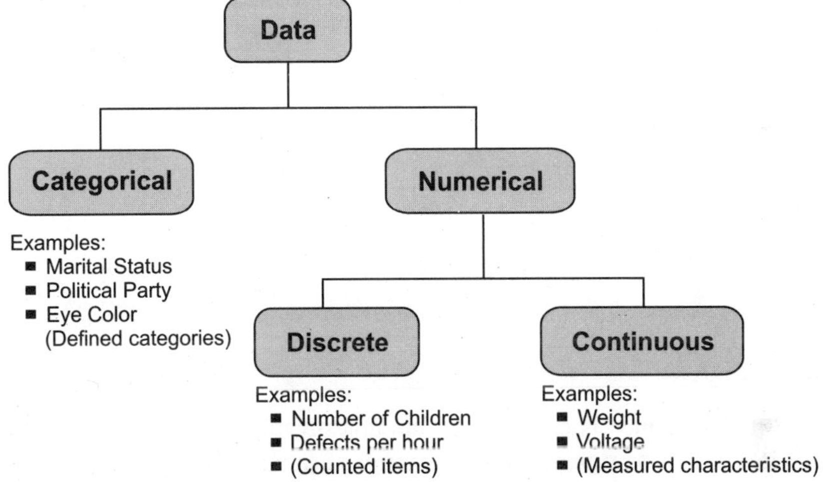

Fig. 2.1: Types of data.

Among the first activities in statistical analysis is to count or measure. Counting/measurement theory is concerned with the connection between data and reality. A set of data is a representation (i.e., a model) of the reality based on numerical and measurable scales. Data are called "*primary type*" data if the analyst has been involved in collecting the data relevant to his/her investigation. Otherwise, it is called "*secondary type*" data.

Data come in the forms of **N**ominal, **O**rdinal, **I**nterval, and **R**atio (remember the French word NOIR for the color black). Data can be either continuous or discrete.

	Levels of Measurements		
	Nominal	**Ordinal**	**Interval/Ratio**
Ranking?	No	Yes	Yes
Numerical difference	No	No	Yes

Both the zero point and the units of measurement are arbitrary on the Interval scale. While the unit of measurement is arbitrary on the Ratio scale, its zero point is a natural attribute. The categorical variable is measured on an ordinal or nominal scale.

Counting/measurement theory is concerned with the connection between data and reality. Both statistical theory and counting/measurement theory are necessary to make inferences about reality.

Since statisticians live for precision, they prefer Interval/Ratio levels of measurement.

2.4 CATEGORIES OF DATA

Any statistical data can be classified under two categories depending upon the sources utilized. These categories are

1. Primary data
2. Secondary data

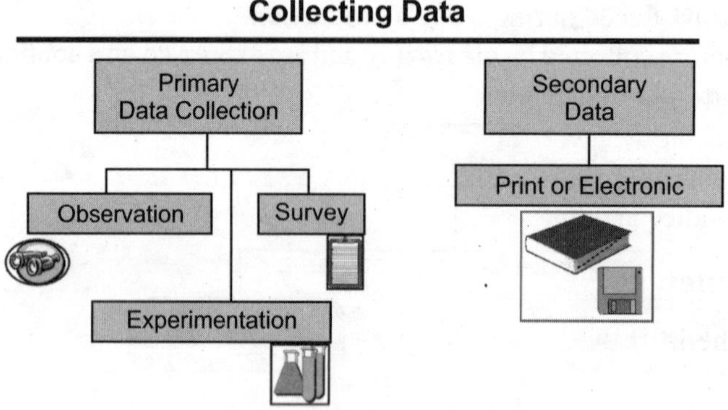

Fig. 2.2: Categories of data.

2.5 PRIMARY DATA

Primary data is the one, which is collected by the investigator himself for the purpose of a specific inquiry or study. Such data is original in character and is generated by survey conducted by individuals or research institution or any organisation.

***Example*:** If a researcher is interested to know the impact of noon-meal scheme for the school children, he has to undertake a survey and collect data on the opinion of parents and children by asking relevant questions. Such a data collected for the purpose is called primary data.

The primary data can be collected by the following five methods.

1. Direct personal interviews.
2. Indirect Oral interviews.
3. Information from correspondents.
4. Mailed questionnaire method.
5. Schedules sent through enumerators.

1. Direct Personal Interviews

The persons from whom information are collected are known as informants. The investigator personally meets them and asks questions to gather the necessary information. It is the suitable method for intensive rather than extensive field surveys. It suits best for intensive study of the limited field.

Merits —

1. People willingly supply information because they are approached personally. Hence, more response noticed in this method than in any other method.
2. The collected information is likely to be uniform and accurate. The investigator is there to clear the doubts of the informants.
3. Supplementary information on informant's personal aspects can be noted. Information on character and environment may help later to interpret some of the results.
4. Answers for questions about which the informant is likely to be sensitive can be gathered by this method.
5. The wordings in one or more questions can be altered to suit any informant. Explanations may be given in other languages also. Inconvenience and misinterpretations are thereby avoided.

Limitations —

1. It is very costly and time consuming.
2. It is very difficult, when the number of persons to be interviewed is large and the persons are spread over a wide area.
3. Personal prejudice and bias are greater under this method.

2. *Indirect Oral Interviews*

Under this method the investigator contacts witnesses or neighbours or friends or some other third parties who are capable of supplying the necessary information. This method is preferred if the required information is on addiction or cause of fire or theft or murder etc., If a fire has broken out a certain place, the persons living in neighbourhood and witnesses are likely to give information on the cause of fire. In some cases, police interrogated third parties who are supposed to have knowledge of a theft or a murder and get some clues. Enquiry committees appointed by governments generally adopt this method and get people's views and all possible details of facts relating to the enquiry. This method is suitable whenever direct sources do not exist or cannot be relied upon or would be unwilling to part with the information.

The validity of the results depends upon a few factors, such as the nature of the person whose evidence is being recorded, the ability of the interviewer to draw out information from the third parties by means of appropriate questions and cross examinations, and the number of persons interviewed. For the success of this method one person or one group alone should not be relied upon.

3. *Information from Correspondents*

The investigator appoints local agents or correspondents in different places and compiles the information sent by them. Information to Newspapers and some departments of Government come by this method. The advantage of this method is that it is cheap and appropriate for extensive investigations. But it may not ensure accurate results because the correspondents are likely to be negligent, prejudiced and biased. This method is adopted in those cases where information is to be collected periodically from a wide area for a long time.

4. *Mailed Questionnaire Method*

Under this method a list of questions is prepared and is sent to all the informants by post. The list of questions is technically called questionnaire. A covering letter accompanying the questionnaire explains the purpose of the investigation and the importance of correct information and request the informants to fill in the blank spaces provided and to return the form within a specified time. This method is appropriate in those cases where the informants are literates and are spread over a wide area.

Merits —

1. It is relatively cheap.
2. It is preferable when the informants are spread over the wide area.

Limitations —

1. The greatest limitation is that the informants should be literates who are able to understand and reply the questions.
2. It is possible that some of the persons who receive the questionnaires do not return them.
3. It is difficult to verify the correctness of the information furnished by the respondents.

With the view of minimizing non-respondents and collecting correct information, the questionnaire should be carefully drafted. There is no hard and fast rule. But the following general principles may be helpful in framing the questionnaire. A covering letter and a self addressed and stamped envelope should accompany the questionnaire. The covering letter should politely point out the purpose of the survey and privilege of the respondent who is one among the few associated with the investigation. It should assure that the information would be kept confidential and would never be misused. It may promise a copy of the findings or free gifts or concessions etc.

5. Schedules sent through Enumerators

Under this method enumerators or interviewers take the schedules, meet the informants and filling their replies. Often distinction is made between the schedule and a questionnaire. A schedule is filled by the interviewers in a face-to-face situation with the informant. A questionnaire is filled by the information which he receives and returns by post. It is suitable for extensive surveys.

Merits —

1. It can be adopted even if the informants are illiterates.
2. Answers for questions of personal and pecuniary nature can be collected.
3. Non-response is minimum as enumerators go personally and contact the informants.
4. The information collected is reliable. The enumerators can be properly trained for the same.
5. It is the most popular method.

Limitations —

1. It is the costliest method.
2. Extensive training is to be given to the enumerators for collecting correct and uniform information.
3. Interviewing requires experience. Unskilled investigators are likely to fail in their work.

Before the actual survey, a pilot survey is conducted. The questionnaire/Schedule is pre-tested in a pilot survey. A few among the people from whom actual information is needed are asked to reply. If they misunderstand a question or find it difficult to answer or do not like its wordings etc., it is to be altered. Further it is to be ensured that every question fetches the desired answer.

Merits and Demerits of Primary Data

1. The collection of data by the method of personal survey is possible only if the area covered by the investigator is small. Collection of data by sending the enumerator is bound to be expensive.

Care should be taken twice that the enumerator record correct information provided by the informants.

2. Collection of primary data by framing a schedule or distributing and collecting questionnaires by post is less expensive and can be completed in shorter time.
3. Suppose the questions are embarrassing or of complicated nature or the questions probe into personnel affairs of individuals, then the schedules may not be filled with accurate and correct information and hence this method is unsuitable.
4. The information collected for primary data is mere reliable than those collected from the secondary data.

2.6 DRAFTING A QUESTIONNAIRE

The sources of the questionnaires method depends to a large extent on proper drafting of the questionnaire. It is highly specialised job and needs lot of skill and experience.

DO YOU KNOW?

There is no hard and fast rule for preparing a questionnaire. The only objective of questionnaire is to get candid response from the respondent.

Questionnaires are an inexpensive way to gather data from a potentially large number of respondents. Often they are the only feasible way to reach a number of reviewers large enough to allow statistically analysis of the results. A well-designed questionnaire that is used effectively can gather information on both the overall performance of the test system as well as information on specific components of the system. If the questionnaire includes demographic questions on the participants, they can be used to correlate performance and satisfaction with the test system among different groups of users.

It is important to remember that a questionnaire should be viewed as a multi-stage process beginning with definition of the aspects to be examined and ending with interpretation of the results. Every step needs to be designed carefully because the final results are only as good as the weakest link in the questionnaire process. Although questionnaires may be cheap to administer compared to other data collection methods, they are every bit as expensive in terms of design, time and interpretation.

The steps required to design and administer a questionnaire include —

1. Defining the Objectives of the survey
2. Determining the Sampling Group
3. Writing the Questionnaire
4. Administering the Questionnaire
5. Interpretation of the Results

This topic will concentrate on how to formulate objectives and write the questionnaire. Before these steps are examined in detail, it is good to consider what questionnaires are good at measuring characteristics of quesionaaires and when it is appropriate to use questionnaires.

2.6.1 What can questionnaires measure?

Questionnaires are quite flexible in what they can measure, however they are not equally suited to measuring all types of data. We can classify data in two ways, ***Subjective vs. Objective*** and ***Quantitative vs. Qualitative.***

Questions may be designed to gather either qualitative or quantitative data. By their vary nature, quantitative questions are more exact then qualitative. ***For example***, the word "easy" and "difficult" can mean radically different things to different people. Any question must be carefully crafted, but in particular questions that assess a qualitative measure must be phrased to avoid ambiguity. Qualitative questions may also require more thought on the part of the participant and may cause them to become bored with the questionnaire sooner. In general, we can say that questionnaires can measure both qualitative and quantitative data well, but that qualitative questions require more care in design, administration, and interpretation.

2.6.2 Characteristics of a Good Questionnaire

1. Number of questions should be minimum.
2. Questions should be in logical orders, moving from easy to more difficult questions.
3. Questions should be short and simple. Technical terms and vague expressions capable of different interpretations should be avoided.
4. Questions fetching YES or NO answers are preferable. There may be some multiple choice questions requiring lengthy answers are to be avoided.
5. Personal questions and questions which require memory power and calculations should also be avoided.
6. Question should enable cross check. Deliberate or unconscious mistakes can be detected to an extent.
7. Questions should be carefully framed so as to cover the entire scope of the survey.
8. The wording of the questions should be proper without hurting the feelings or arousing resentment.
9. As far as possible confidential information should not be sought.
10. Physical appearance should be attractive, sufficient space should be provided for answering each question.

2.6.3 When to use a questionnaire?

There is no all encompassing rule for when to use a questionnaire. The choice will be made based on a variety of factors including the type of information to be gathered and the available resources for the experiment. A questionnaire should be considered in the following circumstances.

(a) **When resources and money are limited.** A Questionnaire can be quite inexpensive to administer. Although preparation may be costly, any data collection scheme will have similar preparation expenses. The administration cost per person of a questionnaire can be as low as postage and a few photocopies. Time is also an important resource that questionnaires can maximize. If a questionnaire is self-administering, such as an e-mail questionnaire, potentially several thousand people could respond in a few days. It would be impossible to get a similar number of usability tests completed in the same short time.

(b) **When it is necessary to protect the privacy of the participants.** Questionnaires are easy to administer confidentially. Often confidentiality is necessary to ensure participants will respond honestly if at all. Examples of such cases would include studies that need to ask embarrassing questions about private or personal behaviour.

(c) **When corroborating other findings.** In studies that have resources to pursue other data collection strategies, questionnaires can be a useful confirmation tool. More costly schemes may turn up interesting trends, but occasionally there will not be resources to run these other tests on large enough participant groups to make the results statistically significant. A follow-up large scale questionnaire may be necessary to corroborate these earlier results.

I. Defining the Objectives of the Survey

The importance of well-defined objectives can not be over emphasized. A questionnaire that is written without a clear goal and purpose is inevitably going to overlook important issues and waste participants' time by asking useless questions. The questionnaire may lack a logical flow and thereby cause the participant to lose interest. Consequential, what useful data you may have collected could be further compromised. The problems of a poorly defined questionnaire do not end here, but continue on to the analysis stage. It is difficult to imagine identifying a problem and its cause, let alone its solution, from responses to broad and generalizing questions. In other words, how would it be possible to reach insightful conclusions if one didn't actually know what they had been looking for or planning to observe. That's why it is very imporant to defining the objective of questionnaire.

II. Writing the Questionnaire

At this point, we assume that we have already decided what kind of data we are to measure, formulated the objectives of the investigation, and decided on a participant group. Now we must compose our questions.

If the preceding steps have been faithfully executed, most of the questions will be on obvious topics.

It is important to ask only those background questions that are necessary. Do not ask income of the respondent unless there is at least some rational for suspecting a variance across income levels. There is often only a fine line between background and personal information. You do not want to cross over in to the personal realm unless absolutely necessary. If you need to solicit personal information, phrase your questions as unobtrusively as possible to avoid ruffling your participants and causing them to answer less than truthfully.

What kind of questions do we ask?

In general, there are two types of questions one will ask, ***open format*** or ***closed format.***

Open format questions are those that ask for unprompted opinions. In other words, there are no predetermined set of responses, and the participant is free to answer however he chooses. Open format questions are good for soliciting subjective data or when the range of responses is not tightly defined. An obvious advantage is that the variety of responses should be wider and more truly reflect the opinions of the respondents. This increases the likelihood of you receiving unexpected and insightful suggestions, for it is impossible to predict the full range of opinion. It is common for a questionnaire to end with an open format question asking the respondent for her unabashed ideas for changes or improvements.

Open format questions have several disadvantages. First, their vary nature requires them to be read individually. There is no way to automatically tabulate or perform statistical analysis on them. This is obviously more costly in both time and money, and may not be practical for lower budget or time sensitive evaluations. They are also open to the influence of the reader, for no two people will interpret an answer in precisely the same way. This conflict can be eliminated by using a single reader, but a large number of responses can make this impossible. Finally, open format questions require more thought and time on the part of the respondent. Whenever more is asked of the respondent, the chance of tiring or boring the respondent increases.

Closed format questions usually take the form of a multiple-choice question. They are easy for the respondent.

There is no clear consensus on the number of options that should be given in an closed format question. Obviously, there needs to be sufficient choices to fully cover the range of answers but not so many that the distinction between them becomes blurred. Usually this translates into five to ten possible answers per questions. For questions that measure a single variable or opinion, such as ease of use or liability, over a complete range (easy to difficult, like to dislike), conventional wisdom says that there should be an odd number of alternatives. This allows a neutral or no opinion response. Other schools of thought contend that an even number of choices is best because it forces the respondent to get off the fence. This may induce some inaccuracies for often the respondent may actually have no opinion. However, it is equally arguable that the neutral answer is over utilized, especially by bored questionnaire takers. For larger questionnaires that test opinions on a very large number of items, such as a music test, it may be best to use an even number of choices to prevent large numbers of no-thought neutral answers.

Closed format questions offer many advantages in time and money. By restricting the answer set, it is easy to calculate percentages and other hard statistical data over the whole group or over any subgroup of participants. Modern scanners and computers make it possible to administer, tabulate, and perform preliminary analysis in a matter of days. Closed format questions also make it easier to track opinion over time by administering the same questionnaire to different but similar participant groups at regular intervals. Finally closed format questions allow the researcher to filter out useless or extreme answers that might occur in an open format question.

Researchers use three basic types of questions: multiple choice, numeric open end and text open end (sometimes called "verbatims"). Examples of each kind of question follow:

Multiple Choice

1. Where do you live

   ❑ North ❑ South ❑ East ❑ West

Numeric Open End

2. How much did you spend on groceries this week? ___________

Text Open End

3. How can our company improve its working conditions? ____________________

   ____

Rating Scales and Agreement Scales are two common types of questions that some researchers treat as multiple choice questions and others treat as numeric open end questions. Examples of these kinds of questions are:

Rating Scales

4. How would you rate this product?

   ❑ Excellent ❑ Good ❑ Fair ❑ Poor

5. On a scale where "10" means you have a great amount of interest in a subject and "1" means you have none at all, how would you rate your interest in each of the following topics?

Domestic politics .. ____
Foreign Affairs …… ____
Science & Health .. ____
Business ……… ____

Agreement Scale

6. How much do you agree with each of the following statements:

Agree Agree Disagree Disagree	Strongly Agree	Agree	Agree	Strongly Agree
My manager provides contructive criticism	❑	❑	❑	❑
Our medical plan provides adequate coverage	❑	❑	❑	❑
I would prefer to work longer hours on fewer days	❑	❑	❑	❑

Whether your questions are open or closed format, there are several points that must be considered when writing and interpreting questionnaires:

1. **Clarity** — This is probably the area that causes the greatest source of mistakes in questionnaires. Questions must be clear and unambiguous. The goal is to eliminate the chance that the question will mean different things to different people. If the designers fail to do this, then essentially participants will be answering different questions.
   To this end, it is best to phrase your questions empirically if possible and to avoid the use of necessary adjectives. ***For example***, if asking a question about frequency, rather than supplying choices that are open to interpretation such as:
   1. Very Often
   2. Often
   3. Sometimes
   4. Rarely
   5. Never

   It is better to quantify the choices, such as:

   6. Every Day or More
   7. 2-6 Times a Week
   8. About Once a Week
   9. About Once a Month
   10. Never

   There are other more subtle aspects to consider such as language and culture. Avoid the use of colloquial or ethnic expressions that might not be equally used by all participants. Technical terms that assume a certain background should also be avoided.
2. **Leading Questions** — A leading question is one that forces or implies a certain type of answer. It is easy to make this mistake not in the question, but in the choice of answers. A closed format question must supply answers that not only cover the whole range of responses, but that are also equally distributed throughout the range. All answers should be equally likely. An obvious, nearly comical, example would be a question that supplied these answer choices:
   1. Superb
   2. Excellent
   3. Great

4. Good
5. Fair
6. Not so Great

A less blatant example would be a Yes/No question that asked:

7. Is this the best CAD interface you have ever used?

In this case, even if the participant loved the interface, but had a favourite that was preferred, he/she would be forced to answer No. Clearly, the negative response covers too wide a range of opinions. A better way would be to ask the same question but supply the following choices:

8. Totally Agree
9. Partially Agree
10. Neither Agree or Disagree
11. Partially Disagree
12. Totally Disagree

This example is also poor in the way it asks the question. It's choice of words makes it a leading question and a good example for the next section on phrasing.

3. **Phrasing** — Most adjectives, verbs, and nouns in English have either a positive or negative connotation. Two words may have equivalent meaning, yet one may be a compliment and the other an insult. Consider the two words "child-like" and "childish", which have virtually identical meaning. Child-like is an affectionate term that can be applied to both men and women, and young and old, yet no one wishes to be thought of as childish.

   In the above example of "Is this the best CAD interface you have ever used?" clearly "best" has strong overtones that deny the participant an objective environment to consider the interface. The signal sent the reader is that the designers surely think it is the best interface, and so should everyone else. Though this may seem like an extreme example this kind of superlative question is common practice.

   A more subtle, but no less troublesome, example can be made with verbs that have neither strong negative or positive overtones. Consider the following two questions:

   1. Do you agree with the Governor's plan to oppose increased development of lands?
   2. Do you agree with the Governor's plan to support curtailed development of lands?

   They both ask the same thing, but will likely produce different data. One asks in a positive way, and the other in a negative. It is impossible to predict how the outcomes will vary, so one method to counter this is to be aware of different ways toward questions and provide a mix in your questionnaire. If the participant pool is very large, several versions may be prepared and distributed to cancel out these effects.

4. **Embarrassing Questions** — Embarrassing questions dealing with personal or private matters should be avoided. Your data is only as good as the trust and care that your respondents give you. If you make them feel uncomfortable, you will lose their trust. Do not ask embarrassing questions.

5. **Hypothetical Questions** — Hypothetical are based, at best, on conjecture and, at worst, on fantasy. I simple question such as:

   1. If you were governor, what would you do to stop crime?

   These forces the respondent to give thought to something he may have never considered. This does not produce clear and consistent data representing real opinion. Do not ask hypothetical questions.

6. **Prestige Bias** — Prestige bias is the tendency for respondents to answer in a way that make them feel better. People may not lie directly, but may try to put a better light on themselves. ***For example***, it is not uncommon for people to respond to a political opinion poll by saying they support exact poll programs, but then go on to vote for candidates who oppose those very programs.

Question and Answer Choice Order

There are two broad issues to keep in mind when considering question and answer choice order.

- One is how the question and answer choice order can encourage people to complete your survey.
- The other issue is how the order of questions or the order of answer choices could affect the results of your survey.

Ideally, the early questions in a survey should be easy and pleasant to answer. These kinds of questions encourage people to continue the survey. In telephone or personal interviews they help build rapport with the interviewer. Grouping together questions on the same topic also makes the questionnaire easier to answer.

Whenever possible leave difficult or sensitive questions until near the end of your survey. Any rapport that has been built up will make it more likely, people will answer these questions. If people quit at that point anyway, at least they will have answered most of your questions.

Answer choice order can make individual questions easier or more difficult to answer. Whenever there is a logical or natural order to answer choices, use it. Always present agree-disagree choices in that order. Presenting them in disagree-agree order will seem odd. For the same reason, positive to negative and excellent to poor scales should be presented in those orders. When using numeric rating scales higher numbers should mean a more positive or more agreeing answer.

Question order can affect the results in two ways. One is that mentioning something (an idea, an issue, a brand) in one question can make people think of it while they answer a later question, when they might not have thought of it, if it had not been previously mentioned. In some cases you may be able to reduce this problem by randomizing the order of related questions. Separating related questions with unrelated ones can also reduce this problem, though neither technique will eliminate it.

The order in which the answer choices are presented can also affect the answers given. People tend to pick the choices nearest the start of a list when they read the list themselves on paper or a computer screen. People tend to pick the most recent answer when they hear a list of choices read to them.

As mentioned previously, sometimes answer choices have a natural order (e.g., Yes, followed by No; or Excellent - Good - Fair - Poor). If so, you should use that order. At other times, questions have answers that are obvious to the person that is answering them (e.g., "Which brands of car do you own?"). In these cases, the order in which the answer choices are presented is not likely to affect the answers given.

Other General Tips

- ***Keep the questionnaire as short as possible.*** We mentioned this principle before, but it is so important it is worth repeating. More people will complete a shorter questionnaire, regardless of the interviewing method. If a question is not necessary, do not include it.
- ***Start with a Title*** (e.g., Leisure Activities Survey). Always include a short introduction - who you are and why you are doing the survey. If you are asking about different brands, it is often a good

idea to give the name of the research company rather than the client (e.g., XYZ Research Agency rather than the manufacturer of the product/ service being surveyed). Many firms create a separate research company name (even if it is only a direct phone line to the research department) to disguise themselves. This is to avoid possible bias, since people rarely like to criticize someone to their face and are much more open to a third party.

- In some cases, though, it may help to mention the client. If you are surveying members of an organization, the members may be more likely to respond if they think the organization is asking their opinions on how it can best meet their needs. The same could be true when you are surveying users of a particular service.
- ***The most effective cover letters and invitations include the following elements:*** Ask the recipient to take the survey. Explain why taking it will improve some aspect of the recipient's life (it will help improve a product, make an organization better meet their needs, make their opinions heard). Appeal to the recipient's sense of altruism ("please help"). Ask the recipient again to take the survey.
- You may want to leave a space for the respondent to add their name and title. Some people will put in their names, making it possible for you to re-contact them for clarification or follow-up questions. Indicate that filling in their name is optional. If the questions are sensitive in nature, do not have a space for a name. Some people would become suspicious and not complete the survey.
- If you hand out questionnaires on your premises, you obviously cannot remain anonymous, but keep the bias problem in mind when you consider the answers.
- Do not put two questions into one. Avoid questions such as "Do you buy frozen meat and frozen fish?" A "Yes" answer can mean the respondent buys meat or fish or both. Similarly with a question such as "Have you ever bought Product X and, if so, did you like it?" A "No" answer can mean "never bought" or "bought and disliked." Be as specific as possible. "Do you ever buy pasta?" can include someone who once bought some in 1990. It does not tell you whether the pasta was dried, frozen or canned and may include someone who had pasta in a restaurant. It is better to say "Have you bought pasta (other than in a restaurant) in the last three months?" "If yes, was it frozen, canned or dried?" Few people can remember what they bought more than three months ago unless it was a major purchase such as an automobile or appliance.
- The overriding consideration in questionnaire design is to make sure your questions can accurately tell you what you want to learn. The way you phrase a question can change the answers you get. Try to make sure the wording does not favour one answer choice over another.
- ***Avoid emotionally charged words or leading questions that point towards a certain answer.*** You will get different answers from asking "What do you think of the XYZ proposal?" than from "What do you think of the Republican XYZ proposal?" The word "Republican" in the second question would cause some people to favour or oppose the proposal based on their feelings about Republicans, rather than about the proposal itself. It is very easy to create bias in a questionnaire. This is another good reason to test it before going ahead.
- ***If you are comparing different products to find preferences, give each one a neutral name or reference.*** Do not call one "A" and the second one "B." This immediately brings images of A grades and B grades to mind, with the former being seen as superior to the latter. It is better to give each a "neutral" reference such "M" or "N" that do not have as strong a quality difference image.

- Avoid technical terms and acronyms, unless you are absolutely sure that respondents know they mean. LIC, PF, VAT, EIEIO (Life Insurance Corporation and Provident Fund, Value Added Tex and Engineering Information External Inquiries Officer) are all well-known acronyms to people in those particular fields, but very few people would understand all of them. If you must use an acronym, spell it out the first time it is used.

Make sure your questions accept all the possible answers. A question like "Do you use regular or premium gas in your car?" does not cover all possible answers. The owner may alternate between both types. The question also ignores the possibility of diesel or electric-powered cars. A better way of asking this question would be "Which type(s) of fuel do you use in your cars?" The responses allowed might be :

❑ Regular gasoline
❑ Premium gasoline
❑ Diesel
❑ Other
❑ Do not have a car

If you want only one answer from each person, ensure that the options are mutually exclusive. ***For example***:

In which of the following do you live?

❑ A house
❑ An apartment
❑ The suburbs

This question ignores the possibility of someone living in a house or an apartment in the suburbs.

Score or rating scale questions (e.g., "If '5' means very good and '1' means very poor how would rate this product?") are a particular problem. Researchers are much divided on this issue. Many surveys use a ten-point scale, but there is considerable evidence to suggest that anything over a five point scale is irrelevant. This depends partially on education. Among university graduates a ten point scale will work well. Among people with less than a high school education five points is sufficient. In third world countries, a three-point scale (good/acceptable/bad) may be all some respondents can understand.

Giving a verbal or written label to each point on a scale, instead of just the endpoints, will usually yield higher-quality data, though this may not be practical when there are more than five points on the scale.

Another issue on which researchers differ is whether to use a scale with an odd or even number of points. Some like to force people to give an answer that is clearly positive or negative. This can make the analysis easier. Others feel it is important to offer a neutral, middle option. Your interviewing mode can make a difference here. A good interviewer can often get a answer, but in a self-administered interview, such as a Web page survey, a person who is frustrated by being unable to give a middle answer may leave a question blank or quit the survey altogether.

Be sure any rating scale labels are meaningful. ***For example***:

What do you think about product X?

❑ It's the best on the market
❑ It's about average
❑ It's the worst on the market

A question phrased like the one above will force most answers into the middle category, resulting in very little usable information.

If you have used a particular scale before and need to compare results, use the same scale. Four on a five-point scale is not equivalent to eight on a ten-point scale. Someone who rates an item "4" on a five-point scale might rate that item anywhere between "6" and "9" on a ten-point scale.

- ***Be aware of cultural factors.*** In the Asian countries, respondents have a strong tendency to exaggerate answers. Researchers may be perceived as being government agents, with the power to punish or reward according to the answer given. Accordingly they often give "correct" answers rather than what they really believe. Even when the questions are not overtly political and deal purely with commercial products or services, the desire not to disappoint important visitors with answers that may be considered negative may lead to exaggerated scores.
- ***Always discount "favourable" answers by a significant factor.*** The desire to please is not limited to the third world. Unfortunately, there is no hard and fast rule on how much to do this. It depends on the situation. One factor to consider is the survey mode. People tend to pick the most positive answer on a scale more often when answering telephone surveys than other types of surveys, regardless of the details of the question.
- ***The desire to please translates into a tendency to pick agreeing answers on agreement scales.*** While logically the percentage that strongly agrees that "X is good" should exactly equal the percentage that strongly disagrees that "X is bad," in the real world, this is unlikely to be true. Experiments have shown that more people will agree than disagree. One way to eliminate this problem is to ask half your respondents if they agree that "X is good" and the other half if they agree that "X is bad." You could then reverse the answers given by the second group. This is extra work, but it may be worth it if it is important to get the most accurate percentage of people who really agree with something.

  People sometimes give answers they feel will reflect well on them. This is a constant problem for pre-election polls. More people say they will vote than actually will vote. More people say they go to museums or libraries than actually do. This problem is most significant when your respondents are talking directly to a person. People give more honest answers when answering questions on a computer. Mail surveys are in-between.
- ***Try to keep your answer spaces in a straight line, either horizontally or vertically.*** A single answer choice on each line is best. Eye tracking studies show the best place to use for answer spaces is the right hand edge of the page. It is much easier for a field worker or respondent to follow a logical flow across or down a page. Using the right edge is also easiest for data entry.

Questions and answer choice grids, as in the second of the following examples, are popular with many researchers. They can look attractive and save paper, or computer screen space. They also can avoid a long series of very repetitive question and answer choice lists. Unfortunately, they also are a bit harder than the repeated lists for some people to understand. As always, consider whom you are studying when you create your questionnaire.

Look at the following layouts and decide which you would prefer to use:

Do you agree, disagree or have no opinion that this company has :

	Agree	Not Sure	Disagree
A good vacation policy —	❑	❑	❑
Good management feedback —	❑	❑	❑
High wages —	❑	❑	❑

An alternative layout is :

	Agree	Not sure	Disagree
A good vacation policy —	❑ 1	❑ 2	❑ 3
Good management feedback —	❑ 1	❑ 2	❑ 3
Good medical insurance —	❑ 1	❑ 2	❑ 3
High waves —	❑ 1	❑ 2	❑ 3

The second example shows the answer choices in neat columns and has more space between the lines. It is easier to read. The numbers in the second example will also speed data entry, if you are using a paper questionnaire.

Surveys are a mixture of science and art, and a good researcher will save their cost many times over by knowing how to ask the correct questions.

Pre-test the Questionnaire

The last step in questionnaire design is to test a questionnaire with a small number of interviews before conducting your main interviews. Ideally, you should test the survey on the same kinds of people you will include in the main study. If that is not possible, at least have a few people, other than the question writer, try the questionnaire. This kind of test run can reveal unanticipated problems with question wording, instructions to skip questions, etc. It can help to see if the interviewers understand your questions and giving useful answers.

If you change any questions after a pre-test, you should not combine the results from the pre-test with the results of post-test interviews. The Survey System will invariably provide you with mathematically correct answers to your questions, but choosing sensible questions and administering surveys with sensitivity and common sense will improve the quality of your results dramatically.

SPECIMEN QUESTIONNAIRE

Workplace Assessment : SAMPLE QUESTIONNAIRE

COMPANY NAME : ____________________________

NAME : ____________________________

PHONE NUMBER : ____________________________

ADDRESS : ____________________________

Background information about your worksite

1.

(a) Approximately how many employees are there in your company? *Please tick.*

❑	❑	❑	❑	❑	❑	❑
0-25	26-50	51-100	101-150	151-200	201-300	301+

(b) Approximately how many departments are there in your company? *(Please state.)*

____

2. What proportion of your employees are … *Please tick.*

	All	More than half	Half	Very few	None	Don't know
Women	❑	❑	❑	❑	❑	❑
Full-time (35+ hours/week)	❑	❑	❑	❑	❑	❑
Part-time	❑	❑	❑	❑	❑	❑
Working shifts	❑	❑	❑	❑	❑	❑
Working flexitime	❑	❑	❑	❑	❑	❑
Regularly working at different locations other than main site	❑	❑	❑	❑	❑	❑
Disabled and/or have special needs	❑	❑	❑	❑	❑	❑

3. Does your worksite have any practices or policies that … *(Please tick.)*

	Yes	No
… allow employees to job share	❑	❑
… allow flexible working for employees to be active during the working day	❑	❑

Health promotion in the workplace

4. How is worksite wellness promoted within your workplace? For example, is it through a formal committee and/or occupational health, health and safety or human resources?

____

____

5. Who would you report any health and safety problems to in your workplace? *(Please give job title.)*

____

6.

(a) Is there a specific group or 'champion' responsible for the promotion, supervision or coordination of a physical activity programme?

Yes	No	Don't know
❑	❑	❑

(b) If Yes, do they have a budget?

Yes	No	Don't know
❑	❑	❑

(c) If Yes, are there any constraints on how this money can be spent?

Yes	No	Don't know
❑	❑	❑

(d) If you answered *No* to 6a, are there any employees or local health professionals who are willing to support the programme by volunteering?

Employees	Yes	No.	Don't Know
Health professionals	❑	❑	❑

7. Does your workplace have written policies addressing the following issues? *(Please tick.)*

	Yes	No.	Don't Know
Health and safety	❑	❑	❑
Healthy eating	❑	❑	❑

Physical activity	❑	❑	❑
Stress in the workplace	❑	❑	❑
Smoking in the workplace	❑	❑	❑
Work-life balance, e.g. flexible working and 'family-friendly' practices	❑	❑	❑
Other *(Please state.)*			

____

8. Does your workplace offer, provide or have access to any of the following activities? *(Please tick all that apply.)*

	Yes	No
Lunchtime walks	❑	❑
Active stretch breaks	❑	❑
Walking meetings	❑	❑
Physical activity/sports courses and qualifications	❑	❑
Lunchtime activity groups	❑	❑
Sports or activity clubs	❑	❑
Recreational games for employees at lunchtime or after work	❑	❑
Company leagues or ladders	❑	❑
On-site activity classes	❑	❑
Activity taster sessions	❑	❑
Corporate challenges	❑	❑
Inter-company and/or cross-company competitions	❑	❑
Activity days	❑	❑
Active team-building day for employees	❑	❑
Health-related treatments	❑	❑

9.

(a) Are these applicable to every site of the workplace?

Yes	No
❑	❑

(b) If *No* please state why.

____

____

10. Does the worksite actively encourage employee participation in its health promotion programmes?

Yes	No
❑	❑

11. Which communication channels are available in your workplace to promote physical activity? *(Please tick whichever ones apply.)*

E-mail	❑
Voicemail	❑
E-bulletin boards	❑

Intranet ❑
Weekly e-notices ❑
Employee newsletter ❑
Internal mail system ❑
Notice boards ❑
Displays/signs ❑
Training ❑
Other *(Please state.)* ______________________________

____

Facilities

12.

(a) Does your worksite offer, provide or have access to physical activity facilities in the following ways? *(Please tick.)*

	Yes	No
On-site exercise facilities/programmes	❑	❑
Free, discounted or employer-subsidised memberships for off-site facilities	❑	❑
Free, discounted or employer-subsidised memberships for on-site facilities	❑	❑
Outdoor exercise areas or playing fields for employee use	❑	❑
Access to fitness testing/assessments	❑	❑
Incentives to employees who participate in physical activities/ maintain physical fitness	❑	❑
Showers	❑	❑
Changing areas	❑	❑
Lockers/ storage facilities	❑	❑
A company bicycle pool and storage racks	❑	❑
Stairs	❑	❑

(b) Are these options available outside work hours? *(Please tick.)*

Yes ❑ No ❑

Please give details : ______________________________

____

____

13. Does your worksite offer any of the following potential sites or facilities for activity? *Please tick all that apply.*

Meeting rooms	❑	Space for on-site exercise classes	❑
Grounds for cycling	❑	Access to areas for walking	❑
Trails or paths	❑	Company grounds	❑

Other *(Please state.)* ______________________________

____

14. What improvements could be made to the facilities you have listed in question 13, that would encourage employees to use them more?

You may want to think about :

Cleanliness ❑
Layout ❑
Lightening ❑
Surface ❑
Ventilation ❑

Whether the facilities are :

Aesthetically pleasing ❑
Well designed ❑
Well maintained ❑
Other *(Please state.)* ______________________

____

15. Are there any areas or services in the local community to support physical activity in and around your workplace? *(Please tick.)*

Walking trails ❑
Cycling routes ❑
Parks ❑
Recreation grounds ❑
Health and fitness centres ❑
Exercise groups/ clubs/ classes ❑
Shopping centres ❑
University/college ❑
Local community organisation ❑
Other *(Please state.)* ______________________

____

Thank You.......

2.7 SECONDARY DATA

Secondary data are those data which have been already collected and analysed by some earlier agency for its own use; and later the same data are used by a different agency.

According to ***W.A. Neiswanger***, "A primary source is a publication in which the data are published by the same authority which gathered and analysed them. A secondary source is a publication, reporting the data which have been gathered by other authorities and for which others are responsible".

2.7.1 Sources of Secondary Data

In most of the studies the investigator finds it impracticable to collect first-hand information on all related issues and as such he makes use of the data collected by others. There is a vast amount of published information from which statistical studies may be made and fresh statistics are constantly in a state of production.

The sources of secondary data can broadly be classified under two heads —

1. Published sources, and
2. Unpublished sources.

1. Published Sources

The various sources of published data are :

1. Reports and official publications of
   (i) International bodies such as the International Monetary Fund, International Finance Corporation and United Nations Organisation.
   (ii) Central and State Governments such as the Report of the Tandon Committee and Pay Commission.
2. Semi-official publication of various local bodies such as Municipal Corporations and District Boards.
3. Private publications-such as the publications of –
   (i) Trade and professional bodies such as the Federation of Indian Chambers of Commerce and Institute of Chartered Accountants.
   (ii) Financial and economic journals such as 'Commerce', 'Capital' and 'Indian Finance'.
   (iii) Annual reports of joint stock companies.
   (iv) Publications brought out by research agencies, research scholars, etc.

It should be noted that the publications mentioned above vary with regard to the period of publication. Some are published at regular intervals (yearly, monthly, weekly etc.) whereas others are ad hoc publications, i.e., with no regularity about periodicity of publications.

NOTE: A lot of secondary data is available on the Internet. We can access it at any time for the further studies.

2. Unpublished Sources

All statistical material is not always published. There are various sources of unpublished data such as records maintained by various Government and private offices, studies made by research institutions, scholars, etc. Such sources can also be used where necessary

Precautions in the use of Secondary data

The following are some of the points that are to be considered in the use of secondary data

1. How the data has been collected and processed
2. The accuracy of the data
3. How far the data has been summarized
4. How comparable the data is with other tabulations
5. How to interpret the data, especially when figures collected for one purpose is used for another

Generally speaking, with secondary data, people have to compromise between what they want and what they are able to find.

Merits and Demerits of Secondary Data

1. Secondary data is cheap to obtain. Many government publications are relatively cheap and libraries stock quantities of secondary data produced by the government, by companies and other organisations.
2. Large quantities of secondary data can be got through internet.

3. Much of the secondary data available has been collected for many years and therefore it can be used to plot trends.
4. Secondary data is of value to —
   - The government – help in making decisions and planning future policy.
   - Business and industry – in areas such as marketing, and sales in order to appreciate the general economic and social conditions and to provide information on competitors.
   - Research organisations – by providing social, economical and industrial information.

SELF PRACTICE EXERCISES

I. CHOOSE THE BEST ANSWER

1. The source of data are
   (a) Primary data (b) Secondary data
   (c) primary and secondary both (d) none of these
2. Primary data as compared to secondary data are
   (a) less reliable (b) more reliable
   (c) equally reliable (d) none of these
3. Secondary data
   (a) should never be used
   (b) should be used after careful scrutiny
   (c) no scrutiny is required while using it
   (d) while scrutinising the only thing to see as who collected it
4. Which of the following is not the source of secondary data-
   (a) data published is newspapers
   (b) publications of central and state governments
   (c) the data obtained by a firm in a market survey conducted by it
   (d) data published by World Bank
5. The data obtained from a newspaper are
   (a) primary data (b) secondary data
   (c) both (a) and (b) (d) none of these
6. The number of questions in a questionnaire should be
   (a) 10 (b) 50
   (c) 75 (d) as small as possible in view the purpose of survey
7. The data obtained from Annual Report of any bank
   (a) Primary data (b) secondary
   (c) A and B both (d) none of above
8. Data originally collected for investigation are known as
   (a) primary data (b) secondary data
   (c) original data (d) none of these

II. FILL IN THE BLANKS

1. From the view of collection, data can be divided into two groups .... and ....
2. Data originally collected for an investigation are known as ....

3. .... are already collected and published earlier and the researcher makes use of them.
4. Most statistical analysis rest upon .... data.
5. Indirect oral investigation method should be used, when the area of investigation is .... and where informants are .... to give information.
6. Questionnaire method cannot be used when the informants are ....
7. .... is the first step in a statistical investigation.
8. In .... the investigator contacts the source of information directly.
9. In mailed questionnaire method, the area of investigation may be ....
10. A questionnarie is a set of ....

III. SHORT ANSWER TYPE QUESTIONS

1. Explain Internal and External data and name their sources.
2. Explain various methods of collecting primary and secondary data.
3. What is a questionnaire? Enlist some points, which should be considered in the formation of questionnaire.
4. What are the errors, which appears in the survey methods of collecting data?
5. How many questions should a questionnaire contain?
6. Name few sources of business data.
7. Why pre-testing of questionnaire is desirable?
8. Briefly explain the characteristics of a good questionnaire.
9. Discuss the merits and limitations of collecting primary data through questionnaires.
10. What precautions should be taken while using secondary data?

IV. LONG ANSWER TYPE QUESTIONS

1. Differentiate between primary data and secondary data. Under what circumstances would secondary data be more useful than primary data?
2. Describe a project in which it would be necessary to use primary data rather than secondary data. Give reasons.
3. What are the various modes of data collection? Under what circumstances would each method be more suitable as compared to other methods? Give reasons for your beliefs.
4. Distinguish clearly between primary and secondary data. Discuss the various methods of collecting primary data indicate the situation in which each of these methods should be used. **[MBA, Osmania University, 2001, HPU, 2002, DU 2002, UPTU, 2002]**
5. Discuss the validity of the statement: "A secondary source is not as reliable as primary source."
6. Distinguish between the following:
   - A schedule and a questionnaire,
   - Primary and secondary data, and
   - Survey and an experiment.
7. What are the essential of a good questionnaire? Draft a suitable questionnaire containing not more than 20 questions to find out the efficacy of MBA program. **[MBA, Osmania University, 2001]**
8. You are required to collect data on the extent and nature of graduate unemployment in urban areas in UP, using the sample survey method. How do you proceed?

9. What are the sources of secondary data? Explain some uses and limitations of secondary sources of data. **[MBA, Osmania University, 2002]**
10. Compare and contrast the questionnaire and interview techniques of collecting data. Which technique is more reliable and why?

ANSWERS

I. CHOOSE THE BEST ANSWER

1. (c)	2. (b)	3. (b)	4. (c)	5. (b)
6. (d)	7. (b)	8. (a)		

II. FILL IN THE BLANKS

1. Primary data, secondary data
2. Primary data
3. Secondary data
4. Secondary
5. wide, reluctant
6. illiterate
7. collection of data
8. direct personal interview
9. wide
10. Questions.

CHAPTER 3

Organising Data: Classification and Tabulation

3.1 INTRODUCTION

So far you know how to collect data. So what do we do with the collected data next? Now you have to present the data you have collected, so that they can be of use. Thus the collected data or raw data are always in an unorganised form and need to be organized and presented in a meaningful and readily comprehensible form in order to facilitate further statistical analysis. We can present the collected data in following ways:

1. Classification and Tabulation
2. Diagrammatic Presentation
3. Graphical Presentation

We will discuss all these modes of presentation of data in details. We will start with the first way i.e. "***Classification and Tabulation***"

The first step in a statistics investigation is to collect numerical data (observation) from the given sphere of inquiry, e.g. if we want to find the average height of the students in a college, then, first of all height of all the students will be measured and recorded. This is known as raw data. The magnitude and the volume of raw data depend upon the purpose and nature of the inquiry. Generally these observations are overwhelming mass of information and detail which cannot be easily grasped and analysed. Hence for better understanding and easy grasp of the phenomenon a systematic and proper presentation of the raw data in necessary.

Thus the voluminous raw data is to be reduced in two senses :

(a) The amount of details in raw data are to be reduced as far as possible and

(b) The data is to be arranged in such a way that significant features stand out prominently.

DO YOU KNOW?

Classification and Tabulation are the ways of presenting the raw data in an orderly and systematic manner which helps for further analysis and interpretation of the data.

This is done by the methods of classification and tabulation. The volume and heterogeneity in the raw data are removed by means of ***Tabulation***, but before tabulation the data should be arranged in homogeneous groups by means of ***Classification***.

3.2 CLASSIFICATION OF DATA

The collected data, also known as raw data or ungrouped data are always in an un-organised form and need to be organised and presented in meaningful and readily comprehensible form in order to facilitate further statistical analysis. It is, therefore, essential for an investigator to condense a mass of data into more and more comprehensible and assailable form. The process of grouping into different classes or sub classes according to some characteristics is known as classification.

What is Classification of Data?

Classification is the process of arranging things in the groups according to their resemblance, similarity, or identity. ***For example***, students in your class may be grouped according to their sex, age, marital status etc. Similarly letters in the post office are classified according to their destinations viz., Delhi, Noida, Bareilly, Jaipur, Agra, Kanpur, etc.

Thus classification is the first step in tabulation.

Objects of Classification

The following are main objectives of classifying the data:

1. It condenses the mass of data in an easily assailable form.
2. It eliminates unnecessary details.
3. It facilitates comparison and highlights the significant aspect of data.
4. It enables one to get a mental picture of the information and helps in drawing inferences.
5. It helps in the statistical treatment of the information collected.

Characteristics of good Classification

The classification of any data is done on the basis of nature, scope and purpose of the inquiry. But an ideal classification should posses the following characteristics:

(i) It should be Unambiguous: the different classes should be defined in such a way that no room is itself for doubt or confusion e.g. if the data is divided as literate and illiterate, then the meaning of literate should be clearly defined.

(ii) It should be Stable: if the classification requires changes every time on the repetition of an inquiry than the data would not be fit for comparison. Hence the classification should be stable.

(iii) Flexible: it should be capable of being adjusted in new situations and circumstances. In fact stability does not mean rigidity. There is bound to be change in classes with time.

Thus an ideal classification is one which adjusts itself to the changes in data during course of time and yet retains its stability. For this the raw data should be divided in few major classes and then it should be further sub divided. In that case only small sub classes may need a change and the classification will retain its stable character.

3.3 TYPES OF CLASSIFICATION

Statistical data are classified in respect of their characteristics. Broadly there are four basic types of classification namely

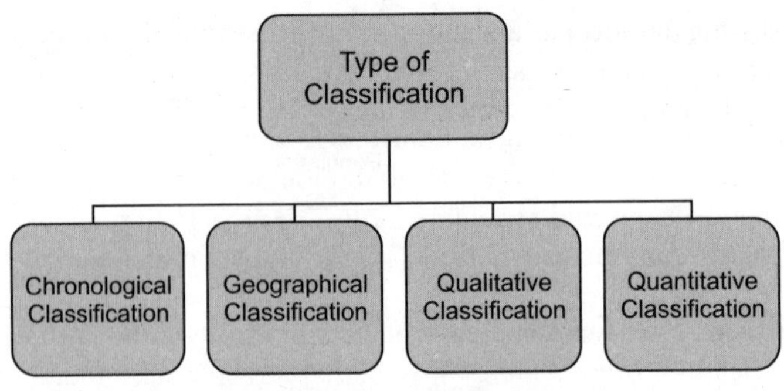

Fig. 3.1: Types of classification

Now we will discuss the above classification in details one by one.

1. Chronological or Temporal Classification

In chronological classification the collected data are arranged according to the order of time expressed in years, months, weeks, etc., the data is generally classified in ascending order of time. ***For example***, the data related with population, sales of a firm, imports and exports of a country are always subjected to chronological classification.

Example: The estimates of birth rates in India during 1970-76 are

Year	1970	1971	1972	1973	1974	1975	1976
Birth rate	36.8	36.9	36.6	34.6	34.5	35.2	34.2

2. Geographical or Spatial Classification

In this type of classification the data are classified according to geographical region or place. For instance, the production of paddy in different states in India, production of wheat in different countries etc.

Example: When names of the countries are in Alphabetical order :

Country	America	China	Denmark	France	India
Yield of Wheat in (kg/acre)	1925	893	225	439	862

Example: When the observations are in descending order :

Country	America	China	India	France	Denmark
Yield of Wheat in (kg/acre)	1925	893	862	439	225

3. Qualitative Classification

In this type of classification data are classified on the basis of same attributes or quality like sex, literacy, religion, employment etc., such attributes cannot be measured along with a scale.

For example, if the population to be classified in respect to one attribute say sex, then we can classify them into two classes namely that of males and females. Similarly, they can also be classified into 'employed' or 'unemployed' on the basis of another attribute 'employment'. Thus when the classification is done with respect to one attribute, which is dichotomous in nature, two classes are formed, one possessing the attribute and the other not possessing the attribute. This type of classification is called simple or dichotomous classification.

A simple classification may be shown as under

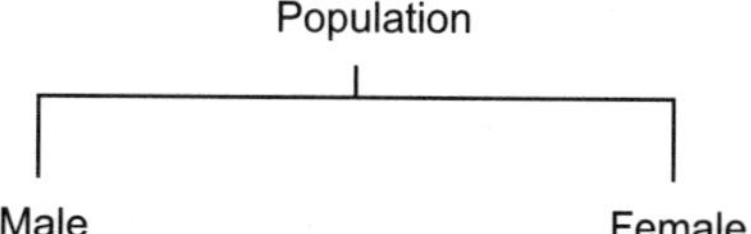

The classification, where two or more attributes are considered and several classes are formed, is called a manifold classification. ***For example***, if we classify population simultaneously with respect to two attributes, e.g sex and employment, then population are first classified with respect to 'sex' into 'males' and 'females'. Each of these classes may then be further classified into 'employment' and 'unemployment' on the basis of attribute 'employment' and as such Population are classified into four classes namely.

(i) Male employed
(ii) Male unemployed
(iii) Female employed
(iv) Female unemployed

Still the classification may be further extended by considering other attributes like marital status etc. This can be explained by the following chart

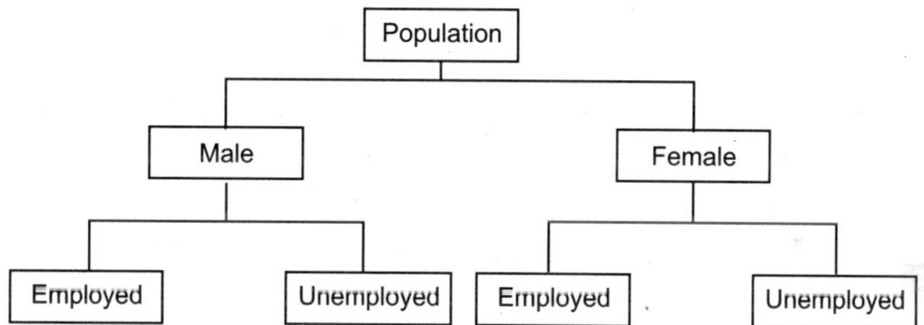

4. Quantitative Classification

Quantitative classification refers to the classification of data according to some characteristics that can be measured such as height, weight, etc., ***For example*** the students of a college may be classified according to weight as given below.

Weight (lbs)	No of Students
90-100	50
100-110	200
110-120	260
130-140	90
140-150	40
Total	**640**

In this type of classification there are two elements, namely

(i) The variable (i.e) the weight in the above example, and
(ii) The frequency in the number of students in each class. There are 50 students having weights ranging from 90 to 100 lb, 200 students having weight ranging between 100 to 110 lb and so on.

3.4 FREQUENCY DISTRIBUTION

Frequency distribution is a series when a number of observations with similar or closely related values are put in separate bunches or groups, each group being in order of magnitude in a series. It is simply a table in which the data are grouped into classes and the numbers of cases which fall in each class are recorded. It shows the frequency of occurrence of different values of a single phenomenon.

A frequency distribution is constructed for three main reasons :

1. To facilitate the analysis of data.
2. To estimate frequencies of the unknown population distribution from the distribution of sample data and
3. To facilitate the computation of various statistical measures

3.4.1 Formation of a Frequency Distribution: Ungrouped Data

In quantitative classification, the collected data are grouped with reference to the characteristics, which can be measured and numerically described such as height, weight, sales, imports, age, income, etc. The first step in the direction of putting observations in some ordered form is to arrange them in ascending or descending order of magnitude. The data are then said to be in an array, which is further described below.

Data Array

Suppose 30 students of your class are asked to toss a coin five times and each one has to record each time whether he gets a head. Suppose the following figure emerge for the 30 students :

3, 2, 0, 4, 1, 2, 3, 2, 5, 3, 3, 1, 1, 3, 5, 4, 2, 2, 3, 1, 0, 4, 3, 2, 2, 4, 2, 3, 3, 1

Now this data need better display. One way of doing this is to show the data in a certain order (ascending or descending). In ascending order we may show the same data as follows:

0, 0, 1, 1, 1, 1, 1, 2, 2, 2, 2, 2, 2, 2, 2, 3, 3, 3, 3, 3, 3, 3, 3, 3, 4, 4, 4, 4, 5, 5

The arrangement of data either in ascending order or in descending order is called an array. One advantage of an array is that you can immediately find the range, that is, difference between the highest and the lowest value. Another advantage of an array is that you can reveal at a glance whether there is tendency of some items to concentrate near a certain value. In our example, we find that there is greater concentration of number three than any other number. Despite these advantages, array is not frequently used because arranging observations in accordance with their respective values needs a good deal of time.

3.4.2 Formation of a Frequency Distribution: Discrete Data

In this form of distribution, the frequency refers to discrete value. Here the data are presented in a way that exact measurements of units are clearly indicated.

There are definite differences between the variables of different groups of items. Each class is distinct and separate from the other class. Non-continuity from one class to another class exists. Data as such facts like the number of rooms in a house, the number of companies registered in a country, the number of children in a family, etc.

The process of preparing this type of distribution is very simple. We have just to count the number of times a particular value is repeated, which is called the frequency of that class. In order to facilitate counting prepare a column of tallies.

In another column, place all possible values of variable from the lowest to the highest. Then put a bar (Vertical line) opposite the particular value to which it relates.

To facilitate counting, blocks of five bars 𝍸 are prepared and some space is left in between each block. We finally count the number of bars and get frequency.

You have noticed that the data relating to the toss of a coin five times by 30 students show that each figure 0 to 5 has occurred a certain number of times. The frequency of their occurrence varies in each case. You can show the same data differently by condensing these data by pairing each value with its frequency.

This you can show in a table as follows: Frequency Distribution for no. of heads obtained by 30 students

Observation(x)	Tally Marks	Frequency
0	II	2
1	𝍸	5
2	𝍸 III	8
3	𝍸 IIII	9
4	IIII	4
5	II	2
	Total	**30**

The arrangement and display of data in this form where the observed value is paired with its frequency is called frequency distribution.

This should be noted that the frequency distribution does not show the details as are shown in an array as it presents the data in more summarized form. It helps the statistician to understand the data in a more meaningful manner.

EXAMPLE 3.1: In a survey of 40 families in a village, the number of children per family was recorded and the following data obtained.

1 0 3 2 1 5 6 2
2 1 0 3 4 2 1 6
3 2 1 5 3 3 2 4
2 2 3 0 2 1 4 5
3 3 4 4 1 2 4 5

Represent the data in the form of a discrete frequency distribution.

Solution : Frequency distribution of the number of children

Number of Children	Tally Marks	Frequency
0	III	3
1	𝍸 II	7
2	𝍸 𝍸	10
3	𝍸 III	8
4	𝍸 I	6
5	IIII	4
6	II	2
	Total	**40**

3.4.3 Formation of Frequency Distribution: Continuous Data

In this form of distribution refers to groups of values. This becomes necessary in the case of some variables which can take any fractional value and in which case an exact measurement is not possible. Hence a discrete variable can be presented in the form of a continuous frequency distribution.

Wage distribution of 100 employees

Weekly Wages (Rs)	Number of Employees
50–100	4
100–150	12
150–200	22
200–250	33
250–300	16
300–350	8
350–400	5
Total	**100**

Nature of Class

Now we will see the formation of frequency table when the data are continuous. But before starting it, we should have a clear idea of following terms:

A. **Class Limits:** These are the lowest and the highest values of a class. ***For example***, take the class 30–50. Here, we find that the lowest limit is 30 and the highest limit is 50. When we categorize individual observations within this class, it is clear that none of the included observation is below 30 or above 50. Take another example; a class 60–79 indicates that no value below 60 can be included here and, likewise, no value above 79 can be included.

B. **Class Interval:** The difference between the upper limit and the lower limit of a class is known as a class interval. It is the width of the class. Thus, the class interval of class 30-50 is 20.The class60-79 has a class interval of 19.

C. **Class Frequency:** The number of observations belonging to a particular class is known as the frequency of that class or class frequency. Suppose there are 20 students who have obtained marks ranging from 30-40 and 44 students have obtained marks ranging from 50–60. In the first case, the class-interval 30–40, the class frequency is 20, while in the second case, in the class interval 50-60, the class frequency is 44. If we add up all the class frequencies, we get the total frequency of the entire series. For instance, if there are 500 students who have been classified in varying class intervals in accordance with their marks in an examination, then the total frequency is 500.

D. **Width or Size of the Class Interval:** The difference between the lower and upper class limits is called Width or size of class interval and is denoted by 'C'

E. **Range:** The difference between largest and smallest value of the observation is called the Range and is denoted by ‘R’ ie

$$R = \text{Largest value} - \text{Smallest value}$$
$$R = L - S$$

F. **Class Mid-Point:** When we add up the lower and the upper class limits of a class interval, we get a certain value. This value is divided by two, which gives us the class mid-point. Thus, the mid-point of class interval 40-60 is (40+60)/ 2 = 50. The formula for obtaining class mid-point is as follows :

$$\text{Class mid-point} = \frac{\text{Lower limit of the Class + Upper limit of the Class}}{2}$$

G. **Number of Class Intervals:** The number of class interval in a frequency is matter of importance. The number of class interval should not be too many.

For an ideal frequency distribution, the number of class intervals can vary from 5 to 15. To decide the number of class intervals for the frequency distribution in the whole data, we choose the lowest and the highest of the values. The difference between them will enable us to decide the class intervals.

Thus the number of class intervals can be fixed arbitrarily keeping in view the nature of problem under study. There is however, ***Struges' formula*** available for guidance. The number of classes can be determined by applying Struges' formula, which is as follows:

$$K = 1 + 3.322 \log_{10} N$$

Where,

N = Total number of observations
log = logarithm of the number
K = Number of class intervals.

Thus if the number of observation is 10, then the number of class intervals is

$$K = 1 + 3.322 \log_{10} 10 = 1 + 3.322 \times 1 = 4.322 \approx 4$$

If 100 observations are being studied, the number of class interval is

$$K = 1 + 3.322 \log_{10} 100 = 1+3.322 \times 2 = 1+6.64 = 7.64 \approx 8 \text{ and so on.}$$

H. **Size of the Class Interval:** Since the size of the class interval is inversely proportional to the number of class interval in a given distribution.

The approximate value of the size (or width or magnitude) of the class interval 'C' is obtained by using Sturges' rule as

$$\text{Size of class interval} = C = \frac{\text{Range}}{\text{Number of class interval}} = \frac{\text{Range}}{1 + 3.322 \log N}$$

Where, Range = Largest Value – Smallest Value in the distribution.

3.4.4 Types of Class Intervals

As we shall see subsequently, the mid-point of each class interval is taken to represent it for the purpose of statistical calculations. One should also know that there are three methods of classifying data into different class-intervals. These are

- Exclusive Method
- Inclusive Method.
- Open-End Classes

1. Exclusive Method

In order to explain this method, let us take some hypothetical data, which are given below:

Profits Earned by Companies	
Profit(Rs Lakh)	**Number of companies**
10–20	12
20–30	17
30–40	30
40–50	25
50–60	16
Total	**100**

This is an exclusive method where the upper limit of one class is shown as the lower limit of the next class. This ensures continuity of data. ***For example***, a company earning a profit of Rs 30 lakh will not be classified in the class-interval 20–30. It will be included in the next class-interval: 30–40. In a field survey, proper instruction should be given to the enumerators where to put a certain response otherwise some enumerators will include a company earning Rs 30 lakh in the 20–30 class while others in the 30–40 class. Obviously, this will lead to erroneous results. It should be noted that if the class intervals are given as shown in the above table, it is presumed that the upper limit is exclusive and that the item of that value is included in the next class interval.

2. Inclusive Method

In the case of inclusive method, the upper limit of one class is included in that class itself. Suppose we have the following frequency distribution:

Profits Earned by Companies	
Profit(Rs Lakh)	**Number of companies**
10–19	12
20–29	17
30–39	30
40–49	25
50–59	16
Total	**100**

In this case, the class intervals are formed on the basis of inclusive method, which shows that the upper limit of the class interval in reality is taken in that class. Thus, a company earning Rs 30 lakh will be in the class 30–39 and another one earning Rs 39 lakh will also be in the same class interval. When a company earns a profit of say, Rs 30.6 lakh, where it should be included? Here we have to use the mid-points of the class interval. We may use the exclusive method and then calculate the mid-points. Thus, we may have classes 10.5–20.5, 20.5–30.5 and so on. The company earning Rs 30.6 lakh will be included in 30.5–40.5 class interval. Another way of classifying it would be 9.5–19.5, 19.5–29.5 and so on.

At this point one may ask: How to decide whether inclusive or exclusive method is to be used? One has to first find out whether the variable under observation is a continuous or discrete. If the variable is a continuous one, then the exclusive method should be used. If, on the other hand, there is a discrete variable, then the inclusive method should be used.

3. Open-End Classes

A class limit is missing either at the lower end of the first class interval or at the upper end of the last class interval or both are not specified. The necessity of open end classes arises in a number of practical situations, particularly relating to economic and medical data when there are few very high values or few very low values which are far apart from the majority of observations.

The example for the open-end classes as follows:

Salary Range	No of workers
Below 2000	7
2000–4000	5
4000–6000	6
6000–8000	4
8000 and above	3

Having made certain terms clear, we now turn to the formation of a grouped frequency table.

3.5 FORMATION OF GROUPED FREQUENCY TABLE

The formation of a frequency distribution table comprises the following steps:

1. Deciding the appropriate number of class groupings
2. Choosing a suitable size or width of a class interval
3. Establishing the boundaries of each class interval
4. Classifying the data into the appropriate classes
5. Counting the number of items (i.e. frequency) in each class.

It will be seen that steps 4 and 5 are purely mechanical. The first three steps assume considerable importance and are discussed as follows.

1. Deciding the Appropriate Number of Class Groupings

The first and the foremost question one confronts is: How many classes should be formed?

The number of class intervals depends mainly on the number of observation as well as their range, as a general rule, the number of classes should not be less than six nor should be more than 15. If the number of observations is small, obviously the classes will be few as we cannot classify small data into 12 or 15 classes. If the classes are too few, then the original data will be so compressed that only limited information will be available.

There is however, struges' formula available for guidance, which we have been discussed.

In practice, the number of classes is determined keeping in mind the requirement in a given problem. It would, therefore, vary from problem to problem and the satisfaction has to decide as to how many classes should be formed in a particular problem. Classes should be chosen in such a way that they cover all the data to be categorized.

2. Choosing a Suitable Size or Width of a Class Interval

Another major consideration while forming a frequency table is the size of the class width. It is desirable to have each class grouping of equal width. In order to ascertain the width of each class, the difference between the highest value and the lowest value, which is known as the range, should be divided by the number of class groupings desired:

$$\text{Width of Class Interval} = \frac{\text{Highest Value} - \text{Lowest Value}}{\text{Number of Class Groupings}}$$

Suppose we have 200 observations pertaining to income of workers where the highest income is Rs. 6, 200 p.m. and lowest is 1, 400 p.m. We have decided that the number of class groupings should be 6.

$$\text{Width} = \frac{6,200 - 1,400}{6}$$

$$= 800$$

At times this value may be in fraction. For the sake of convenience, the width of each class grouping is rounded up to 5.

As far as possible, the class intervals should have equal width. ***For example***, instead of having the class intervals as 1–7 and 8–10, we should have 1–5 and 6–10. Normally, the range should be a multiple of 5, 10 or 100 as it facilitates in computation.

Occasionally, it becomes necessary to have unequal width in class intervals, particularly when there is considerable variation in the individual observations. ***For example***, while dealing with data on income in a certain territory, we may find some extremely high values occurring infrequently while most values are within low or moderate range. In such a case, it is preferable to have larger width in the higher range of class intervals as compared to the width in the lower range values. One has to be careful in dealing with such tables having varying class intervals. In particular, one should ensure that graphs and charts based on such data do not give a distorted picture to the reader.

3. Establishing the Boundaries of the Classes

The next step in the formation of a frequency table is to decide class boundaries for each class-interval so that observations can be placed into one class only. The point to note is that classes should not be overlapping, as it would cause confusion and an observation could be included sometimes in one class and at other times in another class. Suppose we have class boundaries as follows:

0–5
5–10
10–15

In such a case, an observation with value 5 can be included either in 0-5 and 5-10 class. This should be avoided. Instead, we may put the class boundaries as:

Below 5
5 to under 10
10 to under 15

The class boundaries, thus formed, are clear and there will not be any cause of confusion by placing individual observations into different classes where they should belong.

EXAMPLE 3.2: The following data pertain to weights (in kg) of 33 students of a class :

42, 74, 40, 60, 82, 115, 41, 61, 75, 83, 63, 53, 110, 76, 84, 50, 67, 65, 78, 77, 56, 95, 68, 69, 104, 80, 79, 79, 54, 73, 59, 81, and 110

Prepare a suitable frequency table.

Solution : Here, we find that the highest value is 115 and the lowest is 40. We can decide the width of the class-interval. Since the range is 115 – 40 = 75, we may decide there should be 8 classes starting from 40. Thus, class intervals would be as shown in table.

Classification of Students by Weight

Class Intervals	Tally Marks	Frequencies
40 to under 50	IIII	3
50 to under 60	~~IIII~~	5
60 to under 70	~~IIII~~ II	7
70 to under 80	~~IIII~~ III	8
80 to under 90	~~IIII~~	5
90 to under 100	I	1
100 to under 110	I	I
110 to under 120	III	3
	Total	**33**

EXAMPLE 3.3: Given below are the numbers of tools produced by workers in a factory.

43 18 25 18 39 44 19 20 20 26
40 45 38 25 13 14 27 41 42 17
34 31 32 27 33 37 25 26 32 25
33 34 35 46 29 34 31 34 35 24
28 30 41 32 29 28 30 31 30 34
31 35 36 29 26 32 36 35 36 37
32 23 22 29 33 37 33 27 24 36
23 42 29 37 29 23 44 41 45 39
21 21 42 22 28 22 15 16 17 28
22 29 35 31 27 40 23 32 40 37

Construct frequency distribution with inclusive type of class interval. Also find

1. How many workers produced more than 38 tools?
2. How many workers produced less than 23 tools?

Solution : Using sturges formula for determining the number of class intervals, we have

Number of class intervals = $1 + 3.322 \log_{10} N = 1 + 3.322 \log_{10} 100 = 7.6$

$$\text{Size of class interval} = \frac{\text{Range}}{\text{Number of class interval}} = \frac{46-13}{7.6} = 5$$

Hence taking the magnitude of class intervals as 5, we have 7 classes 13-17, 18-22… 43-47 are the classes by inclusive type.

Using tally marks, the required frequency distribution is obtain in the following table

Class Intervals	Tally Marks	Number of tools produced (frequencies)
13–17	~~IIII~~ I	6
18–22	~~IIII~~ ~~IIII~~ I	11
23–27	~~IIII~~ ~~IIII~~ ~~IIII~~ III	18
28–32	~~IIII~~ ~~IIII~~ ~~IIII~~ ~~IIII~~ ~~IIII~~	25
33–37	~~IIII~~ ~~IIII~~ ~~IIII~~ ~~IIII~~ II	22
38–42	~~IIII~~ ~~IIII~~ I	11
43–47	~~IIII~~ II	7
	Total	**100**

We have thus allocated different observations to their respective classes with the help of tallies. The figures on the extreme right are the frequencies.

The main advantage of this frequency distribution table is that it highlights some important characteristics of the data. We find that the range of the data is 75 (115–40). Another point to note is that there is a concentration in the class-interval 70 to under 80 as it contains the highest frequency.

A major limitation of grouped frequency distributions is that some information is lost in this process. We cannot know how the values are within a particular class interval without going to the original source.

A point worth noting is that the selection of class boundaries for frequency distribution tables is very subjective. If the same set of data is given to two persons who are asked to form a frequency table, they nay use different width and number of class intervals. This may be due to shift in the data concentration in the two frequency tables. However, in case the original data relate to a large number of observations, the effect of changes in the class boundaries on the concentration of frequencies would be far less as compared to the data when the data are extremely limited.

3.6 RELATIVE FREQUENCY AND PERCENTAGE DISTRIBUTION

Our discussion so far was confined to absolute frequencies. We can transform the frequency distribution into a relative frequency distribution. The relative frequency may be obtained from

$$\text{Relative frequency} = \frac{\text{Frequency}}{\text{Total number of observations}}$$

Thus, for the data presented in Table, the relative frequency for the class interval 70 to under 80 is obtained from

$$\text{Relative frequency} = \frac{8}{33} = 0.242$$

This relative frequency is the proportion to the total number of observation. By multiplying it by 100, we can change it as a percentage to the total number of observations. This comes to 24.2 percent. In other words, the absolute frequency of 8 in the total number of observation of 33 is 24.2 percent of it. Let us give an example.

EXAMPLE 3.4: A Relative Frequency Table

Class Interval	Frequency	Relative Frequency
10 but less than 20	3	0.055
20 but less than 30	5	0.091
30 but less than 40	9	0.164
40 but less than 50	8	0.327
50 but less than 60	10	0.182
60 but less than 70	8	0.145
70 but less than 80	2	0.036
Total	**55**	**1.000**

The foregoing table can be converted into a percentage frequency distribution by dividing frequency in each class by the total number of observation and multiplying by 100. This percentage distribution is shown in Table.

Size of item	Percentage Frequency
10 but less than 20	5.5
20 but less than 30	9.1
30 but less than 40	16.4
40 but less than 50	32.7
50 but less than 60	18.2
60 but less than 70	14.5
70 but less than 80	3.6
Total	**100.0**

It may be noted that at times the use of relative frequencies is more appropriate than absolute frequencies. Whatever two or more sets of data contain different number of observation, a comparison with absolute frequencies will be erroneous. In such cases, it is necessary to use the relative frequency. Also, the class boundaries should be the same (or at least be multiples of each other) if proper comparisons are to be made.

Let us take another example.

EXAMPLE 3.5: The data given below rate to the number of years those 50 workers of a small factory have worked for :

1.4	2.4	0.6	5.1	4.1	4.8	10.9	3.9	11.6	0.9
11.0	8.6	4.4	0.8	5.7	2.3	1.3	7.6	9.3	14.4
5.4	6.9	8.6	3.2	10.6	6.8	7.1	8.4	2.1	11.3
0.4	4.9	8.2	10.8	15.0	9.3	2.3	0.7	3.9	6.2
2.2	5.7	13.8	10.1	0.7	3.2	4.6	9.8	3.9	2.7

Construct a frequency distribution starting from 0 and under 2.0 and having equal width in each class.

Solution :

Class Intervals	Tally Marks	Frequencies
0 and under 2	𝍸 III	8
2 and under 4	𝍸 𝍸 I	11
4 and under 6	𝍸 IIII	9
6 and under 8	𝍸	5
8 and under 10	𝍸 II	7
10 and under 12	𝍸 II	7
12 and under 14	I	1
14 and under 16	II	2
	Total	**50**

The comparison becomes difficult and at times impossible when the total numbers of items are large and highly different one distribution to other. Under these circumstances percentage frequency distribution facilitates easy comparability. In percentage frequency table, we have to convert the actual frequencies into percentages. The percentages are calculated by using the formula given below :

$$\text{Frequency percentage} = \frac{\text{Actual Frequency}}{\text{Total Frequency}} \times 100$$

It is also called relative frequency table
An example is given below to construct a percentage frequency table.

Marks	No. of students	Frequency percentage
0–10	3	6
10–20	8	16
20–30	12	24
30–40	17	34
40–50	6	12
50–60	4	8
Total	**50**	**100**

3.7 CUMULATIVE FREQUENCY DISTRIBUTION (CFD)

At this stage, we may introduce another concept relating to frequency distribution. This is known as cumulative frequency distribution or simply cumulative distribution. Table gives such a distribution along with original distribution, which is noncumulative.

Cumulative Frequency Distribution			
Marks obtained	**Number of Students**	**Marks obtained**	**Cumulative Frequency**
1	10	Not more than 1	10
2	30	Not more than 2	40
3	35	Not more than 3	75
4	28	Not more than 4	103
5	39	Not more than 5	142
6	20	Not more than 6	162
7	20	Not more than 7	182
8	12	Not more than 8	194
9	6	Not more than 9	200
10	0	Not more than 10	200
Total	**200**		

It may be noted that instead of 'not more than' we could have used the words 'less than'. Such a cumulative frequency table is helpful for knowing the number of students who have scored a certain level of marks. Suppose we want to know the number of students who have scored up to 4 marks, the answer is obvious 103, as shown in the above table. Suppose we want to know the number of students who have scored 60 percent and above marks. Here, from the total number of students, 200, we have to subtract 142, that is, the number of students scoring up to 50 percent marks. This gives us the number of students scoring 60 percent and above marks as 58.

Let us take another example. Suppose we have a grouped frequency distribution as follows:

Class-Interval	0–10	10–20	20–30	20–40	40–50
Frequency	7	10	18	9	6

We can transform this distribution into a cumulative frequency distribution as given below:

Class-Interval	Cumulative Frequency
Less than 10	7
Less than 20	17
Less than 30	35
Less than 40	44
Less than 50	50

The cumulative frequency can be converted into percentage as is given in table.

Class-Interval	Cumulative Frequency
Less than 10	14
Less than 20	34
Less than 30	70
Less than 40	88
Less than 50	100

The cumulative percentage distribution can be used in finding the percent of observation falling below or above a specified value of interest. Thus from Table, we know that 70 percent of the observations are below 30; only 12 percent of the observation lie between sizes 40 and 50; and so on.

3.8 BIVARIATE FREQUENCY DISTRIBUTION (BFD)

In the previous sections, we described frequency distribution involving one variable only. Such frequency distributions are called univariate frequency distribution. In many situations simultaneous study of two variables become necessary. ***For example***, we want to classify data relating to the weights and height of a group of individuals, income and expenditure of a group of individuals, age of husbands and wives. The data so classified on the basis of two variables give rise to the so called bivariate frequency distribution and it can be summarized in the form of a table is called bivariate (two-way) frequency table. While preparing a bivariate frequency distribution, the values of each variable are grouped into

Tablc 3.1 Format of Bivariate Frequency table

<table>
<tr><td colspan="2" rowspan="2">X-series
Y-series</td><td>Class-Intervals</td><td rowspan="2">Marginal frequency of Y</td></tr>
<tr><td>Mid-Values</td></tr>
<tr><td>Class-intervals</td><td>Mid Values</td><td></td><td>f_Y</td></tr>
<tr><td colspan="2">Marginal frequency of X</td><td>f_X</td><td>Total
$\Sigma f_X = \Sigma f_Y = N$</td></tr>
</table>

various classes (not necessarily the same for each variable). If the data corresponding to one variable, say X is grouped into m classes and the data corresponding to the other variable, say Y is grouped into n classes then the bivariate table will consist of m × n cells. By going through the different pairs of the values, (X, Y) of the variables and using tally marks we can find the frequency of each cell and thus, obtain the bivariate frequency table. The format of a bivariate frequency table is given below:

Here *f*(X, Y) is the frequency of the pair (X, Y). The frequency distribution of the values of the variables X together with their frequency total (f_X) is called the marginal distribution of X and the frequency distribution of the values of the variable Y together with the total frequencies (f_Y) is known as the marginal frequency distribution of Y. The total of the values of manual frequencies is called grand total (*N*)

EXAMPLE 3.6: The data given below relate to the height and weight of 20 persons. Construct a bivariate frequency table with class interval of height as 62–64, 64–66… and weight as 115–125, 125–135, write down the marginal distribution of X and Y.

S. No.	Height	Weight	S.No.	Height	Weight
1.	70	170	11.	70	163
2.	65	135	12.	67	139
3.	65	136	13.	63	122
4.	64	137	14.	68	134
5.	69	148	15.	67	140
6.	63	121	16.	69	132
7.	65	117	17.	65	120
8.	70	128	18.	68	148
9.	71	143	19.	67	129
10.	62	129	20.	67	152

Solution : Bivariate frequency table showing height and weight of persons.

Height (X)	62–64	64–66	66–68	68–70	70–72	Total
Weight (Y)						
115–125	II(2)	II(2)				4
125–135	I(1)		I(1)	II(2)	I(1)	5
135–145		III(3)	II(2)		I(1)	6
145–155			I(1)	II(2)		3
155–165					I(1)	1
165–175					I(1)	1
Total	3	5	4	4	4	20

The marginal distribution of height and weight are given in the following table.

Marginal Distribution of height (X)		Marginal distribution of weight (Y)	
CI	frequency	CI	frequency
62–64	3	115–125	4
64–66	5	125–135	5
66–68	4	135–145	6
68–70	4	145–155	3
70–72	4	155–165	1
		165–175	1
Total	20	Total	20

3.9 TABULATION OF DATA

Tabulation is the process of summarizing classified or grouped data in the form of a table so that it is easily understood and an investigator is quickly able to locate the desired information.

A table is a systematic arrangement of classified data in columns and rows. Thus, a statistical table makes it possible for the investigator to present a huge mass of data in a detailed and orderly form. It facilitates comparison and often reveals certain patterns in data which are otherwise not obvious. Classification and 'Tabulation', as a matter of fact, are not two distinct processes.

DO YOU KNOW?

Tabulation is a process between collection and analysis of the data.

Actually they go together. Before tabulation data are classified and then displayed under different columns and rows of a table.

Advantages of Tabulation

Statistical data arranged in a tabular form serve following objectives:

1. It simplifies complex data and the data presented are easily understood.
2. It facilitates comparison of related facts.
3. It facilitates computation of various statistical measures like averages, dispersion, correlation etc.
4. It presents facts in minimum possible space and unnecessary repetitions and explanations are avoided. Moreover, the needed information can be easily located.
5. Tabulated data are good for references and they make it easier to present the information in the form of graphs and diagrams.

Preparing a Table

The making of a compact table itself an art. This should contain all the information needed within the smallest possible space. What the purpose of tabulation is and how the tabulated information is to be used are the main points to be kept in mind while preparing for a statistical table. An ideal table should consist of the following main parts:

1. Table number
2. Title of the table
3. Captions or column headings
4. Stubs or row designation
5. Body of the table
6. Footnotes
7. Sources of data

Table Number

A table should be numbered for easy reference and identification. This number, if possible, should be written in the centre at the top of the table. Sometimes it is also written just before the title of the table.

Title

A good table should have a clearly worded, brief but unambiguous title explaining the nature of data contained in the table. It should also state arrangement of data and the period covered. The title should be placed centrally on the top of a table just below to table number (or just after table number in the same line).

Captions or column Headings

Captions in a table stand for brief and self explanatory headings of vertical columns. Captions may involve headings and sub-headings as well. The unit of data contained should also be given for each column. Usually, a relatively less important and shorter classification should be tabulated in the columns.

Stubs or Row Designations

Stubs stands for brief and self explanatory headings of horizontal rows. Normally, a relatively more important classification is given in rows. Also a variable with a large number of classes is usually represented in rows. ***For example***, rows may stand for score of classes and columns for data related to sex of students. In the process, there will be many rows for scores classes but only two columns for male and female students.

A model structure of a table is given below

Table 3.2

Table number Title of the Table

<table>
<tr><td rowspan="2">Sub Heading</td><td>Caption Headings</td><td rowspan="2">Total</td></tr>
<tr><td>Caption Sub-headings</td></tr>
<tr><td>Stub Sub-headings</td><td>Body</td><td></td></tr>
<tr><td>Total</td><td></td><td></td></tr>
</table>

Body

The body of the table contains the numerical information of frequency of observations in the different cells. This arrangement of data is according to the description of captions and stubs.

Footnotes

Footnotes are given at the foot of the table for explanation of any fact or information included in the table which needs some explanation. Thus, they are meant for explaining or providing further details about the data that have not been covered in title, captions and stubs.

Sources of Data

Lastly one should also mention the source of information from which data are taken. This may preferably include the name of the author, volume, page and the year of publication. This should also state whether the datá contained in the table is of 'primary or secondary' nature.

Requirements of a Good Table

A good statistical table is not merely a careless grouping of columns and rows but should be such that it summarizes the total information in an easily accessible form in minimum possible space. Thus while preparing a table, one must have a clear idea of the information to be presented, the facts to be compared and the points to be stressed.

Though, there is no hard and fast rule for forming a table yet a few general points should be kept in mind:

1. A table should be formed in keeping with the objects of statistical enquiry.
2. A table should be carefully prepared so that it is easily understandable.
3. A table should be formed so as to suit the size of the paper. But such an adjustment should not be at the cost of legibility.
4. If the figures in the table are large, they should be suitably rounded or approximated. The method of approximation and units of measurements too should be specified.
   Rows and columns in a table should be numbered and certain figures to be stressed may be put in 'box' or 'circle' or in bold letters.
6. The arrangements of rows and columns should be in a logical and systematic order. This arrangement may be alphabetical, chronological or according to size.
7. The rows and columns are separated by single, double or thick lines to represent various classes and sub-classes used. The corresponding proportions or percentages should be given in adjoining rows and columns to enable comparison.
   A vertical expansion of the table is generally more convenient than the horizontal one.
8. The averages or totals of different rows should be given at the right of the table and that of columns at the bottom of the table. Totals for every sub-class too should be mentioned.
9. In case it is not possible to accommodate all the information in a single table, it is better to have two or more related tables.

3.9.1 Type of Tables

Tables can be classified according to their purpose, stage of enquiry, nature of data or number of characteristics used. On the basis of the number of characteristics, tables may be classified as follows:

1. Simple or one-way frequency table
2. Two way table
3. Manifold table

1. Simple or One-Way Table

A simple or one-way table is the simplest table which contains data of one characteristic only. A simple table is easy to construct and simple to follow. ***For example***, the blank table given below may be used to show the number of adults in different occupations in a locality.

The number of adults in different occupations in a locality

Occupations	No. of Adults
Total	

2. Two-Way Table

A table, which contains data on two characteristics, is called a two-way table. In such case, therefore, either stub or caption is divided into two co-ordinate parts. In the given table, as an example the caption may be further divided in respect of 'sex'. This subdivision is shown in two-way table, which now contains two characteristics namely, occupation and sex.

The number of adults in a locality in respect of occupation and sex

Occupations	No. of Adults		Total
	Male	Female	
Total			

Manifold Table

Thus, more and more complex tables can be formed by including other characteristics. ***For example***, we may further classify the caption sub-headings in the above table in respect of "marital status", "religion" and "socio-economic status" etc. A table, which has more than two characteristics of data, is considered as a manifold table. For instance, table shown below shows three characteristics namely, occupation, sex and marital status.

Occupations	No. of Adults						Total
	Male			Female			
	M	U	Total	M	U	Total	
Total							

M Stands for Married and U stands for unmarried.

Manifold tables, though complex are good in practice as these enable full information to be incorporated and facilitate analysis of all related facts. Still, as a normal practice, not more than four characteristics should be represented in one table to avoid confusion. Other related tables may be formed to show the remaining characteristics.

Rules of Tabulation

According to ***Bowley***, "In collection and tabulation common sense is the chief requisite and experiences of the chief teacher."

The following are the rules for proper tabulation:

(i) The size of table should suit the size of the paper.

(ii) Captions and stubs should be self explanatory and arranged in a systematic manner.
(iii) Unit of measurements (if any) for each stub and caption should be clearly indicated.
(iv) The table should be precise and easy to understand.
(v) If data is quite large then a number of tables can be prepared for that. In a congested table there is always a chance of committing mistake.
(vi) Rows totals should be shown on extreme right of the table and the column total should be written in the row at the bottom of the table.
(vii) Important figures should be made prominent by placing different signs upon them.
(viii) Miscellaneous column should be provided in the table to represent surplus data (if any).
(ix) There should be proper title, footnote, note etc. in the table.
(x) Percentages and ratios should be clearly shown in the table.

EXAMPLE 3.7: In a sample study about coffee habit in two towns, the following information was received:

Town A : Females were 40%; total coffee drinkers were 45% and male non-coffee drinkers were 20%.

Town B: Males were 55%, male non-coffee drinkers were 30% and female coffee drinkers were 15%.

Represent the above data in a tabular form.

Solution: Table showing the coffee drinking habit of town A and B (In Percentage)

Attribute	Town A			Town B		
	Male	Female	Total	Male	Female	Total
Coffee drinkers	40	5	45	25	15	40
Non-coffee drinkers	20	35	55	30	30	60
Total	**60**	**40**	**100**	**55**	**45**	**100**

Town A: Females = 40%, Males = 60%, Male non-coffee drinkers = 20%, Male coffee drinkers = 60 – 20 = 40%.

Total coffee drinkers = 45%.

∴ Female coffee drinkers = 5%.

LIST OF FORMULAE

1. Range = Largest value – Smallest value
   or R = L – S

2. $$\text{Class Mid-point} = \frac{\text{Lower limit of the class} + \text{Upper limit of the class}}{2}$$

3. Sturges' formula for number of class intervals
   $$K = 1 + 3.222 \log_{10}N$$

4. $$\text{Size of class interval} = C = \frac{\text{Range}}{\text{Numbr of class intervals}} = \frac{\text{Range}}{1 + 3.322 \log_{10}N}$$

   where, Range = Largest value – Smallest value in the distribution

5. Width of class interval = $\dfrac{\text{Highest value} - \text{Lowest value}}{\text{Number of class grouping}}$

6. Relative frequency = $\dfrac{\text{Frequency}}{\text{Total number of observations}}$

7. Frequency percentage = $\dfrac{\text{Actual frequency}}{\text{Total frequency}} \times 100$

SELF PRACTICE EXERCISES

I. CHOOSE THE BEST ANSWER

1. When the collected data is grouped with reference to time, we have:
   (a) Quantitative classification (b) Qualitative classification
   (c) Geographical Classification (d) Chronological classification
2. Most quantitative classifications are:
   (a) Chronological (b) Geographical
   (c) Frequency Distribution (d) None of these
3. Caption stands for:
   (a) A numerical information (b) The column headings
   (c) The row headings (d) The table headings
4. A simple table contains data on:
   (a) Two characteristics (b) Several characteristics
   (c) One characteristic (d) Three characteristics
5. The headings of the rows given in the first column of a table are called:
   (a) Stubs (b) Captions
   (c) Titles (d) Reference notes
6. In an exclusive class interval:
   (a) the upper class limit is exclusive.
   (b) the lower class limit is exclusive.
   (c) the lower and upper class limits are exclusive.
   (d) none of the above.
7. If the lower and upper limits of a class are 10 and 40 respectively, the mid points of the class is:
   (a) 15.0 (b) 12.5
   (c) 25.0 (d) 30.0
8. Class intervals of the type 30-39, 40-49, 50-59 represents:
   (a) inclusive type (b) exclusive type
   (c) open-end type (d) none
9. The class interval of the continuous grouped data is:
   (a) 9 (b) 10
   (c) 14.5 (d) 4.5
10. Raw data means:
    (a) primary data (b) secondary data
    (c) data collected for investigation (d) Well classified data.

II. FILL IN THE BLANKS

1. Geographical classification means, classification of data according to ....
2. The data recorded according to standard of education like illiterate, primary, secondary, graduate, technical etc, will be known as .... classification.
3. An arrangement of data into rows and columns is known as ....
4. Tabulation follows ....
5. In a manifold table we have data on ....
6. H.A.Sturges formula for finding number of classes is ....
7. If the mid-value of a class interval is 20 and the difference between two consecutive midvalues is 10 the class limits are .... and ....
8. The difference between the upper and lower limit of class is called ....
9. The average of the upper and lower limits of a class is known as ....
10. Number of observations falling within a particular class interval is called .... of that class.

III. SHORT ANSWER TYPE QUESTIONS

1. Distinguish between classification and tabulation of data.
2. Define classification.
3. What are the main objects of classification?
4. Write a detail note on the types of classification.
5. Define tabulation.
6. Give the advantages of tabulation.
7. What are the main parts of an ideal table? Explain.
8. What are the essential characteristics of a good table?
9. Define one-way and two-way table.
10. Explain manifold table with example.
11. What is a frequency distribution?
12. What is an array?
13. What is discrete and continuous frequency distribution?
14. Distinguish between with suitable example.
    "Continuous and discrete frequency
    "Exclusive and Inclusive class interval
    "Less than and more than frequency table
    "Simple and Bivariate frequency table.

IV. LONG ANSWER TYPE QUESTIONS

1. Explain the role of tabulation in presenting business data, and discuss briefly the different methods of presentation.
2. What are the chief functions of tabulation? What precautions would you take in tabulating statistical data?
3. What are the objections to unequal class-intervals and to open classes? State the conditions under which the use of unequal class-intervals and open classes is desirable and necessary.

4. What do you understand by classification and tabulation? Discuss their importance.
5. What are the considerations in deciding class limits, the number of class-intervals, the magnitude of class intervals and mid-points of class intervals.
6. Distinguish between frequency distribution and cumulative frequency distribution.
7. Draw the cumulative frequency table for the following data:

Marks	0–4	4–8	8–12	12–16	16–20
No. of students	4	6	10	8	4

8. What is classification? Explain the method of classification by class-intervals in terms of (i) number of classes, (ii) length of a class intervals and (iii) class limits.
9. The following data gives the number of children in 50 families. Construct a discrete frequency table.

4	2	0	2	3	2	2	1	0	2
3	5	1	1	4	2	1	3	4	2
6	1	2	2	2	1	3	4	2	0
1	3	4	1	0	1	2	2	2	5
2	4	3	0	1	3	6	1	0	1

10. In a survey, it was found that 64 families bought milk in the following quantities in a particular month. Quantity of milk (in litres) bought by 64 Families in a month. Construct a continuous frequency distribution making classes of 5–9, 10–14 and so on.

19	16	22	9	22	12	39	19
14	23	6	24	16	18	7	17
20	25	28	18	10	24	20	21
10	7	18	28	24	20	14	23
25	34	22	5	33	23	26	29
13	36	11	26	11	37	30	13
8	15	22	21	32	21	31	17
16	23	12	9	15	27	17	21

ANSWERS

I. CHOOSE THE BEST ANSWER

1. (d) 2. (c) 3. (b) 4. (c) 5. (a) 6. (a) 7. (c) 8. (a) 9. (b) 10. (a)

II. FILL IN THE BLANKS

1. Place
2. Qualitative
3. Tabulation
4. Classification
5. More than two characteristics
6. $k = 1 + 3.322 \log_{10}N$
7. 15 and 25
8. width or size of class
9. Mid-value
10. Frequency.

CHAPTER 4

Presentation of Data: Diagrammatic

4.1 INTRODUCTION

In the previous chapter, we have discussed the techniques of classification and tabulation that help in summarising the collected data and presenting them in a systematic manner. However, these forms of presentation do not always prove to be interesting to the common man. One of the most convincing and appealing ways in which statistical results may be presented is through diagrams and graphs. Just one diagram is enough to represent a given data more effectively than thousand words.

Moreover even a layman who has nothing to do with numbers can also understands diagrams. Evidence of this can be found in newspapers, magazines, journals, advertisement, etc.

An attempt is made in this chapter to illustrate some of the major types of ***diagrams*** and in the next chapter, we will be discussed ***graphs*** frequently used in presenting statistical data.

Significance of Diagrams and Graphs

Diagrams and graphs are extremely useful because of the following reasons:

1. They are attractive and impressive.
2. They make data simple and intelligible.
3. They make comparison possible
4. They save time and labour.
5. They have universal utility.
6. They give more information.
7. They have a great memorizing effect.

4.2 DIAGRAMS

A diagram is a visual form for presentation of statistical data, highlighting their basic facts and relationship. If we draw diagrams on the basis of the data collected they will easily be understood and appreciated by all. It is readily intelligible and save a considerable amount of time and energy.

One of the most convincing and appealing ways in which data may be presented is through diagrams. Evidence of this can be found in the financial pages of newspapers, journals, advertisements, etc.

Pictorial presentation helps in quick understanding of the data. As the number and magnitude of figures increases, they become more confusing and their analysis tends to be more strenuous. A picture is said to be worth 10,000 words, i.e., through pictorial presentation data can be presented in an interesting form. Not only this, diagrams have greater memorizing effect as the impressions created by them last much longer than those created by the figures.

4.2.1 Characteristics of Diagrams

(i) Diagrams are meant only to give a pictorial representation of the quantitative data with a view to make them readily intelligible. Diagrams are not meant for anything beyond it. They prove or disprove a particular fact. They are not suitable for further analysis of data which can be done only from figures. If diagrams are properly drawn they can no doubt give proper emphasis on the different characteristics of the quantitative data. They are capable of focussing attention on the main findings of the enquiry in question. Beyond this, however, they do nothing.

(ii) Data should be homogeneous: Another point to be noted in this connection is that the person drawing the diagrams should make himself sure of figures cannot be suitably represented by means of diagrams. Statistical data which are intended to be diagrammatically represented should be homogeneous and comparable.

(iii) Diagrams are not substitutes for figures. Another very important characteristic of diagrams is that though they represent figures yet the size of a bar or a square or a circle or a picture representing a set of figures, changes with changes in the scale with which they have been drawn. If the same data are represented on two different scales their size would differ and sometimes they may create very misleading impression on the minds of the people.

4.2.2 Rules for Constructing Diagrams

The construction of diagrams is an art, which can be acquired through practice. However, observance of some general guidelines can help in making them more attractive and effective. The diagrammatic presentation of statistical facts will be advantageous provided the following rules are observed in drawing diagrams.

1. A diagram should be neatly drawn and attractive.
2. The measurements of geometrical figures used in diagram should be accurate and proportional.
3. The size of the diagrams should match the size of the paper.
4. Every diagram must have a suitable but short heading.
5. The scale should be mentioned in the diagram.
6. Diagrams should be neatly as well as accurately drawn with the help of drawing instruments.
7. Index must be given for identification so that the reader can easily make out the meaning of the diagram.
8. Footnote must be given at the bottom of the diagram.
9. Economy in cost and energy should be exercised in drawing diagram.

4.2.3 Limitations of Diagrams

- Diagrams are useful only in those situations where the object is to explain the significance of the collected data to general public. For exhaustive investigations and further analysis of the data diagrams are absolutely unsuitable.

- Diagrams should be constructed for these data only which are comparable i.e. related to the same phenomenon and capable of being measured in the same units.
- A single diagram has no value. Comparison can only be made when there are more than one diagram.
- A wrong selection of diagram can lead to fallacious conclusions.

4.3 TYPES OF DIAGRAMS

In practice, a very large variety of diagrams are in use and new ones are constantly being added. For the sake of convenience and simplicity, they may be divided under the following heads:

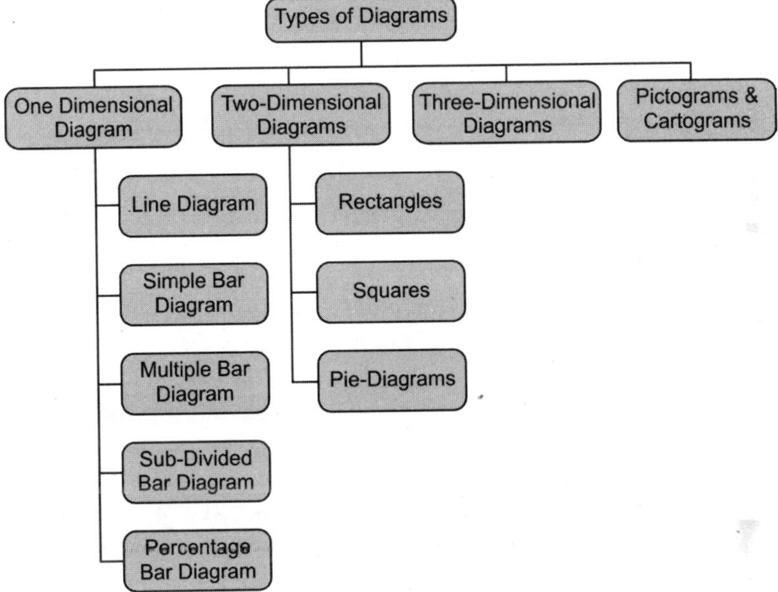

Fig. 4.1: Types of Diagrams

4.4 ONE-DIMENSIONAL DIAGRAMS

In such diagrams, only one-dimensional measurement, i.e height is used and the width is not considered. These diagrams are in the form of bar or line charts and can be classified as

1. Line Diagram
2. Simple Bar Diagram
3. Multiple Bar Diagram
4. Sub-divided Bar Diagram
5. Percentage Bar Diagram

1. Line Diagram

Line diagram is used in case where there are many items to be shown and there is not much difference in their values. Such diagram is prepared by drawing a vertical line for each item according to the scale. The distance between lines is kept uniform. Line diagram makes comparison easy, but it is less attractive.

EXAMPLE 4.1: Show the following data by a line chart:

No. of Children	1	2	3	4	5
Frequency	14	9	6	4	2

Solution:

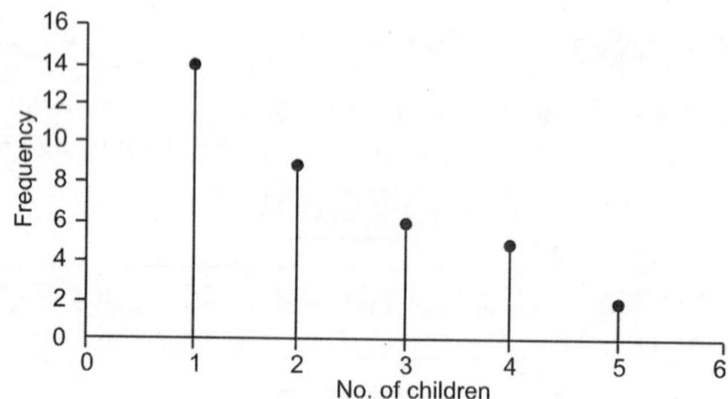

Fig. 4.2: Line Diagram

2. Simple Bar Diagram

Simple bar diagram can be drawn either on ***horizontal*** or ***vertical*** base, but bars on horizontal base more common. Bars must be of uniform width and intervening space between bars must be equal. While constructing a simple bar diagram, the scale is determined on the basis of the highest value in the series.

To make the diagram attractive, the bars can be coloured. Bar diagram are used in business and economics. However, an important limitation of such diagrams is that they can present only one classification or one category of data.

For example, while presenting the population for the last five decades, one can only depict the total population in the simple bar diagrams, and not its sex-wise distribution.

EXAMPLE 4.2: Represent the following data by a bar diagram.

Year	1991	1992	1993	1994	1995
Sugar production (in tonnes)	45	40	42	55	50

Solution:

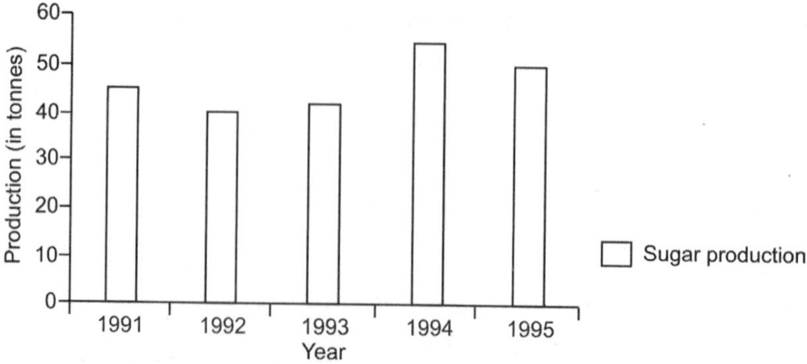

Fig. 4.3: Simple Bar Diagram

Unlike the line diagram, a simple bar diagram shows a width or column. It is used to represent only one variable. Suppose we have the production of an item X for three years. This we can show as in the following Figure 4.4:

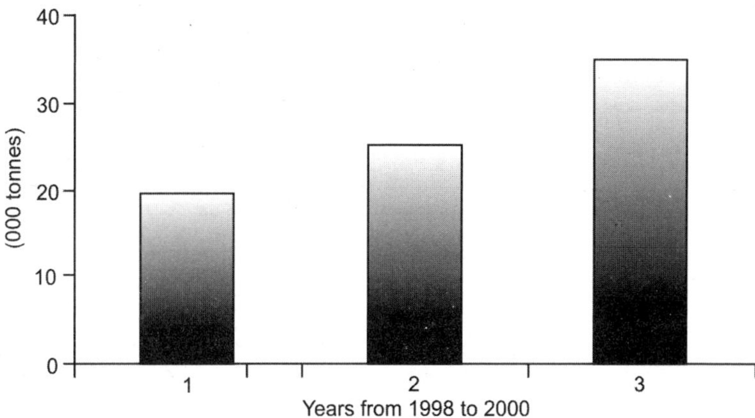

Fig. 4.4 : Simple Vertically Bar Diagram

NOTE: It will be seen that each bar has an equal width but unequal length. The length indicates the magnitude of production.

From such a diagram, it becomes obvious that there is an increase in trend in the production of X commodity. In view of its simplicity and ease of drawing it, a bar diagram is very popular in practice. All the same, it suffers from a major limitation. Such a diagram can display only one classification or one category of data.

It may be noted that the simple bars shown in figure are drawn vertically. They are, therefore, known as vertical bars. But the same bars can be drawn horizontally as shown in figure below.

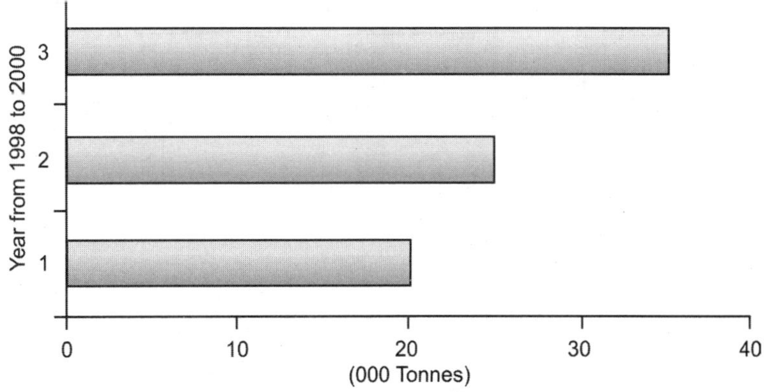

Fig. 4.5: Horizontal Simple Bar Diagram

3. Multiple Bar Diagram

Multiple bar diagram is used for comparing two or more sets of statistical data. Bars are constructed side by side to represent the set of values for comparison. In order to distinguish bars, they may be either differently coloured or there should be different types of crossings or dotting, etc. An index is also prepared to identify the meaning of different colours or dotting.

DO YOU KNOW?

When two or more interrelated series of data are depicted by a bar diagram, then such a diagram is known as a multiple-bar diagram.

It should be noted that multiple bar diagrams are particularly suitable where some comparison is involved. ***For example***, we may represent admission data pertaining to, say, an MBA programme for boys and girls or performance of boys and girls in a particular examination. Similarly, the number of skilled, semi-skilled and unskilled workers in a factory for a couple of years can be represented well by means of a multiple-bar diagram.

EXAMPLE 4.3: Draw a multiple bar diagram for the following data.

Year	Profit before tax (in lakhs of rupees)	Profit after tax (in lakhs of rupees)
1998	195	80
1999	200	87
2000	165	45
2001	140	32

Solution:

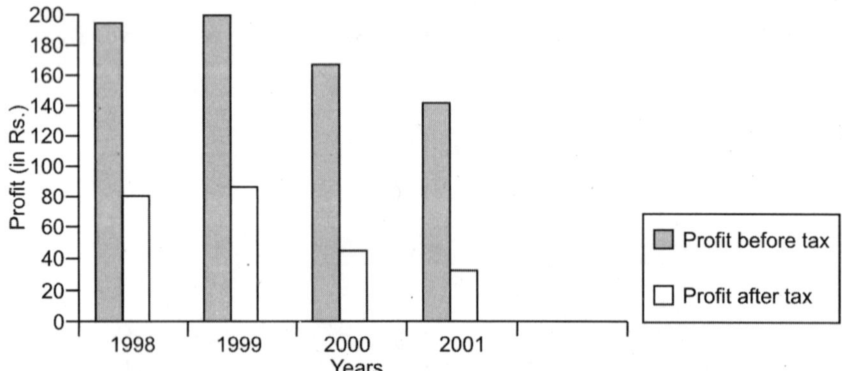

Fig. 4.6: Multiple Bar Diagram

EXAMPLE 4.4: Suppose we have export and import figures for a few years. We can display by two bars close to each other, one representing exports while the other representing imports figure shows such a diagram based on hypothetical data.

Solution :

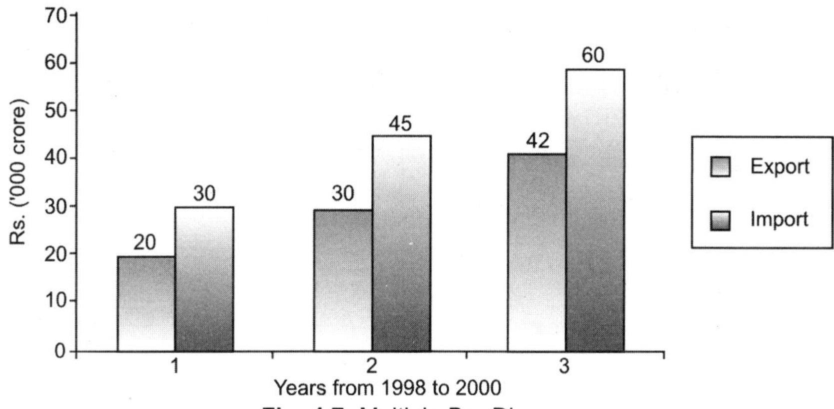

Fig. 4.7: Multiple Bar Diagram

4. Sub-divided Bar Diagram

In a sub-divided bar diagram, the bar is sub-divided into various parts in proportion to the values given in the data and the whole bar represent the total. Such diagrams are also called ***Component Bar diagrams***. The sub divisions are distinguished by different colours or crossings or dotting.

The main defect of such a diagram is that all the parts do not have a common base to enable one to compare accurately the various components of the data.

EXAMPLE 4.5: Represent the following data by a sub-divided bar diagram.

Expenditure items	Monthly expenditure (in Rs.)	
	Family A	Family B
Food	75	95
Clothing	20	25
Education	15	10
Housing Rent	40	65
Miscellaneous	25	35

Solution:

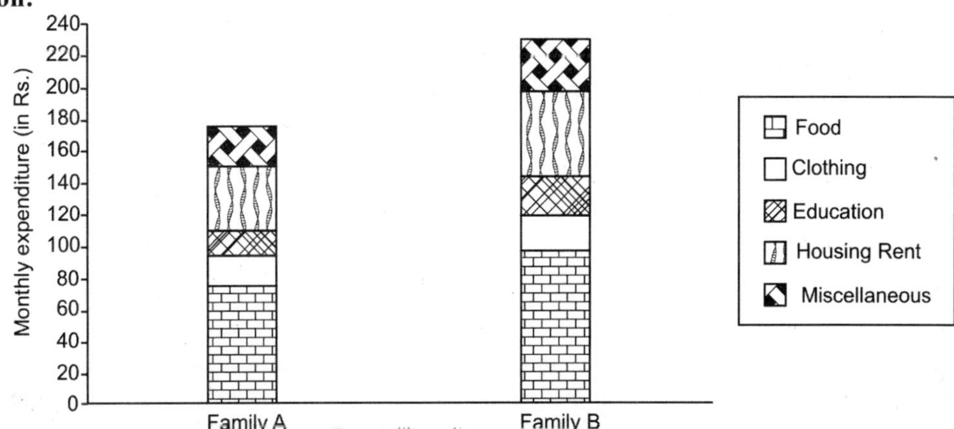

Fig. 4.8: Sub Divided Bar Diagram

Example: A bar diagram may show the composition of revenue expenditure of the Government of India. The components of this bar could be defence expenditure, interest payments, major subsidies, grants to State and Union Territories and others. Such bar diagrams are shown in Fig. 4.9 for two years.

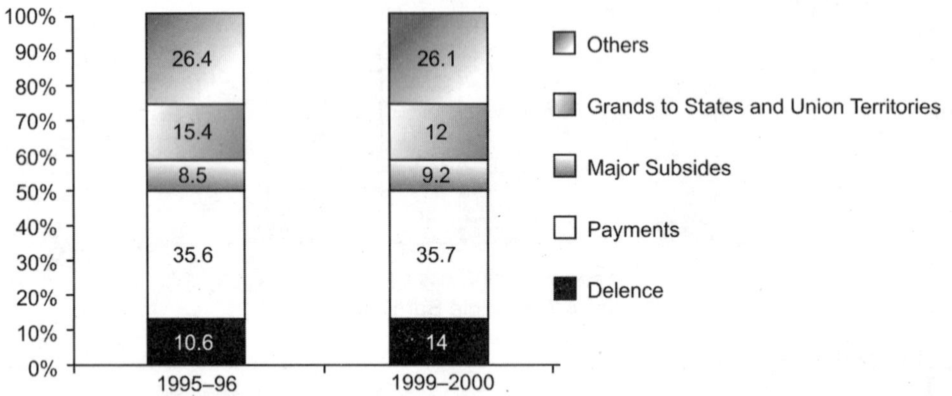

Fig. 4.9: Composition of Revenue Expenditure (Percent)

It will be seen from these bars that the order of components in each bar is the same. This is necessary for proper comparison of two or more bars. It is also to be noted that figure shows the components in percentages. These could have been shown in absolute figures as well, but in such a case the length of each bar would have been different in accordance with the total revenue expenditure of the Government in the two years. Since the bars are in terms of percentages, the length of each bar is the same indicating the total as 100 percent.

In order to distinguish the different components, different colours or shades should be used. This should be accompanied by a legend or key for identifying these components.

Another point worth noting is that such a diagram should not be used when there are too many components or subdivisions. This is because of two reasons.

- ***First,*** it may be difficult to provide so many subdivisions particularly when their magnitudes are small.
- ***Second,*** it may be difficult to understand and interpret such a diagram.

> Component bars can be very suitable mode of presenting data on the enrolment of students by the type of courses such as MBA, MCA, PGDM, M.Com, and B.Com and so on. Likewise, data on the employment of the workers in the public sector, private sector and the total can be suitably displayed by component bars.

5. Percentage Bar Diagram

This is another form of component bar diagram. Here the components are not the actual values but percentages of the whole. The main difference between the sub-divided bar diagram and percentage bar diagram is that in the former the bars are of different heights since their totals may be different whereas in the later the bars are of equal height since each bar represents 100 percent. In the case of data having sub-division, percentage bar diagram will be more appealing than sub-divided bar diagram.

EXAMPLE 4.6: Represent the following data by a percentage bar diagram.

Particular	Factory A	Factory B
Selling Price	400	650
Quantity Sold	240	365
Wages	3500	5000
Materials	2100	3500
Miscellaneous	1400	2100

Solution: Convert the given values into percentages as follows:

Particular	Factory A		Factory B	
	Rs.	%	Rs.	%
Selling Price	400	5	650	6
Quantity Sold	240	3	365	3
Wages	3500	46	5000	43
Materials	2100	28	3500	30
Miscellaneous	1400	18	2100	18
Total	7640	100	11615	100

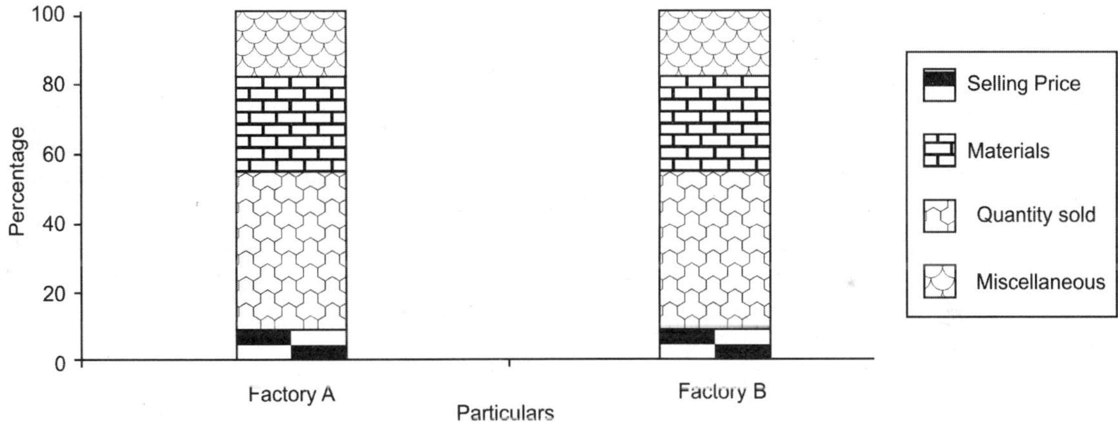

Fig. 4.10: Sub-Divided Percentage Bar Diagram

EXAMPLE 4.7: Suppose we are given the following data pertaining to the monthly expenditure of two families under some heads.

Item of Expenditure	Expenditure in Rupees	
	Family A	Family B
Food	1000	1600
Clothing	500	800
Rent	800	1000
Education	400	800
Recreation	200	500
Miscellaneous	100	300

Solution: Since these data are in absolute terms, we have to convert them into percentages. This has been done in the following table.

Calculation of Percentage Expenditure under Different Heads

Item of Expenditure	Family A		Cumulative percentage	Family B		Cumulative percentage
	Rs.	%	C%	Rs.	%	C%
Food	1000	33.3	33.3	1600	32.0	32.0
Clothing	500	16.7	50.0	800	16.0	48.0
Rent	800	26.7	76.7	1000	20.0	68.0
Education	400	13.3	90.0	800	16.0	84.0
Recreation	200	6.7	96.7	500	10.0	94.0
Miscellaneous	100	3.3	100.0	300	6.0	100.0
Total	**3000**			**5000**		

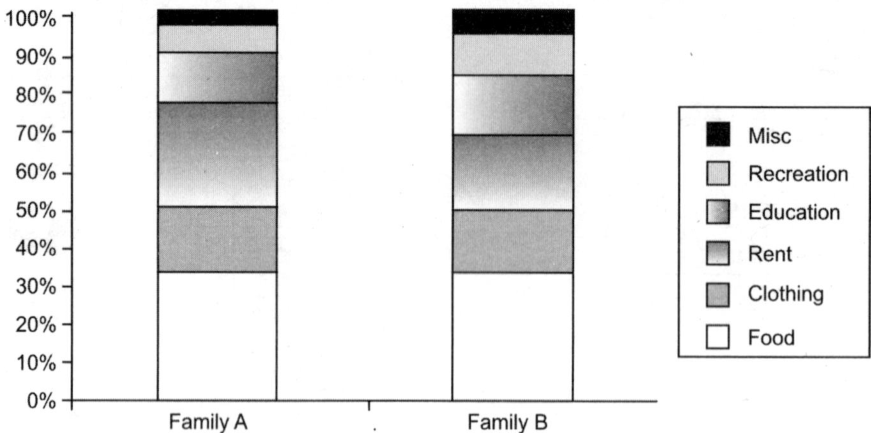

Fig. 4.11: Percentage Subdivided Bars

We may now show the percentage expenditure of the two families by percentage bars. It may be noted that we have calculated cumulative percentages, which have been plotted. Although the above diagram gives some idea of relative expenditure on various items of the two families, a rectangular diagram would be a much better means of displaying the expenditure, which will be taken up later.

> The fundamental characteristic of one dimensional diagram is that the magnitude of various characteristics is proportional to either length or width of the bars.

4.5 TWO-DIMENSIONAL DIAGRAMS

In one-dimensional diagrams, only length 9 is taken into account. But in two-dimensional diagrams the area represents the data and so the length and breadth have both to be taken into account. Such diagrams are also called area diagrams or surface diagrams. The important types of area diagrams are:

1. Rectangles
2. Squares
3. Pie-Diagrams

1. Rectangles

Rectangles are used to represent the relative magnitude of two or more values. The area of the rectangles are kept in proportion to the values. Rectangles are placed side by side for comparison. When two sets of figures are to be represented by rectangles, either of the two methods may be adopted.

We may represent the figures as they are given or may convert them to percentages and then subdivide the length into various components. Thus the percentage sub-divided rectangular diagram is more popular than sub-divided rectangular since it enables comparison to be made on a percentage basis.

EXAMPLE 4.8: Represent the following data by sub-divided percentage rectangular diagram.

Item of Expenditure	Family A (income Rs. 5000)	Family B (income Rs. 8000)
Food	2000	2500
Clothing	1000	2000
House Rent	800	1000
Fuel and lighting	400	500
Miscellaneous	800	2000
Total	**5000**	**8000**

Solution: First of all the figures of family A and family B in each item of expenditure will be converted into percentage. The calculations are shown in the following table.

Item of Expenditure	Family A	Family B
Food	$\frac{2000}{5000} \times 100 = 40$	$\frac{2500}{8000} \times 100 = 31$
Clothing	$\frac{1000}{5000} \times 100 = 20$	$\frac{2000}{8000} \times 100 = 25$
House Rent	$\frac{800}{5000} \times 100 = 16$	$\frac{1000}{8000} \times 100 = 13$
Fuel and lighting	$\frac{400}{5000} \times 100 = 8$	$\frac{500}{8000} \times 100 = 6$
Miscellaneous	$\frac{800}{5000} \times 100 = 16$	$\frac{2000}{8000} \times 100 = 25$

The percentage sub-divided bar diagram will be as follows:

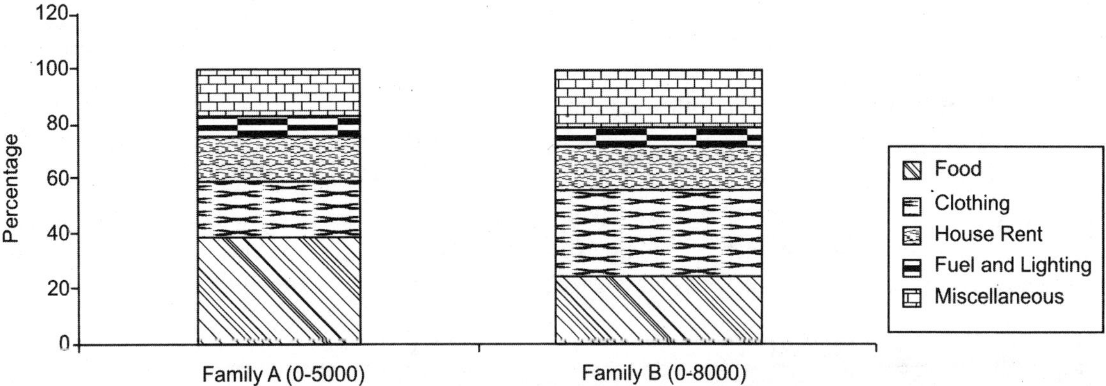

Fig. 5.12: Subdivided Percentage Rectangular Diagram

2. Squares

The rectangular method of diagrammatic presentation is difficult to use where the values of items vary widely. The method of drawing a square diagram is very simple.

In a square diagram the length and width are of the same dimension. Sometimes a square diagram is preferable to rectangle. This is because when a comparison is involved between any two phenomena but their magnitudes are widely different from each other, it is difficult to draw rectangles on the same page. One rectangle would have very wide width while the other a very small width. This apart, a meaningful comparison between the two diagrams would be quite difficult. To overcome this difficulty, square diagrams are preferred.

One has to take the square root of the values of various item that are to be shown in the diagrams and then select a suitable scale to draw the squares.

EXAMPLE 4.9: Yield of rice in Kgs. per acre of five countries are

Country	U.S.A.	Australia	U.K	Canada	India
Yield of rice in Kgs per acre	6400	1600	2500	3600	4900

Solution:

To draw the square diagram we calculate as follows:

Country	Yield	Square root	Side of the square in cm
U.S.A.	6400	80	4
Australia	1600	40	2
U.K.	2500	50	2.5
Canada	3600	60	3
India	4900	70	3.5

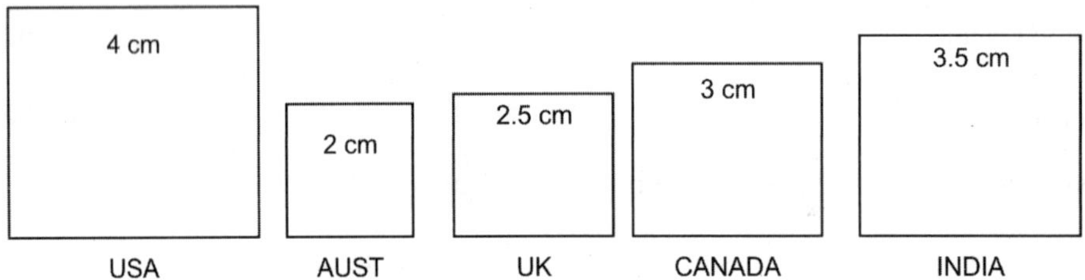

EXAMPLE 4.10: We are given the following data

Year	Production of Food (million tonnes)
1950–51	50.8
1960–61	82.0
1970–71	108.4
1980–81	129.6
1990–91	176.4

As mentioned earlier, first we have to calculate the square roots of these figures. The square roots are as follows:

Year	Production of Food (million tonnes)	Square Roots (million tonnes)
1950–51	50.8	7.12
1960–61	82.0	9.06
1970–71	108.4	10.41
1980–81	129.6	11.38
1990–91	176.4	13.28

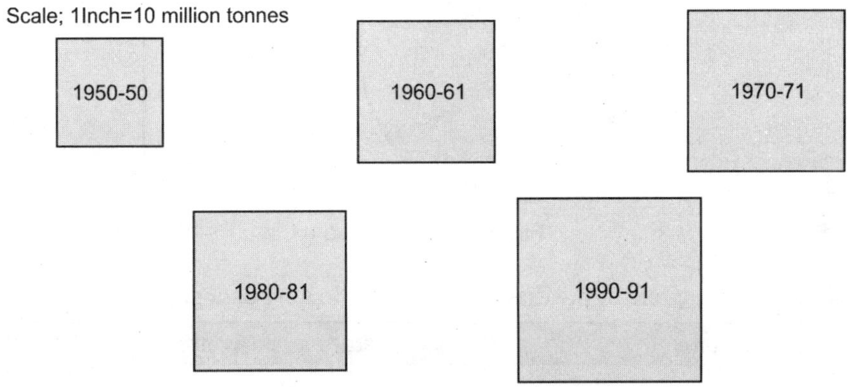

Scale; 1Inch=10 million tonnes

1950-50

1960-61

1970-71

1980-81

1990-91

Fig. 4.13: Square Diagrams

3. Pie Diagram or Circular Diagram

Another way of preparing a two-dimensional diagram is in the form of circles. In such diagrams, both the total and the component parts or sectors can be shown. The area of a circle is proportional to the square of its radius.

While making comparisons, pie diagrams should be used on a percentage basis and not on an absolute basis.

In constructing a pie diagram the first step is to prepare the data so that various components values can be transposed into corresponding degrees on the circle.

The second step is to draw a circle of appropriate size with a compass. The size of the radius depends upon the available space and other factors of presentation. The third step is to measure points on the circle and representing the size of each sector with the help of a protractor.

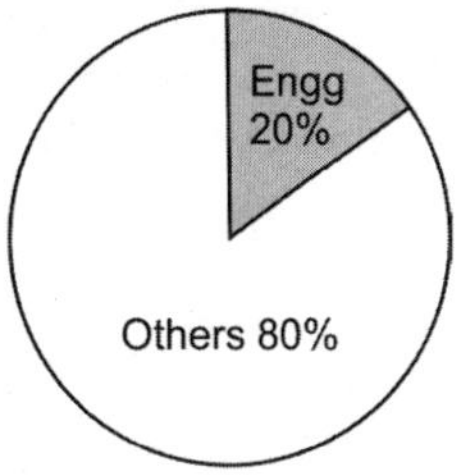

The total angle at the center is 360. ***For example***, suppose 20% of the MBA students in a management institute have engineering background, the angle at the center will be $\frac{20}{100} \times 360 = 72°$, as shown in the pie chart as follows.

Engg 20%

Others 80%

This chart is generally used when the emphasis is on visual presentation of data for easy comprehension.

EXAMPLE 4.11: Draw a Pie diagram for the following data of production of sugar in quintals of various countries.

Country	Cuba	Australia	India	Japan	Egypt
Production of Sugar (in quintals)	50	25	15	10	5

Solution: The values are expressed in terms of degree as follows :

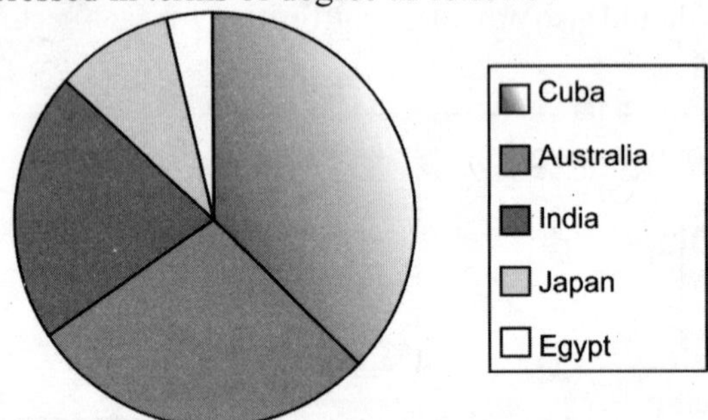

Fig. 4.14: Pie Diagram

EXAMPLE 4.12: Draw a circle or pie diagram for the following data given below:

Items	Expenditure as percent of Total
Food	50
Clothing	15
Housing	10
Fuel and Lighting	5
Education	10
Recreation	5
Miscellaneous	5
Total	100

We have first to calculate the degrees for each of the above mentioned items. These calculations are shown below :

$$\text{Food} = \frac{50}{100} \times 360 = 180°$$

$$\text{Clothing} = \frac{15}{100} \times 360 = 54°$$

$$\text{Housing} = \frac{10}{100} \times 360 = 36°$$

$$\text{Fuel and lighting} = \frac{5}{100} \times 360 = 18°$$

$$\text{Education} = \frac{10}{100} \times 360 = 36°$$

$$\text{Recreation} = \frac{5}{100} \times 360 = 18°$$

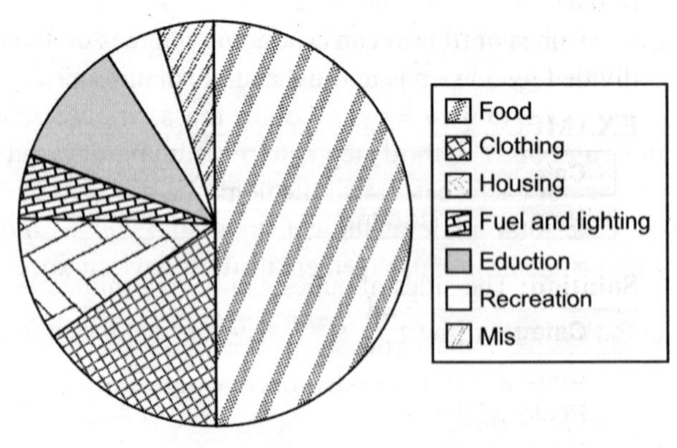

Fig. 4.15: Pie Diagram

$$\text{Miscellaneous} = \frac{5}{100} \times 360 = 18°$$

The total of all these angles will be 360°.

The pie diagram is also known as an ***angular sector diagram*** though in common usage the term pie diagram is used. It is advisable to adopt some logical arrangement, pattern or sequence while laying out the sectors of a pie chart. Usually, the largest sector is given at the top and others in a clock-wise sequence. The pie chart should also provide identification for each sector with some kind of explanatory or descriptive label.

If the space within the chart is sufficient, the labels can be placed inside the sectors, otherwise these should be shown outside the circle, using an arrow or pointing out to the concerned sector.

Limitations of Pie Diagrams

There are certain limitations of pie diagrams.

1. They are not as effective as bar diagrams for accurate reading and interpretation. This limitation becomes all the more obvious when the series are divided into a large number of components or the differences among the components are too small. When a series comprises more than five or six categories, pie chart would not be a proper choice since it would be confusing to differentiate the relative values of several small sectors having more or less the same size.
2. Although pie diagram is frequently used, it turns out to be inferior to a bar diagram whether it is simple bar or a divided bar or a multiple bar.

DO YOU KNOW?

In two dimensional diagrams the area of the diagram is proportional to the magnitude of the items.

4.6 THREE-DIMENSIONAL DIAGRAMS

Three-dimensional diagrams, also known as volume diagram, consist of cubes, cylinders, spheres, etc. In such diagrams three things, namely length, width and height have to be taken into account. Of all the figures, making of cubes is easy. Side of a cube is drawn in proportion to the cube root of the magnitude of data.

Cubes of figures can be ascertained with the help of logarithms. The logarithm of the figures can be divided by 3 and the antilog of that value will be the cube-root.

EXAMPLE 4.13: Represent the following data by volume diagram.

Category	Under graduate	Post graduate	Professionals
Number of Students	64000	27000	8000

Solution: The sides of cubes can be determined as follows :

Category	Number of students	Cube root	Side of cube
Undergradute	64000	40	4 cm
Postgraduate	27000	30	3 cm
Professional	8000	20	2 cm

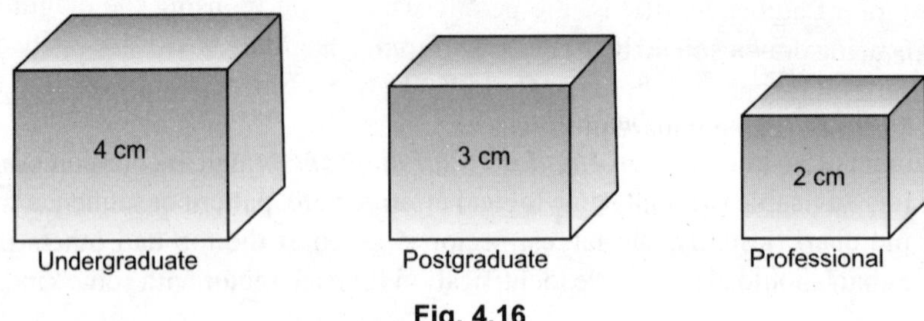

Fig. 4.16

Disadvantage of Three Dimensional Diagrams

The following are the main disadvantage of the three dimensional diagrams

- These are more difficult to construct.
- Cube roots of the figures are not easy to calculate.

4.7 PICTOGRAMS AND CARTOGRAMS

Pictograms are not abstract presentation such as lines or bars but really depict the kind of data we are dealing with. Pictures are attractive and easy to comprehend and as such this method is particularly useful in presenting statistics to the layman. When Pictograms are used, data are represented through a pictorial symbol that is carefully selected.

Cartograms or statistical maps are used to give quantitative information as a geographical basis. They are used to represent spatial distributions. The quantities on the map can be shown in many ways such as through shades or colours or dots or placing pictogram in each geographical unit.

4.8 CHOICE OF A SUITABLE DIAGRAM

The foregoing discussion shows that a variety of diagrams are available, which can be used to display statistical data. At times it may be difficult for one to select a particular type of diagram from among several types. However, there are some major guidelines that should be taken into consideration while deciding on the mode of data presentation. These guidelines are:

1. The nature of data
2. Purpose of the diagrammatic presentation
3. The type of audience or people for whose understanding the diagrammatic presentation is made.

The first consideration is the type of data to be displayed. As we have seen earlier, when there are wide variations in the data, one-dimensional diagrams may not be suitable. Instead, two diagrams seem to be more appropriate.

Apart from the nature of the data, the purpose of the diagram is also a relevant factor while deciding as to how data should be displayed. As far as the data along with the break-up in the form of several components are concerned, subdivided bar diagrams would be suitable. Circle diagrams can also be used in such cases. However, if the magnitudes of components are very small, circular diagrams would not be the right choice as the angles showing the magnitudes would be so small that it would be difficult to show them distinctly.

Finally, the type of audience, that is, the people who would be using the diagram or for whose understanding it is being drawn should be considered. Simple diagrams, which are easily understandable, should be used for the layman. Psychologists hold the view that most people are able to compare bar heights with greater ease than compare pie slices.

As all these considerations are very relevant, one should consider the pros and cons of different modes of display in each case before making a final choice. Above all, one should be aware of a major limitation of diagrams. While they can be useful up to a certain point, they cannot take the place of tabular form of data presentation.

SELF PRACTICE EXERCISES

I. CHOOSE THE BEST ANSWER

1. Which of the following is one dimensional diagram.
   (a) Bar diagram (b) Pie diagram
   (c) Cylinder (d) Histogram
2. Percentage bar diagram has
   (a) Data expressed in percentages (b) Equal width
   (c) Equal interval (d) Equal width and equal interval
3. Two-dimensional diagrams are:
   (a) Linear diagrams (b) Volume diagrams
   (c) Area diagrams (d) None of the above
4. Square is a
   (a) Simple bar diagrams (b) Two-dimensional diagrams
   (c) Volume diagrams (d) None of the above
5. Classification is done:
   (a) Prior to tabulation (b) After tabulation
   (c) No restriction (d) Classification implies tabluation

II. FILL IN THE BLANKS

1. Sub-divided bar diagram are also called .... diagram.
2. In rectangular diagram, comparison is based on .... of the rectangles.
3. Squares are .... dimensional diagrams.
4. Bar diagram are .... dimensional diagrams.
5. Pie-diagram is a .... dimensional diagram.
6. Square-diagram is a .... dimensional diagram.
7. Cartograms are used to give quantitative information on a ....
8. Representation of data by pictures is called ....
9. Multiple bar diagram is .... dimensional diagram.
10. Sub-divided bar diagrams are also called .... bar diagrams.

III. SHORT ANSWER TYPE QUESTIONS

1. What are the advantages of diagrammatic presentation of data?

2. What are the limitations of diagrammatic presentation of data?
3. What is rectangle?
4. What is pictogram?
5. What is pie diagram? Explain the limitations of pie diagrams.

IV. LONG ANSWER TYPE QUESTIONS

1. Discuss the merit and demerits of diagrammatic representation of statistical data.
2. Explain any three important methods used for diagrammatic representation of data.
3. Diagrams do not add anything to the meaning of statistics but when drawn and studied intelligently, they bring to view the salient characteristics of graphs and series". Discuss this statement describing briefly the various types of diagrams.
4. Discuss briefly different types of diagrams generally used to represent numerical data and point out the relative merits and demerits of diagrammatic representation compared to other methods used for the purpose.
5. "Diagrams help us visualize the whole meaning of a numerical complex at a single glance." Comment.
6. State the advantages of a diagrammatic presentation of statistical data. Describe briefly, with suitable examples, a single bar diagram, a multiple bar diagram and a component bar diagram.
7. What are the different types of diagrams used in Statistics? Write a short note on the utility of diagrams in business.
8. What factors would you take into consideration while deciding the type of diagram to be used for a given data set?
9. Name the different types of diagrams commonly used and mention the situations where the use of each type of diagram would be appropriate.
10. "Charts are more effective in attracting attention than are any of the other methods of presenting data." Do you agree? Give reasons for your answer.
11. What are the different types of bar diagrams? Discuss their relative merits and demerits.
12. Point out the usefulness of diagrammatic representation of facts and explain the construction of any one of the different types of diagrams you know.
13. Distinguish between Pie diagram and bar diagrams.
14. Prepare a discrete series from the following data:

62	50	57	58	51	53	62	64	60	61
60	51	64	55	55	52	60	65	58	60
59	52	63	56	56	58	64	63	62	60
58	54	62	54	54	60	65	60	62	59
65	56	63	52	53	62	53	61	61	59

15. If class mid-points in a frequency distribution of a group of persons are 25, 32, 39, 46, 53, 60, 67, 74 and 81, find (a) size of the class interval, and (b) the class boundaries.
16. Change the following into continuous frequency distribution. Also find the less than and more than cumulative frequencies:

Marks (Mid-values)	5	15	25	35	45	55
No. of students	8	12	15	9	4	2

17. Prepare a blank table to show the distribution of students in a college according to marks, sex and two sections.
18. In a sample study about coffee drinking habits in two towns the following information was recorded:
    Town A: Females were 40%. total coffee drinkers were 45% and male non-coffee drinkers were 20%.
    Town B: Male were 55%, male non-coffee drinkers were 30% and female coffee drinkers were 15%.
    Represent the data in a tabular form.
19. The following table shows the marital status of males and females (18 years and older) in a metropolitan city. Draw a pie chart separately for males and females to display

Marital Status	Male (percent of total)	Female (percent of total)
Single	21	16
Married	65	73
Widowed	9	4
Divorced	5	7

20. The following data relate to monthly income and expenditure under different heads for lies. Show these data by a suitable diagram.

Item of Expenditure	Family A (monthly income Rs 12,000)	Family B (monthly income Rs 16,000)
Food	4,000	4,800
Clothing	2,500	3,000
Rent	3,000	4,000
Education	1,500	2,500
Fuel and lighting	400	800
Others	600	900

21. Draw a pie chart for comparing the various costs (Rs in lakh) of the house building activities in two periods, 1984 and 1989.

Item	1984	1989
Land cost	0.75	1.00
Material cost	1.00	1.75
Labour cost	0.60	1.00
Fixtures & furnitures	0.40	0.75
Miscellaneous	0.25	0.50

22. The following data pertain to agricultural production and industrial production, showing age change over previous year.

Year	Agricultural Production	Industrial Production
1996–97	9.3	5.6
1997–98	– 6.1	6.6
1998–99	7.4	4.0
1999 2000	– 2.2	6.2

Show these data by bar diagrams separately for agricultural and industrial production.

23. The data given below pertain to R&D expenditure by public, private and industrial sectors for three years. You are required to draw a suitable diagram to show these data. (You may avoid the fractions by rounding them off.)

Sector	R&D Expenditure (Rs crore)		
	1994–95	1995–96	1996–97
Public	414.61	427.58	536.05
Private	1,318.8	71,627.07	1,796.96
Industry	1,733.33	2,054.65	2,333.01

24. A company having a supermarket chain conducted a survey of its customer's opinion. Respondents were asked to express their opinion regarding the quality of the product sold by the company. The results showed that of the 400 car owners who responded, 220 rated the quality of products 'good', 120 rated it 'fair' and the remaining 'poor'. For non-car owners, the numbers were 147, 108 and 95 respectively.

Tabulate this information adding suitable derived statistics, and draw a diagram or diagrams to show the results.

25. The following information shows the annual growth rate in major sectors of industry.

Year	Mining	Manufacturing	Electricity	General
1996–97	–2.0	6.7	4.0	5.6
1997–98	5.9	6.7	6.6	6.6
1998–99	–1.7	4.3	6.5	4.0

Depict the above information by means of a suitable diagram.

26. The following table shows the sectoral growth rates in GDP (at factor cost) for the two years 1998–99 and 1999–2000.

Sector(s)	Years (Percentage change over the previous year)	
	1998–99	1999–2000
Agriculture & allied	7.2	0.8
Industry	4.0	6.9
Services	8.3	8.2
Total GDP	6.8	5.9

Use the bar charts to show these data.

ANSWERS

I. CHOOSE THE BEST ANSWER

1. (a) 2. (a) 3. (c) 4. (b) 5. (a)

II. FILL IN THE BLANKS

1. Component bar 2. Area 3. Two 4. one 5. two 6. two
7. geographical basis 8. pictogram 9. one 10. component.

CHAPTER 5

Presentation of Data: Graphic

5.1 INTRODUCTION

Diagram discussed in the last chapter are generally used for the purpose of publicity and propaganda. From the purely statistical point of view their importance is not much. No statistical conclusion can be drawn as these provide only an approximate and rough impression about the phenomenon. Diagrams can be used only in those places where two or more quantities have to be compared. If the relationship between two variables is to be studied diagrams would be useless for the purpose. Such studies can be made with the help of graphs only. When we study the relationship between two variables the idea is either to study their cause and effect relationship or to study the extent of change in one variable if the other variable changes by a particular amount. Such study cannot be made by diagrams; graphs are, however, very useful for studying such relationship. Thus for a more rigorous and improved representation of numerical statement graphs and charts are used. The special feature of graphs is that they are more obvious, accurate and precise than diagrams. Thus drawing of graphs is also easier than the drawing of diagrams. Graphs are very useful for studying time series and frequency distributions.

5.2 GRAPHS

Like diagrammatic presentation, graphical presentation also gives a visual effect. Diagrammatic presentation is used to present data classified according to categories and geographical aspects. On the other hand, graphical presentation is used in situations when we observe some functional relationship between the values of two variables.

A graph is a visual form of presentation of statistical data. A graph is more attractive than a table of figure. Even a common man can understand the message of data from the graph. Comparisons can be made between two or more phenomena very easily with the help of a graph.

Charts and graphs represent an extremely useful and flexible medium for explaining, interpreting and analysing numerical facts largely by means of points, lines, areas and other geometric forms and symbols. They make possible the presentation of quantitative data in a simple, clear and effective manner and facilitate comparison of values, trends and relationships.

Graphs are generally drawn with the help of two perpendicular lines known as x-axis and y-axis. The selection of proper scale is of great importance in the construction of graphs.

5.2.1 Construction of Graphs

Before considering the methods of constructing various types of graphs, we first start with the basic approach of dividing a graph sheet into four quadrants.

Let us first use the four quadrants of a graph. Suppose we have to locate on a rectangular coordinate system, the points having coordinates (a) (2,5); (b) (5,2); (c) (-4,3); (d) (2,-4); (e) (-5,-3); (f) (0,-5); and (g) (3,0). We assume that all the given numbers are exact.

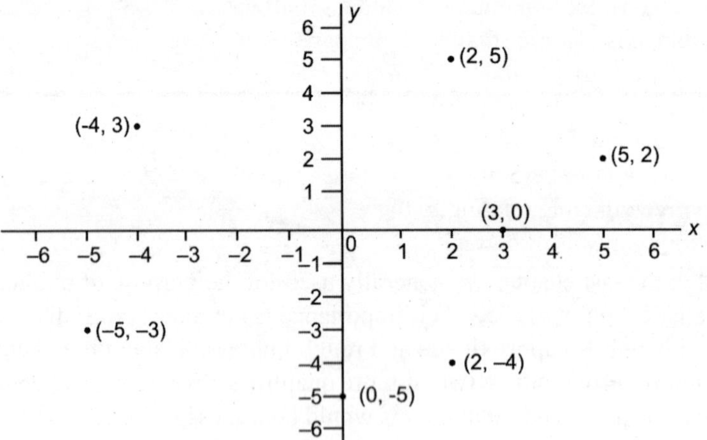

Fig. 5.1: Four Quadrants of a Graph

In the same manner, we can draw graphs of equations. ***For example***, we are given an equation $y = x^2 - 2x + 5$. Here, we assume certain values of x on the basis of which the corresponding values of y can be obtained. This is shown below.

Since all these values are positive, these points will be plotted on the first quadrant where both x and y have positive values only.

This is shown in figure —

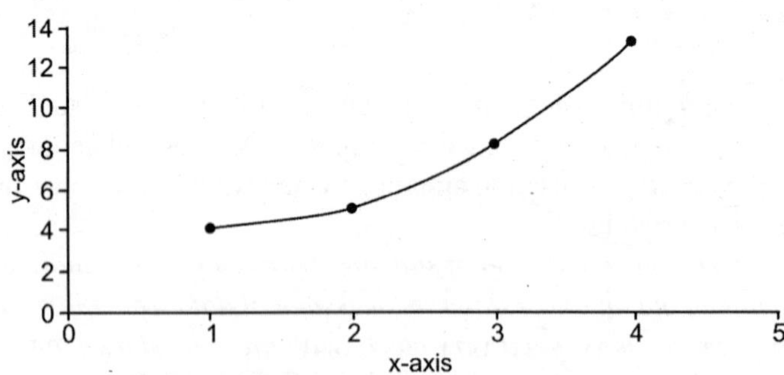

Fig. 5.2: Graph of Equation $y = x^2 - 2x + 5$

x	1	2	3	4
y	4	5	8	13

5.2.2 General Rules for Drawing Graphs

1. **Title:** Every graph must have a clear and comprehensive title so that what facts are presented in the graph may be known.
2. **Structural Framework:** In graph, the main thing is to decide is that which variable is to be taken on x-axis and which on y-axis. Generally, the independent variable or magnitude of the items are taken on x-axis and the corresponding frequencies on y-axis. The scale on y-axis should begin from zero as origin.
3. **Choice of Scale:** The scale should be chosen in such a way that it accommodates the whole data and the whole figure of the graph is visible at a glance.
4. **Use of False Base Line:** Sometimes it happens that the fluctuations in the variables chosen on the axis of x and axis of y are smaller in comparison to their sizes and does not start with zero. In such cases if we start reading the values of x and y on graph from zero then a considerable portion of the graph will remain unutilized and the fluctuations in the data will not be represented prominently in the graph. The problem can be solved by taking a false base line. This is done by showing a break after zero in the continuous vertical or horizontal scales.

Suppose the data given in table relating to the growth of population of a city during the decennial periods are to be shown by means of a graph.

Year	1951	1961	1971	1981	1991	2001
Population (in lakhs)	45	53	60	73	91	115

Now, if we take the starting point zero on the vertical scale (y-axis), we find that we are unable to show all the data, particularly for 1991 and 2001, on account of limitations of space. As such, we use the false base line to get over this difficulty. Figure 5.3 shows the data using the false base line.

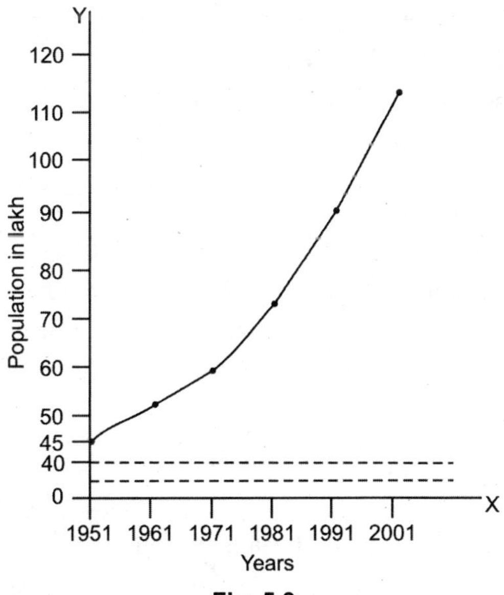

Fig. 5.3

5. **Index:** An index should be given to show the scale and the meaning of different curves.

NOTE: There is a growing feeling that there is no sancity in x-axis and y-axis starting with zero, they can well start from the lowest value or near about from the data given. If that is so the false base line need not be used.

5.2.3 Advantages and Limitations of Graphs

Advantages

1. In the graphical form we may represent the complex data in a simple and easy way.
2. A graph looks more attractive than a table. The features of data become visible at a glance, it becomes easy to grasp the trend and fluctuations, cyclical or otherwise.
3. Graphs helps to save the time and labour of the statisticians as well as the observer. Display of time series and frequency distribution can be made quite effective through a graph.
4. Comparisons between two or more phenomena can be made easily with the help of graph.
5. No special knowledge of mathematics is required to understand the message of data from the graph.
6. Graphic presentation is helpful in interpolation, extrapolation and forecasting. With the help of these one can also determine median, quartiles and mode.

Due to above advantages, graphic presentation of statistical data is becoming more and more popular.

Limitations

Despite of the foregoing advantages of graphs in presenting statistical data, they are subject to certain limitations:

1. A curve simply shows tendency and fluctuations, actual values are not known.
2. Complete accuracy is not possible on a graph.
3. Graphs cannot be quoted and support some statement.
4. Only few characteristics can be depicted on a graph.
5. Graphs should not be regarded as substitutes for classification, tabulation etc. under all circumstances and for all purposes.
6. A great expertise, skill and intelligence is required to select a proper graph to represent the given data. A wrong graph will give fallacious and misleading results.
7. All graphic devices are not simple and straight forward. For understanding ratio graphs and multi-dimensional figures, a good deal of expertise is necessary.

5.3 TYPES OF GRAPHS

In practice, a very large variety of graphs are in use and new ones are constantly being added. For the sake of convenience and simplicity, they may be divided under the following heads:

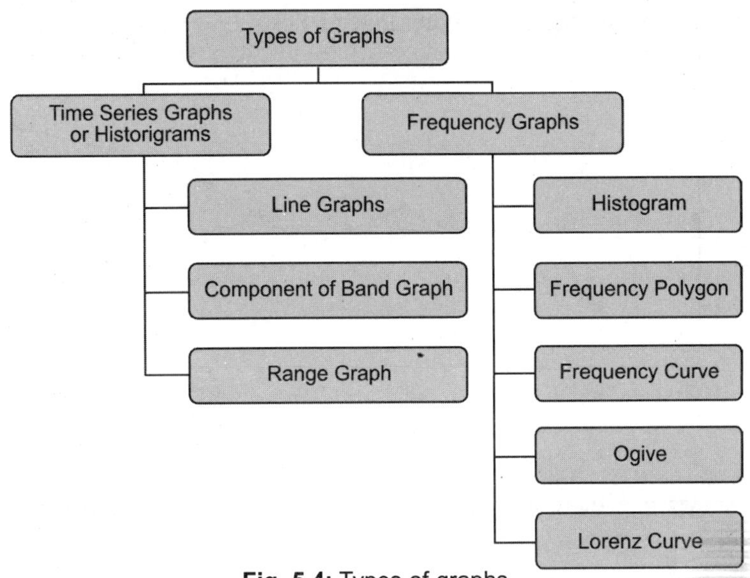

Fig. 5.4: Types of graphs.

5.4 TIME SERIES GRAPHS OR HISTORIGRAMS

Time series graphs, as the name implies, shows the data against time, which could be any measure such as hours, days, weeks, months and years. In time series graph, time is taken as the independent variable on x-axis and the other variables dependent variable on y-axis. The data on population, number of workers in an industrial unit or the entire industry, number of students enrolled in a college, profits earned by a company, scales of a given product are some of the examples where time series can be effectively used to present the given series. Historigrams of two or more variables having same time variable can be plotted on the same graph paper. This makes the comparison easy provided the scale on y-axis for the two variables is same. The plotted points are joined either by straight lines or by free hand curve (if the points are closed). The various types of time series graphs are:

1. Line Graph
2. Component or Band Graph
3. Range or Variation or Zone Graph.

1. Line Graph

Under this graphical presentation, separate lines represent the variables with reference to the time, i.e., the points plotted on graph paper are joined by straight lines. Generally continuous variables are plotted by the line graph. Such graphs are simplest to understand, easiest to make and most adaptable to use. A multiple line graph showing two or more series on the same graph needs more care to accommodate varying values of the different series.

EXAMPLE 5.1: Draw an appropriate graph for the following data:

Years	2001	2002	2003	2004	2005	2006	2007
Sales (in '000 Rs)	5	8	13	10	15	17	20

Solution: The sales data are shown in the figure given below:

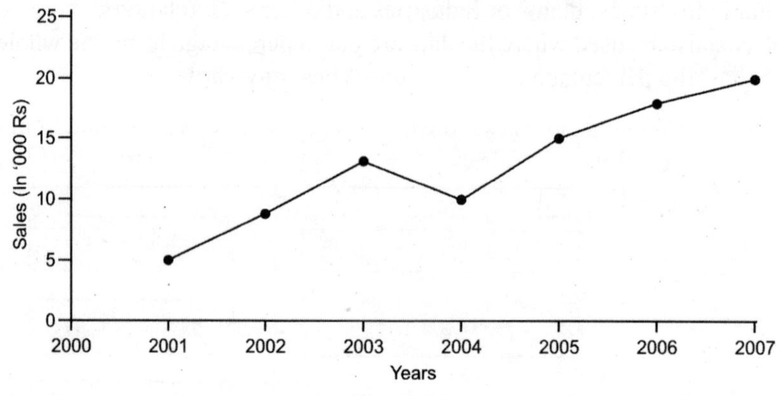

Fig. 5.5

The above graph shows that there was a decline in sales in 2004 while all other years showed an increase in the same.

EXAMPLE 5.2: Following table gives data on the production and sale of a factory (in thousand rupees) between January to June. Make a two-variable line graph.

Month	January	February	March	April	May	June
Production	7.5	10	5	10	12.5	15
Sale	5	7.5	5	10	12.5	156

Solution: Graph of the above data is as under :

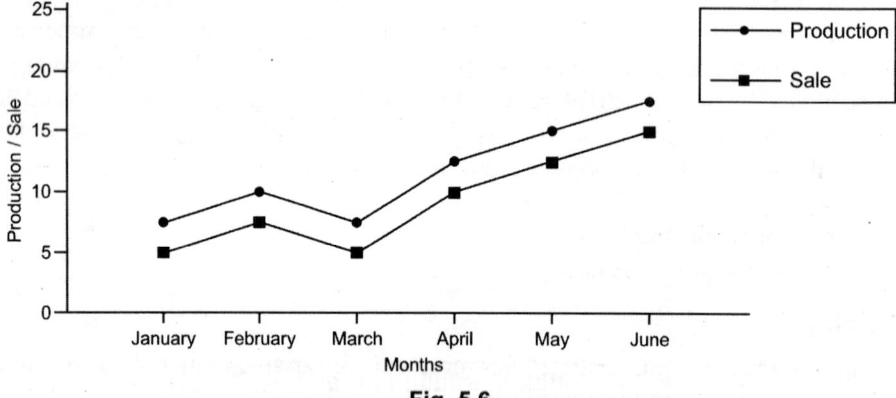

Fig. 5.6

2. Band Graph

Band graph is a graph which is used to present the total for successive time periods broken up into sub-totals for various component parts of the total. The various component parts of the whole are plotted one over the other and in this way there would be as many bands as the number of parts. To distinguish various parts from each other they are either coloured in different colours or the space between them is filled by cross-hatch, vertical or horizontal lines or different types of signs and symbols. This graph is also known as Belt Graph. Such as graph is especially useful in dividing total costs into component cost, total sales into department or district or individual salesman's sales, total production by nature of commodity states, plants or industries and other such relations.

Band graph can also be used where the data are put to percentage form; the whole chart will depict 100% and the bands, the percentage each component bears to whole.

EXAMPLE 5.3: The following table gives the imports of commodity A in India from various countries. Represent the data graphically.

Year ↓ \ Country →	Canada	China	Japan	Iran	Others	Total
1977–78	6.6	5.5	4.6	9.1	5.4	31.2
1978–79	8.2	5.9	7.3	14.9	7.8	44.1
1979–80	7.1	2.4	4.4	8.5	4.7	27.1
1980–81	6.2	8.0	3.6	11.9	24.0	53.7
1981–82	11.9	12.9	1.6	12.1	18.5	57.0
1982–83	10.6	10.9	4.5	10.7	12.6	49.3

Solution:

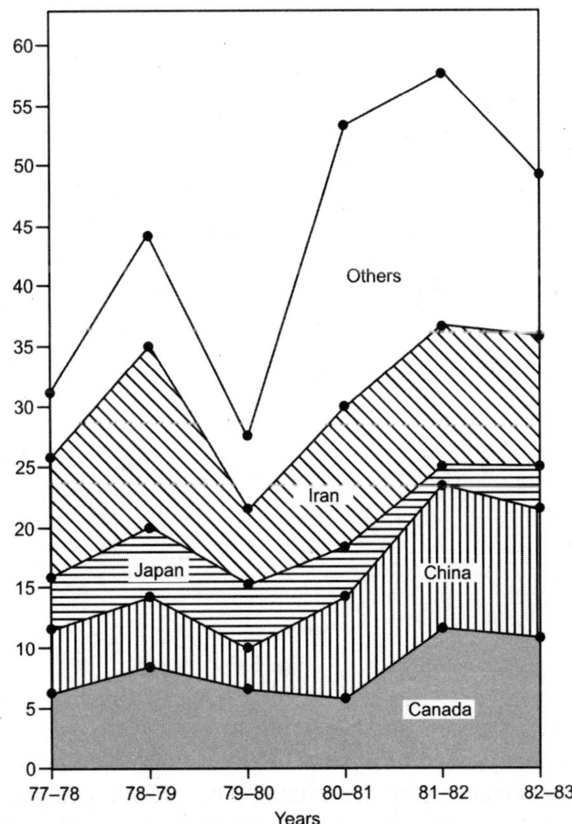

Fig. 5.7: Import of Commodity A in India (1977–78 to 1982–83)

3. Range or Variation or Zone Graph

The range or zone graph, as the name implies, shows the range of variation with reference to each period. If maximum and minimum values for the characteristics are given for a number of years, months, etc. then these can be plotted on the same graph paper with same scale and the difference between the two can be made prominent by drawing a band between the maximum and minimum values for the given years. One can also draw separate Historigrams for the maximum and minimum values of the variable on the same graph and the area between the two Historigrams can be shaded to show the difference. These graphs are known as Range or Zone graph.

DO YOU KNOW?

A graph showing the highest and the lowest values of a certain item under reference is known as range graph.

A range graph may also show the average by taking an average of the two extreme values.

EXAMPLE 5.4: The following table shows the annual price variation in gold over a period 1995–96 to 1998–99. Represent the data graphically.

Year	Highest price	Lowest price	Average price
1995–96	198	177	184
1996–97	574	511	544
1997–98	1730	1305	1522
1998–99	3200	3110	3155

Solution: To draw a range graph, we can take years on x-axis and the prices of gold on y-axis. The data can be displayed as follows:

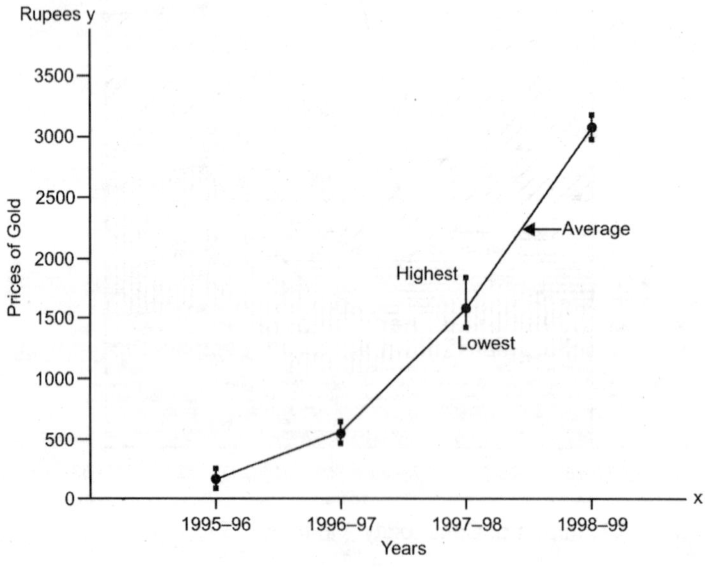

Fig. 5.8

EXAMPLE 5.5: The following table gives the value of imports and exports during a year in crores of rupees. Plot the figures on a graph paper showing the balance of trade.

Months	Imports	Exports	Month	Imports	Exports
April	22	28	October	32	21
May	24	28	November	32	19
June	26	23	December	32	20
July	28	21	January	31	19
August	31	20	February	26	18
September	29	22	March	24	19

Solution: Here balance of trade is to be shown. Hence Range or zone graph will be most appropriate in this case. The months can be taken on x-axis. The maximum and minimum observations are 32 and 18 respectively. Hence we can start with value of 15 on y-axis, using a false base line.

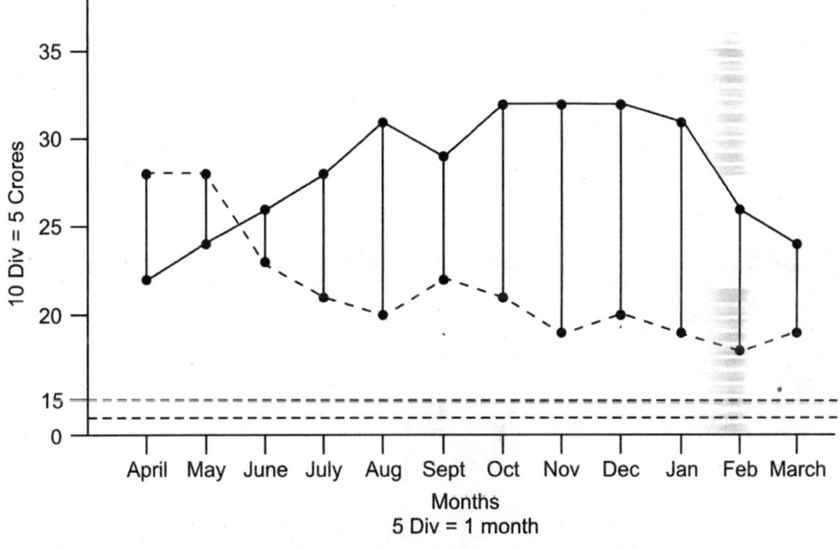

Fig. 5.9

5.5 FREQUENCY GRAPHS

We now come to another category of graphs known as frequency graphs. The following types of frequency graphs are normally used:

1. Histogram
2. Frequency Polygon
3. Frequency Curve
4. Ogive
5. Lorenz Curve

A brief discussion of these along with as follows examples in each case are discussed.

1. Histogram

A histogram is a bar chart or graph showing the frequency of occurrence of each value of the variable being analysed. In histogram, data are plotted as a series of rectangles. Class intervals are shown on the 'X-axis' and the frequencies on the 'Y-axis'.

The height of each rectangle represents the frequency of the class interval. Each rectangle is formed with the other so as to give a continuous picture. Such a graph is also called ***staircase*** or ***block diagram***.

However, we cannot construct a histogram for distribution with open-end classes. It is also quite misleading if the distribution has unequal intervals and suitable adjustments in frequencies are not made.

The total area covered by the histograms for whole frequency distribution is equal to the total number of items in the frequency distribution.

The following points should be kept in mind in drawing a histogram.

1. Histogram can only be drawn for continuous data. If the data is discontinuous i.e. upper limit of one class is not equal to the lower limit of next higher class, then the class-intervals should be first made continuous.
2. Area of the rectangle is always equal to frequency of the corresponding class interval. In case all the class-intervals are of same width, the height of the rectangle can be taken proportional to the frequency of the class interval.
3. In this case of open-end classes, the end class's limits are chosen arbitrarily so that width of the class intervals becomes equal to that of the preceding class.

EXAMPLE 5.6: Draw a histogram for the following data.

Daily Wages (in Rs.)	0–50	50–100	100–150	150–200	200–250	250–300
Number of workers	8	16	27	19	10	6

Solution :

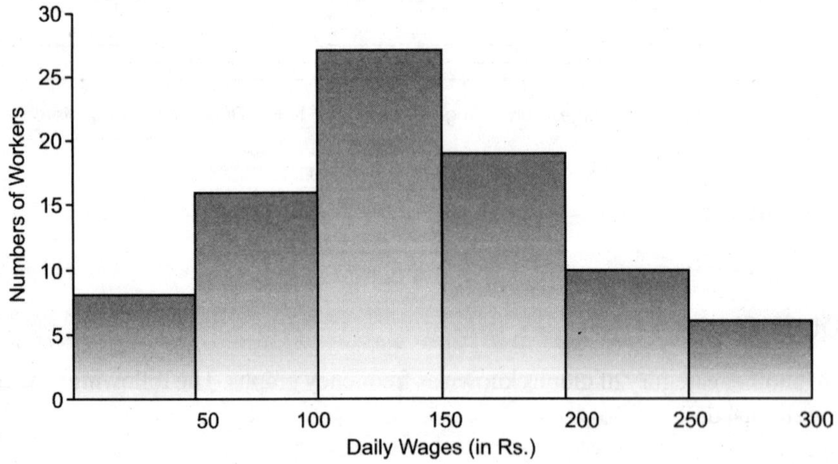

Fig 5.10: Histogram

EXAMPLE 5.7: For the following data, draw a histogram.

Marks	21–30	31–40	41–50	51–60	61–70	70–80
Number of students	6	15	22	31	17	9

Solution: For drawing a histogram, the frequency distribution should be continuous. If it is not continuous, then first make it continuous as follows.

Marks	20.5–30.5	30.5–40.5	40.5–50.5	50.5–60.5	60.5–70.5	70.5–80.5
Number of students	6	15	22	31	17	9

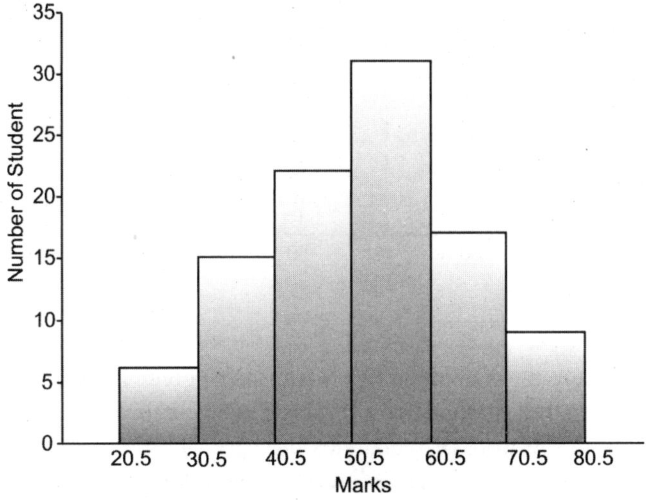

Fig. 5.11: Histogram

EXAMPLE 5.8: Draw a histogram for the following data.

Profits (in lakhs)	0–10	10–20	20–30	30–50	50–80	80–90	90–100
Number of Companies	4	12	24	32	18	9	3

Solution: When the class intervals are unequal, a correction for unequal class intervals must be made. The frequencies are adjusted as follows: The frequency of the class 30-50 shall be divided by two since the class interval is in double. Similarly the class interval 50- 80 can be divided by 3. Then draw the histogram.

Now we rewrite the frequency table as follows.

Profits (in lakhs)	Number of Companies
0–10	4
10–20	12
20–30	24
30–40	16
40–50	16
50–60	6
60–70	6
70–80	6
80–90	9
90–100	3

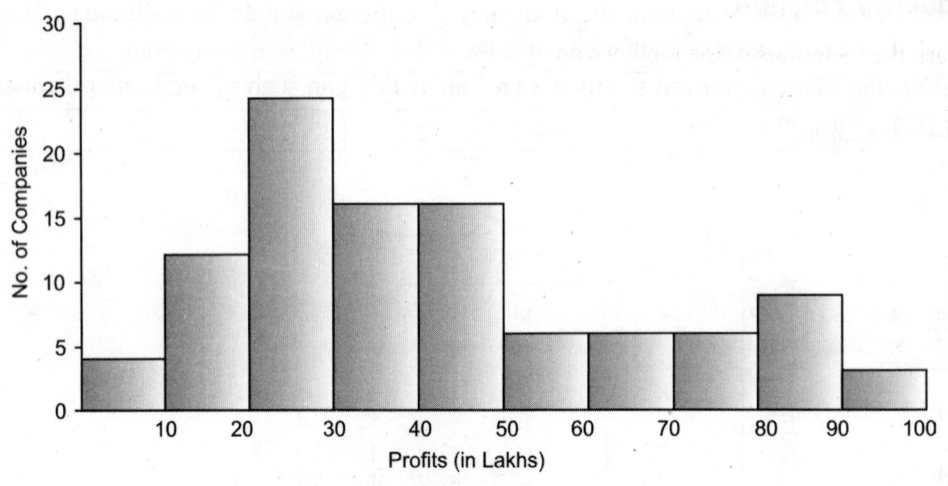

Fig. 5.12

In Histogram, we measure the size of the item in question, given in terms of class intervals, on the axis of X while the corresponding frequencies are shown on the axis of Y. Unlike the line graph, here the frequencies are shown in the form of rectangles the base of which is the class interval. Another feature of this graph is that the rectangles are adjacent to each other without having any gap amongst them. It may be recalled that this was not the case in the line graph where vertical frequency lines were separate and unconnected with each other. This will become clear with an example.

EXAMPLE 5.9: Suppose we are given the following data to be displayed by means of a histogram.

Marks	0–20	20–40	40–60	60–80	80–100
Number of students	10	22	35	28	5

Solution: It will be seen from figure that the area of each rectangle is proportional to the frequency unlike the line graph shown earlier. This is because a histogram generally represents a continuous frequency distribution in contrast to line graph, which represents either a frequency distribution or a time.

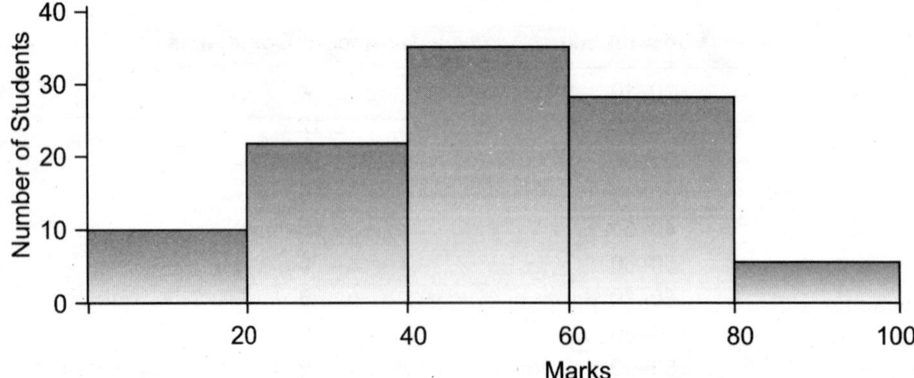

Fig. 5.13: An Example of Histogram

2. Frequency Polygon

If we mark the midpoints of the top horizontal sides of the rectangles in a histogram and join them by a straight line, the figure so formed is called a Frequency Polygon. This is done under the assumption that the frequencies in a class interval are evenly distributed throughout the class. The area of the polygon is equal to the area of the histogram, because the area left outside is just equal to the area included in it.

DO YOU KNOW?

A frequency polygon can also be drawn with the help of histograms by joining the mid-points of the upper side of each rectangle of a histogram.

EXAMPLE 5.10: Draw a frequency polygon for the following data.

Weights (in kg)	30–35	35–40	40–45	45–50	50–55	55–60	60–65
Number of students	4	7	10	18	14	8	3

Solution:

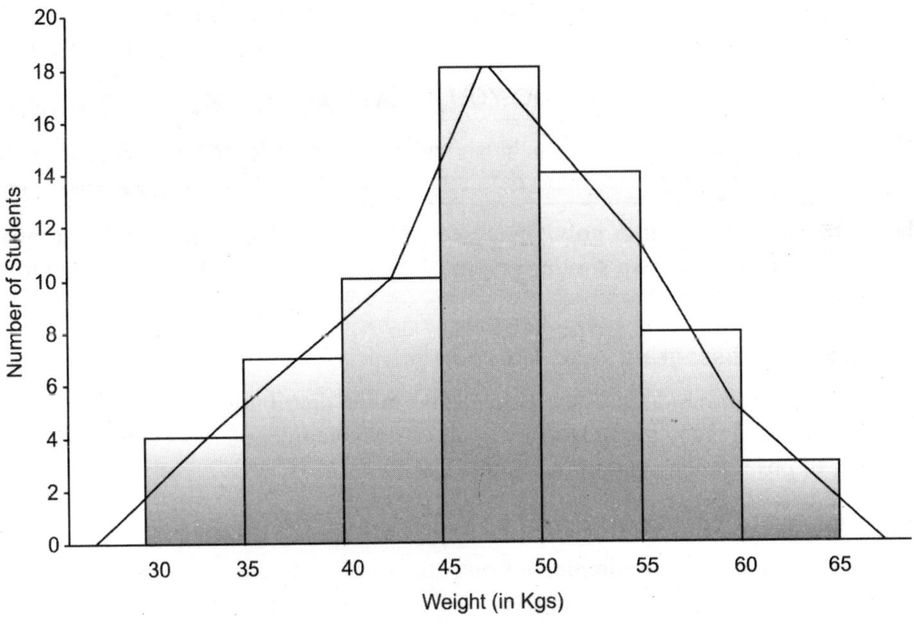

Fig. 5.14: Frequency Polygon

A Frequency Polygon like any polygon consists of many angles. A histogram can be easily transformed into a frequency polygon by joining the mid-points of the rectangles by straight lines.

The preceding Fig. 5.13 has been thus transformed into a frequency polygon as shown in the figure on next page:

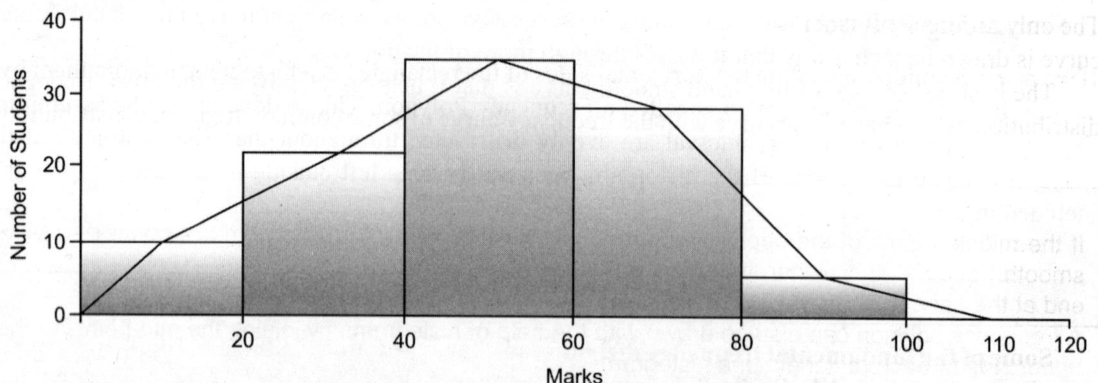

Fig. 5.15: An Example of Frequency Polygon

It may be noted that instead of transforming a histogram into a frequency polygon, one can draw straightaway a frequency polygon by taking the mid-point of each class-interval and by joining the mid-points by the straight lines. Another point to note is that this can be done only when we have a continuous series. In ease of a discrete distribution, this is not possible.

Instead of having a frequency polygon, we can have a relative frequency polygon. While the relative frequency polygon has the same shape as the frequency polygon drawn from the same data, it has a different scale of values on the vertical axis. Instead of having absolute frequencies in the relative frequency polygon will be the number of frequencies in each class as a proportion of the total number of frequencies.

DO YOU KNOW?

A relative frequency distribution is a tabular summary of data showing the fraction or proportion (relative frequency) of observations in the data set in each of several non-overlapping classes.

As the histogram and frequency polygon are very similar graphs, a question that frequently arises is: Why is it necessary to have two similar graphs? It would, therefore, be worthwhile to know their respective advantages.

The Advantages of Histogram over Polygon

1. Each rectangle shows distinctly separate class in the distribution.
2. The area of each rectangle in relation to all other rectangles shows the proportion of the total number of observations pertaining to that class.

Frequency Polygons, too, have certain advantages.

1. The frequency polygon is simpler as compared to a histogram.
2. The frequency polygon shows more vividly an outline of the data pattern.
3. As the number of classes and the number of observations increase, so also the frequency polygon becomes increasingly smooth.

3. Frequency Curve

A frequency curve gives a more realistic representation of the phenomenon than a histogram or a frequency polygon. The method of drawing a frequency curve is similar to frequency polygon.

The only difference is that instead of joining the successive points by straight lines, a free hand smooth curve is drawn in such a way that it passes through more of the points.

The basic advantage of free hand smooth curve is that it helps in classifying the given frequency distribution by comparing the curve with the frequency curve of some common frequency distributions.

DO YOU KNOW?

If the middle points of the upper boundaries of the rectangles of a histogram are connected by a smooth freehand curve, then that diagram is called frequency curve. The curve should begin and end at the base line.

Some of the fundamental frequency distributions have the following form of frequency curves.

(i) **Symmetrical Distribution:** A common characteristic of such distributions is that frequency decreases equally on both sides of the central value having maximum frequency.

(ii) **Moderately Skewed or Slightly Asymmetrical Distributions:** In such distributions the rate of decrease of frequencies on the side of the maximum value is more than the corresponding rate of another side. These are most popular in practice. A asymmetrical curve can be positively skewed if rate of decrease of the frequencies on right side of the maximum is more than that on the left (see fig 5.16 (b)) otherwise the curve is said to be negatively skewed (see fig 5.16 (c)).

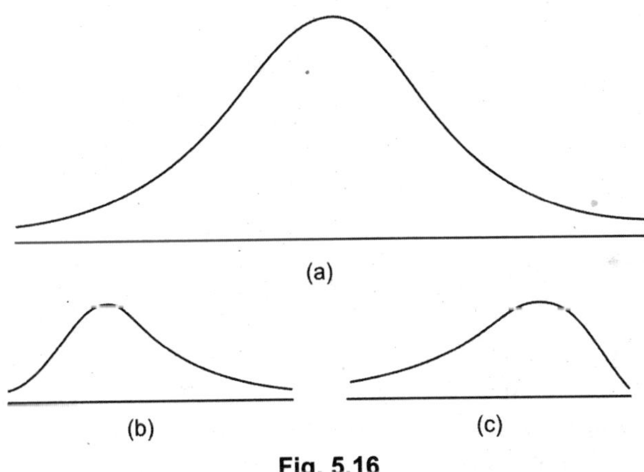

Fig. 5.16

(iii) **J-Shaped or Extremely Skewed Distribution:** Here the frequency is maximum at one end of the distribution.

(iv) **U-Shaped Curve:** In such distribution the frequency is maximum at both ends and minimum in the centre.

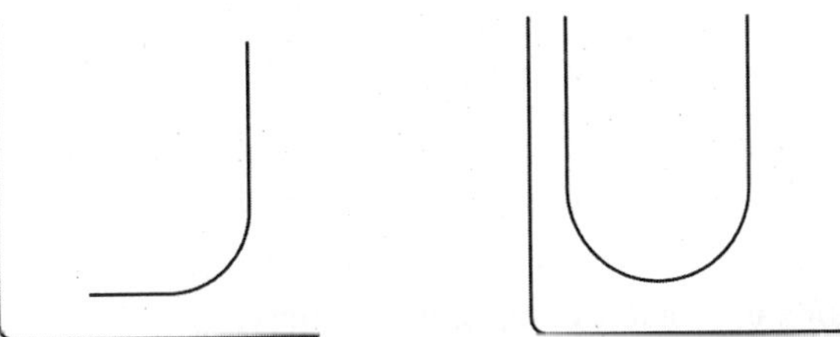

Fig. 5.17

EXAMPLE 5.11: Draw a frequency curve for the following data.

Monthly Wages (in Rs.)	Number of family
0–1000	21
1000–2000	35
2000–3000	56
3000–4000	74
4000–5000	63
5000–6000	40
6000–7000	29
7000–8000	14

Solution:

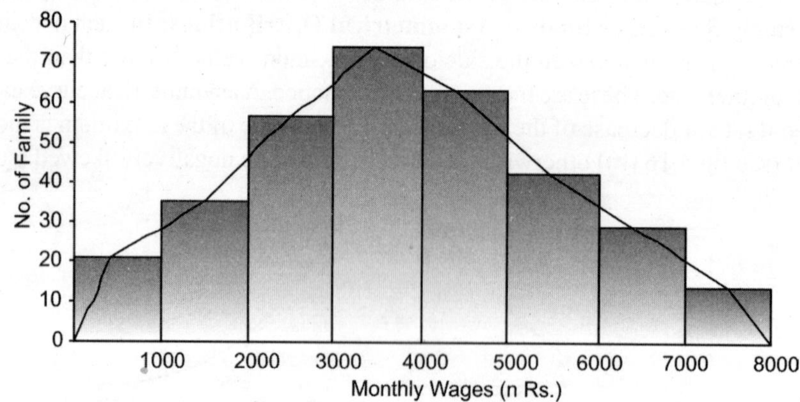

Fig. 5.18: Frequency Curve

A Frequency Polygon is angular as the mid-points of class- intervals ate joined by straight lines. When a frequency polygon is smoothened and rounded at the top, then it known as a Frequency Curve. On account of smoothening angularities of frequency polygon, the frequency curve becomes more suitable for the purpose of interpolation.

4. Ogive or Cumulative Frequency Curve

For a set of observations, we know how to construct a frequency distribution. In some cases we may require the number of observations less than a given value or more than a given value.

This is obtained by a accumulating (adding) the frequencies up to (or above) the give value. This accumulated frequency is called cumulative frequency.

These cumulative frequencies are then listed in a table is called cumulative frequency table. The curve table is obtained by plotting cumulative frequencies is called a cumulative frequency curve or an ogive.

There are two methods of constructing ogive namely:

1. The 'less than ogive' method

2. The 'more than ogive' method.

In less than ogive method we start with the upper limits of the classes and go adding the frequencies. When these frequencies are plotted, we get a rising curve. In more than ogive method, we start with the lower limits of the classes and from the total frequencies we subtract the frequency of each class. When these frequencies are plotted we get a declining curve.

EXAMPLE 5.12: Draw the Ogives for the following data.

Class interval	20–30	30–40	40–50	50–60	60–70	70–80	80–90	90–100
Frequency	4	6	13	25	32	19	8	3

Solution:

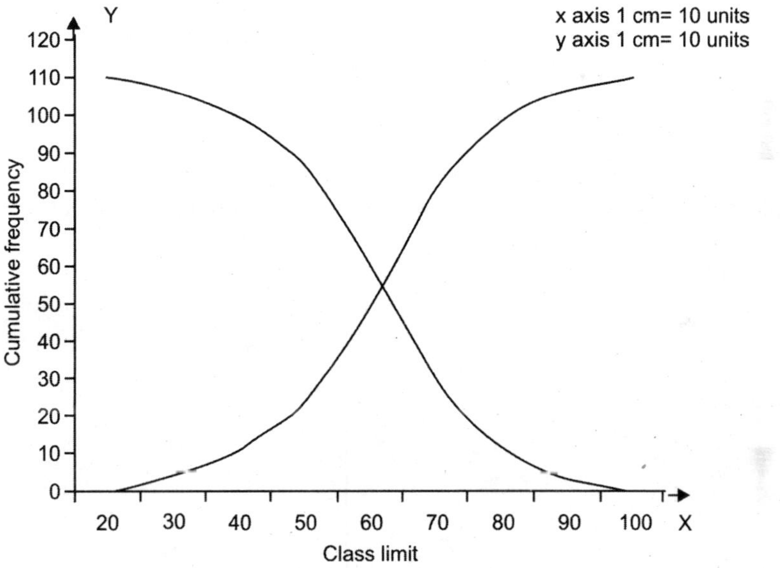

Fig. 5.20: Ogives

Class limit	Less than ogive	More than ogive
20	0	110
30	4	106
40	10	100
50	23	87
60	48	62
70	80	30
80	99	11
90	107	3
100	110	0

EXAMPLE 5.13: Draw the Ogives for the following data :

Weekly Earnings (Rs)	Below 550	550–600	600–650	650–700	700–750	750–800	800–850
No. of Employees	5	10	22	30	16	12	15

Solution: First of all we have to transform the above series into a cumulative series. This can be done in two ways: 'less than' or 'more than' the varying amounts of income. We transform the above data as 'less than' series.

Weekly Earnings (Rs)	Number of Employees
Less than 550	5
Less than 600	15
Less than 650	37
Less than 700	67
Less than 750	83
Less than 800	95
Less than 850	110

We now plot these figures on the graph, which is shown in figure given below.

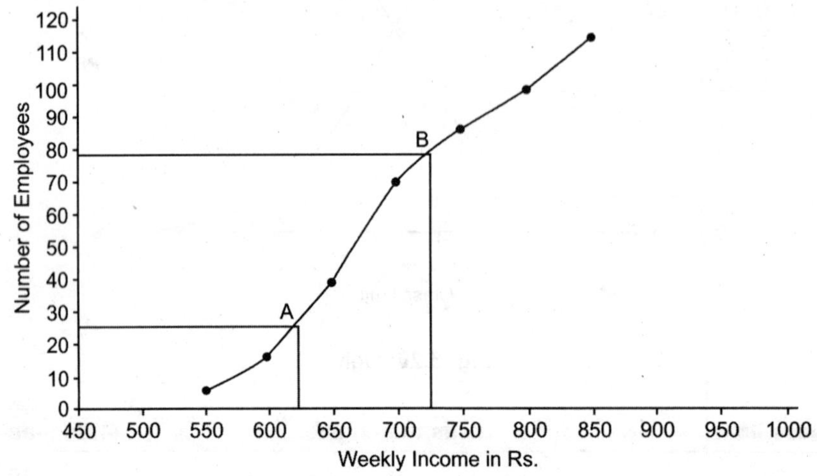

Fig. 5.21: "Less than" Ogive of the Distribution of weekly Income of 110 Employee

It will be seen from figure that 'less than ogive is moving up and to the right. If we plot a 'more than' curve then it would show a declining slope and to the right, as we shall see shortly.

From the ogive of Fig. 5.21, we can find the number of employees earning weekly wages, say, between Rs 625 and Rs 725. What we have to do is to draw arc perpendicular from the horizontal line at Rs 625 meeting the ogive at point A. From this point, a straight line is to be drawn to meet the vertical line. This would give a certain number. Likewise, we have to do with the upper amount of Rs 725. Thus, we would get two figures of number of employees. By subtracting the smaller figure from the higher one, we can find the actual number employees earning between Rs 625 and Rs 725. This has been shown in Fig. 5.21. The upper line which meets the vertical line shows the figure of 76 employees, while the lower line which meets the vertical line shows the figure of 24 employees. Accordingly, the number of employees whose weekly earnings are between Rs 625 and Rs 725 comes to 76–24 = 52.

Similarly, we can find the weekly earnings of the middle 50 percent of the employees.

As we shall see later, we can ascertain graphically the values of median, quartiles, percentiles and so on with the help of a cumulative frequency graph.

Let us take another example where we use 'more than' ogive. We are given the following data and asked to draw an ogive and determine graphically the number of observations lying between 360 and 440.

Size of item	Number of observation
More than 200	400
More than 250	370
More than 300	315
More than 350	220
More than 400	115
More than 450	45
More than 500	15
More than 550	0

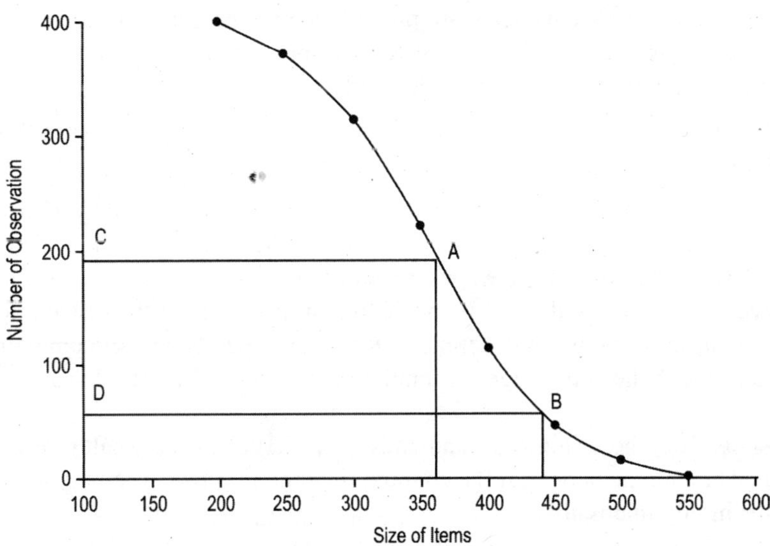

Fig. 5.22: An Example of 'More than' Ogive

We can find out the number of observations lying between 360 and 440 sizes. As described earlier in the case of fig. 5.22, we have drawn the perpendiculars from the two values of 360 and 440 to meet the ogive at points A and B respectively. From these points, straight lines have been drawn to meet the vertical line at points C and D respectively. Now, C gives the value of 195 observations and D gives the value of 57 observations.

Thus, the difference between C and D, that is, C - D gives us the number of observations lying between these values, which his 138 approximately.

It is worthwhile here to recall the steps needed in drawing an ogive after the data have been collected. The data are first arrayed and then a frequency distribution is obtained. Both these steps were discussed in the preceding chapters. From the frequency distribution, we obtain a cumulative frequency distribution on the basis of either 'less than' or 'more than' patterns. The cumulative data are then plotted on the graph, which gives us an ogive. Finally, the ogive curve thus obtained can be used to find graphically the values of any given size or for any given value, the corresponding size. But, we cannot get the exact original data from any of the graphical devices.

Utility of Ogives

From the standpoint of graphic presentation, the ogive is especially used for the following purposes:

1. To determine as well as to portray the number or proportion of cases above or below a given value.
2. To compare two or more frequency distributions. Generally there is less overlapping when comparing several ogives on the same grid than when comparing several simple frequency curves in this manner.
3. Ogives are also drawn for determining certain values graphically, such as median, quartiles, deciles, etc.

NOTE: In ogives cumulative frequencies are plotted against the class-limits (not mid-points) and a smooth free hand curve is drawn. The value of X corresponding to the point where the ogives cut is Median. Ogives can be drawn for continuous data only.

5. Lorenz Curve

Lorenz curve is a graphical method of studying dispersion. It was introduced by ***Max.O.Lorenz***, a great economist and a statistician, to study the distribution of wealth and income. It is also used to study the variability in the distribution of profits, wages, revenue, etc.

Lorenz Curve is specially used to study the degree of inequality in the distribution of income and wealth between countries or between different periods. It is a percentage of cumulative values of one variable in combined with the percentage of cumulative values in other variable and then Lorenz curve is drawn.

The curve starts from the origin (0,0) and ends at (100,100). If the wealth, revenue, land etc. are equally distributed among the people of the country, then the Lorenz curve will be the diagonal of the square. But this is highly impossible.

The deviation of the Lorenz curve from the diagonal shows how the wealth, revenue, land etc. are not equally distributed among people.

EXAMPLE 5.14: In the following table, profit earned is given from the number of companies belonging to two areas A and B. Draw in the same diagram their Lorenz curves and interpret them.

Profit earned (in thousands)	Number of Companies	
	Area A	Area B
5	7	13
26	12	25
65	14	43
89	28	57
110	33	45
155	25	28
180	18	13
200	8	6

Solution :

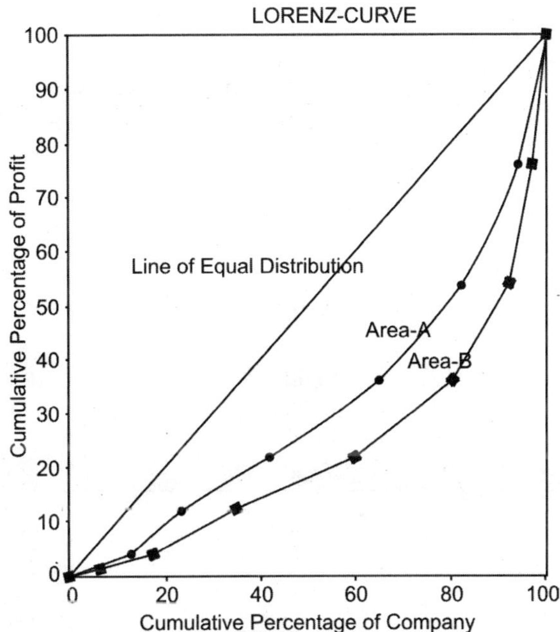

Fig. 5.23: LORENZ - CURVE

Profits			Area A			Area B		
In Rs.	Cumulative profit	Cumulative percentage	No. of companies	Cumulative number	Cumulative percentage	No. of companies	Cumulative number	Cumulative percentage
5	5	1	7	7	5	13	13	16
26	31	4	12	19	13	25	38	17
65	96	12	14	33	23	43	81	35
89	185	22	28	61	42	57	138	60
110	295	36	33	94	65	45	183	80
115	450	54	25	119	82	28	211	92
180	630	79	18	137	94	13	224	97
200	830	100	8	145	100	6	230	100

MISCELLANEOUS SOLVED EXAMPLES

EXAMPLE 5.15: You have conducted a market survey with a sample of size 50 regarding the acceptability of a new product which your company wants to launch. The scores of the respondents on the appropriate scale are as follows:

40	45	41	45	45	30	39	8	48	25
26	9	21	24	26	29	8	40	41	42
39	35	18	25	35	40	42	43	44	36
27	32	28	27	25	26	38	37	36	35
32	28	40	41	43	44	45	40	39	41

Prepare a frequency table and present the same information as a histogram. **[MBA, HPU, 2002]**

Solution: Frequency table of the given data is made as follows :

Frequency Distribution of Scores

Scores	Tally Marks	Frequency
5–10	III	3
10–15	—	—
15–20	I	1
20–25	II	2
25–30	~~IIII~~ ~~IIII~~ I	11
30–35	III	3
35–40	~~IIII~~ ~~IIII~~	10
40–45	~~IIII~~ ~~IIII~~ ~~IIII~~	15
45–50	~~IIII~~	5
	Total	**50**

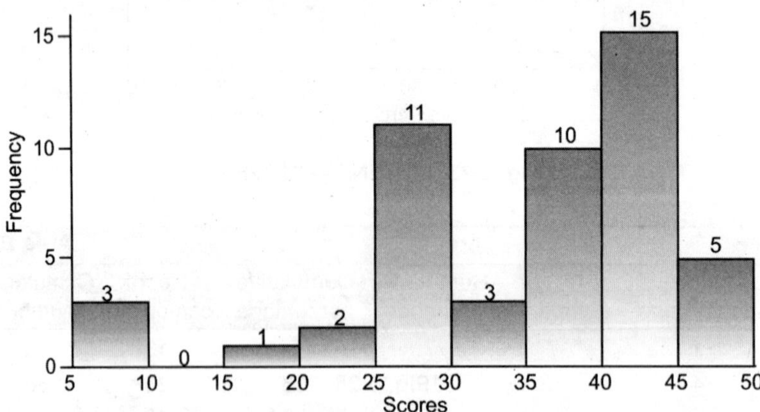

Fig. 5.24: Histogram of the given data.

EXAMPLE 5.16: The following distribution is with regard to weight in grams of mangoes of a given variety. If mangoes of weight less than 443 grams be considered unsuitable for foreign market, what is the percentage of total yield suitable for it? Assume the given frequency distribution to be typical of the variety:

Weight in gms	410–419	420–429	430–439	440–449	450–459	460–469	470–479
No. of Mangoes	10	20	42	54	45	18	7

Draw an ogive of 'more than' type of the above data and deduce how many mangoes will be more than 143 grams.

Solution: Mangoes weighing more than 443 gms, are suitable for foreign market. Number of mangoes weighing more than 443 gms, lies in the last four classes. Number of mangoes weighting between 444 grams and 449 grams would be:

$$\frac{6}{10} \times 54 = \frac{324}{10} = 32.4$$

Total number of mangoes weighing more than 443 gms. = 32.4 + 45 + 18 + 7 = 102.4

$$\text{Percentage} = \frac{102.4}{196} \times 100 = 52.25$$

Therefore, the percentage of the total mangoes suitable for foreign market is 52.25.

Weight more than (gms)	410	420	430	440	450	460	470
No. of Mangoes	196	186	166	124	70	25	7

From the graph, it can be seen that there are 103 mangoes whose weight will be more than 443 gms, and are suitable for foreign market.

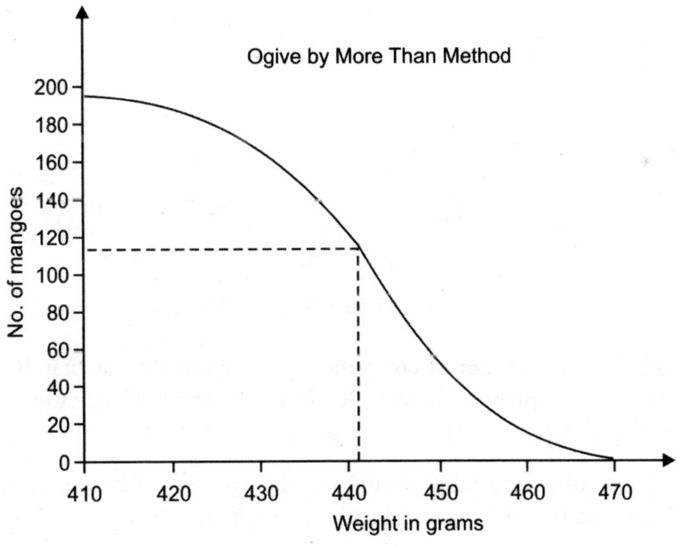

Fig. 5.25

EXAMPLE 5.17: Draw an ogive by less than method and determine the number of companies getting profits between Rs 45 crores and Rs 75 crores: **[MBA, DU, 1999**

Profits (Rs crores)	10–20	20 30	30–40	40–50	50–60	60–70	70–80	80–90	90–100
No. of Companies	8	12	20	24	15	10	7	3	1

Solution:

Ogive by Less Than Method

Profit (Rs crores)	Number of Companies
Less than 20	8
Less than 30	20
Less than 40	40
Less than 50	64
Less than 60	79
Less than 70	89
Less than 80	96
Less than 90	99
Less than 100	100

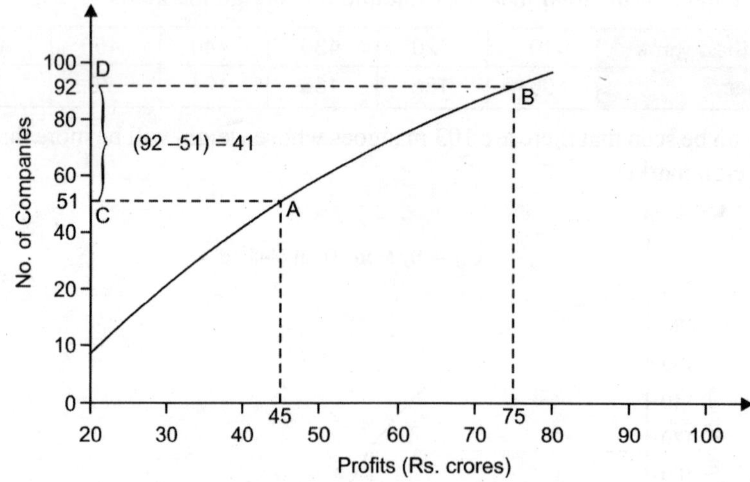

Fig. 5.26: Ogive by less than method.

It is clear from the graph that the number of companies getting profits less than Rs 75 crores is 92 and the number of companies getting profits less than Rs 45 crores is 51. Hence the number of companies getting profits between Rs 45 crores and Rs 75 crores is 92 – 51 = 41.

EXAMPLE 5.18: Find the following table giving the distribution of intelligence quotients (I.Q.) of 905 school children. Draw the two ogives and locale the median. **[B.Sc, Agra, 1967]**

I.Q.	55–64	65–74	75–84	85–94	95–104	105–114	115–124	125–134	135–144
No. of children	3	21	78	182	305	209	81	21	5

Solution: In this case the class-intervals are not continuous. Hence the intervals are made continuous by adding 0.5 to the upper limit and subtracting 0.5 from the lower limit of each class interval. Then the less than and more than cumulative frequencies are calculated for drawing the graph.

I.Q.	No. of children	Less than cumulative frequency	More than cumulative frequency
54.5–64.5	3	3	905
64.5–74.5	21	24	902
74.5–84.5	78	182	881
84.5–94.5	182	284	803
94.5–104.5	305	589	621
104.5–114.5	209	798	316
114.5–124.5	81	879	107
124.5–134.5	21	900	26
134.5–144.5	5	905	5

The graph is drawn in Fig. 5.27.

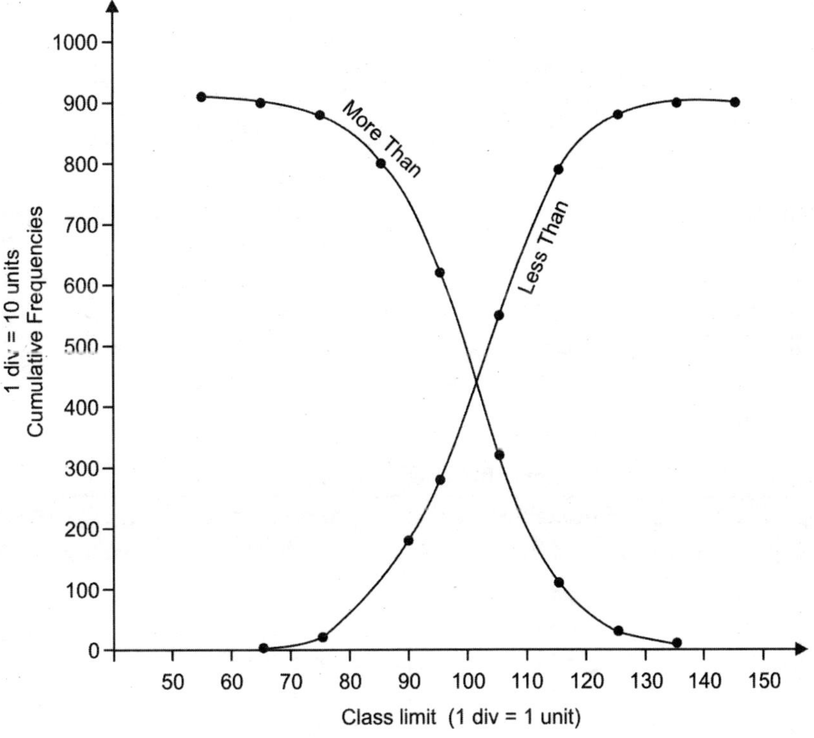

Fig. 5.27

From graph median = 100.

EXAMPLE 5.19: The following table gives the average yearly profits for 580 companies:

Yearly profits (Rs lakh)	No. of companies	Yearly profits (Rs lakh)	No. of companies
80–85	21	120–125	36
85–90	29	125–130	45
90–95	19	130–135	27
95–100	39	135–140	48
100–105	43	140–145	21
105–110	94	145–150	12
110–115	73	150–155	5
115–120	68		

(a) Draw ogives by 'less than' and 'more than' method for the data given above.

(b) Find the number of companies whose yearly profits (in Rs. lakhs) lie between Rs 118 and Rs 148. **[MBA, UPTU, 2003, GGSIP 2000, MBA, DU, 2001]**

Solution: Let us first arrange the frequency distribution for less than and more than methods as given below:

Ogive by Less Than Method			
Yearly profits (Rs lakh)	**Frequency**	**Yearly profits (Rs lakh)**	**Frequency**
Less than 85	21	Less than 125	36
Less than 90	29	Less than 130	45
Less than 95	19	Less than 135	27
Less than 100	39	Less than 140	48
Less than 105	43	Less than 145	21
Less than 110	94	Less than 150	12
Less than 115	73	Less than 155	5
Less than 120	68		

Ogive by More Than Method			
Yearly profits (Rs lakh)	**Frequency**	**Yearly profits (Rs lakh)**	**Frequency**
More than 80	580	More than 120	194
More than 85	559	More than 125	158
More than 90	530	More than 130	113
More than 95	511	More than 135	86
More than 100	472	More than 140	38
More than 105	429	More than 145	17
More than 110	335	More than 150	5
More than 115	262		

With the help of these frequency distribution tables, we can draw ogives by less than and more than method as shown below :

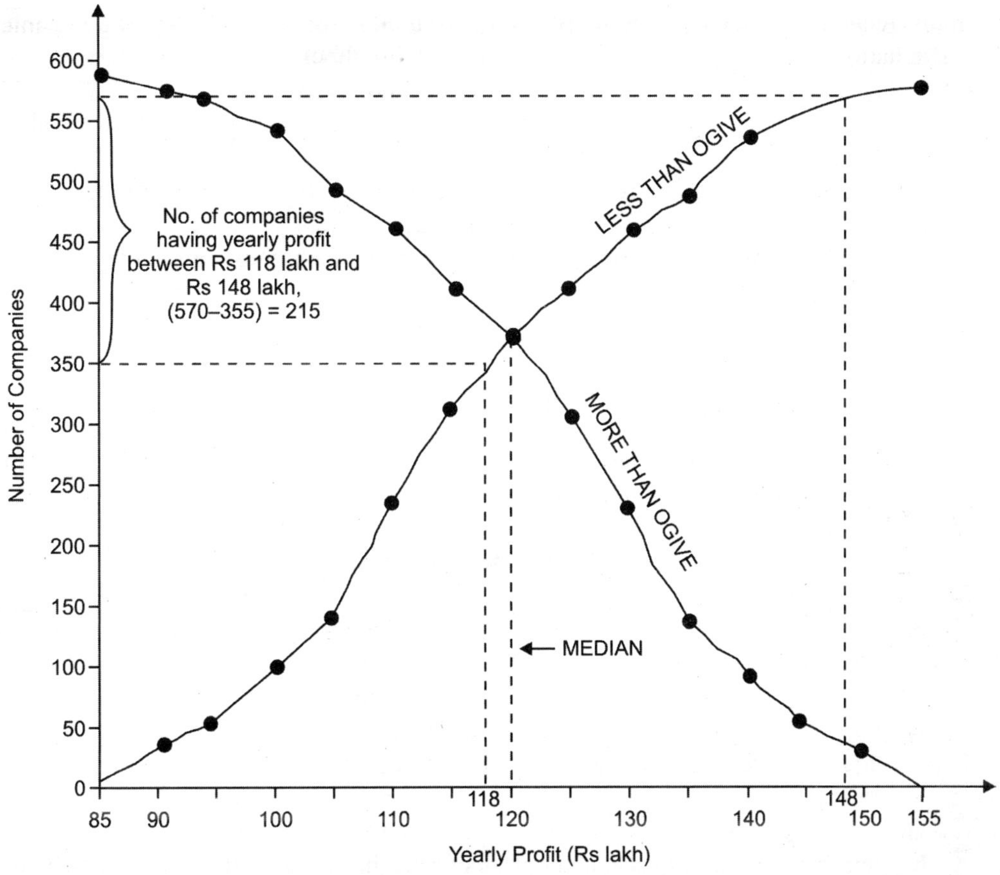

Fig. 5.28: Less than and more than ogive and median.

SELF PRACTICE EXERCISES

I. CHOOSE THE BEST ANSWER

1. Frequency curve:
   (a) begins at the origin (b) passes through the origin
   (c) begins at the horizontal line (d) begins and end at the base line
2. With the help of histogram we can draw:
   (a) frequency polygon (b) frequency curve
   (c) frequency distribution (d) all the above
3. Ogives for 'more than' type and 'less than' type distribution intersect at:
   (a) mean (b) median
   (c) mode (d) origin
4. A graph showing the highest and lowest values of a certain item under reference is known as:
   (a) Band graph (b) Line graph
   (c) Range graph (d) Histogram

5. In histogram the frequencies are shown in the form of:
   (a) squares (b) straight lines
   (c) triangles (d) rectangles
6. In frequency polygon, the area of the graph between the x-axis and two extreme ends of the curve is equal:
   (a) the total frequency of the data (b) half of the total frequency of the data
   (c) zero (d) none of these
7. In frequency polygon, the volume of x corresponding to the highest point in the polygon will be equal to:
   (a) mean (b) median
   (c) mode (d) none of these
8. Various types of graphs of frequency distributions are constructed because they:
   (a) reveal data patterns
   (b) allow easy estimates of values
   (c) increase the possibility of practical applications
   (d) both (a) and (b) but not (c)
9. A graph of a cumulative frequency distribution is called:
   (a) Ogive (b) Frequency polygon
   (c) Frequency curve (d) Pie diagram
10. A line graph indicates:
    (a) Comparison (b) Variation
    (c) Range (d) All of above
11. In the context of income distribution, Lorenz curve depicts:
    (a) Prosperity (b) Poverty
    (c) Growth (d) Inequality
12. As the member of observations and classes increase, the shape of the frequency polygon:
    (a) remains unchanged (b) tends to become jagged
    (c) tends to become smooth (d) none of these

II. FILL IN THE BLANKS

1. The selection of .... is of great importance in the construction of graphs.
2. Historigrams are generally used to represent a data in which the independent variable is ....
3. A frequency polygon can also be drawn with the help of ....
4. The method of drawing a frequency curve is similar to ....
5. Ogives can only be drawn for .... variable.
6. Ogives for more than type and less than type distribution intersects at ....
7. .... curve is graphical method of studying dispersion.
8. A cumulative frequency curve is also known as .... curve.
9. Graphs are very useful for studying .... and ....
10. In time series graph, time is taken as the .... variable.

III. SHORT ANSWER TYPE QUESTIONS

1. What is the use of histogram?
2. What do you mean by frequency curve? State its important characteristics.
3. What is the difference between histogram and frequency polygon?
4. What is a false base line? Under what circumstances should it be used?
5. What are the advantages of using a graph to describe a frequency distribution?
6. Explain briefly some of the uses of graphs and charts in presenting business data, etc.
   [MBA, Osmania University, 1998]
7. Name the various ways of presenting a frequency distribution graphically.
8. Define the following terms:
   (a) Histograms (b) Frequency polygon
   (c) Frequency curve (d) Ogive
9. What do you understand by a cumulative frequency distribution? Point out its special advantages and uses.

IV. LONG ANSWER TYPE QUESTIONS

1. Explain briefly the various methods that are used for graphical presentation of the data.
2. What are different types of graphs and charts known to you? What are their uses?
3. What points should be taken into account in the construction of graph? Discuss in detail.
4. 'Charts are more effective in attracting attention than any of the other methods of presenting data.' Do you agree? Give reasons for your answer.
5. When constructing a graph of a grouped frequency distribution, is it necessary that the resulting distribution be symmetric? Explain.
6. What are the different forms of a frequency curve? Describe their nature in brief.
7. State the advantages and limitations of graphical representation of data.
8. Illustrate graphically the distinction among a frequency polygon, a histogram and an ogive curve. Comment on their uses.
9. What is an ogive? How is it useful in finding the values of median and quartile of the given data?
10. What are less than ogive and more than ogive? What purpose representation of frequency they serve?
11. What is Lorenz curve? Mention its importance.
12. Draw a histogram and frequency polygon for the following data.

Weight (in kg)	40-45	45-50	50-55	55-60	60-65
Number of men	8	14	21	18	10

13. Draw a frequency curve for the following data.

Marks	0-20	20-40	40-60	60-80	80-100
No. of students	7	15	28	17	5

14. Given below are the data on birth rate and death rate (per thousand) in India for a number of years. Graph these data.

Year	Birth Rate	Death Rate
1950–51	39.9	27.4
1960–61	41.7	22.0
1970–71	36.9	14.9
1980–81	33.9	12.5
1990–91	29.5	9.8
1997–98	26.4	8.8

15. Prepare histogram for the following cumulative frequency distribution:

Classes	Frequency
Less than 10	5
Less than 20	8
Less than 30	15
Less than 40	29
Less than 50	36
Less than 60	45
Less than 70	53
Less than 80	60

16. The following table gives the marks of 100 students in the subject 'statistics':

Marks	0–9	10–19	20–29	30–39	40–49	50–59	60–69	70–79
Students	5	15	18	30	15	10	5	2

Draw 'less than' and more than' types ogives. Using these curves find the number of students:
(a) with marks less than 45 (b) with marks more than 65
(c) with marks between 45 and 65.

17. Draw a less than ogive from the following data and estimate the number of employees earning atleast Rs 63 but less than Rs 75.

Wages	50–60	60–70	70–80	80–90	90–100	100–110	110–120
No. of employees	8	10	16	14	10	5	2

18. The following table given the weekly family income in two different region. Draw the Lorenz curve and compare the two regions of incomes.

Income	No. of families	
	Region A	Region B
1000	12	5
1250	18	10
1500	29	17
1750	42	23
2000	20	15
2500	11	8
3000	6	3

19. What is meant by a histogram? State briefly how it is constructed? Indicate clearly how the histogram in respect of the following data can be drawn (only a rough sketch is required). State how you can draw histogram in respect of unequal class-intervals.

Mid-value	Frequency	Mid-value	Frequency
115	6	165	60
125	25	175	38
135	48	185	22
145	72	195	3
155	116		

20. From the following frequency distribution, prepare the less than and more than cumulative frequency curve.

Class-Interval	0–10	10–20	20–30	30–40	40–50	50–60
Frequency	0	12	30	25	18	17

21. The following data indicate the number of foreign tourists arrived in India during the period 1998–2001.

Country	Number of Tourists Arrived		
	1998–1999	1999–2000	2000–2001
USA	2110	2340	2245
UK	5393	6245	6384
Middle East & Gulf	1114	1045	1097
Australia	2432	1849	2249
Western and Eastern Europe	5492	5890	5990

(a) Construct a line graph for the arrival of tourists during 1998–2001.
(b) Construct a histogram for the data.

ANSWERS

I. CHOOSE THE BEST ANSWER

1. (d) 2. (d) 3. (b) 4. (c) 5. (d)
6. (a) 7. (c) 8. (d) 9. (a) 10. (d)
11. (d) 12. (c)

II. FILL IN THE BLANKS

1. Proper scale
2. time
3. histogram
4. frequency polygon
5. continuous
6. median
7. Lorenz
8. Ogive
9. time series, frequency distributions
10. independent.

CHAPTER 6

Measures of Central Tendency

6.1 INTRODUCTION

In the previous chapter, we have studied how to collect raw data, its classification and tabulation in a useful form, which contributes in solving many problems of statistical concern. Yet, this is not sufficient, for in practical purposes, there is need for further consideration, particularly when we want to compare two or more different distributions. We may reduce the entire distribution to one number which represents the distribution.

A single value which can be considered as typical or representative of a set of observations and around which the observations can be considered as centered is called an '*Average*' (or average value) or a *Centre of location*. Since such typical value tends to lie centrally within a set of observations when arranged according to magnitudes, averages are called **measures of central tendency**.

In fact the distribution have a typical value (average) about which, the observations are more or less symmetrically distributed. This is of great importance, both theoretically and practically.

Dr. A.L. Bowley** correctly stated, **"Statistics may rightly be called the science of averages."

Now suppose the students from two or more classes appeared in the examination and we wish to compare the performance of the classes in the examination or wish to compare the performance of the same class after some coaching over a period of time. When making such comparisons, it is not practicable to compare the full frequency distributions of marks. However compactly these may be presented. Therefore, for such statistical analysis, we need a single representative value that describes the entire mass of data given in the frequency distribution. This single representative value is called the central value, measure of location or an average around which individual values of a series cluster. This central value or an average enables us to get a gist of the entire mass of data, and its value lies somewhere in the middle of the two extremes of the given observations. For this reason such a central value or an average is frequently called a ***measure of central tendency***. From the above discussion, it should be clear to you that the concept of a measure of central tendency is concerned only with quantitative variables and is undefined for qualitative variables as these are immeasurable on a scale.

Now we will discuss the various measures of central tendency.

6.2 MEASURES OF CENTRAL TENDENCY

In the study of a population with respect to one in which we are interested we may get a large number of observations. It is not possible to grasp any idea about the characteristic when we look at all the observations. So it is better to get one number for one group.

That number must be a good representative one for all the observations to give a clear picture of that characteristic. Such representative number can be a central value for all these observations. This central value is called a measure of central tendency or an average or a measure of locations.

There are five averages. Among them ***mean, median*** and ***mode*** are called ***simple averages*** and the other two averages ***geometric mean*** and ***harmonic mean*** are called ***special averages***.

The meaning of average is nicely given in the following definitions. "A measure of central tendency is a typical value around which other figures congregate."

6.2.1 Objects of Measures of Central Tendency

(i) **Gives a bird's eye view:** It gives a birds eye view of data huge mass of data, which otherwise are not easily understandable. They set aside unnecessary details of the data and put forward a compact picture of the whole phenomenon e.g. the data giving the height of the students of two colleges will not give any information but if mean height of the students in two colleges is given, then one can easily compare the height of the students.

(ii) **Are representation of the data:** Most of the items in a data cluster around the central value of the data. Thus a measure of central tendency will be a representative of the data.

(iii) **Reduces the complexities of the data:** In order to reduce the complexities of the data and to make it comparable the measures of central tendency reduces each set of data to one figure.

(iv) **Explain the central tendency of the data:** It is obvious that a figure which is used to represent the whole phenomenon should neither have a lowest value nor the highest value. It should have some value lying between the two extremes, possibly in the centre. Thus it gives central tendency of the data.

Thus a statistics average is a measure of central tendency, it represents the entire series by a single value, a value which represents a large number of values which are both above and below it.

6.2.2 Characteristics for a Good Average

The following properties should possess for an ideal average.

1. It should be rigidly defined.
2. It should be easy to understand and compute.
3. It should be based on all items in the data.
4. Its definition shall be in the form of a mathematical formula.
5. It should be capable of further algebraic treatment.
6. It should have sampling stability.
7. It should be capable of being used in further statistical computations or processing.

Besides the above requisites, a good average should represent maximum characteristics of the data; its value should be nearest to the most items of the given series.

6.3 VARIOUS MEASURES OF CENTRAL TENDENCY

A measure of central tendency is also known as measure of first order. There are number of such measures which describe different properties of the data. The various measures of central tendency can be broadly classified in the following categories -

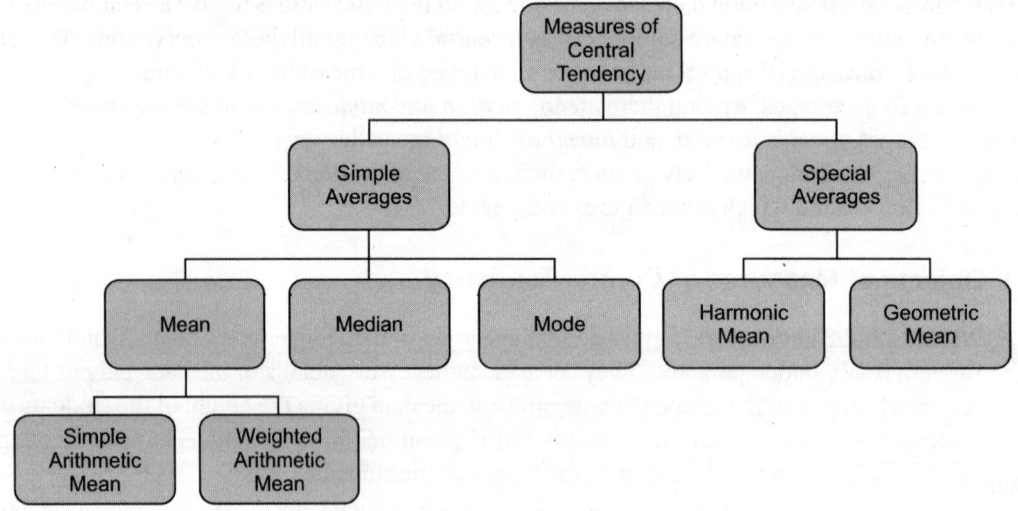

Fig. 6.1: Types of Central Tendency

DO YOU KNOW?

Median and Mode are called the positional measures of an average. These averages are based on the position of the given observations in a series, arranged in an ascending or descending order.

In remaining sections of this chapter the procedure of calculation for the given data, merits and demerits and uses of various measures of central tendency are discussed.

6.4 ARITHMETIC MEAN

Arithmetic mean is the most important among the all averages. It is generally used directly or indirectly by every man. The ***Arithmetic Mean*** of a given set in individual series is their sum divided by the number of observation.

According to ***Horace Secrist***, "The arithmetic mean is the amount secured by dividing the sum of values of the items in a series by their number."

According to ***W.I. King***, "The arithmetic average may be defined as the sum of aggregate of a series of items divided by their number."

"The Arithmetic Mean of a series of items is obtained by adding the values of the items and dividing by the number of items." — ***Croxton & Cowden***

Here the sum or aggregate of a series of items in a series is divided by their number. The simple arithmetic average in the case of individual series (ungrouped data), discrete and continuous series (or grouped data) can be calculated as follow:

6.4.1 Calculation of Arithmetic Mean- Ungrouped or Raw Data

For ungrouped data arithmetic mean may be computed by applying any of the following methods:

1. Direct Method
2. Short-Cut Method

1. **Direct Method:** Arithmetic mean or simply the mean of a variable is defined as the sum of the observations divided by the number of observations. If the variable x assumes n values $x_1, x_2 \ldots x_n$ then the mean, $\overline{X}$*, is given by

$$\overline{X} = \frac{x_1 + x_2 + x_3 + \ldots.. + x_n}{n} = \frac{1}{n}\sum_{i=1}^{n} x_i$$

This formula is for the ungrouped or raw data.

2 **Short-Cut Method:** Under this method an assumed or an arbitrary average (indicated by A) is used as the basis of calculation of deviations from individual values. The formula is

$$\overline{X} = A + \frac{\Sigma d}{n}$$

Where, A = the assumed mean or any value in x

$d = (x - A)$ the deviation of each value from the assumed mean

n = number of items

Σd = sum of deviations

EXAMPLE 6.1: The monthly income of 5 employees working in a firm is as follows:

12000 10000 5000 8000 6000

Find the average monthly income.

Solution: Average monthly income of 5 employees be

$$\overline{X} = \frac{12000 + 10000 + 5000 + 8000 + 6000}{5}$$

$$= \frac{41000}{5} = 8200.$$

EXAMPLE 6.2: A student's marks in 5 subjects are 75, 68, 80, 92, 56. Find his average mark.

Solution:

x	75	68	80	92	56	
d = x – A	7	0	12	24	–12	Σd = 31

$$\overline{X} = A + \frac{\Sigma d}{n}$$

$$= 68 + \frac{31}{5} = 68 + 6.2 = 74.2$$

* For arithmatic mean, we can use both symbols $\bar{x}$ and $\overline{X}$ as they have same meaning. But in this book, we have used only $\overline{X}$ for representing the arithmatic mean.

6.4.2 Calculation of Arithmetic Mean-Discrete Series

In this case also there are two methods of calculating the arithmetic average i.e. For grouped data, arithmetic mean may be calculated by applying any of the following methods:

1. Direct method
2. Short-cut method

1. Direct Method:

Here every term is multiplied by the corresponding frequency and the sum of these products is divided by the sum of frequencies to obtain the arithmetic average. The mean for grouped data is obtained from the following formula :

$$\bar{X} = \frac{\Sigma fx}{N}$$

Where,

x = the mid-point of individual class
f = the frequency of individual class
N = the sum of the frequencies or total frequencies.

2. Short-Cut Method:

In this method we consider an assumed mean and find the deviation of each item from this assumed mean and then use the formula. When short cut method is used, the following formula is applied.

$$\bar{X} = A + \frac{\Sigma fd}{N}$$

Where,

$d = x - A$
f = the frequency of individual class
A = any value in x
N = total frequency

When an arbitrary number 'A' is uniformly subtracted from each observation, it is known as shift of origin of the observation from zero to the point 'A' i.e., the origin becomes A rather than 0. This is usually done for the same of simplifying calculations.

Mean of Original Data = Mean of New Observations + A (origin)

EXAMPLE 6.3: Given the following marks and no. of students, calculate the arithmetic mean:

Marks	64	63	62	61	60	59
Number of Students	8	18	12	9	7	6

Solution :

x	f	fx	d = x − A	fd
64	8	512	2	16
63	18	1134	1	18
62 A	12	744	0	0
61	9	549	− 1	− 9
60	7	420	− 2	− 14
59	6	354	− 3	− 18
	N = 60	Σfx = 3713		Σfd = − 7

Direct Method

$$\bar{X} = \frac{\Sigma fx}{N} = \frac{3713}{60} = 61.68$$

Short-Cut Method

$$\bar{X} = A + \frac{\Sigma fd}{N} = 62 - \frac{7}{60} = 61.88$$

6.4.3 Calculation of Arithmetic Mean-Continuous Series

For grouped data, arithmetic mean may be calculated by applying any of the following methods:

1. Direct method
2. Short-cut method
3. Step Deviation Method

1. **Direct Method:** When the classes are given in the frequency distribution, then the mid-value of each class is taken as x and the remaining method of calculation is the same as that in the discrete series.
2. **Short cut method:** Here we simply transform the given series into an artificially discrete series by replacing each class with its mid-value and then the method of procedure is the same as given in case 6.4.2.

EXAMPLE 6.4: Calculate the arithmetic mean for the following frequency table:

Intervals	20–30	30–40	40–50	50–60	60–70
f	8	26	30	20	16

Here we have

Intervals (C.I.)	f	Mid-value of C.I. (x)	fx	d = x–A	df
20–30	8	25	200	25-45 = – 20	– 160
30–40	26	35	910	35-45 = – 10	– 260
40–50	30	A 45	1350	45-45 = 0	0
50–60	20	55	1100	55-45 = 10	200
60–70	16	65	1040	65-45 = 20	320
	N = 100		Σfx = 4600		Σdf = 100

Direct Method

The required arithmetic mean $= \frac{\Sigma fx}{N} = \frac{4600}{100} = 46$

Short cut Method

The required arithmetic mean = $A + \frac{\Sigma fd}{N} = 45 + \frac{100}{100} = 45 + 1 = 46.$

3. **Step Deviation Method:** This method is used as an auxiliary method of the short-cut method given above, but only in the cases where the widths of the classes are equal. When step Deviation Method is used, the following formula is applied.

$$\bar{X} = A + \frac{\Sigma fd'}{N} \times c$$

Where,

$$d' = \frac{x - A}{c} \qquad [x = A + cd']$$

A = any value in x
N = total frequency
c = width of the interval (upper limit – lower limit)

Like change in origin is made for the save of convenience, sometimes, the original observations are scaled or divided by a number to reduce the value of original observations.

For example, if the original observations are 5, 10 and 15, these can be scaled by a factor of 5 or which is the some thing as dividing the observations by 5, to get the new data as 1, 2 and 3. The A.M. of the new observations is 2, which can be obtained by dividing the original mean 10 by the scaling factor 5.

EXAMPLE 6.5: Following is the distribution of persons according to different income groups. Calculate arithmetic mean.

Income Rs (100)	0–10	10–20	20–30	30–40	40–50	50–60	60–70
Number of Person	6	8	10	12	7	4	3

Solution:

Income	Number of Persons (*f*)	Mid *x*	*d'* = (*x* – *A*)/*c*	*fd'*
0–10	6	5	– 3	– 18
10–20	8	15	– 2	– 16
20–30	10	25	– 1	– 10
30–40	12	**A** 35	0	0
40–50	7	45	1	7
50–60	4	55	2	8
60–70	3	65	3	9
	***N* = 50**			**Σ*fd'* = – 20**

$$\text{Mean} = \bar{X} = A + \frac{\Sigma fd'}{N} \times c \qquad [A = 35] \; [c = 30 - 40 = 10]$$

$$= 35 - \frac{20}{50} \times 10 = 35 - 4 = 31$$

6.4.4 Charlier's Accuracy Check

Charlier has suggested the following checks for the accuracy of results:

1. $\boxed{\Sigma f(x-A) = \Sigma\left[f\{(x-a)+1\}\right]-\Sigma f}$ if short cut method is adopted.

2. $\boxed{\Sigma fd' = \Sigma\left[f(d'+1)\right]-\Sigma f}$ if step – deviation method is adopted.

Where, $d' = \dfrac{x-A}{c}$

Application of this check:

A. Take **example 6.4** on short cut method. Here we have

Interval	*f*	*x*	*d = x – A*	*df*	(*x – A*) + 1	*f* {(*x – A*) +1}
20–30	8	25	25 – 45 = – 20	– 160	– 19	– 152
30–40	26	35	35 – 45 = – 10	– 260	– 9	– 234
40–50	30	45	45 – 45 = 0	0	1	30
50–60	20	55	55 – 45 = 10	200	11	220
60–70	16	65	65 – 45 = 20	320	21	336
	N = 100			= 100		= 200

Now as,

L.H.S $\Sigma f(x-A) = 100$

R.H.S $\Sigma[f\{(x-A)+1\}] - \Sigma f = 200 - 100 = 100$

L.H.S = R.H.S

Therefore the calculations made in example referred above are correct.

B. Take the **example 6.5** on step deviation method. Here we have

Income (CI)	Number of Persons (*f*)	Mid *x*	*d'* = (*x – A*)/*c*	*fd'*	*d'* + 1	*f*(*d'* + 1)
0–10	6	5	–3	–18	–2	–12
10–20	8	15	–2	–16	–1	–8
20–30	10	25	–1	–10	0	0
30–40	12	35	0	0	1	12
40–50	7	45	1	7	2	14
50–60	4	55	2	8	3	12
60–70	3	65	3	9	4	12
	N = 50			Σ*fd'* = – 20		Σ*f*(*d'* + 1) = 30

Now as,

L.H.S $\Sigma fd' = -20$

R.H.S $\Sigma[f(d'+1)] - \Sigma f = 30 - 50 = -20$

L.H.S = R.H.S

Therefore the calculations made in example referred above are correct.

6.4.5 Properties of Arithmetic Mean

1. The sum of the deviations, of all the values of x, from their arithmetic mean, is zero.

Justification :

$$\Sigma f_i\left(x_i - \bar{X}\right) = \Sigma f_i x_i - \bar{X}\,\Sigma f_i = 0$$

$$\bar{X} = \frac{\Sigma f_i x_i}{\Sigma f_i} \quad \therefore\ \Sigma f_i x_i = \bar{X}\,\Sigma f_i$$

Since $\bar{X}$ is a constant,

2. The product of the arithmetic mean and the number of items gives the total of all items.
Justification:

$$\bar{X} = \frac{\Sigma f_i x_i}{\Sigma f_i} \Rightarrow \Sigma f_i x_i = \bar{X}\,\Sigma f_i$$

or

$$\bar{X} = \frac{\Sigma x_i}{n} \Rightarrow \bar{X}\cdot n = \Sigma x_i$$

3. If $\bar{X}_1$ and $\bar{X}_2$ are the arithmetic mean of two samples of sizes n_1 and n_2 respectively then, the arithmetic mean of the distribution combining the two can be calculated as

$$\boxed{\bar{X} = \frac{n_1\bar{X}_1 + n_2\bar{X}_2}{n_1 + n_2}}$$

This formula can be extended for still more groups or samples.
Justification:

$$\bar{X}_1 = \frac{\Sigma x_{1i}}{n_1} \Rightarrow \Sigma x_{1i} = n_1\bar{X}_1 = \text{total of the observations of the first sample.}$$

Similarly $\Sigma x_{2i} = n_2\bar{X}_2$ = total of the observations of the second sample.

The combined mean of the two samples

$$= \frac{\text{combined total}}{n_1 + n_2}$$

$$\bar{\bar{X}}_1 = \frac{n_1\bar{X}_1 + n_2\bar{X}_2}{n_1 + n_2}$$

The advantage of combined arithmetic mean is that, we can determine the over, all mean of the combined data without going back to the original data.

4. It a constant amount is added or subtracted from each value in the series, mean is also added or subtracted by the same constant amount.
Let the values be 3, 5, 9, 15, 16

The AM of these values $= 3 + 5 + 9 + 15 + 16 = \frac{48}{5} = 9.6$

it we add 2 to each value, the value becomes

5, 7, 11, 17, 18

New mean $= \frac{5+7+11+17+18}{5} = \frac{58}{5} = 11.6 = 9.6 + 2$

i.e, the mean is also added by 2.

5. If each value in a series is multiplied or divided by a constant the mean is also multiplied or divided by a contstant.
   The mean of the values 3, 5, 9, 15, 16 is 9.6.
   If we multiply each value by 3, the values become

   9, 15, 27, 45, 48

   $$\text{Mean} = \frac{9+15+27+45+48}{5} = \frac{144}{5} = 28.8 = 9.6 \times 3$$

   i.e., the mean is also multiplied by 3.

EXAMPLE 6.6: Find the combined mean for the data given below

$$n_1 = 20, x_1 = 4, n_2 = 30, x_2 = 3$$

Solution:

$$\text{Combined mean } \bar{X} = \left[\frac{n_1\bar{X}_1 + n_2\bar{X}_2}{n_1 + n_2}\right]$$

$$= \left[\frac{20\times4+30\times3}{20+30}\right]$$

$$= \left[\frac{80+90}{50}\right] = \left[\frac{170}{50}\right] = 3.4.$$

EXAMPLE 6.7: There are two units of an automobile company in two different cities employing 760 and 800 persons, respectively. The arithmetic means of monthly salaries paid to person in these two units are Rs 18,750 and Rs 16,950 respectively. Find the combined arithmetic mean of salaries of the employees in both the units.

Solution: Let n_1 and n_2 be the number of persons working in unit 1 and 2 respectively and x_1 and x_2 be the arithmetic mean of salaries paid to those persons respectively. We are given that :

Unit 1 — $n_1 = 760; x_1 = \text{Rs } 18{,}750$

Unit 2 — $n_2 - 800; x_2 = \text{Rs } 16{,}950$

Thus the combined mean of salaries paid by the company is —

$$\text{Combined mean } \bar{\bar{X}} = \left[\frac{n_1\bar{X}_1 + n_2\bar{X}_2}{n_1 + n_2}\right]$$

$$\text{Combined mean} = \frac{760\times18750+800\times16950}{760+800} = 17826.92 \text{ Rs Per Month}$$

EXAMPLE 6.8: Two groups of size 40 and 50 respectively have their means 100 and 70. Find the mean of the combined group of size 90.

Solution: $\text{The required mean} = \dfrac{(40\times100)+(50\times70)}{40+50}$

$$= \frac{4000+3500}{900} = \frac{75}{9} = 8.333$$

6.4.6 Some Special Types of Problems in Arithmetic Mean and their Solutions

CASE — 1: Frequencies are given in cumulative form, that is, either 'more then type' or 'less than type'

As we know that the 'more than type' cumulative frequencies are calculated by adding frequencies from bottom to top, so that the first class interval has the highest cumulative frequency and it goes on decreasing in subsequent classes. But in case of 'less than cumulative frequencies', the cumulating is done downward so that the first class interval gas the lowest cumulative frequency and it goes on increasing in the subsequent classes.

In both of these cases, data are first converted into inclusive class intervals or exclusive class intervals. Then the calculations for AM are done in the usual manner as discussed earlier.

EXAMPLE 6.9: Find the average marks of students from the following table:

Marks Above	No. of students	Marks Above	No. of students
Above 0	80	Above 60	28
Above 10	77	Above 70	16
Above 20	72	Above 80	10
Above 30	65	Above 90	8
Above 40	55	Above 100	0
Above 50	43		

Solution: Here we first arrange the data in the form of the following frequency table:

Marks Above	No. of students	Marks Above	No. of students
0–10	80 – 77 = 3	50–60	43 – 28 = 15
10–20	77 – 72 = 5	60–70	28 – 16 = 12
20–30	72 – 65 = 7	70–80	16 – 10 = 6
30–40	65 – 55 = 10	80–90	10 – 8 = 2
40–50	55 – 43 = 12	90–100	8 – 0 = 8

Now we can compute the required average by direct method, short cut method or step deviation method.

EXAMPLE 6.10: Find the average marks of students from the following (cumulative frequency) table:

Marks Below	No. of students	Marks Below	No. of students
Below 10	15	Below 50	96
Below 20	35	Below 60	127
Below 30	60	Below 70	198
Below 40	84	Below 80	250

Solution: Here we first arrange the data in the form of the following frequency table:-

Marks	No. of students	Marks	No. of students
0–10	15	40–50	96 – 84 = 12
10–20	35 – 15 = 20	50–60	127 – 96 = 31
20–30	60 – 35 = 25	60–70	198 – 127 = 71
30–40	84 – 60 = 24	70–80	250 – 198 = 52

Now we can compute the required average by direct method, short cut method or step deviation method.

CASE — 2: Frequencies are not given but have to be calculated from the given data

EXAMPLE 6.11: Calculate the missing frequency from the following data :-

No. of tablets	4–8	8–12	12–16	16–20	20–24	24–28	28–32	32–36	36–40
No. of person	11	13	16	14	?	9	17	6	4

The average number of tablets to cure fever was 19.9.

Solution: Take 18 as the assumed mean A and u as the required missing frequency, then we have

No. of tables	No. of persons	Mid value	$d = x - A$	fd
4–8	11	6	–12	–132
8–12	13	10	–8	–104
12–16	16	14	–4	–64
16–20	14	18	0	0
20–24	u	22	4	$4u$
24–28	9	26	8	72
28–32	17	30	12	204
32–36	6	34	16	96
36–40	4	38	20	80
	$N = 90 + u$			$\Sigma fd = 152 + 4u$

The arithmetic Mean $\quad \bar{X} = A + \dfrac{\Sigma fd}{N}$

$$19.9 = 18 + \frac{(152 + 4u)}{(90 + u)}$$

$$(19.9 - 18)(90 - u) = (152 + 4u)$$

$$1.9(90 + u) = (152 + 4u)$$

$$(4 - 1.9)u = 171 - 152$$

$$2.1u = 19$$

$$u = \frac{19}{2.1} = 9.5.$$

CASE — 3: Method of calculating unknown value

If arithmetic mean of discrete and continuous series be given and we are to find the missing item or frequency, then we use the direct or short cut methods.

EXAMPLE 6.12: If the arithmetic mean of data given below be 165 rupees, find the missing term.

Monthly wages in rupees	100	150	200	?	300	500
No. of Labourers	30	20	15	10	4	1

Solution:

X	f	fx
100	30	3000
150	20	3000
200	15	3000
z	10	10z
300	4	1200
500	1	500
	N = 80	Σfx = 10700 + 10z

Now from,

$$AM = \frac{\Sigma fx}{N}$$

$$165 = \frac{(10700 + 10z)}{80}$$

$$165 \times 80 = 10700 + 10z$$

$$10z = 13200 - 10700$$

$$10z = 2500$$

$$Z = 250$$

CASE — 4: To find Arithmetic Mean when Class Intervals are Irregular

If the width of the class-intervals is not equal then the class intervals are said to be irregular and in such cases we should first of all make them regular (if possible) and then use the methods.

EXAMPLE 6.13: Find the arithmetic mean from the following data:

0–5	5–8	8–10	10–12	12–15	15–17	17–20	20–25	25–30
2	5	7	5	6	4	4	9	6

Solution: Making the class intervals regular we can rearrange the given data as follows:

0–5	5–10	10–15	15–20	20–25	25–30
2	12	11	8	9	6

Class Interval	f	x	fx
0–5	2	2.5	5.0
5–10	12	7.5	90.5
10–15	11	12.5	137.5
15–20	8	17.5	140.0
20–25	9	22.5	202.5
25–30	6	27.5	165.0
	N = 48		Σfx = 740

Required

$$AM = \frac{\Sigma fx}{N}$$

$$= \frac{740}{48} = 15.417.$$

CASE-5: Correcting Incorrect Values

It sometimes happens that due to an oversight or mistake in copying certain wrong values are taken while calculating the mean. The problem is how to find out the correct mean. The process is very simple. From Σx deduct wrong observations and add correct observations and then divide the correct Σx by the number of observations and the result so obtained will give the value of the correct mean.

EXAMPLE 6.14: The average weekly for a group of 25 persons working in a factory was calculated to be Rs 378.40. It was later discovered that one figure was misread as 160 instead of the correct value Rs 200. Calculate average wage.

Solution:

$$\Sigma x = N\bar{X} = 25 \times 378.4 = 9460$$

$$\text{Incorrect figure} = 160$$

$$\text{Correct figure} = 200$$

$$\therefore \quad \text{Correct } \Sigma x = 9460 - 160 + 200 = 9500$$

Hence,

$$\text{correct average wage} = \frac{9500}{25} = 380$$

EXAMPLE 6.15: The mean of 200 observations was 50. Later on, it was discovered that two observations were wrongly read as 92 and 8 instead of 192 and 88. Find out the correct mean.

Solution: Here,

$$\bar{X} = 50 \text{ and } N = 200$$

$$\Sigma x = 200 \times 50 = 10{,}000$$

$$\text{Incorrect observations} = 92, 8$$

$$\text{Correct observations} = 192, 88$$

$$\therefore \quad \text{Correct } \Sigma x = 10{,}000 - (92 + 8) + (192 + 88)$$

$$= 10{,}000 - 100 + 280$$

$$= 10{,}180$$

Hence

$$\text{correct mean} = \frac{10{,}180}{200} = 50.9$$

6.4.7 Merits and Demerits of Arithmetic Mean

Merits

1. It is rigidly defined.
2. It is easy to understand and easy to calculate.
3. If the number of items is sufficiently large, it is more accurate and more reliable.
4. It is a calculated value and is not based on its position in the series.
5. It is possible to calculate even if some of the details of the data are lacking.
6. Of all averages, it is affected least by fluctuations of sampling.
7. It provides a good basis for comparison.

Demerits

1. It cannot be obtained by inspection nor located through a frequency graph.
2. It cannot be in the study of qualitative phenomena not capable of numerical measurement i.e., Intelligence, beauty, honesty etc.
3. It can ignore any single item only at the risk of losing its accuracy.

4. It is affected very much by extreme values.
5. It cannot be calculated for open-end classes.
6. It may lead to fallacious conclusions, if the details of the data from which it is computed are not given.

6.4.8 Limitations of Arithmetic Mean

The arithmetic mean should not be used in the following cases:

- In distributions with open end intervals.
- When values of items are in geometric progression.
- When items are very large or very small, since arithmetic mean is affected by extreme values.
- When rates are to be averaged.
- When change over a period of item is required.
- When an average rate of growth is required.

Some Examples based on the drawback of Arithmetic Mean.

1. Let us consider the following marks obtained by three students: Swati, Surbhi, Shweta in three tests respectively.

	I Test	II Test	III Test	Average Marks
Swati	54%	61%	65%	60%
Surbhi	66%	59%	55%	60%
Shweta	68%	54%	58%	60%

The average marks obtained by each of the students at the end of the year is 60%. We can conclude that the level of intelligence of the students at the end is same.
This is a fallacious conclusion since we find that from the data Swati has improved consistently while Surbhi has deteriorated consistently and Shweta has shown average performance.

2. Let us consider a company situations where the average salary of workers (III grade and IV grade) is, say, Rs 6000 per month and the average salary of workers (I grade and II grade) is say, Rs 35,000. Thus we say that average salary of all workers in the company is, say, Rs 15,000 p.m. It gives a very good impression and one is tempted to think that the workers are well paid and their standard of living is good but the really picture is entirely different. Thus in the case of extreme observations, the arithmetic mean gives the destroyed picture.

6.4.9 Weighted Arithmetic Mean

For calculating simple mean, we suppose that all the values or the sizes of items in the distribution have equal importance. But, in practical life this may not be so. In case some items are more important than others, a simple average computed is not representative of the distribution. Proper weightage has to be given to the various items. ***For example***, to have an idea of the change in cost of living of a certain group of persons, the simple average of the prices of the commodities consumed by them will not do because all the commodities are not equally important, e.g rice, wheat and pulses are more important than tea, confectionery etc., It is the weighted arithmetic average which helps in finding out the average value of the series after giving proper weight to each group.

Weight mean should be applied under following situations:

(a) When the importance of each item in the frequency distribution is not same.

(b) The number of items in different groups of the data is widely different.

(c) In the calculation of ratios, percentages or rates a weighted average is more representative.

(d) When the change in the size of items is accompanied by the change in relative proportion of the number of items.

One of the limitations of the arithmetic mean is that it gives equal importance (weight) to all the items in the series. But there are cases where the relative importance of all the items is not equal. ***Weighted Arithmetic Mean*** is the correct tool for measuring the Central Tendency of the given observations in such cases. Here, the term weight stands for the relative importance of different items or observations.

The average whose component items are being multiplied by certain values known as "weights" and the aggregate of the multiplied results are being divided by the total sum of their "weight".

In other words, importance assigned to different items with the help of figures according to priority is known as weights. ***For example***, it is wrong to give equal weight to different categories of employees in a firm viz., manager, clerks, labourer, etc., for calculating mean salary, as there may be only one manager, 30 clerks and 1000 labourers. In such cases, salaries paid should be weighted according to relative importance, which may be number of different categories of employees in the firm.

If $x_1, x_2 \ldots x_n$ be the values of a variable x with respective weights of $w_1, w_2 \ldots w_n$ assigned to them, then

$$\text{Weighted A.M} = \bar{X}_w = \frac{w_1 x_1 + w_2 x_2 + \ldots\ldots w_n x_n}{w_1 + w_2 + \ldots\ldots w_n}$$

$$= \frac{\Sigma w_i x_i}{\Sigma w_i}$$

6.4.9.1 Uses at the Weighted Mean

Weighted arithmetic mean is used in:

a. Construction of index numbers.

b. Comparison of results of two or more universities where number of students differ.

c. Computation of standardized death and birth rates.

EXAMPLE 6.16: Calculate weighted average from the following data:

Designation	Monthly Salary (in Rs)	Strength of The Cadre
Class 1 officers	1500	10
Class 2 officers	800	20
Subordinate staff	500	70
Clerical staff	250	100
Lower staff	100	150

Solution:

Designation	Monthly salary, *x*	Strength of the cadre, *w*	*wx*
Class 1 officers	1,500	10	15,000
Class 2 officers	800	20	16,000
Subordinate staff	500	70	35,000
Clerical staff	250	100	25,000
Lower staff	100	150	15,000
		$\Sigma w = 350$	$\Sigma wx = 1{,}06{,}000$

Weighted average,
$$\bar{X}_w = \frac{\Sigma wx}{\Sigma w}$$
$$= \frac{106000}{350} = \text{Rs } 302.86.$$

EXAMPLE 6.17: Comment on the performance of the students in three universities given below, using simple and weighted averages:

University / Course of study	Delhi		Agra		Punjab	
	% of pass	No. of students (in '00s)	% of pass	No. of students (in '00s)	% of pass	No. of students (in '00s)
MBA	71	3	82	2	81	2
MCA	83	4	76	3	76	3.5
BBA	73	5	73	6	74	4.5
BCA	74	2	76	7	58	2
B.Tech	65	3	65	3	70	7
B.Pharma	66	3	66	7	73	2

Solution: The computation of simple and weighted averages is as below:

University / Course of study	Delhi			Agra			Punjab		
	Pass % (x_1)	No. of students (in '00s) (w_1)	(w_1x_1)	Pass % (x_2)	No. of students (in '00s) (w_2)	(w_2x_2)	Pass % (x_3)	No. of students (in 00's) (w_3)	(w_3x_3)
MBA	71	3	213	82	2	164	81	2	162
MCA	83	4	332	76	3	228	76	3.5	266
BBA	73	5	365	73	6	438	74	4.5	333
BCA	74	2	148	76	7	532	58	2	116
B.Tech	65	3	195	65	3	195	70	7	490
B.Pharma	66	3	198	60	7	420	73	2	146
Total	**432**	**20**	**1451**	**432**	**28**	**1977**	**432**	**21**	**1513**

For Delhi University,

$$\text{Simple Average} = \frac{\Sigma x_1}{6} = \frac{432}{6} = 72$$

$$\text{and weighted average} = \frac{\Sigma w_1 x_1}{\Sigma w_1} = \frac{1451}{20} = 72.55$$

For Agra University,

$$\text{Simple Average} = \frac{\Sigma x_2}{6} = \frac{432}{6} = 72$$

$$\text{and Weighted Average} = \frac{\Sigma w_2 x_2}{\Sigma w_2} = \frac{1977}{28} = 70.61$$

For Punjab University,

$$\text{Simple Average} = \frac{\Sigma x_3}{6} = \frac{432}{6} = 72$$

$$\text{and Weighted Average} = \frac{\Sigma w_3 x_3}{\Sigma w_3} = \frac{1513}{21} = 72.05$$

On the basis of the simple average which comes out to be same for each University viz., 72, we cannot distinguish between the pass percentage of the students in the three universities. However, the weighted averages show that the results are the best in Delhi University (which has highest) weighted average of 72.55), followed by Punjab University (which has weighted average 72.05), while Agra University shows the lowest performance.

6.5 MEDIAN

Median is defined as the value of the middle item (or the mean of the values of the two middle items) when the data are arranged in an ascending or descending order of magnitude. Thus, in an ungrouped frequency distribution if the n values are arranged in ascending or descending order of magnitude, the median is the middle value if n is odd. When n is even, the median is the mean of the two middle values.

DO YOU KNOW?

The median is that value of the variant which divides the group into two equal parts, one part comprising all values greater, and the other, all values less than median.

In ***Connor's*** words - "The median is that value of the variable which divides the group into two equal parts, one part comprising all values greater and the other all values lesser than the median."

For example, the daily wages of 7 workers are 5, 7, 9, 11, 12, 14 and 15 dollars. This series contains 7 terms. The fourth term i.e. $11 is the median.

The Median is the middle value in an ***ordered*** array of observations. If there is an even number of observations in the array, the median is the ***average*** of the two middle numbers. If there is an odd number of data in the array, the median is the ***middle*** number. The median is often used to summarize the distribution of an outcome.

6.5.1 Calculation of Median-Ungrouped or Raw Data

In this case the terms of the series should first of all be written in ascending or descending order. Let n be the number of terms.

CASE — 1: If n is odd, the middle term of the series is $\frac{(n+1)}{2}$ ***th and its value is the median.***

By formula,

$$\text{Median} = M_e = \left(\frac{n+1}{2}\right)^{\text{th}} \text{ item.}$$

CASE — 2: If n is even, then there are two middle terms viz. $\left(\frac{n}{2}\right)^{th}$ ***and*** $\left(\frac{(n+2)}{2}\right)^{th}$***. The mean of their values is the median in this case.***

By formula,

$$\text{Median} = M_e = \frac{1}{2}\left[\begin{array}{l}\text{size of } \left(\frac{n}{2}\right)^{\text{th}} \text{ observations} \\ + \text{ size of } \left(\frac{n+2}{2}\right)^{\text{th}} \text{ observations}\end{array}\right]$$

EXAMPLE 6.18: When odd number of values are given. Find median for the following data 25, 18, 27, 10, 8, 30, 42, 20, 53.

Solution: Arranging the data in the increasing order 8, 10, 18, 20, 25, 27, 30, 42, 53.

Since total number of items $\boxed{\boldsymbol{n = 9\,(\text{odd})}}$. The middle value is the 5th item i.e., 25 is the median.

Using formula,

$$\begin{aligned} M_e &= \left(\frac{n+1}{2}\right)^{\text{th}} \text{ item.} \\ &= \left(\frac{9+1}{2}\right)^{\text{th}} \text{ item} \\ &= \left(\frac{10}{2}\right)^{\text{th}} \text{ item} \\ &= 5^{\text{th}} \text{ item} = 25. \end{aligned}$$

EXAMPLE 6.19: The population (in thousands) of 36 cities are as follows:

2468, 591, 437, 20, 213, 143, 1490, 407, 284, 176, 263, 19, 181, 777, 387, 302, 213, 204, 153, 733, 391, 176 178, 122, 532, 360, 65, 260, 193, 92, 672, 258, 239, 160, 147, 151.
Calculate the median.

Solution: Arranging the terms in the ascending order as :

20, 65, 92, 131, 142, 143, 147, 151, 153, 160, 169, 176, 178, 181, 193, 204, (213, 39), 258, 263, 260, 384, 302, 360, 387, 391, 407, 437, 522, 591, 672, 733, 777, 1490, 2468.

Since total number of items $\boxed{\boldsymbol{n = 36} \textbf{ (Even)}}$.

$$\text{The median} = \frac{1}{2}\left[\text{size of } \left(\frac{n}{2}\right)^{\text{th}} \text{ item} + \text{size of } \left(\frac{n+2}{2}\right)^{\text{th}} \text{ item}\right]$$

$$= \frac{1}{2} \text{ [size of } 18^{\text{th}} \text{ item} + \text{size of } 19^{\text{th}} \text{ item]}$$

$$= \frac{1}{2} [213 + 239]$$

$$= \frac{1}{2} [252] = 226 \text{ thousands.}$$

EXAMPLE 6.20: The numbers of books issued on the consecutive days from a library are 75, 80, 96, 92, 89, 94, 100, 82, 63, 105.

Solution: Arranging the terms in ascending order, we get
63, 75, 80, 82, 89, 92, 94, 96, 100, 105

Hence the number of terms $\boxed{\boldsymbol{n = 10} \textbf{ (Even)}}$.

There will be two middle terms viz.

$$\text{Median} = (M_e) = \frac{\left(\frac{n}{2}\right)^{\text{th}} + \left(\frac{n+2}{2}\right)^{\text{th}}}{2}$$

$$M_e = \frac{\frac{10}{2} + \left(\frac{10+2}{2}\right)}{2} = \frac{5^{\text{th}} + 6^{\text{th}}}{2}$$

Now we get 5th term = 89 and 6th term = 92

$$M_e = \frac{89 + 92}{2} = \frac{181}{2} = 90.5$$

EXAMPLE 6.21: The following table represents the marks obtained by a batch of 10 students in certain class tests in statistics and Accountancy.

Serial No.	1	2	3	4	5	6	7	8	9	10
Marks (Statistics)	53	55	52	32	30	60	47	46	35	28
Marks (Accountancy)	57	45	24	31	25	84	43	80	32	72

Indicate in which subject is the level of knowledge higher?

Solution: For such question, median is the most suitable measure of central tendency. The mark in the two subjects is first arranged in increasing order as follows:

$$\boxed{\boldsymbol{n = 10} \textbf{ (Even)}}$$

Serial No.	1	2	3	4	5	6	7	8	9	10
Marks(Statistics)	28	30	32	35	46	47	52	53	55	60
Marks(Accountancy)	24	25	31	32	43	45	57	72	80	84

$$\text{Median} = \left(\frac{n+1}{2}\right)^{\text{th}} \text{item} = \left(\frac{10+1}{2}\right)^{\text{th}} \text{item} = 5.5^{\text{th}} \text{ item}$$

$$= \frac{\text{Value of } 5^{\text{th}} \text{ item } + \text{ value of } 6^{\text{th}} \text{ item}}{2}$$

$$M_e\,(\text{statistics}) = \frac{46+47}{2} = 46.5$$

$$M_e\,(\text{accountancy}) = \frac{43+45}{2} = 44$$

Therefore the level of knowledge in Statistics is higher than that in Accountancy.

6.5.2 Calculation of Median-Discrete Series

The steps given below are followed for the calculation of median in discrete series.

Working Steps

Step 1: Find Cumulative Frequencies
Step 2: Find $(N + 1)/2$
Step 3: See in the cumulative frequencies the value just greater than $(N + 1)/2$
Step 4: Then the corresponding value of x is median.

EXAMPLE 6.22: The following data pertaining to the number of members in a family. Find median size of the family.

Number of Members *x*	1	2	3	4	5	6	7	8	9	10	11	12
Frequency *f*	1	3	5	6	10	13	9	5	3	2	2	1

Solution:

x	*f*	*cf*
1	1	1
2	3	4
3	5	9
4	6	15
5	10	25
6	13	38
7	9	47
8	5	52
9	3	55
10	2	57
11	2	59
12	1	60
	N = 60	

Here **$N = 60$ (Even)**. Therefore there will be two middle terms $N/2$ and $(N+2)/2$ i.e 30th and 31st. Now from the above table we observe that both 30th and 31st terms come under the cumulative frequency 38 and in the row of cumulative frequency 38, then value of x is 6

OR

$$\text{Median} = \text{size of } \left(\frac{N+1}{2}\right)^{\text{th}} \text{ item}$$

$$= \text{size of } \left(\frac{60+1}{2}\right)^{\text{th}} \text{ item} = 30.5^{\text{th}} \text{ item}$$

The cumulative frequency just greater than 30.5 is 38 and the value of x corresponding to 38 is 6. Hence the median size is 6 members per family.

NOTE: It is an appropriate method because a fractional value given by mean does not indicate the average number of members in a family.

6.5.3 Calculation of Median — Continuous Series

The steps given below are followed for the calculation of median in continuous series.

Working Steps

Step 1: Find cumulative frequencies.

Step 2: Find $\left(\frac{N}{2}\right)$

Step 3: See in the cumulative frequency the value first greater than $\left(\frac{N}{2}\right)$, then the corresponding class interval is called the Median class. Then apply the formula

$$\text{Median} = l_1 + \frac{\frac{N}{2} - m}{f} \times c$$

Where,
l_1 = Lower limit of the median class
m = Cumulative frequency of preceding the median
c = Width of the median class, f = frequency

NOTE: If the class intervals are given in inclusive type convert them into exclusive type and call it as true class interval and consider lower limit in this.

EXAMPLE 6.23: The following table gives the frequency distribution of 325 workers of a factory, according to their average monthly income in a certain year.

Income group	No. of Workers	Income group	No. of Workers
Below 100	1	350–400	30
100–150	20	400–450	25
150–200	42	450–500	15
200–250	55	500–550	18
250–300	62	550–600	10
300–350	45	600 and above	2

Calculate median income.

Solution:

Income group (class-interval)	No of Workers (frequency)	Cumulative Frequency (Cf)
Below 100	1	1
100–150	20	21
150–200	42	63
200–250	55	m 118
250 – 300	f 62	180
300–350	45	225
350–400	30	255
400–450	25	280
450–500	15	295
500–550	18	313
550–600	10	323
600 and above	2	325
	$N = 325$	

Here **$N = 325$ (Odd)**.

Median number = $\left(\frac{N+1}{2}\right)^{\text{th}}$ item = $\left(\frac{325+1}{2}\right)^{\text{th}}$ item = 163, which is in the class 250–300 (see the row of cumulative frequency 180, which contains 163).

Hence ***median class is 250–300***

We have
l_1 = lower limit of median class = 250
f = frequency of median class = 62
m = preceding cumulative frequency = 118
C = difference between upper and lower class = 300–250 = 50

$$\frac{N}{2} = \frac{325}{2} = 162.5$$

Here

$$\text{Median} = l_1 + \frac{\frac{N}{2} - m}{f} \times c$$

$$= 250 + \left(\frac{162.5 - 118}{62}\right) \times 50 = 250 + 35.89 = 285.89$$

EXAMPLE 6.24: Following are the daily wages of workers in a textile. Find the median.

Wages (in Rs)	Number of workers	Wages (in Rs)	Number of workers
Less than 100	5	Less than 600	45
Less than 200	12	Less than 700	52
Less than 300	20	Less than 800	60
Less than 400	32	Less than 900	68
Less than 500	40	Less than 1000	75

Solution: We are given upper limit and less than cumulative frequencies. First find the class-intervals and the frequencies. Since the values are increasing by 100, hence the width of the class interval equal to 100.

Wages (class-interval)	No of Workers (frequency)	Cumulative Frequency (*Cf*)
0–100	5	5
100–200	7	12
200–300	8	20
300–400	12	*m* 32
400 – 500	*f* 8	40
500–600	5	45
600–700	7	52
700–800	8	60
800–900	8	68
900–1000	7	75
	***N* = 75**	

Here **$N = 75$ (Odd)**, Median $= \left(\frac{N+1}{2}\right)^{\text{th}} = \left(\frac{75+1}{2}\right)^{\text{th}} = 38^{\text{th}}$ which is in class 400–500.

Hence Median class 400–500.

$$\left(\frac{N}{2}\right) = \left(\frac{75}{2}\right) = 37.5, \ f = 8, \ m = 32, \ c = 100, \ l_1 = 400$$

$$M_e = l + \left(\frac{\frac{N}{2} - m}{f}\right) \times c = 400 + \left(\frac{37.5 - 32}{8}\right) \times 100 = 400 + 68.75 = 468.75.$$

EXAMPLE 6.25: Find median for the data given below :

Marks	Number of students	Marks	Number of students
Greater than 10	70	Greater than 60	24
Greater than 20	62	Greater than 70	17
Greater than 30	50	Greater than 80	9
Greater than 40	38	Greater than 90	4
Greater than 50	30		

Solution: Here we are given lower limit and more than cumulative frequencies.

Class interval	*f*	More than *c.f*	Less than *c.f*
10–20	8	70	8
20–30	12	62	32
30–40	12	50	*m* 32
40–50	*f* 8	38	40
50–60	6	30	46
60–70	7	24	53
70–80	8	17	61
80–90	5	9	66
90–100	4	4	70
	***N* = 70**		

Here, Median class 40–50, $\left(\frac{N}{2}\right) = \left(\frac{70}{2}\right) = 35, \ f = 8, \ m = 32, \ c = 10, \ l_1 = 40$

$$M_e = l + \left(\frac{\frac{N}{2} - m}{f} \times c \right) = 40 + \left(\frac{35-32}{8} \right) \times 10$$

$$= 40 + 3.75 = 43.75$$

6.5.4 Graphic Method for Location of Median

Median can be located with the help of the cumulative frequency curve or 'ogive'. The procedure for locating median in a grouped data is as follows:

Working Steps

Step 1: The class boundaries, where there are no gaps between consecutive classes, are represented on the horizontal axis (x-axis).

Step 2: The cumulative frequency corresponding to different classes is plotted on the vertical axis (y-axis) against the upper limit of the class interval (or against the variate value in the case of a discrete series.)

Step 3: The curve obtained on joining the points by means of freehand drawing is called the 'ogive'. The ogive so drawn may be either a (i) less than ogive or a (ii) more than ogive.

Step 4: The value of $\frac{n}{2}$ or $\frac{n+1}{2}$ is marked on the y-axis, where n is the total frequency.

Step 5: A horizontal straight line is drawn from the point $n/2$ or $n+1/2$ on the y-axis parallel to x-axis to meet the ogive.

Step 6: A vertical straight line is drawn from the point of intersection perpendicular to the horizontal axis.

Step 7: The point of intersection of the perpendicular to the x-axis gives the value of the median.

Remarks

1. From the point of intersection of 'less than' and 'more than' ogive, if a perpendicular is drawn on the x-axis, the point so obtained on the horizontal axis gives the value of the median.
2. If ogive is drawn using cumulative percentage frequencies, then we draw a straight line from the point intersecting 50 percent cumulative frequency on the y-axis parallel to the x-axis to intersect the ogive. A perpendicular drawn from this point of intersection on the horizontal axis gives the value of the median.

EXAMPLE 6.26: Draw an ogive of 'less than' type on the data given below and hence find median.

Weight(lbs)	Number of Persons
100–109	8
110–119	15
120–129	21
130–139	34
140–149	45
150–159	26
160–169	20
170–179	15
180–189	10
190–199	6

Solution:

Class interval	No. of persons	True class interval	Less than *c.f*
100–109	8	99.5–109.5	8
110–119	15	109.5–119.5	23
120–129	21	119.5–129.5	44
130–139	34	129.5–139.5	78
140–149	45	139.5–149.5	123
150–159	26	149.5–159.5	149
160–169	20	159.5–169.5	169
170–179	15	169.5–179.5	184
180–189	10	179.5–189.5	194
190–199	6	189.5–199.5	200

Y Less than Ogive

X axis 1 cm = 10 units

Y axis 1 cm = 25 units

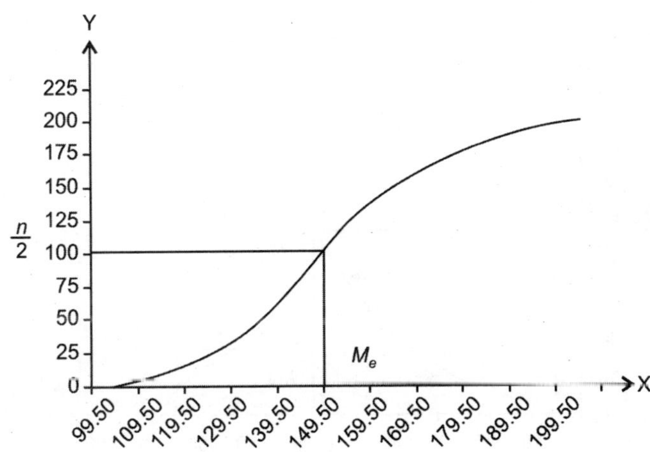

Fig. 6.2: Less than ogive

EXAMPLE 6.27: Draw an ogive for the following frequency distribution and hence find median.

Marks	Number of Students
0–10	5
10–20	4
20–30	8
30–40	12
40–50	16
50–60	25
60–70	10
70–80	8
80–90	5
90–100	2

Solution:

Class Boundary	Cumulative Frequency	
	Less than	More than
0	0	95
10	5	90
20	9	86
30	17	78
40	29	66
50	45	50
60	70	25
70	80	15
80	88	7
90	93	2
100	95	0

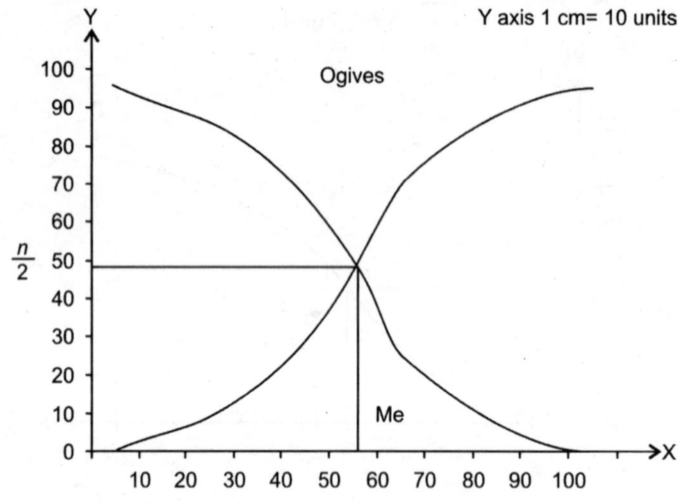

Fig. 6.3: Less than or More than ogive

6.5.5 Merits and Demerits of Median

Merits

1. Median is not influenced by extreme values because it is a positional average.
2. Median can be calculated in case of distribution with opened intervals.
3. Median can be located even if the data are incomplete.
4. Median can be located even for qualitative factors such as ability, honesty etc.

Demerits

1. A slight change in the series may bring drastic change in median value.
2. In case of even number of items or continuous series, median is an estimated value other than any value in the series.
3. It is not suitable for further mathematical treatment except its use in mean deviation.
4. It is not taken into account of all the observations.

6.5.6 Uses of the Median

- The Median is generally used, if
- There are extreme deviations
- The data is heterogeneous (or skewed)
- A quick estimate of average is required.
- Relative comparisons are to be made and
- The distributions are with open end intervals

6.5.7 Measurements depending upon Median

The fundamental purpose of various measures of central tendency is to get as much information about the formulation of the series as possible.

We know that the median divides the given items of a series, arranging in ascending or descending order of magnitude, into two equal parts. Similarly the items of a series can be divided into many other equal parts e.g. in four, five, eight, ten or hundred equal parts and these measurements are known as quartile, octile, decile and percentile respectively.

6.6 QUARTILES

The quartiles divide the distribution in four parts. There are three quartiles. The second quartile Q_2 divides the distribution into two halves and therefore is the same as the median. The ***lower quartile*** (Q_1) marks off the first one-fourth, the ***upper quartile*** (Q_3) marks off the three-fourth.

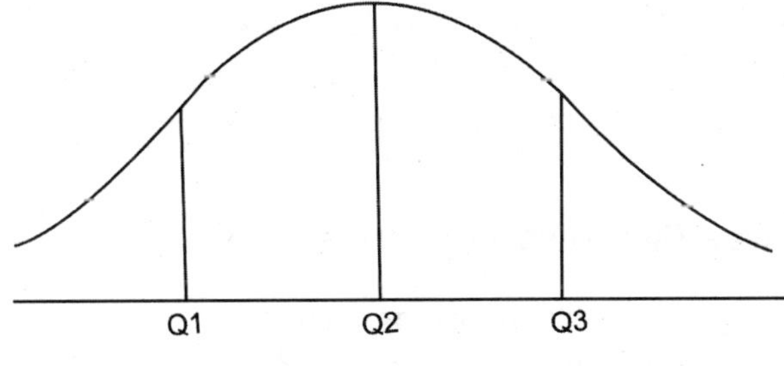

Fig. 6.4

- Q_1 known as **1st quartile** is that value of the variate which divides the data in such a way that $\frac{n}{4}$ items have a value less than Q_1 and $\frac{3n}{4}$ have a value more than Q_1.
- Q_2 known as **2nd quartile** divides the whole distribution in two equal parts and is equal to median.
- Q_3 known as **3rd quartile** is that value of the variate which divides the data in such a way that $\frac{3n}{4}$ items have a value less that Q_3 and $\frac{n}{4}$ have a value more than Q_3.

6.6.1 Calculation of Quartiles-Ungrouped Data or Raw Data

First arrange the given data in the increasing order and use the formula for Q_1 and Q_3

$$Q_1 = \left(\frac{n+1}{4}\right)^{th} \text{item} \quad \text{and} \quad Q_3 = 3\left(\frac{n+1}{4}\right)^{th} \text{item}$$

EXAMPLE 6.28: Compute quartiles for the data given below 25, 18, 30, 8, 15, 5, 10, 35, 40, 45.

Solution:

5, 8, 10, 15, 18, 25, 30, 35, 40, 45

Here number of item $n = 10$.

Now,

$$Q_1 = \left(\frac{n+1}{4}\right)^{th} \text{item} = \left(\frac{10+1}{4}\right)^{th} \text{item}$$

$$= 2^{nd} \text{ item} + \left(\frac{3}{4}\right)(3^{rd} \text{ item} - 2^{nd} \text{ item})$$

$$= 8 + \frac{3}{4}(10-8)$$

$$= 8 + 1.5 = 9.5$$

$$Q_3 = 3\left(\frac{n+1}{4}\right)^{th} \text{item}$$

$$= 3 \times (2.75)^{th} \text{ item} = (8.25)^{th} \text{ item}$$

$$= 8^{th} \text{ item} + \frac{1}{4}(9^{th} \text{ item} - 8^{th} \text{ item})$$

$$= 35 + \frac{1}{4}(40-35) = 35 + 1.25 = 36.25$$

6.6.2 Calculation of Quartiles-Discrete Series

Working Steps

Step 1: Find cumulative frequencies.

Step 2: Find $\left(\frac{N+1}{4}\right)$

Step 3: See in the cumulative frequencies, the value just greater than $\left(\frac{N+1}{4}\right)$, then the corresponding value of x is Q_1.

Step 4: Find $3\left(\frac{N+1}{4}\right)$.

Step 5: See in cumulative frequencies, the value just greater than $3\left(\frac{N+1}{4}\right)$, then the corresponding value of x is Q_3.

EXAMPLE 6.29: Compute quartiles for the data given below:

x	5	8	12	15	19	24	30
f	4	3	2	4	5	2	4

Solution :

x	f	c.f
5	4	4
8	3	7
12	2	9
15	4	13
19	5	18
24	2	20
30	4	24
Total	N = 24	

$$Q_1 = \left(\frac{N+1}{4}\right)^{th} \text{ item} = \left(\frac{24+1}{4}\right) = \left(\frac{25}{4}\right) = 6.25^{th} \text{ item}$$

$$Q_3 = 3\left(\frac{N+1}{4}\right)^{th} \text{ item} = 3\left(\frac{24+1}{4}\right) = 18.75^{th} \text{ item}$$

$\therefore \quad Q_1 = 8, Q_3 = 24$

6.6.3 Calculation of Quartiles-Continuous Series

Working Steps

Step 1: Find cumulative frequencies

Step 2: Find $\left(\frac{N}{4}\right)$

Step 3: See in the cumulative frequencies, the value just greater than $\left(\frac{N}{4}\right)$, then the corresponding class interval is called first quartile class.

Step 4: Find $3\left(\frac{N}{4}\right)$ see in the cumulative frequencies the value just greater than $3\left(\frac{N}{4}\right)$ then the corresponding class interval is called 3rd quartile class. Then apply the respective formulae.

$$Q_1 = l_1 + \frac{\frac{N}{4} - m_1}{f_1} \times c$$

$$Q_3 = l_3 + \frac{3\left(\frac{N}{4}\right) - m_3}{f_3} \times c$$

Where,
l_1 = lower limit of the first quartile class
l_3 = lower limit of the third quartile class
f_1 = frequency of the first quartile class
f_3 = frequency of third quartile class
m_1 = c.f. preceding the 1st quartile class
m_3 = c.f preceding the 3rd quartile class
c = class interval of quartile class

EXAMPLE 6.30: The following series relates to the marks secured by students in an examination.

Marks	0–10	10–20	20–30	30–40	40–50	50–60	60–70	70–80	80–90	90–100
No. of students	11	18	25	28	30	33	22	15	12	10

Find the quartiles.

Solution:

Class-interval	No of students (frequency)	Cumulative Frequency (Cf)
0–10	11	11
10–20	18	m_1 29
20 – 30	f_1 25	54
30–40	28	82
40–50	30	112
50–60	33	m_2 145
60 – 70	f_2 22	167
70–80	15	182
80–90	12	194
90–100	10	204
	$N = 204$	

$$\left(\frac{N}{4}\right) = \left(\frac{204}{4}\right) = 51, \quad 3\left(\frac{N}{4}\right) = \left(\frac{612}{4}\right) = 153$$

Here Model class = 20–30 (for Q_1), Model class = 60–70 (for Q_3)

$\left(\frac{N}{4}\right)$ = 51, see in the cumulative frequency, value lies on 54, then we can say that

$$f_1 = 25,\ l_1 = 20,\ m_1 = 29,\ c_1 = 30 - 20 = 10$$

$$Q_1 = l_1 + \frac{\frac{N}{4} - m_1}{f_1} \times c_1 = 20 + \frac{51 - 29}{25} \times 10 = 20 + 8.8 = 28.8$$

$3\left(\frac{N}{4}\right)$ = 153, see in the cumulative frequency, value lies on 167, then we can say that

$$f_3 = 22,\ l_3 = 60,\ m_3 = 145,\ c_3 = 70 - 60 = 10$$

$$Q_3 = l_3 + \frac{3\left(\frac{N}{4}\right) - m_3}{f_3} \times c_3 = 60 + \frac{153 - 145}{22} \times 12 = 60 + 4.36 = 64.36.$$

6.7 DECILES

These are the values, which divide the total number of observation into 10 equal parts. These are 9 deciles $D_1, D_2 \ldots D_9$.

These are all called first deciles, second deciles …etc.

6.7.1 Calculation of Deciles-Ungrouped Data or Raw Data

The first decile (D_1) comes points to $\left(\frac{n}{10}\right)^{\text{th}}$ item value, D_2 to $2\left(\frac{n}{10}\right)$, D_3 to $3\left(\frac{n}{10}\right)$……, D_9 to $9\left(\frac{n}{10}\right)$ item value when the data is arranged in an ascending or descending order.

EXAMPLE 6.31: Compute D_5 for the data given below 5, 24, 36, 12, 20, 8

Solution : Arranging the given values in the increasing order 5, 8, 12, 20, 24, 36

$n = 6$

$$D_5 = \left(\frac{5(n+1)}{10}\right)^{\text{th}} \text{ observation}$$

$$= \left(\frac{5(6+1)}{10}\right)^{\text{th}} \text{ observation}$$

$$= (3.5)^{\text{th}} \text{ observation}$$

$$= 3^{\text{rd}} \text{ item} + \frac{1}{2}\ [4^{\text{th}} \text{ item} - 3^{\text{rd}} \text{ item}]$$

$$= 12 + \frac{1}{2}[20 - 12]$$

$$= 12 + 4 = 16.$$

6.7.2 Calculation of Deciles- Continuous Data

For grouped data the following formula is used for interpolation

$$D_i = l_i + \frac{i\left(\frac{N}{10}\right) - m_i}{f_i} \times c$$

Where, $i = 1, 2, 3, 4, 5$ ….9. The symbols having usual meaning. ***Note that*** D_5 will be as median.

EXAMPLE 6.32: Calculate D_3 and D_7 for the data given below

Class-Interval	1–10	10–20	20–30	30–40	40–50	50–60	60–70
Frequency	5	7	12	16	10	8	4

Solution:

Class-interval	Frequency (f)	Cumulative Frequency (Cf)
0–10	5	5
10–20	7	m_3 12
20 – 30	f_3 12	24
30–40	16	m_7 40
40 – 50	f_7 10	50
50–60	8	58
60–70	4	62
	$N = 62$	

$$D_3 \text{ item} = \left(\frac{3N}{10}\right)^{\text{th}} \text{item}$$

$$= \left(\frac{3 \times 62}{10}\right)^{\text{th}} \text{item} = \left(\frac{186}{10}\right)^{\text{th}} \text{item} = 18.6 \text{ item}.$$

which lies in the interval (20–30)

$$\therefore \quad D_3 \text{ item} = l_3 + \frac{\left(\frac{3N}{10}\right) - m_3}{f_3} \times c$$

$$= 20 + \frac{18.6 - 12}{12} \times 10 = 20 + 5.5 = 25.5$$

$$D_7 \text{ item} = \left(\frac{7 \times N}{10}\right)^{\text{th}} \text{item}$$

$$= \left(\frac{7 \times 62}{10}\right)^{\text{th}} \text{item} = \left(\frac{434}{10}\right)^{\text{th}} \text{item} = (43.4)^{\text{th}} \text{ item}$$

which lies in the interval (40–50)

$$D_7 \text{ item} = l_1 + \frac{\left(\frac{7N}{10}\right) - m_1}{f_1} \times c$$

$$= 40 + \frac{43.4 - 40}{10} \times 10 = 40 + 3.4 = 43.4.$$

6.8 PERCENTILES

The percentile values divide the distribution into 100 parts each containing 1 percent of the cases. The percentile (P_k) is that value of the variable up to which lies exactly k% of the total number of observations.

Relationship:

$$P_{25} = Q_1; P_{50} = D_5 = Q_2 = \text{Median and } P_{75} = Q_3$$

6.8.1 Calculation of Percentile-Ungrouped Data or Raw Data

The first percentile (P_1) comes points to $\left(\frac{n}{100}\right)^{th}$ item value, P_2 to $2\left(\frac{n}{100}\right)^{th}$, P_3 to $3\left(\frac{n}{100}\right)^{th}$ ......, P_{99} to $99\left(\frac{n}{100}\right)^{th}$ item value when the data is arranged in an ascending or descending order.

EXAMPLE 6.33: Calculate P_{15} for the data given below: 5, 24, 36, 12, 20, 8

Solution: Arranging the given values in the increasing order. 5, 8, 12, 20, 24, 36

Here $n = 6$

$$P_{15} = \left(\frac{15(n+1)}{100}\right)^{th} \text{ item}$$

$$= \left(\frac{15 \times 7)}{100}\right)^{th} \text{ item} = (1.05)^{th} \text{ item}$$

$$= 1^{st} \text{ item} + 0.05\ (2^{nd} \text{ item} - 1^{st} \text{ item})$$

$$= 5 + 0.05\ (8 - 5) = 5.0 + 0.15 = 5.15.$$

6.8.2 Calculation of Percentile-Continuous Data

For grouped data the following formula is used for interpolation

$$P_i = l_i + \frac{i\left(\frac{N}{100}\right) - m_i}{f_i} \times c$$

Where, i – 1, 2, 3, 4, 5....99. The symbols having usual meaning. The methods for the calculation of partition values are illustrated by the following examples.

EXAMPLE 6.34 : Find P_{53} for the following frequency distribution.

Class-Interval	0–5	5–10	10–15	15–20	20–25	25–30	30–35	35–40
Frequency	5	8	12	16	20	10	4	3

Solution:

Class-interval	Frequency (*f*)	Cumulative Frequency (*Cf*)
0–5	5	5
5–10	8	13
10–15	12	25
15–20	16	*m* 41
20 – 25	*f* 20	61
25–30	10	71
30–35	4	75
35–40	3	78
Total	***N* = 78**	

$$P_{53} = l_{53} + \frac{53\left(\frac{N}{10}\right) - m_{53}}{f_{53}} \times c$$

$$= 20 + \frac{41.34 - 41}{20} \times 5$$

$$= 20 + 0.085 = 20.085.$$

6.9 MODE

The mode refers to that value in a distribution, which occur most frequently. It is an actual value, which has the highest concentration of items in and around it.

According to Professor ***Kenney and Keeping***, "*the value of the variable which occurs most frequently in a distribution is called the mode.*"

According to ***Croxton and Cowden*** "*The mode of a distribution is the value at the point around which the items tend to be most heavily concentrated. It may be regarded at the most typical of a series of values*".

It shows the centre of concentration of the frequency in around a given value. Therefore, where the purpose is to know the point of the highest concentration it is preferred. It is, thus, a positional measure. Its importance is very great in marketing studies where a manager is interested in knowing about the size, which has the highest concentration of items. ***For example***, in placing an order for shoes or ready-made garments the modal size helps because these sizes and other sizes around in common demand.

The ***Mode*** is the most frequently occurring value in a set of observations. Why use the mode? The classic example is the shirt/shoe manufacturer who wants to decide what sizes to introduce. Data may have two modes. In this case, we say the data are ***bimodal***, and sets of observations with more than two modes are referred to as ***multimodal***.

For example, if the data is

Size of Shoes	6	7	8	9	10	11
No. of Person (thousand)	10	20	40	42	23	5

then the model size is '9' since it occurs maximum number of times in the above data. Then we can draw the conclusion that size of shoes which maximum person wear is 9.

The mode is poor measure of central tendency when most frequency occurring values of an observation do not appear close to the centre of the data. The mode need even be unique value. Consider the frequency distributions shown in Fig. 6.5(a) and 6.5(b). The distribution in Fig. 6.5(a) has its mode at the lowest class and certainly cannot be considered representative of central location. The distribution shown Fig. 6.5(b) has two modes. Obviously neither of these values appears to be representative of the central location of the data. For these reasons the mode has limited use as a measure of central tendency for decision-making. However, for descriptive analysis, mode is a useful measure of central tendency.

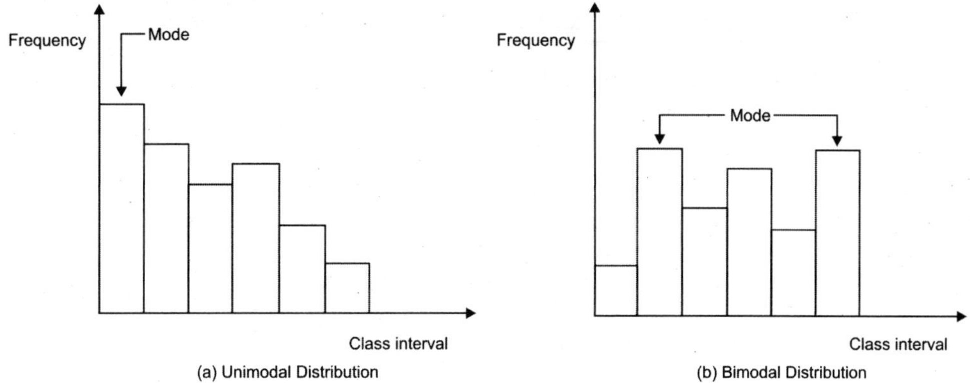

Fig. 6.5

6.9.1 Calculation of Mode- Ungrouped or Raw Data

For ungrouped data or a series of individual observations, mode is often found by mere inspection.

EXAMPLE 6.35: 2, 7, 10, 15, 10, 17, 8, 10, 2

Solution: Mode = M_0 = 10

In some cases the mode may be absent while in some cases there may be more than one mode.

1 : 12, 10, 15, 24, 30 (no mode)

2 : 7, 10, 15, 12, 7, 14, 24, 10, 7, 20, 10

The modes are 7 and 10

If in any series, two or more numbers have the maximum frequency, then the mode will be difficult to calculate. Such series are called as ***Bi-modal***, ***Tri-modal*** or ***Multi-modal*** series.

EXAMPLE 6.36: The following figures relate to the preferences with regard to size of screen (in inches) of T.V sets of 30 persons selected at random from a locality. Find the model size of the T.V screen

12	20	12	24	29
20	12	20	29	24
24	20	12	20	24
29	24	24	20	24
24	20	24	24	12
24	20	29	24	24

Solution: The calculation of model size is as below:

Size in inches	Tally	Frequency
12	𝍸	5
20	𝍸 III	8
24	𝍸 𝍸 III	13
29	IIII	4
		Total 30

Since size 24 occurs the maximum number of time, therefore, the model size of TV screen is 24 inches.

6.9.2 Calculation of Mode-Discrete and Continuous Distribution

(i) Discrete distribution: For Discrete distribution, see the highest frequency and corresponding value of x is mode.

(ii) Continuous Distribution: See the highest frequency then the corresponding value of class interval is called the modal class. Then apply the formula.

$$\text{Mode} = M_0 = l + \frac{\Delta_1}{\Delta_1 + \Delta_2} \times c$$

Where,

l_1 = Lower limit of the model class
$\Delta_1 = f_1 - f_0$
$\Delta_2 = f_1 - f_2$

f_1 = frequency of the modal class
f_0 = frequency of the class preceding the modal class
f_2 = frequency of the class succeeding the modal class
c = $(l_2 - l_1)$. [The difference between upper limit and lower limit of modal class.]

The above formula can also be written as

$$\text{Mode} = l_1 + \frac{f_1 - f_0}{2f_1 - f_0 - f_2} \times c$$

Remarks

1. If $(2f_1 - f_0 - f_2)$ comes out to be zero, then mode is obtained by the following formula taking absolute differences within vertical lines.
2. Mode $= l + \dfrac{(f_1 - f_0)}{|f_1 - f_0| + |f_1 - f_2|} \times c$
3. If mode lies in the first class interval, then f_0 is taken as zero.
4. The computation of mode poses no problem in distributions with open-end classes, unless the modal value lies in the open-end class.

EXAMPLE 6.37: Calculate mode for the following:

CI	*f*	*CI*	*f*
0–50	5	250–300	87
50–100	14	300–350	60
100–150	40	350–400	38
150–200	91	400 and above	15
200 – 250	150		

Solution: The highest frequency is 150 and corresponding class interval is 200–250, which is the modal class.

Here $l = 200, f_1 = 150, f_0 = 91, f_2 = 87, c = 50$ [250–200]

$$\text{Mode} = l_i + \frac{f_1 - f_0}{2f_1 - f_0 - f_2} \times c$$

$$= 200 + \frac{150 - 91}{2 \times 150 - 91 - 87} \times 50$$

$$= 200 + \frac{2950}{122} = 200 + 24.18 = 224.18.$$

EXAMPLE 6.38: Calculate the modal class & mode also.

Daily Wages	20–25	25–30	30–35	35–40	40–45	45–50
No. of workers	1	3	8	12	7	5

Solution: Here the maximum frequency is 12, corresponding to the class interval (35–40) which is the modal class.

Therefore $l_1 = 35, l_2 = 40, f_0 = 8, f_1 = 12, f_2 = 7$

$$\text{Mode} = l_1 + \left[\frac{f_1 - f_0}{2f_1 - f_0 - f_2}\right](l_2 - l_1)$$

$$= 40 + \left[\frac{12 - 8}{24 - 8 - 7}\right](40 - 35) = 40 + \left[\frac{4}{9}\right] \times 5 = 40 + 2.22 = 37.22$$

Modal wages is $37.22.

6.9.3 Determination of Modal Class

For a frequency distribution modal class corresponds to the maximum frequency. But in any one (or more) of the following cases

- If the maximum frequency is repeated
- If the maximum frequency occurs in the beginning or at the end of the distribution
- If there are irregularities in the distribution, the modal class is determined by the method of grouping.

Find the modal class, the valves are first arranged in ascending order and their frequencies are noted. Normally, the grouping table has the following six columns:

Working Steps

We prepare a grouping table with 6 columns

1. In ***Column I***, we write down the given frequencies.
2. ***Column II*** is obtained by combining the frequencies two by two.
3. Leave the 1st frequency and combine the remaining frequencies two by two and write in ***Column III***.
4. ***Column IV*** is obtained by combining the frequencies three by three.
5. Leave the 1st frequency and combine the remaining frequencies three by three and write in ***Column V***.
6. Leave the 1st and 2nd frequencies and combine the remaining frequencies three by three and write in ***Column VI***.

Mark the highest frequency in each column. Then form an analysis table to find the modal class. After finding the modal class use the formula to calculate the modal value.

EXAMPLE 6.39: Calculate mode for the following frequency distribution.

Class-Interval	0–5	5–10	10–15	15–20	20–25	25–30	30–35	35–40
Frequency	9	12	15	16	17	15	10	13

Grouping Table

CI	f	2	3	4	5	6
0–5	9	21				
5–10	12		27	36		
10–15	15	31			43	
15–20	16		33			48
20–25	17	32		48		
25–30	15		25		42	
30–35	10	23				38
35–40	13					

Analysis Table

Columns	0–5	5–10	10–15	15–20	20–25	25–30	30–35	35–40
1						1		
2						1	1	
3					1	1		
4					1	1	1	
5			1	1	1			
6				1	1	1		
Total			1	2	4	5	2	

The maximum occurred corresponding to 20–25, and hence it is the modal class.

$$\text{Mode} = M_0 = l + \frac{\Delta_1}{\Delta_1 + \Delta_2} \times c$$

Here $l = 20$; $\Delta_1 = f_1 - f_0 = 17 - 16 = 1$; $\Delta_2 = f_1 - f_2 = 17 - 15 = 2$

$$\therefore \quad M_0 = 20 + \frac{1}{1+2} \times 5$$

$$= 20 + 1.67$$

$$= 21.67$$

6.9.4 Graphic Location of Mode

Mode is calculated graphically with the help of the curve called histogram.

Working Steps

Step 1: Draw a histogram of the given distribution.

Step 2: Join the rectangle corner of the highest rectangle (modal class rectangle) by a straight line to the top right corner of the preceding rectangle. Similarly the top left corner of the highest rectangle is joined to the top left corner of the rectangle on the right.

Step 3: From the point of intersection of these two diagonal lines, draw a perpendicular to the x-axis.

Step 4: Read the value in x-axis gives the mode.

EXAMPLE 6.40: Locate the modal value graphically for the following frequency distribution.

Class-Interval	0–10	10–20	20–30	30–40	40–50	50–60
Frequency	5	8	12	7	5	3

Solution:

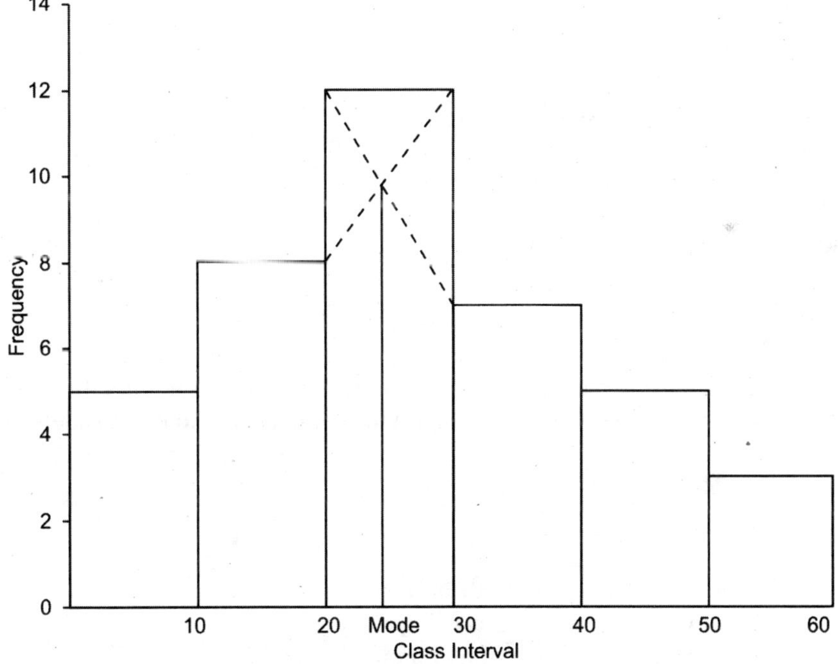

Fig. 6.6: Histogram

Direct Calculation

Mode lies in the class 20–30, then

$$l_1 = 20,\ f_1 = 12,\ f_0 = 8,\ f_2 = 7,\ c = 10$$

$$\text{Mode} = l_1 + \left[\frac{f_1 - f_0}{2f_1 - f_0 - f_2}\right] \times c$$

$$= 20 + \frac{12-8}{24-8-7} \times 10$$

$$= 20 + \frac{4}{9} \times 10 = 20 + \frac{40}{9} = 20 + 4.44 = 24.44.$$

From the above diagram the model value is also 24.44. Hence by both the methods we get the same valve of note.

DO YOU KNOW?

Graphic method of determining mode can be used only where there is one class containing the highest frequency. If two or more classes have the same highest frequency, mode cannot be determined graphically.

6.9.5 Merits and Demerits of Mode

Merits

1. It is easy to calculate and in some cases it can be located mere inspection
2. Mode is not at all affected by extreme values.
3. It can be calculated for open-end classes.
4. It is usually an actual value of an important part of the series.
5. In some circumstances it is the best representative of data.

Demerits

1. It is not based on all observations.
2. It is not capable of further mathematical treatment.
3. Mode is ill-defined generally; it is not possible to find mode in some cases.
4. As compared with mean, mode is affected to a great extent, by sampling fluctuations.
5. It is unsuitable in cases where relative importance of items has to be considered.

6.9.6 Uses of the Mode

The mode is generally used in:

- The study of most popular size in trade or industry,
- The distributions with outstanding large frequency,
- The problems involving the expression of preference and
- The case of qualitative data.

6.10 EMPIRICAL RELATIONSHIP AMONG AVERAGES

A distribution in which the values of mean, median and mode coincide (i.e. mean = median = mode) is known as a symmetrical distribution. Conversely, when values of mean, median and mode are not equal the distribution is known as asymmetrical or skewed distribution. In moderately skewed or asymmetrical distribution a very important relationship exists among these three measures of central tendency.

In such distributions the distance between the mean and median is about one-third of the distance between the mean and mode, as will be clear from the Figs. 6.1, 6.2 and 6.3. Karl Pearson expressed this relationship as:

$$\text{Mode} = \text{mean} - 3\,[\text{mean} - \text{median}]$$

$$\text{Mode} = 3\,\text{median} - 2\,\text{mean}$$

and

$$\text{Median} = \text{mode} + \frac{2}{3}\,[\text{mean} - \text{mode}]$$

Knowing any two values, the third can be computed.

EXAMPLE 6.41: Given Median = 20.6, Mode = 26 Find Mean.

Solution: Mode = 3 Median – 2 Mean

$$\therefore \quad \text{Mean} = \frac{1}{2}\,[3\,\text{median} - \text{mode}]$$

$$\therefore \quad \text{Mean} = \frac{1}{2}\,[3(20.6) - (26)]$$

$$\therefore \quad \text{Mean} = \frac{1}{2}\,[35.8]$$

$$\therefore \quad \text{Mean} = 17.9$$

EXAMPLE 6.42: If the mean and median of a moderately asymmetrical series are 26.8 and 27.9 respectively, what would be its most probable mode?

Solution: Using the empirical formula

$$\begin{aligned}\text{Mode} &= 3\,\text{median} - 2\,\text{mean}\\ &= 3 \times 27.9 - 2 \times 26.8\\ &= 30.1\end{aligned}$$

EXAMPLE 6.43: In a moderately asymmetrical distribution the values of mode and mean are 32.1 and 35.4 respectively. Find the median value.

Solution: Using Empirical Formula

$$\begin{aligned}\text{Median} &= \text{mode} + \frac{2}{3}\,[\,\text{mean} - \text{mode}\,]\\ &= 32.1 + \frac{2}{3}[35.4 - 32.1]\\ &= 32.1 + \left(\frac{2 \times 3.3}{3}\right)\\ &= 32.1 + \frac{6.6}{3} = 32.1 + 2.2 = 34.3.\end{aligned}$$

6.11 COMPARISON OF THE MEAN, MEDIAN AND MODE

Having discussed mean, median and mode, we now turn to the relationship amongst these three measures of central tendency. We shall discuss the relationship assuming that there is a uni-modal frequency distribution.

When a distribution is symmetrical, the mean, median and mode are the same,

Mean = Median = Mode

as is shown below in figure.

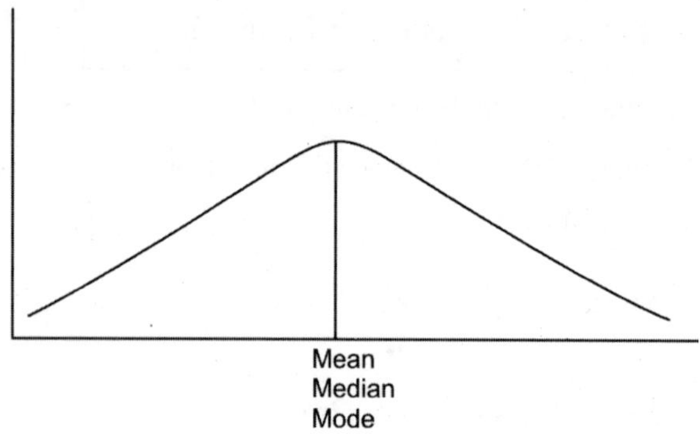

Fig. 6.7: A symmetrical Distribution

In case, a distribution is skewed to the right, then

Mean > Median > Mode

Generally, income distribution is skewed to the right where a large number of families have relatively low income and a small number of families have extremely high income. In such a case, the mean is pulled up by the extreme high incomes and the relation among these three measures is as shown in figure. Here, we find that mean > median >mode.

When a distribution is skewed to the left, then

Mode > Median > Mean.

This is because here mean is pulled down below the median by extremely low values. This is shown in figure

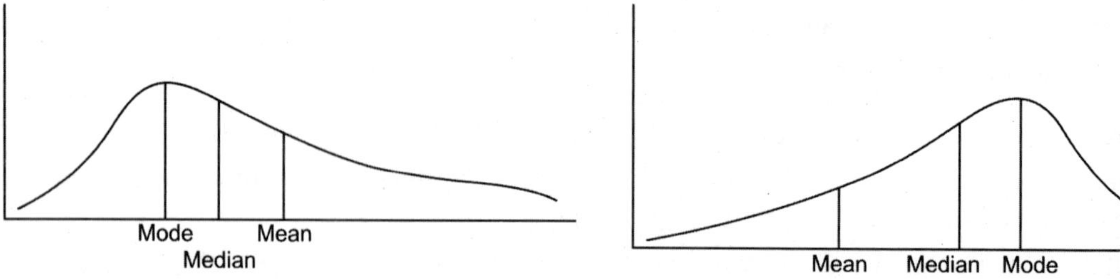

Fig. 6.8: Skewed to the Right (Positively Skewed)

Fig. 6.9: Skewed to the Left (Negatively Skewed)

Given the mean and median of a unimodal distribution, we can determine whether it is skewed to the right or left. When mean >median, it is skewed to the right; when median > mean, it is skewed to the left. It may be noted that the median is always in the middle between mean and mode.

6.12 SELECTING AMONG THE MODE, MEDIAN AND MEAN

It is a common mistake to specify the wrong index for central tenancy.

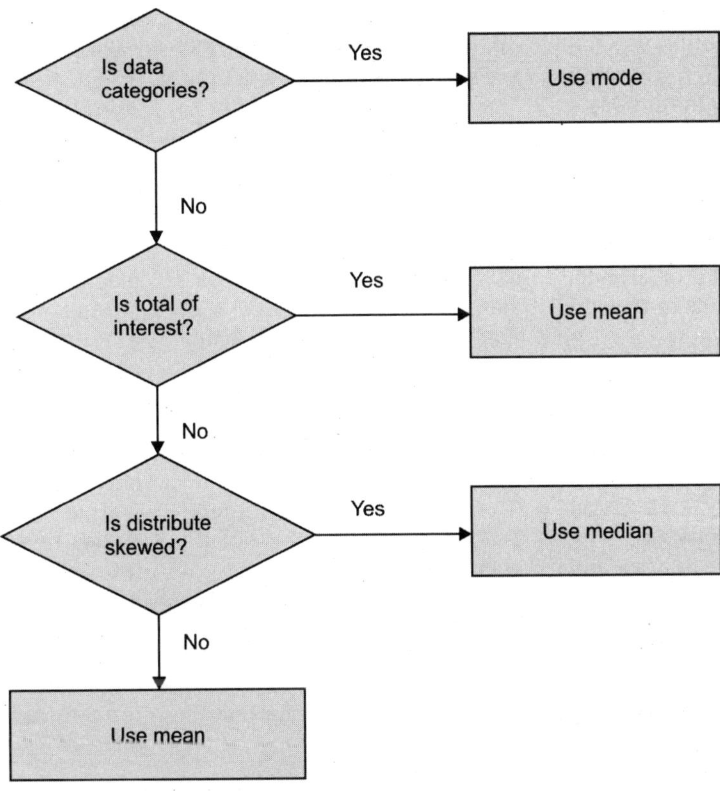

Fig. 6.10: Selecting Among the Mode, Median, and Mean

The first consideration is the type of data, if the variable is categorical; the mode is the single measure that best describes that data.

The second consideration in selecting the index is to ask whether the total of all observations is of any interest. If the answer is yes, then the mean is the proper index of central tendency.

If the total is of no interest, then depending on whether the histogram is symmetric or skewed one must use either mean or median, respectively.

In all cases the histogram must be unimodal. However, notice that, e.g., a Uniform distribution has uncountable number of modes having equal density value; therefore it is considered as a homogeneous population.

Notice also that:

$$|\textbf{Mean - Median}| \leq \sigma$$

6.13 DIFFERENCE AMONG MODE, MEDIAN AND MEAN

Mode	Median	Mean
1. It is the most frequent value in the distribution; it is the point of greatest density.	1. It is the value of the middle point of the array (not midpoint of range), such that half the item are above and half below it.	1. It is the value in a given aggregate which would obtain if all the values were equal.
2. The value of the mode is established by the predominant frequency, not by the value in the distribution.	2. The value of the media is fixed by its position in the array and doesn't reflect the individual value.	2. The sum of deviations on either side of the mean are equal hence, the algebraic sum of the deviation is equal zero.
3. It is the most probable value, hence the most typical.	3. The aggregate distance between the median point and all the value in the array is less than from any other point.	3. It reflect the magnitude of every value.
4. A distribution may have 2 or more modes. On the other hand, there is no mode in a rectangular distribution.	4. Each array has one and only one median.	4. An array has one and only one mean.
5. The mode does not reflect the degree of modality.	5. It cannot be manipulated algebraically: medians of subgroups cannot be weighted and combined.	5. Means may be manipulated algebraically: means of subgroups may be combined when properly weighted.
6. It cannot be manipulated algebraically: modes of subgroups cannot be combined.	6. It is stable in that grouping procedures do not affect it appreciably.	6. It may be calculated even when individual values are unknown, provided the sum of the values and the sample size n are known.
7. It is unstable that it is influenced by grouping procedures.	7. Value must be ordered, and may be grouped, for computation.	7. Values need not be ordered or grouped for this calculation.
8. Values must be ordered and group for its compilation.	8. It can be compute when ends are open.	8. It cannot be calculated from a frequency table when ends are open.
9. It can be calculated when table ends are open.	9. It is not applicable to qualitative data.	9. It is stable in that grouping procedures do not seriously affected it.

6.14 WHICH OF THE THREE MEASURES IS THE BEST?

At this stage, one may ask as to which of these three measure of central tendency is the best. There is no simple answer to this question. It is because these three measures are based upon different concepts. The arithmetic mean is the sum of the values divided by the total number of observations in the series. The median is the value of the value of the middle observations tend to concentrate, As such; the use of a particular measure will largely depend on the purpose of the study and the nature of the data. ***For example***, when we are interested in knowing the consumers' preferences for different brands of television sets or kinds of advertising, the choice should go in favour of mode. The use of mean and median would not be proper. However, the median can sometimes be used in the case of qualitative data when such data can be arranged in an ascending or descending order.

Let us take another example. Suppose we invite applications for a certain vacancy in our company. A large number of candidates apply for that post. We are now interested to know as to which age or age group has the largest concentration of applicants. Her, obviously the mode will be the most appropriate choice. The arithmetic mean may not be appropriate as it may be influenced by some extreme values.

- Where we wish to make total value estimates, mean is themost appropriate average, e.g., per capital income of a country.

- If the data is qualitative, e.g., beauty, honesty, efficiency intelligence, etc., then only median will be most appropriate average.
- In case of business situations, where selection of 'most common', e.g., most common size of shoes for certain age group, most common size of garments, etc., is to be made, then mode is the only average.

6.15 HARMONIC MEAN (H.M)

Harmonic mean of a set of observations is defined as the reciprocal of the arithmetic average of the reciprocal of the given values. If $x_1, x_2 \ldots . x_n$ are n observations,

$$\text{H.M} = \frac{n}{\frac{1}{x_1} + \frac{1}{x_2} + \frac{1}{x_3} \ldots\ldots \frac{1}{x_n}} = \frac{n}{\left(\frac{1}{x_i}\right)}$$

For a frequency distribution

$$\text{H.M} = \frac{n}{\sum_{i=l}^{n} f\left(\frac{1}{x_i}\right)}$$

The harmonic mean is particularly useful for computation of average rates and ratio. Such rates and ratios are generally used to express relations between two different types of measuring units that can be expressed reciprocally. ***For example***, distance (in km), and time (in hours).

An Application: Suppose 4 machines in a machine shop are used to produce the same part. However, each of the four machines takes 2.5, 2.0, 1.5, and 6.0 minutes to make one part, respectively. What is the average rate of speed?

The harmonic means is: $\text{H.M} = \frac{4}{\left[\left(\frac{1}{2.5}\right) + \left(\frac{1}{2.0}\right) + \frac{1}{(1.5)} + \left(\frac{1}{6.0}\right)\right]} = 2.31$ minutes.

If all machines working for one hour, how many parts will be produced? Since four machines running for one hour represent 240 minutes of operating time, then: 240 / 2.31 = 104 parts will be produced.

DO YOU KNOW?

The harmonic mean is a measure of central tendency for data expressed as rates, such as kms, per hour, tonnes per day, quantity per litre, miles per fortnight, etc. It is useful for computing the average rate of increase of profit or average speed at which a journey has been performed or the average price at which an article has been sold.

EXAMPLE 6.44 : From the given data calculate H.M 5, 10, 17, 24, 30.

x	5	10	17	24	30	**Total**
$\frac{1}{x}$	0.2000	0.1000	0.0588	0.0417	0.0333	$\Sigma \frac{1}{x}$ = **0.4338**

Solution: $$\text{H.M} = \frac{n}{\Sigma\left[\frac{1}{x}\right]} = \frac{5}{0.4338} = 11.526.$$

EXAMPLE 6.45: The marks secured by some students of a class are given below. Calculate the harmonic mean.

Marks	20	21	22	23	24	25
Number of students	4	2	7	1	3	1

Solution:

Marks	No. of students	$\frac{1}{x}$	$f\left(\frac{1}{x}\right)$
20	4	0.0500	0.2000
21	2	0.0476	0.0952
22	7	0.0454	0.3178
23	1	0.0435	0.0435
24	3	0.0417	0.1251
25	1	0.0400	0.0400
	18		**0.8216**

$$\text{H.M} = \frac{n}{\Sigma f\left[\frac{1}{x}\right]} = \frac{18}{0.1968} = 21.91.$$

EXAMPLE 6.46: In a small company, two typists are employed. Typist A types one page in ten minutes while typist B takes twenty minutes for the same.

(a) Both are asked to type 10 pages. What is the average time taken for typing one page?
(b) Both are asked to type for one hour. What is the average time taken by them for typing one page?

Solution:

(a) $$\text{A.M} = \frac{(10\times 10)+(20\times 10)\text{ (minutes)}}{10\times 2\text{ (pages)}} = 15\text{ minutes}$$

(b) $$\text{H.M} = \frac{60\times 2\text{(minutes)}}{60/10+60/20\text{ (pages)}} = \frac{120}{\frac{120+60}{20}} = \frac{40}{3}$$

$$= 13\text{ minutes and }20\text{ seconds.}$$

EXAMPLE 6.47: In a certain factory a unit of work is completed by A in 4 minutes, by B in 5 minutes, by C in 6 minutes, by D in 10 minutes and by E in 12 minutes.

(a) What is the average number of units of work completed per minute?
(b) At this rate how many units will they complete in a six–hour day?

Solution:

(a) The average number of units per minute will be obtained by calculating the harmonic mean.

x	4	5	6	10	12	**Total**
$\frac{1}{x}$	0.250	0.200	0.167	0.100	0.083	$\Sigma\frac{1}{x} = 0.8$

$$\text{H.M} = \frac{n}{\Sigma\left(\frac{1}{x}\right)} = \frac{5}{0.8} = 6.25$$

Hence the average number of units completed per minute = 6.25.

(b) The average units per minute = $\frac{1}{6.25} = 0.16$

In 6 hours, i.e 360 minutes, total number of units produced will be $360 \times 0.16 \times 5 = 288$ by all the five workers combined.

EXAMPLE 6.48: It takes ship A 10 days to cross the Pacific Ocean; ship B takes 15 days and ship C takes 20 days.

(a) What is the average number of days taken by a ship to cross the Pacific Ocean?

(b) What is the average number of days taken by a cargo to cross the Pacific Ocean when the ships are hired for 60 days.

Solution:

(a) $$\text{A.M} = \frac{10 + 15 + 20}{3} = 15 \text{ days.}$$

(b) $$\text{H.M} = \frac{60 \times 3 \text{ (days)}}{60/10 + 60/15 + 60/20}$$

$$= \frac{180}{\frac{360 + 240 + 180}{60}} = 13.8 \text{ days approx.}$$

6.15.1 Merits and Demerits of Harmonic Mean

Merits

1. It is rigidly defined.
2. It is defined on all observations.
3. It is amenable to further algebraic treatment.
4. It is the most suitable average when it is desired to give greater weight to smaller observations and less weight to the larger ones.

Demerits

1. It is not easily understood.
2. It is difficult to compute.
3. It is only a summary figure and may not be the actual item in the series
4. It gives greater importance to small items and is therefore, useful only when small items have to be given greater weightage.

6.16 GEOMETRIC MEAN (G.M)

In many business and economics problems, we deal with quantities that change over a period of time. In such cases the aim is to know an average rate of change rather than simple average value to represent the average growth or decline rate in a data set over a period of time. Thus we need to calculate another measure of central tendency called geometric mean (G.M)

The geometric mean of a series containing n observations is the nth root of the product of the values. If $x_1, x_2 \ldots, x_n$ are observations then

$$\text{G.M} = \sqrt[n]{x_1.x_2....x_n} = \left(x_1.x_2....x_n\right)^{1/n} \quad ......(1)$$

$$\log \text{G.M} = \frac{1}{n}\log(x_1.x_2...x_n)$$

$$= \frac{1}{n}(\log x_1 + \log x_2 + \log x_n)$$

$$= \frac{\Sigma \log x_1}{n}$$

$$\text{G.M} = \text{Antilog}\frac{\Sigma \log x_1}{n} \quad ......(2)$$

For Grouped Data

$$\text{G.M} = \text{Antilog}\left[\frac{\Sigma f \log x_1}{N}\right] \quad ......(3)$$

The formulae 1, 2 are used in the case of individual series and the formulae 3 are used in the case of discrete or continuous series. In the case of continuous series mid-values of classes are taken as x's.

The concept of G.M is used in the construction of index numbers. Since G.M < A.M, therefore G.M is useful in those cases where smaller observations are to be given importance. Such cases usually occur in social and economic areas of study.

An Application

Suppose sales of a certain item increase to 110% in the first year and to 50% of that in the second year. For simplicity, assume you sold 100 items initially. Then the number sold in the first year is 110 and the number sold in the second is 150% × 110 = 165. The arithmetic average of 110% and 150% is 130% so that we would incorrectly estimate that the number sold in the first year is 130 and the number in the second year is 169. The geometric mean of 110% and 150% is G = (1.65)1/2 so that we would correctly estimate that we would sell 100 $(G)^2$ = 165 items in the second year.

DO YOU KNOW?

Geometric mean is theoretically considered to be the best average in the construction of index numbers. It is an average which is most suitable when large weights have to be given to small values of observations and small weights to large values of observations, situations which we usually come across in social and economic fields.

EXAMPLE 6.49: Calculate the geometric mean of the following series of monthly income of a batch of families 180, 250, 490, 1400, 1050

x	180	250	490	140	1050	Total
log x	2.2553	2.3979	2.6902	3.1461	3.0212	13.5107

Solution:

$$G.M = \text{Antilog}\left[\frac{\Sigma \log x}{n}\right]$$

$$= \text{Antilog}\ \frac{13.5107}{5} = 2.7021 = 503.6.$$

EXAMPLE 6.50: Calculate the average income per head from the data given below .Use geometric mean.

Class of people	Number of families	Monthly income per head (Rs)
Landlords	2	5000
Cultivators	100	400
Landless - labours	50	200
Money - lenders	4	3750
Office Assistants	6	3000
Shop keepers	8	750
Carpenters	6	600
Weavers	10	300

Solution:

Class of people	Annual income (Rs) x	Number of families (*f*)	Log x	*f* log x
Landlords	5000	2	3.6990	7.398
Cultivators	400	100	2.6021	260.210
Landless - labours	200	50	2.3010	115.050
Money - lenders	3750	4	3.5740	14.296
Office Assistants	3000	6	3.4771	20.863
Shop keepers	750	8	2.8751	23.2008
Carpenters	600	6	2.7782	16.669
Weavers	300	10	2.4771	24.771
		186		**482.257**

$$G.M = \text{Antilog}\left[\frac{\Sigma f \log x}{N}\right]$$

$$= \text{Antilog}\left[\frac{482.257}{186}\right]$$

$$= \text{Antilog}\ (2.5928) = \text{Rs } 391.50.$$

EXAMPLE 6.51: A person has invested Rs 5,000 in the stock market. At the end of the first year the amount has grown to Rs 6,250, he had a 25 percent profit. If at the end of the second year his principal has grown to Rs 8,750, the rate of increase is 40 percent for the year. What is the average rate of increase of his investment during the two years?

Solution: $G.M = \sqrt{1.25 \times 1.40} = \sqrt{1.75} = 1.323$

The average rate of increase in the value of investment is therefore 1.323 – 1 = 0.323, which if multiplied by 100, gives the rate of increase as 32.3 percent.

EXAMPLE 6.52: Compared to the previous year the overhead expenses went up by 32% in 2002; by 50% in the following year. Calculate the average rate of increase in the overhead expenses over the three years.

Solution: In average ratios and percentages, geometric mean is more appropriate. Applying geometric mean here:

% Rise	Expenses at the end of the year taking preceding year as 100	Log *x*
32	132	2.1206
40	140	2.1461
50	150	2.1761
		Σ log x = 6.4428

$$G.M = A.L\left(\frac{\Sigma \log x}{N}\right) = A.L\left(\frac{6.4428}{3}\right)$$

$$= A.L\ 2.1476 = 140.5$$

Average rate of increase in overhead expenses = 140.5 – 100 = 40.5%.

6.16.1 Merits and Demerits of Geometric Mean

Merits

1. It is rigidly defined
2. It is based on all items
3. It is very suitable for averaging ratios, rates and percentages
4. It is capable of further mathematical treatment.
5. Unlike AM, it is not affected much by the presence of extreme values

Demerits

1. It cannot be used when the values are negative or if any of the observations is zero
2. It is difficult to calculate particularly when the items are very large or when there is a frequency distribution.
3. It brings out the property of the ratio of the change and not the absolute difference of change as the case in arithmetic mean.
4. The GM may not be the actual value of the series.

6.17 DEFINING THE ARITHMETIC, GEOMETRIC AND HARMONIC MEANS

The tables give examples of final results calculated using harmonic, arithmetic, and geometric means to illustrate the differences.

Suppose that the examination mark, expressed as a percentage, is x, and the assignment mark, again as a percentage, is y.

Mean	Simplest formula	Most informative formula
Arithmetic mean of x and y	$\frac{(x+y)}{2}$	$0.5x + 0.5y$
Geometric mean of x and y	$\sqrt{(xy)}$	$x^{0.5} \times y^{0.5}$
Harmonic mean of x and y	$\frac{2xy}{(x+y)}$	$\frac{1}{\left(\frac{0.5}{x}+\frac{0.5}{y}\right)}$

Examples (to nearest whole percent)

x	*y*	Mean	Geometric Mean	Harmonic Mean
50	50	50	50	50
40	60	50	49	48
30	70	50	46	42
20	80	50	40	32

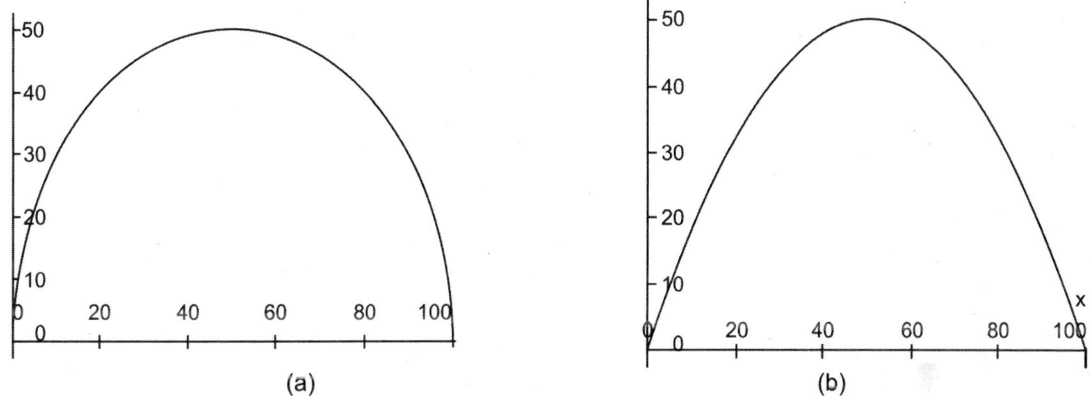

Fig. 6.11: (a) Geometric means of an exam of x with an assignment mark of $100 - x$; (b) Harmonic means of an exam of x with assignment mark of $100 - x$.

Notice that the arithmetic mean is in all cases 50.

Clearly the geometric and harmonic means penalise uneven performances, but the harmonic mean penalises them more heavily. Reasons that lecturers might wish to do this include

(1) Preventing students, who have obtained high marks on the assignments by undetected plagiarism, from passing or doing well: such students are unlikely to do well in the exam, and

(2) preventing students who cannot succeed at the programming assignments, but who are good at the theory, or at exam technique, or at memorising facts, from passing or doing well.

By doing this, lecturers are maintaining the standard of the qualification towards which you are working. If students who cheat, or who cannot program, get through School of CSE degrees, eventually the word will spread to employers, and the value of your qualification will decline.

6.18 RELATIONSHIP AMONG A.M, G.M AND H.M

For any set of observations, it's A.M, G.M and H.M are related to each other in the relationship

$$\boxed{\textbf{A.M} \geq \textbf{G.M} \geq \textbf{H.M}}$$

The sign of '=' holds if and only if all the observations are identical.

If observations in a data set take the values $a, ar, ar^2, ar^3, \ldots ar^{n-1}$, each with single frequency, then

$$\boxed{(G.M)^2 = A.M \times H.M}$$

MISCELLANEOUS SOLVED EXAMPLES

EXAMPLE 6.53: The following are the hourly salaries in rupees of 20 employees of a firm:

130	62	145	118	125	76	151	142	110	98
65	116	100	103	71	85	80	122	132	95

The firm gives bonuses of Rs 10,15, 20, 25 and 30 for individuals in the respective salary group exceeding Rs 60 but not exceeding Rs 80, exceeding Rs 80 but not exceeding Rs 100 and so on up in exceeding Rs 140 but not exceeding Rs 160 . Find the average hourly bonus paid per employee.

Solution: First we shall express the given data in the form of a grouped frequency distribution with salaries (in Rupees) in the class intervals 61–80, 81–100, 101–120, 121–140 and 141–160. The firm value in the above distribution is 130, so we put a tally mark against the class interval 121–140; next value is 62, so we put a tally mark against the class 61–80 and so on. Thus the grouped frequency distribution as follows:

COMPUTATION OF AVERAGE HOURLY BONUS PER EMPLOYEE

Salary (in Rs)	Tally Marks	Frequency (f)	Bonus (in Rs) (X)	fX
61– 80	~~IIII~~	5	10	50
81 –100	IIII	4	15	60
101–120	IIII	4	20	80
121–140	IIII	4	25	100
140 –160	III	3	30	90
Total		$\Sigma f = 20$		$\Sigma fx = 380$

$$\therefore \text{ Average hourly bonus paid per employee} = \frac{\Sigma fx}{\Sigma f} = \frac{380}{20} = \text{Rs } 19.$$

EXAMPLE 6.54: The table below shows the number of skilled and unskilled workers in two small communities, together with their average hourly wages:

Worker category	Ram Nagar		Shyam Nagar	
	Number	Wage per hour	Number	Wage per hour
Skilled	150	Rs 180	350	Rs 175
Unskilled	850	Rs 130	650	Rs 125

Determine the average hourly wage for each community. Also give reasons why the results show that the average hourly wage in Shyam Nagar exceeds the hourly wage in Ram Nagar even though in Shyam Nagar the average hourly wage of both categories of workers is lower. **[MBA, UPTU, 2002]**

Solution: Let n_1 and n_2 denote the number, and x_1 and x_2 denote the wages (in rupees) per hour of the skilled and unskilled workers respectively in the community. Let $\overline{X}$ be the mean wages of all the workers in the community.

Ram Nagar. We have:

$n_1 = 150, \quad \overline{X}_1 = \text{Rs } 180$

$n_2 = 850, \quad \overline{X}_2 = \text{Rs } 130$

$$\therefore \quad \overline{X} = \frac{n_1\overline{X}_1 + n_2\overline{X}}{n_1 + n_2} = \frac{150 \times 180 + 850 \times 130}{150 + 850}$$

$$= \frac{27000 + 110500}{1000} = \frac{137500}{1000} = \text{Rs } 137.50$$

Shyam Nagar. We have:

$n_1 = 350, \quad \overline{X}_1 = 175$

$n_2 = 650, \quad \overline{X}_2 = 125$

$$\therefore \quad \overline{X} = \frac{n_1\overline{X}_1 + n_2\overline{X}_2}{n_1 + n_2} = \frac{350 \times 175 + 650 \times 125}{350 + 650}$$

$$= \frac{61250 + 81250}{1000} = \frac{142500}{1000} = \text{Rs } 142.50$$

Thus, we see that the average wage per hour for all the workers combined is higher in Shyam Nagar than in Ram Nagar, although the average hourly wages of both types of workers are lower in Shyam Nagar. The reasons for this somewhat strange looking result may be assigned as follows:

(a) For skilled workers is Rs (180 – 175) = Rs 5

(b) For unskilled workers is Rs (130 –125) = Rs 5

Thus, although the difference in the wages of skilled and unskilled workers in both the communities is same viz, Rs 5, the number of skilled workers getting relatively higher wages than the unskilled workers is much more in Shyam Nagar than in Ram Nagar and the number of unskilled workers getting relatively less wages is much less in Shyam Nagar than in Ram Nagar. In fact, the ratio of skilled workers to unskilled workers in Ram Nagar is 150 : 850 i.e. 3:17 while in Shyam Nagar, it is 350 : 650 i.e. 7:13.

EXAMPLE 6.55: The mean age of a combined group of men and women is 30 years of mean age of the group of women is 25, find out the percentage of men and women in the group.

Solution: Let n_1 represent percentage of men and n_2 represent percentage of women so that $n_1 + n_2 = 100$.

We have $\overline{\overline{X}} = 30$

$\overline{X}_1 = 32$ [Mean age of group of men]

$\overline{X}_2 = 25$ [Mean age of group of women]

Now, $$\overline{\overline{X}} = \frac{n_1\overline{X}_1 + n_2\overline{X}_2}{n_1 + n_2}$$

or $$30 = \frac{n_1(32) + n_2)(25)}{100}$$

or $3000 = 32n_1 + (100 - n_1)\, 25$

or $3000 = 32n_1 + 2500 - 25n_1$

or $7n_1 = 500$

or $n_1 = 71.43$

$\therefore$ $n_2 = 100 - 71.43 = 28.57$

Hence the percentage of men and women is 71,43 and 28.57 respectively.

EXAMPLE 6.56: The mean of marks in statistics of 100 students of a class was 72. The mean of marks of boys was 75, while their number was 70. Find out the mean marks of girls in the class?

Solution:

Here n = Total numbers of students = 100

$\overline{\overline{X}}$ = Combined mean = 72

$\overline{X}_1$ = Mean marks of boys = 75

n_1 = Number of boys = 70

∴ n_2 = Number of girls = 100–70 = 30

Let mean marks of girls = $\overline{X}_2$

Now, $$\overline{X} = \frac{n_1\overline{X}_1 + n_2\overline{X}_2}{n_1 + n_2}$$

or $$72 = \frac{70 \times 75 + 30x_2}{n_1 + n_2}$$

or $$72 = \frac{5250 + 30x_2}{100}$$

or $$7200 = 5250 + 30x_2$$

or $$30x_2 = 1950$$

or $$x_2 = \frac{1950}{30} = 65$$

Hence mean marks of girls in the class = 65.

EXAMPLE 6.57: The mean salary paid to 1,000 employees of an establishment was found to Rs 180 – 40. Later on, after disbursement of salary, it was discovered that the salary of two employees we wrongly entered as Rs 297 and 165. Their correct salaries were Rs 197 and Rs 185. Find the correct Arithmetic Mean.

Solution: Let the variable x denote the salary (in rupees) of an employee. Then we are given:

$$\overline{X} = \frac{\Sigma x}{1000} = 180 - 40 \quad \Rightarrow \quad \Sigma x = 180400$$

Thus the total salary disbursed to all the employees in the establishment is Rs 1,80,400. After incorporating the corrections we have:

$$\begin{aligned}\text{Corrected } \Sigma x &= 180400 - (\text{sum of wrong salaries}) + (\text{sum of correct salaries})\\ &= 180400 - (297 + 165) + (197 + 185)\\ &= 180400 - 462 + 382\\ &= 180320\end{aligned}$$

∴ $$\text{Corrected mean salary} = \frac{180320}{1000} = \text{Rs } 180.32.$$

EXAMPLE 6.58: The average daily wage of all workers in a factory is Rs 444. If the average daily wages paid to male and female workers are Rs 480 and Rs 360 respectively, find the percentage of male and female workers in the factory.

Solution: Let n_1 and n_2 denote respectively the number of make and female workers in the factory and $\overline{X}_1$ and $\overline{X}_2$ denote respectively their average daily salary (in Rupees). Let $\overline{\overline{X}}$ denote the average salary of all the workers in the factory. Then we are given that:

$$\bar{X}_1 = 480, \qquad \bar{X}_2 = 360 \qquad \text{and} \qquad \bar{\bar{X}} = 444$$

We have $\bar{\bar{X}} = \dfrac{n_1\bar{X}_1 + n_2\bar{X}_2}{n_1 + n_2} \quad \Rightarrow \quad (n_1 + n_2)\bar{X} = n_1\bar{X}_1 + n_2\bar{X}_2$

$\Rightarrow \quad 444\,(n_1 + n_2) = 480n_1 + 360n_2 \quad \Rightarrow \quad (480 - 444)n_1 = (444 - 360)n_2$

$\therefore \quad 36n_1 = 84n_2 \quad \Rightarrow \quad \dfrac{n_1}{n_2} = \dfrac{84}{36} = \dfrac{7}{3}$

Hence, the male workers in the factory are: $\dfrac{7}{7+3} \times 100 = \dfrac{7}{10} \times 100 = 70\%$

and the female workers in the factory are: $\dfrac{3}{7+3} \times 100 = \dfrac{3}{10} \times 100 = 30\%$.

EXAMPLE 6.59: A limited company wants to pay bonus to workers. The bonus is to be paid as under:

Weekly salary (Rs)	Bonus (Rs)
300 but not exceeding 400	100
400 but not exceeding 500	120
500 but not exceeding 600	140
600 but not exceeding 700	160
700 but not exceeding 800	180
800 but not exceeding 900	200
900 but not exceeding 1,000	220
1,000 but not exceeding 1,100	240

Actual salary drawn by the workers is given below:

325	378	420	620	455	620	660	630	725	863
832	942	952	800	1002	1028	1100	610	625	763
382	540	463	578	723	690.				

How much the company would need to pay by way of bonus? What shall be the average bonus paid for member of the staff? **[MBA, Osamania, University, 2001, M.Com, AMU, 2004]**

Solution: For determining the figure of total and average bonus, first ascertain the number of persons in each salary group.

Weekly salary (Rs)	Frequency *f*	Bonus (Rs) *x*	Total Bonus *fx*
300–400	3	100	300
400–500	3	120	360
500–600	2	140	280
600–700	6	160	960
700–800	3	180	540
800–900	3	200	600
900–1,000	2	220	440
1,000 and above	3	240	720
	$N = 25$		$\Sigma fx = 4,200$

From the above table, we find that the company would need Rs 4,200 to pay bonus.

Average bonus per worker $= \dfrac{4,200}{25} = \text{Rs } 168.$

EXAMPLE 6.60: From the results of two colleges A and B below state which of them is better and why?

Name of Examination	College A		College B	
	Appeared	Passed	Appeared	Passed
MBA	300	250	1000	200
MCA	500	450	1200	950
BAA	2000	1500	1000	700
BCA	1200	750	800	50
Total	**4000**	**2950**	**4000**	**2950**

Solution:

Name of Examination	College A			College B		
	Appeared (W_A)	Passed	Pass % age (x_A)	Appeared (W_A)	Passed	Pass % age (x_A)
MBA	300	250	$\frac{250}{300} \times 100 = 83.33$	1000	800	$\frac{800}{1000} \times 100 = 80$
MCA	500	450	$\frac{450}{500} \times 100 = 90$	1200	950	$\frac{950}{1200} \times 100 = 79.17$
BBA	2000	1500	$\frac{1500}{2000} \times 100 = 75$	1000	700	$\frac{700}{1000} \times 100 = 70$
BCA	1200	750	$\frac{750}{1200} \times 100 = 62.5$	800	500	$\frac{500}{800} \times 100 = 62.5$
Total	**4000**	**2950**	$\frac{2950}{4000} \times 100 = 73.75$	**4000**	**2950**	$\frac{2950}{4000} \times 100 = 73.75$

On the basis of the given information, it is not possible to decide which college is better as the criterion for 'better college' is not defined. Let us try to solve the problem by taking the 'Higher Pass Percentage' as criterion for 'better college'. From the above table, we find that the pass percentage in MBA, MCA, BBA is better in College A than in College B whereas the pass percentage in BCA is same in both the colleges. The arithmetic mean of pass percentage in all the four courses is:

$$\bar{X}_A = \frac{83.33 + 90 + 75 + 62.50}{4} = \frac{310.83}{4} = 77.71$$

and
$$\bar{X}_B = \frac{80 + 79.17 + 70 + 62.50}{4} = \frac{291.67}{4} = 72.92$$

Since the mean pass percentage is higher for college A than for college B , we are tempted to conclude that college A is better than college B. However, this conclusion is not valid since the average pass percentage is affected by the number of students appearing in the examination in different courses. An appropriate average would be the weighted average of pass percentages in different courses, the corresponding weights being the number of students appearing in the examination. The weighted arithmetic means are:

$$\bar{X}_w(A) = \frac{\Sigma w_A x_A}{\Sigma w_A} \times = \frac{2950}{4000} \times 100 = 73.75$$

$$\bar{X}_w(B) = \frac{\Sigma w_B x_B}{\Sigma w_B} \times 100 = \frac{2950}{4000} \times 100 = 73.75$$

On comparing the weighted means, we conclude that both the colleges A and B are equally good on the basis of the criterion of higher pass percentage for all the students taken together.

LIST OF FORMULAE

1. Sample Arithmetic Mean of individual observation (ungrouped or Raw Data)

   (a) Direct Method: $\bar{X} = \frac{\Sigma x}{N}$

   (b) Short-cut Method: $\bar{X} = A + \frac{\Sigma d}{N}$; $[d = x - A]$

2. Sample Arithmetic Mean of a Discrete Series

   (a) Direct Method: $\bar{X} = \frac{\Sigma fx}{N}$

   (b) Short –cut Method: $\bar{X} = A + \frac{\Sigma fd}{N}$

3. Sample Arithmetic Mean of a Continuous Series

   (a) Direct Method: $\bar{X} = \frac{\Sigma fx}{N}$

   (b) Short-cut Method: $\bar{X} = A + \frac{\Sigma fd}{N}$

   (c) Step-deviation method $\bar{X} = A + \frac{\Sigma fd^1}{N} \times c$ $[d^1 = \frac{x - A}{c}]$

   Where c is the width of the interval.

4. Charlier's Accuracy check

   (a) For short-cut method, $\Sigma f(x - A) = \Sigma[f\{x - A) + 1\}] - \Sigma f$

   (b) For step-deviation method $\Sigma fd^1 - \Sigma[f(d^1 \mid 1)] - \Sigma f$

5. Combined mean of two series $\bar{X} = \frac{n_1 \bar{X}_1 + n_2 \bar{X}_2}{n_1 + n_2}$

6. Weighted arithmetic mean $\bar{X}_w = \frac{w_1 x_1 + w_2 x_2 + \ldots + w_n x_n}{w_1 + w_2 + \ldots + w_n} = \frac{\Sigma wx}{\Sigma w}$

   Where w stands for weight

7. Medias of individual observations

   (a) If n is odd

$$\text{Median} = \left(\frac{n+1}{2}\right)^{\text{th}} \text{ term}$$

(b) If n is even

$$\text{Median} = \frac{\left[\left(\frac{n}{2}\right)^{\text{th}} \text{term} + \left(\frac{n+2}{2}\right)^{\text{th}} \text{term}\right]}{2}$$

or

$$\text{Median} = \frac{\left[\left(\frac{n}{2}\right)^{\text{th}} \text{term} + \left(\frac{n}{2}+1\right)^{\text{th}} \text{term}\right]}{2}$$

8. Median of a Continuous Series

$$\text{Median} = l_1 + \frac{\frac{N}{2} - m}{f} \times c$$

Where, l_1 is lower limit of the median class, m is cumulative frequency of preceding, median class c is the width of median class and f is the frequency of median class.

9. Quartile of individual observations

Lower quartile $(Q_1) = \left(\frac{n+1}{4}\right)^{\text{th}}$ item

Upper quartile $(Q_3) = 3\left(\frac{n+1}{4}\right)^{\text{th}}$ item

10. Quartile of the Continuous Series

Lower quartile $Q_1 = l_1 + \frac{\frac{n}{4} - m_1}{f_1} \times c$

Upper quartile $Q_3 = l_3 + \frac{3\left(\frac{n}{4}\right) - m_3}{f_3} \times c$

Where, f_1 and f_3 are the frequency of 1st and 3rd quartile class respectively, l_1 and l_3 are the lower limit of 1st and 3rd quartile class and c is the class interval of quartile class.

11. Deciles of Individual Observations

First Decile $(D_1) = \left(\frac{n}{10}\right)^{\text{th}}$ item

⋮ ⋮ ⋮

Tenth Decile $(D_g) = 9\left(\frac{n}{10}\right)^{\text{th}}$ item

12. Deciles of Continuous Series $D_1 = l_1 + \frac{i\left(\frac{n}{10}\right) - m_i}{f_i} \times c$ Where $i = 1, 2, 3, 4 \ldots 9$.

13. Percentile of Individual Observations

$$\text{First percentile} \quad (P_1) = \left(\frac{N}{100}\right)^{\text{th}} \text{ item}$$

$$\vdots \qquad \vdots \qquad \vdots$$

$$\text{Hundredth percentile} \quad (P_{99}) = 99\left(\frac{N}{100}\right)^{\text{th}} \text{ item}$$

14. Percentile of Continuous Series

$$P_i = l_i + \frac{i\left(\frac{N}{100}\right) - m_i}{f_1} \times c$$

15. Mode of the continuous series

$$\text{Mode} = l_1 + \frac{\Delta_1}{\Delta_1 + \Delta_2} \times c$$

Where $D_1 = f_1 - f_0$; $D_2 = f_1 - f_2$

Here f_0 is the frequency of the class preceding the modal class, f_1 is the frequency of modal class and f_2 is the frequency of the class succeeding the modal class.

or $$\text{Mode} = l_1 + \frac{f_1 - f_0}{2f_1 - f_0 - f_2} \times c$$

16. Empirical relationship among averages

$$\text{Mode} = 3 \text{ Median} - 2 \text{ Mean}$$

17. Harmonic Mean of Individual Observations

$$\text{H.M} = \frac{n}{\Sigma\left(\frac{1}{x}\right)}$$

18. Harmonic Mean of Grouped Data (discrete or continuous series)

$$\text{H.M} = \frac{n}{\Sigma f\left(\frac{1}{x}\right)}$$

19. Geometric Mean of Individual Observations

$$\text{G.M} = \sqrt[n]{x_1 . x_2 ... x_n}$$

or $$\text{G.M} = \text{Antilog}\left[\frac{\Sigma \log x}{n}\right]$$

20. Geometric Mean of Grouped Data (Discrete or Continuous Series)

$$\text{G.M} = \text{Antilog}\left[\frac{\Sigma f \log x}{N}\right]$$

21. Relationship among A.M, G.M and H.M

$$\text{A.M} \geq \text{G.M} \geq \text{H.M}$$

If observations in *a* data set take the values $a, ar, ar^2, ar^3, \dots ar^{n-1}$, each with single frequency then

$$(G.M)^2 = A.M \times H.M$$

SELF PRACTICE EXERCISES

I. CHOOSE THE BEST ANSWER

1. Which of the following represents median?
   (a) First Quartile (b) Fiftieth Percentile
   (c) Sixth deciles (d) Third quartile
2. If the grouped data has open-end classes, one can not calculate:
   (a) median (b) mode
   (c) mean (d) quartile
3. Geometric mean of two numbers $\left(\frac{1}{16}\right)$ and $\left(\frac{4}{25}\right)$ is:
   (a) $\left(\frac{1}{10}\right)$ (b) $\left(\frac{1}{100}\right)$
   (c) 10 (d) 100
4. In a symmetric distribution:
   (a) mean = median = mode (b) mean = median = mode
   (c) mean > median > mode (d) mean < median < mode
5. If modal value is not clear in a distribution, it can be ascertained by the method of:
   (a) grouping (b) guessing
   (c) summarizing (d) trial and error
6. Shoe size of most of the people in India is No. 7. Which measure of central value does it represent?
   (a) mean (b) second quartile
   (c) eighth decile (d) mode
7. The middle value of an ordered series is called:
   (a) 2nd quartile (b) 5th decile
   (c) 50th percentile (d) all the above
8. The variate values which divide a series (frequency distribution) into ten equal parts are called:
   (a) quartiles (b) deciles
   (c) octiles (d) percentiles
9. For percentiles, the total numbers of partition values are:
   (a) 10 (b) 59
   (c) 100 (d) 99
10. The first quartile divides a frequency distribution in the ratio:
    (a) 4 : 1 (b) 1 : 4
    (c) 3 : 1 (d) 1 : 3

11. Sum of the deviations about mean is:
    (a) Zero (b) minimum
    (c) maximum (d) one
12. Histogram is useful to determine graphically the value of:
    (a) mean (b) median
    (c) mode (d) all the above
13. Median can be located graphically with the help of:
    (a) Histogram (b) ogives
    (c) bar diagram (d) scatter diagram
14. Sixth deciles is same as:
    (a) median (b) 50th percentile
    (c) 60th percentile (d) first quartile
15. What percentage of values lies between 5th and 25th percentiles?
    (a) 5% (b) 20%
    (c) 30% (d) 75%

II. FILL IN THE BLANKS

1. If 5 is subtracted from each observation of a set, then the mean of the observation is reduced by ....
2. The arithmetic mean of n natural numbers from 1 to n is ....
3. Geometric mean cannot be calculated if any value of the set is ....
4. Median is a more suited average for grouped data with .... classes.
5. 3rd quartile and .... percentile are the same.
6. .... can be calculated from a frequency distribution with open end classes.
7. In the calculation of ...., all the observations are taken into consideration.
8. .... is not affected by extreme observations.
9. The sum of absolute deviations is minimum when taken from ....
10. Median = ... Quartile.
11. For studying phenomenon like intelligence and honesty .... is a better average to be used while for phenomenon like size of shoes or readymade garments the average to be preferred is ....
12. Typist A can type a sheet in 5 minutes, typist B in 6 minutes and typist C in 8 minutes. The average number of sheets typed per hour per typist is ....
13. Relationship between Md, Q_1, Q_2 and Q_3 is ....
14. The empirical relationship between mean, median and mode for a moderately as symmetrical distribution is ....

III. SHORT ANSWER TYPE QUESTIONS

1. What is arithmetic mean? **[MBA, MK, University, 2001]**
2. When is mode useful over other average?
3. Is harmonic mean reciprocal of arithmetic mean?
4. What are model classes?

5. What is weighted mean?
6. What is the relationship among mean, median and mode? **[MBA, UPTU (CO), 2005, MK, University, 2001]**
7. What are percentiles and deciles?
8. Define average. Write down the properties of an average.
9. What is the arithmetic mean of first n natural number 1, 2, 3, 4,……*n*? Show that it is equal to the median? **[MBA, UPTU (MO), 2005, MK, University, 2007]**
10. What are the uses of geometric mean and harmonic mean?

IV. LONG ANSWER TYPE QUESTIONS

1. What do you understand by measures of central tendency?
2. What are the desirable characteristics of a good measure of central tendency?
3. What is the object of an average?
4. State the meaning of 'Measures of Central Tendency'?
5. Give two examples where (i) Geometric mean and (ii) Harmonic mean would be most suitable averages.
6. Define median. Discuss its advantages and disadvantages as an average.
7. Define arithmetic mean. Discuss its merits and demerits.
8. Why the arithmetic mean is most commonly used measure of a central value?
9. Enlist the mathematical properties of mean.
10. Define weighted arithmetic mean. Discuss its importance.
11. How would you account for the predominant choice of arithmetic mean as a measure of central tendency? Under what Circumstances would it be appropriate to use mode, median, geometric mean and harmonic mean? **[MBA, DU, 2001]**
12. Under what circumstances would it be appropriate to use arithmetic mean, median or mode? Discuss. **[MBA, UPTU (CO), 2002, DU, 1998]**
13. "Every average has its own peculiar characteristics. It is difficult to say which average is the best." Comment briefly. **[MBA, UPTU, 2007, HP, University, 1997]**
14. Explain the properties of good average. In the light of these properties which average do you think is the best and why? **[MBA, Jodhpur University, 1996]**
15. Define an average and describe its properties which average would be more suitable in the following cases:

    "Average size of ready-made garments.
    "Average intelligence of students in a class.
    "Average change in the cost of living of workers.
    "Average production per shift in a factory.
    "Average rate of growth of population per decade.

16. Prove that the sums of the deviations of the values X taken from their mean X is zero.
17. State two instances when arithmetic mean is not an appropriate measure of central tendency for data which describe some measurements.
18. Given the two reasons why statisticians prefer arithmetic mean to the medians.
19. What should be an appropriate measure of location for a frequency distribution with an open end? Why?

20. (a) Which best possible average would you use for determining the average daily customers at a restaurant for purposes of estimating (i) the total monthly income and (ii) the number of bearers needed on any given day? State the reason.
    (b) Which best possible average would you use for determining the average height of the water hut so that school children could drink water standing? State the reason.
26. The monthly income of ten families (in rupees) in a certain locality is given below.

Family	A	B	C	D	E	F	G
Income (in Rupees)	30	70	60	100	200	150	300

Calculate the arithmetic average by (a) Direct method and (b) Short-cut method

27. Calculate the mean for the data

X	5	8	12	15	20	24
f	3	4	6	5	3	2

28. The following table gives the distribution of the number of workers according to the weekly wage in a company.

Weekly wage (in Rs. 100's)	0–10	10–20	20–30	30–40	40–50	50–60	60–70	70–80
Numbers of workers	5	10	15	18	7	8	5	3

Obtain the mean weekly wage.

29. Mean of 20 values is 45. If one of these values is to be taken 64 instead of 46, find the corrected mean.
30. From the following data, find the missing frequency when mean is 15.38

Size	10	12	14	16	18	20
Frequency	3	7	-----	20	8	5

31. The following table gives the weekly wages in rupees of workers in a certain commercial organization. The frequency of the class-interval 49–52 is missing.

Weekly wage (in Rs. 100s)	40–43	43–46	49–49	49–52	52–55
Numbers of workers	31	58	60	-----	27

distribution is Rs 47.2. Find the missing frequency.

32. Find combined mean from the following data $x_1 = 210$; $n_1 = 50$; $x_2 = 150$; $n_2 = 100$.
33. Find combined mean from the following data:

Group	1	2	3
Number	200	250	300
Mean	25	10	15

34. Average monthly production of a certain factory for the first 9 months is 2584, and for remaining three months it is 2416 units. Calculate average monthly production for the year.

35. The marks of a student in written and oral tests in subjects A, B and C are as follows. The written test marks are out of 75 and the oral test marks are out of 25. Find the weighted mean of the marks in written test taking the marks in oral test as weight. The marks of written test and oral test respectively as follows: 27, 24, 43 and 5, 10, 15.

36. The monthly income of 8 families is given below. Find G.M.

Family	A	B	C	D	E	F	G	H
Income (Rs.)	70	10	500	75	8	250	8	42

37. The following table gives the diameters of screws obtained in a sample inquiry. Calculate the mean diameter using geometric average.

Diameter (m.m)	130	135	140	145	146	148	149	150	157
No. of Screws	3	4	6	6	3	5	2	1	1

38. An investor buys Rs. 1,200 worth of shares in a company each month. During the first 5 months he bought the shares at a price of Rs. 10, Rs. 12, Rs. 15, Rs. 20 and Rs. 24 per share. After 5 months what is the average price paid for the shares by him.

39. Determine median from the following data 25, 20, 15, 45, 18, 7, 10, 38, 12

40. Find median of the following data:

Weekly wage (in Rs.)	60–70	50–60	40–50	30–40	20–30
Numbers of workers	7	21	11	6	5

41. The table below gives the relative frequency distribution of annual pay roll for 100 small retail establishments in a city.

Annual pay roll (1000 rupees)	Establishments
Less than 10	8
10 and Less than 20	12
20 and Less than 30	18
30 and Less than 40	30
40 and Less than 50	20
50 and Less than 60	12
	100

Calculate Median pay.

42. Calculate the median from the data given below:

Wages in (Rs.)	Number of workers	Wages in (Rs.)	Number of workers
Above 30	520	Above 70	105
Above 40	470	Above 80	45
Above 50	399	Above 90	7
Above 60	210		

43. From the following data, compute the values of upper and lower quartiles, median, D_6, P_{20}.

Marks	No. of students	Marks	No. of Students
Below 10	5	40–50	90
10–20	25	50–60	40
20–30	40	60–70	20
30–40	70	Above 70	10

44. Draw an ogive curve from the following data to find out the values of median and upper and lower quartiles.

Classes	90–100	100–110	110–120	120–130	130–140	140–150	150–160
Frequency	16	22	45	60	50	24	10

45. Calculate mode from the following data

Income (Rs.)	10–20	20–30	30–40	40–50	50–60	60–70	70–80
No. of Persons	24	42	56	66	108	130	154

46. Represent the following data by means of histogram and from it, obtain value of mode.

Weekly wage (in Rs.)	10–15	15–20	20–25	25–30	30–35	35–40	40–45
No. of workers	7	9	27	15	12	12	8

ANSWERS

I. CHOOSE THE BEST ANSWER

1. (b) 2. (c) 3. (a) 4. (b) 5. (a)
6. (d) 7. (d) 8. (b) 9. (c) 10. (d)
11. (a) 12. (c) 13. (b) 14. (c) 15. (b)

II. FILL IN THE BLANKS

1. 5 2. $(n + 1)/2$ 3. 0 and negative 4. Open end 5. 75th
6. Mode 7. Mean 8. Mode 9. Median 10. Second
11. Median, Mode 12. 9.47 13. $a_1 < a_2 = \text{MD} < Q_3$
14. Mo = 3 Md – 2 M

IV. LONG ANSWER TYPE QUESTIONS

26. 130 27. 13.13 28. 35 29. 44.1 30. 12
31. 44 32. 170 33. 16 34. 2542 35. 34
36. G.M = 45.27 37. 142.5 mm 38. Rs. 14.63 39. MD = 18 40. 51.42
41. 34 42. 57.3
43. $Q_1 = 30.714$; $Q_2 = 19.44$; MD = 41.11; $D_6 = 44.44$; $P_{20} = 27.5$
44. MD = 125.08; $Q_1 = 114.18$; $Q_3 = 135.45$ 45. Mode = 71.34.

CHAPTER 7

Measures of Dispersion (Variation)

7.1 INTRODUCTION

In earlier Chapters we have studied that collection of data is represented in different forms. From the data we have learnt to calculate the measures of the central tendency like mean, median and mode. These central measures do not give us all the details about the distribution. Further descriptions of the data called measures of dispersion are necessary. According to ***A.L. Bowley***, "Dispersion is the measure of the variation of the individual item". That is the dispersion is used to indicate the extent to which the data is spread.

The measures of central tendency (i.e. mean) indicate the general magnitude of the data and tries to locate only the centre of the distribution of measures. They do not establish the degree of variability or the spread out or scatter of the individual items and their deviation from (or the difference with) the means.

The measures of central tendency serve to locate the centre of the distribution, but they do not reveal how the items are spread out on either side of the centre. This characteristic of a distribution is commonly referred to as ***dispersion.*** In a series all the items may not be equal. There may be difference or variation among the values. The degree of variation is evaluated by various measures of dispersion. Small dispersion indicates high uniformity of the items, while large dispersion indicates less uniformity.

According to ***Nciswanger***, "Two distributions of statistical data may be symmetrical and have common means, medians and modes and identical frequencies in the modal class. Yet with these points in common they may differ widely in the scatter or in their values about the measures of central tendencies." ***Simpson and Kafka*** said, "An average alone does not tell the full story. It is hardly fully representative of a mass, unless we know the manner in which the individual item. Scatter around it .... a further description of a series is necessary, if we are to gauge how representative the average is."

7.2 MEASURES OF DISPERSION

From this discussion we now focus our attention on the scatter or variability which is known as ***dispersion***. Let us take the following three sets.

Students	Group X	Group Y	Group Z
1	50	45	30
2	50	50	45
3	50	55	75
Mean $\bar{X}$	**50**	**50**	**50**

Thus, the three groups have same mean i.e. 50. In fact the median of group X and Y are also equal. Now if one would say that the students from the three groups are of equal capabilities, it is totally a wrong conclusion then. Close examination reveals that in group X students have equal marks as the mean, students from group Y are very close to the mean but in the third group Z, the marks are widely scattered. ***It is thus clear that the measures of the central tendency is alone not sufficient to describe the data.***

In another example, consider the following marks of two students:

Student I	68	75	65	67	70
Student II	85	90	80	25	65

Both have got a total of 345 and an average of 69 each. The fact is that the second student has failed in one paper. When the averages alone are considered, the two students are equal. But first student has less variation than second student.

Thus, a measure of central tendency does not supply complete information about some distribution and we should know some other measures to supplement the information. One such measure is known as dispersion which gives an idea about the scattering of values around the central value of the data and helps in getting an idea about the composition of the series.

> Statistical measures of variation are numerical values that indicate the ***variability*** inherent in a set of data measurements. A small value for a measure of dispersion indicates that the data are concentrated around the mean; therefore, the mean is a good representative of the data set. On the other hand, a large measure of dispersion indicates that the mean is not a good representative of the data set. Also, measures of dispersion can be used when we want to compare the distributions of two or more sets of data.

Quality of a data set is measured by its variability: *Larger variability indicates lower quality.* That is why high variation makes the manager very worried. Your job, as a statistician, is to measure the variation, and if it is too high and unacceptable, then it is the job of the technical staff, such as engineers, to fix the process.

7.2.1 Definition of Dispersion

The variation of the observed values of the distribution about the central value is known as dispersion literal meaning of dispersion is '***spread***' or '***scatteredness***'. Dispersion is also known as the 'average of second degree' as in the calculation of measures of dispersion we average values derived by the use of the averages of the first order (i.e mean, median, mode, geometric mean, etc.)

Some important definitions of dispersion are given below:

1. 'Dispersion or spread is the degree of the scatter or variation of the variable about a central value'. ***[Brooks and Dick]***

2. 'A measure of variation or dispersion describes the degree of scatter shown by the observations and is usually measured as an average deviation about some central value or by an order statistic.".
3. "Measures of variability are usually used to indicate how tightly bunched the sample values are around the mean." ***[Dyckman and Thomas]***
4. "Dispersion is the measure of the extent of which the individual items vary" ***[Conor]***

7.2.2 Objects of Measuring Dispersion or Variability

Measures of variations are computed to serve the following purposes:

1. For judging the reliability of averages. Measures of dispersion enable us to know whether an average is really representative of the series. If the dispersion or variability in the values of various items in a series is large, the average may be unrepresentative of the series. If on the other hand, the variability is small, the average would be a representative value. No variation indicates perfect uniformity and, therefore values in the data set are identical.
2. To identify the causes of variability with a view to control it. A study of dispersion helps in identifying the causes of variability and in taking remedial measures. ***Spurr and Bonimi*** have very rightly observed that, "In matters of health, variations in body temperature, pulse beats and blood pressure are basic guides to diagnosis. Prescribed treatment is designed to control their variation. In industrial production efficient operation requires control of quality variation, the causes of which are sought through inspection and quality control programmes." In social sciences where we have to study the problems relating to inequality in income and wealth, measures of dispersion are of immense help.
3. To make a comparative study of the variability of two series. Measures of dispersion are also useful in comparing two or more distributions in respect to disparities. A greater degree of dispersion would mean lack of uniformity or consistency or homogeneity in the data while a low degree of dispersion stands for uniformity, consistency or homogeneity.
4. To serve as a basis for further statistical analysis. Measures of dispersion are necessary for studying correlation, regression, testing of hypothesis, analysis of fluctuations in a time series and production and cost control etc.

7.2.3 Characteristics for an Ideal Measure of Dispersion

An ideal measure of dispersion is expected to possess the following properties

1. It should be rigidly defined
2. It should be based on all the items.
3. It should not be unduly affected by extreme items.
4. It should lend itself for algebraic manipulation.
5. It should be simple to understand and easy to calculate

7.3 METHODS FOR MEASURES OF DISPERSION

In measuring dispersion, it is imperative to know the amount of variation (absolute measure) and the degree of variation (relative measure).

There are two kinds of measures of dispersion, namely

1. Absolute measure of dispersion
2. Relative measure of dispersion.

Absolute measure of dispersion indicates the amount of variation in a set of values in terms of units of observations. ***For example***, when rainfalls on different days are available in mm, any absolute measure of dispersion gives the variation in rainfall in mm. On the other hand relative measures of dispersion are free from the units of measurements of the observations. They are pure numbers. They are used to compare the variation in two or more sets, which are having different units of measurements of observations.

The various absolute and relative measures of dispersion are listed below.

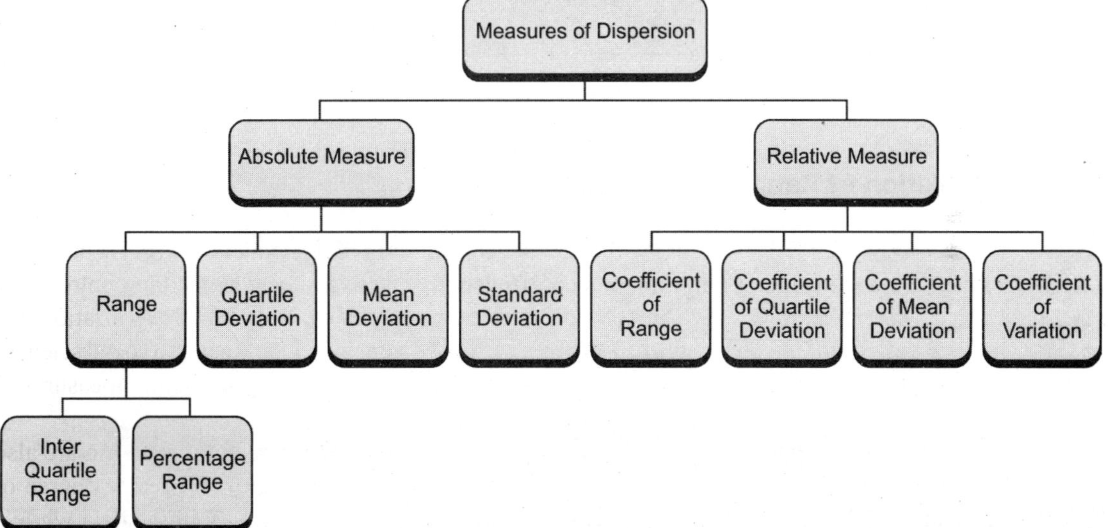

Fig. 7.1: Measures of Dispersion

The various measures of dispersion are discussed in detail in the remaining sections of this chapter.

7.4 RANGE AND COEFFICIENT OF RANGE

Range

This is the simplest possible measure of dispersion and is defined as the difference between the largest and smallest values of the variable. It is based solely on two values, not on the entire data set. In addition, it cannot be defined for open-ended distributions such as normal distribution.

In symbols,

$$\boxed{\text{Range} = L - S}$$

Where, L = Largest value.
S = Smallest value.

DO YOU KNOW?

In any statistical series, the difference between the largest and the smallest values is called as the range.

Thus if in a lightest student has a weight of 40 kg and the heaviest of 100 kg the value of range would be 60 kg. This figure indicates the variability in the weight of students.

Coefficient of Range

Range as calculated above is an absolute measure of dispersion which is unfit purpose of comparison if the distributions are in different units. ***For example***, the range of the weights of students cannot be compared with the range of their height measurements as the range of weights would be in kg and that at heights in centimetres. Sometimes, for purpose of comparison, a relative measure of range is calculated. If range is divided by the sum of the extreme items, the resulting figure is called "The Ratio of the Range" or "The coefficient of Range".

$$\text{Coefficient of Range} = \frac{L-S}{L+S}$$

7.4.1 Calculation of Range — Individual series

For the raw data we can calculate the difference between the largest and smallest value of the data.

EXAMPLE 7.1: Find the value of range and it's co-efficient for the following data: 7, 9, 6, 8, 11, 10, 4.

Solution:

$$L = 11, S = 4.$$

$$\text{Range} = L - S = 11 - 4 = 7$$

$$\text{Co-efficient of Range} = \frac{L-S}{L+S} = \frac{11-4}{11+4} = \frac{7}{15} = 0.4667$$

EXAMPLE 7.2: Find the range and the co-efficient of the range of the following items: 110, 117, 129, 197, 190, 100, 100, 178, 255, 790.

Solution:

$$L = 790, S = 100$$

$$R = L - S = 790 - 100 = 690$$

$$\text{Co-efficient of Range} = \frac{L-S}{L+S} = \frac{790-100}{790+100} = \frac{690}{890} = 0.78$$

EXAMPLE 7.3: The largest value of a data is 98. If the range of the data is 73, find the smallest value of the data.

Solution:

Largest value $\quad L = 98$; Range = 73

$$\text{Range} = L - S$$

or $\quad 73 = 98 - S$

or $\quad S = 98 - 73 = 25$

The smallest value $\quad = 25$

EXAMPLE 7.4: The least score of a cricket player of the school team is 5 runs in a series of ten matches. If his range of scores is 87, find his highest score in the series.

Solution:

Least Score $S = 5$; Range = 87

$$\text{Range} = L - S$$

or $87 = L - 5$

or $L = 87 + 5 = 92$

The highest score = 92 runs.

7.4.2 Calculation of Range — Discrete Series

For the discrete series we can calculate the difference between the largest and smallest value of the series.

EXAMPLE 7.5: The profits of a Company for the last 7 years are given below. Calculate the range and its Co-efficient:

Year	1981	1982	1983	1984	1985	1986	1987
Profits (crores)	40	30	80	140	145	90	200

Solution:

$$\text{Range} = L - S$$

where $L = 200$

and $S = 30$

$$\text{Range} = 200–30 = 170$$

$$\text{Coefficient of Range} = \frac{L - S}{L + S} = \frac{200 - 30}{200 + 30}$$

$$= \frac{170}{230} = 0.74$$

7.4.3 Calculation of Range — Continuous Series

When the data are available in the form of a continuous frequency distributions, then range is calculated by any one of the following two methods.

Method 1: By subtracting the lower limit of the lowest class from the upper limit of the highest class.

Method 2: By subtracting the mid-value of the lowest class from mid–value of the highest class.

EXAMPLE 7.6: Find the range and its co-efficient from the following data.

Size	10–20	20–30	30–40	40–50	50–60
Frequency	2	3	5	4	2

Solution:

Method 1: $L = 60, S = 10$

$$R = L - S = 60 - 10 = 50$$

$$\text{Co-efficient of Range} = \frac{L - S}{L + S} = \frac{60 - 10}{60 + 10} = \frac{50}{70}$$

$$= 0.71$$

Method 2: Largest value = 55 [middle value of the last class interval]

Smallest value = 15 [middle value of first class intervals]

Therefore, $R = L - S = 55 - 15 = 40$

$$\text{Coefficient of Range} = \frac{L-S}{L+S} = \frac{55-15}{55+15} = \frac{40}{70} = 0.57$$

EXAMPLE 7.7: Calculate range and its co-efficient from the following distribution.

Size	60–63	63–66	66–69	69–72	72–75
Number	5	18	42	27	8

Solution:

L = Upper boundary of the highest class = 75

S = Lower boundary of the lowest class = 60

Range = $L - S = 75 - 60 = 15$

$$\text{Co-efficient of Range} = \frac{L-S}{L+S} = \frac{75-60}{75+60} = \frac{15}{135} = 0.1111$$

7.4.4 Quartile and Interquartile Range

Quartiles

When we order the data, ***for example*** in ascending order, we may divide the data into quarters, $Q_1 \ldots Q_4$, known as quartiles. The first Quartile (Q_1) is that value where 25% of the values are smaller and 75% are larger. The second Quartile (Q_2) is that value where 50% of the values are smaller and 50% are larger. The third Quartile (Q_3) is that value where 75% of the values are smaller and 25% are larger.

Interquartiles Range

If we concentrate on two extreme values (as in the case of range), we don't get any idea about the scatter of the data within the range (i.e. the two extreme values). If we discard these two values the limited range thus available might be more informative. For this reason the concept of ***interquartile range*** is developed. It is the range which includes middle 50% of the distribution. Here 1/4 (one quarter of the lower end) and 1/4 (one quarter) of the upper end of the observations are excluded.

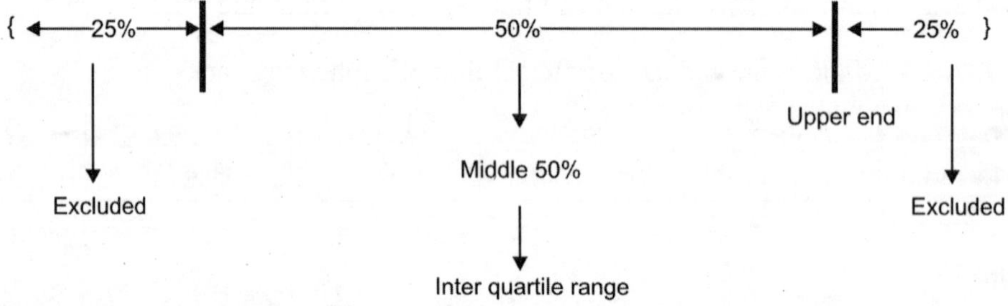

Now the lower quartile (Q_1) is the 25th percentile and the upper quartile (Q_3) is the 75th percentile. It is interesting to note that the 50th percentile is the middle quartile (Q_2) which is in fact what you have studied under the title "Median". Thus symbolically

$$\text{Interquartile Range } (IQR) = Q_3 - Q_1$$

If we divide $(Q_3 - Q_1)$ by 2 we get what is known as Semi-interquartile range.

$$\text{Semi-Interquartile Range} = \frac{Q_3 - Q_1}{2}$$

It is known as Quartile deviation (*Q.D* or *SI Q.R*).

7.4.5 Percentile and Percentile Range

Percentile

Percentiles have a similar concept and therefore, are related; e.g., the 25th percentile corresponds to the first quartile Q_1, etc. The advantage of percentiles is that they may be subdivided into 100 parts.

The nth percentile is that value (or size) such that n% of values of the whole data lies below it. ***For example***, a score of 7% from the topmost score would be 93 the percentile as it is above 93% of the other scores.

000 111111 222222 4444 55 666 7777 8 999 (10) 11 11 etc

← 93% of scores →

93th percentile

Percentile Range

It is used as one of the measure of dispersion. It is a set of data and is defined as $P_{90} - P_{10}$ where P_{90} and P_{10} are the 90th and 10th percentile respectively.

$$\text{Percentile Range} = P_{90} - P_{10}$$

$$\text{Semi-percentile Range} = \left(\frac{P_{90} - P_{10}}{2}\right)$$

7.4.6 Merits and Demerits of Range

Merits

1. It is simple to understand.
2. It is easy to calculate.
3. In certain types of problems like quality control, weather forecasts, share price analysis, etc., range is most widely used.

Demerits

1. It is very much affected by the extreme items.
2. It is based on only two extreme observations.
3. It cannot be calculated from open-end class intervals.
4. It is not suitable for mathematical treatment.

For example, observe the following three groups:

Group A	6	46	46	46	46	46	46	46
Group B	6	6	6	6	46	46	46	46
Group C	6	10	15	25	30	32	40	46

In all the three groups range is the same (i.e. 46 – 6 = 40), but it does not mean that the distributions are alike. The range takes no account on the form of the distribution within the range. Range is, therefore, most unreliable as a guide to the variation of the values within a distribution.

7.4.7 Uses of Range

1. Range is commonly used in the field of statistical Quality Control. In quality control of manufactured products, range is used to study the variation in the quality of the units manufactured. Even with the most modern mechanical equipment there may be a small, almost insignificant, difference in the different units of a commodity manufactured. Thus, if a company is manufacturing bottles of a particular type, there may be a slight variation in the size or shape of the bottles manufactured. In such cases a range is usually determined, and all the units which fall within these limits are accepted while those which fall outside the limits are rejected.
2. Variations in money rates, share values, gold prices and exchange rates are commonly studied through range because the fluctuations in them are not very large. In fact range as a measure of dispersion should be generally used only when variations in the value of the variable are not much.
3. Range is also used for weather forecasting. It gives an idea of the variation between maximum and minimum levels of temperature. From day to day the range would not vary much and it is helpful in studying the vagaries of nature if variations suddenly rise or fall.

7.5 QUARTILE DEVIATION AND COEFFICIENT OF QUARTILE DEVIATION

Quartile Deviation (Q.D)

Quartile Deviation is half of the difference between the first and third quartiles. Hence, it is called Semi Inter Quartile Range.

$$Q.D = \frac{Q_3 - Q_1}{2}$$

Among the quartiles Q_1, Q_2 and Q_3, the range $Q_3 - Q_1$ is called inter quartile range and $\frac{Q_3 - Q_1}{2}$, Semi inter quartile range.

Also note that Q_1 and Q_3 are equidistance from the median. In any perfect symmetrical distribution (in future we will call it as the normal distribution).

$$\text{Median} - Q_1 = Q_3 - \text{Median}$$

i.e. $$2\text{ Median} = Q_3 + Q_1$$

$\Rightarrow$ $$\text{Median} = \frac{Q_3 + Q_1}{2}$$

which covers exactly 50% of the observations.

Co-efficient of Quartile Deviation

Since quartile deviation is an absolute measure of variation, therefore its value gets affected by the size and number of observed values in the data set. Thus, the QD of two or more than sets of data may differ. Due to this reason, to compare the degree of variation in different sets of data, we compute the relative measure corresponding to *QD*, called the coefficient of *QD*, and it is calculated as follow:

$$\text{Co-efficient of } Q.D = \frac{Q_3 - Q_1}{Q_3 + Q_1}$$

7.5.1 Calculation of Quartile Deviation — Individual Series

EXAMPLE 7.8: Find the Quartile Deviation for the following data:

391 384 591 407 672 522 777 733 1490 2488

Solution: Arrange the given values in ascending order.

384 391 407 522 591 672 733 777 1490 2488

$$\text{Position of } Q_1 \text{ is } \frac{n+1}{4} = \frac{10+1}{4} = 2.75^{\text{th}} \text{ item}$$

$$Q_1 = 2^{\text{nd}} \text{ value} + 0.75 \text{ (3rd value} - 2^{\text{nd}} \text{ value)}$$

$$= 391 + 0.75\ (407 - 391)$$

$$= 391 + 0.75 \times 16$$

$$= 391 + 12$$

$$= 403$$

$$\text{Position } Q_3 \text{ is } 3\frac{n+1}{4} = 3 \times 2.75 = 8.25^{\text{th}} \text{ item}$$

$$Q_3 = 8^{\text{th}} \text{ value} + 0.25\ (9^{\text{th}} \text{ value} - 8^{\text{th}} \text{ value})$$

$$= 777 + 0.25\ (1490 - 777)$$

$$- 777 + 0.25\ (713)$$

$$= 777 + 178.25 = 955.25$$

$$\text{Q.D} = \frac{Q_3 - Q_1}{2}$$

$$= \frac{955.25 - 403}{2}$$

$$= 276.125$$

7.5.2 Calculation of Quartile Deviation — Discrete Series

EXAMPLE 7.9: Weekly wages of labours are given below. Calculated *Q.D* and coefficient of *Q.D*.

Weekly Wage (Rs)	100	200	400	500	600
No. of Weeks	5	8	21	12	6

Solution:

Weekly Wage (Rs)	No. of Weeks	Cum. No. of Weeks
100	5	5
200	8	13
400	21	34
500	12	46
600	6	52
Total	$N = 52$	

$$\text{Position of } Q_1 \text{ in } \frac{N+1}{4} = \frac{52+1}{4} = 13.25^{\text{th}} \text{ item}$$

$$\begin{aligned} Q_1 &= 13^{\text{th}} \text{ value} + 0.25\,(14^{\text{th}} \text{ Value} - 13^{\text{th}} \text{ value}) \\ &= 13^{\text{th}} \text{ value} + 0.25\,(400 - 200) \\ &= 200 + 0.25\,(400 - 200) \\ &= 200 + 0.25\,(200) \\ &= 200 + 50 = 250 \end{aligned}$$

$$\text{Position of } Q_3 \text{ is } 3\left(\frac{N+1}{4}\right) = 3 \times 13.25 = 39.75^{\text{th}} \text{ item}$$

$$\begin{aligned} Q_3 &= 39^{\text{th}} \text{ value} + 0.75\,(40^{\text{th}} \text{ value} - 39^{\text{th}} \text{ value}) \\ &= 500 + 0.75\,(500 - 500) \\ &= 500 + 0.75 \times 0 = 500 \end{aligned}$$

$$\begin{aligned} Q.D &= \frac{Q_3 - Q_1}{2} \\ &= \frac{500 - 250}{2} = \frac{250}{2} = 125 \end{aligned}$$

$$\text{Coefficient of } Q.D = \frac{Q_3 - Q_1}{Q_3 + Q_1} = \frac{500 - 250}{500 + 250} = \frac{250}{750} = \frac{1}{3} = 0.33$$

7.5.3 Calculation of Quartile Deviation — Continuous Series

For continuous series (grouped data), the formula for calculating Q_1 and Q_2 are same as the median (Q_2).

i.e.

$$Q_1 = l_1 + \frac{\frac{N}{4} - m_1}{f_1} \times c$$

$$Q_3 = l_3 + \frac{3\left(\frac{N}{4}\right) - m_3}{f_3} \times c$$

EXAMPLE 7.10: For the data given below, given the quartile deviation and coefficient of quartile deviation.

x	351–500	501–650	651–800	801–950	951–1100
f	48	189	88	4	28

Solution:

x	f	True class Intervals	Cumulative frequency
351–500	48	350.5–500.5	48
501–650	189	500.5–650.5	237
651–800	88	650.5–800.5	325
801–950	47	800.5–950.5	372
951–1100	28	950.5–1100.5	400
Total	N = 400		

$$Q_1 = l_1 + \frac{\frac{N}{4} - m_1}{f_1} \times c$$

$$\frac{N}{4} = \frac{400}{4} = 100$$

Q_1 class is 500.5–650.5

$$[\, l_1 = 500.5; \quad m_1 = 48; \quad f_1 = 189; \quad c = 150]$$

$$\therefore \quad Q_1 = 500.5 + \frac{100 - 48}{189} \times 150$$

$$= 500.5 + \frac{52 \times 150}{189}$$

$$= 500.5 + 41.27$$

$$= 541.77$$

$$Q_3 = l_3 = \frac{3\frac{N}{4} - m_3}{f_3} \times c$$

$$3\frac{n}{4} = 3 \times 100 = 300$$

Q_3 Class is 650.5–800.5

$$l_3 = 650.5; \quad m_3 = 237; \quad f_3 = 88; \quad c = 150$$

$$\therefore \quad Q_3 = 650.5 + \frac{300 - 237}{88} \times 150$$

$$= 650.5 + \frac{63 \times 150}{88}$$

$$= 650 + 107.39 = 757.89$$

$$\therefore \quad Q.D = \frac{Q_3 - Q_1}{2}$$

$$= \frac{757.89 - 541.77}{2} = \frac{216.12}{2} = 108.06$$

$$\text{Coefficient of } Q.D = \frac{Q_3 - Q_1}{Q_3 + Q_1}$$

$$= \frac{757.89 - 541.77}{757.89 + 541.77} = \frac{216.12}{1299.66} = 0.1663$$

7.5.4 Merits and Demerits of Quartile Deviation

Merits

1. It is Simple to understand and easy to calculate
2. It is not affected by extreme values.
3. It can be calculated for data with open end classes also.

Demerits

1. It is not based on all the items. It is based on two positional values Q_1 and Q_3 and ignores the extreme 50% of the items
2. It is not amenable to further mathematical treatment.
3. It is affected by sampling fluctuations.

Due to its easy calculations it is generally used in elementary descriptive statistics. It can be used safety when the distribution is open and where it is impossible to find other measures of dispersion.

Quartile deviation is a better measure than range as it makes use of 50% of the data. But since it does not take into account the rest 50% of the data, it cannot be regarded as a reliable measure of dispersion.

7.6 MEAN DEVIATION AND COEFFICIENT OF MEAN DEVIATION

Mean Deviation

Average deviations (mean deviation) is the average amount of variations (scatter) of the items in a distribution from either the mean or the median or the mode, ignoring the signs of these deviations by ***Clark and Senkade***.

The range and quartile deviation are not based on all observations. They are positional measures of dispersion. They do not show any scatter of the observations from an average. The mean deviation is measure of dispersion based on all items in a distribution.

DO YOU KNOW?

Mean deviation is the arithmetic mean of the deviations of a series computed from any measure of central tendency; i.e., the mean, median or mode, all the deviations are taken as positive i.e., signs are ignored.

We usually compute mean deviation about any one of the three averages mean, median or mode. Some times mode may be ill defined and as such mean deviation is computed from mean and median. Median is preferred as a choice between mean and median. But in general practice and due to wide applications of mean, the mean deviation is generally computed from mean. M.D can be used to denote mean deviation.

The mean deviation is defined as the average distance between the mean and each point in the distribution. It is the arithmetic mean of the deviations of each point to the mean. Points smaller than the mean will have negative signs and those which are larger than the mean will have positive signs.

Coefficient of Mean Deviation

Mean deviation calculated by any measure of central tendency is an absolute measure. For the purpose of comparing variation among different series, a relative mean deviation is required. The relative mean deviation is obtained by dividing the mean deviation by the average used for calculating mean deviation.

$$\text{Coefficient of Mean Deviation} = \frac{\text{Mean deviation}}{\text{Mean or Median or Mode}}$$

If the result is desired in percentage, the coefficient of mean

$$\text{Coefficient of Mean Deviation} = \frac{\text{Mean deviation}}{\text{Mean or Median or Mode}} \times 100$$

7.6.1 Calculation of Mean Deviation — Ungrouped or Raw Data

To measure the variation about the sample mean $\overline{X}$, the distance from each data value (i.e. $x - \overline{X}$) has been computed and then divided by the total number of points (n). Thus,

$$\text{Mean Deviation(M.D.)} = \frac{\Sigma|x - \overline{X}|}{n}$$

Where x = Actual data

$\overline{X}$ = Mean

$|x - \overline{X}|$ = Deviation without plus sign

Σ = Sign of Summation (of the observation)

n = number of points (observations)

In this relation, we will replace $\overline{X}$ by Median (M_e) and by Mode (M_o), we will obtain Mean deviation about Median and Mean deviation about mode respectively.

$$\text{Mean Deviation (M.D)}\ \delta M_e = \frac{\Sigma|x - M_e|}{n}$$

$$\text{Mean Deviation (M.D)}\ \delta M_o = \frac{\Sigma|x - M_o|}{n}$$

There are two methods of calculating mean deviation from a series of individual observation

1. Direct Method
2. Short–cut Method

1. **Direct Method:** In the direct method, the mean deviation would be calculated by totalling the deviations from the mean, motion or mode and diving the total by the number of items.

Working Steps

1. Find the mean or median or mode of the given series.
2. Using and one of three, find the deviations (differences) of the items of the series from them.
   i.e. $x_i - X, x_i - M_e$ and $i_i - M_o$.
3. Find the absolute values of these deviations i.e. ignore there positive (+) and negative (-) signs.
   i.e. $|x_i - \bar{X}|, |x_i - M_e|$ and $x_i - M_o|$.
4. Find the sum of these absolute deviations.
   i.e. $\Sigma|x_i - \bar{X}|, \Sigma|x_i - M_e|$, and $\Sigma| x_i - M_o|$
5. Divide this total obtained by the number of items.

EXAMPLE 7.11: Calculate mean deviation for the data given in the table.

x : 4 6 8 10 22

Data of points x	$x - \bar{X}$	$\lvert x - \bar{X}\rvert$
4	–6	6
6	–4	4
8	–2	2
10	0	0
22	12	12
	$\Sigma(x - \bar{X}) = 0$	$\Sigma[x - \bar{X}] = 24$

$$\bar{X} = \frac{\Sigma x}{n} = \frac{4+6+8+10+22}{5} = \frac{50}{5} = 10$$

To get the average, divide $\Sigma|x - \bar{X}|$ by the total number of points which is 5 for the above example.

Hence, Mean Deviation (M.D) $= \frac{\Sigma|x - \bar{X}|}{n} = \frac{24}{5} = 4.8$

EXAMPLE 7.12: Calculate Mean deviation and its co-efficient for the following salaries:

$ 1030, $ 500, $ 680, $ 1100, $ 1080, $ 1740. $ 1050, $ 1000, $ 2000, $ 2250, $ 3500 and $ 1030.

Solution:

S.No.	Salary ($) x_i	Deviation from M_e (1080) ± ignored $\lvert x_i - M_e\rvert$
1	500	580
2	680	400
3	1030	50
4	1030	50
5	1050	30
6	1080	0
7	1100	20
8	1500	420
9	1740	660
10	2000	920
11	2250	1170
12	3500	2420
$N = 13$		$\Sigma\lvert x_i - M_e\rvert = 6770$

Calculation: Here Median = 1080 (Middle value of series)

(i) Median (M_e) = size of $\left(\frac{n+1}{2}\right)^{th}$ item = size of 7th item.

(ii) $$\text{M.D. } (\delta\, M_e) = \frac{\Sigma|x_i - M_e|}{n}$$

$$= \frac{6770}{13} = \$\ 520.76$$

(iii) $$\text{Co-efficient of } \delta\, M_e = \frac{\delta M_e}{M_e} = \frac{52076}{1080} = 482$$

EXAMPLE 7.13: Calculate Mean Deviation and state which series is more variable:

Series A	100	150	300	200	400	350	800
Series B	50	20	40	45	25	30	15

Solution: In question there is no guide line for calculating the mean deviation. So, we should calculate the mean deviation with the help of median. Because among mean, median and mode, median is the most appropriate method for calculating mean deviation.

So, for calculating mean deviation firstly arrange the series A and series B in ascending order.

S.No.	Series A	$\|x_i - M_e\|$	Series B	$\|x_i - M_e\|$
1	100	200	15	15
2	150	150	20	1
3	200	100	25	5
4	300	0	30	0
5	350	50	40	10
6	400	100	45	15
7	800	500	50	20
$n = 7$		$\Sigma\|x_i - M_e\| = 1100$		$\Sigma\|x_i - M_e\| = 75$

Median

Series A:

$$M_e = \text{The size of } \left(\frac{n+1}{2}\right)^{\text{th}} \text{ item}$$

$$= \text{The size of } \left(\frac{7+1}{2}\right)^{\text{th}} \text{ item}$$

$$M_e = 4^{\text{th}} \text{ item} = 300$$

Series B:

$$M_e = \text{The size of } \left(\frac{n+1}{2}\right)^{\text{th}} \text{ item}$$

$$= \text{The size of } \left(\frac{7+1}{2}\right)^{\text{th}} \text{ item}$$

$$M_e = 4^{\text{th}} \text{ item} = 30$$

Mean Deviation from Median

Series A: $\delta M_e = \dfrac{|x_i - M_e|}{n} = \dfrac{1100}{7} = 157.14$

Series B: $\delta M_e = \dfrac{|x_i - M_e|}{n} = \dfrac{75}{7} = 10.71$ size

Coefficient of Mean Deviation from Median

Series A: $\text{C at } \delta M_e = \dfrac{\delta M_e}{M_e} = \dfrac{157.14}{300} = 0.52$

Series B: $\text{C at } \delta M_e = \dfrac{\delta M_e}{M_e} = \dfrac{10.71}{30} = 0.36$

Since the coefficient at mean deviation for series A is more than the series B. So, there is more variability and less stability in series A than series B.

2. **Shortcut Method:** In the short–cut method, mean or median is calculated and the total of the values of the items below the mean or median and the above it are found out. The former is subtracted from the latter and divided by the number of items. The resulting figure is the mean deviation:

(a) Mean deviation about Mean

$$\delta \bar{X} = \frac{\Sigma XA - \Sigma XB - (NA - NB)\bar{X}}{n}$$

where,
ΣXA = Total of items above the arithmetic mean
ΣXB = Total of items below the arithmetic mean
NA = Number of items above the arithmetic mean
NB = Number of items below the arithmetic mean
$\bar{X}$ = Arithmetic average
n = Total number of items

(b) Mean deviation about Median

$$\delta M_e = \frac{\Sigma XA - \Sigma XB}{n}$$

where,
ΣXA = Total of items more than median
ΣXB = Total of items less than median
n = Total number of items

In this formula, $NA - NB$ can not be written because there difference is mostly zero. The reason is that the median lies in the middle due to which the number of items more and less than median are equal. But if NA and NB are not equal in the distribution than we will use the complete formula.

EXAMPLE 7.14: Calculate mean deviation from mean and median by both direct and short cut methods from the following data:

15 20 40 50 80 100 130 200 250 320 335

Solution:

S.No.	Size (x)	$(x-\bar{X})$ ± signs ignored	$(x-M_e)$ (±signs ignored)
1	15	125	85
2	20	120	80
3	40	100	60
4	50	90	50
5	80	60	20
6	100	40	0
7	130	10	30
8	200	60	100
9	250	110	150
10	320	180	220
11	335	195	235
$n = 11$	$\Sigma x = 1540$	$\Sigma(x-\bar{X}) = 1090$	$\Sigma(x-M_e) = 1030$

$$\bar{X} = \frac{\Sigma x}{n} = \frac{1540}{11} = 140$$

$$M_e = \text{The size of the } \left(\frac{n+1}{2}\right)^{\text{th}} \text{ item}$$

$$= \text{The size of } \left(\frac{11+1}{2}\right)^{\text{th}} = 6^{\text{th}} \text{ item} = 100$$

(a) Calculation of Mean Deviation by Direct Method

(i) Mean deviation from mean,

$$\delta\bar{X} = \frac{\Sigma(x-\bar{X})}{n} = \frac{1090}{11} = 99.09 \text{ size}$$

(ii) Mean deviation from median,

$$\delta M = \frac{\Sigma(x-M_e)}{n} = \frac{1030}{11} = 93.64 \text{ size}$$

(b) Calculation of Mean Deviation by Short Cut Method

(i) Mean deviation from mean

$$\delta\bar{X} = \frac{\Sigma XA - \Sigma XB - (NA - NB)\bar{X}}{n}$$

where,

ΣXA = Total of items more than mean = 200 + 250 + 320 + 335 = 1105

ΣXB = Total of items less than mean = 15 + 20 + 40 + 50 + 80 + 100 + 130 = 435

NA = Number of items more than mean = 200, 250, 320, 335 = 4

NB = Number of items less than mean = 15, 20, 40, 50, 80, 100, 130 = 7

X = Mean = 140

n = Total number of items = 11

Substituting the values in above formula, we get:

$$\delta\bar{X} = \frac{1105 - 435 - (4 - 7)140}{11}$$

$$= \frac{670 - (1 - 3)140}{11}$$

$$= \frac{670 + 420}{11} = \frac{1090}{11} = 99.09 \text{ size}$$

(ii) Mean deviation from Median:

$$\delta M = \frac{\Sigma XA - \Sigma XB}{n}$$

where, ΣXA = Total of items more than median = 130 + 200 + 250 + 320 + 335 = 1235

ΣXB = Total of items less than median = 15 + 20 + 40 + 50 + 80 = 205

Substituting the values in the above formula we get:

$$\delta M = \frac{1235 - 205}{11}$$

$$= \frac{1030}{11} = 93.64 \text{ size}$$

7.6.2 Calculation of Mean Deviation — Discrete Series

In discrete series the calculation of mean deviation involves the following steps:

Working Steps

1. Find the mean or median of the given series.
2. Using and one of three, find the deviations (differences) of the items of the series from them.

   i.e. $d = x_i - \bar{X}$, or $d = x_i - M_e$
3. Find the absolute values of these deviations i.e. ignore there positive (+) and negative(-) signs.

   i.e. $|d| = |x_i - \bar{X}|$ or $|d| = |x_i - M_e|$
4. Multiply the deviations with the respective frequencies

   i.e. $|d|f = f \times |x_i - \bar{X}|$ or $|d|f = f \times |x_i - M_e|$
5. Find the sum of these absolute deviations.

   i.e. $\Sigma|d|f = \Sigma f|x_i - \bar{X}|$ or $\Sigma|d|f = \Sigma f|x_i - M_e|$
6. Divide this total obtained by the number of items. This will be the value of Mean Deviation.

Thus, symbolically,

$$\text{Mean Deviation from Mean} = \frac{\Sigma f|d|}{N} = \frac{\Sigma f|x_i - \bar{X}|}{N}$$

$$\text{Mean Deviation from Median} = \frac{\Sigma f|d|}{N} = \frac{\Sigma f|x_i - M_e|}{N}$$

7.6.3 Calculation of Mean Deviation — Continuous Series

The calculation of mean deviation in continuous series is done by the same procedure by which it is done in discrete series.

EXAMPLE 7.15: Calculate mean deviation from median for the following data. Also compute the coefficient of mean deviation.

Size	2	4	6	8	10	12	14	16
Frequency	2	2	4	5	3	2	1	1

Solution: First we determine median of the given discrete series

Size (x)	Frequency (f)	*c.f.*	$\lvert x - M_e \rvert$	$f \lvert x - M_e \rvert$
2	2	2	6	12
4	2	4	4	8
6	4	8	2	8
8	5	13	0	0
10	3	16	2	6
12	2	18	4	8
14	1	19	6	6
16	1	20	8	6
	$N = 20$			$\Sigma f \lvert x - M_e \rvert = 56$

Here, $N = 20$ i.e., even

$$\text{Median} = \frac{\left(\frac{N}{2}\right)^{\text{th}} \text{item} + \left(\frac{N}{2}+1\right)^{\text{th}} \text{item}}{2}$$

$$= \frac{\left(\frac{20}{2}\right)^{\text{th}} \text{item} + \left(\frac{20}{2}+1\right)^{\text{th}} \text{item}}{2}$$

$$= \frac{10^{\text{th}} \text{ item} + \left(\frac{20}{2}+1\right)^{\text{th}} \text{item}}{2}$$

$$= \frac{8+8}{2} = \frac{16}{2} = 8$$

Now,

$$\text{Mean deviation from mean} = \frac{\Sigma f \lvert X - M_e \rvert}{N}$$

$$= \frac{56}{20} = 2.8$$

$$\text{Coefficient of Mean Deviation} = \frac{M.D}{M_e}$$

$$= \frac{2.8}{8} = 0.35$$

EXAMPLE 7.16: Calculate the mean deviation for the following data:

Class Interval	0–10	10–20	20–30	30–40	40–50	50–60	60–70
Frequency	8	12	10	8	3	2	7

(a) Find mean deviation about mean
(b) Also find the mean deviation about median
(c) Compare the results obtained in (a) and (b).

Solution: The calculation for M.D about mean and median is as follows:

C.I.	Mid–value (x)	Frequency (f)	c.f	fx	For Mean $(x-\bar{X}) = \lvert x-29 \rvert$	$f(x-\bar{X})$	For Median $\lvert x-M_e \rvert = \lvert x-22 \rvert$	$f\lvert x-M_e \rvert$
0–10	5	8	8	40	24	192	17	136
10–20	15	12	20	180	14	168	7	84
20–30	25	10	30	250	4	40	3	30
30–40	35	8	38	280	6	48	13	104
40–50	45	3	41	135	16	48	23	69
50–60	55	2	43	110	26	52	33	66
60–70	65	7	50	455	36	252	43	301
Total		N = 50		Σfx = 1450		$\Sigma f(x-\bar{X})$ = 800		$\Sigma f\lvert x-M_e \rvert$ =790

(a) Mean $\bar{X} = \frac{\Sigma fx}{N} = \frac{1450}{50} = 29$

Mean deviation about mean $= \frac{\Sigma f\lvert x-\bar{X}\rvert}{N} = \frac{800}{50} = 16$

(b) Here $\frac{N}{2} = \frac{50}{2} = 25$

The c.f. first greater than 25 is 30. Hence median class is 20–30
Now,

$$\text{Median} = l_1 + \frac{\frac{N}{2} - m_1}{f} \times c$$

$$= 20 + \frac{(25-20)}{25} \times 10 = 20 + 2 = 22$$

Mean deviation about median $= \frac{\Sigma f\lvert x - M_e\rvert}{N} = \frac{790}{50} = 15.8$

(c) From (a) and (b), we observe that
M.D about median < M.D about mean. In fact, we have the following general result:

"Mean deviation is least when taken about median".

7.6.4 Merits and Demerits of Mean Deviation

Merits

1. Mean deviation is rigidly defined and is easy to understand and calculate.
2. Mean deviation is based on all the observations and is thus definitely a better measure of dispersion than the range and quartile deviation.
3. The averaging of the absolute deviations from an average irons out the irregularities in the distribution and thus mean deviation provides an accurate and true measure of dispersion.
4. As compared with standard deviation, it is less affected by extreme observations.
5. Since mean deviation is based on the deviations about an average, it provides a better measure for comparison about the formation of different distributions.

Demerits

1. The strongest objection against mean deviation is that while computing its value we take the absolute value of the deviations about an average and ignore the signs of the deviations.
2. The step of ignoring the signs of the deviations is mathematically sound and illogical. It creates artificially and renders mean deviation useless for further mathematical treatment. This drawback necessitates the requirement of another measure of variability which, in addition to being based on all the observations is also amenable to further algebraic manipulations.
3. It gives accurate results only when deviations are taken from median. It is not a satisfactory measure when taken about mode or while dealing with a fairly skewed distribution.
4. It cannot be computed for distributions with open end classes.

7.6.5 Uses of Mean Deviation

1. Inspite of its mathematical drawbacks, mean duration has found favour with economists and business statisticians because of its simplicity in calculation, accuracy and also on account of the fact that standard deviation gives greater weightage to deviations of extreme observations.
2. For forecasting of business cycles this measure has been found more useful than other.
3. It is also good for small sample studies where elaborate statistical analysis is not needed.

7.7 STANDARD DEVIATION (S.D)

The measures of dispersion discussed so far are useful in elementary situations and in most of the cases are not suitable. In the calculation of mean deviation the algebraic signs of deviations are made artificially positive without any justification. These short comings are removed by another measure of dispersion known as standard Deviations. This is the most important measure and occupies a significant place in the theory of statistics.

The concept of standard deviation was first used by ***Karl Pearson*** in the year 1893. It is most commonly used measure of dispersion. It satisfies most of the properties laid down for an ideal measure of dispersion.

DO YOU KNOW?

Standard deviation is the square root of the arithmetic average of the squares of the deviations measured from the mean.

The standard deviation of a variate x is defined to be the positive square root of the arithmetic mean of the sum of the square of the deviation of the variate values $x_1, x_2, x_3, \ldots x_n$ from their arithmetic mean $\bar{X}$. It is generally denoted by the Green letter σ. Thus we have

$$S.D(\sigma) = \sqrt{\frac{\Sigma(x_i - \bar{X})^2}{n}}$$

where $\bar{X} = \frac{\Sigma x}{n}$, is the arithmetic mean of the given values.

or

$$\sigma = \sqrt{\frac{\Sigma d^2}{n}}$$

where $d = x - \bar{X}$

Standard deviation is also called the root-mean square deviation.

Coefficient of Standard Deviation

The standard deviation is an absolute measure of dispersion and is expressed in terms of the units of the variable.

For example standard deviation of incomes would be in rupees, of heights in centimeters, and of weights in parts. For purpose of comparative studies a relative measure of dispersion is calculated.

$$\text{Coefficient of Standard Deviation} = \frac{\sigma}{X}$$

or standard deviation divided by mean.

7.7.1 Difference between Mean Deviation and Standard Deviation

Though both these measures are based on all the items of a variable yet they differ in the following ways:

- Mean Deviation does not take into account the algebraic sign (plus or minus) in its calculation which is illogical. The standard deviation takes these into account.
- Mean deviation can be computed from Median, Note or Mean and its value differs in these cases. The standard deviation is always calculated from the arithmetic mean.
- The mathematical properties possessed by standard deviation are for greater than these possessed by Mean Deviation.

7.7.2 Calculation of Standard Deviation — Ungrouped or Raw Data

For ungrouped data standard deviation may be computed any of the following method

1. Direct Method
2. Actual Mean Method
3. Assumed Mean Method
4. Step-Deviation Method

1. **Direct Method:** By definition, the standard deviation is calculated by the formula

$$\sigma = \sqrt{\frac{\Sigma(x-\bar{X})^2}{n}}$$

Here $$\frac{\Sigma(x-\bar{X})^2}{n} = \frac{\Sigma(x^2 - 2x\bar{X} + \bar{X}^2)}{n} = \frac{\Sigma x^2}{n} - 2\bar{x}\frac{\Sigma x}{n} + \frac{\Sigma \bar{X}^2}{n}$$

$$= \frac{\Sigma x^2}{n} - 2\bar{X} \times \bar{X} + \frac{n\bar{X}^2}{n}$$

$$= \frac{\Sigma x^2}{n} - 2\bar{X}^2 + \bar{X}^2 = \frac{\Sigma x^2}{n} - \bar{X}^2 = \frac{\Sigma x^2}{n} - \left(\frac{\Sigma x}{n}\right)^2$$

Therefore

$$\boxed{\sigma = \sqrt{\frac{\Sigma x^2}{n} - \left(\frac{\Sigma x}{n}\right)^2}}$$

This formula is used to find S.D in direct method

NOTE: In this method, there is no need to calculate the mean of the distribution. We take only the square of each item, so that it is easy to calculate the standard deviation of the deviation by direct method.

EXAMPLE 7.17: Calculate the standard deviation for the 14, 22, 9, 15, 20, 17, 12, 11.

Solution:

x	x^2
14	196
22	484
9	81
15	225
20	400
17	289
12	144
11	121
$\Sigma x = 120$	$\Sigma x^2 = 1940$

$$\sigma = \sqrt{\frac{\Sigma x^2}{n} - \left(\frac{\Sigma x}{n}\right)^2}$$

$$= \sqrt{\frac{1940}{8} = \left(\frac{120}{8}\right)^2}$$

$$= \sqrt{242.5 - 225}$$

$$= \sqrt{17.5}$$

$$\sigma = 4.18$$

```
         4.18
    4 | 17.5000
      | 16
   81 |  150
      |   81
  828 |  6900
      |  6624
      |   276
```

2. **Actual Mean Method:** The formula used in this method is $\sigma = \sqrt{\dfrac{\Sigma(x-\bar{X})^2}{n}}$

or $$\sigma = \sqrt{\frac{\Sigma d^2}{n}} \text{ where } d = x - \bar{X}$$

- Calculate the mean $\bar{X} = \dfrac{\Sigma x}{n}$
- Calculate the deviation $d = x - \bar{X}$ for each value of the series and find Σd^2.
- Substitute Σd^2, n in the formula and calculate $\sigma = \sqrt{\dfrac{\Sigma d^2}{n}}$

EXAMPLE 7.18: The marks obtained by 10 students in a class test out of 100 marks are 62, 49, 71, 75, 33, 41, 100, 88, 50, 31. Calculate the standard deviation.

Solution: $\bar{X} = \dfrac{\Sigma x}{n} = \dfrac{62+49+71+75+33+41+100+88+50+31}{10} = \dfrac{600}{10} = 60$

x	$d = x - \bar{X} = x - 60$	d^2
62	2	4
49	–11	121
71	11	121
75	15	225
33	–27	729
41	–19	361
100	40	1600
88	28	784
50	–10	100
31	–29	841
	$\Sigma d = 0$	$\Sigma d^2 = 4886$

$$\sigma = \sqrt{\frac{\Sigma d^2}{n}} = \sqrt{\frac{4886}{10}} = \sqrt{488.6} = 22.10$$

Therefore standard deviation is 22.10.

3. **Assumed Mean Method:** When the data is large or the mean is not an integer we use assumed mean method to calculate the standard deviation.
   Choose one of the items nearer to the middle value in the data say A as the assumed mean
   - Calculate deviation $d = x - A$ for each value of the series and find Σd, Σd^2
   - Substitute Σd, Σd^2 and n in the formula and calculate the standard deviation.

   The formula for standard deviation is

$$\boxed{\sigma = \sqrt{\frac{\Sigma d^2}{n} - \left(\frac{\Sigma d}{n}\right)^2}}$$

where $d = x - A$

EXAMPLE 7.19: The following are the bowling rate per over of a player in 12 cricket matches: 6.5, 5.0, 5.2, 5.3, 5.5, 5.0, 4.7, 4.5, 6.3, 3.0, 4.0, 9.0. Find the standard deviation.

Solution: Take the assumed mean $A = 5$

Bowling rate per over	$d = x - A$ $= x - 5$	d^2
6.5	1.5	2.25
5.0	0	0
5.2	0.2	0.04
5.3	0.3	0.09
5.5	0.5	0.25
5.0	0	0
4.7	–0.3	0.09
4.5	–0.5	0.25
6.3	1.3	1.69
3.0	–2.0	4.00
4.0	–1.0	1.00
9.0	4.0	16.00
	$\Sigma d = 4.0$	$\Sigma d^2 = 25.66$

$\Sigma d = 4$, $\Sigma d^2 = 25.66$, $n = 12$

$$\sigma = \sqrt{\frac{\Sigma d^2}{n} - \left(\frac{\Sigma d}{n}\right)^2}$$

$$= \sqrt{\frac{25.66}{12} - \left(\frac{4}{12}\right)^2}$$

$$= \sqrt{2.1383 - 0.1089} = \sqrt{2.0294} = 1.42$$

4. Step Deviation Method

- Choose one of the nearest middle values in the series as the assumed mean A
- Calculate $d = x = A$ for each value of the series
- Find $d' = \dfrac{x - A}{c}$ where e is the common factor of all 'd'
- Find $\Sigma d' \cdot \Sigma d'^2$
- Substitute the values of $\Sigma d'$, $\Sigma d'^2$, c and n in the formula and calculate the standard deviation.

The formula for standard deviation is

$$\sigma = \sqrt{\frac{\Sigma d'^2}{n} - \left(\frac{\Sigma d'}{n}\right)^2} \times c$$

where $d' = \dfrac{x - A}{c}$

EXAMPLE 7.20: The following are the income (in Rs) of ten employees of a firm 600, 620, 640, 620, 680, 670, 680, 640, 700, 650. Calculate the standard deviation of the income.

Solution: Take assumed mean $A = 640$; Common factor $c = 10$

Income (in Rs)	$d = x - 640$	$d' = \frac{x - 640}{10}$	d'^2
600	–40	–4	16
620	–20	–2	4
640	0	0	0
620	–20	–2	4
680	40	4	16
670	30	3	9
680	40	4	16
640	0	0	0
700	60	6	36
650	10	1	1
		$\Sigma d' = 10$	$\Sigma d'^2 = 102$

$$n = 10, \Sigma d' = 10, \Sigma d'^2 = 102$$

$$\sigma = \sqrt{\frac{\Sigma d'^2}{n} - \left(\frac{\Sigma d'}{n}\right)^2} \times c$$

$$= \sqrt{\left(\frac{102}{10}\right) - \left(\frac{10}{10}\right)^2} \times 10$$

$$= \sqrt{10.2 - 1} \times 10 = \sqrt{9.2} \times 10 = 3.033 \times 10$$

$$\sigma = \text{Rs } 30.33$$

EXAMPLE 7.21: Find standard deviation for the following values: 30, 80, 60, 70, 20, 40, 50

Solution: (i) Direct Method:

x	x^2
30	900
80	6400
60	3600
70	4900
20	400
40	1600
50	2500
$\Sigma x = 350$	$\Sigma x^2 = 20300$

$$\sigma = \sqrt{\frac{\Sigma x^2}{n} - \left(\frac{\Sigma x}{n}\right)^2}$$

$$= \sqrt{\frac{20300}{7} - \left(\frac{350}{7}\right)^2} = \sqrt{400} = 20$$

(ii) Actual Mean Method:

$$\bar{X} = \frac{\Sigma x}{n} = \frac{30 + 80 + 60 + 70 + 20 + 40 + 50}{7} = \frac{350}{7} = 50$$

x	$d = x - 50$	d^2
30	–20	400
80	30	900
60	10	100
70	20	400
20	–30	900
40	–10	100
50	0	0
	$\Sigma d = 0$	$\Sigma d^2 = 2800$

$$\sigma = \sqrt{\frac{\Sigma d^2}{n}} = \sqrt{\frac{2800}{7}} = \sqrt{400} = 20$$

(iii) Assumed Mean Method: Take assumed mean $A = 40$

x	$d = x - 40$	d^2
30	–10	100
80	40	1600
60	20	400
70	30	900
20	–20	400
A 40	0	0
50	10	100
	$\Sigma d = 70$	$\Sigma d^2 = 3500$

$$\sigma = \sqrt{\frac{\Sigma d^2}{n} - \left(\frac{\Sigma d}{n}\right)^2}$$

$$= \sqrt{\frac{3500}{7} - \left(\frac{70}{7}\right)^2} = \sqrt{500 - 10^2} = \sqrt{400} = 20$$

(iv) Step Deviation Method: Take $A = 60$, $c = 10$

x	$d = x - 60$	$d' = \frac{x - 60}{10}$	d'^2
30	–30	–3	9
80	20	2	4
60	0	0	0
70	10	1	1
20	–40	–4	16
40	–20	–2	4
50	–10	–1	1
		$\Sigma d' = -7$	$\Sigma d'^2 = 35$

$$\sigma = \sqrt{\frac{\Sigma d'^2}{n} - \left(\frac{\Sigma d'}{n}\right)^2} \times c$$

$$= \sqrt{\frac{35}{7} - \left(\frac{-7}{7}\right)^2} \times 10 = \sqrt{5 - 1} \times 10 = \sqrt{4} \times 10 = 20$$

In all the four methods we get the same standard deviation $\sigma = 20$.

EXAMPLE 7.22: A school has the strength of 1600 students. The no. of absentees to the school on 10 different days are as follows: 26, 34, 26, 41, 48, 22, 36, 26. Calculate the S.D.

Solution: Take the assumed mean $A = 30$

Marks x	$d = x - A = x - 30$	d^2
26	– 4	16
34	4	16
22	–8	64
36	6	36
26	–4	16
41	11	121
48	18	324
22	–8	64
36	6	36
26	–4	16
	$\Sigma d = 17$	$\Sigma d^2 = 709$

$$\sigma^2 = \sqrt{\frac{\Sigma d^2}{n} - \left(\frac{\Sigma d}{n}\right)^2}$$

$$= \sqrt{\frac{709}{10} - \left(\frac{17}{10}\right)^2} = \sqrt{70.9 - 2.89} = \sqrt{68.01}$$

S.D $\quad \sigma = \sqrt{68.01} = 8.24$

7.7.3 Calculation of Standard Deviation — Discrete Series

For the discrete series, standard deviation may be calculated by any of the following method:

1. **Direct Method:** When deviations are taken from direct method, the following method is used:

$$\sigma = \sqrt{\frac{\Sigma fx^2}{N} - \left(\frac{\Sigma fx}{N}\right)^2}$$

or

$$\sigma = \sqrt{\frac{\Sigma fx^2}{N} - (\overline{X})^2}$$

2. **Actual Mean Method:** The formula used in this method is

$$\sigma = \sqrt{\frac{\Sigma f(x - \overline{X})^2}{N}}$$

3. **Assumed Mean Method:** The formula used in this method is

$$\sigma = \sqrt{\frac{\Sigma fd^2}{N} - \left(\frac{\Sigma fd}{N}\right)^2}$$

where, $d = x - A$

4. Step-Deviation Method: The formula used in this method is

$$\sigma = \sqrt{\frac{\Sigma fd'^2}{N} - \left(\frac{\Sigma fd'}{N}\right)^2} \times c$$

where, $d' = \frac{x - A}{c}$

EXAMPLE 7.23: Compute Standard deviation from the following data

Marks	10	20	30	40	50	60
No. of Students	8	12	20	10	7	3

Solution:

Marks x	f	$d' = \frac{x - 30}{10}$	fd'	fd'^2
10	8	–2	–16	32
20	12	–1	–12	12
30	20	0	0	0
40	10	1	10	10
50	7	2	14	28
60	3	3	9	27
	$N = 60$		$\Sigma fd' = 5$	$\Sigma fd'^2 = 109$

$$\sigma = \sqrt{\frac{\Sigma fd'^2}{N} - \left(\frac{\Sigma fd'}{N}\right)^2} \times C$$

$$= \sqrt{\frac{109}{60} - \left(\frac{5}{60}\right)^2} \times 10$$

$$= \sqrt{1.82 - 0.01 \times 10}$$

$$= \sqrt{1.8101} \times 10$$

$$= 1.345 \times 10$$

$$= 13.45$$

7.7.4 Calculation of Standard Deviation — Continuous Series

In the continuous series the method of calculating standard deviation is almost the same as in a discrete series. But in a continuous series, mid-values of the class intervals are to be found out. The step-deviation method is widely used.

The formula is

$$\sigma = \sqrt{\frac{\Sigma fd'^2}{N} - \left(\frac{\Sigma fd'}{N}\right)^2} \times c$$

$$d' = \frac{x - A}{c}, c - \text{Class interval}$$

Working Steps

1. Find out the mid-value of each class.
2. Assume the center value as an assumed mean and denote it by A.
3. Find out $d' = \dfrac{x - A}{c}$.
4. Multiply the deviations d by the respective frequencies and get $\Sigma fd'$.
5. Square the deviations and get d'^2.
6. Multiply the squared deviations (d'^2) by the respective frequencies and get $\Sigma fd'^2$.
7. Substituting the values in the following formula to get the standard deviation.

$$\sigma = \sqrt{\frac{\Sigma fd'^2}{N} - \left(\frac{\Sigma fd'}{N}\right)^2} \times c$$

EXAMPLE 7.24: The daily temperature recorded in a city in Russia in a year is given below:

Temperature C°	No. of days
– 40 to –30	10
–30 to –20	18
–20 to –10	30
–10 to 0	42
0 to 10	65
10 to 20	180
20 to 30	20
	365

Calculate Standard Deviation.

Solution:

Temperature	Mid value (x)	No. of days f	$d = \dfrac{x-(-5)}{10}$	fd'	fd'^2
–40 to –30	–35	10	–3	–30	90
–30 to –20	–25	18	–2	–36	72
–20 to –10	–15	30	–1	–30	30
–10 to –0	–5	42	0	0	0
0 to 10	5	65	1	65	65
10 to 20	15	180	2	360	720
20 to 30	25	20	3	60	180
		$N = 365$		$\Sigma fd' = 389$	$\Sigma fd'^2 = 1157$

$$\sigma = \sqrt{\frac{\Sigma fd'^2}{N} - \left(\frac{\Sigma fd'}{N}\right)^2} \times c$$

$$= \sqrt{\frac{1157}{365} - \left(\frac{389}{365}\right)^2} \times 10$$

$$= \sqrt{3.17 - 1.14} \times 10$$

$$= \sqrt{2.0341} \times 10 = 1.4262 \times 10$$

$$= 14.26° \text{ C}$$

7.7.5 Charlier's Check of Accuracy

Just as in case of arithmetic average we check the accuracy of calculation by a formula given by charlier. Similarly the accuracy of the calculation of standard deviation can be checked by another formula given by Charlier.

It is as follows:

$$\boxed{\Sigma f(d'+1)^2 - \Sigma fd'^2 - 2\Sigma fd = \Sigma f}$$

If step deviation method is adopted where

$$d' = \frac{x - A}{c}$$

Thus, if in **example 7.24** we add +1 to d', and then after squaring if we multiply by 'f' and total all values we will get $\Sigma f(d' + 1)^2$.

Thus $\Sigma f(d' + 1)^2 = 2300$ $\Sigma f(d'^2 = 1157$ $fd' = 389$

Substituting the value, we get,

$$2300 - 1157 - 2\,(389) = 365$$
$$2300 - 1157 - 778 = 365$$
$$2300 - 1935 = 365$$
$$365 = 365$$

Since the rule has been satisfied the calculation of standard deviation is correct.

7.7.6 Calculation of Standard deviation from Summation Method

If in a continuous series, the class intervals are same then we can calculate the standard deviation by summation method. For calculating the standard deviation by summation method, the following formula is used:

$$\boxed{\sigma = c \times \sqrt{2F_2 - F_1 - F_1^2}}$$

where, $F_1 = \dfrac{\Sigma cf_1}{n}$, cf_1 is the first cumulative frequency

$F_2 = \dfrac{\Sigma cf_2}{n}$, cf_2 is the second accumulative frequency.

c = Width of class-interval

EXAMPLE 7.25: Calculation the standard deviation of the following series by using summation method:

Age in years	0–10	10–20	20–30	30–40	40–50	50–60	60–70
No. of Person	8	12	25	30	15	6	4

Solution:

Age (in years)	No. of person (f)	Cf_1	Cf_2
0–10	8	8	8
10–20	12	20	28
20–30	25	45	73
30–40	30	75	148
40–50	15	90	238
50–60	6	96	334
60–70	4	100	434
Total	$N = 100$	$\Sigma Cf_1 = 434$	$\Sigma Cf_2 = 1263$

$$F_1 = \frac{\Sigma cf_1}{N} = \frac{434}{100} = 4.34$$

$$F_2 = \frac{\Sigma cf_2}{N} = \frac{1263}{100} = 12.63$$

Substituting the values in the following formula of S.D

$$\sigma = c \times \sqrt{2F_2 - F_1 - F_1^2}$$

$$= 10 \times \sqrt{2 \times 12.63 - 4.34 - (4.34)^2}$$

$$= 10 \times \sqrt{25.26 - 4.34 - 18.8356}$$

$$= 10 \times \sqrt{25.26 - 23.1756}$$

$$= 10 \times \sqrt{2.0844} = 10 \times 1.4437$$

$= 14.437 = 14.44$ **[Age 14 years]**

7.7.7 Mathematical Properties of Standard Deviation

Standard Deviation possesses a number of interesting and important mathematical properties which are given below:

1. Standard deviation is independent of change of origin but not of scale.
2. Standard deviation is the minimum value of the root mean square deviation
3. S.D $\leq$ Range i.e $\sigma < X_{max} - X_{min}$
4. The standard deviation of a series gets multiplied or divided by a quantity K if each value is multiplied or divided by K.
5. The standard deviation of a series remains unchanged when each value is added or subtracted by the same quantity
6. Standard deviation is suitable for further mathematical treatment. If we know the sizes means and standard deviations of two or more groups, then we can obtain the standard deviation of the group obtained on combining all the groups.
7. The standard deviation of the first and natural numbers viz. 1, 2, 3, ... n is

$$\boxed{\sigma = \sqrt{\frac{n^2 - 1}{12}}}$$

8. The sum of the squares of the deviations of all the observations from their arithmetic mean is minimum.
   In other words, the sum of the squares of the deviations of observations from a value other than the arithmetic mean would always be greater. This is the reason, why standard deviation is always computed from the arithmetic mean.

Some Examples Based on Mathematical Properties of S.D

EXAMPLE 7.26: Find the standard deviation of the following data 5,10, 15, 20, 25. Add 3 to each item and find the new standard deviation.

Solution: Here $c = 5$ and take assumed mean $A = 15$

x	$d' = \frac{x-15}{5}$	d'^2
5	–2	4
10	–1	1
15	0	0
20	1	1
25	2	4
	$\Sigma d' = 0$	$\Sigma d'^2 = 10$

$$\sigma = \sqrt{\frac{\Sigma d'^2}{n} - \left(\frac{\Sigma d'}{n}\right)^2} \times c$$

$$= \sqrt{\frac{10}{5} - 0} \times 5 = \sqrt{2} \times 5 = 5\sqrt{2}$$

When we add 3 to each value we get 8, 13, 18, 23, 28

x	$d' = \frac{x-18}{5}$	d'^2
8	–2	4
13	–1	1
18	0	0
23	1	1
28	2	4
	$\Sigma d' = 0$	$\Sigma d'^2 = 10$

$$\sigma = \sqrt{\frac{\Sigma d'^2}{n} - \left(\frac{\Sigma d'}{n}\right)^2} \times c$$

$$= \sqrt{\frac{10}{5} - 0} \times 5 = \sqrt{2} \times 5 = 5\sqrt{2}$$

From the above example we conclude:

> The standard deviation of a series remains unchanged when each value is added or subtracted by the same quantity.

EXAMPLE 7.27: The marks of 5 students scored out of 50 are 20, 25, 30, 35, 40. Find the standard deviation of the marks. When we convert the marks to 100 find the new standard deviation.

Solution: Take the assumed mean $A = 30$, $c = 5$

x	$d' = \frac{x-30}{5}$	d'^2
20	–2	4
25	–1	1
30	0	0
35	1	1
40	2	1
	$\Sigma d' = 0$	$\Sigma d'^2 = 10$

$$\sigma = \sqrt{\frac{\Sigma d'^2}{n} - \left(\frac{\Sigma d'}{n}\right)^2} \times c = \sqrt{\frac{10}{5} - 0} \times 5 = \sqrt{2} \times 5 = 5\sqrt{2}$$

To convert the marks out of 100, it is enough to multiply the marks by 2. Then

x	$d' = \frac{x-60}{5}$	d'^2
40	–2	4
50	–1	1
60	0	0
70	1	1
80	2	4
	$\Sigma d' = 0$	$\Sigma d'^2 = 10$

$$\sigma = \sqrt{\frac{\Sigma d'^2}{n} - \left(\frac{\Sigma d'}{n}\right)^2} \times c$$

$$= \sqrt{\frac{10}{5} - 0} \times 10 = \sqrt{2} \times 10 = 10\sqrt{2}$$

From the above example we conclude the following result:

The standard deviation of a series gets multiplied or divided by the quantity k if each value is multiplied or divided by k.

EXAMPLE 7.28: The standard deviation of 10 values is 4. If each value is increased by 3, find the standard deviation and the variance of the new set of values.

Solution: S.D of given 10 values = 4; Increment in each value = 3

S.D is unchanged by the increments in the values Variance = $\sqrt{\sigma} = \sqrt{4} = 2$

7.7.8 Calculation of Missing items and Missing Frequencies

For calculating the missing items and missing frequencies, the following formulas are used:

$$\sigma = \sqrt{\frac{\Sigma x^2}{n} - (\overline{X})^2}$$

$$\sigma^2 = \frac{\Sigma x^2}{n} - (\overline{X})^2 \qquad \text{[From formula]}$$

$$\sigma^2 + \bar{X}^2 = \frac{\Sigma x^2}{n} \quad \text{....(A)}$$

$$\bar{X}^2 = \frac{\Sigma x^2}{n} - \sigma^2$$

$$\boxed{\bar{X} = \sqrt{\frac{\Sigma x^2}{n} - \sigma^2}}$$

$$n = \frac{\Sigma x^2}{\bar{X} + \sigma^2} \qquad \left[\sigma^2 + \bar{X}^2 = \frac{\Sigma x^2}{n}\right]$$

$$\boxed{\Sigma x^2 = n(\bar{X}^2 + \sigma^2)} \qquad \text{[from (A)]}$$

$$\Sigma x = \sqrt{n(\bar{X}^2 + \sigma^2)}$$

$$\Sigma x^2 = n \cdot \bar{X} \cdot \bar{X} + n \cdot \sigma^2 \qquad \sqrt{n(\bar{X}^2 + \sigma^2)}$$

$$\left[\begin{array}{l} \bar{X} = \frac{\Sigma x}{n}, \ \Sigma x = n\bar{X} \\ \sigma = \sqrt{\frac{\Sigma d^2}{n}}, \ n\sigma^2 = \Sigma d^2 \end{array}\right]$$

$$\boxed{\Sigma x^2 = \Sigma x \cdot \bar{X} + \Sigma d^2}$$

$$\Sigma x^2 = n \cdot (\bar{X})^2 + \Sigma d^2$$

for discrete and continuous series

$$\sigma = \sqrt{\frac{\Sigma x^2 f}{n} - (\bar{x})^2}$$

$$\bar{X} = \frac{\Sigma x^2 f}{n} - \sigma^2$$

$$n = \frac{\Sigma x^2 f}{\bar{X}^2 + \sigma^2}$$

$$\boxed{\Sigma x^2 f = n(\bar{X}^2 + \sigma^2)}$$

$$\boxed{\Sigma x^2 f = \Sigma x \cdot \bar{X} + \Sigma f d^2}$$

$$\Sigma x^2 f = n(\bar{X})^2 + \Sigma f d^2$$

EXAMPLE 7.29:

1. Find out the value of arithmetic mean, if $\Sigma x^2 = 560$, $n = 10$, $\sigma = 2.65$
2. Find out the numbers of item (n), if $\Sigma x^2 = 560$, $\bar{X} = 7$, $\sigma = 2.65$
3. Find out the value of Σx^2, if $n = 10$, $\bar{X} = 70$, $\sigma = 2.65$

Solution:

(i)
$$\bar{X} = \sqrt{\frac{\Sigma x^2}{n} - \sigma^2}$$
$$= \sqrt{\frac{560}{10} - (2.65)^2} = \sqrt{56-7} = \sqrt{49} = 7$$

Thus arithmetic mean = 7

(ii)
$$n = \frac{\Sigma x^2}{\bar{X}^2 + \sigma^2}$$
$$= \frac{560}{(7)^2 + (265)^2} = \frac{560}{49+7} = \frac{560}{56} = 10$$

Thus the number of items is 10

(iii)
$$\Sigma x^2 = n(\bar{X}^2 + \sigma^2)$$
$$= 10\,[(7)^2 + (2.65)^2] = 10\,[49 + 7)]$$
$$= 10 \times 56 = 560$$

Thus the value of $\Sigma x^2 = 560$

7.7.9 Calculation of Corrected Standard Deviation

Mistakes in calculations are always possible. Sometimes it so happens that while calculating mean and standard deviation. We unconsciously copy out wrong observations. In such case, if the entire calculations are done again, it would become too difficult a task. By adopting a very simple procedure we can correct the incorrect values of mean and standard deviation.

EXAMPLE 7.30: The mean and standard deviation of a sample of 10 items were calculated as 5 and 2. Later on it was found that one item '8' was misread as 4. Find out correct mean and standard deviation.

Solution: Calculation of Correct Mean:

$$n = 10,\ \bar{X} = 5$$
$$\bar{X} = \frac{\Sigma x}{n}$$
$$\Sigma x = n.\bar{X}$$
$$= 10.5 = 50$$

Since the item '8' was misread as 4, the correct Σx will be:

$$\Sigma x = 50 + 8 - 4 = 54$$

Therefore correct mean:

$$\text{Correct } \bar{X} = \frac{\Sigma x}{n} = \frac{54}{10} = 5.4$$

Calculation of correct standard deviation:

We know

$$\Sigma x^2 = n(\sigma^2 + \bar{X}^2)$$

$$\begin{bmatrix} \sigma = 2 \\ \bar{X} = 5 \end{bmatrix}$$

$= 10\,[\,(2)^2 + (5)^2]$

$= 10\,[\,4 + 25]$

$\Sigma x^2 = 290$

Corrected $\Sigma x^2 = 290 + (8)^2 - (4)^2$

$= 290 + 64 - 16$

$= 354 - 16 = 338$

Now corrected standard deviation

$$\sigma = \sqrt{\frac{\Sigma x^2}{n} - (\bar{X})^2}$$

$$= \sqrt{\frac{338}{10} - (5.4)^2}$$

$$= \sqrt{33.8 - 29.16}$$

$$= \sqrt{4.64} = 2.15$$

EXAMPLE 7.31: For a frequency distribution of marks in History of 200 candidates (grouped in intervals 0–5, 5–10.....etc.) the mean and standard deviation were found to be 40 and 15. Later on it was discovered that the score 43 was misread as 53 in obtaining the frequency distribution. Find the corrected mean and standard deviation corresponding to the corrected frequency distribution.

Solution: In this question following values are given:

$$n = 200, \quad \bar{X} = 40, \quad \sigma = 15$$

Calculation of Corrected $\bar{X}$

The correct mark (43) lies in the group 40–45, the middle value (x) of which is 42.5 ((40 + 45)/2) similarly the incorrect mark (53) belongs to the group of 50–55 the middle value of which is 52.5.

$$\bar{X} = \frac{\Sigma x}{n}$$

Total of item $(\Sigma x) = 200 \times 40 = 8000$

Corrected $\Sigma x = 8000 - 52.5 + 42.5 = 7990$

Therefore, Corrected $\bar{X} = \frac{\Sigma x}{n} = \frac{7990}{200} = 39.95$

Calculation of Corrected σ

In order to find out correct σ we will have to determine the correct total of product of frequency and the square of measurements (x) i.e. $\Sigma x^2 f$.

$\Sigma x^2 f = n(\sigma^2 + \bar{X}^2)$

$= 200\,(225 + 1600) = 36{,}50{,}000$

Corrected $\Sigma x^2 f = \text{Incorrect } \Sigma x^2 f - (52.5)^2 + (42.5)^2$

$= 36{,}50{,}000 - 2756.25 + 1806.25$

$= 3{,}64{,}050$

Therefore, Corrected $\sigma = \sqrt{\dfrac{\Sigma x^2 f}{n} - (\bar{X})^2}$

$$= \sqrt{\frac{364050}{200} - (39.95)^2}$$

$$= \sqrt{1820.25 - 1596.0025}$$

$$= \sqrt{224.2475} = 14.97$$

Thus,

Corrected $\bar{X}$ = 39.95
Corrected σ = 14.97

7.7.10 Combined Standard Deviation

Let the means and standard deviations of two series be known. Then the two series are taken together as one group. Its mean and standard deviation can be calculated without considering the actual series.

The means and standard deviations of the two series containing n_1, n_2 values respectively are $\bar{X}_1$, $\bar{X}_2$ and σ_1, σ_2. The mean and standard deviation of the whole group are calculated by the formula.

Combined S.D $\quad \sigma = \sqrt{\dfrac{n_1\,\sigma_1^2 + n_2\,\sigma_2^2 + n_1\,d_1^2 + n_2\,d_2^2}{n_1 + n_2}}$

where $d_1 = \bar{X}_1 - \bar{X}$ and $d_2 = \bar{X}_2 - \bar{X}$

Combined mean $\quad \bar{X} = \dfrac{n_1\bar{X}_1 + n_2\bar{X}_2}{n_1 + n_2}$

EXAMPLE 7.32: The following details give the mean and standard deviation of two series of values

	No. of values	Mean	S.D
A	50	61	8
B	100	70	9

Find the mean and standard deviation of the combined group of both *A* and *B*.

[MBA, Kurukshetra University, 2003]

Solution: Here $n_1 = 50$, $\bar{X}_1 = 61$, $\sigma_1 = 8$

$n_2 = 100$, $\bar{X}_2 = 70$, $\sigma_2 = 9$

Mean of the combined group

$$\bar{X} = \frac{n_1\bar{X}_1 + n_2\bar{X}_2}{n_1 + n_2} = \frac{50 \times 61 + 100 \times 70}{50 + 100} = \frac{3050 + 7000}{150} = \frac{10050}{150} = 67$$

Now, $\quad d_1 = \bar{X}_1 - \bar{X} = 61 - 67 = -6$;

$$d_2 = \bar{X}_2 - \bar{X} = 70 - 67 = 3$$

Standard deviation of the combined group

$$\sigma = \sqrt{\frac{n_1\sigma_1^2 + n_2\sigma_2^2 + n_1 d_1^2 + n_2 d_2^2}{n_1 + n_2}}$$

$$= \sqrt{\frac{50 \times 64 + 100 \times 81 + 50 \times 36 + 100 \times 9}{50 + 100}}$$

$$= \sqrt{\frac{3200 + 8100 + 1800 + 900}{150}} = \sqrt{\frac{14000}{150}}$$

$$= \sqrt{93.3333} = 9.66$$

EXAMPLE 7.33: The first of the two samples has 100 items with mean 15 and standard deviation 3. If the combined group has 250 items with mean 15.6 and standard deviation 13.44 , find the mean and standard deviations of the second group. **[MBA, Vikram University, 2001]**

Solution: Here

$n_1 = 100,\ \bar{X}_1 = 15, \sigma_1 = 3,\ \bar{X} = 15.6.\ \sigma = \sqrt{13.44}\ \ n_1 + n_2 = 250$

Therefore $n_2 = 250 - 100 = 150$

Combined mean $\bar{X} = \dfrac{n_1\bar{X}_1 + n_2\bar{X}_2}{n_1 + n_2}$; $\quad 15.6 = \dfrac{100 \times 15 + 150\bar{x}_2}{250}$

$$150\,\bar{X}_2 = (15.6 \times 250) - (100 \times 15) = 3900 - 1500 = 2400$$

$$\Rightarrow \quad \bar{X}_2 = \frac{2400}{150} = 16$$

$$d_1 = \bar{X}_1 - \bar{X} = 15 - 15.6 = 0.6$$

$$d_2 = \bar{X}_2 - \bar{X} = 16 - 15.6 = 0.4$$

S.D of the combined group $= \sqrt{\dfrac{n_1\,\sigma_1^2 + n_2\,\sigma_2^2 + n_1\,d_1^2 + n_2\,d_2^2}{n_1 + n_2}}$

$$\sqrt{13.44} = \sqrt{\frac{900 + 150\sigma_2^2 + 36 + 24}{250}}$$

$$\Rightarrow \quad 3360 = 960 + 150\sigma_2^2$$

$$150\sigma_2^2 = 3360 - 960 = 2400;$$

$$\sigma_2^2 = \frac{2400}{150}$$

$$\Rightarrow \quad \sigma^2 = 4$$

7.7.11 Setting the limits through Standard Deviation

With the help of standard deviation and arithmetic mean, we can set such minimum and maximum limits between which there is possibility of lying certain pre cent of observations of a series.

For a symmetrical distribution, the following area relationship hold good.

Mean ± 1 σ covers 68.27% observations.
Mean ± 2 σ covers 95.45% observations.
Mean ± 3 σ covers 99.73% observations.

If a Normal Frequency Distribution is shown through a curve then it is called a Normal curve and it can be shown as follows:

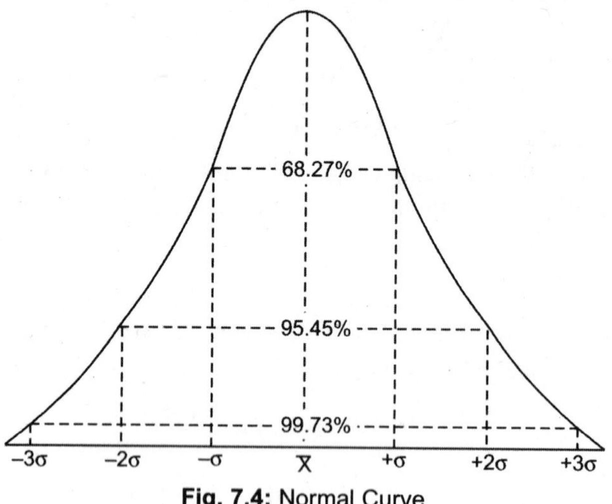

Fig. 7.4: Normal Curve

Further it should be noted that in symmetrical or moderately asymmetrical series a range which is 6 times of the standard deviation usually covers at least 99% of the observations. This property gives a concrete meaning of standard deviation and it is the property which leads to the above relationship shown in the graph.

(i) **Setting the limits of the units of a group:** The limits of the units of a whole group can be set through the standard deviation and arithmetic mean of a normal distribution. It can be understood through an example.

A sample of 100 students is taken from a group of 10,000 students. Let the arithmetic mean S.D of the marks obtained by these 100 students in statistics is 50 and 5 respectively. If the marks obtained by 10,000 students are normally distributed then we can say that:

⇒ 68.27% (6827 out of 10,000) students lie between the limits $\bar{X} \pm \sigma$ (between $50 \pm 5 = 45$ and 55). It means nearly 6827 students will get marks between 45 and 55.

⇒ 95.45% students lie between the limits $\bar{X} \pm 2\sigma$ (i.e $50 \pm 2 \times 5 = 40$ and 60). It means nearly 9545 students will obtain marks between 40 and 60.

⇒ 99.73% students lie between the limits $\bar{X} \pm 30$ (i.e. $50 \pm 3 \times 5 = 35$ and 65). It means nearly 9973 students (all students approximately) will obtain marks between 35 and 65.

(ii) **For comparing the different items of different distributions:** We can compare the individual items of different distributions on the basis of the relationship between standard deviation and arithmetic mean. *z*-statistic technique is used for this purpose. The *z*-statistic is obtained on dividing the difference of individual item (x) and mean ($\bar{X}$) by standard deviation.

i.e.

$$z = \frac{x - \overline{X}}{\sigma}$$

(Here $\overline{X}$ is the arithmetic mean and s is the standard deviation of the sample).

If the sum of individual items in two or more conditions is equal then z-statistic technique is useful in such cases. We can easily take the decision about any special case to be good or bad on the basis of the sum of z-statistics.

EXAMPLE 7.34: Two candidates in a certain examination had the same aggregate and were bracketed equal. Use the following data to determine whether this placing was equitable or whether one of the candidates has better performance.

Candidate	Marks in		Total
	Statistics	Marketing	
X	90	85	175
Y	84	91	175

Average marks for statistics = 82
Average marks for marketing = 76
Standard Deviation for statistics = 10
Standard Deviation for Income tax = 15

Solution: Because in both conditions there is equal total. So, we can compare marks with the help of z–statistics

$$z = \frac{x - \overline{X}}{\sigma}$$

In Case of Candidate *X*	In case of Candidate *Y*
(i) Statistics $= z = \frac{90 - 82}{10} = 0.8$	(i) Statistics $= z = \frac{84 - 82}{10} = 0.2$
(ii) Marketing $= z = \frac{85 - 76}{15} = 0.6$	(ii) Marketing $= z = \frac{91 - 76}{15} = 1.0$
Total z-score $= 0.8 + 0.6 = 1.4$	**Total z-score** $= 0.2 + 1.0 = 1.2$

On the basis of total z-score we can say that candidate '*X*' has better performance.

7.7.12 Variance and Coefficient of Variance

Variance

The term variance was used to describe the square of the standard deviation, R.A Fisher in 1913. The concept of variance is of great importance in advanced work where it is possible to split the total into several parts, each attributable to one of the factors causing variations in their original series.

Variance is defined as follows:

$$\text{Variance } (\sigma^2) = \frac{\Sigma(x - \overline{X})^2}{n}$$

where x = Actual data
$\overline{X}$ = Mean
n = Number of points (observations)

Coefficient of Variation (C.V)

The Standard deviation is an absolute measure of dispersion. It is expressed in terms of units in which the original figures are collected and stated. The standard deviation of heights of students cannot be compared with the standard deviation of weights of students, as both are expressed in different units, i.e heights in centimeter and weights in kilograms. Therefore the standard deviation must be converted into a relative measure of dispersion for the purpose of comparison. The relative measure is known as the coefficient of variation.

The coefficient of variation is obtained by dividing the standard deviation by the mean and multiply it by 100.

Symbolically,

$$\text{C.V} = \frac{\sigma}{\overline{X}} \times 100$$

where, σ is the S.D,
$\overline{X}$ is the mean of the given data. It is also called relative standard deviation.

This measure is most commonly used for a comparative study of the variability or consistence of two or more series.

If we wish to compare the variability of two or more series, we can use the coefficient of variation. The series of data for which the coefficient of variation is large indicates that the group is ***more variable*** (less stable/less uniform/less consistent). If the coefficient of variation is small it indicates that the group is ***less variable*** (more stable / more uniform / more consistent).

Remark: It is given as a percentage and is used to compare the consistency or variability of two more series. The higher the C.V, the higher the variability and lower the C. V, the higher is the consistency of the data.

EXAMPLE 7.35: In two factories A and B located in the same industrial area, the average weekly wages (in rupees) and the standard deviations are as follows:

Factory	Average	Standard Deviation	No. of workers
A	34.5	5	476
B	28.5	4.5	524

1. Which factory A or B pays out a larger amount as weekly wages?
2. Which factory A or B has greater variability in individual wages?

Solution: Given $n_1 = 476,\ \overline{X}_1 = 34.5,\ \sigma_1 = 5$

$n_2 = 524,\ \overline{X}_2 = 28.5,\ \sigma_2 = 5$

1. Total wages paid by factory A

$= 34.5 \times 476 =$ Rs 16.422.

Total wages paid by factory B

$= 28.5 \times 524 =$ Rs 14,934.

Therefore factory A pays out larger amount as weekly wages.

2. C.V of distribution of weekly wages of factory A and B are

$$\text{C.V (A)} = \frac{\sigma_1}{\bar{X}_1} \times 100 = \frac{5}{34.5} \times 100 = 14.49$$

$$\text{C.V (B)} = \frac{\sigma_2}{\bar{X}_2} \times 100 = \frac{4.5}{28.5} \times 100 = 15.79$$

Factory B has greater variability in individual wages, since C.V of factory B is greater than C.V of factory A.

EXAMPLE 7.36: Prices of a particular commodity in five years in two cities are given below:

Price in city A	20	22	19	23	16
Price in city B	10	20	18	12	15

Which city has more stable prices?

Solution: Actual mean method

City A			City B		
Prices (x)	Deviations from $\bar{X} = 20$ dx	dx^2	Prices (y)	Deviations from $\bar{Y} = 15$ dy	dy^2
20	0	0	10	–5	25
22	2	4	20	5	25
19	–1	1	18	3	9
23	3	9	12	–3	9
16	–4	16	15	0	0
$\Sigma x = 100$	$\Sigma dx = 0$	$\Sigma dx^2 = 30$	$\Sigma y = 75$	$\Sigma dy = 0$	$\Sigma dy^2 = 68$

City A:

$$\bar{X} = \frac{\Sigma x}{n} = \frac{100}{5} = 20$$

$$\sigma_x = \sqrt{\frac{\Sigma(x-\bar{X})^2}{n}} = \sqrt{\frac{\Sigma dx^2}{n}} = \sqrt{\frac{30}{5}} = \sqrt{6} = 2.45$$

$$\text{C.V }(x) = \frac{\sigma_x}{\bar{X}} \times 100 = \frac{2.45}{20} \times 100 = 12.25\%$$

City B:

$$\bar{Y} = \frac{\Sigma y}{n} = \frac{75}{5} = 15$$

$$\sigma_y = \sqrt{\frac{\Sigma(y-\bar{Y})^2}{n}} = \sqrt{\frac{\Sigma dy^2}{n}} = \sqrt{\frac{68}{5}} = \sqrt{13.6} = 3.69$$

$$\text{C.V }(y) = \frac{\sigma_y}{\bar{Y}} \times 100$$

$$= \frac{3.69}{15} \times 100 = 24.6\%$$

City A had more stable prices than City B, because the coefficient of variation is less in City A.
A had more stable prices than City B, because the coefficient of variation is less in City A.

EXAMPLE 7.37: Find the coefficient of variation of the following data: 16, 13, 17, 21, 18.

Solution:

$$\text{Mean } \overline{X} = \frac{16+13+17+21+18}{5} = \frac{85}{5} = 17$$

x	d = x – 17	d^2
16	–1	1
13	–4	16
17	0	0
21	4	16
18	1	1
	$\Sigma d = 0$	$\Sigma d^2 = 34$

S.D $$\sigma = \sqrt{\frac{\Sigma d^2}{n}} = \sqrt{\frac{34}{5}} = \sqrt{6.8}$$

$$C.V = \frac{\sigma}{\overline{X}} \times 100 = \frac{2.61}{17} \times 100$$

$$C.V = 15.35$$

NOTE: Of the three values $\overline{X}$, σ, C.V if we are given then the third can be calculated using the C.V formula.

EXAMPLE 7.38: The coefficient of variation of a series is 69 and its standard deviation is 15.6. Find the arithmetic mean of the series.

Solution:

$$\text{Coefficient of variation } C.V = \frac{\sigma}{\overline{X}} \times 100$$

$$\Rightarrow \quad \overline{X} = \frac{\sigma}{C.V} \times 100$$

Arithmetic mean of the series

$$\overline{X} = \frac{15.6}{69} \times 100 = 22.6$$

EXAMPLE 7.39: A group of 100 candidates have their average height 163.8 cm with coefficient of variation 3.2. What is the standard deviation of their height?

Solution:

$$C.V = \frac{\sigma}{\overline{X}} \times 100$$

$$\sigma = \frac{\overline{X}}{100} \times C.V = \frac{163.8}{100} \times 3.2 = 5.24$$

EXAMPLE 7.40: A factory has two sections with 50 and 60 employees respectively. Their average weekly wages are Rs. 386 and Rs. 475. The standard deviations are 9 and 10.

(i) Which section has a larger wage bill?

(ii) Which section has greater variability in wages?

Solution:

(i) Wage bill for section A = 50 × 386 = Rs. 19,300.
Wage bill for section B = 60 × 475 = Rs. 28,500. ⇒ Section B has larger wage bill.

(ii) C.V for section A $= \frac{9}{386} \times 100 = 2.33$; C.V for section B $= \frac{10}{475} \times 100 = 2.11$

EXAMPLE 7.41: The mean of the runs scored by three batsmen A, B and C in the same series of 10 innings are 58, 48 and 14 respectively. The S.D. of their runs is 15, 12 and 2 respectively who is the most consistent batsman?

Solution:

Player	Mean	S.D.
A	58	15
B	48	12
C	14	2

$$\text{C.V for A} = \frac{15}{58} \times 100 = 25.86$$

$$\text{C.V for B} = \frac{12}{48} \times 100 = 25.0$$

$$\text{C.V for C} = \frac{2}{14} \times 100 = 14.29$$

Since C.V for C is the least ⇒ C is the most consistent batsman.

EXAMPLE 7.42: The following are the marks obtained by two students in six tests conducted for 100 marks:

A	58	64	60	65	76	52
B	56	87	89	48	93	65

Find who is more consistent in his performance.

Solution: For student A

x	$d = x - 60$	d^2
58	–2	4
64	4	16
60	0	0
65	5	25
76	16	256
52	–8	64
	$\Sigma d = 15$	$\Sigma d^2 = 365$

$$\bar{X} = A + \frac{\Sigma d}{n} = 60 + \frac{15}{6} = 62.5$$

$$\sigma = \sqrt{\frac{\Sigma d^2}{n} - \left(\frac{\Sigma d}{n}\right)^2} = \sqrt{\frac{365}{6} - \left(\frac{15}{6}\right)^2} = \sqrt{54.58} = 7.38$$

$$\text{C.V} = \frac{\sigma}{\bar{X}} \times 100 = \frac{7.38}{62.5} \times 100 = 11.81$$

For student B

x	$d = x - 80$	d^2
56	–24	576
87	7	49
89	9	81
48	–32	1024
93	13	169
65	–15	225
	$\Sigma d = 42$	$\Sigma d^2 = 2124$

$$\bar{X} = A + \frac{\Sigma d}{n} = 80 - \frac{42}{6} = 73$$

$$\sigma = \sqrt{\frac{2124}{6} - \left(\frac{-42}{6}\right)^2} = \sqrt{354 - 49}$$

$$= \sqrt{305} = 17.46$$

$$\text{C.V} = \frac{17.46}{73} \times 100 = 23.91$$

EXAMPLE 7.43: Calculate the standard deviation and its co-efficient from the following data.

A	B	C	D	E	F	G	H	I	J
10	12	16	8	25	30	14	11	13	11

Solution:

No	x_i	$(x_i - \bar{X})$	$(x_i - \bar{X})^2$
A	10	–5	25
B	12	–3	9
C	16	+1	1
D	8	–7	49
E	25	+10	100
F	30	+15	225
G	14	–1	1
H	11	–5	16
I	13	–2	4
J	11	–4	16
$n = 10$	$\Sigma x_i = 150$		$\Sigma \mid x_i - \bar{X} \mid 2 = 446$

Calculations:

(i) $$\bar{X} = \frac{\Sigma x_i}{n} = \frac{150}{10} = 15$$

(ii) $$\text{S.D } (\sigma_x) = \sqrt{\frac{\Sigma (x_i - \bar{X})^2}{n}} = \sqrt{\frac{446}{10}} = 6.7$$

(iii) $$\text{Co-efficient of S.D} = \frac{\sigma_x}{\bar{X}} = \frac{6.7}{15} = 0.45$$

7.7.13 Other Measures based upon Standard Deviation

1. **Probable Error:** It is equal to .6745 or $\frac{2}{3}$ of standard deviation

i.e.
$$\boxed{\begin{array}{l} \text{P.E} = \cdot 6745 \times \sigma \\ \text{P.E} = \frac{2}{3}\sigma \end{array}}$$

2. **Modulus:** Modulus is the square root of twice the second moment of dispersion about the mean. It is generally denoted by *C*.
   Thus,
$$\boxed{C = \sqrt{\frac{2fd^2}{n}}}$$
   Modulus is equal to standard deviation multiplied by the square root of 2

   or
$$\boxed{C = \sigma \times \sqrt{2}}$$
   Like standard deviation this measure is also based on the second moment about the mean.
3. **Precision:** It is reciprocal of modulus.

   Thus precision $= \frac{1}{C} = \frac{1}{\sqrt{\frac{2fd^2}{n}}} = \frac{1}{\sigma \times \sqrt{2}}$
4. **Fluctuation:** It is the square of modulus. Symbolically fluctuations
$$F = C^2 = \frac{2fd^2}{n}$$

7.7.14 Merits and Demerits of Standard Deviation

Merits

1. Standard deviation is rigidly defined and its value is always definite.
2. It is based on all the observation of the data
3. It is amendable to algebraic treatment and is less affected by fluctuations of sampling then most other measures of dispersion.
4. It is possible to calculate the combined standard deviation of two or more sets of data.
5. Standard deviation is useful in further statistical investigation such as in comparing skewness correlation and in sampling theory etc.
6. Standard deviation has a definite relationship with the area under the symmetric curve of a frequency distribution. Due to this reason, it is called a standard measure of variation.

Demerits

1. Standard deviation is comparatively not easy to calculate, nor it is easily understood.
2. It is also affected by the extreme values. It gives undue importance to the items away from the arithmetic mean, and less importance to the items near the mean.

3. The chief limitation of S. D is that it can not be used for comparing the dispersion of two or more series of observations given in different units.

7.7.15 Uses of Standard Deviation

1. The standard deviation may be used as a measure of greatest stability
2. It plays a great role in sampling theory
3. It is widely applied in other statistical operations.

7.8 RELATIONSHIP BETWEEN MEASURES OF DISPERSION

In a normal distribution the relationship between Quartile Deviation, Mean Deviation and Standard Deviation is fixed. The reason is that in a normal distribution Median, Mode and Arithmetic Mean have the same value, and further the two quartiles are equidistant from the Median. In such a situation:

Quartile Deviation is .6745 of Standard Deviation.
Mean Deviation is .7979 of Standard Deviation.

A.

$$\text{Quartile Deviation (Q.D)} = \frac{2}{3}\sigma$$

$$\text{Quartile Deviation (Q.D)} = \frac{5}{6}\delta$$

B.

$$\text{Mean Deviation (M.D) } \delta = \frac{4}{6}\sigma$$

$$\text{Mean Deviation (M.D) } \delta = \frac{6}{5}\text{Q.D}$$

C.

$$\text{Standard Deviation (S.D) } \sigma = \frac{5}{4}\delta$$

$$\text{Standard Deviation (S D) } \sigma = \frac{3}{2}\text{Q.D}$$

So we can say

$$\boxed{6\sigma = 9\,\text{Q.D} = 7.5\,\delta}$$

Further, in such distribution

(a) Arithmetic Mean ± Q.D would cover 50% of the items.
(b) Arithmetic Mean ± Mean Deviation would cover 57.51% the items
(c) Arithmetic Mean ± standard Deviation would cover 68.27% of the items

The above relationships are applicable to normal distribution only, but can be applied to moderately/ asymmetrical distributions for certain purposes.

7.9 SELECTING AMONG THE Q.D, M.D AND S.D

A general guideline for selecting a suitable statistic in describing the dispersion in a population includes consideration of the following factors:

- The concept of dispersion required by the problem. Is a single pair of values adequate, such as the two extremes or the two quartiles (range or Q)?
- The type of data available. If they are few in numbers, or contain extreme value, avoid the standard deviation. If they are generally skewed, avoid the mean absolute deviation as well. If they have a gap around the quartile, the quartile deviation should be avoided.
- The peculiarity of the dispersion measures them. These are summarized under "The Main Characteristics of the Quartile Deviation, the Mean Absolute Deviation, and the Standard deviation" below.

The Main Characteristics of the Quartile Deviation, the Mean Absolute Deviation, and the Standard Deviation are:

Fact No.	The Quartile Deviation	The Mean Absolute Deviation	The Standard Deviation
1.	The quartile deviation is also easy to calculate and to understand. However, it is unreliable if there are gaps in the data around the quartiles.	The mean absolute deviation has the advantage of giving equal weight to the deviation of every value form the mean or median.	The standard deviation is usually more useful and better adapted to further analysis than the mean absolute deviation.
2.	It depends on only 2 values, which include the middle half of the items.	Therefore, it is a more sensitive measure of dispersion than those described above and ordinarily has a smaller sampling error.	It is more reliable as an estimator of the population dispersion than other measures, provided the distribution is normal.
3.	It is usually superior to the range as a rough measure of dispersion.	It is also easier to compute and to understand and is less affected by extreme values than the standard deviation.	It is the most widely used measure of dispersion and the easiest to handle algebraically.
4.	It may be determined in an open-end distribution, or one in which the data may be ranked but not measured quantitatively.	Unfortunately, it is difficult to handle algebraically, since minus signs must be ignored in its computation.	Compared with the others, it is harder to compute and more difficult to understand.
5.	It also useful in badly skewed distributions or those in which other measures of dispersion would be warped by extreme values.	Its main application is in modeling accuracy for comparative forecasting techniques.	It is generally affected by extreme values that may be due to skewness of data

MISCELLANEOUS SOLVED EXAMPLES

EXAMPLE 7.44: Explain the term 'dispersion' What purpose does a measure of dispersion serve? What are the different measures of dispersion? **[MBA, Mangalore University]**

Solution: A measure of dispersion is designed to state the extent to which individual observations (or items) vary from their average. Here we shall account only the amount of variation and not the direction.

Purpose:

1. To assess the reliability of an average
2. To serve as a basis for control of variability

3. To compare two or more series regarding variability between the items in each series
4. For facilitating the use of other statistical measures.

EXAMPLE 7.45: Twenty passengers were found ticketless on a bus. The sum of the squares and the S.D of the amount found in their pockets were Rs. 2,000, and Rs. 6 respectively. If the total find imposed on these passengers is equal to the total amount recovered from them and the fine imposed in uniform, what is the amount each one of them has to pay as fine. What difficulties do you visualise if such a system of penalty were imposed.

Solution: $\text{S.D} = \sqrt{\frac{\Sigma x^2}{n} - \left(\frac{\Sigma x}{n}\right)^2} \Rightarrow 6 = \sqrt{\frac{2,000}{20} - \left(\frac{\Sigma x}{20}\right)^2}$

$\Rightarrow 36 = 100 - \left(\frac{\Sigma x}{20}\right)^2 \Rightarrow \left(\frac{\Sigma x}{20}\right)^2 = 64$

$\Rightarrow \frac{\Sigma x}{20} = 8$

i.e. each passenger will have to pay Rs. 8 as fine. In such a system, the persons having money in their pockets may object.

EXAMPLE 7.46: The mean weight of 150 students is 60 kg. The mean weight of boys is 70 kg with a standard deviation of 10 kg for the girls the mean weight is 55 kg and the standard deviation is 15 kg. Find the number of boys and the combined standard deviation.

Solution:

Let the number of boys = n_1

Then the number of girls = $150 - n_1$

Total weight of 150 students = $150 \times 60 = 9,000$ kg

Total weight of boys = $70\, n_1$ kg

Total weight of girls = $(150 - n_1)\, 55$ kg

$9,000 = 70n_1 + 150 \times 55 - 55n_1 \Rightarrow 750 = 15n_1 \Rightarrow n_1 = 50$

The number of boys = 50

The number of girls = 100

$$\text{Combined S.D} = \sqrt{\frac{50 \times 100 + 100 \times 225}{150} + \frac{50 \times 100}{(150)^2} \times 225}$$

$$= \sqrt{\frac{5000 + 22,500}{150} + \frac{50}{9}} = \sqrt{\frac{27,500}{150} + 50}$$

$$= \sqrt{\frac{550}{3} + 50} = \sqrt{\frac{700}{2}} = 15.275$$

EXAMPLE 7.47: Mr. X wants to invest Rs. 10,000 in one of the two companies A and B. Average return in a year from company A is Rs. 4,000 with a standard deviation of Rs. 25, while in company B the average return in a year is Rs. 5,000 with a standard deviation of Rs. 40.

Which company will you recommend to Mr. X for investment? Justify your answer.

Solution: Coefficient of variation for company A $= \dfrac{25}{4,000} \times 100$

$= 0.625$

Coefficient of variation for company B $= \dfrac{40}{5,000} \times 100$

$= 0.8$

Since the coefficient of variation for company A is less, company A is more consistent and Mr Basu should invest in company A.

EXAMPLE 7.48: State whether the following statements are true or false:

(i) For any data, larger the mean larger is the standard deviation
(ii) If every item of a distribution of 10 values is 35, then standard deviation is 1.
(iii) Standard deviation can be defined as the mean of the square root of the sum of squared deviations about the mean.
(iv) The variance of 10 observations is 4, their S.D is + 2 or –2. **[MBA, UPTU, (CO), 2003]**

Solution:

(i) Not always, Mean depends on the value whereas S.D depends on the deviations if the values are close mean may be more but S.D will be very small.
(ii) No, S.D will be zero because if every item is 35, mean will also be 35 and $\sqrt{\dfrac{\Sigma(x-\bar{X})^2}{n}}$ will be zero.
(iii) No, it is defined as the square root of the mean of the squared deviations about the mean
(iv) No, S.D is always positive. Therefore the S.D = +2

EXAMPLE 7.49: Two workers on the same job show the following results over a long period of time:

	Worker A	Worker B
Mean time of completing the job (minutes)	30	25
Standard deviation (minutes)	6	4

(i) Which worker appears to be more consistent in the time he requires to complete the job?
(ii) Which worker appears to be faster in completing the job? Explain

Solution: C.V for worker A $= \dfrac{6}{30} \times 100 = 20\%$

C.V for worker B $= \dfrac{4}{25} \times 100 = 16\%$

∴ Worker B is more consistent. Since average time for completing the job by B is less than the average time for completing the job by A, the worker B is faster than worker A.

EXAMPLE 7.50: Which shares are more stable if the prices of shares A and B are as follows:

A	55	54	52	53	56	58	52	50	51	49
B	108	107	105	105	106	107	104	103	104	101

Solution:

Calculation of Co-efficient of Variation					
A shares			B Shares		
x	*dx* (56)	*dx*²	*x*	*dx* (106)	*dx*²
55	–1	1	108	+2	4
54	–2	4	107	+1	1
52	–4	16	105	–1	1
53	–3	9	105	–1	1
56	0	0	106	0	0
58	+2	4	107	+1	1
52	–4	16	104	–2	4
50	–6	36	103	–3	9
51	–5	25	104	–2	4
49	–7	49	101	–5	25
n = 10	–30	160	*n*=10	–10	50

A-Shares

$$\bar{X} = A + \frac{\Sigma dx}{n} = 56 + \frac{-30}{10} = -3 = 53$$

$$\sigma = \sqrt{\frac{\Sigma dx^2}{n} - \left(\frac{\Sigma dx}{n}\right)^2} = \sqrt{\frac{160}{10} - \left(\frac{-30}{10}\right)^2}$$

$$= \sqrt{(16-9)} = \sqrt{7} = 2.646$$

$$\text{Co-efficient of Variation, or C.V} = \frac{\text{S.D}}{\text{Mean}} \times 100$$

$$= \frac{2.646}{33} \times 100 = 4.99\%$$

B-Shares

$$\bar{X} = A \pm \frac{\Sigma dx}{N} = 106 + \frac{-10}{10} = 105 - 1 = 105$$

$$\sigma = \sqrt{\frac{\Sigma dx^2}{n} - \left(\frac{\Sigma dx}{n}\right)^2} = \sqrt{\frac{50}{10} - \left(\frac{-10}{10}\right)^2}$$

$$= \sqrt{(5-1)} = \sqrt{4} = 2$$

$$\text{Co-efficient of Variation, or C.V} = \frac{\text{S.D}}{\text{Mean}} \times 100$$

$$= \frac{2}{105} \times 100 = 1.90\%$$

Since the C.V in case of B–shares is less, it can be said that B–shares are more stable in price.

EXAMPLE 7.51: The number of workers, employed, the mean wage (in Rs.) per month and standard deviation (in Rs.) in each section of a factory are given below. Calculate the mean wages and standard deviation of all the workers taken together.

Section	No. of workers employed	Mean Wage in (Rs)	Standard Deviation (in Rs)
A	50	113	6
B	60	120	7
C	90	115	8

Solution:

$$\bar{X} = \frac{n_1 \bar{X}_1 + n_2 \bar{X}_2 + n_2 \bar{X}_3}{n_1 + n_2 + n_3} = \frac{(50 \times 113) + (60 \times 120) + (90 \times 115)}{50 + 60 + 90}$$

$$= \frac{23,200}{200} = \text{Rs. } 116$$

$$\sigma = \sqrt{\frac{n_1(\sigma_1^2 + d_1^2) + n_2(\sigma_2^2 + d_2^2) + n_2(\sigma_3^2 + d_3^2)}{n_1 + n_2 + n_3}}$$

$$d_1 = \bar{X}_1 - \bar{X}_{123} = 113 - 116 = -3$$

$$d_2 = \bar{X}_2 - \bar{X}_{123} = 120 - 116 = +3$$

$$d_3 = \bar{X}_3 - \bar{X}_{123} = 115 - 116 = -1$$

$$\sigma = \sqrt{\frac{50[6^2 + (-3^2) + 60[7^2 + (+4)^2] + 90[8^2 + (-1)^2]}{50 + 60 + 90}}$$

$$= \sqrt{\frac{(50 \times 36) + (50 \times 9) + (60 \times 49) + (60 \times 16) + (90 \times 64) + (90 \times 1)}{200}}$$

$$= \sqrt{\frac{1800 + 450 + 2940 + 960 + 5760 + 90}{200}}$$

$$= \sqrt{\frac{12,000}{200}} = \sqrt{60} = 7.75 \text{ rupees.}$$

EXAMPLE 7.52: You are incharge of rationing in a State affected by food shortage. The following reports arrive from local investigators:

Daily caloric value of food available per adult during current period:

Area	Mean	Standard Deviation
A	2,500	400
B	2,000	200

The estimated requirement of an adult is taken at 2,800 calories daily and the absolute minimum is 1,350. Comment on the reported figures, and determine which area, in your opinion, need more urgent attention.

Solution: We know that $\bar{X} \pm 1\sigma$ covers 68.2% cases; $\bar{X} \pm 2\sigma$ covers 95;45% cases and $\bar{X} \pm 3\sigma$ covers 93.73% cases. In the given problem, if we take into consideration 99.73% i.e. almost the whole of the population, the limits would be $\bar{X} \pm 3\sigma$

For Area A, these limits are:

$$\bar{X} + 3\sigma = 2{,}500 + (3 \times 400) = 3{,}700$$

$$\bar{X} - 3\sigma = 2{,}500 - (3 \times 400) = 1{,}300$$

For Area B, these limits are:

$$\bar{X} + 3\sigma = 2{,}000 + (3 \times 200) = 2{,}600$$

$$\bar{X} - 3\sigma = 2{,}000 - (3 \times 2000) = 1{,}400$$

It is clear from above that in Area A there are some persons who are getting 1300 calories, i.e., below the minimum which is 1,350. But in case of area B there is no one who is getting less than the minimum. Hence area *A* needs more urgent attention.

EXAMPLE 7.53: The prices of a Tea Company shares in Mumbai and Koklkata markets during the last ten months are recorded below:

Month	Mumbai	Kolkata	Month	Mumbai	Kolkata
January	105	108	June	127	125
February	120	117	July	109	125
March	115	120	August	110	120
April	118	130	September	104	110
May	130	100	October	112	135

Determine the Arithmetic Mean and Standard Deviation of the prices of shares. In which market are the share prices stable? **[MBA, HPU, 2002]**

Solution: For determining in which market prices of shares are more stable, we shall compare the coefficient of variation. Let prices in Mumbai and Kolkata be denoted by *X* and *Y* respectively:

Calculation of Coefficient Variation

X	$(X-\bar{X})=x$	x^2	Y	$(Y-\bar{Y})=y$	y^2
105	–10	100	108	–11	121
120	+5	25	117	–2	4
115	0	0	120	+1	1
118	+3	9	130	+11	121
130	+15	225	100	–19	361
127	+12	144	125	+6	36
109	–6	36	125	+6	36
110	–5	25	120	+1	1
104	–11	121	110	–9	81
112	–3	9	135	+16	256
$\Sigma X = 1150$	$\Sigma x = 0$	$\Sigma x^2 = 694$	$\Sigma Y = 1190$	$\Sigma y = 0$	$\Sigma y^2 = 1018$

Mumbai: $C.V = \frac{\sigma}{\bar{X}} \times 100$

$$\bar{X} = \frac{\Sigma X}{n} = \frac{1150}{10} = 115$$

$$\sigma = \sqrt{\frac{\Sigma x^2}{n}} = \sqrt{\frac{694}{10}} = 8.33$$

Kolkata: $C.V = \frac{\sigma}{\bar{Y}} \times 100$

$$\bar{Y} = \frac{\Sigma Y}{n} = \frac{1190}{10} = 119$$

$$\sigma = \sqrt{\frac{\Sigma y^2}{n}} = \sqrt{\frac{1018}{10}} = 10.09$$

$$\text{C.V} = \frac{8.33}{115} \times 100 = 7.24 \qquad \text{C.V} = \frac{10.09}{119} \times 100 = 8.48$$

Since the coefficient of variation is less in Mumbai, hence the share price in Mumbai market shows greater stability.

EXAMPLE 7.54: The salaries paid to the managers of a company has a mean of Rs. 20,000 with a standard deviation of Rs. 3,000. What will be the mean and standard deviation if all the salaries are increased by (i) 10% (ii) 10% of the existing mean?

Which policy would you recommend if the management does not want to have increased disparities in waves?

Solution: Increasing all the salaries by 10% $\Rightarrow$ multiplying each salary by 1.1. Hence the mean is also multiplied by 1.1. Since the S.D depends on change of scale. S.D is also multiplied by 1.1.

$\therefore$ When all salaries are increased by 10-% the S.D also increased by 10%

If each salary is increased by 10% the mean is also increased by 10%.

Increasing all the salaries by 10% of the existing mean $\Rightarrow$ Adding a constant amount to each salary.

Since S.D is independent of the change of origin, if we remain unchanged if each salary is increased by 10% of the mean. But mean will increase by 10% of the original mean.

If the management do not want to have increased disparities, it showed increase the salary of the workers by 10% of the existing mean.

EXAMPLE 7.55: A company has three establishments E_1, E_2 and E_3 in three cities. Analysis of the daily wages paid to the employees in the three establishments is given below:

	E_1	E_2	E_3
Number of employees	20	25	40
Average daily wage (Rs)	305	300	340
Standard deviation (Rs)	50	40	45

Find the average and the standard deviation of the wages of all the 85 employees in the company.

Solution:

$$\bar{X} = \frac{n_1\bar{X}_1 + n_2\bar{X}_2 + n_3\bar{X}_3}{n_1 + n_2 + n_3}$$

$$= \frac{(20 \times 305) + (25 \times 300) + (40 \times 340)}{20 + 25 + 40}$$

$$= \frac{6100 + 7500 + 13600}{85} = \frac{27200}{85} = 320$$

$$\sigma = \sqrt{\frac{n_1\sigma_1^2 + n_2\sigma_2^2 + n_3\sigma_3^2 + n_1d_1^2 + n_2d_2^2 + n_3\,d_3^2}{n_1 + n_2 + n_3}}$$

$$d_1 = |\bar{X}_1 - \bar{X}| = |305 - 320| = 15$$

$$d_2 = |\bar{X}_2 - \bar{X}| = |1300 - 320| = 20$$

$$d_3 = |\bar{X}_3 - \bar{X}| = |340 - 320| = 20$$

$$\sigma = \sqrt{\frac{20(50)^2 + 25(40)^2 + 40(45)^2 + 20(15)^2 + 25(20)^2 + 40(20)^2}{20 + 25 + 40}}$$

$$= \sqrt{\frac{50000 + 40000 + 81000 + 4500 + 10000 + 16000}{85}}$$

$$= \sqrt{\frac{201500}{85}} = \sqrt{237059} = 48.69.$$

Thus the combined average wage is Rs. 320 and the combined standard deviation is Rs. 48.69.

EXAMPLE 7.56: The following table relates to the profits and losses of 100 firms. Calculate the average profits and the standard deviation of profits.

Profits	Number of Firms
5000 to 6000	8
4000 to 5000	12
3000 to 4000	30
2000 to 3000	10
1000 to 2000	5
0 to 1000	5
– 1000 to 0	6
–2000 to 1000	8
–3000 to 2000	9
–4000 to 3000	7

Solution:

Calculation of Mean Profit and Standard Deviation

Profit	No. of firms	Step–Deviation from 1500 (c = 1000)		
(X)	(f)	dx	fdx	fdx²
5000 to 6000	8	+4	+32	128
4000 to 5000	12	+3	+36	108
3000 to 4000	30	+2	+ 60	120
2000 to 3000	10	+1	+ 10	
1000 to 2000	5	0	0	0
0 to 1000	5	–1	– 5	5
–1000 to 0	6	–2	–12	24
–2000 to 1000	8	–3	–24	72
–3000 to 2000	9	–4	–36	144
–4000 to 3000	7	–5	–35	175
	N = 100		Σfdx = +26	Σfdx² = 786

Mean or $\bar{X} = A + \left(\frac{\Sigma fdx}{N}\right) \times i = 1500 + \left(\frac{+26}{100} \times 1000\right)$

$= 1500 + 260 = 1760$ rupees.

Standard Deviation or $\sigma = \sqrt{\frac{\Sigma\, fdx^2}{N} - \left(\frac{\Sigma\, fdx}{N}\right)^2} \times c$

$$= \sqrt{\frac{786}{100} - \left(\frac{26}{100}\right)^2} \times 1000$$

$$= \sqrt{7.79} \times 1000$$

$$= 2.791 \times 1000$$

$$= 2791 \text{ rupees}$$

It should be noted that here Standard Deviation is more than mean because of negative values of profits and wide variation in profits ranging from — 4000 to 6000 rupees.

LIST OF FORMULAE

1. Range = L – S
2. Coefficient of range $= \frac{L - S}{L + S}$
3. Inter Quartile Range (IQR) = $Q_3 - Q_1$
4. Semi-inter Quartile Range $= \frac{Q_3 - Q_1}{2}$
5. Percentile Range = $P_{90} - P_{10}$
6. Semi-percentile Range $= \frac{P_{90} - P_{10}}{2}$
7. Quartile Deviation $= \frac{Q_3 - Q_1}{2}$
8. Coefficient of Quartile Deviation $= \frac{Q_3 - Q_1}{Q_3 + Q_1}$
9. Mean-Deviation,

   About Mean, $M.D = \frac{\Sigma |x - \bar{X}|}{n}$ [$\bar{X}$ = Mean]

   About Median, $M.D = \frac{\Sigma |x - M_e|}{n}$ [M_e = Mean]

   About Mode, $M.D = \frac{\Sigma |x - M_o|}{n}$ [M_o = Mode]
10. Coefficient of Mean Deviation $= \frac{\text{Mean Deviation}}{\text{Mean or Median or Mode}}$
11. Mean Deviation by short –cut method

    About Mean, $\delta\bar{X} = \frac{\Sigma XA - \Sigma XB - (nA - nB)\bar{X}}{n}$

    About Median, $\delta M_e = \frac{\Sigma XA - \Sigma XB}{n}$

12. Mean Deviation for Discrete and continuous series:

About Mean, $\delta\bar{X} = \dfrac{\Sigma f\,|x - \bar{X}|}{N} = \dfrac{\Sigma f\,|d|}{N}$

About Median, $\delta M_e = \dfrac{\Sigma f\,|x - M_e|}{N} = \dfrac{\Sigma f\,|d|}{N}$

13. Standard Deviation $(\sigma) = \sqrt{\dfrac{\Sigma(x_i - \bar{X})^2}{n}} = \sqrt{\dfrac{\Sigma d^2}{n}}$, where $d = x_i - \bar{X}$

or Direct method, $\sigma = \sqrt{\dfrac{\Sigma x^2}{n} - \left(\dfrac{\Sigma x}{n}\right)^2}$

or step-deviation method, $\sigma = \sqrt{\dfrac{\Sigma d'^2}{n} - \left(\dfrac{\Sigma d'}{n}\right)^2} \times c$, where $d' = \dfrac{x - A}{c}$

14. Standard Deviation for Discrete and Continuous series:

Direct Method, $\sigma = \sqrt{\dfrac{\Sigma fx^2}{N} - \left(\dfrac{\Sigma fx}{N}\right)^2}$

or $\sigma = \sqrt{\dfrac{\Sigma fx^2}{N} - (\bar{X})^2}$

Actual Mean Method, $\sigma = \sqrt{\dfrac{\Sigma f(x - \bar{X})^2}{N}}$

Assumed Mean Method, $\sigma = \sqrt{\dfrac{\Sigma fd^2}{N} - \left(\dfrac{\Sigma fd}{N}\right)^2}$, where $d = x - A$

Step-Deviation Method, $\sigma = \sqrt{\dfrac{\Sigma fd'^2}{N} - \left(\dfrac{\Sigma fd'}{N}\right)^2} \times c$, where $d' = \dfrac{x - A}{c}$

15. Charler's Check of accuracy

$$\Sigma f(d' + 1)^2 - \Sigma f d'^2 - 2\Sigma f d = \Sigma f$$

If step-deviation method is adopted, where

$$d' = \frac{x - A}{c}$$

16. Standard-deviation from summation method:

$$\sigma = c \times \sqrt{2F_2 - F_1 - F_1^2}$$

where $F_1 = \dfrac{\Sigma cf_1}{N}$, $F_2 = \dfrac{\Sigma cf_2}{N}$

17. Variance $\sigma^2 = \dfrac{\Sigma(x - \bar{X})^2}{n} = \dfrac{\Sigma d^2}{n}$

18. Coefficient of variance (C.V) $= \dfrac{\sigma}{\bar{X}} \times 100$

19. Combined standard deviation

$$\sigma = \sqrt{\frac{n_1\sigma_1^2 + n_2\sigma_2^2 + n_1d_1^2 + n_2d_2^2}{n_1 + n_2}}$$

where, $d_1 = \bar{X}_1 - \bar{X}$, $d_2 = \bar{X}_2 - \bar{X}$

20. Relationship among S.D, Q.D and M.D

$$6\sigma = 9\text{ Q.D.} = 7.5\ \delta$$

SELF PRACTICE EXERCISES

I. CHOOSE THE BEST ANSWER

1. Standard deviation is always computed from:
   (a) mean (b) mode
   (c) median (d) geometric mean
2. Which of the following measures is least affected by extreme items:
   (a) quartile deviation (b) range
   (c) standard deviation (d) mean deviation
3. Mean deviation is:
   (a) less than S.D. (b) more than S.D
   (c) not related to S.D (d) equal to standard deviation
4. Coefficient of variation is given by:
   (a) $\frac{\sigma}{\bar{X}}$ (b) $\frac{\bar{X}}{\sigma}$
   (c) $\frac{\bar{X}}{\sigma} \times 100$ (d) $\frac{\sigma}{\bar{X}} \times 100$
5. Quartile deviation is based on the:
   (a) the highest 50% of the items (b) the lowest 25% of the items
   (c) the highest 25% of the items (d) middle 50% of the items
6. If 25% of the items are less than 20 and 25% are more than 40, the quartile deviation is:
   (a) 20 (b) 30
   (c) 40 (d) 10
7. The sum of squares of deviations for 10 observations taken from mean 50 is 25. The coefficient of variation is:
   (a) 50% (b) 10%
   (c) 40% (d) 10
8. The mean of squared deviations about the mean is called:
   (a) S.D (b) Variance
   (c) M.D (d) None of these
9. The mean of absolute deviations from an average is called:
   (a) S.D (b) 50% of the items
   (c) Variance (d) Q.D

10. The range includes:
    (a) 100% of the items
    (b) 50% of the items
    (c) 25% of the items
    (d) None of these
11. The interquartile range excludes:
    (a) 50% of the values
    (b) 100% of the values
    (c) 25% of the values
    (d) None of these
12. A measure of dispersion is an indicator of the reliability of:
    (a) An average
    (b) Variability
    (c) Median class
    (d) None of these
13. Mean ± 3 s covers:
    (a) 90% items
    (b) 99.73% items
    (c) 95% items
    (d) None of these
14. Algebraic sum of deviations from mean is:
    (a) positive
    (b) negative
    (c) zero
    (d) different for each other
15. Sum of squares of deviations is minimum when taken from:
    (a) mean
    (b) median
    (c) mode
    (d) none of these
16. Sum of absolute deviations is minimum when measured from:
    (a) mean
    (b) median
    (c) mode
    (d) none of these
17. For a normal distribution, the range mean ± 1.s covers:
    (a) 65%
    (b) 6826%
    (c) 85%
    (d) 95% of the items
18. If the distribution is approximately normal, then:
    (a) $M.D = \frac{2}{5}\sigma$
    (b) $M.D = \frac{3}{5}\sigma$
    (c) $M.D = \frac{4}{5}\sigma$
    (d) None of these
19. In case of open end classes, an appropriate measure of dispersion to be used is:
    (a) Range
    (b) Q.D
    (c) M.D
    (d) S.D
20. Measure of dispersion which is affected must by extreme observations is:
    (a) Range
    (b) Q.D
    (c) M.D
    (d) S.D

II. FILL IN THE BLANKS

1. Algebraic sum of deviations is zero from ....
2. The sum of absolute deviations is minimum from ....
3. Standard deviation is always .... than range
4. Standard deviation is always .... than mean deviation
5. Mean deviation is .... than standard deviation

6. $\overline{X} \pm \sigma$ includes .... per cent of the items
7. If in a series coefficient of variation is 64 and mean is 10, the standard deviation shall be ....
8. Variance is always .... negative
9. If each of the 10 values of a set are equal to 5, the standard deviation will be equal to ....
10. All relative measures of dispersion are .... from units of measurement
11. Variance is the .... value of mean square deviation
12, Quartile deviation is .... measure of dispersion
13. If $Q_1 = 20$ and $Q_3 = 50$, the coefficient of quartile deviation is ....
14. If in a series, coefficient of variation is 64 and mean 10, the standard deviation shall be ....

III. SHORT ANSWER TYPE QUESTIONS

1. What is the formula for Coefficient of variation? **[MBA, Madurai Kamaraj University, 2003]**
2. Explain the term variation what purpose toes a measure of variation serve? In the light of these comment on some of the well–known measures of variation? **[MBA, Delhi University, 1996, 2000]**
3. What is coefficient of variation? What purpose does it serve? Also distinguish between 'variance' and coefficient of variation'.
4. What is the importance of dispersion?
5. What are two characteristics of standard deviation
6. Write the characteristics of a good measure of dispersion
7. Explain mean deviation and coefficient of mean deviation?
8. Why standard deviation is preferred do mean deviation?
9. Under what circumstances range is more meaningful than any other measure of variation? **[MBA, HPU, 2001]**
10. What do you understand by standard deviation? Explain its usefulness. Highlight its important properties

IV. LONG ANSWER TYPE QUESTIONS

1. Explain with suitable examples the term / variation. Mention some common measures of variation and describe the one which you think is the most important. **[MBA, DU, 1993]**
2. Critically examine the different methods of measuring variation which of these do you consider as the best and why? **[MBA, Jodhpur Univ., 2002, HPU, 1998, Ku, 2004]**
3. Describe the various methods of measuring variation along with their respective merits and demerits. **[MBA, Delhi University, 2002]**
4. Explain and illustrate how the measures of variation afford a supplement to the information, about frequency distribution furnished by averages. **[MBA, BIT Ranchi, 1994, MBA, Delhi]**
5. What are merits and demerits of quartile deviation?
6. Why measures of dispersion are called averages of second order?
7. Find the standard deviation for a set of items 3, 4, 6, 7,15.25.
8. Find out the standard deviation and variance from the following frequency distribution:

Marks	0–4	4–8	8–12	12–16
No. of Students	4	8	2	1

9. For a group of 50 male workers, the mean and standard deviation of their daily wages are Rs 72 and Rs 9 respectively. For another group of 40 female workers these are Rs 54 and Rs 6 respectively. Find the standard deviation for the combined group of 90 workers.
10. The mean and S.D of 200 items was found to be 60 and 20 respectively. If at the time of calculations, two items were wrongly recorded as 3 and 67 instead of 13 and 17, find the correct mean, correct S.D and correct coefficient of variation.
11. A factory produces two types of electric lamps A and B. In an experiment relating to their life, the following results were obtained:

Length of life (in hours)	No. of lamps (A)	No. of Lamps (B)
500– 700	5	4
700– 900	11	30
900–1100	26	12
1100–1300	10	8
1300–1500	8	6

Compare the variability of the life of the two types using coefficient of variation.

[MBA, Kurukshetra University, 2004]

ANSWERS

I. CHOOSE THE BEST ANSWER

1. (a)	2. (a)	3. (a)	4. (d)	5. (d)
6. (d)	7. (d)	8. (b)	9. (b)	10. (a)
11. (a)	12. (a)	13. (b)	14. (c)	15. (a)
16. (b)	17. (b)	18. (c)	19. (b)	20. (a)

II. FILL IN THE BLANKS

1. Arithmetic mean		2. Median	3. Less	4. Greater
5. Less	6. 68.26	7. 6.4	8. None	9. Zero
10. Free	11. Minimum	12. Absolute	13. 0.375	14. 6.4

IV. LONG ANSWER TYPE QUESTIONS

7. 7.7 8. S.D = .3.27, Variance = 10.67 10. 59.8, 20.09, 33.6%

11. $C.V_A = 21.64$, $C.V_B = 23.41$

CHAPTER 8

Skewness, Moments and Kurtosis

8.1 INTRODUCTION

The measures of central tendency and variation discussed in previous chapter do not reveal the entire story about frequency distribution. Two distributions may have the same mean and standard deviation but may differ in their shape of the distribution. Further description of their characteristics is necessary that is provided by measures of skewness and kurtosis. Which we shall discuss in the following sections. Skewness helps us to study the shape i.e symmetry or asymmetry of the distribution while kurtosis refers to the flatness or peakedness of the curve which can be drawn with the help of the given data. These four measures viz., central tendency, dispersion, skewness and kurtosis are sufficient to describe a frequency distribution completely.

8.2 SKEWNESS

Skewness means '***lack of symmetry***'. We study skewness to have an idea about the shape of the curve which we can draw with the help of the given data. If in a distribution

$$\boxed{\text{Mean} = \text{Median} = \text{Mode}}$$

then that distribution is known as symmetrical distribution. If in a distribution

$$\boxed{\text{Mean} \neq \text{Median} \neq \text{Mode}}$$

then it is not a symmetrical distribution and it is called a skewed distribution and such a distribution could either be positively skewed or negatively skewed.

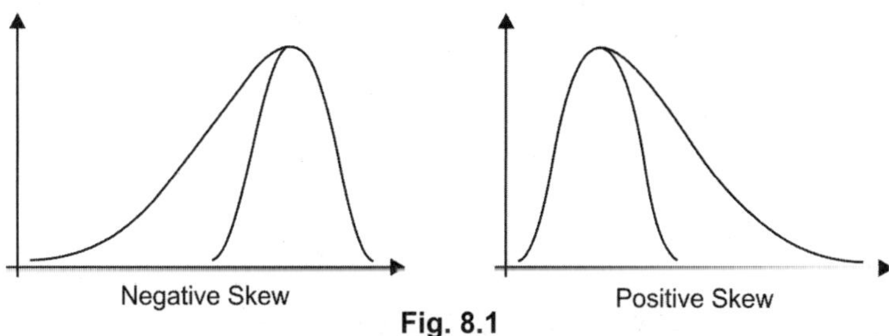

Fig. 8.1

Skewness is opposite of symmetry and its presence tells us that a particular distribution is not symmetrical or in other words it is skewed. Thus averages tell us about the concentration of items around the central value and measures of skewness tell us whether the dispersal of items from an average is symmetrical.

In everyday language, the terms "skewed" and "askew" are used to refer to something that is out of line or distorted on one side. When referring to the shape of frequency or probability distributions, "skewness" refers to asymmetry of the distribution. A distribution with an asymmetric tail extending out to the right is referred to as "positively skewed" or "skewed to the right," while a distribution with an asymmetric tail extending out to the left is referred to as "negatively skewed" or "skewed to the left." Skewness can range from minus infinity to positive infinity.

DO YOU KNOW?

Measures of skewness tells us the direction and the extent of skewness. In symmetrical distribution the mean, median and mode are identical. The more the mean moves away from the mode, the larger the asymmetry or skewness.

8.2.1 Type of Skewness

The following types would give an idea about the shape of symmetrical and asymmetrical curves.

(a) Symmetrical Distribution

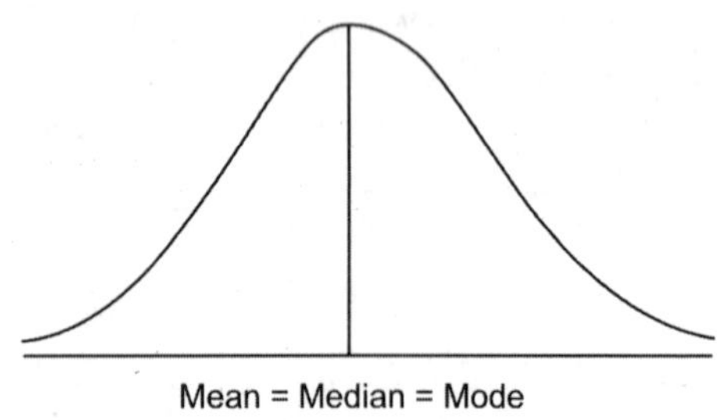

Fig. 8.2: Symmetrical Distribution

It is clear from the Fig. 8.2 that in a symmetrical distribution the values of mean, median and mode coincide. The spread of the frequencies is the same on both sides of the center point of the curve.

(b) Positively Skewed Distribution

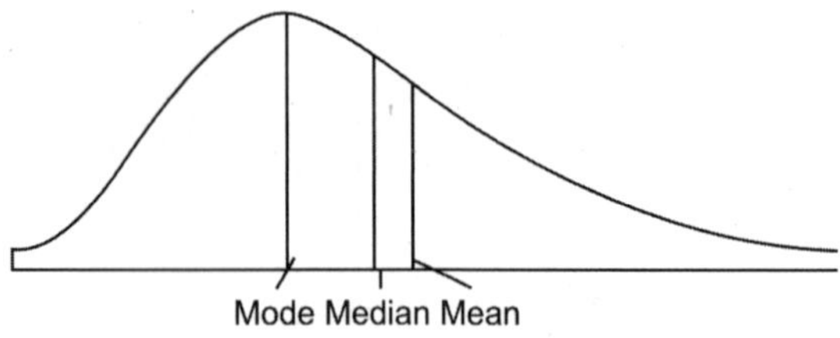

Fig. 8.3: Positively Skewed Distribution

It is clear from the Fig. 8.3, in a positively skewed distribution, the value of the mean is maximum and that of the mode is least, the median lies in between the two. In the positively skewed distribution the frequencies are spread out over a greater range of values on the right hand side than they are on the left hand side.

(c) Negatively Skewed Distribution

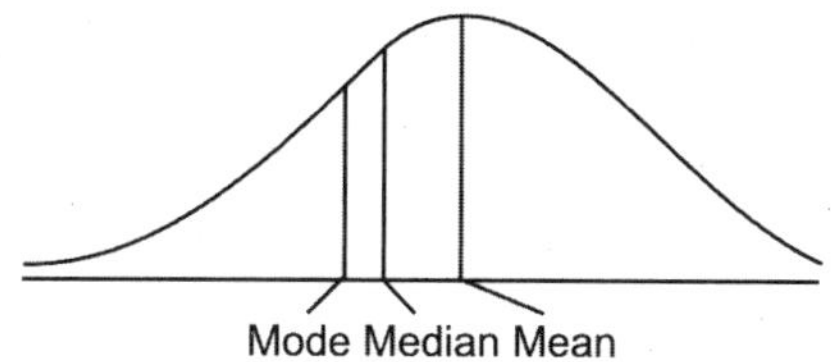

Fig. 8.4: Negatively Skewed Distribution

It is clear from the Fig. 8.4, in a negatively skewed distribution, the value of the mode is maximum and that of the mean is least. The median lies in between the two. In the negatively skewed distribution the frequencies are spread out over a greater range of values on the left hand side than they are on the right hand side.

> ***Concept —***
>
> - In Symmetrical distribution — Mean = Median = Mode
> - In a Positively Skewed distribution. — Mean > Median > Mode
> - In a Negatively Skewed distribution — Mean < Median < Mode

8.2.2 Comparison between Symmetrical and Skewed Distribution

S.No.	Symmetrical Distribution	S.No.	Skewed (Asymmetrical) Distribution
1.	Mean = Median = Mode	1.	Mean, Median, Mode do not coincide, i.e. Mean ≠ Median ≠ Mode
2.	The sum of the positive deviations from the median or mode is equal to the sum of the negative deviations	2.	The sum of the positive deviations from the median or mode is not equal to the sum of the negative deviations. The amount of difference between the sum of positive and negative deviations determines the amount of skewness
3.	Q_3 – Median = Median – Q_1 D_9 – Median = Median – D_1 P_{90} – Median = Median – P_{10} where *D* and *P* denotes deciles and percentiles	3.	Q_3 – Median ≠ Median – Q_1 D_9 – Median ≠ Median – D_1 P_{90} – Median ≠ Median – P_{10}
4.	Frequencies on either side of the mode are equal	4.	Frequencies on either side of the mode are not equal

8.2.3 Test of Skewness

In order to find out whether a particular distribution is skewed, certain tests are usually applied. They are as follows:

(a) In a skew distribution values of mean, median and mode would not coincide. The mean and mode would be pulled wide apart and median would usually lie between them. In a moderately asymmetrical distribution.

$$\text{Mean} - \text{Mode} = 3\,(\text{Mean} - \text{Median})$$

$$\Rightarrow \quad 3\,\text{Median} = 3\,\text{Mean} + \text{Mode} - \text{Mean}$$

$$= 2\,\text{Mean} + \text{Mode}$$

$$= 2\,\text{Mean} + \text{Mode} + 2\,\text{Mode} - 2\,\text{Mode}$$

$$= \text{Mode} + 2\,(\text{Mean} - \text{Mode})$$

$$\Rightarrow \quad \text{Median} = \text{Mode} + \frac{2}{3}\,(\text{Mean} - \text{Mode})$$

(b) In a skewed distribution the two quartiles would not be equidistant from the median or in other words $(Q_3 - M_e) - (M_e - Q)$ would not be zero.

(c) A skewed distribution when plotted on a graph paper would not give a symmetrical bell shaped curve.

(d) The sum of positive deviations from the Median is not equal to the sum of negative deviations.

(e) Frequencies are not equally distributed at various points which are equidistant from the Mode. In an asymmetrical distribution.
Mean – Median = 3 (Mean – Mode) on either side.

8.2.4 Difference between Dispersion and Skewness

1. Dispersion deals with the spread of values around central value whereas skewness deals with symmetry of distribution around central value.
2. Dispersion deals with the amount of variation and skewness deals with the direction of variation and the extend to which central tendency departs from symmetry.
3. Dispersion helps us to find the extend to which a central value is a representative of the whole distribution. But skewness deals with the nature of variations on either side of a central value.

8.3 MEASURES OF SKEWNESS

The above test mentioned tests would indicate whether a particular distribution is skewed or not. If a particular distribution is found to be skewed the next problem that arises is to measure the extent of skewness.

Measure of skewness can be both absolute as well as relative. For purpose of comparison it is necessary to have relative measures of skewness. Relative measures of skewness are obtained by dividing the absolute measures by any one of the measures of dispersion. The absolute measures of skewness should not be divided by a measure of central tendency or average. The purpose of studying skewness is to find out how much more or less do the items on one side deviate from the items on the other side of a central value. So, absolute measures of skewness should be divided by a measure of dispersion rather than a measure of central tendency. They also called first measures of skewness. The important measures of skewness are:

1. Karl-Pearson's coefficient of skewness
2. Bowley's coefficient of skewness
3. Kelly's coefficient of skewness
4. Measure of skewness based on moments

8.3.1 Karl-Pearson's Coefficient of Skewness

According to Karl-Pearson, the absolute measure of skewness = Mean – Mode. This measure is not suitable for making valid comparison of the skewness in two or more distributions because the unit of measurement may be different in different series. To avoid this difficulty use relative measure of skewness called Karl-Pearson's coefficient of skewness given by:

$$\boxed{\text{Karl – Pearson's Coefficient of Skewness} = \frac{\text{Mean} - \text{Mode}}{\text{S.D}}} \quad .....(I)$$

In case of mode is ill – defined, the coefficient can be determined by the formula:

$$\boxed{\text{Coefficient of Skewness} = \frac{3(\text{Mean} - \text{Median})}{\text{S.D}}} \quad .....(II)$$

Remark

1. Theoretical limits for (I) are ± 1 and for (II) are ± 3 but they never reached in actual practice.
2. From (I) and (II), skewness is zero if $\bar{X} = M_e = M_o$. In other words, for a symmetrical distribution mean, mode and median coincide.
3. $Sk > 0$ if $\bar{X} > M_e > M_o$ or if $M_o < M_e < \bar{X}$

   Thus, for a positively skewed distribution, the value of the mean is the greatest of the three measures and the value of mode is the least of the three measures.
4. $Sk < 0$, if $\bar{X} < M_e < M_o$ or if $M_o > M_e > \bar{X}$

   Thus, for a negatively skewed distribution, the value of mode is the greatest and value of mean is the least of the three measures of central tendency.

EXAMPLE 8.1: Calculate Karl-Pearson's coefficient of skewness for the following data.

25, 15, 23, 40, 27, 25, 23, 25, 20

Solution: Computation of Mean and Standard deviation:

Short-cut method.

Size	$d = x - A$	d^2
25	0	0
15	– 10	100
23	– 2	4
40	15	225
27	2	4
25 A	0	0
23	– 2	4
25	0	0
20	– 5	25
$n = 9$	$\Sigma d = -2$	$\Sigma d^2 = 362$

$$\text{Mean }(\bar{X}) = A + \frac{\Sigma d}{n} = 25 + \frac{-2}{9}$$

$$= 25 - 0.22 = 24.78$$

$$\text{Standard Dev. }(\sigma) = \sqrt{\frac{\Sigma d^2}{n} - \left(\frac{\Sigma d}{n}\right)^2} = \sqrt{\frac{362}{9} - \left(\frac{-2}{9}\right)^2}$$

$$= \sqrt{40.22 - 0.05} = \sqrt{40.17} = 6.3.$$

Mode = 25, as this size of item repeats 3 times

Karl-Pearson's coefficient of skewness

$$= \frac{\text{Mean} - \text{Mode}}{\text{S.D}} = \frac{24.78 - 25}{6.3}$$

$$= \frac{-0.22}{6.3} = -0.03.$$

EXAMPLE 8.2: Find the coefficient of skewness from the data given below

Size	3	4	5	6	7	8	9	10
Frequency	7	10	14	35	102	136	43	8

Solution:

Size	Frequency(*f*)	*d* = *x* – *A*	d^2	*fd*	fd^2
3	7	–3	9	–21	63
4	10	–2	4	–20	40
5	14	–1	1	–14	14
6 *A*	35	0	0	0	0
7	102	1	1	102	102
8	136	2	4	272	544
9	43	3	9	129	387
10	8	4	16	32	128
	N = 355			Σ*fd* = 480	Σfd^2 = 1278

$$\text{Mean} = A + \frac{\Sigma fd}{N} = 6 + \frac{480}{355}$$

$$= 6 + 1.35 = 7.35$$

$$\text{Mode} = 8$$

[Mode lies in size 8 which contains the maximum frequency]

$$\sigma = \sqrt{\frac{\Sigma fd^2}{N} - \left(\frac{\Sigma fd}{N}\right)^2} = \sqrt{\frac{1278}{355} - \left(\frac{480}{355}\right)^2}$$

$$= \sqrt{3.6 - 1.82} = \sqrt{1.78} = 1.33.$$

$$\text{Coefficient of skewness} = \frac{\text{Mean} - \text{Mode}}{\text{S.D}} = \frac{7.35 - 8}{1.33} = \frac{0.65}{1.33} = -0.5.$$

EXAMPLE 8.3: Find Karl-Pearson's coefficient of skewness for the given distribution:

X	0–50	5–10	10–15	15–20	20–25	25–30	30–35	35–40
f	2	5	7	13	21	16	8	3

Solution:

Mode lies in 20–25 group which contains the maximum frequency

$$\text{Mode} = l+\frac{f_1-f_0}{2f_1-f_0-f_2}\times c$$

$$l=20,\ f_1=21,\ f_0=13,\ f_2=16,\ c=5$$

$$\text{Mode} = 20+\frac{21-13}{2\times 21-13-16}\times 5$$

$$= 20+\frac{8\times 5}{42-29} = 20+\frac{40}{13}$$

$$= 20+3.08 = 23.08$$

Computation of Mean and Standard deviation

X	Mid-point (*x*)	Frequency (*f*)	Deviation $\left(d=\frac{x-22.5}{5}\right)$	*fd'*	*d'*^{2}	*fd'*^{2}
0-5	2.5	2	–4	–8	16	32
5-10	7.5	5	–3	–16	9	45
10-15	12.5	7	–2	–14	4	28
15-20	17.5	13	–1	–13	1	13
20-25	22.5	21	0	0	0	0
25-30	27.5	16	1	16	1	16
30-35	32.5	8	2	16	4	32
35-40	37.7	3	3	9	9	27
	N = 75			$\Sigma fd' = -9$	$\Sigma fd'^2 = 193$	

$$\text{Mean} = A+\frac{\Sigma fd'}{N}\times c = 22.5+\frac{-9}{75}\times 5$$

$$= 22.5-\frac{45}{75}$$

$$\sigma = \sqrt{\frac{\Sigma fd'^2}{N}-\left(\frac{\Sigma fd'}{N}\right)^2}\times c = \sqrt{\frac{193}{75}-\left(\frac{-9}{75}\right)}\times 5$$

$$= \sqrt{2.57-0.0144}\times 5 = \sqrt{2.5556}\times 5$$

$$= 1.5986\times 5 = 7.99$$

Karl-Pearson's coefficient of Skewness

$$= \frac{\text{Mean}-\text{Mode}}{\text{S.D}} = \frac{21.9-23.08}{7.99}$$

$$= \frac{-1.18}{7.99} = -0.1477.$$

8.3.2 Bowley's Coefficient of Skewness

In Karl-Pearson's method of measuring skewness the whole of the series is needed. Prof. Bowley's has suggested a formula based on relative position of quartiles. In a symmetrical distribution, the quartiles are equidistant from the value of the median; ie., Median $- Q_1 = Q_3 -$ Median. But in a skewed distribution, the quartiles will not be equidistant from the median. Hence Bowley's has suggested the following formula:

$$\text{Bowley's Coefficient of Skewness } (sk) = \frac{Q_3 + Q_1 - 2 \text{ Median}}{Q_3 - Q_1}$$

The value of this coefficient will be zero if it is a symmetrical distribution. If the value is greater than zero, it is positively skewed and if the value is less than zero, it is negatively skewed distribution.

This method is particularly useful in case of open-end distribution and where extreme values are present. Also when positional measures are called for, skewness should be measured by the Bowley's method.

EXAMPLE 8.4: Find the Bowley's coefficient of skewness for the following series.

2, 4, 6, 8, 10, 12, 14, 16, 18, 20, 22

Solution: The given data in order 2, 4, 6, 10, 12, 14, 16, 18, 20, 22

$$Q_1 = \text{size of } \left(\frac{n+1}{4}\right)^{\text{th}} \text{ item}$$

$$= \text{size of } \left(\frac{11+1}{4}\right)^{\text{th}} \text{ item} = \text{size of } 3^{\text{rd}} \text{ item} = 6$$

$$Q_3 = \text{size of } 3\left(\frac{n+1}{4}\right)^{\text{th}} \text{ item}$$

$$= \text{size of } 3\left(\frac{11+1}{4}\right)^{\text{th}} \text{ item} = \text{size of } 9^{\text{th}} \text{ item} = 18$$

$$\text{Median} = \text{size of } \left(\frac{n+1}{2}\right)^{\text{th}} \text{ item}$$

$$= \text{size of } \left(\frac{11+1}{2}\right)^{\text{th}} \text{ item} = \text{size of } 6^{\text{th}} \text{ item} = 12$$

$$\text{Bowley's Coefficient of Skewness } (sk) = \frac{Q_3 + Q_1 - 2 \text{ Median}}{Q_3 - Q_1} = \frac{18 + 6 - 2 \times 12}{18 - 6} = 0$$

Since $sk = 0$, the given series is a symmetrical data.

EXAMPLE 8.5: Find Bowley's coefficient of skewness of the following series:

Size	4	4.5	5	5.5	6	6.5	7	7.5	8
Frequency	10	18	22	25	40	15	10	8	7

Solution:

Size	f	c.f
4	10	10
4.5	18	28
5	22	50
5.5	25	75
6	40	115
6.5	15	130
7	10	140
7.5	8	148
8	7	155

$$Q_1 = \text{size of } \left(\frac{N+1}{4}\right)^{\text{th}} \text{ item} = \text{size of } \left(\frac{155+1}{4}\right)^{\text{th}} \text{ item}$$

$$= \text{size of } 39^{\text{th}} \text{ item} = 5$$

$$Q_2 = \text{size of } \left(\frac{N+1}{2}\right)^{\text{th}} \text{ item} = \text{size of } \left(\frac{155+1}{2}\right)^{\text{th}} \text{ item}$$

$$= \text{size of } 78^{\text{th}} \text{ item} = 6$$

$$Q_3 = \text{size of } 3\left(\frac{N+1}{4}\right)^{\text{th}} \text{ item} = \text{size of } 3\left(\frac{155+1}{4}\right)^{\text{th}} \text{ item}$$

$$= \text{size of } 117^{\text{th}} \text{ item} = 6.5$$

$$\text{Bowley's Coefficient of Skewness } (sk) = \frac{Q_3 + Q_1 - 2 \text{ Median}}{Q_3 - Q_1}$$

$$= \frac{6.5 + 5 - 2 \times 6}{6.5 - 5} = \frac{11.5 - 12}{1.5} = \frac{0.5}{1.5}$$

$$= 0.33$$

EXAMPLE 8.6: Calculate the value of the Bowley's coefficient of skewness from the following series:

Wages (Rs)	10–20	20–30	30–40	40–50	50–60	60–70	70–80
No. of Persons	1	3	11	21	43	32	9

Solution:

Wages (Rs)	f	c.f
10–20	1	1
20–30	3	4
30–40	11	15
40–50	21	36
50–60	43	79
60–70	32	111
70 80	9	120
	N = 120	

$$Q_1 = l_1 + \frac{\frac{N}{4} - m_1}{f_1} \times c_1$$

$$\frac{N}{4} = \frac{120}{4} = 30$$

Q_1 class = 40–50, $l_1 = 40$, $m_1 = 15$, $f_1 = 21$, $c_1 = 10$

$$\therefore \quad Q_1 = 40 + \frac{30 - 15}{21} \times 10 = 40 + \frac{150}{21}$$

$$= 40 + 7.14 = 47.14$$

$$Q_2 = \text{Median} = l + \frac{\frac{N}{2} - m}{f} \times c$$

$$\frac{N}{2} = \frac{120}{2} = 60$$

Medianal class = 50–60, $l = 50$, $m = 36$, $f = 43$, $c = 10$

$$\text{Median} = 50 + \frac{60 - 36}{43} \times 10 = 50 + \frac{240}{43}$$

$$= 50 + 5.58 = 55.58$$

$$Q_3 = l_3 + \frac{3\frac{N}{4} - m_3}{f_3} \times c_3$$

$$3\frac{N}{4} = 3 \times \frac{120}{4} = 90$$

Q_3 class = 60–70, $l_3 = 60$, $m_3 = 79$, $f_3 = 32$, $c_3 = 10$

$$\therefore \quad Q_3 = 60 + \frac{90 - 79}{32} \times 10 = 60 + \frac{110}{32}$$

$$= 60 + 3.44 = 63.44$$

Bowley's Coefficient of Skewness (*sk*) $= \dfrac{Q_3 + Q_1 - 2\text{ Median}}{Q_3 - Q_1}$

$$= \frac{63.44 + 47.14 - 2 \times 55.58}{63.44 - 47.14}$$

$$= \frac{110.58 - 111.16}{16.30}$$

$$= \frac{-0.58}{16.30} = -0.0356$$

Uses and Limitation of Bowley's Coefficient of Skewness

Uses

Bowley's coefficient of skewness is also known as quartile coefficient of skewness and is especially useful in situations where quartiles and median are used:

(i) When the mode is ill–defined and extreme observations are present in the data.
(ii) when the distribution has open end classes or unequal class intervals.

In these situations, Pearson's coefficient of skewness can not be used.

Limitations

Limitations of Bowley's coefficient of skewness are:

(i) The only and perhaps quite serious limitations of this coefficient is that it is based only on the central 50% of the data and ignores the remaining 50% of the data towards the extremes.
(ii) It should be clearly understood that the values of the coefficient of skewness obtained by Bowley's formula and Pearson's formula are not comparable, although in each case, $SK = 0$ implies the absence of skewness i.e. the distribution is symmetrical way even happen that one of them positive skewness while the other gives negative skewness.

8.3.3 Kelly's Coefficient of Skewness

The drawback of Bowley's coefficient of skewness i.e ignore the 50% of the data towards the extremes, can be partially removed by taking two deciles or percentiles equidistant from the median value. The refinement was suggested by Kelly. Kelly's percentile (or decile) measure of skewness is given by:

$$SK = (P_{90} - P_{50}) - (P_{50} - P_{10}) \qquad \text{.....(I)}$$
$$= P_{90} + P_{10} - 2P_{50}$$

But $P_{90} = D_9$ and $P_{10} = D_1$. Hence eq (I) can be re–written as:

$$SK = (D_9 - D_5) - (D_5 - D_1) \qquad \text{.....(II)}$$
$$= D_9 + D_1 - 2D_5$$

eq (I) and (II) gives an absolute measure of skewness. However, for practical purposes, we generally compute the coefficient of skewness, which is given by

$$\boxed{SK = \frac{P_{90} + P_{10} - 2P_{50}}{P_{90} - P_{10}}} \qquad \text{.....(A)}$$

and for decile

$$\boxed{SK = \frac{D_9 + D_1 - 2D_5}{D_9 - D_1}} \qquad \text{.....(B)}$$

we have $D_5 = P_{50}$ Median Hence from (A) and (B), we get

$$\boxed{SK = \frac{P_{90} + P_{10} - 2M_e}{P_{90} - P_{10}} = \frac{D_9 + D_1 - 2M_e}{D_9 - D_1}}$$

EXAMPLE 8.7: In a frequency distribution the coefficients of skewness based on quartiles is 0.6 if the sum of upper and lower quartiles is 100 and median is 38, find the upper and lower quartiles.

Solution:

$$SK = \frac{Q_3 + Q_1 - 2M_e}{Q_3 - Q_1} = 0.6$$

$$Q_3 + Q_1 = 100 \text{ and } M_e = 38$$

Now, $$\frac{100 - 2 \times 38}{Q_3 - Q_1} = 0.6$$

$$Q_3 - Q_1 = \frac{100 - 76}{0.6} = \frac{24}{0.6} = 40$$

Then $$Q_3 + Q_1 = 100 \text{ and } Q_3 - Q_1 = 40$$

So, $$2Q_3 = 140 \qquad Q_3 = 70$$

$$2Q_1 = 60 \qquad Q_1 = 30$$

Hence, the value of the upper and lower quartiles are 70 and 30 respectively.

EXAMPLE 8.8: From the information given below. Calculate Karl-Pearson's coefficient of skewness and also Bowley coefficient of skewness:

Measure	Group *A*	Group *B*
Mean	150	140
Median	142	155
Standard Deviation	30	55
Third quartile (Q_3)	195	260
First quartile (Q_1)	62	80

Solution:

Group *A*:

$$\text{Karl Pearson } (SK_A) = \frac{3(\bar{X} - M_e)}{\sigma}$$

$$= \frac{3(150 - 142)}{30}$$

$$= \frac{8}{10} = +0.8$$

$$\text{Bowly } (SK_A) = \frac{Q_3 + Q_1 - 2M_e}{Q_3 - Q_1}$$

$$= \frac{195 + 62 - 2 \times 142}{195 - 62}$$

$$= \frac{257 - 284}{133} = -0.203$$

Group *B*:

$$\text{Karl Pearson } (SK_B) = \frac{3(\bar{X} - M_e)}{\sigma}$$

$$= \frac{3(140 - 155)}{55} = \frac{3X(-15)}{55} = 0.82$$

$$\text{Bowly } (SK_B) = \frac{Q_3 + Q_1 - 2M_e}{Q_3 - Q_1} = \frac{260 + 80 - 2 \times 155}{260 - 80}$$

$$= \frac{340 - 310}{180} = 0.167$$

8.3.4 Measure of Skewness based on Moments

The measure of skewness based on moments is denoted by β_1 and is given by:

$$\boxed{\beta_1 = \frac{{\mu_3}^2}{{\mu_2}^3}}$$

if μ_3 is negative, then β_1 is negative.

∴ Moment coefficient of skewness can also be written as

$$= \frac{\mu_3}{\sqrt{{\mu_2}^3}} = \pm\sqrt{\frac{\mu_3}{{\mu_2}^3}} = \pm\sqrt{\beta_1}$$

The moment coefficient of skewness is also denoted by γ_1

$$\boxed{\gamma_1 = \sqrt{\beta_1} = \pm\sqrt{\frac{{\mu_3}^2}{{\mu_2}^3}} = \frac{\mu_3}{\sqrt{{\mu_2}^3}}}$$

However this method would be more discussed later when we study moments.

8.4 MOMENTS

Moment is a familiar mechanical term for the measure of a force with reference to its tendency to produce rotation. In statistics moments are used to describe the various characteristics of a frequency distribution like centre tendency, variation, skewness and kurtosis.

Moments are calculated using the arithmetic mean. According to ***Waugh***, "The arithmetic mean of the various powers of these deviations in any distribution is called the moments of the distribution".

Let 'x' be the deviation of any item in a distribution from the arithmetic mean of that distribution. The arithmetic mean of the various powers of these deviations is the moments of the distribution. If we take the mean of the 1st power of the deviations, we get the 1st moment about the mean, the mean of the squares of the deviations gives the second moment about the mean, and the mean of the cubes gives the third moment about the mean and so on. The moments about mean are called the "central moment".

Moments can be defined as the arithmetic mean of various powers of deviations taken from the mean of a distribution. These moments are known as central moments. The Greek letter μ (pronounced as 'mu') is generally used to denote the moments.

8.4.1 Moment about Mean

The first four moments about arithmetic mean or central moments are defined below:

	Individual Series	Discrete Series
First moments about the mean ; μ_1	$\frac{\Sigma(x-\bar{X})}{n}=0$	$\frac{\Sigma f(x-\bar{X})}{N}=0$
Second moments about the mean ; μ_2	$\frac{\Sigma(x-\bar{X})^2}{n}=\sigma^2$	$\frac{\Sigma f(x-\bar{X})^2}{N}$
Third moments about the mean ; μ_3	$\frac{\Sigma(x-\bar{X})^3}{n}$	$\frac{\Sigma f(x-\bar{X})^3}{N}$
Fourth moment about the mean ; μ_4	$\frac{\Sigma(x-\bar{X})^4}{n}$	$\frac{\Sigma f(x-\bar{X})^4}{N}$

8.4.2 Moment about Arbitrary Point

If the mean is a fractional value, then it becomes a difficult task to work out the moments. In such cases, we can calculate moments about a working origin and then change it into moments about the actual mean. The moments about an origin are known as raw moments.

The first four raw moments - Individual Series* —

$$\mu'_1=\frac{\Sigma(x-A)}{n}=\frac{\Sigma d}{n} \qquad \mu'_2=\frac{\Sigma(x-A)^2}{n}=\frac{\Sigma d^2}{n}$$

$$\mu'_3=\frac{\Sigma(x-A)^3}{n}=\frac{\Sigma d^3}{n} \qquad \mu'_4=\frac{\Sigma(x-A)^4}{n}=\frac{\Sigma d^4}{n}$$

Where A – any origin, $d=x-A$

The first four raw Moments - Discrete and Continuous Series (Step — Deviation Method)**

$$\mu'_1=\frac{\Sigma fd'}{N}\times c \qquad \mu'_2=\frac{\Sigma fd'^2}{N}\times c^2$$

$$\mu'_3=\frac{\Sigma fd'^3}{N}\times c^3 \qquad \mu'_4=\frac{\Sigma fd'^4}{N}\times c^4$$

Where $d=\frac{x-A}{c}$, A – origin, c – Common point

* The rth moment of a variable x about any arbitrary point A is given $\mu'_r=\frac{1}{n}\Sigma(x-A)^r$

** The rth moment of a variable x about any arbitrary point A (for discrete and continue series) $\mu'_r=\frac{1}{n}\Sigma f(x-A)^r$

8.4.3 Relationship between Raw Moments and Central Moments

Relation between moments about arithmetic mean and moments about an origin are given below.

$$\mu_1 = \mu'_1 - \mu'_1 = 0$$
$$\mu_2 = \mu'_2 - (\mu'_1)^2$$
$$\mu_3 = \mu'_3 - 3\mu'_1\mu'_2 + 2(\mu'_1)^3$$
$$\mu_4 = \mu'_4 - 4\mu'_1\mu'_3 + 6\mu'_2\mu'^{\,2}_1 - 3\mu'^{\,4}_1$$

8.4.4 Coefficients of Skewness based on Moments

Karl-Pearson has given β_1, β_2 coefficients and γ_1, γ_2 coefficients based on moments, they are as follows:

(i) $\boxed{\beta_1 = \dfrac{\mu_3^2}{\mu_2^3}}$ (ii) $\boxed{\beta_2 = \dfrac{\mu_4}{\mu_2^2} = \dfrac{\mu_4}{\sigma^4}}$

(iii) $\boxed{\gamma_1 = \sqrt{\beta_1} = \dfrac{\mu_3^2}{\mu_2^3} = \sqrt{\dfrac{\mu_3}{\mu_2^3}}}$ $[\mu_2 = \sigma^2]$

(iv) $\boxed{\gamma_2 = \beta_2 - 3 = \dfrac{\mu_4}{\mu_2^2} - 3}$

The coefficients are pure numbers not connected with the unit of measurement and as such can be used for comparative studies. They are used for measuring skewness and also kurtosis.
NOTE: If there is no skewness in a distribution the value of $\beta_1 = 0$. If the value of β_1 is more than zero it is an indication of skewness and the greater the value of β_1 the greater is the extent of skewness.

DO YOU KNOW?

β_1 cannot assume a negative value because $\beta_1 = \dfrac{\mu_3^2}{\mu_2^3}$. Now μ_3 can be either positive or negative but the square of μ_3 would always be positive. Similarly μ_2 is always a positive value.

The great drawback of β_1 as a measure of skewness be in the fact that it does not indicate whether skewness is positive or negative.

This drawback is removed by Karl Pearson's gamma one (γ_1) coefficient.

$\gamma_1 = +\sqrt{\beta_1}$ [Which is taken the positive square root of β_1]

EXAMPLE 8.9: Calculate first four moments from the following data.

Size	0	1	2	3	4	5	6	7	8
Frequency	5	10	15	20	25	20	15	10	5

Solution:

X	f	fx	d = x − $\bar{X}$ (x − 4)	fd	fd^2	fd^3	fd^4
0	5	0	−4	−20	80	−320	1280
1	10	10	−3	−30	90	−270	810
2	15	30	−2	−30	60	−120	240
3	20	60	−1	−20	20	−20	20
4	25	100	0	0	0	0	0
5	20	100	1	20	20	20	20
6	15	90	2	30	60	120	240
7	10	70	3	30	90	270	810
8	5	40	4	20	80	320	1280
	N = 125	Σfx = 500	Σd = 0	Σfd = 0	Σfd^2 = 500	Σfd^3 = 0	Σfd^4 = 4700

$$\bar{X} = \frac{\Sigma fx}{N} = \frac{500}{125} = 4$$

$$\mu_1 = \frac{\Sigma fd}{N} = \frac{0}{125} = 0$$

$$\mu_2 = \frac{\Sigma fd^2}{N} = \frac{500}{125} = 4$$

$$\mu_3 = \frac{\Sigma fd^3}{N} = \frac{0}{125} = 0$$

$$\mu_4 = \frac{\Sigma fd^4}{N} = \frac{4700}{125} = 37.6$$

EXAMPLE 8.10: From the data given below, first calculate the first four moments about an arbitrary origin and then calculate the first four moments about the mean.

X	30–33	33–36	36–39	39–42	42–45	45–48
f	2	4	26	47	15	6

X	*Midvalues (x)*	*f*	$d = \frac{(x - 37.5)}{3}$	*fd*	fd^2	fd^3	fd^4
30–33	31.5	2	-2	-4	8	16	32
33–36	34.5	4	1	4	4	4	4
36–39	37.5	26	0	0	0	0	0
39–42	40.5	47	1	47	47	47	47
42–45	43.5	15	2	30	60	120	240
45–48	46.5	6	3	18	54	162	486
		N = 100		Σfd' = 87	Σfd^2 = 173	Σfd^3 = 309	Σfd^4 = 809

$$\mu'_1 = \frac{\Sigma fd'}{N} \times c = \frac{87}{100} \times c = \frac{261}{100} = 2.61$$

$$\mu'_2 = \frac{\Sigma fd'^2}{N} \times c^2 = \frac{173}{100} \times 9 = \frac{1557}{100} = 15.57$$

$$\mu'_3 = \frac{\Sigma fd'^3}{N} \times c^3 = \frac{309}{100} \times 27 = \frac{8343}{100} = 83.43$$

$$\mu'_4 = \frac{\Sigma fd'^4}{N} \times c^4 = \frac{809}{100} \times 81 = \frac{65529}{100} = 655.29$$

Moments about Mean

$$\mu_1 = 0$$

$$\mu_2 = \mu'_2 - (\mu'_1)^2$$
$$= 15.57 - (2.61)^2$$
$$= 15.57 - 6.81 = 8.76$$

$$\mu_3 = \mu'_3 - 3\mu'_2\mu'_1 + 2(\mu'_1)^3$$
$$= 83.43 - 3(2.61)\,(15.57) + 2(2.61)^2$$
$$= 83.43 - 121.9 + 35.56 = -2.91$$

$$\mu_4 = \mu'_4 - 4\mu'_3\mu'_1 + 6\mu'_2\mu'^2_1 - 3\mu'^4_1$$
$$= 655.29 - 4(83.43)\,(2.61) + 6(15.57)\,(2.61)^2 - 3(2.61)^4$$
$$= 655.29 - 871.01 + 636.39 - 139.214 = 291.454$$

8.5 KURTOSIS

The expression 'Kurtosis' is used to describe the peakedness of a curve. It has its origin in the Greek word "Bulginess". The three measures – central tendency, dispersion and skewness describe the characteristics of frequency distributions. But these studies will not give us a clear picture of the characteristics of a distribution. As far as the measurement of shape is concerned, we have two characteristics – skewness which refers to asymmetry of a series and kurtosis which measures the peakedness of a normal curve. All the frequency curves expose different degrees of flatness or peakedness. This characteristic of frequency curve is termed as kurtosis.

According to ***Simpson and Kafka***, "Kurtosis refers to degree of peakedness or plotness in the region about the mode in a frequency curve. The degree of kurtosis of a distribution is measured relative to the peakedness of a normal curve.".

According to ***Croxton and Cowden***, "A measure of Kurtosis indicates the degree to which a curve of the frequency distribution is peaked or flat topped".

Different symmetrical curves, even having the same range may have different shapes of their peaks. Measure of Kurtosis enables us to have an idea about the shape and nature of the middle part of a frequency distribution. The following figure explaining the Kurtosis.

Measure of Kurtosis denotes the shape of top of a frequency curve. Measure of Kurtosis tell us the extent to which a distribution is more peaked or more flat topped than the normal curve,

- If a curve is symmetrical and bell-shaped, is designated as Mosokurtic. (In Fig. 8.5 type M)
- If a curve is relatively more narrow and peaked at the top, it is designated as Leptohurtic. (In Fig. 8.5 type L)
- If a curve is more falt than normal curves designated as platykurtic. (In Fig. 8.5 type P)

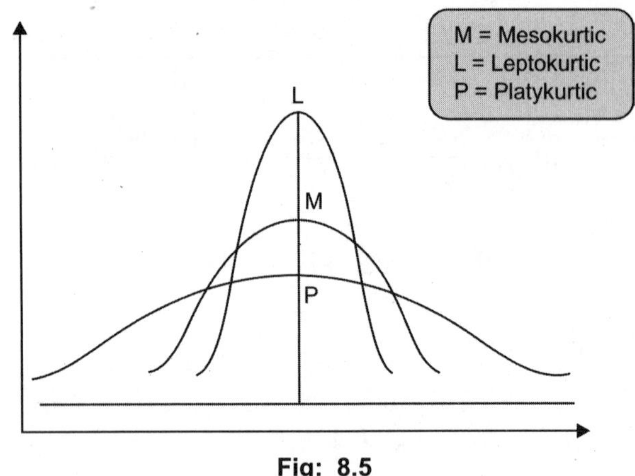

Fig: 8.5

8.5.1 Measure of Kurtosis

The measure of kurtosis of a frequency distribution based moments is denoted by β_2 and is given by

$$\boxed{\beta_2 = \frac{\mu_4}{\mu_2^{\ 2}}}$$

Concept —

If $\beta_2 = 3$, the distribution is said to be normal and the curve is ***mesokurtic***.
If $\beta_2 > 3$, the distribution is said to be more peaked and the curve is ***leptokurtic***.
If $\beta_2 < 3$, the distribution is said to be flat topped and the curve is ***platykurtic***.

EXAMPLE 8.11: From the data given below, calculate the first four moments about an arbitrary origin and then calculate the first four central moments.

Solution: Refer Example 8.10 of page 268 and get the values of first four moments about the origin and the first four moments about the mean. Then using these values find the values of β_1 and β_2.

$\mu_1 = 0, \quad \mu_2 = 8.76, \quad \mu_3 = -2.91, \quad \mu_4 = 291.454$

$$\beta_1 = \frac{\mu^2{}_3}{\mu^3{}_2}$$

$$\beta_1 = \frac{(-2.91)^2}{(8.76)^3} = \frac{8.47}{672.24} = 0.0126$$

$$\beta_2 = \frac{\mu_4}{\mu_2^{\ 2}}$$

$$\beta_1 = \frac{291.454}{(8.76)^2} = 3.70$$

Since $\beta_2 > 3$, the curve is leptokurtic.

EXAMPLE 8.12: Calculate β_1 and β_2 for the following data.

X	0	1	2	3	4	5	6	7	8
F	5	10	15	20	25	20	15	10	5

Solution: Refer Example 8.10 of page 268 and get the values of first four central moments and then proceed to find β_1 and β_2.

$$\mu_1 = 0 \qquad \mu_2 = \frac{\Sigma fd^2}{N} = \frac{500}{125} = 4$$

$$\mu_3 = \frac{\Sigma fd^3}{N} = 0 \qquad \mu_4 = \frac{\Sigma fd^4}{N} = \frac{4700}{125} = 37.6$$

$$\therefore \qquad \beta_1 = \frac{\mu^2{}_3}{\mu^3{}_2} = \frac{0}{64} = 0$$

$$\beta_2 = \frac{\mu_4}{\mu_2{}^2} = \frac{37.6}{4^2} = \frac{37.6}{16} = 2.35.$$

The value of β_2 is less than 3, hence the curve is platykurtic.

8.5.2 Difference between skewness and Kurtosis

Measures of skewness study about the shape of the series and the cluster of deviating above and below a central tendency. In a normal distribution (or symmetrical distribution) the deviations below and above an average (central tendency) are equal while in an asymmetrical distribution they are not equal. kurtosis studies the concentration of items at the central part of a series. If the items concentrate too much in centre, the curve becomes leptokurtic and if the concentration at the centre is comparatively small the curves becomes platykurtic Normal curve is mesokurtic.

MISCELLANEOUS SOLVED EXAMPLES

EXAMPLE 8.13: Find an appropriate measure of skewness from the following distribution:

Age (yrs)	Below 20	20–25	25–30	30–35	35–40	40–45	45–50	50 and above
No. of employees	13	29	46	60	112	94	45	21

Solution: Since it is an open–end distribution, therefore appropriate measure of skewness would be Bowley's coefficient of skewness. **[MBA, Osmania University, 1997, Bun. Univ., 2001]**

Calculation Of Bowley's Coefficient

Age (Yrs.)	No. of employees (*f*)	*c.f.*
Below 20	13	13
20–25	29	42
25–30	46	88
30–35	60	148
35–40	112	260
40–45	94	354
45–50	45	399
50 and above	21	420
	N = 420	

$$Sk_B = \frac{Q_3 + Q_1 - 2\text{Med.}}{Q_3 - Q_1}$$

$$Q_1 = \text{Size of } \frac{N}{4}^{\text{th}} \text{ observation} = \frac{420}{4} = 105^{\text{th}} \text{ observation}$$

Q_1 lies in the class 30–35.

$$Q_1 = l + \frac{N/4 - m}{f} \times i = 30 + \frac{105 - 88}{60} \times 5 = 30 + 1.42 = 31.42$$

$$Q_1 = \text{Size of } \frac{3N}{4}^{\text{th}} \text{ observation} = \frac{3 \times 420}{4} = 315^{\text{th}} \text{ observation}$$

Q_3 lies in the class 40–45.

$$Q_3 = l + \frac{3N/4 - m}{f} \times i = 40 + \frac{315 - 260}{94} \times 5 = 40 + 2.93 = 42.93$$

$$\text{Med.} = \text{Size of } \frac{N}{2}^{\text{th}} \text{ observation} = \frac{420}{2} = 210^{\text{th}} \text{ observation}$$

Median lies in the class 35–40.

$$\text{Med.} = l + \frac{N/2 - m}{f} \times i = 35 + \frac{210 - 148}{112} \times 5 = 35 + 2.77 = 37.77$$

$$Sk_B = \frac{42.93 + 31.42 - (2 \times 37.77)}{42.93 - 31.42} = \frac{-1.19}{11.51} = -0.103$$

EXAMPLE 8.14: (a) The sum of 50 observations is 500, its sum of squares is 6,000 and median 12. Find the coefficient of variation and coefficient of skewness.

(b) For a moderately skewed distribution, the arithmetic mean is 100 and coefficient of variation is 35, and Pearson's coefficient of skewness is 0.2. Find the mode and the median.

Solution:

(a) $n = 50, \quad \Sigma X = 500, \quad \Sigma X^2 = 6{,}000, \quad \text{Med.} = 12$

$$\bar{X} = \frac{\Sigma X}{n} = \frac{500}{50} = 10;$$

and

$$\sigma = \sqrt{\frac{\Sigma X^2}{n} - (\bar{X})^2} = \sqrt{\frac{6{,}000}{50} - (10)^2} = 4.47$$

$$\text{C.V} = \frac{\sigma}{\bar{X}} \times 100 = \frac{4.47}{10} \times 100 = 44.7 \text{ per cent}$$

$$\text{Mode} = 3 \text{ Median} - 2 \text{ Mean} = 3 \times 12 - 2 \times 10 = 16$$

$$Sk_B = \frac{\text{Mean} - \text{Mode}}{\sigma} = \frac{10 - 16}{4.47} = -1.34$$

(b) $\bar{X} = 100, \quad \text{C.V} = 35, \quad Sk_P = 0.2$

$$\text{C.V} = \frac{\sigma}{\bar{X}} \times 100$$

$$35 = \frac{\sigma}{100} \times 100 \text{ or } \sigma = 35$$

$$Sk_P = \frac{\bar{X} - \text{Mode}}{\sigma} \text{ or } 0.2 = \frac{100 - \text{Mode}}{35}$$

$$7 = 100 - \text{Mode or Mode} = 93$$

$$\text{Mode} = 3 \text{ Med.} - 2 \text{ Mean}$$

$$93 = 3 \text{ Med.} - 2 \times 100 \text{ or } 3 \text{ Med.} - 200 = 93$$

$$3 \text{ Med.} = 293$$

$$\therefore \quad \text{Med.} = 97.7$$

Hence, Mode = 93 and Median = 97.7

EXAMPLE 8.15: Find out quartile coefficient of skewness in a series where $Q_1 = 18$, $Q_3 = 25$, Mode = 21 and Mean = 18.

Solution: In a moderately asymmetric distribution,

$$\text{Mean} - \text{Mode} = 3 \text{ (Mean} - \text{Median)}$$

$$\Rightarrow \quad 18 - 21 = 3 \text{ (18} - \text{Median)}$$

$$\Rightarrow \quad \frac{-3}{3} = 18 - \text{Median}$$

$$\Rightarrow \quad -1 = 18 - \text{Median}$$

$$\Rightarrow \quad \text{Median} = 19$$

Quartile coefficient of skewness = [Bowley's coefficient of skewness]

$$= \frac{Q_3 + Q_1 - 2M_e}{Q_3 - Q_1}$$

Where M_e = Median = Q_2 , Q_1 and Q_3 are first and third quartiles respectively

$$= \frac{25 + 18 - 2 \times 19}{25 - 18} = \frac{5}{7} = 0.71$$

EXAMPLE 8.16: Distribution of wage rates in the cotton textile industry when compared with wage rates in all manufacturing industries in 1999 show the following results:

	Mean monthly wages in Rs	Median monthly wages in Rs	S.D
Cotton Text.	57.00	55.00	1.2
All manufacturers	54.00	53.00	1.2

Give your comments on the structure of the distribution

Solution: Pearson's coefficient of skewness for cotton industries

$$= \frac{3(\text{Mean} - \text{Median})}{\text{S.D}} = \frac{3(57 - 55)}{1.2} = 5$$

Coefficient of skewness for all manufacturers $= \dfrac{3(54 - 53)}{1.2} = 2.5$

Since the coefficient of skewness is more for cotton industries, the wage rates in cotton industries are more asymmetrical as compared to wage rates for all industries.

EXAMPLE 8.17: You are given the following frequency distribution of the daily earnings of employees in a company:

Earnings (in Rs.)	50–70	70–90	90–110	110–130	130–150	150–170	170–190
No. of workers	4	8	12	20	6	7	3

Calculate the first four moments about the point 120. Convert the result into moments about the mean. Compute the value of γ_1 and γ_2 comment on the result. **[MBA, DU, 2002, HPU, 2005]**

Solution: Moment about some arbitrary point is given by

$$\mu_r' = \frac{1}{n}\Sigma f(X - A)^r$$

Here $A = 120$ and X are the mid–points. To get the first four moments, put $r = 1$, 2,3 and 4 in the above formula.

Computation of First Four Moments

Earnings (Rs)	m.p. X	f	(X – 120)/20 d	fd	fd^2	fd^3	fd^4
50–70	60	4	–3	–12	46	108	324
70–90	80	8	–2	–16	32	–64	128
90–110	100	12	–1	–12	12	–12	12
110–130	**120**	20	0	0	0	0	0
130–150	140	6	+1	+6	6	+6	6
150–170	160	7	+2	14	28	+56	112
170–190	180	3	+3	+9	27	+81	243
		N = 60		**Σfd = –11**	**Σfd^2 = 141**	**Σfd^3 = –41**	**Σfd^4 = 825**

Moments about the arbitrary point = 120

$$\mu'_1 = \frac{\Sigma fd}{N} \times c = \frac{-11}{60} \times 20 = -3.6667$$

$$\mu'_2 = \frac{\Sigma fd^2}{N} \times c^2 = \frac{141}{60} \times (20)^2 = 940$$

$$\mu'_3 = \frac{\Sigma fd^3}{N} \times c^3 = \frac{-41}{60} \times (20)^3 = -5466.6667$$

$$\mu'_4 = \frac{\Sigma fd^4}{N} \times c^4 = \frac{825}{60} \times (20)^4 = 22,00,000$$

Moments about mean:

μ_1 = 0 (since the sum of the deviations from the mean is zero).

$$\mu_2 = \mu'_2 - \mu'^2_1 = 940 - (-3.6667)^2 = 926.5553 \text{ or } \sigma = \sqrt{\mu_2} = 30.4394$$

$$\mu_3 = \mu'_3 - 3\mu'_1\mu'_2 + 2\mu'^3_1$$
$$= -5466.6667 - 3(940)(-3.6667) + 2(-3.6667)^3$$
$$= -5466.6667 + 10340.094 - 98.5953 = 4774.832$$

$$\mu_4 = \mu'_4 - 4\mu'_1\mu'_3 + 6\mu'_2\mu'^2_1 - 2\mu'^4_1$$
$$= 2200000 - 4(-3.6667)\ (-5466.6667) + 6(940)\ (-3.6667)^2 - 2(-3.6667)^4$$
$$= -2200000 - 80178.507 + 75828.045 - 542.2789 = 2195107.3$$

$$\gamma_1 = \sqrt{\beta_1} = \frac{\mu_3}{\sigma^3} = \frac{4774.83}{(30.4394)^3} = 0.1693$$

$$\beta_2 = \frac{\mu_4}{\mu_2^2} = \frac{2195107.3}{(926.56)^2} = 2.56, \quad \gamma_2 = \beta_2 - 3 = -0.44$$

The value of γ_1 indicates that the distribution is slightly skewed to the right, i.e., it is not perfectly symmetrical. Since the value of γ_2 is less than zero, therefore, the distribution is platykurtic.

LIST OF FORMULAE

1. For symmetric distribution

$$\text{Mean} = \text{Median} = \text{Mode}$$

2. For positively skewed distribution

$$\text{Mean} > \text{Median} > \text{Mode}$$

3. For negatively skewed distribution

$$\text{Mean} < \text{Median} < \text{Mode}$$

4. Karl –Pearson's coefficient of skewness $= \dfrac{\text{Mean} - \text{Mode}}{\text{S.D}}$

$$= \frac{3(\text{Mean} - \text{Median})}{\text{S.D}}$$

5. Bowley's coefficient of skewness $= \dfrac{Q_3 + Q_1 - 2\text{Median}}{Q_3 - Q_1}$

6. Kelly's coefficient of skewness,

For percentile, $$Sk = \frac{P_{90} + P_{10} - 2P_{50}}{P_{90} - P_{10}}$$

For Decile, $$Sk = \frac{D_9 + D_1 - 2D_5}{D_9 - D_1}$$

7. Measurement of skewness based on Moments:

$$\beta_1 = \frac{\mu_3^2}{\mu_2^3}$$

$$\gamma_1 = \sqrt{\beta_1} = \pm\sqrt{\frac{\mu_3^2}{\mu_2^3}} = \pm\frac{\mu_3}{\sqrt{\mu_2^3}}$$

$$\beta_2 = \frac{\mu_4}{\mu_2^2} = \frac{\mu_4}{\sigma^4}$$

$$\gamma_2 = \beta_2 - 3 = \frac{\mu_2}{\mu_2^2} - 3$$

8. Moment about Mean

$$\mu_1 = \frac{\Sigma(x - \bar{X})}{n} = 0$$

$$\mu_2 = \frac{\Sigma(x - \bar{X})^2}{n} = \sigma^2$$

$$\mu_n = \frac{\Sigma(x - \bar{X})^n}{n}$$

9. Moment about Arbitrary Point (for Raw Data)

$$\mu_1^1 = \frac{\Sigma d}{n} = \frac{\Sigma(x - A)}{n}$$

$$\mu_2^1 = \frac{\Sigma d^2}{n} = \frac{\Sigma(x - A)^2}{n}$$

$$\mu_n^1 = \frac{\Sigma d^n}{n} = \frac{1}{n}\Sigma(x - A)^2$$

10. Moment about Arbitrary Point (For Discrete and continuous series)

$$\mu_1' = \frac{\Sigma fd'}{N} \times c = \frac{\Sigma f(x - A)}{N}$$

$$\mu_2' = \frac{\Sigma fd'^2}{N} \times c = \frac{\Sigma f(x - A)^2}{N}$$

$$\mu_n' = \frac{1}{N}\left[\Sigma fd'^n\right] \times c = \frac{\Sigma f(n - A)^n}{N}$$

Where, $$d' = \frac{x - A}{c}$$

SELF PRACTICE EXERCISES

I. CHOOSE THE BEST ANSWER

1. Which of the following is a unitless measure of dispersion?
   (a) Standard deviation (b) Mean deviation
   (c) Coefficient of variation (d) Range
2. Absolute sum of deviations is minimum from:
   (a) Mode (b) Median
   (c) Mean (d) None of the above
3. In a distribution S.D = 6. All observation multiplied by 2 would give the result to S.D is:
   (a) 12 (b) 6
   (c) 18 (d) 6
4. For a negatively skewed distribution, the correct inequality is:
   (a) Mode < Median (b) Mean < Median
   (c) Mean < Mode (d) None of the above
5. In case of positive skewed distribution, the extreme values lie in the
   (a) Left tail (b) Right tail
   (c) Middle (d) Any where

6. Which one is the formula for relative skewness?
   (a) Mean – Mode (b) $(Q_3 - Q_2) - (Q_2 - Q_1)$
   (c) $\dfrac{Q_3 + Q_1 - 2M_e}{Q_3 - Q_1}$ (d) None of the above
7. Which one of the following is measure of skewness?
   (a) First moment (b) Second moment
   (c) Third moment (d) Fourth moment
   (e) None of these
8. Which one of the curves is more peaked than the normal curve?
   (a) Mesokurtic (b) Platykurtic
   (c) Laptokurtic (d) None of these
9. A curve which is elougated to the right, shows that it is:
   (a) Skewed to the left (b) symmetrical
   (c) Positively skewed (d) None of these
10. For a distribution, Mean = 43.71, Median = 43.82 and standard deviation = –0.33, the coefficient of skewness is:
   (a) 0.05 (b) 0.2
   (c) –0.02 (d) None of these
11. The shape of a probability distribution is such that it tails off to right end when the distribution is:
   (a) Symmetrical (b) Skewed left
   (c) Positively skewed (d) None of the above
12. Normal curve is:
   (a) Mesokurtic (b) Platykurtic
   (c) Leptokurtic (d) None of these
13. Second moment about the mean is:
   (a) Variance (b) Mean
   (c) Standard deviation (d) Mean deviation
14. First moment about the origin is:
   (a) Mean (b) Standard deviation
   (c) Mean deviation (d) Nonc of these
15. Fourth moment about the mean measures:
   (a) Skewness (b) Kurtosis
   (c) Standard deviation (d) Quartile deviation

II. FILL IN THE BLANKS

1. Relative measure of dispersion is free from ....
2. .... is suitable for open end distributions.
3. The mean of absolute deviations from an average is called ....
4. The second central moment is always a ....
5. If $x = 50$, mode = 48, $s = 20$, the coefficient of skewness shall be ....
6. In a symmetrical distribution the coefficient of skewness is ....
7. If $\beta_2 = 3$ the distribution is called ....

III. SHORT ANSWER TYPE QUESTIONS

1. What do you understand by skewness? What are the various measures of skewness?
2. What do you understand by kurtosis? What is the measure of measuring kurtosis?
3. Distinguish between skewness and kurtosis and bring out their importance in describing frequency distribution.
4. Define moments. Also distinguish between raw moments and central moments.
5. Mention the relationship between raw moments and central moments for the first four moments.
6. Explain briefly the different methods of measuring skewness. **[MBA, Kumavn Univ., 2000]**
7. What do you understand by the terms skewness and Kurtosis? Point out their role in analysing a frequency distribution. **[MBA, Delhi University, 1994]**
8. Distinguish between Karl Pearson's and Bowley's measure of skewness. Which one of these would you prefer and why? **[MBA, Delhi University, 2000, 2002]**
9. Karl Pearson's coefficient of skewness is 0.32. Its S.D is 6.5 and mean 29.6. Find the value of mode and median
10. Show by calculation whether the group is negatively skewed or positively skewed if median = 24, mean = 26.
11. For a distribution S.D = 2. What should be the value of μ_4 so that the distribution is:
    (i) Platykurtic (ii) Mesokurtic (iii) Leptokurtic?

IV. LONG ANSWER TYPE QUESTIONS

1. Particulars regarding the income of two villages are given below :

	Village A	Village B
Number of people	600	500
Average income (in Rs)	175	186
Variance of income (in Rs)	100	81

In which village is the variation in income greater)

2. From the following table calculate the Karl-Pearson' s coefficient of Skewness

Daily Wages (in Rs)	150	200	250	300	350	400	450
No. of People	3	25	19	16	4	5	6

3. Compute Bowley's coefficient of skewness from the following data:

Size	5–7	8–10	11–13	14–16	17–16
Frequency	14	24	38	20	4

4. Using moments calculate β_1 and β_2 from the following data:

Daily Wages	70–90	90–110	110–130	130–150	150–170
No. of Workers	8	11	18	9	4

5. Locate the mode and calculate mean and standard deviation of the following distribution and using your results comment on the skewness of the distribution: **[MBA, DU, 2002, 2005]**

Scores	Frequency	Scores	Frequency
10–15	2	35–40	6
15–20	8	40–45	4
20–25	6	45–50	3
25–30	12	50–55	1
30–35	7	55–60	1

6. A survey was conducted by a manufacturing company to enquire the maximum price at which persons would be willing to buy their product. The following table gives the stated prices (in rupees) by persons:

Price (in Rs)	80–90	90–100	100–110	110–120	120–130
No. of persons	11	29	18	27	15

Calculate Bowley's coefficient of skewness. **[MBA, Delhi University, 2002]**

7. Calculate the first four moments about mean and find the values of β_1 and β_2 and comment on the result: **[MBA, Kumavu University, 1998]**

Profit (Rs lakhs)	0–10	10–20	20–30	30–40	40–50	50–60	60–70
No. of companies	8	12	20	30	15	10	5

8. Compute the first 3 moments about the arithmetic mean from the following data:

Variable value	5	10	15	20	25	30	35
Frequency	8	15	20	32	23	17	5

[MBA, Lucknow University, 2001]

ANSWERS

I. CHOOSE THE BEST ANSWER

1. (c) 2. (c) 3. (a) 4. (c) 5. (b) 6. (c) 7. (c) 8. (c)
9. (c) 10. (c) 11. (c) 12. (a) 13. (a) 14. (a) 15. (b)

II. FILL IN THE BLANKS

1. units 2. Q.D 3. M.D. 4. Variance 5. 0.1 6. zero 7. Mesokurtic

III. SHORT ANSWER TYPE QUESTIONS

10. Mode = 27.52, Median = 28.91
11. Positively skewed
12. For mesokurtic, $\mu_u = 48$
For leptokurtic, $\mu_u = 748$ and For platykurtic, $\mu_u < 48$.

IV. LONG ANSWER TYPE QUESTIONS

1. $C.V_A = 5.71\%$, $C.V_B = 4.84\%$
2. Sk = 0.88
3. Sk = –0.13
4. $\beta_1 = 0.006$, $\beta_2 = 2.305$
5. $\bar{X} = 30.1$, $M_o = 27.73$, $\sigma = 10.45$, Sk = 0.227
6. 30.35
7. $\mu_1 = 20$, $\mu_2 = 18$, $\mu_3 = 30$

CHAPTER 9

Index Numbers

9.1 INTRODUCTION

An index number is a statistical device for comparing the general level of magnitude of a group of related variables in two or more situation. If we want to compare the price level of 2000 with what it was in 1990, we shall have to consider a group of variables such as price of wheat, rice, vegetables, cloth, house rent etc., If the changes are in the same ratio and the same direction, we face no difficulty to find out the general price level. But practically, if we think changes in different variables are different and that too, upward or downward, then the price is quoted in different units i.e milk for litre, rice or wheat for kilogram, rent for square feet, etc We want one figure to indicate the changes of different commodities as a whole. This is called an ***index number***. Index Number is a number which indicate the changes in magnitudes.

M. Spiegel say, "An index number is a statistical measure designed to show changes in variable or a group of related variables with respect to time, geographic location or other characteristic".

In general, index numbers are used to measure changes over time in magnitude which are not capable of direct measurement.

"An ***Index Number*** is a single ratio (usually in percentages) which measures the (combined average) change of several variables between two different times, places and situations" — ***Alva. M. Tuttle.***

Index numbers are the devices for measuring differences in the magnitude of a group of related variables, over two different situations or defined as a measure of the average change in a group of related variables over two different situations. ***For example***, the price of commodities at two different places or two different time periods at the same location. We need Index Numbers to compare the cost of living at different times or in different locations.

9.2 DEFINITION OF INDEX NUMBERS

Some definitions of the index numbers are —

A series of index numbers is a series which reflects its trend and fluctuation the movement of some quantity to which it is related. — ***Dr. A. L. Bowley***

Index Numbers are derives for measuring differences in the magnitude of a group of related variables. — ***Croxton & Cowden***

Index numbers are a series of numbers by which changes in the magnitude of phenomena are measured from time to time or from place to place. — ***Hores Secrist***

An Index Numbers is, as its name suggests, an indicator of the general trend of a set of figures. — ***Boddington***

The above definitions clarify the characteristics of index number and the purpose they serve. It is obvious that index numbers study relative changes over a period of time or geographical locations or some other characteristics. ***For example***, when it is said the price index number for the year 2005 was 345 as compared to the year 2000 when it was 200, it gives an idea about the change in the price level between two periods. Similarly when it is said that the Indian national income index increased by 5 percent in the year 1990 as compared to the year 1989, and in America the rise in national income during these two periods was 12 per cent. We are making a comparison both on the basis of time and geographical location.

If the variation in the level of a single item is being studied the index number would be called an univariate index. The index numbers of wheat production in India during the last 10 years would be an example of a univariate index. On the other hand if the changes in average level of a number of items is being studied together this index number of agricultural production in India would be an example of a composite index.

9.3 USES OF INDEX NUMBERS

The first index number was constructed by an Italian. ***Mr. Carli*** in 1764 to compare the change in price for the year 1750 (current year) with the price level in 1500 (base year) in order to study the effect of discovery of America on the price level in Italy. Through originally designed to study the general level of prices or accordingly purchasing power of money, today index numbers are extensively used for a variety of purposes in economics, business, management etc and for quantitative data relating to production, consumption, profits, personnel and financial matters etc., for comparing changes in the level of phenomenon for two periods, places etc. In fact, there is hardly any field of quantitative measurements where index numbers are not constructed. They are used in almost all sciences -natural, social and physical and index numbers are indispensable tools of economic and business analysis. They are particular useful in measuring relative changes. Their uses can be appreciated by the following points.

- Provide economic indicators like prices of commodities and financial instruments like shares, output like industrial and agricultural production, exports, imports etc.
- Policy formulation at state, national and international levels.
- Measuring and comparing the purchasing power of money.
- In India, as also in various other countries, consumer price index number is used to decide the amount of dearness allowance to the employees of public and organised sectors.
- The index numbers are also used for deflating time series data on wages, cost of living, national income etc.
- The wholesale price indicator is used as a benchmark for deciding the interest rate on Government securities, bank rate for the Reserve Bank's lending to commercial banks, the rates for deposits and loans of commercial bank's etc.

9.4 CHARACTERISTICS OF INDEX NUMBERS

On the basis of study and analysis of the definition given above, the following characteristics of index numbers are apparent.

1. Index numbers are specified averages.
2. Index numbers are expressed in percentage.
3. Index numbers measure changes not capable of direct measurement.
4. Index numbers are for comparison.

9.5 LIMITATIONS OF INDEX NUMBERS

Even though index numbers are very useful devices for measuring relative changes, and are very widely used for the purpose, but they suffer from limitations which should always be kept in mind.
These limitations are :

(i) They are only approximate indicators of the relative level of a phenomenon, and should be interpreted as such.

(ii) Index numbers use only limited number of items in their calculation and may not reflect the true picture of the problem under study, if the items chosen are not representative of the universe.

(iii) The quality of the product is very difficult to be accounted for in the construction of index numbers. In modern times when qualities of various products undergo quick changes the index numbers may not reflect the relative change appropriately if the quality level of the items has changed.

(iv) Indices constructed for one purpose cannot be used for another purpose. Every index number is constructed by a technique which is appropriate for the objective with which the index is constructed. It cannot be used to serve a different objective. A wholesale price index number cannot measure cost of living. An index of production cannot measure productivity. As such index numbers should be used with caution.

(v) Index numbers are liable to be misused. If a wrong base has been chosen, or if weights are not assigned rationally or if the appropriate formula for the construction of the indices has not been chosen the results could be highly misleading and mischievous.

9.6 TYPES OF INDEX NUMBERS

There are various types of index numbers, but in brief, we shall take three kinds and they are

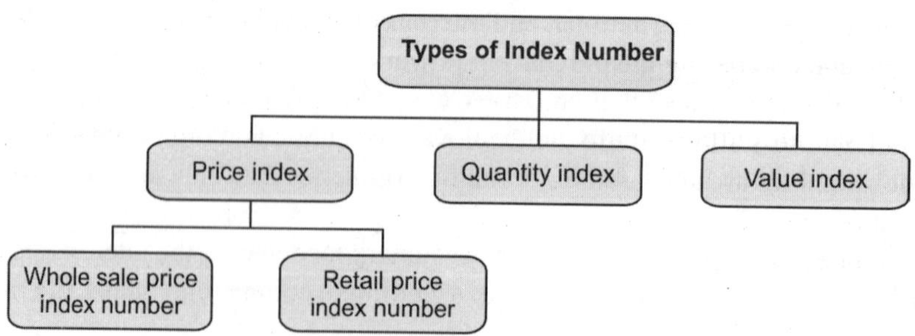

Fig. 9.1: Types of Index Number

A. Price Index

For measuring the value of money, in general, price index is used. It is an index number which compares the prices for a group of commodities at a certain time as at a place with prices of a base period. There are two price index numbers such as whole sale price index numbers and retail price index numbers. The wholesale price index reveals the changes into general price level of a country, but the retail price index reveals the changes in the retail price of commodities such as consumption of goods, bank deposits, etc.

B. Quantity Index

Quantity index number is the changes in the volume of goods produced, purchased or consumed. They are useful and helpful to study the output in an economy.

Like the indices of agricultural production, industrial production, imports and exports etc. They are extremely helpful in studying the level of physical output in an economy, during a given period compared with any other period.

C. Value Index

Value index numbers compare the total value of a certain period with total value in the base period. Here total value is equal to the price of commodity multiplied by the quantity consumed.

Notation and Terminology used in Index Number

For any index number, two time periods are needed for comparison. These are called the ***Base period*** and the ***Current period***. The period of the year which is used as a basis for comparison is called the base year and the other is the current year. The various notations used are as given below:

Notation	
	p_1 = Price of current year,
	p_0 = Price of base year,
	q_1 = Quantity of current year,
	q_0 = Quantity of base year,
	P_{01} = Price Index Number for the current year w.r.t the base year,
	P_{10} = Price Index Number for the base year w.r.t the current year,
	Q_{01} = Quantity Index Number for the current year w.r.t the base year,
	Q_{10} = Quantity Index Number for the base year w.r.t. the current year.

9.7 PROBLEMS IN THE CONSTRUCTION OF INDEX NUMBERS

No index number is an all purpose index number. Hence, there are many problems involved in the construction of index numbers, which are to be tackled by an economist or statistician. They are

1. Purpose of the index numbers
2. Selection of base period
3. Selection of items
4. Selection of source of data
5. Collection of data
6. Selection of average
7. System of weighting

9.8 METHOD OF CONSTRUCTION OF INDEX NUMBERS

Index numbers may be constructed by various methods as shown below:

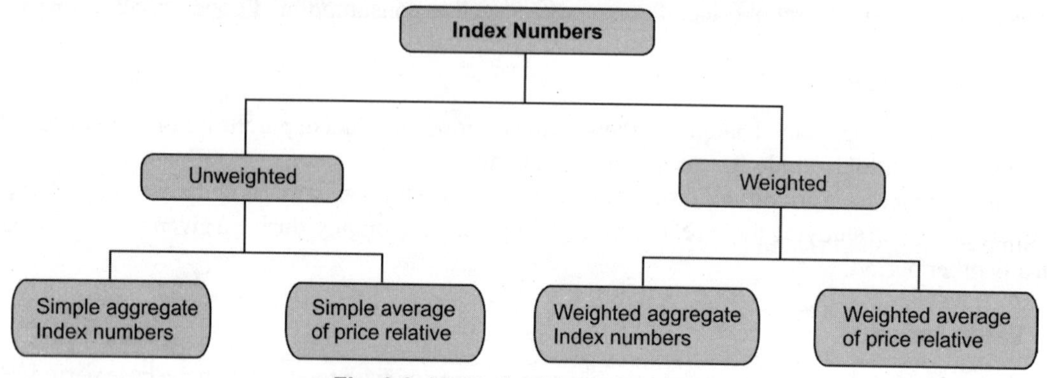

Fig. 9.2: Methods of Index Numbers

9.9 UN-WEIGHTED INDEX NUMBERS

In unweighted index numbers each item is supposed to have the same weight. Unweight index numbers can be further divided in two categories on the basis of construction techniques as follows:

A. Simple Aggregate Index Number

This is the simplest method of construction of index numbers. The prices of the different commodities of the current year are added and the sum is divided by the sum of the prices of those commodities by 100. Symbolically, Simple aggregate price index

$$P_{01} = \frac{\Sigma p_1}{\Sigma P_0} \times 100$$

Where,

ΣP_{01} = Index number of the current year

Σp_1 = Total prices for the current year

ΣP_0 = Total prices for the base year

The following example will illustrate the application of the above rules.

EXAMPLE 9.1: Calculate index numbers from the following data by simple aggregate method taking prices of 2000 as base.

Commodity	Price per unit (in Rupees)	
	2000	2004
A	80	95
B	50	60
C	90	100
D	30	45

Solution:

Commodity	Price per unit (in Rupees)	
	2000 (P_0)	2004 (P_1)
A	80	95
B	50	60
C	90	100
D	30	45
Total	**250**	**300**

$$\text{Simple aggregate Price index} = P_{01} = \frac{\Sigma p_1}{\Sigma p_0} \times 100$$

$$= \frac{300}{250} \times 100 = 120.$$

Limitations of the Aggregative Method

This method, though simple, has the following limitations:

1. The prices of various commodities may be quoted in different units, e.g., cereals may be quoted in Rs Per quintal, liquids like milk, petrol, kerosene may be quoted in Rs Per litre; cloth may be quoted in Rs Per metre and so on. Thus the index is influenced very much by the units in which commodities are quoted and accordingly some of the commodities may get more importance because they are quoted in a particular unit.
2. In this method the various commodities are weighted according to the magnitudes of their prices and accordingly commodities which are highly priced exert a greater influence on the value of the index than the commodities which are low priced.
3. The relative importance in use of various commodities is not taken into consideration.

B. Simple Average Price Relative Index

In this method, first calculate the price relative for the various commodities and then average of these relative is obtained by using arithmetic mean and geometric mean. When arithmetic mean is used for average of price relative, the formula for computing the index is

(a) Using Arithmetic Mean

Simple average of price relative by arithmetic mean

$$P_{01} = \frac{\Sigma\left(\frac{p_1}{p_0} \times 100\right)}{n}$$

Where,

p_1 = Prices of current year
p_0 = Prices of base year
n = Number of items or commodities

(b) Using Geometric Mean

When geometric mean is used for average of price relative, the formula for obtaining the index is Simple average of price relative by geometric Mean

$$P_{01} = \text{Antilog}\left(\frac{\Sigma \log \frac{P_1}{P_0} \times 100}{n}\right)$$

The following example will illustrate the application of the above rules.

EXAMPLE 9.2: From the following data, construct an index for 1998 taking 1997 as base by the average of price relative using (a) arithmetic mean and (b) Geometric mean

Commodity	Price in 1997	Price in 1998
A	50	70
B	40	60
C	80	100
D	20	30

Solution:

(a) Price relative index number using Arithmetic Mean

Commodity	Price in 1997(p_0)	Price in 1998(p_1)	$\frac{p_1}{p_0} \times 100$
A	50	70	140
B	40	60	150
C	80	100	125
D	20	30	150
			Total = 565

Simple average of price relative index =

$$P_{01} = \frac{\Sigma\left(\frac{p_1}{p_0} \times 100\right)}{n} = \frac{565}{4} = 141.25$$

(b) Price Relative Index Number using Geometric Mean

Commodity	Price in 1997(p_0)	Price in 1998(p_1)	$\frac{p_1}{p_0} \times 100$	$\log\left(\frac{p_1}{p_0} \times 100\right)$
A	50	70	140	2.1461
B	40	60	150	2.1761
C	80	100	125	2.0969
D	20	30	150	2.1761
		Total	**565**	**8.5952**

Simple average of price Relative index =

$$P_{01} = \text{Antilog}\ \frac{\Sigma \log\left(\frac{p_1}{p_0} \times 100\right)}{n} = \text{Antilog}\ \frac{8.5952}{4}$$

$$= \text{Antilog}\ [2.1488] = 140.9.$$

It should be noted that since arithmetic mean gives greater weightage to bigger items the index which uses arithmetic mean would be higher than the index using geometric mean.

Limitations of the Average of Relatives Method

Limitation of this method is the choice of the average to be used. As already discussed, G.M, though difficult to compute, is theoretically a better average as A.M. However, because of the computational ease, A.M is used in practice. Some economists, notably F.Y. Edgeworth advocated the use of harmonic mean for averaging the price relatives but it did not find favour with others and is not in use.

The main limitations of the method are:

(i) Since it is an unweighted average the importance of all items is assumed to be the same.
(ii) The index constructed by this method does not satisfy all the criteria laid down for an ideal index.

Advantages over the simple Aggregative Method

The method has three advantages over the simple aggregative method. They are:

(i) It is not affected by the units in which prices are quoted. It is also not affected by absolute values of prices as prices are converted into price relatives.
(ii) It gives equal importance to all items and extreme items do not unduly affect the index number.
(iii) The index number calculated by the method satisfies the unit test.*

9.10 WEIGHT INDEX NUMBER

The unweighted index numbers discussed so far are not unweighted in the true sense of the term. They assign equal importance to all the items included in the index and so such they are in reality weighted, weights being implicit rather than explicit. As discussed earlier, in case of unweighted indices it is possible to get different results by changing the importance of different items by quoting prices relative to different units, implicit weighting is far from realistic in most of the cases. Construction of useful index numbers requires a conscious effort to assign to each commodity a weight in accordance with its importance in the total phenomenon that the index is supposed to describe.

Weight index number can be further divided in two categories on the basis of construction techniques as follows:

A. Weighted Aggregate Index Numbers

In order to attribute appropriate importance to each of the items used in an aggregate index number some reasonable weights must be used. There are various methods of assigning weights and consequently a large number of formulae for constructing index numbers have been devised of which some of the most important ones are

1. **Laspeyre's method**
2. **Paasche's method**
3. **Fisher's ideal method**
4. **Bowley's method**
5. **Marshall-Edgeworth method**
6. **Kelly's method**

* Discuss later in this chapter.

1. Laspeyre's Method

The method is named after a German economist ***Etienne Laspeyres*** who formulated it in 1871. The Laspeyre's price index is a weighted aggregate price index, where the weights are determined by quantities in the base period and is given by

$$\text{Laspeyre's price index} = P_{01}^{\ L} = \frac{\Sigma p_1 q_0}{\Sigma p_0 q_0} \times 100$$

It is necessary to bear in mind that without having a constant weight or quantity the clear effect of change in price will not be reflected in the price index because the quantity demanded is likely to be affected in the two periods by a change in price. The constant weight helps in excluding the effect of price elasticity of demand.

2. Paasche's Method

The Paasche's price index is a weighted aggregate price index in which the weights are determined by the quantities in the current year. The formulae for constructing the index is

$$\text{Paasche's price index number} = P_{01}^{\ P} = \frac{\Sigma p_1 q_1}{\Sigma p_0 q_1} \times 100$$

The steps in the construction of an index number by this method are the same as those used in Laspeyre's method with only charge that instead of base year's weights, the weights of the current year are used. The main drawback in Paasche's method is that every time an index number is constructed weights have to be determined. This is a tedious and expensive task. Hence this method even though scientific is not in popular use.

Laspeyre's Vs Paasche's Method

Laspeyre's method has an advantage over Paasche's method because in the former weights are constant while in the latter weights have to be determined every time an index number is constructed which is a cumbersome task.

Laspeyre	Paasche
1. Compares cost of buying base year quantities at current year prices with base year prices.	1. Compares cost of buying current year quantities at current year prices with year prices.
2. Assumes that if prices had risen would still purchase same base year. (Overestimates inflation)	2. Assumes that if prices had risen would have bought same quantities as in current year. (Underestimates inflation)
3. Easy to calculate as weights fixed.	3. Difficult, expensive and time consuming to keep re-calculating weights.
4. Same basket of goods so are directly comparable.	4. Difficult to make comparisons as different years changes in index reflect both changes in price and weights.

3. Fisher's Ideal Method

Fisher's Price index number is the geometric mean of the Laspeyre's and Paasche's indices.

Symbolically

$$\text{Fisher's ideal index number} = P_{01}^{F} = \sqrt{L \times P} = \sqrt{\frac{\Sigma p_1 q_0}{\Sigma p_0 q_0} \times \frac{\Sigma p_1 q_1}{\Sigma p_0 q_1}} \times 100$$

Merits and Demerits of Fisher's Method

Merits

The formula is known as "Ideal" due to the following reasons:

1. ***It is free from bias***, since the upward bias of Laspeyres' index number is balanced to a great extent by the downward bias of Passche's index number.
2. ***It is based on the geometric mean***, theoretically which is considered to be the best average for constructing index numbers.
3. ***It conforms to certain tests of consistency*** which we will discuss later.
4. This formula takes into account the influence of the ***current year as well as the base year***.

Demerits

1. The ideal index number is a hybrid of two index numbers. It is difficult to say what exactly it is supposed to measure.
2. The ideal index number requires the quantities of both the base and the current year. The determination of these quantities is a difficult task, involving a lot of labour, expense and time. Index numbers which involve shifting weights fail to give a truly comparable picture.

4. Bowley's Method

To take into account the influence of both the base as well as current periods, Bowley suggested the arithmetic average of the Laspeyre's and Paasche's indices.

$$\text{Bowley's price index number} = P_{01}^{B} = \frac{L+P}{2} = \frac{1}{2}\left[\frac{\Sigma p_1 q_0}{\Sigma p_0 q_0} + \frac{\Sigma p_1 q_1}{\Sigma p_0 q_1}\right] \times 100$$

5. Marshall-Edgeworth Method

In this method also both current year as well as base year prices and quantities are considered. The formula for constructing the index is Marshall Edgeworth price index

$$\text{Marshall-Edgeworth index number} = P_{01}^{ME} = \frac{\Sigma(q_0 + q_1)p_1}{\Sigma(q_0 + q_1)p_0} \times 100 = \frac{\Sigma p_1 q_0 + \Sigma p_1 q_1}{\Sigma p_0 q_0 + \Sigma p_0 q_1} \times 100$$

NOTE: It may be remarked that both Fisher's Ideal Index and Marshall-Edgeworth Index lie between Laspeyre's and Paasche's indices.

This formula also suffers from the same defect, as the Fisher's ideal formula and Paasche's formula as it also needs current weights every time an index number is constructed.

6. Kelly's Method

Kelly has suggested the following formula for constructing the index number

$$\text{Kelly's price index number} = P_{01}{}^{k} = \frac{\Sigma p_1 q}{\Sigma p_0 q} \times 100$$

Where, $q = \dfrac{q_0 + q_1}{2}$

Here the average of the quantities of two years is used as weights. The following examples will illustrate the application of the above rules.

EXAMPLE 9.3: Construct price index number from the following data by applying

1. Laspeyre's method
2. Paasche's method
3. Fisher's ideal method

Commodity	2000		2001	
	Price	Qty	Price	Qty
A	2	8	4	5
B	5	12	6	10
C	4	15	5	12
D	2	18	4	20

Solution:

Commodity	p_0	q_0	p_1	q_1	p_0q_0	p_0q_1	p_1q_0	p_1q_1
A	2	8	4	5	16	10	32	20
B	5	12	6	10	60	50	72	60
C	4	15	5	12	60	48	75	60
D	2	18	4	20	36	40	72	80
					172	**148**	**151**	**220**

$$\textbf{Laspeyre's price index} = P_{01}{}^{L} = \frac{\Sigma p_1 q_0}{\Sigma p_0 q_0} \times 100 = \frac{251}{172} \times 100 = 145.93$$

$$\textbf{Paasche's price index number} = P_{01}{}^{P} = \frac{\Sigma p_1 q_1}{\Sigma p_0 q_1} \times 100 = \frac{220}{148} \times 100 = 148.7$$

$$\textbf{Fisher's ideal index number} = \sqrt{L \times P} = \sqrt{(145.9) \times (148.7)}$$

$$= \sqrt{21695.33} = 147.3$$

OR

$$\textbf{Fisher's ideal index number} = \sqrt{\frac{\Sigma p_1 q_0}{\Sigma p_0 q_0} \times \frac{\Sigma p_1 q_1}{\Sigma p_0 q_1}} \times 100$$

$$= \sqrt{\frac{251}{172} \times \frac{220}{148}} \times 100 = \sqrt{(1.459) \times (1.487)} \times 100$$

$$= \sqrt{2.170} \times 100 = 1.473 \times 100 = 147.3.$$

Interpretation: The results can be interpreted as follows:

If 100 rupees were used in the base year to buy the given commodities, we have to use Rs 145.90 in the current year to buy the same amount of the commodities as per the Laspeyre's formula. Other values give similar meaning.

EXAMPLE 9.4: Calculate the index number from the following data by applying (a) Bowley's price index (b) Marshall-Edgeworth price index.

Commodity	Base year		Current year	
	Quantity	Price	Quantity	Price
A	10	3	8	4
B	20	15	15	20
C	2	25	3	30

Solution:

Commodity	p_0	q_0	p_1	q_1	p_0q_0	p_0q_1	p_1q_0	p_1q_1
A	10	3	8	4	30	24	40	32
B	20	15	15	20	300	225	400	300
C	2	25	3	30	50	75	60	90
					380	**324**	**500**	**422**

(a) **Bowley's price index number** $= \frac{1}{2}\left[\frac{\Sigma p_1q_0}{\Sigma p_0q_0}+\frac{\Sigma p_1q_1}{\Sigma p_0q_1}\right]\times 100 = \frac{1}{2}\left[\frac{500}{380}+\frac{422}{324}\right]\times 100$

$$= \frac{1}{2}[1.316+1.302]\times 100$$

$$= \frac{1}{2}[2.168]\times 100 = 1.309 \times 100 = 130.9$$

(b) **Marshall Edgeworths price index Number** $= P_{01}^{ME} = \frac{\Sigma(q_0+q_1)p_1}{\Sigma(q_0+q_1)p_0}\times 100$

$$= \left[\frac{500}{380}+\frac{422}{324}\right]\times 100 = \left[\frac{922}{704}\right]\times 100 = 131.0$$

EXAMPLE 9.5: Calculate a suitable price index from the following data

Commodity	Quantity	Price	
		1995	1997
A	20	2	4
B	15	5	6
C	8	3	2

Solution: Here the quantities are given in common we can use Kelly's index price number and is given by Kelly's Price index number =

$$P_{01}^{k} = \frac{\Sigma p_1 q}{\Sigma p_0 q}\times 100$$

Commodity	q	p_0	p_1	p_0q	p_1q
A	20	2	4	40	80
B	15	5	6	75	90
C	8	3	2	24	16
			Total	139	186

$$\text{Kelly's price index number} = P_{01}^{\ k} = \frac{\Sigma p_1 q}{\Sigma p_0 q} \times 100 = \frac{186}{139} \times 100 = 133.81$$

EXAMPLE 9.6: Compute Laspeyre's, Paasche's and Fisher's price index number for 2005. Using the following data concerning three commodities:

Commodity	2004		2005	
	Price (Rs)	Quantity (kg)	Price (Rs)	Quantity (kg)
A	15	15	22	12
B	20	5	27	4
C	4	10	7	5

Solution:

Calculation of Various Indices

Commodity	p_0	q_0	p_1	q_1	p_1q_0	p_0q_0	p_1q_1	p_0q_1
A	15	15	22	12	330	225	264	180
B	20	5	27	4	135	100	108	80
C	4	10	7	5	70	40	35	20
					535	365	407	280

Laspeyre's Index: $p_{01} = \dfrac{\Sigma p_1 q_1}{\Sigma p_0 q_0} \times 100$

$$= \frac{535}{365} \times 100 = 146.58$$

Paasche's Index: $p_{01} = \dfrac{\Sigma p_1 q_1}{\Sigma p_0 q_1} \times 100$

$$= \frac{407}{280} \times 100 = 145.36$$

Fisher's Index: $\sqrt{L \times p} = \sqrt{146.58 \times 145.36} = 145.97.$

EXAMPLE 9.7: Calculate the index from the following data using Fisher's Ideal formula:

Commodity	2004		2005	
	Price (Rs)	Quantity (kg)	Price (Rs)	Quantity (kg)
A	10	50	12	60
B	8	30	9	32
C	5	35	7	40

Solution:

Calculation of Fisher's Ideal Index

Commodity	p_0	q_0	p_1	q_1	p_0q_0	p_1q_0	p_0q_1	p_1q_1
A	10	50	12	60	500	600	600	720
B	8	30	9	32	240	270	256	288
C	5	35	7	40	175	245	200	280
					915	**1,115**	**1,056**	**1,288**

Using Fisher's ideal index formula,

$$P_{01} = \sqrt{\frac{\Sigma p_1q_0}{\Sigma p_0q_0} \times \frac{\Sigma p_1q_1}{\Sigma p_0q_1}} \times 100 = \sqrt{\frac{1115}{915} \times \frac{1288}{1056}} \times 100$$

$$= \sqrt{1.4863} \times 100 = 1.219 \times 100 = 121.91$$

B. Weighted Average of Price Relative Index

When the specific weights are given for each commodity, the weighted index number is calculated by the formula.

$$\text{Weighted Average of Price Relative index} = \frac{\Sigma Pw}{\Sigma w}$$

or

$$p_{01} = \frac{\Sigma\left(\frac{p_1}{p_0} \times 100\right) w}{\Sigma w}$$

Where, w = the weight of the commodity

p = the price relative index

$= \frac{p_1}{p_0} \times 100$

When the base year value p_0q_0 is taken as the weight i.e. $w = p_0q_0$ then the formula is

$$\text{Weighted Average of Price Relative index} = \frac{\Sigma\left(\frac{p_1}{p_0} \times 100\right) \times p_0q_0}{\Sigma p_0q_0} = \frac{\Sigma p_1q_0}{\Sigma p_0q_0} \times 100$$

This is nothing but Laspeyre's formula.

When the weights are taken as $w = p_0q_1$, the formula is

$$\text{Weighted Average of Price Relative index} = \frac{\Sigma\left(\frac{p_1}{p_0} \times 100\right) \times p_0q_1}{\Sigma p_0q_1} = \frac{\Sigma p_1q_1}{\Sigma p_0q_1} \times 100$$

This is nothing but Paasche's formula.

The following examples would illustrate the application of the above formula.

EXAMPLE 9.8: Compute the weighted index number for the following data.

Commodity	Price		Weight
	Current Year	Base Year	
A	5	4	60
B	3	2	50
C	2	1	30

Solution:

Commodity	p_1	p_0	w	$p = \frac{p_1}{p_0} \times 100$	pw
A	5	4	60	125	7500
B	3	2	50	150	7500
C	2	1	30	200	6000
			140		**21000**

$$\text{Weighted average of price relative index} = \frac{\Sigma pw}{\Sigma w} = \frac{21000}{140} = 150$$

Merits of Weighted Average of Price Relatives Method

The following are the advantages of weighted average of relative indices over weighted aggregative indices.

(i) When different index numbers are constructed by the average of price relatives method, all of which have the same base, they can be combined to form a new index.

(ii) The price or quantity relatives for each single item in the aggregate are, in effect, themselves a simple index that often yields valuable information for analysis.

(iii) When a new commodity is introduced to replace the one formerly used, the relative for the new item may be spliced to the relative for the old one, using the former value weights.

9.11 QUANTITY OR VOLUME INDEX NUMBER

Price index numbers measure and permit comparison of the price of certain goods. On the other hand, the quantity index numbers measure the physical volume of production, employment and etc. The most common type of the quantity index is that of quantity produced.

Thus if a quantity index number is prepared by using:

1. Laspeyre's quantity index number

$$Q_{01}^{L} = \frac{\Sigma q_1 p_0}{\Sigma q_0 p_0} \times 100$$

2. Paasche's quantity index number

$$Q_{01}^{P} = \frac{\Sigma q_1 p_1}{\Sigma q_0 p_1} \times 100$$

3. Fisher's quantity index number

$$Q_{01}^F = \sqrt{L \times P} = \sqrt{\frac{\Sigma q_1 p_0}{\Sigma q_0 p_0} \times \frac{\Sigma q_1 p_1}{\Sigma q_0 p_1}} \times 100$$

These formulae represent the quantity index in which quantities of the different commodities are weighted by their prices. The following examples would illustrate the computation of quality index numbers.

EXAMPLE 9.9: From the following data compute quantity indices by (i) Laspeyre's method, (ii) Paasche's method and (iii) Fisher's method.

Commodity	2000		2002	
	Price	Total value	Price	Total value
A	10	100	12	180
B	12	240	15	450
C	15	225	17	340

Solution:

Here instead of quantity, total values are given. Hence first find quantities of base year and current year, i.e. Quantity = total value price

Commodity	p_0	q_0	p_1	q_1	p_0q_0	p_0q_1	p_1q_0	p_1q_1
A	10	10	12	15	100	150	120	180
B	12	20	15	30	240	360	300	450
C	15	15	17	20	225	30	255	340
					565	**810**	**675**	**970**

$$\text{Laspeyre's quantity index number} = Q_{01}{}^L = \frac{\Sigma q_1 p_0}{\Sigma q_0 p_0} \times 100 = \frac{810}{565} \times 100 = 143.4$$

$$\text{Paasche's quantity index number} = Q_{01}{}^P = \frac{\Sigma q_1 p_1}{\Sigma q_0 p_1} \times 100 = \frac{970}{675} \times 100 = 143.7$$

$$\text{Fisher's quantity index number} = Q_{01}{}^F = \sqrt{L \times P}$$

OR

$$Q_{01}{}^F = \sqrt{\frac{\Sigma q_1 p_0}{\Sigma q_0 p_0} \times \frac{\Sigma q_1 p_1}{\Sigma q_0 p_1}} \times 100$$

$$= \sqrt{\frac{810}{565} \times \frac{970}{675}} \times 100 = \sqrt{1.434 \times 1.437} \times 100$$

$$= 1.436 \times 100 = 143.6$$

9.12 VALUE INDEX NUMBERS

The value index numbers are very easy to calculate. Value is the product of price and quantity. A simple value ratio is equal to the value of the current year divided by the value of the base year. If this ratio is multiplied by 100 we get the value index number.

Thus a value index number.

$$V = \frac{\Sigma p_1 q_1}{\Sigma p_0 q_0} \times 100$$

Where V is the value index, Number if the values are given directly then the value index number or

$$V = \frac{\Sigma \upsilon_1}{\Sigma \upsilon_0}$$

Such index numbers are not weighted because they take account both the price and quantity. These index numbers are however not very popular, because the situation revealed by price and quantities are not fully revealed by the values.

9.13 TESTS OF CONSISTENCY OF INDEX NUMBERS

From statistical point of view, the system of calculation of index numbers should be such that it satisfies certain mathematical tests.

Several formulae have been studied for the construction of index number. The question arises as to which formula is appropriate to a given problem. A number of tests have been developed and the important among these are:

1. Unit test
2. Time Reversal test
3. Factor Reversal test
4. Circular or Cyclical Test

A brief discussion on each of these tests is given below:

Unit Test

The unit test requires that the formula for constructing an index should be independent of the units in which prices and quantities are quoted. Except for the simple aggregate index (unweighted), all other formulae discussed in this chapter satisfy this test.

Time Reversal Test

Time Reversal test is a test to determine whether a given method will work both ways in time, forward and backward.

This criterion stipulates that if the base and current years are interchanged, the Index number so formed is the reciprocal of the index formed with the original base and current year. In other words, this test stipulates that if the time subscripts of a price index formula are interchanged to form another index number, the product of the new formula with the original formula should be equal to 1.

In the words of ***Fisher***, "the formula for calculating the index number should be such that it gives the same ratio between one point of comparison and the other, no matter which of the two is taken as base".

Symbolically, the following relation should be satisfied.

$$P_{01} \times P_{10} = 1$$

Where P_{01} is the index for time '1' as time '0' as base and P_{01} is the index for time '0' as time '1' as base. If the product is not unity, there is said to be a time bias is the method.

Fisher's ideal index satisfies the time reversal test.

$$P_{01} = \sqrt{\frac{\Sigma p_1 q_0}{\Sigma p_0 q_0} \times \frac{\Sigma p_1 q_1}{\Sigma p_0 q_1}}$$

$$P_{10} = \sqrt{\frac{\Sigma p_0 q_1}{\Sigma p_1 q_1} \times \frac{\Sigma p_0 q_0}{\Sigma p_1 q_0}}$$

Then $$P_{01} \times P_{10} = \sqrt{\frac{\Sigma p_1 q_0}{\Sigma p_0 q_0} \times \frac{\Sigma p_1 q_1}{\Sigma p_0 q_1} \times \frac{\Sigma p_0 q_1}{\Sigma p_1 q_1} \times \frac{\Sigma p_0 q_0}{\Sigma p_1 q_0}} = \sqrt{1} = 1$$

Therefore Fisher ideal index satisfies the time reversal test.

This test is not satisfied by Laspeyres Index and by Paasche's Index. The methods which satisfy the time reversal test are:

- Fisher's Ideal Formula
- Simple Geometric Mean of Price Relatives
- Aggregatives with Fixed Weights
- Marshall Edgeworth Method
- Weighted Geometric Mean of price relatives if fixed weighted are used.

Factor Reversal Test

Another test suggested by Fisher is known as factor reversal test. It holds that the product of a price index and the quantity index should be equal to the corresponding value index.

In the words of ***Fisher***, "Just as each formula should permit the interchange of the two times without giving inconsistent results, so it ought to permit interchanging the prices and quantities without giving inconsistent result, i e, the two results multiplied together should give the true value ratio.

In other words, if P_{01} represent the changes in price in the current year and Q_{01} represent the changes in quantity in the current year, then

$$P_{01} \times Q_{01} = \frac{\Sigma p_1 q_1}{\Sigma p_0 q_0}$$

Thus based on this test, if the product is not equal to the value ratio, there is an error in one or both of the index number.

The Factor reversal test is satisfied by the Fisher's ideal index.

i.e. $$P_{01} = \sqrt{\frac{\Sigma p_1 q_0}{\Sigma p_0 q_0} \times \frac{\Sigma p_1 q_1}{\Sigma p_0 q_1}}$$

$$Q_{01} = \sqrt{\frac{\Sigma q_1 p_0}{\Sigma q_0 p_0} \times \frac{\Sigma q_1 p_1}{\Sigma q_0 p_1}}$$

Then $$P_{01} \times Q_{01} = \sqrt{\frac{\Sigma p_1 q_0}{\Sigma p_0 q_0} \times \frac{\Sigma p_1 q_1}{\Sigma p_0 q_1} \times \frac{\Sigma q_1 p_0}{\Sigma q_0 p_0} \times \frac{\Sigma q_1 p_1}{\Sigma q_0 p_1}} = \sqrt{\left(\frac{\Sigma p_1 q_1}{\Sigma p_0 q_0}\right)^2} = \frac{\Sigma p_1 q_1}{\Sigma p_0 q_0}$$

$$\text{Since } P_{01} \times Q_{01} = \frac{\Sigma p_1 q_1}{\Sigma p_0 q_0}$$

The factor reversal test is satisfied by the Fisher's ideal index.

Circular Test

Another test applied in index number studies in the circular test. It is a sort of extension of the time reversal test. Suppose an index number is constructed for the year 2005 with base of 2004 and another index number for 2004 on the base of 2003, then it should be possible for us to directly get an index number for 2005 on the base of 2003.

If the index number calculated directly does not give an inconsistent value, the circular test is said to be satisfied.

If P_{01} represents the price change of the current year on the base year and P_{12} the price change of the base year on some other base and P_{20} the price change of the current year on this second base then the following equation should be satisfied:

$$\boxed{P_{01} \times P_{12} \times P_{20} = 1}$$

This test is not fulfilled by most of the common formulae used in the construction of index numbers. Even Fisher's ideal formula does not satisfy this test. This test is fulfilled by unweighted or fixed weighted aggregative or by index numbers which use simple geometric mean.

The following example is a numerical illustration of calculation of Laspeyre's, Paasche's and Fisher's index numbers as also testing the adequacy of Fisher's index number for Time Reversal and Factor Reversal tests.

EXAMPLE 9.10: Show that Laspeyre's Index and Paasche's Index do not satisfy the Time Reversal Test.

Solution:

In Laspeyre's Index.

$$P_{01} = \frac{\Sigma p_1 q_0}{\Sigma p_0 q_0} \text{ and } P_{10} = \frac{\Sigma p_0 q_1}{\Sigma p_1 q_1}$$

$$P_{01} \times P_{10} = \frac{\Sigma p_1 q_0}{\Sigma p_0 q_0} \times \frac{\Sigma p_0 q_1}{\Sigma p_1 q_1} \neq 1$$

Hence Time Reversal Test is not satisfied. In Paasche's Index

$$P_{01} = \frac{\Sigma p_1 q_1}{\Sigma p_0 q_1} \text{ and } P_{10} = \frac{\Sigma p_0 q_0}{\Sigma p_1 q_0}$$

$$P_{01} \times P_{10} = \frac{\Sigma p_1 q_1}{\Sigma p_0 q_1} \times \frac{\Sigma p_0 q_0}{\Sigma p_1 q_0} \neq 1$$

Hence Time Reversal Test is not satisfied.

EXAMPLE 9.11: Show that:

(i) Simple Aggregative index numbers
(ii) Marshall-Edgeworth index number

Satisfy the Time Reversal Test.

Solution:

(i) In Simple Aggregative Method (without the factor 100)

$$P_{01} = \frac{\Sigma p_1}{\Sigma p_0} \text{ and } P_{10} = \frac{\Sigma p_0}{\Sigma p_1}$$

$$P_{01} \times P_{10} = \frac{\Sigma p_1}{\Sigma p_0} \times \frac{\Sigma p_0}{\Sigma p_1} = 1$$

Hence Time Reversal Test is satisfied.

(ii) In Marshall-Edgeworth Index Number

$$P_{10} = \frac{\Sigma p(q_0 + q_1)}{\Sigma p_0(q_0 + q_1)} \text{ and } P_{10} = \frac{\Sigma p(q_1 + q_0)}{\Sigma p_1(q_1 + q_0)}$$

$$P_{01} \times P_{10} = \frac{\Sigma p_1(q_0 + q_1)}{\Sigma p_0(q_0 + q_1)} \times \frac{\Sigma p_0(q_1 + q_0)}{\Sigma p_1(q_1 + q_0)} = 1$$

Hence Time Reversal Test is satisfied.

EXAMPLE 9.12: Calculate Fisher's Ideal Number from the data given below and show that it satisfies Time Reversal Test.

Commodity	1979		1980	
	Price	Quantity	Price	Quantity
A	10	49	12	50
B	12	25	15	20
C	18	10	20	12
D	20	5	40	2

Solution:

Calculation of Fisher's Ideal Index

Commodity	1979		1980					
	p_0	q_0	p_1	q_1	p_1q_0	p_0q_0	p_1q_1	p_0q_1
A	10	49	12	50	588	490	600	500
B	12	25	15	20	375	300	300	240
C	18	10	20	12	200	180	240	216
D	20	5	40	2	200	100	80	40
					1363	**1070**	**1220**	**996**

$$\text{Fishers Index } P_{01} = \sqrt{\frac{\Sigma p_1 q_0}{\Sigma p_o q_0} \times \frac{\Sigma p_1 q_1}{\Sigma p_0 q_1}} \times 100$$

$$= \sqrt{\frac{1363}{1070} \times \frac{1220}{996}} \times 100 = 124.9$$

Time Reversal Test is satisfied if

$$P_{01} \times P_{10} = 1$$

$$P_{10} = \sqrt{\frac{\Sigma p_0 q_1}{\Sigma p_1 q_1} \times \frac{\Sigma p_0 q_0}{\Sigma p_1 q_0}}$$

$$P_{01} \times P_{10} = \sqrt{\frac{\Sigma p_1 q_0}{\Sigma p_0 q_0} \times \frac{\Sigma p_1 q_1}{\Sigma p_0 q_1} \times \frac{\Sigma p_0 q_1}{\Sigma p_1 q_1} \times \frac{\Sigma p_0 q_0}{\Sigma p_1 q_0}}$$

$$= \sqrt{\frac{1363}{1070} \times \frac{1220}{996} \times \frac{996}{1220} \times \frac{1070}{1363}} = \sqrt{1} = 1$$

Hence Time Reversal Test is satisfied.

EXAMPLE 9.13: Show that the Laspeyre's and Paasche's index numbers do not satisfy the Factor Reversal test.

Solution:

For Laspeyre's Index Numbers:

It is defined as

$$\frac{\Sigma p_1 q_0}{\Sigma p_0 q_0}$$

Intercharing the factors p and q with each other, it becomes

$$\frac{\Sigma q_1 p_o}{\Sigma q_0 p_0}$$

which is a quantity index number. Multiplying this number with the original price index number, we have,

$$\frac{\Sigma q_1 p_o}{\Sigma q_0 p_0} \times \frac{\Sigma p_1 q_0}{\Sigma p_0 q_0}$$

The square root of this product is $= \sqrt{\dfrac{(\Sigma p_1 q_0)\,(\Sigma q_1 p_0)}{\Sigma p_0 q_0}}$

which is not equal to $\dfrac{\Sigma p_1 q_1}{\Sigma p_0 q_0}$

Thus the factor reversal criterion is not satisfied by the Laspeyre's Index number.

For Paasche's Index Number:

It is defined as $\dfrac{\Sigma p_1 q_1}{\Sigma p_0 q_1}$

Interchanging the factors p and q with each other, it becomes

$$\frac{\Sigma q_1 p_1}{\Sigma q_0 p_1}$$

which is a quantity index number. Multiplying this number with the original price index number, we have

$$\frac{\Sigma q_1 p_1}{\Sigma q_0 p_1} \times \frac{\Sigma p_1 q_1}{\Sigma p_0 q_1}$$

The square root of this product is = $\dfrac{\Sigma q_1 p_1}{\sqrt{\Sigma(p_1 q_0)(\Sigma q_1 p_0)}}$

which is not equal to $\dfrac{\Sigma p_1 q_1}{\Sigma p_0 q_0}$

Thus the factor reversal criterion is not satisfied by the Paasche's Index Number.

EXAMPLE 9.14: Construct Fisher's ideal index for the Following data. Test whether it satisfies time reversal test and factor reversal test.

Commodity	Base Year		Current Year	
	Quantity	Price	Quantity	Price
A	12	10	15	12
B	15	7	20	5
C	5	5	8	9

Solution:

Commodity	q_0	p_0	q_1	p_1	p_0q_0	p_0q_1	p_1q_0	p_1q_1
A	12	10	15	12	120	150	144	180
B	15	7	20	5	105	140	75	100
C	5	5	8	9	25	40	45	72
					250	**330**	**264**	**352**

Fisher ideal index number

$$P_{01}^{F} = \sqrt{\frac{\Sigma p_1 q_0}{\Sigma p_0 q_0} \times \frac{\Sigma p_1 q_1}{\Sigma p_0 q_1}} \times 100$$

$$= \sqrt{\frac{264}{250} \times \frac{352}{330}} \times 100$$

$$= \sqrt{(1.056) \times (1.067)} \times 100 = 1.062 \times 100 = 106.2.$$

Time Reversal Test

Time Reversal test is satisfied when $P_{01} \times P_{10} = 1$

$$P_{01} = \sqrt{\frac{\Sigma p_1 q_0}{\Sigma p_0 q_0} \times \frac{\Sigma p_1 q_1}{\Sigma p_0 q_1}} = \sqrt{\frac{264}{250} \times \frac{352}{330}}$$

$$P_{10} = \sqrt{\frac{\Sigma p_0 q_1}{\Sigma p_1 q_1} \times \frac{\Sigma p_0 q_0}{\Sigma p_1 q_0}} = \sqrt{\frac{\Sigma p_1 q_0}{\Sigma p_0 q_0} \times \frac{\Sigma p_1 q_1}{\Sigma p_0 q_1}}$$

Now $$P_{01} \times P_{10} = \sqrt{\frac{264}{250} \times \frac{352}{330} \times \frac{330}{352} \times \frac{250}{264}} = \sqrt{1} = 1.$$

Hence Fisher ideal index satisfy the time reversal test.

Factor Reversal Test

Factor Reversal test is satisfied when

$$P_{01} \times Q_{01} = \frac{\Sigma p_1 q_1}{\Sigma p_0 q_0}$$

Now $$P_{01} = \sqrt{\frac{\Sigma p_1 q_0}{\Sigma p_0 q_0} \times \frac{\Sigma p_1 q_1}{\Sigma p_0 q_1}} = \sqrt{\frac{264}{250} \times \frac{352}{330}}$$

$$Q_{01} = \sqrt{\frac{\Sigma q_1 p_0}{\Sigma q_0 p_0} \times \frac{\Sigma q_1 p_1}{\Sigma q_0 p_1}} = \sqrt{\frac{330}{250} \times \frac{352}{264}}$$

Then $$P_{01} \times Q_{01} = \sqrt{\frac{264}{250} \times \frac{352}{330} \times \frac{330}{250} \times \frac{352}{264}} = \sqrt{\left(\frac{352}{250}\right)^2}$$

$$= \frac{352}{250} = \frac{\Sigma p_1 q_1}{\Sigma p_0 q_0}$$

Hence Fisher ideal index number satisfies the factor reversal test.

9.14 CHAIN INDEX NUMBERS

The various formulae discussed for the construction of index numbers are based on the fixed base method and they reflect changes in the level of a phenomenon in any period called current period with its changes in some particular fixed year called the base year.

Fixed base indices, though simple to construct have their limitations, some of which are outlined below:

(i) Due to the dynamic pace of events these days, there may be a considerable change in the tastes, customer, fashion, etc, of the society and consequently in the consumption pattern of the people. Hence, if the base year is quite distant from the current year, the comparisons on the basis of fixed base indices may be unrealistic unreliable and may even be misleading.

(ii) Because of the inherent changes in the consumption patterns of the people due to time lag, the relative importance of the various commodities in the two period may change considerably, thus, necessitating a revision in the original weights.

Keeping these limitations in mind, it was felt that the data for the two periods being compared should be as homogeneous as possible and this is best attained by taking two adjacent periods. In chain index numbers there is no fixed base. A chain base index number is an index number with previous year as base. This means that for the index of 2008 the base would be 2007 and for the index of 2007 the base would be 2006.

Such index numbers are very useful in comparing current year figures with the preceding year's figures. Fixed, base index in such case does not give an appropriate comparison, since all prices are tied to the base year which may be remote or for away from the current year of the preceding year.

The figures for each year are first expressed as percentages of the figures for the preceding year. These percentages are then chained together by successive multiplication to form a chain index.

$$\text{Chain index for current year} = \frac{\text{Link Relative of current year} \times \text{Chain index of previous year}}{100}$$

NOTE: The figure of a particular year expressed as a percentage of the preceding year's figure is called link relative.

The chain index numbers are useful for long term comparison whereas link relatives are used to have a comparison with the immediately preceding year. The fixed base index numbers compiled from the original data and the chain index numbers compiled from link relatives give the same value of the index provided there is only one commodity.

Chain base index for 2008 with 2000 as base is give by

$$p_{2000,\,2008} = p_{2000,\,2001},\ p_{2001,\,2002} \cdots\cdots p_{2007,\,2008}$$

Conversion of Chain Base Index into Fixed Base Index

A chain base index number can be converted into a fixed base index number by the following rule.

$$\text{Current Years Fixed Base Index} = \frac{\text{Current years C.B.I} \times \text{Previous Years F.B.I}}{100}$$

where,

F.B.I = Fixed Base Index
C.B.I = Chain Base Index

Conversion of Fixed Base Index into Chain Base Index

A fixed base index can be converted into a chain base index by the following rule. For the first year the value would be 100.

$$\text{Chain Base Index} = \frac{\text{Current Years F.B.I} \times 100}{\text{previous Years F.B.I}}$$

Remarks:

Obviously, the techniques of computing the index number by the 'fixed base' and the 'chain base' methods are different the former (F.B.I) using the original (raw) data while the letter (U.B.I) using the link Relatives.

If there is only one series of observations, i.e., if we re given the prices (quantities) of only one commodity (item) for different years, then the fixed base indices and the chain base indices will always be same.

Hence, in such a case we should always use the fixed base method since it requires much less calculations as compared with chain base method.

However, if there are more than two series, then the chain base indices and fixed base indices would usually be different except for the first two years, for which they will always be equal.

EXAMPLE 9.15: Compute the chain index numbers with 2000 prices as base, from the following table giving the average wholesale prices of the commodities *A, B* and *C* for the years 2000 to 21004.

	Average Wholesale Price (Rs)				
Commodity	**2000**	**2001**	**2002**	**2003**	**2004**
A	20	16	28	35	21
B	25	30	24	36	45
C	20	25	30	24	30

Solution:

	Relatives based on preceding year				
Commodity	**2000**	**2001**	**2002**	**2003**	**2004**
A	100	$\frac{16}{20} \times 100 = 80$	$\frac{28}{16} \times 100 = 175$	$\frac{35}{28} \times 100 = 125$	$\frac{21}{35} \times 100 = 60$
B	100	$\frac{30}{25} \times 100 = 120$	$\frac{24}{30} \times 100 = 80$	$\frac{36}{24} \times 100 = 150$	$\frac{45}{36} \times 100 = 125$
C	100	$\frac{25}{36} \times 100 = 125$	$\frac{30}{25} \times 100 = 120$	$\frac{24}{30} \times 100 = 80$	$\frac{30}{24} \times 100 = 125$
Average of link relatives	300	325	375	355	310
Average of relatives	100	108.33	125	118.33	103.33
Chain index	100	$\frac{108.33 \times 100}{100}$ = 108.33	$\frac{125 \times 108.33}{100}$ = 135.41	$\frac{118.33 \times 135.41}{100}$ = 60.23	$\frac{103.33 \times 160.23}{100}$ = 165.57

EXAMPLE 9.16: From the chain base index numbers given below. Find fixed base index numbers:

Year	1995	1996	1997	1998	1999
Chain Base Index	80	40	120	90	140

Solution: The formula for converting Chain Base Index Number to Fixed Base Index Numbers is

$$\text{Current year } F.B.I = \frac{\text{Current years C.B.I} \times \text{Previous year F.B.I}}{100}$$

The first F.B.I. would always be the same as the Chain Base Index Number

	Conversion of FBI to CBI	
Year	**Chain Base Index**	**Fixed Base Index**
1995	80	80
1996	110	$\frac{110 \times 80}{100} = 88$
1997	120	$\frac{120 \times 88}{100} = 105.60$
1998	90	$\frac{90 \times 105.6}{100} = 95.04$
1999	140	$\frac{140 \times 95.04}{100} = 133.06$

EXAMPLE 9.17: Convert the fixed base index numbers derived in the last example. i.e., Example 9.16 into Chain Base Index Numbers.

Solution: The formula for conversion of Fixed Base Index Numbers to Chain Base Index Number is

$$\text{Current Year's C.B.I} = \frac{\text{Current year's F.B.I} \times 100}{\text{Previous Year's F.B.I}}$$

Conversion of F.B.I to C.B.I

Year	Fixed Base Index	Chain Base Index
1995	80	80
1996	88	$\frac{88}{80} \times 100 = 110$
1997	105.6	$\frac{105.6}{88} \times 100 = 120$
1998	95.04	$\frac{95.0}{105.6} \times 100 = 90$
1999	133.06	$\frac{133.06}{95.05} \times 100 = 140$

Thus we have obtained the values of the Chain Base Index from the Fixed Index.

Uses and Limitations of Chain Base Index Numbers

Uses

In the chain base method the comparison are made with the immediate past (preceding year) and accordingly the data (for the two periods being compared) are relatively homogeneous. The comparisons are, therefore, more valid and meaningful and the resulting index is more representative of the current trends in the tastes, habits, customs and fashions of the society. Hence, the chain base indices are specially useful to a businessman who is basically interested in comparison between the values of a phenomenon of two consecutive periods rather than the values of the phenomenon at any period with its value in some distant fixed base period.

In the chain base method, new commodities or items may be deleted without impairing comparability and without requiring the recalculation of the entire series of index numbers, which is necessary in case of fixed base and method.

Limitations

The chain indices are relatively tedious and time consuming to calculate as compared with fixed base indices. They are suitable only for short range comparisons and the long range comparisons of the chain indices are not really valid. It is very difficult to understand the significance of these indices, and give physical interpretations to them.

9.15 BASE SHIFTING OF INDEX NUMBERS

Base shifting means the changing of the given base period (Year) of a series of index numbers and recasting them into a new series based on some recent new base period.

For example, one may have consumer price indices from 1961 onwards with base year as 1960 right up to 2003. But, one way line to have the series with base as 2000 i.e the beginning of the 21 century to have a better comprehension of the changes in prices during 21 century. Such change of reference base year is referred to as "Base" shifting and is usually done for three purpose:

(i) The existing base year is very old and, therefore, might have lost its relevance.

(ii) If we want to compare series of index numbers with different base periods, to make quick and valid comparisons both the series must be expressed with a common base period.

Base shifting requires the recomputation of the entire series of the index numbers with the new base. However, this is a very difficult and time consuming job. A relatively much simple, though approximate method consists in taking the index number of the new base year as 100 and then expressing the given series of index numbers as a percentage of the index number of the time period selected as the new base year. Thus, the series of index numbers, recast with a new base is obtained by the formula:

$$\text{New Index of any Year} = \frac{\text{Old Index of the year}}{\text{Index Number of the new base}} \times 100$$

$$= \left(\frac{100}{\text{Index of the New Base}}\right) \times (\text{Old Index of the year})$$

In other words of the new index numbers are obtained by multiplying the old indices with a common factor which is 100 divided by the index of the new base. The following examples would illustrate the technique of base shifting.

EXAMPLE 9.18: The following are the index number of prices (Base 1961 = 100)

Year	1970	1971	1972	1973	1974	1975	1976	1977
Index Numbers	140	200	210	230	250	260	280	300

Shift the base from 1961 to 1971.

Solution: The common factor by which these indices should be multiplied is

$$\frac{100}{\text{The Index of the New Base}} \text{ or } \frac{100}{200}$$

The result would be the index on the new base of 1971.

Shifting of the Base from 1961 to 1971

Year	Old Index (1961 = 100)	New Index (1971 = 100)	Year	Old Index (1961 = 100)	New Index (1971 = 100)
1970	140	$\frac{100}{200} \times 140 = 70$	1971	200	 100
1972	210	$\frac{100}{200} \times 210 = 105$	1973	230	$\frac{100}{200} \times 230 = 115$
1974	250	$\frac{100}{200} \times 250 = 125$	1975	260	$\frac{100}{200} \times 260 = 130$
1976	280	$\frac{100}{200} \times 280 = 140$	1977	300	$\frac{100}{200} \times 300 = 150$

EXAMPLE 9.19: An index is at 100 in 1961. It rises 4% in 1962, falls 6% in 1963, falls 4% in 1964 and rises 3% in 1965. Calculate the index number for 5 years with 1963 as the base.

Solution: First we will have to calculate the index at the old base of 1961 and the construct the new series with 1963 as the base. This is done in the following table:

Index Number with the new base of 1963

Year	Old Index (1961 = 100)	New Index (1963 = 100)
1961	100	$\frac{100}{97.76} \times 100 = 102.32$
1962	100 + 4 = 104	$\frac{100}{97.76} \times 104 = 106.40$
1963	$\frac{94}{100} \times 104 = 97.76$	100.00
1964	$\frac{96}{100} \times 97.76 = 93.85$	$\frac{100}{97.76} \times 93.85 = 96.00$
1965	$\frac{103}{100} \times 93.85 = 96.66$	$\frac{100}{97.76} \times 96.66 = 98.88$

9.16 SPLICING OF INDEX NUMBERS

By splicing of index numbers we mean combining two or more series of over lapping index numbers to obtain a single index number on a common base. This is done by the same technique as used in base shifting splicing of index numbers can be done only if the index numbers are constructed with the same items, and have an overlapping year.

For example, following arc two series of consumer price index numbers for various years. The first one has base year as 1960 and the second has base year as 1994-95.

Year	Consumer Price Index
1990–91	369
1991–92	413
1992–93	446
1993–94	492
	[Base Year 1960 = 100]

Year	Consumer Price Index
1993–94	92
1994–95	100
1995–96	107
1996–87	115
1997–98	126
	[Base Year 1994–95]

For splicing or interlinking the two series, we note that for the year 1993–94, the index is 492 with base year as 1960, and 92 with base year as 1993–94. Thus the indices 1994–95 to 1997–98 can be derived by multiplying each of these index numbers by the factor 492/92 i.e. 5.348. Doing so, the required indices with base year 1960 are obtained as follows:

1994–95 = 100 × 5.348 = 535

1995–96 = 107 × 5.348 = 572

1996–97 = 115 × 5.348 = 615

1997–98 = 126 × 5.348 = 674

Similarly, the indices for the years 1990–91 to 1992–93 with base year as 1994–95 = 100, can be derived by multiplying each of the index by 92/492 = 0.187. Thus, the required indices are:

1990–91 = 369 × 0.187 = 69.0

1991–92 = 413 × 0.187 = 77.2

1992–93 = 446 × 0.187 = 83.4

Splicing is generally done when an old index number with an old base is being discontinued and a new index with a new base is being started. To have continuity of comparison the new index number is spliced to the old index number in the over lapping year. Splicing can be the other way round also when the old index is spliced to the new index. In splicing of index numbers we find a common factor by which the spliced index number series is multiplied to give a common base.

NOTE: Splicing like base shifting will give accurate result if the index numbers use simple geometric mean on if they use fixed weights and thus satisfy the circular test.

The following examples would illustrate the technique of splicing.

EXAMPLE 9.20: A price index number series was started in 1967 as base. By 1971 it rose by 25%. The link relative for relative for 1972 was 95. In this year a new series was started. This new series rose by 15 points by next year. But during next four years the rise was not rapid. During 1977 the price level was only 5% higher than 1975 and in 1975 they were 8% higher than 1973. Splice the two series and calculate the index numbers for the various years shifting the base to 1973.

Solution:

Splicing of the Index Numbers

Year	Index No (1967 = 100)	Index No (1972 = 100)	Old Index Spliced to new one (1972 = 100)
1967	100		$\frac{100}{118.75} \times 100 = 84.21$
1971	125		$\frac{100}{118.75} \times 125 = 105.26$
1972	$\left(\frac{95}{100} \times 125\right) = 118.75$	100	100
1973		115	115
1975		$\left(\frac{115 \times 108}{100}\right) = 124.2$	124.2
1977		$\left(\frac{124.2 \times 105}{100}\right) = 130.41$	130.41

Base Shifting to 1973			
Year	Index Number	Year	Index Number
1967	$\frac{100}{115} \times 84.21 = 73.23$	1971	$\frac{100}{115} \times 105.26 = 91.53$
1972	$\frac{100}{115} \times 100 = 86.96$	1973	$\frac{100}{115} \times 115 = 100.00$
1975	$\frac{100}{115} \times 124.2 = 108.00$	1977	$\frac{100}{115} \times 130.41 = 113.40$

EXAMPLE 9.21: Splice the following two index number series, continuing series *A* forward and series *B* backwards.

Year	1968	1969	1970	1971	1972	1973
Series *A*	100	120	150			
Series *B*			100	110	120	150

Solution:

Splicing of Two Index numbers				
Year	Series *A*	Series *B*	Series *B* Spliced to *A*	Series *A* Spliced to *B*
1968	100			$\frac{100}{150} \times 100 = 66.6$
1969	120			$\frac{100}{150} \times 120 = 80.00$
1970	150	100	$\frac{150}{100} \times 100 = 150$	$\frac{100}{150} \times 150 = 100.00$
1971		110	$\frac{150}{100} \times 110 = 165$	
1972		120	$\frac{150}{100} \times 120 = 180$	
1973		150	$\frac{150}{100} \times 150 = 225$	

EXAMPLE 9.22: In 1960 an index with a base of 1950 had the following values:

Year	1950	1955	1960
Index	100	120	200

In 1961 the index was reconstructed with a base of the year 1960. The values of the index were

Year	1960	1965
Index	100	150

In 1966 the index was reconstructed again on a base of 1965. The values of this index were

Year	1965	1970	1975
Index	100	120	150

Obtain a continuous series with the base of 1965 by splicing the three series.

Solution:

Splicing of Three Index Number Series

Year	First Series Base 1950	Second Series Base 1960	Third Series Base 1965
1950	100	$\frac{100}{200} \times 100 = 50$	$\frac{100}{150} \times 50 = 33.33$
1955	120	$\frac{100}{200} \times 120 = 60$	$\frac{100}{150} \times 60 = 40.00$
1960	200	$\frac{100}{200} \times 200 = 100$	$\frac{100}{150} \times 100 = 66.67$
1965		150	100.00
1970			120.00
1975			150.00

In the above problem the first series is spliced to the second one.

For this the multiplying factor is $\frac{100}{200}$.

After this the second series (spliced) is spliced to the third series (Base 1965). Here the multiplying factor is $\frac{100}{150}$.

9.17 DEFLATING OF INDEX NUMBERS

Deflating means adjusting, correcting or reducing a value which is inflated. Hence, by deflating of the price index numbers we mean adjusting them after having allowance for the effect of changing price levels. This is particularly desirable in the case of an economy which has inflationary trends because in such an economy, the increase in the prices of commodities or items over a period of years means a fall in their real incomes (which is defined as the purchasing power of money), accordingly a rise in their money income or nominal income may not amount to a rise in their real income.

Thus, it becomes necessary to adjust or correct nominal wages in accordance with the rise in the corresponding price index to arrive at the real income.

The purchasing power is given by the reciprocal of the index number and consequently the real income (or wages) is obtained on dividing the money or nominal income by the corresponding appropriate price index and multiplying the result by 100.

Symbolically,

$$\text{Real Wages} = \frac{\text{Money or Nominal wages}}{\text{Price Index}} \times 100$$

The real income is also known as deflated income.

This technique is extensively used to deflate value series or value indices, rupee sales, inventories, incomes, wages and so on.

The following examples would clarify the process of deflating index numbers.

EXAMPLE 9.23: The annual wages (in Rs) of workers are given along with Consumer Price Indices. Find (i) the real wages and (ii) the real wage indices.

Year	1980	1981	1982	1983
Wages	1800	2200	3400	3600
Consumer Price Indices	100	170	300	320

Solution:

Construction of Real Wage Indices				
Year	Wages (Rs)	Price Index	Real Wages	Real Wage Indices 1980 = 100
1980	1800	100	$\frac{1800}{100} \times 100 = 1800$	100
1981	2200	170	$\frac{2200}{170} \times 100 = 1294.1$	$\frac{1294.1}{1800} \times 100 = 71.89$
1982	3400	300	$\frac{3400}{300} \times 100 = 1133.3$	$\frac{1333.3}{1800} \times 100 = 62.96$
1983	3600	320	$\frac{3600}{320} \times 100 = 1125.00$	$\frac{1125}{1800} \times 100 = 62.50$

EXAMPLE 9.24: The employees of the Australian Steel Ltd have presented the following data in support of their contention that they are entitled to a wage adjustment. Dollar amounts shown represent the average weekly take home pay of the group. **[B.Com., Punjab University, 1978]**

Year	1973	1974	1975	1976
Pay	$ 260.50	$ 260.80	$ 274.0	$ 282.50
Index	126.8	129.5	136.2	141.2

(a) Compute the real wages based on the take home pay and the price indices given

(b) Compute the amount of pay needed in 1976 to provide buying power equal to that employed in 1973.

Solution:

(a)

Computation of Real Wages			
Year (i)	Pay (in dollars) (ii)	Price Index (iii)	Real Wages $\frac{\text{Col (ii)}}{\text{Col (iii)}} \times 100$ (iv)
1973	260.50	126.8	$\frac{260.50}{126.8} \times 100 = 205.44$
1974	263.80	129.5	$\frac{263.80}{129.5} \times 100 = 203.71$
1975	274.00	136.2	$\frac{274.00}{136.2} \times 100 = 201.17$
1976	282.50	141.2	$\frac{282.50}{141.2} \times 100 = 200.07$

(b) In order that the employees have the same buying power in 1976 as they had in 1973 the pay in 1976 should be

$$\frac{260.50}{126.8} \times 141.2 = 290.08 \text{ dollars}$$

EXAMPLE 9.25: The consumer price index for a group of workers was 250 in 1994 with 1980 as the base.

(i) Compute the purchasing power of a rupee in 1994 compared to 1980.
(ii) At what value of consumer price index would the purchasing power of a rupee by 25 paise?

Solution:

(i) Purchasing power (pp) of a rupee in 1994 with respect to the base period 1980 is given by:

$$\text{Purchasing Power of rupee} = \frac{100}{\text{Consumer price index for 1994 (base 1980)}} \qquad ...(1)$$

$$= \frac{100}{250} = 0.40$$

This implies that if a person was spending 0.40 (i.e. 40 paise) to buy a certain basket of goods in 1980s, in 1994 he has to spend 1 Rs to buy the same basket of goods.

(ii) If we want the purchasing power of a rupee to be 0.25 Rs in 1994, then from eq (i), we get

$$\text{Consumer price index for 1994 with respect to base 1980} = \frac{100}{\text{pp of rupee}} = \frac{100}{0.25} = 400$$

9.18 CONSUMER PRICE INDEX (COST OF LIVING INDEX)

Consumer Price index is also called the ***cost of living index***. It represents the average change over time in the prices paid by the ultimate consumer of a specified basket of goods and services. A change in the price level affects the costs of living of different classes of people differently. The general index number fails to reveal this. So there is the need to construct consumer price index. People consume different types of commodities. People's consumption habit is also different from man to man, place to place and class to class i.e richer class, middle class and poor class. The scope of consumer price is necessary, to specify the population group covered. ***For example***, working class, poor class, middle class, richer class, etc and the geographical areas must be covered as urban, rural, town, city etc.

DO YOU KNOW?

Cost of living index numbers are constructed to study the effect of changes in the prices of a basket of goods and services on the purchasing power of a particular class of people during current period as compared with some base period.

Change in the cost of living of an individual between two periods means the change in his money income which will be necessary for him to maintain the same standard of living in both periods. Thus the cost of living index numbers are intended to measure the average increase in the cost of maintaining the same standard in a given year as in the base year.

Use of Cost of Living Index

The consumer price indices are of great significance and are given below.

1. This is very useful in wage negotiations, wage contracts and dearness allowance adjustment in many countries.
2. At government level, the index numbers are used for wage policy, price policy, rent control, taxation and general economic policies.
3. Change in the purchasing power of money and real income can be measured.
4. Index numbers are also used for analysing market price for particular kinds of goods and services.
5. Cost of living index numbers indicate whether the real wages are rising or falling, money wages remaining unchanged. In other words they are used for the calculation of real wages and for determining the change in the purchasing power of the money.

$$\text{Purchasing Power of Money} = \frac{1}{\text{Cost of living Index Number}}$$

$$\text{Real Wages} = \frac{\text{Money Wages}}{\text{Cost of Living Index}} \times 100$$

6. These indices are also used for deflation of income and value series in national accounts.
7. Cost of living indices are used for the regulation of dearness allowance or the grant of bonus to the workers so as to enable them to meet the increased cost of living.

Steps in the Construction of Cost of Living Index Number

The following are the steps in the construction of cost of living index numbers.

1. **Scope and Coverage:** Select the class of people (low income, high income, labour class, industrial worker, agricultural worker, etc). For whom the index is desired. In addition to the class of people, the geographical area such as rural area, urban area, city or town, or a locality of a town etc, should also be clearly defined.
2. **Family Budget Enquiry:** After step (1), the next step is to conduct a sample family budget enquiry. This is done by selections a sample of adequate number of representative families from the class of people for whom the index is designed. The enquiry should be conducted in a normal period of economic stability. The objective of the enquiry is to find out the expenses which an average family incurs of different items of consumption. The enquiry furnishes the information on the following points:

   (a). The nature, quality and quantity of the commodities by given class of people. The commodities are broadly classified into the following five major groups.

   (i) Food (ii) Clothing (iii) Fuel and Lighting
   (iv) House Rent (v) Miscellaneous

   Each of these major groups is further sub-divided into smaller groups termed as sub-groups.

   (b) The retail prices of different commodities selected for the index. The price quotations for the selected commodities should be obtained from 'local markets' where the class of people reside or from super bazar, fair price shops or cooperative stores or departmental stores from where they usually do their shopping.

Method of Constructing Consumer Price Index

There are two methods of constructing consumer price index. They are

1. Aggregate Expenditure method (or) Aggregate method.
2. Family Budget method (or) Method of Weighted Relative method.

1. Aggregate Expenditure Method

This method is based upon the Laspeyre's method. It is widely used. The quantities of commodities consumed by a particular group in the base year are the weight.

$$\text{Consumer Price Index number} = \frac{\Sigma p_1 q_0}{\Sigma p_0 q_0} \times 100$$

$$= \frac{\text{Total Expenditure in current year}}{\text{Total Expenditure in base year}} \times 100$$

2. Family Budget Method or Method of Weighted Relatives

This method is estimated an aggregate expenditure of an average family on various items and it is weighted.

$$\text{Consumer Price index number} = \frac{\Sigma pw}{\Sigma w}$$

Where $P = \frac{p_1}{p_0} \times 100$ for each item w = value weight (i.e.) $p_0 q_0$

"Weighted average price relative method" which we have studied before and "Family Budget method" are the same for finding out consumer price index.

EXAMPLE 9.26: Construct the consumer price index number for 1996 on the basis of 1993 from the following data using Aggregate expenditure method.

Commodity	Quantity Consumed	Price in	
		1993	1996
A	100	8	12
B	25	6	7
C	10	5	8
D	20	15	18

Solution:

Commodity	q_0	p_0	q_1	$p_0 q_0$	$p_1 q_0$
A	100	8	12	800	1200
B	25	6	7	150	175
C	10	5	8	50	80
D	20	15	18	300	360
			Total	1300	1815

Consumer price index by Aggregate expenditure method

$$= \frac{\Sigma p_1 q_0}{\Sigma p_0 q_0} \times 100$$

$$= \frac{1815}{1300} \times 100$$

EXAMPLE 9.27: Calculate consumer price index by using Family Budget method for year 1993 with 1990 as base year from the following data.

Items	Weights	Price in	
		1990 (Rs)	1993 (Rs)
Food	35	150	140
Rent	20	75	90
Clothing	10	25	30
Fuel and lighting	15	50	60
Miscellaneous	20	60	80

Solution:

Items	W	p_0	p_1	$P = \frac{p_1}{p_0} \times 100$	PW
Food	35	150	140	93.33	3266.55
Rent	20	75	90	120.00	2400.00
Clothing	10	25	30	120.00	1200.00
Fuel and lighting	15	50	60	120.00	1800.00
Miscellaneous	20	60	80	133.33	2666.60
	100				**11333.15**

$$\text{Consumer Price Index} = \frac{\Sigma pw}{\Sigma w} = \frac{11333.15}{100} = 113.33$$

Uses of Cost of Living Numbers

1. Cost of living index numbers are used to determine the purchasing power of money and for computing the real wages from the nominal or money wages. We have

$$\text{Purchasing Power of Money} = \frac{1}{\text{Cost of Living Index Number}}$$

$$\text{Real wages} = \frac{\text{Money Wages}}{\text{Cost of Living Index}} \times 100$$

Thus, cost of living index number enables us to find if the real wages are rising or falling, the money wages remaining unchanged.

2. Cost of living indices are used for deflating income and value series in national accounts
3. Cost of living index numbers are used widely in wage negotiations and wage contracts. ***For example***, they are used for automatic adjustment of wages under 'Escalator clause' in collective bargaining agreements. Escalator clause provides for certain point automatic increase in the wages corresponding to a unit increase in the consumer price index.

MISCELLANEOUS SOLVED EXAMPLES

EXAMPLE 9.28: Construct the cost of living index number from the following group data:

Group	Weights	Group Index No.
Food	47	247
Fuel and Lighting	7	293
Clothing	8	289
House Rent	13	100
Misc.	14	236

Solution: **[MBA, Vikram University, 1994]**

Calculation of Cost of Living Index

Group	Weights (*W*)	Group Index (*I*)	*IW*
Food	47	247	11609
Fuel and Lighting	7	293	2051
Clothing	8	289	2312
House Rent	13	100	1300
Misc.	14	236	3304
	$\Sigma W = 89$		$\Sigma IW = 20576$

$$\text{Cost of living index} = \frac{\Sigma IW}{\Sigma W} = \frac{20576}{89} = 231.19$$

EXAMPLE 9.29: Compute a Price Index for the following by (a) simple aggregative method (b) average of price relatives method by using both arithmetic mean and geometric mean.

Commodity	*A*	*B*	*C*	*D*	*E*	*F*
Price in 1971 (Rs)	20	30	10	25	40	50
Price in 1981 (Rs)	25	30	15	35	45	55

Solution: **[M.Com., AMU, 2000]**

Calculation of Price Index

Commodity	p_0	p_1	$p = \frac{p_1}{p_0} \times 100$	Log *P*
A	20	25	125	2.0969
B	30	30	100	2.0000
C	10	15	150	2.1761
D	25	35	140	2.1461
E	40	45	112.5	2.0511
F	50	55	110	2.0414
Total	**175**	**205**	**737.5**	**12.5116**

(a) Simple aggregative Index $= \frac{\Sigma p_1}{\Sigma p_0} \times 100 = \frac{205}{175} \times 100 = 117.143$

(b) Arithmetic Mean of Price Relatives $= \frac{\Sigma P}{n} = \frac{737.5}{6} = 122.92$

(c) Geometric Mean of Price Relatives $= A.L.\left[\dfrac{\Sigma \log P}{n}\right]$

$$= A.L.\left(\frac{12/5116}{6}\right)$$

$$= A.L.\ 2.0853 = 121.7$$

EXAMPLE 9.30: Calculate index number of prices for 1995 on the basis of 1990 from the data given below:

Commodity	Weight	Price per unit 1990 (Rs)	Price per unit 1995 (Rs)
A	40	16	20
B	25	40	50
C	20	12	15
D	15	2	3

If the weights of commodities A, B, C, D are increased in the ratio 1 : 2 : 3 : 4, what will be increase in index number?

Solution:

Commodity	Weight (w)	Price of 1990 (p_0)	Price of 1995 (p_1)	$\frac{p_1}{p_0} \times 100$	Increased wt. (w)
A	40	16	20	$\frac{20}{16} \times 100 = 125$	44
B	25	40	50	$\frac{50}{40} \times 100 = 125$	30
C	20	12	15	$\frac{15}{12} \times 100 = 125$	26
D	15	2	3	$\frac{3}{2} \times 100 = 150$	21

Index number of price for 1995 on the basis of 1990:

$$= \frac{\Sigma\left(\frac{p_1}{p_0} \times 100\right)w}{\Sigma w}$$

$$= \frac{40 \times 125 + 25 \times 125 + 20 \times 125 + 15 \times 150}{40 + 25 + 20 + 15} = 128.75.$$

The weights of commodities A, B, C and D are increased in the ratio 1 : 2 : 3 : 4, i.e. new weights are:

$$40\left(1+\frac{1}{10}\right) = 44;\ 25\left(1+\frac{2}{10}\right) = 30;\ 20\left(1+\frac{30}{10}\right) = 26 \text{ and } 15\left(1+\frac{4}{10}\right) = 21.$$

$$\text{So the new index number is} = \frac{44 \times 125 + 30 \times 125 + 26 \times 125 + 21 \times 150}{44 + 30 + 26 + 21}$$

$$= \frac{5500 + 3750 + 3250 + 3150}{121}$$

$$= \frac{15650}{121} = 129.33$$

So increase in index number is 129.33 – 128.75 = 0.58%.

EXAMPLE 9.31: Using Fisher's form find price index number of the following data:

Commodity	Unit	Base Year Price	Base Year Total Value (Rs)	Current Year Quantity	Current Year Total Value (Rs)
A	kg.	12.5	125	12	156
B	kg.	14	112	9	135
C	metre	11	88	9	108
D	kg.	13	78	6	90

Solution: p_0, p_1 ⇒ Prices of base and current year;

q_0, q_1 ⇒ Quantity consumed of base and current year.

Commodity	Base Year p_0	Base Year q_0	Current Year p_1	Current Year q_1	p_0q_0	p_0q_1	p_1q_0	p_1q_1
A	12.5	10	13	12	125	150	130	156
B	14	8	15	9	112	126	120	135
C	11	8	12	9	88	99	96	108
D	13	6	15	6	78	78	90	90
					403	**453**	**436**	**489**

$$\text{Base year quantity} = \frac{\text{Total value for Base Year}}{\text{Price per unit in Base Year}}$$

$$\text{Current year price / unit} = \frac{\text{Total value for Current Year}}{\text{Quantity for Current Year}}$$

Hence, Price Index by Fisher's Method

$$= \sqrt{\frac{\Sigma p_1q_0}{\Sigma p_0q_0} \times \frac{\Sigma p_1q_1}{\Sigma p_0q_1}} \times 100 = \sqrt{\frac{436}{403} \times \frac{489}{453}} \times 100$$

$$= \sqrt{1.0819 \times 1.0795} \times 100 = \sqrt{1.1679} \times 100 = 108.07\%.$$

EXAMPLE 9.32: A company spent Rs 50, Rs 48, Rs 18 and Rs 42 during 1998. The company increased the expenditure to Rs 100, Rs 98, Rs 60 and Rs 102 during 1999 respectively on four commodities. If the units of four commodities purchased during 1998 and 1999 are identical i.e., 5, 2, 6 and 17, compute the price index for 1999 by the most suitable method.

Solution: Most suitable method here will be the method of weighted aggregate of prices.

∴ Price index for 1999 with 1998 as base

$$= \frac{\text{Sum of the prices in 1999}}{\text{Weighted sum of the prices in 1998}} \times 100$$

$$= \frac{100 + 98 + 60 + 102}{50 + 48 + 18 + 42}$$

$$= \frac{360}{158} \times 100 = 227.84$$

EXAMPLE 9.33: An enquiry into the budgets of middle class families in a village near Hyderabad gave the following information.

Expenses on :	**Food**	**Rent**	**Clothing**	**Education**	**Miscellaneous**
	30%	25%	15%	10%	20%
Price (Rs) 2004	1800	1000	700	400	700
Price (Rs) 2005	2000	1200	900	500	1000

Construct cost of living index and comment on the change in the cost of living in 2005 as compared to 2004.

Solution:

Construction of Living Index

Expenses on	**2004 (p_0)**	**2005 (p_1)**	$\frac{p_1}{p_0} \times 100$ **(p)**	***W***	***PW***
Food	1800	2000	111.11	30	3333.30
Rent	1000	200	120.00	25	3000.00
Clothing	700	900	128.57	15	1928.55
Education	400	500	125.00	10	1250.00
Misc.	700	1000	142.86	20	2857.20
				ΣW = 100	**Σ*PW* = 12369.05**

$$\text{Cost of Living Index (for 2004)} - \frac{\Sigma PW}{\Sigma W} = \frac{12369.05}{100} = 123.69$$

EXAMPLE 9.34: A textile worker in the city of Mumbai earns Rs 3,500 per month. The cost of living index for a particular month is given as 136. Using the following information, find out the amount of money he spent on house rent and clothing:

Group	**Expenditure**	**Group Index**
Food	1,400	180
Clothing	?	150
House Rent	?	100
Fuel and Lighting	560	110
Miscellaneous	630	80

Solution: Let the expenditure on clothing and house rent = Rs x and Rs y respectively.

Then $1400 + x + y + 560 + 630 = 3{,}500$

$$\Rightarrow \quad x + y = 3{,}500 - 1{,}400 - 560 - 630$$

$$\Rightarrow \quad x + y = 910$$

$$\Rightarrow \quad y = 910 - x$$

Then

$$136 = \frac{180 \times 1{,}400 + 150 \times x + 100(910 - x) + 110 \times 560 + 80 \times 630}{3{,}500}$$

As per the question

$$\frac{20 + 5x}{15} \times \frac{7}{10 + 2x} = \frac{28}{27}$$

$$\Rightarrow \quad \frac{4 + x}{10 + 2x} = \frac{4}{9}$$

$$\Rightarrow \quad 36 + 9x = 40 + 8x$$

$$\Rightarrow \quad x = 4$$

EXAMPLE 9.35: Construct the consumer price index number for 2000 on the basis of 1999 from the following data using:

(i) Family Budget method

(ii) Aggregative expenditure method.

Commodity	Rice	Wheat	Pulses	Ghee	Oil
Weights	40	20	15	20	5
Price (per unit) 1999 (Rs)	16.00	40.00	0.50	5.12	2.00
Price (per unit) 2000 (Rs)	20.00	60.00	0.50	6.25	1.50

Solution: (i)

Constructing Consumer Price Index Number (Family Budget Method)

Commodity	Weights (W)	Price (Rs) (per unit) 1999 (p_0)	Price (Rs) (per unit) 2000 (p_1)	Price Relative $\frac{p_1}{p_0} \times 100$ (I)	Weighted Relatives (IW)
Rice	40	16.00	20.00	125	5,000
Wheat	20	40.00	60.00	150	3,000
Pulses	15	0.50	0.50	100	1,500
Ghee	20	5.12	6.25	122	2,440
Oil	5	2.00	1.50	75	375
	$\Sigma W = 1000$				$\Sigma IW = 12{,}315$

$$\text{Cost of Living Index for 2000} = \frac{\Sigma IW}{\Sigma W} = \frac{12{,}315}{100} = 123.15$$

Thus, there is an increase of 23.15% in prices of 2000 with that of 1999.

(ii)

(Aggregative Expenditure Method)					
Commodity	**Weights (*W*)**	**Price (Rs) 1999**	**Price (Rs) 2000**		
	q_0	p_0	p_1	p_0q_0	p_1q_0
Rice	40	16.00	20.00	640.00	800.00
Wheat	20	40.00	60.00	800.00	1,200.00
Pulses	15	0.50	0.50	7.50	7.50
Ghee	20	5.12	6.25	102.40	125.00
Oil	5	2.00	1.50	10.00	7.50
				1,559.90	**2,140.00**

$$\text{Consumer Price Index for 2000} = \frac{\Sigma p_1 q_0}{\Sigma p_0 q_0} \times 100 = \frac{2,140}{1,559.9} \times 100 = 137.188$$

Thus, there is increase of 37.188 in prices of 2000 with that of 1999.

EXAMPLE 9.36: A company has three major items that it produces, say items A, B and C. The table below prices and units sold in each of three years, i.e., 1991, 1992, 1993. **[MBA, Osmania Univ., 2001]**

	1991		1992		1993	
Items	**Price**	**Qty.**	**Price**	**Qty.**	**Price**	**Qty.**
A	0.50	30	0.75	30	1.00	35
B	2.00	25	4.00	20	3.00	25
C	3.00	20	3.50	25	3.50	20

Use 1991 as the base and answer the following:

(a) The unweighted aggregate price index for 1993.
(b) The unweighted aggregate quantity index for 1993.
(c) The weighted aggregate index for 1993, using Laspeyre's Method to calculate weights.
(d) The weighted aggregate index for 1993, using Paasche's Method to calculate weights.
(e) The weighted average of relatives price index for 1993, using 1991 values as weights.
(f) The unweighted average for relatives quantity index for 1993.

Solution:

	1991		1993					
Items	**Price**	**Qty.**	**Price**	**Qty.**				
	p_0	q_0	p_1	q_1	$p_0\,q_0$	$p_1\,q_0$	$p_1\,q_1$	$p_0\,q_1$
A	0.50	30	1.00	35	15	30	35.00	17.50
B	2.00	25	3.00	25	50	75	75.00	50.00
C	3.00	20	3.50	20	60	70	70.00	60.00
	5.50	**75**	**7.50**	**80**	**125**	**175**	**180.00**	**127.50**

(a) Unweighted aggregate price index for 1993 $= \dfrac{7.50}{5.50} \times 100 = 136$

(b) Unweighted aggregate quantity index for 1993 $= \frac{80}{75} \times 100 = 107$

(c) Weighted aggregate index for 1993 using Laspeyre's Method

$$= \frac{\Sigma p_1 q_0}{\Sigma p_0 q_0} \times 100 = \frac{175}{125} \times 100 = 140$$

(d) Weighted aggregate index for 1993 using Paasche's Method

$$= \frac{\Sigma p_1 q_1}{\Sigma p_0 q_1} \times 100 = \frac{180}{127.50} \times 100 = 141$$

(e) Weighted average of relative price indexes for 1993 using 1991 values as weights

$$= \frac{\left[\Sigma \frac{p_1}{p_0} \times p_0 q_0\right] \times 100}{\Sigma p_0 q_0}$$

$$= \frac{\left[\frac{1.00}{0.50} \times 15 + \frac{3.00}{2.00} \times 50 + \frac{3.50}{3.00} \times 60\right] \times 100}{(15 + 50 + 60)}$$

$$= \frac{17.500}{125} \times 100 = 140$$

(f) Unweighted average for relative quantity indexes for 1993

$$= \frac{\Sigma \frac{q_1}{q_0}}{3} \times 100$$

$$= \frac{\left[\frac{35}{30} + \frac{25}{25} + \frac{20}{20}\right]}{3} \times 100 \frac{317}{3} = 106.$$

EXAMPLE 9.37: The following table gives the weekly wages (in Rs) of a worker and the general index number of prices during 1996-2004. Prepare the index number to show the changes in the real weekly wages of the worker.

Year	Weekly Wages (Rs)	Price Index No.
1996	360	100
1997	420	104
1998	500	115
1999	550	160
2000	600	280
2001	640	290
2002	680	300
2003	720	320
2004	750	330

Solution:

Index Number Showing Changes in the Real Weekly Wages to the Worker				
Year	**Weekly Wages (in Rs)**	**Price Index**	**Real Weekly Wages**	**Real Weekly Wages**
1996	360	100	$\frac{360}{100} \times 100 = 360.00$	100.00
1997	420	104	$\frac{420}{104} \times 100 = 403.85$	112.18
1998	500	115	$\frac{500}{115} \times 100 = 434.78$	120.77
1999	550	160	$\frac{550}{160} \times 100 = 343.75$	95.49
2000	600	280	$\frac{600}{280} \times 100 = 214.29$	59.53
2001	640	290	$\frac{640}{290} \times 100 = 220.69$	61.30
2002	680	300	$\frac{680}{300} \times 100 = 226.67$	62.96
2003	720	320	$\frac{720}{320} \times 100 = 225.00$	62.50
2004	750	330	$\frac{750}{330} \times 100 = 227.27$	63.13

EXAMPLE 9.38: Compute index number from the following data using Fisher's ideal index formula:

	Base Year		Current Year	
Commodity	**Qty.**	**Price**	**Qty.**	**Price**
A	12	10	15	12
B	15	7	20	5
C	24	5	20	9
D	5	16	5	14

Solution:

Calculation of Disher's Indeal Index								
Commodity	**Base year**		**Current year**					
	p_0	q_0	p_1	q_1	p_1q_0	p_0q_0	p_1q_1	p_0q_1
A	12	10	15	12	144	120	180	150
B	15	7	20	5	75	105	100	140
C	24	5	20	9	216	120	180	100
D	5	16	5	14	70	80	70	80
					505	**425**	**530**	**470**

$$p_{01} = \sqrt{\frac{\Sigma p_1 q_0}{\Sigma p_0 q_0} \times \frac{\Sigma p_1 q_1}{\Sigma p_0 q_1}} \times 100$$

$$= \sqrt{\frac{505}{425} \times \frac{530}{470}} \times 100$$

$$= \sqrt{1.1576} \times 100 = 115.76.$$

LIST OF FORMULAE

1. Price Relative $= p_{01} = \dfrac{p_1}{p_0} \times 100$

   Quantity Relative $= Q_{01} = \dfrac{q_1}{q_0} \times 100$

2. Unweighted Index Numbers:

   (a) simple Aggregate Price Index $= p_{01} = \dfrac{\Sigma p_1}{\Sigma p_0} \times 100$

   (b) simple Average of Price Relative

   (i) Using Arithmetic Mean $p_{01} = \dfrac{\Sigma\left(\dfrac{p_1}{p_0} \times 100\right)}{n}$

   (ii) Using Geometric Mean $p_{01} = \text{Antilog}\left(\dfrac{\Sigma \log \dfrac{p_1}{p_0} \times 100}{n}\right)$

3. Weighted Index Numbers:

   (a) Laspeyre's Price Index $= p_{01}^{L} = \dfrac{\Sigma p_1 q_0}{\Sigma p_0 q_0} \times 100$

   (b) Paaschae's Index Numbers $= p_{01}^{P} = \dfrac{\Sigma p_1 q_1}{\Sigma p_0 q_1} \times 100$

   (c) Fisher's Ideal Index $= p_{01}^{F} = \sqrt{L \times P} = \sqrt{\dfrac{\Sigma p_1 q_0}{\Sigma p_0 q_0} \times \dfrac{\Sigma p_1 q_1}{\Sigma p_0 q_1}} \times 100$

   (d) Bowley's Price Index $= p_{01}^{B} = \dfrac{L+P}{2} = \dfrac{1}{2}\left[\dfrac{\Sigma p_1 q_0}{\Sigma p_0 q_0} + \dfrac{\Sigma p_1 q_1}{\Sigma p_0 q_1}\right] \times 100$

   (e) Marshall-Edgeworth Index

$$p_{01}^{ME} = \frac{\Sigma(q_0 + q_1)p_1}{\Sigma(q_0 + q_1)p_0} \times 100 = \frac{\Sigma p_1 q_0 + \Sigma p_1 q_1}{\Sigma p_0 q_0 + \Sigma p_0 q_1} \times 100$$

(f) Kellys Price Index $= p_{01}^{K} = \dfrac{\Sigma p_1 q}{\Sigma p_0 q} \times 100$

where, $q = \dfrac{q_0 + q_1}{2}$

4. Weighted Average of Price Relatives:

$$\text{Weighted Average of Price Relatives} = p_{01} = \frac{\Sigma\left(\frac{p_1}{p_0} \times 100\right) w}{\Sigma w}$$

Weighted Average of Price Relatives (base year values as weights)

$$p_{01} = \frac{\Sigma\left(\frac{p_1}{p_0} \times 100\right) p_0 q_0}{\Sigma p_0 q_0} = \frac{\Sigma p_1 q_0}{\Sigma p_0 q_0} \times 100$$

Weighted Average of Price Relatives (current year values as weights)

$$p_{01} = \frac{\Sigma\left(\frac{p_1}{p_0} \times 100\right) p_1 q_1}{\Sigma p_1 q_1}$$

5. Quantity (Volume) Index Number:

(a) Laspeyre's Quantity Index Number

$$Q_{01}^{L} = \frac{\Sigma q_1 p_0}{\Sigma q_0 p_0} \times 100$$

(b) Paaschae's Quantity Index Number

$$Q_{01}^{P} = \frac{\Sigma q_1 p_1}{\Sigma q_0 p_1} \times 100$$

(c) Fisher's Quantity Index Number

$$Q_{01}^{F} = \sqrt{L \times P} = \sqrt{\frac{\Sigma q_1 p_0}{\Sigma q_0 p_0} \times \frac{\Sigma q_1 p_1}{\Sigma q_0 p_1}} \times 100$$

6. Chain Index for current year

$$= \frac{\text{Link Relative of current year} \times \text{Chain Index of previous year}}{100}$$

SELF PRACTICE EXERCISES

I. CHOOSE THE BEST ANSWER

1. Index number is a:

(a) Measure of relative changes
(b) A special type of an average
(c) A percentage relative
(d) All of the above

2. Most preferred type of average for index number is:
   (a) Arithmetic mean (b) Geometric mean
   (c) Harmonic mean (d) None of the above
3. Laspeyre's index formula uses the weights of the:
   (a) base year
   (b) current year
   (c) average of the weights of a number of years
   (d) none of the above
4. The geometric mean of Laspeyre's and Passche's price indices is also known as:
   (a) Fisher's price index (b) Kelly's price index
   (c) Marshall-Edgeworth index number (d) Bowley's price index
5. The condition for the time reversal test to hold good with usual notations is:
   (a) $P_{01} \times P_{10} = 1$ (b) $P_{10} \times P_{01} = 0$
   (c) $\frac{P_{01}}{P_{10}} = 1$ (d) $P_{01} + P_{10} = 1$
6. An appropriate method for working out consumer price index is:
   (a) weighted aggregate expenditure method
   (b) family budget method
   (c) price relative method
   (d) none of the above
7. The weights used in Passche's formula belong to:
   (a) The base period (b) The given period
   (c) To any arbitrary chosen period (d) None of the above
8. Index number provides a tool for comparing values of a variable over a period of time. The variable could be:
   (a) Price (b) Quantity
   (c) Value (d) Any one of the above
9. The base year should be selected such that the prices in that year are:
   (a) High (b) Low
   (c) Stable (d) Exceptional
10. If the reference of the base year of an index number is changed, it is referred to as:
    (a) Splicing (b) Base shifting
    (c) Linking (d) None of above

II. FILL IN THE BLANKS

1. Index numbers help in framing of ....
2. Fisher's ideal index number is the .... of Laspeyre's and Paasche's index numbers
3. Index numbers are expressed in ....
4. .... is known as Ideal index number.
5. In family budget method, the cost of living index number is ....
6. Index numbers are called .... of economic changes
7. The base period should always be ....

8. .... is the most, appropriate average for constructing the index.
9. Quantity index reflects .... changes from one period to another.
10. .... test is satisfied both by Fisher's and Kelly's formula.

III. SHORT ANSWER TYPE QUESTIONS

1. What is Index? **[MBA, Madurai-Kamraj, 2001]**
2. Laspeyre's price index generally shows an upward trend in the price changes while Paasche's method shows a downward trend on them elucidate the statement. **[MBA, DU, 1997, 2005]**
3. What is Fisher's index ? Why is it called ideal?
4. "Since the value of the base is always 100, it does not make any difference which period is selected as the base on which to construct an index." Comment.
5. Explain Time Reversal Test and Factor Reversal Test with the help of a suitable example. **[MBA, HPU, Osmania University, 1998]**
6. It is said that index numbers are a specialized type of averages. How far do you agree with this statement. Explain briefly time reversal and factor reversal tests. **[MBA, Osmania, 1998]**

IV. LONG ANSWER TYPE QUESTIONS

1. What are the uses of Index Numbers? What are the problems in their construction? **[MBA, Vikram University, 2002]**
2. What are the Fisher's Ideal Index? Why is it called ideal? Show that it satisfies both the time reversal test as well as the factor reversal test. **[MBA, HPU, 1998]**
3. Laspeyre's price index generally shows an upward trend in the price changes while Paasche's method shows a downward trend on them. Elucidate the statement. **[MBA, Delhi University, 1997]**
4. Explain Time Reversal Test and Factor Reversal Test with the help of a suitable example. **[MBA, HPU, MBA, Osmania University, 1998]**
5. What is an index number? What are the uses of index numbers?
6. Explain Time Reversal Test and Factor Reversal test.
7. What is meant by consumer price index number? What are its uses?
8. What is an index numbers? Explain its uses in industry. Examine the various problems involved in the construction of an index number of prices.
9. What is implied by "weighting" in the process of index number construction? Why is it necessary? What are the commonly proposed weighting schemes?
10. "In the construction of index numbers, the advantages of Geometric mean are greater than those of the Arithmetic mean." Discuss
16. Calculate price index number by
    (i) Laspeyre's method
    (ii) Paasche's method
    (iii) Fisher's ideal index method.

Commodity	1990		1995	
	Price	Quantity	Price	Quantity
A	20	15	30	20
B	15	10	20	15
C	30	20	25	10
D	10	5	12	10

17. Calculate Fisher ideal index for the following data. Also test whether it satisfies time reversal test and factor reversal test.

Commodity	Price		Quantity	
	2000	2002	2000	2002
A	6	35	10	40
B	10	25	12	30
C	12	15	8	20

18. Calculate the cost of living index number from the following data.

	Price		
Item	Base Year	Current Year	Weight
Food	30	45	4
Fuel	10	15	2
Clothing	15	20	1
House Rent	20	15	3
Miscellaneous	25	20	2

ANSWERS

I. CHOOSE THE BEST ANSWER

1. (d) 2. (b) 3. (a) 4. (a) 5. (a)
6. (b) 7. (b) 8. (d) 9. (d) 10. (b)

II. FILL IN THE BLANKS

1. Polices 2. Geometric mean 3. Percentage 4. Fisher's index number
5. "pw/"w 6. Barometers 7. normal 8. GM
9. quantity 10. Factor reversal

IV. LONG ANSWER TYPE QUESTIONS

16. (i) L = 110 (ii) P = 123.9 (iii) F = 116.7
17. 296 18. 118.2

CHAPTER 10

Correlation Analysis

10.1 INTRODUCTION

So far we have considered only univariate distributions. By the averages, dispersion and skewness of distribution, we get a complete idea about the structure of the distribution. Many a time, we come across problems which involve two or more variables. If we carefully study the figures of rain fall and production of paddy, figures of accidents and motor cars in a city, of demand and supply of a commodity, of sales and profit, we may find that there is some relationship between the two variables. On the other hand, if we compare the figures of rainfall in India and the production of cars in Japan, we may find that there is no relationship between the two variables. If there is any relation between two variables i.e. when one variable changes the other also changes in the same or in the opposite direction, we say that the two variables are correlated.

The term correlation is used by a common man without knowing that he/she is making use of the term correlation. ***For example*** when parents advice their children to work hard so that they may get good marks, they are correlating good marks with hard work.

The study related to the characteristics of only variable such as height, weight, ages, marks, wages, etc., is known as univariate analysis. The statistical Analysis related to the study of the relationship between two variables is known as Bi-Variate Analysis. Some times the variables may be inter-related. In health sciences we study the relationship between blood pressure and age, consumption level of some nutrient and weight gain, total income and medical expenditure, etc., the nature and strength of relationship may be examined by ***Correlation*** and ***Regression Analysis***.*

Thus Correlation refers to the relationship of two variables or more. e.g. relation between height of father and son, yield and rainfall, wage and price index, share and debentures etc.

Correlation is statistical analysis which measures and analyses the degree or extent to which the two variables fluctuate with reference to each other. The word relationship is important. It indicates that there is some connection between the variables. It measures the closeness of the relationship. Correlation does not indicate cause and effect relationship. Price and supply, income and expenditure are correlated.

---

* We will discuss about Regression Analysis in next chapter.

10.2 MEANING OF CORRELATION

Correction is a statistical technique which measures and analysis the degree or extent to which two or more variable fluctuate with reference to one another. Correction thus denotes the inter-dependence amongst variable. The degrees are expressed by a coefficient which 'ranges, between -1 and +1. The direction of change is indicated by +1 or – 1 signs; the former, refers to the sympathetic movement in the same direction and the latter, in opposite direction. An absence of correction is indicated by zero. Correction thus expresses the relationship through a relative measure of change and it has nothing to do with units in which the variables are expressed.

NOTE: Two variables are said to be correlated if the change in one variable results in a corresponding change in the other variable.

10.3 DEFINITION OF CORRELATION

Some important definitions of correction are given below:

1. Correlation Analysis attempts to determine the degree of relationship between variables. — ***Ya-Kun-Chou.***
2. Correlation is an analysis of the covariation between two or more variables. — ***A.M.Tuttle.***
3. "Correction means that between two series or groups of data there exists some casual connection." — ***W. L. King***
4. "When the relationship is of a quantitative nature, the appropriate statistical tool for discovering and measuring the relationship and expressing it in a brief formula is known as correlation." — ***Croxton and Cowden***

Correlation expresses the inter-dependence of two sets of variables upon each other. One variable may be called as (subject) independent and the other relative variable (dependent). Relative variable is measured in terms of subject.

10.4 USES OF CORRELATION

The use of correction is there both in physical and social sciences but we will confine ourselves to the latter and particularly to the fields of business and economics.

1. It is used in physical and social sciences.
2. It is useful for economists to study the relationship between variables like price, quantity etc. Businessmen estimates costs, sales, price etc. using correlation.
3. It is helpful in measuring the degree of relationship between the variables like income and expenditure, price and supply, supply and demand etc.
4. Sampling error can be calculated.
5. The concept of regression and ratio of variation are also based upon the measure of correlation.

10.5 TYPES OF CORRELATION

Correlation is classified into various types. The most important ones are:

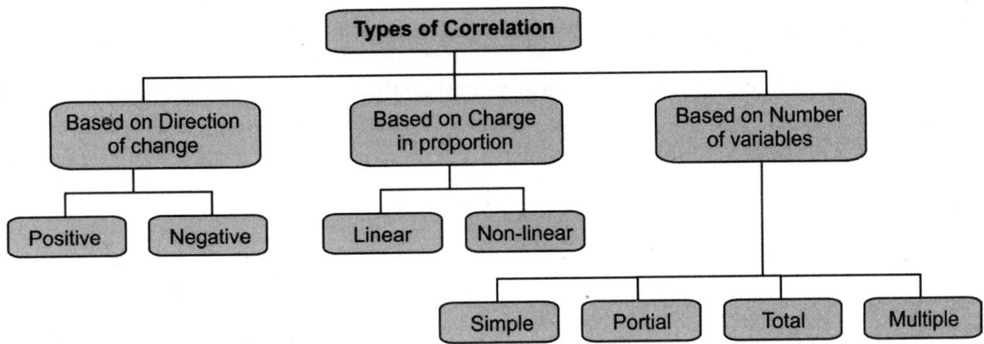

Fig. 10.1: Types of Correlation

(A) Positive and Negative Correlation

It depends upon the direction of change of the variables. If the two variables tend to move together in the same direction (ie) an increase in the value of one variable is accompanied by an increase in the value of the other, (or) a decrease in the value of one variable is accompanied by a decrease in the value of other, then the correlation is called positive or direct correlation. Price and supply, height and weight, yield and rainfall, are some examples of positive correlation.

If the two variables tend to move together in opposite directions so that increase (or) decrease in the value of one variable is accompanied by a decrease or increase in the value of the other variable, then the correlation is called negative (or) inverse correlation. Price and demand, yield of crop and price, are examples of negative correlation.

- If two variables change in the same direction (i.e. if one increases the other also increases, or if one decreases, the other also decreases), then this is called a ***Positive Correlation***. Some examples of series of positive correlation are:
  (i) Advertising and sales
  (ii) Heights and Weights
  (iii) The family income and expenditure on luxury items
  (iv) Amount of rainfall and yield of crop
  (v) Price and supply of a commodity and so on.
- If two variables change in the opposite direction (i.e. if one increases, the other decreases and vice versa), then the correlation is called a ***Negative Correlation***. Some examples of series of negative correlation are:
  (i) T.V registrations and cinema attendance
  (ii) Price and demand of a commodity
  (iii) Sale of woollen garments and the day temperature, and so on.

(B) Linear and Non-Linear Correlation

If the ratio of change between the two variables is a constant then there will be linear correlation between them. Consider the following.

X	2	4	6	8	10	12
Y	3	6	9	12	15	18

Here the ratio of change between the two variables is the same. If we plot these points on a graph we get a straight line. If the amount of change in one variable does not bear a constant ratio of the amount of change in the other. Then the relation is called "***Curvi-linear*** (or) ***non-linear correlation***". The graph will be a curve.

The nature of the graph gives us the idea of the linear type of correlation between two variables. If the graph is in a straight line, the correlation is called a "***linear correlation***" and if the graph is not in a straight line, the correlation is ***non-linear*** or ***curvi-linear.***

For example, if variable x changes by a constant quantity, say 20 then y also changes by a constant quantity, say 4. The ratio between the two always remains the same (1/5 in this case). In case of a curvi-linear correlation this ratio does not remain constant.

(C) Simple and Multiple Correlation

When we study only two variables, the relationship is ***Simple Correlation***. ***For example***, quantity of money and price level, demand and price. But in a multiple correlation we study more than two variables simultaneously. The relationship of price, demand and supply of a commodity are an example for ***Multiple Correlations***.

(D) Partial and Total Correlation

The study of two variables excluding some other variable is called ***Partial Correlation***. ***For example***, we study price and demand eliminating supply side. In total correlation all facts are taken into account.

10.6 METHODS OF CORRELATION

Initially, we confine ourselves to simple linear correction. The various methods employed are classified broadly into the following categories:

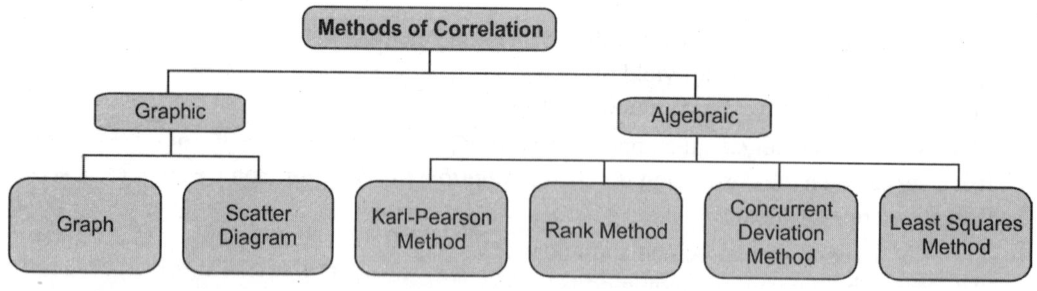

Fig. 10.2: Methods of Correlation

1. Graphic Method

The pure graphic method is the extension of graphic methods explained earlier. Under this method, two or more variable are plotted on a graph paper-arithmetic or semi-logarithmic. The latter one is preferred when the size magnitudes of the variable differ a great deal and our interest lies mainly in finding out the relative changes in two or more variable.

Scatter Diagram

It is the simplest method of studying the relationship between two variables diagrammatically. One variable is represented along the horizontal axis and the second variable along the vertical axis. For each pair of observations of two variables, we put a dot in the plane. There are as many dots in the plane as the number of paired observations of two variables. The direction of dots shows the scatter or concentration of various points. This will show the type of correlation.

(i) If all points lie on a rising straight line the correlation is perfectly positive and $r = +1$ (see 1)

(ii) If all points lie on a falling straight line the correlation is perfectly negative and $r = -1$ (see 2)

(iii) If the points lie in narrow strip, rising upwards, the correlation is high degree of positive (see 3)

(iv) If the points lie in a narrow strip, falling downwards, the correlation is high degree of negative (see 4)

(v) If the points are spread widely over a broad strip, rising upwards, the correlation is low degree positive (see 5)

(vi) If the points are spread widely over a broad strip, falling downward, the correlation is low degree negative (see 6)

(vii) If the points are spread (scattered) without any specific pattern, the correlation is absent, i.e. $r = 0$. (see 7).

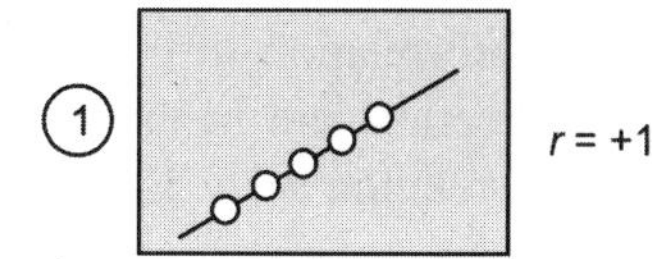

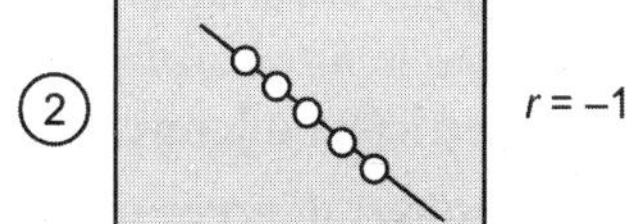

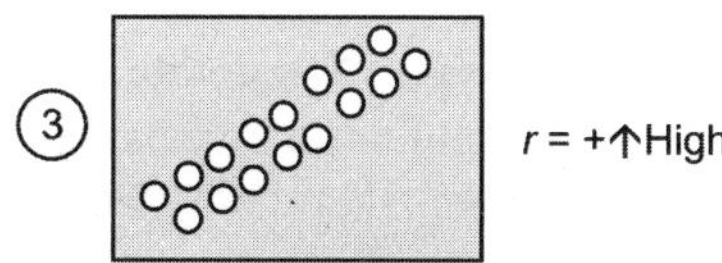

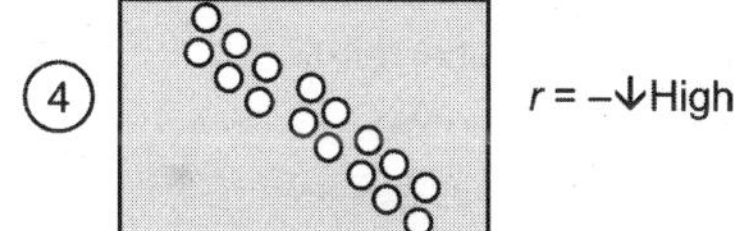

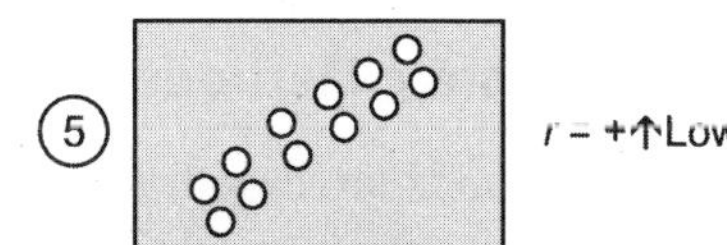

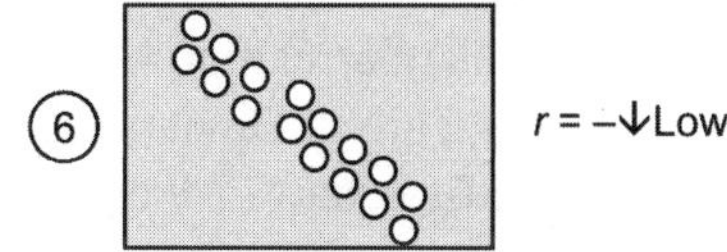

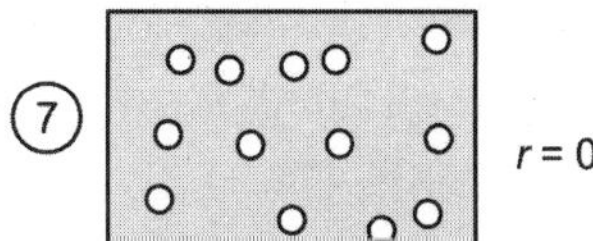

Fig. 10.3

Though this method is simple and is a rough idea about the existence and the degree of correlation, it is not reliable. As it is not a mathematical method, it cannot measure the degree of correlation.

Merits and Demerits of Scatter Diagram

Merits

1. It is a simplest and attractive method of finding the nature of correlation between the two variables.
2. It is a non-mathematical method of studying correlation. It is easy to understand.
3. It is not affected by extreme items.
4. It is the first step in finding out the relation between the two variables.
5. We can have a rough idea at a glance whether it is a positive correlation or negative correlation.

Demerits

By this method we cannot get the exact degree or correlation between the two variables.

Degree of Correlation

Through the coefficient of correlation, we can measure the degree or extent of the correlation between two variables. On the basis of the coefficient of correlation we can also determine whether the correlation is positive or negative and also its degree or extent.

1. **Perfect Correlation:** If two variables changes in the same direction and in the same proportion, the correlation between the two is ***perfect positive***. According to Karl Pearson the coefficient of correlation in this case is +1. On the other hand if the variables change in the opposite direction and in the same proportion, the correlation is ***perfect negative***. Its coefficient of correlation is –1. In practice we rarely come across these types of correlations.
2. **Absence of Correlation:** If two series of two variables exhibit no relations between them or change in variable does not lead to a change in the other variable, then we can firmly say that there is ***no correlation*** or ***absurd correlation*** between the two variables. In such a case the coefficient of correlation is 0.
3. **Limited degrees of Correlation:** If two variables are not perfectly correlated or is there a perfect absence of correlation, then we term the correlation as limited correlation. It may be positive, negative or zero but lies with the limits ± 1.

High degree, moderate degree or low degrees are the three categories of this kind of correlation. The following table reveals the effect (or degree) of coefficient or correlation.

Degrees	Positive	Negative
Absence of correlation	0	0
Perfect correlation	+1	–1
High degree	+0.75 to +1	0.75 to –1
Moderate degree	+0.25 to + 0.75	– 0.25 to – 0.75
Low degree	0 to 0.25	0 to –0.25

2. Algebraic Methods

These methods are based on mathematical formulae. The relationship is expressed by coefficient of correlation in the range ± 1. The relationship is, thus, expressed in precise terms and has not to be guessed by visual inspection as in the case of graphic methods. The following are the main algebraic methods:

(i) Karl Pearson's or Covariance Method
(ii) Rank Correlation Method
(iii) Concurrent Deviation Methods
(iv) Least Squares Method*

10.7 KARL-PEARSON'S METHOD

Karl-Pearson's method of calculating coefficient of correlation is based on covariance of the concerned variables.

* The method is discussed in detail in next chapter.

Computation of Correlation

When there exists some relationship between two variables, we have to measure the degree of relationship. This measure is called the measure of correlation (or) correlation coefficient and it is denoted by 'r'.

Co-Variation

The covariation between the variables X and Y is defined as

$$\text{Cov}(X,Y) = \frac{\Sigma(X-\bar{X})(Y-\bar{Y})}{n}$$

Where $\bar{X}$, $\bar{Y}$ are respectively means of X and Y and 'n' is the number of pairs of observations.

Karl-Pearson's Coefficient of Correlation

Karl-pearson, a great biometrician and statistician, suggested a mathematical method for measuring the magnitude of linear relationship between the two variables. It is most widely used method in practice and it is known as pearsonian coefficient of correlation. It is denoted by 'r'.

For ungrouped data, Karl-Pearson's coefficient of correlation can be obtained by using any of the following three methods:

(i) Actual Mean Method

(ii) Direct Method

(iii) Short-cut Method

(i) Actual Mean Method

It this method, we make use of the following formula for computing correlation i.e.

$$r = \frac{Cov(X,Y)}{\sigma_X \cdot \sigma_Y} \qquad ...(i)$$

where, σ_X and σ_Y are S.D of X and Y respectively. Putting the value of covariation in eq (i), we get

$$r = \frac{\Sigma(X-\bar{X})(Y-\bar{Y})}{n\sigma_X\sigma_Y} \qquad ...(ii)$$

Putting the value of standard deviation, σ_X and σ_Y in eq (ii), we get

$$r = \frac{\left[\Sigma(X-\bar{X})(Y-\bar{Y})\right]/n}{\sqrt{\frac{\Sigma(X-\bar{X})^2}{n}}\cdot\sqrt{\frac{\Sigma(Y-\bar{Y})^2}{n}}}$$

$$r = \frac{\Sigma(X-\bar{X})(Y-\bar{Y})}{\sqrt{\Sigma(X-\bar{X})^2}\cdot\sqrt{\Sigma(Y-\bar{Y})^2}}$$

Putting $X-\bar{X} = x$ and $Y-\bar{Y} = y$, we get

$$r = \frac{\Sigma xy}{\sqrt{\Sigma x^2 \cdot \Sigma y^2}} \qquad ...(iii)$$

When the deviations are taken from the actual mean we can apply any one of these methods. Simple formula is the third one. The third formula is easy to calculate, and it is not necessary to calculate the standard deviations of X and Y series respectively.

Working Steps

The various steps involved are as follows:

1. Calculate arithmetic means of X and Y series.
2. Take deviations of the two series from x and y

$$x = X - \bar{X}, \quad y = Y - \bar{Y}.$$

3. Square the deviations and get the total of the respective squares of deviations of x and y and denote by Σx^2 and Σy^2 respectively.
4. Multiply these calculated deviations of x and y and get the total and divide by n. This is covariance.

The following example will explain the application of these formula:

EXAMPLE 10.1: Find Karl Pearson's coefficient of correlation from the following data between height of father (x) and son (y).

X	64	65	66	67	68	69	70
Y	66	67	65	68	70	68	72

Comment on the result.

Solution:

X	Y	$x = X - \bar{X}$ $x = X - 67$	x^2	$y = Y - \bar{Y}$ $y = Y - 68$	y^2	xy
64	66	–3	9	–2	4	6
65	67	–2	4	–1	1	2
66	65	–1	1	–3	9	3
67	68	0	0	0	0	0
68	70	1	1	2	4	2
69	68	2	4	0	0	0
70	72	3	9	4	16	12
469	**476**	**0**	**28**	**0**	**34**	**25**

$$\bar{X} = \frac{469}{7} = 67; \quad \bar{Y} = \frac{476}{7} = 68$$

$$r = \frac{\Sigma xy}{\sqrt{\Sigma x^2 \cdot \Sigma y^2}} = \frac{25}{\sqrt{28 \times 34}} = \frac{25}{\sqrt{952}} = \frac{25}{30.85} = 0.81$$

Since $r = +\,0.81$, the variables are highly positively correlated. (ie) Tall fathers have tall sons.

(ii) Direct Method

In case there are a small number of items in the two series the correlation can be found out by ***product moment method***.

In modern literature, it has also been indicated as Product Moment Formula of coefficient of correlation because it is based on the product of the first moment around mean in the two series.

We can also find r with the following formula

We have $$r = \frac{\text{Cov}(X,Y)}{\sigma_X, \sigma_Y}$$

$$\text{Cov}(X, Y) = \frac{\Sigma(X-\bar{X})(Y-\bar{Y})}{n} = \frac{\Sigma(XY + \bar{X}Y - \bar{Y}X - \bar{X}\,\bar{Y})}{n}$$

$$= \frac{\Sigma XY}{n} - \frac{\bar{Y}\Sigma X}{n} - \frac{\bar{X}\Sigma Y}{n} + \frac{\Sigma\bar{X}\,\bar{Y}}{n}$$

$$\text{Cov}(X, Y) = \frac{\Sigma XY}{n} - \bar{Y}\bar{X} - \bar{X}\,\bar{Y} + \bar{X}\bar{Y} = \frac{\Sigma XY}{n} - \bar{X}\,\bar{Y}$$

$$\sigma_X^2 = \frac{\Sigma X^2}{n} - \bar{X}^2, \quad \sigma_Y^2 = \frac{\Sigma Y^2}{n} - \bar{Y}^2$$

Now $$r = \frac{\text{Cov}(X,Y)}{\sigma_X, \sigma_Y}$$

$$r = \frac{\frac{\Sigma XY}{n} - \bar{X}\,\bar{Y}}{\sqrt{\left(\frac{\Sigma X^2}{n} - \bar{X}^2\right)}\sqrt{\left(\frac{\Sigma Y^2}{n} - \bar{Y}^2\right)}} \qquad \left[\begin{array}{l} \because \bar{X} = \frac{\Sigma X}{n}, \bar{Y} = \frac{\Sigma Y}{n} \\ \therefore \Sigma X = n\bar{X}, \Sigma Y = n\bar{Y} \end{array}\right]$$

Multiply n^2 in both denominator and numerator.

$$\boxed{r = \frac{n\Sigma XY - (\Sigma X)(\Sigma Y)}{\sqrt{[n\Sigma X^2 - (\Sigma X)^2][n\Sigma Y^2 - (\Sigma Y)^2]}}}$$

NOTE: In the above method we need not find mean or standard deviation of variables separately.

The following examples will explain the application of this formula:

EXAMPLE 10.2: Calculate coefficient of correlation from the following data.

X	1	2	3	4	5	6	7	8	9
Y	9	8	10	12	11	13	14	16	15

Solution:

X	*Y*	*X*²	*Y*²	*XY*
1	9	1	81	9
2	8	4	64	16
3	10	9	100	30
4	12	16	144	48
5	11	25	121	55
6	13	36	169	78
7	14	49	196	98
8	16	64	256	128
9	15	81	225	135
45	**108**	**285**	**1356**	**597**

$$r = \frac{n\Sigma XY - (\Sigma X)(\Sigma Y)}{\sqrt{[n\Sigma X^2 - (\Sigma X)^2][n\Sigma Y^2 - (\Sigma Y)^2]}}$$

$$r = \frac{9 \times 597 - 45 \times 108}{\sqrt{9 \times 285 - (45)^2 .(9 \times 1356 - (108)^2)}}$$

$$r = \frac{5373 - 4860}{\sqrt{(2565 - 2025)(12204 - 11664)}}$$

$$= \frac{513}{\sqrt{540 \times 540}} = \frac{513}{540} = 0.95$$

EXAMPLE 10.3: The Personnel Manager of a large chain of retail stores is interested in studying the relationship between the experience of his sales personnel and their sales performance. For this purpose, he took a sample of 5 sales personnel at random and recorded data regarding their experience in years and sales in Rs lakhs as follows:

Sales Personnel	Experience (in yrs.)	Sales performance (Rs lakhs)
1	2	20
2	4	12
3	6	18
4	8	10
5	10	40

Calculate Karl-Pearson's coefficient of correlation between the experience and sales performance of the sales personnel.

Solution: Let the experience be denoted by x and sales performance be denoted by y.

Let us form the table as:

X	Y	XY	X^2	Y^2
2	20	40	4	400
4	12	48	16	144
6	18	108	36	324
8	100	80	64	100
10	40	400	100	1600
ΣX = 30	**ΣY = 100**	**ΣXY = 676**	**ΣX^2 = 220**	**ΣY^2 = 2568**

Here, $n = 5$

Karl Pearson's Coeff. of correlation is given by

$$r = \frac{n\Sigma XY - \Sigma X \Sigma Y}{\sqrt{n\Sigma X^2 - (\Sigma X)^2}\sqrt{n\Sigma Y^2 - (\Sigma Y)^2}}$$

$$= \frac{(5 \times 676) - (30 \times 100)}{\sqrt{(5 \times 220) - (30)^2}\sqrt{(5 \times 2568) - (100)^2}}$$

$$= \frac{3380 - 3000}{\sqrt{1100 - 900}\sqrt{12840 - 10000}}$$

$$= \frac{380}{\sqrt{200}\sqrt{2840}} = 0.5042$$

(iii) Shortcut Method

Under this method, the deviations are taken from assumed mean. The need for this method arises when the means of both the series are not in whole numbers.

The coefficient correlation is obtained by using the following formula.

We have $$r = \frac{\text{Cov}(X,Y)}{\sigma_X \cdot \sigma_Y}$$

Where $$\text{Cov}(X, Y) = \frac{\Sigma(X - \bar{X})(Y - \bar{Y})}{n}$$

Take the deviation from x as $X - A$ and the deviation from y as $Y - B$

$$\text{Cov}(X, Y) = \frac{\Sigma[(X - A) - (\bar{X} - A)][(Y - B) - (\bar{Y} - B)]}{n}$$

$$= \frac{1}{n}\Sigma[(X - A)(Y - B) - (\bar{X} - A)(\bar{Y} - B) - (\bar{X} - A)(\bar{Y} - B) + (\bar{X} - A)(\bar{Y} - B)]$$

$$= \frac{1}{n}\Sigma[(X - A)(Y - B)] - (\bar{Y} - B)\frac{\Sigma(X - A)}{n} - (\bar{X} - A)\frac{\Sigma(Y - B)}{n} + \frac{\Sigma(\bar{X} - A)(\bar{Y} - B)}{n}$$

$$= \left[\frac{\Sigma(X - A)(Y - B)}{n} - (\bar{Y} - B)(\bar{X} - \frac{nA}{n}) - (\bar{X} - A)(\bar{Y} - \frac{nB}{n}) + (\bar{X} - A)(\bar{Y} - B)\right]$$

$$= \left[\frac{\Sigma(X - A)(Y - B)}{n} - (\bar{Y} - B)(\bar{X} - A) - \cancel{(\bar{X} - A)(\bar{Y} - B)} + \cancel{(\bar{X} - A)(\bar{Y} - B)}\right]$$

$$\text{Cov}(X, Y) = \frac{\Sigma(X - A)(Y - B)}{n} - (\bar{X} - A)(\bar{Y} - B)$$

Let $X - A = u$; $Y - B = v$; $\bar{X} - A = \bar{u}$; $\bar{Y} - B = \bar{v}$

$$\therefore \quad \text{Cov}(X, Y) = \frac{\Sigma uv}{n} - \bar{u}\,\bar{v}$$

$$\sigma_X^2 = \frac{\Sigma u^2}{n} - \bar{u}^2 = \sigma_u^2$$

$$\sigma_Y^2 = \frac{\Sigma v^2}{n} - \bar{v}^2 = \sigma_v^2$$

$$\therefore \quad \boxed{r^* = \frac{n\Sigma uv - (\Sigma u)(\Sigma v)}{\sqrt{[n\Sigma u^2 - (\Sigma u)^2].[(n\Sigma v^2) - (\Sigma v)^2]}}}$$

* See the footnote in the next page

Working Steps

The various steps involved are as follows:

1. Some convenient values are taken as assumed means in series X and Y (say A and B)
2. Deviations (denoted by the symbols u and v) are obtained from the assumed means of the X-series and Y-series from their respective individual values, i.e., $u = X - A$, $v = Y - B$
3. Σv, sum of the deviations of X series from the assumed mean and Σv, the sum of the deviations of Y series from the assumed mean are obtained.
4. The deviations u and v are squared up and their total Σu^2 and Σv^2 are obtained.
5. Lastly Σuv, which is the sum of the product of the deviations of X and Y series from their assumed means are obtained.

NOTE: Actual Mean Method is used when actual mean is a whole number. Short-cut Method is used when the actual mean is a fraction and the observations have large values.

EXAMPLE 10.4: Calculate Pearson's Coefficient of correlation.

X	45	55	56	58	60	65	68	70	75	80	85
Y	56	50	48	60	62	64	65	70	74	82	90

X	Y	$u = X - A$	$v = Y - B$	u^2	v^2	uv
45	56	–20	–14	400	196	280
55	50	–10	–20	100	400	200
56	48	–9	–22	81	484	198
58	60	–7	–10	49	100	70
60	62	–5	–8	25	64	40
A 65	64	0	–6	0	36	0
68	65	3	–5	9	25	–15
70	B 70	5	0	25	0	0
75	74	10	4	100	16	40
80	82	15	12	225	144	180
85	90	20	20	400	400	400
		2	–49	1414	1865	1393

$$r = \frac{n\Sigma uv - (\Sigma u)(\Sigma v)}{\sqrt{[n\Sigma u^2 - (\Sigma u^2)][n\Sigma v^2 - (\Sigma v)^2]}}$$

---

* Some authors use d_X and d_Y instead of u and v resp.
Then formula is:

$$r = \frac{n\Sigma d_X d_Y - \Sigma d_X \Sigma d_Y}{\sqrt{nd_X^2 - (\Sigma d_X)^2} \cdot \sqrt{n\Sigma d_Y^2 - (\Sigma d_Y^2)}}$$

where $d_X = (X - A)$ and $d_Y = (Y - B)$

$$r = \frac{11 \times 1393 - 2 \times (-49)}{\sqrt{(1414 \times 11 - (2)^2 \times [1865 \times 11 - (-49)^2]}}$$

$$r = \frac{15421}{\sqrt{15550 \times 18114}}$$

$$= \frac{15421}{16783.11} = +0.92$$

EXAMPLE 10.5: The following data relate to the age of 10 employees and the number of days which they reported sick month:

Age	20	30	32	35	40	46	52	55	58	62
Sick days	11	12	10	13	14	16	15	17	18	19

Solution: Let age and sick days be represented by variable X and Y respectively

Calculation Correlation Coefficient

Age X	$(X-43)$ d_X	Sick days d_X^2	$(Y-14)$ Y	d_Y	d_Y^2	$d_X d_Y$
20	–23	529	11	–3	9	+69
30	–13	169	12	–2	4	+26
32	–11	121	10	–4	16	+44
35	–8	64	13	–1	1	+8
40	–3	9	14	0	0	0
46	+3	9	16	+2	4	+6
52	+9	81	15	+1	1	+9
55	+12	144	17	+3	9	+36
58	+15	225	18	+4	16	+60
62	+19	361	19	+5	25	+45
$\Sigma X = 430$	$\Sigma d_X = 0$	$\Sigma d_X^2 = 1712$	$\Sigma Y = 145$	$\Sigma d_Y = 5$	$\Sigma d_Y^2 = 85$	$\Sigma d_X d_Y = 353$

$$r = \frac{n\Sigma d_X d_Y - \Sigma d_X \Sigma d_Y}{\sqrt{n\Sigma d_X^2 - (\Sigma d_X)^2}\sqrt{n\Sigma d_Y^2 - (\Sigma d_Y)^2}}$$

$$= \frac{10 \times 353 - (0)(-5)}{\sqrt{10 \times 1712 - (0)^2}\sqrt{10 \times 85 - (-5)^2}}$$

$$= \frac{3530}{\sqrt{17120}\sqrt{825}}$$

$$= \frac{3530}{130.85 \times 28.72} = 0.939$$

Thus, there is a very high degree of positive correlation between age and sick days taken. Hence, we can conclude that as the age of an employee increases, he is liable to be sick more often than others.

Merits and Demerits of Karl-Pearson's Coefficient of Correlation

Merits

1. It is important and popular method of measuring the relationship between two variables. It gives a precise and quantitative value indicating the degree of relationship existing between the two variables. The value of r is easily interpretable.
2. It measures the direction as well as the relationship between the two variables.

Demerits

1. The value of the coefficient is affected by extreme items
2. Its computational procedure is difficult as compared to other methods
3. It assumes the ***linear relationship*** between the two variables.

10.8 PROPERTIES OF CORRELATION COEFFICIENT

The following are the important properties of the coefficient of correlation:

1. The coefficient of correlation r lies between -1 and $+1$, i.e., $-1 \leq r \leq 1$, i.e., a number between -1 and 1 both inclusive that describes the linear relationship between pairs of quantitative variables.
2. The correlation coefficient is independent of the change of origin and scale.
3. The correlation coefficient is the ratio of two quantities having same units, thus it is a pure number having no units.
4. The value of r does not change if all the values of either variable are converted to a different scale. ***For example***, if the units of X are changed from feet to meters, the value of r does not change.
5. The value of r is not affected by the choice of X or Y. Interchange of all X and Y values will not change the value of r, i.e., the correlation coefficient between X and Y is equal to the correlation coefficient between Y and X.
6. r measures the strength of linear relationship. It is not designated to measure the strength of a relationship that is not linear.
7. If the sign of all the values of one of the variables is changed, the sign of the correlation coefficient changes, i.e., the correlation between X and Y is opposite in sign to the correlation between $-X$ and Y or X and $-Y$.
8. If each value of X and (or) Y a constant amount is added or subtracted, the correlation coefficient remains unchanged, i.e., correlation coefficient is independent of the change of origin.
9. If each value of X and (or) Y a constant amount is added or subtracted, the correlation coefficient remains unchanged, i.e., the correlation coefficient is independent of the change of scale.

NOTES: 1. The change of origin means adding or subtracting a constant amount from given observations of the variables X and Y and the change of scale means multiplying or dividing the values of X and Y by some constant amount. The constant amount can be chosen arbitrarily as per convenience. It may be same or different for X and Y.

2. Property II is very useful for reducing computational work involved in the calculation of coefficient of correlation and forms the basis for short-cut method.

10.9 CORRELATION OF BIVARIATE GROUPED DATA

When the number of observations is very large, the data is classified into two way frequency distribution or correlation table. The class intervals for '*Y*' are in the column headings and for '*X*' in the stubs. The order can also be reversed. The frequencies for each cell of the table are obtained. The formula for calculation of correlation coefficient '*r*' is

$$r = \frac{\text{cov}(X,Y)}{\sigma_X \cdot \sigma_Y}$$

Where
$$\text{cov}(X, Y) = \frac{\Sigma f(X-\bar{X})(Y-\bar{Y})}{N} = \frac{\Sigma fXY}{N} - \overline{X}\,\overline{Y}$$

$$\sigma_X^2 = \frac{\Sigma fX^2}{N} - \bar{X}^2; \quad \sigma_Y^2 = \frac{\Sigma fY^2}{N} - \bar{Y}^2;$$

N = Total frequency

$$r = \frac{N\Sigma fXY - (\Sigma fX)(\Sigma fY)}{\sqrt{[N\Sigma fX^2 - (\Sigma fX)^2][N\Sigma fY^2 - (\Sigma fY)^2]}} \qquad \text{...(I)}$$

Theorem: The correlation coefficient is not affected by change of origin and scale.

If
$$u = \frac{X-A}{c}; \quad v = \frac{Y-B}{d}$$

then
$$r_{XY} = r_{uv}$$

Proof:
$$u = \frac{X-A}{c}$$

$$cu = X - A$$

$$X = cu + A \qquad \bar{X} = [A + \bar{u}c]$$

$$v = \frac{Y-B}{d}$$

$$vd = Y - B$$

$$Y = B + ud; \qquad \bar{Y} = [B + \bar{u}d]$$

$$\sigma_X = c\sigma_u; \qquad \sigma_Y = d\sigma_u$$

$$\sigma_{XY} = \frac{\text{cov}(X,Y)}{\sigma_X \sigma_Y}$$

$$\text{cov}(X, Y) = \frac{\Sigma f(X-\bar{X})(Y-\bar{Y})}{N}$$

$$\frac{1}{n}\Sigma f[(cu + A) - (c\bar{u} + A)][(dv + B) - (d\bar{v} + B)] = \frac{1}{N}\Sigma f[cu - c\bar{u}][(dv - d\bar{v})]$$

$$= \frac{1}{N}\Sigma f[c(u - \bar{u}][(d(v - \bar{v})]$$

$$= \frac{1}{N}\Sigma fcd[u - \bar{u}][v - \bar{v}]$$

$$= \frac{1}{N} cd\Sigma f(u - \bar{u})(v - \bar{v})$$

$$= cd \frac{\Sigma f(u - \bar{u})(v - \bar{v})}{N} = cd \ \text{cov}(u, v)$$

∴ $\text{cov}(X, Y) = cd \ \text{cov}(u.v)$

∴ $$r_{XY} = \frac{\text{cov}(X,Y)}{\sigma_X \sigma_Y} = \frac{cd \ \text{cov}(u,v)}{c\sigma u \cdot d\sigma_Y} = r_{uv}$$

∴ $$\boxed{r_{XY} = r_{uv}}$$

So, from eq (1), we can also write

$$r = \frac{N\Sigma fuv - (\Sigma fu)(\Sigma fv)}{\sqrt{[N\Sigma fu^2 - (\Sigma fu)^2]} \cdot \sqrt{[N\Sigma fv^2 - (\Sigma fv)^2]}}$$

or, $$r = \frac{N\Sigma fd_X d_Y - (\Sigma fd_X)(\Sigma fd_Y)}{\sqrt{N\Sigma fd_X^2 - (\Sigma fd_X)^2} \cdot \sqrt{N\Sigma fd_Y^2 - (\Sigma fd_Y)^2}}$$

Working Steps

1. Take the step deviations of the variable *X* and denote these deviations by *u*.
2. Take the step deviations of the variable *Y* and denote these deviations by *v*.
3. Multiply uv and the respective frequency of each cell and unite the figure obtained in the right hand bottom corner of each cell.
4. Add the corrected (all) as calculated in step 3 and obtain the total Σfuv.
5. Multiply the frequencies of the variable *X* by the deviations of *X* and obtain the total Σfu.
6. Take the squares of the step deviations of the variable *X* and multiply them by the respective frequencies and obtain the Σfu^2 similarly get Σfv and Σfv^2. Then substitute these values in the formula 1 and get the value of '*r*'.

The following examples will explain the application of this formula.

EXAMPLE 10.6: The following are the marks obtained by 132 students in two tests.

Test-1 → / Test-2 ↓	30–40	40–50	50–60	60–70	70–80	Total
20–30	2	5	3			**10**
30–40	1	8	12	6		**27**
40–50		5	22	14	1	**42**
50–60		2	16	9	2	**29**
60–70		1	8	6	1	**16**
70–80			2	4	2	**8**
Total	**3**	**21**	**63**	**39**	**6**	**132**

Calculate the correlation coefficient. **[MBA, Kuman University, MK. University,]**

Solution: Lex X denote Test 1 marks and Y denote Test 2 marks.

mid X → / mid Y ↓	35	45	55	65	75	f	v	fv	fv²	fuv
25	2 / 8	5 / 10	0 / 1 / 0			10	–2	–20	40	18
35	2 / 1 / 2	1 / 8 / 8	0 / 12 / 0	–1 / 6 / –6	—	27	–1	–27	27	4
45		0 / 5 / 0	0 / 22 / 0	0 / 14 / 0	0 / 1 / 0	42	0	0	0	0
55		–1 / 2 / –2	0 / 16 / 0	1 / 9 / 9	2 / 2 / 4	29	1	29	29	11
65		–2 / 1 / –2	0 / 8 / 0	2 / 6 / 12	4 / 1 / 4	16	2	32	64	14
75			0 / 2 / 0	3 / 4 / 12	6 / 2 / 12	8	3	24	72	24
f	3	21	63	39	6	**132**	**3**	**38**	**232**	**71**
u	–2	–1	0	1	2	**0**				
fu	–6	–21	0	39	12	**24**				
fu²	12	21	0	39	24	**96**				
fuv	10	14	0	27	20	**71**				

$$r = \frac{N\Sigma fuv - (\Sigma fu)(\Sigma fv)}{\sqrt{[N\Sigma fu^2 - (\Sigma fu)^2][N\Sigma fv^2 - (\Sigma fv)^2]}}$$

$$= \frac{132 \times 71 - 24 \times 38}{\sqrt{\{132 \times 96 - (24)^2\}[132 \times 232 - (38)^2]}} = \frac{9372 - 912}{\sqrt{(12672 - 576)(30624 - 1444)}}$$

$$= \frac{8460}{109.96 \times 170.82} = \frac{8460}{18786.78} = 0.4503$$

EXAMPLE 10.7: Calculate Karl-Pearson's coefficient of correlation from the data given below:

Age in years → / Marks ↓	18	19	20	21	22
0–5	—	—	—	3	1
5–10	—	—	—	3	2
10–15	—	—	7	10	—
15–20	—	5	4	—	—
20–25	3	2	—	—	—

$$u = \frac{X - 12.5}{5}, \quad v = \frac{Y - 20}{1}$$

Y → / mid X ↓	18	19	20	21	22	f	v	fv	fv²	fuv
2.5	—	—	—	2 3 -6	-4 1 -4	4	-2	-8	16	-10
7.5	—	—	—	-1 3 -3	-2 2 -4	5	—	-5	5	-7
12.5	—	—	0 7 -0	0 10 0	—	17	0	0	0	0
17.5	—	-1 5 -5	0 4 0	—	—	0	1	9	9	-5
22.5	-4 3 -12	-2 2 -4	—	—	—	5	2	10	20	-16
f	3	7	11	16	3	**40**	**0**	**6**	**50**	**-38**
u	-2	-1	0	1	2	**0**				
fu	-6	-7	0	16	6	**9**				
fu²	12	7	0	16	6	**9**				
fuv	-12	-9	0	-9	-8	**-38**				

$$r = \frac{N\Sigma fuv - (\Sigma fu)(\Sigma fv)}{\sqrt{[N\Sigma fu^2 - (\Sigma fu)^2][N\Sigma fv^2 - (\Sigma fv)^2]}}$$

$$= \frac{40(-38) - 6 \times 9}{\sqrt{[40 \times 50 - 6^2][40 \times 47 - 9^2]}}$$

$$= \frac{-1520 - 54}{\sqrt{(2000 - 36) \times (1880 - 81)}} = \frac{-1574}{\sqrt{1964 \times 1799}} = 0.8373.$$

10.10 PROBABLE ERROR

Probable error is an old measure of ascertaining the reliability of the value of Pearson coefficient of correlation.

According to ***Weldon***, "Probable error defines the limits above and below the size of the coefficient determined within which there is an equal change that coefficient of correlation similarly calculated from other sample will fall."

It is used to help in the determination of the Karl-Pearson's coefficient of correlation 'r'. Due to this 'r' is corrected to a great extent but note that 'r' depends on the random sampling and its conditions. It is given by

$$P.E = 0.6745 \left[\frac{1 - r^2}{\sqrt{n}}\right]$$

The reason for taking the factor 0.6745 is that in a normal distribution 50% of the observations lie in the range $\mu \pm 0.6745\ \sigma$, where μ is the mean and σ is the S.D.

A few rules for the interpretation of the significance of correlation are as follows:

(i) If the value of r is less than P.E ($r <$ P.E), then there is no evidence of correlation i.e. r is not significant.

(ii) If r is more than 6 times the P.E ($r >$ 6 P.E) 'r' is practically certain .i.e. significant.

(iii) In other situations, nothing can be stated with certainty.

(iv) By adding or subtracting P.E. to 'r', we get the upper and Lower limits within which 'r' of the population can be expected to lie.

Symbolically $e = r \pm$ P.E

NOTE:

1. P.E may lead to fallacious conclusions particularly when n (the number of observation) is small.
2. P.E is meaningful only when the following conditions exist
   (i) The data must have been drawn from normal population.
   (ii) The selected sample observations are obtained by random sampling method.

EXAMPLE 10.8: If $r = 0.6$ and $n = 64$ find out the probable error of the coefficient of correlation.

Solution:

$$\text{P.E} = 0.6745 \left[\frac{1 - r^2}{\sqrt{n}}\right] = 0.6745 \left[\frac{1 - (-0.6)^2}{\sqrt{64}}\right]$$

$$= \frac{0.6745 - 0.64}{8} = 0.57.$$

10.11 RANK CORRELATION

There are many occasions in problems related with business and industry where it is not possible to measure the variable under consideration quantitatively or where the statistical series is composed of items, the exact magnitudes of which cannot be ascertained. ***For example***, it may be possible for the two judges to rank six different brands of cigarettes in terms of taste, whereas it may be different to give them a numerical grade in terms of taste.

Similarly, it may possible for two foremen to rank their ten employees for promotion, but it may be difficult to assign them a numerical grade. In such cases, it is not possible to measure the relationship between the attributes by coefficient of correlation discussed earlier. If the two series are ranked according to two attributes, the correction coefficient between their ranks is called the ***"Rank Correlation"***.

This method is based on the ranks of the items rather than on their actual values. The advantage of this method over the others in that it can be used even when the actual values of items are unknown. ***For example*** if you want to know the correlation between honesty and wisdom of the boys of your class, you can use this method by giving ranks to the boys. It can also be used to find the degree of agreements between the judgements of two examiners or two judges.

DO YOU KNOW?

The method of ascertaining the coefficient of correlation by ranks was devised by ***Charles Edwards Spearman*** in 1904. It is studied when no assumption about the parameters of the population is made. This method is based on ranks. It is useful to study the qualitative measure of attributes like honesty, colour, beauty, intelligence, character, morality etc.

Method of Calculation

The individuals in the group can be arranged in order and there on, obtaining for each individual a number showing his/her rank in the group.

This method was developed by Edward Spearman in 1904. It is defined as

$$r = \frac{6\Sigma D^2}{n^3 - n}$$

where, r^* = rank correlation coefficient.

ΣD^2 = sum of squares of differences between the pairs of ranks.

n = number of pairs of observations.

Working Steps

To calculate the rank correlation coefficient. The various steps involved are as follows:

1. We first rank the two series say X's and Y's individually among themselves, giving rank 1 to the largest (or smallest) value, rank 2 to be second largest (or second smallest) and so on in each series separately.
2. Find the differences 'D' of the corresponding ranks of X and Y.
3. Square these differences and find the sum of the squares of these differences, i.e. ΣD^2.
4. Calculate rank correlation coefficient by using the formula.

The value of r lies between –1 and +1. If $r = +1$, there is complete agreement in order of ranks and the direction of ranks is also same. If $r = -1$, then there is complete disagreement in order of ranks and they are in opposite directions.

10.11.1 Computation for Tied Observations

There may be two or more items having equal values. In such case the same rank is to be given. The ranking is said to be tied. In such circumstances an average rank is to be given to each individual item. ***For example*** if the value so is repeated twice at the 5th rank, the common rank to be assigned to each item is (5 + 6)/ 2= 5.5 which is the average of 5 and 6 given as 5.5, appeared twice.

If the ranks are tied, it is required to apply a correction factor which is $\frac{1}{12}(m^3 - m)$

Where m is the number of times an item (or rank) has repeated.

A slightly different formula is used when there is more than one item having the same value.

* Some authors use the symbol ρ for rank correlation.

The formula is $$r = 1 - \frac{6[\Sigma D^2 + \frac{1}{12}(m^3 - m) + \frac{1}{12}(m^3 - m) + ..]}{n^3 - n}$$

Where m is the number of items whose ranks are common and should be repeated as many times as there are tied observations.

The following examples will explain the application of these formulas:

EXAMPLE 10.9: In a marketing survey the price of tea and coffee in a town based on quality was found as shown below. Could you find any relation between and tea and coffee price.

Price of tea	88	90	95	70	60	75	50
Price of coffee	120	134	150	115	110	140	100

Solution:

Price of tea	Rank	Price of coffee	Rank	D	D^2
88	3	120	4	1	1
90	2	134	3	1	1
95	1	150	1	0	0
70	5	115	5	0	0
60	6	110	6	0	0
75	4	140	2	2	4
50	7	100	7	0	0
					$\Sigma D^2 = 6$

$$r = 1 - \frac{6\Sigma D^2}{n^3 - n} = 1 - \frac{6 \times 6}{7^3 - 7} = 1 - \frac{36}{336} = 1 - 0.1071 = 0.8929$$

The relation between price of tea and coffee is positive at 0.89. Based on quality the association between price of tea and price of coffee is highly positive.

EXAMPLE 10.10: In an evaluation of answer script the following marks are awarded by the examiners.

1st	88	95	70	60	50	80	75	85
2nd	84	90	88	55	48	85	82	75

Do you agree the evaluation by the two examiners is fair?

Solution:

X	R_1	Y	R_2	D	D^2
88	2	84	4	2	4
95	1	90	1	0	0
70	6	88	2	4	16
60	7	55	7	0	0
50	8	48	8	0	0
80	4	85	3	1	1
75	5	82	5	0	0
85	3	75	6	3	9
					$\Sigma D^2 = 30$

$$r = 1 - \frac{6\Sigma D^2}{n^3 - n} = 1 - \frac{6 \times 30}{8^3 - 8} = 1 - \frac{180}{540} = 1 - 0.357 = 0.643$$

$r = 0.643$ shows fair in awarding marks in the sense that uniformity has arisen in evaluating the answer scripts between the two examiners.

EXAMPLE 10.11: Calculate coefficient of correlation between X and Y by the method of rank differences:

X	48	33	40	9	16	16	65	24	16	57
Y	13	13	24	6	15	4	20	9	6	19

Solution:

X	R_X	Y	R_Y	$R_X - R_Y = D$	D^2
48	3	13	5.5	–2.5	6.25
33	5	13	5.5	–0.5	0.25
40	4	24	1	3.0	9.00
9	10	6	8.5	1.5	2.25
16	8	15	4	4	16.00
16	8	4	10	–2	4.00
65	1	20	2	–1	1.00
24	6	9	7	–1	1.00
16	8	6	8.5	–0.5	0.25
57	2	19	3	–1	1.00
				$\Sigma D = 0$	$\Sigma D^2 = 41$

In this question, in *X*-series, the value 16 is repeated thrice. The common rank given to the value 16 is 8, which is the average of 7, 8 and 9 ranks which these values would have assumed if they were different. Here $m = 3$, so the correction factor to be added for this value will be $\frac{1}{12}(3^3 - 3)$. In series-*Y*, the value 13 and 6 are repeated twice. The average rank for the value 6 is 8.5 while for the value 13 it is 5.5. In both these cases, the correction factor will be $\frac{1}{12}(2^3 - 2)$.

Thus, the rank correlations is:

$$r = 1 - \frac{6[\Sigma D^2 + \frac{1}{12}(m^3 - m) + \frac{1}{12}(m^3 - m) + \frac{1}{12}(m^3 - m)]}{n(n^2 - 1)}$$

$$= 1 - \frac{6[41 + \frac{1}{12}(3^3 - 3) + \frac{1}{2}(2^3 - 2) + \frac{1}{12}(2^3 - 2)]}{10(10^2 - 1)}$$

$$= 1 - \frac{6[41 + 2 + .5 + .5]}{990}$$

$$= 1 - \frac{264}{990} = 1 - .267 = 0.733$$

EXAMPLE 10.12: Rank Correlation for tied observations. Following are the marks obtained by 10 students in a class in two tests.

Students	A	B	C	D	E	F	G	H	I	J
Test 1	70	68	67	55	60	60	75	63	60	72
Test 2	65	65	80	60	68	58	75	63	60	70

Calculate the rank correlation coefficient between the marks of two tests.

Solution:

Students	Test 1	R_1	Test 2	R_2	D	D^2
A	70	3	65	5.5	–2.5	6.25
B	68	4	65	5.5	–1.5	2.25
C	67	5	80	1.0	4.0	16.00
D	55	10	60	8.5	1.5	2.25
E	60	8	68	4.0	4.0	16.00
F	60	8	58	10.0	–2.0	4.00
G	75	1	75	2.0	–1.0	1.00
H	63	6	62	7.0	–1.0	1.00
I	60	8	60	8.5	0.5	0.25
J	72	2	70	3.0	–1.0	1.00
						ΣD^2 = **50.00**

60 is repeated 3 times in test 1. 60, 65 is repeated twice in test 2.
$m = 3$; $m = 2$; $m = 2$

$$r = 1 - \frac{6[\Sigma D^2 + \frac{1}{12}(m^3 - m) + \frac{1}{12}(m^3 - m) + \frac{1}{12}(m^3 - m)}{n^3 - n}$$

$$= 1 - \frac{6[50 + \frac{1}{12}(3^3 - 3) + \frac{1}{12}(2^3 - 2) + \frac{1}{12}(2^3 - 2)]}{10^3 - 10}$$

$$= 1 - \frac{6[50 + 2 + 0.5 + 0.5]}{990}$$

$$= 1 - \frac{6 \times 53}{990} = \frac{672}{990} = 0.68$$

There is uniformity in the performance of students in the two tests.

EXAMPLE 10.13: Rank correlation co-efficient of marks obtained by 10 students in Mathematics and English was found to be 0.5. It was later discovered that the difference in ranks in two subjects obtained by one of the students was wrongly taken as 3 instead of 7. Find the correct rank correlation co-efficient.

Solution: Incorrect $r_k = 0.5$, $n = 10$

$$\therefore \quad \text{Incorrect } \Sigma D^2 = \frac{n(n^2 - 1)(1 - r_k)}{6} = \frac{10 \times 99 \times 0.5}{6} = 82.5$$

Now, correct ΣD^2 = Incorrect $\Sigma d^2 - (3)^2 + (7)^2 = 82.5 - 9 + 49 = 122.5$

$$\therefore \qquad \text{Correct } r_k = 1 - \left\{\frac{6\Sigma D^2}{n(n^2-1)}\right\} = 1 - \left\{\frac{6 \times 122.5}{10(100-1)}\right\} = 0.2676$$

EXAMPLE 10.14: The competitors in a beauty contest were ranked by three judges in the following orders:

First Judge	1	6	5	10	3	2	4	9	7	8
Second Judge	3	5	8	4	7	10	2	1	6	9
Third Judge	6	4	9	8	1	2	3	10	5	7

Use the method of rank correlation to determine which pair of judges has the nearest approach to common taste in beauty?

Solution: Let R_1, R_2, R_3 be the ranks given by three judges.

Calculation of Rank Correlation Coefficient

Competitor	R_1	R_2	R_3	$D_{12} = R_1 - R_2$	$D_{13} = R_1 - R_3$	$D_{23} = R_2 - R_3$	D_{12}^2	D_{13}^2	D_{23}^2
A	1	3	6	−2	−5	−3	4	25	9
B	6	5	4	1	2	1	1	4	1
C	5	8	9	−3	−4	−1	9	16	1
D	10	4	8	6	2	−4	36	4	16
E	3	7	1	−4	2	6	16	4	36
F	2	10	2	−8	0	8	64	0	64
G	4	2	3	2	1	−1	4	1	1
H	9	1	10	8	−1	−9	64	1	81
I	7	6	5	1	2	1	1	4	1
J	8	9	7	−1	1	2	1	1	4
N = 10							ΣD_{12}^2 **= 200**	ΣD_{13}^2 **= 60**	ΣD_{23}^2 **= 214**

Rank correlation coefficient between first and second judges,

$$r_{12} = 1 - \left\{\frac{6\Sigma D_{13}^2}{N(N^2-1)}\right\} = 1 - \left\{\frac{6 \times 200}{10(99)}\right\} = 0.212$$

Rank correlation coefficient between first and third judges,

$$r_{13} = 1 - \left\{\frac{6\Sigma D_{13}^2}{N(N^2-1)}\right\} = 1 - \left\{\frac{6 \times 60}{10 \times 99}\right\} = 0.636$$

Rank correlation coefficient between second and third judges,

$$r_{23} = 1 - \left\{\frac{6\Sigma D_{23}^2}{N(N^2-1)}\right\} = 1 - \left\{\frac{6 \times 214}{10 \times 99}\right\} = -0.297$$

Correlation between first and second judges is negative i.e., their opinions regarding beauty test are opposite to each other. Similarly opinions of second and third judges are opposite to each other, but the opinions of first and third judges are of similar type as their correlation is positive. It means their likings and dislikings are very much common.

EXAMPLE 10.15: Calculate Spearman's rank correlation coefficient between the series *A* and *B* based on the following informations:

Ranks of Series-*A*	2.5	5	6	7	8	9	1	4	2.5
Ranks of Series-*B*	3	5	6.5	6.5	9	8	1	4	2

Solution:

R_X	R_Y	D	D^2
2.5	3	–0.5	0.25
5	5	0	0
6	6.6	–0.5	0.25
7	6.5	0.5	0.25
8	9	–1	1
9	8	1	1
1	1	0	0
4	4	0	0
2.5	2	0.5	0.25
			$\Sigma D^2 = 3$

$$r_r = 1 - \frac{6\left[\Sigma D^2 + \frac{1}{12}(m^3 - m) + \frac{1}{12}(m^3 - m)\right]}{n(n^2 - 1)}$$

$$= 1 - \frac{6\left[3 + \frac{1}{12}(2^3 - 2) + \frac{1}{12}(2^3 - 2)\right]}{9(9^2 - 1)}$$

$$= 1 - \frac{6[3 + .5 + .5]}{9 \times 80} = 1 - \frac{6 \times 4}{720}$$

$$= 1 - 0.033 = 0.967.$$

Merits and Demerits of Rank Correlation Method

Merits

1. This method is simple to understand and easy to apply compared with Karl Pearson's method. The laborious calculations for the product- moment are replaced by rankings.
2. This method can conveniently be used as a measure of the degree of association between two attributes where measurements on characteristics are not available, but the individuals can be ranked in some order without difficulty. ***For example***, in a group of salesmen, the extent of association between "intelligence" and "efficiency" can be easily obtained by arranging the individuals in order of proficiency assessed.
3. Even when exact measurements are given, the rank correlation method can be applied to ascertain rough estimate of the degree of correlation.
4. The method can conveniently be used when the data are irregular or when the extreme items are erratic or inaccurate because rank correlation coefficient is not based on the assumption of normality of data.

Demerits

1. This method is applicable only to individual observations rather than to grouped frequency distributions.
2. Under the ranking method, original values are not taken into account; therefore the result obtained is only approximate.
3. When the number of observations exceeds 30, the calculations become quite tedious.

10.12 COEFFICIENT OF CONCURRENT DEVIATIONS

When much of precision is not required and our interest is simply to know whether the two variables move in the same direction or opposite direction, the method of concurrent deviations can be conveniently used to study the correlation between two variables or series. In this method, the deviation of each value is taken from its previous value in each series separately and only the direction (sign) of the deviations and not the magnitude is taken into account for calculations. *The deviations having the same sign at the corresponding places in the two series are called concurrent deviations.* The coefficient of concurrent deviations is calculated from the following formula:

$$r_c = \pm\sqrt{\frac{2c - n}{n}}$$

where n = number of pairs of deviations.

Note that **n is not equal to the number of item** in each series. If each series contains the same number of items or values then n = (number of values in each series –1) and c = number of concurrent deviations, *i.e.*, deviations having the same sign at the corresponding places in the two series. + or – sign in r_c is taken according as the actual value of $\frac{2c - n}{n}$ is positive or negative.

EXAMPLE 10.16: Compute the coefficient of concurrent deviations from the following data:

Year	1988	1989	1990	1991	1992	1993	1994
Supply	152	158	169	182	160	166	182
Price (Rs)	198	178	167	156	180	170	162

Solution:

Calculation of Coefficient Deviations

Year	Supply	Direction	Price (Rs)	Direction	
	X	d_X	Y	d_Y	$d_X d_Y$
1988	152		198		
1989	158	+	178	–	–
1990	169	+	167	–	–
1991	182	+	156	–	–
1992	160	–	180	+	–
1993	166	+	170	–	–
1994	182	+	162	–	–
					c = 0

Coefficient of concurrent deviation:

$$r_c = \pm\sqrt{\frac{(2c - n)}{n}} \quad \text{here, } c = 0,\ n = 7 - 1 = 6$$

Substituting these values, we get

$$r_c = \pm\sqrt{\frac{2 \times 0 - 6}{6}} = -1 \qquad [\therefore 2c - n \text{ is negative}]$$

Thus the coefficient of concurrent deviations is – 1.

EXAMPLE 10.17: Calculate the coefficient of correlation, using the method of concurrent deviations, between supply and demand given the following data. Also comment on your result: **[CA., Nov., 1991]**

Years	1990	1991	1992	1993	1994	1995	1996	1997	1998	1999
Supply ('000 tons)	120	110	120	119	140	125	127	119	140	160
Demand ('000 tons)	240	250	260	266	232	245	255	267	268	239

Solution:

Calculation of Correlation by Concurrent Deviation Method

Year	Supply X	Direction of Change in X d_x	Demand Y	Direction of Change in Y d_y	$d_x d_y$
1990	120		240		
1991	110	–	250	+	–
1992	120	+	260	+	+
1993	119	–	266	+	–
1994	140	+	232	–	–
1995	125	–	245	+	+
1996	127	+	255	+	+
1997	119	–	267	+	–
1998	140	+	268	+	+
1999	160	+	239	–	–
					$c = 3$

$$r_c = \pm\sqrt{\frac{2c - n}{n}} \quad \text{here, } c = 3,\ n = 10 - 1 = 9$$

Substituting these values, we get

$$r_c = \pm\sqrt{\frac{(2 \times 3) - 9}{n}} = -0.333 \qquad [\therefore 2c - n \text{ is negative}]$$

The results show that supply and demand are negatively correlated, i.e., they move in opposite directions.

MISCELLANEOUS SOLVED EXAMPLES

EXAMPLE 10.18: Find the correlation coefficient between age and playing habits of the following students:

Age	15	16	17	18	19	20
No. of students	250	200	150	120	100	80
Regular players	200	150	90	48	30	12

Solution: Let us find the percentage of regular players and then calculate coefficient of correlation between age and percentage. **[MBA, Madras University, 2000]**

X	$(X-17)$ d_x	d_x^2	No. of Students	Regular Players Y	% of Regular Players	$(Y-50)$ d_y	d_y^2	$d_x d_y$
15	–2	4	250	200	80	+30	900	–60
16	–1	1	200	150	75	+25	625	–25
17	0	0	150	90	60	+10	100	0
18	+1	1	120	48	40	–10	100	–10
19	2	4	100	30	30	–20	400	–40
20	3	9	80	12	15	–35	1225	–105
	$\Sigma d_x = +3$	$\Sigma d_x^2 = 19$				$\Sigma d_y = 0$	$\Sigma d_y^2 = 3350$	$\Sigma d_x d_y = -240$

$$r = \frac{n\Sigma d_x d_y - \Sigma d_x \Sigma d_y}{\sqrt{n\Sigma d_x^2 - (\Sigma d_x)^2}\ \sqrt{n\Sigma d_y^2 - (\Sigma d_y)^2}}$$

$$= \frac{6(-240) - (3)(0)}{\sqrt{6 \times 19 - (3)^2}\ \sqrt{6 \times 3350 - (0)^2}} = \frac{-1440}{\sqrt{105 \times 20100}} = -0.991$$

Thus there is a high degree of negative correlation between age and playing habits.

EXAMPLE 10.19: Calculate Karl-Pearson's coefficient of correlation from the following data and interpret its value:

Roll No.	1	2	3	4	5
Marks in Accountancy	48	35	17	23	47
Marks in Statistics	45	20	40	25	45

Solution: Let marks in accountancy be denoted by X and that is statistics by Y.

Calculation of Coefficient of Correlation

X	$(X-34)$ x	x^2	Y	$(Y-35)$ y	y^2	xy
48	+14	196	45	+10	100	+140
35	1	1	20	–15	225	–15
17	–17	289	40	+5	25	–85
23	–11	121	25	–10	100	+110
47	+13	169	45	+10	100	+130
$\Sigma X = 170$	$\Sigma x = 0$	$\Sigma x^2 = 776$	$\Sigma Y = 175$	$\Sigma y = 0$	$\Sigma y^2 = 550$	$\Sigma xy = 280$

$$r = \frac{\Sigma xy}{\sqrt{\Sigma x^2\ \Sigma y^2}} = \frac{280}{\sqrt{776 \times 550}} = \frac{280}{6533} = +0.429$$

It is moderate case of positive correlation between marks in accountancy and statistics.

EXAMPLE 10.20: Calculate the coefficient of correlation and its probable error from the following:

S.No.	Subject	% marks in final year exams.	% marks in sessionals
1.	Hindi	75	62
2.	English	81	68
3.	Physics	70	65
4.	Chemistry	76	60
5.	Maths	77	69
6.	Statistics	81	72
7.	Botany	84	76
8.	Zoology	75	72

Solution: Let % marks in final year exams be denoted by *X* and % marks in sessional by *Y*.

Calculation of Coefficient of Correlation

X	$(X-77)\ d_x$	d_x^2	Y	$(Y-68)\ d_y$	d_y^2	$d_x d_y$
75	–2	4	62	–6	36	+12
81	+4	16	68	0	0	0
70	–7	49	65	–3	9	+21
76	–1	1	60	–8	64	+8
77	0	0	69	+1	1	0
81	+4	16	72	+4	16	+16
84	+7	49	76	+8	64	+56
75	–2	4	72	+4	16	–8
$\Sigma X = 619$	$\Sigma d_x = 3$	$\Sigma d_x^2 = 139$	$\Sigma Y = 544$	$\Sigma d_y = 0$	$\Sigma d_y^2 = 206$	$\Sigma d_x d_y = 105$

$$r = \frac{n\Sigma d_x d_y - \Sigma d_x \Sigma d_y}{\sqrt{n\Sigma d_x^2 - (\Sigma d_x)^2}\ \sqrt{N\Sigma d_y^2 - (\Sigma d_y)^2}}$$

$$= \frac{8 \times 105 - (3 \times 0)}{\sqrt{8 \times 139 - (3)^2}\ \sqrt{8 \times 206}} = \frac{840}{\sqrt{1103 \times 1648}} = \frac{840}{1348.237} = 0.623$$

Probable error is given by:

$$\text{P.E}r = .6745\ \frac{I - r^2}{\sqrt{n}}$$

$$= .6745\frac{1-(.623)^2}{\sqrt{8}} = \frac{.6745 \times .6119}{2.8284} = 0.164$$

EXAMPLE 10.21: Following figures give the rainfall in inches for the year and the production in 00's of kgs or the Rabi crop and Kharif crop. Calculate the Karl-Pearson's coefficient of correlation between rainfall and total production.

Rainfall	20	22	24	26	28	30	32
Rabi Production	15	18	20	32	40	39	40
Kharif Production	15	17	20	18	20	21	15

Solution: Let rainfall be denoted by X and production by Y.

Calculation of Correlation of Coefficient

X	$(X-26)\ d_x$	d_x^2	Y	$(Y-47)\ d_y$	d_y^2	$d_x d_y$
20	–6	36	30	–17	289	+102
22	–4	16	35	–12	144	+48
24	–2	4	40	–7	49	+14
26	0	0	50	+3	9	0
28	+2	4	60	+13	169	+26
30	+4	16	60	+13	169	+52
32	+6	36	55	+8	64	+48
$\Sigma X = 182$	$\Sigma d_x = 0$	$\Sigma d_x^2 = 112$	$\Sigma Y = 330$	$\Sigma d_y = 1$	$\Sigma d_y^2 = 893$	$\Sigma d_x d_y = 290$

$$r = \frac{n\Sigma d_x d_y - \Sigma d_x \Sigma d_y}{\sqrt{n\Sigma d_x^2 - (\Sigma d_x)^2}\sqrt{n\Sigma d_y^2 - (\Sigma d_y)^2}}$$

$$= \frac{(7)(290) - (0)(1)}{\sqrt{(7)(112) - (0)^2}\sqrt{(7)(893) - (1)^2}}$$

$$= \frac{2030}{\sqrt{784}\sqrt{6250}} = \frac{2030}{2213.594} = 0.917$$

It is a case of very high degree of positive correlation between rainfall and Agricultural production.

EXAMPLE 10.22: Find the rank correlation from the following data:

Candidate	1	2	3	4	5	6	7
Marks awarded by Judge I	86	59	64	74	48	70	94
Marks awarded by Judge II	90	45	72	64	59	60	80

Solution: Since ranks are not given, we first assign ranks and then calculate the rank correlation coefficient.

Candidate	Marks by Judge I	R_1	Marks by Judger II	R_2	$(R_1 - R_2)^2\ D^2$
1	86	6	90	7	1
2	59	2	45	1	1
3	64	3	72	5	4
4	74	5	64	4	1
5	48	1	59	2	1
6	70	4	60	3	1
7	94	7	80	6	1
$N = 7$					$\Sigma D^2 = 10$

$$R = 1 - \frac{6\Sigma D^2}{N^3 - N} = 1 - \frac{6 \times 10}{7^3 - 7} = 1 - \frac{60}{336}$$

$$= 1 - 0.179 = 0.821$$

EXAMPLE 10.23: A panel of men and a panel of women were asked by a consumer testing organisation to rank 8 brands of tea according to taste. A rank of 1 was given to the best tasting tea and a rank of 8 to the worst.

Brand	A	B	C	D	E	F	G	H
Panel of Women (*X*)	5	4	3	6	7	8	1	2
Panel of Men (*Y*)	4	5	6	3	8	7	2	1

Determine how closely men's and women's tastes in tea are related.

Solution:

Calculation of Rank Correlation Coefficient

R_1	R_2	$(R_1 - R_2)^2$
5	4	1
4	5	1
3	6	9
6	3	9
7	8	1
8	7	1
1	2	1
2	1	1
		$\Sigma D^2 = 24$

$$R = 1 - \frac{6\Sigma D^2}{n^3 - n} = 1 - \frac{6 \times 24}{8^3 - 8}$$

$$= 1 - \frac{144}{512 - 8} = 1 - 0.286 = 0.714$$

There is a high degree of positive correlation between the tastes of men and women in tea.

LIST OF FORMULAE

1. Co-variation between x and y

$$\text{Cov}(x, y) = \frac{\Sigma(X - \bar{X})(Y - \bar{Y})}{n}$$

2. Karl Pearson's coefficient of correlation

(a) Actual Mean Method:

$$r = \frac{\text{Cov}(X, Y)}{\sigma_X \cdot \sigma_Y} \qquad \text{...(i)}$$

where σ_x and σ_y are S.D.

or, $$r = \frac{\Sigma(X - \overline{X})(Y - \overline{Y})}{n\sigma_X \cdot \sigma_Y} \quad \text{...(ii)}$$

or, $$r = \frac{\Sigma xy}{\sqrt{\Sigma x^2 \cdot \Sigma y^2}} \quad \text{...(iii)}$$

where $x = X - \overline{X}$ and $y = Y - \overline{Y}$

(b) Direct Method:

$$r = \frac{n\Sigma XY - (\Sigma X)(\Sigma Y)}{\sqrt{[n\Sigma X^2 - (\Sigma X)^2][n\Sigma Y^2 - (\Sigma Y)^2]}}$$

(c) Short-cut Method:

$$r = \frac{n\Sigma uv - (\Sigma u)(\Sigma v)}{\sqrt{[n\Sigma u^2 - (\Sigma u)^2] \cdot [n\Sigma v^2 - (\Sigma v)^2]}}$$

3. Correlation of Bivariate Grouped data:

$$r = \frac{N\Sigma fXY - (\Sigma fX)(\Sigma fY)}{\sqrt{[N\Sigma fX^2 - (\Sigma fX)^2][N\Sigma fY^2 - (\Sigma fY)^2]}}$$

4. By change of origin and scale,

$$r = \frac{N\Sigma fuv - (\Sigma fu)(\Sigma fv)}{\sqrt{[N\Sigma fu^2 - (\Sigma fu)^2][N\Sigma fv^2 - (\Sigma fv)^2]}}$$

5. Rank Correlation

$$r = \frac{6\Sigma D^2}{n^3 - n}$$

where ΣD^2 = sum of squares of differences between the pairs of ranks.
n = number of pairs of observations

6. For Tied observations, rank correlation

$$r = 1 - \frac{6[\Sigma D^2 + \frac{1}{12}(m^3 - m) + \frac{1}{12}(m^3 - m) + ...)}{n^3 - n}$$

where m is the number of items whose ranks are common.

7. Coefficient of concurrent deviations

$$r_e = \pm\sqrt{\left|\frac{2c - n}{n}\right|}$$

8. Probable error

$$\text{P.E} = 0.6745 \left[\frac{1 - r^2}{\sqrt{n}}\right]$$

SELF PRACTICE EXERCISES

I. CHOOSE THE BEST ANSWER

1. Limits for correlation coefficient:
   (a) $-1 \le r \le 1$ (b) $0 \le r \le 1$
   (c) $-1 \le r \le 0$ (d) $1 \le r \le 2$
2. The coefficient of correlation:
   (a) cannot be negative (b) cannot be positive
   (c) always positive (d) can either be positive or negative
3. The product moment correlation coefficient is obtained by:
   (a) $r = \frac{\Sigma xy}{xy}$ (b) $r = \frac{\Sigma XY}{n \sigma_x, \sigma_y}$
   (c) $r = \frac{\Sigma XY}{n \sigma_x}$ (d) none of these
4. If cov $(X, Y) = 0$ then:
   (a) X and Y are correlated (b) X and Y are uncorrelated
   (c) none (d) X and Y are linearly related
5. If $r = 0$ the cov (x, y) is:
   (a) 0 (b) -1
   (c) 1 (d) 0.2
6. Rank correlation coefficient is given by:
   (a) $1 + \frac{6\Sigma D^3}{n^3 - n}$ (b) $1 - \frac{6\Sigma D^2}{n^2 - n}$
   (c) $1 - \frac{6\Sigma D^2}{n^3 - n}$ (d) $1 - \frac{6\Sigma D^2}{n^3 + n}$
7. If cov $(X, Y) = \sigma_X \sigma_Y$ then:
   (a) $r = +1$ (b) $r = 0$
   (c) $r = 2$ (d) $r = -1$
8. If $D_2 = 0$ rank correlation is:
   (a) 0 (b) 1
   (c) 0.5 (d) -1
9. Correlation coefficient is independent of change of:
   (a) Origin (b) Scale
   (c) Origin and Scale (d) None
10. Rank Correlation was found by:
    (a) Pearson (b) Spearman
    (c) Galton (d) Fisher

II. FILL IN THE BLANKS

1. Correlation coefficient is free from ....
2. The diagrammatic representation of two variables is called ....

3. The relationship between three or more variables is studied with the help of .... correlation.
4. Product moment correlations was found by ....
5. When $r = +1$, there is .... correlation.
6. If $r_{xy} = r_{yx}$, correlation between x and y is ....
7. Rank Correlation is useful to study .... characteristics.
8. The nature of correlation for shoe size and IQ is ....

III. SHORT ANSWER TYPE QUESTIONS

1. What is correlation?
2. Distinguish between positive and negative correlation.
3. Define Karl-Pearson's coefficient of correlation. Interpret r, when $r = 1, -1$ and 0.
4. Mention important properties of correlation coefficient.
5. Prove that correlation coefficient lies between –1 and +1.
6. What is Rank correlation? What are its merits and demerits?
7. Distinguish between linear and non-linear correlation. **[MBA, MK, 2003]**
8. Explain the meaning and significance of the term correlation. **[MBA, DU, 2000]**
9. What is a scatter diagram? How does it help in studying the correlation between two variables, in respect of both its direction and degree? **[MBA, DU, 2002]**
10. Does correlation always signify a cause and effect relationship between variables?

IV. LONG ANSWER TYPE QUESTION

1. What are the advantages of Spearman's rank correlation coefficient over Karl-Pearson's Correlation? Explain the method of calculating Spearman's correlation coefficient.
2. What is a scatter diagram? How is it useful in the study of Correlation? **[MBA, UPTU, 2004]**
3. Show that correlation coefficient is independent of change of origin and scale. **[MBA, DU, 2001]**
4. Explain different types of correlation with examples.
5. Distinguish between Karl-Pearson's coefficient of correlation and Spearman's correlation coefficient.
6. For 10 observations □$\Sigma x = 130$; $\Sigma y = 220$; $\Sigma x^2 = 2290$; $\Sigma y^2 = 5510$; $\Sigma xy = 3467$. Find 'r.
7. Cov $(x, y) = 18.6$; var $(x) = 20.2$; var $(y) = 23.7$. Find 'r'.
8. Given that $r = 0.42$ cov $(x, y) = 10.5$ $v(x) = 16$; Find the standard deviation of y.
9. Rank correlation coefficient $r = 0.8$. $\Sigma D^2 = 33$. Find 'n'.

Karl-Pearson Correlation

10. Compute the coefficient of correlation of the following score of A and B.

A	5	10	5	11	12	4	3	2	7	1
B	1	6	2	8	5	1	4	6	5	2

11. Calculate coefficient of Correlation between price and supply. Interpret the value of correlation coefficient.

Price	8	10	15	17	20	22	24	25
Supply	25	30	32	35	37	40	42	45

12. Find out Karl-Pearson's coefficient of correlation in the following series relating to prices and supply of a commodity:

Price (Rs)	11	12	13	14	15	16	17	18	19	20
Supply (Rs)	30	29	29	25	24	24	24	21	18	15

13. Find the correlation coefficient between the marks obtained by ten students in economics and statistics.

Marks (in economics)	70	68	67	55	60	60	75	63	60	72
Marks (in statistics)	65	65	80	60	68	58	75	62	60	70

14. Compute the coefficient of correlation from the following data:

Age of workers	40	34	22	28	36	32	24	46	26	30
Days absent	2.5	3	5	4	2.5	3	4.5	2.5	4	3.5

15. Find out correlation coefficient between height of father and son from the following data:

Height of father	65	66	67	67	68	69	70	72
Height of son	67	68	65	68	72	72	69	71

Bi-variate Correlation

16. Calculate Karl-Pearson's coefficient of correlation for the following data:

Class → / **Interval ↓**	**0**	**1**	**2**	**3**	**4**	**5**	**6**	**7**	**8**	**Total**
20–29	2	1	2	2	–	1	–	1	1	**10**
30–39	–	2	–	1	–	2	–	1	2	**8**
40–49	–	2	–	2	–	–	1	–	1	**6**
50–59	1	–	2	–	–	–	–	1	–	**4**
60–69	–	–	–	–	–	1	–	1	–	**2**

17. Calculate the coefficient of correlation and comment upon your result.

Age of Wives → / **Age of Husband ↓**	**15–25**	**25–35**	**35–45**	**45–55**	**55–65**	**65–75**	**Total**
15–25	1	1	–	–	–	–	**2**
25–35	2	12	1	–	–	–	**15**
35–45	–	4	10	1	–	–	**15**
45–55	–	–	3	6	1	–	**10**
55–65	–	–	–	2	4	2	**8**
65–75	–	–	–	–	1	2	**3**
Total	**3**	**17**	**14**	**9**	**6**	**4**	**53**

18. The following table gives class frequency distribution of 45 clerks in a business office according to age and pay. Find correlation between age and pay if any.

Pay → / Age ↓	60–70	70–80	80–90	90–100	100–110	Total
20–30	4	3	1	–	–	**8**
30–40	2	5	2	1	–	**10**
40–50	1	2	3	2	1	**9**
50–60	–	1	3	5	2	**11**
60–70	–	–	1	1	5	**7**
Total	**7**	**11**	**10**	**9**	**8**	**45**

19. Find the correlation coefficient between two subjects marks scored by 60 candidates.

Marks in Statistics → / Marks in Economics ↓	5–15	15–25	25–35	35–45	Total
0–10	1	1	–	–	**2**
10–20	3	6	5	1	**15**
20–30	1	8	9	2	**20**
30–40	–	3	9	3	**15**
40–50	–	–	4	4	**8**
Total	**5**	**18**	**27**	**10**	**60**

20. Compute the correlation coefficient for the following data.

Advertisement Exp. (' 000) → / Sales Revenue (Rs 000) ↓	5 –15	15–25	25–35	35–45	Total
75–125	4	1	–	–	**5**
125–175	7	6	2	1	**16**
175–225	1	3	4	2	**10**
225–275	1	1	3	4	**9**
Total	**13**	**11**	**9**	**7**	**40**

21. The following table gives the no. of students having different heights and weights. Do you find any relation between height and weight.

Weights in Kg → / Height in cms ↓	55–60	60–65	65–70	70–75	75–80	Total
150–155	1	3	7	5	2	**18**
155–160	2	4	10	7	4	**27**
160–165	1	5	12	10	7	**35**
165–170	–	3	8	6	3	**20**
Total	**4**	**15**	**37**	**28**	**16**	**100**

Rank Correlation

22. Two judges gave the following ranks to eight competitors in a beauty contest. Examine the relationship between their judgements.

Judge A	4	5	1	2	3	6	7	8
Judge B	8	6	2	3	1	4	5	7

23. From the following data, calculate the coefficient of rank correlation.

X	36	36	20	65	42	33	44	50	15	60
Y	50	35	70	25	58	75	60	45	80	38

24. Calculate spearman's coefficient of Rank correlation for the following data.

X	53	98	95	81	75	71	59	55
Y	47	25	32	37	30	40	39	45

25. Apply spearman's Rank difference method and calculate coefficient of correlation between *X* and *Y* from the data given below.

X	22	28	31	23	29	31	27	22	31	18
Y	18	25	25	37	31	35	31	29	18	20

26. Find the rank correlation coefficients.

Marks in Test 1	70	68	67	55	60	60	75	63	60	72
Marks in Test II	65	65	80	60	68	58	75	62	60	70

27. Calculate spearman's Rank correlation coefficient for the following table of marks of students in two subjects.

First subject :	80	64	54	49	48	35	32	29	20	18	15	10
Second subject :	36	38	39	41	27	43	45	52	51	42	40	52

ANSWERS

I. CHOOSE THE CORRECT ANSWERS

1. (a) 2. (d) 3. (b) 4. (b) 5. (a) 6. (c) 7. (a) 8. (b) 9. (c) 10. (b)

II. FILL IN THE BLANKS

1. Units
2. Scatter diagram
3. Multiple
4. Pearson
5. Positive perfect
6. Symmetric
7. Qualitative
8. No correlation

IV. LONG ANSWER TYPE QUESTIONS

6. $r = 0.9574$ 31. $r = 0.85$ 32. $y = 6.25$
9. $n = 10$ 34. $r = +0.58$ 35. $r = +0.98$
12. $r = -0.96$ 37. $r = +0.68$ 38. $r = -0.92$
15. $r = +0.64$ 40. $r = +0.1$ 41. $r = +0.98$
18. $r - +0.746$ 43. $r - +0.533$ 44. $r - +0.596$
21. $r = +0.0945$ 46. $r = +0.62$ 47. $r = -0.93$
24. $r = -0.905$ 49. $r = 0.34$ 50. $r = 0.679$
27. $r = 0.685$

CHAPTER 11

Regression Analysis

11.1 INTRODUCTION

In the last chapter we have discussed correlation analysis, which seeks to determine the degree of linear relationship or correlation between two variables in bivariate distributions. The coefficient of correlation indicates whether the variables are linearly related and if so, how strong the relationship is.

The statistical method that helps to formulate an algebraic relationship between two or more variables in the form of an equation to estimate the value of a continuous random variable, given the value of another variable, is called ***regression analysis*** and in this chapter we will discuss linear regression analysis in detail.

11.2 MEANING OF REGRESSION

The term ***'regression'*** was first used by ***Sir Francis Galton*** (1822-1911), a British Biometrician in connection with the height of parents and their offspring's.

The literal meaning of regression is ***"moving backward"*** or ***"stepping back towards the average"***. But now-a-days the term "regression" stands for some sort of functional relationship between two or more related variable.

The regression analysis is mathematical measure of the average relationship between two or more variables, it terms of the original units of the data.

After knowing the relationship between two variables we may be interested in estimating (predicting) the value of one variable given the value of another. The variable predicted on the basis of other variables is called the ***"dependent"*** or the 'explained' variable and the other the ***'independent'*** or the 'predicting' variable. The prediction is based on average relationship derived statistically by regression analysis. The equation, linear or otherwise, is called the ***regression equation*** or the explaining equation.

DO YOU KNOW?

Regression is the measure of the average relationship between two or more variables in terms of the original units of the data.

For example, if we know that advertising and sales are correlated we may find out expected amount of sales for a given advertising expenditure or the required amount of expenditure for attaining a given amount of sales. The relationship between two variables can be considered between, say, rainfall and agricultural production, price of an input and the overall cost of product, consumer expenditure and disposable income. Thus, regression analysis reveals average relationship between two variables and this makes possible estimation or prediction.

For example, A sales manager may want to determine whether product price, advertising budgets and competitor's prices have any effect on total sales. A regression analysis determines, within a certain error bound, how well the variables "fit" together, and which ones have the most effect on total sales.

Purposes of the Regression

Regression analysis is used to understand the statistical dependence of one variable on other variables. The technique can show what proportion of variance between variables is due to the dependent variable, and what proportion is due to the independent variables. The relation between the variables can be illustrated graphically, or more usually using an equation.

People use regression on an intuitive level every day. In business, a well-dressed man is thought to be financially successful. A mother knows that more sugar in her children's diet results in higher energy levels. The ease of waking up in the morning often depends on how late you went to bed the night before. Quantitative regression adds precision by developing a mathematical formula that can be used for predictive purposes.

For example, a medical researcher might want to use body weight (independent variable) to predict the most appropriate dose for a new drug (dependent variable). The purpose of running the regression is to find a formula that fits the relationship between the two variables. Then you can use that formula to predict values for the dependent variable when only the independent variable is known. A doctor could prescribe the proper dose based on a person's body weight.

An Application: A company wants to know if there is a significant relationship between its advertising expenditures and its sales volume. The independent variable is advertising budget and the dependent variable is sales volume. A lag time of one month will be used because sales are expected to lag behind actual advertising expenditures. Data was collected for a six month period. All figures are in thousands of Rs. Is there a significant relationship between advertising budget and sales volume?

Independent Variable	4.2	6.1	3.9	5.7	7.3	5.9
Dependent Variable	27.1	30.4	25.0	29.7	40.1	28.8

$$Y = 10.079 + (3.700\,X) + \text{error}$$

Standard error of the estimate = 2.568

t-test for the significance of the slope = 4.095

Degrees of freedom = 4

Two-tailed probability = .0149

r-squared = .807

You might make a Statement in a Report like this: A simple linear regression was performed on six months of data to determine if there was a significant relationship between advertising expenditures and sales volume. The *t*-statistic for the slope was significant at the .05 critical alpha level, $t(4) = 4.10$, $p = .015$. Thus, we reject the null hypothesis and conclude that there was a positive significant relationship between advertising expenditures and sales volume. Furthermore, 80.7% of the variability in sales volume could be explained by advertising expenditures.

11.3 USES OF REGRESSION ANALYSIS

1. Regression analysis helps in establishing a functional relationship between two or more variables.
2. Since most of the problems of economic analysis are based on cause and effect relationships, the regression analysis is a highly valuable tool in economic and business research.
3. Regression analysis predicts the values of dependent variables from the values of independent variables.
4. We can calculate coefficient of correlation (r) and coefficient of determination (r_2) with the help of regression coefficients.
5. In statistical analysis of demand curves, supply curves, production function, cost function, consumption function etc., regression analysis is widely used.

11.4 DIFFERENCE BETWEEN CORRELATION AND REGRESSION

S.No.	Correlation	Regression
1.	Correlation is the relationship between two or more variables, which vary in sympathy with the other in the same or the opposite direction.	Regression means going back and it is a mathematical measure showing the average relationship between two variables
2.	Both the variables *X* and *Y* are random variables.	Here *X* is a random variable and *Y* is a fixed variable. Sometimes both the variables may be random variables.
3.	It finds out the degree of relationship between two variables and not the cause and effect of the variables.	It indicates the causes and effect relationship between the variables and establishes functional relationship.
4.	It is used for testing and verifying the relation between two variables and gives limited information.	Besides verification it is used for the prediction of one value, in relationship to the other given value.
5.	The coefficient of correlation is a relative measure. The range of relationship lies between –1 and +1.	Regression coefficient is an absolute figure. If we know the value of the independent variable, we can find the value of the dependent variable.
6.	There may be spurious correlation between two variables.	In regression there is no such spurious regression.
7.	It has limited application, because it is confined only to linear relationship between the variables.	It has wider application, as it studies linear and nonlinear relationship between the variables.
8.	It is not very useful for further mathematical treatment.	It is widely used for further mathematical treatment.
9.	If the coefficient of correlation is positive, then the two variables are positively correlated and vice-versa.	The regression coefficient explains that the decrease in one variable is associated with the increase in the other variable.

11.5 TYPE OF REGRESSION

The regression analysis can be classified into:

(i) Simple and Multiple (ii) Linear and Non-Linear (iii) Total and Partial

(i) Simple and Multiple: In case of simple relationship only two variables are considered, ***for example***, the influence of advertising expenditure on sales turnover. In the case of multiple relationships, more than two variables are involved. On this while one variable is a dependent variable the remaining variables are independent ones.
For example, the turnover (y) may depend on advertising expenditure (x) and the income of the people (z). Then the functional relationship can be expressed as $y = f(x,z)$.

(ii) Linear and Non-linear: The linear relationships are based on straight-line trend, the equation of which has no-power higher than one. But, remember a linear relationship can be both simple and multiple. Normally a linear relationship is taken into account because besides its simplicity, it has a better predictive value; a linear trend can be easily projected into the future. In the case of non-linear relationship curved trend lines are derived. The equations of these are parabolic.

(iii) Total and Partial: In the case of total relationships all the important variables are considered. Normally, they take the form of a multiple relationships because most economic and business phenomena are affected by multiplicity of cases. In the case of partial relationship one or more variables are considered, but not all, thus excluding the influence of those not found relevant for a given purpose.

11.6 LINEAR REGRESSION EQUATION

If two variables have linear relationship then as the independent variable (X) changes, the dependent variable (Y) also changes. If the different values of X and Y are plotted, then the two straight lines of best fit can be made to pass through the plotted points. These two lines are known as ***regression lines***. Again, these regression lines are based on two equations known as ***regression equations.*** These equations show best estimate of one variable for the known value of the other. The equations are linear.

Linear regression equation of ***Y* on *X*** is

$$Y = a + bX \quad \text{... (1)}$$

And ***X* on *Y*** is

$$X = a + bY \quad \text{...(2)}$$

a, b are constants.

From (1) We can estimate Y for known value of X. (2) We can estimate X for known value of Y.

11.6.1 Regression Lines

For regression analysis of two variables there are two regression lines, namely Y on X and X on Y.

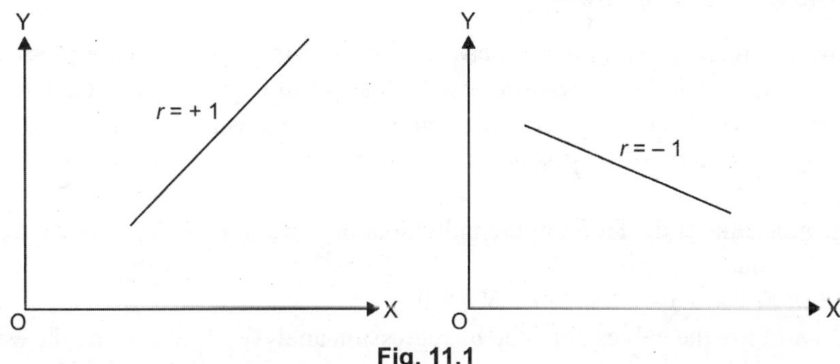

Fig. 11.1

The two regression lines show the average relationship between the two variables. For perfect correlation, positive or negative i.e., $r = + 1$, the two lines coincide i.e., we will find only one straight line. If $r = 0$, i.e., both the variables are independent then the two lines will cut each other at right angle. In this case the two lines will be parallel to X and Y-axis.

Lastly the two lines intersect at the point of means of X and Y. From this point of intersection, if a straight line is drawn on X-axis, it will touch at the mean value of X. Similarly, a perpendicular drawn from the point of intersection of two regression lines on Y-axis will touch the mean value of Y.

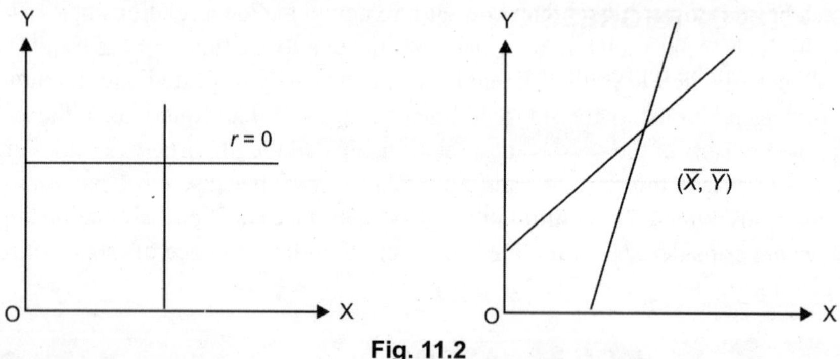

Fig. 11.2

Thus we get two lines of regressions as shown in the figure 11.3(a) and 11.3(b).

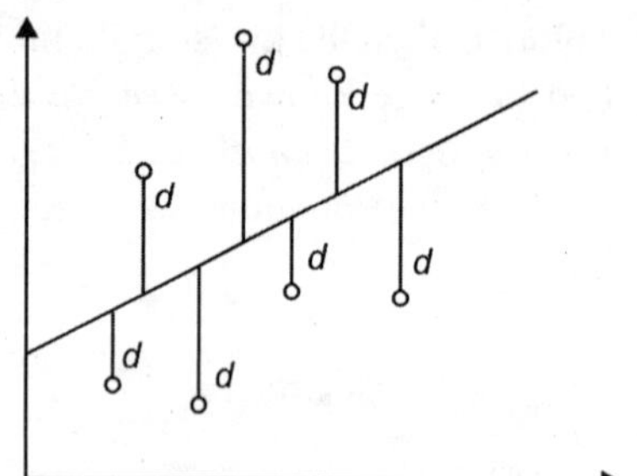

Fig. 11.3(a): Line of regression of Y and X
Its form is $Y = a + b X$
It is used to estimate
Y when X is given

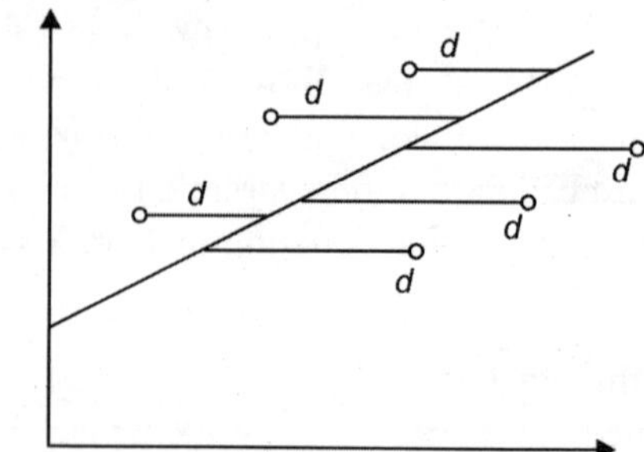

Fig. 11.3(b): Line of regression of X and Y
Its form is $X = a + b Y$
It is used to estimate
X when Y is given

11.6.2 Principle of 'Least Squares'

Regression shows an average relationship between two variables, which is expressed by a line of regression drawn by the method of ***"least squares"***. This line of regression can be derived graphically or algebraically. Before we discuss the various methods let us understand the meaning of least squares.

A line fitted by the method of least squares is known as the line of best fit. The line adapts to the following rules:

(i) The algebraic sum of deviation in the individual observations with reference to the regression line may be equal to zero. i.e.,

$$\Sigma(X - X_e) = 0 \text{ or } \Sigma(Y - Y_e) = 0$$

where X and Y are the values obtained by regression analysis. X_e and Y_e are the estimated values of X and Y variables.

(ii) The sum of the squares of these deviations is less than the sum of squares of deviations from any other line. i.e.,

$$\Sigma (Y - Y_e)^2 < \Sigma (Y - A_i)^2$$

where A_i = corresponding values of any other straight line.

(iii) The lines of regression (best fit) intersect at the mean values of the variables X and Y, i.e., intersecting point is $\overline{X}$, $\overline{Y}$.

11.7 METHODS OF REGRESSION ANALYSIS

The various methods can be represented in the form of chart given below:

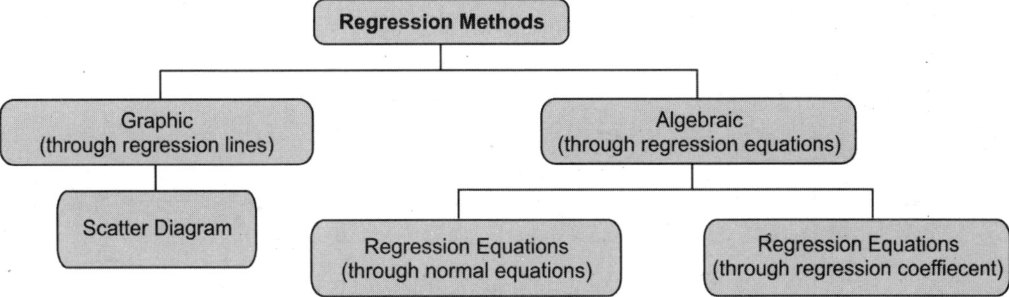

Fig. 11.4: Methods of Regression Analysis

11.8 GRAPHIC METHOD

Scatter Diagram

Under this method the points are plotted on a graph paper representing various parts of values of the concerned variables. These points give a picture of a scatter diagram with several points spread over. A regression line may be drawn in between these points either by free hand or by a scale rule in such a way that the squares of the vertical or the horizontal distances (as the case may be) between the points and the line of regression so drawn is the least. In other words, it should be drawn faithfully as the line of best fit leaving equal number of points on both sides in such a manner that the sum of the squares of the distances is the best.

When we study the relationship between two variables, X and Y, the very first step we should take is to plot the given data on the graph. For each pair of X and Y values, there will be a point on the graph. (Figure 11.5).

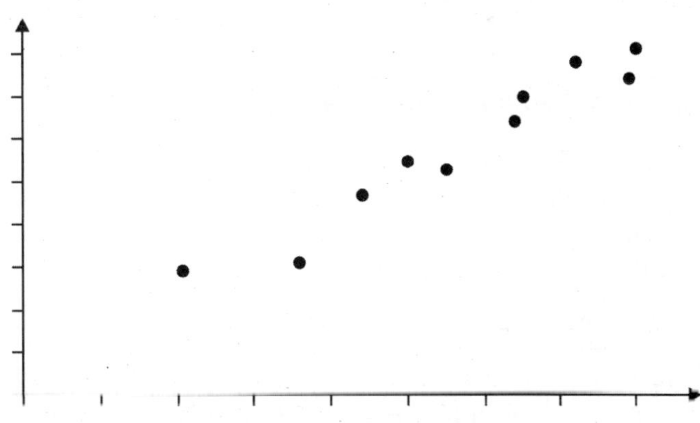

Fig. 11.5: Scatter Diagram

For example, here is a table showing the results of two examinations set to students that I teach. I set them a Maths exam and DBMS exam and record the scores that they get in both:

	Sumit	Vikas	Anu	Arvind	Garima	Swati	Monica	Ankit	Sachin	Udit
Maths score	72	65	80	36	50	21	79	64	44	55
DBMS score	78	70	81	31	55	29	74	64	47	53

We take a piece of graph paper and draw two axes. The horizontal axis will represent the score on the DBMS exam. The vertical axis will represent the score on the Maths exam. For each student, we then mark a small dot at the co-ordinates representing their two scores. Below, I have done this:

You can see that the points follow a fairly strong pattern. People who are good at maths tend to be good at English as well. The marks lie fairly close to an imaginary straight line that we can draw on the graph. In the diagram below, I have drawn in this straight line, and also included another point (in white) which I will explain later:

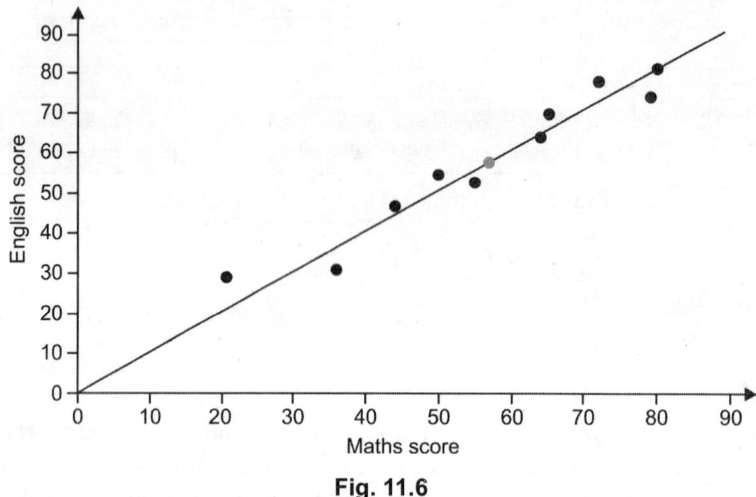

Fig. 11.6

The fact that the points lie close to the straight line is called a strong correlation. The fact that this line points upwards to right — indicating that the DBMS mark tends to increase as the maths mark increases — is called a positive correlation.

Line of Best Fit (Regression Line)

The straight line that we draw through the points is called either the *line of best fit* or the *regression line*. It describes the relationship between the two variables (the quantities compared) mathematically. There is a standard way to draw this line to ensure that it fits as closely to the data points as possible. Later on, we will investigate exactly what that mathematical way is. For now, we only have to remember one thing:

The regression line goes through the point whose co-ordinates are the *mean values* of the variables.

The arithmetic means are found by adding the relevant scores, and dividing by 10. This is because there are ten students in the table. We work out the arithmetic mean of the maths scores:

$$\text{Mean Maths score} = (72 + 65 + 80 + 36 + 50 + 21 + 79 + 64 + 44 + 55) / 10$$
$$= 56.6$$

then we work out the arithmetic mean of the DBMS scores

Mean DBMS score = (78 + 70 + 81 + 31 + 55 + 29 + 74 + 64 + 47 + 53) / 10
= 58.2

and we can be sure that the line must go through the point (56.6, 58.2). This is the point marked in red on the graph above. You will notice that there are roughly the same numbers of data point lying above this line as there are below it.

We can use the regression line to make predictions. For instance, what DBMS mark would we expect someone to receive if they received a maths mark of 30. If we look at the straight line, we can see that when the maths mark is 30, the DBMS mark is approximately 28. Similarly, we can assume that anyone who got an English mark of 40, would also get a maths mark of about 40. However, there are limits on the predictions that we can make, as you will see later on.

11.9 ALGEBRAIC METHODS

11.9.1 Regression Equations

Regression equations are algebraic expressions of the regression lines. Since there are two regression lines, there are two regression equations – the regression equation of X and Y is used to describe the variations in the values of X for given changes in Y and the regression equation of Y on X is used to describe the variation in the values of Y for given changes in X.

(A) Line of Regression of X on Y

To obtain of regression of X on Y, we shall assume X as dependent variable and Y as independent variable.

Let

$$X = a + bY$$

Where, X, Y are variable and a, b are constants whose values are to be determined. The values of a and b are found by the method of least squares.

For the equation $X = a + bY$, the normal eq^n are

$$\boxed{\Sigma X = na + b\Sigma Y} \quad ...(1)$$

and

$$\boxed{\Sigma XY = a\Sigma Y + b\Sigma Y^2} \quad ...(2)$$

eq^n (1) and eq^n (2) are called ***Normal equations***.

Solving (1) and (2) for 'a' and 'b', we get

$$b\Sigma Y^2 = \Sigma XY - a\Sigma Y \quad \text{[From eq}^n\text{ (2)]}$$

Putting the value of 'a' from eq (1), we get

$$b\Sigma Y^2 = \Sigma XY - \left[\frac{\Sigma X}{n} - \frac{b\Sigma Y}{n}\right]\Sigma Y$$

$$nb\Sigma Y^2 = n\Sigma XY - \Sigma X\Sigma Y - b\,(\Sigma Y)^2$$

Solving the eq^n for the value of '*b*', we get

$$b = \frac{n\Sigma XY - \Sigma X\Sigma Y}{n\Sigma Y^2 - (\Sigma Y)^2} \quad ...(3)$$

Now, from eq (1)

$$na = \Sigma X - b\Sigma Y$$

$$a = \frac{\Sigma X}{n} - b\frac{\Sigma Y}{n}$$

$$a = \bar{X} - b\bar{Y} \qquad \left[\bar{X} = \frac{\Sigma X}{n}, \bar{Y} = \frac{\Sigma Y}{n}\right]$$

$$\bar{X} = a + b\bar{Y} \quad ...(4)$$

Hence $X = a + bY$ line passes through point ($\bar{X}, \bar{Y}$)

Putting $a = \bar{X} - b\bar{Y}$ in eq^n of line $X = a + bY$
we get

$$X - \bar{X} = b(Y - \bar{Y}) \quad ...(5)$$

eq^n (5) is called regression line of *X* and *Y*. '*b*' is called the regression coefficient of *X* on *Y* and is usually denoted by b_{XY} (for *X* on *Y*). Hence eq^n (5) can be rewritten as

$$\boxed{X - \bar{X} = b_{XY}(Y - \bar{Y})} \quad ...(6)$$

Where $\bar{X}$ and $\bar{Y}$ are mean values while

$$\boxed{b_{XY} = \frac{n\Sigma XY - \Sigma X\Sigma Y}{n\Sigma Y^2 - (\Sigma Y)^2}}$$

(B) Line of Regression of Y on X

Proceeding in the same way, we can derive normal equations for *Y* on *X*.

$$\Sigma Y = na + b\Sigma X$$

and

$$\Sigma XY = a\Sigma X + b\Sigma X^2$$

and the regression line of *Y* of *X* as

$$\boxed{Y - \bar{Y} = b_{YX}(X - \bar{X})} \quad ...(7)$$

where $\bar{X}$ and $\bar{Y}$ are mean values while

$$\boxed{b_{YX} = \frac{n\Sigma XY - \Sigma X\Sigma Y}{n\Sigma X^2 - (\Sigma X)^2}}$$

11.9.2 Regression Coefficients

The quantity *b* in the regression equations is called the 'regression coefficient' or 'slope coefficient' since there are two regression equations, therefore, there are two regression coefficients – regression coefficient of *X* on *Y* and regression coefficient of *Y* on *X*.

(A) Regression Coefficient of X on Y

The regression coefficient of X on Y is represented by the symbol b_{XY} or b_1. It measures the amount of change in X corresponding to a unit change in Y. In eq^n (2), page no 373 (11.9.1), shifting the origin to $(\bar{X}, \bar{Y})$.

We get

$$\Sigma(X - \bar{X})(Y - \bar{Y}) = a\Sigma(Y - \bar{Y}) + b\Sigma(Y - \bar{Y})^2 \quad ...(1)$$

We know that

$$\Sigma(Y - \bar{Y}) = 0, \frac{1}{n}\Sigma(Y - \bar{Y})^2 = \sigma_Y^2$$

$$\frac{\Sigma(X - \bar{X})(Y - \bar{Y})}{n\sigma_X \cdot \sigma_Y} = r$$

So

$\Rightarrow$
$$nr\ \sigma_X\ \sigma_Y = a\,(o) + bn\,\sigma_Y^2 \quad \text{[From eq (1)]}$$

$$b = r\frac{\sigma_X}{\sigma_Y}$$

Hence regression coefficient b_{XY} can also be defined

$$\boxed{b_{XY} = r\frac{\sigma_X}{\sigma_Y}} \quad ...(2)$$

where r is the coefficient of correlation σ_X and σ_Y are the standard deviations of X and Y series respectively.

When deviations are taken from the means of X and Y, the regression coefficient is obtained by

$$b_{XY} = \frac{n\Sigma XY - \Sigma X\Sigma Y}{n\Sigma Y^2 - (\Sigma Y)^2}$$

$r\frac{\sigma_X}{\sigma_Y}$ is called regression coefficient of X on Y and is denoted by b_{XY}. Thus

$$b_{XY} = r\frac{\sigma_X}{\sigma_Y} = \frac{\Sigma(X - \bar{X})(Y - \bar{Y})}{n\sigma_X \cdot \sigma_Y} \cdot \frac{\sigma_X}{\sigma_Y}$$

Let
$$x = X - \bar{X} \text{ and } y = Y - \bar{Y}$$

Then

$$b_{XY} = \frac{\Sigma xy}{n\sigma_y^2} = \frac{\Sigma xy}{n \cdot \left(\frac{\Sigma y^2}{n}\right)} \qquad \left[\sigma_y = \frac{\Sigma(Y - \bar{Y})^2}{n}\right]$$

$$\boxed{b_{XY} = \frac{\Sigma xy}{\Sigma y^2}}$$

Thus instead of finding out the values of r, σ_X and σ_Y we can directly find out the value of b_{XY} by dividing the product of the deviations of X and Y series from their respective means by the sum of the squares of the deviations of the Y series from its mean.

(B) Regression Coefficient of Y on X

The regression coefficient of Y on X is represented by b_{YX} or b_2. It measures the amount of change in Y corresponding to a unit change in X. The value of b_{YX} is given by

$$b_{YX} = r\frac{\sigma_Y}{\sigma_X}$$

When deviations are taken from actual means X and Y, the regression coefficient is obtained by

$$b_{YX} = \frac{n\Sigma XY - \Sigma X \Sigma Y}{n\Sigma X^2 - (\Sigma X)^2}$$

Its value is $\frac{\Sigma xy}{\Sigma x^2}$ in the same manner as proved above.

Thus $$b_{YX} = \frac{\Sigma xy}{\Sigma x^2}, \text{ where } x = X - \bar{X} \text{ and } y = Y - \bar{Y}$$

Thus the two regression equations would take the following shape:

Regression equation of X on Y

$$\left(X - \bar{X}\right) = r\frac{\sigma_X}{\sigma_Y}\left(Y - \bar{Y}\right) \quad \text{Or} \quad \left(X - \bar{X}\right) = \frac{\Sigma xy}{\Sigma y^2}\left(Y - \bar{Y}\right)$$

Regression equation of Y or X

$$\left(Y - \bar{Y}\right) = r\frac{\sigma_Y}{\sigma_X}\left(X - \bar{X}\right) \quad \text{Or} \quad (Y - \bar{Y}) = \frac{\Sigma xy}{\Sigma x^2}\left(X - \bar{X}\right)$$

Find the regression equation from this method is called ***deviations from the means***.

The method of obtaining regression equations by the method of least squares is very tedious and involves lot of calculation work. The following examples will explain the application of these equations.

EXAMPLE 11.1: From the following data obtain the two regression equation.

X	2	4	6	8	10
Y	5	7	9	8	11

Solution:

X	Y	XY	X^2	Y^2
2	5	10	4	25
4	7	28	16	49
6	9	54	36	81
8	8	64	64	64
10	11	110	100	121
ΣX=30	ΣY=40	ΣXY=266	ΣX^2 = 220	ΣY^2 = 340

Regression Equations Y on X is of the form

$$Y = a + bX$$

and the normal equations are

$$\Sigma Y = na + b\Sigma X$$

$$\Sigma XY = a\Sigma X = b\Sigma X^2$$

Substituting the value from the table, we get

$$40 = 5a + 30b \qquad ...(1)$$

$$266 = 30a + 220b \qquad ...(2)$$

Multiplying equation (1) by 6 we get

$$240 = 30a + 180b \qquad ...(3)$$

Subtracting equation (3) from equation (2), we get

$$40b = 26 \quad \text{or} \quad b = 0.65$$

Subtracting the value of b in equation (1), we get

$$40 = 5a + 19.5 \quad \text{or} \quad 5a = 20.5$$

$\Rightarrow$ $$a = 4.1$$

Substituting the value of a and b in the regression

Equation Y on X, we get $\boxed{Y = 4.1 + 0.65X}$

This is the Regression equation of Y or X.

Again, Regression equation of X or Y is

$$X = a + bY \quad \text{and}$$

Normal equation are

$$\Sigma X = na + b\Sigma Y$$

$$\Sigma XY = a\Sigma Y + b\Sigma Y^2$$

Substituting the values in these equations, we get

$$30 = 5a + 40b \qquad ...(4)$$

$$266 = 40a + 340b \qquad ...(5)$$

Multiplying equation (4) by 8 we get

$$240 = 40a + 320b \qquad ...(6)$$

Substracting (6) from (5), we get

$$20b = 26$$

$\Rightarrow$ $$b = 1.3$$

Substituting the value of b in equation (1), we get

$$30 = 5a + 52$$

$$5a = -22$$

$\Rightarrow$ $$a = 4.4$$

Substituting the values of a and b in the regression equation, we get

$$\boxed{X = -4.4 + 1.3Y}$$

This is the regression equation of X or Y.

EXAMPLE 11.2: From the data given in example 11.1 obtain the regression equations by taking deviations from the actual means of *X* and *Y* series.

Solution:

X	X − X̄ (x)	x^2	Y	Y − Ȳ (y)	(y^2)	xy
2	−4	16	5	−3	9	+12
4	−2	4	7	−1	1	+2
6	0	0	9	+1	1	0
8	+2	4	8	0	0	0
10	+4	16	11	+3	9	+12
ΣX=30 Mean = 6	Σx = 0	Σx^2 = 40	Σy = 40	Σy = 0 Mean = 8	Σy^2 = 20	Σxy = 26

Regression equation of *X* or *Y* is

$$\left[\bar{X} = \frac{\Sigma X}{n} = \frac{30}{5} = 6 \qquad \bar{Y} = \frac{\Sigma Y}{n} = \frac{40}{5} = 8\right]$$

$$(X - \bar{X}) = r\frac{\sigma_x}{\sigma_y}(Y - \bar{Y})$$

or $$(X - \bar{X}) = \frac{\Sigma xy}{\Sigma y^2}(Y - \bar{Y})$$

or $$X - 6 = \frac{26}{20}(Y - 8)$$

$\Rightarrow$ $$X - 6 = 1.3\ (Y - 8)$$

$\Rightarrow$ $$X - 6 = 1.3Y - 10.4$$

$\Rightarrow$ $$\boxed{X = 1.3\,Y - 4.4}$$

Regression Equation of *Y* or *X* is

$$(Y - \bar{Y}) = r\frac{\sigma_y}{\sigma_x}(X - \bar{X})$$

or $$(Y - \bar{Y}) = \frac{\Sigma xy}{x^2}\ (X - \bar{X})$$

or $$Y - 8 = \frac{26}{40}(X - 6)$$

$\Rightarrow$ $$Y - 8 = 0.65\ (X - 6)$$

$\Rightarrow$ $$Y - 8 = 0.65\,X - 3.90$$

$\Rightarrow$ $$\boxed{Y = 0.65\,X - 4.10}$$

It would be observed that these regression equations are same as those obtained by the method of least squares is example 11.1.

EXAMPLE 11.3: The following table gives the aptitude test scores and productivity indices of 10 workers selected at random:

Aptitude scores	60	62	65	70	72	48	53	73	65	82
Productivity index	68	60	62	80	85	40	52	62	60	81

Estimate: (i) the productivity index of a worker whose test score is 92,
(ii) the test score of a worker whose productivity index is 75.

Solution: Since productivity depends on aptitude scores, let Y denote the productivity and X the aptitude score.

Calculation of Regression Equations

Aptitude Score X	$(X-65)$ $\bar{X}=65$ x	x^2	Productivity Index Y	$(Y-65)$ $\bar{Y}=65$ y	y^2	xy
60	–5	25	68	+3	9	–15
62	–3	9	60	–5	25	+15
65	0	0	62	–3	9	0
70	+5	25	80	+15	225	+75
72	+7	49	85	+20	400	+140
48	–17	289	40	–25	625	+425
53	–12	144	52	–13	169	+156
73	+8	64	62	–3	9	24
65	0	0	60	–5	25	0
82	+17	289	81	+16	256	+272
$\Sigma X = 650$	$\Sigma x = 0$	$\Sigma x^2 = 894$	$\Sigma Y = 650$	$\Sigma y = 0$	$\Sigma y^2 = 1752$	$\Sigma xy = 1044$

(i) We have to fit a regression equation of Y on X.

$$Y - \bar{Y} = b_{yx}\left(X - \bar{X}\right)$$

$$\bar{X} = \frac{\Sigma X}{n} = \frac{650}{10} = 65; \quad \bar{Y} = \frac{\Sigma Y}{n} = \frac{650}{10} = 65$$

$$b_{yx} = \frac{\Sigma xy}{\Sigma x^2} = \frac{1044}{894} = 1.168 \qquad [x = X - \bar{X}\ ;\ y = Y - \bar{Y}]$$

$$Y - 65 = 1.168\,(X - 65)$$

$$Y - 65 = 1.168X - 75.92 \quad \text{or} \quad Y = 1.168X - 10.92$$

$$Y_{92} = 1.168\,(92) - 10.92$$

$$= 107.456 - 10.92 = 96.536$$

(ii) We have to fit a regression equation of X on Y.

$$X - \bar{X} = b_{xy}\left(Y - \bar{Y}\right)$$

$$b_{xy} = \frac{\Sigma xy}{\Sigma y^2} = \frac{1044}{1752} = 0.596$$

$$X - 65 = 0.596\,(Y - 65)$$

$$X - 65 = 0.596Y - 38.74 \quad \text{or} \quad X = 0.596Y + 26.26$$

$$Y_{75} = .596\,(75) + 26.26$$

$$= 44.7 + 26.26 = 70.96.$$

EXAMPLE 11.4: The following data show the experience of machine operators and their performance ratings as given by the number of good parts turned out per 100 pieces:

Operator	1	2	3	4	5	6	7	8
Experience (*X*)	16	12	18	4	3	10	5	12
Performance Rating (*Y*)87	88	89	68	78	80	75	83	

Calculate the regression line of performance ratings on experience and estimate the probable performance if an operator has 10 years' experience.

Solution: Let performance rating be denoted by *Y* and experience by *X*. We have to calculate the regression line of *Y* on *X*.

Experience	(*X* – 10)		Performance	(*Y* – 81)		
X	*x*	x^2	*Y*	*y*	y^2	*xy*
16	+6	36	87	+6	36	+36
12	+2	4	88	+7	49	+14
18	+8	64	89	+8	64	64
4	–6	36	68	–13	169	+78
3	–7	49	78	–3	9	+21
10	0	0	80	–1	1	0
5	–5	25	75	–6	36	+30
12	+2	4	83	+2	4	+4
$\Sigma X = 80$	$\Sigma x = 0$	$\Sigma x^2 = 218$	$\Sigma Y = 648$	$\Sigma y = 0$	$\Sigma y^2 = 368$	$\Sigma xy = 247$

Regression equation of *Y* on *X*: $Y - \bar{Y} = b_{yx}\left(X - \bar{X}\right)$

$$\bar{X} = \frac{80}{8} = 10 \qquad \bar{Y} = \frac{648}{8} = 81$$

$$b_{yx} = \frac{\Sigma xy}{\Sigma x^2} = \frac{247}{218} = 1.133$$

$\therefore$

$$Y - 81 = 1.133\,(X - 10) = 1.133\,X - 11.33$$

$$Y = 69.67 + 1.133\,X$$

When $X = 10$ [Given]

$$Y = 69.67 + 1.133\,(10) = 69.67 + 11.33 = 81$$

Thus the probable performance of an operator who has 10 years' experience is 81 good parts out of 100.

EXAMPLE 11.5: Find the regression equation showing the regression equation of capacity utilisation on production from the following data:

	Average	**Standard deviation**
Production (in lakh units)	35.6	10.5
Capacity utilisation (in percentage)	84.8	8.5

$r = 0.62$

Estimate the production when the capacity utilisation is 70 per cent.

Solution: Let production be denoted by the variable X and capacity utilisation by Y. Then the regression equation showing the regression equation of capacity utilisation of production will be given by the following formula:

$$Y - \bar{Y} = b_{YX}\left(X - \bar{X}\right)$$

where $$b_{YX} = r\frac{\sigma_Y}{\sigma_X} = 0.62 \times \frac{8.5}{10.5} = \frac{527}{105} = 0.5019$$

and $$\bar{X} = 35.6\ ;\ \bar{Y} = 84.8$$

Substituting all these values in the above equation, we get

$$Y - 84.8 = 0.5019\ (X - 35.6)$$

or $$Y = 84.8 + 0.5019\ X - 17.8676$$

or $$Y = 66.9324 + 0.5019X$$

which is the required regression of capacity utilisation on production.

To estimate the production, we shall have to find the regression equation of X on Y. i.e.,

$$X - \bar{X} = b_{XY}\left(Y - \bar{Y}\right)$$

where $$b_{XY} = r\frac{\sigma_X}{\sigma_Y} = 0.62 \times \frac{10.5}{8.5} = \frac{6.51}{8.50} = 0.7659$$

Substituting the values, we have

$$(X - 35.6) = 0.7659\ (Y - 84.8)$$

or $$X = 35.6 + 0.7659\ Y - 64.9483$$

$$= -29.3483 + 0.7659\ Y$$

when $$Y = 70,\ X = -29.3483 + 0.7659\ (70)$$

$$= -29.3483 + 53.613 = 24.2647$$

Hence the estimated production is 2,42,647 units when the capacity utilisation is 70 per cent.

11.9.3 Deviations taken from Assumed Means

If the means of both the variable X and Y come out to be in fractions, the deviation from the actual means create a problem and it is advisable to take deviations from the assumed mean.

Thus when deviations are taken from assumed means, the b_{XY} and b_{YX} are given by

$$b_{XY} = \frac{\left[\Sigma d_X d_Y - (\Sigma d_X) \times (\Sigma d_Y)\right]/n}{\Sigma d_Y^2 - (\Sigma d_Y)^2/n}$$

and $$b_{YX} = \frac{\left[\Sigma d_X\ d_Y - \left(\Sigma d_X\right) \times \left(\Sigma d_Y\right)\right]/n}{\Sigma d_X^2 - \left(\Sigma d_X\right)^2/n}$$

These can also be written as

$$\boxed{b_{XY} = \frac{n\Sigma d_X d_Y \quad (\Sigma d_X) \times (\Sigma d_Y)}{n\Sigma d_Y^2 - (\Sigma d_Y)^2}}$$

and
$$b_{YX} = \frac{n\Sigma d_X d_Y - (\Sigma d_X) \times (\Sigma d_Y)}{n\Sigma d_X^2 - (\Sigma d_X)^2}$$

where $d_X = (X - A)$ and $d_Y = (Y - B)$

EXAMPLE 11.6: The personnel manager of an electronic manufacturing company devises a manual dexterity test for job applicants to predict their production rating in the assembly department. In order to do this he selects a random sample of 10 applicants. They are given the test and later assigned a production rating. Results are as follows:

Worker	A	B	C	D	E	F	G	H	I	J
Test Score	53	36	88	84	86	64	45	48	39	69
Production Rating	45	43	89	79	84	66	49	48	43	76

Fit a linear least square regression equation of production rating on test score.

Solution: Let test score be denoted by *X* and production rating by *Y*. We have to fit a regression of *Y* on *X*.

Fitting Regression Equation of *Y* on *X*

Worker	X	(X – 61) d_x	d_x^2	Y	(Y – 62) d_y	$d_x d_y$
A	53	–8	64	45	–17	+136
B	36	–25	625	43	–19	+475
C	88	+27	729	89	+27	+729
D	84	+23	529	79	+17	+391
E	86	+25	625	84	+22	+350
F	64	+3	9	66	+4	+12
G	45	–16	256	49	–13	+208
H	48	–13	169	48	–14	+182
I	39	–22	484	43	–19	+418
J	69	+8	64	76	+14	+112
	$\Sigma X = 612$	$\Sigma d_x = 2$	$\Sigma d_x^2 = 3554$	$\Sigma Y = 622$	$\Sigma d_y = 2$	$\Sigma d_x d_y = 3213$

Regression Equation of *Y* on *X* : $Y - \bar{Y} = b_{yx}(X - \bar{X})$ [Let $A = 61$; $B = 62$]

$$b_{YX} = \frac{n\Sigma d_X d_Y - \Sigma d_X \Sigma d_Y}{n\Sigma d_X^2 - (\Sigma d_X)^2} = \frac{10 \times 3213 - 2 \times 2}{10 \times 3554 - (2)^2}$$

$$= \frac{32130 - 4}{35536} = \frac{32126}{35536} = +0.904$$

$$\bar{Y} = \frac{\Sigma Y}{n} = \frac{622}{10} = 62.2 \quad \text{or} \quad \bar{X} = \frac{\Sigma X}{n} = \frac{612}{10} = 61.2$$

Hence
$$Y - 62.2 = 0.904\ (X - 61.2)$$
$$Y = .904X - 55.325 + 62.2$$
$$Y = 6.875 + 0.904X$$

is the required regression equation to predict production rating on test score.

Example 11.7: Suppose that you are interested in using past expenditure on research and development by a firm to predict current expenditure on *R* and *D*. You got the following data by taking a random sample of firms, where *X* is the amount of *R* and *D* (in lakhs of rupees) 5 years ago and *Y* is the amount spent on *R* and *D* (in lakhs of rupees) in the current year:

X	30	50	20	80	10	20	20	40
Y	50	80	30	110	20	20	40	50

(i) Find the regression equation of *Y* on *X*.

(ii) If a firm is chosen random and $X = 10$, can you use the regression to predict the value of *Y*? Discuss. **[MBA, Madurai Kamraj University, 2000]**

Solution:

Calculation of Regression Equation

X	(X – 33) d_x	d_x^2	Y	(Y – 50) d_y	d_y^2	$d_x d_y$
30	–3	–9	50	0	0	0
50	+17	289	80	+30	900	510
20	–13	169	30	–20	400	+260
80	+47	2209	110	+60	3600	+2820
10	–23	529	20	–30	900	+690
20	–13	169	20	–30	900	+390
20	–13	169	40	–10	100	+130
40	+7	49	50	0	0	0
$\Sigma X = 270$	$\Sigma d_x = +6$	$\Sigma d_x^2 = 3592$	$\Sigma Y = 400$	$\Sigma d_y = 0$	$\Sigma d_y^2 = 6800$	$\Sigma d_x d_y = 4800$

(i) Regression equation of *Y* on *X*: $Y - \bar{Y} = b_{yx}(X - \bar{X})$ [Let $A = 33$; $B = 50$]

$$\bar{X} = \frac{\Sigma X}{n} = \frac{270}{8} = 33.75; \quad Y = \frac{\Sigma Y}{n} = \frac{400}{8} = 50$$

$$b_{yx} = \frac{n\Sigma d_x d_y - \Sigma d_x \Sigma d_y}{n\Sigma d_x^2 - (\Sigma d_x)^2} = \frac{8 \times 4800 - 6 \times 0}{8 \times 3592 - (6)^2} = \frac{38400}{28700} = 1.338$$

$$Y - 50 = 1.338\,(X - 33.75) \text{ or } \boxed{Y = 4.84 + 1.338\,X}$$

(ii) When *X* is 10:

$$Y = 4.84 + 1.338\,(10) = 18.22$$

EXAMPLE 11.8: In trying to evaluate the effectiveness in its advertising campaign, a firm complied the following information:

Year	1996	1997	1998	1999	2000	2001	2002	2003
Adv. Expenditure ('000 Rs)	12	15	15	23	24	38	42	48
Sales (Lakh Rs)	5.0	5.6	5.8	7.0	7.2	8.8	9.2	9.5

Calculate the regression equation of sales on advertising expenditure. Estimate the probable sales when advertisement expenditure is Rs 60 thousand.

Solution:

Calculation of Regression Equation

X	$(X-24)\ d_x$	d_x^2	Y	$(Y-7.0)\ d_y$	d_y^2	d_xd_y
12	–12	144	5.0	–2.0	4.00	24.0
15	–9	81	5.6	–1.4	1.96	12.6
15	–9	81	5.8	–1.2	1.44	10.8
23	–1	1	7.0	0	0	0
24	0	0	7.2	+0.2	.04	0
38	+14	196	8.8	+1.8	3.24	25.2
42	+18	324	9.2	+2.2	4.84	39.6
48	+24	576	9.5	+2.5	6.25	60.0
$\Sigma X = 217$	$\Sigma d_x = 25$	$\Sigma d_x^2 = 1403$	$\Sigma Y = 58.1$	$\Sigma d_y = 2.1$	$\Sigma d_y^2 = 21.17$	$\Sigma d_xd_y = 172.2$

Let $A = 24$ and $B = 7.0$

$$\overline{X} = \frac{\Sigma X}{n} = \frac{217}{8} = 27.125;\quad \overline{Y} = \frac{\Sigma Y}{n} = \frac{58.1}{8} = 7.26$$

Regression equation of sales on advertisement exp. is given by:

$$(Y - \overline{Y}) = b_{yx}\left(X - \overline{X}\right)$$

Where

$$b_{YX} = \frac{n\Sigma d_X d_Y - (\Sigma d_X)(\Sigma d_Y)}{n\Sigma d_X^2 - (\Sigma d_X)^2}$$

$$= \frac{8(172.2) - (25)(2.1)}{8(1403) - (25)^2} = \frac{1377.6 - 525}{11224 - 625} = \frac{1325.1}{10599} = 0.125$$

Substituting the values, we have

$$Y - 7.2625 = 0.125\,(X - 27.125)$$

$$Y - 7.2625 = 0.125X - 3.3906$$

$$Y = 3.8719 + 0.1250X$$

When $X = 60$, the estimated value of Y shall be:

$$Y = 3.8719 + 0.1250\,(60) = 3.8719 + 75 = 11.37$$

11.9.4 Regression Equation in Group Frequency Distribution

Like correlation analysis, the regression analysis of a grouped frequency distribution requires a two – way correlation table in which the values of one of the variables is represented horizontally in the first row and values of the other variable is represented vertically in the first column. We find out the values of $\overline{X}$, $\overline{Y}$ and the two regression coefficients and then proceed in the usual manner. The modified formula for calculating regression coefficients are:

$$b_{XY} = \left[\frac{\Sigma fd_X\, d_Y - \dfrac{(\Sigma fd_X)\times(\Sigma fd_Y)}{N}}{\Sigma fd_Y{}^2 - \dfrac{(\Sigma fd_Y)^2}{N}}\right] \times \frac{c_x}{c_y}$$

and
$$b_{YX} = \left[\frac{\Sigma f d_X d_Y - \frac{(\Sigma f d_X) \times (\Sigma f d_Y)}{N}}{\Sigma f d_X^2 - \frac{(\Sigma f d_X)^2}{N}}\right] \times \frac{c_y}{c_x}$$

where c_x = width of the class interval of the X – variable
and c_y = width of the class-interval of Y – variable

11.10 PROPERTIES OF REGRESSION COEFFICIENT

1. Both regression coefficients must have the same sign, i.e., either it will be positive or negative.
2. Correlation coefficient is the geometric mean of the regression coefficients ie, $r = \pm\sqrt{b_1 b_2}$.
3. The correlation coefficient will have the same sign as that of the regression coefficients.
4. If one regression coefficient is greater than unity, then other regression coefficient must be less than unity.
5. Regression coefficients are independent of origin but not of scale.
6. Arithmetic mean of b_1 and b_2 is equal to or greater than the coefficient of correlation. Symbolically $\frac{b_1 + b_2}{2} \geq r$.
7. If r = 0, the variables are uncorrelated, the lines of regression become perpendicular to each other.
8. If r = +1, the two lines of regression either coincide or parallel to each other
9. Angle between the two regression lines is $\theta = \tan^{-1}\left[\frac{m_1 - m_2}{1 + m_1 m_2}\right]$.
   Where m_1 and m_2 are the slopes of the regression lines X on Y and Y on X respectively.
10. The angle between the regression lines indicates the degree of dependence between the variables.
11. Both the regression cannot be more than 1.

EXAMPLE 11.9: If 2 regression coefficients are b_1= 4/5 and b_2 = 9/20. What would be the value of r?

Solution: The correlation coefficient,

$$r = \pm\sqrt{b_1 b_2}$$
$$= \sqrt{\frac{4}{5} \times \frac{9}{20}} = \sqrt{\frac{36}{100}} = \frac{6}{10} = 0.6$$

EXAMPLE 11.10: Given $b_1 = \frac{15}{8}$ and $b_2 = \frac{3}{5}$, find r.

Solution:
$$r = \pm\sqrt{b_1 b_2}$$
$$= \sqrt{\frac{15}{8} \times \frac{3}{5}} = \sqrt{\frac{45}{40}} = \frac{9}{8} = 1.06$$

It is not possible since r, cannot be greater than one. So the given values are wrong.

EXAMPLE 11.11: Regression equations of two correlated variables X and Y are $5X - 6Y + 90 = 0$ and $15X - 8Y - 130 = 0$. Find correlation coefficient.

Solution: Let $5X - 6Y + 90 = 0$ represents the regression equation of X on Y and other for Y on X.

Now $$X = \frac{6}{5}Y - \frac{90}{5}$$

$$b_{XY} = b_2 = \frac{6}{5}$$

For $$15X - 8Y - 130 = 0$$

$$Y = \frac{15}{8}X - \frac{130}{8}$$

$$b_{YX} = b_1 = \frac{15}{8}$$

$$r = \pm\sqrt{b_1 b_2}$$

$$= \sqrt{\frac{15}{8} \times \frac{6}{5}} = \sqrt{2.25} = 1.5 > 1$$

It is not possible. So our assumption is wrong. So let us take the first equation as Y on X and second equation as X on Y.

From the equation $5X - 6Y + 90 = 0$,

$$Y = \frac{5}{6}X - \frac{90}{6}$$

$$b_{YX} = \frac{5}{6}$$

From the equation $15X - 8Y - 130 = 0$,

$$X = \frac{8}{15}Y + \frac{130}{15}$$

$$b_{YX} = \frac{8}{15}$$

Correlation coefficient, $$r = \pm\sqrt{b_1 b_2}$$

$$= \sqrt{\frac{5}{6} \times \frac{8}{15}} = \sqrt{\frac{40}{90}} = \frac{2}{3} = 0.67$$

EXAMPLE 11.12: The lines of regression of Y on X and X on Y are respectively, $Y = X + 5$ and $16X = 9Y - 94$. Find the variance of X if the variance of Y is 19. Also find the covariance of X and Y.

Solution: From regression line Y on X,

$$Y = X + 5$$

We get $$b_{YX} = 1$$

From regression line X on Y,

$$16X = 9Y - 94$$

$$X = \frac{9}{16}Y - \frac{94}{16},$$

we get $$b_{XY} = \frac{9}{16}$$

$$r = \pm\sqrt{b_1 b_2}$$

$$= \sqrt{1 \times \frac{9}{16}} = \frac{3}{4}$$

Again, $$b_{YX} = r\frac{\sigma_Y}{\sigma_X}$$

i.e., $$1 = \frac{3}{4} \times \frac{4}{\sigma_X}$$ [Since $\sigma_Y^2 = 16$, $\sigma Y = 4$]

$$\sigma_X = 3.$$

Variance of X $$= \sigma_X^2 = 9$$

Again, $$b_{YX} = \frac{\text{cov}(X,Y)}{\sigma_X^2}$$

$$1 = \frac{\text{cov}(X,Y)}{9} \quad \text{or} \quad \text{cov}(X,Y) = 9.$$

EXAMPLE 11.13: Is it possible for two regression lines to be as follows:

$$Y = -1.5X + 7, \quad X = 0.6Y + 9\text{ ? Give reasons.}$$

Solution: The regression coefficient of Y on X is $b_1 = b_{yx} = -1.5$

The regression coefficient of X on Y is $b_2 - b_{xy} - 0.6$

Both the regression coefficients are of different sign, which is a contrary. So the given equations cannot be regression lines.

EXAMPLE 11.14: In a correlation study, the following values are obtained

	X	**Y**
Mean	65	67
S.D	2.5	3.5

Co-efficient of correlation = 0.8. **[MBA, IGNOU, 2001, Osmania Univ., 2004]**

Find the two regression equations that are associated with the above values.

Solution: Given, $\bar{X} = 65$, $\bar{Y} = 67$, $\sigma_X = 2.5$, $\sigma_Y = 3.5$, $r = 0.8$

The regression co-efficient of Y on X is

$$b_{YX} = b_1 = r\frac{\sigma_Y}{\sigma_X}$$

$$= 0.8 \times \frac{3.5}{2.5} = 1.12$$

The regression coefficient of X on Y is

$$b_{XY} = b_2 = r\frac{\sigma_X}{\sigma_Y}$$

$$= 0.8 \times \frac{2.5}{3.5} = 0.57$$

Hence, the regression equation of Y on X is

$$Y_e = \bar{Y} + b_1 (X - \bar{X})$$
$$= 67 + 1.12\ (X - 65)$$
$$= 67 + 1.12X - 72.8$$
$$= 1.12X - 5.8$$

Hence, the regression equation of X on Y is

$$X_e = \bar{X} + b_2 (X - \bar{Y})$$
$$= 65 + 0.57\ (Y - 67)$$
$$= 65 + 0.57Y - 38.19$$
$$= 26.81 + 0.57Y$$

NOTE: Suppose, we are given two regression equations and we have not been mentioned the regression equations of Y on X and X on Y. To identify, always assume that the first equation is Y on X then calculate the regression co-efficient $b_{YX} = b_1$ and $b_{XY} = b_2$. If these two are satisfied the properties of regression co-efficient, our assumption is correct, otherwise interchange these two equations.

11.11 STANDARD ERROR OF AN ESTIMATE

Standard error of estimate is analogous to standard deviation (which is a measure of scatter of the observations about the average of the distribution) and gives us a measure of the scatter of the observation about the line of regression.

Thus S_{YX} = S.E of estimate of Y for given X

$$= \sqrt{\frac{\Sigma(Y - Y_e)^2}{n}}$$

$$= \sqrt{\frac{\text{Un-explained variation in } Y}{n}}$$

Similarly $$S_{XY} = \sqrt{\frac{\Sigma(X - X_e)^2}{n}}$$

where Y_e and X_e are the estimated values of Y and X variables obtained from the line of regression of Y on X and X on Y respectively.

A simpler method of computing S_{YX} and S_{XY} is to use formulae:

$$S_{YX} = \sqrt{\frac{\Sigma Y^2 - a\Sigma Y - b\Sigma XY}{n}}$$

and $$S_{XY} = \sqrt{\frac{\Sigma X^2 - a\Sigma X - b\Sigma XY}{n}}$$

Coefficient of Determination

The total variation can be divided into two:

(a) The explained variation, i.e. the variation which is explained by the variable X.

(b) The unexplained variation i.e., the variation which is unexplained by the variables X and is due to some other factors.

Thus, $$\Sigma(Y - \bar{Y})^2 = \Sigma[(Y - Y_e) + (Y_e - \bar{Y})]^2$$
$$= \Sigma(Y - Y_e)^2 + \Sigma(Y_e - \bar{Y})^2 \qquad ...(1)$$

The product term variables, since

$$\Sigma(Y - Y_e) = 0$$

In equation (1), $\Sigma(Y - Y_e)^2$ is called the unexplained variation and $\Sigma(Y_e - \bar{Y})^2$ is called the ***explained variation***.

A similar relationship we may have for variable X in terms of Y.

$$\Sigma(X - \bar{X})^2 = \Sigma(X - X_e)^2 + \Sigma(X_e - \bar{X})^2$$

The ratio of the explained variation to the total variation is known as the ***coefficient of determination*** (r^2) i.e.

$$r_e^2 = \frac{\text{Explained variation}}{\text{Total variation}} = \frac{\Sigma(Y_e - \bar{Y})^2}{\Sigma(Y - \bar{Y})} = \frac{S_{ye}^{\ 2}}{\sigma_y^2}$$

When $r^2 = 1$, the whole of the total variation is explained by regression, so that the unexplained variation is zero and each $Y_e = Y_i$ i.e., all the points on the scatter diagram lie on the regression line which also indicates a perfect correlation.

When $r^2 = 0$, the explained variation is zero and in such a case there is no relationship between the variables.

Further, when each side of equation (i) is divided by n, we have

$$\frac{\Sigma(Y - \bar{Y})}{n} = \frac{\Sigma(Y - Y_e)^2}{n} + \frac{\Sigma(Y_e - \bar{Y})^2}{n}$$

$$\Rightarrow \qquad \sigma_X^{\ 2} = S_{YX}^2 + S_{Y_e}^2$$

Now $$r_e^{\ 2} = \frac{S_{Y_e}^2}{\sigma_Y^2} = \frac{\sigma_Y^2 - S_{YX}^2}{\sigma_Y^2}$$

$$\Rightarrow \qquad r_e = \sqrt{\frac{1 - S_{YX}^2}{\sigma_Y^2}}$$

On simplification, we get

$$S_{YX} = \sigma_Y \sqrt{1 - r_c^2}$$

Similarly, by considering the total variation in X, we get

$$S_{XY} = \sigma_x \sqrt{1 - r_c^2}$$

EXAMPLE 11.15: In a partially destroyed record, for the estimation of the two lines of regression from a bivariate data (X, Y), the following results were available:

Coefficient of regression of Y on $X = -1.6$
Coefficient of regression of X on $Y = -0.4$
Standard error of the estimate of Y on $X = 3$

Find:

(a) Coefficient of correlation between X and Y.
(b) Standard deviations σ_x and σ_Y.
(c) Standard error of the estimate of X on Y. **[BA, Delhi University, 1998]**

Solution: In the usual notations, we are given:

$$b_{YX} = -1.6; \quad b_{XY} = -0.4; \quad S_{YX} = 3 \qquad ...(1)$$

(i) Coefficient of correlation $r = r(X, Y)$ is given by:

$$r^2 = b_{YX} \cdot b_{XY} = (-1.6) \times (-0.4) = 0.64$$

$$\Rightarrow \quad r = \pm\sqrt{0.64} = \pm 0.8$$

Since the regression coefficients are negative, r is also negative.

$$\therefore \quad r = 0.8 \qquad ...(2)$$

(ii) The standard error of estimate of Y on X is given by

$$S_{YX} = \sigma_Y (1 - r^2)^{1/2}$$

$$\Rightarrow \quad \sigma_Y = \frac{S_{YX}}{(1 - r^2)^{1/2}}$$

$$\therefore \quad \sigma_Y = \frac{3}{\sqrt{1 - 0.64}} = \frac{3}{\sqrt{0.36}} = \frac{3}{0.6} = 5 \qquad \text{[From (1), (2)]} \quad ...(3)$$

Also

$$b_{YX} = \frac{r\sigma_Y}{\sigma_X}$$

$$\Rightarrow \quad \sigma_X = \frac{r\sigma_Y}{b_{YX}}$$

$$\therefore \quad \sigma_X = \frac{(-0.8) \times 5}{-1.6} = 2.5 \qquad \text{[From (1), (2) and (3)]}$$

(iii) Standard error of estimate of X on Y is given by:

$$S_{xy} = \sigma_x (1 - r^2)^{1/2} = 2.5\,(1 - 0.64)^{1/2} = 2.5 \times 0.6 = 1.5$$

11.12 STRENGTHS AND LIMITATIONS OF THE REGRESSION

Strengths

- Regression analysis provides an opportunity to specify hypotheses concerning the nature of effects (action theory), as well as explanatory factors.
- When it is successfully executed (with a statistically valid adjustment), regression analysis can produce a quantitative estimate of net effects.

Limitations

- The technique is demanding because it requires quantitative data relating to several thousand individuals.
- Implementing the data collection can be time-consuming and expensive.
- Regression analysis is likely to reach the conclusion that there is a strong link between two variables; whereas the influence of other, more important, variables may not have been estimated (this error is called "data snooping"). The tool should therefore be used with care.
- Relations between the different explained and explanatory variables are often circular (X explains Y and Y explains X). In this case, the method is inapplicable.

The observations must present sufficiently contrasted evolutions to allow for adjustment. ***For example***, if all the observations concern the 30–40 age groups, it will not be possible to estimate the influence of age on employment.

MISCELLANEOUS SOLVED EXAMPLES

EXAMPLE 11.16: Calculate linear regression coefficient from the following: **[MCA, UPTU, 2001]**

X	1	2	3	4	5	6	7	8
Y	3	7	10	12	14	17	20	24

Solution: linear regression coefficients are given by

$$b_{YX} = \frac{n\Sigma XY - \Sigma X \Sigma Y}{n\Sigma X^2 - (\Sigma X)^2}$$

and

$$b_{XY} = \frac{n\Sigma XY - \Sigma X \Sigma Y}{n\Sigma Y^2 - (\Sigma Y)^2}$$

The calculation is as below:

X	Y	X²	Y²	XY
1	3	1	9	3
2	7	4	49	14
3	10	9	100	30
4	12	16	144	48
5	14	25	196	70
6	17	36	289	102
7	20	49	400	140
8	24	64	576	192
ΣX = 36	**ΣY = 107**	**ΣX² = 204**	**ΣY² = 1763**	**ΣXY = 599**

Here $n = 8$

$$b_{YX} = \frac{(8 \times 599) - (36 \times 107)}{(8 \times 204) - (36)^2} = \frac{4792 - 3852}{1632 - 1296} = \frac{940}{336} = 2.7976$$

$$b_{XY} = \frac{(8 \times 599) - (36 \times 107)}{(8 \times 1763) - (107)^2} = \frac{940}{2655} = 0.3540$$

EXAMPLE 11.17: In a partially destroyed laboratory record of an analysis of a correlation data, the following results only are eligible:

Variance of $X = 9$

Regression equations: $8X - 10Y + 66 = 0$, $40X - 18Y = 214$.

What were: (a) The mean values of X and Y; (b) The standard deviation of Y and the coefficient of correlation between X and Y. **[B.Tech., UPTU, 2003]**

Solution:

(a) Since both the lines of regression pass through the point $(\bar{X}, \bar{Y})$ therefore, we have

$$8\bar{X} - 10\bar{Y} + 66 = 0 \quad ...(1)$$

$$40\bar{X} - 18\bar{Y} - 214 = 0 \quad ...(2)$$

Multiplying equation (1) by 5, we have

$$40\bar{X} - 50\bar{Y} + 330 = 0 \quad ...(3)$$

Subtracting equation (3) from equation (2), we have

$$32\bar{Y} - 544 = 0 \Rightarrow \bar{Y} = 17$$

$\therefore$ From (1), $8\bar{X} - 170 + 66 = 0$

or $8\bar{X} = 104$

$\Rightarrow$ $\bar{X} = 13$

Hence $\bar{X} = 13$, $\bar{Y} = 17$

(b) Variance of $X = \sigma_x^2 = 9$ (given)

$\therefore$ $\sigma_x = 3$

The equations of lines of regression can be written as

$$Y = 8X + 6.6$$

and $$X = .45\,Y + 5.35$$

$\therefore$ The regression co-efficient of Y on X is $\dfrac{r\sigma_y}{\sigma_x} = .8$ ...(4)

The regression co-efficient of X on Y is $\dfrac{r\sigma_x}{\sigma_y} = .45$ ...(5)

Multiplying (4) and (5), $r^2 = .8 \times .45 = .36$

$\Rightarrow$ $r = 0.6$

(+ve sign with square root is taken because regression coefficients are +ve).

From (4), $\sigma_Y = \dfrac{.8\sigma_x}{r} = \dfrac{.8 \times 3}{0.6} = 4$

$$Y = 1.015\,(16) + 8.805$$
$$= 25.045 \text{ units.}$$

EXAMPLE 11.18: A study of prices of a certain commodity at Hapur and Kanpur yields the following data:

	Hapur (Rs)	Kanpur (Rs)
Average price / Kilo	2.463	2.797
Standard deviation	0.326	0.207

'r' between prices at Hapur and Kanpur is 0.774.

Estimate, from the above data, the most likely price at Hapur corresponding to the price of Rs 3.052 per kilo at Kanpur.

Solution: Here, $\bar{X} = 2.463$, $\bar{Y} = 2.797$, $\sigma_X = 0.326$, $\sigma_Y = 0.26$ and $r = 0.774$.

Regression coefficient

$$b_{XY} = r\frac{\sigma_X}{\sigma_Y} = (0.774)\left(\frac{0.326}{0.207}\right) = 1.218956522$$

Regression line of X on Y is given by

$$X - \bar{X} = b_{XY}(Y - \bar{Y})$$

$$\Rightarrow \quad X - 2.463 = 1.218956522\,(Y - 2.797)$$

$$\Rightarrow \quad X = 1.218956522\,Y - 0.9464213$$

When $Y = 3.052$, $\quad X = 1.218956522\,(3.052) - 0.9464213 = 2.7738$

Hence the most likely price at Hapur is Rs 2.7730 per kilo, corresponding to the given price at Kanpur.

EXAMPLE 11.19: Given below are data relating to prices of a share in Kolkata and Mumbai Stock Exchanges:

Particulars	Kolkata (*X*)	Mumbai (*Y*)
Average Price	Rs 130	Rs 134
Standard Deviation	Rs 5	Rs 7

Coefficient of correlations between the prices of the share in Kolkata and Mumbai is +0.8. Fit the two lines of regression and find the most likely price of the share in the Mumbai Stock Exchange corresponding to a price of Rs 140 in Kolkata. **[MBA, UPTU, 2003, HPU, 2000]**

Solution: We have, $\bar{X} = 130$, $\bar{Y} = 134$, $\sigma_X = 5$, $\sigma_Y = 7$, $r = 0.8$

Regression line of Y on X is

$$Y - \bar{Y} = r\frac{\sigma_Y}{\sigma_X}\left(X - \bar{X}\right)$$

$$Y - 134 = (0.8)\left(\frac{7}{5}\right)(X - 130) = 1.12\,(X - 130) = 1.12X - 145.6$$

$$\boxed{Y = 1.12X - 11.6} \quad \text{...(1)}$$

Regression line of X on Y is

$$X - \bar{X} = r\frac{\sigma_X}{\sigma_Y}\left(Y - \bar{Y}\right)$$

$$\Rightarrow \quad X - 130 = (0.8)\left(\frac{5}{7}\right)(Y - 134)$$

$$\Rightarrow \quad 7X - 910 = 4Y - 536$$

$$\Rightarrow \quad \boxed{7X = 4Y + 374} \quad \text{...(2)}$$

To find most likely price of share in Mumbai Stock Exchange corresponding to given price of share in Kolkata Stock Exchange, we shall use the regression line of Y on X.

Regression line of Y on X is

$$Y = 1.12 \times - 11.6 \qquad \text{[From (1)]}$$

When $X = 140$,

$$Y = 1.12\,(140) - 11.6$$
$$= 156.8 - 11.6 = 145.2$$

Hence, the most likely price of share in Mumbai Stock Exchange is Rs 145.2 corresponding to a price of Rs 140 in Kolkata Stock Exchange.

EXAMPLE 11.20: The coefficient of correlation between the ages of husbands and wives in a community was found to be + 0.8, the average of husbands age was 25 years and that of wives age 22 years. Their standard deviations were 4 and 5 years respectively. Find with the help of regression equations:

(a) The expected age of husband when wife's age is 16 years, and
(b) The expected age of wife when husband's age is 33 years.

Solution: Let age of wife be denoted by Y and age of husband by X. We are given

$$\bar{X} = 25, \quad \bar{Y} = 22, \quad \sigma_X = 4, \quad \sigma_Y = 5, \quad r = 0.8$$

For answering part (a) we have to fit a regression equation X on Y.

$$X - \bar{X} = r\frac{\sigma_X}{\sigma_Y}\left(Y - \bar{Y}\right)$$

$$X - 25 = .8\,\frac{4}{5}\,(Y - 22) \text{ or } X - 25 = .64\,(Y - 22)$$

$$X - 25 = .64Y - 14.08 \text{ or } X = 10.92 + 0.64Y$$

When $Y = 16$

$$X = 10.92 + 0.64\,(16)$$
$$= 10.92 + 10.24 = 21.16$$

Thus, the expected age of husband when wife's age is 16 years shall be 21.16 years.

For answering part (*b*) we have to fit a regression equation of Y on X.

$$Y - \bar{Y} = r\frac{\sigma_Y}{\sigma_X}\left(X - \bar{X}\right)$$

$$Y - 22 = .8\,\frac{5}{4}\,(X - 25)$$

$$Y - 22 = (X - 25) \text{ or } Y = -3 + X$$

When $X = 33$

$$Y = -3 + 33 = 30$$

Thus, the expected age of wife when husband's age is 33 is 30 years.

LIST OF FORMULAE

1. Simple linear regression equation

   (a) Line of Regression of X on Y

$$X = a + bY$$

and normal equation

$$\Sigma X = na + b\Sigma Y$$
$$\Sigma XY = a\Sigma Y + b\Sigma Y^2$$

(b) Line of Regression of Y on X

$$Y = a + bX$$

and normal equation

$$\Sigma Y = na + b\Sigma X$$

$$\Sigma XY = a\Sigma X + b\Sigma X^2$$

2. Regression equation of X on Y

$$X - \bar{X} = b_{XY}\left(Y - \bar{Y}\right)$$

or $$X - \bar{X} = r \cdot \frac{\sigma_X}{\sigma_Y}\left(Y - \bar{Y}\right)$$

3. Regression Equation of Y on X

$$Y - \bar{Y} = b_{YX}(X - \bar{X})$$

or $$(Y - \bar{Y}) = r \cdot \frac{\sigma_Y}{\sigma_X}\left(X - \bar{X}\right)$$

4. Slope of the best fitting regression line

$$b_{XY} = \frac{nXY - \Sigma X \Sigma Y}{n\Sigma Y^2 - (\Sigma Y)^2}$$ [for X on Y]

and $$b_{YX} = \frac{n\Sigma XY - \Sigma X \Sigma Y}{n\Sigma X^2 - (\Sigma X)^2}$$

5. Regression coefficient

(a) X on Y

$$b_{XY} = r \cdot \frac{\sigma_X}{\sigma_Y} = b_2$$

or $$b_{XY} = \frac{\Sigma xy}{\Sigma y^2}$$

where $x = X - \bar{X}$ and $y = Y - \bar{Y}$

(b) Y on X

$$b_{YX} = r \cdot \frac{\sigma_Y}{\sigma_X} = b_1$$

or $$b_{YX} = \frac{\Sigma xy}{\Sigma x^2}$$

6. Coefficient of correlation based on the two regression coefficients.

$$r = \sqrt{b_{XY} \cdot b_{YX}}$$

7. Regression equation with the help of Deviations taken from assumed means

(a) X on Y

$$(X - \bar{X}) = b_{XY}(Y - \bar{Y})$$

where $$b_{XY} - \frac{\left[\Sigma d_X d_Y - \left(\Sigma d_X\right) \times (\Sigma d_Y)\right]/n}{\Sigma d_Y^2 - (\Sigma d_Y)^2/n}$$

(b) *Y* on *X*

$$\left(Y - \bar{Y}\right) = b_{YX}(X - \bar{X})$$

where
$$b_{YX} = \frac{\left[\Sigma d_X d_Y - \left(\Sigma d_X\right) \times \left(\Sigma d_Y\right)\right] / n}{\Sigma d_X^2 - \left(\Sigma d_X\right)^2 / n}$$

8. Regression equation in Group. Frequency distribution

$$b_{XY} = \left[\frac{\Sigma f d_X d_Y - (\Sigma f d_X) \times \left(\Sigma f d_Y\right)}{\Sigma f d_Y^2 - \frac{(\Sigma f d_Y)^2}{n}}\right] \times \frac{C_X}{C_Y}$$

and
$$b_{YX} = \left[\frac{\Sigma f d_X d_Y - \frac{(\Sigma f d_X) \times (\Sigma f d_Y)}{n}}{\Sigma f d_X^2 - \frac{(\Sigma f d_X)^2}{n}}\right] \times \frac{C_Y}{C_X}$$

where C_X = width of the class-interval of X – variable

C_Y = Width of the class-interval of Y – variable

9. Standard Error of Estimate

$$S_{YX} = \sqrt{\frac{\Sigma(Y - Y_e)^2}{n}}$$

and
$$S_{XY} = \sqrt{\frac{\Sigma(X - X_e)^2}{n}}$$

or
$$S_{YX} = \sqrt{\frac{\Sigma Y^2 - a\Sigma Y - b\Sigma XY}{n}}$$

and
$$S_{XY} = \sqrt{\frac{\Sigma X^2 - a\Sigma X - b\Sigma XY}{n}}$$

10. Coefficient of determination

$$r_c = \sqrt{1 - \frac{S_{YX}^2}{\sigma_Y^2}}$$

or
$$S_{YX} = \sigma_Y \sqrt{1 - r_c^2}$$

and
$$S_{XY} = \sigma_X \sqrt{1 - r_c^2}$$

SELF PRACTICE EXERCISES

I. CHOOSE THE BEST ANSWER

1. When the correlation coefficient $r = +1$, then the two regression lines:
   (a) are perpendicular to each other (b) coincide
   (c) are parallel to each other (d) none of these
2. If one regression coefficient is greater than unity then the other must be:
   (a) greater than unity (b) equal to unity
   (c) less than unity (d) none of these
3. Regression equation is also named as:
   (a) predication equation (b) estimating equation
   (c) line of average relationship (d) all the above
4. The lines of regression intersect at the point:
   (a) (X, Y) (b) (X, Y)
   (c) $(0, 0)$ (d) $(1, 1)$
5. If $r = 0$, the lines of regression are:
   (a) coincide (b) perpendicular to each other
   (c) parallel to each other (d) none of the above
6. Regression coefficient is independent of:
   (a) origin (b) scale
   (c) both origin and scale (d) neither origin nor scale.
7. The geometric mean of the two-regression coefficients $b_{YX}$and b_{XY} is equal to:
   (a) r (b) r^2
   (c) 1 (d) r
8. Given the two lines of regression as $3X - 4Y + 8 = 0$ and $4X - 3Y = 1$, the means of X and Y are:
   (a) $X = 4, Y = 5$ (b) $X = 3, Y = 4$
   (c) $X = 2, Y = 2$ (d) $X = \frac{4}{3}, Y = \frac{5}{3}$
9. If the two lines of regression are $X + 2Y - 5 = 0$ and $2X + 3Y - 8 = 0$, the means of X and Y are:
   (a) $X = -3, Y = 4$ (b) $X = 2, Y = 4$
   (c) $X = 1, Y = 2$ (d) $X = -1, Y = 2$
10. If $b_{YX} = -\frac{3}{2}, b_{XY} = -\frac{3}{2}$ then the correlation coefficient, r is:
    (a) $\frac{3}{2}$ (b) $-\frac{3}{2}$
    (c) $\frac{9}{4}$ (d) $-\frac{9}{4}$

II. FILL IN THE BLANKS

1. The regression analysis measures .... between X and Y.
2. The purpose of regression is to study .... between variables.
3. If one of the regression coefficients is .... unity, the other must be .... unity.

4. The farther the two regression lines cut each other, the .... be the degree of correlation.
5. When one regression coefficient is positive, the other would also be ....
6. The sign of regression coefficient is .... as that of correlation coefficient.

III. SHORT ANSWER TYPE QUESTIONS

1. Define regression and write down the two regression equations
2. Describe different types of regression.
3. Explain principle of least squares.
4. Explain:
   (i) graphic method (ii) Algebraic method.
5. What are regressions co-efficient?
6. State the properties of regression coefficients.
7. Why there are two regression equations?
8. What are the uses of regression analysis?
9. Distinguish between correlation and regression.
10. What do you mean by regression line of Y on X and regression line of X on Y?

IV. LONG ANSWER TYPE QUESTIONS

1. From the following data, find the regression equation

$$“X = 21, \quad “Y = 20, \quad “X^2 = 91, \quad “XY = 74, \quad n = 7$$

2. From the following data find the regression equation of Y on X. If $X = 15$, find Y?

X	8	11	7	10	12	5	4	6
Y	11	30	25	44	38	25	20	27

3. Find the two regression equations from the following data.

X	25	22	28	26	35	20	22	40	20	18
Y	18	15	20	17	22	14	16	21	15	14

4. Find S.D (Y), given that variance of $X = 36$, $b_{XY} = 0.8$, $r = 0.5$
5. In a correlation study, the following values are obtained

	X	Y
Mean	68	60
S.D	2.5	3.5

   Coefficient of correlation, $r = 0.6$ Find the two regression equations.

6. In a correlation studies, the following values are obtained:

	X	Y
Mean	12	15
S.D	2	3

   $r = 0.5$ Find the two regression equations.

7. The correlation coefficient of bivariate X and Y is $r = 0.6$, variance of X and Y are respectively, 2.25 and 4.00, X=10, Y=20. From the above data, find the two regression lines.

8. For the following lines of regression find the mean values of X and Y and the two regression coefficients $8X - 10Y + 66 = 0$; $40X - 18Y = 214$.
9. Given $X = 90$, $Y = 70$, $b_{xy} = 1.36$, $b_{YX} = 0.61$.
   Find:
   (a) the most probable values of X, when $Y = 50$ and
   (b) the coefficient of correlation between X and Y 36.

   You are supplied with the following data:

   $$4X - 5Y + 33 = 0 \quad \text{and} \quad 20X - 9Y - 107 = 0, \quad \text{variance of } Y = 4.$$

   Calculate:
   (i) Mean values of x and y;
   (ii) S.D. of X;
   (iii) Correlation coefficients between X and Y.
10. The average number of people in a family that received welfare for various years is given below:

Year	1969	1973	1975	1979	1983	1988	1991
Welfare family size	4.0	3.6	3.2	3.0	3.0	3.0	2.9

   (a) Using "year" as the independent variable and "welfare family size" as the dependent variable, make a scatter plot of the data.
   (b) Calculate the least squares line. Put the equation in the form of: $y = a + bx$
   (c) Find the correlation coefficient. Is it significant?
   (d) Pick two years between 1969 and 1991 and find the estimated welfare family sizes.
   (e) Use the two points in (d) to plot the least squares line on your graph from (b).
   (f) Based on the above data, is there a linear relationship between the year and the average number of people in a welfare family?
   (g) Using the least squares line, estimate the welfare family sizes for 1960 and 1995. Does the least squares line give an accurate estimate for those years? Explain why or why not.
   (h) Are there any outliers in the above data?
   (i) What is the estimated average welfare family size for 1986? Does the least squares line give an accurate estimate for that year? Explain why or why not.
   (j) What is the slope of the least squares (best-fit) line? Interpret the slope.
11. The height (sidewalk to roof) of notable tall buildings in America is compared to the number of stories of the building (beginning at street level).

Height (in feet)	1050	428	362	529	790	401	380	1454	1127	700
Stories	57	28	26	40	60	22	38	110	100	46

   (a) Using "stories" as the independent variable and "height" as the dependent variable, make a scatter plot of the data.
   (b) Does it appear from inspection that there is a relationship between the variables?
   (c) Calculate the least squares line. Put the equation in the form of: $y = a + bx$
   (d) Find the correlation coefficient. Is it significant?

(e) Find the estimated heights for 32 stories and for 94 stories.

(f) Use the two points in (e) to plot the least squares line on your graph from (b).

(g) Based on the above data, is there a linear relationship between the number of stories in tall buildings and the height of the buildings?

(h) Are there any outliers in the above data? If so, which point(s)?

(i) What is the estimated height of a building with 6 stories? Does the least squares line give an accurate estimate of height? Explain why or why not.

(j) Based on the least squares line, adding an extra story adds about how many feet to a building?

(k) What is the slope of the least squares (best-fit) line? Interpret the slope.

ANSWERS

I. CHOOSE THE BEST ANSWERS

1. (b) 2. (c) 3. (d) 4. (b) 5. (b) 6. (a) 7. (a) 8. (a) 9. (c) 10. (b)

II. FILL IN THE BLANKS

1. Dependence
2. Dependence
3. More than, Less than
4. Lesser
5. Positive
6. Same.

IV. LONG ANSWER TYPE QUESTIONS

1. $Y = 0.498X + 1.366$
2. $Y = 1.98X + 12.9$; $Y = 42.6$
3. 3.75
4. $Y = 2.88 + 0.84X$, $X = 42.2 + 0.43Y$
5. $Y = 6 + 0.75X$; $X = 7 + 0.33Y$
6. $Y = 0.8X + 12$, $X = 0.45Y + 1$
7. $X = 13$, $Y = 17$, $b_{yx} = 9/20$, $bxy = 4/5$
8. (i) 62.8, (ii) 0.91
9. $X = 13$, $Y = 17$, S.D(X) = 9, $r = 0.6$
10. (b) $y = 88.7206 - 0.0432x$, (c) –0.8533, Yes
    (g) No (h) No
    (i) 2.97, Yes (j) slope = –0.0432.
    As the year increases by one, the welfare family size decreases by 0.0432 people.
11. (b) Yes (c) $y = 102.4287 + 11.7585x$
    (d) 0.9436; Yes (e) 478.70 feet; 1207.73 feet
    (g) Yes (h) Yes; (57,1050)
    (i) 172.98; No (j) 11.7585 feet
    (k) slope = 11.7585
    As the number of stories increases by one, the height of the building increases by 11.7585 feet

CHAPTER 12

Time Series Analysis and Forecasting

12.1 INTRODUCTION

Whenever one looks at an economic situation, whether it relates to an individual firm, industry or a nation as a whole, one will find a continuous movement of economic activity. In order to describe this flow of economic activity, the statistician uses a time series. The term 'time series' indicates a set of observations concerning any activity against different periods of time. The duration of time period may be hourly, daily, weekly, monthly or yearly. The following are few examples of time series data:

1. Profits earned by a company for each of the past five years.
2. Workers employed by a company for each of the past 15 years.
3. Number of students registered for the MBA programme of an institute for each of the past five years.
4. The weekly wholesale price index for each of the past 30 weeks.
5. Number of fatal road accidents in Delhi for each day for the past two months.

One can thus think of several types of time series relating to various aspects. Before we proceed further to the analysis of time series, it is necessary to understand the importance of a time series analysis.

A time series consists of data pertaining to a given unit or entity at a number of points in time. ***For example***, the accounting department of Sears generates time series on sales, costs, taxes, profits, assets, debts, dividends, and many other variables. Often our aim is to forecast the value of a variable (say, sales) for a particular month in the future. In order to do this statisticians have developed certain techniques for describing and analyzing time series data. They have developed procedures to break down a time series into such elements as its trend, seasonal variation, and cyclical variation. Depending on the purpose, an analyst may be interested only in one or more of these components. ***For example***, when the Social Security Administration studies the long-term viability of its trust fund, it will only be interested in the long term trend of the trust fund, and not in its within-year variations. On the other hand, a roadside hotdog vendor will be interested in its sales figures for each day of the week.

12.2 IMPORTANCE OF TIME SERIES ANALYSIS

There are several reasons for undertaking a time series analysis.

1. The analysis of a time series enables us to ***understand the past behaviour*** or ***performance***. We can know how the data have changed over time and find out the probable reasons responsible for such changes. If the past performance, say, of a company, has been poor, it can take corrective measures to arrest the poor performance.
2. A time series analysis helps directly in business planning. A firm can know the long-term trend in the sale of its products. It can find out at what rate sales have been increasing over the years. This may help it in making projections of its sales for the next few years and plan the procurement of raw material, equipment and manpower accordingly.
3. A time series analysis enables one to study such movements or cycles that fluctuate around the trend. Knowledge of cyclical pattern in certain series of data will be helpful in making generalisations in the concerned business or industry.
4. A time series analysis enables one to make meaningful comparisons in two or more series regarding the rate or type of growth. ***For example***, growth in consumption at the national level can be compared with that in the national income over specified period. Such comparisons are of considerable importance to business and industry.

The foregoing advantages of a time series analysis clearly point out its utility to business and industry. However, we should be clear about forecasts based on such analyses. Since a number of unknown factors influence the projections of a certain activity or phenomenon, it is just possible that projections based on time series data may turn out to be wrong. As such, we should not take the projections as absolutely correct, though we must always aim at improving these projections so that the error can be minimised. Having looked into the major advantages of a time series analysis, we now turn to the components of a time series.

12.3 TIME SERIES DEFINITIONS

1. "A time series is a set of data collected at successive points in time or over successive periods of time. A sequence of monthly data on new housing starts and a sequence of weekly data on product sales are examples of time series. Usually the data in a time series are collected at equally spaced periods of time, such as hour, day, week, month, or year."
2. "***Time series:*** Values of a variable recorded, usually at a regular interval, over a long period of time. The observed movement and fluctuations of many such series are composed of four different components, secular trend, seasonal variation, cyclical variation, and irregular variation. An example from medicine is the incidence of a disease recorded yearly over several decades. Such data usually require special methods for their analysis because of the presence of serial correlation between the separate observations." ***Everitt*** (The Cambridge Dictionary of Statistics, 1998).
3. "Time Series analysis deals with records that are collected over time." ***Fan and Yao*** (2003)
4. "A Time Series is a set of ordered observations on a quantitative characteristic of an individual or collective phenomenon taken at different points of time. Although it is not essential, it is common for these points to be equidistant in time. The essential quality of the series is the order of the observations according to the time variable, as distinct from those which are not ordered at all, e.g. in a random sample chosen simultaneously or are ordered according to their internal properties e.g. a set arranged in order of magnitude." ***Marriott*** (A Dictionary of Statistical Terms, 1990)
5. "***Time-series analysis*** techniques used in statistics to study data, often economic, collected over a period of time, e.g. quarterly sales figures for cars over a number of years. Time series

are used mainly for prediction purposes. To make useful predictions, allowance must be made for seasonal variation; this gives seasonally adjusted data. Interest then centres on any trend in the series. Typically, for car sales there may be a steady, or accelerating, increase or decrease in demand. Properties such as a five-year periodicity in sales may also be of interest." ***Daintith and Nelson*** (The Penguin Dictionary of Mathematics, 1989)

12.4 COMPONENTS OF TIME SERIES

A time series may contain one or more of the following four components:

- Secular trend
- Seasonal variation
- Cyclical variation
- Irregular variation

1. **Secular Trend:** The word secular is derived from Latin word '***SAECULUM***' which means generation or age. Sometimes a time-series displays a steady tendency of either upward or downward movement in the average (or mean) value of the forecast variable y over time. Such a tendency is called secular trend or simply trend. When observations are plotted against time, a straight line describes the increase or decrease in the time series over a period of time.
2. **Seasonal Variations:** Seasonal variations refer to rhythmic forces of change inherent in most time series showing a regular or a periodic pattern of movement over a span of less than a year and has the same or almost the same pattern year after year.
   The seasonal variations are usually measured in an interval within the calendar year. These may be hourly, daily, weekly, monthly or quarterly.
3. **Cyclical Variations:** Cyclical variations are oscillatory movements in a time series with period of oscillation greater than one year. These variations do not follow any regular pattern and move in somewhat unpredictable manner. These are upswings and downswings in the time series that are observable over extended periods of time called cycles. Cycles of 8 or 9 years duration called trade cycles. Cycles occurring after a time interval of 3 to 4 years are known as minor cycles.
4. **Irregular Variations:** Irregular variations are rapid changes or bleeps in the data caused by short-term unanticipated and non-securing factors. Irregular or random fluctuations can happen as often as day to day.

12.5 ANALYSIS OF TIME SERIES (MODELS OF DECOMPOSITION)

Analysis of time series essentially involves decomposition of the time series into four components. The main purpose of the analysis of time series is to estimate and separate the above four types of variations and to bring out the relative impact of each on the overall behaviour of the time series independently. There are many models by which a time series can be analysed; two models commonly used for decomposition of a time series are discussed below:

- Additive model
- Multiplicative model

Let us discuss each model.

Additive Model

The analysis of time series greatly depends on the hypothesis as to how the components interact.

In simplest case, we assume that the relationship amongst these components is additive, that is,

$$\boxed{Y = T + S + C + I}$$

Where,

Y is the result of the four components, T = trend, S = seasonal variation, C = cyclical variation and I = irregular variation.

Multiplicative Model

Here we assume that there is a multiplicative relationship amongst these four components. In symbols this can be written as

$$\boxed{Y = T \times S \times C \times I}$$

There is no unanimity amongst statisticians in this regard. The effects of these components might be multiplicative, additive or might be a combination of several other forms. On account of this, different assumptions will give different results. Having said this, we may add that the assumption that the time series consists of multiplicative components is most frequently used.

12.6 PRELIMINARY ADJUSTMENTS

Before analysing a time series it is necessary to make certain adjustments in the raw data. The procedure of making such adjustments is called editing of time series. The adjustments are necessary to bring about homogeneity in data in the following points:

1. Adjustment in calendar variations
2. Adjustment in population changes
3. Adjustment in Price changes
4. Adjustment for comparability of the data.

1. **Adjustment in Calendar Variations:** Most of the time series data is available in monthly form. But the number of days in a calendar month are not uniform and if the number of holidays and weekends are considered the variation may be even larger. Thus, as compared with February, the production in March may be more, not because of any increase in production activity but because of the fact that March has a larger number of days as compared with February. Obviously, the monthly production data need some adjustment for ensuring comparability. The adjustment for such calendar variations may be made by dividing the monthly data by the number of days in a month.
2. **Adjustment in Population Changes:** The data regarding income, consumption, production, etc. need to be adjusted for population changes because such changes are bound to distort comparisons in the phenomenon under study. If we are studying national income figures or figures of output such adjustments become necessary. National income may be rising due to change in the number of working population or output may be going down because the number of workers has declined. In such cases the easiest adjustment is to divide the income or output by the number of persons concerned. We can have per capita income figures or figures of output per worker.
3. **Adjustment in Price Variations:** The sale value of a commodity is the product of price and quantity sold. Now, in a situation when we have a value series and wish to study quantity changes alone, an adjustment for price changes becomes necessary.

For example, let in 1990, 500 units of commodity priced at Rs 20 are sold, the total value will be 500 × 20 = Rs 10,000. Again, in 1991, the commodity was priced at Rs 22. Obviously for the same demand of 500 units, the total sale value in 1991 comes to be 500 × 22 = Rs 11,000. This increase of Rs 1000 in sale value is due to price rise and not because of an increase in demand. Obviously, to have the desired comparability, in quantity changes, adjustments for price changes become necessary. For eliminating the influence of price changes on sale value, we make use of the following formula

$$\text{Quantity Sold} = \frac{\text{Sale value}}{\text{Price of the commodity}}$$

4. **Adjustment in Comparability of the data:** In order that valid conclusions are drawn the data which are being analysed should be comparable. However, when we are dealing with the analysis of time series which involves data relating to past, homogeneity of data is always a difficult proposition. Sometimes the definitions of the term change, sometimes there is a change in the size of the sample or sometimes the geographical coverage changes so that it becomes difficult to have strictly comparable data. In the Indian population census the definition of 'literate' and many other concepts has been changing. As such the figures of literates in various censuses are not comparable. Before partition of the country the geographical coverage of the national data was different than what it is after partition. In all such cases as far as possible, figures must be adjusted to make the data as homogeneous and comparable as possible.

As a time series involves the methods by which the different components can be separated, we shall now discuss these methods beginning with the trend. Let us discuss each of these components of time series independently.

12.7 SECULAR TREND

The trend is the long-term movement of a time series. In other words, an increase or decrease in the values of a variable occurring over a period of several years gives a trend. If the values of a variable remain stationery over several years, then we can say that there is no trend in that time series. When we study the growth in industrial production for the time period say 1990 to 2000, we are trying to find the trend in industrial production for this time period. The trend may be increasing or decreasing, as will be clear from two graphs presented below:

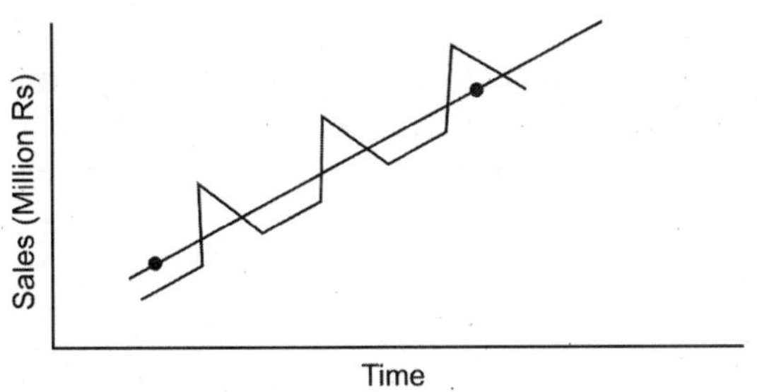

Fig. 12.1: Trend of Time Series
(Rising Trend)

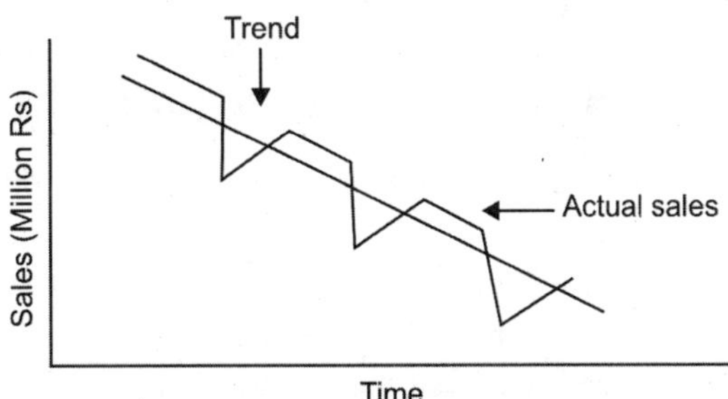

Fig. 12.2: Trend of a time service
(Declining Trend)

DO YOU KNOW?

The word secular is derived from the Latin word '***Saeculum***' which means generation or age, hence secular trend is that characteristic of a time series which extends consistently throughout the entire period of time under consideration. It shows a long term tendency of an activity to grow or to decline.

It will be seen that Fig. 12.1 shows both actual sales and the trend. It is a graph of increasing trend as is shown by a straight line passing through the actual sales data. In contrast, Fig. 12.2 shows a decreasing trend as sales have declined over time.

Thus, the general tendency of the data to grow or decline over a long period of time is technically called 'secular trend' or simply 'trend'. It should be noted that when we talk of trend, we mean thereby smooth, regular long-term movement of the data-sudden and erratic movements either in upward or in downward direction have nothing to do with the trend.

General trend is the result of such forces which are more or less constant for a long period of time or which change very gradually or slowly. The term 'long period of time' is a relative term. What constitutes a long period of time is a question which cannot be answered easily. The answer would depend upon the nature of data under study. If we are studying the trend of say national income, agricultural production, exports or imports, a period of 4 to 5 years may not be sufficient. In such cases the time series should be of a longer duration. However, if we are studying the effect of a medicine designed to regulate the human pulse rate, and if readings are done every 15 seconds and we have 40 such readings spread over 10 hours, they are enough to study the trend of the pulse rate. Hence it depends on nature of data whether a particular period would be called as long or not.

Generally speaking, the longer the time period of a series the better would be the results. As a minimum safeguard, the time period should cover two to three complete cycles.

It is not necessary that a time series should always have a rising or falling tendency. Some time series are such whose values fluctuate around a constant reading, which normally does not change with the passage of time. The temperature of human body would always fluctuate around a constant figure of 98.6° F. Similarly the temperature of a city would generally vary between more or less constant limits in various seasons of a year.

A trend can be linear or non-linear. If the values of the phenomenon under study when plotted on a graph paper duster more or less around a straight line, the trend is said to be linear or a straight line trend otherwise it is called non-linear or curvi-linear.

There are some other types of trend such as parabolic and logarithmic. We are concerned here with only the straight-line trends.

12.8 METHODS FOR MEASURING TRENDS

There are various methods of fitting a straight line to a time series. Some of these are given below:

1. Freehand Method.
2. The Method of semi-averages
3. The Method of moving averages,
4. The Method of least squares.

Let us discuss each of these methods independently

1. The Freehand Method

This is the simplest method of finding a trend line. The procedure involves first the plotting of the time series on a graph and then fitting a straight line through the plotted points in such a way that the straight line shows the trend of the time series.

When a trend line is fitted by the freehand method, the following points must be kept in mind-

(i) the curve should be smooth
(ii) the number of points above the line or curve are equal to the points below it
(iii) the sum of vertical deviations of the points above the smoothed line is equal to the sum of the vertical deviations of the points below the line.
(iv) the sum of the squares of the vertical deviations from the trend line curve is minimum.

The hypothetical data given below will illustrate the fitting of a freehand curve to set of time series value:

Year (*X*)	1995	1996	1997	1998	1999	2000	2001
Sale (*Y*) Million Rs	10	20	15	25	37	35	40

Let *X* show the year, starting with 1995, and *Y* show the sale of a product in million rupees. The sale figures are plotted in Fig. 12.3. We now join the points thereby getting the production line from 1995 to 2001. We draw a straight line by observation that gives a broad trend of the sales. It may be noted that the freehand method is not an accurate method of fitting a trend as different persons may fit different trend lines to the same set of data.

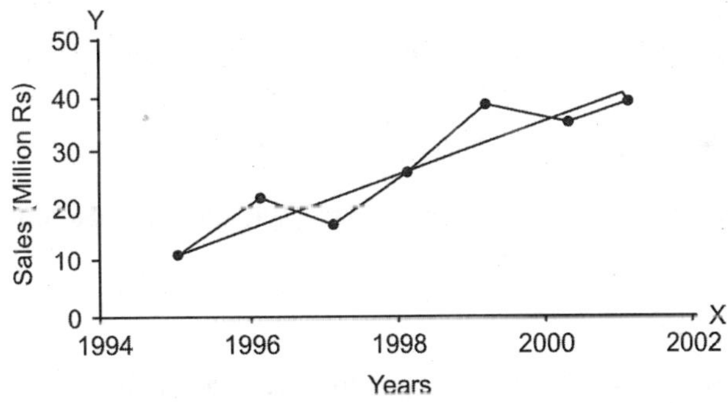

Fig. 12.3: Trend by Free Hand Method

Let us assume that the trend line goes through the points for 1995 and 2000. Now, the trend line can be found by setting up the equation for the straight line that passes through the two points 1995 and 2000.

In order to ascertain the required equation, we first assign a sequence to the different years for which the data are given, starting from 1995, which is indicated by zero, that is, the year of origin. Then 1996 is 1, 1997 is 2 and so forth. Since the straight line connects two points, let us assume that these two points are at the point of origin and at the end of 2001. Thus, the coordinates of the two points selected become (0,10) and (6,40). On the basis of this information, we may formulate the following two equations for a straight line:

$$Y = a + bX$$

Putting the value of X and Y

$$10 = a + 0b \qquad [X = 0, Y = 10]$$

$$40 = a + 6b \qquad [X = 6, Y = 40]$$

Solving the two equations gives $a = 10$ and $b = 5$. This gives the equation for the trend line as

$$Y_c = 10 + 5X$$

Origin: 1st July 1995

X: 1- year units

It may be noted that we have used the symbol Y_c instead of Y. This is because the values of Y obtained from the equation are the computed or the estimated values and are not the actual ones. Another point to note is that it is necessary to specify the origin as well as the units of X. The general practice is to take the middle of the year (i.e., 1st July) as the point to represent the data for that year.

Advantages and Limitations of the Freehand Method

Advantages

1. The Freehand method is a very simple method of estimating trend.
2. There is flexibility in this method as it can be used regardless whether the trend is a straight line or non-linear.
3. If the statistician is well-conversant with the movement of the particular variable involved in the time series, the use of this method may even give a better expression to the long-term movement than the trend fitted by a rigid mathematical formula.

Limitations

1. This is a highly subjective method as the trend line fitted to the same set of data by this method will vary from one person to another.
2. In view of the trend line being highly subjective, it is not an appropriate method for making predictions.
3. It means very long experience on the part of the statistician to use this method, otherwise, the trend fitted would not be of much use.

2. The Method of Semi-Averages

When the method of semi-averages is used, the given time series is divided into two parts preferably with the same number of years. The average of each part is calculated and then a trend line through these averages is fitted. This is illustrated with the data given in table.

Production from 1994–2001

Year	X	Y	Average
1994	0	10	
1995	1	12	60/4 = 15
1996	2	18	
1997	3	20	
1998	4	20	
1999	5	25	
2000	6	23	100/4 = 25
2001	7	32	

The average of first part of the data is 15 and that of the second part is 25. Since 15 is the average of 1994, 1995, 1996 and 1997, 15 are plotted in between 1995 and 1996, which is the middle of the 4-year period. Likewise, 25 are plotted in between 1999 and 2000. Then these points are joined by a straight line, which is a semi-average trend line. This is shown in Fig. 12.4.

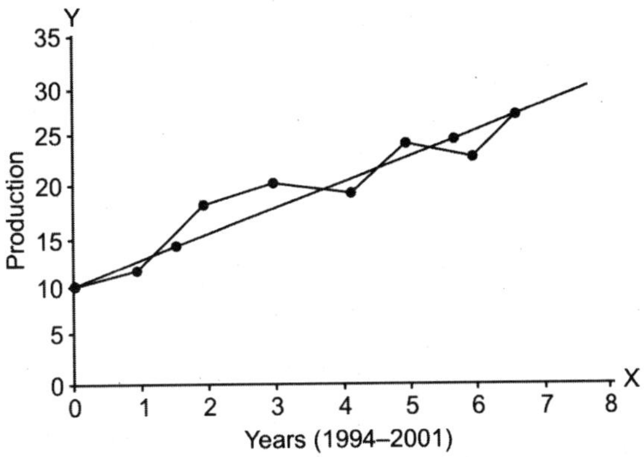

Fig. 12.4: Trend line by the Method of Semi-Average

On the basis of the semi-average trend line, the following two simultaneous equations are arrived at

$$15 = a + b \quad ...(1)$$

$$25 = a + 4b \quad ...(2)$$

Solving for a and b gives us $a = 11.67$ and $b = 3.33$. This gives the equation of the trend line

$$Y_c = 11.67 + 3.33X$$

Origin: 1st July 1994

X: 1-year units

Applying this equation to estimate the production for 1996,

$$Y_c = 11.67 + (3.33 \times 2) = 18.33$$

As we know, the actual production in 1996 was 18. This shows that the discrepancy between actual and estimated production is

$$Y_c 96 - Y96 = 18.33 - 18 = 0.33$$

It will be seen that there was a very close fit in this example because of a very negligible difference between the actual and the estimated figures.

It may be noted that in case of a time series pertaining to odd number of years, either the middle year is excluded from the computation or the series may be split in two unequal parts. A point worth emphasising is that in case a particular year has been an abnormal year on account of such factors as a prolonged strike disrupting production, it is advisable to omit that year so that the trend line may be more realistic.

Advantages and Limitations of the Semi-Average Method

Advantages

1. The method of semi-averages is simple to use as anyone can use it conveniently.
2. This is an objective method as anyone applying it to the given set of data would get the same trend line.

Limitations

1. This method will always give a straight line trend regardless of the nature of the given set of data. Thus, it assumes a straight line relationship, which may not be true.
2. This method may give wrong trend-line on account of the limitations of arithmetic average. In case there is an extreme value in either half or both halves of the time series, then the trend line will not give a realistic growth of the phenomenon being measured. In order to overcome this problem, it is necessary to ensure that the data do not have extreme values.

3. The Method of Moving Averages

The method of moving averages is a simple device of reducing fluctuations and obtaining trend values with a fair degree of accuracy. It issued not only to fit trend lines but also to seasonal and cyclical variations. The following example illustrates how the method is used.

EXAMPLE 12.1: Suppose we are given a time series data for 12 years-1989 to 2000 relating to sales of a certain business firm. These data are given below:

Year	Sales (Million Rs)	Year	Sales (Million Rs)
1989	10 .	1995	15
1990	15	1996	24
1991	20	1997	15
1992	25	1998	21
1993	15	1999	15
1994	12	2000	24

We are asked to find out the three-year moving averages, starting from 1989.

Solution: Table 3 shows these figures. Taking the first three years — 1989, 1990 and 1991, we add up their sales — 10 + 15 + 20 = 45. This figure is written in column 3 of Table 20.3 against the mid-year, that is, 1990. Now, we drop the year 1989 and include the year 1992 in our calculation. Thus, the total of three years 1990, 1991 and 1992, which comes to 60, is entered in the third column against 1991. This process is continued until we reach the last three years — 1998, 1999 and 2000. It may be noted that the Table does not have a total for the first year, 1989 and the last year, 2000.

The next step involves the calculation of moving averages by dividing the moving totals by 3. The moving averages are shown in the last column of table.

Calculation of Moving Averages 1995

Year	Sales (Million Rs)	Three year Moving Total	Three year Moving Average
1989	10		
1990	15	45	15
1991	20	60	20
1992	25	60	20
1993	15	52	17
1994	12	42	14
1995	15	51	17
1996	24	54	18
1997	15	60	20
1998	21	54	18
1999	18	63	21
2000	24		

The moving averages have been plotted on a graph as shown in Fig. 12.5. In order to fit a trend line to these moving average points on the graph, the freehand method, the semi-average method, the method of least squares (which is discussed later in this chapter) may be used. We have joined two points of moving averages to fit a trend line.

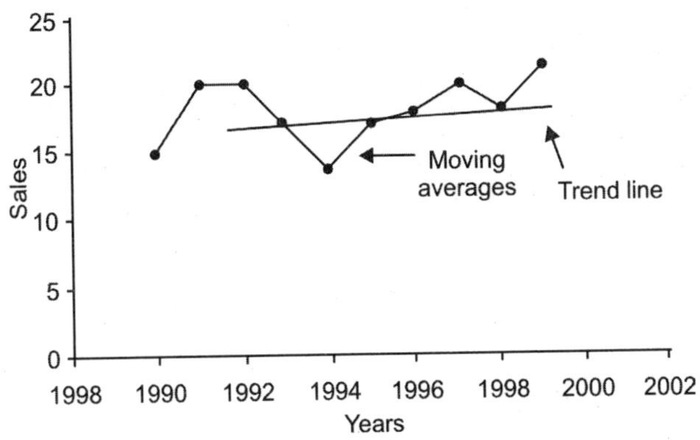

Fig. 12.5: Graph showing moving average and the trend line

In order to ensure that the moving average method is appropriate and it is applied effectively, it is necessary to ascertain first whether a regular, periodic cycle in the time series exists. In several cases, one would find that there is certain regularity in the series to allow the use of the moving average method. It may also be noted that if the basic nature of the time series is linear, it will give a linear trend. In case it is curvilinear, then its trend will be a curve. Another point to note is that the use of the moving average method is not confined to trend lines alone but is also extended to varying types of data that show regular periodic fluctuations. Later, we shall use it for removing seasonal fluctuations from a time series.

Advantages and Limitations of the Moving Average Method

Advantages

1. The method of moving averages is simpler method than the method of least quares.
2. The general movement of the data is reflected in the moving averages. As such, the trend line is based on the data rather than on the statistician's choice of a mathematical function.
3. In case the period of moving averages coincides with that of cyclical fluctuations in the data, this method automatically removes such fluctuations.

Limitations

1. The method does not cover all the years so far as trend values are concerned.
2. It needs to be exercised very carefully as there are no definite rules regarding the period of moving averages.
3. This method cannot be used for forecasting as it is not represented by a mathematical function.
4. If the trend is non-linear, the moving averages may considerably deviate from it.

4. The Method of Least Squares

Among the methods of fitting a straight line to a series of data, this is the most frequently used method. As we have seen earlier that the equation of a straight line is $Y = a + bX$, where Y is the time period, say, year, X is the value of the item measured against time, a is the Y-intercept and b is the coefficient of X that shows the slope of the straight line. In order to find out the values of a and b, the following two equations are solved:

$$\Sigma Y = na + b\Sigma X$$

$$\Sigma XY = a\Sigma X + b\Sigma X^2$$

Where n is the total number of observations in a series. These equations are called the ***normal equations***.

This method, discussed in Chapter 11 Regression Analysis, is known as the method of least squares because deviations of the observed points (actual data) from the trend line (computed values) are the least, if it is used.

The following example will show how the method of least squares is used.

An example of the series having odd numbers

Year *X*	*Y*
1996	270
1997	285
1998	295
1999	315
2000	330

We are required to fit a trend to these data, using the method of least squares.

Solution: We know from the normal equations that we need the values of ΣY, ΣX, ΣXY, and ΣX^2 so that the normal equations can be solved. In order to get these values, the following worksheet is set up.

The values are: $\Sigma X = 0$, $\Sigma Y = 1495$, $\Sigma XY = 150$ and $\Sigma X^2 = 10$

Substituting these values in the two normal equations, we get

$$1495 = 5a + b\,(0) \qquad ...(1)$$

$$150 = a\,(0) + b(10) \qquad ...(2)$$

Equation (1) gives the value of a as 1495/5 = 299 and equation (2) gives the value of b as 150/10 = 15.

Worksheet

Year	*X*	*Y*	*XY*	X^2
1996	–2	270	–540	4
1997	–1	285	–285	1
1998	0	295	0	0
1999	1	315	315	1
2000	2	330	660	4
Total	**0**	**1,495**	**150**	**10**

Thus, the straight line trend that we get is

$$Y_c = 299 + 15X$$

Origin: 1-7-1998

X: 1-year unit

Now, in order to fit the trend to the original data on a graph, first we plot the original values against the respective years. We then decide location of any two points as two points are needed to draw a straight line. Let us compute the value of *X* for 1997 and 2000.

$$Y_c 1997 = a + bX = 299 + 15\,(-1) = 284$$
$$Y_c 2000 = a + bX = 299 + 15\,(2) = 329$$

We now draw a straight line with the help of these two calculated values. This is shown in Figure 12.6. We now take another example, which consists of even number of years.

An Example of the Series Having Even Numbers Example

Suppose we have the following data.

Year (X)	1995	1996	1997	1998	1999	2000
Y	15	14	18	20	17	24

We have to fit a trend to these data, again using the method of least squares

Solution: We set up the following worksheet.

Worksheet

Year	X	Y	XY	X^2
1995	–5	15	–75	25
1996	–3	14	–42	9
1997	–1	18	–18	1
1998	1	20	20	1
1999	3	17	51	9
2000	5	24	120	25
Total	**0**	**108**	**56**	**70**

The two normal equations are:

$$\Sigma Y = na + b\Sigma X$$
$$\Sigma XY = a\Sigma X + b\Sigma X^2$$

Substituting the values in the two equations, we get

$$108 = 6\,a + b\,(0)$$
$$56 = a\,(0) + b\,(70)$$

The first equation gives $a = 108/6 = 18$ and the second equation gives $b = 56/70 = 0.8$. Thus, the trend line is

$$Y_c = 18 + 0.8X$$

Origin: 1-1-1998

X: half-year units

A comparison of this equation with that in the earlier example will show that there are two changes here. *First,* unlike in the previous example, the origin is halfway between 1st July 1997 and 1st July 1998, that is, 1st January 1998. *Second,* the *X*s are in half-year units. This is because the *X*s are indicated as 1, 3, 5 and each year varies by 2 units. Thus, to move from 1st July 1998 to 1st July 1999, *X* has to move from 1 to 3. When *X* has to move from 1 to 2, it means it moves only half year, that is, from 1st July 1998 to 1st January 1999.

Figure shows the plot of original data along with the trend line. If we want to avoid half-year units and would like to retain one-year X units, then we may multiply the X values by 1/2. In this example, the X has been given the values as:

Years	1995	1996	1997	1998	1999	2000
	–5 –2.5	–3 –1.5	–1 –0.5	1 0.5	3 1.5	5 2.5

The last row in the above table shows the revised values of X, where X unit becomes 1 year instead of half-year.

Changing the Unit Value: So far our discussion related to the trend equation pertaining to annual data. But in many cases the time series are given as annual monthly averages and monthly data. The trend line equation will be different in the three cases viz. the annual total, annual monthly average and monthly data. An illustration will bring out this distinction clearly.

EXAMPLE 12.2: Suppose the annual salary of a person for 1998 was Rs 24,000, which was raised to Rs 27,600 in 1999 and to Rs 31,200 in 2000.

Using this information, explain how the trend line equation will be different in case of annual total, annual monthly average and monthly data.

Solution: This means that his monthly average salary was Rs 2,000 for 1998, Rs 2,300 for 1999 and Rs 2,600 for 2000. Thus, the annual increase of the monthly average salary was Rs 300. The monthly increase of the monthly average salary was Rs 300/12 = Rs 25.

On the basis of these data, the following three equations can be constructed.

1. The annual total equation:

$$Y_c = \text{Rs } 24{,}000 + 3{,}600\,X$$
$$X = 0 \text{ at July 1, 1999}$$

where X is in 1-year units

2. The monthly average equation:

$$Y_c = (\text{Rs } 24{,}000/12) + (3{,}600/12)\,X$$
$$Y_c = \text{Rs } 2{,}000 + 300\,X$$
$$X = 0 \text{ at July 1, 1999}$$

where X is in I-year units

3. The monthly equation:

$$Y_c = (\text{Rs } 24{,}000/12) + [3{,}600/(12 \times 12)]X$$
$$Y_c = \text{Rs } 2{,}000 + 25X$$
$$X = 0 \text{ at July 1, 1999}$$

where X is in 1-month units

It may be noted that the b coefficient in equation (2), which is Rs 3,600/12 = 300, shows the annual increase of the monthly average salary. In equation (3), the b coefficient is Rs [3,600/(12*12)] = 25, which shows the monthly increase of the monthly average salary.

In keeping with our earlier approach of using the middle of the year to represent the annual data, it is necessary to use the same approach for monthly data. That is, the origin should be July 15 instead of July 1 as shown in equation (3).

In order to shift the origin from July 1, 1999 to July 15, the value of 'a' (in the equation $Y = a + bX$) has to be changed.

$$Y_c = \text{Rs } 2{,}000 + 25 \times 1/2$$
$$= 2{,}000 + 12.5 = 2012.5$$

This will give the monthly equation for 15th July 1999 as

$$Y_c = \text{Rs } 2{,}012.5 + 25X$$

Origin: 15-7-1999
X: 1-month units

Shifting the Origin: The monthly average equation used in the preceding section was

$$Y_c = \text{Rs } 2{,}000 + 300X$$

Origin: July 1, 1999
X: 1-year units

Suppose we are interested in shifting the origin to July 1, 2001. This can be done by finding the new Y-intercept a_{2001}. This is

$$a_{2001} = 2{,}000 + (300 \times 2) = 2{,}600$$

Thus, the equation becomes

$$Y_c = 2{,}600 + 300X$$

Origin: July 1,2001
X: 1-year units

In the same manner, we can shift the trend value to January 1999 instead of July 1999. What we have to do is to subtract the value of X for a six-month period from the value of Y-intercept.

Taking our earlier example,

$$Y_c = 2{,}600 + 300X$$

Origin: July 1, 2001
X: 1-year units

We can rewrite thus

$$Y_c = 2600 - (300 \times 1/2) + 300X$$

or
$$Y_c = 2450 + 300X$$

Origin: January 1, 2001
X: 1-year units

Second-degree Polynomial

A second-degree polynomial is also known as a ***quadratic trend*** or parabola. It is given by the equation

$$\boxed{Y = a + bX + cX^2}$$

Given a set of data, the trend can be obtained by the usual least square method. We explain this by taking an example.

EXAMPLE 12.3: *Suppose we have the following data:*

Years	1995	1996	1997	1998	1999
Production of TV sets ('000)	2	4	8	14	22

In the second degree parabola, there will be three normal equations as shown below:

$$\Sigma Y = na + b\Sigma X + c\Sigma X^2$$

$$\Sigma XY = a\Sigma X + b\Sigma X^2 + c\Sigma X^3$$

$$\Sigma X^2Y = a\Sigma X^2 + b\Sigma X^3 + c\Sigma X^4$$

If we put $\Sigma X = 0$, the above normal equations become

$$\Sigma Y = na + c\Sigma X^2$$

$$\Sigma XY = b\Sigma X^2$$

$$\Sigma X^2Y = a\Sigma X^2 + c\Sigma X^4$$

Let us set up a worksheet to obtain the numerical values of these terms.

Years	X	X^2	Y	XY	X^2Y	X^3	X^4
1995	–2	4	2	–4	8	–8	16
1996	–1	1	4	–4	4	–1	1
1997	0	0	8	0	0	0	0
1998	1	1	14	14	14	1	1
1999	2	4	22	44	88	8	16
Total	**0**	**10**	**50**	**500**	**114**	**0**	**34**

Applying these values in the above equations, we get

$$50 = 5a + 10c \quad ...(1)$$

$$50 = 10b \quad ...(2)$$

$$114 = 10\,a + 34c \quad ...(3)$$

Solving these we get: $a = 8$, $b = 5$, $c = 1$.

Now, we have $a = 8$, $b = 5$ and $c = 1$

$$Y = a + bX + cX^2$$

or $$Y = 8 + 5X + 1X^2$$

Origin: July 1, 1997

X: 1 -year units

If we have to find out the trend value for the year 2000, then

$$X = 3$$

$$Y = a + \text{b}X + cX^2$$

or $$Y = 8 + (3 \times 5) + (9 \times 1)$$

or $$Y = 32$$

Let us see how well the second degree parabola has fitted to the time series data. It will be seen that the parabolic trend has fitted extremely well to the original data. In fact, the Y_c values, if calculated, turn out to be the same as the original values.

On the basis of the parabola fitted to the time series, we can say that the production of TV sets in that firm would be 32,000 in the year 2000. A word of caution is necessary here. One has to be more careful while using a parabola for forecasting when one is using a linear trend. This is because the slope of the second degree curve is continually increasing. Further, it is sometimes risky to use a parabola to forecast further into the future. In order to have a realistic forecast, one has to be fully aware of factors that may either increase or slacken the growth rate. In case a given time series has an even number of elements, we can proceed in the same manner as was shown earlier for a linear trend. In such a case, the origin will shift to 1st January of the concerned year and X would be in half-year units.

Exponential Curves for Trend Values

The equation of the exponential curve is of the following form:

$$Y = AB^X$$

Taking the logarithm of both sides, we get $\log Y = \log A + X \log B$

To obtain the values of the constants A and B the two normal equations are:

$$\Sigma \log Y = N \log A + \log B \Sigma X$$

$$\Sigma(X \log Y) = \log A \Sigma X + \log B \Sigma X^2$$

When deviations are taken from the middle year so that $\Sigma(X - \bar{X}) = \Sigma x = 0$ the above equations are simplified and assume the following form:

$$\Sigma \log Y = N \operatorname{Log} A \Rightarrow \log A = \frac{\Sigma \log Y}{N}$$

$$\Sigma(x \log Y) = \log B \Sigma x^2 \Rightarrow \log B = \frac{\Sigma(x \log Y)}{\Sigma x^2}$$

To fit an equation of the above type we need the values of x, Y, $\log Y$, Σx^2 and values of A and B along with their logs.

To get these values the following steps are necessary.

(i) x = Deviation of the X-series from its mid value. Find these time deviations and square these values and total the squares to get the value of Σx^2.

(ii) Obtain the logarithms of the values of Y.

(iii) Multiply $\log Y$ with corresponding values of x, total these products to get $\Sigma (x \log Y)$.

(iv) Obtain the value of $\log A$ by dividing $\Sigma \log Y$ by N.

(v) Obtain the value of log B by dividing $\Sigma (x \log Y)$ by Σx^2. This would be the ***slope of the line*** or the ***value of growth.***

The values of A and B can be obtained by taking antilogarithms.

The required equation would be $Y = AB^X = AB(X - \bar{X})$

The following examples would illustrate the above rules.

EXAMPLE 12.4: Calculate the trend values by the method of least squares from the data given below and estimate the sales for the year 2001.

Years	1992	1993	1994	1995	1996
Sales of TV sets (in '000)	12	18	20	23	125

Solution:

Calculation of Trend Values by Least Squares Method

Years X	Sales Y	X-1994 x	xY	x^2	Trend Values Y_c
1992	12	–2	–24	4	13.0
1993	18	–1	–18	4	16.5
1994	20	0	0	0	20.0
1995	23	+1	+23	1	23.5
1996	27	+2	+54	4	27.0
$n = 5$	$\Sigma Y = 100$	$\Sigma x = 0$	$\Sigma xY = 35$	$\Sigma x^2 = 10$	

Equation of Straight line = $Y_c = A + B\ (X–1994)$

Since $\Sigma x = 0$, Value of $a = \frac{\Sigma Y}{n} = \frac{100}{5} = 20$

Value of $b = \frac{\Sigma xY}{\Sigma x^2} = \frac{35}{10} = 3.5$

Equation of Straight line = $Y_c = A + B\ (X - 1994)$ or $Y_c = 20 + 3.5x$.

When $X = 1992$, $Y_c = 20 + (3.5 \times -2) = 13$

When $X = 1993$, $Y_c = 20 + (3.5 \times -1) = 16.5$

When $X = 1994$, $Y_c = 20$

When $X = 1995$, $Y_c = 20 + (3.5 \times 1) = 23.5$

When $X = 1996$, $Y_c = 20 + (3.5 \times 2) = 27.0$

Now for 2001 the value of x would be 7 and $Y_c = 20 + (3.5 \times 7) = 44.5$

Thus the likely sale of T.Vs in 2001 is 44.5 thousands.

EXAMPLE 12.5: Fit a logarithmic straight line to the following data:

Years	2000	2001	2002	2003	2004	2005
Production (m. tonnes of steel)	64	70	75	82	88	95

Solution:

Fitting of Logarithmic Straight Line

Years	Production Y	X	log Y	X^2	X.log Y
2000	64	–3	1.8062	9	–5.4186
2001	70	–2	1.8451	4	–3.6902
2002	75	–1	1.8751	1	–1.8751
2003	82	0	1.9138	0	0
2004	88	+1	1.9445	1	+1.9445
2005	95	+2	1.9777	4	+3.9554
$n = 6$	$\Sigma Y = 474$	$\Sigma X = -3$	$\Sigma \log Y = 11.3624$	$\Sigma X^2 = 19$	$\Sigma X \log Y = 5.084$

The logarithmic straight line trend is given by

$$\log Y = \log A + X \log B$$

The two normal equations are:

$$\Sigma \log Y = n \log A + \log B \Sigma X$$

$$\Sigma X \log Y = \log A \Sigma X + \log B \Sigma X^2$$

Substituting the values

$$11.3624 = 6 \log A - 3 \log B \quad \text{...(i)}$$

$$-5.084 = -3 \log A + 19 \log B \quad \text{...(ii)}$$

Multiplying eq. (ii) by 2 and adding to (i),

$$11.3624 = 6 \log A - 3 \log B$$

$$-10.168 = -6 \log A - 38 \log B$$

$$35 \log B = 1.1944$$

$$\log B = \frac{1.1944}{35} = 0.034$$

Putting the value of log b in eqn. (i)

$$11.3264 = 6 \log A - 0.102$$

$$6 \log A = 11.4644$$

$$\log A = 1.911$$

Hence $\qquad \log Y = 1.911 - 0.034\, X$

Advantages and Limitations of the Moving Average Method

Advantages

1. It is a mathematical method which does not leave any scope of subjectivity, i.e., it is free from any bias.
2. Unlike the method of moving averages, this method provides trend values for all given time points in the series.
3. The fitted trend equation can be used for purposes of estimation, prediction and forecasting.

Limitations

1. The method involves lots of calculations as compared to other methods of trend determination.
2. It is not flexible in the sense that an addition of even a single value to initial data needs fresh calculations for determining the trend equation.
3. Predictions or forecasts are based only on long-term variations, i.e. trend, while the impact of remaining (cyclical, seasonal and irregular) variations is ignored.
4. The choice of a particular trend equation or curve is largely a subjective matter. In the absence of no hard and fast rule, the choice of the equation depends on the person concerned.

Detrending

The process of eliminating trend from the time series is known as detrending. After eliminating trend, the remaining components are short-term variations namely, seasonal, cyclical and irregular. In terms of time series models a time series after detrending may be expressed as:

1. Under additive model : $Y = S + C + I$
2. Under multiplicative model : $Y = S \times C \times I$

12.9 SEASONAL VARIATION

A seasonal variation is a recurring fluctuation that has duration of one year. Some examples of seasonal variation are the consumption of soft drinks, sale of woolen cloth, sale of dry fruits, and so on. Soft drinks are taken during the summer season and during winter months their consumption is extremely low. In contrast, the woolens are in great demand during the winter season only. The same is the case of dry fruits, which are largely consumed in winter. Again, on account of major festivals there are fluctuations in the sale and consumption of certain items. ***For example***, during Diwali festival, one finds that the sale of cloth is the maximum. In West Bengal, this pattern is noticeable during the Durga Pooja festival.

Why is it necessary to Measure Seasonal Variation?

If one knows in advance that the sales of a specific product are bound to be high in a particular month or week, one may hold a larger stock of it to match the increased demand in that month or week. In the same manner, if one knows that the price of some commodity moves in a particular fashion, one may buy it while the price is low and hold it for subsequent use or sale when the price is high. This will be true for any raw material that goes into the production of finished goods.

Yet another reason for measuring seasonal variation is to adjust the data statistically for such variation. It is easier to interpret seasonally adjusted data as it would reduce the confusion, which might otherwise arise. For instance, if the data on sale of some commodity are not seasonally adjusted, a seasonal upswing in those data may be taken as an improved performance. This would obviously be wrong. Our main concern here is with periodic series that have a period of one year. We will now focus on the methods used for measuring seasonal variation.

12.10 METHODS OF MEASURING SEASONAL VARIATION

There are four methods of measuring seasonal variation:

1. The method of simple averages
2. The ratio to trend method
3. The moving average method
4. The link relative method

We will discuss all of them, one by one, with suitable examples.

1. The Method of Simple Averages

According to this method the data for each month (if monthly data is given) are expressed as percentage of the average for the year.

This method can be better explained with the help of an example. Suppose we are given monthly data for two years as shown in the first two columns of given table.

Consumption of Electricity (KWhrs)					
Month	**1999 (1)**	**2000 (2)**	**Total (3) (1999 + 2000)**	**A. Mean (4)**	**Seasonal (5)**
January	342	392	734	367	116.48
February	309	349	658	329	104.42
March	299	343	642	321	101.88
April	268	312	580	290	92.04
May	250	290	540	270	85,69
June	236	274	510	255	80.93
July	242	282	524	262	83.15
August	263	305	568	284	90.14
September	288	328	616	308	97.75
October	321	365	686	343	108.86
November	343	379	722	361	114.58
December	365	417	782	391	124.10
			Total	**3,781**	**1,200.00**
			Average	**315.08**	**100.00**

It may be noted that

(i) Column (3) gives the total of two months for 1999 and 2000

(ii) Column (4) shows the arithmetic mean for the two months.

(iii) The total of column (4) comes to 3,781. This is divided by 12 in order to obtain the monthly average, which is 315.08.

(iv) In order to obtain the seasonal variation S, figures given in column (4) are divided by 315.08 and multiplied by 100, as it is customary to express the seasonal factor as a base of 100.

The values of S are shown in the last column of the table.

NOTE: The above illustration consists of only two years because our purpose is to explain the method for computing seasonal variation. In real life, one may have to use a longer time series. Moreover, it is advisable to use a longer time series, which will give more realistic results. It may be noted that above series is related to monthly data but the method, explained above, can be applied to any series with weekly or quarterly data.

Advantages and Limitations of the Method of Simple Averages

This method is the simplest method for determining seasonal indices. However, it assumes that the time series is free from the trend component or the trend is assumed to have little impact on the time series. These assumptions, however, are not always true. Most economic and business series have definite trends and as such this method is not suitable for analysing business and economic data. This method also tries to eliminate the effect of irregular or random variables by averaging process but this in itself is not enough. To arrive at dependable seasonal indices it is necessary that the effect of trend should first be removed from the original data before seasonal variations are studied.

2. The Ratio to Trend Method

Another method of measuring seasonal variation is the ratio to trend method (also known as Percentage — to — Trend Method). This method is an improvement over the method of simple averages. It involves a number of steps as indicated below:

(i) By using the method of least squares, the trend values are obtained.
(ii) The original time series is to be divided by the trend values obtained earlier. These figures are to be transformed into percentages. Now these percentage figures have three components of the time series, viz. seasonal, cyclical and irregular as the trend has been eliminated.
(iii) The percentages are to be averaged for each month or quarter or for any other time period in which the original data are available. This process will eliminate the effects of both cyclical and irregular movements. It may be noted that while averaging the percentages, median should be preferred to the arithmetic mean. This is because the later gives undue weightage to extreme values, which are mainly on account of seasonal swings.
(iv) The figures obtained in (iii) above need to be adjusted to a total of 1,200 for the monthly series and to 400 for the quarterly series. This adjustment is carried out by multiplying each figure by a constant 'K'. The formula for this adjustment is:
   (a) For the monthly series: K =1,200/Sum of the indices
   (b) For the quarterly series: K= 400/Sum of the indices

Let us take an example that uses this method for measuring seasonal variation.

EXAMPLE 12.6: Find seasonal variation by the ratio-to-trend method for the following data:

Year	Quarters			
	1st	2nd	3rd	4th
1997	75	60	54	59
1998	88	65	63	80
2000	100	78	73	93
2001	118	100	88	110

Solution: For calculating the trend values, we have to use the method of least squares. For straight-line trend, $Y = a + bX,$ the two normal equations are:

$$\Sigma Y = na + b\Sigma X$$

$$\Sigma XY = a\Sigma X + b\Sigma X^2$$

In order to find the numerical values for these terms, we have to set up worksheet, which is given in table.

Computation of Straight-line Trend

Year	Year X	Annual total of Q. data	Quarterly average for the year Y	XY	X^2	Trend values
1997	–2	248	62	–124	4	62
1998	–1	296	74	–74	1	71.6
1999	0	320	80	0	0	81.2
2000	1	344	86	86	1	90.8
2001	0	416	104	208	4	100.4
Total	**0**	**1,624**	**406**	**96**	**10**	

Applying these values in the two normal equations,

$$406 = 5a + 0b \quad ...(1)$$

$$96 = 0a + 10b \quad ...(2)$$

From equation (1), $a = 406/5 = 81.2$

From equation (2), $b = 96/10 = 9.6$

From the above we get the trend line

$$Y_c = 81.2 + 9.6X$$

Origin: July 1, 1999

X 1-year: units

As can be seen, yearly increment in the trend value is $b = 9.6$.

Hence the increment per quarter is $9.6/4 = 2.4$. On this basis, we now determine the quarterly trend values, which are shown in table.

Quarterly Trend Values

Year	Quarters			
	1st	2nd	3rd	4th
1997	58.4	60.8	63.2	65.6
1998	68.0	70.4	72.8	75.2
1999	77.6	80.0	82.4	84.8
2000	87.2	89.6	92.0	94.4
2001	96.8	99.2	101.6	104.0

For 1st July 1997, the trend value is $81.2 + (9.6 \times -2) = 62$. As the quarterly increment is 2.4, half of quarterly increment is 1.2.

We obtain the trend values for 2nd and 3rd quarters of 1997 as $62 - 1.2$ and $62 + 1.2$, that is, 60.8 and 63.2 respectively. As a result, the trend value for the 1st quarter of 1997 would be $60.8 - 2.4 = 58.4$ and for the 4th quarter is $63.2 + 2.4 = 65.6$.

Trend Eliminated Values (Quarterly Values as percentage of Trend Values)

Year	Quarters			
	1st	2nd	3rd	4th
1997	128.42	98.68	85.44	89.94
1998	129.41	92.33	86.54	106.38
1999	122.42	92.50	79.14	100.24
2000	114.68	87.64	79.35	98.52
2001	121.90	100.81	86.61	105.77
Total	**616.83**	**471.96**	**417.08**	**500.85**
A. Mean	**123.37**	**94.39**	**83.42**	**100.17**

As the total of arithmetic means of the four quarters (i.e. 123.37 + 94.39 + 83.42 + 100.17) is 401.35, it should be 400 for the quarterly series. It is, therefore, necessary to make some adjustment. This adjustment can be made by using the following formula:

$$K = \frac{400}{\text{Sum of the quarterly indices}} = \frac{400}{401.35} = 0.996636$$

If we multiply the unadjusted indices by 0.996636, we will get the seasonal indices. Applying this adjustment factor, we get the following seasonal indices:

	Q_1	Q_2	Q_3	Q_4
Seasonal Index	122.96	94.07	83.14	99.83

It will be seen that these four seasonal indices add to 400.

Advantages and Limitations of Ratio-to-Trend Method

Advantages

1. It is simple to compute and easy to understand.
2. The obvious advantage of this method over the moving, average method lies in the fact that 'ratio to trend' can be obtained for each month for which the data are available and as such, unlike the 'ratio to moving average' method, there is no loss of data.

Limitations

This method does not effectively tackle the elimination of cyclical movements. If the series exhibits pronounced cyclical swings, the trend values can never follow the actual data as closely as a 12-month moving average does and as such the seasonal indices obtained by 'ratio to trend' method are liable to be more biased than those obtained by 'ratio-to-moving average' method.

3. Ratio to Moving Average Method

This method is also known as '***percentage of moving average***' method. This method consists of expressing the original time series data as percentages of moving averages instead of percentages of trend values as in 'ratio-to-trend' method, while rest of the steps are essentially the same.

This method uses either of the two relationships

1. $Y \times S \times C \times I$ 2. $Y \times T \times S \times I$

In the second relationship, T is the trend cycle, that is, it consists of both T and C of (1) above.

To begin with, we assume that the seasonal component S has a 12-month period and that its pattern is the same each year. In case we use quarterly data, our assumption is the same-the seasonal component is the same each year. We make another assumption that the irregular variations I are independent for different years. In view of these assumptions, if a 12-month moving average is applied to a series, it will smooth out $S \times I$ and the remainder will be $T \times C$. In other words, the use of the moving average gives the trend and cycle, $T \times C$.

Symbolically,
$$\frac{T \times S \times C \times I}{T \times C} = S \times I$$

Where the numerator is the original data and the denominator is the moving average, in the first term (T).

An example will help us in understanding this process clearly.

EXAMPLE 12.7: Given the following quarterly data, you are asked to calculate the seasonal index.

Year	Q_1	Q_2	Q_3	Q_4
1	68	62	61	63
2	65	58	56	61
3	68	63	63	67
4	70	59	56	62
5	60	55	31	58

Solution: The method is the same whether the monthly data or quarterly data are to be used for measuring the seasonal variation. We set up the following worksheet.

Worksheet for Measuring Seasonal Variation

Year (1)	Quarters (2)	Given Figures (3)	4–Fig. Moving Total (4)	2–Fig. Moving Total (5)	Moving Average (5)/8 (6)	Given Figs. as % of Moving Average (7)
1	1	68				
	2	62	254			
	3	61	251	505	63.1	96.7
	4	63	247	498	62.2	101.3
2	1	63	242	489	61.1	106.4
	2	36	240	482	60.2	96.3
	3	36	243	483	60.4	92.7
	4	61	248	491	61.4	99.3
3	1	68	255	303	62.9	106.2
	2	63	261	516	64.5	97.7
	3	63	263	524	65.5	96.2
	4	67	259	522	65.2	102.8
4	1	70	252	511	63.9	109.5
	2	59	247	439	62.4	94.6
	3	36	237	434	60.5	92.6
	4	62	233	470	50.0	105.4
5	1	60	228	461	57.6	104.2
	2	55	224	452	56.5	97.3
	3	51				
	4	58				

Calculation of Seasonal Index

	Percentage to Moving Average				
Year	**1Q**	**IIQ**	**IIIQ**	**IVQ**	**Total**
1			96.7	101.3	
2	106.4	96.3	92.7	99.3	
3	108.1	97.7	96.2	102.8	
4	109.5	94.6	92.6	105.4	
5	104.2	97.3	-	-	
Total	**428.2**	**385.9**	**378.2**	**408.8**	**1,601.1**
Average	**107.1**	**96.5**	**94.5**	**102.2**	**400.3**
Seasonal Index	**107.1**	**96.4**	**94.4**	**102.1**	**400**

It may be noted that in table, the starting figure 96.7 is the original figure (61) taken as a percentage of the corresponding moving average (63.1). This figure of 96.7 is shown in the last column of table against third quarter of the 1st Year.

Seasonal index is obtained by multiplying each quarterly average by an adjustment factor 400/400.3.

Advantages and Limitations of Ratio-to-Moving Average Method

Advantages

Of all the methods of measuring seasonal variations, this method is the most satisfactory, flexible and widely used method. These indices do not fluctuate so much as the indices by the ratio-to-trend method.

Limitations

This method does not completely utilise the data e.g., in the case of 12-month moving average seasonal indices cannot be obtained for the first 6 months and for the last 6 months.

4. The Link Relative Method

This method, also known as the ***Pearson's method,*** is relatively complex as it involves the averaging of the link relatives. The use of this method to calculate seasonal indices involves the following steps:

(i) As a first step, link relatives of the seasonal figures are to be calculated. A link relative is the value of one season expressed as a percentage of the preceding season. Suppose our data are monthly, then

$$\text{Link Relative} = \frac{\text{Figure for the current month}}{\text{Figure for the preceding month}} \times 100$$

In case the data are quarterly, then

$$\text{Link Relative} = \frac{\text{Figure for the current quarter}}{\text{Figure for the preceding quarter}} \times 100$$

(ii) The link relatives for each month or quarter are to be averaged. For this purpose, we can use either the mean or the extreme values, the median is preferable.

(iii) The average link relatives are now to be converted into chain relatives on the basis of the first season (month or quarter).

The formula to calculate chain relatives is:

$$\frac{\text{Link relative of the current month} \times \text{Chain relative of the preceding month}}{100}$$

In case of quarterly data,

$$\frac{\text{Link relative of the current quarter} \times \text{Chain relative of the preceding quarter}}{100}$$

As this will not add to 100 due to trend effect, some adjustment is needed.

(iv) The adjustment can be done by subtracting a 'correction factor' from each chain relative. ***For example***, the correction factor (CF) for January will be CF(d) = 1/12 [second (new) CR for January - 100], CF for February will be 2d, for March 3d, and so forth. In quarterly series, the CF(d) will be 1/4 (second new CR for lst Q-100); For 2nd Q 1d; for 3rd Q 2d and for 4th Q 3d will be the correction factor). This correction factor is used on the assumption that there is a linear trend.

(v) This is the final step wherein we have to ensure that the adjusted chain relatives add up to 1,200 if the data are monthly or to 400 if the data are quarterly. The figures thus arrived at are the required seasonal indices.

Let us take an example to illustrate the use of link relative method.

EXAMPLE 12.8: Calculate the seasonal indices from the following data using the link relative method.

Year	Q_1	Q_2	Q_3	Q_4
1996	68	63	63	67
1997	70	59	56	52
1998	60	55	51	58

Solution: We have to first calculate the link relatives. This has been done by dividing the figure for 2nd quarter by the 1st quarter-figure and then multiplied by 100. ***For example***, take the case of 1995 2nd quarter, for which the link relative is $(58/65) \times 100 = 89.23$.

In the same manner, link relatives for all quarters have been calculated. Table shows these link relatives.

Computation of Seasonal Indices by the Method of Link Relatives

Year	Quarters			
	1st	2nd	3rd	4th
1995	–	89.23	96.55	108.90
1996	111.48	92.65	100.00	106.35
1997	104.48	84.29	94.92	92.86
1998	115.38	91.67	92.73	113.73
Total	**331.34**	**357.84**	**384.20**	**421.87**
Average of LR	110.45	89.46	96.05	105.47
Chain relatives	100	$\frac{89.46 \times 100}{100} = 89.46$	$\frac{96.05 \times 89.46}{100} = 85.93$	$\frac{105.46 \times 85.926}{100} = 90.62$
Adjusted CR	100.09	89.43	85.90	90.55
Seasonal indices	109.33	97.78	93.89	99.00

The new (second) CR for 1st quarter

$$= \frac{\text{LR of 1st quarter} \times \text{CR of last (4th) quarter}}{100}$$

$$= \frac{110.45 \times 90.62}{100} = 100.09$$

The difference between these chain relatives $= 100.09 - 100 = 0.09$

Difference per quarter $= 0.09/4 = 0.0241$

Adjustment factor, $d = 0.0241$

Adjusted CR for 2nd, 3rd and 4th quarters are obtained by subtracting d, 2d and 3d from the corresponding CRs Finally, seasonal indices are obtained by adjusting the corrected CRs to a total of 400. This is done by multiplying each index by a constant factor K = 400/365.97. This is because the total of seasonal indices for the four quarters should be 400. The total of adjusted CR for the four quarters is 365.97. Hence, the constant factor K is 400/365.97. The adjusted seasonal indices are shown in the last row of Table.

As can be seen, this method is somewhat cumbersome on account of a number of calculations involved for link relatives followed by adjustments to be made.

Advantages and Limitations of Link Relative Method

The computational procedure involved in this method is much simpler as compared to that in the 'Ratio to Trend' or in 'Ratio-to-Moving Average' method. In this method, only one LR of the first period is lost whereas in the 'Ratio-to-Trend' a number of values in the beginning and at the end are lost. The method provides good estimates of seasonal indices in a situation when the trend in the time series is linear.

The question now is

Which of these four methods we should use in order to compute seasonal indices? Each method gives different indices. To a large extent, our choice will depend on the nature of data and the purpose of measuring seasonal variation. Without going further in details, we may say that the ratio-to-moving average method should be preferable as it has certain advantages over other methods.

12.11 DESEASONALISATION OF DATA

Deseasonalisation means removing the effects of seasonal factors from the given time series values. It is very helpful in the analysis of time series as it helps to adjust the time series for seasonal variations leaving us with only three components viz., trend, cyclical variations and irregular variation. If trend is also removed from the original data we are left with only cyclical and random variations which can also be isolated from each other.

Deseasonalisation is helpful to business executives in planning production and marketing programmes. It is also helpful in the proper interpretation of data.

In an additive model where $Y = T + S + C + I$ deseasonalisation can be done by subtracting the seasonal variations from the values of Y. Thus a deseasonalised series would be

$$Y - S = T + C + I.$$

In a multiplicative model where $Y = T \times S \times C \times I$ the deseasonalised values are obtained by dividing the given values by corresponding indices of seasonal variations. Thus in a multiplicative model deseasonalised values would be

$$\frac{Y}{S} = \frac{TSCI}{S} = TCI$$

EXAMPLE 12.9: A company estimate its sales for a particular year to be Rs 24,00,000., The seasonal indices for sales are as follows:

Month	Seasonal Index	Month	Seasonal Index
January	75	July	102
February	80	August	104
March	98	September	100
April	128	October	100
May	137	November	82
June	119	December	73

Using this information, calculate estimates of monthly sales of the company. Assume that there is no trend.

[B.Com. (Hon.), Delhi University, 1979]

Solution: Annual sales = Rs 24,00,000 Therefore

$$\text{Monthly sales} = \text{Rs}\ \frac{24,00,000}{12} = \text{Rs}\ 2,00,000$$

$$\text{Seasonal effect} = \frac{\text{Seasonal Index}}{100}$$

The estimated sale for any months would be Rs 2,00,000 × Seasonal Effect.

Budget Estimates of Monthly Sales for the Company

Month (1)	Seasonal Index (2)	Seasonal Effect Col.(2) ÷ 100 (3)	Estimated Sales Col.(3) × 2,00,000 (4)
January	75	0.75	1,50,000
February	80	0.80	1,60,000
March	98	0.98	1,96,000
April	128	1.28	2,56,000
May	137	1.37	2,74,000
June	119	1.19	2,38,000
July	102	1.02	2,04,000
August	104	1.04	2,08,000
September	100	1.00	2,00,000
October	102	1.02	2,04,000
November	82	0.82	1,64,000
December	73	0.73	1,46,000
Total	**1200**	**12.00**	**24,00,000**

It should be noted that the total of seasonal indices should be 1200 and the total of seasonal effects should be 12.

EXAMPLE 12.10: The sales of a company rose from Rs 30,000 in the month of February to Rs 35,000 in the month of March. The seasonal indices for these two months are 105 and 140 respectively. The owner of the company was not satisfied by this increase of Rs 5000 in the month of March. He expected much more because of the seasonal index. How much could he expect on the basis of the seasonal index?

Solution:

On the basis of the seasonal index for the month of March the estimated sales in March could be expected to be

$$\text{Rs}\ \frac{30,000 \times 140}{105} = \text{Rs}\ 40,000$$

Alternatively we can say that the actual sales for February were Rs 30,000 and the seasonal index was 105 or the seasonal effect was 1.05. As such the expected sales for February were

$$\text{Rs}\ \frac{30,000}{1.05}\ \text{or Rs}\ 28571.428$$

Seasonal effect for March is 1.40 hence the expected sales in March were

$$\text{Rs}\ \frac{30,000}{1.05} \times 1.40\ \text{or}\ (28571.428 \times 1.40) = \text{Rs}\ 40,000$$

Thus the owner could have expected a sale of Rs 40,000 in the month of March.

12.12 CYCLICAL VARIATION

The oscillatory movements in a time series with period of oscillation more than one year are termed as cyclic fluctuations. One complete period is called a 'cycle'. The cyclic movements in a time series are generally, attributed to the so called 'Business Cycle', which may also be referred to as the 'four-phase cycle' composed of prosperity, recession, depression and recovery and normally lasts from seven to eleven years. The upswings and downswings in business depend upon the cumulative nature of the economic forces and the interaction between them. Most of the economic and commercial series e.g., series relating to prices, production and wages etc, are affected by business cycles. Cyclic fluctuations, though more or less regular, are not periodic.

12.13 METHODS FOR MEASURING CYCLICAL FLUCTUATIONS

Measurement of cyclical fluctuations is a difficult proposition. There is no well recognised method of isolating the cyclical fluctuations though a number of methods have been suggested by *Croxton and Cowden* in their work entitled '*Applied General Statistics*'.

After the seasonal variations have been estimated and the trend values have been isolated we are left with the cyclical and irregular variations. The problem is to identify the cyclical variations and to isolate them so that in the end we are left only with irregular variations.

Croxton and Cowden have suggested the following four methods of measuring cyclical variations.

1. Residual Method
2. Direct Method
3. Reference cycle analysis method
4. Harmonic Analysis Method.

1. Residual Method

We shall discuss only the residual method which is crude but easy to understand and is widely used. In this method first the effect of trend and seasonal variations are eliminated from the original data.

In a multiplicative model

$$Y = TSCI \quad \text{so}$$

$$\boxed{\frac{Y}{T \times S} = \frac{TSCI}{TS} = CI}$$

Thus we are left with cyclical and irregular fluctuations only, if we isolate the trend and seasonal variations. Now if it is assumed that irregular fluctuations are to be ignored or if we assume that their effect is negligible then the values CI may be taken to reflect cyclical fluctuations. However this is generally not done and an attempt is made to identify cyclical fluctuations and irregular fluctuations separately. Irregular movements by nature are such that there cannot be set procedure for measuring them, and as such cyclical fluctuations are identified and whatever residual is left after making adjustments for trend, seasonal variations and cyclical variations is taken as irregular variations. An attempt is made to smoothen the irregular component by taking a moving average of CI values.

Thus under the Residual Method the following steps are involved:

(i) Obtain trend values (T) and the seasonal indices (S)

(ii) Divide the original data by T to get SCI and then divide SCI by S to get CI

(iii) Take the moving total of CI values for monthly series, generally 3 monthly moving total is taken.

The moving total is generally taken by giving weights of 1, 2, 1, to the three months.

After this the weighted moving total is divided by 4 (which is the total of weights 1 + 2 + 1) to get the moving average. If a five monthly moving average is taken then the weights are 1, 2, 4, 2, 1.

These moving averages are the cyclical variation of the series. Now to get the irregular variations the *CI* values can be divided by the cyclical variations. These would be the irregular variations.

2. Direct Analysis

In this method the values of each month are expressed as percentages of the values of the same month in the previous year. This roughly results in eliminating seasonal variation and trend. However in these percentages an element of trend and seasonal variations is included because the effect of *T* and *S* are not completely eliminated by these percentages. A variations in this method is possible if the figures of a month are not expressed as percentages of the figures of the same months in previous year, but as percentage of the average of the same months for a number of years. Thus the figures of January, 1983 will be expressed as a percentage of the average figure of the months of January for a number of years.

3. Harmonic Analysis

When the cyclical movements in a series are of the same duration and amplitude a sine-cosine or a curve of a similar type may be fitted. Such a curve is fitted to the *CI* data or the data after the irregular movements have been smoothed. However this method is not of much use in business and economic problems as the cycles are not of the same duration nor are their amplitudes common.

4. Reference Cycle Analysis

When several time series are being studied it is possible to compare the cyclical movements of one series with the cyclical movements of the other series. The National Bureau of Economic Research, U.S.A has evolved a procedure involving 'reference data' which allows each series to be compared with a standard set of data and also makes it possible to compare the results of various individual series. In this method the following steps are involved.

(a) Select reference data which are the data of peaks and troughs of a business cycle. Here business cycle refers to general business movements – not the business cycle of particular series.

(b) Obtain a cyclical pattern for each series for the period between each two successive troughs. Each period is the same for all series so that inter-series comparison may be possible.

(c) To obtain a cyclical pattern for a series, the data are adjusted for seasonal variations. These are then divided into reference cycle segments, for each segment the monthly values are expressed as percentages of the average of all values in the segment. These are called 'reference cycle relatives'. This step converts the series into percentages and eliminates inter-cycle trend. This however does not eliminate intra-cycle trend.

(d) Each reference -cycle segment is broken into nine stages to correspond to the same nine stages in the business cycle and the reference cycle relatives are averaged for each of the nine stages.

The nine stages identified are:

(i) The three months centered on the initial trough

(ii) The first third of the expansion period

(iii) The second third of the expansion period
(iv) The last third of the expansion period
(v) The three months centered on the peak.
(vi) The first third of the contraction period
(vii) The second third of the contraction period
(viii) The last third of the contraction period
(ix) The three months centered on the terminal trough.

The nine stage average for each reference -cycle segment reduce the erratic movements in a series. They thus give a reference cycle pattern for the particular series under consideration.

12.14 IRREGULAR VARIATION

Apart from the regular variations, almost all the series contain another factor called the random or irregular or residual fluctuations which are not accounted for by secular trend and seasonal and cyclic variations. These fluctuations are purely random, erratic unforeseen, unpredictable and are due to numerous non-recurring and irregular circumstances which are beyond the control of human hand but at the same time are a part of our system such as earthquakes, wars, floods, famines revolutions, epidemics etc. These isolated or irregular but powerful fluctuations due to floods, revolution political upheaval, famines etc are also called episodic fluctuations. In some cases the importance of irregular fluctuations may not be significant while in others these may be very effective and might give rise to cyclic movements.

12.15 METHODS FOR MEASURING IRREGULAR VARIATIONS

By the very nature of these movements which are erratic no specific formula can be suggested to isolate and identify the irregular fluctuations. Generally the three other components of a time series i.e., Trend (*T*), Seasonal variations (*S*) and cyclical variation (*C*) are obtained and the residual is taken as the irregular variations.

In a multiplicative model

$$\frac{Y}{TSC} \text{ or } \frac{\text{TSCI}}{TSC} = I$$

Where *S* and *C* are in fractional form and not in percentages.

In an additive model the irregular variations are

$$Y - (T + S + C) \text{ or}$$
$$T + S + C + I - (T + S + C)$$

However in actual practice only the Trend and Seasonal variations are isolated and the cyclical and irregular fluctuations are kept together because cycles differ in periods and amplitude and irregular fluctuations are so mixed up with cyclical fluctuations that it is almost impossible to separate them in a meaningful manner.

12.16 FORECASTING

The growing competition, rapidity of change in circumstances and the trend towards automation demand that decisions in business are not based purely on guesses and hunches rather on a careful analysis of data concerning the future course of events. More time and attention is given to the future than to the past and the question "what is likely to happen" ? takes precedence over "what has happened"? though no attempt to answer the first can be taken without the facts and figures being available to answer the second.

When estimates of future conditions are made on a systematic basis, the process is referred to as '***forecasting***' and the figure or statement obtained is known as a "forecast". In a world where the future is not known with certainty, virtually every business and economic decision rests upon a forecast of future conditions.

In fact, when a man assumes the responsibility of running a business, he automatically takes the responsibility for attempting to forecast the future and to a very large extent; his success or failure would depend upon the ability to forecast successfully the future course of events. Forecasting aims at reducing the areas of uncertainty that surround management decision making with respect to costs, profit, sales, production, pricing, capital investment and so forth. If the future were known with certainty forecasting would be unnecessary.

Decisions could be made and plans formulated on a once-and for- all basis, without the need for subsequent revision. But uncertainty does exist, future outcomes are rarely assured and, therefore, organised system of forecasting is necessary rather than the establishment of predictions that are based on hunches, intuition or guesses. In fact, a good manager is not so much one who can minimize the effect of past mistakes but rather one who can successfully manage the future. The forecasts may be wrong, but they must be made.

The question is not 'forecast or no forecast?' Instead it is: "What kind of forecast?" It may be noted that the value of a forecast is not merely its accuracy but the fact that making it requires a balanced consideration of factors influencing future developments, right or wrong.

Role of Forecasting in Business

It should be realized at the outset that the object of business forecasting is not to determine a curve or series of figures that will tell exactly what will happen, say, a year in advance, but it is to make analysis based on definite statistical data which will enable and execute to take advantage of future conditions to a greater extent than he could do without them. In many respects, the future tends to move like the past. This is a good thing, since without some element of continuity between past, present and future, there would be little possibility of successful prediction. But history is not likely to repeat itself and we would hardly expect economic conditions next year or over the next ten years to follow a clear-cut precedent. Yet, frequently past patterns prevail sufficiently to justify using the past as a basis for predicting the future.

While forecasting, one should note that it is impossible to forecast the future precisely there always must be some range of error allowed for in the forecast. Statistical forecasts are those in which we can use the mathematical theory of probability of measure the risks of errors in predictions.

Steps in Forecasting

Forecasting business change involves more than analysis of statistical data-it also embodies the prediction of economic change such as secular trend, seasonal variations, cyclical variations and a consideration of cause and effect. Broadly speaking, the forecasting of business fluctuations consists of the following steps:

Understanding why changes in the past have occurred

One of the basic principles of statistical forecasting-indeed of all forecasting when historical data are available-is that the forecaster should use the data on past performance to get a "speedometer reading" of the current rate (say, of sales) and of how fast this rate is increasing or decreasing. The current rate and changes in the rate-"acceleration" and "deceleration"- constitute the basis of forecasting. Once they are known, various mathematical techniques can develop projections from them. If an attempt is made to forecast business fluctuations without understanding why past changes have taken place, the forecast will be purely mechanical based solely upon the application of mathematical formulae and subject to serious error.

Observation and analysis of the past behaviour is one of the most vital parts of forecasting. However, it should be carefully noted that though future may be some sort of extension of the past, it may not be an exact replica. Changes in business and economic activity are caused by numerous forces or factors, which are often difficult to discover and measure. Not only this, they may appear in all kinds of combinations and may be constantly changing. Hence in making forecasts, we should not assume that history repeats itself. Rather, we should believe that there are certain regularities in the past behaviour, which can be observed and used as a basis for reducing the uncertainties of the future. It is often said that the past, imperfect indicator of the future though it is the best guide we have in attempting to make predictions.

Determining which phases of business activity must be measured

After it is known why business fluctuations have occurred, or if there is a reasonable supposition, it is necessary to measure certain phases of business activity in order to predict what changes will probably follow the present level of activity.

Selecting and compiling data to be used as measuring devices

There is an interdependent relationship between the selection of statistical data and determination of why business fluctuations occur. Statistical data cannot be collected and analyzed in an intelligent manner unless there is a sufficient understanding of business fluctuations; likewise, it is important that reasons for business fluctuations be stated in such a manner that it is possible to secure data that are related to the reasons.

Analysing the data

In this last step, the data are analysed in the light of one's understanding of the reason why change occurs. ***For example***, if it is reasoned that a certain combination of forces will result in a given change, the statistical part of the problem is to measure these forces and from the data available, to draw conclusions on the future course of action. The methods of drawing conclusions may be called forecasting techniques and they represent any one of a large number of analytical devices for summarising data and drawing inferences from the summaries.

12.17 METHODS OF FORECASTING

There is nothing new about business forecasting as, for centuries, the businessmen have tried to adjust themselves in such a manner as to make the best out of the future conditions. The rule-of-thumb method has been widely practiced in business. It consists of deciding about the future in terms of past experience and familiarity with the problem at hand. Even today, this method is very widely used in business. However, it can lead to absurd conclusions if employed by the inexperienced. In recent years, the techniques of forecasting have improved to a marked degree and are applicable to almost every sphere of business activity. Attempts are being made to make forecasting as scientific as possible. The base of scientific forecasting is statistics, i.e., numerical data on business trends, which many businessmen fail to acquaint themselves with. However, forecasting business change involves more than an analysis of statistical data. It also embodies the prediction of economic change, such as secular trend, seasonal variation and a consideration of cause and effect. To handle the increasing variety of managerial forecasting problems, several forecasting techniques have been developed in recent years. Forecasting techniques vary from simple expert guesses to complex analyses of mass data. Each technique has its special use and care must be taken to select the correct technique for a particular situation. Also before applying a method of forecasting, the following questions should be answered:

1. What is the purpose of the forecast-how is it to be used?
2. What are the dynamics and components of the system for which the forecast will be made?
3. How important is the past in estimating the future?

The following are some of the important methods of forecasting:

1. Business Barometers
2. Extrapolation
3. Regression Analysis
4. Econometric Models
5. Forecasting by the use of Time Series Analysis
6. Opinion Polling
7. Causal Models
8. Exponential Smoothing

A forecast is usually a combination of several techniques. Now we will discuss each in detail.

1. Business Barometers

Of great assistance in practical forecasting is a series that can be used "index" or "indicator" is also, widely, though loosely, used in business statistics; sometimes the term is used to mean simply an indicator of the present economic situations and sometimes it is designate an indicator of future conditions.

The following are some of the important series, which aid businessmen in forecasting:

1. Gross national product
2. Employment
3. Wholesale prices
4. Consumer prices
5. Industrial production
6. Volume of bank deposits and currency outstanding
7. Consumer credit
8. Disposable personal income
9. Departmental store sales
10. Stock prices
11. Bond yields

This list is by no means exhaustive, nor is the arrangement necessarily in order of importance. Several of the above series are composite average or total-or indexes of these averages or totals. Analysis also should be made of the major components of these series.

Index numbers relating to different activities in the field of production, trade, finance, etc., may also be combined into a general index of Business Activity. This general index refers to the general conditions of trade and industry. But the behaviour of individual industries of trades might show a different trend from that of the Composite Business Activity Index. Also general boom or depression may be reflected in a majority of separate industries and trades, yet some industries and trades might show quite contrary tendencies. Hence the study of general business conditions, as revealed by the Composite Business Index, should be supplemented by special studies of individual business based on separate indices. The trends indicated by barometers will guide the businessmen as to whether the stocks of goods should be increased or released or whether to increase investment or not, etc.

2. Extrapolation

Extrapolation is the simplest yet often a useful method of forecasting. In many forecasting situations the most reasonable expectation is that the variable will follow its already established path, Extrapolation relies on the relative constancy in the pattern of past movements in some time series. Strictly speaking, nothing needs to be known about causation-why the series moves as it does. But in practice the justification does involve the nature of the growth process being described. Extrapolation is used frequently for sales forecasts and for other estimates when "better" forecasting methods may not be justified. Since extrapolation assumes that the variable will follow its established pattern of growth, the problem is to determine accurately the appropriate trend curve and the values of its parameters. Numerous alternative trend curves can be used for the purpose of business forecasting. Some of the most useful ones are:

(a) **Arithmetic trend:** The straight-line arithmetic trend assumes that growth will be by a constant absolute amount each year.

(b) **Semi-log trend:** The semi-logarithmic trend assumes a constant percentage increase each year. Since the annual increment is constant in logarithms, this line translates into a straight line when drawn on paper within a logarithmic vertical scale.

(c) **Modified exponential trend:** This curve assumes that each increment of growth will be a constant per cent less than 100 of the previous one. The line tends generally to approach, but never quite reach a constant asymptote, which may be thought of as an upper limit.

(d) **Logistic curve:** The logistic curve has both an upper asymptote and a lower asymptote. It assumes a 'law of growth' involving increasing increments from an initial low value and then gradual slowing down of growth as 'maturity' is approached.

(e) **The Gompertz curve:** The Gompertz is a curve with similar properties as described above and is often used to describe growth of industrial output. Selection of an appropriate growth curve can be by empirical and theoretical considerations. Empirically, it is a question of selecting the curve that best fits the past movement of the data. Theoretical matters, which intervene in logic, may support a particular growth pattern. ***For example***, population growth, when there are no restraints, implies a geometric pattern of growth, as has been known since Malthus. With limited resources, however, population is sometimes thought to grow along a logistic curve. Lest these theoretical notions be taken too seriously, it should be emphasised that empirical consideration may lead us quickly to a more realistic and less restrictive notion of the relevant growth curve.

3. Regression Analysis

The regression approach offers many valuable contributions to the solution of the forecasting problem. It is the means by which we select from among the many possible or theoretically suggestive relationships between variable in a complex economy those which will be useful for forecasting. With it, one makes the jump from intuitive evaluation on the relationship between two variables to precise quantified knowledge. If two variables are functionally related then a knowledge of one will make possible an estimate of the other. ***For example***, if we know that advertising expenditure and sales are correlated then for a given advertising expenditure, we can find out the probable increase in sales or *vice versa.*

Regression relationship may involve one predicted or dependent and one independent variable-simple regression, or it may involve relationship between the variable to be forecast and several independent variables-multiple regression. Statistical techniques to estimate the regression equations are often fairly complex and time-consuming but there are many computer programmes now available that estimate simple and multiple regressions quickly. Regression analysis is also the econometrician's standard tool in his research. With the help of regression analysis, the level of industry sales is usually forecasted first and the company forecast is then made on the basis of predicted behaviour of the whole industry. The demand for most commodities often depends upon multiplicity of aggregate economic variables such as GNP, disposable income, prices, population, employment, industrial production. A careful analysis of these factors is made. It may be pointed out that the factors selected for analysis should be kept as low as possible because the danger of seriously imprecise results is multiplied as regressions are made more complex or if curvilinear relationships are used.

There are two dangers in using regression analysis for forecasting

1. There is possibility of a mechanistic approach accepting with little question the relationship which the calculations reveal perhaps that with the highest r2 -and applying it to the forecast. There are many possibilities for spurious correlation among time series as many series move together over time even where there is no conceivable connection between them.
2. There is the risk that the estimated regression is false. The forecaster must always use his judgement and knowledge of the facts and of the underlying theory.

4. Econometric Models

Econometric techniques, which originated in the eighteenth century, have recently gained in popularity for forecasting. Much of the revival of econometrics is attributed to the growth of computer technology.

The *term* econometrics refers *to the* application of mathematical economic *theory* and statistical procedures *to* economic data in order *to* verify economic theorems and *to* establish quantitative results in economics. An econometrician is, therefore, an economist, a statistician and a mathematician, all in one. Econometric models take the *form* of a set of simultaneous equations.

The values of the constants in such equations are supplied, by a study of statistical time series and a large number of equations may be necessary *to* produce an adequate model. The work of computations is greatly facilitated by electronic data processing equipment like computer, etc.

At the present time, most short-term forecasting uses only statistical methods with little qualitative information. However, in the years *to* come when most large companies develop and refine econometric models of their major business, this tool of forecasting will become more popular. However, it should be remembered that the development of an econometric model requires sufficient data so that the correct relationships can be established. Hence, when data are scarce —***for example***, when a product is first introduced into the market — this method cannot profitably be employed.

The econometric model is, in principle, the most formal, since the forecast is based on an explicit mathematical model. The model states in detail and in quantitative *terms,* the way in which the various aspects of the economy are interrelated. Theoretically, the model makes possible a wholly mechanical forecast, because once values have been estimated *for* the exogenous variables, *the* solution of the model gives specific values *for the* predicted variables. But in actual practice, qualitative and quantitative forecasters have tended *to* come together. The 'artist' forecaster has become fully aware of the fact that he needs quantitative relationships, while *the* econometric forecaster has learnt that in some instances, quantitative relationships have *to* be modified by qualitative factors. The econometric model provides the forecaster with a record of the prediction with a clear statement of the assumptions concerning exogenous variables and *the* solution of *the* model-it is often possible or at least it is made easier *to* trace and reproduce *the* causes *for* success as well as failures. One can learn just where errors were made and, hopefully, where improvements can be made. Thus, discredited hypothesis may be dropped and new ones can be substituted which ultimately will lead *to* better understanding of the economic system and business fluctuations.

The econometric models are not very popular in practice because it is probably neither necessary nor feasible *for* every business forecaster *to* construct his own model of *the* economy. The effort and cost involved in a fully developed econometric model are well beyond most forecasting operations. Thus, most forecasters will probably rely *for* some time on the basic aggregate model developed at research institutes or at universities. These models may be used *to* make predictions and *to test* out alternative assumptions about Government policy or the other exogenous aspects of *the* economy. With the help of *the* models and, hopefully, sector analysis of his own industry *the* business forecaster will be in a better position *to* augment other more familiar approaches. The greater the understanding of the various forecasting methods and of their inter-relationships, *the* better *the* forecasts will be.

5. Forecasting by the Use of Time Series Analysis

Time series analysis helps *to* identify and explain:

Any regular or systematic variation in the series of data which is due *to* seasonality-the "Seasonals".

1. Cyclical patterns
2. Trends in the data.

Growth rates of these trends. Unfortunately, most existing methods identify only the seasonals, the combined effect of trends and cycles and the irregular or chance component. That is they do not separate trend from cycles. This is not to say that those other effects are not to some degree manageable. The suggestion is rather that the analysis for trend and seasonal effects and the projection of these two sets of forces should be understood to be the first step in the forecast and that, taking into account such cyclical and residual forces as may be manageable, further refinements may be made. Many statisticians consider time series analysis a somewhat useless tool. One critic, M.J. Moroney, said that "Economic forecasting like weather forecasting in England is only valid for the next six hours or so. Beyond that it is sheer guesswork."

In any event, although the limitation of time series analysis must be understood, the importance and usefulness of the procedures should not be underestimated. The analysis serves two purposes:

1. It does provide an initial approximation forecast that takes into account those empirical regularities which may, with reasonable assurance, be expected to persist.
2. After the trend and seasonal effects have been identified and measured, the original data may be adjusted for these influences, yielding a new historical time series consisting of the trend and seasonally adjusted data. This new time series may be helpful in the analysis and interpretation of cyclical and residual influences.

It should be noted that this method of forecasting can be used only when several years' data for a product or product line are available and when relationships and trends are both clear and relatively stable.

6. Opinion Polling

Opinion poll is the survey of opinion of experts, i.e., knowledgeable persons in the field whose views carry lot of weight.

For example, a survey of opinion of sales representatives, wholesalers, retailers, etc. shall be of great help in formulating demand projections. The Survey Research Centre of the University of Michigan conducts an annual pool regarding the future plans of consumers. The answers to many questions are translated into short-run demand for colour television sets, automobiles and other consumer products.

7. Causal Models

A causal model is the most sophisticated kind of forecasting tool. It expresses mathematically the relevant causal relationships, and may include pipeline considerations (*i.e.,* inventories) and market survey information. It may also directly incorporate the results of a time-analysis. The causal model takes into account everything known of the dynamics of the flow system and utilises predictions of related events such as competitive action, strikes and promotions. If the data are available, the model generally includes factors for each location in the flow chart and connects these by questions to describe overall product flow. If certain kinds of data are lacking, initially it may be necessary to make assumptions about some of the relationships and then track what is happening to determine if the assumptions are true: Typically, a causal model is continually revised as more knowledge about the system becomes available.

8. Exponential Smoothing

This method is an outgrowth of the recent attempts to maintain the smoothing function of moving averages without their corresponding drawbacks and limitations.

DO YOU KNOW?

Exponential smoothing is a type of moving average forecasting technique which weights past data from previous time periods with exponentially decreasing importance in the forecast so that the most recent data carries more weight in the moving average.

Two major limitations to the use of moving averages are:

(i) to compute a moving average forecast it is necessary to store the last N observation values. This takes up considerable space which in many computer systems is costly;

(ii) the method of moving averages gives equal weight to each of the last N observed and no weight at all to observations before period $(t - N)$; that is, the weight given to each of the last N observations is $1/N$ and 0 (zero) for any previous observations.

In principle, exponential smoothing operates in a manner analogous to moving averages by "smoothing" historical observations to eliminate randomness. The mathematical procedure for performing this smoothing, however, is somewhat different from that used in moving averages. The basic principle and the application of this device are quite simple. If we wish to forecast the value of a time series for the period $t + 1$ on the basis of information available just after period t, and the forecast is best considered as a function of two components: the actual value of the series for period, t, and the forecasted value for the same period made in the previous period $t - 1$. The use of both realised and estimated values available now for predicting future values is better than the use of either alone.

The exponential smoothing models can be either single exponential smoothing model or double exponential smoothing model, the former being applicable in the absence of trend, and the latter being applicable when the time series is exhibiting some type of growth pattern.

When we talk of single exponential smoothing model, the forecasted value of the series at time period t, $\hat{y}_i$ is equal to a fraction of the forecast error of the previous period. $(y_{t-1} - \hat{y}_{t-1})$, plus the forecasted values of the previous period. Thus to predict the value of the time series at time $t + 1$, we use

$$y_{t+1} = a\ (y_t - \hat{y}_t) + \hat{y}_t$$

It should be noted that exponential smoothing, a special kind of weighted moving average, is found to be useful in short-term forecasting for inventories and sales. Exponential smoothing can also be employed for projections over long terms. Because of several computational advantages over the simple moving average, the exponential smoothing time series model is perhaps the most widely used time series forecasting technique today.

Some experts have been critical of exponential smoothing procedures on the ground that they are empirically inadequate when major policy decisions undergo change. They also object to the assumption that differing weights should be assigned to observations depending solely upon their relative recency. The exponential smoothing as a technique for prediction has very limited applications for sales items that have many wide variations in expected demand.

MISCELLANEOUS SOLVED EXAMPLES

EXAMPLE 12.11: Given below are the figures of production (in thousand maunds) of a Sugar factory:

Year	1991	1992	1993	1994	1995	1996	1997
Production ('000 maunds)	40	45	46	42	47	50	46

Fit Straight trend by the least squares method and tabulate the trend. **[Osmania University, 2001]**

Solution:

Calculation of Trend Values by Least Square Method

Years t	Production ('000 maunds) Y	$t - 1994$ X	X^2	XY	Trend Values Y_c
1991	40	−3	9	−120	42.035
1992	45	−2	4	−90	43.071
1993	46	−1	1	−46	44.107
1994	42	0	0	0	45.143
1995	47	+1	1	+47	46.179
1996	50	+2	4	+100	47.215
1997	46	+3	9	+138	48.250
$N = 7$	$\Sigma Y = 316$	$\Sigma X = 0$	$\Sigma X^2 = 28$	$\Sigma XY = +29$	$\Sigma Y_c = 316$

$$Y_c = a + bX = a + b\,(t - 1994)$$

$$a = \frac{\Sigma Y}{N} = \frac{316}{7} = 45.143$$

$$b = \frac{\Sigma XY}{\Sigma X^2} = \frac{29}{28} = 1.036$$

$$Y_c = 45.143 + 1.036X$$

When $X=-3$, $Y_c=45.143+[1.036\times(-3)]=42.035$, similarly we can calculate trend values for other years.

EXAMPLE 12.12: Below are given the figures of production (in million tonnes) of a cement factory:

Year	1997	1998	2000	2001	2002	2003	2004
Production (in m. tonnes)	77	88	94	85	91	98	90

(i) Fit a straight line trend by the 'least squares method' and tabulate the trend values

(ii) Eliminate the trend. What components of the Time Series are thus left over?

(iii) What is monthly increase in the production of cement?

Solution:

Fitting Straight Line Trend by The Method of Least Squares

Year	Production (in m. tonnes) Y	Deviations from 1998 X	XY	X^2	Trend values Y_c
1997	77	−4	−308	16	83.299
1999	88	−2	−176	4	86.051
2000	94	−1	−94	1	87.427
2001	85	0	0	0	88.803
2002	91	+1	+91	1	90.179
2003	98	+2	+196	4	91.555
2004	90	+5	+450	26	95.683
$N = 7$	$\Sigma Y = 623$	$\Sigma X = 1$	$\Sigma XY = 159$	$\Sigma X^2 = 51$	

(i) The equation of the straight line trend is $Y_c = a + bX$. Since ΣX is not zero, we will solve the two normal equations.

$$\Sigma Y = Na + b\Sigma X$$
$$\Sigma XY = a\,\Sigma X + b\Sigma X^2$$
$$623 = 7a + b \qquad \text{...(i)}$$
$$159 = a + 515 \qquad \text{...(ii)}$$

Multiplying eq. (ii) by 7 and subtracting from eq. (i), we get $b = 1.376$

Putting the value of b in eq. (i)

$$7a + 1.376 = 623 \quad \text{or} \quad 7a = 621.624 \text{ or a} = 88.803$$

Hence $\quad Y = 88.803 + 1.376\;\; X$ is the equation of the straight line

$$Y_{1997} = 88.803 + 1.376\,(-4) = 88.803\; - 5.504$$
$$Y_{1999} = 88.803 + 1.376\,(-2) = 88.803 - 2.752 = 86.051$$
$$Y_{2000} = 88.803 + 1.376\,(-1) = 88.803 - 1.376 = 87.427$$
$$Y_{2001} = 88.803$$
$$Y_{2002} = 88.803 + 1.376\,(+1) = 88.803 + 1.376 = 90.179$$

$$Y_{2003} = 88.803 + 1.376\,(+2) = 88.803 + 2.752 - 91.555$$
$$Y_{2004} = 88.803 + 1.376\,(+5) = 88.803 + 6.88 = 95.683$$

(i) After eliminating the trend we are left with seasonal, cyclical and irregular variations.

(ii) Monthly increase in the production of cement shall be given by

$$\frac{b}{12} = \frac{1.376}{12} = 0.115$$

EXAMPLE 12.13: Compute the quadratic trend of the form $Y = a + bX + cX^2$ for the data showing the production of an item, over a 7 years period: **[CA, Foundation, 1996]**

Year	1995	1996	1997	1998	1999	2000	2001
Production (in '000 nos.)	10	11	12	9	10	13	11

Solution:

Year x	X $X = (x - 1998)$	Y	XY	X^2	X^2Y	X^3	X^4
1995	−3	10	−30	9	90	−27	81
1996	−2	11	−22	4	44	−8	16
1997	−1	12	−12	1	12	−1	1
1998	0	9	0	0	0	0	0
1999	1	10	10	1	10	1	1
2000	2	13	26	4	52	8	16
2001	3	11	33	9	99	27	81
$N = 7$	$\Sigma X = 0$	$\Sigma Y = 76$	$\Sigma XY = 5$	$\Sigma X^2 = 28$	$\Sigma X^2 Y = 307$	$\Sigma X^3 = 0$	$\Sigma X^4 = 196$

Normal equations are :

$$\Sigma Y = Na + b\Sigma X + c\Sigma X^2$$
$$\Sigma XY = a\Sigma X + b\Sigma X^2 + c\Sigma X^3$$
$$\Sigma X^2\,Y = a\Sigma X^2 + b\Sigma X^3 + c\Sigma X^4$$

Hence $76 = 7a + 28c$, $5 = 28b$ and $307 = 28\,a + 196c$

Solving these 3 equations, we get

$$a = \frac{75}{7} = 10.71,\; b = \frac{5}{28} = 0.178 \approx 0.18 \text{ and } c = \frac{3}{84} = 0.0357 \approx 0.036$$

Hence the quadratic trend is

$$Y = a + bX + cX^2$$
$$= 10.71 + 0.18\,X + 0.036\,X^2$$

where $X = 0$ for 1998

EXAMPLE 12.14: The following table gives the total expenditure of the Govt. of India during 1994–95 to 2000–01:

Year	1994–95	1995–96	1996–97	1997–98	1998–99	1999–2000	2000–01
Expenditure (in crores)	177.2	185.0	224.9	254.0	304.9	359.9	438.8

Fit an exponential trend curve $y = ab^x$ to the data **[CA, Foundation, 2000]**

Solution: We have to fit curve $y = ab^x$

Taking logarithm of both the sides, we get, $\log y = \log a + x \log b$

Year	Mid.Value X	Expenditure Y	X – 1997.5 = x	x^2	Log Y	x Log Y
1994–95	1994.5	177.2	–3	9	2.2485	– 6.7455
1995–96	1995.5	185.0	– 2	4	2.2672	– 4.5344
1996–97	1996.5	224.9	–1	1	2.352	– 2.352
1997–98	1997.5	254.0	0	0	2.4048	0
1998–99	1998.5	304.9	1	1	2.4842	2.4842
1999–2000	1999.5	359.9	2	4	2.5562	5.1124
2000–01	2000.5	438.8	3	9	2.6423	7.9269
		1944.7	**0**	**28**	**16.9552**	**1.8916**

Normal equations by the method of least squares are

$$\Sigma \log\ y = n\ \log\ a + \log b\ \ [\Sigma\, x]$$

$$\Sigma x \log y = \log \text{a}\ [\Sigma\, x] + \log \text{b}\ [\Sigma\, x^2]$$

$$\log\ a = \frac{\Sigma \log y}{n} = \frac{16.9552}{7} = 2.4222 \Rightarrow a = \text{Antilog } 2.4222 = 264.36$$

$$\log b = \frac{1.8916}{28} = 0.06755 \qquad \Rightarrow b = \text{ Antilog } 0.06755 = 1.168$$

Thus exponential trend curve is given by $y_c = 264.36 \times 1.168^x$ when $x = X - 1997.5$.

EXAMPLE 12.15: (i) Given the trend equation: $Y_c = 35 + 5X + 3X^2$

(Origin: 1998, X unit = 1 year) change the origin of the equation to 2004.

(ii) Given the equation $Y_c = 10\ (1.5)^X$

(Origin: 1998, X unit = 1 year)

Shift the origin forward by two years.

(iii) The trend of the annual sales of an Aluminium Company is described by the following equation:

$$Y_c = 12 + 0.7X$$

(Origin: 1998, X unit = 1 year and Y unit = annual production)

Shift the origin to January, 2004 and write the equation on monthly basis.

Solution:

(i) To shift the origin from 1998 to 2004, i.e. 6 years forward, put $X = 6$ in the equation.

$$Y_c = 35 + 5\ (6) + 3\ (6)^2 = 35 + 30 + 108 = 173$$

The new trend equation is

$$Y_c = 173 + 5X + 3\ X^2$$

(Origin: 1998, X unit = 1 year)

(ii) For shifting the origin forward by two years, we put $X + 2$ instead of X in the given equation. The new trend equation is

$$Y_c = 10\ (1.5)^{X+2}$$

$$= 10\ (1.5)^2\ (1.5)^X = 22.5\ (1.5)^X$$

(iii) To shift the origin to January, 2004, we should subtract $1/2b$ from trend value of July, 2004.

$$1/2b = 0.7/2 = 0.35;\ \text{therefore, } a = 12 - 0.35 = 11.65$$

The new trend equation is

$$Y_c = 11.65 + 0.7\ X$$

(Origin: January, 2004, X unit = 1 year)

To obtain the equation on monthly basis, we divide the value of a by 12 and value of b by 144.

The new trend equation on monthly basis can be written as:

$$Y_c = \frac{11.65}{12} + \frac{0.7}{144}X = 0.971 + .0049X$$

(Origin: January 2004, X unit = 1 month)

EXAMPLE 12.16: The following table gives the profits of a concern for 5–years ending 2001.

Year	1997	1998	1999	2000	2001
Profit ('000 Rs)	1.6	4.5	13.8	40.2	125.0

Find out the trend values by using the equation $Y_c = AB^X$

Solution:

Trend Values by the Equation $Y_c = AB^X$

Year t	Profits ('000 Rs) Y	$t-1999 = X$	Trend Values Log Y	X^2	$X \log Y$	Y_c
1997	1.6	–2	0.2041	4	–0.4082	1.56
1998	4.5	–1	0.6532	1	–0.6532	4.63
1999	13.8	0	1.1399	0	0.000	13.79
2000	40.2	+1	1.6042	1	1.6042	41.05
2001	125.0	+2	2.0969	4	4.1938	122.21
$n = 5$	–	$\Sigma X = 0$	$\Sigma \log Y = 5.6983$	$\Sigma X^2 = 10$	$\Sigma(X \log Y) = 4.7366$	

Since $\Sigma X = 0$; the value of $\log A = \frac{\Sigma \log Y}{n} = \frac{5.6983}{5} = 1.1397$

The value of $\log B = \frac{\Sigma(X \log Y)}{\Sigma X^2} = \frac{4.7366}{10} = 0.47366$

Therefore A = Antilog 1.1397 = 13.79

B = Antilog 0.47366 = 2.977

The equation $Y_c = A.\, B^X$, now would be

$$Y_c = 13.79 \times (2.977)^X$$

Now when $t = 1979$, $X = -2$, the value of $Y_c = 13.79 \times (2.977)^{(-2)}$

$$= \frac{13.79 \times 1}{(2.977)^2} = \frac{13.79}{8.8625} = 1.56$$

Similarly when $X = -1$ the value of $Y_c = 13.79 \times (2.977)^{-1} = \frac{13.79}{2.977} = 4.$

When $X = 1$ the value of $Y_c = 13.79 \times (2.97)^1 = 41.05$

When $X = 2$ the value of $Y_c = 13.79 \times (2.977)^2 = 13.79 \times 8.8625 = 122.21$

The above values have been shown in the last column of the table. The value of Y_c when $X = 0$ is 13.79 which is the value of A.

EXAMPLE 12.17: The seasonal indices of a commodity manufactured by a company for four quarters of a year are respectively 100, 90, 80, and 130. If the total sale in the first quarter is worth Rs 25,000 , how much worth of sale is expected during the whole year?

Solution:

Quarter	I	II	III	IV
Seasonal index	100	9	80	130
Estimated sales (Rs)	25,000	22,500	20,000	32,500

$$\text{Estimated sales for 2}^{\text{nd}}\text{ Qtr.} = \frac{\text{Figure for 1st Qtr.}}{\text{S.I. for 1st Qtr.}} \times \text{S.I for 2nd Qtr.}$$

$$= \frac{25{,}000 \times 90}{100} = 20{,}000$$

$$\text{Estimated sales for 3}^{\text{rd}}\text{ Qtr.} = \frac{\text{Figure for 1st Qtr.}}{\text{S.I. for 1st Qtr.}} \times \text{S.I for 3rd Qtr.}$$

$$= \frac{25{,}000 \times 80}{100} = 20{,}000$$

$$\text{Estimated sales for 4}^{\text{th}}\text{ Qtr.} = \frac{25{,}000 \times 130}{100} = 32{,}500.$$

EXAMPLE 12.18: The time series given below shows the number of tables sold by a small company since it started.

Years	1994	1995	1996	1997	1998	1999	2000	2001	2002	2003
Tables sold	42	50	61	75	92	111	120	127	140	138

Find the linear equation that describes the trend in the number of tables sold. Also estimate the sale of tables in 2005. **[MBA, IGNOU, 2003]**

Solution:

Fitting Linear Equation

Year	Tables Sold Y	Taking deviations from 1998.5	Multiplying deviations by 2 X	XY	X
1994	42	– 4.5	– 9	– 378	81
1995	50	– 3.5	–7	– 350	49
1996	61	– 2.5	– 5	– 305	25
1997	75	– 1.5	–3	–225	9
1998	92	– 0.5	–1	– 92	1
1999	111	+ 0.5	+1	+ 111	1
2000	120	+ 1.5	+3	+ 360	9
2001	127	+ 2.5	+ 5	+ 635	25
2002	140	+ 3.5	+ 7	+ 980	49
2003	138	+ 4.5	+ 9	+1242	81
$N = 10$	$\Sigma Y = 956$		$\Sigma X = 0$	$\Sigma XY = 1978$	$\Sigma X^2 = 330$

The linear equation would be of the form:

$$Y = a + bX$$

The two normal equations shall be

$$\Sigma Y = Na + b\Sigma X$$

$$\Sigma XY = a\,\Sigma X + b\Sigma X^2$$

Since $\Sigma X = 0$

$$a = \frac{\Sigma Y}{N} = \frac{956}{10} = 95.6;$$

and $$b = \frac{\Sigma XY}{\Sigma X^2} = \frac{1979}{330} = 5.994$$

Thus the linear equation is

$$Y_c = 95.6 + 5.994$$

For 2005, X would be + 13.

$$Y_{2005} = 95.6 + 5.994\,(13)$$

$$= 95.6 + 77.92$$

$$= 173.52 \text{ or } 174$$

Hence the expected number of tables that would be sold in 2005 shall be 174.

LIST OF FORMULAE

1. Additive time series model:

   $$Y = T + C + S + I$$

   where T, C, S and I are the trend, cyclical seasonal and irregular components respectively and Y is the value of the time series at a given time.

2. Multiplicative time series model:

   $$Y = T \times C \times S \times I$$

3. Regression model for linear trend:

   $$Y = a + bX \qquad ...(1)$$

   where Y is the time period, X is the value of the item measured against time, a is the Y - intercept and b is the Normal equations of (1) are

   $$\Sigma Y = na + b\Sigma X$$

   $$\Sigma XY = a\,\Sigma X + b\Sigma X^2$$

   where n is the total number of observations.

4. Computed or estimated linear trend line:

   $$Y_c = a + bX$$

   Where Y_c is the completed or estimated value of a time series.

5. Multiplicative time series for annual data (i.e. no seasonal variation is involved):

   $$Y = T \times C \times I$$

6. Parabolic or quadratic trend:

   $$Y = a + bX + CX^2$$

Its normal equations are:

$$\Sigma Y = na + b\Sigma X + c\Sigma X^2$$

$$\Sigma XY = a\,\Sigma X + b\,\Sigma X^2 + c\,\Sigma X^3$$

$$\Sigma X^2 = a\,\Sigma X^2 + b\Sigma X^3 + c\,\Sigma X^4$$

7. Exponential trend

$$Y = AB^X$$

Its normal equations are

$$\Sigma \log Y = N \log A + \log B\,\Sigma X$$

$$\Sigma\ (X \log Y) = \log A\Sigma X + \log B\,\Sigma X^2$$

8. After detrending, additive time series model:

$$Y = S + C + I$$

9. After detrending, multiplicative time series model:

$$Y = S \times C \times I$$

10. Link relative (*a*) when the data are monthly

$$\text{Link relative} = \frac{\text{Figure for the current month}}{\text{Figure for the preceding month}} \times 100$$

(b) when the data are quarterly

$$\text{Link relative} = \frac{\text{Figure for the current quarter}}{\text{Figure for the preceding quarter}} \times 100$$

11. Chain relative:

(a) In case of monthly data,

$$C.R = \frac{\text{Link relative of current month} \times \text{C.R. of preceding month}}{100}$$

(b) In case of quarterly data.

$$C.R. = \frac{L.R\text{of current quarter} \times C.R\text{ of preceding quarter}}{100}$$

12. Deseasonalised value for an additive model

$$Y - S = T + C + I$$

13. Deseasonalised value for multiplicative model

$$\frac{Y}{S} = TCI$$

SELF PRACTICE EXERCISES

I. CHOOSE THE BEST ANSWER

1. An overall tendency of rise or fall in a time series is called:
   (a) Seasonal (b) Trend
   (c) Cyclical (d) Irregular
2. The component useful for short-term forecasting is:
   (a) Cyclical (b) Trend
   (c) Seasonal (d) Irregular

3. The component useful for long-term forecasting is:
   (a) Trend (b) Seasonal
   (c) Cyclical (d) Irregular
4. If annual data are given, the time series is representable by the additive model in:
   (a) $Y = T \times S \times C \times I$ (b) $Y = T + S + C + I$
   (c) $Y = T + C + I$ (d) $Y = S + C + I$
5. In an additive model, the component measurements are:
   (a) positive (b) negative
   (c) absolute (d) None of these
6. A trend of the form $Y = a + bX + cX^2$ is called:
   (a) Linear (b) Parabolic
   (c) Exponential (d) None of these
7. With a change in origin, the value of b in a linear trend $y = a + bx$:
   (a) also changes (b) remains the same
   (c) is always positive (d) is always negative
8. After detrending, the time series multiplicative model is:
   (a) $Y = T \times S \times C \times I$ (b) $Y = S \times C \times I$
   (c) $Y = T \times S \times I$ (d) None of these
9. In a multiplicative model, *C, S* and *I* have:
   (a) positive value (b) positive or negative values
   (c) absolute values (d) indexing values
10. The method of moving averages is useful for determining:
    (a) trend (b) seasonal indices
    (c) irregular variations (d) None of these
11. Seasonal variations repeat with in:
    (a) Five years (b) Seven years
    (c) Two years (d) A year
12. If trend is not present in the time series, the seasonal indices are obtained by using:
    (a) Method of simple averages (b) Ratio-to-trend method
    (c) Moving average method (d) Method of least squares
13. An increase in harvesting time is associated to:
    (a) trend (b) seasonal component
    (c) cyclical component (d) irregular component
14. A recession in industry is associated to the:
    (a) trend (b) seasonal component
    (c) cyclical component (d) irregular component
15. A boom in business activity is associated to the:
    (a) cyclical component (b) seasonal component
    (c) random component (d) trend
16. Decline in mortality rate due to improvements in science is associated to the:
    (a) seasonal component (b) cyclical component
    (c) trend (d) None of these

17. Decline in steel production due to worker's strike is associated to the:
    (a) random component (b) cyclical component
    (c) trend (d) seasonal component
18. The first step in the analysis of time series is:
    (a) to obtain trend (b) to obtain seasonal variations
    (c) to edit the series (d) none of these
19. Cyclical fluctuations are caused by:
    (a) strikes and lockouts (b) floods
    (c) wars (d) None of these
20. Forecasting time horizons include:
    (a) large range (b) medium range
    (c) short range (d) all of these
21. A forecast that projects company's sales is the:
    (a) economic forecast (b) technological forecast
    (c) demand forecast (d) None of these
22. Quantitative methods of forecasting include:
    (a) salesforce composite (b) consumer market survey
    (c) smoothing approach (d) all of these
23. With regard to regression based forecast, the standard error of estimate gives a measure of:
    (a) overall accuracy of the forecast
    (b) time period for which the forecast is valid
    (c) maximum error of the forecast
    (d) all of these

II. FILL IN THE BLANKS

1. An over-all tendency of rise or fall in a time series is called the ....
2. The component useful for long-term forecasting is ....
3. Analysis of time series greatly helps in ....
4. Editing of time series is necessary before its ....
5. .... means the process of eliminating the trend.
6. In an yearly data, we have no ....
7. The process of eliminating seasonal variations is called .... of data.
8. Period of moving averages is determined by the .... for the time series
9. The moving averages are greatly affected by .... in the time series.
10. For yearly data, the additive model will be ....
11. Periodic movements with duration longer than a year are called ....
12. When estimates of future conditions are made on a systematic basis, the process is referred to as ....

III. SHORT ANSWER TYPE QUESTIONS

1. What is a time series? Explain the objectives of the analysis of a time series.
2. Suggest the important adjustments to be made before analysing time series.
3. Describe the components of a time series. Illustrate them with suitable examples.

4. Define trend in a time series. What are the objectives behind the study of trend in a time series?
5. Distinguish between the seasonal and cyclical variations.
6. Explain the method of moving averages for determining trend. Describe the merits and demerits of this method.
7. How does analysis of time series helps in making business forecast?
8. Explain the way an exponential trend of the type $y = ab^x$ is fitted to time series data.
9. What are cyclical fluctuations? How are they measured?
10. Write a short note on least squares method.
11. Write short note on Link relative method of measuring seasonal variations.
12. What are irregular movements? Explain the residual method of estimating irregular components in a time series.
13. With which characteristic movement of a time series would you mainly associate the following:
    (i) An era of prosperity
    (ii) The sale before Deepawali in a departmental store
    (iii) A fire in a factory delaying production for two months
    (iv) A need for increased wheat production due to estimated increase in population
    (v) Strike in a factory
14. Explain the meaning of deseasonalisation of data? Why do we deseasonalize data
15. What is Business forecasting? Explain clearly its role and limitations.

IV. LONG ANSWER TYPE QUESTIONS

1. Explain clearly the meaning of Time series Analysis? Mention its important components. Explain these components with examples, indicating the importance of each component in business. **[B.Com., Andhra University, 2003]**
2. Explain the term Time-series. Why is Time Series considered to be an effective tool of forecasting. **[MBA, BHU, 2002]**
3. What is forecasting? Discuss in brief the various theories and methods of business forecasting. **[MBA, Delhi University, 1998, 2001]**
4. Explain briefly the additive and multiplicative models of time series. Which of these models is more popular in practice and why? **[MBA, Osmania University, 1998]**
5. Explain briefly the different methods of measuring trend. **[MBA, Madras University, 2002]**
6. Distinguish between ratio-to-trend and ratio-to-moving average methods of measuring seasonal variations. Which is better and why?
7. How would you eliminate seasonal influences? Illustrate with the help of an example.
8. Fit a trend line to the following data by the freehand method:

Year	Production of steel (million tonnes)	Year	Production of steel (million tonnes)
1995	20	2000	25
1996	22	2001	23
1997	24	2002	26
1998	21	2003	25
1999	23		

9. Calculate the three-month moving averages from the following data:

Jan.	Feb.	March	April	May	June
57	65	63	72	69	78
July	**Aug.**	**Sept.**	**Oct.**	**Nov.**	**Dec.**
82	81	90	93	95	97

10. Fit a straight line trend by the method of least squares to the following data:

Year (*X*)	1997–98	1998–99	1999–00	2000–01	2001–02	2002–03	2003–04
Sales (in lakhs Rs) (*Y*)	278	309	335	378	424	481	521

(clearly specify the origin and the units of the variables in the trend equation obtained).

11. Use method of least squares to determine sales for the year 2004. **[MBA, Anna University, 2002]**

Year	1997	1999	2000	2001	2002
Sales	100	110	130	125	160

12. The following table gives the total expenditure of the Government during 1996-2003. Fit a quadratic trend to the data: **[MBA, Anna University, 2003]**

Year	1996–97	1997–98	1998–99	1999–00	2000–01	2001–02	2002–03
Expenditure	177.2	185.0	224.9	254.0	304.9	359.9	438.8

13. Calculate seasonal indices by the 'ratio to moving average method' from the following data:

Year	Quarter			
	I	II	III	IV
2002	68	62	61	63
2003	65	58	66	61
2004	68	63	63	67

14. The following table gives the number of patients visiting an out patient department of a hospital during a course of 4 weeks. (From Monday to Saturday)

Week	M	T	W	Th	F	S
I	352	307	285	270	275	314
II	325	318	300	280	275	310
III	335	324	290	276	282	318
IV	324	315	285	274	288	322

Find the seasonal indices by link relative method.

15. Deseasonalise the following data using multiplicative model.

Quarter	1	2	3	4
Sales (Rs '000)	65.4	25.2	23.7	12.4
Seasonal Index	148	124	78	50

[ICWA, Dec., 1998]

16. The following table gives the profits of a concern for five years ending 2004:

Year (X)	2000	2001	2002	2003	2004
Profit (in Rs '000) (Y)	1.6	4.5	13.8	40.2	125

Find the trend values for the years 200 –2004 using an equation of the form $Y = ab^x$.

ANSWERS

I. CHOOSE THE BEST ANSWERS

1. (b) 2. (c) 3. (a) 4. (c) 5. (c) 6. (b) 7. (b) 8. (b)
9. (d) 10. (a) 11. (d) 12. (a) 13. (b) 14. (c) 15. (a) 16. (c)
17. (d) 18. (c) 19. (d) 20. (d) 21. (c) 22. (c) 23. (a)

II. FILL IN THE BLANKS

1. secular trend 2. seasonal 3. forecasting 4. analysis
5. Detrending 6. Seasonal variation 7. deseasonalisation 8. periodicity
9. extreme values 10. $Y = T + C + I$ 11. cyclical movements 12. forecasting

IV. LONG ANSWER TYPE QUESTIONS

10. $Y = 389.43 + 41.5\,X$
13. 105.30, 95.21, 100.97, 98.52
14. 110.42, 104.80, 96.38, 91.60, 93.45, 103.35
15. 44.19, 20.32, 30.38,. 42.80
16. 1.56, 4.63, 13.79, 41.06, 122.22

CHAPTER 13

Probability and Mathematical Expectation

13.1 INTRODUCTION

The word ***'Probability'*** and chance are quite familiar to everyone. Many a time we come across statements like "our cricket team is likely to win the World Cup". "I have a good chance of getting selected in the College team". "Probably I may meet the Prime Minister today".

In the above sentences, the word likely, chance, probably, etc., convey some sense of uncertainty about the occurrence of some events. Ordinarily, it may appear that there cannot be any exact measurement for these uncertainties. But in Mathematics, we do have methods for calculating the degree of certainty of events in numerical values, provided certain conditions are satisfied. In order to think about and measure uncertainty, we turn to a branch of Mathematics called ***Probability.***

Probability theory is an important part of statistical theory that bridges descriptive and inferential statistics. It is the science of uncertainty or chance, or likelihood.

A probability value ranges between 0 and 1 inclusive and represents the likelihood that a particular event will happen. A probability value of 0 means there is no chance that an event will happen and a value of 1 means there is 100 percent chance that the event will happen.

The Theory of Probability provides a numerical measure of the element of uncertainty. It enables us to take decision under conditions of uncertainty with a calculated risk. The theory of probability was developed towards the end of the 18th century and its history suggests that it developed with the study of games and chance, such as rolling a dice, drawing a card, flipping a coin etc.

History of Probability

The theory of probability has its origin in the games of chance related to gambling such as tossing of a coin, throwing of a die, drawing cards from a pack of cards etc. ***Jerame Cardon***, an Italian Mathematician wrote 'A book on games of chance' which was published on 1663. Starting with games of chance, probability has become one of the basic tools of statistics. The knowledge of probability theory makes it possible to interpret statistical results, since many statistical procedures involve conclusions based on samples.

The Theory of Probability provides a numerical measure of the element of uncertainty. It enables us to take decision under conditions of uncertainty with a calculated risk.

The theory of probability was developed towards the end of the 18th century and its history suggests that it developed with the study of games and chance, such as rolling a dice, drawing a card, flipping a coin etc.

Understanding probability is helpful for decision-making. Probability theory is being applied in the solution of social, economic, business problems. Today the concept of probability has assumed greater importance and the mathematical theory of probability has become the basis for statistical applications in both social and decision-making research. Probability theory, in fact, is the foundation of statistical inferences.

13.2 BASIC CONCEPT

Before we give definitions of the word probability as looked upon by various schools of thought it is necessary that we familiarise ourselves with following definitions and terms that are used in studying the theory of probability.

Random Experiments and Sample Space

When we toss (or flip) a coin once, the coin may turn up in either of the two ways - ***'Head'*** or ***'Tail'***. We call Head or Tail as an ***outcome*** of this activity. The set S of all possible outcomes is given by $S = \{H, T\}$ where H stands for Head and T stands for Tail. The set S is called the ***sample space*** (of the activity of tossing a coin). This activity (of tossing a coin) is called a ***random experiment.***

Thus we define the following:

- **Random Experiment:** Any experiment whose outcomes cannot be predicted in advance or determine in advance is a random experiment.
- **Trial:** Each performance of the random experiment is called a trial.
- **Outcomes:** The results of a random experiment are called its outcomes. When two coins are tossed the possible outcomes are HH, HT, TH, TT.
- **Sample Space:** The set of all possible outcomes of a random experiment is called a sample space and is denoted by S.
- **Sample Point:** Each element of the sample space is called a sample point.

Event

An event is a subset of a sample space.

A boy throws a die. Suppose he reports that the number appeared on the die is a square number. Can we guess what number he could get? Certainly the answer is 1 or 4 as these are the only square numbers in the sample space $S = \{1, 2, 3, 4, 5, 6\}$. Thus the set $E = \{1, 4\}$ is an event of this experiment.

When a coin is tossed, getting a head is an event, getting a tail is another event. Here $S = \{H, T\}$ is the sample space.

$E = \{H\}$ and $F = \{T\}$ are the events. Note that E and F are subsets of the sample space S.

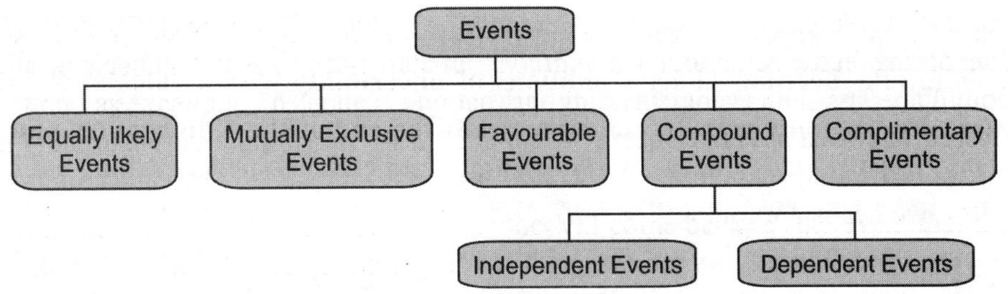

Fig. 13.1: Types of events

Equally Likely Events

Two or more events are said to be equally likely if each one of them has an equal chance of occurring.

For example, in tossing a coin, getting a head and getting a tail are equally likely events.

Mutually Exclusive Events

Two events A and B are said to be mutually exclusive events if the occurrence of any one of them excludes the occurrence of the other event. i.e., they cannot occur simultaneously.

For example, A business can't be bankrupt, break-even and profitable at the same. It can only be one of the three. Similarly, being a male or female are mutually exclusive and collectively exhaustive events. None one is both and everyone is one or the other.

In terms of sets, this means A and B are disjoint. ***For example***, in drawing a single card from a well-shuffled standard deck of playing cards, the events,

A: Card is a heart,

B: Card is a diamond

are mutually exclusive because a card cannot be both a heart and a diamond at the same time.

But if the events are

A: Card is a heart;

B: Card is a king,

then A and B are not mutually exclusive because we have a king of hearts.

Similarly, if we roll a die, we will get either an "odd number" or an "even number". The event A "getting an odd number" excludes the event B "getting an even number" and vice-versa. Here A and B are mutually exclusive $A = \{1, 3, 5\}$, $B = \{2, 4, 6\}$ and $A \cap B = 0$

Favourable Events or Cases

The numbers of outcomes or cases which entail the occurrence of the event in an experiment are called favourable events or favourable cases.

For example, when two dice are thrown the number of cases favourable to the event of getting a sum 5 is (1, 4), (2, 3), (3, 2), (4, 1). There are 4 cases favourable to an event of sum = 5.

Compound (Joint) Events

The joint occurrence of two or more events is called compound events. Thus compound events imply the simultaneous occurrence of two or more simple events.

For example, driving autos is one event and talking on the cell phone is another event. When you see someone talking on the cell phone while driving an automobile it is a joint event. In tossing of two fair coins simultaneously, the event of getting "atleast one head" is a compound event as it consists of joint occurrence of two simple events.

Event A = one head appears ie $A = \{HT, TH\}$ and

Event B = two heads appears ie $B = \{HH\}$

Similarly, if a bag contains 6 white and 6 red balls and we make a draw of 2 balls at random, then the events that 'both are white' or 'one is white and one is red' are compound events.

The compound events may be further classified as

1. Independent Events
2. Dependent Events

(A) Independent Events

If two or more events occur in such a way that the occurrence of one does not affect the occurrence of another, they are said to be independent events.

For example, if a coin is tossed twice, the results of the second throw would in no way be affected by the results of the first throw.

Similarly, if a bag contains 5 white and 7 red balls and then two balls are drawn one by one in such a way that the first ball is replaced before the second one is drawn. In this situation, the two events, 'the first ball is white' and 'second ball is red', will be independent, since the composition of the balls in the bag remains unchanged before a second draw is made.

(B) Dependent Events

If the occurrence of one event influences the occurrence of the other, then the second event is said to be dependent on the first. In the above example, if we do not replace the first ball drawn, this will change the composition of balls in the bag while making the second draw and therefore the event of 'drawing a red ball' in the second will depend on event (first ball is red or white) occurring in first draw.

Similarly, if a person draw a card from a full pack and does not replace it, the result of the draw made afterwards will be dependent on the first draw.

Independent Events: Two events are said to be independent if the occurrence of any event does not affect the occurrence of the other event. ***For example*** in tossing of a coin, the events corresponding to the two successive tosses of it are independent. The flip of one penny does not affect in any way the flip of a nickel.

Dependent Events: If the occurrence or non-occurrence of any event affects the happening of the other, then the events are said to be dependent events. ***For example***, in drawing a card from a pack of cards, let the event A be the occurrence of a king in the 1st draw and B be the occurrence of a king in the 1st draw and B be the occurrence of a king in the second draw. If the card drawn at the first trial is not replaced then events A and B are independent events.

NOTES:

1. If an event contains a single simple point i.e. it is a singleton set, then this event is called an elementary or a simple event.
2. An event corresponding to the empty set is an "impossible event".
3. An event corresponding to the entire sample space is called a "certain event".

Complementary Events

Let S be the sample space for an experiment and A be an event in S. Then A is a subset of S. Hence $\bar{A}$, the complement of A in S is also an event in S which contains the outcomes which are not favourable to the occurrence of A i.e. if A occurs, then the outcome of the experiment belongs to A, but if A does not occur, then the outcomes of the experiment belongs to $\bar{A}$

It is obvious that A and $\bar{A}$ are mutually exclusive. $A \cap \bar{A} = 0$ and $A \cup \bar{A} = S$.

If S contains n equally likely, mutually exclusive and exhaustive points and A contains m out of these n points then $\bar{A}$ contains $(n - m)$ sample points.

Mutually Exclusive versus Independent Events

Mutually Exclusive (ME): Event A and B are ME if both cannot occur simultaneously. That is, $P[A \text{ and } B] = 0$.

Independency (Ind.): Events A and B are independent if having the information that B already occurred does not change the probability that A will occur. That is $P[A \text{ given } B \text{ occurred}] = P[A]$.

- ***If two events are ME they are also Dependent:*** $P(A \text{ given } B) = P[A \text{ and } B]$, $P[B]$, and since $P[A \text{ and } B] = 0$ (by ME), then $P[A \text{ given } B] = 0$. Similarly,
- If two events are Independent then they are also not ME.
- If two events are Dependent then they may or may not be ME.
- If two events are not ME, then they may or may not be Independent.

The following Figure contains all possibilities. The notations used in this table are as follows: ***X*** means does not imply, question mark? means it may or may not imply, while the **check mark** means it implies.

Notice that the (probabilistic) pairwise independency and mutual independency for a collection of events $A_1, \ldots, A_n$ are two different notions.

EXAMPLE 13.1: A coin is tossed three times. Write its sample space.

Solution: We denote the head by H and tail by T.

$$S = \{HHH, HHT, HTH, THH, HTT, THT, TTH, TTT\}$$

EXAMPLE 13.2: A die is thrown twice. Find out the sample space.

Solution:

Sample space = (1, 1), (1, 2), (1, 3), (1, 4), (1, 5), (1, 6),
(2, 1), (2, 2), (2, 3), (2, 4), (2, 5), (2, 6),
(3, 1), (3, 2), (3, 3), (3, 4), (3, 5), (3, 6),
(4, 1), (4, 2), (4, 3), (4, 4), (4, 5), (4, 6),
(5, 1), (5, 2), (5, 3), (5, 4), (5, 5), (5, 6),
(6, 1), (6, 2), (6, 3), (6, 4), (6, 5), (6, 6) }

EXAMPLE 13.3: From a leap year selected at random, what would be the sample space for the two odd days?

Solution: Since the leap year has 366 days which means 52 weeks and two extra days, which are known as odd days.

Sample space = {(Sunday, Monday), (Monday, Tuesday), (Tuesday, Wednesday), (Wednesday, Thursday), (Thursday, Friday), (Friday, Saturday), (Saturday, Sunday)}

13.3 DEFINITIONS OF PROBABILITY

We shall now consider three definitions of probability:

- Mathematical or a priori or classical.
- Statistical or empirical.
- The Axiomatic approach, and

1. Mathematical (or A Priori or Classic) Definition

If the probability of an event can be calculated even before the actual happening of the event, that is, even before conducting the experiment, it is called ***Mathematical probability****.

If there are '*n*' exhaustive, mutually exclusive and equally likely cases and m of them are favourable to an event *A*, the probability of a happening is defined as the ratio m/n

Expressed as a formula:

$$P(A) = \frac{m}{n} = \frac{\text{number of favourable outcomes}}{\text{total number of possible outcomes}}$$

If *A* is a favourable event, which is a subset of the sample space S of the experiment, then the probability of A denoted by *P* (*A*) is defined by

$$P(A) = \frac{n(A)}{n(S)}$$

Where *n* (*A*), *n* (*S*) are the cardinal number of sets *A* and *S* provided the members of the set *S* are equally likely.

Mathematical probability is often called ***classical probability*** or a ***priori probability*** because if we keep using the examples of tossing of fair coin, dice etc., we can state the answer in advance (*prior*), without tossing of coins or without rolling the dice etc.,

The above definition of probability is widely used, but it cannot be applied under the following situations:

1. If it is not possible to enumerate all the possible outcomes for an experiment.
2. If the sample points (outcomes) are not mutually independent.
3. If the total number of outcomes is infinite.
4. If each and every outcome is not equally likely.

For example, the probability of randomly drawing taking from a well-shuffled deck of cards is 4/52. Since 4 is the number of favourable outcomes (i.e. 4 kings of diamond, spade, club and heart) and 52 is the number of total outcomes (the number of cards in a deck).

---

* The probability of the occurrence of any event always lies between 0 and 1 and these are the two limits of probability.

If A is any event of sample space having probability P, then clearly, P is a positive number (expressed as a fraction or usually as a decimal) not greater than unity. $0 \leq P \leq 1$ i.e. 0 (no chance or for impossible event) to a high of 1 (certainty). Since the number of cases not favourable to A are $(n - m)$, the probability q that event A will not happen is, $q = \frac{n - m}{n}$ or $q = 1 - \frac{m}{n}$ or $q = 1 - p$.

Now note that the probability q is nothing but the probability of the complementary event A i.e. $\bar{A}$ Thus,

$$P(A) + P(\bar{A}) = 1$$
$$P(\bar{A}) = 1 - P(A)$$

The probability of certain events is already known or the resulting probabilities are definitive.

For example:

1. The chance that a woman gives birth to a male or female baby ($p = 0.50$ or ½),
2. The chance that tail or head appears in a toss of coin ($p = 0.50$ or ½), and
3. The chance that one spot will appear in die-rolling ($p = 0.16$ or 1/6).

NOTES:

(a) If the events are mutually exclusive and exhaustive, the sum of their individual probabilities of occurrence, is equal to one.
For example, if A, B, C are three mutually exclusive and exhaustive events then

$$P(A) + P(B) + P(C) = 1$$

(b) The probability of the occurrence of one particular event is also called Marginal probability of that event.

(c) To choose an object at random from N objects means that each object has the same probability $\frac{1}{n}$ of being choose.

Demerits of Mathematical Definition of Probability

The mathematical definition of probability of possible following demerits:

- This definition fails if the total number of possible results (or outcomes) is infinite.
- This definition gives the values of probability only in the form of rational numbers.
- This definition fails if the cases are not equally likely. ***For example*** if a coin is biased in favour of heads i.e. if this coin is tossed then head will appear more likely on its upper face when it falls. In such cases this definition will not give the probability of a head in a toss of this coin.

2. Relative Frequency Definition

If the probability of an event can be determined only after the actual happening of the event, it is called ***Statistical probability.***

If an event occurs m times out of n, its relative frequency is m/n.

In the limiting case, when n becomes sufficiently large it corresponds to a number which is called the probability of that event.

In symbol,

$$P(A) = \underset{n \to \infty}{\text{Limit}}\ (m/n)$$

The above definition of probability involves a concept which has a long term consequence. This approach was initiated by the mathematician ***Von Mises.***

For example:

1. 383 of 751 business graduates were employed in the past. The probability that a particular graduate will be employed in his or her major area is 383/751 = 0.51 or 51%.
2. The probability that your income tax return will be audited if there are two million mailed to your district office and 2,400 are to be audited is 2,400/2,000,000 = 0.0012 or 0.12%.

If a coin is tossed 10 times we may get 6 heads and 4 tails or 4 heads and 6 tails or any other result. In these cases the probability of getting a head is **not 0.5** as we consider in mathematical probability.

However, if the experiment is carried out a large number of times we should expect approximately equal number of heads and tails and we can see that the probability of getting head approaches 0.5. The Statistical probability calculated by conducting an actual experiment is also called a ***posteriori probability*** or ***empirical probability.***

3. Axiomatic Approach to Probability

The modern approach to probability is purely axiomatic and it is based on the set theory. The axiomatic approach to probability was introduced by the Russian mathematician ***A.N. Kolmogorov*** in the year 1933.

Axioms of Probability

Let S be a sample space and A be an event in S and $P(A)$ is the probability satisfying the following axioms:

1. The probability of any event ranges from zero to one, i.e $0 \leq P(A) \leq 1$
2. The probability of the entire space is 1, i.e $P(S) = 1$
3. If $A_1, A_2...$ is a sequence of mutually exclusive events in S, then
$$P(A_1 \cup A_2 \cup ..) = P(A_1) + P(A_2) + ...$$

13.4 SOME BASIC CONCEPTS OF SET THEORY

Set: A fundamental concept in the study of probability and statistics is the set. A set is a well-defined collection of distinct objects or members.

For example, the letters in the alphabet, the number of points on the dice, the books in a departmental library, the citizens of India etc.

Each object in a set is called an element or member of the set. The set must be well-defined, i.e., we are given a rule by which we can determine whether a particular element is a member of the set or not under consideration. The elements of the set are distinct in the sense that no two elements in a set are the same. Usually the sets are denoted by capital letters A, B, C, D ... and the small letters $a.,b, c,d$ ... denotes the elements of a set.

The set can be written in two ways. Firstly, if the set has a finite number of members, we may list the members, separated by commas and enclosed in brackets. ***For example***, the set A has the elements 1, 2, 3, 4 and 5, it may be written as

$$A = \{1, 2, 3, 4, 5\}$$

Secondly the set may be described by a statement or rule, i.e.,

$$A = \{X \mid x \text{ is a natural number from 1 to 5}\}$$
$$A = \{X \mid x \text{ is a vowel in the English Alphabet}\}$$

We read this as "A is a set of all X such that x is a vowel in the English Alphabet".

Null or Empty or Void Set: A set which contains no element, is called a Null set or Empty set or void set, denoted by ϕ. ***For example:*** the set of people who have travelled from earth to Mars is a Null set.

Universal set: A set U consisting of all the elements under consideration is called a universal set.

Equal sets: Two sets A and B are said to be equal if all the elements of set A belong to set B and all the elements of set B belong to set A.

Subset: From a given set we may form new sets, called the subsets of the given set. If each element of the set X is also an element of Y, then X is called a sub-set of Y and we write $X \subseteq Y$.

The notation $\subseteq$ stands for "set inclusion or contains in".

For example; if Y is a set of all integers and X is a set of positive integers, then X is contained in Y. Therefore, X is a subset of Y i.e. $X \subseteq Y$.

The set inclusion is a Transitive relation, because if $X \subseteq Y$, $Y \subseteq Z$ then $X \subseteq Z$.

If $X \subseteq Y$ and $Y \subseteq X$, we have $X = Y$.

If there is at least one element of Y which is not in X, then X is a proper subset of Y, written as $X \subset Y$. According to the definition every set is a subset of itself also.

Operation with Sets: We shall now consider certain operations on sets which will result the new sets: The new sets will be the subset of the universal set U.

Intersection of Sets: The intersection of two sets A and B is the set of elements which are common to both A and B. The intersection of the sets is denoted by $\cap$ [cap]. The intersection of the sets A and B, written as $A \cap B$ is given by

$$A \cap B = \{X \mid x \in A \text{ and } x \in B\}$$

In the Venn diagram the intersection of the sets A and B is shown by the shaded portion.

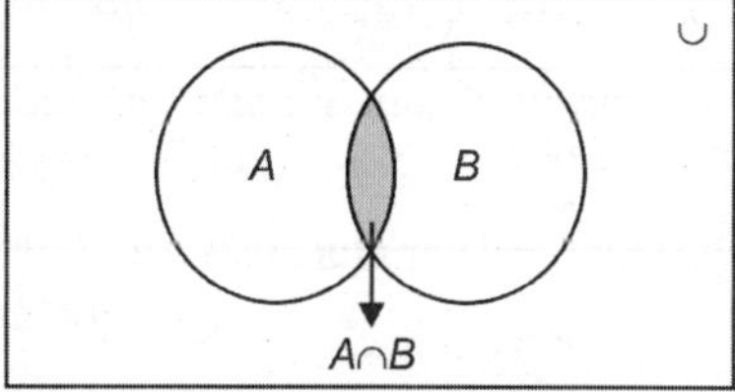

Fig. 13.2: Intersection of Sets A and B

Disjoint or Mutually Exclusive Sets: Two sets A and B are said to be disjoint or mutually exclusive, if they have no elements in common i.e. $A \cap B = \phi$. In the Venn diagram the disjoint sets are represented.

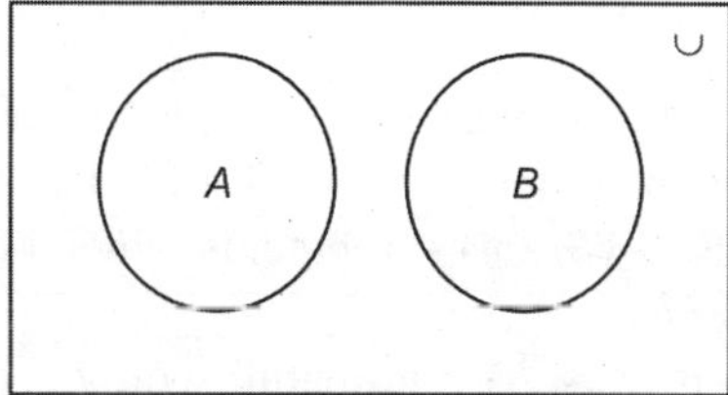

Fig.13.3: Disjoint Sets

Union of Sets: The union of two sets A and B is the set of elements that belong either to A or B or both. This is written as $A \cup B$ ($\cup$ is called cup).

i.e. $$A \cup B = \{X \mid x \in A \quad \text{or} \quad x \in B\}$$

In the following diagram, the union of set A and B is represented by the shaded portion.

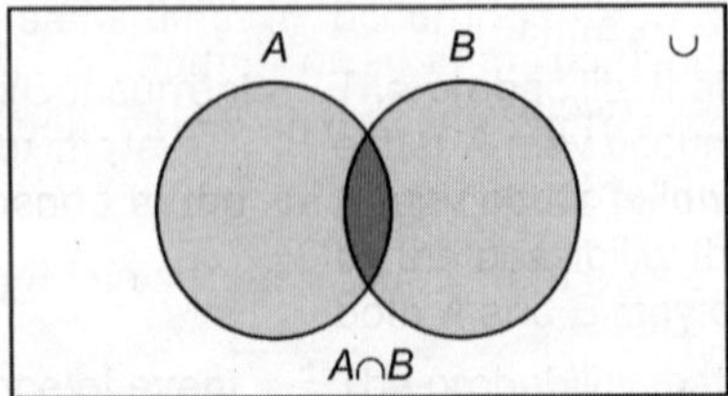

Fig. 13.4: Union of Sets A and B

Complement of a Set: If A is the subset of the universal set $\cup$, then the set of the elements that are not in A, is called the complement of the set A, denoted by $\overline{A}$ or A'.

i.e. $\overline{A}$ or $A' = \cup - A = \{X \mid x \notin A\}$

The complement of A is shown by the shaded portion in the following diagram.

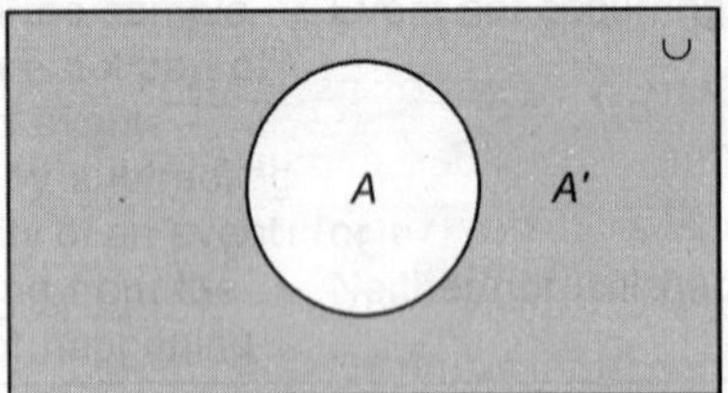

Fig.13.5: Complement of Set A

NOTES:

1. A and A' do not intersect i.e. $A \cap A' = \phi$ so, A and A' are disjoint or mutually exclusive sets.
2. Also, $A \cup A' = \cup$. Thus A and A' are completely exhaustive]

Difference of Two Sets

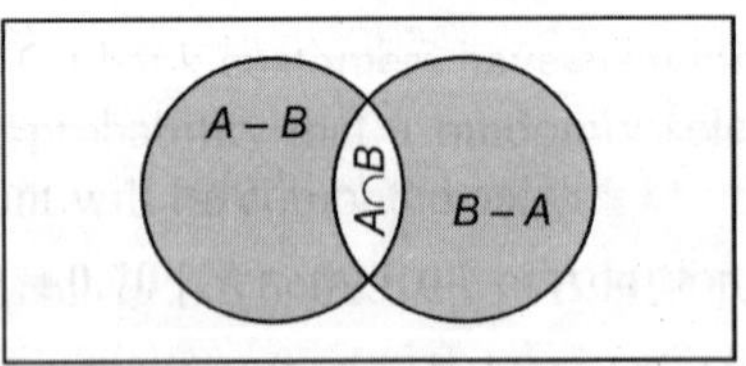

Fig. 13.6

Elements of $(A - B)$ = Elements belonging only to A = Elements of A – Elements of $(A \cap B)$

Elements of $(B - A)$ = Elements belonging only to B = Elements of B – Elements of $(A \cap B)$

Elements of $(A - B)$ + Elements of $(B - A)$ = Elements which belong only to A or only to B.

Probability of the occurrence of $(A - B)$ i.e.,

$$P(A - B) = P(A) - P(A \cap B) = \text{Probability only } A \text{ occurs.}$$

Probability of the occurrence of $(B - A)$ i.e.

$$P(B - A) = P(B) - P(A \cap B) = \text{Probability only } B \text{ occurs.}$$

Probability only one of the events A or B occurs = $P(A - B) + P(B - A)$.

This formula is applicable whether events are independent or not. But if the events are independent then we can also apply the following formula.

Probability that only one of A or B occurs = $P(A)\,P(\bar{B}) + P(B)\,P(\bar{A})$ ...(1)

NOTE: The above formula (I) is applicable only if the events are independent.

Symmetric Difference of Two Sets

If A and B are two sets, we define their symmetric difference as the set of all elements that belong to A or to B but not to both A and B and we denote it by $A \oplus B$. Thus,

$$A \oplus B = \{x\}\{x \in A \text{ and } x \notin B\} \text{ or } \{x \in B \text{ and } x \notin A\}$$
$$= (A - B) \cup (B - A)$$

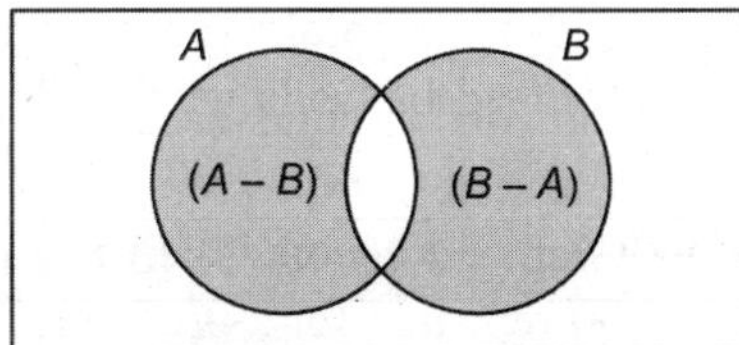

Fig. 13.7

The shaded region in above figure represents $A \oplus B$.

Interpretation of Statistical Statements in Terms of Set Theory

$S \Rightarrow$ Sample space

$\bar{A} \Rightarrow A$ does not occur

$A \cup \bar{A} - S$

$A \cap B = \phi \Rightarrow A$ and B are mutually exclusive.

$A \cup B \Rightarrow$ Event A occurs or B occurs or both A and B occur.

$\Rightarrow$ (at least one of the events A or B occurs)

$A \cap B \Rightarrow$ Both the events A and B occur

$\bar{A} \cap \bar{B} \Rightarrow$ Neither A nor B occurs

$A \cap \bar{B} \Rightarrow$ Event A occurs and B does not occur

$\bar{A} \cap B \Rightarrow$ Event A does not occur and B occur.

13.5 HOW TO ASSIGN PROBABILITIES?

Probability is an instrument to measure the likelihood of the occurrence of an event. There are four major approaches of assigning probability: Classical Approach, Subjective Approach, Anchoring, and the Delphi Technique:

Classical Approach: Classical probability is predicated on the condition that the outcomes of an experiment are equally likely to happen. The classical probability utilizes the idea that the lack of knowledge implies that all possibilities are equally likely. The classical probability is applied when the events have the same chance of occurring

The classical definition of probability has a disadvantage i.e. the words 'equally likely' are vague. In fact, since these words seem to be synonymous with "equally probable". This definition is circular as it is defining (in terms) of itself. Therefore, the estimated or empirical probability of an event is taken as the relative frequency of the occurrence of the event when the number of observations is very large.

Subjective Approach: The subjective probability is based on personal judgment and experience. ***For example,***

Events that require computing subjective probability are —

- Medical doctors sometimes assign subjective probability to the length of life expectancy for a person who has cancer.
- Estimating the probability that a person wins a jackpot lottery.
- Estimating the probability that the GM will lose its first ranking in car sales.

Anchoring: is the practice of assigning a value obtained from a prior experience and adjusting the value in consideration of current expectations or circumstances

The Delphi Technique: It consists of a series of questionnaires. Each series is one "round". The responses from the first "round" are gathered and become the basis for the questions and feedback of the second "round". The process is usually repeated for a predetermined number of "rounds" or until the responses are such that a pattern is observed. This process allows expert opinion to be circulated to all members of the group and eliminates the bandwagon effect of majority opinion.

Delphi Analysis is used in decision making processes, in particular in forecasting. Several "experts" sit together and try to compromise on something upon which they cannot agree.

EXAMPLE 13.4: Find the probability of drawing a red ball from a bag containing 4 white and 6 black balls.

Solution:

$$n\ (S) = 4 + 6$$

$$n\ (S) = 10$$

Let A denote the event of drawing a red ball

$$n\ (A) = 0$$

Because the event of drawing a red ball is an impossible event.

$$P(A) = \frac{n(A)}{n(S)} = \frac{0}{10} = 0$$

EXAMPLE 13.5: What is the probability that a number selected from the first 25 natural numbers is a prime number. **[MBA, IGNOU, 2000]**

Solution:

$$S = \{1, 2, 3, 4, 5, \ldots 25\}$$

$$n\ (S) = 25$$

Let A denote the event of getting a prime number.

$$A = \{2, 3, 5, 7, 11, 13, 17, 19, 23\}$$

$$n\ (A) = 9$$

$$P\ (A) = \frac{n(A)}{n(S)} = \frac{0}{10} = 0$$

EXAMPLE 13.6: A coin is tossed twice. Find the probability of getting exactly one head.

Solution: Sample space = $\{HH, TT, TH, HT\}$

Let A denote the event of getting exactly one head.

$$A = \{TH, HT\}$$
$$n(A) = 2$$
$$P(A) = \frac{n(A)}{n(S)} = \frac{2}{4} = \frac{1}{2}$$

EXAMPLE 13.7: Three horses A, B and C are in a race. A is twice as likely to win as B and B is twice as likely to win as C. What are their respective probabilities of winning? **[MBA, HPU, 2001]**

Solution: Let the probability of winning of horse $C = P$. Then the probability of winning of B and will be $2P$ and $4P$ respectively.

Since the events of winning of horses are mutually exclusive and exhaustive, we have

$$P + 2P + 4P = 1 \Rightarrow P = \frac{1}{7}$$

∴ Respective probabilities of winning of A, B, C are $\frac{4}{7}, \frac{2}{7}$ and $\frac{1}{7}$.

NOTE: In the above example the events are mutually exclusive because only one horse can win. The events are exhaustive because there is no other horse.

EXAMPLE 13.8: A, B and C are bidding for a contract. It is believed that A had exactly half the chance that B has, B in turn is $\frac{4}{5}$ as likely as C to win the contract. What is the probability for each to win the contract?

Solution:

Let $P(A)$ = probability that A wins the contract
$P(B)$ = probability that B wins the contract
$P(C)$ = probability that C wins the contract

Let $P(C) = p$, then $P(B) = \frac{4}{5}p$, $P(A) = \frac{2}{5}p$

Since there are only three persons bidding for a contract, and one and only one of them must win, the events, A, B, C can be taken as mutually exclusive and exhaustive.

$$\therefore \quad P(A) + P(B) + P(C) = 1 \Rightarrow p + \frac{4}{5}p + \frac{2}{5}p = 1$$

$$\Rightarrow \quad \frac{11p}{5} = 1 \Rightarrow p = \frac{5}{11}$$

$$\therefore \quad P(A) = \frac{2}{11}, P(B) = \frac{4}{11}, P(C) = \frac{5}{11}.$$

EXAMPLE 13.9: A man wants to marry a girl having qualities white complexion — The probability of having such a girl is 1 in twenty; Handsome dowry — the probability of getting this is one in fifty; Westernised manners and etiquettes, the probability here is one in hundred. Find out the probability of his getting married to such a girl when the possession of these three attributes is independent.

Solution: In other words, the question reduces to saying that there are three independent events, i.e., white complexion, handsome dowry and westernised manners and etiquettes and we are to find the probability that all these three events occur simultaneously.

$$\therefore \quad \text{Required probability} = \frac{1}{20} \times \frac{1}{50} \times \frac{1}{100} = 10^{-5}$$

EXAMPLE 13.10: From 20 tickets marked with first 20 numerals one is drawn at random, what is the probability that it is a multiple of 3 or 7.

Solution: In first 20 numerals multiples of 3 are 3, 6, 9, 12, 15, 18. Total numbers = 6 and multiples of 7 are 7, 14. Total numbers = 2

$$\text{Required Probability} = \frac{6+2}{20} = \frac{8}{20} = \frac{2}{5}$$

EXAMPLE 13.11: There are four hotels in a certain town. If three men check into hotels in a day. What is the probability that each checks into a different hotel.

Solution: Three persons can check into 4 hotels in 4 × 4 × 4 = 64 ways

The number of ways that three person check into 4 hotels, in such a way that each checks into a different hotel = 4 × 3 × 2 = 24 ways.

$$\text{Required probability} = \frac{24}{64} = \frac{3}{8}.$$

13.6 GENERAL COMPUTATIONAL PROBABILITY RULES

There are various laws that can ease our task of computing probabilities. In this section, we will discuss two of the fundamental laws of computing probabilities i.e., Addition law and Multiplication law.

13.6.1 Addition Theorem on Probabilities

We shall discuss the addition theorem on probabilities for mutually exclusive events and not mutually exclusive events.

(A) For Mutually Exclusive Events

If two events A and B are mutually exclusive, the probability of the occurrence of either A or B is the sum of individual probabilities of A and B. ie

$$\boxed{P(A \cup B) = P(A) + P(B)}$$

This is clearly stated in axioms of probability.

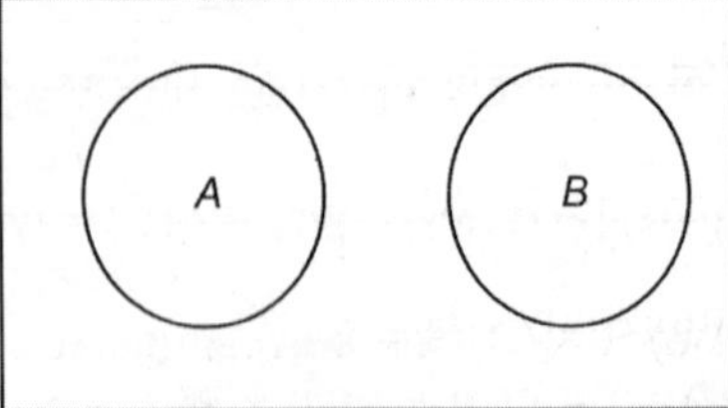

Fig. 13.8

NOTE: In case of three events A, B, C, $\quad P(A \cup B \cup C) = P(A) + P(B) + P(C)$

(B) For Non-Mutually Exclusive Events

If two events *A* and *B* are non-mutually exclusive, the probability of the event that either *A* or *B* or both occur is given as

$$\boxed{P(A \cup B) = P(A) + P(B) - P(A \cap B)}$$

Proof: Let us take a random experiment with a sample space *S* of *N* sample points. Then by the definition of probability,

$$P(A \cup B) = \frac{n(A \cup B)}{n(S)} = \frac{n(A \cup B)}{n}$$

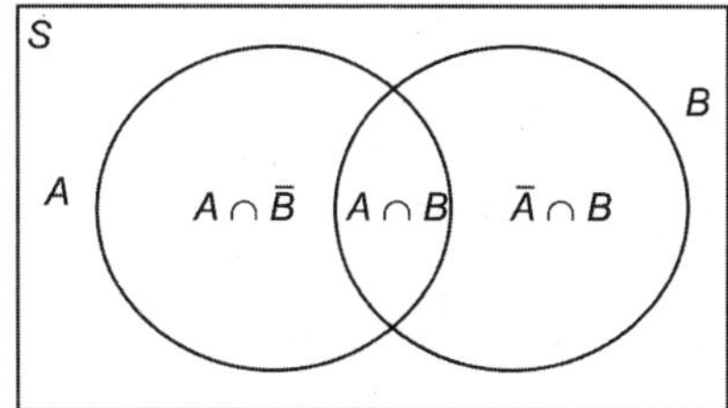

Fig. 13.9

From the diagram, using the axiom for the mutually exclusive events, we write

$$P(A \cup B) = \frac{n(A) + n(\bar{A} \cap B)}{n}$$

Adding and subtracting $(\bar{A} \cap B)$ in the numerator.

$$= \frac{n(A) + n(\bar{A} \cap B) + n(A \cap B) - n(A \cap B)}{n}$$

$$= \frac{n(A) + n(B) - n(A \cap B)}{n}$$

$$= \frac{n(A)}{n} + \frac{n(B)}{n} - \frac{n(A \cap B)}{n}$$

$$P(A \cup B) = P(A) + P(B) - P(A \cap B)$$

NOTE: In the case of three events *A*, *B*, *C*,

$$P(A \cup B \cup C) = P(A) + P(B) + P(C) - P(A \cap B) - P(A \cap B) - P(A \cap B)$$
$$+ P(B \cap C) + P(A \cap B \cap C)$$

EXAMPLE 13.12: Three coins are tossed together. Find the probability that either only 2 heads or only 2 tails turns up.

Solution: Sample space $(S) = \{HHH, TTT, THH, HTT, HTH, THT, HHT, TTH\}$

Let *A* denote the event of getting only 2 heads

$$A = \{THH, HTH, HHT\}$$

$$P(A) = \frac{n(A)}{n(S)} = \frac{3}{8}$$

Let B denote the event of getting only 2 tails.

$$B = \{HTT, THT, TTH\}$$

$$n(B) = 3$$

$$P(B) = \frac{n(B)}{n(S)} = \frac{3}{8}$$

Both the events are mutually exclusive.

$$P(A \cup B) = p(A) + p(B)$$

$$= \frac{3}{8} + \frac{3}{8} = \frac{6}{8} = \frac{3}{4}$$

Probability of getting only two heads or only two tails is 3/4.

EXAMPLE 13.13: Two dice are thrown together. What is the probability of getting a total 8 or a product 12.

Solution: For sample space refer example 13.2

We have, $n(S) = 36$

Let A denote the event of getting a total of 8.

$$A = \{(2, 6), (3, 5), (4, 4), (5, 3), (6, 2)\}$$

$$n(A) = 5$$

$$P(A) = \frac{n(A)}{n(S)} = \frac{5}{36}$$

Let B denote the event of getting a product of 12.

$$B = \{(2, 6), (3, 4), (4, 3), (6, 2)\}$$

$$n(B) = 4$$

$$P(B) = \frac{n(B)}{n(S)} = \frac{4}{36}$$

Now $A \cap B = \{(2,6), (6,2)\}$

$$n(A \cap B) = 2$$

$$P(A \cap B) = \frac{n(A \cap B)}{n(S)} = \frac{2}{36}$$

$$P(A \cup B) = P(I) + P(B) - P(A \cap B)$$

$$= \frac{5}{36} + \frac{4}{36} - \frac{2}{36} = \frac{7}{36}$$

Probability of getting a total 8 or a product 12 when two is 7/36

EXAMPLE 13.14: A number is selected at random from 40 to 80. Find the probability that it is divisible by 6 or 9.

Solution: Sample space $(S) = \{40, 41, ...80\}$

$$n(S) = 41$$

Let A denote the event of getting a number divisible by 6.

$$A = \{42, 48, 54, 60, 66, 72, 78\}$$

$$n(A) = 7$$

$$P(A) = \frac{n(A)}{n(S)} = \frac{7}{41}$$

Let B denote the event of getting a number divisible by 9.

$$B = \{45, 54, 63, 72\}$$

$$n(B) = 4$$

$$P(B) = \frac{n(B)}{n(S)} = \frac{4}{41}$$

We have, $A \cap B = \{54, 72\}$

$$n(A \cap B) = 2$$

$$P(A \cap B) = \frac{n(A \cap B)}{n(S)} = \frac{2}{41}$$

$$P(A \cup B) = P(A) + P(B) - P(A \cap B)$$

$$= \frac{7}{41} + \frac{4}{41} - \frac{2}{41}$$

$\therefore$ Required probability is $\frac{9}{41}$

EXAMPLE 13.15: It is 8 to 5 against a person who is now 40 years old living till he is 70 and 4 to 3 against a person now 50 living till he is 80. Find the probability that at least one of these persons would be alive 30 years hence. **[MBA, Anna University, 2002]**

Solution: Probability that a man now 40 years old will live till he is 70 = $\frac{5}{13}$ = $Pp(A)$ (say)

Probability that a man now 50 years old living till he is 80 = $\frac{3}{7}$ = $P(B)$ (say)

Then $P(A \cup E) - P(A) + P(B) - P(A \cap B)$

$$= \frac{5}{13} + \frac{3}{7} - \frac{5}{13} \times \frac{3}{7} = \frac{35 + 39 - 15}{91} = \frac{59}{91}.$$

EXAMPLE 13.16: A candidate is called for interview by the three companies. For the first company there are 12 candidates and for the there second are 15 candidates and for the third there are 10 candidates. What are the chances of his getting at least one of the components.

Solution: **[MBA, Madras Univ., 2003]**

Let $P(A)$ = Probability of getting first company by the candidate

$P(B)$ and $P(C)$ the probabilities of getting second and third company respectively then

$$P(A \cup B \cup C) = P(A) + P(B) + P(C) - P(A \cap B) - P(A \cap C) - P(B \cap C) + P(A \cap B \cap C)$$

$$= \frac{1}{12} + \frac{1}{15} + \frac{1}{10} - \frac{1}{12} \times \frac{1}{15} - \frac{1}{12} \times \frac{1}{10} - \frac{1}{15} \times \frac{1}{10} + \frac{1}{12} \times \frac{1}{15} \times \frac{1}{10}$$

$$= \frac{150 + 120 + 180 - 10 - 15 - 12 + 1}{1800} = \frac{144}{1800} = \frac{207}{900}.$$

EXAMPLE 13.17: City residents were surveyed recently to determine readership of newspapers available. 50% of the residents read the morning paper, 60% read the evening paper and 20% read both newspapers. Find the probability that a resident selected read either the morning or evening paper or both the papers.

Solution: Let A and B represent that the resident read morning and evening paper respectively.

Then $$P(A) = 0.50;\ P(B) = 0.60 \text{ and } P(A \cap B) = 0.20$$

The probability that the resident reads either the morning or evening or both the papers is given by

$$P(A \cup B) = P(A) + P(B) - P(A \cap B) = 0.50 + 0.60 - 0.20 = 0.90.$$

EXAMPLE 13.18: A can solve 80% of the problems given in Statistics book, B can solve 6-%. What is the probability that at least one of them will solve a problem selected at random?

Solution: This type of question can be solved in three ways. **[M.Com., MK, Univ., 2005]**

Method 1:

Probability that A cannot solve the problem = 1 – 0.80 = 0.20
Probability that B cannot solve the problem = 1 – 0.6 = 0.4
Probability that A and B both cannot solve the problem = 0.20 × 0.40 = 0.08
Probability that at least one of them will solve the problem = 1 – 0.08 = 0.92.

Method 2:

Probability that both will solve the problem = 0.8 × 0.6 = 0.48 [∴ events are independent]
Probability that at least one of them will solve the problem

$$P(A \cup B) = P(A) + P(B) - P(A \cap B) = 0.8 + 0.6 - 0.48 = 0.92.$$

Method 3:

Required probability = Probability that A will solve the problem but not B + Probability that B will solve the problem but not A + probability that A and B both will solve the problem

$$= 0.8 \times 0.4 + 0.6 \times 0.2 + 0.48 = 0.32 + 0.12 + 0.48 = 0.92.$$

EXAMPLE 13.19: The probability that a trainee will remain with a company is 0.8. The probability that an employee earns more than Rs 20,000 per year is 0.4. The probability that an employee, who was a trainee and remained with the company or who earns more than Rs 20,000 per year is 0.9.

What is the probability that an employee earns more than Rs 20,000 per year given that he is a trainee who stayed with the company?

Solution: Let A be the event that a trainee will remain with the company and B the event that an employee earns more than Rs 20,000 per year. Then

$$P(A) = 0.8,\ P(B) = 0.4 \text{ and } P(A \cup B) = 0.9$$

$$P(A \cup B) = P(A) + P(B) - P(A \cap B)$$

$$\Rightarrow \quad P(A \cap B) = P(A) + P(B) - P(A \cup B)$$

$$= 0.8 + 0.4 - 0.9 = 0.3$$

$$P(B/A) = \frac{P(A \cap B)}{P(A)} = \frac{3}{8}$$

EXAMPLE 13.20: The Nickels restaurant chain regularly conducts surveys of its customers. Respondents are asked to assess food quality, service, and price. The responses are

Excellent Good Fair

They are also asked whether they would come back. After analysing the responses, an expert in probability determined that 76% of customers say that they will return. Of those who so indicate, 57% rate the restaurant as excellent, 36% rate it as good, and the remainder rate is as fair. Of those who say tht they won't return, the probabilities are 14%, 32% snd 54% respectively. What proportion of customers rate the restaurant as good?

Solution: Let B_1 be the event that the customer say he will come back, B_2 the event that the customer says he will not come back. Let A be the event that the customer rate the Restaurant as good. Then,

$$P(B_1) = 0.76,\ P(B_2) = 1 - 0.76 = 0.24,\ P(A/B_1) = 0.36,\ P(A/B_2) = 0.32$$

$$\text{Required Probability} = 0.76 \times 0.36 + 0.24 \times 0.32$$

$$= 0.2736 + 0.0768 = 0.3504$$

EXAMPLE 13.21: The probability that a contractor will get a plumbing contract is 2/3, and the probability that he will not get an electric contract is 5/9. If the probability of getting at least one contract is 4/5 what is the probability that he will get both the contracts?

Solution: Let A and B denote the events of getting the plumbing and electric contracts respectively, then

$$P(A) = \text{The probability that the contractor will plumbing contract} = \frac{2}{3}$$

$$P(B) = \text{The probability that the contractor will get electric contract} = 1 - \frac{5}{9} = \frac{4}{9}$$

$$\text{The probability that the contractor will get at least one contractor} = P(A \cup B) = \frac{4}{5}$$

$$P(A \text{ or } B) = P(A) + P(B) - P(A \cap B) = \frac{4}{5}$$

or
$$\frac{2}{3} + \frac{4}{9} - P(A \cap B) = \frac{4}{5}$$

$$P(A \cap B) \text{ or } P(AB) = \frac{2}{3} + \frac{4}{9} - \frac{4}{5} = \frac{30 + 20 - 36}{45} = \frac{14}{45}.$$

Thus the probability of the contractor getting both the contracts is 14/45.

EXAMPLE 13.22: The probability that a student passes English test is 2/3, the probability that he passes both English and Technical test is 11/15 . The probability that he passes atleast one test is 1/3. What is the probability that he passes the Technical test?

Solution : Given $P(E) = \frac{2}{3},\quad P(E \cap T) = \frac{11}{15}$ and $P(E \cup T) = \frac{1}{3}$

Where E stands for English T stands for Technical.

$$P(E \cup T) = \frac{1}{3}$$

$$P(E \cup T) = P(E) + P(T) - P(E \cap T) \Rightarrow \frac{1}{3} = \frac{2}{3} + P(T) - \frac{11}{15}$$

$$P(T) = \frac{2}{5}$$

Probability that the student passes the technical test is 2/5.

13.6.2 Multiplication Theorem on Probabilities

We shall discuss multiplication theorem on probabilities for both independent and dependent events.

(A) For Independent Events

If two events A and B are independent, the probability that both of them occur is equal to the product of their individual probabilities. i.e

$$\boxed{P(A \cap B) = P(A) \cdot P(B)}$$

Proof: Out of n_1 possible cases let m_1 cases be favourable for the occurrence of the event A.

$$\therefore \qquad P(A) = \frac{m_1}{n_1}$$

Out of n_2 possible cases, let m_2 cases be favourable for the occurrence of the event B

$$\therefore \qquad P(B) = \frac{m_2}{n_2}$$

Each of n_1 possible cases can be associated with each of the n_2 possible cases.

Therefore the total number of possible cases for the occurrence of the event 'A' and 'B' is $n_1 \times n_2$. Similarly each of the m_1 favourable cases can be associated with each of the m_2 favourable cases. So the total number of favourable cases for the event 'A' and 'B' is $m_1 \times m_2$

$$\therefore \qquad P(A \cap B) = \frac{m_1 n_1}{n_1 n_2} = \frac{m_1}{n_1}\frac{m_2}{n_2} = P(A)\,P(B)$$

NOTES:

1. The theorem can be extended to three or more independent events. If A, B, C....... be independent events, then
$$P(A \cap B \cap C.......) = P(A) \cdot P(B) \cdot P(C).......$$
2. If A and B are independent then the complements of A and B are also independent. i.e
$$P(\bar{A} \cap \bar{B}) = P(\bar{A})\,P(\bar{B})$$

(B) For Dependent Events

If A and B be two dependent events, i.e the occurrence of one event is affected by the occurrence of the other event, then the probability that both A and B will occur is

$$\boxed{P(A \cap B) = P(A)P(B/A)}$$

or

$$\boxed{P(A \cap B) = P(A/B) \cdot P(B)}$$

Proof: Suppose an experiment results in n exhaustive, mutually exclusive and equally likely outcomes, m of them being favourable to the occurrence of the event A.

Out of these n outcomes let m_1 be favourable to the occurrence of another event B.

Then the outcomes favourable to the happening of the events 'A and B' are m_1.

$$\therefore \qquad P(A \cap B) = \frac{m_1}{n} = \frac{m_1}{n} \times \frac{m}{m} = \frac{mm_1}{nn_1} = \frac{m}{n} \times \frac{m_1}{m}$$

$$\therefore \qquad P(A \cap B) = P(A) \cdot P(B/A)$$

NOTE: In the case of three events A, B, C.

$$P(A \cap B \cap C) = P(A) \, . \, P(B/A) \cdot P(C/A \cap B).$$

ie., the probability of occurrence of A, B and C is equal to the probability of A times the probability of B given that A has occurred, times the probability of C given that both A and B have occurred.

EXAMPLE 13.23: A candidate is selected for interview of management trainees for 3 companies. For the first company there are 12 candidates, for the second there re 15 candidates and for the third there are 10 candidates. What are the chances of his getting job at least at one of the company?

Solution: The probability that the candidate gets the job at least at one company = 1 – probability that the candidates does not get the job in any company.

Probability that the candidate does not get the job in the first company = $1 - \frac{1}{12} = \frac{11}{12}$

Probability that the candidate does not get the job in the second company = $1 - \frac{1}{15} = \frac{14}{15}$

Probability that the candidate does not get the job in the third company = $1 - \frac{1}{10} = \frac{9}{10}$

Since the events are independent, therefore, the probability that the candidate does not get any job in any of the three companies = $\frac{11}{12} \times \frac{14}{15} \times \frac{9}{10} = \frac{231}{300} = 0.77$

Hence the required probability = 1 – 0.77 = 0.23.

13.7 CONDITIONAL PROBABILITY

Let A be any event with $p(A) > 0$. The probability that an event B occurs subject to the condition that A has already occurred is known as the conditional probability of occurrence of the event B on the assumption that the event A has already occurred and is denoted by the symbol $p(B/\text{A})$ or $p(B/A)$ and is read as the probability of B given A.

The same definition can be given as follows also: Two events A and B are said to be dependent when A can occur only when B is known to have occurred (or vice versa). The probability attached to such an event is called the ***conditional probability*** and is denoted by $P(B/A)$ or, in other words, probability of B given that A has occurred

A conditional probability is denoted by $P(A/B)$. This phrase is read: the probability that A will occur **given that** B is known to have occurred.

Conditional probabilities are based on knowledge of one of the variables. The conditional probability of an event, such as A, occurring given that another event, such as B, has occurred is expressed as:

$$P\left(\frac{A}{B}\right) = \frac{P(A \cap B)}{P(B)} \qquad P(B) \neq 0$$

Similarly

$$P\left(\frac{B}{A}\right) = \frac{P(A \cap B)}{P(A)} \qquad P(A) \neq 0$$

provided $P(B)$ is not zero. Note that when using the conditional rule of probability, you always divide the joint probability by the probability of the event after the word given. Thus, to get $P(A$ given $B)$, you divide the joint probability of A and B by the unconditional probability of B. In other words, the above equation is used to find the conditional probability for any two **dependent** events.

NOTE: If two events, such as A and B, are **independent,** that is the probability of occurrence of any one of them

$$P(A/B) = P(A)$$

and

$$P(B/A) = P(B)$$

13.8 BAYES' THEOREM

The concept of conditional probability discussed earlier takes into account information about the occurrence of one event to predict the probability of another event. This concept can be extended to revise probabilities based on new information and to determine the probability that a particular effect was due to specific cause. The procedure for revising these probabilities is known as Bayes theorem.

The Principle was given by ***Thomas Bayes*** in 1763. By this principle, assuming certain prior probabilities, the posteriori probabilities are obtained. That is why Bayes' probabilities are also called posteriori probabilities.

Let $A_1, A_2, A_3, \ldots\ldots A_i, \ldots\ldots$An be a set of n mutually exclusive and collectively exhaustive events and $P(A_1), P(A_2) \ldots, P(A_n)$ are their corresponding probabilities. If B is another event such that $P(B)$ is not zero and the priori probabilities $P(B|A_i)$ $i = 1,2\ldots, n$ are also known. Then

$$P(A_i / B) = \frac{P(A_i / B)\, P(B / A_i)}{\sum_{i=1}^{n} P(A_i)\, P(B / A_i)}$$

$$= \frac{P(A_i)\,(B / A_i)}{P(A_1)\, P(B / A_1) + P(A_2)\, P(B / A_2) + \ldots P(A_n)\, P(B / A_n)}$$

EXAMPLE 13.24: Suppose a black ball has been drawn from one of three bags, the first containing three black balls and seven white, the second black balls and three white, the third eight black balls and four white: what is the probability that it was drawn from the first bag? **[MBA, Vikram Univ., 2002]**

Solution: Let B_1, B_2 and B_3 are the events that first, second and third bags respectively are selected. Let A be the event that ball drawn in Black.

Then $$P(B_1) = P(B_2) = P(B_3) = \frac{1}{3}$$

$P(A / B_1)$ = Probability of drawing a black ball given that first bag is selected $= \dfrac{3}{10}$

$$P(A / B_2) = \frac{5}{8},\ P(A / B_3) = \frac{8}{12}$$

$$P(B_1/ A) = \frac{P(B_1)\, P(A/B_1)}{P(B_1)\, P(A/B_1) + P(B_2)\, P(A/B_2) + P(B_3)\, p(A/B_3)}$$

$$= \frac{\frac{1}{3} \times \frac{3}{10}}{\frac{1}{3} \times \frac{3}{10} + \frac{1}{3} + \frac{5}{8} + \frac{1}{3} \times \frac{8}{12}} = \frac{36}{191}$$

EXAMPLE 13.25: A company launches an advertising campaign of its new product on TV, radio and in print media in an area where 30% watch TV, 50% listen to the radio and the rest rely on newspapers for all information. It is estimated that a person who sees the advertisement on TV will buy the product with probability 0.6. A person who has heard it on radio is expected to buy the product with probability 0.3 and seeing the advertisement in print will convince a person to buy the product with probability 0.1. A consumer, chosen at random, is found to have purchased the product. What is the probability she heard about the product on radio? **[MBA, DU, 1999]**

Solution: Let B_1, B_2 and B_3 be the events that the campaign is done on TV, radio and in print media. Let A be the event that the person will buy the product. Then

$$P(B_1) = 0.3,\ P(B_2) = 0.5 \text{ and } P(B_3) = 0.2$$

$$P(A/\ B_1) = 0.6,\ P(A/\ B_2) = 0.3,\ P(A\ /\ B_3) = 0.1$$

$$P(B_2\ /\ A) = \frac{P(B_2)\,P(A/B_2)}{P(B_1)\,P(A/B_1) + P(B_2)\,P(A/B_2) + P(B_3)\,P(A/B_3)}$$

$$= \frac{0.5 \times 0.3}{0.3 \times 0.6 + 0.5 \times 0.3 + 0.2 \times 0.1} = \frac{0.15}{0.18 + 0.15 + 0.02}$$

$$= \frac{0.15}{0.35} = \frac{3}{7} = 0.428$$

EXAMPLE 13.26: A speaks the truth 2 out of 3 times and *B*, 4 out of 5 times. They agree that from a bag of 6 balls of different colours, a black ball has been drawn. Find the probability that the statement is true.

Solution: They will agree when both of them tell a lie or speak the truth.

Probability that both of them tell a lie $= \frac{1}{3} \times \frac{1}{5} \times \frac{1}{6}$

Probability that both of them speak truth $= \frac{2}{3} \times \frac{4}{5} \times \frac{1}{6}$

$$\text{Required Probability} = \frac{\frac{2}{3} \times \frac{4}{5} \times \frac{1}{6}}{\frac{2}{3} \times \frac{4}{5} \times \frac{1}{6} + \frac{1}{3} \times \frac{1}{5} \times \frac{1}{6}} = \frac{8}{9}$$

EXAMPLE 13.27: Suppose the probability that a particular student will get a first division in the annual examination is $\frac{1}{10}$. Suppose he appeared in 10 class tests and obtained first division in 4 of them. What is the probability now that the student will get a first division in the annual examination?

Solution:

Let stand for getting first division in annual examination. Then

$$P(A) = \frac{1}{10} \text{ and } P(\text{Not } A) = \frac{9}{10}$$

These are prior probabilities.

Let B stand for the probability of getting first division in class tests. When the probability of getting a first division in the annual examination is known. Then

$$P(B/A) = \frac{4}{10} \text{ and } P(B/\text{No. } 4) = \frac{6}{10}$$

Thus $$P(A) = \frac{1}{10},\ P(\text{Not } A) = \frac{9}{10},\ P(B/A) = \frac{4}{10},\ P(B\ /\ \text{Not } A) = \frac{6}{10}$$

Now the posterior probability of getting a first division in the annual examination (after knowing the results of the class-tests) would be

$$P(A\ /\ B) = \frac{P(A)\ P(B\ /\ A)}{P(A)\ P(B\ /\ A)\ +(\text{not } A)\ P(B\ /\text{not } A)}$$

$$= \frac{\frac{1}{10} \times \frac{4}{10}}{\left(\frac{1}{10} \times \frac{4}{10}\right) + \left(\frac{9}{10} \times \frac{5}{10}\right)} = \frac{4/100}{58/100} = \frac{4}{58} = 0.069$$

The prior probability was $\frac{1}{10}$ or 0.1

The posterior probability is $\frac{4}{58}$ or 0.069

The posterior probability is thus revised downwards. The result of the candidate in class-tests has adversary affected the chances of his getting first division at the annual examination.

EXAMPLE 13.28: Suppose the probability of A' s winning a prize in a Lottery is $\frac{1}{10}$. Suppose C, who speaks truth 2 times out of 3 informs A that he has won a prize. What is the probability the A has actually won a prize after C's information. **[MBA, Mangalore Univ.]**

Solution: Let B_1 be the event that A wins prize and B_2 the event that A does not win the prize. Let S be the event that C reports that A has won the prize $P(B_1) = \frac{1}{10}$, $P(B_2) = \left(1 - \frac{1}{10}\right) = \frac{9}{10}$

$P(S\ /B_1)$ = Conditional Probability that C reports that A has won when A has actually won = $\frac{2}{3}$

$P(S\ /B_2)$ = Conditional Probability that C reports that A has won when A has not actually won = $\frac{1}{3}$

$P(B_1/S)$ = Conditional Probability that has won when C is known to have reported that A has won

$$= \frac{P(B_1)\ P(S\ /\ B_1)}{P(B_1)\ P(S\ /\ B_1)\ +P(B_2)\ P(S\ /\ B_2)} = \frac{\frac{1}{10} \times \frac{2}{3}}{\frac{1}{10} \times \frac{2}{3} + \frac{9}{10} \times \frac{1}{3}} = \frac{\frac{1}{15}}{\frac{11}{30}} = \frac{2}{11}.$$

EXAMPLE 13.29: A Certain production process produces items that are 10% defective. Each item is inspected before being supplied to customers but the inspector incorrectly classifies an item 10% of the time. Only items classified as good are supplied. If 820 items in all are supplied, how many of them are expected to be defective.

Solution: There are two cases

(i) The item is good and the inspector also declared is good for which the

$$\text{Probability} = \frac{9}{10} \times \frac{9}{10} = \frac{81}{100}$$

(ii) The item is defective and the inspector declares in good for which the

$$\text{Probability} = \frac{1}{10} \times \frac{1}{10} = \frac{1}{100}$$

The number of defective items supplied in a lot of 820 items $= 820 \times \dfrac{\frac{1}{100}}{\frac{81}{100} + \frac{1}{100}} = 10.$

Second Method:

This question can be done by Baye's theorem also. Let B_1, B_2 be the events that item is acceptable and not acceptable, then

$P(B_1) = \dfrac{9}{10}$ = Probability that the item is acceptable,

$P(B_2) = \dfrac{1}{10}$ = Probability that the item is defective or unacceptable.

Let A be the event that the inspector declares the item as good.

$P(A / B_1)$ = The conditional probability that item is declared as good by the inspector when the item is actually good

$= \dfrac{9}{10}$

$P(A / B_2) = \dfrac{1}{10}$

= Conditional Probability that the inspector declares the items as good when the item is actually defective.

$P(B_2 / A)$ = Conditional Probability that item is supplied (declared good by the inspector) when the item is defective.

$$= \frac{P(B_2)\, P(A/B_2)}{P(B_1)\, P(A/B_1) + P(B_2)\, P(A/B_2)}$$

$$= \frac{\frac{1}{10} \times \frac{1}{10}}{\frac{9}{10} \times \frac{9}{10} + \frac{1}{10} \times \frac{1}{10}} = \frac{1}{82}$$

= No. of defective item supplied as good in 820 items

$$= \frac{1}{82} \times 820 = 10.$$

13.9 BASIC RULES OF PROBABILITY

1. Mutually exclusive	No overlapping events if one event happens the other one can't occur at the same time	The probability of *A* occurring or the probability of *B* occurring	Special rule of addition	$p(A \text{ or } B) = p(A) + P(B)$
2. Not mutually exclusive (Joint/ compound)	Overlapping/Concurrent events-two or more events happened at the same time	The probability that either *A* may occur or *B* may occur followed by the possibility that both *A* and *B* may occur	General rule of addition	$p(A \text{ or } B) = p(A) + P(B) - p(A \text{ and } B)$
3. Independent	The occurence of event *A* has no effect on the occurence of another event *B*	The probability that *A* and *B* will occur	Special rule of multiplication	$p(A \text{ and } B) = p(A \text{ and } B) = p(A)\,P(B)$
4. Conditional	Dependent events-the probability of a particular event occurring given that	$p(B/A)$-probability that event *B* will occur given that event *A* has already occurred	General rule of multiplication	$p(A \text{ and } B) = p(A)\,P(B\|A)$
5. Complement	All events in the sample space that are not part of the specified event-determined by subtracting the probability of an event not happening from the probability of happening	Event not occurring or Neither/nor will happen	Complement rule	$p(A) = 1 - p(\sim A)$

Some Common Business Application Problem

EXAMPLE 13.30: The two most common primary causes of death in the US are heart attack and cancer. Heart attack is the cause for one-third (0.33) of the Americans who die each year and cancer is the cause for one-fifth (0.20) of the deaths each year. If 2003 is like 2002, the probability that a randomly selected American will die of either a heart attack or cancer is the sum of these two probabilities.

0.33 + 0.20 = 0.53. [Special Rule of Addition].

EXAMPLE 13.31: If 90% of the Citibank customers have a saving account, 40% have a market rate account, and 60% have both, the probability that a randomly selected Citibank customer will have either saving or market rate account will be computed as:

0.90 + 0.40 – 0.60 = 0.70 [General Rule of Addition].

EXAMPLE 13.32: Suppose the probability that a student gets an "*A*" grade is **0.50** in statistics and **0.60** in History. Assume that the grade received in statistics is independent of the grade received in History. The probability that the student will receive an "*A*" grade in both subjects (statistics and History) is computed as:

(0.50) *x* (0.60) = 0.30 [Special Rule of Multiplication].

EXAMPLE 13.33: Two traffic lights on Broadway Road operate independently. Your probability of being stopped at the first one is 0.4 and your probability of being stopped at the second one is 0.7.

The probability of being stopped at:

(A) both lights = **0.4 × 0.7 = 0.28** (B) neither light = **0.6 × 0.3 = 0.18**
(C) the first but not the second = **0.4 × 0.3 = 0.12**
(D) the second but not the first = **0.7 × 0.6 = 0.42**

EXAMPLE 13.34: Three defective electric toothbrushes were accidentally shipped to a drugstore by Clean-brush products along with 17 non-defective ones.

(A) What is the probability that the first two electric toothbrushes sold will be returned to the drugstore because they are defective?

(3/20) + (2/19) = 6/380 = 0.01579 [General Rule of Multiplication].

(B) What is the probability that the first two electric toothbrushes sold will not be defective?

(17/20) + (16/19) = 272/380 = 0.7158 [General Rule of Multiplication].

EXAMPLE 13.35: Suppose the probability that mortgage loans are approved by lenders in your state is 0.70 (70%). By the complement rule, the probability that loans may not be approved for a randomly selected applicant is 0.30 (30%). **1 – .70 = .30**

EXAMPLE 13.36: An airline company completed an on-board passenger survey of 400 customers in an attempt to measure the number of bags checked by those traveling on business or for pleasure. Results are shown in the table below:

Passenger	0 Checked	1 Checked	2 Checked	3 or more	Total
Business	50	60	30	10	**150**
Pleasure	20	80	90	60	**250**
Total	**70**	**140**	**120**	**70**	**400**

1. The probability that a customer checks exactly 2 bags

   120/400 = **0.30**

2. The probability that a passenger who responded to the survey was a business customer is

   150/400 = **0.375**

3. The probability that a customer checked fewer than 2 bags

   70/400 + 140/400 = 210/400 = **0.525**

4. The probability that a customer checked more than one bag is

   120/400 + 70/400 = 190/400 = **0.47**

The breakdown of the simple and joint probabilities can be displayed graphically using the *tree diagram*.

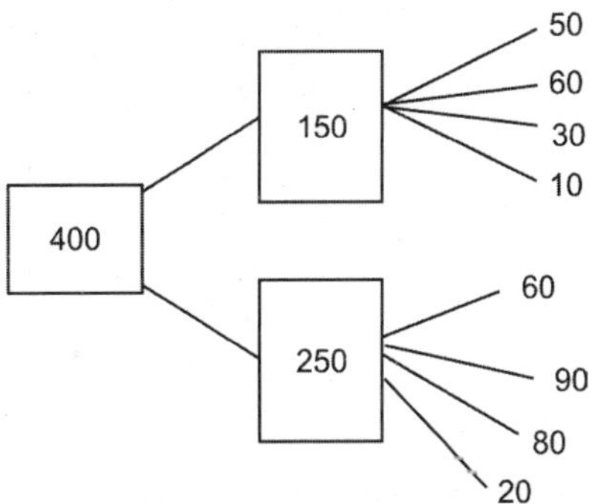

Fig. 13.10: Tree Diagram for Airlines Passengers

EXAMPLE 13.37: Suppose two machines *A* and *B*, produce identical parts. Machine A has probability 0.1 of producing a defective each time, whereas Machine *B* has probability 0.4 of producing a defective. Each machine produces one part. One of these parts is selected at random, tested, and found to be defective. What is the probability that it was produced by Machine *B*?

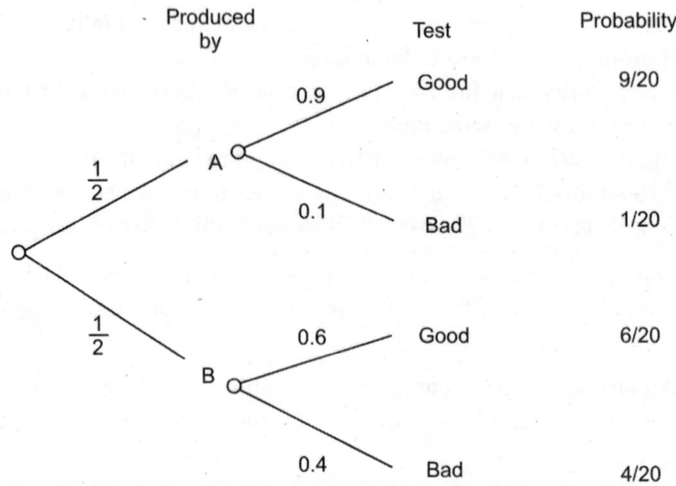

Fig. 13.11: Conditional Probabilities

Probability Tree Diagrams depict events or sequences of events as branches of a tree. Tree diagrams are useful for visualizing the conditional probabilities:

The probabilities at the end of each branch are the probability that events leading to that end will happen simultaneously. The above tree diagram indicates that the probability of a part testing Good is 9/20 + 6/20 = 3/4, therefore the probability of Bad is 1/4. Thus, *P*(made by *B*|it is bad) = (4/20)/(1/4) = **4/5**.

Now using the Bayes' Rule we are able to obtain useful information such as:

P(it is bad | made by *B*) = 1/4(4/5) / [1/4(4/5) + 3/4(2/5)] = **2/5**.

Equivalently, using the above conditional probability, results in:

P(it is bad | made by *B*) = *P*(it is bad and made by *B*) / *P*(made by *B*) = (4/20) / (1/2) = **2/5**.

EXAMPLE 13.38: A surveys show that 70% of all convenience store shoppers buy milk and 55% buy bread. If 45% buy both bread and milk, what percentage buys neither?

Solution: The Venn diagram model for this problem is depicted below:

The solution is readily available from the above Venn diagram model, i.e.

P [buy neither] = 1 – [0.25 + 0.45 + 0.1]
= **20%**

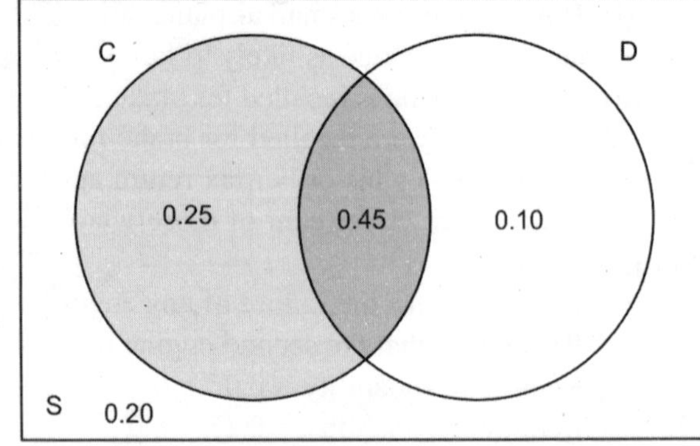

Fig. 13.12: (A) Probability Diagram

Another approach is to use both, first the Complement Probability Rule and then the Addition Probability Rule, i.e.

P [buy neither] = 1 – *P*[bread OR milk] = 1 - [0.70 + 0.55 – 0.45] = **20%**

It is up to you to decide which approach is "nicer" and more transparent.

EXAMPLE 13.39:

(i) The traffic light at a certain road crossing is set in the following fashion. It starts green at 06 : 00 and continues to be green till 6 : 02 and again turns green at 6 : 06 and continues green till 6 : 08. This cycle is repeated throughout the day. What percentage of the time during any given hour, traffic light will be green?

(ii) If your arrival time at this crossing is random and uniform over the interval 16 : 55 to 17 : 05, what is the probability that you will have to stop at this light?

Solution:

(i) In every 6 minutes the light remains green for 2 minutes.

$$\text{Required percentage} = \frac{2}{6} \times 100 = 33.3\%$$

(ii) During 16:55 to 17:05 the light will remain green for three minutes and the total interval is 10 minutes. Required Probability $= \dfrac{10 - 3}{10} = 0.7.$

EXAMPLE 13.40: The probability that a driver stopping at a petrol station will have his car tyres checked is 0.012, the probability that he will have oil checked is 0.29 and probability that he will have both oil and tyres checked is 0.07. What is the probability that a driver stopping at this station will have neither his car tyres nor oil checked?

Solution: Let A be the event that the driver will have tyres checked and *B* the event that he will have Petrol checked.

$P(A \cup B)$ = Probability that he will either get tyres checked or oil checked.

$= P(A) + P(B) - P(A \cap B) = 0.012 + 0.29 - 0.07 = 0.232$

Required Probability $= 1 - P(A \cup B)$

$= 1 - 0.232 = 0.768.$

EXAMPLE 13.41: Determine the probability that:

(i) Both engines on a small airplane fail, given that each engine fails with probability 0.05 and that an engine is twice as likely to fail when it is the only engine working.

(ii) An automobile is recalled for brake failure and has steering problems, given that 15 per cent of that model were recalled for brake failure and 2 per cent has steering problems.

(iii) A citizen files his or her tax return and cheats on it, given that 70 per cent of all citizens file returns and 25 per cent of those who file cheat. **[M.Com., AMU, 1996]**

Solution:

(i) Probability for the failure of any engine = 0.05

Probability that the second engine fails when one engine has already failed = $0.05 \times 2 = 0.1$

Required Probability $= 0.05 \times 0.1 = 0.005$

(ii) Required Probability $= 0.15 \times 0.02 = 0.03$

(iii) Required Probability $= 0.7 \times 0.25 = 0.175$

EXAMPLE 13.42 : An anti-aircraft gun can take maximum of four shots of an enemy plane moving away from it. The probabilities the plane at the first, second, third and fourth shot are 0.4, 0.3, 0.2 and 0.2 respectively. What is the probability that the plane gets hit?

Solution: Plane gets hit if at least one of the shorts hits

$$\begin{aligned}\text{Required Probability} &= 1 - \text{None of the shots hit}\\ &= 1 - (1 - 0.4)\ (1 - 0.3)\ (1 - 0.2)\ (1 - 0.2)\\ &= 1 - 0.6 \times 0.7 \times 0.8 \times 0.8 = 1 - 0.2688 = 0.7312.\end{aligned}$$

EXAMPLE 13.43: The results of an investigation by an expert on a fire accident are summarised below:

(i) The probability that there could have been a short circuit = 0.8
(ii) The probability of LPG explosion in a cylinder = 0.2
(iii) Chance of fire accident is 30% given a short circuit and 95% of given an LPG explosion.

Based on these what do you think is the most probable cause of fire. **[B.Com. (Hons.) DU, 2007]**

Solution: $P\ (SC) = 0.8$, p (LPGE) = 0.2

Let A denotes the event of fire accident then

$$P\ (A\ /SC) = 0.3, \quad P\ (A/LPGE) = 0.95$$

$$P\ (SC)\ P\ (A/SC) = 0.8 \times 0.3 = 0.24$$

$$P\ (LPGE)\ P\ (A/LPGE) = 0.2 \times 0.95 = 0.19$$

∴ The most probable cause of fire accident is short circuit.

EXAMPLE 13.44:

(a) The chances that a famous tutor will train a student is 70%. The chances that the student will improve by his coaching and get selected for the engineering stream is 60%. The chances that the student getting selected even if he does not get the assistance of the coach is 20%.
  (i) What is the probability that the student gets selected?
  (ii) If the student has been selected, what is the probability that he has been assisted by that tutor?

(b) In a college it is observed tht 60% of all students play cricket and 40% of all students play football. Both games are played by 24% of all students. If a student is selected at random, what is the probability that he will
  (i) Play cricket or football?
  (ii) Play neither of the sports?

Solution:

(a) Probability of getting coached = $P\ (C) = 0.70$

Probability of not getting coached = $P\ (NC) = 0.3$

Probability that the student has been selected, given that he has been coached by the particular tutor = $P\ (S\ /C) = 0.60$

Probability that the student has been selected, given that he has not been coached by the particular tutor = $P\ (S/NC) = 0.20$

(i) $P\ (S)$ = Probability of being selected = $P\ (C) \times P\ (S\ /\ C) + P\ (NC) \times P\ (S\ /\ NC)$

$$= 0.70 \times 0.60 + 0.30 \times 0.20 = 0.42 + 0.06 = 0.48$$

(ii) $\dfrac{0.42}{0.48} = \dfrac{7}{8}$

(b) The Probability that the student plays cricket = 0.6
The Probability that the student plays football = 0.4
The Probability that the student plays both the games = 0.24.

13.10 PRINCIPAL OF PERMUTATION AND COMBINATION

Factorial

The consecutive product of first n natural numbers is known as ***factorial n*** and is denoted as ***n*!**.

That is $n! = 1 * 2 * 3 * 4 * 5 *...* n$

$3! = 3 * 2 * 1$

$4! = 4 * 3 * 2 * 1$

$5! = 5 * 4 * 3 * 2 * 1$

Also $5! = 5 * (4 * 3 *2 * 1) = 5 * (4!)$

Therefore this can be algebraically written as $n! = n * (n - 1)!$

Note that $1! = 1$ and $0! = 1$.

Permutations

Permutation means arrangement of things in different ways. Out of three things A, B, C taking two at a time, we can arrange them in the following manner.

$AB \quad BA$

$AC \quad CA$

$BC \quad CB$

Here we find 6 arrangements. In these arrangements order of arrangement is considered. The arrangement AB and the other arrangement BA are different.

The number of arrangements of the above is given as the number of permutations of 3 things taken 2 at a time which gives the value 6. This is written symbolically, ${}^3P_2 = 6$

Thus the number of arrangements that can be made out of n things taken r at a time is known as the number of permutation of n things taken r at a time and is denoted as ${}^nP_r$.

The expansion of ${}^nP_r$ is given below:

$${}^nP_r = n\,(n-1)(n-2)\ \ldots\ldots\ldots\ldots\ldots[n \quad (r \quad 1)]$$

The same can be written in factorial notation as follows:

$${}^nP_r = \frac{n!}{(n-r)!}$$

For example, to find ${}^{10}P_3$ we write this as follows:

$${}^{10}P_3 = 10\,(10 - 1)\,(10-2) = 10 \times 9 \times 8 = 720$$

To find ${}^{10}P_3$, Start with 10, write the product of 3 consecutive natural numbers in the descending order.

Simplifying ${}^{10}P_3$ using factorial notation.

$${}^{10}P_3 = \frac{10!}{(10-3)!} = \frac{10 \times 9 \times 8 \times 7 \times 6 \times 5 \times 4 \times 3 \times 2 \times 1}{7 \times 6 \times 5 \times 4 \times 3 \times 2 \times 1} = 10 \times 9 \times 8 = 720$$

Note that ${}^nP_o = 1$, ${}^nP_1 = n$, ${}^nP_n = n!$

Combinations

A combination is a selection of objects without considering the order of arrangements.

For example, out of three things *A*, *B*, *C* we have to select two things at a time.

This can be selected in three different ways as follows:

AB *AC* *BC*

Here the selection of the object *A B* and *B A* are one and the same. Hence the order of arrangement is not considered in combination. Here the number of combinations from 3 different things taken 2 at a time is 3.

This is written symbolically ${}^3C_2 = 3$

Thus the number of combination of n different things, taken

r at a time is given by ${}^nC_r = \frac{{}^nP_r}{r!}$

or $${}^nC_r = \frac{n!}{(n-r)!r!}$$

Note that ${}^nC_0 = 1$, ${}^nC_1 = n$, ${}^nC_n = 1$

Find ${}^{10}C_3$. $${}^{10}C_3 = \frac{{}^{10}P_3}{3!} = \frac{10 \times 9 \times 8}{1 \times 2 \times 3} = 120$$

Find ${}^8C_4$ $${}^8C_4 = \frac{8 \times 7 \times 6 \times 5}{1 \times 2 \times 3 \times 4} = 70$$

NOTE: To find ${}^8C_4$: In the numerator, first write the product of 4 natural numbers starting with 8 in descending order and in the denominator write the factorial 4 and then simplify.

Compare ${}^{10}C_8$ and ${}^{10}C_2$

$${}^{10}C_8 = \frac{10 \times 9 \times 8 \times 7 \times 6 \times 5 \times 4 \times 3}{1 \times 2 \times 3 \times 4 \times 5 \times 6 \times 7 \times 8} = \frac{10 \times 9}{1 \times 2} = 45$$

$${}^{10}C_2 = \frac{10 \times 9}{1 \times 2} = 45$$

From the above, we find ${}^{10}C_8 = {}^{10}C_2$

This can be got by the following method also:

$${}^{10}C_8 = {}^{10}C_{(10-8)} = {}^{10}C_2$$

This method is very useful, when the difference between *n* and *r* is very high in ${}^nC_r$.

This property of the combination is written as ${}^nC_r = {}^nC_{(n-r)}$.

To find $200C_{198}$ we can use the above formula as follows:

$${}^{200}C_{198} = {}^{200}C_{(200-198)} = {}^{200}C_2 = \frac{200 \times 199}{1 \times 2} = 19900$$

EXAMPLE 13.45: Out of 13 players, 11 players are to be selected for a cricket team. In how many ways can this be done? Out of 13 players, 11 players are selected in 13 C 11 ways

i.e $${}^{13}C_{11} = {}^{13}C_2 = \frac{13 \times 12}{1 \times 2} = 78$$

EXAMPLE 13.46: Library received 20 books including 8 Hindi novels. If 2 of these books are selected at random. What is the probability that none of them is a Hindi novel.

Solution: The number of ways in which 2 books can be selected from 20 books = ${}^{20}C_2$

$$\text{Required Probability} = \frac{{}^{12}C_2}{{}^{20}C_2} = \frac{66}{190} = \frac{33}{95} = 0.347.$$

EXAMPLE 13.47: Six radios out of a batch of 100 are defective. Two are selected at random. How many points have sample space? If A be the event that one is defective, how many sample points are in? Hence find $p\ (A)$.

Solution: Number of sample points when two radios are selected out of 100 radios.

$$= {}^{100}C_2 = \frac{1001}{2!98!} = \frac{100 \times 99}{2} = 4950$$

Number of sample points when one defective radio is selected and one good radio is selected

$$= {}^{6}C_1 \times {}^{94}C_1 = 6 \times 94 = 564$$

$$P\ (A) = \frac{564}{4950} = 0.114.$$

EXAMPLE 13.48: A bag contains 5 red and 8 black balls. Two draws of three balls each are made. The ball being replaced after the first draw. What is the chance that in the first draw the balls were red the second black?

Solution: Required Probability $= \frac{{}^{5}C_3}{{}^{13}C_3} \times \frac{{}^{8}C_3}{{}^{13}C_3}$.

EXAMPLE 13.49: A sub-committee of 6 members is to be formed out of a group of 7 men and 4 ladies. Calculate the probability that the sub-committee will consist of (i) exactly 2 ladies and (ii) at least two ladies.

Solution:

(i) There are 7 + 4 = 11 members.

A sub-committee of 6 can be formed out of these 11 members in ${}^{11}C_6$

or $$\frac{11!}{6!5!} = \frac{11 \times 10 \times 9 \times 8 \times 7}{5 \times 4 \times 3 \times 2}$$

Two ladies out of 4, and four men out of 7 can be selected in ${}^{4}C_2 \times {}^{7}C_4$ ways

$$= \frac{4!}{2!2!} \times \frac{4!}{4!3!} = \frac{4 \times 3}{2} \times \frac{7 \times 6 \times 5}{3 \times 2}$$

$$= 6 \times 35 = 210 \text{ ways.}$$

Thus the probability that the sub-committee will contain exactly two ladies $= \frac{210}{462} = \frac{5}{11}$.

(ii) The sub-committee will consist of at least 2 ladies if there are 2, 3 or 4 ladies in it and in that case the number of men would be 4, 3 and 2 respectively.

The probability of having exactly 2 ladies in the committee is already calculated in (i) and $\frac{210}{462}$.

The probability of having 3 ladies in the committee with 3 men

$$= \frac{{}^4C_3 \times {}^7C_3}{{}^{11}C_6} = \frac{\frac{4!}{3!} \times \frac{7!}{3!4!}}{\frac{111}{6!5!}}$$

$$= \frac{4 \times 7 \times 6 \times 5 \times 5 \times 4 \times 3 \times 2 \times 1}{6 \times 11 \times 10 \times 9 \times 8 \times 7} = \frac{10}{23} = \frac{140}{462}$$

The probability of having 4 ladies and 2 men

$$= \frac{C_4 \times {}^7C_2}{{}^{11}C_6} = \frac{\frac{7!}{2!5!}}{\frac{11!}{6!5!}} = \frac{21}{462}$$

The combined probability of having either 2 or 3 or 4 ladies in the committee, by the rule of addition.

$$= \frac{210}{462} + \frac{140}{462} + \frac{21}{462} = \frac{371}{462} = \frac{53}{66} \quad [\therefore \text{ The events are mutually exclusive}]$$

MISCELLANEOUS SOLVED EXAMPLES

EXAMPLE 13.50: The probability that A will live upto 60 years is $\frac{3}{4}$ and probability that *B* will live up to 60 years is $\frac{2}{3}$. What is the probability (i) that both *A* and *B* will live upto sixty years (ii) that both dice before reaching 60 years. **[B.Com., Andhra Univ., 1999]**

Solution: The events in question are independent of each other and the rule of multiplication would be applied.

(i) The probability that both *A* and *B* live up to 60 years i.e.,

$$P(A \text{ and } B) = P(A) \times P(B) = \frac{3}{4} \times \frac{2}{3} = \frac{6}{12} = \frac{1}{2}$$

(ii) Since the probabilities of the survival of *A* and *B* upto 60 years are $\frac{3}{4}$ and $\frac{2}{3}$ respectively, therefore the probabilities of their death would be $\left(1 - \frac{3}{4}\right) = \frac{1}{4}$ and $\left(1 - \frac{2}{3}\right) = \frac{1}{3}$ respectively.

Now the probability that both *A* and *B* would dice before reaching 60 years, would be $\frac{1}{4} \times \frac{1}{3} = 12$.

EXAMPLE 13.51: The manager of a chemical plant located near a River knows that some court case had been filed against the company for polluting the river and if found guilty, the company will be required to install a water purification system, pay a fine, or both. So far, only 10 per cent of the companies involved in similar cases have been both find and required to install the purification system. In addition, when the court's ruling has not involved both penalties, a company has been 2 times more likely to be fined than to be required to install the purification system. If 28 per cent of the companies have been found guilty so far, what is the probability that this company will be required to (i) install a purification system, (ii) Pay the fine.

Solution: Let A denotes the event that the company is required to install a water purification system. B denotes the event the company is required to pay the fine.

Then AB is the event that the company is required to pay the fine and install a water purification system.

$$P(A) + P(B) + P(AB) = 0.28$$

$$\Rightarrow \quad P(A) + P(B) = 0.28 - 0.10 = 0.18$$

$$\Rightarrow \quad P(A) + 2P(A) = 0.18$$

$$P(A) = 0.06$$

The company will be required to instal a purification system if

(i) The court decides that the company should instal a purification system if

(ii) The court decides that the company should install a purification system and pay the fine also.

(i) The required Probability = $P(A) + P(AB) = 0.06 + 0.1 = 0.16$.

(ii) Required Probability = $P(B) + P(AB) = 2P(A) + P(AB) = 0.12 + 0.1 = 0.22$.

EXAMPLE 13.52: The records of 400 examinees are given below:

Score	Educational Qualification			Total
	BA	B.Sc	B.Com.	
Below 50	90	30	60	**180**
Between 50 and 60	20	70	70	**160**
Above 60	10	30	20	**60**
Total	**120**	**130**	**150**	**400**

If an examinee is selected from this group of examinees, find

(i) The probability that he is a commerce graduate

(ii) The probability that he is a science graduate given that his score is above 60.

(iii) The probability that his score is below 50, given that he is a $B.A$.

Solution:

(i) Total number of commerce graduates = 150

$$\therefore \quad \text{Required probability} = \frac{150}{400} = \frac{3}{8}.$$

(ii) Total number of examinees having score above 60 = 60

$$\therefore \quad \text{Required probability} = \frac{30}{60} = \frac{1}{2}.$$

(iii) Total number of students doing B.A = 120

$$\therefore \quad \text{Required probability} = \frac{90}{120} = \frac{3}{4}.$$

EXAMPLE 13.53: The probability that a contractor will get a contract for road construction in 4/9 and the probability that he will get contract for the construction of a water tank is 5/7. What is the probability of getting at least one of the contract?

Solution: Required probability $= \frac{4}{9} + \frac{5}{7} + \frac{4}{9} \times \frac{5}{7} = \frac{28 + 45 - 20}{63} = \frac{53}{63}$.

EXAMPLE 13.54: A company tenders for two contracts *A* and *B*. The probability that it will obtain contract *A* is $\frac{1}{3}$ and the probability that it will obtain contract B is $\frac{1}{4}$. Find the probability that the company will (i) obtain Both contracts (ii) obtain only one contract.

Solution: (i) $\frac{1}{3} \times \frac{1}{4}$ (ii) $\frac{1}{3} \times \frac{3}{4} + \frac{1}{4} \times \frac{2}{3}$.

EXAMPLE 13.55: A problem in STATISTIC is given to two students. The odds is favour of *A* solving a problem are 6 to 9 and the odds in against *B* solving the same problem are 12 to 10. What is the probability that if both of them try the problem would be solved?

Solution: The problem would be solved if

(a) Both *A* and *B* solve it
(b) *A* solves but *B* fails to solve it
(c) *B* solves but *A* fails to solve it

When it is said that the *odds* is favour of A solving the problem are 6 to 9 it means that the probability of solving the problem is $\frac{6}{15}$ or the probability of not solving it is $I - \frac{6}{15} = \frac{8}{15}$, i.e.,

$$P(A) = \frac{6}{15}, \text{ and } P(\bar{A}) = \frac{9}{15}$$

Similarly when it is said odds against B solving the problem are 12 to 10 it means that the probability of not solving is $\frac{12}{22} = P(\bar{B})$ and of solving is $I - \frac{12}{22} = \frac{10}{22} = p(B)$

Probability that both *A* and *B* solve $= \frac{6}{15} \times \frac{10}{22} = \frac{2}{11}$

Probability of *A* solving and *B* failing $= P(A)\, P(\bar{B}) = \frac{6}{15} \times \frac{12}{22} = \frac{12}{55}$

Probability of *B* solving and *A* failing $= P(B)\, P(\bar{A}) = \frac{10}{22} \times \frac{9}{15} = \frac{3}{11}$

$\therefore$ Probability that the problem is solved $= \frac{2}{11} + \frac{12}{55} + \frac{3}{11} = \frac{37}{55}$.

Second Method

The probability that the problem is solved is one minus the probability that the problem not solved.

The probability that A would fail $= q_1 = \frac{9}{15}$ and that *B* would fail $= q_2 = \frac{12}{22}$

$\therefore$ The probability that both fail to solve the problem when they try independently

$$= q_1\, q_2 = \frac{9}{15} \times \frac{12}{22} = \frac{18}{55}$$

$\therefore$ The probability that the problem is solved $= 1 - \frac{18}{55} = \frac{37}{55}$.

This is a more convenient way of solving such problems.

Third Method

The problem will be solved if at least one of them is able to solve the problems i.e.,

$$P(A \cup B) = P(A) + P(B) - P(A \cap B)$$

$$= \frac{6}{15} + \frac{10}{22} - \frac{6}{15} \times \frac{10}{22}$$

$$= \frac{132 + 150 - 60}{15 \times 22} = \frac{37}{35}.$$

EXAMPLE 13.56: A university has to select an examiner from the list of 50 persons 20 of them women and 30 men, 10 of them knowing Hindi and 40 not, 15 of the being teachers and the remaining 35 not. What is the probability of the university selecting a Hindi knowing woman teacher?

Solution: Probability that the selected candidate is a women $= \frac{20}{50} = \frac{2}{5}$

Probability that the selected candidate is a Hindi knowing $= \frac{10}{50} = \frac{1}{5}$

Probability that the selected candidate is a teacher $= \frac{15}{50} = \frac{3}{10}$

Probability of selecting a Hindi knowing woman teacher $= \frac{2}{5} \times \frac{1}{5} \times \frac{3}{10} = \frac{6}{250} = \frac{3}{125}$

[$\therefore$ events are independent]

EXAMPLE 13.57: In a survey of 100 readers, it was found that 40 read magazine A, 15 read magazine B, 10 read both. What is the probability of a person reading at least one of the magazines.

Solution: Required probability = 0.40 + 0.15 – 0.10 = 0.45

EXAMPLE 13.58: A husband and a wife appear in an interview for two vacancies in the same post. The probability of husband selection is $\frac{1}{7}$ and that of wife's selection is $\frac{1}{5}$. What is the probability that:

(a) both of them will be selected;
(b) only one of them will be selected;
(c) none of them will be selected

Solution:

(a) Let A and B denote the events of husband's and wife selection respectively.

Let $P(A) = p_1, \; P(B) = p_2$

$\therefore \quad p_1 = \frac{1}{7}, \; p_2 = \frac{1}{5}$

$P(\bar{A})$ = Probability of husband's rejection $= 1 - p_1 = 1 - \frac{1}{7} = \frac{6}{7} = q_1$

$P(\bar{B})$ = Probability of wife's rejection $= 1 - p_2 = 1 - \frac{1}{5} = \frac{4}{5} = q_2$

Probability that husband and wife both are selected: $P(A)\,P(B) = \frac{1}{7} = \frac{1}{5} = \frac{1}{35}$.

[$\therefore$ the events are independent]

(b) Probability that only one of them will be selected = $P(A)\,P(\bar{B}) + P(\bar{A})\,P(B)$

$$= \frac{1}{7} \times \frac{4}{5} + \frac{6}{7} \times \frac{1}{5} = \frac{10}{35} = \frac{2}{7}.$$

(c) Probability that both are rejected = $P(\bar{A})\,P(\bar{B}) = \frac{6}{7} \times \frac{4}{5} = \frac{24}{35}.$

EXAMPLE 13.59: A problem in statistics is given to three students *A, B* and *C* whose chances of solving are $\frac{1}{2}, \frac{1}{3}, \frac{1}{4}$ respectively. What is the probability that the problem is solved.

Solution: The respective probabilities of student *A, B* and *C* not solving the problem are

$$\left(1 - \frac{1}{2}\right), \left(1 - \frac{1}{3}\right) \text{ and } \left(1 - \frac{1}{4}\right).$$

The problem will be solved if at least one student solves the problem

Required Probability = 1 – None of the students solves the problem

$$= 1 - \left(1 - \frac{1}{2}\right)\left(1 - \frac{1}{3}\right)\left(1 - \frac{1}{4}\right)$$

$$= 1 - \frac{1}{2} \times \frac{2}{3} \times \frac{3}{4} = \frac{3}{4}$$

EXAMPLE 13.60: If *N* people are seated at a round table, what is the probability that two named individuals will be neighbours?

Solution: If one of the named individuals is seated, the other one can sit in $(N-1)$ places. Out of these, two seats would make him a neighbour of the first named individual.

Hence the required probability = $\frac{2}{N-1}$

EXAMPLE 13.61: Find the probability that a man asked to form a two digit number out of 2, 3, 5, 7,9 would form 79 when,

(a) repetitions are not allowed
(b) repetitions are allowed

Solution:

(a) **When repetitions are not allowed**

Out of the 5 digit a 2 digit number can be formed in ${}^5P_2$ ways. [It is a question of arrangement or permutation, because any two digits will give 2 different (2 digit) numbers. Like 2 and 3 can give 23, or 32 as two digit numbers.

$${}^5P_2 = \frac{5!}{(5-2)!} = \frac{5 \times 4 \times 3 \times 2 \times 1}{3 \times 2 \times 1} = 20$$

This is the exhaustive number of cases. Out of this 79 is one number.

Hence the required probability would be $\frac{1}{20}$.

(b) **When repetitions are allowed**

Out of the 5 digits, 2 digit numbers can be formed in 5 × 5 or 25 ways (as each digit can be repeated) out of which 79 is one possibility. Hence the required probability = $\frac{1}{25}$.

EXAMPLE 13.62: Given $P(A) = \frac{3}{8}$, $P(B) = \frac{5}{8}$ and $P(A \cup B) = \frac{3}{4}$. Find $P(A / B)$ and $P(B/A)$, show whether A and B are independent. **[B.Com., Kurukshetra, Univ., 1994]**

Solution: $P(A \cup B) = P(A) + P(B) - P(A \cap B)$

$$\frac{3}{4} = \frac{3}{8} + \frac{5}{8} - P(A \cap B)$$

$$\Rightarrow \quad P(A \cap B) = \frac{3}{8} + \frac{5}{8} - \frac{3}{4} = \frac{2}{8} = \frac{1}{4}$$

$$P(A \cap B) = P(A)\,P(B/A) = P(B)\,P(A/B)$$

$$\Rightarrow \quad \frac{1}{4} = \frac{3}{8} \times P(B/A) \Rightarrow P(B/A) = \frac{2}{3}$$

or $$\frac{1}{4} = \frac{5}{8} \times P(A/B) \Rightarrow P(A/B) = \frac{2}{5}$$

Since $P(B / A) \neq P(B)$ and $P(A / B) \neq P(A)$. The events A and B are not independent.

EXAMPLE 13.63: A Problem in statistics is given to two students A and B. The odds in favour of A solving the problem are 6 to 9 and against B solving the problem are 12 to 10. If both A and B attempt, find the probability of the problem being solve.

Solution: Probability that A solves the problem $P(A) = \frac{6}{15}$

Probability that B solves the problem $P(B) = \frac{10}{22}$

Probability that problem is solved = Probability that at least one of them solves the problem

$$= P(A) + P(B) - P(A)\,P(B)$$

$$= \frac{6}{15} + \frac{10}{22} - \frac{6 \times 10}{22 \times 15}$$

$$= \frac{132 + 150 - 60}{330} = \frac{222}{330} = 0.672.$$

EXAMPLE 13.64: A print shop has three presses: p_1, p_2 and p_3. Each press is shut down 10 per cent of the time. The probability of any press being shut down not influenced by the operating conditions of the other two. Determine the probability that

(i) All the three presses are shut down

(ii) At least one press is shut down

(iii) p_1 or p_2 or both are shut down.

Solution: The probability of any press shut down is not influenced by the operating condition of the other two implies that the events are independent.

∴ Probability of shut down of a press = 0.1

(i) The probability that all the three presses are shut down = 0.1 × 0.1 × 0.1 = 0.001

(ii) Required Probability = 1 – Probability that none of the presses is shut down.

$= 1 - 0.9 \times 0.9 = 1 - 0.729 = 0.271$

Second Method for part (ii)

The probability that only press p_1 is shut down and p_2, p_3 are working = 0.1 × 0.9 × 0.9 = 0.081.

The probability that only press p_2 is shut down and p_1, p_3 are working = 0.9 × 0.1 × 0.9 = 0.081

The probability that only press p_3 is shut down and p_1, p_2 are working = 0.9 × 0.9 × 0.1 = 0.081

The probability that press p_1 and p_2 are shut down and p_3 is working = the probability that press p_2, p_3 are shut down and p_1 is working

= the Probability that press p_1, p_3 are shut down and p_2 is working

= 0.1 × 0.1 × 0.9 = 0.009

Required probability = Probability that only p_1 is shut down + Probability that only p_2 is shut down + Probability that only p_3 is shut down + Probability that only p_1 , p_2 are shut down + Probability that only p_2, p_3 are shut down + Probability that only p_1, p_3 are shut down + Probability that p_1, p_2, p_3 all the three are shut down.

= 3 × 0.081 + 3 × 0.009 + 0.001

= 0.243 + 0.027 + 0.001 = 0.271

(iii) Required probability = 0.081 + 0.081 + 0.009 = 0.171.

EXAMPLE 13.65: Three coins are tossed simultaneously Find the probability that (i) no head (ii) one head (iii) two heads (iv) atleast two heads. (v) atmost two heads appear.

Solution: The sample space for the 3 coins is

$S = \{HHH, HHT, HTH, HTT, THH, THT, TTH, TTT\}$; $n(S) = 8$

(i) No head appear $A = \{TTT\}$; $n(A) = 1$

$P(A) = 1/8$

(ii) One head appear $B = \{HTT, THT, TTH\}$; $n(B) = 3$

$P(B) = 3/8$

(iii) Two heads appear $C = \{HHT, HTH, THH\}$; $n(c) = 3$

$P(C) = 3/8$

(iv) Atleast two heads appear $D = \{HHT, HTH, THH, HHH\}$; $n(D) = 4$

$P(D) = 4/8$

(v) Atmost two heads appear $E = \{TTT, HTT, THT, TTH, HHT, HTH, THH\}$

$n(E) = 7$

$P(E) = 7/8$

EXAMPLE 13.66: A ball is drawn at random from a box containing 5 green, 6 red, and 4 yellow balls. Determine the probability that the ball drawn is (i) Green (ii) Red (iii) Yellow (iv) Green or Red (v) not Yellow.

Solution: Total number of balls in the box = 5 + 6 + 4 = 15 balls

(i) Probability of drawing a green ball = 5/15 = 1/3

(ii) Probability of drawing a red ball = 6/15 = 2/5

(iii) Probability of drawing a yellow ball = 4/15

(iv) Probability of drawing a Green or a Red ball = 5/15 + 6/15 = 11/15

(v) Probability of getting not yellow = 1 – p (yellow) = 1 – 4/15 = 11/15

EXAMPLE 13.67: Two persons A and B appeared for an interview for a job. The probability of selection of A is 1/3 and that of B is 1/2. Find the probability that

(i) both of them will be selected

(ii) only one of them will be selected

(iii) none of them will be selected

Solution:
$$P(A) = \frac{1}{3}, P(B) = \frac{1}{2}$$

$$P(\bar{A}) = \frac{2}{3} \text{ and } P(\bar{B}) = \frac{1}{2}$$

Selection or non-selection of any one of the candidate is not affecting the selection of the other. Therefore A and B are independent events.

(i) Probability of selecting both A and B

$$P(A \cap B) = P(A), P(B) = \frac{1}{3} \times \frac{1}{2} = \frac{1}{6}$$

(ii) Probability of selecting any one of them

= P (selecting A and not selecting B) + P (not selecting A and selecting B)

i.e. $P(A \cap \bar{B}) + (\bar{A} \cap B) = P(A), P(\bar{B}) + P(\bar{A})\ P(B)$

$$= \frac{1}{3} \times \frac{1}{2} + \frac{2}{3} \times \frac{1}{2}$$

$$= \frac{1}{6} \times \frac{2}{6} = \frac{3}{6} \times \frac{1}{2}$$

(iii) Probability of not selecting both A and B

i.e. $P(\bar{A} \cap \bar{B}) = P(\bar{A}), P(\bar{B}) = \frac{2}{3}, \frac{1}{2} = \frac{1}{3}$

EXAMPLE 13.68: There are three T.V programmes A, B and C which can be received in a city of 2000 families. The following information is available on the basis of survey.

1200 families listen to Programme A

1100 families listen to Programme B

800 families listen to Programme C

765 families listen to Programme A and B

450 families listen to Programme A and C

400 families listen to Programme B and C

100 families listen to Programme A, B and C

Find the probability that a family selected at random listens atleast one or more T.V Programmes.

Solution: Total number of families $n(S)$= 2000

Let $n(A) = 1200$

$n(B) = 1100$

$n(C) = 800$

$n(A \cap B) = 765$

$n(A \cap C) = 450$

$n(B \cap C) = 400$

$n(A \cap B \cap C) = 100$

Let us first find $n(A \, U \, B \, U \, C)$.

$$n(AUBUC) = n(A) + n(B) + n(C) - n(A \cap B) - n(A \cap C) - n(B \cap C) + n(A \cap B \cap C)$$

$$= 1200 + 1100 + 800 - 765 - 450 - 400 + 100$$

$$n(AUBUC) = 1585$$

now $$P(AUBUC) = \frac{n(AUBUC)}{n(S)} = \frac{1585}{2000} = 0.792$$

Therefore about 79% chance that a family selected at random listens to one or more T.V. Programmes.

EXAMPLE 13.69: A stockist has 20 items in a lot. Out of which 12 are no defective and 8 are defective. A customer selects 3 items from the lot. What is the probability that out of these three items (i) three items are non-defective (ii) two are non defective and one is Defective

Solution:

(i) Let the event, that all the three items are non-defective, be denoted by E_1. There are 12 non-defective items and out of them 3 can be selected in $^{12}C_3$ ways ie $n(E_1) = {}^{12}C_3$

Total numbers of ways in which 3 items can be selected are $^{20}C_3$

i.e. $$n(S) = {}^{20}C_3$$

$\therefore$ $$P(E_1) = \frac{n(E_1)}{n(S)} = \frac{^{12}C_3}{^{20}C_3}$$

$$= \frac{12 \times 11 \times 10}{20 \times 19 \times 18} = 0.193$$

(ii) Let the event, that two items are non-defective and one is defective be denoted by E_2.

Two non-defective items out of 12 can be selected in $^{12}C_2$ ways. One item out of 8 defective can be selected in $^{8}C_1$ ways.

Thus $$n(E_2) = {}^{12}C_2 \cdot {}^{8}C_1$$

Two non-defective items out of 12 can be selected in $^{12}C_2$ ways. One item out of 8 defective can be selected in $^{8}C_1$ ways.

Thus $$n(E_2) = {}^{12}C_2, {}^{8}C_1$$

Then the probability

$$P(E_2) = \frac{n(E_2)}{n(S)} = \frac{^{12}C_2 . {}^{8}C_1}{^{20}C_3} = \frac{12 \times 11 \times 8 \times 3}{20 \times 19 \times 18} = 0.463.$$

EXAMPLE 13.70: A test paper containing 10 problems is given to three students *A*, *B*, *C*. It is considered that student A can solve 60% problems, student B can solve 40% problems and student *C* can solve 30% problems. Find the probability that the problem chosen from the test paper will be solved by all the three students.

Solution:

Probability of solving the problem by $A = 60\%$

Probability of solving the problem by $B = 40\%$

Probability of solving the problem by $C = 30\%$

Solving the problem by a student is independent of solving the problem by the other students.

Hence, $P(A \cap B \cap C) = P(A) \,.\, P(B) \,.\, P(C)$

$$= \frac{60}{100} \times \frac{40}{100} \times \frac{30}{100}$$

$$= 0.6 \times 0.4 \times 0.3 = 0.072$$

EXAMPLE 13.71: From a pack of 52 cards, 2 cards are drawn at random. Find the probability that one is king and the other is queen.

Solution: From a pack of 52 cards 2 cards are drawn $n(S) = {}^{52}C_2$

Selection of one king is in ${}^4C_1$ ways

Selection of one queen is in ${}^4C_1$ ways

Selection of one king and one queen is in ${}^4C_1 \cdot {}^4C_1$ ways

ie $n(E) = {}^4C_1 \cdot {}^4C_1$

$\therefore$ $$P(E) = \frac{n(E)}{n(S)} = \frac{{}^4C_1 {}^4C_1}{{}^{52}C_2}$$

$$= 4 \times 4 + \frac{52 \times 51}{1 \times 2} = \frac{4 \times 4 \times 2}{52 \times 51} = \frac{8}{663}$$

EXAMPLE 13.72: An urn contains 4 black balls and 6 white balls. If 3 balls are drawn at random, find the probability that (i) all are black (ii) all are white

Solution: Total number of balls = 10

Total number ways of selecting 3 balls $= {}^{10}C_3$

(i) Number of ways of drawing 3 black balls $= {}^4C_3$

Probability of drawing 3 black balls $= \frac{{}^4C_3}{{}^{10}C_3}$

$$= \frac{4 \times 3 \times 2}{1 \times 2 \times 3} + \frac{10 \times 9 \times 8}{1 \times 2 \times 3} = \frac{4 \times 3 \times 2}{10 \times 9 \times 8} = \frac{1}{30}$$

(ii) Number of ways of drawing 3 white balls $= {}^6C_3$

Probability of drawing 3 white balls $= \frac{{}^6C_3}{{}^{10}C_3} = \frac{6 \times 5 \times 4}{10 \times 9 \times 8} = \frac{1}{6}$.

EXAMPLE 13.73: A box containing 5 green balls and 3 red colour balls. Find the probability of selecting 3 green colour balls one by one (i) without replacement (ii) with replacement

Solution: (i) Selection without replacement: Selecting 3 balls out of 8 balls = $^8C_3$ ways

i.e n (S) = $^8C_3$

Selecting 3 green balls in $^5C_3$ ways

(ii) Selection with replacement: When a ball is drawn and replaced before the next draw, the number of balls in the box remains the same. Also the 3 events of drawing a green ball in each case are independent.

Probability of drawing a green ball in each case is 5

The event of selecting a green ball in the first, second and third event are same,

$\therefore$ Probability of drawing 3 green balls $= \frac{5}{8} \times \frac{5}{8} \times \frac{5}{8} = \frac{125}{512}$

EXAMPLE 13.74: A box contains 5 red and 4 white marbles. Two marbles are rawn successively from the box without replacement and it is noted that the second one is white. What is the probability that the first is also white?

Solution: If w_1, w_2 are the events 'white on the first draw', 'white on the second draw' respectively.

Now we are looking for $P\ (w_1/w_2)$

$$P\ (w_1/\ w_2) = \frac{P(w_1 \cap w_2)}{P(w_2)} = \frac{P(w_1)\ p(w_2)}{P(w_2)}$$

$$= \frac{(4/9)\ (3/8)}{(3/8)} = \frac{4}{9}$$

EXAMPLE 13.75: In a certain town, males and females form 50 percent of the population. It is known that 20 percent of the males and 5 percent of the females are unemployed. A research student studying the employment situation selects unemployed persons at random. What is the probability that the person selected is (i) a male (ii) a female?

Solution: Out of 50% of the population 20% of the males are unemployed. i.e

$$\frac{50}{100} \times \frac{20}{100} = \frac{10}{100} = 0.10$$

Out of 50% the population 5% of the females are unemployed.

i.e. $$\frac{50}{100} \times \frac{5}{100} = \frac{25}{1000} = 0.025$$

Based on the above data we can form the table as follows:

	Employed	Unemployed	Total
Males	0.400	0.100	**0.50**
Females	0.475	0.025	**0.50**
Total	**0.875**	**0.125**	**1.00**

Let a male chosen be denoted by M and a female chosen be denoted by F

Let U denotes the number of unemployed persons then

(i) $P\ (M\ /\ U) = \frac{P(M \cap U)}{P(U)} = \frac{0.10}{0.125} = 0.80$

(ii) $P\ (F\ /\ U) = \frac{P(F \cap U)}{P(U)} = \frac{0.025}{0.125} = 0.20$

13.11 RANDOM VARIABLE

A variable whose value is a number determined by the outcome of a random experiment is called a random variable. We can also say that a random variable is a function defined over the sample space of an experiment and generally assumes different values with a definite probability associated with each value. Generally, a random variable is denoted by capital letters like X, Y, Z….., where as the values of the random variable are denoted by the corresponding small letters like x, y, z …….

Suppose that two coins are tossed so that the sample space is $S = \{HH, HT, TH, TT\}$

Suppose X represent the number of heads which can come up, with each sample point we can associate a number for X as shown in the table below:

Sample point	*HH*	*HT*	*TH*	*TT*
X	2	1	1	0

Thus the random variable X takes the values 0, 1,2 for this random experiment.

The above example takes only a finite number of values and for each random value we can associate a probability as shown in the table.

Usually, for each random variable x_i, the probability of respective random variable is denoted by $p(x_i)$ or simply p_i .

X	$x_1 = 0$	$x_2 = 1$	$x_3 = 2$
P (x$_i$)	$P(x_i) = \frac{1}{4}$	$P(x_i) = \frac{2}{4}$	$P(x_i) = \frac{1}{4}$

Observe that the sum of the probabilities of all the random variable is equal to one. ie

$$P(x_1) + P(x_2) + P(x_3) = \frac{1}{4} + \frac{2}{4} + \frac{1}{4} = 1$$

Thus the probability distribution for a random variable provides a probability for each possible value and that these probabilities must sum to 1.

Similarly if 3 coins are tossed, the random variable for getting head will be $X = 0$, $X = 1$, $X = 2$, $X = 3$ and sum of their respective probabilities i.e $\Sigma\ p(x_i) = 1$.

If two dice are rolled then the sample space S consists of 36 sample points. Let X denotes the sum of the numbers on the two dice. Then X is a function defined on S by the rule $X(i, j) = i + j$.

Then X is a random variable which can takes the values 2,3,4……12. That is the range of X is {2,3,4……12}

(A) Discrete Random Variable

If a random variable takes only a finite or a countable number of values, it is called a discrete random variable. ***For example***, when 3 coins are tossed, the number of heads obtained is the random variable X assumes the values 0,1,2,3 which form a countable set. Such a variable is a discrete random variable.

(B) Continuous Random Variable

A random variable X which can take any value between certain intervals is called a continuous random variable.

Note that the probability of any single value at x, value of X is zero. i.e $p\ (X = x) = 0$ Thus continuous random variable takes value only between two given limits.

For example the height of students in a particular class lies between 4 feet to 6 feet.

We write this as $X = \{x \mid 4 \leq x \leq 6\}$

The maximum life of electric bulbs is 2000 hours. For this the continuous random variable will be $X = \{x \mid 0 \leq x \leq 2000\}$

13.12 PROBABILITY MASS FUNCTION (PMS)

Let X be a discrete random variable which assumes the values $x_1, x_2, \ldots x_n$ with each of these values, we associate a number called the probability $P_i = P\ (X = x_i),\ i = 1,2,3\ldots n$ This is called probability of x_i satisfying the following conditions.

(i) $P_i \geq 0$ for all i, ie P_i' s are all non-negative

(ii) $\Sigma p_i = p_1 + p_2 + \ldots p_n = 1$

ie the total probability is one.

This function P_i or $P\ (x_i)$ is called the ***Probability Mass Function*** of the discrete random variable X.

The set of all possible ordered pairs $(x, P\ (x))$ is called the probability distribution of the random variable X.

NOTE: The concept of probability distribution is similar to that of frequency distribution. Just as frequency distribution tells us how the total frequency is distributed among different values (or classes) of the variable, a probability distribution tells us how total probability 1 is distributed among the various values which the random variable can take. It is usually represented in a tabular form given below:

X	x_1	x_2	x_3	...	x_n
P(X = x)	$P(x_1)$	$P(x_2)$	$P(x_3)$	...	$P(x_n)$

13.13 PROBABILITY DENSITY FUNCTION (PDF)

A function f is said to be the probability density function of a continuous random variable X if it satisfies the following properties.

(i) $f\ (x) \geq 0 \quad -\infty < x < \infty$ (ii) $\int_{-\infty}^{\infty} f(x)dx = 1$

Remark: In case of a discrete random variable, the probability at a point ie $p\ (x = a)$ is not zero for some fixed 'a' However in case of continuous random variables the probability at a point is always zero

i.e. $$P\ (X = a) = \int_a^a f(x)dx = 0$$

Hence $P\ (a \leq X \leq b) = P\ (a < X < b) = P\ (a \leq X < b) = P\ (a < X \leq b)$

The probability that x lies in the interval (a, b) is given by

$$P\ (a < X < b) = \int_a^b f(x)dx$$

Distribution functions for continuous random variable.

If X is a continuous random variable with $p.d.\ f(x)$, then the distribution function is given by

(i) $F(x) = \int_{-\infty}^{x} f(x)dx = p(X \le x) : -\infty < x < \infty$

(ii) $F(b) - F(a) = \int_{a}^{b} f(x)dx = p(a \le X \le b)$

EXAMPLE 13.76: Find the probability distribution of the number of sixes in throwing two dice once.

Solution: When two dice are thrown the total number of sample points is 36. Let X denotes the number of sixes obtained in throwing two dice once. Then X is the random variable, which can take the values 0,1,2.

Let A denote the success of getting a six in throwing a die and A denote not getting a six.

Then probability getting a six

$$P(A) = \frac{1}{6}$$

Probability not getting a six $P(\bar{A}) = \frac{5}{6}$

No sixes:

$$\therefore \quad P(x = 0) = P(\bar{A} \text{ and } \bar{A})$$

$$= P(\bar{A}) \cdot P(\bar{A})$$

$$= \frac{5}{6} \cdot \frac{5}{6} = \frac{25}{36}$$

EXAMPLE 13.77: A random variable has the following probability distribution

Values of X	0	1	2	3	4	5	6	7	8
p (x)	a	3a	5a	7a	9a	11a	13a	15a	17a

1. Determine the value of a
2. Find:

   (i) $P(x < 3)$ (ii) $P(x \le 3)$
   (iii) $P(x > 7)$ (iv) $P(2 \le x \le 5)$
   (v) $P(2 < x < 5)$
3. Find the cumulative distribution function of x.

Solution:

1. Since p_i is the probability mass functions of discrete random variable X,

   We have $\Sigma p_i = 1$

$$\therefore \quad a + 3a + 5a + 7a + 9a + 11a + 13a + 15a + 17a = 1$$

$$81a = 1$$

$$a = 1/81$$

2. (i) $P(x < 3) = P(x = 0) + P(x = 1) + P(x = 2)$

$$= a + 3a + 5a = 9a$$

$$= 9\left(\frac{1}{81}\right) = \frac{1}{9}$$

(ii) $P(x \leq 3) = P(x = 0) + P(x = 1) + P(x = 2) + P(x = 3)$

$$= a + 3a + 5a + 7a = 16a = \frac{16}{81}$$

(iii) $P(x > 7) = P(x = 8) = 17a = \frac{17}{81}$

(iv) $P(2 \leq x \leq 5) = P(x = 2) + P(x = 3) + P(x = 4) + P(x = 5)$

$$= 5a + 7a + 9a + 11a$$

$$= 32a = \frac{32}{81}$$

(v) $P(2 < x < 5) = P(x = 3) + P(x = 4)$

$$= 7a + 9a$$

$$= 16a = \frac{16}{81}$$

3. The distribution function is as follows:

$X = x$ $F(x) = P(X \leq x)$	0 a	1 $4a$	2 $9a$	3 $16a$	4 $25a$	5 $36a$	6 $49a$	7 $64a$	8 $81a$
(or) $F(x)$	$\frac{1}{81}$	$\frac{4}{81}$	$\frac{9}{81}$	$\frac{16}{81}$	$\frac{25}{81}$	$\frac{36}{81}$	$\frac{49}{81}$	$\frac{64}{81}$	$\frac{81}{81}$

EXAMPLE 13.78: An urn contains 6 red and 4 white balls. Three balls are drawn at random. Obtain the probability distribution of the number of white balls drawn.

Solution: The total number of balls in the urn is 10 Let X denote the number of white balls drawn. If three balls are drawn, the random variable takes the value X= 0, 1, 2, 3

Probability of getting white balls from the urn containing 10 balls (red and white) with the following combination are

$$P(\text{no white, 3 red balls}) = \frac{{}^4C_0\,{}^6C_3}{{}^{10}C_3} = \frac{1 \times 120}{720} = \frac{5}{30}$$

$$P(\text{1 white, 2 red}) = \frac{{}^4C_1\,{}^6C_1}{{}^{10}C_3} = \frac{15}{30}$$

$$P(\text{2 white, 1 red}) = \frac{{}^4C_2\,{}^6C_1}{{}^{10}C_3} = \frac{9}{30}$$

$$P(\text{3 white, no red}) = \frac{{}^4C_3\,{}^6C_0}{{}^{10}C_3} = \frac{1}{30}$$

Hence the probability distribution of X is given by

C	0	1	2	3
$P(X=x)$	$\frac{5}{30}$	$\frac{15}{30}$	$\frac{9}{30}$	$\frac{1}{30}$

13.14 MATHEMATICAL EXPECTATION

Expectation is a very basic concept and is employed widely in decision theory, management science, system analysis, theory of games and many other fields. Some of these applications will be discussed in the chapter on Decision Theory.

The expected value or mathematical expectation of a random variable X is the weighted average of the values that X can assume with probabilities of its various values as weights. Thus the expected value of a random variable is obtained by considering the various values that the variable can take multiplying these by their corresponding probabilities and summing these products. Expectation of X is denoted by $E(X)$.

Expectation of a Discrete Random Variable

Let X be a discrete random variable which can assume any of the values of $x_1, x_2, x_3 \ldots\ldots x_n$ with respective probabilities $p_1, p_2, p_3 \ldots\ldots p_n$. Then the mathematical expectation of X is given by

$$E(x) = E(x) = x_1 p_1 + x_2 p_2 + x_3 p_3 + \ldots\ldots x_n p_n = \sum_{i=1}^{n} x_i P_i$$

Where, $\sum_{i=1}^{n} P_i = 1$

NOTE: Mathematical expectation of a random variable is also known as its arithmetic mean. We shall give some useful theorems on expectation without proof.

Theorems on Expectation

1. For two random variable X and Y if $E(X)$ and $E(Y)$ exist, $E(X + Y) = E(X) + E(Y)$. This is known as addition theorem on expectation.
2. For two independent random variable X and Y, $E(XY) = E(X).E(Y)$ provided all expectation exist. This is known as multiplication theorem on expectation.
3. The expectation of a constant is the constant it self. ie $E(C) = C$
4. $E(cX) = cE(X)$, where c is constant.
5. $E(aX + b) = aE(X) + b$
6. Variance of constant is zero. ie Var $(c) = 0$
7. $\text{Var}(X + c) = \text{Var } X$

NOTE: This theorem gives that variance is independent of change of origin.

8. Var $(aX) = a_2$ var(X)

NOTE: This theorem gives that change of scale affects the variance.

9. Var $(aX + b) = a_2$Var (X)
10. Var $(b - ax) = a_2$ Var (x)

Let $f(x)$ be a function of random variable X. Then expectation of $f(x)$ is given by

$$E[f(x)] = \Sigma f(x)\, p(X = x)$$

where $P(X = x)$ is the probability function of x.

Particular Cases

1. If we take $f(x) = X^r$, then $E(X^r) = \Sigma x^r\, P(x)$ is defined as the rth moment about origin or r^{th} raw moment of the probability distribution. It is denoted by μ'.

Thus
$$\mu' = E(X^r)$$
$$\mu_1' = E(X)$$
$$\mu_2' = E(X^2)$$

Hence
$$\text{mean} = \bar{X} = \mu_1' = E(X)$$

$$\text{Variance} = \frac{\Sigma X^2}{n} \cdot \left[\frac{\Sigma X}{n}\right]^2$$
$$= E(X^2) - [E(X)]^2$$
$$= \mu_2' - (\mu_1')^2$$

Variance is denoted by μ_2

2. If we take $f(x) = (X - \bar{X})^r$ then $E(X - \bar{X})^r = \Sigma (X - \bar{X})^r P(x)$ which is μ_r the rth moment about mean or r^{th} central moment.
In particular if $r = 2$, we get

$$\mu_2 = E(X - \bar{X})^2 = \Sigma (X - \bar{X})^2 P(X)$$
$$= E(X - E(X)]^2$$

These two formulae give the variance of probability distribution in terms of expectations.

EXAMPLE 13.79: Find the expected value of x, where x represents the outcome when a die is thrown.

Solution: Here each of the outcome (ie., number) 1, 2, 3, 4, 5 and 6 occurs with probability 1/6. Thus the probability distribution of X will be

x	1	2	3	4	5	6
p (x)	$\frac{1}{6}$	$\frac{1}{6}$	$\frac{1}{6}$	$\frac{1}{6}$	$\frac{1}{6}$	$\frac{1}{6}$

Thus the expected value of X is

$$E(X) = \Sigma x_i p_i = x_1\, p_1 + x_2\, p_2 + x_3\, p_3 + x_4\, p_4 + x_5\, p_5 + x_6 p_6$$

$$E(X) = \left[1 \times \frac{1}{6}\right] + \left[2 \times \frac{1}{6}\right] + \left[3 \times \frac{1}{6}\right] + \left[4 \times \frac{1}{6}\right] + \left[5 \times \frac{1}{6}\right] + \left[6 \times \frac{1}{6}\right] = \frac{7}{2}$$

$$E(X) = 3.5$$

Remark: In the games of chance, the expected value of the game is defined as the value of the game to the player.

The game is said to be favourable to the player if the expected value of the game is positive, and unfavourable, if value of the game is negative. The game is called a fair game if the expected value of the game is zero.

EXAMPLE 13.80: A player throws a fair die. If a prime number occurs he wins that number of rupees but if a non-prime number occurs he loses that number of rupees. Find the expected gain of the player and conclude.

Solution: Here each of the six outcomes in throwing a die have been assigned certain amount of loss or gain. So to find the expected gain of the player, these assigned gains (loss is considered as negative gain) will be denoted as X.

These can be written as follows:

Outcome on a die **Associated gain to the outcome (x_i)**	1 –1	2 2	3 3	4 –4	5 5	6 –6
$P(x_i)$	$\frac{1}{6}$	$\frac{1}{6}$	$\frac{1}{6}$	$\frac{1}{6}$	$\frac{1}{6}$	$\frac{1}{6}$

Note that 2,3 and 5 are prime numbers now the expected gain is

$$E(x)\ \sum_{i=1}^{6} x_i P_i = (-1)\left[\frac{1}{6}\right]+(2)\left[\frac{1}{6}\right]+(3)\left[\frac{1}{6}\right]+(-4)\left[\frac{1}{6}\right]+(5)\left[\frac{1}{6}\right]+(-6)\left[\frac{1}{6}\right] = -\left[\frac{1}{6}\right]$$

Since the expected value of the game is negative, the game is unfavourable to the player.

EXAMPLE 13.81: An urn contains 7 white and 3 red balls. Two balls are drawn together at random from the urn. Find the expected number of white balls drawn.

Solution: *F*rom the urn containing 7 white and 3 red balls, two balls can be drawn in $10C_2$ ways. Let X denote the number of white balls drawn, X can take the values 0, 1 and 2.

The probability distribution of X is obtained as follows:

$P(0)$ = Probability that neither of two balls is white.

= Probability that both balls drawn are red.

$$\frac{{}^3C_2}{{}^{10}C_2} = \frac{3\times 2}{10\times 9} = \frac{1}{15}$$

$P(1)$ = Probability of getting 1 white and 1 red ball.

$$= \frac{{}^7C_1\times{}^3C_1}{{}^{10}C_2} = \frac{7\times 3\times 2}{10\times 9} = \frac{7}{15}$$

$P(2)$ = Probability of getting two white balls

$$= \frac{{}^7C_2}{{}^{10}C_2} = \frac{7\times 6}{10\times 9} = \frac{7}{15}$$

Hence expected number of white balls drawn is

$$E(x) = \Sigma x_i P(x_i) = \left[0\times\frac{1}{15}\right]+\left[1\times\frac{7}{15}\right]+\left[2\times\frac{7}{15}\right]$$

$$= \frac{7}{5} = 1.4$$

EXAMPLE 13.82: A dealer in television sets estimates from his past experience the probabilities of his selling television sets in a day is given below. Find the expected number of sales in a day.

Number of TV sold in a day	0	1	2	3	4	5	6
Probability	0.02	0.10	0.21	0.32	0.20	0.09	0.06

Solution: We observe that the number of television sets sold in a day is a random variable which can assume the values 0, 1,2, 3,4,5,6 with the respective probabilities given in the table.

Now the expectation of $x = E(X) = x_i\ P_i$

$$= x_1 p_1 + x_2 p_2 + x_3 p_3 + x_4 p_4 + x_5 p_5 + x_6 p_6$$

$$= (0)(0.02) + (1)(0.010) + 2(0.21) + (3)(0.32) + 4(0.20) + (5)(0.09) + (6)(0.06)$$

$$E(X) = 3.09$$

The expected number of sales per day is 3.

EXAMPLE 13.83: Let x be a discrete random variable with the following probability distribution

X	–3	6	9
$P(X=x)$	1/6	1/2	1/3

Find the mean and variance

Solution:

$$E(X) = \Sigma x_i\ P_i$$

$$= (-3)\left[\frac{1}{6}\right] + (6)\left[\frac{1}{2}\right] + 9\left[\frac{1}{3}\right] = \left[\frac{11}{2}\right]$$

$$E(x^2) = \Sigma x_i^2 P_i$$

$$= (-3)^2\left[\frac{1}{6}\right] + (6)^2\left[\frac{1}{2}\right] + (9)^2\left[\frac{1}{3}\right] = \left[\frac{93}{2}\right]$$

$$\text{Var}(X) = E(X^2) - [E(X)]^2$$

$$= \left[\frac{93}{2}\right] - \left[\frac{11}{2}\right]^2 = \left[\frac{93}{2}\right] - \left[\frac{121}{4}\right]$$

$$= \frac{186 - 121}{4} = \frac{65}{4}$$

Expectation of a Continuous Random Variable

Let X is a continuous random variable with probability density function $f(x)$, then the mathematical expectation of x is defined as

$$\boxed{E(x) = \int_{-x}^{x} x f(x) dx},$$

provided the integral exists.

Remark: If $g(x)$ is function of a random variable and $E[g(x)]$ exists.

then
$$E[(g(x)] = \int_{-\infty}^{\infty} g(x) f(x)\, dx$$

13.15 MOMENT GENERATING FUNCTION (MGF)

To find out the moments, the moment generating function is a good device. The moment generating function is a special form of mathematical expectation and is very useful in deriving the moments of a probability distribution.

If X is a random variable, then the expected value of etx is known as the moment generating functions, provided the expected value exists for every value of t in an interval, $-h < t < h$, where h is some positive real value.

The moment generating function is denoted as $Mx\ (t)$ For discrete

$$M_x(t) = E\ (e_{tx})$$

$$= \Sigma \left[1 + 1x + \frac{(tx)^2}{2!} + \frac{(tx)^3}{3!} + \ldots\right] p_x(X)$$

$$M_x(t) = \left[1 + t\mu_1' + \frac{t^2}{2!}\mu_2' + \frac{t^3}{3!}\mu_3' + \ldots\right] = \sum_{r=0}^{x} \frac{t^1}{r!}\mu_1'$$

In the above expression, the rth raw moment is the coefficient of $\frac{t^r}{r!}$ in the above expanded sum. To find out the moments differentiate the moment generating function with respect to t once, twice, thrice… and put $t = 0$ in the first, second, third, ... derivatives to obtain the first, second, third,........ moments.

From the resulting expression, we get the raw moments about the origin. The central moments are obtained by using the relationship between raw moments and central moments.

Characteristic Function

In the above expression, the rth raw moment is the coefficient of $\frac{t^1}{r!}$ in the above expanded sum. To find out the moments differentiate the moment generating function with respect to t once, twice, thrice .. and put $t = 0$ in the first, second, third, ... derivatives to obtain the first, second, third, ... moments.

From the resulting expression, we get the raw moments about the origin. The central moments are obtained by using the relationship between raw moments and central moments. The moment generating function does not exist for every distribution. Hence another function, which always exists for all the distributions, is known as characteristic function.

It is the expected value of e^{itx}, where $i = \sqrt{-1}$ and t has a real value and the characteristic function of a random variable X is denoted by $0x(t)$

For a discrete variable X having the probability function $P(x)$, the characteristic function is

$$\phi_x\ (t) = \Sigma\ e^{itx}\ P\ (x)$$

For a continuous variable X having density function $f(x)$, such that $a < x < b$, the characteristic function

$$\phi_x\ (t) = \int_x^b e^{itx}\ f'(x)\ dx$$

LIST OF FORMULAE

1. Probability of an event *A*

$$P(A) = \frac{m}{n} = \frac{\text{Number of favourable outcomes}}{\text{Total number of possible outcomes}}$$

2. Probability of Mutually Exclusive Events *A* and *B*

$$P(A \cup B) = P(A) + P(B)$$

3. Probability of non-mutually exclusive events *A* and *B*

$$P(A \cup B) = P(A) + P(B) - P(A \cap B)$$

4. Probability of two independent event *A* and *B*.

$$P(A \cap B) = P(A)\ P(B)$$

5. Probability of two dependent events *A* and *B*

$$P(A \cap B) = P(A)\ P(B/A)$$

6. Bayes' Theorem

$$P(A_i / B) = \frac{P(A_i / B)\ p(B / A_i)}{\sum_{i=1}^{n} P(A_i)\ P(B / A_i)}$$

7. Conditional Probability

$$P(A / B) = \frac{P(A \cap B)}{P(B)},\ P(B) \neq 0$$

$$P(B / A) = \frac{P(A \cap B)}{P(A)},\ P(A) \neq 0$$

SELF PRACTICE EXERCISES

I. CHOOSE THE BEST ANSWER

1. Probability is expressed as:
   (a) ratio
   (b) percentage
   (c) Proportion
   (d) all the above
2. Probability can take values from:
   (a) $-\infty$ to $+\infty$
   (b) $-\infty$ to 1
   (c) 0 to +1
   (d) –1 to +1
3. Two events are said to be independent if:
   (a) each out come has equal chance of occurrence
   (b) there is the common point in between them
   (c) one does not affect the occurrence of the other.
   (d) both events have only one point

4. Classical probability is also known as:
   (a) Statistical probability
   (b) A priori probability
   (c) Empirical probability
   (d) None of the above
5. When a coin and a die are thrown, the number of all possible cases is:
   (a) 7
   (b) 8
   (c) 12
   (d) 0
6. Probability of drawing a spade queen from a well shuffled pack of cards is:
   (a) 1/13
   (b) 1/52
   (c) 4/13
   (d) 1
7. Three dice are thrown simultaneously the probability that sum being 3 is:
   (a) 0
   (b) 1/216
   (c) 2/216
   (d) 3/216
8. An integer is chosen from 1 to 20. The probability that the number is divisible by 4 is:
   (a) 1/4
   (b) 1/3
   (c) 1/2
   (d) 1/10
9. The conditional probability of B given A is:
   (a) $\frac{P(A \cap B)}{P(B)}$
   (b) $\frac{P(A \cap B)}{P(A)}$
   (c) $\frac{P(A \cup B)}{P(B)}$
   (d) $\frac{P(A \cup B)}{P(A)}$
10. $P(X) = 0.15$, $P(Y) = 0.25$, $P(X\,)”\,Y) = 0.10$ then $P(X \cup Y)$ is:
    (a) 0.10
    (b) 0.20
    (c) 0.30
    (d) 0.40
11. If $P(A) = 0.5$, $P(B) = 0.3$ and the events A and B are independent then $P(A \cap B)$ is:
    (a) 0.8
    (b) 0.15
    (c) 0.08
    (d) 0.015
12. If $P(A) = 0.4$, $P(B) = 0.5$ and $P(AI\ B) = 0.2$ then $P(B/A)$ is:
    (a) 1/2
    (b) 1/3
    (c) 4/5
    (d) 2/5
13. A coin is tossed 6 times. Find the number of points in the sample space.
    (a) 12
    (b) 6
    (c) 32
    (d) 64
14. When a single die is thrown the event of getting odd number or even number are:
    (a) Mutually exclusive events
    (b) Not-mutually exclusive events
    (c) Independent event
    (d) Dependent event
15. The probability of not getting 2, when a die is thrown is:
    (a) 1/3
    (b) 2/3
    (c) 1/6
    (d) 5/6

II. FILL IN THE BLANKS

1. The probability of a sure event is ....
2. The probability of an impossible event is ....

3. Mathematical probability is also called a .... probability.
4. The joint occurrence of two or more events is called ....
5. If A and B are mutually exclusive events, then $P(A \cup B) =$ ....
6. If A and B are independent events then $P(A \cap B) =$ ....
7. If A and B are dependent events then $P(A/B) =$ ....
8. If A and B are mutually exclusive events $P(A \cap B) =$ ....
9. When three coins are tossed the probability of getting 3 heads is ....
10. When three dice are thrown the probability of sum being 17 is ....
11. If $f(x)$ is a distribution function, then $F(+\infty)$ is equal to ....
12. If $F(x)$ is a cumulative distribution function of a continuous random variable x with p.d.f $f(x)$ then $F'(x) =$ ....
13. $f(x)$ is the probability density function of a continuous random variable X.

    $\int_{-\infty}^{\infty} f(x)\, dx$ is equal to ....
14. Mathematical expectation of a random variable X is also known as ....
15. Variance of a constant is ....
16. Var $(12x)$ is ....
17. Var $(4x + 7)$ is ....
18. If x is a discrete random variable with the probabilities pi, then the expected value of x^2 is ....
19. If $f(x)$ is the p.d.f of the continuous random variable X, then the expectation of X is given by ....
20. The moment generating function for the discrete random variable is given by ....

III. SHORT ANSWER TYPE QUESTIONS

1. Define the following terms:
   Event, equally likely events, mutually exclusive events, exhaustive events, sample space.
2. Define dependent and independent events.
3. Define mathematical probability.
4. Define statistical probability.
5. State the axioms of probability.
6. Explain addition theorem on probability for any two events. **[MBA, MK, Univ., 2001]**
7. State the multiplication theorem on probability.
8. Define conditional probability.
9. State Bayes' Rule. **[MBA, Bharathidasan University, 2002, IGNOU, 2002]**
10. What you mean by probability? Discuss the importance of probability? **[MBA, Delhi University, 2002]**
11. Explain the conditional probability. **[MBA, Delhi University, 1999]**

IV. LONG ANSWER TYPE QUESTIONS

1. Describe briefly the various schools of through on probability. How does the concept of probability help decision-maker to improve his decisions? **[MBA, HPU, 1998, DU, 1999]**

2. Examine critically the different schools of through on probability.
3. State the multiplicative theorem of probability. How is the result modified when the events are independent? **[Delhi University, 1999]**
4. Explain what do you mean by the term "mathematical expectation". How is it useful for a businessman? Given an example to illustrate its usefulness. **[Delhi University, 1997]**
5. Give three real-life or business examples for each of the following:
   (a) Mutually exclusive events (b) Joint events
   (c) Independent events (d) Conditional events
6. There are 5 items defective in a sample of 30 items. Find the probability that an item chosen at random from the sample is (i) defective, (ii) non-defective
7. Four coins are tossed simultaneously what is the probability of getting (i) 2 heads (ii) 3 heads (iii) atleast 3 heads
8. Two dice are thrown. What is probability of getting
   (i) the sum is 10, (ii) atleast 10
9. Three dice are rolled once. What is the chance that the sum of the face numbers on the dice is
   (i) exactly 18, (ii) exactly 17, (iii) atmost 17.
10. An integer is chosen from 20 to 30. Find the probability that it is a prime number.
11. An integer is chosen from 1 to 50. Find the probability that it is multiple of 5 or multiply of 7.
12. From a pack of cards find the probability of drawing a spade card or a diamond card.
13. Find the probability that a leap year selected at random will contain 53 Sundays.
14. Find the probability that a non-leap year selected at random will contain either 53 Sundays or 53 Mondays.
15. If two events A and B are not mutually exclusive and are not connected with one random experiment $P(A)= 1/4$, $P(B) =2/5$ and $P(A \cup B) = 1/2$ then find the value of $P(B/A)$
16. For two independent events A and B for which $p(A) = 1/2$ and $p(B) = 1/3$. Find the probability that one of them occur.
17. For two events A and B, $P(A) =1/3 = P(B)$, $P(B/A) =1/4$ find $P(A/B)$
18. A box contains 4 red pens and 5 black pens. Find the probability of drawing 3 black pens one by one: (i) with replacement . (ii) without replacement
19. An urn contains 5 red and 7 green balls. Another urn contains 6 red and 9 green balls. If a ball is drawn from any one of the two urns, find the probability that the ball drawn is green.
20. Two cards are drawn at random from a pack of 52 cards. Find the probability that the cards drawn are:
    (i) a diamond and a spade (ii) a king and a queen (iii) 2 aces
21. A problem in statistics is given to two students A and B. The probability that A solves the problem is 1/2 and that of B' s to solve it is 2/3. Find the probability that the problem is solved.
22. A bag contains 6 white, 4 green and 10 yellow balls. Two balls are drawn at random. Find the probability that both will be yellow.
23. In a certain class there are 21 students in subject A, 17 in subject B and 10 in subject C. Of these 12 attend subjects A and B, 5 attend subjects B and C, 6 attend subjects A and C. These include 2 students who attend all the three subjects. Find the probability that a student studies one subject alone.
24. If $P(A) = 0.3$, $P(B) = 0.2$ and $P(C) = 0.1$ and A, B, C are independent events, find the probability of occurrence of at least one of the three events A , B and C.

25. The odds that A speaks the truth are 3:2 and the odds that B speaks the truth 5:3. In what percentage of cases are they likely to contradict each other on an identical point?
26. The chances of X, Y and Z becoming managers of a certain company are 4:2:3. The probabilities that bonus scheme will be introduced if X, Y and Z become managers are 0.3, 0.5 and 0.4 respectively. If the bonus scheme has been introduced what is the probability that Z is appointed as the manager?
27. A manufacturing firm produces steel pipes in three plants with daily production volumes of 500, 1000 and 2000 units respectively. According to past experience, it is known that the fractions of defective outputs produced by the three plants are respectively, 0.005, 0.008 and 0.010. If a pipe is selected from days total production and found to be defective, what is the probability that it came from the
   (i) first plant (ii) the second plant (iii) the third plant?

ANSWERS

I. CHOOSE THE BEST ANSWERS

1. (d)	2. (c)	3. (c)	4. (b)	5. (c)
6. (b)	7. (b)	8. (a)	9. (b)	10. (c)
11. (b)	12. (a)	13. (d)	14. (a)	15. (d)

II. FILL IN THE BLANKS

1. 1	2. zero	3. priori	4. Compound events
5. $P(A) + P(B)$	6. $P(A) \cdot P(B)$	7. $P(A \cap B) / P(B)$	8. 0
9. 1/8	10. 3/216	11. 1	12. $f(x)$
13. 1	14. Mean	15. Zero	16. 144 var (x)
17. 16 var (x)	18. $\Sigma x^2 p_i$	19. $\int_{-\infty}^{\infty} x f(x) dx$	20. $\sum_{t-0}^{x} \frac{t^t}{r!} \mu!_t$

IV. LONG ANSWER TYPE QUESTIONS

16. $\frac{1}{6} \cdot \frac{5}{6}$	17. $\frac{3}{8}; \frac{1}{4}; \frac{5}{16}$	18. $\frac{1}{12}; \frac{1}{6}$
19. $\frac{1}{216}, \frac{3}{216}, \frac{215}{216}$	20. $\frac{2}{11}$	21. $\frac{8}{25}$
22. $\frac{1}{2}$	23. $\frac{2}{7}$	24. $\frac{2}{7}$

25. $P(A \cap B) = 3/20$; $P(B/A) = 3/5$

26. $\frac{1}{2}$

27. $P(A \cap B) = 1/12$; $P(A/B) = 1/8$

CHAPTER 14

Probability Theoretical Distributions

14.1 INTRODUCTION

Frequency distribution can be obtained in two ways viz., (i) by compiling actual frequencies through collection of data or by conducting experiments, (ii) by deriving the frequencies on the basis of some mathematical relationship.

In chapters on Measures of Central Tendency, Dispersion, Correlation and Regression we dealt with observed frequency distributions where frequencies were arrived at by collection, tabulation and classification of data. When ***for example***, we have a frequency distribution relating to the wages of workers in a factory, or marks obtained by students in an examination or the heights or weights of a group of individuals, we are dealing with observed frequency distribution (also called ***empirical*** or ***experimental*** distribution). These distributions are used to estimate certain values in the universe on the basis of sample studies. Thus when we are finding the average height of adult males through a sample study our purpose is to estimate the average height of the adult males in the universe from which the sample has been taken.

However there are certain situations where we can derive expected values on the basis of some mathematical relationships. ***For example*** if toss a coin we know that the probability of a head is ½ and of a tail is also ½. If we toss a coin 200 times the expected number of heads is 100. This is the theoretical or ***derived frequency*** of heads. In actual practice if we toss a coin 200 times and heads come up 130 times then this is the ***observed frequency*** of heads. Thus in such a case we have an observed frequency of 130 and an expected frequency of 100. If we toss 20 coins 100 times we can have a set of observed frequencies by conducting the experiment and getting observed frequencies. This distribution would be called a ***Theoretical Frequency Distribution*** or a ***Probability Distribution***.

We can define theoretical or probability distributions as such distributions which are not obtained by actual observations or experiments but are mathematically deduced on certain assumptions.

Empirical vs. Theoretical Distribution

An ***empirical distribution*** is one composed of some set of variates — that is, values of X_i— that have either been observed or are capable in principle of being observed. If you were to measure the level of serum cholesterol of 100 adult Canadian males, the resulting 100 values of X_i would constitute an empirical distribution. If you were to speak of the distribution of serum cholesterol levels among adult Canadian males ***in general***, that too would be an empirical distribution, even though you might not have observed all or even most of the multitudinous X_i values of which this distribution is composed.

A ***theoretical distribution***, on the other hand, is one that is derived from certain basic facts, principles, or assumptions, by logical and mathematical reasoning, formulas and logic involving a more or less complex sequence of conditional statements of the general form "***If*** such-and-such is true, ***then*** so-and-so must also be true." In general, the procedures of inferential statistics begin with one or more empirical distributions and conclude by making reference to a theoretical probability distribution.

Theoretical distribution is used in statistics to determine probabilities. When empirical and theoretical distributions correspond, you can use the theoretical one to determine probabilities of an outcome, which will lead to inferential statistics. The main point to retain is that theoretical distributions represent the ***"best estimate"*** of how events would actually occur. As with all estimates, a theoretical distribution may produce predictions that vary from observation, but will produce good estimates. Theoretical Distribution is also called as "Expected or probability or Model frequency Distribution". We may define theoretical distribution as a distribution of frequencies which is not based on actual experiments or observations but is constructed through expected frequencies obtained by mathematical computation based on certain hypothesis. Theoretical distributions are used it statistics to determine probabilities. ***For example***, what is the probability it will rain today? When there is correspondence between an empirical and theoretical distribution, you can use the theoretical distribution to make probabilities (predictions) about future empirical even

14.2 TYPE OF THEORETICAL DISTRIBUTIONS

Distributions are of many types. We will however discuss here only two such distributions which are more popular than others and are widely used. These are

14.2.1 Discrete Probability Distributions

The probability distributions of discrete random variable, termed discrete probability distributions that arise from statistical experiments. The populations that arise from statistical experiments are similar in nature and have the same probability distribution. In this chapter we will study Binomial and Poisson discrete probability distributions that describe most populations encountered in practice.

14.2.2 Continuous Probability Distributions

The random variable X, defined on the sample space S containing an infinite or uncountable infinite numbers of real values, is called a continuous Random variable and their probability distributions are called continuous Probability distribution.

Many types of data are continuous in nature, because the observations are obtained by measurements, made to any degree of accuracy desired. Continuous random variables are usually associated with experiments, related with the measurements. Measurements of time, distance, height, weight, lengths, temperatures and velocities are the continuous random variables, since the successive measurements may differ only by a very small amount. The values of such variables are really rounded a point, but an interval in which the measurement falls. ***For example***, if we write $a \le X \le b$, then X is continuous random variable. The probability distribution of a continuous random variable X is represented by the functional notation $f(X)$ called usually the density function.

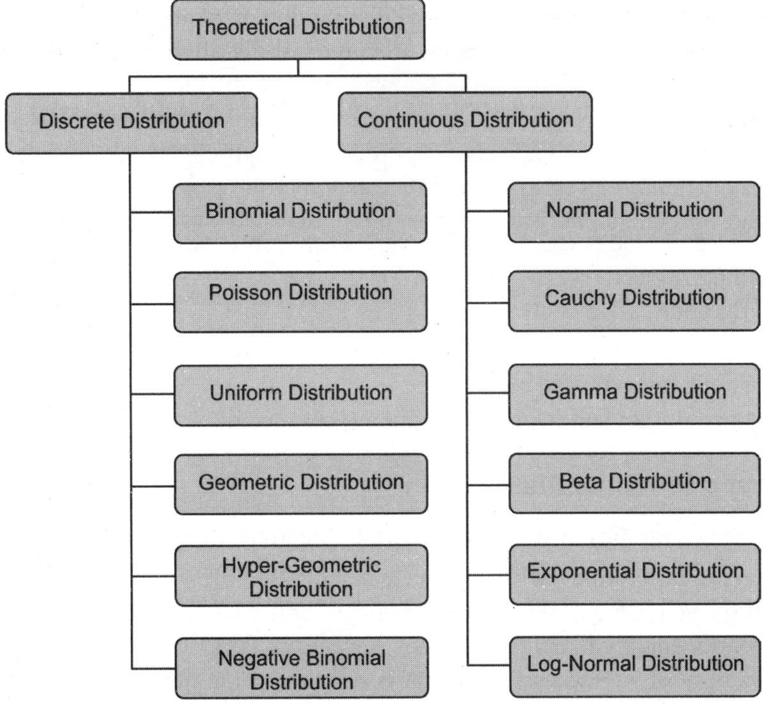

Fig. 14.1: Types of Distribution

In this chapter we will study Binomial Distribution, Poisson Distribution and Normal Continuous Probability Distributions only.

14.3 BINOMIAL DISTRIBUTION

The Binomial distribution is a discrete distribution expressing the probability of a set of dichotomous alternative i.e., ***success*** or ***failure***. This distribution has been used to describe a wide variety of process in business and social sciences as well as other areas.

DO YOU KNOW?

Binomial Distribution is associated with the name of Swiss Mathematician James Bernoulli (1954-1705). However, it was published in 1713, eight years after his death. It is also known as Bernoulli's Distribution. Trial or Process, the literal meaning of the word "Binomial" is two groups or dichotomous alternatives. Hence, in this distribution frequencies are divided on the basis of two aspects or two possible outcomes, which for the sake of convenience are called as success and failure.

Bernoulli's Trials

A series of independent trials which can be resulted in one of the two mutually exclusive possibilities 'successes' or 'failures' such that the probability of the success (or failures) in each trials is constant, then such repeated independent trials are called as "***Bernoulli's trials***".

A discrete variable which can results in only one of the two outcomes (success or failure) is called ***Binomial***.

For example, a coin flips the result of an examination success or failures, the result of a game - win or loss etc. The Binomial distribution is also known as Bernoulli's distribution, which expresses probabilities of events of dichotomous nature in repeated trials.

A random variable X which takes two values 0 and 1 with probabilities q and p i.e.,

$$\boxed{P(x=1)=p \quad \text{and} \quad P(x=0)=q,}$$

$q = 1 - p$

is called a Bernoulli variate and is said to be a Bernoulli Distribution, where p and q takes the probabilities for success and failure respectively.

Examples of Bernoulli's Trails are:

1. Toss of a coin (head or tail)
2. Throw of a die (even or odd number)
3. Performance of a student in an examination (pass or fail)

When do we get a Binomial Distribution?

The following are the conditions in which probabilities are given by binomial distribution.

1. A trial is repeated 'n' times where n are finite and all 'n' trials are identical.
2. Each trial (or you can call it an event) results in only two mutually exclusive, exhaustive but not necessarily equally likely possibilities, success or failure.
3. The probability of a "success" outcome is equal to some percentage which is identified as proportion, p
4. This proportion p, remains constant throughout all events (or trials). It is defined as the ratio of the number of successes to the number of trials.
5. The events (or trials) are independent.
6. If probability of success is p, then the probability of failures is $1 - p$ this is denoted by q. Thus $p + q = 1$.

Suppose a coin is flipped twice. Let p be the probability of getting heads and q the probability of tails, such that $p + q = 1$ (note that $p = q = 1/2$ if the coin is fair) Then there are three possible outcomes which are given below.

Sr. No.	First flip	Second flip	Probability
1.	Tail	Tail	$q \times q = q^2$
2.	Head or Tail	Tail or Head	$p \times q$ or $q \times p = 2pq$
3.	Head	Head	$p \times p = p^2$

The sum of all these probabilities is $q^2 + 2\,pq + p^2 = (q + p)^2$. The terms of $(q + p)^2$ in its expansion give the probabilities of getting 0, 1, 2 heads.

The result obtained above can be generalized to find the probability of getting 'x' heads in flipping n coins simultaneously.

The probabilities of getting 0, 1, 2, 3, ..., r... n heads in a flip of 'n' coins are the terms of the expansion $(q + p)^n$. Since the expansion is given by the Binomial Theorem, the distribution is called Binomial Distribution.

Thus, *A* random variable X is said to follow binomial distribution, if its probability mass function is given by

$$P(X = x) = P(x)^* = \begin{cases} {}^nC_x p^x q^{n-x} & : x = 0, 1, 2, \ldots n \\ 0 & : \text{ otherwise} \end{cases} \quad \ldots(1)$$

Here, the two independent constants n and p are known as the '***parameters***' of the distribution. The distribution is completely determined if n and p are known. x refers the number of successes.

OR

$$p(x = r) = {}^nC_r q^{n-r} p^r$$

$$\text{i.e. } p(x = r) = \frac{n!}{r!(n-r)!} q^{n-r} p^r$$

Where $n! = n(n-1)(n-2) \ldots\ldots\ldots\ldots 3 \,.\, 2 \,.\, 1$

p = Probability of Success,

q = Probability of failure $(1 - p)$

n = Number of trials,

x or r = number of successes in n trial

From (1), we have

Probability of exactly zero success $= {}^nC_0 \; P^0 q^n = {}^nC_0 \; q^n = q^n$

Probability of exactly one success $= {}^nC_1 \; P^1 q^{n-1} = {}^nC_1 \; q^{n-1} P$

Probability of exactly r success $= {}^nC_r \; q^{n-r} P^r$

Probability of exactly n success $= {}^nC_n \; q^{n-n} P^r = {}^nC_n \; P^n$

Sum of the probabilities of exactly zero success, one success, two success and so on upto n success

$$= {}^nC_0 P^0 q^n + {}^nC_1 P q^{n-1} + {}^nC_2 P^2 q^{n-2} + \ldots + {}^nC_r \; P^r q^{n-r} + \ldots + {}^nC_n \; P^n q^0$$

$$= {}^nC_0 \; q^n P^0 + {}^nC_1 q^{n-1} P + {}^nC_2 \; q^{n-2} P^2 + \ldots + {}^nC_n P^n$$

$$= (q + P)^n = (1)^n = 1$$

The Probability of at least one success

= The probability of non-zero success

= Probability of positive success

= 1 – probability of zero success

$= 1 - {}^nC_0 \, q^n = 1 - q^n$

The Probability of at least *r* success (*r* < *n*)

= Probability of exactly r success + probability of exactly $(r + 1)$ success + ... + probability of exactly n success. e.g. probability of at least two success

$= P(2) + P(3) + \ldots P(n)$

$= 1 - [P(0) + P(1)]$ $\qquad [\because (q + P)^n = 1]$

Probability of at most *r* success

$= P(0) + P(1) + \ldots + P(r)$

e.g. probability of at most two success

$= P(0) + P(1) + P(2)$

---

* equal to probability of exactly x success and $(n - x)$ failures in a series of n independent trials.

14.3.1 Condition for Binomial Distribution

We get the Binomial distribution under the following experimental conditions.

1. **Finite number of trails:** The number of trials 'n' is finite and should be fixed.
2. **All trials independent:** The trials are independent of each other.
3. **Same probability in each trail:** The probability of success 'p' is constant for each trial.
4. **Mutually exclusive outcomes:** In each trail, there must be only two possible outcomes of the event which are mutually exclusive. ***For example***, when we toss a coin there are only two possible outcomes-Head or Tail and one of them must happen.
5. **Discrete variable:** The variable should be discrete, i.e., failure or success should be in whole numbers.

The problems relating to tossing of coins or throwing of dice or drawing cards from a pack of cards with replacement lead to binomial probability distribution.

$X \sim B(n, p)$ denotes that the random variable X follows Binomial distribution with parameters n and p.

14.3.2 Constants of Binomial Distribution

For the binomial distribution with parameters n and p.

(i) Mean of Binomial Distribution is

$$\text{mean} = np$$

(ii) Standard deviation of a Binomial Distribution

$$SD(\sigma) = \sqrt{npq}$$

So the variance is $$\text{Variance}(\sigma^2) = npq$$

(iii) The moment in a binomial distribution are as follows:

$$\mu_1 = 0, \mu_2 = npq$$
$$\mu_3 = npq\,(q - P)$$
$$\mu_4 = 3n^2p^2q^2 + npq(1 - 6pq)$$

(iv) The β_1 and β_2 (on the basis of the above moments) are

$$\beta_1 = \frac{\mu_3^2}{\mu_2^3} = \frac{n^2p^2q^2(q-p)^2}{x^3p^3q^3} = \frac{(q-p)^2}{npq}$$

If $\beta_1 = 0$ the distribution is symmetrical

$$\beta_2 = \frac{\mu_4}{\mu_2^2} = \frac{3n^2p^2q^2 + npq(1-6pq)}{n^2p^2q^2} = 3 + \frac{(1-6pq)}{npq}$$

(v) The value of γ_1 and γ_2 are

$$\gamma_1 = \sqrt{\beta_1} = \sqrt{\frac{(p-q)^2}{npq}} = \frac{q-p}{\sqrt{npq}} = \text{skewness}$$

$$\gamma_2 = \beta_{2-3} = 3 + \frac{1-6pq}{npq} - 3$$

$$= \frac{1-6pq}{npq} = \text{Kurtosis}$$

If distribution is normal both γ_1 and γ_2 would be zero.

NOTES:

1. Since q is the probability of failure, we always have $0 < q < 1$

$$\text{Variance} = np \times q < np$$

i.e. $\boxed{\text{Variance} < \text{Mean}}$ [Mean $= np$]

In a Binomial Distribution variance would always be less than the mean.

2. $$\text{Var}(X) = npq = np(1-p)$$

Var (X) is maximum when $p = \frac{1}{2}$

$$\Rightarrow \quad q = 1 - p = 1 - \frac{1}{2} = \frac{1}{2}$$

Maximum variance $(nqP) = n \times \frac{1}{2} \times \frac{1}{2} = \frac{n}{4}$

i.e. for the Binomial Distribution with parameters n and p variance cannot exceed $\frac{n}{4}$.

3. "Binomial Distribution is symmetrical if $p = q = 0.5$ It is positively skewed if $p < 0.5$ and negatively skewed if $p > 0.5$"

14.3.3 Characteristics of Binomial Distribution

1. Binomial distribution is a discrete distribution in which the random variable X (the number of success) assumes the values 0, 1, 2, ...n, where n is finite.
2. The mode of the binomial distribution is that value of the variable which occurs with the largest probability. It may have either one or two modes.
3. If two independent random variables X and Y follow binomial distribution with parameter (n_1, p) and (n_2, p) respectively, then their sum $(X + Y)$ also follows Binomial distribution with parameter $(n_1 + n_2, p)$
4. **Expected frequencies:** If n independent trials are repeated N times, N sets of n trials are obtained and the expected frequency of x success is $N\,({}^nC_x\, p^x\, q^{n-x})$. The expected frequencies of 0, 1, 2... n success are the successive terms of the binomial distribution of $N\,(q + p)^n$.
5. **Sequence of p and q:** The number of successes can be placed in ascending or descending order and according to sequence, the expression shall be as follows:

$$0,1,2,3,4,5,6,7,8,9,\ldots\ldots\ldots\ldots,n = (q + p)^n$$
$$n\ldots\ldots\ldots\ldots9,8,7,6,5,4,3,2,1,0 = (p + q)^n$$

EXAMPLE 14.1: Eight coins are tossed simultaneously. Find the probability of getting atleast six heads.

Solution: Here number of trials, $n = 8$, p denotes the probability of getting a head.

$$\therefore \quad p = \frac{1}{2} \text{ and } q = \frac{1}{2}$$

If the random variable X denotes the number of heads, then the probability of a success in n trials is given by

$$P(X = x) = {}^{n}c_{x}\, p^{x}\, q^{n-x},\ x = 0, 1, 2, \ldots n$$

$$= {}^{8}C_{x}\left(\frac{1}{2}\right)^{x}\left(\frac{1}{2}\right)^{8-x} = {}^{8}C_{x}\left(\frac{1}{2}\right)^{8} = \frac{1}{2^{8}}\,{}^{8}C_{x}$$

Probability of getting atleast six heads is given by

$$P(x^{3} \geq 6) = P(x = 6) + P(x = 7) + P(x = 8)$$

$$= \frac{1}{2^{8}}\,{}^{8}C_{6} + \frac{1}{2^{8}}\,{}^{8}C_{7} + \frac{1}{2^{8}}\,{}^{8}C_{8}$$

$$= \frac{1}{2^{8}}[{}^{8}C_{6} + {}^{8}C_{7} + {}^{8}C_{8}]$$

$$= \frac{1}{2^{8}}[28 + 8 + 1] = \frac{37}{256}$$

EXAMPLE 14.2: Ten coins are tossed simultaneously. Find the probability of getting (i) atleast seven heads (ii) exactly seven heads (iii) atmost seven heads.

Solution:

$$p = \text{Probability of getting a head} = \frac{1}{2}$$

$$q = \text{Probability of not getting a head} = \frac{1}{2}$$

The probability of getting x heads throwing 10 coins simultaneously is given by

$$P(X = x) = {}^{n}C_{x}\, p^{x}\, q^{n-x}.,\ x = 0, 1, 2, .. n$$

$$= {}^{10}C_{x}\left(\frac{1}{2}\right)^{x}\left(\frac{1}{2}\right)^{10-x} = \frac{1}{2^{10}}\,{}^{10}C_{x}$$

(i) Probability of getting atleast seven heads

$$P(x^{3} \geq 7) = P(x = 7) + P(x = 8) + P(x = 9) + P(x = 10)$$

$$= \frac{1}{2^{10}}[{}^{10}C_{7} + {}^{10}C_{8} + {}^{10}C_{9} + {}^{10}C_{10}]$$

$$= \frac{1}{1024}[120 + 45 + 10 + 1] = \frac{176}{1024}$$

(ii) Probability of getting exactly 7 heads 11

$$P(x = 7) = \frac{1}{2^{10}}\,{}^{10}C_{7} = \frac{1}{2^{10}}(120) = \frac{120}{1024}$$

(iii) Probability of getting atmost 7 heads

$$P(x \leq 7) = 1 - P(x > 7)$$

$$= 1 - \{P(x = 8) + P(x = 9) + P(x = 10)\}$$

$$= 1 - \frac{1}{2^{10}}\{{}^{10}C_{8} + {}^{10}C_{9} + {}^{10}C_{10})$$

$$= 1 - \frac{1}{2^{10}}[45 + 10 + 1] = 1 - \frac{56}{1024} = \frac{968}{1024}.$$

EXAMPLE 14.3: 20 wrist watches in a box of 100 are defective. If 10 watches are selected at random, find the probability that (i) 10 are defective (ii) 10 are good (iii) at least one watch is defective (iv) at most 3 are defective. **[MBA, Manglore University, 2002]**

Solution: 20 out of 100 wrist watches are defective

Probability of defective wrist watch,

$$p = \frac{20}{100} = \frac{1}{5}$$

$$\therefore \qquad q = 1 - p = \frac{4}{5}$$

Since 10 watches are selected at random, $n = 10$

$$P(X = x) = {}^nC_x p^x q^{n-x}, \quad x = 0, 1, 2 .. 10$$

$$= {}^{10}C_x \left(\frac{1}{5}\right)^x \left(\frac{4}{5}\right)^{10-x}$$

(i) Probability of selecting 10 defective watches

$$P(x = 10) = {}^{10}C_{10} \left(\frac{1}{5}\right)^{10} \left(\frac{4}{5}\right)^0$$

$$= 1 \cdot \frac{1}{5^{10}} \cdot 1 = \frac{1}{5^{10}}$$

(ii) Probability of selecting 10 good watches (i.e. no defective)

$$P(x = 0) = {}^{10}C_0 \left(\frac{1}{5}\right)^0 \left(\frac{4}{5}\right)^{10}$$

$$= 1.1 \cdot \left(\frac{4}{5}\right)^{10} - \left(\frac{4}{5}\right)^{10}$$

(iii) Probability of selecting at least one defective watch

$$P(x \leq 1) = 1 - P(x < 1)$$

$$= 1 - P(x = 0)$$

$$= 1 - {}^{10}C_0 \left(\frac{1}{5}\right)^0 \left(\frac{4}{5}\right)^{10}$$

$$= 1 - \left(\frac{4}{5}\right)^{10}$$

(iv) Probability of selecting at most 3 defective watches

$$p(x \leq 3) = P(x = 0) + P(x = 1) + P(x = 2) + P(x = 3)$$

$$= {}^{10}C_0 \left(\frac{1}{5}\right)^0 \left(\frac{4}{5}\right)^{10} + {}^{10}C_1 \left(\frac{1}{5}\right)^1 \left(\frac{4}{5}\right)^9 + {}^{10}C_2 \left(\frac{1}{5}\right)^2 \left(\frac{4}{5}\right)^8 + {}^{10}C_3 \left(\frac{1}{5}\right)^3 \left(\frac{4}{5}\right)^7$$

$$= 1.1 \left(\frac{4}{5}\right)^{10} + 10 \left(\frac{1}{5}\right)^1 \left(\frac{4}{5}\right)^9 + \frac{10.9}{1.2} \left(\frac{1}{5}\right)^2 \left(\frac{4}{5}\right)^8 + \frac{10.9.8}{1.2.3} \left(\frac{1}{5}\right)^3 \left(\frac{4}{5}\right)^7$$

$$= 1.\,(0.107) + 10\,(0.026) + 45\,(0.0062) + 120\,(0.0016) = 0.859 \text{ (approx.)}$$

EXAMPLE 14.4: With the usual notation find p for binomial random variable X if $n = 6$ and $9\,P(X = 4) = P(X = 2)$

Solution: The probability mass function of binomial random variable X is given by

$$P(X = x) = {}^{n}C_{x}\, p^{x}\, q^{n-x}., \qquad [x = 0, 1, 2, ..., n]$$

Here $n = 6$

$$\therefore \quad P(X = x) = {}^{6}C_{x}\, p^{x}\, q_{2}^{6-x}$$

$$P(x = 4) = {}^{6}C_{4}\, p^{4} q^{2}$$

$$P(x = 2) = {}^{6}C_{2}\, p^{2} q^{4}$$

Given that,

$$9.P(x = 4) = P(x = 2)$$

$$9.{}^{6}C_{4}\, p^{4}\, q^{2} = {}^{6}C_{2}\, p^{2}\, q^{4}$$

$$\Rightarrow \quad 9 \times 15\, p^{2} = 15\, q^{2}$$

$$9p^{2} = q^{2}$$

Taking positive square root on both sides we get.

$$3p = q = 1 - p$$

$$4p = 1$$

$$\therefore \quad p = \frac{1}{4} = 0.25$$

EXAMPLE 14.5: Suppose that the half of the population of town are consumers of rice. One hundred investigators are appointed to find out its truth. Each investigator interviewed 10 individuals. How many investigators do you expect to report that three or less of the people interviewed are consumers of rice?

Solution: Probability of a person being consumer of rice is $P = 1/2$, $q = 1/2$. Probability that three people or less are consumers of rice is given by

$$P[X \le 3] = P[X = 0] + [X = 1] + P[X = 2] + P[X = 3]$$

$$= q^{10} + {}^{10}C_{1}\, q^{9}\, p^{1} + {}^{10}C_{2}\, q^{8}\, p^{2} + {}^{10}C_{3}\, q^{7}\, p^{3}$$

$$= \left(\frac{1}{2}\right)^{10} + 10\left(\frac{1}{2}\right)^{10} + 45\left(\frac{1}{2}\right)^{10} + 120\left(\frac{1}{2}\right)^{10}$$

$$= \left(\frac{1}{2}\right)^{10} (1 + 10 + 45 + 120) = \frac{176}{1024}$$

Therefore, the number of investigators to report that three or less people are consumers of rice is given by $= \frac{176}{1024} \times 100 = 17.2 \approx 17$ approx.

EXAMPLE 14.6: The incidence of occupational disease in an industry is such that the workers have a 20% chance of suffering from it. What is the probability that out of six workers 4 or more will contract disease?

[MBA, Lucknow University, 1998, DU, 2002]

Solution: The probability of a worker who is suffering from the disease, i.e., $p = \frac{20}{100} = \frac{1}{5}$

The probability of a worker who is not suffering from the disease i.e., $q = 1 - P = 1 - \frac{1}{5} = \frac{4}{5}$

The probability of 4 or more. i.e, 4, 5 or 6 will contract disease is given by

$$P[X \leq 4] = P[4] + P[5] + P[6]$$

$$= ({}^6C_4)\left(\frac{1}{5}\right)^4 + ({}^6C_5)\left(\frac{1}{5}\right)^5\left(\frac{4}{5}\right) + ({}^6C_6)\left(\frac{1}{5}\right)^6$$

$$= 15\left(\frac{1}{5}\right)^4\left(\frac{4}{5}\right)^2 + 6\left(\frac{1}{5}\right)^5\left(\frac{4}{5}\right) + \left(\frac{1}{5}\right)^6$$

$$= \frac{15 \times 16}{15625} + \frac{6 \times 4}{15625} \times \frac{1}{15625}$$

$$= \frac{1}{15625}[240 + 24 + 1] = \frac{265}{15625} = \frac{53}{3125} = 0.01696$$

EXAMPLE 14.7: Assume that on an average one telephone number out of fifteen is busy. What is the probability that if six randomly selected telephone numbers are called

(a) not more than three will be busy?
(b) at least three of them will be busy?

Solution: p = probability that a telephone number is busy $= \frac{1}{15}$

$$q = 1 - p = 1 - \frac{1}{15} = \frac{14}{15}; \text{ and } n = 6.$$

(a) The probability that out of six randomly selected telephone numbers not more than three numbers are busy is given by

$$P[X \leq 3] - P(0) + P(1) + P(2) + P(3)$$

$$= ({}^6C_0)\left(\frac{14}{15}\right)^6 + ({}^6C_1)\left(\frac{14}{15}\right)^5\left(\frac{1}{15}\right)^1 + ({}^6C_2)\left(\frac{14}{15}\right)^4\left(\frac{1}{15}\right)^2 + ({}^6C_3)\left(\frac{14}{15}\right)^3\left(\frac{1}{15}\right)^3$$

$$= \left(\frac{1}{15}\right)^6[(14)^6 + 6(14)^5 + 15(14)^4 + 20(14)^3]$$

$$= \frac{(14)^3}{(15)^6}[(14)^3 + 6(14)^2 + 15(14) + 20]$$

EXAMPLE 14.8: Four candidates *A, B, C* and *D* are contesting for an election. The probabilities that a voter will vote for *A, B, C* and *D* respectively are 0.3, 0.1, 0.2 and 0.4. What is the probability that out of 4 voters, three or more will vote for *B*?

Solution: Probability that a voter will vote for $B = 0.1$ = Probability of success for *B*.

Probability that a voter will not vote for $B = 1 - 0.1 = 0.9$ = Probability of *B*'s failure.

Required Probability = Probability of three successes + Probability of four successes

$$= {}^4C_3\, qp^3 + {}^4C_4\, p^4$$

$$= 4\,(0.9)\,(0.1)^3 + (0.1)^4 = 4 \times 0.9 \times 0.001 + 0.0001$$

$$= 4 \times 0.0009 + 0.0001 = 0.0036 + 0.0001 = 0.0037.$$

EXAMPLE 14.9: If the probabilities of having a male or female child are both 0.50, find the probabilities that

(a) a family's fourth child is their first son;
(b) a family's seventh child is their second daughter;
(c) a family's tenth child is their fourth or fifth son.

Solution:

(a) The required Probability is the probability that there is no son in the first three children and the Probability that fourth child is son

$$= {}^3C_0 \left(\frac{1}{2}\right)^3 \left(\frac{1}{2}\right)^0 \times \frac{1}{2} = \frac{1}{16}$$

(b) Required Probability = The Probability that there is only one daughter in the first six children and the seventh child is daughter

$$= {}^6C_1 \left(\frac{1}{2}\right)^5 \times \frac{1}{2} \times \frac{1}{2} = 6 \times \frac{1}{128} = \frac{6}{128}$$

(c) Required Probability $= {}^9C_3 \left(\frac{1}{2}\right)^6 \times \left(\frac{1}{2}\right)^3 \times \frac{1}{2} + {}^9C_4 \left(\frac{1}{2}\right)^5 \times \left(\frac{1}{2}\right)^4 \times \frac{1}{2}$

$$= \frac{9 \times 8 \times 7}{6} \times \frac{1}{1024} + \frac{9 \times 8 \times 7 \times 6}{24} \times \frac{1}{1024}$$

$$= \left[\frac{84}{1024} + \frac{126}{1024}\right] = \frac{210}{1024} = 0.205$$

EXAMPLE 14.10: What is the expression of heads if an unbiased coin is tossed 12 times?

Solution: Since the expression of x in a binomial distribution is given by, $E(x) = np$

Where $n = 12$ and $p = 0.5$

We could expect $12 \times 0.5 = 6$ heads

EXAMPLE 14.11: For a Binomial distribution, mean is 2 and standard deviation is 1. Find all the constants of the distribution.

Solution: We are given, Mean $(m) = n\,p = 2$ and S.D $= \sqrt{npq}$

Therefore, $\frac{npq}{np} = \frac{1}{2}$

$q = 0.5$

Also, $p = 1 - q = 1.0.5 = 0.5$

Again $np = 2 \Rightarrow n \times 0.5 = 2$

$n = 4$

Hence the constants of the distribution are $n = 4$, $p = 0.5$ and $q = 0.5$

EXAMPLE 14.12: Comment on the following: "The mean of a binomial distribution is 5 and its variance is 9"

Solution: The parameters of the binomial distribution are n and p

We have mean » $np = 5$

Variance » $npq = 9$

$$\therefore \quad q = \frac{npq}{np} = \frac{9}{5}$$

$$q = \frac{9}{5} > 1$$

Which is not admissible since q cannot exceed unity? Hence the given statement is wrong.

EXAMPLE 14.13: For a Binomial distribution, mean is 2 and standard deviation is 1. Find all the constants of the distribution.

Solution: We are given, Mean $(m) = n\,p = 2$ and S.D = $\sqrt{npq}$

Therefore, $$\frac{npq}{np} = \frac{1}{2}$$

$$q = 0.5$$

Also, $p = 1, q = 1.0.5 = 0.5$

Again $np = 2 \Rightarrow n \times 0.5 = 2$

$$n = 4$$

Hence the constants of the distribution are $n = 4$, $p = 0.5$ and $q = 0.5$

EXAMPLE 14.14: If the probability of a defective bulb is 0.4. Find the mean and the standard deviation for the distribution of the defective bulbs in a lot of 1000 bulbs. What is the expected number of defective bulbs in the lot?

Solution: We have $p = 0.4$, $n = 1000$ and $q = 1 - p = 1 - 0.4 = 0.6$

Mean $(m) = np = 1000 \times 0.2 = 200$

Fitting of Binomial Distribution

When a binomial distribution is to be fitted to an observed data, the following procedure is adopted.

1. Find Mean $(\bar{X}) = \frac{\Sigma fx}{\Sigma f} = np$

   □ $P = \frac{\bar{X}}{n}$ [n is number of trials]

2. Determine the value of q. [$q = 1 - p$]
3. The probability function is

   $$P\ (x) = {}^nC_x\ p^x\ q^{n-x}$$

   put $x = 0$, we get

   $P\ (0) = q^n$ and

   $f(0) = N \times P\ (0)$

4. Expand the binomial $(q + p)^n$. The power n is equal to one less than the number of terms in the expanded binomial. Thus, when $n = 2$ there will be three terms in the binomial. Similarly, when $n = 4$ there will be five terms.
5. Multiply each term of the expanded binomial by N (the total frequency), in order to obtain the expected frequency in each category.

It is convenient to use the following recurrence relation for fitting of binomial distribution:

$$f(x) = p\,[X = x] = {}^nC_x\; p^x\; q^{n-x}$$

$$f(x+1) = p\,[X = x+1] = {}^nC_{x+1}\, p^{x+1}\; q^{n-(x+1)}$$

$$\therefore \quad \frac{f(x+1)}{f(x)} = \frac{p}{q}\,\frac{n-x}{x+1}$$

$$\boxed{f(x+1) = \frac{p}{q}\,\frac{n-x}{x+1}\,f(x)}$$

When $x = 0$, $\quad f(1) = \frac{p}{q}\,\frac{n-0}{0+1}\,f(0) = \frac{p}{q}\,nf(0)$

$x = 1$, $\quad f(2) = \frac{p}{q}\,\frac{n-1}{2}\,f(1) = \left(\frac{p}{q}\right)^2 \frac{n(n-1)}{2!}\,f(0)$

$x = 2$, $\quad f(3) = \frac{p}{q}\,\frac{n-1}{3}\,f(2) = \left(\frac{p}{q}\right)^3 \frac{n(n-1)(n-2)}{3!}\,f(0)$ and so on.

This formula provides us a very convenient method for fitting the binomial distribution. The only probability we need to calculate is $f(0)$ which is equal to q^n, where q can be estimated from the given data.

EXAMPLE 14.15: A set of three similar coins are tossed 100 times with the following results

Number of heads	0	1	2	3
Frequency	36	40	22	2

Solution:

X	f	fx
0	36	0
1	40	40
2	22	44
3	2	6
	Σf = 100	Σfx = 90

$$\text{Mean } \bar{X} = \frac{\Sigma fx}{\Sigma f} = \frac{90}{100} = 0.9$$

$$p = \frac{x}{n} = \frac{0.9}{3} = 0.3$$

$$q = 1 - 0.3 = 0.7$$

The probability function is $P(x) = {}^nC_x\, p^x\, q^{n-x}$

Here $n = 3$, $p = 0.3$ $q = 0.7$

$$\therefore \quad P(x) = {}^3C_x\,(0.3)^x\,(0.7)^{3-x}$$

$$P(0) = {}^3C_0\,(0.3)^0\,(0.7)^3 = (0.7)^3 = 0.343$$

$$\therefore \quad f(0) = N \times P(0) = 0.343 \times 100 = 34.3$$

The other frequencies are obtained by using the recurrence formula

$$f(1) = \frac{3-0}{0+1}\left(\frac{p}{q}\right) \times 34.3 = 3 \times (0.43) \times 34.3 = 44.247$$

$$f(2) = \frac{3-1}{1+1}\left(\frac{p}{q}\right) f(1) = \frac{2}{2}(0.43) \times 44.247 = 19.03$$

$$f(3) = \frac{3-2}{2+1}\left(\frac{p}{q}\right) f(2) = \frac{1}{3}(0.43) \times 19.03 = 2.727$$

the observed and theoretical (expected) frequencies are tabulated below:

					Total
Observed frequencies	36	40	22	2	**100**
Expected frequencies	34	44	19	3	**100**

The observed and theoretical (expected) frequencies are tabulated below:

EXAMPLE 14.16: 4 coins are tossed and number of heads noted. The experiment is repeated 200 times and the following distribution is obtained.

Number of heads (x)	0	1	2	3	4
Frequencies (f)	62	85	40	11	2

Solution:

x	0	1	2	3	4	**Total**
f	62	85	40	11	2	**200**
fx	0	85	80	33	8	**206**

$$\text{Mean } (\bar{X}) = \frac{\Sigma fx}{\Sigma f} = \frac{206}{200} = 1.03$$

$$p = \frac{x}{n} = \frac{1.03}{4} = 0.2575$$

$\therefore$ $$q = 1 - 0.2575 = 0.7425$$

Here $$n = 4, p = 0.2575; q = 0.7425$$

The probability function of binomial distribution is

$$P(x) = {}^nC_x p^x q^{n-x}$$

The binomial probability function is

$$P(x) = {}^4C_x (0.2575)^x (0.7425)^{4-x}$$

$$P(0) = (0.7425)^4 = 0.3039$$

$\therefore$ $$f(0) = NP(0) = 200 \times 0.3039 = 60.78$$

The other frequencies are calculated using the recurrence formula

$$f(x+1) = \frac{n-x}{x+1}\left(\frac{p}{q}\right) f(x)$$

By putting $x = 0,1, 2, 3$ then the expected frequencies are calculated as follows:
Put $x = 0$, we get

$$f(1) = \frac{4-0}{0+1}(0.3468)(60.78) = 84.3140$$

$$f(2) = \frac{4-1}{1+1}(0.3468)(84.3140) = 43.8601$$

$$f(3) = \frac{4-2}{2+1}(0.3468)(43.8601) = 10.1394$$

$$f(4) = \frac{4-3}{3+1}(0.3468)(10.1394) = 0.8791$$

The theoretical and expected frequencies are tabulated below:

						Total
Observed frequencies	62	85	40	11	2	200
Expected frequencies	61	84	44	10	1	200

14.4 POISSON DISTRIBUTION

Poisson distribution is also a discrete distribution. He derived it as a limiting case of Binomial distribution. For n-trials the binomial distribution is $(q+p)\,n$; the probability of x successes is given by $P(X=x) = nCx\,px\,qn-x$. If the number of trials n is very large and the probability of success 'p' is very small so that the product $np = m^*$ is non – negative and finite. The probability of x success is given by

$$P(X=x) = \begin{cases} \dfrac{e^{-m} m^x}{x!} & \text{for } x = 0,1,2... \\ 0 & ;\text{otherwise} \end{cases}$$

DO YOU KNOW?

Poisson distribution was discovered by a French Mathematician-cum-Physicist Simeon Denis Poisson in 1837.

Here m is known as parameter of the distribution so that $m > 0$. Since number of trials is very large and the probability of success p is very small, it is clear that the event is a rare event.

Therefore Poisson distribution relates to rare events.

NOTES:

1. e is given by $e = 1 + \frac{1}{11} + \frac{1}{2!} + \frac{1}{3!} + ... = 2.71828$

* Some author use λ instead of m.

2. $P(X=0) = \dfrac{e^{-m}m^6}{0!}$ [0! = 1 and 1! = 1]

3. $P(X=1) = \dfrac{e^{-m}m^1}{1!}$

Poisson distribution is an approximation of binomial distribution when n (number of trials) is large and p, the probability of success is very close to zero with np as constant.

14.4.1 Areas Where Poisson Distribution is Applied

1. The number of blinds born in a town in a particular year.
2. Number of mistakes committed in a typed page.
3. The number of students scoring very high marks in all subjects
4. The number of plane accidents in a particular week.
5. The number of defective screws in a box of 100, manufactured by a reputed company.
6. Number of suicides reported in a particular day.
7. Number of accidents on road
8. Number of printing mistakes in a book
9. Number of suicides reported in a particular city.

An important class of decision problems under uncertainty is characterized by the small chance of the occurrence of a particular event, such as an accident. Poisson probability function computes the probability of exactly x independent occurrences during a given period of time, if events take place independently and at a constant rate. Poisson probability function also represents number of occurrences over constant areas or volumes: Poisson probabilities are often used; ***for example*** in quality control, software and hardware reliability, insurance claim, number of incoming telephone calls, and queuing theory.

It is used frequently in quality control, reliability, queuing theory, and so on.

Used to represent distribution of number of defects in a piece of material, customer arrivals, insurance claims, incoming telephone calls, alpha particles emitted, and so on.

A process that creates fabric is monitored. If the number of defects (X) per meter of fabric exceeds 5 then the process is stopped for diagnosis. The random variable X follows a Poisson distribution with rate = number of defects per meter of fabric.

One of the most useful applications of the Poisson distribution is in the field of queuing theory. In many situations where queues occur it has been shown that the number of people joining the queue in a given time period follows the Poisson model.

14.4.2 Conditions for Poisson Distribution

Poisson distribution is the limiting case of binomial distribution under the following conditions:

1. The number of trials n is indefinitely large i.e., $n \rightarrow \infty$
2. The probability of success 'p' for each trial is very small; i.e., $p \rightarrow 0$
3. $np = m$ (say) is finite , $m > 0$

14.4.3 Constants of Poisson Distribution

For the Poisson Distribution with parameters m

(i) Mean of Poisson Distribution is

$$\boxed{\text{Mean} = m}$$

(ii) Standard deviation of a Poisson Distribution is

$$\boxed{\text{S.D}\,(\sigma) = \sqrt{m}}$$

so the variance is

$$\boxed{\text{Variance}(\sigma)^2 = m}$$

Thus, the variance of the Poisson Distribution is also equal to mean

$$\boxed{\text{Variance} = \text{Mean}}$$

14.4.4 Characteristics of Poisson Distribution

The following are the characteristics of Poisson Distribution

1. **Discrete distribution:** Poisson distribution is a discrete distribution like Binomial distribution, where the random variable assumes as a countable infinite number of values 0, 1, 2 ….
2. **The values of p and q:** It is applied in situation where the probability of success p of an event is very small and that of failure q is very high almost equal to 1 and n is very large.
3. **The parameter:** The parameter of the Poisson distribution is m. If the value of m is known, all the probabilities of the Poisson distribution can be ascertained.
4. **Additive Property:** If X and Y are two independent Poisson distributions with parameter m_1 and m_2 respectively. Then $(X+Y)$ also follows the Poisson distribution with parameter $(m_1 + m_2)$
5. **As an approximation to binomial distribution:** Poisson distribution can be taken as a limiting form of Binomial distribution when n is large and p is very small in such a way that product $np = m$ remains constant.
6. **Assumptions:** The Poisson distribution is based on the following assumptions.
   - The occurrence or non-occurrence of an event does not influence the occurrence or non-occurrence of any other event.
   - The probability of success for a short time interval or a small region of space is proportional to the length of the time interval or space as the case may be.
   - The probability of the happening of more than one event is a very small interval is negligible.

EXAMPLE 14.17: Find the probability that atmost 5 defective fuses will be found in a box of 200 fuses if experience shows that 2 percent of such fuses are defective. ($e^{-4} = 0.0183$)

Solution:

$$p = \text{probability that a fuse is defective} = \frac{2}{100}$$

$$n = 200$$

$$\therefore \quad m = np = \frac{2}{100} \times 200 = 4$$

Let X denote the number of defective fuses found in a box.

Then the distribution is given by

$$P[X = x] = p(x) = \frac{e^{-4}4^x}{x!}$$

So, probability that atmost 5 defective fuses will be found in a box of 200 fuses.

$$= P(X \leq 5)$$

$$= P(X=0) + P(X=1) + P(X=2) + P(X=3) + P(X=4) + P(X=5)$$

$$= e^{-4} + \frac{e^{-4}}{1!} + \frac{e^{-4}4^2}{2!} + \frac{e^{-4}4^3}{3!} + \frac{e^{-4}4^4}{4!} + \frac{e^{-4}4^5}{5!}$$

$$= e^{-1}(1 + \frac{4}{1!} + \frac{4^2}{2!} + \frac{4^3}{3!} + \frac{4^4}{4!} + \frac{4^5}{5!})$$

$$= 0.0183 \times \frac{643}{15} = 0.785$$

EXAMPLE 14.18: Suppose on an average 1 house in 1000 in a certain district has a fire during a year. If there are 2000 houses in that district, what is the probability that exactly 5 houses will have a fire during the year? [given that $e^{-2} = 0.13534$] **[MBA, Rohalkhand University, 1999]**

$$\text{Mean } (m) = np,\ n = 2000 \text{ and } p = 1/1000$$

$$= 2000 \times \frac{1}{1000}$$

$$m = 2$$

The Poisson distribution is

$$P(X = x) = \frac{e^{-m}m^x}{x!}$$

The probability that exactly 5 houses will have a fire during the year is

$$\therefore \quad P(X = 5) = \frac{e^{-2}2^5}{5!} = \frac{(0.13534) \times 32}{120} = 0.036$$

EXAMPLE 14.19: In a Poisson distribution $3P(X = 2) = P(X = 4)$. Find the parameter 'm'.

Solution: Poisson distribution is given by

$$P(X = x) = \frac{e^{-m}m^x}{x!}$$

Given that $3P(x = 2) = P(x = 4)$

$$3 \cdot \frac{e^{-m}m^2}{2!} = \frac{e^m m^4}{4!}$$

$$m^2 = \frac{3 \times 4!}{2!}$$

$$\therefore \quad m = \pm 6$$

Since mean is always positive $m = 6$

EXAMPLE 14.20: If 2% of electric bulbs manufactured by a certain company are defective. Find the probability that in a sample of 200 bulbs (i) less than 2 bulbs (ii) more than 3 bulbs are defective. $[e^{-4} = 0.0183]$ **[MBA, Jodhpur University, 1998]**

Solution: The probability of a defective bulb

$$p = \frac{2}{100} = 0.02$$

Given that $n = 200$ since p is small and n is large

We use the Poisson distribution

$$\text{mean } (m) = np = 200 \times 0.02 = 4$$

Now, Poisson Probability function,

$$P(X = x) = \frac{e^{-m} m^x}{x!}$$

(i) Probability of less than 2 bulbs are defective

$$= P(X < 2)$$
$$= P(x = 0) + P(x = 1)$$
$$= \frac{e^{-4} 4^0}{0!} + \frac{e^{-4} 4^1}{1!}$$
$$= e^{-4} + e^{-4}(4)$$
$$= e^{-4}(1 + 4) = 0.0183 \times 5 = 0.0915$$

(ii) Probability of getting more than 3 defective bulbs

$$P(x > 3) = 1 - P(x \leq 3)$$
$$= 1 - \{P(x = 0) + P(x = 1) + P(x = 2) + P(x = 3)\}$$
$$= 1 - e^{-4}\{1 + 4 + \frac{4^2}{2!} + \frac{4^3}{3!}\}$$
$$= 1 - \{0.0183 \times (1 + 4 + 8 + 10.67)\}$$
$$= 0.567$$

EXAMPLE 14.21: The number of accidents in a year attributed to taxi drivers in a city follows poisson distribution with mean 3. Out of 1000 taxi drivers, find the approximate number of drivers with

(i) no accident in a year

(ii) more than 3 accidents in a year

Solution:

Here
$$m = np = 3$$
$$n = 1000$$

Then the distribution is

$$P[X = x] = \frac{e^{-3} 3^r}{x!} \text{ where } X \text{ denotes the number accidents}$$

(i) P (no accidents in a year) $= P(X = 0)$

$$= e^{-3} = 0.05$$

$\therefore$ Number of drivers with no accident $= 1000 \times 0.05 = 50$

(ii) P (that more than 3 accident in a year) = $P(X > 3)$

$$= 1 - P(X \leq 3)$$

$$= 1 - \left[e^{-3} + \frac{e^{-3}3^1}{1!} + \frac{e^3 3^2}{2!} + \frac{e^{-3}3^3}{3!} \right]$$

$$= 1 - e^{-3} [1 + 3 + 4.5 + 4.5]$$

$$= 1 - e^{-3} (13) = 1 = .65 = .35$$

$\therefore$ Number of drivers with more than 3 accidents = 1000 × 0.35 = 350

EXAMPLE 14.22: A local electrical appliances shop has found from experience that the demand for tube lights is distributed as Poisson with a mean of 4 tube lights per week. If the shop keeps 6 tubes during a particular week, what is the probability that the demand will exceed the supply during that week? ($e^{-4} = 0.0183$).

Hint: Let the demand for the tube be taken as success.

Probability that the demand will exceed the supply

$$= 1 - e^4 \left[\frac{4^0}{0!} + \frac{4!}{1!} + \frac{4^2}{2!} + \frac{4^3}{3!} + \frac{4^4}{4!} + \frac{4^5}{5!} + \frac{4^6}{6!} \right] = 0.1114.$$

EXAMPLE 14.23: In a certain factory blades are manufactured in a package of 10. There is a 0.2% probability for any blade to be defective. Using Poisson distribution calculate approximately the number of packets containing two defective blades in a consignment of 20,000 packets (given $e^{-0.02} = 0.9802$).

Solution: Average number of defective blades in a packet of 10 blades

$$= 10 \times \frac{0.2}{100} = 0.02$$

$$\text{Required number of packets} = 20{,}000 \times \frac{e^{-0.02} \times (0.02)^2}{2}$$

$$= 20{,}000 \times \frac{0.9802 \times 0.0004}{2} = 3.9208 = 4 \text{(approx.)}$$

EXAMPLE 14.24: A manufacture of pins knows that on an average 5% of his product is defective. He sells pins in boxes of 100, and guarantees that not more than 4 pins will be defective. What is the probability that a box will meet the guaranteed quality? ($e^{-5} = 0.0067$).

Solution: $m = 100 \times \frac{5}{100} = 5$

Required Probability = $P(X = 0) + P(X = 1) + P(X = 2) + P(X = 3) + P(X = 4)$

EXAMPLE 14.25: A manufacturer who produces medicine bottles finds that 0.1% of the bottles are defective. The bottles are packed in boxes containing 500 bottles. A drug manufacturer buys 100 boxes from the producer of bottles. Using Poisson distribution, find how many boxes will contain:

(i) no defective

(ii) at least two defectives [given $e^{-0.5} = 0.6065$]

Solution: $m = np = 500 \times \frac{0.1}{100} = 0.5$; n = no. of units = 100

(i) $P(0) \times n = ne^{-m} = 100 \times 0.6065 = 61$ (approx.)

= Number of boxes containing no defective.

(ii) $P(1) \times n = \dfrac{e^{-m} \cdot m^1}{1!} \times 100 = e^{-0.5} \times 100 = 0.6065 \times 0.5 \times 100 = 30$

= Number of boxes containing one defective

Number of boxes containing at least two defectives = 100 – (61 + 30) = 9.

EXAMPLE 14.26: The number of accidents in a year attributed to taxi drivers in a city follows Poisson distribution with mean 3. Out of 1,000 taxi drivers, find approximately the number of drivers with (i) no accident in a year and (ii) more than 3 accidents in a year (given $e^{-1} = 0.3670$, $e^{-2} = 0.1353$, $e^{-3} = 0.0498$).

Solution: For Poisson distribution, the probability of x successes is given by

$$P(x) = \frac{e^{-m} \cdot m^x}{x!}, \quad m \text{ being the mean of the distribution.}$$

For the Poisson distribution with $m = 3$, we have

$$P(x) = e^{-3}\left(\frac{3x}{x!}\right)$$

(i) ∴ $P(x = 0 = \dfrac{3^0}{0!} e^{-3} = e^{-3} = 0.0498$

Hence, the number of drivers with no accident in a year = 0.0498 × 1,000 = 49.8 = 50

(ii) $P(x > 3) = 1 - \{P(x = 0) + P(x = 1) + P(x = 2) + P(x = 3)\}$

$$= 1 - \left(\frac{e^{-3} \cdot 3^0}{0!} + \frac{e^{-3} \cdot 3^1}{1!} + \frac{e^{-3} \cdot 3^2}{2!} + \frac{e^{-3} \cdot 3^3}{3!}\right)$$

$$= 1 - e^{-3}\left(1 + 3 + \frac{9}{2} + \frac{9}{2}\right) = 1 - 0.0498 \times 13$$

$$= 1 - 0.647 = 0.353$$

Thus, the number of drivers with more than 3 accidents in a year = 0.353 × 1000 = 353.

14.4.5 Fitting of Poisson Distribution

The process of fitting of Poisson distribution for the probabilities of $x = 0, 1, 2, \ldots$ success are given below:

1. Find mean $(\bar{X}) = \dfrac{\Sigma fx}{\Sigma f} = m$
2. Find the value of e^{-m} is obtained from table
3. By using the formula $P(X = x) = \dfrac{e^{-m} m^x}{x!}$

Putting $x = 0$, we get $P(0) = \dfrac{e^{-m} m^0}{0!} = e^{-m}$

Then $f(0) = N \times P(0)$

It is convenient to use the following recurrence relation for fitting of Poisson distribution

$$f(x) = \frac{e^{-m} m^x}{x!}$$

$$f(n+1) = \frac{e^{-m} m^{x+1}}{(n+1)!}$$

$$\therefore \quad \frac{f(n+1)}{f(x)} = \frac{m}{(x+1)}$$

$$\boxed{f(x+1) = \frac{m}{(x+1)} f(x)}$$

When $x = 0, \quad f(1) = mf(0)$

$x = 1, \quad f(2) = \frac{m}{2} f(0) = \frac{m^2}{2} f(0)$

$x = 2, \quad f(3) = \frac{m}{2} f(2) = \frac{m^3}{6} f(0)$

This recurrence relation provides a very convenient method for fitting the Poisson distribution. The only probability we need to know is $f(0) = e^{-m}$, where m is the only parameter of the Poisson distribution.

Multiplying by N (the total frequency) each probability of the Poisson distribution, we get the expected frequencies for respective probabilities.

EXAMPLE 14.27: The following mistakes per page were observed in a book.

Number of mistakes (per page)	0	1	2	3	4
Number of pages	211	90	19	5	0

Fit a Poisson distribution to the above data.

Solution:

x_i	f_i	$f_i x_i$
0	211	0
1	90	90
2	19	38
3	5	15
4	0	0
	$N = 325$	**$\Sigma fx = 143$**

Mean $\quad (\bar{X}) = \frac{\Sigma fx}{N}$

$$= \frac{143}{325} = 0.44 = m$$

Then $e^{-m} \Rightarrow e^{-0.44}\square = 0.6440$

Probability mass function of Poisson distribution is

$$P(x) = e^{-m} \frac{m^x}{x!}$$

Put $x = 0$. $\quad P(0) = e^{-0.44} \frac{44^o}{0!} = e^{-0.44} = 0.6440$

$\therefore \quad f(0) = nP(0)$

$= 325 \times 0.6440 = 209.43$

The other expected frequencies will be obtained by using the recurrence formula

$$f(x+1) = \frac{m}{x+1} f(x)$$

By putting $x = 0,1,2,3$ we get the expected frequencies and are calculated as follows.

$$f(1) = 0.44 \times 209.43 = 92.15$$

$$f(2) = \frac{0.44}{2} \times 92.15 = 20.27$$

$$f(3) = \frac{0.44}{3} \times 20.27 = 2.97$$

$$f(4) = \frac{0.44}{4} \times 2.97 = 0.33$$

						Total
Observed frequencies	211	90	19	5	0	**325**
Expected frequencies	210	92	20	3	0	**325**

EXAMPLE 14.28: Find mean and variance to the following data which gives the frequency of the number of deaths due to horse kick in 10 corps per army per annum over twenty years.

X	0	1	2	3	4	**Total**
F	109	65	22	3	0	**325**

Solution: Let us calculate the mean and variance of the given data

x_i	f_i	$f_i x_i$	$f_i x^2$
0	109	0	0
1	65	65	65
2	22	44	88
3	3	9	27
4	1	4	16
Total	$N = 200$	$\Sigma fx = 122$	$\Sigma fx^2 = 196$

Mean $\quad (\bar{X}) = \frac{\Sigma_i f_i x}{N} = \frac{122}{200} = 0.61$

$$\text{Variance} = \sigma^2 = \frac{\Sigma_i f_i^2 x}{n} - (\bar{X})^2$$

$$= \frac{196}{200} - (0.61)^2 = 0.61$$

Hence, Mean = variance = 0.61

EXAMPLE 14.29: 100 car radios are inspected as they come off the production line and number of defects per set is recorded below:

No. of defects	0	1	2	3	4
No. of sets	79	18	2	1	0

Fit a Poisson distribution and find expected frequencies

Solution:

x	*f*	*fx*
0	79	0
1	18	18
2	2	4
3	1	3
4	0	0
	***N* = 100**	**Σ*fx* = 25**

$$\text{Mean} = \frac{\Sigma fx}{N} = \frac{25}{100}$$

∴ $m = .25$

Then $e^{-m} = e^{-0.25} = 0.7788 = 0.779$

Poisson probability function is given by

$$P(x) = \frac{e^{-m} m^x}{x!}$$

$$P(0) = \frac{e^{-0.25}(0.25)^0}{0!} = (0.779)$$

Other frequencies are calculated using the recurrence formula

$$f(x-1) = \frac{m}{x+1} f(x)$$

By putting $x = 0,1,2,3$, we get the expected frequencies and are calculated as follows.

$$f(1) = f(0+1) = \frac{m}{0+1} f(0)$$

$$f(1) = \frac{0.25}{1}(77.9) = 19.46$$

$$f(2) = \frac{0.25}{2}(19.46) = 2.43$$

$$f(3) = \frac{0.25}{3}(2.43) = 0.203$$

$$f(4) = \frac{0.25}{4}(0.203) = 0.013.$$

Observed frequencies	79	18	2	1	0	100
Expected frequencies	78	20	2	0	0	100

EXAMPLE 14.30: Assuming that one in 80 births in a case of twins, calculate the probability of 2 or more sets of twins on a day when 30 births occurs. Compare the results obtained by using (i) the binomial and (ii) Poisson distribution.

Solution: (i) Using Binomial distribution

$$\text{Probability of twins birth} = p = \frac{1}{80} = 0.0125$$

$$q = 1 - p - 1 = 0.0125 = 0.9875$$

$$n = 30$$

Binomial distribution is given by

$$P(x) = {}^nC_x\, p^x\, q^{n-x}$$

$$P(x \geq 2) = 1 - P(x < 2)$$

$$= 1 - \{P(x = 0) + P(x = 1)$$

$$= 1 - \{{}^{30}C_0 (0.0125)^0 (0.9875)^{30} + {}^{30}C_1 (0.0125)^1 (0.9875)^{29}\}$$

$$= 1 - \{1.1(0.9875)^{30} + 3(0.125)(0.9875)^{29}\}$$

$$= 1 - \{0.6839 + 0.2597] = 1 - 0.9436$$

$$P(x \geq 2) = 0.0564$$

(ii) By using Poisson distribution:

The probability mass function of Poisson distribution is given by

$$P(x) = \frac{e^{-m} m^x}{x!}$$

$$\text{Mean} = m = np = 30\,(0.0125) = 0.375$$

$$P(x \geq 2) = 1 - P(x < 2) = 1 - \{P(x = 0) + P(x = 1)\}$$

$$= 1 - \left\{\frac{e^{-0.375}(0.375)^0}{0!} + \frac{e^{-0.375}(0.375)^1}{1!}\right\}$$

$$= 1 - e^{-0.375}(1 + 0.375)$$

$$= 1 - (0.6873)(1.375) = 1 - 0.945 = 0.055$$

14.5 NORMAL DISTRIBUTION

In the preceding sections we have discussed the discrete distributions, the Binomial and Poisson distribution. In this section we deal with the most important continuous distribution, known as normal probability distribution or simply normal distribution. It is important for the reason that it plays a vital role in the theoretical and applied statistics.

A continuous random variable X is said to follow normal distribution with mean μ and standard deviation σ, if its probability density function

$$f(x) = \frac{1}{\sigma\sqrt{2\pi}} e^{-\frac{1}{2}\left(\frac{x-\mu}{\sigma}\right)^2}$$

$-\infty < x < \infty, -\infty < \mu < \infty, \sigma > 0$

NOTE: The mean μ and standard deviation σ^2 are called the parameters of Normal distribution. The normal distribution is expressed by $X \sim N(\mu, \sigma^2)$.

DO YOU KNOW?

Normal Distribution is considered to be the most important and powerful of all the distributions in statistics. The normal distribution was first discovered by DeMoivre (English mathematician) in 1733 as limiting case of binomial distribution. Later it was applied in natural and social science by Laplace (French Mathematician) in 1777. The normal distribution is also known as Gaussian distribution in honour of Karl Friedrich Gauss(1809).

14.5.1 Condition of Normal Distribution

(i) Normal distribution is a limiting form of the binomial distribution under the following conditions.
   (a) n, the number of trials is indefinitely large ie., $n \to \infty$ and
   (b) Neither p nor q is very small.

(ii) Normal distribution can also be obtained as a limiting form of Poisson distribution with parameter $m \to \infty$

(iii) Constants of normal distribution are mean = μ , variation = σ^2, Standard deviation = μ .

14.5.2 Constants of Normal Distribution

1. Mean, median, and mode of the distribution are coincide i.e., Mean = Median = Mode = μ
2. It has only one mode at $x = \mu$ (i.e., unimodal)
3. Since the curve is symmetrical, Skewness = $\beta_1 = 0$ and Kurtosis = $\beta_2 = 3$.

14.5.3 Normal Probability Curve

The curve representing the normal distribution is called the normal probability curve. The curve is symmetrical about the mean (?), bell-shaped and the two tails on the right and left sides of the mean extends to the infinity. The shape of the curve is shown in the following figure.

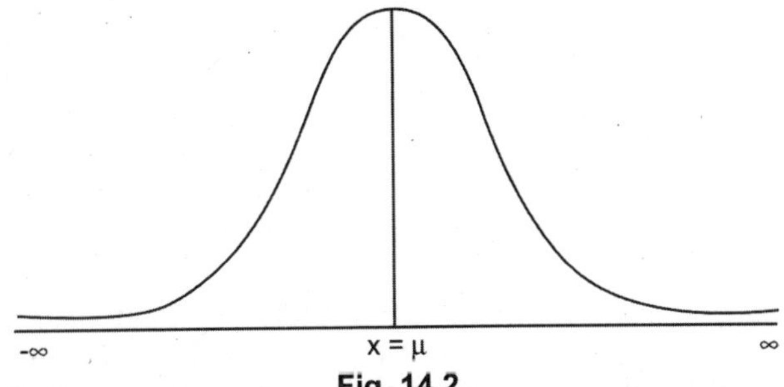

Fig. 14.2

NOTE: The graph of the p.d.f of the normal distribution is called the Normal curve.

14.4.4 Characteristics of Normal Distribution

1. The normal curve is bell shaped and is symmetric at $x = \mu$.
2. Mean, median, and mode of the distribution are coincide, i.e., Mean = Median = Mode = μ
3. It has only one mode at $x = \mu$ (i.e., unimodal)
4. Since the curve is symmetrical, Skewness = $\beta_1 = 0$ and Kurtosis = $\beta_2 = 3$.
5. The points of inflection are at $x = \mu + \sigma$
6. The maximum ordinate occurs at $x = \mu$ and its value is = $\frac{1}{\sigma\sqrt{2\pi}}$
7. The x axis is an asymptote to the curve (i.e. the curve continues to approach but never touches the *x*-axis)
8. The first and third quartiles are equidistant from median.
9. The mean deviation about mean is 0.8 s
10. Quartile deviation = 0.6745 σ
11. If X and Y are independent normal variates with mean σ_1 and σ_2, and variance σ_{12} and σ_{22} respectively then their sum $(X + Y)$ is also a normal variate with mean $(\mu_1 + \mu_2)$ and variance $(\sigma_{12} + \sigma_{22})$
12. Area Property
    $P(\mu - \sigma < x < \mu + \sigma) = 0.6826$
    $P(\mu - 2\sigma < x < \mu + 2\sigma) = 0.9544$
    $P(\mu - 3\sigma < x < \mu + 3\sigma) = 0.9973$

It may be appreciated that μ lies at the centre of the curve and indicates the central value of the normal distribution. On the other hand, σ is a measure of the extent of dispersion of the values of X from the central value μ. In other words, while μ fixes the position or the level of the distribution on the X– axis, σ determines the extent of spread of the distribution along X–axis on both sides of the central value.

The following three situations are explained diagrammatically below:

(i) A change in μ, standard deviation σ remaining the same, shift the curve along the X–axis without changing its shape or spread. This is shown in figure below:

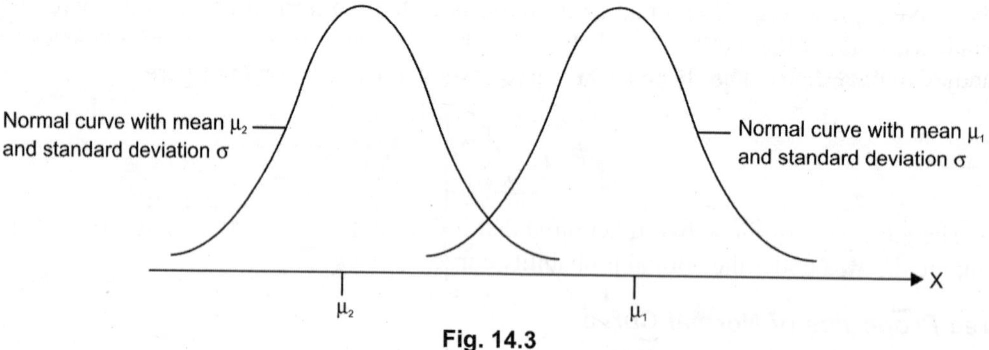

Fig. 14.3

NOTE: Two normal curves with different means and equal standard deviations. If μ_1 is greater than μ_2, the normal curve with mean μ_1 is centered farther to the right.

(ii) A change in σ, means μ remaining the same, changes the shape or spread of the normal curve. This is shown in figure below. The more the standard deviation, the more is the spread.

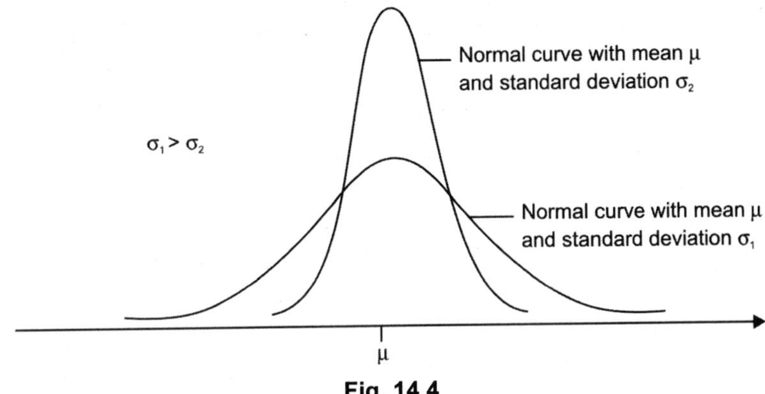

Fig. 14.4

NOTE: Two normal curves with the same means and different standard deviations. If σ, is greater than σ_2, the normal curve with standard deviation σ_1 is flatter and more spread out.

(iii) As may again be noticed from above figure an increase in s increases the spread of the normal curve equally on both sides of the central value. As a result, the normal curve is lowered in height irrespective of whether or not an increase in σ is associated with any change in μ. A decrease in σ, on the other hand, reduces the spread of the normal curve and increases its height. This inverse relationship between the extent of spread of the normal curve and its height at the central value is because the total area under any normal curve has always to be 1 i.e., if the speed increases the height will decrease so that the total area remains equal to 1.

14.4.5 Standard Normal Distribution

Let *X* be random variable which follows normal distribution with mean μ and variance σ^2. The standard normal variate is defined as

$$Z = \frac{X - \mu}{\sigma}$$

which follows standard normal distribution with mean 0 and standard deviation 1 i.e., $Z \sim N(0,1)$. The standard normal distribution is given by

$$\boxed{\phi(z) = \frac{1}{\sqrt{2\pi}} e^{\frac{-1}{2}z^2} \; ; -\infty < z < \infty}$$

The advantage of the above function is that it does not contain any parameter. This enable us to compute the area under the normal probability curve.

Area Properties of Normal Curve

The total area under the normal probability curve is 1. The curve is also called standard probability curve. The area under the curve between the ordinates at $x = a$ and $x = b$ where $a < b$, represents the probabilities that x lies between $x = a$ and $x = b$ i.e., $P(a \le x \le b)$

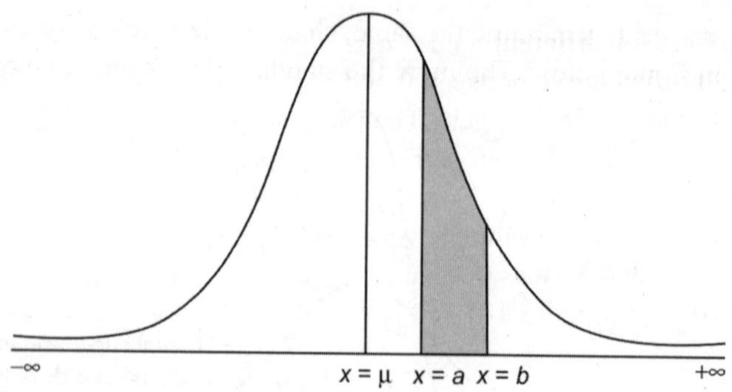

Fig. 14.5

To find any probability value of x, we first standardize it by using

$$Z = \frac{X - \mu}{\sigma}$$

and use the area probability normal table.

A Table of Areas under the Standard Normal Curve (Normal Table)

z	0.00	0.01	0.02	0.03	0.04	0.05	0.06	0.07	0.08	0.09
0.0	0.0000	0.0040	0.0080	0.0120	0.0160	0.0199	0.0239	0.0279	0.0319	0.0359
0.1	0.0398	0.0438	0.0478	0.0517	0.0557	0.0596	0.0636	0.0675	0.0714	0.0753
0.2	0.0793	0.0832	0.0871	0.0910	0.0948	0.0987	0.1026	0.1064	0.1103	0.1141
0.3	0.1179	0.1217	0.1255	0.1293	0.1331	0.1368	0.1406	0.1443	0.1480	0.1517
0.4	0.1554	0.1591	0.1628	0.1664	0.1700	0.1736	0.1772	0.1808	0.1844	0.1879
0.5	0.1915	0.1950	0.1985	0.2019	0.2054	0.2088	0.2123	0.2157	0.2190	0.2224
0.6	0.2257	0.2291	0.2324	0.2357	0.2389	0.2422	0.2454	0.2486	0.2517	0.2549
0.7	0.2580	0.2611	0.2642	0.2673	0.2704	0.2734	0.2764	0.2794	0.2823	0.2852
0.8	0.2881	0.2910	0.2939	0.2967	0.2995	0.3023	0.3051	0.3078	0.3106	0.3133
0.9	0.3159	0.3186	0.3212	0.3238	0.3264	0.3289	0.3315	0.3340	0.3365	0.3389
1.0	0.3413	0.3438	0.3461	0.3485	0.3508	0.3531	0.3554	0.3577	0.3599	0.3621
1.1	0.3643	0.3665	0.3686	0.3708	0.3729	0.3749	0.3770	0.3790	0.3810	0.3830
1.2	0.3849	0.3869	0.3888	0.3907	0.3925	0.3944	0.3962	0.3980	0.3997	0.4015
1.3	0.4032	0.4049	0.4066	0.4082	0.4099	0.4115	0.4131	0.4147	0.4162	0.4177
1.4	0.4192	0.4207	0.4222	0.4236	0.4251	0.4265	0.4279	0.4292	0.4306	0.4319
1.5	0.4332	0.4345	0.4357	0.4370	0.4382	0.4394	0.4406	0.4418	0.4429	0.4441
1.6	0.4452	0.4463	0.4474	0.4484	0.4495	0.4505	0.4515	0.4525	0.4535	0.4545
1.7	0.4554	0.4564	0.4573	0.4582	0.4591	0.4599	0.4608	0.4616	0.4625	0.4633
1.8	0.4641	0.4649	0.4656	0.4664	0.4671	0.4678	0.4686	0.4693	0.4699	0.4706
1.9	0.4713	0.4719	0.4726	0.4732	0.4738	0.4744	0.4750	0.4756	0.4761	0.4767
2.0	0.4772	0.4778	0.4783	0.4788	0.4793	0.4798	0.4803	0.4808	0.4812	0.4817
2.1	0.4821	0.4826	0.4830	0.4834	0.4838	0.4842	0.4846	0.4850	0.4854	0.4857
2.2	0.4861	0.4864	0.4868	0.4871	0.4875	0.4878	0.4881	0.4884	0.4887	0.4890
2.3	0.4893	0.4896	0.4898	0.4901	0.4904	0.4906	0.4909	0.4911	0.4913	0.4916
2.4	0.4918	0.4920	0.4922	0.4925	0.4927	0.4929	0.4931	0.4932	0.4934	0.4936
2.5	0.4938	0.4940	0.4941	0.4943	0.4945	0.4946	0.4948	0.4949	0.4951	0.4952
2.6	0.4953	0.4955	0.4956	0.4957	0.4959	0.4960	0.4961	0.4962	0.4963	0.4964
2.7	0.4965	0.4966	0.4967	0.4968	0.4969	0.4970	0.4971	0.4972	0.4973	0.4974
2.8	0.4974	0.4975	0.4976	0.4977	0.4977	0.4978	0.4979	0.4979	0.4980	0.4981
2.9	0.4981	0.4982	0.4982	0.4983	0.4984	0.4984	0.4985	0.4985	0.4986	0.4986
3.0	0.4987	0.4987	0.4987	0.4988	0.4988	0.4989	0.4989	0.4989	0.4990	0.4990

The normal table gives, for different values of z, the area under the standard normal curve between 0 and z.

Such an area is the shaded area in the figure. The values of z in the table range from 0.00 to 3.09 in increments of 0.01.

However, because the table lists no values beyond 3.09, we approximate any area beyond 3.10 as 0. That is,

$$P(Z > 3.10) = P(Z < -3.10) \approx 0$$

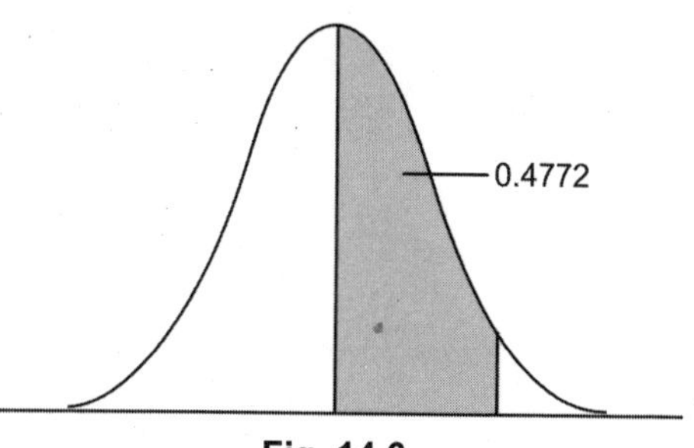

Fig. 14.6

For Example:

(i) The probability that the normal random variable x to lie in the interval $(\mu - \sigma, \mu + \sigma)$ is given by

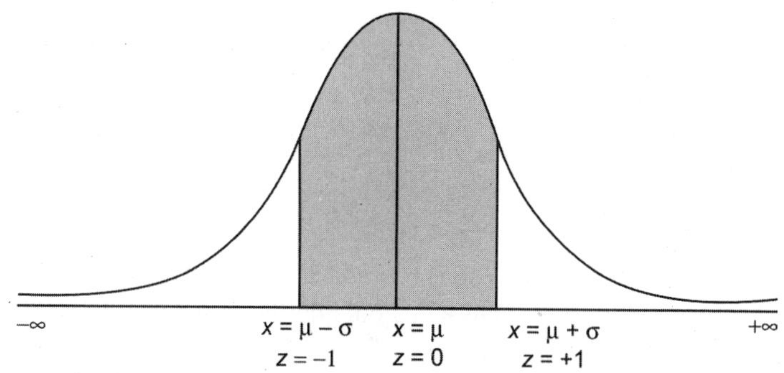

Fig. 14.7

$$\begin{aligned} P(\mu - \sigma < x < \mu + \sigma) &= P(-1 \le z \le 1) = 2P(0 < z < 1) \\ &= 2\,(0.3413) \qquad \text{[From Table-using row } z = 1 \text{ and column 0.00]} \\ &= 0.6826 \end{aligned}$$

(ii) The probability that the normal random variable x to lie in the interval $(\mu - 2\sigma, \mu + 2\sigma)$ is given by

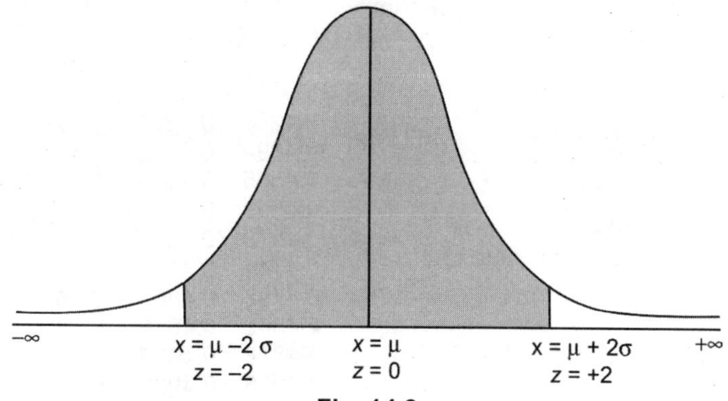

Fig. 14.8

$$\begin{aligned} P(\mu - 2\sigma < x < \mu + 2\sigma) &= P(-2 < z < 2) \\ &= 2P(0 < z < 2) \\ &= 2\,(0.4772) \\ &= 0.9544 \end{aligned}$$

(iiii) The probability that the normal random variable x to lie in the interval $(\mu - 3\sigma, \mu + 3\sigma)$ is given by

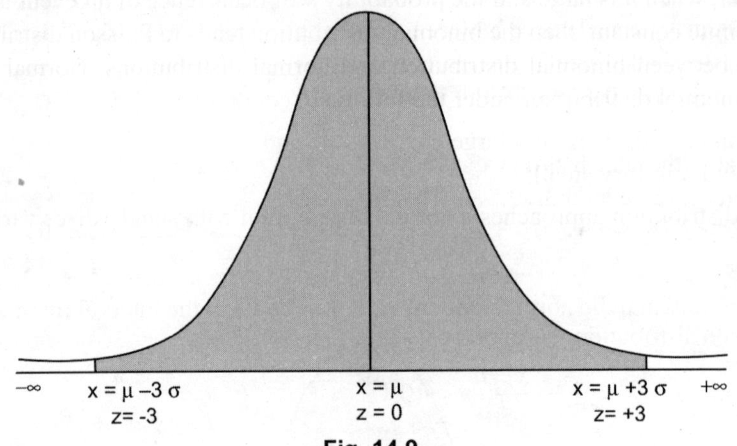

Fig. 14.9

$$P(\mu - 3\sigma < x < (\mu + 3\sigma) = P(-3 < z < 3)$$
$$= 2P(0 < z < 3)$$
$$= 2(0.49865) = 0.9973 \quad \text{[From Table]}$$

(iv) The probability that a normal variate x lies outside the range $\mu + 3\sigma$ is given by

$$P(|x - \mu| > 3\sigma) = P(|z| > 3)$$
$$= 1 - P(-3 \le z \le 3) \quad \text{[From (iii)]}$$
$$= 1 - 0.9773 = 0.0027$$

Thus we expect that the values in a normal probability curve will lie between the range $\mu + 3\sigma$, though theoretically it range from $-\infty$ to ∞.

NOTE: Z-value measures the number of standard deviations that a data value is from the population mean. *A* negative *Z*-value shows that the random variable is located to the left of *Z* and a positive *Z*-value means the random variable is located to the right of the centre.

The rules for solving different normal probability problems are given below.

Rules for Solving Normal Probability Problems Manually

Rule	To Find	Area under the curve	Look Up
1.	$P(Z < z)$	below a value of *Z*	The Z-value and use the table directly
2.	$P(Z > z)$	above a value of *Z*	The Z-value and subtract the value in the table from 1 OR the negative of the *Z*-value and use the table directly
3.	$P(z_1 < Z < z_2)$	Between two values of *Z*	Both Z-values and subtract the lower value from the higher value
4.	$P(Z = z)$	exactly the value of *Z*	The *Z*-value in table directly (left side of the curve if *Z*-value is negative (right side of the curve of *Z*-value is positive) in *table*.

Approximation of Binomial and Poisson Distribution to Normal Distribution

The three distribution, namely Binomial, Poisson and Normal are very closely related to each other.

As explained earlier, when n is large and the probability p of occurrence of an event is close to zero so that np remains a finite constant, then the binomial distribution tends to Poisson distribution. Similarly, there is a relation between binomial distribution and normal distributions. Normal distribution is a limiting form of binomial distribution under the following conditions:

(i) n , the number of trials is very large, i.e., $n \rightarrow \alpha$ and
(ii) neither p and q is very small.

The binomial distribution approaches a normal distribution with standardizes variable that is,

$$z = \frac{x - np}{\sqrt{npq}} \sim n(0,1)$$

Similarly, Poisson distribution also approaches a normal distribution with standardized variable, that is,

$$z = \frac{x - m}{\sqrt{m}} \sim n(0,1)$$

EXAMPLE 14.31: Find the probability that the standard normal variate lies between 0 and 1.56

Solution:

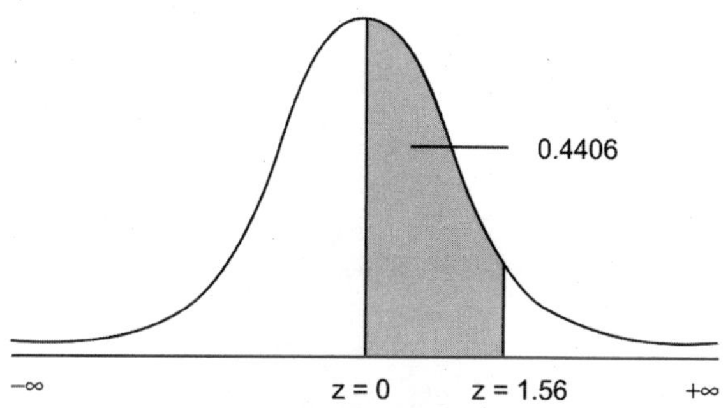

Fig. 14.10

$P(0 < z < 1.56)$ = Area between $z = 0$ and $z = 1.56 = 0.4406$ [From table]

EXAMPLE 14.32: Find the area of the standard normal variate from –1.96 to 0.

Solution:

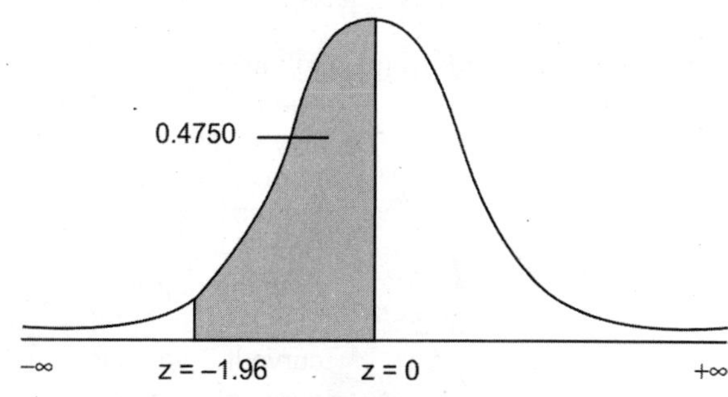

Fig. 14.11

Area between $z = 0$ & $z = 1.96$ is same as the area $z = -1.96$ to $z = 0$

$$P(-1.96 < z < 0) = P(0 < z < 1.96)$$ [By symmetry]

$$= 0.4750$$ [From the table]

EXAMPLE 14.33: Find the area to the right of $z = 0.25$

Solution:

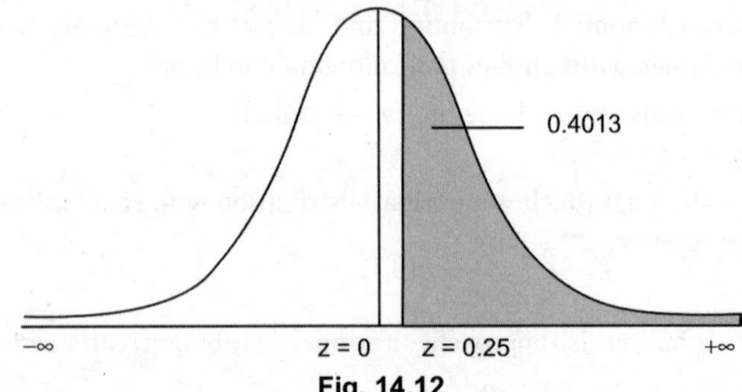

Fig. 14.12

$$\begin{aligned} P(z > 0.25) &= P(0 < z < \infty) - P(0 < z < 0.25) \\ &= 0.5000 - 0.0987 = 0.4013 \end{aligned}$$ [From the table]

EXAMPLE 14.34: Find the area to the left of $z = 1.5$

Solution:

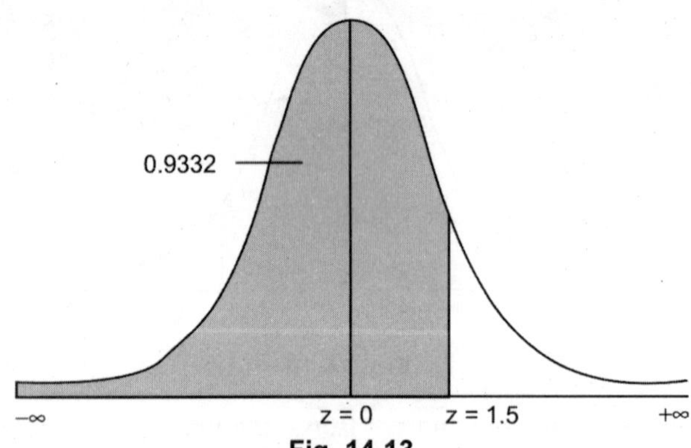

Fig. 14.13

$$\begin{aligned} P(z < 1.5) &= P(-\infty < z < 0) + P(0 < z < 1.5) \\ &= 0.5 + 0.4332 = 0.9332 \end{aligned}$$ [From the table]

EXAMPLE 14.35: Find the area of the standard normal variate between −1.96 and 1.5

Solution:

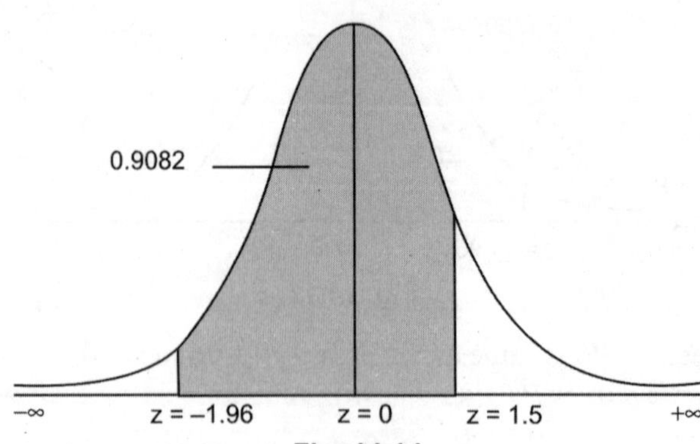

Fig. 14.14

$$P(-1.96 < z < 1.5) = P(-1.96 < z < 0) + P(0 < z < 1.5)$$
$$= P(0 < z < 1.96) + P(0 < z < 1.5)$$
$$= 0.4750 + 0.4332 = 0.9082 \qquad \text{[From the table]}$$

EXAMPLE 14.36: Given a normal distribution with $\mu = 50$ and $\sigma = 8$, find the probability that x assumes a value between 42 and 64.

Solution:

Given that $\mu = 50$ and $\sigma = 8$

The standard normal variate

$$z = \frac{x - \mu}{\sigma}$$

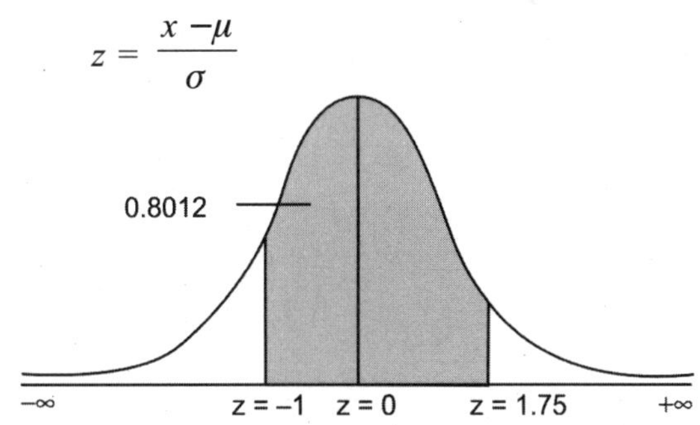

Fig. 14.15

If $X = 42,\ Z_1 = \dfrac{42 - 50}{8} = \dfrac{-8}{8} = -1$

If $X = 64,\ Z_2 = \dfrac{64 - 50}{8} = \dfrac{14}{8} = 1.75$

$\therefore$ $P(42 < x < 64) = P(-1 < z < 1.75)$

$= P(-1 < z < 0) + P(0 < z < 1.95)$

$= P(0 < z < 1) + P(0 < z < 1.75)$ [By symmetry]

$= 0.3413 + 0.4599 = 0.8012$ [From the table]

EXAMPLE 14.37: Students of a class were given an aptitude test. Their marks were found to be normally distributed with mean 60 and standard deviation 5. What percentage of students scored? (i) More than 60 marks (ii) Less than 56 marks (iii) Between 45 and 65 marks

Solution:

Given that mean (μ) = 60 and standard deviation = $\sigma = 5$

(i) The standard normal variate $Z = \dfrac{x - \mu}{\sigma}$

If $X = 60,\ Z = \dfrac{x - \mu}{\sigma} = \dfrac{60 - 60}{5} = 0$

$\therefore$ $P(x > 60) = P(z > 0)$

$= P(0 < z < \infty)$

$= 0.5000$

Hence the percentage of students scored more than 60 marks is 0.5000 (100) = 50%.

Fig. 14.16

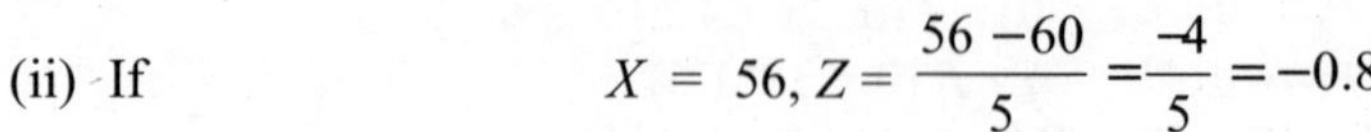

(ii) If $X = 56, Z = \frac{56-60}{5} = \frac{-4}{5} = -0.8$

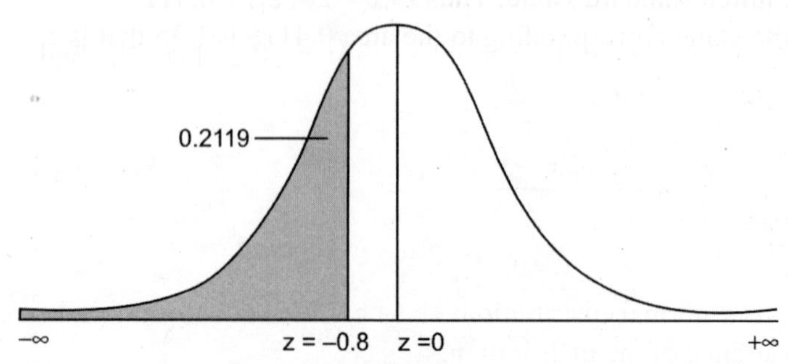

Fig. 14.17

$$\begin{aligned} P(x < 56) &= P(z < -0.8) \\ &= P(-\infty < z < 0) - P(-.8 < z < 0) && \text{[By symmetry]} \\ &= P(0 < 2 < \infty) - P(0 < z < 0.8) \\ &= 0.5 - 0.2881 && \text{[From the table]} \\ &= 0.2119 \end{aligned}$$

Hence the percentage of students score less than 56 marks is 0.2119 (100) = 21.19%.

(iii) If $X = 45$, then $z = \frac{45-60}{5} = \frac{15}{5} = -3$

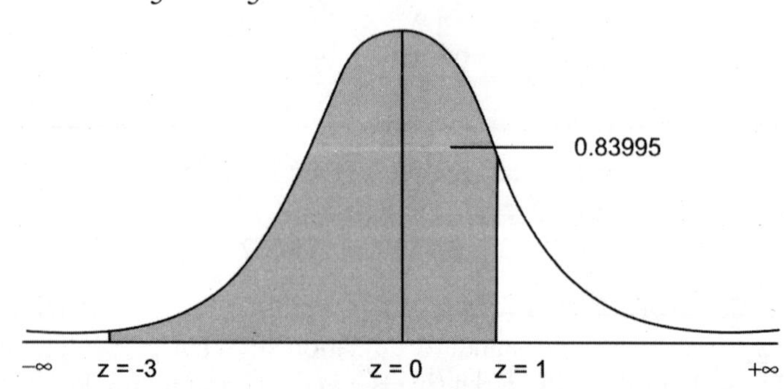

Fig. 14.18

$X = 65$ then $z = \frac{65-60}{5} = \frac{5}{5} = 1$

$$\begin{aligned} P(45 < x < 65) &= P(-3 < z < 1) \\ &= P(-3 < z < 0) + P(0 < z < 1) \\ &= P(0 < z < 3) + P(0 < z < 1) && \text{[By symmetry]} \\ &= 0.4986 + 0.3413 && \text{[From the table]} \\ &= 0.8399 \end{aligned}$$

Hence the percentage of students scored between 45 and 65 marks is 0.8399(100) = 83.99 %

EXAMPLE 14.38: X is normal distribution with mean 2 and standard deviation 3. Find the value of the variable x such that the probability of the interval from mean to that value is 0.4115

Solution:

Given μ = 2, σ = 3

Suppose z_1 is required standard value, Thus $P(0 < z < z_1) = 0.4115$

From the table the value corresponding to the area 0.4115 is 1.35 that is $z_1 = 1.35$

Here
$$z_1 = \frac{x-\mu}{\sigma}$$
$$1.35 = \frac{x-2}{3}$$
$$x = 3(1.35) + 2 = 4.05 + 2 = 6.05$$

EXAMPLE 14.39: In a normal distribution 31 % of the items are under 45 and 8 % are over 64. Find the mean and variance of the distribution.

Solution: Let x denotes the items are given and it follows the normal distribution with mean μ and standard deviation σ. The points $x = 45$ and $x = 64$ are located as shown in the figure.

(i) Since 31 % of items are under $x = 45$, position of x into the left of the ordinate $x = \mu$

(ii) Since 8 % of items are above $x = 64$, position of this x is to the right of ordinate $x = \mu$

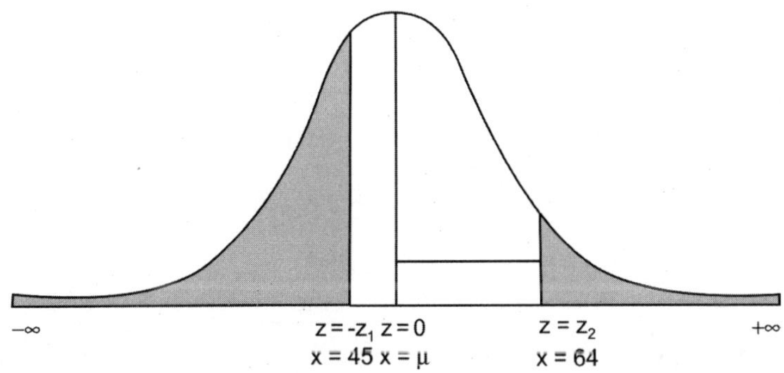

Fig. 14.19

When $x = 45$, $z = \frac{x-\mu}{\sigma} = \frac{45-\mu}{\sigma} = -z_1 \text{(say)}$

Since x is left of $x = \mu$, z_1 is taken as negative

When $x = 64$. $z = \frac{64-\mu}{\sigma} = z_2 \text{(say)}$

From the diagram $P(x < 45) = 0.31$
$$P(z < -z_1) = 0.31$$
$$P(-z_1 < z < 0) = P(-\infty < z < 0) - p(-\infty < z < z_1)$$
$$\sigma = 0.5 - 0.31 = 0.19$$
$$P(0 < z < z_1) = 0.19 \quad \text{[By symmetry]}$$
$$z_1 = 0.50 \quad \text{[From the table]}$$

Also from the diagram $p(x > 64) = 0.08$
$$P(0 < z < z_2) = P(0 < z < \infty) - P(z_2 < z < \infty)$$
$$= 0.5 - 0.08 = 0.42$$
$$z_2 = 1.40 \quad \text{[From the table]}$$

Substituting the values of z_1 and z_2 we get

$$\frac{45-\mu}{\sigma} = 0.50 \text{ and } \frac{64-\mu}{\sigma} = 1.40$$

Solving $\mu - 0.50\,\sigma = 45$ ...(1)

$\mu + 1.40\,\sigma = 64$ ...(2)

$(2) - (1) \rightarrow 1.90\,\sigma = 19 \rightarrow \sigma = 10$

Substituting $\sigma = 10$ in (1)

$$\mu = 45 + 0.050\,(10) = 45 + 5.0 = 50.0$$

Hence mean = 50 and variance = $\sigma^2 = 100$

MISCELLANEOUS SOLVED EXAMPLES

EXAMPLE 14.40: A post-graduate student in commerce is trying to decide on the number of firms to which he should apply. Given his work experience and grades, he can expect to receive a job offer from 80% of the firms to which he applies. The student decides to apply to only four firms.

(i) What is the probability that he received no job offers?

(ii) What is the probability that he received more than two offers? **[MBA, UPTU (CO), 2004]**

Solution: Let p be the probability of receiving a job offer and $q = 1 - p$, the probability of not receiving a job offer, then $p = 0.8$, $q = 1 - 0.8 = 0.2$

(i) Required Probability $= {}^4C_0\, q^4 p^0 = {}^4C_0\,(0.2)^4\,(0.8)^0 = 0.0016$

(ii) Required Probability $= {}^4C_3\, q^{4-3}\, p^3 + {}^4C_4\, q^{4-4}\, p^4$

$= 4 \times 0.2 \times (0.8)3 + (0.2)0\,(0.8)4 = 4 \times 0.1024 + 0.4096$

$= 0.4096 + 0.4096 = 0.8192$

= Probability he received three offers or four offers.

EXAMPLE 14.41: The output of a production process is 10 per cent defective. What is the probability of getting exactly two defectives in a sample of five?

Solution: Probability that the output is defective = 0.1

Probability that the output is good = 0.9

Required Probability $= {}^5C_2\,(0.9)^3\,(0.1)^2$

$$= \frac{5!}{(2!)\,(3!)} \times 0.729 \times 0.01 = 729 \times 0.01 = 0.0729.$$

EXAMPLE 10.42: The telephone company reports that among 5000 telephones installed in a new subdivision 4000 have push buttons. If 10 people are called at random, what is the probability that exactly 3 will be talking on dial telephones?

Solution: Probability that a telephone has a push button $= \frac{4000}{5000} = 0.8$

Probability that a telephone is a dial telephone (i.e., Telephone without push button) = 0.2

Required Probability $= {}^{10}C_3\,(0.8)^7\,(0.2)^3$

$$= \frac{10!}{(7!)\,(3!)}\,(0.2097)\,(0.008) = \frac{10 \times 9 \times 8}{8} \times 0.2097 \times 0.008 = 0.2013.$$

EXAMPLE 10.43: One -fourth of the female freshmen entering a Hindu College are out-of-state students. If the students are assigned at random to the dormitories, 3 to a room, what is the probability that in one room at most 2 of the 3 room-mates are out-of-state students? **[MBA, IGNOU, 1996]**

Solution: Probability that a freshman is out-of-state student $= \frac{1}{4} = p$

Probability that a student is not out-of-state student $= 1 - \frac{1}{4} = \frac{3}{4}$

$$\text{Required Probability} = 1 - {}^3C_3\, p^3$$

$$= 1 - {}^3C_3 \left(\frac{1}{4}\right)^3 = 1 - \frac{1}{64} = \frac{63}{64}.$$

Alternative Method

$$\text{Required Probability} = P(x = 0) + P(x = 1) + P(x = 2)$$

$$= {}^3C_0\, q^3 + {}^3C_1\, pq^2 + {}^3C_2\, p^2 q^1$$

$$= \left(\frac{3}{4}\right)^3 + 3\left(\frac{1}{4}\right) \times \left(\frac{3}{4}\right)^2 + 3\left(\frac{1}{4}\right)^2 \times \frac{3}{4} = \frac{27}{64} + \frac{27}{64} + \frac{9}{64} = \frac{63}{64}$$

EXAMPLE 10.44: In a shipment of 25 hard disks, six are defective. If five of the disks are selected at random, what is the probability that

(i) exactly one is defective?
(ii) at least one is defective?
(iii) no less than two are defective? (At least two are defective)

What is the average number of defective hard disks that you would expect to find in the sample of five hard disk drives?

Solution: Probability of getting a defective hard disk $= \frac{6}{25} = p$

∴ Probability of not getting a defective hard disk $= 1 - \frac{6}{25} = \frac{19}{25}$

(i) Required Probability $= {}^5C_1 \left(\frac{19}{25}\right)^4 \left(\frac{6}{25}\right) = 5 \times \frac{6 \times (19)^4}{(25)^5} = 0.4$

(ii) Required Probability = 1 – Probability that none is defective

$$= 1 - \left(\frac{19}{25}\right)^5$$

(iii) Required Probability $= 1 - P(0) - P(1)$

$$= 1 - \left(\frac{19}{25}\right)^5 - {}^5C_1 \left(\frac{19}{25}\right)^4 \left(\frac{6}{25}\right)$$

$$= 1 - \left(\frac{19}{25}\right)^4 \left[\frac{19}{25} + \frac{5 \times 6}{25}\right] = 1 - \left(\frac{19}{25}\right)\left(\frac{49}{25}\right)$$

(iv) Probability that no disk is defective = $^5C_0 \left(\frac{19}{25}\right)^5$

Probability that only one disk is defective = $^5C_1 \left(\frac{19}{25}\right)^4 \left(\frac{6}{25}\right)$

Probability that two disk are defective = $^5C_2 \left(\frac{19}{25}\right)^3 \left(\frac{6}{25}\right)^2$

Probability that three disks are defective = $^5C_3 \left(\frac{19}{25}\right)^2 \left(\frac{6}{25}\right)^3$

Probability that four disks are defective = $^5C_4 \left(\frac{19}{25}\right) \left(\frac{6}{25}\right)^4$

Probability that four disks are defective = $^5C_5 \left(\frac{6}{25}\right)^5$

Expected number of defective disks

$$= 0 \times {}^5C_0 \left(\frac{19}{25}\right)^5 + 1 \times {}^5C_1 \left(\frac{19}{25}\right)^4 \left(\frac{6}{25}\right) + 2 \times {}^5C_2 \left(\frac{19}{25}\right)^3 \left(\frac{6}{25}\right)^2 + 3 \times {}^5C_3 \left(\frac{19}{25}\right)^2 \left(\frac{6}{25}\right)^3$$

$$+ 4 \times {}^5C_4 \left(\frac{19}{25}\right) \left(\frac{6}{25}\right)^4 + 5 \times {}^5C_5 \left(\frac{6}{25}\right)^2$$

$$= \frac{1}{(25)^5} (5 \times 781926 + 20 \times 246924 + 30 \times 77976 + 20 \times 24624 + 5 \times 7776)$$

$$= \frac{1}{(25)^5} (39, 09, 630 + 49, 38, 480 + 23, 39, 280 + 4,92,480 + 38,880) = 1.2$$

EXAMPLE 14.45: The odds in favour of *A* winning a game of chess against *B* are 3:2. If 3 games are to be played, what are the odds (i) in favour of *A*'s winning at least two games out of three, (ii) against *A* losing the first two games to *B*? **[MBA, Madras Univ.]**

Solution: Probability of *A*'s winning the game = $\frac{3}{5} = \frac{3}{3+2}$

Probability of *A*'s losing the game = $\frac{2}{5}$ = Probability of *B*'s winning the game.

If *A*'s winning is taken as success and *p* denotes the probability of success and *q* that of failure then

$$p = \frac{3}{5}, \quad q = \frac{2}{5}$$

(i) Probability that *A* will win at least two games

$$= {}^3C_2\, q^{(3-2)}\, p^2 + {}^3C_3\, q^0\, p^3$$

$$= 3 \times \frac{2}{5} \times \left(\frac{3}{5}\right)^2 + \left(\frac{3}{5}\right)^3 = \left(\frac{3}{5}\right)^3 (2+1) = \frac{81}{125} = \frac{81}{81+44}$$

Odds in favour of *A*'s winning at least two games = 81 : 44.

(ii) If A loses first two games, then there are two cases.

(a) A loses third game also

(b) A wins third game.

$$\therefore P(A \text{ loses first two games}) = \left(\frac{2}{5}\right)^3 + \left(\frac{2}{5}\right)^2 \times \frac{3}{5} = \frac{8+12}{125} = \frac{20}{125} = \frac{4}{25}$$

∴ Odds against A losing first two games = 21 : 4.

EXAMPLE 14.46: Multiple choice test consists of eight questions and three answers to each question (of which only one is correct). If a student answers each question by rolling a balanced die and marking the first answer if he gets 1 or 2, the second answer if he gets 3 or 4 and the third answer if he gets 5 or 6, what is the probability that he will get exactly four correct answers? **[B.Com., Andhra Uniov., 2001]**

Solution : Probability that the students marks first answer = $\frac{1}{3}$

Probability that the student marks second answer = $\frac{1}{3}$

Probability that the student marks third answer = $\frac{1}{3}$

Since there is equal probability of marking first, second or third answer, we can presume that the marking made by the student is random. Therefore the probability of any marking being correct $= \frac{1}{3}$.

∴ The Probability of success = $\frac{1}{3}$

The Probability of failure = $\frac{2}{3}$

Probability of getting exactly four correct answers = ${}^8C_4 \left(\frac{1}{3}\right)^4 \left(\frac{2}{3}\right)^4$

$$= \frac{8!}{(4!)(4!)}\left[\frac{1}{81} \times \frac{16}{81}\right]$$

$$= \frac{8 \times 7 \times 6 \times 5}{4 \times 3 \times 2 \times 1} \times \frac{16}{81 \times 81}$$

$$= \frac{70 \times 16}{81 \times 81} = 0.1707.$$

EXAMPLE 14.47: Five hundred television sets are inspected as they come off the production line and the number of defects per set is recorded below:

No. of defects (X)	0	1	2	3	4
No. of sets	368	72	52	7	1

Estimate the average number of defects per set and expected frequencies of 0, 1, 2, 3 and 4 defects assuming Poisson distribution.

Solution: For finding the average number of defects, we make the following table:

X	*f*	*fX*
0	368	0
1	72	72
2	52	104
3	7	21
4	1	4
	***N* = 500**	**Σ*f X* = 201**

Therefore, $\bar{X} = \frac{\Sigma fX}{N} = \frac{201}{500} = 0.402$

Thus, average number of defects per set is $m = 0.402$

The expected frequency of getting 0 defect $= nP(0) = 500 \times e^{-0.402}$

But $e^{-0.402} = 0.6689$ [From the table]

Therefore, $nP(0) = 500 \times 0.6689 = 334.45$

Expected frequency of getting one defect

$$nP(1) = m.nP(0) = 0.402 \times 334.45 = 134.45$$

Expected frequency of getting 2 defects

$$nP(2) = \frac{m}{2} \cdot nP(1) = \frac{0.402}{2} \times 134.45 = 201 \times 134.45 = 27.02$$

Expected frequency of getting 3 defects

$$nP(3) = \frac{m}{3} \cdot nP(2) = \frac{0.402}{2} \times 27.02 = 0.134 \times 27.02 = 3.62$$

Expected frequency of getting 4 defects

$$nP(4) = \frac{m}{4} \cdot nP(3) = \frac{0.402}{4} \times 3.62 = 0.1005 \times 3.62 = 0.364$$

LIST OF FORMULAE

1. Binomial Distribution

$$P(x = r) = {}^nC_r \; q^{n-r} \; p^r$$

2. Mean of Binomial Distribution

$$\mu = np$$

3. Standard Deviation of Binomial Distribution

$$\text{S.D} = \sqrt{npq}$$

So the, variance $= npq$

4. Poisson Distribution

$$P(X = x) = \frac{e^{-m} m^x}{x!}$$

5. Mean of Poisson Distribution

$$\text{Mean} = m$$

6. Standard Deviation of Poisson Distribution

$$\text{SD} = \sqrt{m}$$

7. The binomial distribution approaches a normal distribution

$$z = \frac{x - np}{\sqrt{npq}}$$

8. Normal Distribution

$$f(x) = \frac{1}{\sigma\sqrt{2\pi}} e^{-\frac{1}{2}\left(\frac{x-\mu}{\sigma}\right)^2}.$$

9. Standard Normal Distribution

$$z = \frac{x - \mu}{\sigma}$$

SELF PRACTICE EXERCISES

I. CHOOSE THE BEST ANSWER

1. Which of the following is not a continuous random variable?
   (a) Life of Electric bulbs (b) Sales revenue of a store
   (c) Number of televisions sold by a store (d) Price of a company's store
2. Which of the following is not a discrete variable?
   (a) Number of bicycles in a cycle stand
   (b) Number of shoppers in a store
   (c) Number of cinema houses in a city
   (d) Percentage of marks of a student in an examination
3. Number of parameters in a probability distribution could be:
   (a) 1 (b) 2
   (c) 3 (d) All of the above
4. In which of the following situations, Binomial distribution is not applicable?
   (a) Sex of a new born baby (b) Result in an examination
   (c) Rating of a new movie (d) Result of a tennis match
5. The mean of the binomial distribution is:
   (a) P (b) nP
   (c) nPq (d) P^2
6. For a Poisson distribution $P(1) = P(2)$, its variance is :
   (a) 3 (b) 4
   (c) 6 (d) 2
7. For a binomial probability distribution, we observe that:
   (a) mean > variance (b) mean < variance
   (c) mean = variance (d) None of these

8. The mean of a normal distribution is 50, its mode will be:
   (a) 25 (b) 40
   (c) 50 (d) None of these
9. For a Poisson distribution:
   (a) Mean = Variance (b) Mean = Standard Deviation
   (c) Mean < Variance (d) Man > Variance
10. If n is large, neither P nor q is a small, the limiting form of the binomial distribution is:
    (a) Binomial (b) Poisson
    (c) Normal (d) None of these
11. Approximately 60% of the observations in a normal distribution fall within the range of:
    (a) $\mu \pm 0.52s$ (b) $\mu \pm 0.67$ s
    (c) $\mu \pm 1.04$ s (d) $\mu \pm 1.28$ s.
12. The standard normal distribution has a:
    (a) Mean = 1 and standard deviation = 0
    (b) Mean = 1 and standard deviation = 1
    (c) Mean = 0 and standard deviation = 1
    (d) Mean = 0 and standard deviation = 0
    (e) Mean = –1 and standard deviation = 0.
13. Which of the following is not true?
    (a) The standard normal distribution is a normal distribution
    (b) The standard normal distribution has a variance of 1.
    (c) The normal distribution remains the same for all sample sizes
    (d) The t-distribution approximates the normal distribution as the sample size increases.
14. Which of the following is true with regard to a Bernoulli process?
    (a) It is related with a continuous random variable
    (b) Each trial has two or more possible outcomes
    (c) The probability of the outcome of any trial remains constant over time
    (d) The outcome of one trial influences the outcome of another trial
    (e) None of the above.
15. The normal distribution:
    (a) Is a discrete distribution
    (b) Is multimodal
    (c) Is a symmetrical distribution
    (d) Has mean, median and mode which are different from each other
    (e) Touches the horizontal axis at a finite distance from the mean.

II. FILL IN THE BLANKS

1. In binomial distribution, the number of trials is ....
2. The binomial distribution is symmetrical if ....
3. In binomial distribution .... and .... are the two parameters
4. A family of parametric distribution in which mean is equal to variance is ....
5. For a poisson distribution $P(x)$ = ..., x = 0, 1 .... the S.D is ....
6. The shape of the normal curve is ....

7. The area under normal curve beyond the distance $\mu \pm 3\sigma$ is only .... percent.
8. The parameters of normal distribution are ....
9. $x \pm 3\sigma$ range of a normal distribution curve covers .... percent area of the curve. **[MBA, UPTU, 2002]**
10. The mean ± 2 standard deviation is called .... percent of the area under the normal curve. **[MBA, UPTU, 2001]**

III. SHORT ANSWER TYPE QUESTIONS

1. Define Poisson distribution and state its uses. **[M. Com., MK Univ., 2004]**
2. Define Normal distribution? What are the main characteristics of Normal distribution?
3. What is Binomial distribution? Under what conditions will it trend to Normal distribution?
4. Explain, what is meant by Probability distribution of a discrete random variable.
5. What are the chief properties of Normal distribution? Describe briefly the importance of Normal distribution in statistical analysis. **[MBA, Delhi University, 1997]**
6. In what ways, Binomial, Poisson and normal distribution are related.
7. When can Poisson distribution be a reasonable approximation of the binomial? **[M.Com., DU, 1999]**

IV. LONG ANSWER TYPE QUESTIONS

1. What is Poisson distribution? Point out its role in business decision -making. Under what conditions will it tend to normal distribution? **[MBA, Kamau Univ., 1998]**
2. Define binomial distribution stating its parameters, mean and standard deviation and give any two examples where such a distribution is ideally suited. **[CA Foundation, 1994]**
3. Discuss the distinctive features of the binomial poisson and normal distribution when does a binomial distribution tend to become a normal distribution? **[MBA, Sukhadia Univ., 95, Kamau, 2000]**
4. What do you understand by theoretical distributions? Discuss their utility in statistics?
5. "A binomial distribution need not necessarily be a symmetrical distribution". Do you agree with the statement?
6. Name the six situations where Poisson distribution can have applications.
7. A certain type of plastic bag in the past has burst under a pressure of 10 pounds 30% of the time. If a prospective buyer tests 5 bags chosen at random, what is the probability that exactly one will burst?
8. The distribution of typing mistakes committed by a typist is given below. Assuming a poisson model, find out the expected frequencies: **[MBA, Sukhadia Univ., 1995]**

Mistakes per page	0	1	2	3	4	5
No. of pages	142	156	69	27	5	1

9. In a normal distribution, 7% of the observations are under 35 and 8.9% are under 63. What are the mean and standard deviation of distribution?
10. Daily demand for a product is approximately normally distributed with mean sales of 12 units per day and standard deviation of 4 units. Now many units must be on hand in the morning to assure no more than one chance in 5 of running out of stock during the day? **[MBA, DU, 2003]**

11. One hundred car radio sits are inspected as they come off the production line and number of defects per set is recorded below:

No. of defects	0	1	2	3	4
No. of sets	79	18	2	1	0

Fit a Poisson distribution to the above data. **[MBA, DU, 1999]**

12. For a binomial distribution the mean is 4 and variance 2. Find the probability of getting
    (i) at least 2 successes (ii) at most 2 successes. **[MBA, DU, 2002]**

13. Proof reading of 200 pages of a book containing 500 pages gave the following results:

No. of mistakes per page	0	1	2	3	4	5
Frequency	113	62	20	3	1	1
Cost per page for checking	1.0	1.5	2.5	3.0	3.5	4.0

(a) Fit a Poisson distribution
(b) Estimate the total cost of correcting the whole book. **[MBA, MD Univ., 1995]**

14. An insurance salesman sells policies to 5 men, all of an identical age and in good health. According to actuarial tables, the probability that a man of this particular age will be alive 30 years hence is 2/3. Find the probability that 30 years hence:
    (i) at least 1 man will be alive (ii) at least 3 men will be alive. **[MBA, IGNOU, 2002]**

15. The local authorities in a certain city install 10,000 electric lamps in the streets of the city. Of these lamps have an average life of 1000 burning hours with a standard deviation of 200 hours, assuming normality, what number of lamps might be expected to fail in the first 800 burning hours? **[MBA, IGNOU, 2002]**

ANSWERS

I. CHOOSE THE BEST ANSWERS

1. (c) 2. (d) 3. (d) 4. (c) 5. (b)
6. (d) 7. (a) 8. (c) 9. (a) 10. (c)
11. (e) 12. (c) 13. (d) 14. (c) 15. (c)

II. FILL IN THE BLANKS

1. Finite 2. $P = q$ 3. n and P 4. Poisson distribution
5. 4 6. Symmetrical 7. 0.27% 8. μ and σ
9. 99.73 10. 95. 45

IV. LONG ANSWER TYPE QUESTIONS

7. 0.302
8. 147.12, 147.12, 73.56, 2452, 6.13, 1.22
9. $\mu = 50.28$, $\sigma = 10.25$
10. 16
11. 77.88, 19.47, 2.43, 0.2028, 0.1267
12. (i) 0.9648 (ii) 0.1445
13. (a) 109.76, 65.85, 19.15, 3.95, 0.592, 0.0711 (b) 272.139

CHAPTER 15

Sampling, Sampling Distributions and Estimation

15.1 INTRODUCTION

Sampling is being used in our everyday life without knowing about it. For examples, a cook tests a small quantity of rice to see whether it has been well cooked and a grain merchant does not examine each grain of what he intends to purchase, but inspects only a small quantity of grains. Most of our decisions are based on the examination of a few items only.

A doctor examines a few drops of blood as sample and draws conclusion about the blood constitution of the whole body. Thus most of our investigations are based on samples. In this chapter, let us see the importance of sampling and the various methods of sample selections from the population.

15.2 POPULATION

In a statistical investigation, the interest usually lies in the assessment of general magnitude and the study of variation with respect to one or more characteristics relating to individuals belonging to a group. This group of individuals or units under study is called ***population*** or ***universe.*** Thus in statistics, population is an aggregate of objects or units under study. The population may be finite or infinite.

Sometimes it is possible and practical to examine every person or item in the population we wish to describe. We call this a ***complete enumeration***, or ***census***. We use ***sampling*** when it is not possible to measure every item in the population. Statisticians use the word population to refer not only to people but to all items that have been chosen for study.

15.2.1 Finite Population and Infinite Population

A population is said to be finite if it consists of finite number of units. Number of workers in a factory, production of articles in a particular day for a company are examples of finite population. The total number of units in a population is called population size. A population is said to be infinite if it has infinite number of units. For example the number of stars in the sky, the number of people seeing the Television programmes etc.

15.3 CENSUS METHOD

Information on population can be collected in two ways – census method and sample method. In census method every element of the population is included in the investigation. ***For example***, if we study the average annual income of the families of a particular village or area, and if there are 1000 families in that area, we must study the income of all 1000 families. In this method no family is left out, as each family is a unit.

15.3.1 Merits and Limitations of Census Method

Merits

1. The data are collected from each and every item of the population.
2. The results are more accurate and reliable, because every item of the universe is required.
3. Intensive study is possible.
4. The data collected may be used for various surveys, analyses etc.
5. It is an appropriate method of obtaining information on rare events such as areas under some crops and yield thereof, the number a' persons of certain age groups, their distribution by sex, educational, level of people, etc. This is the reason why throughout the world the population data are obtained by conducting a census generally every 10 years by the census method.
6. Data of complete enumeration census can be widely used as a basis for various surveys.

Limitations

1. It requires a large number of enumerators and it is a costly method
2. It requires more money, labour, time energy etc.
3. It is not possible in some circumstances where the population is infinite.

15.4 SAMPLING AND SAMPLE

Sampling is a method of selecting units for analysis such as households, consumers, companies etc. from the respective population under statistical investigation. The theory of sampling is based on the principle of statistical regularity. According to this principle, a moderately large number of items chosen at random from a large group are almost sure on an average to possess the characteristics of the larger group.

A smallest non-divisible part of the population is called a unit. A unit should be well defined and should not be ambiguous. For example, if we define unit as a household, then it should be defined that a person should not belong to two households nor should it leave out persons belonging to the population.

A finite subset of a population is called a sample and the number of units in a sample is called its sample size.

The process of selecting a sample from a population is called sampling. In sampling, a representative sample of elements of a population is selected and then analysed.

By analysing the data collected from the sample one can draw inference about the population under study.

15.4.1 Need for Sampling

Suppose that the raw materials department in a company receives items in lots and issues them to the production department as and when required. Before accepting these items, the inspection department inspects or tests them to make sure that they meet the required specifications. Thus

(i) It could inspect all items in the lot or

(ii) It could take a sample and inspect the sample for defectives and then estimate the total number of defectives for the population as a whole.

The first approach is called ***complete enumeration*** (***census***). It has two major disadvantages namely, the time consumed and the cost involved in it. The second approach that uses sampling has two major advantages. (i) It is significantly less expensive. (ii) It takes least possible time with best possible results.

There are situations that involve destruction procedure where sampling is the only answer. A well-designed statistical sampling methodology would give accurate results and at the same time will result in cost reduction and least time. Thus sampling is the best available tool to decision makers.

15.4.2 Elements of Sampling Plan

The main steps involved in the planning and execution of sample survey are:

(i) **Objectives:** The first task is to lay down in concrete terms the basic objectives of the survey. Failure to define the objective(s) will clearly undermine the purpose of carrying out the survey itself. For example, if a nationalised bank wants to study savings bank account holders perception of the service quality rendered over a period of one year, the objective of the sampling is, here, to analyse the perception of the account holders in the bank.

(ii) **Population to be covered:** Based on the objectives of the survey, the population should be well defined. The characteristics concerning the population under study should also be clearly defined. For example, to analyse the perception of the savings bank account holders about the service rendered by the bank, all the account holders in the bank constitute the population to be investigated.

(iii) **Sampling frame:** In order to cover the population decided upon, there should be some list, map or other acceptable material (called the ***frame***) which serves as a guide to the population to be covered. The list or map must be examined to be sure that it is reasonably free from defects. The sampling frame will help us in the selection of sample. All the account numbers of the savings bank account holders in the bank are the sampling frame in the analysis of perception of the customers regarding the service rendered by the bank.
For adopting any sampling procedure it is essential to have a list identifying each sampling unit by a number. Such a list or map is called ***sampling frame.*** A list of voters, a list of house holders, a list of villages in a district, a list of farmers etc. are a few examples of sampling frame.

(iv) **Sampling unit:** For the purpose of sample selection, the population should be capable of being divided up into sampling units. The division of the population into sampling units should be unambiguous. Every element of the population should belong to just one sampling unit.
Each account holder of the savings bank account in the bank, form a unit of the sample as all the savings bank account holders in the bank constitute the population.
The constituents of a population which are individuals to be sampled from the population and cannot be further subdivided for the purpose of the sampling at a time are called ***sampling units.*** For example, to know the average income per family, the head of the family is a sampling unit. To know the average yield of rice, each farm owner's yield of rice is a sampling unit.

(v) **Sample selection:** The size of the sample and the manner of selecting the sample should be defined based on the objectives of the statistical investigation. The estimation of population parameter along with their margin of uncertainty is some of the important aspects to be followed in sample selection.

(vi) **Collection of Data:** The method of collecting the information has to be decided, keeping in view the costs involved and the accuracy aimed at. Physical observation, interviewing respondents and collecting data through mail are some of the methods that can be followed in collection of data.

(vii) **Analysis of Data:** The collected data should be properly classified and subjected to an appropriate analysis. The conclusions are drawn based on the results of the analysis.

15.4.3 Principles of Sampling

Samples have to provide good estimates. The following principle tell us that the sample methods provide such good estimates

- **Principle of Statistical Regularity:** A moderately large number of units chosen at random from a large group are almost sure on the average to possess the characteristics of the large group.
- **Principle of Inertia of Large Numbers:** Other things being equal, as the sample size increases, the results tend to be more accurate and reliable.
- **Principle of Validity:** This states that the sampling methods provide valid estimates about the population units (parameters).
- **Principle of Optimisation:** This principle takes into account the desirability of obtaining a sampling design which gives optimum results. This minimizes the risk or loss of the sampling design. The foremost purpose of sampling is to gather maximum information about the population under consideration at minimum cost, time and human power. This is best achieved when the sample contains all the properties of the population.

15.4.4 Sampling With and Without Replacement

Before we proceed further, it is necessary at this stage to know that we can choose a simple random sample with and without replacement.

Sampling with replacement

Sampling with replacement implies that an element once chosen is returned to the population and as such it is available to be chosen again. This means that an element can be selected more than once when sampling with replacement is adopted.

In a population containing N observations, the number of samples each containing n observations = N^n if the sampling is done with replacement.

For example, if we have four numbers 3, 4, 6, 7, constitute a population. We have to choose a sample of 2 elements from this population.

Samples with replacement = [3,3], [3,4], [3,6], [3,7], [4,3], [4,4], [4,6], [4,7], [6,3], [6,4], [6,6], [6,7], [7,3], [7,4], [7,6], [7,7],

= 16 = $(4)^2$

Sampling without replacement

In case of sampling without replacement, before choosing the first element from the population, every element has an equal chance ($1/N$) of being included in the sample. But once the first element has been chosen, it is not replaced in the population. This means that the second element is selected from the remaining N–1 elements of the population. Hence each element has a chance of $1/(N–1)$ to be included in the sample.

In a population containing N observations, the number of samples each containing n observations $= {}^{N}C_{n}$ if the sampling is done with replacement.

For example, if four numbers 3, 4, 6, 7, constitute a population. We have to choose a sample of 2 elements from this population.

$$\text{Samples with replacement} = [3,4], [3,6], [3,7], [4,6], [4,7], [6,7]$$
$$= 6 = {}^{4}C_{2}$$

15.4.5 Advantages and Limitation of Sampling

Advantages

There are many advantages of sampling methods over census method. They are as follows:

1. Sampling saves time and labour.
2. It results in reduction of cost in terms of money and man-hour.
3. Sampling ends up with greater accuracy of results.
4. It has greater scope.
5. It has greater adaptability.
6. If the population is too large, or hypothetical or destroyable sampling is the only method to be used.

Limitations

The limitations of sampling are given below:

1. Sampling is to be done by qualified and experienced persons. Otherwise, the information will be unbelievable.
2. Sample method may give the extreme values sometimes instead of the mixed values.
3. There is the possibility of sampling errors. Census survey is free from sampling error.

15.5 POPULATION PARAMETERS AND SAMPLE STATISTICS

Parameters

Unknown measure (or value) which describes the entire population or process characteristics is called a parameters. *For example,* quantities such as mean μ, variance σ^2, standard deviation σ, median, mode and proportion p computed from a data set (population) are called parameters. A parameter is usually denoted with letters of the lower case Greek alphabet such as mean μ and standard deviation σ.

Samples

A measure found from analysing sample data is called a sample statistic or simply a statistic. Inferential statistical methods attempt to estimate population parameters using sample statistics.

Sample statistics are usually denoted by Roman letters such as mean $\overline{X}$, standard deviation s, variance s^2 and proportion $\overline{p}$.

NOTE: The value of every statistic varies randomly from one sample to another whereas the value of a parameter is considered as constant.

Key Statistical Concepts

Population — a ***population*** is the group of **all** items of interest to a statistics practitioner.
— Frequently very large; sometimes infinite. e.g. All 5 million Delhi voters,

Sample — A ***sample*** is a set of data drawn from the population.
— Potentially very large, but less than the population. e.g. a sample of 765 voters exit polled on election day.

Parameter — A descriptive measure of a ***population.***

Statistic — A descriptive measure of a ***sample.***

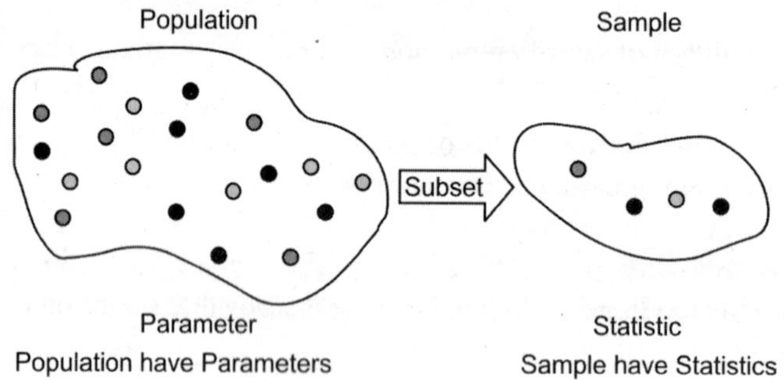

Fig. 15.1

Inferential or inductive statistics helps us in making an educated guess about the population parameters based on the statistics of its random sample.

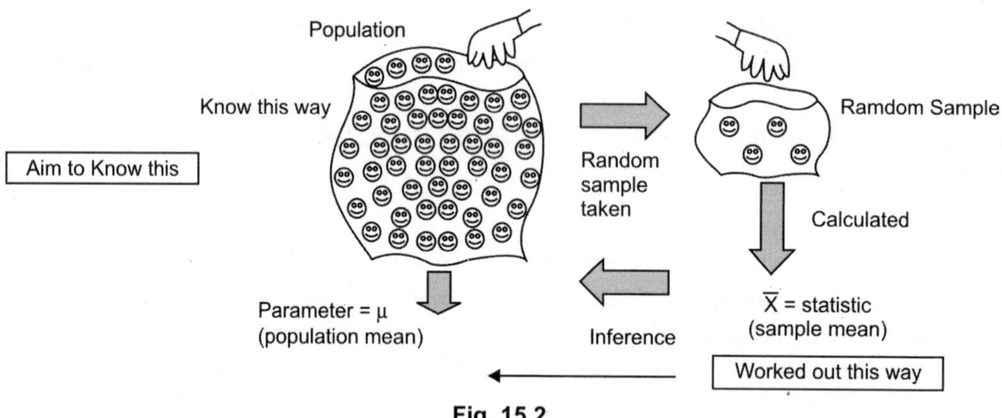

Fig. 15.2

For instance, say

Aim to know: The average (mean) income of families living in the area "Park avenue" in the year 1997-1998. i.e. The population parameter m (in dollars).

Work out this way: Draw a random sample of 200 families and compute their mean income. i.e. the statistic of sample x say \$ 120000.

Conclusion (or inference): The population mean (parameter) is close to sample mean (statistic) i.e. mean income of the families living in the area 'Park Avenue' is \$ 120000.

15.6 CENSUS VERSUS SAMPLE METHOD

Statistical data can be collected either on the basis of census type of enquiry or on the basis of sample Method.

Census Method

In the census type of enquiry there is complete enumeration of all the items of the population and the question of taking a sample does not arise. Normally, a census method should give exact and accurate results, but this method suffers from certain limitations which are:

- It is very expensive, particularly if the size of the population is large;
- It requires more time for competition.
- It needs substantial manpower and administrative control.

The census method is, however, used in certain cases where

- Complete information is needed about the entire population.
- Where the size of the population is not big and the need for accurate results great.
- In case of manufacturing process in industry, if the occurrence of a defects may cause damage to the machine itself or to the life of person or persons operating it. Hundred percent inspections would be recommended.

Sample Method

Sample Method of study, as has already been stated, is one where we study some selected items from the population for drawing general inferences.

This method has many advantages over Census Method. R A Fisher has summed up the advantages of sampling technique over census technique in just four words:

Speed, Economy, Adaptability, and Scientific Approach

Why Statistical Sampling?

Sampling is the selection of part of an aggregate or totality known as population, on the basis of which a decision concerning the population is made.

The following are the advantages and/or necessities for sampling in statistical decision making:

- **Cost:** Cost is one of the main arguments in favour of sampling, because often a sample can furnish data of sufficient accuracy and at much lower cost than a census.
- **Accuracy:** Much better control over data collection errors is possible with sampling than with a census, because a sample is a smaller-scale undertaking.
- **Timeliness:** Another advantage of a sample over a census is that the sample produces information faster. This is important for timely decision making.
- **Amount of Information:** More detailed information can be obtained from a sample survey than from a census, because it take less time, is less costly, and allows us to take more care in the data processing stage.
- **Destructive Tests:** When a test involves the destruction of an item under study, sampling must be used. Statistical sampling determination can be used to find the optimal sample size within an acceptable cost.

15.7 TYPES OF SAMPLING

The technique of selecting a sample from a population usually depends on ***the nature of the data*** and ***the type of enquiry***. The procedure of sampling may be broadly classified under the following heads:

(i) Probability Sampling or Random Sampling and
(ii) Non-Probability Sampling or non-Random Sampling.

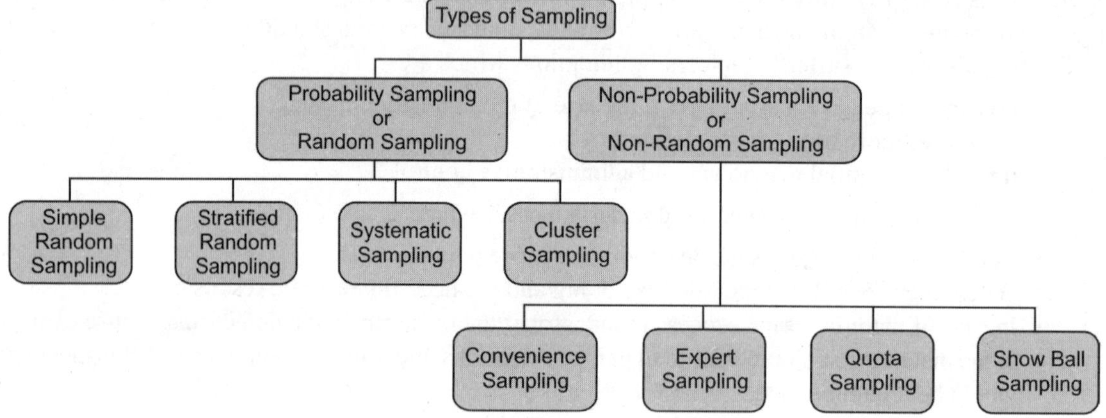

Fig. 15.3: Types of sampling

15.7.1 Difference Between Non-probability and Probability Sampling

The difference between Non-probability and Probability Sampling is that non-probability sampling does not involve ***random*** selection and probability sampling does. Does that mean that Non-probability samples aren't representative of the population? Not necessarily. But it does mean that Non-probability samples cannot depend upon the rationale of probability theory. At least with a probabilistic sample, we know the odds or probability that we have represented the population well. We are able to estimate confidence intervals for the statistic. With Non-probability samples, we may or may not represent the population well, and it will often be hard for us to know how well we've done so. In general, researchers prefer probabilistic or random sampling methods over Non-probabilistic ones, and consider them to be more accurate and rigorous. However, in applied social research there may be circumstances where it is not feasible, practical or theoretically sensible to do random sampling. Here, we consider a wide range of Non-probabilistic alternatives.

15.8 PROBABILITY SAMPLING

Probability sampling is a method of sampling that ensures that every unit in the population has a known ***non-zero chance*** of being included in the sample.

Before We can explain the various probability methods we have to define some basic terms. These are:

$$^{N}C_{n} = \text{the number of combinations (subsets) of } n \text{ from } N$$

$$f = n / N = \text{the sampling fraction}$$

Where, N = the number of cases in the sampling frame and n = the number of cases in the sample.

That's it. With those terms defined we can begin to define the different probability sampling methods.

The different methods of random sampling are:

15.8.1 Simple Random Sampling

Simple random sampling is the foundation of probability sampling. It is a special case of probability sampling in which every unit in the population has an ***equal chance*** of being included in a sample. Simple random sampling also makes the selection of every possible combination of the desired number of units equally likely.

Sampling may be done with or without replacement. It may be noted that when the sampling is with replacement, the units drawn are replaced before the next selection is made. The population size remains constant when the sampling is with replacement.

If one wants to select n units from a population of size N without replacement, then every possible selection of n units must have the same probability. Thus there are ${}^{N}c_{n}$ possible ways to pick up n units from the population of size N. Simple random sampling guarantees that a sample of n units has the same probability $1/{}^{N}c_{n}$ of being selected.

Example: A bank wants to study the Savings Bank account holders perception of the service quality rendered over a period of one year. The bank has to prepare a complete list of savings bank account holders, called as ***sampling frame,*** say 500. Now the process involves selecting a sample of 50 out of 500 and interviewing them. This could be achieved in many ways. Two common ways are:

1. **Lottery Method:** Select 50 slips from a box containing well shuffled 500 slips of account numbers without replacement. This method can be applied when the population is small enough to handle.
2. **Random Numbers Method:** When the population size is very large, the most practical and inexpensive method of selecting a simple random sample is by using the random number tables.

Methods of Selection of a Simple Random Sampling

The following are some methods of selection of a simple random sampling.

(a) Lottery Method: This is the most popular and simplest method. In this method all the items of the population are numbered on separate slips of paper of same size, shape and colour. They are folded and mixed up in a container. The required numbers of slips are selected at random for the desire sample size. For example, if we want to select 5 students, out of 50 students, then we must write their names or their roll numbers of all the 50 students on slips and mix them. Then we make a random selection of 5 students.

This method is mostly used in lottery draws. If the population is infinite this method is inapplicable.

(b) Table of Random Numbers: As the lottery method cannot be used, when the population is infinite, the alternative method is that of using the table of random numbers. There are several standard tables of random numbers.

1. Tippett's table
2. Fisher and Yates' table
3. Kendall and Smith's table are the three tables among them.
4. Rand Corporation Table
5. C R Rao Mitra & Mathai Table

NOTE: Tippett's random numbers are by far the most popular ones and very much in use.

A random number table is so constructed that all digits 0 to 9 appear independent of each other with equal frequency. If we have to select a sample from population of size N= 100, then the numbers can be combined three by three to give the numbers from 001 to 100.

Merits and Limitations of using Random Numbers

Merits

1. Personal bias is eliminated as a selection depends solely on chance.
2. A random sample is in general a representative sample for a homogenous population.
3. There is no need for the thorough knowledge of the units of the population.
4. The accuracy of a sample can be tested by examining another sample from the same population when the population is unknown.
5. This method is also used in other methods of sampling.

Limitations

1. Preparing lots or using random number tables is tedious when the population is large.
2. When there is large difference between the units of population, the simple random sampling may not be a representative sample.
3. The size of the sample required under this method is more than that required by stratified random sampling.
4. It is generally seen that the units of a simple random sample lie apart geographically. The cost and time of collection of data are more.

15.8.2 Stratified Random Sampling

Stratified random sampling involves dividing the population into a number of groups called ***strata*** in such a manner that the units within a stratum are ***homogeneous*** and the units between the strata are ***heterogeneous***. The next step involves selecting a simple random sample of appropriate size from each stratum. The sample size in each stratum is usually of (a) equal size, (b) proportionate to the number of units in the stratum.

For example, a marketing manager in a consumer product company wants to study the customer's attitude towards a new product in order to improve the sales. Then three typical cities that will influence the sales will be considered as three strata. The customers within a city are similar but between the cities are vastly different. Selection of the customers for the study from each city has to be a random sample to draw meaningful inference on the whole population.

A stratified sampling approach is most effective when three conditions are met:

- Variability within strata are minimized
- Variability between strata are maximized
- The variables upon which the population is stratified are strongly correlated with the desired dependent variable.

Types of Stratified Sampling

There are two types of stratified sampling. They are ***proportional*** and ***non-proportional***. In the proportional sampling equal and proportionate representation is given to subgroups or strata. If the number of items is large, the sample will have a higher size and vice versa.

The population size is denoted by N and the sample size is denoted by ' n' the sample size is allocated to each stratum in such a way that the sample fractions is a constant for each stratum. That is given by $n/N = c$. So in this method each stratum is represented according to its size.

In non-proportionate sample, equal representation is given to all the sub-strata regardless of their existence in the population.

EXAMPLE 15.1: A sample of 50 students is to be drawn from a population consisting of 500 students belonging to two institutions A and B. The number of students in the institution A is 200 and the institution B is 300. How will you draw the sample using proportional allocation? **[MBA, HPU, 2001]**

Solution: There are two strata in this case with sizes $N_1 = 200$ and $N_2 = 300$ and the total population $N = N_1 + N_2 = 500$. The sample size is 50.

If n_1 and n_2 are the sample sizes,

$$n_1 = \frac{n}{N} \times N_1 = \frac{50}{500} \times 200 = 20$$

$$n_2 = \frac{n}{N} \times N_2 = \frac{50}{500} \times 300 = 30$$

The sample sizes are 20 from A and 30 from B. Then the units from each institution are to be selected by simple random sampling.

EXAMPLE 15.2: You are given the following data relating to the number of workers and their wages.

Wages	Number of workers			
per Months	Unskilled	Semi-skilled	Skilled	Total
Less than Rs. 1000	300	90	10	**400**
Rs. 1,000 – 5000	200	80	10	**290**
1500–2000	100	180	30	**310**
Total	**600**	**350**	**50**	**1000**

(i) Find out the number of unskilled, semi-skilled and skilled workers that would be selected in a sample of 10% if stratified proportionate sampling method is used;

(ii) What would be their distribution if unskilled and skilled workers are to be selected in the ratio of 5.4.1 and further weight-age to income groups (beginning with less than 400) is to be in ratio of 3:2:1. **[MBA, Manglore University, 2000]**

Solution:

(i) The sample size would be 100 which is 10% of the total. Since proportionate stratified sampling method has to be used 10% of the units in each of the nine strata have to be picked up. The units selected would be as follows:

Wages per Months	Unskilled	Semi-skilled	Skilled	Total
Less than Rs. 400	30	9	1	**40**
Rs. 400 – 800	20	8	1	**29**
Rs. 800–1200	10	18	3	**31**
Total	**60**	**35**	**5**	**100**

(ii) In the second case also the size of the sample is 10% hence 100 workers have to be selected but this time the unskilled, semi-skilled and to their strength but in proportion of 5 : 4 : 1 and further these proportions have to be weighted on the basis of wages, the weights being in proportion of 3 : 2 : 1 for unskilled, semi-skilled and skilled workers.

The number of wage earners in various strata would be as follows:

Wages per Months	Unskilled	Semi-skilled	Skilled	Total	Ratio
Less than Rs. 400	25	20	5	**50**	**3**
Rs. 400 – 800	17	13	3	**33**	**2**
Rs. 800–1200	8	7	2	**17**	**1**
Total	**50**	**40**	**10**	**100**	
Ratio	**5**	**4**	**1**		

Thus unskilled workers, semi-skilled workers and skilled workers are 50, 40 and 10 in the sample. They are in the ratio of 5 : 4 : 1. Of the 50 unskilled workers those having an income of less than Rs 400, 400–800 and 800–1200, are 25, 17 and 8 respectively. Their numbers are

$$\frac{(50 \times 3)}{6} = 25, \quad \frac{(50 \times 2)}{6} = 17, \text{ and } \frac{(50 \times 1)}{6} = 8.$$

Since they have to be in the ratio of 3 : 2 : 1, the actual figures have been rounded off as the ratios gave fractional values.

Merits and Limitations of Stratified Sampling

Merits

1. It is more representative.
2. It ensures greater accuracy.
3. It is easy to administer as the population is sub - divided.
4. Greater geographical concentration reduces time and expenses.
5. When the original population is badly skewed, this method is appropriate.
6. For non – homogeneous population, it may field good results.

Limitations

1. To divide the population into homogeneous strata, it requires more money, time and statistical experience which are a difficult one.
2. Improper stratification leads to bias, if the different strata overlap such a sample will not be a representative one.

15.8.3 Systematic Sampling (Quasi-Random Sampling)

Systematic Sampling is a convenient way of selecting a sample. It requires less time and cost when compared to simple random sampling.

In this method, the units are selected from the population at a uniform interval. To facilitate this we arrange the items in numerical, alphabetical, geographical or any other order. When a complete list of the population is available, this method is used.

NOTE: This method is widely employed because of its ease and convenience. A frequently used method of sampling when a complete list of the population is available is ***systematic sampling***. It is also called ***Quasi-random sampling***.

Step for Systematic Random Sample

Here are the steps you need to follow in order to achieve a systematic random sample:

- number the units in the population from 1 to N
- decide on the n (sample size) that you want or need

$$k = \frac{N}{n} = \frac{\text{Population size}}{\text{Sample size}} = \text{the interval size}$$

- randomly select an integer between 1 to k
- then take every kth unit

For Example, if we want to select a sample of 9 students out of 105 students numbered as 1, 2, ..., 105 , select a student among 1, 2, ... , 11 at random (say at 3rd position). Here $k = 105/10 = 10.5$ and $k = 11$. Hence students at the positions 3, 14, 25, 36, 47, 58, 69, 80, 91 form a random sample of size 9.

For Example:

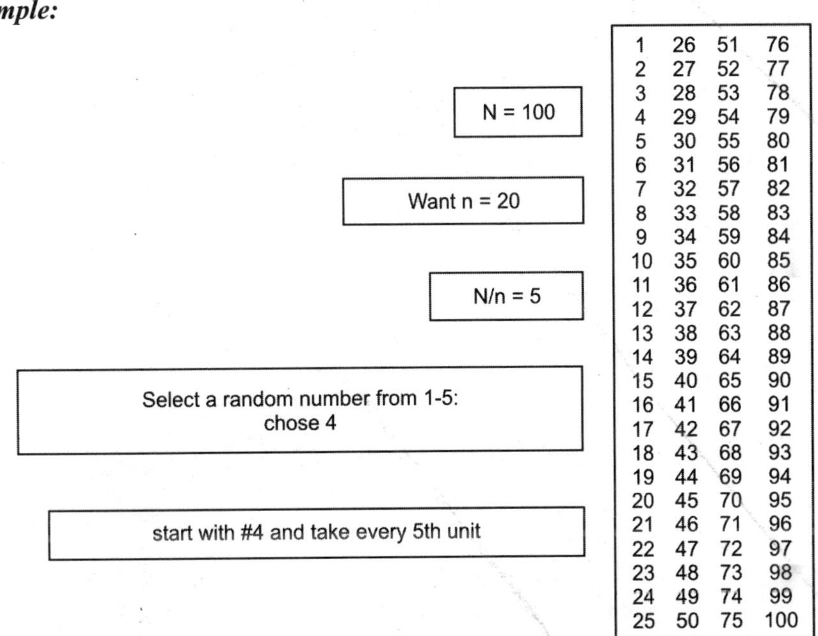

All of this will be much clearer with an example. Let's assume that we have a population that only has N=100 people in it and that you want to take a sample of n =20. To use systematic sampling, the population must be listed in a random order. The sampling fraction would be $f = 20/100 = 20\%$. In this case, the interval size, k, is equal to $N/n = 100/20 = 5$. Now, select a random integer from 1 to 5. In our example, imagine that you chose 4. Now, to select the sample, start with the 4th unit in the list and take every k-th unit (every 5th, because k =5). You would be sampling units 4, 9, 14, 19, and so on to 100 and you would wind up with 20 units in your sample.

Merits and Limitations of Systematic Sampling

Merits

1. This method is simple and convenient.
2. Time and work is reduced much.
3. If proper care is taken result will be accurate.
4. It can be used in infinite population.

Limitations

1. Systematic sampling may not represent the whole population.
2. There is a chance of personal bias of the investigators.

Systematic sampling is preferably used when the information is to be collected from trees in a forest, house in blocks, entries in a register which are in a serial order etc.

15.8.4 Cluster Sampling

Cluster sampling is used when the population is divided into ***groups*** or ***clusters*** such that each cluster is a representative of the population.

If a study has to be done to find out the number of children that each family in Chennai has, then the city can be divided into several clusters and a few clusters can be chosen at random. Every family in the chosen clusters can be a sample unit. In using cluster sampling the following points should be noted

(a) For getting precise results clusters should be as small as possible consistent with the cost and limitations of the survey and
(b) The number of units in each cluster must be more or less equal.

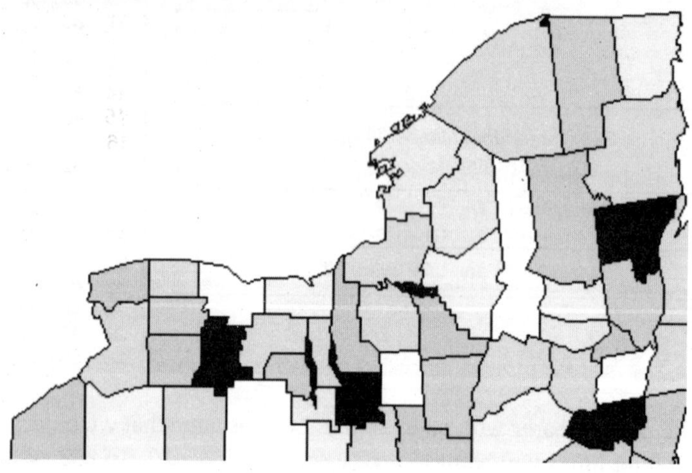

Fig. 15.4

For example, in the figure we see a map of the a particular city. Let's say that we have to do a survey of blocks that will require us going to the blocks personally. If we do simple random samples state-wide we'll have to cover the entire capital geographically. Instead, we decide to do a cluster sampling of five blocks (marked in red in the figure). Once these are selected, we go to *every block* in the five areas to give opinion on a particular issue.

Clearly this strategy will help us to economize on our mileage. Cluster or area sampling, then, is useful in situations like this, and is done primarily for efficiency of administration. Note also, that we probably don't have to worry about using this approach if we are conducting a mail or telephone survey because it doesn't matter as much (or cost more or raise inefficiency) where we call or send letters to.

This method is commonly used in collecting data about some common characteristics of the population.

Cluster Sampling is an example of ***'two-stage sampling'*** or ***'multistage sampling'***: in the first stage a sample of areas is chosen; in the second stage a sample of respondent *within* those areas is selected. This can reduce travel and other administrative costs. It also means that one does not need a sampling frame listing all elements in the target population. Instead, clusters can be chosen from a cluster-level frame, with an element-level frame created only for the selected clusters. Cluster sampling generally increases the variability of sample estimates above that of simple random sampling, depending on how the clusters differ between themselves, as compared with the within-cluster variation.

In cluster sampling, we follow these steps:

- divide population into clusters (usually along geographic boundaries)
- randomly sample clusters
- measure all units within sampled clusters

Merits and Limitations of Cluster Sampling

Merits

1. Whether or not a particular aggregate of units should be called a cluster will depend on circumstances of each case.
2. It is not necessary that clusters should always be natural aggregates such as blocks, polling constituencies, schools or colleges. Artificial clusters may be formed.
3. Various levels of clusters may be used in any one sample design.

Limitations

1. Estimates based on cluster samples are generally not as reliable as those based on simple random samples of the same size.
2. A major limitations of cluster sampling is the high degree of intra-cluster homogeneity.

Since both stratified sampling and cluster sampling have some subgroups, a pertinent question may be asked: How do they differ from each other? The following three considerations clearly bring out the difference between the two types of sample designs:

Stratified Sampling	Cluster Sampling
1. Population is divided into a few subgroups, each having many elements. The selection of subgroups is made on the basis of some criterion, which is related to the variables under study.	1. Population is divided into many subgroups, each having a few elements. Here, the selection of subgroups is made on the basis of some criterion of ease or availability of requisite data.
2. In selecting the sample, homogeneity within subgroups and heterogeneity between subgroups are aimed at.	2. Here, the approach is just the opposite as in selecting the sample heterogeneity within subgroups and homogeneity between subgroups are aimed at.
3. Elements are randomly selected from within each subgroup.	3. Only a few sbubgroups are randomly selected and then all elements within those subgroups are covered in the study.

15.9 NON-PROBABILITY SAMPLING

The fundamental difference between probability sampling and non-probability sampling is that in non-probability sampling procedure, the selection of the sample units does not ensure a known to the units being selected. In other words the units are selected without using the ***principle of probability.*** Even though the non-probability sampling has advantages such as reduced cost, speed and convenience in implementation, it lacks accuracy in view of the selection bias. Non-probability sampling is suitable for pilot studies and exploratory research

The methods of ***Non-Random sampling*** are:

Purposive Sampling

In this sampling, the sample is selected with definite purpose in view and the choice of the sampling units depends entirely on the discretion and judgement of the investigator.

For example, if an investigator wants to give the picture that the standard of living has increased in the city of Madurai, he may take the individuals in the sample from the posh localities and ignore the localities where low income group and middle class families live.

Quota Sampling

This is a restricted type of purposive sampling. This consists in specifying quotas of the samples to be drawn from different groups and then drawing the required samples from these groups by purposive sampling. Quota sampling is widely used in opinion and market research surveys.

In quota sampling, you select people non-randomly according to some fixed quota. There are two types of quota sampling: ***proportional*** and ***non proportional***.

In proportional quota sampling you want to represent the major characteristics of the population by sampling a proportional amount of each. For instance, if you know the population has 40% women and 60% men, and that you want a total sample size of 100, you will continue sampling until you get those percentages and then you will stop. So, if you've already got the 40 women for your sample, but not the sixty men, you will continue to sample men but even if legitimate women respondents come along, you will not sample them because you have already "met your quota." The problem here (as in much purposive sampling) is that you have to decide the specific characteristics on which you will base the quota. Will it be by gender, age, education race, religion, etc.?

Expert Opinion Sampling or Expert Sampling

Expert opinion sampling involves gathering a set of people who have the knowledge and expertise in certain key areas that are crucial to decision making. The advantage of this sampling is that it acts as a support mechanism for some of our decisions in situations where virtually no data are available. The major disadvantage is that even the experts can have prejudices, likes and dislikes that might distort the results.

Snowball Sampling

In snowball sampling, you begin by identifying someone who meets the criteria for inclusion in your study. You then ask them to recommend others who they may know who also meet the criteria.

Although this method would hardly lead to representative samples, there are times when it may be the best method available. Snowball sampling is especially useful when you are trying to reach populations that are inaccessible or hard to find. For instance, if you are studying the homeless, you are not likely to be able to find good lists of homeless people within a specific geographical area. However, if you go to that area and identify one or two, you may find that they know very well who the other homeless people in their vicinity are and how you can find them.

Heterogeneity Sampling

We sample for heterogeneity when we want to include all opinions or views, and we aren't concerned about representing these views proportionately. Another term for this is sampling for *diversity*. In many brainstorming or nominal group processes (including concept mapping), we would use some form of heterogeneity sampling because our primary interest is in getting broad spectrum of ideas, not identifying the "average" or "modal instance" ones. In effect, what we would like to be sampling is not people, but ideas. We imagine that there is a population of all possible ideas relevant to some topic and that we want to sample this population, not the population of people who have the ideas. Clearly, in order to get all of the ideas, and especially the "outlier" or unusual ones, we have to include a broad and diverse range of participants. Heterogeneity sampling is, in this sense, almost the opposite of modal instance sampling.

15.10 CHOICE OF SAMPLING TECHNIQUES

It is very difficult to say that any one of the techniques discussed above would always be better than the rest. In different situations different techniques would be found appropriate. Factors like nature of the problem, size of the universe, size of the sample, availability of resources and time, would affect the choice of an appropriate method.

However, it should not be thought that random sampling is always better than non-random sampling. One should weight the uncertainties of purpose sampling with those of random sampling. In studies where the size of the sample is small is small in relation to the size of universe, purposive sampling would be better than random sampling, but as the size of the sample increases, the importance of random sampling also goes up.

It should also be kept in mind that even in small size samples purposive sampling can give better estimates only about the means of a series and not about its dispersion or Skewness. The reason for this is that in non random sampling such units are selected whose values are around the mean value. Extreme items are avoided and therefore the extent of dispersion or Skewness items are avoided and therefore the extent of dispersion or Skewness cannot be properly estimated if purposive sampling is used.

In many situations, stratified sampling may give better results than simple random sampling or non-sampling. (See figure 15.5 on next page.)

15.11 SAMPLING AND NON-SAMPLING ERRORS

The errors involved in the collection of data, processing and analysis of data may be broadly classified as

- Sampling Errors
- Non-Sampling Errors

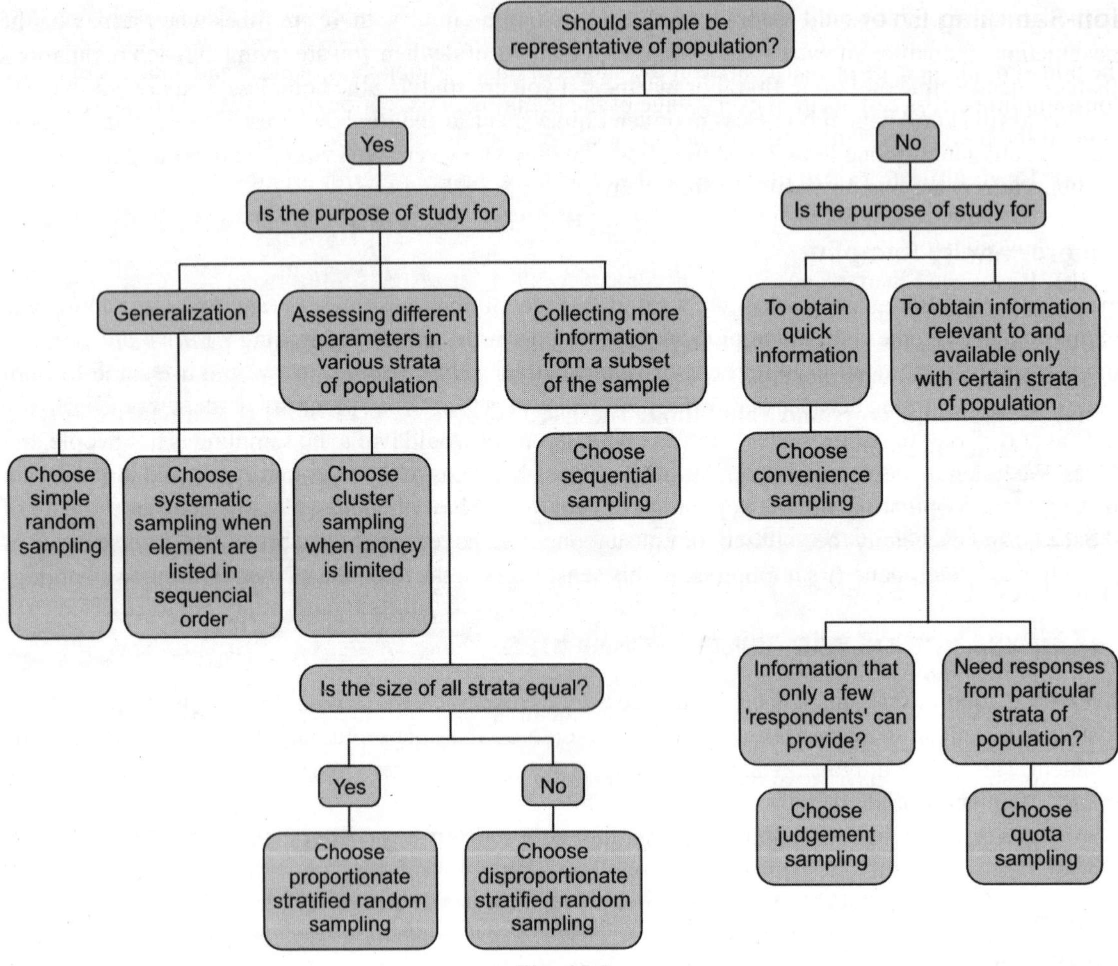

Fig. 15.5

Sampling Errors

Sampling errors have their origin in sampling and arise due to the fact that only a part of the population has been used to estimate population parameters and draw inference about the population. Increasing in the sample size usually results in decrease in the sampling error. Sampling errors are primarily due to some of the following reasons:

(a) **Faulty Selection of the Sample:** Some of the bias is introduced by the use of defective sampling technique for the selection of a sample in which the investigator deliberately selects a representative sample to obtain certain results.

(b) **Substitution:** If difficulty arises in enumerating a particular sampling unit included in the random sample, the investigators usually substitute a convenient member of the population leading to sampling error.

(c) **Faulty demarcation of Sampling Units :** Bias due to defective demarcation of sampling units is particularly significant in area surveys such as agricultural experiments. Thus faulty demarcation could cause sampling error.

Non-Sampling Errors

The non-sampling errors primarily arise at the stages of observation, classification and analysis of data. Non-sampling errors can occur at every stage of the planning or execution of census or sample surveys. Some of the more important non-sampling errors arise from the following factors:

(a) **Errors due to faulty planning and definitions:** Sampling error arises due to improper data specification, error in location of units, measurement of characteristics and lack of trained investigators.
(b) **Response Errors:** These errors occur as a result of the responses furnished by the respondents.
(c) **Non-Response bias:** Non-response biases occur due to incomplete information on all the sampling units.
(d) **Errors in Coverage:** These errors occur in the coverage of sampling units.
(e) **Compiling Errors and Tabulation:** These errors arise due to compilation such as editing and coding of responses.

15.12 SAMPLING DISTRIBUTIONS

There are two basic questions asked by inferential statistics:

- How close is the value of a statistic to the corresponding parameter of the entire population? For example, if we have a sample of 30 elements from a population and we find that $\bar{X} = 17.6$, we would like to know how far this might be from the mean μ of the entire population.
- In many cases, someone has hypothesized a particular value for the parameter of a population or some relationship between the parameters of two or more populations. For example, experience may show that the mean *IQ* of all people is 100 and someone may want to test whether a particular teaching method leads to higher mean *IQ*. Similarly, someone may wonder if mean *IQ* of men (call it μ_1) is the same as that for women (call it μ_2).

Both of these inferential questions are answered using an idea called the ***sampling distribution of a transformed statistic*** which we study in this section.

Before discuss in detail about sampling distributions, it is necessary to understand the following two probability distributions, their characteristics and relations:

(i) The population distribution
(ii) The sample distribution

Population Distribution

When we talk of population distribution, we assume that we have investigated the population and have full knowledge of its mean and standard deviation.

Sample Distribution

When we talk of a sample distribution, we take a sample from population. A sample distribution may take any shape. Each sample distribution is a discrete distribution because the value of the sample mean would vary from sample to sample. This variability serves as the basis for the random sampling distribution. In given figure only five such samples are shown, however there could be various such cases.

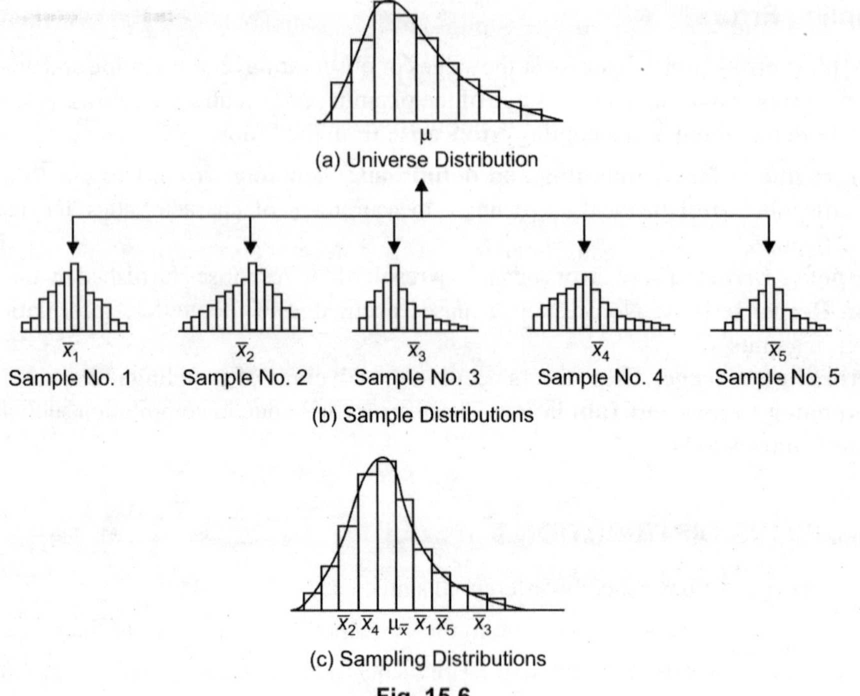

Fig. 15.6

Sampling distributions constitute the theoretical basis of statistical inference and are of considerable importance in business decision-making.

If we take numerous different samples of equal size from the same population, the probability of all the possible values of a given statistic from all the distinct possible samples of equal size is called a sampling distribution. (See figure 15.6.)

DO YOU KNOW?

Mean of a sampling distribution of sample means is the same as the mean of the population distribution from which the samples were taken.

The aim of the theory of sampling is to get as much information as possible, ideally all the information about the population from which the sample has been drawn. From the parent population, in particular, we would like to estimate the parameters of the population or specify the limits or ranges within which the population parameters are expected to lie with a specified degree of confidence.

The logic of the sampling theory is the logic of induction, that is, we go from particular (i.e. sample) to general (i.e. population). Normally all results will have to be expressed in terms of probability. In the theory of sampling, we often come across two words, '***parameters***' and '***statistics***'.

Different symbols are used for sampling distribution are:

n = **sample size**	μ = **population mean**	$p, \bar{p}$ = **sample proportion**
n_1, n_2 = **sample 1, 2 size**	μ_0 = **hypothesized population mean**	p_0 = **hypothesized proportion**

$\bar{X}$ = **sample mean** s = **sample standard deviation** s^2 = **sample variance** s^1, s^2 = **sample 1, 2 SD**	μ_1, μ_2 = **population 1, 2 mean** σ = **population SD** σ^2 = **population variance**	p_1, p_2 = **proportion 1, 2** N = **population size**

For example, Consider a finite population of 4000 students of a certain college. Of this 200 students are selected randomly and their mean weight is calculated. It was computed as $x = 135$ lbs. If we draw 20 different samples of 200 students, instead of just one as we did previously. We can't expect the same mean weight of these 20 samples chosen randomly. It is due to sampling variability i.e. each sample drawn randomly from the same population differs from each other in their computed '***statistic***'.

The mean computed is listed as

130	137	140	131	132	133	128	125	129	138
133	134	142	145	136	134	128	143	137	136

These 20 values from what is known as a part of the sampling distribution of a ***statistic 'mean' weight***. Therefore, the sampling distribution is the statistic calculated for a large number of random samples drawn from the same population.

Alternatively, consider all possible samples of size 'n' which can be drawn randomly from the same population, and for each one, compute the aimed statistic. In this manner we obtain the distribution of the statistic, which is the sampling distribution.

Now we compute mean of this sampling which is 134.55 lb (note that is obtained using the formula)

$$\bar{X} = \frac{\Sigma x_i}{n} = \frac{2691}{20} = 134.55$$

Now we are told that the population mean (μ) i.e. mean weight of 4000 students is 134.21 lb (In case of infinite population, this is not known). Therefore, 135 lb is not a bad estimate of the population mean. But 134.55 lb is a still better estimation. We thus conclude that the more the sample means (statistics) included in the sampling distribution, the more correct the chances of the mean of the sampling distribution becoming an estimate of the population mean (parameter). The following graphical representation supports this argument.

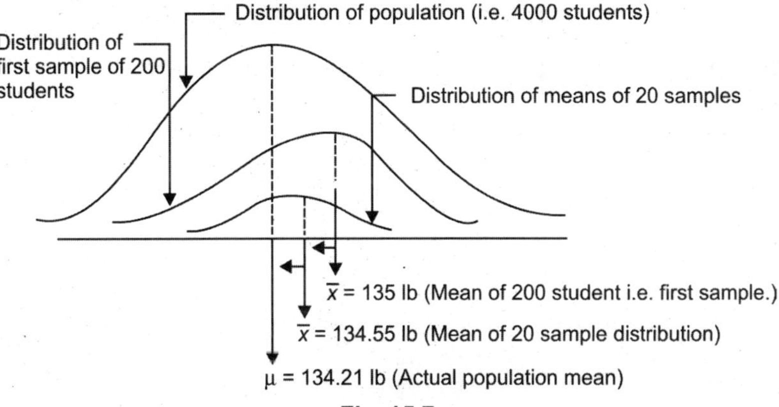

Fig. 15.7

Now recall the list of means computed for 20 random samples. We observe that the 20 sample means differed form the true population mean μ = 134.21 lbs. The means 137, 140, 138, 133, 142, 136, 143, 147, 136 are clearly above the true mean while 130, 131, 133, 132, 128, 125, 129, 133, 134, 134, 128 are below the true mean. These deviations or differences from true value are due to the variability of samples. This is known as '***Random error***' in statistical estimation. Note that the mean of 20 random sample means is slightly greater than the true population mean. If we take 20 more samples of 200 students, the mean of this new sampling distribution might be lower than the true population mean.

Other than random error, error arises due to the tendency of consistent under estimating or over estimating a true value. This is known as systematic error or bias.

Suppose in the example discussed above, an investigator is investigating only those students who are healthy and fit. He would most likely overestimate the population mean. Generally healthy bodies have reasonable weights. Clearly the investigator's choice is one of bias.

This is an example from one of the bias that occurs in estimation.

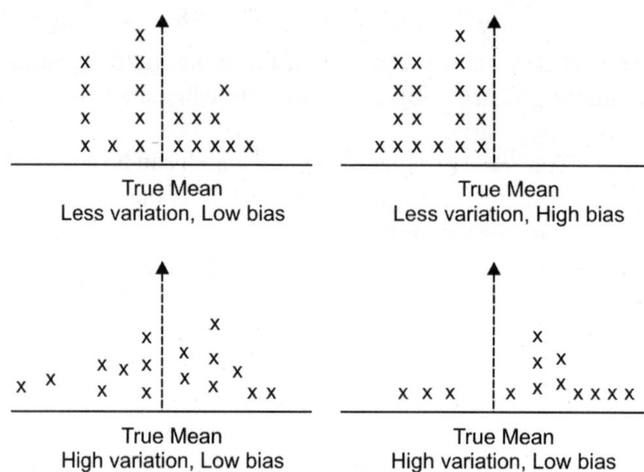

Fig. 15.8

15.12.1 Properties of Sampling Distribution

Sampling distribution statistics is based on the following properties:

(i) The mean μ of the distribution of sample means will be exactly equal to the population mean if we are able to select all possible samples of the same size from a given population that is

$$\boxed{\mu_{\bar{X}} = \mu}$$

(ii) The sampling distribution has a standard deviation* equal to the population standard deviation divided by the square root of the sample size, that is,

$$\boxed{\sigma_{\bar{X}} = \frac{\sigma}{\sqrt{n}}}$$

(iii) The sampling distribution of sample mean values from normally distributed populations is the normal distribution for samples of all sizes.

---

* The standard deviatin of the sampling distribution of means given a special name, standard error of mean.

(iv) Large sample size provides a more reliable estimate of population mean for the same level of precision in other words, smaller the value of $\sigma_{\bar{x}}$ the more accurate will be the sample result (see fig. 15.7).

The accuracy of the sample result depends not only upon the sample size but also on the degree of variability in the population itself, i.e, standard deviation of the population.

15.12.2 Sampling Distribution of Sample Mean

In general, the sampling distribution of sample means depending on the distribution of the population or process from which samples are drawn.

> For any given series, there can be only one value of μ. But is case of sampling distribution, we cannot say that the sampling mean is constant. As different samples of the same size can be selected from the same population, they will give different values of the sample mean $\bar{X}$.

The value of sample mean for any one sample will depend on the elements included in that sample. This means that the sample mean $\bar{X}$ is a random variable and it possesses a probability distribution, which is usually known as the sampling distribution of $\bar{X}$.

NOTE: Other sample statistics such as the median, mode and standard deviation also possess sampling distribution.

Let us take an example, suppose there are 5 workers A, B, C, D and E-Comprising the population. Their monthly wages in thousand rupees are:

A	B	C	D	E
3	5	7	7	8

$$\text{Mean of the population} = \frac{3+5+7+7+8}{5} = \frac{30}{5} = 6$$

Further, suppose we have to select a sample of size 3 out of 5 workers. As we have seen earlier, there can be in all to samples of size 3 out of a population size of 5.

Sample	Wages in the sample	Sample Mean ($\bar{X}$)
ABC	3, 5, 7	5.00
ABD	3, 5, 7	5.00
ABE	3, 5, 8	5.33
ACD	3, 7, 7	5.67
ACE	3, 7, 8	6.00
ADE	3, 7, 8	6.00
BCD	5, 7, 7	6.33
BCE	5, 7, 8	6.67
BDE	5, 7, 8	6.67
CDE	7, 7, 8	7.33

Sample Distribution of Means

Mean	5.0	5.33	5.67	6.0	6.33	6.67	7.33
Frequency	2	1	1	2	1	2	1

Mean of sampling distribution of means

$$= \frac{5 \times 2 + 5.33 \times 1 + 5.67 \times 1 + 6 \times 2 + 6.33 \times 1 + 6.67 \times 2 + 7.33 \times 1}{2 + 1 + 1 + 2 + 1 + 2 + 1}$$

$$= \frac{10 + 5.33 + 5.67 + 12 + 6.33 + 13.34 + 7.33}{10}$$

$$= \frac{60}{10} = 6 = \text{Mean of the population}$$

The mean of the population and the mean of the sampling distribution of the mean is the same but the SD of population and the SD of the sampling distribution of the mean are not the same.

Now, by diving the frequencies of different $\bar{X}$ values by the total number of frequencies, we obtain the relative frequencies of the classes. The relative frequencies are used as probabilities of classes.

15.12.3 Sampling Distribution of Mean When Population has Non-normal Distribution

In must of the cases the population from which a sample is taken is not normally distributed. If population is not normally distributed. Then we make use of the central limit theorem to describe the random nature of the sample mean for large samples without knowledge of the population distribution.

15.12.4 Central Limit Theorem (CLT)

The central limit theorem states that as sample size acts large enough, the sampling distribution of the mean can be approximated by the normal distribution. This is true regardless of the distribution of the population from which the random sample is drawn.

According to ***Rice***, "The central limit theorem states that the re-averaged sum of a sufficiently large number of identically distributed independent random variables each with finite mean and variance will be approximately normally distributed.

When the random samples of observations are drawn from a non-normal population with finite mean μ and standard deviation σ, and as the sample size n is increased, the sampling distribution of sample mean $\bar{X}$ is approximately normally distributed, with mean and standard deviation as:

$$\mu_{\bar{X}} = \mu \text{ and } \sigma_{\bar{X}} = \frac{\sigma}{\sqrt{n}}$$

The question here is: which sample size is considered large enough? In general, when a sample size of 30 and more element, it is considered large enough for the application of the central limit theorem.

Thus, the central limit theorem is a hall mark of statistical inference about the population parameter based on random samples drawn from population that are not necessarily normally distributed.

When the population distribution is very different from a normal distribution, it is necessary to have a large minimum sample size for a good normal approximation. By the same, when the population distribution is close to a normal distribution, even a smaller minimum sample size is considered sufficient.

In short, the larger the sample size, the better is the approximation, to the normal distribution and vice versa.

Fig. 15.9 shows a number of situations with varying sample sizes. It will be seen from Fig. 15.9 (b), (c) and (d). Show the shape of sampling distributions with different sample sizes.

The figure shown that as the sample size increases, the shape of the sampling distribution undergoes change and it tends to be more and more approximate to normal distribution.

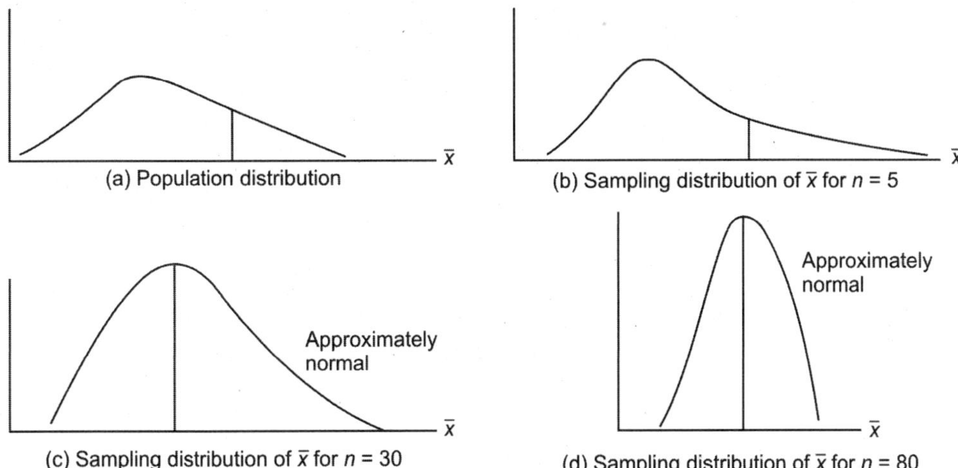

(a) Population distribution (b) Sampling distribution of $\bar{x}$ for $n = 5$

(c) Sampling distribution of $\bar{x}$ for $n = 30$ (d) Sampling distribution of $\bar{x}$ for $n = 80$

Fig. 15.9

EXAMPLE 15.3: In a certain locality, the average rent paid by all tenants amounts to Rs 1,500 pm with a standard deviation of Rs 450. However, the population distribution of rents pertaining to all tenants in that city is positively skewed. Find out the mean and standard deviation of $\bar{X}$ when the sample size is (i) 30 and (ii) 100. Also describe the shape of its sampling distribution in both the cases.

Solution: Given that the population distribution is not normal, but the sample size in both the cases is large as $n \geq 30$, the central limit theorem can be applied to infer the shape of the sampling distribution of $\bar{X}$.

(i) Let $\bar{X}$ be the average rent paid by a sample of 30 tenants. Then, the sampling distribution of $\bar{X}$ is approximately normal with the values of the mean and standard deviation as a

$$\mu_{\bar{X}} = \mu = \text{Rs } 1500 \text{ and } \sigma_{\bar{X}} = \frac{\sigma}{\sqrt{n}} = \frac{450}{\sqrt{30}} = 82.16$$

Fig. 15.10 shows the population distribution and the sampling distribution of $\bar{X}$.

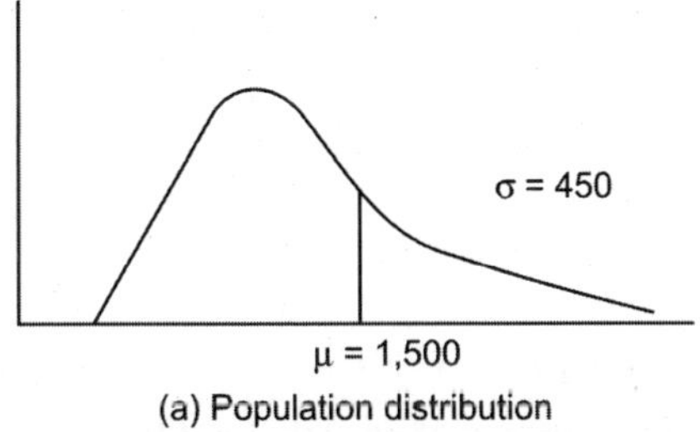

μ = 1,500

(a) Population distribution

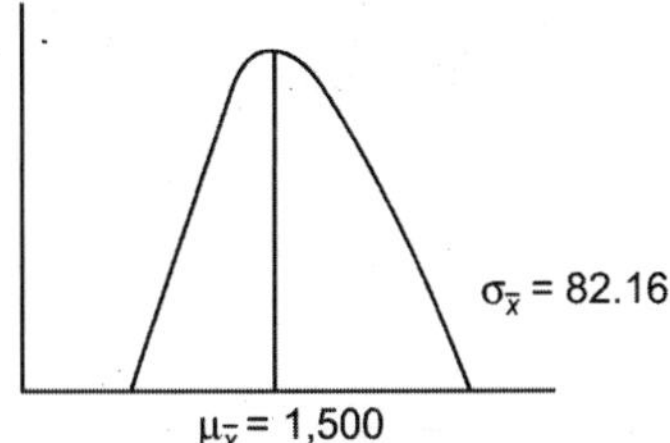

$\mu_{\bar{x}}$ = 1,500

(b) Sampling distribution of $\bar{x}$ for $n = 30$

Fig. 15.10

(b) Let $\overline{X}$ be the average rent paid by a sample of 100 tenants. Then, the sampling distribution of $\overline{X}$ is approximately normal with the values of the mean and standard deviation as

$$\mu_{\overline{X}} = \mu = \text{Rs } 1500 \text{ and } \sigma_{\overline{X}} = \frac{\sigma}{\sqrt{n}} = \frac{450}{\sqrt{100}} = 45$$

Fig. 15.11 shows the population distribution and the sampling distribution of $\overline{X}$.

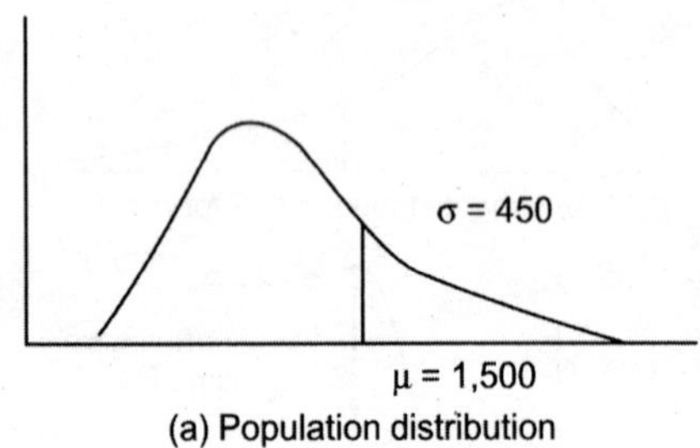

(a) Population distribution

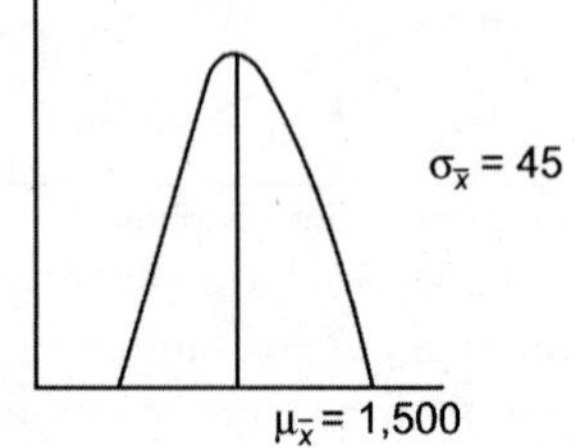

(b) Sampling distribution of $\bar{x}$ for n = 100

Fig. 15.11

> In respect of the central limit theorem, the following three aspects need to be noted:
> - when the sample size is large enough, the sampling distribution of $\overline{X}$ is normal.
> - the expected value of $\overline{X}$ is μ.
> - the standard deviation of $\overline{X}$ is $\frac{\sigma}{\sqrt{n}}$.

From above example and Fig.15.10. When the sample size is 30, $\sigma_{\overline{X}} = 82.16$. In contrast, when the sample size is increased to 100, $\sigma_{\overline{X}}$ is much lower, being only 45.

NOTE: When the sample size increase, the variance between $\overline{X}$ and its mean m decreases.

15.12.5 Sampling Distribution of Mean When Population has Normal Distribution

1. Population standard deviation σ is known

The sampling distribution of a mean of a sample taken from a normal population shows two important properties.

- First, the sampling distribution has a mean that is equal to the population mean.
  It symbols $\mu_{\overline{X}} = \mu$.
- Second, the sampling distribution has a standard deviation (a standard error) that is equal to the population. Standard deviation divided by the square root of sample size. This can be written in symbolic form

$$\boxed{\sigma_{\overline{X}} = \frac{\sigma}{\sqrt{n}}}$$

Where,
$\sigma_{\overline{X}}$ = standard error of the mean
σ = population standard deviation
n = sample size

If all possible samples of size n are drawn with replacement from a population having normal distribution with mean μ and standard deviation σ, then it can be shown that the sampling distribution of mean $\bar{X}$ and standard error $\sigma_{\bar{X}}$ will also be normally distributed irrespective of the size of the sample.

For this purpose, the value of sample mean $\bar{X}$ is first converted into a value z on the standard normal distribution is known how any single mean value deviated from the mean $\bar{X}$ of sample mean values, by using the formula

$$Z = \frac{\bar{X} - \mu_{\bar{X}}}{\sigma_{\bar{X}}} = \frac{\bar{X} - \mu}{\sigma / \sqrt{n}}$$

The procedure for making statistical inference using sampling distribution about the population mean μ based on mean $\bar{X}$ of sample means is summarized as follows:

- if the population standard deviation σ value is known and either
  (i) population distribution is normal, or
  (ii) population distribution is not normal, but the sample size n is large ($n \geq 30$), then the sample distribution of mean $\mu_{\bar{X}} = \mu$ and standard deviation $\sigma_{\bar{X}} = \sigma / \sqrt{n}$, is very close to the standard normal distribution given by

$$Z = \frac{\bar{X} = \mu_{\bar{X}}}{\sigma_{\bar{X}}} = \frac{\bar{X} - \mu}{\sigma / \sqrt{n}}$$

- If the ***population is finite with N elements*** whose mean is μ and variance is σ^2 and the samples of fixed size n are drawn without replacement, then the standard deviation (also called standard error) of sampling distribution of mean $\bar{X}$ can be modified to adjust the continued change in the size of the population N due to the several draws of samples of size $\boldsymbol{n}$ as follows:

$$\sigma_{\bar{X}} = \frac{\sigma}{\sqrt{n}} \sqrt{\frac{N - n}{N - 1}}$$

The term $\sqrt{(N - n)/(N - 1)}$ is called the finite population correction factor (*fpc*).

NOTE: This factor has little effect on reduting the amount of sampling error when the size of the sample is less than 5 percent of the population size. But if N is large relative to the sample size n, $\sqrt{(N - n)/(N - 1)}$ is approximately equal to 1.

2. Population standards deviation (σ) is not known

While calculating standard error $\sigma_{\bar{X}}$ of normally distributed sampling distribution, so far we have assumed that the population standard deviation σ is known.

However, if σ is not known, the value of the normal variate z cannot be calculated for a specific sample. In such a case, the standard deviation of population σ must be estimated using the sample standard deviation σ.

Thus the standard error of the sampling distribution of mean $\bar{X}$ becomes

$$\sigma_{\bar{X}} = \frac{s}{\sqrt{n}}$$

since the value of $\sigma_{\bar{X}}$ varies according to each sample standard deviation, therefore we use following formula, called 'student's *t*-distribution'

$$t = \frac{\bar{X} - \mu}{s/\sqrt{n}}$$

Where, $$s = \sqrt{\frac{\Sigma(x - \bar{X})^2}{(n-1)}}$$

EXAMPLE 15.4: Ten oil tins are taken at random from an automatic filling machine. The mean weight of the tins is 15.8 kg and standard deviation is 0.50 kg. Does the sample mean differ significantly from the intended weight of 16 kg? **[MBA, DU, 1996, 1999]**

Solution: Let the null hypothesis be that the sample mean weight is not different from the intended weight.

Given that $n = 10,\ \bar{X} = 15.8,\ s = 0.50,\ \mu = 16$

Using the *t*-test, we have $$t = \frac{\bar{X} - \mu}{s/\sqrt{n}} = \frac{15.8 - 16}{0.50/\sqrt{10}} - \frac{0.2}{0.158} = -1.266$$

The table value of *t* for 9 d.f. at 5% level of significance is 2.26. The computed value of *t* is smaller than the table value of *t*. Therefore, the difference is insignificant and the null hypothesis is accepted. Hence the difference between sample mean weight and the intended weight is insignificant.

EXAMPLE 15.5: Suppose in a normally distributed population, average income per household is Rs 10,000 pm with the standard deviation of Rs 800. A survey based on a random sample of 100 households is undertaken. What is the probability that the sample mean will be between Rs 9,800 and Rs 10,100? **[MBA, Anna Univ., 2004]**

Solution: As this is a question relating to the sampling distribution of the mean, we have to first calculate the standard error of the mean. In order to calculate it, we use the formula given earlier:

$$\sigma_{\bar{X}} = \frac{\sigma}{\sqrt{n}}$$

Substituting the two values in the above formula, we get

$$\sigma_{\bar{X}} = \frac{800}{\sqrt{100}}$$

$= \text{Rs } 80$ — Standard error of the mean.

Having obtained the standard error of the mean, we now use the following formula

$$Z = \frac{\bar{X} - \mu}{\sigma_{\bar{X}}}$$

This formula transforms any normal random variable to a standard normal random variable. Since we have been given the range within which the sample mean will lie, we have to use the formula for the two values.

For $\bar{X} = 9{,}800$, $$Z = \frac{\bar{X} - \mu}{\sigma_{\bar{X}}} = \frac{\text{Rs } 9{,}800 - 10{,}000}{\text{Rs } 80} = -2.5$$

For $\bar{X} = 10{,}100$, $\quad Z = \dfrac{\bar{X} - \mu}{\sigma_{\bar{X}}} = \dfrac{\text{Rs } 10{,}100 - 10{,}000}{\text{Rs } 80} = 1.25$

Now, we have to use the table on the Standard Normal Probability Distribution (Appendix Table). We find that the table gives an area of 0.0062 corresponding to a Z value of -2.5, and an area of 0.1056 corresponding to a Z value of 1.25. It may be noted that the former figure relates to the left-tail of the normal curve while the latter figure relates to its right-tail. As such, each figure is to be subtracted from 0.5 which is the total area of one-half of the curve. Thus, we get $0.5 - 0.0062 = 0.4938$ and $0.5 - 0.1056 = 0.3944$. Adding these two values, we get

$$0.4938 + 0.3944 = 0.8882$$

This is the probability that the sample mean will lie between Rs 9,800 and Rs 10,100. This is shown in Fig. 15.12.

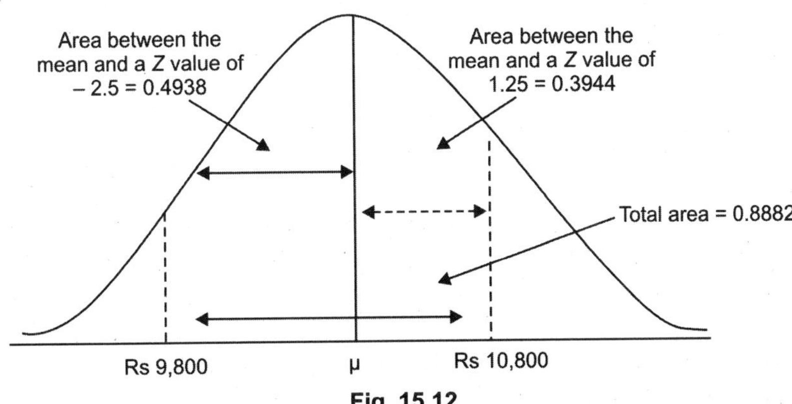

Fig. 15.12

EXAMPLE 15.6: Suppose we are interested in 15 electronic companies of the same size. All these companies are confronting a serious problem in the form of excessive turnover of their employees. It has been found that the standard deviation of the distribution of annual turnover is 60 employees. Take a sample of 3 electronic companies, without replacement, and determine the standard error of the mean. **[MBA, Madurai-Kamra, Univ., 2003]**

Solution: Out calculations would be as follows:

$$\sigma_{\bar{X}} = \frac{\sigma}{\sqrt{n}} \times \sqrt{\frac{N-n}{N-1}} = \frac{60}{\sqrt{3}} \times \sqrt{\frac{15-3}{15-1}}$$

$$= \frac{60}{1.7321} \times \sqrt{0.8571} = \frac{60}{1.7321} \times 0.9258$$

$$= 34.64 \times 0.9258 = 32.07$$

Thus, the standard error is 32.07. It will be seen that in this case the fpc factor of 0.9258 reduced the standard error from 34.64 to 32.07.

EXAMPLE 15.7: The mean length of life of a certain cutting tool is 41.5 hours with a standard deviation of 2.5 hours. What is the probability that a simple random sample of size 50 drawn from this population will have a mean between 40.5 hours and 42 hours? **[MBA, DU, 2003]**

Solution: We are given the following information

$$\mu = 41.5 \text{ hours}, \quad \sigma = 2.5 \text{ hours, and } n = 50$$

It is required to find the probability that the mean length of life, $\bar{X}$, of the cutting tool lies between 40.5 hours and 42 hours, that is, $P(40.5 \leq \bar{X} \leq 42)$.

Based upon the given information, the statistics of the sampling distribution are computed as:

$$\mu_{\bar{X}} = \mu = 41.5$$

and
$$\sigma_{\bar{X}} = \frac{\sigma}{\sqrt{n}} = \frac{2.5}{\sqrt{50}} = \frac{2.5}{7.0711} = 0.3536$$

The population distribution is unknown, but sample size $n = 50$ is large enough to apply the central limit theorem. Hence, the normal distribution can be used to find the required probability as shown by the shaded area in fig. 15.13.

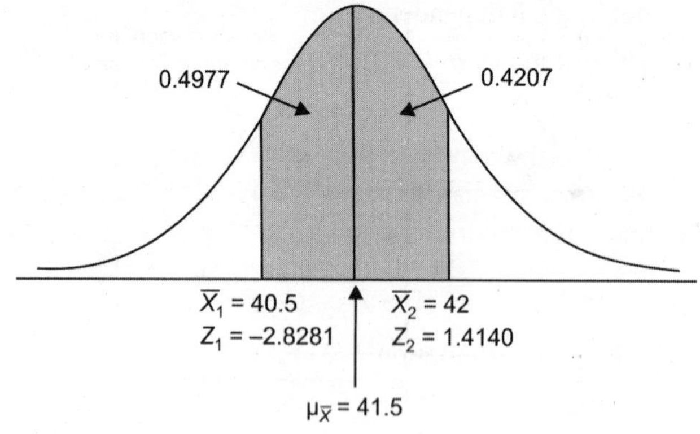

Fig. 15.13

$$P(40.5 \leq \bar{X} \leq 42) = P\left[\frac{\bar{X}_1 - \mu}{\sigma_{\bar{X}}} \leq z \leq \frac{\bar{X}_2 - \mu}{\sigma_{\bar{X}}}\right]$$

$$= P\left[\frac{40.5 - 41.5}{0.3536} \leq z \leq \frac{42 - 415}{0.3536}\right]$$

$$= P[-2.8281 \leq z \leq 1.4140]$$

$$= P[z \geq -2.8281] + P[z \leq 1.4140]$$

$$= 0.4977 + 0.4207 = 0.9184$$

Thus 0.9184 is the probability of the tool of having a mean life between the required hours.

15.12.6 Sampling Distribution of Difference Between Two Sample Means

The concept of sampling distribution of sample mean introduced earlier in this chapter can also be used to compare a population of size N_1 having mean μ_1 and standard deviation σ_1 with another similar type of population of size N_2 having mean μ_2 and standard deviation σ_2.

Let $\bar{X}_1$ and $\bar{X}_2$ be the mean of sampling distribution of mean of two populations respectively. Then the difference between their mean values μ_1 and μ_2 can be estimated by generalizing the formula of standard normal variable as follows:

$$z = \frac{(\bar{X}_1 - \bar{X}_2) - (\mu_{\bar{X}_1} - \mu_{\bar{X}_2})}{\sigma_{\bar{X}_1 - \bar{X}_2}} = \frac{(\bar{X}_1 - \bar{X}_2) - (\mu_1 - \mu_2)}{\sigma_{\bar{X}_1 - \bar{X}_2}}$$

where, $\mu_{\bar{X}_1 - \bar{X}_2} = \mu_{\bar{X}_1} - \mu_{\bar{X}_2} = \mu_1 - \mu_2$ (mean of sampling distribution of difference of two means)

$$\sigma_{\bar{X}_1 - \bar{X}_2} = \sqrt{\sigma^2_{\bar{X}_1} + \sigma^2_{\bar{X}_2}} = \sqrt{\frac{\sigma_1^2}{n_1} + \frac{\sigma_2^2}{n_2}}$$

(Standard error of sampling distribution of two means)

n_1, n_2 = independent random samples drawn from first and second population, respectively.

Since random samples are drawn independently from two populations with replacement, therefore the sampling distribution of the difference of two means $\bar{X}_1 - \bar{X}_2$ will be normal provided sample size of sufficiently large.

EXAMPLE 15.8: Car stereos of manufacturer A have a mean lifetime of 1400 hours with a standard deviation of 200 hours, while those of manufacturer B have a mean lifetime of 1200 hours with a standard deviation of 100 hours. If a random sample of 125 stereos of each manufacturer are tested, what is the probability that manufacturer A's stereos will have a mean lifetime which is at least 160 hours than manufacturer B's stereos. **[MBA, DU, 1999]**

Solution: We are given the following information

Manufacturer A: μ_1 = 1400 hours, σ_1 = 200 hours, and n_1 = 125

Manufacturer B: μ_2 = 1200 hours, σ_2 = 100 hours, and n_2 = 125

Thus, $\mu_{\bar{X}_1 - \bar{X}_2} = \mu_{\bar{X}_1} - \mu_{\bar{X}_2} = \mu_1 - \mu_2 = 1400 - 1200 = 200$

$$\sigma_{\bar{X}_1 - \bar{X}_2} = \sqrt{\frac{\sigma_1^2}{n_1} + \frac{\sigma_2^2}{n_2}} = \sqrt{\frac{(200)^2}{125} + \frac{(100)^2}{125}} = \sqrt{80 + 320} = \sqrt{400} = 20$$

Let $\bar{X}_1 - \bar{X}_2$ be the difference in mean lifetime of stereo manufactured by the two manufacturers. Then we are required to find the probability that this difference is more than or equal to 160 hours, as shown in fig. 15.14. That is,

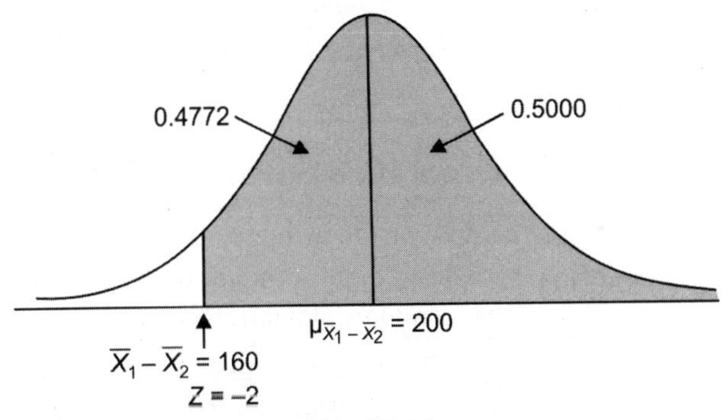

Fig. 15.14

$$P[(\bar{X}_1 - \bar{X}_2) \geq 160] = P\left[z \geq \frac{(\bar{X}_1 - \bar{X}_2) - (\mu_1 - \mu_2)}{\sigma_{\bar{X}_1 - \bar{X}_2}}\right]$$

$$= P\left[z \geq \frac{160 - 200}{20}\right]$$

$$= P[z \geq -2]$$

$$= 0.5000 + 0.4772 = 0.9772 \text{ (Area under normal curve)}$$

Hence, the probability is very high that the mean lifetime of the stereos of A is 160 hours more than that of B.

15.12.7 Sampling Distribution of Sample Proportion

Our discuss so far was confined to the sampling distribution of the sample mean $\bar{X}$. We will now discuss the distribution of the sample proportion $\bar{p}$.

In previous chapter, we discussed the binomial distribution where p is taken as the success while $q = 1 - p$ is taken as the failure.

Suppose we take a random sample of n persons from population and if x of these persons are doctors then the sample proportion

$$\bar{p} = \frac{\text{Elements of sample}}{\text{Sample size}} = \frac{x}{n}$$

is used to estimate the population proportion p.

When the sample size n is large ($n \geq 30$), this sampling distribution of the sample proportion can be approximated by a normal distribution.

The mean of the sampling distribution $\bar{p}$ of is given by

$$\boxed{\mu_{\bar{p}} = p}$$

and its standard deviation (standard error) is

$$\boxed{\sigma_{\bar{p}} = \sqrt{\frac{p(1-p)}{n}} = \frac{pq}{n}}$$

The mean and standard deviation (error) of the sampling distribution of proportion are valid for a finite population in which sampling is with replacement. However, for finite population in which sampling is done without replacement, we have

$$\boxed{\mu_{\bar{p}} = p \text{ and } \sigma_{\bar{p}} = \sqrt{\frac{pq}{n}}\sqrt{\frac{N-n}{N-1}}}$$

Where, $q = 1 - p$

To standardize sample proportion $\bar{p}$, the standard normal variable: '

$$\boxed{Z = \frac{\bar{p} - \mu_{\bar{p}}}{\sigma_{\bar{p}}} = \frac{\bar{p} - p}{\sqrt{p(1-p)/n}}}$$

is approximately the standard normal distribution.

EXAMPLE 15.9: A manufacturer of watches has determined from experience that 3 per cent of the watches he produces are defective. If a random sample of 300 watches is examined, what is the probability that the proportion defective is between 0.02 and 0.035? **[MBA, DU, 1990]**

Solution: We are given the following information

$$\mu_{\bar{p}} = p = 0.03, \quad \bar{p}_1 = 0.02, \quad \bar{p}_2 = 0.035, \text{ and } n = 300$$

Thus standard error of proportion is given by

$$\sigma_{\bar{p}} = \sqrt{\frac{p(1-p)}{\sqrt{n}}} = \sqrt{\frac{0.03 \times 0.97}{300}} = \sqrt{0.000097} = 0.0098$$

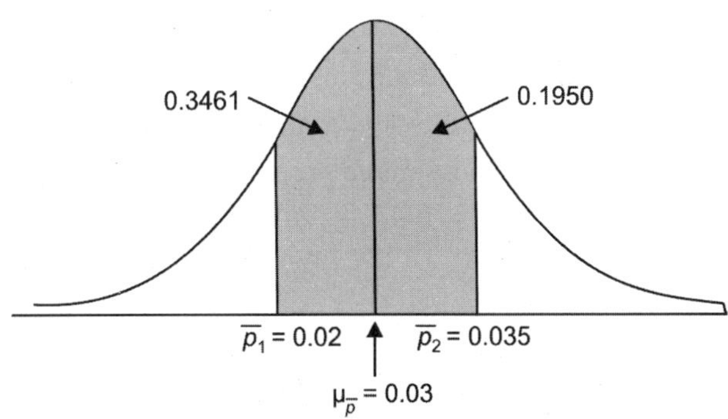

Fig. 15.15

For calculating the desired probability, we apply the following formula

$$P[0.02 \le \bar{p} \le 0.035] = P\left[\frac{\bar{p}_1 - p}{\sigma_{\bar{p}}} \le z \le \frac{\bar{P}_2 - p}{\sigma_{\bar{p}}}\right]$$

$$= P\left[\frac{0.02 - 0.03}{0.0098} \le z \le \frac{0.035 - 0.03}{0.0098}\right]$$

$$= P[-1.02 \le z \le 0.51]$$

$$= P[z \ge -1.02] + P[z \le 0.51]$$

$$= 0.3461 + 0.1950 = 0.5411 \quad \text{[From table]}$$

Hence, the probability that the proportion of defectives will lie between 0.02 and 0.035 is 0.5411.

15.12.8 Sampling Distribution of the Difference of Two Proportions

Suppose two populations of size N_1 and N_2 are given. For each sample of size n_1 from first population, compute sample proportion $\bar{p}_1$ and standard deviation $\sigma_{\bar{p}_1}$. Similarly for each sample of size n_2 from second population, compute sample proportion $\bar{p}_2$ and standard deviation $\sigma_{\bar{p}_2}$.

For all combinations of these samples from these populations, we can obtain a sampling distribution of the difference $\bar{p}_1 - \bar{p}_2$ of samples proportions. Such a distribution is called ***sampling distribution of difference of two proportions***. The mean and standard deviation of this distribution are given by

$$\mu_{\bar{p}_1-\bar{p}_2} = \mu_{\bar{p}_1} - \mu_{\bar{p}_2} = p_1 - p_2$$

and
$$\sigma_{\bar{p}_1-\bar{p}_2} = \sqrt{\sigma^2_{\bar{p}_1} + \sigma^2_{\bar{p}_2}} = \sqrt{\frac{p_1(1-p_1)}{n_1} + \frac{p_2(1-p_2)}{n_2}}$$

If sample size n_1 and n_2 are large, that is $n_1 \geq 30$ and $n_2 \geq 30$, then the sampling distribution of difference of proportions is closely approximated by a normal distribution.

EXAMPLE 15.10: Ten per cent of machines produced by company A are defective and five per cent of those produced by company B are defective. A random sample of 250 machines is taken from company A and a random sample of 300 machines from company B. What is the probability that the difference in sample proportion is less than or equal to 0.02?

Solution: We are given the following information

$\mu_{\bar{p}_1-\bar{p}_2} = \mu_{\bar{p}_1} - \mu_{\bar{p}_2} = p_1 - p_2 = 0.10 - 0.05 = 0.05;\ n_1 = 250$ and $n_2 = 300$

Thus standard error of the difference in a sample proportion is given by

$$\mu_{\bar{p}_1-\bar{p}_2} = \sqrt{\frac{p_1(1-p_1)}{n_1} + \frac{p_2(1-p_2)}{n_2}} = \sqrt{\frac{0.10 \times 0.90}{250} + \frac{0.05 \times 0.95}{300}}$$

$$= \sqrt{\frac{0.90}{250} + \frac{0.0475}{300}} = \sqrt{0.00052} = 0.0228$$

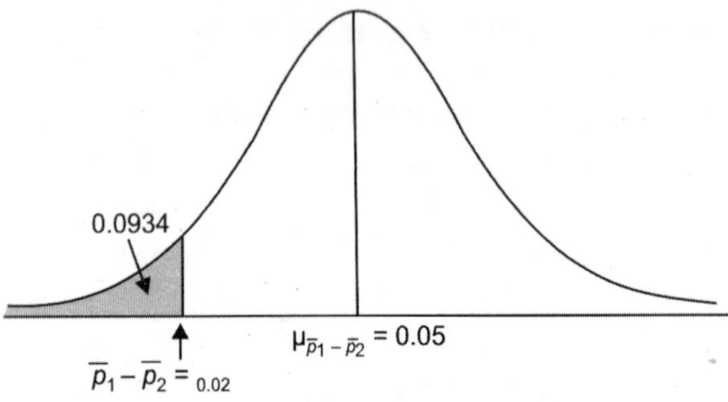

Fig. 15.16

The desired probability of difference in sample proportion is given by

$$P[(\bar{p}_1 - \bar{p}_2) \leq 0.02] = P\left[z \leq \frac{(\bar{p}_1 - \bar{p}_2) - (p_1 - p_2)}{\sigma_{\bar{p}_1-\bar{p}_2}}\right] = P\left[z \leq \frac{0.02 - 0.05}{0.0228}\right]$$

$$= p[z \leq -1.32] = 0.5000 + 0.4066 = 0.0934$$

Hence, the desired probability for the difference in sample proportion is 0.0934.

15.12.9 Standard Error

The standard deviation of the sampling distribution of a statistic is called the standard error of the statistic. The standard deviation of the distribution of the sample means is called the standard error of the mean. Likewise, the standard deviation of the distribution of the sample proportions is called the standard error of the proportion.

The standard error is popularly known as sampling error. Sampling error throws light on the precision and accuracy of the estimate. The standard error is inversely proportional to the sample size i.e. the larger the sample size the smaller the standard error.

The standard error measures the dispersion of all possible values of the statistic in repeated samples of a fixed size from a given population. It is used to set up confidence limits for population parameters in tests of significance. Thus the standard errors of sample mean X and sample proportion p are used to find confidence limits for the population mean μ and the population proportion P respectively.

Statistic	Standard error	Remarks
Sample mean	$\frac{\sigma}{\sqrt{n}}$	Population size is infinite or sample with replacement.
$\overline{X}$	$\frac{\sigma}{\sqrt{n}}\sqrt{\frac{N-n}{N-1}}$	Population size N finite or sample without replacement
Sample proportion	$\sqrt{\frac{pq}{n}}$	Population size is infinite or sample with replacement.
	$\sqrt{\frac{pq}{n}}\sqrt{\frac{N-n}{N-1}}$	Population size N finite or sample without replacement.

EXAMPLE 15.11: A population consists of the five numbers 2, 3, 6, 8, 11. Consider all possible samples of size 2 which can be drawn with replacement from this population. Find (i) mean of the population, (i) the standard deviation of the population (iii) the mean of the sample distribution of means and (iv) the standard error of means.

Solution:

(i) The population mean $\mu = \Sigma x / N = (2 + 3 + 6 + 8 + 11) / 5 = 6$

(ii) The variance of the population $\sigma^2 = 1/ N\, \Sigma(x - \mu)^2$

$= 1/5\{(2 - 6)^2 + (3 - 6)^2 + (6 - 6)^2 + (8 - 6)^2 + (11 - 6)^2\} = 10.8$

the standard deviation of the population $\sigma = 3.29$

(iii) There are 25 samples of size two which can be drawn with replacement. They are

(2, 2)	(2, 3)	(2, 6)	(2, 8)	(2,11)
(3, 2)	(3, 3)	(3, 6)	(3, 8)	(3,11)
(6, 2)	(6, 3)	(6, 6)	(6, 8)	(6, 11)
(8, 2)	(8, 3)	(8, 6)	(8, 8)	(8,11)
(11, 2)	(11, 3)	(11, 6)	(11,8)	(11,11)

The corresponding sample means are

2.0	2.5	4.0	5.0	6.5
2.5	3.0	4.5	5.5	7.0
4.0	4.5	6.0	7.0	8.5
5.0	5.5	7.0	8.0	9.5
6.5	7.0	8.5	9.5	11.0

The mean of sampling distribution of means

$$\mu_{x} = \frac{\text{sum of all sample means}}{25} = \frac{150}{25} = 6.0$$

(iv) The variance $\sigma^2_{\overline{X}}$ of the sampling distribution of means is obtained as follows:

$$\sigma^2_{\overline{X}} = \frac{1}{25}\{(2-6)^2 + (2.5-6)^2 + ... + (6.5-6)^2 + ... + (9.5-6)^2 + (11-6)^2\}$$

$$= \frac{135}{25} = 5.4$$

∴ the standard error of means $\sigma = \sqrt{5.4} = 2.32$

EXAMPLE 15.12: Assume that the monthly savings of 1000 employees working in a factory are normally distributed with mean Rs. 2000 and standard deviation Rs. 50 If 25 samples consisting of 4 employees each are obtained, what would be the mean and standard deviation of the resulting sampling distribution of means if sampling were done (i) with replacement, (ii) without replacement.

Solution: **[MBA, Osmania University., 2002]**

Given $N = 1000$, $\mu = 2000$, $\sigma = 50$, $n = 4$

(i) $\mu_{\bar{x}} = \mu = 2000$

$$\sigma_{\bar{x}} = \frac{\sigma}{\sqrt{n}} = \frac{50}{\sqrt{4}} = 25$$

(ii) Sampling without replacement

The mean of the sampling distribution of the means is

$$\mu_{\bar{x}} = \mu = 2000$$

The standard deviation of the sampling distribution of means is

$$\sigma_{\bar{x}} = \frac{\sigma}{\sqrt{n}}\sqrt{\frac{N-n}{N-1}} = \frac{50}{\sqrt{4}}\sqrt{\frac{100-4}{1000-1}}$$

$$= (25)\sqrt{\frac{996}{999}} = 25\left(\sqrt{.996}\right)$$

$$= (25)\,(0.9984) = 24.96$$

EXAMPLE 15.13: The marks obtained by students in an aptitude test are normally distributed with a mean of 60 and a standard deviation of 30. A random sample of 36 students is drawn from this population.

(i) What is the standard error of the sampling mean?

(ii) What is the probability that the mean of a sample of 16 students will be either less than 50 or greater than 80?

[P (0 < Z < 4) = 0.4999]

Solution:

(i) The standard error of the sample mean X is given by

$$\sigma_{\bar{x}} = \frac{\sigma}{\sqrt{n}} = \frac{30}{\sqrt{36}} = 5 \quad (N \text{ is not given})$$

(ii) The random variable $\overline{X}$ follows normal distribution with mean $\mu_{\bar{x}}$ and standard deviation $\frac{\sigma}{\sqrt{n}}$

To find $p\,(\overline{X} < 50 \text{ or } \overline{X} > 80)$.

$$p(\bar{X} < 50 \text{ or } \bar{X} > 80) = p(\bar{X} < 50) + P(\bar{X} > 80)$$
$$= p\left(\frac{\bar{X} - \mu_X}{\sigma_X} < \frac{50 - 60}{5}\right) + p\left(\frac{\bar{X} - \mu_X}{\sigma_X} > \frac{80 - 60}{5}\right)$$
$$= p(Z < -2) + p(Z > 4)$$
$$= [0.5 - p(0 < Z 2)] + [0.5 - p(0 < Z < 4)]$$
$$= (0.5 - 0.4772) + (0.5 - 0.4999)$$
$= .02283$, which is the required probability.

EXAMPLE 15.14: 2% of the screws produced by a machine are defective. What is the probability that in a consignment of 400 such screws, 3% or more will be defective.

Solution: Here N is not given, but $n = 400$

Population proportion $p = 2\% = 0.02$

$\therefore$ $q = 1 - p = 0.98$

The sample size is large

$\therefore$ The sample proportion is normally distributed with mean

$$\mu_p = 0.02$$

and $$S.D = \sqrt{\frac{pq}{n}} = \sqrt{\frac{0.02 \times 0.98}{400}} = 0.007$$

Probability that the sample proportion $p \geq 0.03$

= Area under the normal curve to the right of $Z = 1.43$

$$Z = \frac{p - p}{S.D} = \frac{0.03 - 0.02}{0.007} = 1.43$$

$\therefore$ Required probability = 0.5 – Area between $Z = 0$ to $Z = 1.43$

= 0.5 – 0.4236 = 0.0764

15.13 STATISTICAL INFERENCE

Inferential statistics is also a set of methods, but it is used to draw conclusions or inferences about characteristics of populations based on data from a sample.

Statistical Inference is the ***process*** of making an estimate, prediction, or decision about a population BASED sample.

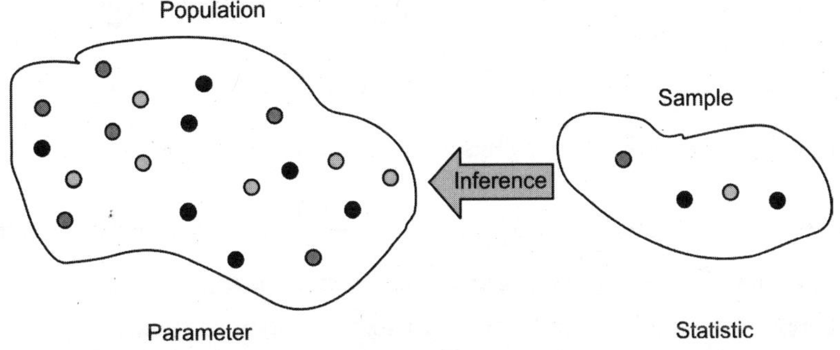

Fig. 15.17

What can we *infer* about a Population's Parameters based on a Sample's Statistics?

The technique used for generalising the results of the sample to the population is provided by an important branch of statistics called ***Statistical Inference.*** The concept of statistical inference deals with two basic aspects namely (a) ***Estimation*** and (b) ***Testing of Hypothesis.***

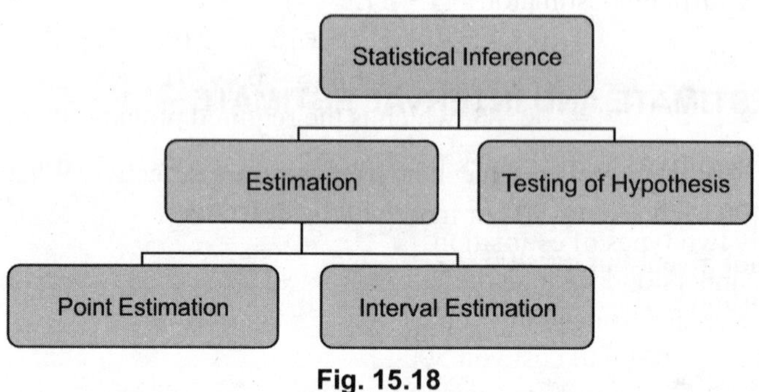

Fig. 15.18

In statistics, estimation is concerned with making inference about the parameters of the population using information available in the samples. The parameter estimation is very much needed in the decision making process. The estimation of population parameters such as mean, variance, proportion, etc. from the corresponding sample statistics is an important function of statistical inference.

15.14 ESTIMATION

To estimate means to esteem (to give value to). An estimator is any quantity calculated from the sample data which is used to give information about an unknown quantity in the population. For example, the sample mean is an estimator of the population mean μ.

Results of estimation can be expressed as a single value; known as a point estimate, or a range of values, referred to as a confidence interval. Whenever we use point estimation, we calculate the margin of error associated with that point estimation

15.14.1 Estimator

A sample statistic which is used to estimate a population parameter is known as ***estimator.*** A good estimator is one which is as close to the true value of population parameter as possible. A good estimator possesses the following properties:

(i) Unbiasedness : As estimate is said to be unbiased if its expected value is equal to its parameter. The sample mean $\bar{X} = \frac{\Sigma x}{n}$ is an unbiased estimator of population mean μ. For a sample of size n, drawn from a population of size N, $s^2 = \frac{\Sigma(x - \bar{X})^2}{n - 1}$ is an unbiased estimator of population variance. Hence s^2 is used in ***estimation*** and in ***testing of hypothesis.***

(ii) Consistency: An estimator is said to be consistent if the estimate tends to approach the parameter as the sample size increases.

(iii) Efficiency: If we have two unbiased estimators for the same population parameter, the first estimator is said to be more efficient than the second estimator if the standard error of the first estimator is smaller than that of the second estimator for the same sample size.

(iv) Sufficiency: If an estimator possesses all information regarding the parameter, then the estimator is said to be a sufficient estimator.

15.15 POINT ESTIMATE AND INTERVAL ESTIMATE

It is possible to find two types of estimates for a population parameter. They are ***point estimate*** and ***interval estimate.***

There are actually two types of estimation.

They can be first understood through the following analogy: Let's say that you take your car to your local car dealer's service department and you ask the service manager how much it will cost to repair your car. If the manager says it will cost you 5000 Rs. then He/She is providing a ***point estimate.*** If the manager says it will cost somewhere between 4000 and 6000 then he/she is providing an ***interval estimate.***

In other words, a point estimate is a single number, and an interval estimate is a range of numbers.

- A point estimate is the value of your sample statistic (e.g., your sample mean or sample correlation), and it is used to estimate the population parameter (e.g., the population mean or the population correlation). For example, if you take a random sample from adults living an the Delhi and you find that the average income for the people in your sample is 45,000, then your best guess or your point estimate for the population of adults in the New Delhi will be 45,000.

In the above example, you used the value of the sample mean as the estimate of the population mean.

- Again, whenever you engage in point estimation, all you need to do is to use the value of your sample statistic as your "best guess" (i.e., as your estimate) of the (unknown) population parameter.

Often times, we like to put an interval around our point estimates so that we realize that the actual population value is somewhat different from our point estimate because sampling error is always present in sampling.

An interval estimate (also called a confidence interval) is a range of numbers inferred from the sample that has a known probability of capturing the population parameter over the long run (i.e., over repeated sampling).

Point Estimate

An estimate of a population parameter given by a single number is called a point estimator of the parameter. Mean (x) and the sample variance are the examples of point estimates.

A point estimate will rarely coincide with the true population parameter value.

Interval Estimate

An estimate of a population parameter given by two numbers between which the parameter is expected to lie is called an interval estimate of the paramcter.

Interval estimate indicates the accuracy of an estimate and is therefore preferable to point estimate.

As point estimate provides a single value for the population parameter it may not be suitable in some situation.

For example, if we say that a distance is measured as 5.28 mm, we are giving a point estimate. On the other hand, if we say that the distance is 5.28 + 0.03 mm i.e. the distance lies between 5.25 and 5.31 mm, we are giving an interval estimate.

15.16 CONFIDENCE INTERVAL FOR POPULATION MEAN AND PROPORTION

The interval within which the unknown value of parameter is expected to lie is called ***confidence interval.*** The limits so determined are called ***confidence limits.*** Confidence intervals indicate the probability that the population parameter lies within a specified range.

Computation of Confidence Interval

To compute confidence interval we require

(i) the sample statistic,
(ii) the standard error (S.E) of sampling distribution of the statistic
(iii) the degree of accuracy reflected by the z-value.

If the size of sample is sufficiently large, then the sampling distribution is approximately normal. Therefore, the sample value can be used in estimation of standard error in the place of population value. The z-distribution is used in case of large samples to estimate the confidence limits.

We give below values of z corresponding to some confidence levels.

Confidence Level (I – α) (%)	Acceptable Error Level, α	α/2	$Z_{\alpha/2}$
90%	0.10	0.050	±1.64
95%	0.05	0.025	±1.96
98%	0.02	0.010	±2.33
99%	0.01	0.005	±2.58

15.16.1 Interval Estimation of Population Mean

1. Population Standard Deviation (σ) is known

Let μ and σ be the population mean and standard deviation of the population. Let $\overline{X}$ and s be the sample mean and standard deviation of the sampling distribution of a statistic.

The value of the estimator, the sample mean is given by

$$\overline{X} = \frac{\Sigma x}{n}$$

and $$\sigma_{\overline{X}} = \frac{\sigma}{\sqrt{n}}$$

Then for a large sample size n, the sample mean $\overline{X}$ is the best point estimator for the population mean μ. Since sampling distribution is approximately normal, it can be used to compute confidence interval of population mean μ as follows:

$$\bar{X} \pm Z_{\alpha/2}\sigma_{\bar{X}} \quad \text{or} \quad \bar{X} \pm Z_{\alpha/2}\frac{\sigma}{\sqrt{n}}$$

or

$$\bar{X} - Z_{\alpha/2}\frac{\sigma}{\sqrt{n}} \le \mu \le \bar{X} + Z_{\alpha/2}\frac{\sigma}{\sqrt{n}}$$

for example, the 95% confidence interval for mean is

$$\bar{X} - 1.96\frac{\sigma}{\sqrt{n}} \quad \text{to} \quad \bar{X} + 1.96\frac{\sigma}{\sqrt{n}}$$ [from table]

The interpretation of this confidence interval is that if there is a variable x which is normally distributed with mean μ and S.D σ, and a sample mean of n observations of the variable is calculated as $\bar{X}$, then we are 95%. Confident that the mean μ would lie in the above interval.

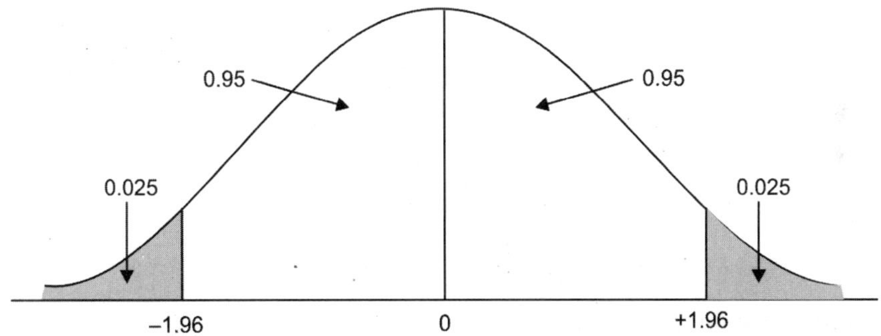

Fig.15.19: Area under Standard Normal Curve

in general (100 – α)%. Confidence interval is derived by finding these values of Z, under standard normal curve, such that they contain (100 – α)% at the area. Such values of Z are written as $Z_{\alpha/2}$. The sum of area upto $-Z_{\alpha/2}$ and area beyond $Z_{\alpha/2}$ is equal to α.

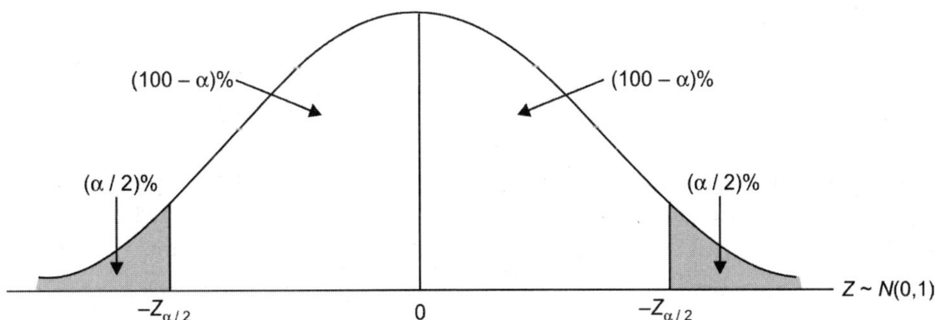

Fig.15.20: Area under Standard Normal Curve

EXAMPLE 15.15: In order to introduce some incentive for higher balance in savings accounts, a random sample of size 64-savings accounts at a bank's branch was studied to estimate the average monthly balance in savings bank accounts. The mean and standard deviation were found to be Rs. 8,500 and Rs. 2000, respectively. Find (i) 90%, (ii) 95%, (iii) 99% confidence intervals for the population mean. **[MBA, UPTU, (CO), 2005]**

Solution: Confidence limits with confidence level (100 – α)% (or 100 – α)% confidence limits) for average monthly balance in savings accounts are given as:

(i) 90% confidence limits:

$$\bar{X} \pm 1.645\frac{\sigma}{\sqrt{n}}$$

$$8500 \pm 1.645\frac{2000}{\sqrt{64}}$$

$$8500 \pm \frac{3290}{8}$$

$$\text{Rs. } 8500 \pm 411.25$$

(ii) 85% confidence limits:

$$\bar{X} \pm 1.96\frac{\sigma}{\sqrt{n}}$$

$$8500 \pm 1.96\frac{2000}{\sqrt{64}}$$

$$8500 \mp \frac{3920}{8}$$

$$\text{Rs. } 8500 \pm 490$$

(iii) 99% confidence limits:

$$\bar{X} \pm 2.575\frac{\sigma}{\sqrt{n}}$$

$$8500 \pm 2.575\frac{2000}{\sqrt{64}}$$

$$8500 \pm \frac{5150}{8}$$

$$\text{Rs. } 8500 \pm 644$$

It may be noted that the interval or limits get wider as the desired level of confidence is increased.

EXAMPLE 15.16: The average monthly electricity consumption for a sample of 100 families is 1250 units. Assuming the standard deviation of electric consumption of all families is 150 units, construct a 95 per cent confidence interval estimate of the actual mean electric consumption.

Solution: The information given is : $\bar{X}$ = 1250, σ = 150, n = 100 and confidence level (1– α) = 95 per cent. Using the 'Standard Normal Curve' we find that the half of 0.95 yields a confidence coefficient $Z_{\alpha/2}$ = 1.96. Thus confidence limits with = $Z_{\alpha/2}$ = ± 1.96 for 95 per cent confidence are given by

$$\bar{X} \pm z_{\alpha/2}\frac{\sigma}{\sqrt{n}} = 1250 \pm 1.96\ \frac{150}{\sqrt{100}}$$

$$= 1250 \pm 29.40 \text{ units}$$

Thus for 95 per cent level of confidence, the population mean μ is likely to fall between 1220.60 units and 1274.40 units, that is, 1220.60 μ ≤ 1274.40.

EXAMPLE 15.17*:* A survey conducted by a shopping mall group showed that a family in a metro-city spends an average of Rs. 500 on clothes every month. Suppose a sample of 81 families resulted in a sample mean of Rs. 540 per month and a sample standard deviation of Rs. 150, develop a 95 per cent confidence interval estimator of the mean amount spent per month by a family.

Solution: The information given is: $\bar{X} = 540$, $\sigma = 150$, $n = 81$ and $Z_{\alpha/2} = 1.96$ for 95 per cent confidence level. Thus confidence limits with $Z_{\alpha/2} = \pm\ 1.96$ are given by

$$\bar{X} \pm z_{\alpha/2}\sigma_{\bar{X}} = \bar{X} \pm z_{\alpha/2}\frac{\sigma}{\sqrt{n}} = 540 \pm 1.96\frac{150}{\sqrt{81}}$$

Hence for 95 per cent of confidence, the population mean μ is likely to fall between Rs. 499.33 and Rs. 580.67, i.e. $499.33 \le \mu \le 580.67$.

2. Population Standard Deviation (σ) is unknown

In the above examples, the value of population standard deviation was given. If not given, it has to be estimated from the sample itself. In that case, we use the '*t*' distribution. So, instead of referring to Table for normal distribution, we refer to the table for '*t*' distribution.

Thus, the interval estimate of a population mean when the sample size is small ($n \le 30$) with confidence coefficient $(1 - \alpha)$, is given by

$$\bar{X} \pm t_{\alpha/2}\sigma_{\bar{X}} \quad \text{or} \quad \bar{X} \pm t_{\alpha/2}\frac{s}{\sqrt{n}}$$

or

$$\bar{X} - t_{\alpha/2}\frac{s}{\sqrt{n}} \le \mu \le \bar{X} + t_{\alpha/2}\frac{s}{\sqrt{n}}$$

where, $\bar{X}$ and s are the mean and the standard deviation of the observations in a sample of size n, and $t_{\alpha/2}$ is the value of student's '*t*' with $(n-1)$ *d.f.*, area beyond which, on either side is $\alpha/2$.

where, $$s = \sqrt{\frac{\Sigma(x - \bar{X})^2}{n-1}}$$

The procedure of the confidence interval estimation of population mean μ when population standard deviation is unknown and sample size is large or small, is summarized in table.

Sample size	Interval Estimate of Population Mean μ
Large	
• σ is known	$\bar{x} \pm z_{\alpha/2}\frac{\sigma}{\sqrt{n}}$
• σ estimated by *s*	$\bar{x} \pm z_{\alpha/2}\frac{s}{\sqrt{n}}$
Small	
• σ is known	$\bar{x} \pm z_{\alpha/2}\frac{\sigma}{\sqrt{n}}$
• σ estimated by *s*	$\bar{x} \pm t_{\alpha/2}\frac{s}{\sqrt{n}}$

For large value of n, say ($n \geq 30$), 't' distribution may be approximated by a normal distribution and we can use normal distribution table and using s in place of σ.

EXAMPLE 15.18: For assessing the number of monthly transactions in credit cards issued by a bank, transactions in 25 cards were analysed. The analysis revealed an average of 7.4 transactions and sample standard deviation of 2.25 transactions. Find confidence limits for the monthly number of transactions by all the credit card holders of the bank?

Solution: When population standard deviation is not known, and values of sample mean and sample standard deviation are given, the 85% confidence interval for the population mean is given by

$$\bar{X} - t_{\alpha/2.(n-1)} \frac{s}{\sqrt{n}} \quad \text{to} \quad \bar{X} + t_{\alpha/2,(n-1)} \frac{s}{\sqrt{n}}$$

where $\bar{X}$ and s are the sample mean and sample standard deviation, respectively, and $t_{\alpha/2,\, n-1}$ is the point in the t distribution with $(n - 1)$ d.f. such that the total area, on both the sides of the curve, beyond which is equal to α. For example if $\alpha = 0.05$ and $n = 25$ (d.f. = 25 – 1 = 24), the value of 't' is 2.06 vide Table relating to 't' distribution.

Since, level of confidence is not given, we assume it to be 95%, and thus $\alpha = .05$. It is given that $\bar{X} = 7.4$, $s = 2.25$, $n = 25$ and $t_{\alpha/2,n-1} = t_{.025.24} = 2.06$.

Thus the confidence limits for the average number of transactions per credit card are

$$\bar{X} \pm 2.06 \frac{2.25}{\sqrt{25}}$$

or, $$7.4 \pm \frac{4.635}{5}$$

or, $$7.4 \pm 0.927$$

or, $$6.473 \text{ to } 8.327$$

For large values of n, say (≥ 30),'t' distribution may be approximated by a normal distribution. Thus, the limits are given by the formula 10.1, using s in place of σ.

EXAMPLE 15.19: A sample of 100 students are drawn from a school. The mean weight and variance of the sample are 67.45 kg and 9 kg. respectively. Find (a) 95% and (b) 99% confidence intervals for estimating the mean weight of the students.

Solution:

Sample size, $n = 100$
The sample mean, $\bar{X} = 67.45$
The sample variance $s^2 = 9$
The sample standard deviation $s = 3$
Let μ be the population mean.

(a) The 95% confidence limits for m are given by $\bar{X} \pm (Z_c)\frac{s}{\sqrt{n}}$

$\Rightarrow 67.45 \pm (1.96)\frac{3}{\sqrt{100}}$ (Here $Z_c = 1.96$ for 95% confidence level)

$\Rightarrow 67.45 \pm 0.588$

Thus the 95% confidence intervals for estimating μ is given by (66.86, 68.04)

(b) The 99% confidence limits for estimating *m* are given by

$$\bar{X} \pm (Z_c)\frac{s}{\sqrt{n}}$$

$$\Rightarrow 67.45 \pm (2.58)\frac{3}{\sqrt{100}} \text{(Here } Z_c = 2.58 \text{ for 99\% confidence level)}$$

$$\Rightarrow 67.45 \pm 0.774$$

Thus the 99% confidence interval for estimating *m* is given by (66.67, 68.22)

EXAMPLE 15.20: A random sample of 50 sales invoices was taken from a large population of sales invoices. The average value was found to be Rs. 2000 with a standard deviation of Rs. 540. Find a 90 per cent confidence interval for the true mean value of all the sales.

Solution: The information given is: $\bar{X}_1 = 2000$, $s = 540$, $n = 64$, and $\alpha = 10$ per cent.

Therefore $$s_{\bar{x}} = \frac{s}{\sqrt{n}} = \frac{540}{\sqrt{64}} = 67.50 \text{ and}$$

$$Z_{\alpha/2} = 1.64$$ [from Normal table]

The required confidence interval of population mean μ is given by

$$\bar{X} \pm z_{\alpha/2}\frac{s}{\sqrt{n}} = 2000 \pm 1.64\,(67.50) = 2000 \pm 110.70$$

Thus the mean of the sales invoices for the whole population is likely to fall between Rs 1889.30 and Rs 2110.70, that is, $1889.30 \le \mu \le 2110.70$.

EXAMPLE 15.21: The personnel department of an organization would like to estimate the family dental expenses of its employees to determine the feasibility of providing a dental insurance plan. A random sample of 10 employees reveals the following family dental expenses (in thousand Rs) in the previous year: 11, 37, 25, 62, 51, 21, 18, 43, 32, 20.

Set up a 99 per cent confidence interval of the average family dental expenses for the employees of this organization.

Solution: The calculations for sample mean $\bar{X}$ and standard deviation are shown in table given below.

Calculation for x and s

Variable, x	$(x - \bar{X}) = (x - 32)$	$(x - \bar{X})^2$
11	–21	441
37	05	25
25	–07	49
62	30	900
51	19	361
21	–11	121
18	–14	196
43	11	121
32	00	00
20	–12	–144
320	**0**	**2358**

From the data in table the sample mean $\bar{X} = \Sigma x/n = 320/10$ = Rs. 32, and the sample standard deviation $s = \sqrt{\Sigma(x - \bar{X})^2 / n - 1} = \sqrt{2358/9}$ = Rs. 5.11. Using this information and $t_{\alpha/2} = 1.833$ at d.f. = 9, we have

$$\bar{X} \pm t_{\alpha/2} \frac{s}{\sqrt{n}} = 32 \pm 1.833 \frac{5.11}{\sqrt{10}} = 32 \pm 2.962$$

Hence the mean expenses per family are likely top fall between Rs. 29.038 and Rs. 34.962, that is, $29.038 \leq \mu \leq 34.962$.

15.16.2 Interval Estimation of Difference of Two Means

If all possible samples of large size n_1 and n_2 are drawn from two different population, then sampling distribution of the difference between two mean $\bar{X}_1$ and $\bar{X}_2$ is approximately normal with mean $(\mu_1 - \mu_2)$ and standard deviation.

1. Population Standard Deviation (σ) is know

$$\sigma_{\bar{X}_1 - \bar{X}_2} = \sqrt{\frac{\sigma_1^2}{n_1} + \frac{\sigma_2^2}{n_c}}$$

For a desired confidence level, the confidence interval limits for the population mean $(\mu_1 - \mu_2)$ are given by

$$\left(\bar{X}_1 - \bar{X}_2\right) \pm Z_{\alpha/2} \sigma_{\bar{X}_1 - X_2} \text{ or } \left(\bar{X}_1 - \bar{X}_2\right) \pm Z_{\alpha/2} \sqrt{\frac{\sigma_1^2}{n_1} + \frac{\sigma_2^2}{n_2}}$$

2. Population Standard Deviation (σ) is unknow

$$\sigma_{\bar{X}_1 - \bar{X}_2} = \sqrt{\frac{S_1^2 - S_2^2}{n_1 + n_2}}$$

$$\left(\bar{X}_1 - \bar{X}_2\right) \pm Z_{\alpha/2} \sigma_{\bar{X}_1 - \bar{X}_2} \text{ or } \left(\bar{X}_1 - \bar{X}_2\right) \pm Z_{\alpha/2} \sqrt{\frac{s_1^2}{n_1} + \frac{s_2^2}{n_2}}$$

EXAMPLE 15.22: The strength of the wire produced by company. A has a mean of 4500 kg and a standard deviation of 200 kg. Company B has a mean of 4000 kg and a standard deviation of 300 kg. A sample of 50 wires of company A and 100 wires of company B are selected at random for testing the strength. Find 99 per cent confidence limits on the difference in the average strength of the populations of wires produced by the two companies. **[MBA, Delhi University, 2002]**

Solution: The following information is given:

Company A: $\bar{X}_1 = 4500, \quad \sigma_1 = 200, \quad n_1 = 50$

Company B: $\bar{X}_2 = 4000, \quad \sigma_2 = 300, \quad n_2 = 100$

Therefore $\bar{X}_1 - \bar{X}_2 = 4500 - 4000 = 500$ and $Z_{\alpha/2} = 2.576$ and

$$\sigma_{\bar{X}_1 - \bar{X}_2} = \sqrt{\frac{\sigma_1^2}{n_1} + \frac{\sigma_2^2}{n_2}} = \sqrt{\frac{40,000}{50} + \frac{90,000}{100}} = 41.23$$

The required 99 per cent confidence interval limits are given by

$$(\bar{X}_1 - \bar{X}_2) \pm z_{\alpha/2}\, \sigma_{\bar{X}_1 - \bar{X}_2} = 500 \pm 2.576\ (41.23) = 500 \pm 106.20$$

Hence, the 99 per cent confidence limits on the difference in the average strength of wires produced by the two companies are likely to fall in the interval 393.80 ≤ μ ≤ 606.20.

15.16.3 Interval Estimation for Population Proportion

When the sample size is large, the sample proportion $\bar{p} = x/n$ is the best point estimator for the population proportion p. Since the sampling distribution of sample proportion $\bar{p}$ is approximately normal with mean $\mu_{\bar{p}}$ and standard error $\sqrt{pq/n}$, the confidence interval for a population proportion at 1– α confidence coefficient is given by

$$\bar{p} \pm Z_{\alpha/2}\sigma_{\bar{p}} \quad \text{or} \quad \bar{p} \pm Z_{\alpha/2}\sqrt{\frac{pq}{n}}$$
$$\bar{p} - Z_{\alpha/2}\sigma_{\bar{p}} \le p \le \bar{p} \pm Z_{\alpha/2}\sigma_{\bar{p}}$$

Where $q = 1 - p$ and $Z_{\alpha/2}$ is the Z –value corresponding to an area of α/2 in the right fail of the standard normal probability distribution and quantity $Z_{\alpha/2}\ \sigma_{\bar{p}}$ is the margin of error.

$$\sigma_{\bar{p}} = \sqrt{\frac{\bar{p}\bar{q}}{n}} = \sqrt{\frac{\bar{p}(1-\bar{p})}{n}}$$

A sample proportion, the standard error denoted by SE $(\bar{p})$.

EXAMPLE 15.23: A random sample of size 50 with mean 67.9 is drawn from a normal population. If it is known that the standard error of the sample mean is 0.7, find 95% confidence interval for the population mean.

Solution:

$n = 50$, sample mean $X = 67.9$

95% confidence limits for population mean m are:

$$\bar{X} + (Z_c)\ \{\ S.E\ (X)\ \}$$

$\Rightarrow$ 67.9 + (1.96) (0.7)

$\Rightarrow$ 67.9 + 1.64

Thus the 95% confidence intervals for estimating m are given by (66.2, 69.54)

EXAMPLE 15.24: A random sample of 500 apples was taken from large consignment and 45 of them were found to be bad. Find the limits at which the bad apples lie at 99% confidence level.

Solution:

We shall find confidence limits for the proportion of bad apples.

Sample size $n = 500$

Proportion of bad apples in the sample = 45/500 = 0.09

$p = 0.09$

Proportion of good apples in the sample $q = 1 - p = 0.91$.

The confidence limits for the population proportion P of bad apples are given by

$$P \pm (Z_c)\left(\sqrt{\frac{pq}{n}}\right)$$

$$\Rightarrow \qquad 0.09 \pm (2.58)\sqrt{\frac{(.09)(0.91)}{500}} \quad \Rightarrow \quad 0.09 \pm 0.033$$

Thus, the bad apples in the consignment lie between 5.7% and 12.3%

EXAMPLE 15.25: Out of 1000 TV viewers, 320 watched a particular programme. Find 95% confidence limits for TV viewers who watched this programme.

Solution:

Sample size $n = 1000$

Sample proportion of TV viewers

$$p = \frac{x}{n} = \frac{320}{1000} = .32$$

$$\therefore \qquad q = 1 - p = .68$$

$$S.E\,(p) = \sqrt{\frac{pq}{n}} = 0.0147$$

The 95% confidence limits for population proportion P are given by

$$P \pm (1.96)\, S.E\,(p) = 0.32 \pm 0.028$$

$\Rightarrow$ 0.292 and 0.348

TV viewers of this programme lie between 29.2% and 34.8%

EXAMPLE 15.26: Out of 1500 school students, a sample of 150 selected at random to test the accuracy of solving a problem in business mathematics and of them 10 did a mistake. Find the limits within which the number of students who did the problem wrongly in whole universe of 1500 students at 99% confidence level.

Solution:

Population size, $N = 1500$

Sample size, $n = 150$

Sample proportion, $p = 10/150 = 0.07$

$q = 1 - p = 0.93$

Standard error of p, $SE\,(p) = \sqrt{\frac{pq}{n}} = 0.02$

The 99% confidence limits for population proportion P are given by

$$p \pm (Z_c)\sqrt{\frac{pq}{n}}\sqrt{\frac{N-n}{N-1}}$$

$$\Rightarrow \qquad 0.07 \pm (2.58)(0.02)\sqrt{\frac{1500-150}{1500-1}} \Rightarrow 0.07 \pm 0.048$$

The confidence interval for P is (0.022, 0.118)

The number of students who did the problem wrongly in the population of 1500 lies between

$$.022 \times 1500 = 33 \quad \text{and} \quad 0.118 \times 1500 = 177.$$

Determination of a Proper Sample Size

In this section, we discuss the methodology for deciding the sample size which is required to meet the criteria for level of confidence and margin of error or tolerance. The sample size, so determined is the minimum size as any sample size more than this value would automatically satisfy all the criteria.

The method of determining a proper sample size, n is given for the following two cases:

1. Sample Size Required For Estimating Mean

In this case, the problem involves finding the sample size required to be confident to the extent of (100 – α%) that the sample mean will not deviate from the population mean by more than specified margin; when the distribution of sample mean $\bar{X}$ is normal, the standard normal variable z is given as

$$Z = \frac{\bar{X} - \mu}{\sigma / \sqrt{n}}$$

The value of Z will be positive or negative, depending on whether the sample mean $\bar{X}$ is larger or smaller the population mean μ. This difference between $\bar{X}$ and μ is called the sampling error or margin of error (E).

The confidence interval formula is given by

$$\bar{X} \pm Z \frac{\sigma}{\sqrt{n}}$$

or

$$\bar{X} \pm E$$

Where,

$$\boxed{E = Z \frac{\sigma}{\sqrt{n}}}$$

is the maximum allowable sampling error. Solving for n yields a formula that can be used to determine sample size

$$\sqrt{n} = \frac{Z\sigma}{E}$$

$$\boxed{n = \left(\frac{Z\sigma}{E}\right)^2}$$

This formula for sample size n will provide the tolerable margin of error E, at the chosen confidence level 1 – α with known or estimated population standard deviation σ.

EXAMPLE 15.27: A cigarette manufacturer wishes to use a random sample to estimate the average nicotine content. The sampling error should not be more than one milligram above or below the true mean, with a 99 per cent confidence coefficient. The population standard deviation is 4 milligrams. What sample size should the company use in order to satisfy these requirements?

Solution: Here $E = 1$, $Z = 2.58$ and $\sigma = 4$

Sample size formula is $$n = \left(\frac{Z\sigma}{E}\right)^2 = \left(\frac{2.58 \times 4}{1}\right)^2$$

$$= 106.56$$

Hence, the required sample size is $n = 107$ which the company should use for their requirement to be fulfilled.

2. Sample Size Required For Estimating Proportion

The confidence interval formula for proportion is given by

$$p \mp Z\sqrt{\frac{pq}{n}}$$

Using E to represent the maximum allowable sampling error, we may write the above as

$$p \pm E$$

where,
$$E = Z\sqrt{\frac{pq}{n}}$$

Solving for n, we get
$$\boxed{n = \frac{Z^2 pq}{E^2}}$$

This formula for n will provide the desired margin of error (E) at the chosen confidence level $1 - \alpha$ with known or estimated population proportion p.

EXAMPLE 15.28: A firm wishes to estimate with a maximum allowable error of 0.05 and a 95 per cent level of confidence, the proportion of consumers who prefer its product. How large a sample will be required in order to make such an estimate if the preliminary sales reports indicate that 25 percent of all consumers prefer the firm's product? **[MBA, UPTU, 2002]**

Solution: Here $E = 0.05$, $p = 0.25$ and $z = 2.33$

Substituting these values in the formula

$$n = \frac{Z^2 pq}{E^2} \qquad [p = 0.25,\ q = 1 - p = 0.75]$$

$$= \frac{(2.33)^2 \times (0.25) \times (0.75)}{(0.05)^2} = \frac{5.4289 \times 0.1875}{0.0025} = 407.16$$

Hence the required sample size $n = 407$.

LIST OF FORMULAE

1. Standard deviation of sampling distribution of mean, $\bar{X}$
   - Infinite population $\sigma_{\bar{X}} = \frac{\sigma}{\sqrt{n}}$
   - Finite population $\sigma_{\bar{X}} = \frac{\sigma}{\sqrt{n}}\sqrt{\frac{N-n}{N-1}}$
2. Estimate of $\sigma_{\bar{x}}$ when population standard deviation is not known
   - Infinite population $s_{\bar{X}} = \frac{s}{\sqrt{n}}$
   - Finite population $\sigma_{\bar{X}} = \frac{s}{\sqrt{n}}\sqrt{\frac{N-n}{N-1}}$

3. Standard deviation of difference between two

Sample means $\sigma_{\bar{X}_1 - \bar{X}_2} = \sqrt{\frac{\sigma_1^2}{n_1} + \frac{\sigma_2^2}{n_2}}$

4. Standard Deviation of sampling distribution of proportion

• Infinite population $\sigma_{\bar{p}} = \sqrt{\frac{p(1-p)}{n}}$

• Finite population $\sigma_{\bar{p}} = \sqrt{\frac{p(1-p)}{n}}\sqrt{\frac{N-n}{N-1}}$

5. Standard deviation of sampling distribution of the Difference between two proportions

$$\sigma_{\bar{p}_1 - \bar{p}_2} = \sqrt{\frac{p_1(1-p_1)}{n_1} + \frac{p_2(1-p_2)}{n_2}}$$

6. Interval Estimation of population Mean

• σ know $\bar{X} \pm Z_{\alpha/2}\,\sigma_{\bar{X}}$ or $\bar{X} + Z_{\alpha/2}\frac{\sigma}{\sqrt{n}}$

$$\bar{X} - Z_{\alpha/2}\frac{\sigma}{\sqrt{n}} \le \mu \le \bar{X} + Z_{\alpha/2}\frac{\sigma}{\sqrt{n}}$$

• σ Unknown $\bar{X} \pm t_{\alpha/2}\sigma_{\bar{X}}$ or $\bar{X} \pm t_{\alpha/2}\frac{\sigma}{\sqrt{n}}$

$$\bar{X} - t_{\alpha/2}\frac{s}{\sqrt{n}} \le \mu \le \bar{X} + t_{\alpha/2}\frac{s}{\sqrt{n}}$$

• Difference of two Means

$$(\bar{X}_1 - \bar{X}_2) \pm Z_{\alpha/2}\sigma_{\bar{X}_1 - \bar{X}_2} \quad \text{or} \quad (\bar{X}_1 - \bar{X}_2) \pm Z_{\alpha/2}\sqrt{\frac{\sigma_1^2}{n_1} + \frac{\sigma_2^2}{n_2}}$$

7. Interval Estimation for population Proportion

$$\bar{p} \pm Z_{\alpha/2}\sigma_{\bar{p}} \quad \text{or} \quad \bar{p} \pm Z_{\alpha/2}\sqrt{\frac{pq}{n}}$$

$$\bar{p} - Z_{\alpha/2}\sigma_{\bar{p}} \le p \le \bar{p} \pm Z_{\alpha/2}\sigma_{\bar{p}}$$

8. Sample size when estimating
   • Population Mean, μ

$$n = \frac{(Z)^2\sigma^2}{E^2}$$

   • Population proportion, *p*

$$n = \frac{(Z)^2 pq}{E^2}$$

SELF PRACTICE EXERCISES

I. CHOOSE THE BEST ANSWER

1. Sampling is inevitable in the situations:
   (a) Blood test of a person (b) When the population is infinite
   (c) Testing of life of dry battery cells (d) All the above
2. The difference between sample estimate and population parameter is termed as:
   (a) Human error (b) Sampling error
   (c) Non-sampling error (d) None of the above
3. If each and every unit of population has equal chance of being included in the sample, it is known as:
   (a) Restricted sampling (b) Purposive sampling
   (c) Simple random sampling (d) None of the above
4. Simple random sample can be drawn with the help of:
   (a) Slip method (b) Random number table
   (c) Calculator (d) All the above
5. A selection procedure of a sample having no involvement of probability is known as:
   (a) Purposive sampling (b) Judgement sampling
   (c) Subjective sampling (d) All the above
6. Five establishments are to be selected from a list of 50 establishments by systematic random sampling. If the first number is 7, the next one is:
   (a) 8 (b) 16
   (c) 17 (d) 21

II. FILL IN THE BLANKS

1. A population consisting of an unlimited number of units is called an .... population
2. If all the units of a population are surveyed it is called ....
3. The discrepancy between a parameter and its estimate due to sampling process is known as ....
4. The list of all the items of a population is known as ....
5. Stratified sampling is appropriate when population is ....
6. When the items are perishable under investigation it is not possible to do ....
7. When the population consists of units arranged in a sequence would prefer .... sampling
8. For a homogeneous population, ... sampling is better than stratified random sampling.

III. SHORT ANSWER TYPE QUESTIONS

1. Define a population.
2. Define finite and infinite populations with examples
3. What is sampling?
4. Define the following terms:
   (a) Sample (b) Sample size (c) census
   (d) Sampling unit (e) Sampling frame

5. Distinguish between census and sampling
6. What are the advantages of sampling over complete enumeration.
7. Why do we resort to sampling?
8. What are the limitations of sampling?
9. State the principles of sampling
10. What are probability and non-probability sampling?
11. Define purposive sampling. Where it is used?
12. What is called mixed sampling?
13. Define a simple random sampling.
14. Explain the selection procedure of simple random Sampling.
15. Explain the two methods of selecting a simple random sampling.
16. What is a random number table? How will you select the random numbers?
17. What are the merits and limitations of simple random sampling?
18. What circumstances stratified random sampling is used?
19. Discuss the procedure of stratified random sampling. Give examples.
20. What is the objective of stratification?
21. What are the merits and limitations of stratified random sampling?
22. Explain systematic sampling.
23. Discuss the advantages and disadvantages of systematic random sampling
24. Give illustrations of situations where systematic sampling is used.
25. A population of size 800 is divided into 3 strata of sizes 300, 200, 300 respectively. A stratified sample size of 160 is to be drawn from the population. Determine the sizes of the samples from each stratum under proportional allocation.
26. There are 50 houses in a street. Select a sample of 10 houses for a particular study using systematic sampling.

IV. LONG ANSWER TYPE QUESTIONS

1. A population consists of four numbers 3, 7, 11 and 15. Consider all possible samples of size two which can be drawn without replacement from this population. Find
   - the population mean
   - the population standard deviation.
   - the mean of the sampling distribution of mean
   - the standard deviation of the sampling distribution of mean.
2. The weights of 1500 iron rods are normally distributed with mean of 22.4 kgs. and standard deviation of 0.048 kg. If 300 random samples of size 36 are drawn from this population, determine the mean and standard deviation of the sampling distribution of mean when sampling is done
   - with replacement
   - without replacement.
3. 1% of the outgoing +2 students in a school have joined I.I.T. Madras. What is the probability that in a group of 500 such students 2% or more will be joining I.I.T. Madras.
4. A sample of five measurements of the diameter of a sphere were recorded by a scientist as 6.33, 6.37, 6.36, 6.32 and 6.37 mm. Determine the point estimate of (a) mean, (b) variance.

5. Measurements of the weights of a random sample of 200 ball bearings made by a certain machine during one week showed mean of 0.824 newtons and a standard deviation of 0.042 newtons. Find (a) 95% and (b) 99% confidence limits for the mean weight of all the ball bearings.
6. A random sample of 50 branches of State Bank of India out of 200 branches in a district showed a mean annual profit of Rs. 75 lakhs and a standard deviation of 10 lakhs. Find the 95% confidence limits for the estimate of mean profit of 200 branches.
7. A random sample of marks in mathematics secured by 50 students out of 200 students showed a mean of 75 and a standard deviation of 10. Find the 95% confidence limits for the estimate of their mean marks.
8. Out of 10000 customer's ledger accounts, a sample of 200 accounts was taken to test the accuracy of posting and balancing wherein 35 mistakes were found. Find 95% confidence limits within which the number of defective cases can be expected to lie.
9. A sample poll of 100 voters chosen at random from all voters in a given district indicated that 55% of them were in favour of a particular candidate. Find (a) 95% confidence limits, (b) 99% confidence limits for the proportion of all voters in favour of this candidate.

ANSWERS

I. CHOOSE THE CORRECT ANSWERS

1. (d) 2. (b) 3. (c) 4. (d) 5. (d) 6. (c)

II. FILL IN THE BLANKS

1. infinite
2. complete enumeration or census
3. sampling error
4. sampling frame
5. heterogeneous or Non- homogeneous
6. complete enumeration
7. systematic
8. simple random

CHAPTER 16

Test of Hypothesis

16.1 INTRODUCTION

A hypothesis is a tentative statement that proposes a possible explanation to some phenomenon or event. A useful hypothesis is a testable statement which may include a prediction. A hypothesis should not be confused with a theory. Theories are general explanations based on a large amount of data. For example, the theory of evolution applies to all living things and is based on wide range of observations. However, there are many things about evolution that are not fully understood such as gaps in the fossil record. Many hypotheses have been proposed and tested.

When Are Hypothesis Used?

The key word is testable. That is, you will perform a test of how two variables might be related. This is when you are doing a real experiment. You are testing variables. Usually, a hypothesis is based on some previous observation such as noticing that in November many trees undergo colour changes in their leaves and the average daily temperatures are dropping. Are these two events connected? How?
Any laboratory procedure you follow without a hypothesis is really not an experiment. It is just an exercise or demonstration of what is already known.

16.2 HYPOTHESIS AND HYPOTHESIS TEST

There are many problems in which, besides estimating the value of a parameter of the population, we must decide whether a statement concerning a parameter is true or false; that is, we must test a hypothesis about a parameter. To illustrate the general concepts involved in this kind of decision problems, suppose that a consumer protection agency wants to test a manufacturer's claim that the average life time of electric bulbs produced by him is 200 hours. So it instructs a member of its staff to take 50 electric bulbs from the go down of the company and test them for their lifetime continuously with the intention of rejecting the claim if the mean life time of the bulbs is below 180 hours (say); otherwise it will accept the claim.

Hypothesis

Hypothesis is an assumption that we make about an unknown population parameter. We can collect sample data from the population, arrive at the sample statistic and then test if the hypothesis about the population parameter is true.

Hypothesis Test

"The basic idea of hypothesis testing is to examine the probability that the result of a study could have been obtained even if the actual situation was that the experimental treatment or comparison made NO difference."

16.3 NULL HYPOTHESIS AND ALTERNATIVE HYPOTHESIS

Null Hypothesis

A hypothesis of no difference is called null hypothesis and is usually denoted by $\boldsymbol{H_0}$.

The Capital letter H stands for hypothesis and the subscript 'zero' implies 'no difference' between sample statistic and the parameter value. The null hypothesis is always expressed in the form of mathematical statement.

$$H_0 = \mu(\geq = \leq)\mu_0$$

where μ is population mean and μ_0 represents a hypothesized value of μ.

According to ***R.A. Fisher***, "Null hypothesis is the hypothesis which is tested for possible rejection under the assumpting that it is true."

It is very useful tool in test of significance. For example: If we want to find out whether the special classes (for MBA Students) after college hours has benefited the students or not. We shall set up a null hypothesis that

H_0: special classes after college hours has not benefited the students.

We give special consideration to the null hypothesis. This is due to the fact that the null hypothesis relates to the statement being tested, whereas the alternative hypothesis relates to the statement to be accepted if when the null is rejected.

Alternative Hypothesis

Any hypothesis, which is complementary to the null hypothesis, is called an alternative hypothesis, usually denoted by $\boldsymbol{H_1}$. That is, an alternative hypothesis must be true when the null hypothesis is found to be false.

The alternative hypothesis, $\boldsymbol{H_1}$, is a statement of what a statistical hypothesis test is set up to establish.

The final conclusion once the test has been carried out is always given in terms of the null hypothesis. We either "Reject H_0 in favour of H_1" or "Do not reject H_0"; we never conclude "Reject H_1", or even "Accept H_1".

If we conclude "Do not reject H_0", this does not necessarily mean that the null hypothesis is true; it only suggests that there is not sufficient evidence against H_0 in favour of H_1. Rejecting the null hypothesis then, suggests that the alternative hypothesis may be true.

If we want to test the null hypothesis that the population has a specified mean μ_0 (say), i.e.,

Step 1: Null hypothesis H_0: $\mu = \mu_0$ then
Step 2: Alternative hypothesis H_1 may be
(i) H_1: $\mu \neq \mu_0$ (ii) H_1: $\mu > \mu_0$ (iii) H_1: $\mu < \mu_0$

16.4 LEVEL OF SIGNIFICANCE AND CRITICAL VALUES

Level of Significance (α)

In testing a given hypothesis, the maximum probability with which we would be willing to take risk is called level of significance of the test. This probability often denoted by "α" is generally specified before samples are drawn. The level of significance usually employed in testing of significance are 0.05 (or 5 %) and 0.01 (or 1 %).

If for example a 0.05 or 5 % level of significance is chosen in deriving a test of hypothesis, then there are about 5 chances in 100 that we would reject the hypothesis when it should be accepted. (i.e.,) we are about 95 % confident that we made the right decision. In such a case we say that the hypothesis has been rejected at 5 % level of significance which means that we could be wrong with probability 0.05.

Given Fig. 16.1 illustrates the region in which we could accept or reject the null hypothesis when it is being tested at 5 % level of significance and a two-tailed test is employed.

Critical Value

The value of test statistic which separates the critical (or rejection) region and the acceptance region is called the critical value or significant value. It depends upon

(i) The level of significance used and
(ii) The alternative hypothesis, whether it is two-tailed or single-tailed. For large samples the standard normal variate corresponding to the statistic t,

$$\boxed{Z = \left|\frac{t - E(t)}{S.E.(t)}\right| \sim N(0,1)} \qquad [\text{Asymptotically as } n \to \alpha]$$

The value of Z under the null hypothesis is known as test statistic. The critical value of the test statistic at the level of significance Z_α for a two - tailed test is given by $Z_{\alpha/2}$ and for a one tailed test by Z_α where Z_α is determined by equation $P(|Z| > Z_\alpha) = \alpha$

Z_α is the value so that the total area of the critical region on both tails is α.

$P(Z > Z_\alpha) = \alpha/2$. Area of each tail is $\alpha/2$.

Z_α is the value such that area to the right of $+Z_\alpha$ and to the left of $-Z_\alpha$ is $\alpha/2$ as shown in the Fig. 16.1.

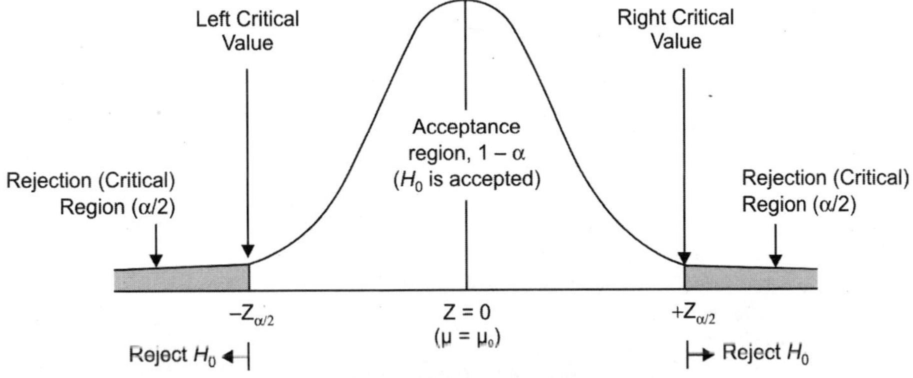

Fig. 16.1

16.5 CRITICAL AND REJECTION REGION

The area under the sampling distribution curve of the test statistic is divided into two mutually exclusive regions (areas). These regions are called the acceptance region and the rejection (or critical) region as shown in Fig. 16.1.

The Acceptance Region

The acceptance region is a range of the sample statistic spread around the null hypothesized population parameter.

If values of the sample statistic fall within the limits of acceptance region, the null hypothesis is accepted, otherwise it is rejected.

The Rejection Region

The rejection region is the range of sample statistic values within which if values of the sample statistic falls (i.e. outside the limits of the acceptance region), then null hypothesis is rejected.

If probability of H_0 is being true is less than or equal to the significance level, α the reject H_0, otherwise accept H_0, i.e., the level at significance α is used as the cut off point which separates the area of acceptance form the area of rejection.

16.6 TYPES OF TESTS — ONE AND TWO TAILED TEST

Tests of hypothesis can be carried out on one or two samples. One sample tests are used to test if the population parameter (μ) is different from a specified value. Two sample tests are used to detect the difference between the parameters of two populations (μ_1 and μ_2).

Two sample tests can further be classified as unpaired or paired two sample tests. While in unpaired two sample tests the sample data are not related, in paired two sample tests the sample data are paired according to some identifiable characteristic. For example, when testing hypothesis about the effect of a treatment on (say) a landfill, we would like to pair the data taken at different points before and after implementation of the treatment.

In any test, the critical region is represented by a portion of the area under the probability curve of the sampling distribution of the test statistic.

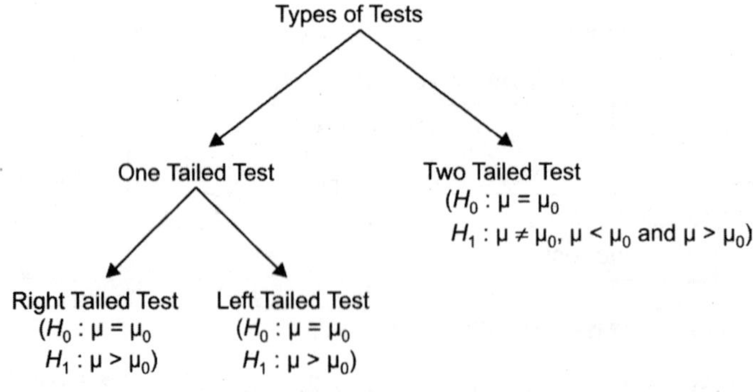

Fig. 16.2: Types of tests

One Tailed Test

The alternate hypothesis H_1 is one-sided and we test whether the test statistic falls in the critical region on only one side of the distribution.

A test of any statistical hypothesis where the alternative hypothesis is one tailed (right tailed or left tailed) is called a one tailed test.

For testing the mean of a population

H_0: $\mu = \mu_0$

then H_1: $\mu > \mu_0$ [Right Tailed Test]

or H_1: $\mu < \mu_0$ [Left Tailed Test]

In the ***right – tailed test*** H_1: $\mu > \mu_0$ the critical region lies entirely in right tail of the sampling distribution of x, while for the ***left – tailed test*** H_1: $\mu < \mu_0$ the critical region is entirely in the left of the distribution of x. (see Fig. 16.3)

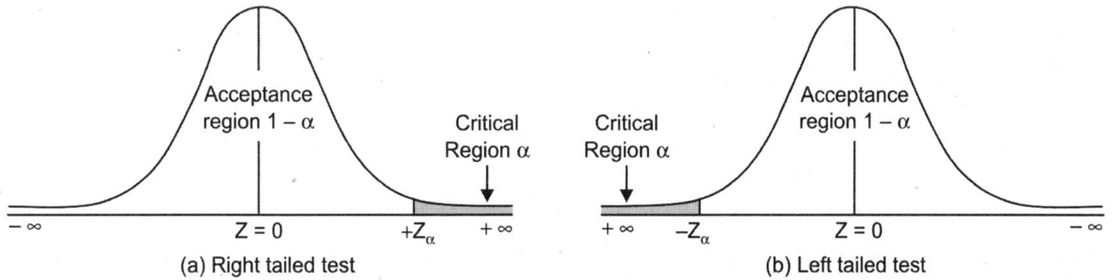

Fig. 16.3

Two Tailed Test

A test of statistical hypothesis where the alternative hypothesis is two tailed such as,

H_0: $\mu = \mu_0$ against the alternative hypothesis

H_1: $\mu \neq \mu_0$ [Two Tailed Test]

($\mu > \mu_0$ and $\mu < \mu_0$)

is known as two tailed test and in such a case the critical region is given by the portion of the area lying in both the tails of the probability curve of test of statistic.

Here the alternate hypothesis H_1 is formulated to test for difference in either direction, i.e., for either an increase or a decrease in the random variable. Hence the test statistic is tested for occurrence within either of the two critical regions on the two extremes of the distribution.

Critical value (Z_α) of Z				
Level of significance α	**0.05 or 5%**		**0.01 or 1%**	
	Left	**Right**	**Left**	**Right**
Critical values of Z_α for one tailed Tests	—1.645	+1.645	–2.33	+2.33
Critical values of $Z_{\alpha/2}$ for two tailed tests	–1.96	+1.96	–2.58	+2.58

16.7 ERRORS IN HYPOTHESIS TESTING

For testing the hypothesis, we take a sample from the population, and on the basis of the sample result obtained, we decide whether to accept or reject the hypothesis.

Here, two types of **errors** are possible. A null hypothesis could be rejected when it is true. This is called **Type I error** and the probability of committing type I error is denoted by α.

Alternatively, an error could result by accepting a null hypothesis when it is false. This is known as **Type II error** and the probability of committing type II error is denoted by β.

TYPE I AND TYPE II ERROR

When choosing a probability level of 95%, there is always a 5% chance that one rejects the null hypothesis when it was actually correct. This is called **Type I error**, represented by the Greek letter α. It is possible to error in the opposite way if one fails to reject the null hypothesis when it is, in fact, incorrect. This is called **Type II error,** represented by the Greek letter β.

This is illustrated in the following table

Actual	Decision based on sampling	Error and its probability
H_0 is True	Rejecting H_0	Type 1 error; $\alpha = P\{H_1/H_0\}$
H_0 is False	Accepting H_0	Type II error; $\alpha\beta = P\{H_0/H_1\}$

As a convention in statistics, Type I error is always denoted by α, and Type II error by β. α is also referred to as level of significance, and 1-α is called confidence coefficient.

16.8 POWER OF A TEST AND THE SIZE EFFECT

The power of a test plays the same role in hypothesis testing that standard error played in estimation. It is measuring tool for assessing the accuracy of a test or in comparing two competing test procedures.

The power of a test is the probability of rejecting a false null hypothesis when the null hypothesis is false. The probability is inversely related to the probability of making a Type II error, not rejecting the null hypothesis when it is false. Recall that we choose the probability of making a Type I error when the set α. If we decrease the probability of making a Type I error, then we increase the probability of making a Type II error.

Evaluating the goodness of a statistical test is the look at the complement of Type-II error, which is states as:

$$1 - \beta = P \quad \text{[Reject } H_0 \text{ when } H_1 \text{ is true]}$$

The complement $1 - \beta$ of β, i.e., the probability of Type-II error, is called the power of a statistical test because H measures the probability of rejecting H_1, when it is true.

Power and Alpha (α): Thus, the probability of not rejecting a true null has the same relationship to Type I errors as the probability of correctly rejecting an untrue null does to Type II error. Yet, as we mentioned if we decrease the odds of making one type of error we increase the odds of making the other type of error. What is the relationship between Type I and Type II errors? For a fixed sample size, decreasing one Type of error increases the size of the other one.

Power and the Size Effect: Anytime we test whether a sample differs from a population, or whether two samples come from 2 separate populations, there is the condition that each of the populations we are comparing has its own mean and standard deviation (even if we do not know it). The distance between the two population means will affect the power of our test. This is known as the size of treatment, also known as the effect size.

Power and the Size of Variance (s^2): The greater the variance s^2, the lower the power $1-\beta$. Anything that effects the extent to which the two distributions share common values will increase β (the likelihood of making a Type II error).

Power and the Sample Size: The smaller the sample size *n*, the lower the power. Very small *n* produces power so low that false hypothesis are accepted.

The following is a list of four factors influencing the power:

- Effect size (for example, the difference between the means)
- Variance s^2
- Significance level a
- Number of observations, or the sample size *n*

In practice, the first three factors are often fixed. Only the sample size can be controlled by the statistician and that only within budget constraint. There exists a tradeoff between budget and achievement of desirable accuracy in any analysis.

16.9 STEPS IN HYPOTHESIS TESTING

Steps for testing hypothesis are given below. (For both large sample and small sample tests)

Test Procedure

1. **Null Hypothesis:** set up null hypothesis H_0.
2. **Alternative Hypothesis:** Set up alternative hypothesis H_1, which is complementary to H_0 which will indicate whether one tailed (right or left tailed) or two tailed test is to be applied.
3. **Level of Significance:** Choose an appropriate level of significance α (alpha), is fixed in advance.
4. **Establish Critical or Rejection Region:** Sample space of the experiment which corresponds to the area under the sampling distribution curve of the test statistic is divided into two mutually exclusive as shown in Fig. 16.1. These regions are called the acceptance region and the rejection or critical region.
5. **Test Statistic (or Test of Criterian):** The value of test statistic is calculate from the distribution of sample statistic by using the following formula

$$\text{Test Statistics} = \frac{\text{Value of sample statistic-Value of hypothesized population parameter}}{\text{Standard error of the sample statistic}}$$

$$Z = \frac{t - E(t)}{S.E.(t)}$$

under the null hypothesis, where t is the sample statistic.

Select the test statistic and determine its value from the sample data. This value is called the observed value of the test statistic. Remember that a t statistic is usually appropriate for a small number of samples; for larger number of samples, a z statistic can work well if data are normally distributed.

6. **Inference (Reach a Conclusion):** We compare the computed value of Z_o (in absolute value) with the significant value (critical value) $Z_{\alpha/2}$ (or Z_α).
   - If $|Z_o| > Z_\alpha$ we reject the null hypothesis H_0 at α % level of significance and
   - If $|Z_o| >= Z_\alpha$ we accept H_0 at α % level of significance.

In other words, if the calculated absolute value of a test statistic is more than or equal to its critical value (or table value), then reject the null hypothesis, otherwise, accept it.

16.10 TEST OF SIGNIFICANCE

Tests of significance have great importance in the study and research on the basis of samples; and from the view of such tests, samples may be divided as follows:

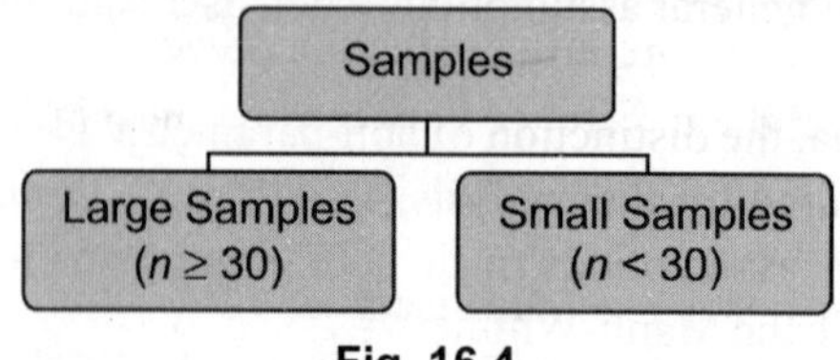

Fig. 16.4

The tests of significance are:

(a) Test of significance for large samples and

(b) Test of significance for small samples.

The tests of significance or test statistic are classified into two categories: ***parametric*** and ***non-parametric*** test. Parametric tests are more powerful because their data are derived from interval and ration measurements. Non parametric tests are used to test hypothesis with nominal and ordinal data.

Parametric Test

Parametric techniques are the tests of choice provided certain assumptions are met. Assumptions for parametric tests are as follows:

- The selection of any element from the population should not affect the chance for any other to be included in the sample to be drawn from the population.
- The samples should be drawn from normally distributed populations.
- Populations under study should have equal variance.

Various test of significance have been developed to meet various types of requirements in social, economical, financial, operational and business environments, etc. we have selected the following tests for discussion in this chapter.

- ***Z*-test** based on Normal Distribution
- **'*t*'-test** based on Student's '*t*'-Distribution
- **'*F*'-test** based on Fisher's *F*' Distribution

Remember that, in the *t*-tests for differences in means, there is a condition of equal population variances that must be examined. One way to test for possible differences in variances is to do an *F* test. However, the *F* test is very sensitive to violations of the normality condition; i.e., if populations appear not to be normal, then the *F* test will tend to reject too often the null of no differences in population variances.

Non-Parametric Test

One must use a statistical technique called non-parametric if it satisfies at least one of the following five types of criteria:

1. The data entering the analysis are enumerative; that is, counted data represent the number of observations in each category or cross-category.
2. The data are measured and/or analyzed using a nominal scale of measurement.
3. The data are measured and/or analyzed using an ordinal scale of measurement.

4. The inference does not concern a parameter in the population distribution; for example, the hypothesis that a time-ordered set of observations exhibits a random pattern.
5. The probability of the statistic upon which the analysis is based is not dependent upon specific information or conditions (i.e., assumptions) about the population(s) from which the sample(s) are drawn, but only upon general assumptions, such as a continuous and/or symmetric population distribution.

According to these criteria, the distinction of non-parametric is accorded either because of the level of measurement used or required for the analysis, as in types 1 through 3; the type of infernece, as in type 4, or the generality of the assumptions made about the population distribution, as in type 5.

For example, one may use the Mann-Whitney Rank Test as a non-parametric alternative to Students *T*-test when one does not have normally distributed data.

- **Chi-Square Test** based on the χ^2 distribution.
- **Mann-Whitney:** To be used with independent groups (analogous to the independent groups *t*-test).
- **Wilcoxon:** To be used with two related (i.e., matched or repeated) groups (analogous to the related samples *t*-test).
- **Kruskall-Wallis:** To be used with two or more independent groups (analogous to the single-factor between-subjects ANOVA).
- **Friedmann:** To be used with two or more related groups (analogous to the single-factor within-subjects ANOVA).

NOTE: In this book, we will discuss only Chi-Square Non-Parametric Test in the next chapter. **(See CD for Non-Parametric Test)**

The following decision chart provides a guide in selecting an appropriate test-statistic concerning the means μ's for both, one and two populations.

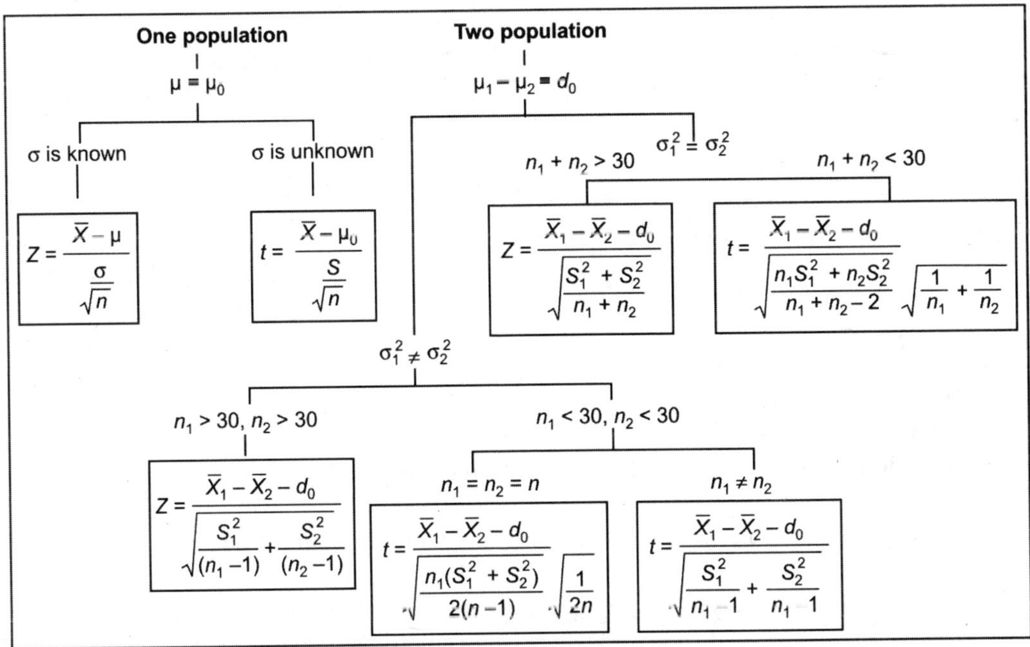

16.11 HYPOTHESIS TESTING FOR LARGE SAMPLES (N>30)

The tests of significance used for problems of large samples are different from those used in case of small samples as the assumptions used in both cases are different. The following assumptions are made for problems dealing with large samples:

(i) Almost all the sampling distributions follow normal asymptotically.

(ii) The sample values are approximately close to the population values.

For larger sample size (>30), all the distributions like Binomial, Poisson etc., are approximated by normal distribution. Thus normal probability curve can be used for testing of hypothesis.

For the test Statistic Z (standard normal variate), the critical region at 5% level is given by $|Z| > 1.96$ and hence the acceptance region is $|Z| < 1.96$. Where as the critical region for Z at 1% level is $|Z| > 2.58$ and the acceptance region is $|Z| < 2.58$.

The following tests are discussed in large sample tests.

(i) Test of significance for mean

(ii) Test of significance for difference between two means.

(iii) Test of significance for proportion

(iv) Test of significance for difference between two proportions

16.11.1 Test of Significance of Single Mean

If standard deviation σ of the population is known, then based on the central limit theorem, then the sampling distribution of mean X would follow the standard normal distribution for a larger size. The z-test statistic is given by

$$z = \frac{\bar{X} - \mu}{\sigma_{\bar{X}}} = \frac{\bar{X} - \mu}{\sigma / \sqrt{n}} \qquad \left[\sigma_{\bar{X}} = \frac{\sigma}{\sqrt{n}}\right]$$

In this formula, the numerator $X - \mu$, measures how far (in an absolute sense) the observed sample mean X is from the hypothesized mean μ. The denominator σ is the standard error of the mean, so the z-test statistic represents how many standard errors x is from μ.

If the population standard deviation σ is not known, then a sample standard deviation s is used to estimate σ. The value of the test statistic is

$$t = \frac{\bar{X} - \mu}{s / \sqrt{n}}$$

[for more detail see the t-Distribution]

Test Procedure

1. **Null and Alternative Hypotheses:** H_0: $\mu = \mu_0$. H_1: $\mu \neq \mu_0$ ($\mu > \mu_0$ or $\mu < \mu_0$)
2. **Level of Significance:** Let $\alpha = 0.05$ or 0.01
3. **Calculation of Statistic:** Under H_0, the test statistic is

$$Z_0 = \frac{\bar{X} - E(\bar{X})}{S.E(x)} = \frac{\bar{X} - \mu}{\sigma / \sqrt{n}} \qquad [Z_0 = \text{Calculated value}]$$

4. **Expected value:** $$Z_c = \frac{\bar{X} - \mu}{\sigma / \sqrt{n}} = N(0.1) \qquad [Z_e = \text{Table value}]$$

$= 1.96$ for α
$= 0.05$ (1.645)
or $= 2.58$ for α
$= 0.01$ (2.33)

5. Inference:

- If $Z_0 \leq Z_e$, we accept our null hypothesis and conclude that the sample is drawn from a population with mean $\mu = \mu_0$
- If $Z_0 > Z_e$ we reject our H_0 and conclude that the sample is not drawn from a population with mean $\mu = \mu_0$

(a) H_0: $\mu = \mu_0$
H_1: $\mu \neq \mu_0$

EXAMPLE 16.1: A random sample of 100 students from the current year's batch give the mean CGPA as 3.55 and variance 0.04. Can we say that this is same as the mean CGPA of the previous batch which was 3.5? **[MBA, Osmania Univ., 2002]**

Solution: Since we have to test the hypothesis that the population mean is equal to 3.5, the null and alternative hypotheses are set up as

H_0: $\mu = 3.5$
H_1: $\mu \neq 3.5$

Even though population variance is not given, but the sample size is so large that the sample variance can be taken to be equal to population variance i.e. 0.04. Thus, the test statistic used is

$$Z = \frac{\bar{X} - \mu}{\sigma / \sqrt{n}} \quad \text{which is distributed as } N(0, 1)$$

We are given, $\bar{X} = 3.55$, $m_0 = 3.5$, $n - 100$ and $\sigma = \sqrt{0.04} = 0.2$

Therefore,

$$Z = \frac{3.55 - 3.5}{0.2/\sqrt{100}}$$

$$= \frac{0.05}{0.2/10} = \frac{0.05}{0.02} = 2.5$$

Since, the total calculated value of Z (2.5) is more than the tabulated value of Z, at 5% level of significance, 1.96 the null hypothesis is rejected, as shown below:

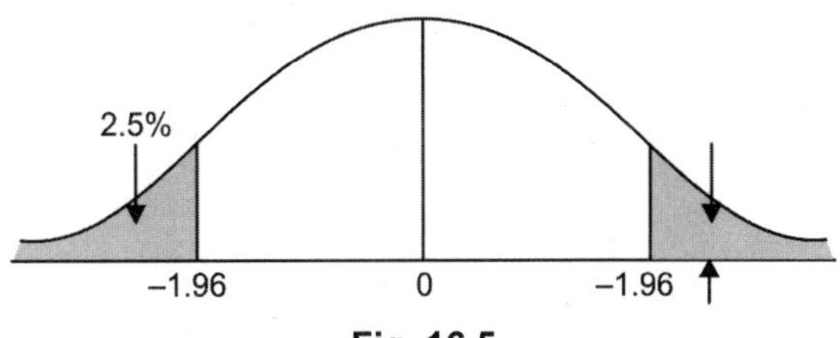

Fig. 16.5

Thus the current year's mean CGPA is not the same as the last year's mean CGPA.

EXAMPLE 16.2: A company markets car tyres. Their lives are normally distributed with a mean of 50000 kilometers and standard deviation of 2000 kilometers. A test sample of 64 tyres has a mean life of 51250 kms. Can you conclude that the sample mean differs significantly from the population mean? (Test at 5% level).

Solution:

Sample size, $n = 64$

Sample Mean, $\bar{X} = 51250$

H_0 : population mean $\mu = 50000$

H_1 : $\mu_1 \neq 50000$

Under H_0 the test statistic $Z = \dfrac{\bar{X} - \mu}{\dfrac{\sigma}{\sqrt{n}}} \sim N(0,1)$

$$Z = \frac{51250 - 50000}{\dfrac{2000}{\sqrt{64}}} = 5$$

Since the calculated Z is much greater than 1.96, it is highly significant.

∴ $H_0 : \mu = 50000$ is rejected

∴ The sample mean differs significantly from the population mean.

(b) H_0: $\mu = \mu_0$
H_1: $\mu < \mu_0$ **[Left Talid Test]**

EXAMPLE 16.3: It has been found from experience that the mean breaking strength of a brand of thread is 500 gms. with a s.d. of 40 gms. From the supplies, received during the last month, a sample of 16 pieces of thread was tested which showed a mean strength of 450 gms. Can we conclude that the thread supplied is inferior?

Solution: In this case

H_0: $\mu = 500$

H_1: $\mu < 500$

The test statistics is $Z = \dfrac{\bar{X} - \mu}{\sigma / \sqrt{n}}$ which is distributed as $N(0, 1)$

We are given that $\bar{X} = 450$, $\mu = 500$, $n = 16$ and $\sigma = 40$,

Therefore,

$$Z = \frac{450 - 500}{40/\sqrt{16}}$$

$$= \frac{-50}{40/4}$$

$$= \frac{-50}{10} = -5.0$$

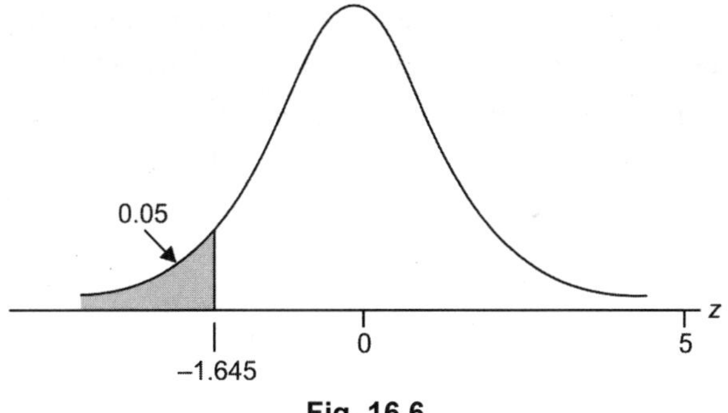

Fig. 16.6

Here the test statistic falls in the rejection region, and hence we reject the null hypothesis i.e. the sample indicates that the thread is inferior.

(c) H_0: $\mu = \mu_0$
H_1: $\mu > \mu_0$

EXAMPLE 16.4: A telephone company's records indicate that individual customers pay on an average Rs. 155 per month for long-distance telephone calls with standard deviation Rs. 45. A random sample of 40 customers' bills during a given month produces a sample mean of 160 for long-distance calls. At 5% significance, can we say that the company's records indicate lesser mean than the actual i.e. actual mean is more than 155 mts.?

Solution: Here the two hypotheses are set up as follows:

H_0: $\mu = 155$
H_1: $\mu < 155$

The test statistics is $Z = \dfrac{\bar{X} - \mu}{\sigma / \sqrt{n}}$ which is distributed as $N(0, 1)$

We are given that $\bar{X} = 160, \mu = 155, n = 40$ and $\sigma = 45$,

Therefore,

$$Z = \frac{160 - 155}{45/\sqrt{40}}$$

$$= \frac{5}{45/6.325} = \frac{5}{7.115} = 0.703$$

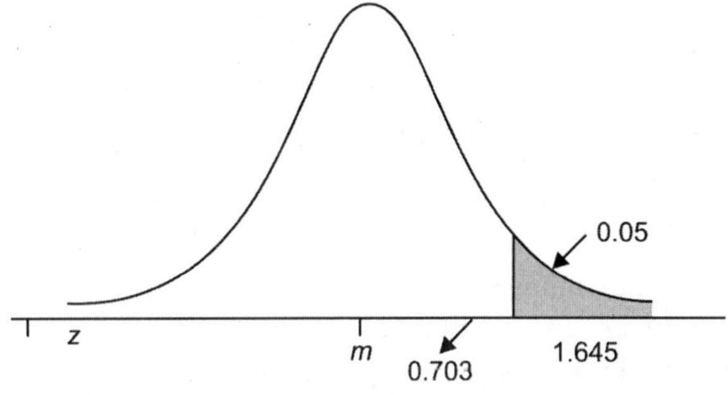

Fig. 16.7

Here, the test statistic falls in the acceptance region. Hence we do not reject the null hypothesis i.e. there is no evidence to infer that records indicate lesser mean than the actual.

EXAMPLE 16.5: A sample of 400 students is found to have a mean height of 171.38 cms. Can it reasonably be regarded as a sample from a large population with mean height of 171.17 cms and standard deviation of 3, 3 cms. (Test at 5% level)

Solution:

Sample size, $n = 400$

Sample mean, $\bar{X} = 171.38$

Population mean, $\mu = 171.17$

Sample standard deviation, $s = 33$

Population standard deviation,

$\sigma = 3.3$

Set $H_0: \mu = 171.38$

The test statistic, $$Z = \frac{\bar{X} - \mu}{\frac{\sigma}{\sqrt{n}}} \sim N(0,1)$$

$$= \frac{\bar{X} - \mu}{\sigma / \sqrt{n}}$$ [since the sample is large $s = \sigma$]

$$= \frac{171.38 - 171.17}{\frac{33}{\sqrt{400}}}$$

$$= 1.273$$

Since $|Z| = 1.273 < 1.96$, we accept the null hypothesis at 5% level of significance. Thus the sample of 400 has come from the population with mean height of 171.17 cms.

16.11.2 *p*-Valve Approach to Test Hypothesis of Single Mean

The p valve is another approach for hypothesis testing of population mean based on a large sample. This is after referred to as the observed significance level, that is, the smallest significance level and for which null hypothesis H_0 can be rejected.

> In other words, p-valve is probability of observing a sample valve as extreme as or more extreme than, the value of test statistic, given that the null hypothesis H_0 is true.

The advantage of this approach is that the p-valve can be compared directly to the level of significance α.

This value indicates the maximum level of significance at which the Null hypothesis would be accepted. if the level of significance is specified as 5% and the p-value generated by computer is 0.02, i.e. less than .05, the null hypothesis is rejected.

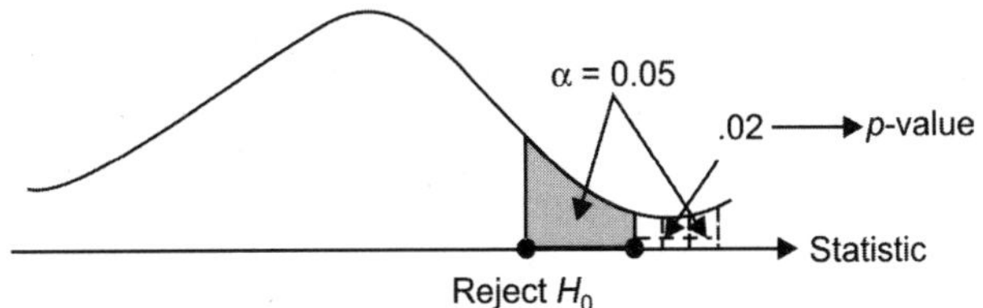

Fig. 16.8: Critical region and *p*-value

If the *p*-value is 0.10 i.e. ≥ 0.05, the null hypothesis is accepted.

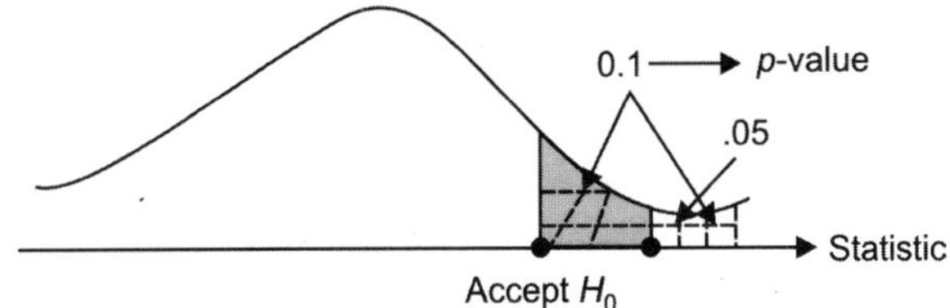

Fig. 16.9: Critical region and *p*-value

The *p*-value is the probability of getting the given sample when the null hypothesis is true. The smaller the *p*-value, the less likely it is that the observed sample would have come from the assumed population i.e. when the nul hypothesis is tue. The computer packages provide the *p*-value associated with any test of significance. Thus, one can compare the *p*-value to the level of significance, and conclude without referring to statistical tables.

The use of ***p***-value in testing of hypotheses is explained with the help of the following example.

EXAMPLE 16.6: A random sample of 100 students from the current year's batch gives the mean CGPA as 3.55 and variance 0.04. Can we say that this is same as the CGPA of the previous batch which was 3.5?

Solution: Since we have to test the hypothesis that the population mean is equal to 3.5, the null and alternative hypotheses are set up as

$$H_0: \quad \mu = 3.5$$
$$H_1: \quad \mu \neq 3.5$$

Even though population variance is not given, but the sample size is so large that the sample variance can be taken to be equal to population variance i.e. 0.04. Thus, the test statistic used is

$$Z = \frac{\overline{X} - \mu}{\sigma / \sqrt{n}} \quad \text{which is distributed as } N(0, 1)$$

We are given that $\overline{X} = 3.55$, $\mu = 3.5$, $n = 100$ and $\sigma = \sqrt{0.04} = 0.2$,

Therefore,
$$Z = \frac{3.55 - 3.5}{0.2/\sqrt{100}}$$
$$= \frac{0.05}{0.2/10} = \frac{0.05}{0.02}$$
$$= 2.5$$

Since, the calculated value of *z* (2.5) is more than the tabulated value of *z*, at 5% level of significance, 1.96, the null hypothesis is rejected, as shown below:

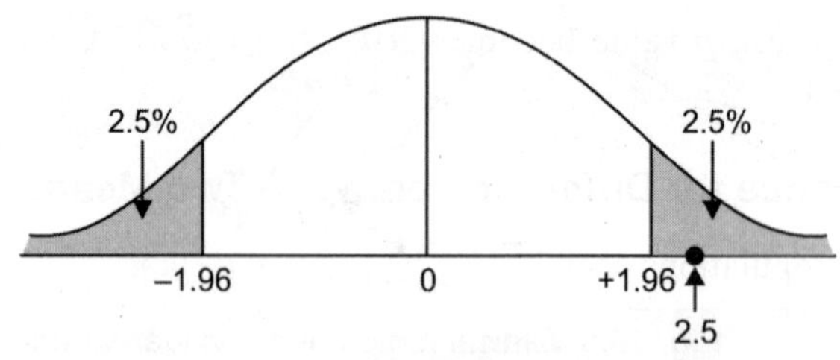

Fig. 16.10

Thus the current year's CGPA is not same as the last year's CGPA.

The p-value for this example works out to 0.0124 which is less than 0.05 (assumed level of significance). Hence the null hypothesis is rejected by this method as well.

EXAMPLE 16.7: An auto company decided to introduce a new six cylinder car whose mean petrol consumption is claimed to be lower than that of the exiting auto engine. It was found that the mean petrol consumption for 50 cars was 10 km per litre with a standard deviation of 3.5 km per litre. Test for the company at 5 per cent level of significance, the clain that in the new car petrol consumption is 9.5 km per litre on the average. **[MBA, DU, 1998, HPU, 1989]**

Solution: Let us assume the null hypothesis H_0 that there is no significant difference between the company's claim and the sample average value, that is,

$H_0 = \mu = 9.5$ km/litre and $H_1 : \mu \neq 9.5$ km/litre

Given $\bar{X} = 10$, $n = 50$, $s = 3.5$, and $Z_{\alpha/2} = 1.96$ at a = 0.05 level of significance. Thus using the Z-test statistic

$$Z = \frac{\bar{X} - \mu}{\sigma_{\bar{X}}} = \frac{\bar{X} - \mu}{s/\sqrt{n}}$$

$$= \frac{10 - 9.5}{3.5/\sqrt{50}} = 1.010$$

Since $Z_e = 1.010$ is less than its critical value $z_{\alpha/2} = 1.96$ at $\alpha = 0.05$ level of significance, the null hypothesis is accepted. Hence we can conclude that the new car's petrol consumption is 9.5 km/litre.

The p-value approach: The null hypothesis accepted H_0 because $Z_e = 1.010$ lies in the acceptance region. The probability of finding $Z_e = 1.010$ or more is 0.3437 (from normal table). The p-value is the area to the right as well as left of the calculated value of z-test statistic (for two-tailed test). Since $z$cal = 1.010, then the area to its right is 0.5000 – 0.3437 = 0.1563 as shown in Fig. 16.11.

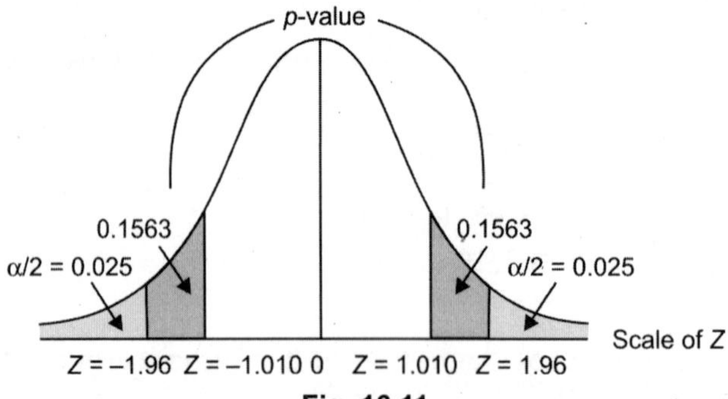

Fig. 16.11

Since it is the two-tailed test, p-value becomes 2(0.1563) = 0.3126. Since 0.3126 > α = 0.05, null hypothesis H_0 is accepted.

16.11.3 Test of Significance for Difference between Two Means

If we have two independent populations each having its mean and standard deviation as:

Population	Mean	Standard Deviation
1	μ_1	σ_1
2	μ_2	σ_2

Let two independent random samples of large size n_1 and n_2 be drawn from the first and second population, respectively.

Let the sample means so calculated be $\bar{X}_1$ and $\bar{X}_2$.

The z-test statistic used to determine the difference between the population means ($\mu_1 - \mu_2$) is based on the difference between the sample means $(\bar{X}_1 - \bar{X}_2)$.

The standard deviation of the sampling distribution of $(\bar{X}_1 - \bar{X}_2)$ is given by

$$\sigma^2_{\bar{X}_1 - \bar{X}_2} = \text{Var}[\bar{X}_1 - \bar{X}_2] = \text{Var}[\bar{X}_1] + \text{Var}[\bar{X}_2]$$

$$\sigma^2_{\bar{X}_1 - \bar{X}_2} = \frac{\sigma_1^2}{n_1} + \frac{\sigma_2^2}{n_2}$$

$$\sigma = \sqrt{\frac{n_2\sigma_1^2 + n_2\sigma_2^2}{n_1 + n_2}}$$

Therefore, the Z statistic is given by

$$Z = \frac{(\bar{X}_1 - \bar{X}_2) - (\mu_1 - \mu_2)}{\sigma_{\bar{X}_1 - \bar{X}_2}}$$

Test statistic for the difference between two means are

$$\boxed{Z = \frac{(X_1 - X_2) - (\mu_1 - \mu_2)}{\sqrt{\frac{\sigma_1^2}{n_1} + \frac{\sigma_2^2}{n_2}}}}$$

NOTE: In case σ_1^2 and σ_2^2 are not known then for large sample, S_1^2 and S_2^2 can be used instead.

Test Procedure

1. **Null and Alternative Hypotheses:** H_0: $\mu_1 = \mu_2$; H_1: $\mu_1 \neq \mu_2$ ($\mu_1 > \mu_2$ or $\mu_1 < \mu_2$)
2. **Level of Significance:** Let α %
3. **Calculation of Statistic:** Under H_0 the test statistic is

$$Z_0 = \frac{\bar{X}_1 - \bar{X}_2}{\sqrt{\frac{\sigma_1^2}{n_1} + \frac{\sigma_2^2}{n_2}}} \qquad [\mu_1 = \mu_2]$$

If $\sigma_1^2 = \sigma_2^2 = \sigma^2$ (i.e) if the samples have been drawn from the population with common S.D. σ then under $H_0 : \mu_1 = \mu_2$

$$Z_0 = \frac{\bar{X}_1 - \bar{X}_2}{\sigma\sqrt{\frac{1}{n_1} + \frac{1}{n_2}}}$$

Expected value: $$Z_e = \frac{\bar{X}_1 - \bar{X}_2}{S.E(x_1 - x_2)} \sim N(0.1)$$

Inference:

- If $Z_0 < Z_e$ we accept the H_0
- If $Z_0 > Z_e$ we reject the H_0

(a) H_0: $\mu_1 = \mu_2$
H_1: $\mu_1 \neq \mu_2$

EXAMPLE 16.8: A test of the breaking strengths of two different types of cables was conducted using samples of $n_1 = n_2 = 100$ pieces of each type of cable.

Cable I	Cable II
$\bar{X}_1 = 1925$	$\bar{X}_2 = 1905$
$\sigma_1 = 40$	$\sigma_2 = 30$

Do the data provide sufficient evidence to indicate a difference between the mean breaking strengths of the two cables? [Use 0.01 level of significance.]

Solution: We are given

$$\bar{X}_1 = 1925 \qquad \bar{X}_2 = 1905 \qquad \sigma_1 = 40 \qquad \sigma_2 = 30$$

Null Hypothesis: $H_0 : \mu_1 = \mu_2$ .i.e. There is no significant difference between the mean breaking strengths of the two cables.

Alternative Hypothesis: $H_1 : \mu_1 \neq \mu_2$ (Two tailed alternative)

Level of Significance: Let $\alpha = 0.01$ or 1%

Calculation of Statistic: Under H_0 the test statistic is

$$Z_0 = \frac{\bar{X}_1 - \bar{X}_2}{\sqrt{\frac{\sigma_1^2}{n_1} + \frac{\sigma_2^2}{n_2}}}$$

$$= \frac{1925 - 1905}{\sqrt{\frac{40^2}{100} + \frac{30^2}{100}}} = \frac{30}{5} = 4 \qquad \text{[Calculated value]}$$

Inference:

- Since $Z_0 > Z_e$, we reject the H_0. Hence the formulated null hypothesis is wrong i.e. there is a significant difference in the breaking strengths of two cables.

EXAMPLE 16.9: The means of two large samples of 1000 and 2000 items are 67.5 cms and 68.0 cms respectively. Can the samples be regarded as drawn from the population with standard deviation 2.5 cms. Test at 5% level of significance.

Solution: We are given

$n_1 = 1000 \quad n_2 = 2000 \quad \bar{X}_1 = 67.5$ cms $\quad \bar{X}_2 = 68.0$ cms $\quad \sigma = 2.5$ cms

Null Hypothesis: H_0: $\mu_1 = \mu_2$ (i.e ,) the sample have been drawn from the same population.

Alternative Hypothesis: H_1 : $\mu_1 \neq \mu_2$ (Two tailed alternative)

Level of Significance: Let $\alpha = 5\%$

Calculation of Statistic: Under H_0 the test statistic is

$$Z_0 = \frac{\bar{X}_1 - \bar{X}_2}{\sigma\sqrt{\frac{1}{n_1} + \frac{1}{n_2}}}$$

$$= \frac{67.5 - 68.0}{2.5\sqrt{\frac{1}{1000} + \frac{1}{2000}}} = \frac{0.5 \times 20}{2.5\sqrt{3/5}}$$

$$= 5.1$$

Inference:

- Since $Z_0 > Z_e$ we reject the H_0 at 5% level of significance and conclude that the samples have not come from the same population.

EXAMPLE 16.10: An automobile company is interested in testing the mileage given by one of the car brands in two different cities, Mumbai and Delhi. The company surveyed 100 car owners in Mumbai and found that the average mileage is 12 kms. per litre. Out of 150 car owners in Delhi, the mileage averages to 12.5 kms, per litre. The standard deviation for mileage of this brand of car is known to be 0.9. **[MBA, Rohalkhand University, 1999]**

Solution: The hypotheses to be tested are:

H_0: $\mu_1 = \mu_2$ (μ_1 and μ_2 being average mileages of

H_0: $\mu_1 \neq \mu_2$ the cars in Mumbai and Delhi, respectively)

Since the significance level is not given we assume it to be 5%

The 'Z' statistic to be calculated is as follows, ($\sigma_1 = \sigma_2 = \sigma$ known)

$$Z = \frac{\bar{X}_1 - \bar{X}_2}{\sigma\sqrt{\left(\frac{1}{n_1} + \frac{1}{n_2}\right)}} \quad Z \sim N(0, 1)$$

where x_1 denotes the average mileage in Mumbai

x_2 denotes the average mileage in Delhi

n_1 and n_2 are number of observations for Mumbai and Delhi

Here $\bar{X}_1 = 12$

$\bar{X}_2 = 12.5$

$$\sigma_1 = \sigma_2 = 0.9$$
$$n_1 = 100$$
$$n_2 = 150$$

Substituting in the above formula, we get

$$Z = \frac{12 - 12.5}{0.9\sqrt{\left(\frac{1}{100} + \frac{1}{150}\right)}}$$

$$Z = \frac{-0.5}{0.9 \times 0.129} = -4.31$$

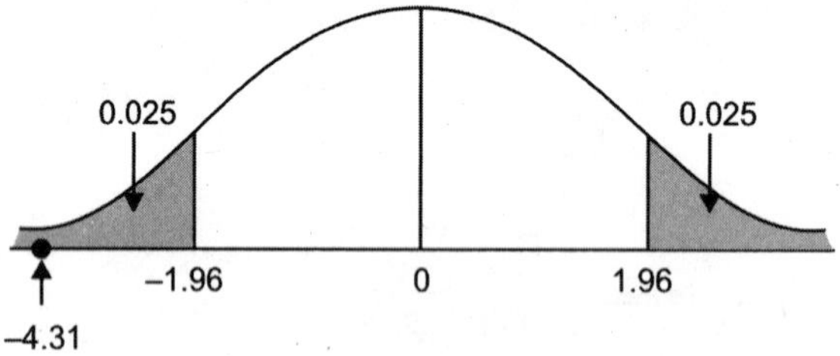

0.025 0.025

−1.96 0 1.96

−4.31

Fig. 16.12

This calculated value of 'Z' is less than the tabulated value of Z (–19.6) which lies in the shaded region, which is the rejection region. Therefore, the null hypothesis that $m_1 = m_2$ is rejected. Thus, the two cities do not have same mileage for the car.

(b) For H_0: $\mu_1 = \mu_2$

H_1: $\mu_1 \neq \mu_2$ **or** $\mu_1 < \mu_2$

See the 't'-distribution

16.11.4 Test of Significance of Single Proportion

Sometimes instead of testing a hypothesis pertaining to a population mean, a population proportion p of values in a particular category is considered. For this a random sample of size n is selected to compute the proportion of successes in the particular sample as follows:

$$\bar{p}^* = \frac{\text{Number of successes in the sample}}{\text{Sample size}} = \frac{x}{n}$$

The value of this statistic is compared with a hypothesized population proportion p_0 so as arrive at a conclusion about the hypothesis.

To conduct a test of a hypothesis, it is assumed that the sampling distribution of a proportion follows a standardized normal distribution. Then, using the value of the sample proportion $\bar{p}$ and its standard deviation $\sigma_{\bar{p}}$, we compute a value for the z-test statistics as follow:

*We can use $\bar{p}$ or $\hat{p}$ for sample proportion and p_0 or p is hypotheses population proportion.

$$Z = \frac{\bar{p} - p_o}{\sigma_p} = \frac{\bar{p} - p_o}{\sqrt{\dfrac{p_0(1-p_0)}{n}}}$$

where $\bar{p}$ is the sample proportion and
p_0 is the hypothesized population proportion

Test Procedure

1. **Null and Alternative Hypotheses:** H_0: $p = p_0$ H_1: $p \neq p_0$ ($p > p_0$ or $p < p_0$)
2. **Level of significance:** Let $\sigma = 0\ .05$ or 0.01
3. **Calculation of statistic:** Under H_0 the test statistic is

$$Z_0 = \frac{p - p}{\sqrt{\dfrac{p_0(1-p_0)}{n}}} = \frac{\bar{p} - p_0}{\sqrt{\dfrac{p_0 q_0}{n}}} \qquad [q_0 = 1 - p_0]$$

4. **Expected value:**

$$Z_0 = \frac{\bar{p} - p_0}{\sqrt{\dfrac{p_0(1-p_0)}{n}}} \sim N(0,1)$$

$= 1.96$ for $\alpha = 0.05$ (1.645)
$= 2.58$ for $\alpha = 0.01$ (2.33)

5. **Inference:**
   - If the computed value of $Z_0 \leq Z_e$ we accept the null hypothesis and conclude that the sample is drawn from the population with proportion of success p_0.
   - If $Z_0 > Z_e$ we reject the null hypothesis and conclude that the sample has not been taken from the population whose population proportion of success is p_0.

(a) $\boldsymbol{H_0: \; p_1 = p_0}$
$\boldsymbol{H_1: \; p \neq p_0}$

EXAMPLE 16.11: A cable TV operator claims that 50% of the homes in a city have opted for his services. Before sponsoring advertisement on the local cable channel; a company conducted a survey, and found that 280 out of 600 persons were found to have cable TV services from the operator. On the basis of this data can we accept the claim of the cable TV operator? **[MBA, UPTU, (CO), 2004]**

Solution: Since we want to ascertain whether the proportional of homes with cable TV in the city, is 0.5, we set up the null and alternative hypothesis as follows:

$$H_0: \; p = 0.5$$
$$H_1: \; p \neq 0.5$$

The appropriate test statisitic to be used is:

$$Z = \sqrt{\frac{\bar{p} - p_0}{p_0 q_0 / n}} \sim N(0, 1)$$

In this given situation,

$$p_0 = 0.5$$
$$n = 600$$
$$q_0 = 1 - p_0 = 0.5$$
$$\hat{p} = \frac{280}{600} = 0.4667$$

Therefore,
$$Z = \frac{0.4667 - 0.5}{\sqrt{\frac{0.5 \times 0.5}{600}}} = \frac{-0.0333}{0.0204}$$
$$= -1.63$$

Now, since z is a standard normal variable, we find the value of Z such that the total area under the standard normal curve beyond that point on either side of the curve is 5%.

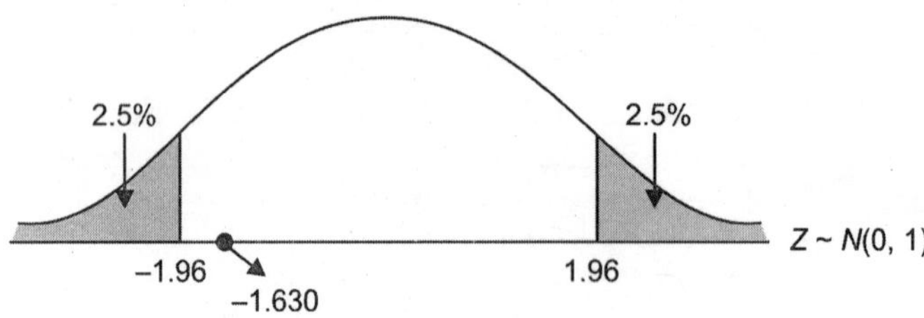

Fig. 16.13: Critical region

Since the calculated value (–1.63) of Z falls in the acceptance region we conclude that the null hypothesis is to be accepted. Thus, the claim of the cable TV operator is to accepted as we do not have sufficient evidence to disapprove his statement.

EXAMPLE 16.12: In a random sample of 400 persons from a large population 120 are females. Can it be said that males and females are in the ratio 5:3 in the population? Use 1% level of significance.

Solution: We are given $n = 400$ and x = No. of female in the sample = 120

$\bar{p}$ = observed proportion of females in the sample = 120/400 = 0.30

Null Hypothesis: The males and females in the population are in the ratio 5:3 i.e.,

H_0: $\bar{p}_0$ = Proportion of females in the population = 3/8 = 0.375

Alternative Hypothesis: H_1: $p_0 \neq 0.375$ (two-tailed)

Level of significance: α = 1 % or 0.01

Calculation of Statistic:

Under H_o, the test statistic is
$$Z_0 = \frac{\bar{p} - p_0}{\sqrt{\frac{p_0(1 - p_0)}{n}}}$$
$$= \frac{0.300 - 0.375}{\sqrt{\frac{0.375 \times 0.625}{400}}} \qquad [(1 - p_0) = 0.625]$$
$$= \frac{0.075}{\sqrt{0.000586}} = \frac{0.075}{0.024} = 3.125$$

Inference:

- Since the calculated $Z_0 > Z_e$ we reject our null hypothesis at 1% level of significance and conclude that the males and females in the population are not in the ratio 5:3.

(b) H_0: $p = p_0$
H_1: $p > p_0$

EXAMPLE 16.13: In a sample of 400 parts manufactured by a factory, the number of defective parts was found to be 30. The company, however, claimed that only 5% of their product is defective. Is the claim tenable?

Solution: We are given $n = 400$, x = No. of defectives in the sample = 30

$\bar{p}$ = proportion of defectives in the sample = $x/n = 30/400 = 0.075$

Null Hypothesis: The claim of the company is tenable H_0: $\bar{p}_0 = 0.05$

Alternative Hypothesis: H_1: $\bar{p}_0 > 0.05$ (Right tailed Alternative)

Level of Significance: 5%

Calculation of Statistic: Under H_0, the test statistic is

$$Z_0 = \frac{\bar{p} - p_0}{\sqrt{\frac{p_0(1-p_0)}{n}}}$$

$$= \frac{0.075 - 0.050}{\sqrt{\frac{0.05 \times 0.95}{400}}} \qquad [(1 - p_0) = 0.95]$$

$$= \frac{0.025}{\sqrt{0.0001187}} = 2.27$$

Inference

- Since the calculated $Z_0 > Z_e$ we reject our null hypothesis at 5% level of significance and we conclude that the company's claim is not tenable.

EXAMPLE 16.14: In a Departmental store, 380 customers out of a random sample of 800 customers were found to be using Visa credit card. Discuss whether this information supports the view that the majority of customers of the store are using cares other than Visa. **[MBA, UPTU, 2005]**

Solution: Let p denote the proportion of customers using cards other than Visa. Then the alternative hypothesis that majority of customers are not using Visa card would be

$$H_1: \; p > 0.5$$

while the null hypothesis is set up as,

$$H_0: \; p = 0.5$$

It is given that the proportion of visa card used is $380/800 = 0.475$, and, therefore, the proportion of other card users is $420/800$ i.e 0.525. While this sample proportion of other card users is more than 0.5, we have to test whether the value 0.525 is significantly more than 0.5. The test statistic is

$$Z = \frac{\hat{p} - p_0}{\sqrt{\frac{p_0 q_0}{n}}}$$

which is distributed as Normal with mean as 0 and s.d. as 1, and where, $\hat{p}$ is the sample proportion, p_0 is the proportion as per H_0 and n is the sample size.

It is given that

$$n = 800$$
$$p_0 = 0.5$$
$$q_0 = 1 - p_0 = 0.5$$
$$\hat{p} = 0.525$$

Therefore,

$$Z = \frac{0.525 - 0.5}{\sqrt{\frac{0.5 \times 0.5}{800}}} = \frac{0.7071}{0.5}$$

$$= 1.41$$

Since, level of significance is not given, we presume it to be 0.05. From the table of area under normal curve, we note the value beyond which the area, to the right, is 0.05 is 1.645, as shown below:

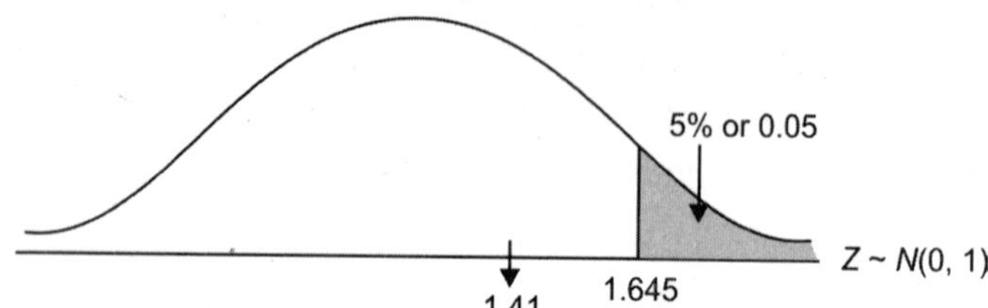

Fig. 16.14: Critical region under normal curve

It may be noted that the entire critical region is on the right as the alternative hypothesis is one sided.

Since the calculated value 1.41 is less than the tabulated value, and it falls in the acceptance region, we accept H_0 and reject H_1. Thus there is no sufficient evidence to conclude that the majority of customers of the store are users of cards other than Visa.

(c) H_0: $p = p_0$
H_1: $p < p_0$

EXAMPLE 16.15: A manufacturer of LCD TV claims that it is becoming quite popular, and that about 5% homes are having LCD TV. However, a dealer of conventional TVs claims that the percentage of homes with LCD TV is less than 5%. A sample of 400 household is surveyed, and it is found that only 18 households have LCD TV. Test at 1% level of significance whether the claim of the company is tenable.

[MBA, Osmania University, 1996, Anna Univ., 2000]

Solution: Let p be the proportion of derfective parts.

In this case, we take the null hypothesis as the claim of the Company is 5%, that is to be tested against the alternative that the percentage of LCD TV is less than 5%. Thus, the null and alternative hypotheses are set up as follows:

$$H_0: \; p = 0.05$$
$$H_1: \; p < 0.05$$

The appropriate test statistic to be used is:

$$Z = \frac{\bar{p} - p_0}{\sqrt{\frac{p_0 q_0}{n}}} \sim N(0, 1)$$

In this given situation,

$$p_0 = 0.05$$
$$n = 400$$
$$q_0 = 1 - p_0 = 0.95$$
$$\hat{p} = \frac{18}{400} = -0.045$$

Therefore,

$$Z = \frac{0.045 - 0.05}{\sqrt{\frac{0.05 \times 0.95}{400}}}$$
$$= \frac{-0.005}{0.011} = -0.4545$$

Now, since z is a standard normal variable, we find the value of z such that the total area under the standard normal curve beyond that point is 1%.

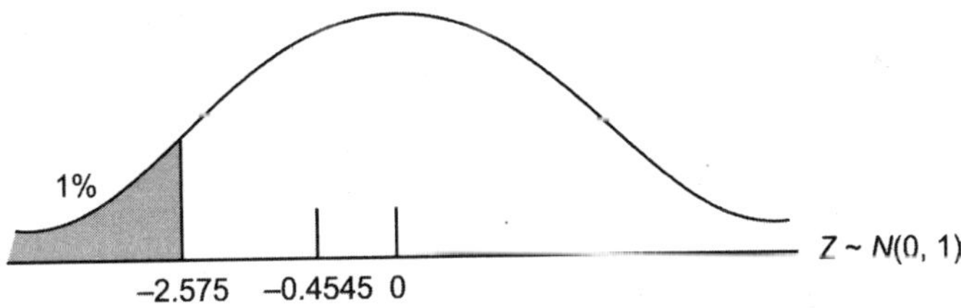

Fig. 16.15: Critical region under normal curve

Since the calculated value (–1.63) of Z falls in the acceptance region we conclude that the null hypothesis is to be accepted. Thus, the claim of the cable TV operator is to accepted as we do not have sufficient evidence to disapprove his statement.

16.11.5 Test of Significance for Difference between Proportions of Two Populations

Let two independent populations each having proportion and standard deviation of an attribute be as follow:

Population	Proportion	Standard Deviation
1	p_1	σ_{p_1}
2	p_2	σ_{p_2}

The hypothesis testing concepts developed in the previous section can be extended to test whether there is any difference between the proportions of these populations. The null hypothesis that there is no difference between two population proportions is stated as:

$H_0: p_1 = p_2$ or $p_1 - p_2 = 0$ and $H_1: p_1 \neq p_2$

The sampling distribution of difference in sample proportions $p_1 - p_2$ is based on the assumption that the difference between two population proportions, $p_1 - p_2$ is normally distributed. The standard deviation (or error) of sampling distribution of $p_1 - p_2$ is given by

$$\sigma_{\bar{p}_1 - \bar{p}_2} = \sqrt{\frac{p_1 q}{n_1} + \frac{p_2 q_2}{n_2}}$$

where $q_1 = 1 - p_1$, and $q_2 = 1 - p_2$

$$= \sqrt{\frac{p_1(1-p_1)}{n_1} + \frac{p_2(1-p_2)}{n_2}}$$

Therefore, the statistic is

$$Z = \frac{(\bar{p}_1 - \bar{p}_2) - (p_1 - p_2)}{\sigma_{\bar{p}_1 - \bar{p}_2}}$$

The statistic for the difference between two proportions are:

$$\boxed{Z = \frac{(\bar{p}_1 - \bar{p}_2) - (p_1 - p_2)}{\sqrt{\frac{p_1(1-p_1)}{n_1} + \frac{p_2(1-p_2)}{n_2}}}}$$

Test Procedure

1. Set up the Null and Alternative Hypotheses:

$$H_0: p_1 = p_2 = p \text{ (say)}$$

$$H_1: p_1 \neq p_2 \ (p_1 > p_2 \text{ or } p_1 < P_2)$$

2. Level of Significance: Let $\alpha = 0.05$ or 0.01

3. Calculation of Statistic: Under H_0, the test statistic is

$$Z_0 = \frac{\bar{p}_1 - \bar{p}_2}{\sqrt{\frac{p_1 q_1}{n_1} + \frac{p_2 q_2}{n_2}}} \quad (p_1 \text{ and } p_2 \text{ are known}) \qquad [p_1 = p_2]$$

$$= \frac{\bar{p}_1 - \bar{p}_1}{\sqrt{\bar{p}\bar{q}\left(\frac{1}{n_1} + \frac{1}{n_2}\right)}} \quad (p_1 \text{ and } p_2 \text{ are not known}) \qquad [\bar{q} = 1 - \bar{p}]$$

Where Pooled Estimate $\bar{p} = \frac{n_1\bar{p}_1 + n_2\bar{p}_2}{n_1 + n_2} = \frac{x_1 + x_2}{n_1 + n_2}$

4. Expected value: $Z_0 = \frac{\bar{p}_1 - \bar{p}_2}{S.E(\bar{p}_1 - \bar{p}_2)} \sim N(0.1)$

5. Inference:

- If $Z_0 \leq Z_e$ we accept the null hypothesis and conclude that the difference between proportions are due to sampling fluctuations.
- If $Z_0 > Z_e$ we reject the null hypothesis and conclude that the difference between proportions cannot be due to sampling fluctuations.

(a) H_0: $p_1 = p_2$
H_1: $p_1 \neq p_2$

EXAMPLE 16.16: In a referendum submitted to the 'student body' at a university, 850 men and 550 women voted. 530 of the men and 310 of the women voted 'yes'. Does this indicate a significant difference of the opinion on the matter between men and women students?

Solution: We are given

$n_1 = 850 \quad n_2 = 550 \quad x_1 = 530 \quad x_2 = 310$

$$\bar{p}_1 = \frac{530}{850} = 0.62\,; \quad \bar{p}_2 = \frac{310}{550} = 0.56$$

$$\bar{p} = \frac{x_1 + x_2}{n_1 + n_2} = \frac{530 + 310}{1400} = 0.60$$

$$\bar{q} = 0.40 \qquad [\bar{q} = 1 - \bar{p}]$$

Null Hypothesis: H_0: $p_1 = p_2$ ie the data does not indicate a significant difference of the opinion on the matter between men and women students.

Alternative Hypothesis: H_1: $p_1 \neq p_2$ (Two tailed Alternative)

Level of Significance: Let $\alpha = 0.05$

Calculation of Statistic: Under H_0, the test statistic is

$$Z_0 = \frac{p_1 - p_2}{\sqrt{\overline{pq}\left(\frac{1}{n_1} + \frac{1}{n_2}\right)}}$$

$$= \frac{0.62 - 0.56}{\sqrt{0.6 \times 0.4\left(\frac{1}{850} + \frac{1}{550}\right)}}$$

$$= \frac{0.06}{0.027} = 2.22$$

Inference: Since $Z_0 > Z_e$ we reject our null hypothesis at 5% level of significance and say that the data indicate a significant difference of the opinion on the matter between men and women students.

EXAMPLE 16.17: In a certain city 125 men in a sample of 500 are found to be self employed. In another city, the number of self employed is 375 in a random sample of 1000. Does this indicate that there is a greater population of self employed in the second city than in the first?

Solution: We are given

$n_1 = 500 \quad n_2 = 1000 \quad x_1 = 125 \quad x_2 = 375$

$$\bar{p}_1 = \frac{125}{500} = 0.25$$

$$\bar{p}_2 = \frac{375}{1000} = 0.375$$

$$\bar{p} = \frac{x_1 + x_2}{n_1 + n_2} = \frac{125 + 375}{500 + 1000}$$

$$= \frac{500}{1500} = \frac{1}{3}$$

$$\bar{q} = 1 - \frac{1}{3} = \frac{2}{3}$$

Null Hypothesis: H_0: $p_1 = p_2$ There is no significant difference between the two population proportions.

Alternative Hypothesis: H_1: $p_1 < p_2$ (left tailed Alternative)

Level of Significance: Let $\alpha = 0.05$

Calculation of Statistic: Under H_0, the test statistic

$$Z_0 = \frac{\bar{p}_1 - \bar{p}_2}{\sqrt{\bar{p}\bar{q}\left(\frac{1}{n_1} + \frac{1}{n_2}\right)}}$$

$$= \frac{0.25 - 0.375}{\sqrt{\frac{1}{3} \times \frac{2}{3}\left(\frac{1}{500} + \frac{1}{1000}\right)}} = \frac{0.125}{0.026} = 4.8$$

Inference: Since $Z_0 > Z_e$ we reject the null hypothesis at 5% level of significance and say that there is a significant difference between the two population proportions.

EXAMPLE 16.18: A firm wanted to choose a popular actor to be the brand ambassador for the firm's product. However, before taking the final decision, the firm conducted a market survey to know the opinion of its customers in Mumbai and Delhi. The surveys conducted in the two cities revealed that while 290 out of 400 customers favoured the choice, in Mumbai, only 160 out of 300 customers favoured the choice in Delhi. Can firm conclude that the proportions of customers who favoured the actor in Mumbai and Delhi are the same?

Solution: Let $\bar{p}_1$ denote the proportion of customers favouring the choice of the actor in Mumbai.

Let $\bar{p}_2$ be proportion of customers favouring the choice of the actor in Delhi.

Then the alternative hypothesis that majority of customers are

$$\bar{p}_1 = 290/400 = 0.725 \quad (n_1 = 400)$$

$$\bar{p}_2 = 160/300 = 0.533 \quad (n_2 = 300)$$

The null and alternate hypothesis are as follows:

$$H_1: \; p_1 \neq p_2$$

$$H_0: \; p_1 = p_2$$

The test statistic is $$Z = \frac{\bar{p}_1 - \bar{p}_2}{\sqrt{\left\{\overline{pq}\left(\frac{1}{n_1}+\frac{1}{n_2}\right)\right\}}}$$

which is distributed as Normal with mean as 0 and s.d. as 1, and where,

$$\bar{p} = \frac{n_1\hat{p}_1 + n_2\hat{p}_2}{n_2 + n_2} = \frac{290+160}{400+300}$$

$$= \frac{450}{700} = 0.643$$

and $$\bar{q} = 1 - \bar{p} = 0.357$$

Therefore, $$Z = \frac{0.725 - 0.533}{\sqrt{0.23\left(\frac{1}{400}+\frac{1}{300}\right)}}$$

$$= \frac{0.192}{0.037} = 5.24$$

Since level of significance is not given, we presume it to be 0.05. From the Table *T*1 of area under normal curve, we note the two tail value for level of significance 0.05 as 1.96, as shown

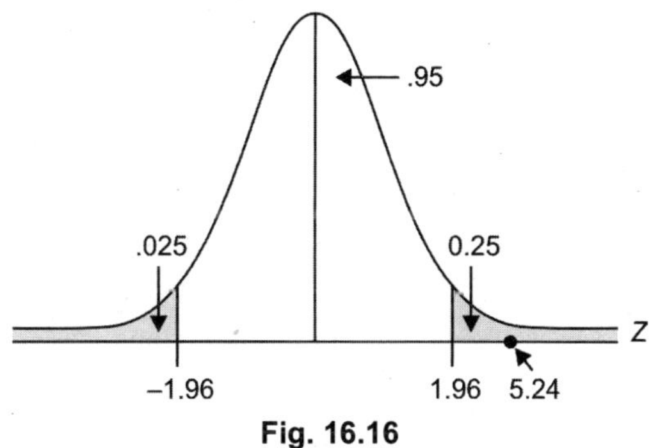

Fig. 16.16

Since the calculated value of *Z* is in the rejection region, the null hypothesis may be rejected. It indicates that there is a significant difference in the customers' responses in the two cities for the choice of the actor.

(b) One Sides or One Tailed

H_0: $p_1 = p_2$

H_1: $p_1 > p_2$

EXAMPLE 16.19: A machine produced 20 defective items in a sample 500. After the machine was overhauled, it produced 5 defective items in a batch of 150. Has the machine improved after overhauling?

Solution: Here the null hypothesis to be tested is that the machine puts out same proportion of defective items before and after overhauling against the alternative hypothesis that the proportion of defective items gets reduced after overhauling.

$$H_0: \ p_1 = p_2$$
$$H_1: \ p_1 > p_2$$

where $\quad p_1$: Proportion of defective before overhaul

p_2: Proportion of defectives after overhaul

The appropriate test statistic here, is the same as for the two sided test, above. However, the entire critical region is on the right:

$$Z = \frac{\bar{p}_1 - \bar{p}_2}{\sqrt{\overline{pq}\left(\frac{1}{n_1} + \frac{1}{n_2}\right)}} \sim N(0, 1)$$

n_1: sample size before overhauling

n_2: sample size after overhauling

$\bar{p}_1$: proportional of defective before overhauling

$\bar{p}_2$: proportion of defective after overhauling

where, $\quad \bar{p}$: $\dfrac{n_1\bar{p}_1 + n_2\bar{p}_2}{n_1 + n_2}$

$\bar{q}$: $\bar{q} = 1 - \bar{p}$

In the given exercise:

$$n_1 = 500, \qquad n_2 = 150$$

$$\bar{p}_1 = \frac{20}{500} = 0.04 \qquad \bar{p}_2 = \frac{5}{150} = 0.033$$

$$\bar{p} = \frac{n_1\hat{p}_1 + n_2\hat{p}_2}{n_1 + n_2}$$

$$= \frac{20 + 5}{500 + 150}$$

$$= \frac{25}{650} = .0385$$

$$\bar{q} = 1 - \bar{p} = 0.9615$$

$$Z = \frac{0.04 - 0.0333}{\sqrt{(0.0385)\,(0.9615)\left(\frac{1}{500} + \frac{1}{150}\right)}}$$

$$= \frac{0.0067}{0.0370\,(0.002 + 0.0067)}$$

$$= \frac{0.00667}{0.0179} = 0.373$$

Since the level of significance is not specified, it is presumed as 0.05.

Further, since z is standard normal variable, we refer to the Table $T1$ of area under standard normal curve, and look for the value of z area beyond which is 5%.

This value is 1.645.

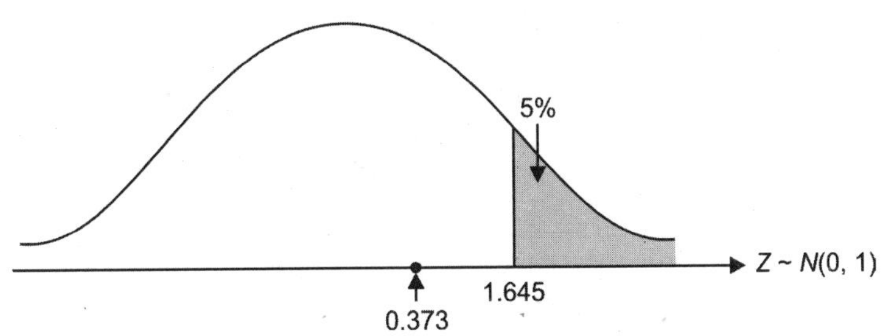

Fig. 16.17: Critical region under normal curve

It may be noted that the entire area of 5% of taken on the right side (tail), as the 'good' the hypothesis is $p_1 > p_2$.

Since the calculated value 0.373 is less than the tabulated value, we do not reject the hypothesis and reject the alternative hypothesis. Thus, we conclude that the machine has improve after overhauling.

(c) One Sided or One Tailed

H_0: $p_1 = p_2$

H_1: $p_1 < p_2$

Just like testing equality of means, choice of p_1 and p_2 is arbitrary. The bigger ratio may be taken as p_1 and the smaller as p_2. Thus, having test for alternative H_1: $p_1 < p_2$ is not necessary.

Confidence Interval for the Difference in the Two Proportions:

EXAMPLE 16.20: A soap manufacturing company wanted to estimate the difference between the proportions of loyal users of its soap in urban and rural areas. In a sample of 1200 users from urban areas, 300 users were found to be loyal users, and in the sample of 1500 from rural areas, 300 were found to be loyal. Let p_1 and p_2 be the proportional of loyal users in urban and rural areas respectively.

(i) What is the point estimate of the difference of proportions of loyal users of the soap in urban and rural areas i.e. $(p_1 - p_2)$, Construct a 95% confidence interval for the proportion of the same.

(ii) At the 1% significance level, can we conclude that the proportion of loyal users of the soap in urban areas is higher than the proportion of loyal users in rural areas?

Solution: Let p_1 and p_2 be the proportions of loyal users of soap from urban and rural areas respectively., From the given information, the estimates of the two sample proportions are calculated as follows:

$$\bar{p}_1 \text{ (urban)} = 300/1200 = 0.25$$

$$\bar{p}_2 \text{ (rural)} = 300/1500 = 0.20$$

Thus $\quad \hat{q}_1 = 1 - 0.25 = 0.75, \quad \hat{q}_2 = 1 - 0.20 = 0.80$

From the above data

(i) The point estimate of $\bar{p}_1 - \bar{p}_2 = 0.05$

The standard error of $(\bar{p}_1 - \bar{p}_2)$ is:

$$S_{\hat{p}_1 - \hat{p}_2} = \sqrt{\frac{\bar{p}_1\bar{q}_1}{n_1} + \frac{\bar{p}_2\bar{q}_2}{n_2}} = \sqrt{\frac{(0.25)(0.75)}{1200} + \frac{(0.20)(0.80)}{1500}} = .0162$$

Thus, the 95% confidence interval for $(p_1 - p_2)$ is:

$(\bar{p}_1 + \bar{p}_2) \pm z_{\sigma/2} s_{\hat{p}_1 - \hat{p}_2} = 0.05 \pm 1.96\ (0.0162) = 0.05 \pm 0.032 =$ **0.018 to 0.082**

(ii) Here, the hypotheses are:

$$H_0:\ p_1 - p_2 = 0 \quad (p_1 \text{ is equal to } p_2)$$
$$H_1:\ (p_1 - p_2) > 0 \quad (p_1 \text{ is greater than } p_2)$$

The test statistic, as given in Example 10.21 is:

$$Z = \frac{\bar{p}_1 - \bar{p}_2}{\sqrt{\left\{\bar{p}\bar{q}\left(\frac{1}{n_1} + \frac{1}{n_2}\right)\right\}}} \sim N(0, 1)$$

where, $$\bar{p} = \frac{300 + 300}{1200 + 1500} = 0.222$$

$\therefore$ $$\bar{q} = 1 - \bar{p} = 1 - 0.222 = 0.778$$

$\therefore$ $$Z = \frac{(0.25 - 0.20)}{.0161} = 3.11$$

Because the value of test statistic $Z = 3.11$ is more than 1.96, and falls in the rejection region, we reject the H_0. Therefore, we conclude that the proportion of loyal users from urban areas is more than that from the rural areas.

16.12 HYPOTHESIS TESTING FOR SMALL SAMPLES ($n < 30$)

In the previous topic we have discussed problems relating to large samples. The large sampling theory is based upon two important assumptions such as

(a) The random sampling distribution of a statistic is approximately normal and

(b) The values given by the sample data are sufficiently close to the population values and can be used in their place for the calculation of the standard error of the estimate.

The above assumptions do not hold well in the theory of small samples. Thus, a new technique is needed to deal with the theory of small samples. A sample is small when it consists of less than 30 items ($n < 30$).

Since in many of the problems it becomes necessary to take a small size sample, considerable attention has been paid in developing suitable tests for dealing with problems of small samples. The greatest contribution to the theory of small samples is that of ***Sir William Gosset*** and ***Prof. R.A. Fisher***. Sir William Gosset published his discovery in 1905 under the pen name 'Student' and later on developed and extended by Prof. R.A. Fisher.

He gave a test popularly known as '***t-test***'.

16.13 STUDENT'S *t*-DISTRIBUTION

If $x_1, x_2, \ldots\ldots x_n$ is a random sample of size n from a normal population with mean μ and variance σ^2, then Student's t-statistic is defined as

$$t = \frac{\bar{x} - \mu}{s/\sqrt{n}}$$

Where $\bar{X} = \frac{\Sigma x}{n}$ is the sample mean

and $s^2 = \frac{1}{n-1}\Sigma(x-\bar{X})^2$

is an unbiased estimate of the population variance σ^2 It follows student's t-distribution with $\upsilon = n - 1$ d.f.

16.13.1 Assumptions for Student's *t*-Test

1. The parent population from which the sample drawn is normal.
2. The sample observations are random and independent.
3. The population standard deviation is not known.

16.13.2 Properties of *t*-Distribution

1. t-distribution ranges from $-\infty$ to ∞ to just as does a normal distribution.
2. Like the normal distribution, t-distribution also symmetrical and has a mean zero.
3. t-distribution has a greater dispersion than the standard normal distribution.
4. As the sample size approaches 30, the t-distribution, approaches the Normal distribution.
5. The t-distribution is more of platykurtic than the normal distribution.

The t-distribution has different shapes depending on the size of the sample. When the sample is quite small, for example if n equals five, the height of the t-distribution is shorter than the normal distribution and the tails are wider. As n nears 30, however, the t-distribution approaches the normal distribution in shape.

Comparison between Normal curve and corresponding *t*-curve:

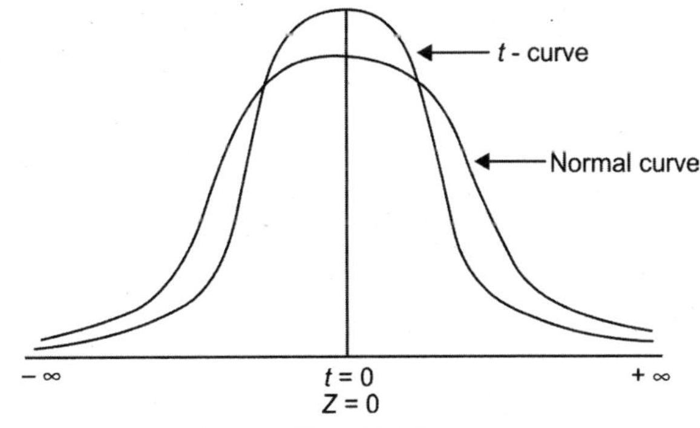

Fig. 16.18

16.13.3 Degrees of Freedom (d.f.)

Suppose it is asked to write any four numbers then one will have all the numbers of his choice. If a restriction is applied or imposed to the choice that the sum of these number should be 50.

Here, we have a choice to select any three numbers, say 10, 15, 20 and the fourth number is 5: [50 – (10 + 15 + 20)]. Thus our choice of freedom is reduced by one, on the condition that the total is 50.

Therefore the restriction placed on the freedom is one and degree of freedom is three. As the restrictions increase, the freedom is reduced.

The number of independent variates which make up the statistic is known as the degrees of freedom and is usually denoted by υ (*Nu*).

The number of degrees of freedom for n observations is $n - k$ where k is the number of independent linear constraint imposed upon them.

For the student's *t*-distribution. The number of degrees of freedom is the sample size minus one. It is denoted by $\upsilon = n - 1$.

When we fit a distribution the number of degrees of freedom is $(n - k - 1)$ where n is number of observations and k is number of parameters estimated from the data.

For e.g., when we fit a Poisson distribution the degrees of freedom is $\upsilon = n - 1 - 1$

In a contingency table the degrees of freedom is $(r - 1)(c - 1)$ where r refers to number rows and c refers to number of columns.

Thus in a 3*4 table the *d.f* are (3 – 1) (4 – 1) = 6 d.f. In a 2*2 contingency table the d.f are (2 – 1) (2 – 1) = 1.

In case of data that are given in the form of series of variables in a row or column the d.f will be the number of observations in a series less one ie $\upsilon = n - 1$

Critical value of t

The column figures in the main body of the table come under the headings $t_{0 \cdot 100}$, $t_{0 \cdot 50}$, $t_{0 \cdot 025}$, $t_{0 \cdot 010}$ and $t_{0 \cdot 005}$. The subscripts give the proportion of the distribution in 'tail' area. Thus for two tailed test at 5% level of significance there will be two rejection areas each containing 2.5% of the total area and the required column is headed $t_{0 \cdot 025}$.

For example,

- $t\upsilon(.05)$ for single tailed test = $t\upsilon(0.025)$ for two tailed test
  $t\upsilon(.01)$ for single tailed test = $t\upsilon(0.005)$ for two tailed test

Thus for one tailed test at 5% level the rejection area lies in one end of the tail of the distribution and the required column is headed $t_{0 \cdot 025}$.

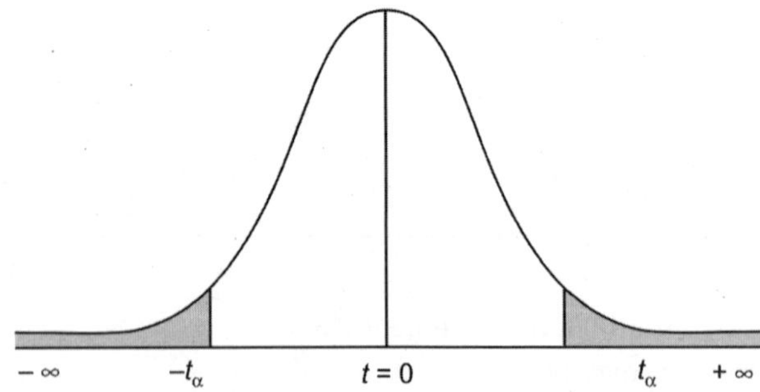

Fig. 16.19: Critical values of *t*-distribution

16.13.4 Applications of *t*-Distribution

The *t*-distribution has a number of applications in statistics of which we shall discuss the following in the coming sections:

- t-test for significance of single mean, population variance being unknown.
- t-test for significance of the difference between two sample means, the population variances being equal but unknown.
  (a) Independent samples
  (b) Related samples: paired t-test

16.13.5 Test of Significance for Mean

When the population distribution is normal and standard deviation s is unknown then "t" statistic is defined as:

$$t = \frac{\bar{X} - \mu}{s_{\bar{X}}} = \frac{\bar{X} - \mu}{s/\sqrt{n}}$$

follows the student's t-distribution with $(n - 1)$ d.f.

Where $\bar{X} = \frac{\Sigma x}{n}$ is the sample mean

μ = hypothesized population mean

n = sample size

and S is the standard deviation of sample calculated by the formula:

$$s = \sqrt{\frac{\Sigma(x - \bar{X})^2}{n - 1}}$$

Test procedure

1. Null and Alternative Hypotheses:

H_0: $\mu = \mu_0$; There is no significant difference between the sample mean and population Mean

H_1: $\mu \neq \mu_0$ ($\mu < \mu_0$ (or) $\mu > \mu_0$)

2. Level of Significance: 5% or 1%

3. Calculation of Statistic: Under H_0 the test statistic is

$$t_0 = \frac{\bar{x} - \mu}{\frac{S}{\sqrt{n}}} \text{ or } \frac{\bar{x} - \mu}{s/\sqrt{n-1}}$$

4. Expected value: $t_e = \frac{\bar{X} - \mu}{\frac{S}{\sqrt{n}}}$ ~ student's t-distribution with $(n - 1)$ d.f.

5. Inference: If $t_0 \leq t_e$ it falls in the acceptance region and the null hypothesis is accepted and if $t_0 > t_e$ the null hypothesis H_0 may be rejected at the given level of significance.

(a) $\boldsymbol{H_0}$: $\mu = \mu_0$

$\mu \neq \mu_0$

EXAMPLE 16.21: A sample size of 10 drawn from a normal population has mean as 31, and variance as 2.25. It is reasonable to assume that the mean of the population is 30? Assume $\alpha = 0.01$.

Solution: This is the situation corresponding to testing the hypothesis that the population mean has a specified value m_0 when s.d. (σ) of the population is not known. The appropriate test is the students '*t*' test with:

$$H_0: \mu = 30$$
$$H_1: \mu \neq 30$$

The test statistic is

$$t = \frac{\bar{X} - \mu_0}{s/\sqrt{n}} \sim \text{students '}t\text{' distribution with } (n-1) \text{ d.f.}$$

where, $\bar{X}$ is the sample mean, and
s is the sample standard deviation

In the given case

$$n = 10$$
$$\bar{X} = 31$$
$$s = \sqrt{2.25} = 1.5$$

Thus,

$$'t' = \frac{31 - 30}{1.5/\sqrt{10}} = \frac{1}{0.474}$$
$$= 2.11$$

The tabulate value of '*t*' with $(n-1) = (10-1) = 9$ d.f. at 1% level of significance vide Table *T*2 is 3.25.

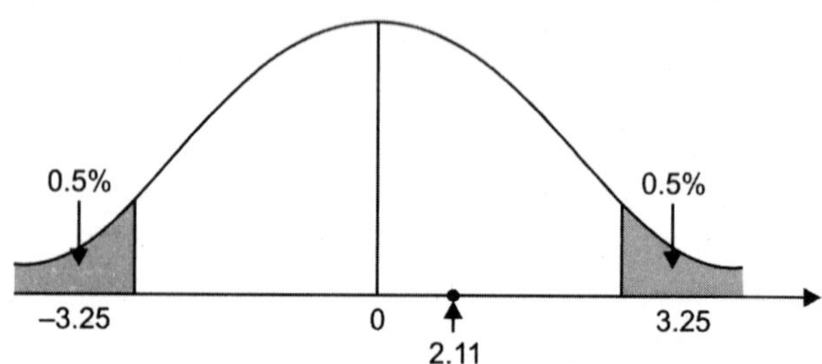

Fig. 16.20: Area under '*t*' distribution

Since the calculated value 2.11 is less than 3.25 and falls in the acceptance region, we do not reject the null hypothesis H_0 that the population mean age of the whole batch is 30. It is therefore reasonable to assume that the population mean is 30.

If the sample size is large say ³ 30, '*t*' distribution may be approximated by the normal distribution and instead of *t* statistic, one may use *Z* statistic $= \frac{\bar{X} - \mu_0}{s/\sqrt{n}} \sim N(0, 1)$.

EXAMPLE 16.22: Certain pesticide is packed into bags by a machine. A random sample of 10 bags is drawn and their contents are found to weigh (in kg) as follows:

50 49 52 44 45 48 46 45 49 45 Test if the average packing can be taken to be 50 kg.

Solution:

Null Hypothesis: H_0: μ = 50 kgs in the average packing is 50 kgs.

Alternative Hypothesis: H_1: μ ≠ 50 kgs (Two-tailed)

Level of Significance: Let $\sigma = 0.05$

Calculation of Sample Mean and S.D

X	d = x – 48	d^2
50	2	4
49	1	1
52	4	16
44	–4	16
45	–3	9
A 48	0	0
46	–2	4
45	–3	9
49	+1	1
45	–3	9
Total	**$\Sigma d = -7$**	**$\Sigma d^2 = 69$**

$$\bar{X} = A + \frac{\Sigma d}{n}$$

$$= 48 + \frac{-7}{10}$$

$$= 48 - 0.7 = 47.3$$

$$s^2 = \frac{1}{n-1}\left[\Sigma d^2 - \frac{(\Sigma d)^2}{n}\right]$$

$$= \frac{1}{9}\left[69 - \frac{(7^2)}{10}\right] = \frac{64.1}{9} = 7.12$$

Calculation of Statistic: Under H_0 the test statistic is:

$$t_0 = \frac{\bar{X} - \mu}{\sqrt{s^2/n}} = \frac{47.3 - 50.0}{\sqrt{7.12/10}}$$

$$= \frac{2.7}{\sqrt{0.712}} = 3.2$$

Expected Value: $t_e = \dfrac{\bar{X} - \mu}{\sqrt{s^2/n}}$ follows t distribution with (10 – 1) d.f.

$$= 2.262$$

Inference: Since $t_0 > t_e$, H_0 is rejected at 5% level of significance and we conclude that the average packing cannot be taken to be 50 kgs.

(b) $\mu = \mu_0$

$\mu > \mu_0$

EXAMPLE 16.23: A soap manufacturing company was distributing a particular brand of soap through a large number of retail shops. Before a heavy advertisement campaign, the mean sales per week per shop was 140 dozens. After the campaign, a sample of 26 shops was taken and the mean sales was found to be 147 dozens with standard deviation 16. Can you consider the advertisement effective?

Solution: We are given $n = 26$; $x = 147$ dozens; $s = 16$

Null Hypothesis: H_0: μ= 140 dozens i.e. Advertisement is not effective.

Alternative Hypothesis: H_1: μ > 140 kgs (Right-tailed)

Calculation of Statistic: Under the null hypothesis H_0, the test statistic is

$$t_0 = \frac{\bar{X} - \mu}{s/\sqrt{n-1}}$$

$$= \frac{147 - 140}{16/\sqrt{25}} = \frac{7 \times 5}{16} = 2.19$$

Expected Value:

$$t_e = \frac{\bar{X} - \mu}{s/\sqrt{n-1}} \text{ follows } t\text{-distribution with } (26-1) - 25 \text{ d.f.}$$

$$= 1.708$$

Inference: Since $t_0 > t_e$, H_0 is rejected at 5% level of significance. Hence we conclude that advertisement is certainly effective in increasing the sales.

EXAMPLE 16.24: A car manufacturer claims that its new car gives a mileage of at least 10 kms. per litre (km.p.l) of petrol. A sample of 10 cars is taken, and their mileage recorded as follows (in km.p.l):

11.2, 10.7, 11.3, 11.0, 10.8, 10.7, 10.6, 10.7, 10.4.

Is there any statistical evidence to support the claim of the manufacturer about the mileage of its car?

Solution: This is the situation when we have to test that the population mean is at least equal to a specified value. The s.d. is not known, and has, therefore, to be estimated from the sample.

Thus, the appropriate hypotheses are:

H_0: μ = 10

H_1: μ > 10

The appropriate statistics is 't' as follows:

$$t = \frac{\bar{X} - \mu_0}{s/\sqrt{n}}$$

which follows student's 't' distribution with $(n - 1)$ d.f.

In the example,

$$n = 10$$

$$\bar{X} = \text{sample mean} = \frac{\Sigma x_i}{n} \frac{108}{10} = 10.8$$

$$s = \text{s.d. of the sample}$$

The calculations are as follows:

$$s = \sqrt{\frac{\Sigma x_i^2 - n(\bar{X})^2}{n-1}}$$

$$s = \sqrt{\frac{1167.12 - 10 \times (10.8)^2}{9}}$$

$$s = \sqrt{\frac{0.72}{9}}$$
$$= 0.283$$

Thus, the 't' statistic is

$$t = \frac{10.8 - 10}{0.283/\sqrt{10}}$$
$$= 8.94$$

The tabulate value of 't' with $(n - 1) = (10 - 1) = 9$ d.f. and 5% level of significance vide Table T2, is 1.83, the entire critical area being on the right side of 1.83.

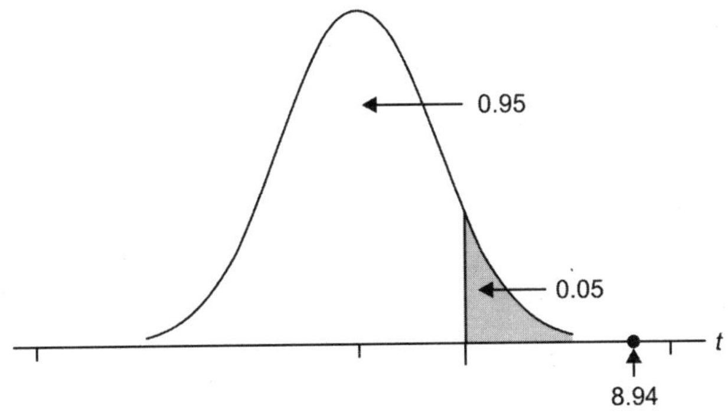

Fig. 16.21

Since the calculated value is more than the tabulated value of $t_{9,\,0.05}(1.83)$ vide Table *T*2, and lies in the critical region, the null hypothesis is rejected i.e. there is sufficient evidence to support the company's claim that the mileage of their car is at least 10 km.p.kl.

(c) H_0: $\mu = \mu_0$
H_1: $\mu < \mu_0$

EXAMPLE 16.25: The mean nicotine content of a brand of cigarette is 20.0 mgs. A new process is proposed to lower the nicotine content without affecting the flavour. To test the new process, 16 cigarettes are selected at random from the week's output from the test plant. The sample mean nicotine content is found to be 18.5 mg. If the s.d. of nicotine contents is calculated to be 2 mgs, is the claim of the new process justified? Use 5% level of significance. **[MBA, 2002, 2003]**

Solution: Since we have to test the hypothesis that the population mean is reduced from 20, the null and alternative hypotheses are set up as

$$H_0: \ \mu = 20.0$$
$$H_1: \ \mu < 20.0$$

The test statistic used is

$$t = \frac{\overline{X} - \mu_0}{s/\sqrt{n}} \quad \text{which is distributed as } t_{15,\,0.05}$$

We are given,

$$\bar{X} = 18.5, \quad \mu_0 = 20, \quad n = 16 \text{ and } s = 2,$$

Therefore,

$$t = \frac{-1.5}{2/\sqrt{16}}$$

$$= \frac{-1.5}{2/4} = -3.0$$

Since, the calculated value of $t(-3.0)$ is less than the tabulated value of $t_{15,\,0.05}$, at 5% level of significance (–1.75), and falls in the critical region, the null hypothesis is rejected, as shown below:

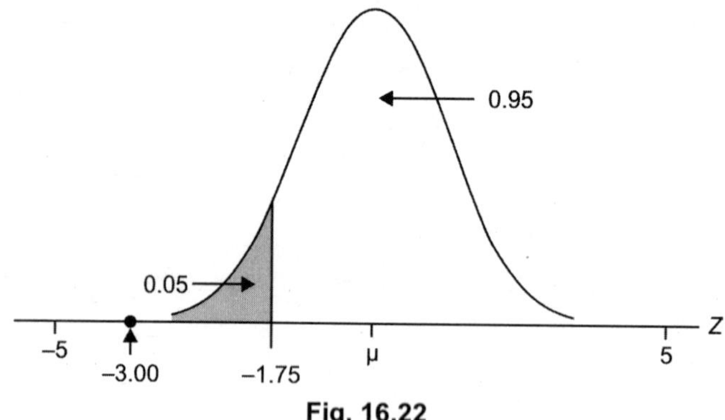

Fig. 16.22

16.13.6 Test of Significance for Difference between Two Means

In testing a hypothesis concerning the difference between the means of two normally distributed populations when the population variance are unknown, the *t*-test can be used in two types of cases:

(a) The case in which variance are equal, i.e. $\sigma_1^2 = \sigma_2^2$.

(b) The case in which variance are not equal, i.e. $\sigma_1^2 \neq \sigma_2^2$.

NOTE: Here we are taking about independent samples.

1. Population Variances are Unknown but Equal

If population variances σ_1^2 and σ_2^2 are unknown but equal, that is, both populations have exactly the same shape and $\sigma_1^2 = \sigma_2^2 = \sigma^2$, then standard error of the difference is two sample means $\bar{X}_1 - \bar{X}_2$ can be written as:

$$\sigma_{\bar{X}_1 - \bar{X}_2} = \sqrt{\frac{\sigma_1^2}{n_1} + \frac{\sigma_2^2}{n_2}} = \sqrt{\sigma^2\left(\frac{1}{n_1} + \frac{1}{n_2}\right)}$$

$$= \sigma\sqrt{\frac{1}{n_1} + \frac{1}{n_2}}$$

In such a case we need not estimate σ_1^2 and σ_2^2 separately and therefore data from two samples can be combined to get a pooled, single estimate of σ^2. If we use the sample estimate s^2 for the population variance s^2, then the pooled variance estimator of σ^2 is given by

$$s^2 = \frac{(n_1 - 1)s_1^2 + (n_2 - 1)s_2^2}{(n_1 - 1) + (n_2 - 1)} = \frac{(n_1 - 1)s_1^2 - (n_2 - 1)\, s_2^2}{n_1 + n_2 - 2}$$

This single variance estimator s^2 is a *weighted average* of the values of s_1^2 and s_2^2 in which weights are based on the degrees of freedom $n_1 - 1$ and $n_2 - 1$. Thus the point estimate of $\sigma_{\bar{X}_1 - \bar{X}_2}$ when $\sigma_1^2 = \sigma_2^2 = \sigma^2$ is given by

$$s_{\bar{X}_1 - \bar{X}_2} = \sqrt{s^2\left(\frac{1}{n_1} + \frac{1}{n_2}\right)} = s\sqrt{\frac{1}{n_1} + \frac{1}{n_2}}$$

Since $s_1 = \sqrt{\dfrac{\Sigma(x_1 - \bar{X}_1)^2}{(n_1 - 1)}}$ and $s_2 = \sqrt{\dfrac{\Sigma(x_2 - \bar{X}_2)^2}{(n_2 - 1)}}$, therefore the pooled variance also be calculated as

$$s^2 = \frac{\Sigma(x_1 - \bar{X}_1)^2 + \Sigma(x_2 - \bar{X}_2)^2}{n_1 + n_2 - 2}$$

Following the same logic as discussed earlier, the t-test statistic is defined as

$$t = \frac{(\bar{X}_1 - \bar{X}_2) - (\mu_1 - \mu_2)}{S_{\bar{X}_1 - \bar{X}_2}}$$

$$\boxed{t = \frac{\bar{X}_1 - \bar{X}_2}{s\sqrt{\dfrac{1}{n_1} + \dfrac{1}{n_2}}} = \frac{\bar{X}_1 - \bar{X}_2}{s}\sqrt{\frac{n_1 n_2}{n_1 + n_2}}}$$

The sampling distribution of this t-statistic is approximated by the t-distribution $n_1 + n_2 - 2$ degrees of freedom.

2. Population Variances are Unknown and Unequal

When two population variances are not equal, we may estimate the standard error $\sigma_{\bar{X}_1 - \bar{X}_2}$ of the statistic $(\bar{X}_1 - \bar{X}_2)$ by sample variances s_1^2 and s_2^2 in place of σ_1^2 and σ_2^2. Thus estimate of standard error of $\bar{X}_1 - \bar{X}_2$ is given by

$$s_{\bar{X}_1 - \bar{X}_2} = \sqrt{\frac{s_1^2}{n_1} + \frac{s_2^2}{n_2}}$$

The sampling distribution of a t-test statistic

$$t = \frac{(\bar{X}_1 - \bar{X}_2) - (\mu_1 - \mu_2)}{s_{\bar{X}_1 - \bar{X}_2}} = \frac{\bar{X}_1 - \bar{X}_2}{s_{\bar{X}_1 - \bar{X}_2}}$$

is approximated by t-distribution with degrees of freedom given by

$$\text{Degrees of freedom (d.f.)} = \frac{[s_1^2/n_1 + s_2^2/n_2]^2}{\frac{(s_1^2/n_1)^2}{n_1 - 1} + \frac{(s_2^2/n_2)^2}{n_2 - 1}}$$

The number of degrees of freedom in this case is less than that obtained is Case 1.

Test Procedure

1. Null Hypothesis:

H_0: $\mu_1 = \mu_2$ i.e. the samples have been drawn from the normal populations with same means.

2. Alternative Hypothesis H_1: $\mu_1 \neq \mu_2$ ($\mu_1 < \mu_2$ or $\mu_1 > \mu_2$)

3. Test statistic: Under the H_0, the test statistic is

$$t_0 = \frac{\bar{X}_1 - \bar{X}_2}{S\sqrt{\frac{1}{n_1} + \frac{1}{n_2}}}$$

Where $\bar{X}_1 = \frac{\Sigma X_1}{n_1}$; $\bar{X}_2 = \frac{\Sigma X_2}{n_2}$

and $s^2 = \frac{1}{n_1 + n_2 - 2}[\Sigma(X_1 - \bar{X}_1)^2 + \Sigma(X_2 - \bar{X}_2)^2]$

$$= \frac{n_1 s_1^2 + n_2 s_2^2}{n_1 + n_2 - 2}$$

4. Expected Value: $t_e = \frac{\bar{X}_1 - \bar{X}_2}{S\sqrt{\frac{1}{n_1} + \frac{1}{n_2}}}$ follows t-distribution with $n_1 + n_2 - 2$ d.f.

5. Inference: If the $t_0 < t_e$ we accept the null hypothesis. If $t_0 > t_e$ we reject the null hypothesis.

EXAMPLE 16.26: A group of 5 patients treated with medicine 'A' weigh 42, 39, 48, 60 and 41 kgs: Second group of 7 patients from the same hospital treated with medicine 'B' weigh 38, 42, 56, 64, 68, 69 and 62 kgs. Do you agree with the claim that medicine 'B' increases the weight significantly?

Solution: Let the weights (in kgs) of the patients treated with medicines A and B be denoted by variables X and Y respectively.

Null hypothesis: H_0: $\mu_1 = \mu_2$

i.e. There is no significant difference between the medicines A and B as regards their effect on increase in weight.

Alternative Hypothesis: H_1: $\mu_1 < \mu_2$ (left – tail) i.e. medicine B increases the weight significantly.

Level of Significance: Let $\alpha = 0.05$

Computation of Sample Means and S.Ds

Medicine A

x_1	$x_1 - \bar{X}_1$	$(x_1 - \bar{X}_1)^2$
42	–4	16
39	–7	49
48	2	4
60	14	196
41	–5	25
230	**0**	**290**

$$\bar{X} = \frac{\Sigma x_1}{n_1} = \frac{230}{5} = 46$$

Medicine B

x_2	$x_2 - \bar{X}_2$	$(x_2 - \bar{X}_2)^2$
38	–19	361
42	–15	225
56	–1	1
64	7	49
68	11	121
69	12	144
62	5	25
399	**0**	**926**

$$\bar{X}_2 = \frac{\Sigma \bar{X}_2}{n_2} = \frac{399}{7} = 57$$

$$s^2 = \frac{1}{n_1 + n_2 - 2}[\Sigma(X_1 - \bar{X}_1)^2 + \Sigma(X_2 - \bar{X}_2)^2]$$

$$= \frac{1}{10}[290 + 926] = 121.6$$

Calculation of Statistics: Under H_0 the test statistic is

$$t_0 = \frac{\bar{X}_1 - \bar{X}_2}{\sqrt{s^2\left(\frac{1}{n_1} + \frac{1}{n_2}\right)}} = \frac{46 - 57}{\sqrt{121.6\left(\frac{1}{5} + \frac{1}{7}\right)}}$$

$$= \frac{11}{\sqrt{121.6 \times \frac{12}{35}}} = \frac{11}{6.57} = 1.7$$

Expected value: $t_e = \dfrac{\bar{x} - \bar{y}}{\sqrt{s^2\left(\frac{1}{n_1} + \frac{1}{n_2}\right)}}$ follows t-distribution with $(5 + 7 - 2) = 10$ d.f.

$= 1.812$

Inference: Since $t_0 < t_e$ it is not significant. Hence H_0 is accepted and we conclude that the medicines A and B do not differ significantly as regards their effect on increase in weight.

EXAMPLE 16.27: Two types of batteries are tested for their length of life and the following data are obtained:

	No. of samples	Mean life (in hrs)	Variance
Type A	9	600	121
Type B	8	640	144

Is there a significant difference in the two means? **[MBA, IGNOU, 2000]**

Solution: We are given $n_1 = 9$; $x_1 = 600$ hrs; $s^2{}_1 = 121$; $n_2 = 8$; $x_2 = 640$ hrs; $s^2{}_2 = 144$

Null Hypothesis: H_0: $\mu_1 = \mu_2$ i.e. Two types of batteries *A* and *B* are identical i.e. there is no significant difference between two types of batteries.

Alternative Hypothesis: H_1: $\mu_1 \neq \mu_2$ (Two-tailed)

Level of Significance: Let $\alpha = 5\%$

Calculation of Statistics: Under H_0, the test statistic is

$$t_0 = \frac{\bar{X}_1 - \bar{X}_2}{\sqrt{s^2\left(\frac{1}{n_1} + \frac{1}{n_2}\right)}}$$

where

$$s^2 = \frac{n_1 s_1^2 + n_2 s_2^2}{n_1 + n_2 - 2} = \frac{9 \times 121 + 8 \times 144}{9 + 8 - 2}$$

$$= \frac{2241}{15} = 149.4$$

∴

$$t_0 = \frac{600 - 640}{\sqrt{149.4\left(\frac{1}{9} + \frac{1}{8}\right)}} = \frac{40}{\sqrt{149.4\left(\frac{17}{72}\right)}} = \frac{40}{5.9391} = 6.735$$

Expected Value:

$$t_e = \frac{\bar{X}_1 - \bar{X}_2}{\sqrt{s^2\left(\frac{1}{n_1} + \frac{1}{n_2}\right)}}$$ follows *t*-distribution with $9 + 8 - 2 = 15$ d.f.

$$= 2.131$$

Inference: Since $t_0 > t_e$ it is highly significant. Hence H_0 is rejected and we conclude that the two types of batteries differ significantly as regards their length of life.

16.13.7 Related Samples–Paired *t*-Test

In the t-test for difference of means, the two samples were independent of each other. Let us now take a particular situations where

(i) The sample sizes are equal; i.e., $n_1 = n_2 = n$ (say), and

(ii) The sample observations x_1, and x_2 are not completely independent but they are dependent in pairs.

That is we are making two observations one before treatment and another after the treatment on the same individual. For example a business concern wants to find if a particular media of promoting sales of a product say door to door canvassing or advertisement in papers or through T.V. is really effective. Similarly a pharmaceutical company wants to test the efficiency of a particular drug, say for inducing sleep after the drug is given. For testing of such claims gives rise to situations in (i) and (ii) above, we apply paired t-test.

If two samples are dependent, they must have the same numbers of units. Instead of obtaining two random samples, we can get one random sample of pairs.

The appropriate test statistic to be used here is

$$t = \frac{\bar{d}}{s/\sqrt{n}}$$

follows t-distribution with $(n - 1)$ d.f. where $\bar{d} = \frac{\Sigma d}{n}$, s is the standard deviation of the differences and is given by

$$s = \sqrt{\frac{\Sigma(d - \bar{d})^2}{n - 1}} = \sqrt{\frac{\Sigma d^2 - n(\bar{d})^2}{n - 1}}$$

$$= \sqrt{\frac{\Sigma d^2}{n - 1} - \frac{(\Sigma d)^2}{n(n - 1)}}$$

and n is the number of paired observations in the samples.

Paired-t-Test

Test Procedure

1. **Null Hypothesis:** H_0: $\mu_1 = \mu_2$ ie the increments are just by chance
2. **Alternative Hypothesis**: H_1: $\mu_1 \neq \mu_2$ ($\mu_1 > \mu_2$ (or) $\mu_1 < \mu_2$)
3. **Calculation of Test Statistic:**

$$t_0 = \frac{\bar{d}}{s/\sqrt{n}}$$

4. **Expected Value:** $t_e = \frac{\bar{d}}{s/\sqrt{n}}$ follows t-distribution with $n - 1$ d.f.
5. **Inference:** By comparing t_0 and t_e at the desired level of significance, usually 5% or 1%, we reject or accept the null hypothesis.

EXAMPLE 16.27: To test the desirability of a certain modification in typists' desks, 9 typists were given two tests of as nearly as possible the same nature, one on the desk in use and the other on the new type. The following difference in the number of words typed per minute were recorded:

Typists	A	B	C	D	E	F	G	H	I
Increase in number of words	2	4	0	3	–1	4	–3	2	5

Do the data indicate the modification in desk promotes speed in typing?

Solution:

Null Hypothesis: $H_0 : \mu_1 = \mu_2$ i.e. the modification in desk does not promote speed in typing.
Alternative Hypothesis: $H_1: \mu_1 < \mu_2$ (Left tailed test)
Level of Significance: Let $\alpha = 0.05$

Typist	d	d^2
A	2	4
B	4	16
C	0	0
D	3	9
E	–1	1
F	4	16
G	–3	9
H	2	4
I	5	25
	$\Sigma d = 16$	$\Sigma d^2 = 84$

$$\bar{d} = \frac{\Sigma d}{n} = \frac{16}{9} = 1.778$$

$$s = \sqrt{\frac{1}{n-1}[\Sigma d^2 - \frac{(\Sigma d)^2}{n}]} = \sqrt{\frac{1}{8}[84 - \frac{(16)^2}{9}]} = \sqrt{6.9} = 2.635$$

Calculation of statistic: Under H_0 the test statistic is

$$t_0 = \left|\frac{\bar{d}.\sqrt{n}}{s}\right| = \frac{1.778 \times 3}{2.635} = 2.024$$

Expected value: $t_e = \dfrac{\bar{d}.\sqrt{n}}{s}$ follows t-distribution $\upsilon = 9 - 1 = 8$, For $\upsilon = 8$, $t_{0.05} = 1.860$

$= 1.860$

Inference: When $t_0 < t_e$ the null hypothesis is accepted. The data does not indicate that the modification in desk promotes speed in typing.

EXAMPLE 16.29: As per Consumer Survey, the consumer confidence indices for some of the cities changed from December 2005 to September 2006, as follows. Is the difference significant?

City	December 2005	September 2006
Delhi	106	83
Jaipur	117	142
Mumbai	112	126
Ahmedabad	123	108
Kolkata	83	84
Bhubaneshwar	137	144
Bangalore	137	138
Kochi	113	134

Solution: The following table gives the data collected and also the calculations required to test the hypothesis that the consumer confidence indices did not change from December 2005 to September 2006.

City	Dec-05	Sep-06	d_i	d_i^2
Delhi	106	83	23	529
Jaipur	117	142	–25	625
Mumbai	112	126	–14	196
Ahmedabad	123	108	15	225
Kolkata	83	84	–1	1
Bhubaneshwar	137	144	–7	49
Bangalore	113	134	–21	441
Sum (Σ)			–31	2067
Average ($\bar{d}$)			**–3.875**	

The statistic to be used is

$$t = \frac{\bar{d}}{s_d \sqrt{n}} \quad \text{is distributed as } t_{n-1} \text{ d.f.}$$

In the above example, $n = 8$, $\bar{d} = -3.875$, and $\Sigma d_i^2 = 2067$

Thus,
$$s_d^2 = \frac{\Sigma(di - \bar{d})^2}{7} = \frac{\Sigma di^2 - 8\bar{d}^2}{7}$$

$$= \frac{2067 - 8 \times (-3.875)^2}{7} = 16.68$$

Therefore,
$$s_d = 5.90$$

$$'t' = \frac{-3.875}{16.68/\sqrt{8}} = \frac{-3.875}{5.90}$$

$$= -0.657$$

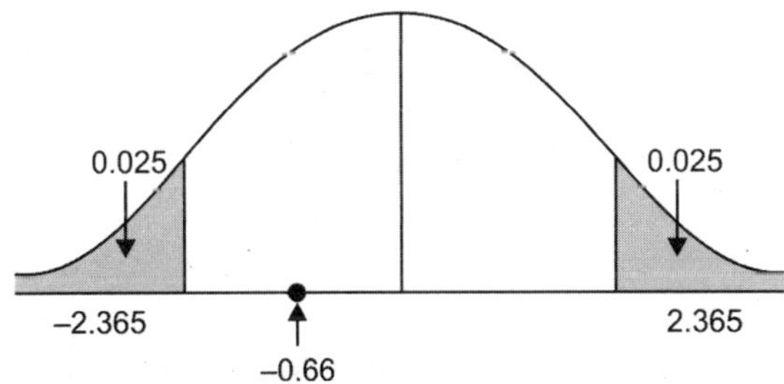

Fig. 16.23: Critical region under '*t*' distribution

The tabulated value of '*t*' at 7 d.fd. and 5% level of significance is 2.365.

Since the calculated value is less than the tabulated value, and it does not fall in the critical region, the null hypothesis is not rejected. This implies that there is no apparent difference in the consumer indices from December 2005 to September 2006.

EXAMPLE 16.30: Five salesmen were imparted a one week specialised training form improving their selling skills. The following data was recorded during the month preceding the training and the month after the training relating to their sales per month. Can we conclude that the training has made any significant impact? **[MBA, Delhi University, 1999]**

Before (Rs. in lakhs)	After (Rs in lakhs)	Difference d_i	d_i^2	$d_i - \bar{d}$	$(d_i - \bar{d})^2$
5	5.5	0.5	0.25	–0.2	0.04
6.2	7	0.8	0.64	0.1	0.01
5.4	5.6	0.2	0.04	–0.5	0.25
4.5	5.5	1	1	0.3	0.09
5.6	6.6	1	1	0.3	0.09
	Sum	**3.5**	**2.93**	**0**	**0.48**
	Average	**0.7**			

The statistic to be used is

$$t = \frac{\bar{d}}{s_d/\sqrt{n}} \text{ distributed as } t_{n-1} \text{ d.f.}$$

In the above example, $n = 5$, $\bar{d} = 0.7$, $\Sigma(d_i - \bar{d})^2 = 0.48$ and $\Sigma d_i^2 = 2.93$

$$s_d^2 = \frac{\Sigma(d_i - \bar{d})^2}{4} \text{ or } \frac{\Sigma d_i^2 - 5(\bar{d}^2)}{4}$$

$$= \frac{2.93 - 5(0.7)^2}{4} = \frac{0.48}{4} = 0.12$$

$$s_d = 0.346 = \frac{0.7}{0.346/\sqrt{5}}$$

Therefore 't' $= \dfrac{0.7}{0.346/\sqrt{5}} = \dfrac{0.7}{0.155}$

The tabulated value of 't' at 5 d.f. and 5% level of significance is 2.78.

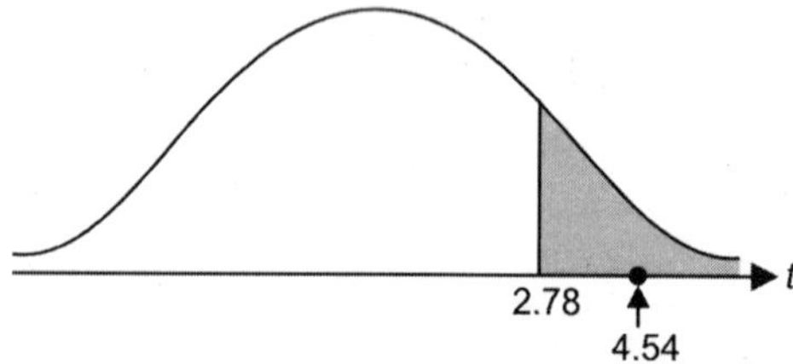

Fig. 16.24: Critical region under 't' distribution

Since the calculated value is more than the tabulated value, it falls in the critical region and the null hypothesis is rejected. Thus, we may conclude that the training has been effective.

16.14 *F*-DISTRIBUTION

The *F*-distribution is named in honour of R.A. Fisher who first studied it in 1924. The distribution is usually defined in term of the ratio of the variances of two normally distributed populations. The quantity

$$\boxed{F = \frac{s_1^2/\sigma_1^2}{s_2^2/\sigma_2^2}}$$

is distributed of *F*-distribution with $\upsilon_1 = n - 1$ and $\upsilon_2 = n_2 - 1$ degrees of freedom.

where $$s_1^2 = \frac{\Sigma(x_1 - \bar{X}_1)^2}{n_1 - 1} \text{ is the unbiased estimator of } \sigma_1^2$$

and $$s_2^2 = \frac{\Sigma(x_2 - \bar{X}_2)^2}{n - 2} \text{ is the unbiased estimator of } \sigma_2^2$$

If $\sigma_1^2 = \sigma_2^2$ then the statistic

$$\boxed{F = \frac{s_1^2}{s_2^2}}$$

follows F-distribution with $n_1 - 1$ and $n_2 - 1$ degree of freedom.

Since F-test is based on the ratio of variances it is also known as the variance ratio test. The ratio of two variances follows a distribution called the F-distribution named after the famous statisticians R.A. Fisher.

The F-distribution depends on the degrees of freedom υ_1 for the numerator and υ_2 for the denominator. Therefore, the parameters for F-distribution are υ_1 and υ_2. For different values of υ_1 and υ_2, we shall have different distribution.

16.14.1 Assumptions for *F*-test

The following assumptions are required for the validity of the 'F'test for comparing variances of two populations.

Normality: The values in each population are normally distributed.

Homogeneity: The variance within each population are equal $(\sigma_1^2 = \sigma_2^2 = \sigma^2)$. The assumption is needed in order to combine or pool the variances within the populations into a single source of variation 'within populations'.

Independence of errors: It stipulates that the error, i.e. variation of each value around its own population mean, should be independent of the value.

16.14.2 Properties of *F*-Distribution

Some of the important properties of F-distribution are given below:

1. If the ratio s_1^2/s_2^2 is nearly equal to 1, then it indicates little evidence that σ_1^2 and σ_2^2 are unequal. On the other hand, a very large or very small value for s_1^2/s_2^2 provides evidence of difference in the population variance.
2. The mean and variance of F-distribution are

$$\text{Mean} = \frac{v_2}{v_2 - 2}, \quad v_2 > 2$$

and $$\text{Variance} = \sigma^2 = \frac{2v_2^2(v_2 + v_2 - 2)}{v_1(v_2 - v_1)^2(v_2 - 4)}, \quad v_2 > 4$$

3. The shape of the F-distribution depends upon the number of degrees of freedom.

4. The variance of F with 1 and n degree of freedom is distributed same as t-distribution with n degrees of freedom.
5. The sample variances S_1^2 and S_2^2 are the unbiased estimates of population variance. Since $S_1 > S_2$. the range of F-distribution curve is from 1 to α.

Test Procedure

1. Null hypothesis: $H_0 = \sigma_1^2 = \sigma_2^2 = \sigma^2$

i.e. population variances are same. In other words H_0 is that the two independent estimates of the common population variance do not differ significantly.

2. Calculation of Statistics: Under H_0, the test statistic is

$$F_0 = \frac{s_1^2}{s_2^2}$$

Where

$$s_1^2 = \frac{1}{n_1 - 1}\Sigma(x - \bar{X})^2 = \frac{n_1 s_1^2}{n_1 - 1}$$

$$s_2^2 = \frac{1}{n_2 - 1}\Sigma(y - \bar{Y})^2 = \frac{n_2 s_2^2}{n_2 - 1}$$

It should be noted that numerator is always greater than the denominator in F-ratio

$$F = \frac{\text{Smaller Variance}}{\text{Larger Variance}}$$

If s_1^2 / s_2^2, and the d.f. for 'F' are $(n_1 - 1)$, $(n_2 - 1)$, then

$$F_0 = \frac{s_1^2}{s_2^2}$$

If S_2^2 / S_1^2, and the d.f. for 'F' are $(n_2 - 1)$, $(n_1 - 1)$, then

$$F_0 = \frac{s_2^2}{s_1^2}$$

3. Expected value: $F_e = \frac{s_1^2}{s_2^2}$ follows F-distribution with $\upsilon_1 = n_1 - 1$, $\upsilon_2 = n_2 - 1$ d.f.

The calculated value of F is compared with the table value for υ_1 and υ_2 at 5% or 1% level of significance If $F_0 > F_e$ then we reject H_0. On the other hand if $F_0 < F_e$ we accept the null hypothesis and it is a inferred that both the samples have come from the population having same variance.

EXAMPLE 16.31: Two random samples drawn from two normal populations Two random samples drawn from two normal populations are:

Sample I	20	16	26	27	22	23	18	24	19	25		
Sample II	27	33	42	35	32	34	38	28	41	43	30	37

Obtain the estimates of the variance of the population and test 5% level of significance whether the two populations have the same variance.

Solution:

Null Hypothesis:

H_0: $\sigma_1^2 = \sigma_2^2$ i.e. The two samples are drawn from two populations having the same variance.

Alternative Hypothesis: $H_1: \sigma_1^2 \neq \sigma_2^2$ (two tailed test)

$$\bar{X}_1 = \frac{\Sigma x_1}{n_1} = \frac{220}{10} = 22$$

$$\bar{X}_2 = \frac{\Sigma x_2}{n_2} = \frac{420}{12} = 35 \qquad [n_1 = 10, n_2 = 12]$$

x_1	$x_1 - \bar{X}_1$	$(x_1 - \bar{X}_1)^2$	x_2	$x_2 - \bar{X}_2$	$(x_2 - \bar{X}_2)^2$
20	–2	4	27	–8	64
16	–6	36	33	–2	4
26	4	16	42	7	49
27	5	25	35	0	0
22	0	0	32	–3	9
23	1	1	34	–1	1
18	–4	16	38	3	9
24	2	4	28	–7	49
19	–3	9	41	6	36
25	3	9	43	8	64
			30	–5	25
			37	2	4
220	**0**	**120**	**420**	**0**	**314**

Level of Significance: 0.05

The statistic F is defined by the ratio

$$F_0 = \frac{s_1^2}{s_2^2}$$

Where

$$s_1^2 = \frac{\Sigma(x_1 - \bar{X}_1)^2}{n_1 - 1} = \frac{120}{9} = 13.33$$

$$s_2^2 = \frac{\Sigma(x_2 - \bar{x}_2)^2}{n_2 - 1} = \frac{314}{11} = 28.54$$

Since $s_2^2 > s_1^2$ larger variance must be put in the numerator and smaller in the denominator

$$F = \frac{28.54}{13.33} = 2.14 \qquad [s_2^2 > s_1^2]$$

Expected Value: $F_e = s_1^2 / s_2^2$ follows F-distribution with

$\upsilon_1 = 12 - 1 = 11$; $\upsilon_2 = 10 - 1 = 9$ d.f = 3.10

Inference: Since $F_0 < F_e$, we accept null hypothesis at 5% level of significance and conclude that the two samples may be regarded as drawn from the populations having same variance.

EXAMPLE 16.32: The following data refer to yield of wheat in quintals on plots of equal area in two agricultural blocks A and B Block A was a controlled block treated in the same way as Block B expect the amount of fertilizers used.

	No. of plots	Mean yield	Variance
Block A	8	60	50
Block B	6	51	40

Use F test to determine whether variance of the two blocks differ significantly?

Solution: We are given that

$n_1 = 8, n_2 = 6, x_1 = 60, x_2 = 51, s_1^2 = 50, s_2^2 = 40$

Null Hypothesis: H_0: $\sigma_1^2 = \sigma_2^2$ ie there is no difference in the variances of yield of wheat.

Alternative Hypothesis: H_1: $\sigma_1^2 \neq \sigma_2^2$ (two tailed test)

Level of Significance: Let $\alpha = 0.05$

Calculation of Statistic:

$$s_1^2 = \frac{n_1 s_1^2}{n_1 - 1} = \frac{8 \times 50}{7} = 57.14$$

$$s_2^2 = \frac{n_2 s_2^2}{n_2 - 1} = \frac{6 \times 40}{5} = 48$$

Since $s_1^2 > s_2^2$

$$F_0 = \frac{s_1^2}{s_2^2} = \frac{57.14}{48} = 1.19$$

Expected Value: $F_e = s_1^2 / s_2^2$ follows F-distribution with

$\upsilon_1 = 8 - 1 = 7$ $\upsilon_2 = 6 - 1 = 5$ d.f = 4.88

Inference: Since $F_0 < F_e$, we accept the null hypothesis and hence infer that there is no difference in the variances of yield of wheat.

LIST OF FORMULAE

1. Type of Test
   - One Tailed Test

     Right Tailed Test

     H_0: $\mu = \mu_0$
     H_1: $\mu > \mu_0$

     Left Tailed Test

     H_0: $\mu = \mu_0$
     H_1: $\mu < \mu_0$

   - Two Tailed Test

     H_0: $\mu = \mu_0$
     H_1: $\mu_1 \neq \mu_2$ ($\mu < \mu_0$ and $\mu > \mu_0$)

2. Test of significance of single mean

 (a) If standard deviation s of the population is known

$$Z = \frac{\bar{X} - \mu}{\sigma_{\bar{X}}} = \frac{\bar{X} - \mu}{s/\sqrt{n}}$$

3. Test of significance for difference between Two Mean

$$Z = \frac{\left(\bar{X}_1 - \bar{X}_2\right) - (\mu_1 - \mu_2)}{\sigma_{\bar{X}_1 - \bar{X}_2}}$$

Where, $\sigma_{\bar{X}_1 - \bar{X}_2} = \sqrt{\frac{\sigma_1^2}{n_1} + \frac{\sigma_2^2}{n_2}}$

If $\sigma_1^2 = \sigma_2^2 = \sigma_2^2$

$$\sigma_{\bar{X}_1 - \bar{X}_2} = \sigma\sqrt{\frac{1}{n_1} + \frac{1}{n_2}}$$

4. Test of significance of single proportion

$$Z = \frac{\bar{p} - p_0}{\sigma_{\bar{p}}} = \frac{\bar{p} - p_0}{\sqrt{\frac{p_o q_o}{n}}}$$

Where, $q_0 = 1 - p_0 \quad \bar{p} = \frac{x}{n}$

5. Test of significance for difference between proportion of two population

$$Z = \frac{\left(\bar{p}_1 - \bar{p}_2\right) - \left(p_1 - p_2\right)}{\sigma_{\bar{p}_1 - \bar{p}_2}}$$

Where, $\sigma_{\bar{p}_1 - \bar{p}_2} = \sqrt{\frac{p_1 q_1}{n_1} + \frac{(p_1 - q_2)}{n_2}}$

If $p_1 q_1 = p_2 q_2 = \bar{p}\,\bar{q}$

$$\sigma_{\bar{p}_1 - \bar{p}_2} = \sqrt{\bar{p}\,\bar{q}\left(\frac{1}{n_1} + \frac{1}{n_2}\right)}$$

6. Test of significance for Mean ($n \leq 30$)

$$t = \frac{\bar{X} - \mu}{\sigma_{\bar{X}}} = \frac{\bar{X} - \mu}{s/\sqrt{n}}$$

7. Test of significance for difference between Two Means ($n \leq 30$)

 - Population variance are unknown but equal

$$s^2 = \sqrt{\frac{(n_1 - 1)s_1^2 + (n_2 - 1)s_2^2}{n_1 + n_2 - 2}}$$

$$= \sqrt{\frac{\left(x_1 - \bar{X}_1\right)^2 + \left(x_2 - \bar{X}_2\right)^2}{n_1 + n_2 - 2}}$$

$$t = \frac{(\bar{X}_1 - \bar{X}_2) - (\mu_1 - \mu_2)}{s_{\bar{X}_1 - \bar{X}_2}}$$

Where, $$s = \sqrt{\frac{(n_1 - 1)s_1^2 + (n_2 - 1)s_2^2}{n_1 + n_2 - 2}}$$

$$= \sqrt{\frac{\left(x_1 - \bar{X}_1\right)^2 + (x_2 - \bar{X}_2)^2}{n_1 + n_2 - 2}}$$

- Population variances are unknown and unequal

$$t_1 = \frac{(x_1 - x_2) - (\mu_1 - \mu_2)}{s_{\bar{X}_1 - \bar{X}_2}}$$

$$= \frac{\bar{X}_1 - \bar{X}_2}{S_{\bar{X}_1 - \bar{X}_2}}$$

Where, $$s_{\bar{X}_1 - \bar{X}_2} = \sqrt{\frac{s_1^2}{n_1} + \frac{s_1^2}{n_2}}$$

8. Paired t-test

$$t = \frac{\bar{d}}{s / \sqrt{n}}$$

Where, $$\bar{d} = \frac{\Sigma d}{n}$$

$$s = \sqrt{\frac{\Sigma(d - \bar{d})^2}{n - 1}} = \sqrt{\frac{\Sigma d^2}{n - 1} - \frac{(\Sigma d)^2}{n(n - 1)}}$$

9. F-test

$$F = \frac{s_1^2 / \sigma_1^2}{s_2^2 / \sigma_2^2}$$

If, $$\sigma_1^2 = \sigma_2^2$$

$$F = \frac{s_1^2}{s_2^2}$$

SELF PRACTICE EXERCISES

I. CHOOSE THE BEST ANSWER

1. Student's '*t*' distribution was pioneered by:
   (a) Karl Pearson (b) Laplace
   (c) R.A. Fisher (d) William S.Gosset
2. While testing the significance of the difference between two sample means in case of small samples, the degree of freedom is:
   (a) $n_1 + n_2$ (b) $n_1 + n_2 - 1$
   (c) $n_1 + n_2 - 2$ (d) $n_1 + n_2 + 2$
3. Paired *t*-test is applicable when the observations in the two samples are:
   (a) Paired (b) Correlated
   (c) Equal in number (d) All the above
4. The mean difference between a paired observations is 15.0 and the standard deviation of differences is 5.0 if $n = 9$, the value of statistic t is:
   (a) 27 (b) 9
   (c) 3 (d) Zero
5. Customarily the larger variance in the variance ratio for *F*-statistic is taken:
   (a) In the denominator (b) In the numerator
   (c) Either way (d) None of the above
6. Large sample theory is applicable when:
   (a) $n > 30$ (b) $n < 30$
   (c) $n < 100$ (d) $n < 1000$

II. FILL IN THE BLANKS

1. The assumption in *t*-test is that the population standard deviation is ....
2. t-values lies in between ....
3. Paired t-test is applicable only when the observations are ....
4. Student t-test is applicable in case of .... samples.
5. Equality of two population variances can be tested by ....
6. F-test is also known as .... ratio test.
7. If $Z_0 < Z_e$ then the null hypothesis is ....
8. When the difference is ...., the null hypothesis is rejected.
9. Test statistic for difference between two proportions is ....
10. The variance of sample mean is ....

III. SHORT ANSWER TYPE QUESTIONS

1. Define students '*t*'-statistic
2. State the assumption of students '*t*' test
3. State the properties of *t*-distribution
4. What are the applications of *t*-distribution?

5. Explain the test procedure to test the significance of mean in case of small samples.
6. What do you understand by paired '*t*' test? What are its assumption.
7. Explain the test procedure of paired—*t*-test
8. Write the variance of difference between two proportions
9. Write the standard error of proportion.
10. Write the test procedure for testing the test of significance for:
    (a) Proportion
    (b) Mean
    (c) Difference between two proportions
    (d) Difference between two mean

IV. LONG ANSWER TYPE QUESTIONS

1. A coin was tossed 400 times and the head turned up 216 times. Test the hypothesis that the coin is unbiased.
2. A person throws 10 dice 500 times and obtains 2560 times 4, 5 or 6. Can this be attributed to fluctuations of sampling?
3. In a hospital 480 female and 520 male babies were born in a week. Does this figure confirm the hypothesis that males and females are born in equal number?
4. In a big city 325 men out of 600 men were found to be self-employed. Does this information support the conclusion that the majority of men in this city are self-employed?
5. A machine puts out 16 imperfect articles in a sample of 500. After machine is overhauled, it puts out 3 imperfect articles in a batch of 100. Has the machine improved?
6. In a random sample of 1000 persons from town A, 400 are found to be consumers of wheat. In a sample of 800 from town B, 400 are found to be consumers of wheat. Do these data reveal a significant difference between town A and town B, so far as the proportion of wheat consumers is concerned?
7. 1000 articles from a factory A are examined and found to have 3% defectives. 1500 similar articles from a second factory B are found to have only 2% defectives. Can it be reasonably concluded that the product of the first factory is inferior to the second?
8. In a sample of 600 students of a certain college, 400 are found to use blue ink. In another college from a sample of 900 students 450 are found to use blue ink. Test whether the two colleges are significantly different with respect to the habit of using blue ink.
9. It is claimed that a random sample of 100 tyres with a mean life of 15269kms is drawn from a population of tyres which has a mean life of 15200 kms and a standard deviation of 1248 kms. Test the validity of the claim.
10. A sample of size 400 was drawn and the sample means B was found to be . Test whether this sample could have come from a normal population with mean 100 and variance 64 at 5% level of significance.
11. The arithmetic mean of a sample 100 items drawn from a large population is 52. If the standard deviation of the population is 7, test the hypothesis that the mean of the population is 55 against the alternative that the mean is not 55. Use 5% level of significance.
12. A company producing light bulbs finds that mean life span of the population of bulbs is 1200 hrs with a standard deviation of 125 hrs. A sample of 100 bulbs produced in a lot is found to have a mean life span of 1150hrs. Test whether the difference between the population and sample means is statistically significant at 5% level of significance.

13. An examination was given to two classes consisting of 40 and 50 students respectively. In the first class the mean mark was 74 with a standard deviation of 8, while in the second class the mean mark was 78 with a standard deviation of 7. Is there a significant difference between the performances of the two classes at a level of significance of 0.05?
14. If 60 M.A. Economics students are found to have a mean height of 63.60 inches and 50 M.Com students a mean height of 69.51 inches. Would you conclude that the commerce students are taller than Economics students? Assume the standard deviation of height of post-graduate students to be 2.48 inches.

ANSWERS

I. CHOOSE THE CORRECT ANSWERS

1. (d) 2. (c) 3. (d) 4. (b) 5. (b) 6. (a)

II. FILL IN THE BLANKS

1. not known
2. $-\infty$ to ∞
3. paired
4. small
5. *F*-test
6. variance
7. accepted
8. significant
9. $\dfrac{P_1 - P_2}{\sqrt{\hat{P}\hat{Q}\left(\dfrac{1}{n_1} + \dfrac{1}{n_2}\right)}}$
10. $\dfrac{\sigma^2}{a}$

IV. LONG ANSWER TYPE QUESTIONS

16. $Z = 1.6$ Accept H_0
15. $Z = 1.265$ Accept H_0
17. $Z = 0.106$ Accept H_0
19. $Z = 1.63$ Accept H_0
21. $Z = 0.5529$ Accept H_0
23. $Z = 4.29$ Reject H_0
25. $Z = 2.49$ Reject H_0
14. $Z = 1.7$ Accept H_0
16. $Z = 2.04$ Accept H_0
18. $Z = 4.247$ Reject H_0
20. $Z = 6.38$ Reject H_0
22. $Z = 2.5$ Reject H_0
24. $Z = 4$ Reject H_0
26. $Z = 12.49$ Reject H_0

CHAPTER 17

CHI-SQUARE TEST

17.1 INTRODUCTION

Various tests of significance described in the previous chapter have mostly applicable to only quantitative data and usually to the data which are approximately normally distributed. It may also happen that we may have data which are not normally distributed. Therefore there arises a need for other methods which are more appropriate for studying the differences between the expected and observed frequencies. The other method is called Non-parametric or distribution free test. A non-parametric test may be defined as a statistical test in which no hypothesis is made about specific values of parameters. Such non-parametric test has assumed great importance in statistical analysis because it is easy to compute.

In this chapter, we will discuss the chi-test which belongs to this category.

17.2 CHI-SQUARE DISTRIBUTION

The square of a standard normal variate is a Chi-square variate with 1 degree of freedom i.e., If χ is normally distributed with mean μ and standard deviation σ, then $\left(\frac{x-\mu}{\sigma}\right)^2$ is a Chi-square variate.

(χ^2) with 1 d.f. The distribution of Chi-square depends on the degrees of freedom. There is a different distribution for each number of degrees of freedom.

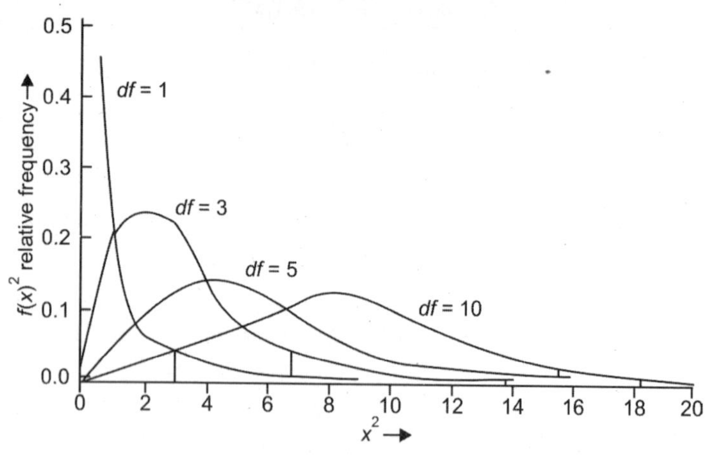

Fig. 17.1

17.3 PROPERTIES OF CHI-SQUARE DISTRIBUTION

1. The Mean of χ^2 distribution is equal to the number of degrees of freedom (n)
2. The variance of χ^2 distribution is equal to $2n$
3. The median of χ^2 distribution divides, the area of the curve into two equal parts, each part being 0.5.
4. The mode of χ^2 distribution is equal to $(n - 2)$
5. Since Chi-square values are always positive, the Chi square curve is always positively skewed.
6. Since Chi-square values increase with the increase in the degrees of freedom, there is a new Chi-square distribution with every increase in the number of degrees of freedom.
7. The lowest value of Chi-square is zero and the highest value is infinity ie $\chi^2 \geq 0$.
8. When Two Chi- squares χ_1^2 and χ_2^2 are independent χ^2 distribution with n_1 and n_2 degrees of freedom and their sum $\chi_1^2 + \chi_2^2$ will follow χ^2 distribution with $(n_1 + n_2)$ degrees of freedom.
9. When n (d.f) > 30, the distribution of $\sqrt{2\chi^2}$ approximately follows normal distribution. The mean of the distribution $\sqrt{2}\,\chi$ is $\sqrt{2}\,n - 1$ and the standard deviation is equal to 1.

17.4 CONDITIONS FOR APPLYING χ^2 TEST

The following conditions should be satisfied before applying χ^2 test

1. N, the total frequency should be reasonably large, say greater than 50.
2. No theoretical cell-frequency should be less than 5. If it is less than 5, the frequencies should be pooled together in order to make it 5 or more than 5.
3. Each of the observations which make up the sample for this test must be independent of each other.
4. χ^2 test is wholly dependent on degrees of freedom.

17.5 THE CHI-SQUARE TEST-STATISTIC

The Chi square (χ^2) test (chi-pronounced as *ki*) is one of the simplest and most widely used non-parametric tests in statistical work.

The χ^2-test was first used by ***Karl Pearson*** in the year 1900. The quantity χ^2 describes the magnitude of the discrepancy between theory and observation. It is defined as:

$$\chi^2 = \sum_{i=1}^{N} \left[\frac{(O_i - E_i)^2}{E_i}\right]$$

Where,

O_i = An observed frequency in a particular category
E_i = An expected frequency for a particular category

The distribution is skewed to the right and the random variable can never take a negative value. Theoretically, its range is from 0 to ∞ as shown in fig. 17.2 values of χ^2 that divide the curve with a proportion of the area is equivalent to ∞ (level of significance) in the right tail.

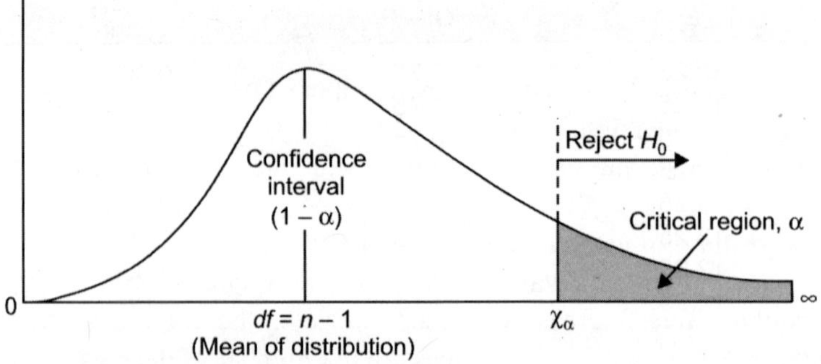

Fig. 17.2

The calculated value of χ^2 is compared with its critical value at a particular level of significance and degrees of freedom. If $\chi_0^2 > \chi_e^2$, then the null hypothesis is rejected in favour of the alternative hypothesis, and it is concluded that the difference between two sets of frequencies is significant.

> If χ^2 is zero, it means that the observed and expected frequencies coincide with each other. The greater the discrepancy between the observed and expected frequencies the greater is the value of χ^2.

Since the mean of χ^2-distribution is equal to the number of degrees of freedom, therefore skewness of this distribution is considerable when the number of degrees of freedom is small, but H reduces as the number of degrees of freedom increases.

EXAMPLE 17.1: The number of breakdowns of machines in a big factory was found as 20, 17, 12, 6, 7, 15, 8, 5, 16 and 14 during the last 10 months period. Test whether these frequencies are in agreement with the belief that occurrence of breakdowns was the same during the 10 months period.

Solution: We are required to test the hypothesis that the observed frequencies of breakdowns during the last 10 months are in equal proportion during the last 10 months. This hypothesis can be tested with the help of χ^2 test, relating to 'goodness of fit'.

The null and alternative hypothesis are as follows:

H_0 : Occurrence of accidents is the same during the last 10 months.
H_1 : Occurrence of accidents is not the same during the last 10 months.

The statistic χ^2 is defined as

$$\chi^2 = \sum \frac{(O_i - E_i)^2}{E_i}$$

where O_i and e_i are the observed and expected frequencies for *i*th month ($i = 1$ to 10), and n is the total frequency. While observed frequencies are:

$$O_i : 20 \quad 17 \quad 12 \quad 6 \quad 8 \quad 5 \quad 16 \quad 14$$

$$n = \Sigma O_i = 98$$

the expected frequencies $e_i s$ are all equal to

$$\frac{n}{8} = \frac{98}{8} = 12.25$$

O_i	E_i	$O_i - E_i$	$(O_i - E_i)^2$	$(O_i - E_i)^2 / E_i$
20	12.25	7.75	60.063	4.903
17	12.25	4.75	22.653	1.842
12	12.25	–0.25	0.0625	0.005
6	12.25	–6.25	39.063	3.189
8	12.25	–4.25	18.063	1.474
5	12.25	–7.25	52.563	4.291
16	12.25	3.75	14.063	4.291
14	12.25	1.75	3.0625	0.25
				$\chi^2 = 17.1$

The χ^2 statistic as calculated in the above table is 17.10.
The d.f. for this χ^2 are $k - 1 = 8 - 1 = 7$.

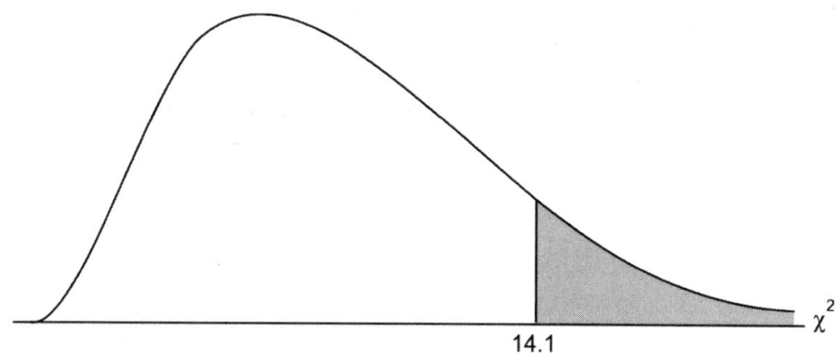

Fig. 17.3: Critical Region Under χ^2 Distribution

Inference: Since the level of significance is not specified, it is taken as 5%. The tabulated value of χ^2 at 5% level of significance and 7b d.f., vide Table T_3, is 14.1. Since the calculated value, 17.1 is more than the tabulated value, and, therefore, lies in the critical region, we reject that occurrence of accidents was the same during the last 10 months.

17.5.1 Grouping When Frequencies Are Small

One or more observations with frequencies less than 1.0 may be grouped together to represent a single category before calculating the difference between observed and expected frequencies. For example, the figure given below are the theoretical (observed) and expected frequencies (based on Poisson distribution) having same mean value and equal number of total frequencies.

Observed frequencies:	125	200	190	180	59	80	9	3
Expected frequencies:	120	210	200	160	60	75	8	4

These 8 frequencies can be reduced to 7 by combining the last two frequencies in both the cases as follows:

Observed frequencies:	125	200	190	180	59	80	12
Expected frequencies:	120	210	200	160	60	75	12

Since the original 8 frequencies have been reduced to 7 by grouping, therefore the revised degree of freedom are d.f. = 6 – 2 = 4, due to two restraints.

17.5.2 Applications of χ^2-Test

A few important application of χ^2-test discussed in this chapter are as follows:

- Test of Goodness-of-fit
- Test of independence
- Yate's correction of continuity

17.6 TEST OF GOODNESS-OF-FIT

Karl Pearson in 1900 developed a test for testing the significance of the discrepancy between experimental values and the theoretical values obtained under some theory or hypothesis. This test is known as χ^2-test of goodness of fit and is used to test if the deviation between observation (experiment) and theory may be attributed to chance or if it is really due to the inadequacy of the theory to fit the observed data.

Under the null hypothesis that there is no significant difference between the observed and the theoretical values. Karl Pearson proved that the statistic

$$\chi^2 = \sum_{i=1}^{n}\left[\frac{(Oi - Ei)^2}{Ei}\right]$$

$$= \frac{(O_1 - E_1)^2}{E_1} + \frac{(O_2 - E_2)^2}{E_2} + \ldots \frac{(O_n - E_n)^2}{E_n}$$

Follows χ^2-distribution with $\upsilon = n - k - 1$ d.f. where O_1, O_2, ...O_n are the observed frequencies, E_1, E_2...E_n, corresponding to the expected frequencies and k is the number of parameters to be estimated from the given data. A test is done by comparing the computed value with the table value of χ^2 for the desired degrees of freedom.

The χ^2-test for goodness-of-fit is a statistical test of how well given data support an assumption about the distribution of a population or random variable of interest. The test determines how well an assumed distribution fits the given data.

Test Procedure

1. **Null Hypothesis (H_0) :** No difference between the observed and expected sets of frequencies.
2. **Alternative Hypothesis (H_1) :** There is a difference.
3. **Level of Significance :** Let α and d.f. = $n - 1$.
4. **Calculation of Statistic :**

$$\chi_0^2 = \sum\frac{(O_i - E_i)^2}{E}$$

- Select a random sample and record the observed frequencies for each category.
- Calculate expected frequencies (E)

5. **Expected Value:**

$$\chi_0^2 = \sum\frac{(O_i - E_i)^2}{E}$$

6. **Inference:**

- If $\chi_0^2 \leq \chi_e^2$, we accept the null hypothesis.
- If $\chi_0^2 > \chi_e^2$, we accept the null hypothesis.

EXAMPLE 17.2: Four coins are tossed simultaneously and the number of heads occurring at each throw was noted. This was repeated 240 times with the following results.

No. of heads	0	1	2	3	4
No. of throws	13	64	85	58	20

Fit a Binomial distribution assuming under the hypothesis that the coins are unbiased.

Solution:

Null Hypothesis:

H_0: The given data fits the Binomial distribution. i.e the coins are unbiased.

$p = q = 1/2$, $n = 4$, $N = 240$

Computation of Expected Frequencies:

No. of heads	$P(X = x) = {}^4C_x p^x q^{n-x}$	Expected frequency N.P $(X = x)$
0	${}^4C_0 \left(\frac{1}{2}\right)^2 \left(\frac{1}{2}\right)^4 = \left(\frac{1}{16}\right)$	$\left(\frac{1}{16}\right) \times 240 = 15$
1	${}^4C_1 \left(\frac{1}{2}\right)^1 \left(\frac{1}{2}\right)^3 = \left(\frac{4}{16}\right)$	$\left(\frac{4}{16}\right)$ $\left(\frac{4}{16}\right) \times 240 = 60$
2	${}^4C_2 \left(\frac{1}{2}\right)^2 \left(\frac{1}{2}\right)^2 = \left(\frac{6}{16}\right)$	$\left(\frac{6}{16}\right)$ $\left(\frac{6}{16}\right) \times 240 = 90$
3	${}^4C_3 \left(\frac{1}{2}\right)^3 \left(\frac{1}{2}\right)^1 = \left(\frac{4}{16}\right)$	$\left(\frac{4}{16}\right) \times 240 = 60$
4	${}^4C_4 \left(\frac{1}{2}\right)^4 \left(\frac{1}{2}\right)^0 = \left(\frac{1}{16}\right)$	$\left(\frac{1}{16}\right) \times 240 = 15$
		240

Computation of Chi-square values

Observed frequency O	Expected frequency E	$(O - E)^2$	$\left(\frac{(O-E)^2}{E}\right)$
13	15	4	0.17
64	60	16	0.27
85	90	25	0.28
58	60	4	0.07
20	15	25	1.67
			2.56

$$\chi_0^2 = \Sigma\left(\frac{(O-E)^2}{E}\right) = 2.56$$

Expected Values: Follows χ^2-distribution with $(n - k - 1)$ d.f. (Here $k = 0$, since no parameter is estimated from the data)

$$= 9.488 \text{ for} = 5 - 1 = 4 \text{ d.f.}$$

Inference: Since $\chi_0^2 < \chi_e^2$ we accept our null hypothesis at 5% level of significance and say that the given data fits Binomial distribution.

EXAMPLE 17.3: The following table shows the distribution of goals in a foot ball

No. of Goals	0	1	2	3	4	5	6	7
No. of Matches	95	158	108	63	40	9	5	2

Fit a Poisson distribution and test the goodness of fit.

Solution:

Null Hypothesis: The given data fits the Poisson distribution.

Level of Significance: Let $\sigma = 0.05$

Computation of Expected Frequencies:

$$m = \frac{812}{480} = 1.7$$

$$P(0) = e^{-1.7}\frac{(1.7)^0}{0!} = 0.183$$

$$f(0) = \text{N.P}(0) = 480 \times 0.183 = 87.84$$

The other expected frequencies will be obtained by using the recurrence formula

$$f(x+1) = \frac{m}{x+1} x\, f(x)$$

Putting $x = 0, 1, 2, \ldots$ we obtain the following frequencies.

$$f(1) = 1.7 \times 87.84 = 149.328$$

$$f(2) = \frac{1.7}{2} \times 149.328 = 126.93$$

$$f(3) = \frac{1.7}{3} \times 126.93 = 71.927$$

$$f(4) = \frac{1.7}{4} \times 71.927 = 30.569$$

$$f(5) = \frac{1.7}{5} \times 30.569 = 10.393$$

$$f(6) = \frac{1.7}{6} \times 10.393 = 2.94$$

$$f(7) = \frac{1.7}{7} \times 2.94 = 0.719$$

No. of goals	0	1	2	3	4	5	6	7	Total
Expected frequency	88	149	127	72	30	10	3	1	480

Computation of Statistic:

Observed frequency *O*	Expected frequency *E*	$(O-E)^2$	$\left(\frac{(O-E)^2}{E}\right)$
95	88	49	0.56
158	150	64	0.43
108	126	324	2.57
63	72	81	1.13
40	30	100	3.33
9, 5, 2 } 16	10, 3, 1 } 14	4	0.29
			8.31

$$\chi_0^2 = \Sigma\left(\frac{(O-E)^2}{E}\right) = 8.31$$

Expected Values: Follows χ^2-distribution with $(n - k - 1)$ d.f. (Here $k = 0$, since no parameter is estimated from the data) = 9.488 for = 6 – 1 – 1= 4 d.f.

Inference: Since $\chi_0^2 < \chi_e^2$ we accept our null hypothesis at 5% level of significance and say that the given data fits Binomial distribution.

EXAMPLE 17.4: A personnel Manager is interested in trying to determine whether absenteeism is greater on one day of the week than on another. His records for the past year show the following sample distributions:

Day of the week	Monday	Tuesday	Wednesday	Thursday	Friday
No. of absentees	66	56	54	48	75

Test whether the absence is uniformly distributed over the week. **[M.Com., Madras University, 1999]**

Solution: Let us assume the null hypothesis that the absence is uniformly distributed over the week.

The number of absentees during a week are 300 and if absenteeism is equally probable on all days, then we should expect 300/5 = 60 absentees on each day of the week. Now arranging the data as follows:

Category	O	E	O – E	(O – E)²	(O – E)²/E
Monday	66	60	6	36	0.60
Tuesday	57	60	–3	9	0.15
Wednesday	54	60	–6	36	0.60
Thursday	48	60	–12	144	2.40
Friday	75	60	–15	225	3.75
					7.50

Inference: The critical value of $\chi^2 = 9.49$ at $\alpha = 0.05$ and d.f. = 5 – 1 = 4. Since calculated value χ_e = 7.50 is less than its critical value, the null hypothesis is accepted.

EXAMPLE 17.5: A survey of 800 families with 4 children each revealed following distribution:

No. of boys	0	1	2	3	4
No. of girls	4	3	2	1	0
No. of families	32	178	290	236	64

Is this result consistent with the hypothesis that male and female births are equally probable?

Solution: Let us assume the null hypothesis that male and female births are equally probable.

The probability of a male or female is $p = q = 1/2$. Since birth of male and female is mutually exclusive and exhaustive, the expected number of families having different combinations of boys and girls can be calculated using binomial probability distribution as follows:

$$P(x = r) = {}^4C_r p^r q^{4-r}\ ;\ r = 0, 1, ..., 4$$

$$= {}^4C_r\ (1/2)4 \text{ since } p = q = 1/2$$

The calculations for expected frequencies for each combination (category) of boy or girl are as shown on next page:

Category (x)	P(x = r)	Expected Frequency, n P(x)
0	${}^4C_0\ (1/2)^4 = 1/16$	800 × (1/16) = 50
1	${}^4C_1\ (1/2)^4 = 4/16$	800 × (4/16) = 200
2	${}^4C_2\ (1/2)^4 = 6/16$	800 × (6/16) = 300
3	${}^4C_3\ (1/2)^4 = 4/16$	800 × (4/16) = 200
4	${}^4C_4\ (1/2)^4 = 1/16$	800 × (1/16) = 50

The apply the χ^2 test, arrange the observed and expected frequencies in the table below:

Category	*O*	*E*	*O* – *E*	$(O-E)^2$	$(O-E)^2/E$
0	32	50	–18	324	6.480
1	178	200	–22	484	2.420
2	290	300	–10	100	0.333
3	236	200	36	1296	6.480
4	75	60	–15	225	3.920
					19.633

Inference: The critical value of $\chi^2 = 9.488$ at $= 0.05$ and d.f. $= 5 - 1 = 4$. Since calculated value of is greater than its table value, the hypothesis is rejected. Hence, we conclude that male and female births do not seem to be equally probable.

17.7 TEST OF INDEPENDENCE: CONTINGENCY ANALYSIS

A different Chi-square test, the Chi-square test of independence, can be used to analyse the frequencies of two variable with the multiple categories to determine whether the two variables are independent.

Many time this type of analysis is desirable.

For example,

- A Market researcher might want to determine whether the type of soft drink preferred by a customer is independence of the consumer's age.
- An organizational behaviourist might want to know whether absenteeism is independent of job classifications.
- Financial investors might want to determine whether type of preferred stock investment is independent of the region where the investor resides.
- Whether voters can be classified by gender is independent of the political affiliation.

The Chi-square test of independence can be used to analyse and level of data measurement, but it particularly useful in analysing nominal data.

Let us suppose that the given population consisting of N items is divided into r mutually disjoint (exclusive) and exhaustive classes $A_1, A_2, \ldots, A_r$ with respect to the attribute A so that randomly selected item belongs to one and only one of the attributes $A_1, A_2, \ldots, A_r$ .Similarly let us suppose that the same population is divided into c mutually disjoint and exhaustive classes $B_1, B_2, \ldots, B_c$ w.r.t another attribute B so that an item selected at random possess one and only one of the attributes $B_1, B_2, \ldots, B_c$. The frequency distribution of the items belonging to the classes $A_1, A_2, \ldots, A_r$ and $B_1, B_2, \ldots, B_c$ can be represented in the following $r \times c$ manifold contingency table.

$r \times c$ manifold contingency table

$A\downarrow$ \ $B\rightarrow$	B_1	B_2	...	B_j	...	B_c	Total
A_1	(A_1B_1)	(A_1B_2)	...	(A_1B_1)	...	(A_1B_c)	(A_1)
A_2	(A_2B_1)	(A_2B_2)	...	(A_2B_1)	...	(A_2B_c)	(A_2)
$\vdots$	$\vdots$	$\vdots$	$\vdots$	$\vdots$	$\vdots$	$\vdots$	$\vdots$
A_i	(A_iB_i)	(A_iB_2)	...	(A_iB_j)	..	(A_iB_c)	(A_i)
$\vdots$	$\vdots$	$\vdots$	$\vdots$	$\vdots$	$\vdots$	$\vdots$	$\vdots$
A_r	(A_rB_1)	(A_rB_2)	...	(A_rB_j)	...	(A_rB_c)	(A_r)
Total	(B_1)	(B_2)	...	(B_j)	...	(B_c)	N

(A_i) is the number of persons possessing the attribute A_i, $(i = 1,2,\ldots r)$, (B_j) is the number of persons possessing the attribute B_j,$(j = 1, 2, 3, \ldots.c)$ and (A_iB_j) is the number of persons possessing both the attributes Ai and B_j $(i = 1, 2,\ldots r, j = 1,2,\ldots c)$.

Also $\Sigma A_i = \Sigma B_j = N$

When observations are classified according to two qualitative variables or attributes and arranged in a table, the display is called contingency table.

Under the null hypothesis that the two attributes A and B are independent, the expected frequency for (A_iB_j) is given by

$$E_{ij} = \frac{\text{Row } i \text{ total}}{\text{Sample size}} \times \frac{\text{Column } J \text{ total}}{\text{Sample size}} \times \text{Grand total}$$

$$= \frac{A_i}{N} \times \frac{B_J}{N} \times N$$

$$\boxed{E_{ij} = \frac{A_i \times B_J}{N}}$$

The analysis of a two-way contingency table helps to answer the question whether the two variables are unrelated or independent of each other.

The null hypothesis for a Chi-square test of independence is that the two variables are independent. If null hypothesis H_0 is rejected, then two variables are not independent but are related.

The χ^2-test statistic measures how much the observed frequencies differ from the expected frequencies when the variable are independent.

Test Procedure

1. **Null Hypothesis (H_0) :** No relationship exists between two variables, that is, they are independent.
2. **Alternative Hypothesis (H_1) :** A relationship exists, that is, they are related.
3. **Level of Significance :** Let α and d.f.
4. **Calculate the expected frequencies:**

$$E = \frac{\text{Row total} \times \text{Column total}}{\text{Grand total}}$$

5. Calculate the degree of freedom:

d.f. = (No. of rows – 1) (No. of column –1) = $(r-1)(c-1)$

6. Calculate of Statistic:

$$\chi_0^2 = \sum \frac{(O_i - E_i)^2}{E_i}$$

7. Inference:

- If $\chi_0^2 \le \chi_e^2$, we accept null hypothesis.
- If $\chi_0^2 > \chi_e^2$, we reject hypothesis.

17.7.1 2 × 2 Contingency Table

Under the null hypothesis of independence of attributes, the value of χ^2 for the 2 × 2 contingency table

			Total
	a	b	a + b
	c	d	c + d
Total	a + c	b + d	N

is given by

$$\chi^2 = \frac{N(ad - bc)^2}{(a+c)(b+d)(a+b)(c+d)}$$

17.8 YATE' S CORRECTION

In a 2 × 2 contingency table, the number of d.f. is (2 – 1) (2–1) =1. If any one of the theoretical cell frequency is less than 5, the use of pooling method will result in d.f = 0 which is meaningless. In this case we apply a correction given by F.Yate (1934) which is usually known as "Yates correction for continuity". This consisting adding 0.5 to cell frequency which is less than 5 and then adjusting for the remaining cell frequencies accordingly. Thus corrected values of χ^2 is given as

$$\chi^2 = \frac{N\left[(a \mp \frac{1}{2})(d \mp \frac{1}{2}) - (b \pm \frac{1}{2})(c \pm \frac{1}{2})\right]^2}{(a+c)(b+d)(a+b)(c+d)}$$

EXAMPLE 17.6: 1000 students at college level were graded according to their I.Q. and the economic conditions of their homes. Use χ^2 test to find out whether there is any association between economic condition at home and I.Q.

Economic Conditions	I.Q.		Total
	High	Low	
Rich	460	140	600
Poor	240	160	400
Total	700	300	1000

Solution: Null Hypothesis: There is no association between economic condition at home and I.Q. i.e. they are independent.

$$E_{11} = \frac{(A)(B)}{N} = \frac{600 \times 700}{1000} = 420$$

The table of expected frequencies shall be as follows.

			Total
	420	180	600
	280	120	400
	700	300	1000
	Total		

Observed frequency *O*	Expected frequency *E*	$(O-E)^2$	$\left(\frac{(O-E)^2}{E}\right)$
460	420	1600	3.81
240	280	1600	5.714
140	180	1600	8.889
160	120	1600	13.333
			31.746

$$\chi_0^2 = \Sigma\left(\frac{(O-E)^2}{E}\right) = 31.746$$

Expected Value: Follow χ^2 distribution with (2 –1) (2 – 1) = 1 d.f. = 3.84

Inference: $\chi_0^2 > \chi_e^2$, hence the hypothesis is rejected at 5 % level of significance. ∴ there is association between economic condition at home and I.Q.

EXAMPLE 17.7: Two hundred randomly selected adults were asked whether TV shows as a whole are primarily entertaining, educational, or a waste of time (only one answer could be chosen). The respondents were categorized by gender. Their responses are given in the following table:

	Opinion			
Gender	**Entertaining**	**Educational**	**Waste f time**	**Total**
Female	52	28	30	110
Male	28	12	50	90
Total	**80**	**40**	**80**	**200**

In this evidence convincing that there is a relationship between gender and opinion in the population interest?

Solution: Let us assume the null hypothesis that the opinion of adults is independent of gender.

The contingency table is of size 2 × 3, the degrees of freedom would be (2 – 1) (3 – 1) = 2, that is, we will have to calculate only two expected frequencies and the other four can be automatically determined as shown below:

$$E_{11} = \frac{\text{Row 1 total} \times \text{Column 1 total}}{\text{Grand total}} = \frac{110 \times 80}{200} = 44$$

$$E_{12} = \frac{\text{Row 1 total} \times \text{Column 2 total}}{\text{Grand total}} = \frac{110 \times 40}{200} = 22$$

$$E_{13} = 110 - (44 + 22) = 44$$
$$E_{21} = 80 - E_{11} = 80 - 44 = 36$$
$$E_{22} = 40 - E_{12} = 40 - 22 = 18$$
$$E_{23} = 80 - E_{13} = 80 - 44 = 36$$

The contingency table of expected frequencies is as follows:

	Opinion			
Gender	**Entertaining**	**Educational**	**Waste f time**	**Total**
Female	44	22	44	110
Male	36	18	36	90
Total	**80**	**40**	**80**	**200**

Arranging the observed and expected frequencies in the following table to calculate the value of χ^2-test statistic.

Observed (O)	Expected (E)	(O – E)	$(O - E)^2$	$(O - E)^2/E$
52	44	8	64	1.454
28	22	6	36	1.636
30	44	14	196	4.455
28	36	–8	64	1.777
12	18	–6	36	2.000
50	36	14	196	5.444
				16.776

Inference: The critical (or table) value of $\chi^2 = 5.99$ at a = 0.05 and *d.f.* = 2. Since the calculated value of $\chi^2 = 16.766$ is more than its critical value, the null hypothesis is rejected. Hence, we conclude that the opinion of adults is not independent of gender.

EXAMPLE 17.8: Of the 1000 workers in a factory exposed to an epidemic,. 700 in all were attacked, 400 had been inoculated, and of these 200 were attacked. On the basis of this information, can it be believed that inoculation and attack are independent?

Solution: Let us assume the null hypothesis that there is no association between inoculation and attack that is, inoculation and attack are independent.

The given information can be arranged in a 2 × 2 contingency table as follows:

Attributes	Attacked	Not attacked	Total
Inoculated	200	200	400
Not inoculated	500	100	600
Total	**700**	**300**	**1000**

Using the result of Section 11.4.3, we have $a = 200$, $b = 200$, $c = 500$, $d = 100$, and $n = 1000$. Thus

$$\chi^2 = \frac{(a+b+c+d)(ab-bc)^2}{(a+b)(c+d)(a+c)(b+d)}$$

$$= \frac{1000(200 \times 100 - 200 \times 500)^2}{(200+200)(500+100)(200+500)(200+100)}$$

$$= \frac{1000 \times (80,000)^2}{400 \times 600 \times 700 \times 300} = \frac{1000 \times 64}{504} = 126.984$$

Inference: The critical value of $\chi^2 = 3.84$ at $\alpha = 0.05$ and d.f. = (2 – 1) (2 – 1) = 1. Since calculated value $\chi^2_e = 126.984$ is more than its critical value, the null hypothesis rejected. Hence, we conclude that inoculation and attack are not independent.

EXAMPLE 17.9: Out of a sample of 120 persons in a village, 76 persons were administered a new drug for preventing influenza and out of them, 24 persons were attacked by influenza. Out of those who were not administered the new drug, 12 persons were not affected by influenza.. Prepare

(i) 2 × 2 table showing actual frequencies.

(ii) Use Chi-square test for finding out whether the new drug is effective or not.

Solution: The above data can be arranged in the following 2 × 2 contingency table.

Table of observed frequencies

	Effect of Influenza		
New drug	**Attacked**	**Not attacked**	**Total**
Administered	24	76 – 24 = 52	76
Not administered	44 –12 = 32	12	120 – 76 = 44
Total	**120 – 64 = 56**	**52 + 12 = 64** **24 + 32 = 56**	**120**

Null Hypothesis: 'Attack of influenza' and the administration of the new drug are independent.

Computation of Statistic:

$$\chi_0^2 = \frac{N(ad - bc)^2}{(a+c)(b+d)(a+b)(c+d)}$$

$$= \frac{120(24 \times 12 - 52 \times 32)^2}{56 \times 64 \times 76 \times 44}$$

$$= \frac{120(-1376)^2}{56 \times 64 \times 76 \times 44} = \frac{120(1376)^2}{56 \times 64 \times 76 \times 44}$$

= Anti log [log 120 + 2 log 1376 – (log 56 + log 64 + log 76 + log 44)]

= Antilog (1.2777) = 18.95

Expected Value: $\chi_e^2 = \Sigma \left(\frac{O - E}{E}\right)^2$ follows χ^2 distribution with (2 –1) × (2 – 1) d.f = 3.84

Inference: Since $\chi_0^2 > \chi_e^2$, H_0 is rejected at 5% level of significance. Hence we conclude that the new drug is definitely effective in controlling (preventing) the disease (influenza).

17.9 TEST FOR POPULATION VARIANCE

The assumption underlying the χ^2-test is that the population from which the samples are drawn is normal.

Suppose we want to test if the given normal population has a specified variance $\sigma^2 = \sigma_0^2$.

Test Procedure

1. **Null Hypothesis:** $H_0: \sigma^2 = \sigma_0^2$ if $x_1, x_2 \ldots x_n$
2. **Level of Significance:** Let α = 5% or 1%
3. **Calculation of Statistic:** $\chi_e^2 = \frac{\sum_{i=1}^{n}(x_i - \bar{x})^2}{\sigma^2} = \frac{ns^2}{\sigma^2}$

Where, $s^2 = \frac{1}{n}\sum_{i=1}^{n}(x_i - \bar{x})^2$

4. **Expected Value:** $\chi_e^2 = \frac{\sum_{i=1}^{n}(x_i - \bar{x})^2}{\sigma_0^2}$ follows c^2 distribution with $(n-1)$ degrees of freedom.
5. **Inference:** If $\chi_0^2 \leq \chi_e^2$ we accept the null hypothesis otherwise if $\chi_0^2 > \chi_e^2$ we reject the null hypothesis.

EXAMPLE 17.10: A random sample of size 20 from a population gives the sample standard deviation of 6. Test the hypothesis that the population Standard deviation is 9.

Solution: We are given $n = 20$ and $s = 6$

Null hypothesis: H_0**:** The population standard deviation is $\sigma = 9$.

Level of Significance: Let α = 5%

Calculation of Statistic: Under null hypothesis H_0:

$$\chi_0^2 = \frac{ns^2}{\sigma^2} = \frac{20 \times 36}{9 \times 9} = 8.89$$

Expected value: $\chi_e^2 = \frac{ns^2}{\sigma^2}$ follows χ^2 distribution 20 – 1

$= 19$ d.f.

$= 30.144$

Inference: Since $\chi_0^2 \leq \chi_0^2$ we accept the null hypothesis at 5% level of significance and conclude that the population standard deviation is 9.

EXAMPLE 17.11: Weights in kgs of 10 students are given below:

38 40 45 53 47 43 55 48 52 and 49.

Can we say that the variance of distribution of weights of all the students from which the above sample of 10 students was drawn is equal to 20 sq kg?

Solution:

Null hypothesis: H_0**:** $\sigma^2 = 20$

Computation of sample variance

Weight in Kg x	$x-\bar{X}$	$(x-\bar{X})^2$
38	–9	81
40	–7	49
45	–2	4
53	6	36
47	0	0
43	–4	16
55	8	64
48	1	1
52	5	25
49	2	4
		280

Sample mean is

$$\bar{X} = \frac{\Sigma x}{n} = \frac{470}{10} = 47$$

Calculation of Statistic: Test statistic is

$$\chi_0^2 = \frac{ns^2}{\sigma^2} = \frac{\Sigma(x-\bar{X})^2}{\sigma^2} = \frac{280}{20} = 14$$

Expected Value: $\chi_e^2 = \frac{ns^2}{\sigma^2}$ follows χ^2 distribution with 10 –1 = 9 d.f. = 16.919

Inference: Since $\chi_0^2 < \chi_e^2$ we accept H_0 and we conclude that the variance of the distribution of weights of all the students in the population is 20 sq. kgs.

LIST OF FORMULAE

1. Chapter 1 test statistic

$$\chi^2 = \sum_{i=1}^{N}\left[\frac{(O_i - E_i)^2}{E_i}\right]$$

2. Expected frequencies for a contingency table

$$E_{ij} = \frac{\text{Row } i \text{ total} \times \text{Column } j \text{ total}}{\text{Sample size}}$$

3. Degree of freedom for a contingency table

d.f. = $(r-1)(c-1)$

SELF PRACTICE EXERCISES

I. CHOOSE THE BEST ANSWER

1. When observed and expected frequencies completely coincide c^2 will be
   (a) –1 (b) +1
   (c) greater than 1 (d) 0

2. For $\upsilon = 2$, $\chi^2_{0.05}$ equals
   (a) 5.9 (b) 5.99
   (c) 5.55 (d) 5.95
3. The calculated value of χ^2 is
   (a) always positive (b) always negative
   (c) can be either positive or negative (d) none of these
4. The Yate's corrections are generally made when the cell frequency is
   (a) 5 (b) < 5
   (c) 1 (d) 4
5. The χ^2 test was derived by
   (a) Fisher (b) Gauss
   (c) Karl Pearson (d) Laplace
6. Degrees of freedom for Chi-square in case of contingency table of order (4 × 3) are
   (a) 12 (b) 9
   (c) 8 (d) 6
7. Customarily the larger variance in the variance ratio for Fstatistic is taken
   (a) in the denominator (b) in the numerator
   (c) either way (d) none of the above
8. The test statistic $F = S_1^2 / S_2^2$ is used for testing
   (a) $H_0: \mu_1 = \mu_2$ (b) $H_0: \sigma_1^2 = \sigma_2^2$
   (c) $H_0: \sigma_1 = \sigma_2$ (d) $H_0: \sigma^2 = \sigma_0^2$

II. FILL IN THE BLANKS

1. The value of χ^2 statistic depends on the difference between .... and .... frequencies .
2. The value of χ^2 varies from .... to ....
3. Equality of two population variance can be tested by ....
4. The χ^2 test is one of the simplest and most widely used .... test.
5. The greater the discrepancy between the observed and expected frequency .... the value of χ^2
6. In a contingency table *n* ....
7. The distribution of the χ^2 depends on the ....
8. The variance of the χ^2 distribution is equal to .... the d.f
9. One condition for application of χ^2 test is that no cell frequency should be ....
10. In a 3 × 2 contingency table, there are .... cells
11. F-test is also known as .... ratio test.

III. SHORT ANSWER TYPE QUESTIONS

1. Define Chi-square distribution. Describe the uses of χ^2 test?
2. What is Yate's corrections?
3. Explain how χ^2 test is used in the test of homogencity.
4. What is χ^2 test of goodness of fit?
5. What precautions should be kept in mind while using the χ^2 test?

IV. LONG ANSWER TYPE QUESTIONS

1. What is χ^2 test of goodness of fit? What cautions are necessary while applying this test?
2. What is χ^2 test? Point out its applications. Under what conditions this test is applicable?
3. Show that the sum of two independent chi-square variables is also a Chi-square variable?
4. Explain Yates's method of correction for small frequencies in contingency table.
5. What is Chi-square test of independence? What cautions are necessary while applying this test?
6. A survey of 320 families with 5 children each revealed the following distribution.

No. of boys	5	4	3	2	1	0
No. of Girls	0	1	2	3	3	5
No. of Families	14	36	110	88	40	12

Is the result consistent with the hypothesis that the male and female births are equally probable?

7. The following mistakes per page were observed in a book.

No. of mistakes per page	0	1	2	3	4	**Total**
No. of pages	211	90	19	5	0	**325**

Fit a Poisson distribution and test the goodness of fit.

8. Out of 800 persons, 25% were literates and 300 had travelled beyond the limits of their district 40% of the literates were among those who had not travelled. Test of 5% level whether there is any relation between travelling and literacy.
9. A random sample of size 10 from a normal population gave the following values

   65 72 68 74 77 61 63 69 73 71

   Test the hypothesis that population variance is 32.
10. A sample of size 15 values shows the s.d to be 6.4. Does this agree with hypothesis that the population s.d is 5, the population being normal.

ANSWERS

I. CHOOSE THE CORRECT ANSWERS

1. (d) 2. (b) 3. (a) 4. (c) 5. (c) 6. (d) 7. (b) 8. (b)

II. FILL IN THE BLANKS

1. Observed, expected 2 0, ∞ 3. F– test 4. non parametric
5. greater 6. $(r-1)(-1)$ 7. degrees of freedom 8. d.f. twice
9. less than 5 10. 6 11. variance

IV. LONG ANSWER TYPE QUESTIONS

6. $\chi^2 = 7.16$ H_0 is accepted
7. $\chi^2 = 0.068$ H_0 is accepted
8. $\chi^2 = 0.0016$ H_0 is accepted
9. $\chi^2 = 7.3156$ H_0 is accepted
10. $\chi^2 = 24.58$ H_0 is rejected

CHAPTER 18

Analysis of Variance (ANOVA)

18.1 INTRODUCTION

In chapters 15 and 16, we studied inference methods concerning a single population mean. In chapter 17, we discussed the comparison of two population means. In this chapter, we develop a method for comparing several population means at the same time. This method is known as *"Analysis of Variance"* through its abbreviated form *'ANOVA'* is more frequently used.

The analysis of variance is a powerful statistical tool for tests of significance. The term Analysis of Variance was introduced by Prof. R.A. Fisher to deal with problems in agricultural research.

The test of significance based on *t*-distribution is an adequate procedure only for testing the significance of the difference between two sample means. In a situation where we have three or more samples to consider at a time, an alternative procedure is needed for testing the hypothesis that all the samples are drawn from the same population, i.e., they have the same mean. For example, five fertilizers are applied to four plots each of wheat and yield of wheat on each of the plot is given. We may be interested in finding out whether the effect of these fertilizers on the yields is significantly different or in other words whether the samples have come from the same normal population. The answer to this problem is provided by the technique of analysis of variance. Thus basic purpose of the analysis of variance is to test the homogeneity of several means.

DO YOU KNOW?

The basic purpose of the analysis of variance is to test the homogeneity of various means.

Variation is inherent in nature. The total variation in any set of numerical data is due to a number of causes which may be classified as:

(i) Assignable causes and (ii) Chance causes

The variation due to assignable causes can be detected and measured whereas the variation due to chance causes is beyond the control of human hand and cannot be traced separately.

According to ***R.A. Fisher***, Analysis of Variance (ANOVA) is the "Separation of Variance ascribable to one group of causes from the variance ascribable to other group".

By this technique the total variation in the sample data is expressed as the sum of its nonnegative components where each of these components is a measure of the variation due to some specific independent source or factor or cause.

Assumptions of ANOVA

For the validity of the F-test in ANOVA the following assumptions are made.

- The observations are independent
- Parent population from which observations are taken is normal and
- Various treatment and environmental effects are additive in nature.

18.2 COMPUTATION OF ANALYSIS OF VARIANCE

The null hypothesis taken while applying analysis of variance technique is that the means of different samples do not differ significantly. The procedure in the analysis of variance would be explained separately for

- One-way classification
- Two-way classification

However, irrespective of the type of classification, the analysis of variance is a technique of partitioning the total sum of squared deviations of all sample values from the grand mean and is divided into two parts-sum of squares between the samples and sum of squares within the samples.

DO YOU KNOW?

Analysis of variance is — The technique implies the analysing or breaking up of variance into portions arising from specified sources and the testing of whether these portions are significantly different.

18.3 ONE WAY CLASSIFICATION

Let us suppose that n observations x_{ij}, $i = 1, 2, \ldots\ldots k\,; j = 1,2\ldots.n_i$) of a random variable X are grouped on some basis, into k classes of sizes $n_1, n_2, \ldots..n_k$ respectively $\left(n = \sum_{i=1}^{k} n_i\right)$ as exhibited below:

				Mean	Total
x_{11}	x_{12}	...	x_1n_1	$\overline{x_1}\bullet$	T_1
x_{21}	x_{22}	...	x_2n_2	$\overline{x_2}\bullet$	T_2
• • •	• • •		• • •	• • •	• • •
x_{i1}	x_{i2}	...	x_in_i	$\overline{x_i}\bullet$	T_i
• • •	• • •		• • •	• • •	• • •
x_{k1}	x_{k2}	...	x_kn_k	$\overline{x_k}\bullet$	T_{ki}
					T

The total variation in the observation x_{ij} can be split into the following two components:

(i) The variation between the classes or the variation due to different bases of classification, commonly known as treatments.

(ii) The variation within the classes i.e., the inherent variation of the random variable within the observations of a class.

The first type of variation is due to assignable causes which can be detected and controlled by human endeavour and the second type of variation due to chance causes which are beyond the control of human hand.

In particular, let us consider the effect of k different rations on the yield in milk of n cows (of the same breed and stock) divided into k classes of sizes $n_1, n_2, \ldots n_k$ respectively.

$$n = \sum_{i=1}^{k} n_i$$

Hence the sources of variation are:

- Effect of the rations
- Error due to chance causes produced by numerous causes that they are not detected and identified.

Calculate Variation between Samples (SST)

This is usually called the '***sum of squares between***' and measures the variation between samples due to treatments. The variance between samples reflects the contribution of both different treatments and chance to inter-sample variability.

The steps in calculating variance between samples will be:

- Calculate the mean of each sample i.e., $\bar{X}_1, \bar{X}_2, \ldots, \bar{X}_k$.
- Calculate the grand mean $\bar{\bar{X}}$.

$$\bar{\bar{X}} = \frac{\bar{X}_1 + \bar{X}_2 + \bar{X}_3 + \ldots + \bar{X}_k}{n_1 + n_2 + n_3 + \ldots + n_k} = \frac{\text{Grand Total}}{\text{Total number of observation}} = \frac{T}{n}$$

- Take the difference between the means as $\bar{X}_1 - \bar{\bar{X}}, \bar{X}_2 - \bar{\bar{X}}, \ldots$
- Square these deviations and obtain the total which will give sum of squares between the samples;

$$\text{Sum of squares between sample (SST)} = \Sigma\Sigma\,(\bar{X}_i - \bar{\bar{X}})^2$$

- Divide the total obtained from above step by the degrees of freedom.

$$\text{Mean sum of squares due to treatments (MSST)} = \frac{\text{SST}}{k-1}$$

Calculate Variation within Samples (SSE)

This is usually called the '***sum of squares within***' and measures the difference within samples due to chance error. The variance within samples measures those inter-sample differences that arise due to change only.

The steps in calculating variance within the samples will be:

- Calculate the mean of each sample i.e., $\bar{X}_1, \bar{X}_2, \ldots, \bar{X}_k$.
- Take the deviations of the various observations in a sample from the mean values of the respective samples.

- Square these deviations and obtain the total which give the sum of squares within the samples;

$$\text{Sum of squares within the sample (SSE)} = \Sigma\Sigma\,(x_{ij} - \bar{X}_j)^2$$

- Divide the total obtained from the above step by the degrees of freedom.

$$\text{Mean sum of squares due to error (MSSE)} = \frac{\text{SSE}}{n-k}$$

Total Variation or Total Sum of Squares

Total variation is represented by the 'total sum of squares' (TSS) and is equal to the sum of the squared differences between each sample value from the grand mean $\bar{\bar{X}}$.

$$\boxed{\text{TSS} = \sum_{i=1}^{k}\sum_{j=1}^{n_j}(xij - \bar{\bar{X}})^2}$$

Where, k = number of sample (or treatment levels)

n_j = size of the sample

This can also be written as,

$$\text{TSS} = \Sigma\Sigma\,(x_{ij} - \bar{X}_i + \bar{X}_i - \bar{\bar{X}})^2$$

or,

$$\boxed{\text{TSS} = \Sigma\Sigma\,(x_{ij} - \bar{X}_i)^2 + \Sigma\Sigma\,(\bar{X}_i - \bar{\bar{X}})^2}$$

[Proof not included]

Thus, we can say that, the total variation is divided into two parts as shown below:

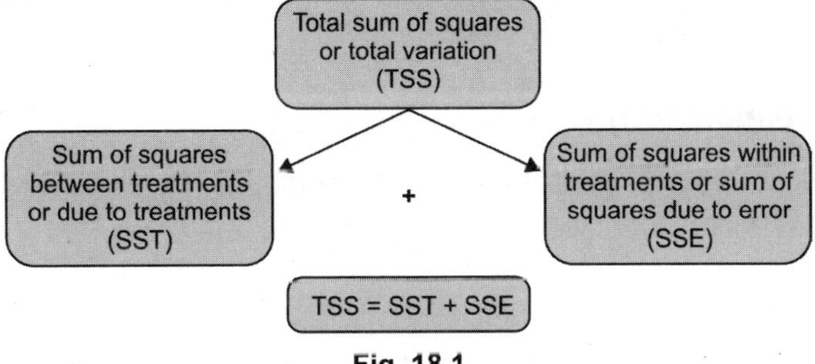

Fig. 18.1

18.4 TEST PROCEDURE FOR ONE-WAY ANALYSIS

The steps involved in carrying out the analysis are:

(1) Null Hypothesis

The first step is to set up of a null hypothesis

H_0: $\mu_1 = \mu_2 = \ldots = \mu_k$

H_1: all μ_i's are not equal ($i = 1, 2, \ldots, k$) [Alternative hypothesis]

(2) Level of Significance

Let α: 0.05

(3) Test Statistic

(a) Calculated the grand total of all observations in samples.

$$T = \Sigma X_1 + \Sigma X_2 + \ldots\ldots + \Sigma X_k$$

(b) Find the sum of values of all the (n) items of the given data. Then correction factor

$$C.F = \frac{T^2}{n} \qquad [n = n_1 + n_2 + \ldots\ldots + n_k]$$

(c) Find the sum of squares of all the individual items (x_{ij}) and then the total sum of squares (TSS) is

$$\text{TSS} = \sum_i \sum_j x_{ij}^2 - C.F$$

(d) Find the sum of squares of all the class totals (or each treatment total) T_i ($i = 1, 2, \ldots, k$) and then the sum of squares between the classes or between the treatments (SST) is

$$\text{SST} = \sum_j \frac{T_i^2}{n_i} - C.F$$

where n_i ($i = 1, 2, \ldots\ldots, k$) is the number of observations in the ith class or number of observations received by ith treatment.

(e) Find the sum of squares within the class or sum of squares due to error (SSE) by subtraction.

$$\text{SSE} = \text{TSS} - \text{SST}$$

(4) Degrees of Freedom (d.f)

The degrees of freedom for total sum of squares (TSS) is ($n - 1$). The degrees of freedom for SST is ($k - 1$) and the degree for SSE is ($n - k$).

(5) Mean Sum of Squares

For testing the equality of means or equal effectiveness of all the k treatments, we compute

(i) Mean Sum of Squares Due to Treatments

$$\text{MST} = \frac{\text{SST}}{k - 1}$$

(ii) Mean Sum of Squares Due to Error

$$\text{MSE} = \frac{\text{SSE}}{n - k}$$

(6) ANOVA Table

The above sum of squares together with their respective degrees of freedom and mean sum of squares will be summarized in the following table.

ANOVA Table for One-Way Classification

Sources of Variation	Degrees of Freedom (d.f)	Sum of Squares (S.S)	Mean Squares (M.S.S)	F-value
Between treatments	$k-1$	SST	$\text{MST} = \dfrac{\text{SST}}{k-1}$	$F = \dfrac{\text{MST}}{\text{MSE}}$
Error	$n-k$	SSE	$\text{MSE} = \dfrac{\text{SSE}}{n-k}$	
Total	$n-1$	**TSS**		

(7) Calculation of Variance Ratio

Variance ratio of F is the ratio between greater variance and smaller variance, thus

$$F = \frac{\text{Variance between the treatment}}{\text{Variance within the treatment}} = \frac{\text{MST}}{\text{MSE}}$$

Important Concept: If variance within the treatment is more than the variance between the treatments, then numerator and denominator should be interchanged and degrees of freedom adjusted accordingly.

(8) Critical Value of *F* or Table Value of *F*

The Critical value of F or table value of F is obtained from F table for $(k-1, n-k)$ d.f at 5% level of significance.

(9) Inference

If calculated F value is less than table value of F, we may accept our null hypothesis H_0 and say that there is no significant difference between treatments.

If calculated F value is greater than table value of F, we reject our H_0 and say that the difference between treatments is significant.

DO YOU KNOW?

If we add, subtract, multiply or divide the given data, the solution will not change.

Coding Method

Something the method for calculating solution takes a lot of computational time due to the magnitude of numerical values of observations. The coding method is based on the fact that the F-test statistic used in the analysis of variance is the ration of variances without unit of measurement. Thus its values does not change if an appropriate constant value is either multiplied, divided, subtracted or added to each of the observations in the sample data. (see example 18.5)

EXAMPLE 18.1: Three processes A, B and C are tested to see whether their outputs are equivalent. The following observations of outputs are made:

A	10	12	13	11	10	14	15	13
B	9	11	10	12	13			
C	11	10	15	14	12	13		

Carry out the analysis of variance and state your conclusion. **[MBA, Anna Univ., 2003]**

Solution: To carry out the analysis of variance, we form the following table

									Total	**Squares**
A	10	12	13	11	10	14	15	13	98	9604
B	9	11	10	12	13				55	3025
C	11	10	15	14	12	13			75	5625
										***T* = 228**

Individual Squares:

A	100	144	169	121	100	196	225	169
B	81	121	100	144	169			
C	121	100	225	196	144	169		
				Total = 2794				

Null Hypothesis: H_0: $\mu_1 = \mu_2 = \mu_3$

i.e., there is no significant difference between the three processes.

Alternative Hypothesis: H_1: $\mu_1 \neq \mu_2 \neq \mu_3$

Level of Significance: Let α: 0.05

Test Statistic:

$$\text{Correct Factor (C.F)} = \frac{T^2}{n}$$

$$= \frac{(228)^2}{19} = \frac{51984}{19} = 2736$$

$$\text{Total sum of squares (TSS)} = \Sigma\Sigma x_{ij}^2 - \text{C.F}$$

$$= 2794 - 2736 = 58$$

$$\text{Sum of squares due to processes} = \text{(SST)}$$

$$= \frac{\sum_{i=1}^{3} T_i^2}{n_i} - \text{C.F}$$

$$= \frac{9604}{8} + \frac{3025}{5} + \frac{5625}{6} - 2736$$

$$= (1200.5 + 605 + 937.5) - 2736$$

$$= 2743 - 2736 = 7$$

$$\text{Sum of squares due to error (SSE)} = \text{TSS} - \text{SST}$$

$$= 58 - 7 = 51$$

ANOVA Table

Sources of Variation	d.f	S.S	M.S.S	*F* ratio
Between Processes	3 –1 = 2	7	7/2 = 3.50	3.5/3.19 = 1.097
Error	16	51	51/16 = 3.19	
Total	**19 – 1 = 18**			

Table Value: Table value of F_e for (2, 16) d.f at 5% level of significance is 3.63

Inference: Since calculated F_0 is less than table value of F_e, we may accept our H_0 and say that there is no significant difference between the three processes.

EXAMPLE 18.2: A test was given to five students taken at random from the fifth class of three schools of a town. The individual scores are:

School I	9	7	6	5	8
School II	7	4	5	4	5
School III	6	5	6	7	6

Carry out the analysis of variance. **[MBA, UPTU, 2002, Kuman Univ., 2004]**

Solution: To carry out the analysis of variance, we form the following tables.

						Total	**Squares**
School I	9	7	6	5	8	35	1225
School II	7	4	5	4	5	25	625
School III	6	5	6	7	6	30	900
					Total	***T* = 90**	**2750**

Individual Squares:

School I	81	49	36	25	64
School II	49	16	25	16	25
School III	36	25	36	49	36
	Total = 568				

Null Hypothesis: $H_0: \mu_1 = \mu_2 = \mu_3$

i.e., there is no significant difference between the performance of schools.

Alternative Hypothesis: $H_1: \mu_1 \neq \mu_2 \neq \mu_3$

Level of Significance: Let α: 0.05

Test Statistic:

$$\text{Correct Factor (C.F)} = \frac{T^2}{n}$$

$$= \frac{(90)^2}{15} = \frac{8100}{15} = 540$$

Total sum of squares (TSS) $= \Sigma\Sigma x_{ij}^2 - \text{C.F}$
$= 568 - 540 = 28$

Sum of squares due to processes $= \dfrac{\Sigma T_i^2}{n_i} - \text{C.F} = \dfrac{2750}{5} - 540$
$= 550 - 540 = 10$

Sum of squares due to error (SSE) = TSS – SST = 28 – 10 = 18.

ANOVA Table

Sources of Variation	d.f	S.S	M.S.S	*F* ratio
Between Schools	3 – 1 = 2	10	10/2 = 5.0	5/1.5 = 3.33
Error	12	18	18/12 = 1.5	
Total	**15 – 1 = 14**			

Table Value: Table value of F_e for (2, 12) d.f at 5% level of significance is 3.8853

Inference: Since calculated F_0 is less than table value of F_e, we may accept our H_0 and say that there is no significant difference between the performance of schools.

18.5 TWO WAY CLASSIFICATION

Let us consider the case when there are two factors which may affect the variate values x_{ij}, e.g the yield of milk may be affected by difference in treatments i.e., rations as well as the difference in variety i.e., breed and stock of the cows. Let us now suppose that the *n* cows are divided into *h* different groups or classes according to their breed and stock, each group containing *k* cows and then let us consider the effect of *k* treatments (i.e., rations given at random to cows in each group) on the yield of milk.

Let the suffix *i* refer to the treatments (rations) and *j* refer to the varieties (breed of the cow), then the yields of milk x_{ij} (i:1,2, …..k; j:1,2….h) of $n = h*k$ cows furnish the data for the comparison of the treatments (rations). The yields may be expressed as variate values in the following $k*h$ two way table.

				Mean	Total
	x_{11}	x_{12}	x_{1j} … x_{1h}	$\overline{X_{1.}}$	$T_{1.}$
	x_{21}	x_{22}	x_{2j} … x_{2h}	$\overline{X_{2.}}$	$T_{2.}$
	• •	• •	• • • •	• •	• •
	x_{i1}	x_{i2}	x_{ij} … x_{ih}	$\overline{X_{i.}}$	$T_{i.}$
	• • •	• • •	• • • • • •	• • •	• • •
	x_{k1}	x_{k2}	x_{kj} … x_{kh}	$\overline{X_{k.}}$	$T_{k.}$
Mean	$\overline{X_{.1}}$	$\overline{X_{.2}}$	… $\overline{X_{.i}}$ … $\overline{X_{.h}}$	$\overline{X}$	
Total	$T_{.1}$	$T_{.2}$	…$T_{.j}$ …$T_{.h}$		T

The total variation in the observation x_{ij} can be split into the following three components:

(i) The variation between the treatments (rations)

(ii) The variation between the varieties (breed and stock)

(iii) The inherent variation within the observations of treatments and within the observations of varieties.

The first two types of variations are due to assignable causes which can be detected and controlled by human endeavour and the third type of variation due to chance causes which are beyond the control of human hand.

18.6 TEST PROCEDURE FOR TWO-WAY ANALYSIS

The steps involved in carrying out the analysis are:

1. Null Hypothesis (H_0)

The first step is to setting up a null hypothesis H_0

$$\mu_{1.} = \mu_{2.} = \ldots = \mu_{k.} = \mu$$
$$\mu_{.1} = \mu_{.2} = \ldots \mu_{.h} = \mu$$

i.e.,

- there is no significant difference between rations
- there is no significant difference between varieties

2. Alternative Hypothesis (H_1)

not all $\mu_{i.}$'s equal

not all $\mu_{.j}$'s equal

3. Level of Significance

Let $\alpha : 0.05$

4. Test Statistic

Various sums of squares are obtained as follows:

(a) Find the sum of values of the entire n $(k \times h)$ items of the given data. Let this grand total represented by 'T'.

Then, $$\text{Correction Factor (C.F)} = \frac{T^2}{n}$$

(b) Find the sum of squares of all the individual items (x_{ij}) and then the

$$\text{Correction Factor (C.F)} = \Sigma\Sigma\, x_{ij}^2 - \text{C.F}$$

(c) Find the sum of squares of all the treatment (rations) totals, i.e., sum of squares of column totals in the $h \times k$ two-ways table. Then the sum of squares between treatments or sum of squares between columns are

$$\text{Sum of squares between columns (SSC)} = \frac{\Sigma T_{i.}^2}{h} - \text{C.F}$$

where h is the number of observations in each column.

(d) Find the sum of squares of all the varieties totals, in the $h \times k$ two-way table. Then the sum of squares between varieties or sum of squares between rows are

$$\text{Sum of squares between rows (SSR)} = \frac{\Sigma T_{.j}^2}{k} - \text{C.F}$$

where k is the number of observations in each row.

(e) Find the sum of squares due to error by subtraction:

$$\text{SSE} = \text{TSS} - (\text{SSR} + \text{SSC})$$

5. Degrees of Freedom (d.f.)

- The degrees of freedom for total sum of squares is $n - 1 = h - k - 1$
- The degrees of freedom for sum of squares between treatments is $k - 1$
- The degree of freedom for sum of squares between varieties is $h - 1$
- The degrees of freedom for error sum of squares is $(k - 1)(h - 1)$

6. Mean Sum of Squares (MSS)

(i) Mean sum of squares for treatments

$$\text{MST} = \frac{\text{SSC}}{(k - 1)}$$

(ii) Mean sum of squares for varieties

$$\text{MSV} = \frac{\text{SSR}}{(h - 1)}$$

(iii) Mean sum of squares for error

$$\text{MSE} = \frac{\text{SSE}}{(h - 1)(k - 1)}$$

7. ANOVA TABLE

ANOVA Table for Two-Way Classification

Sources of Variation	Degrees of Freedom (d.f)	Sum of Squares (S.S)	Mean Squares (M.S.S)	*F*-values
Between treatments (columns)	$k - 1$	SST	MST	$F_c = \frac{\text{MST}}{\text{MSE}}$
Between treatments (rows)	$h - 1$	SSR	MSV	$F_r = \frac{\text{MSV}}{\text{MSE}}$
Error	$(k - 1)(h - 1)$	SSE	MSE	
Total	$n - 1$			

8. Critical values F_e or Table values of F

- The critical value or table value of 'F' for between treatments is obtained from F table for $[(k-1, (k-1)(h-1)]$ d.f at 5% level of significance.
- The critical value or table value of F_e for between varieties is obtained from F table for $[(h-1), (k-1)(h-1)]$ d.f at 5% level of significance.

9. Inference

- If calculated F_0 value is less than or greater than the table value of F_e for between treatments (rows) H_0 may be accepted or rejected accordingly.
- If calculated F_0 value is less than or greater than the table value of F_e for between varieties (column), H_0 may be accepted or rejected accordingly.

EXAMPLE 18.3: To study the performance of three detergents and three different water temperatures, the following 'whiteness' readings were obtained with specially designed equipment:

Water Temperature	Detergent A	Detergent B	Detergent C
Cold water	57	55	67
Warm water	49	52	68
Hot water	54	46	58

Perform a two-way analysis of variance, using 5 per cent level of significance.

[Osmania Univ., MBA, 1998]

Solution:

1. Null Hypothesis (H_0)

$$H_0 : \mu_{1.} = \mu_{2.} = \mu_{3.} = \mu$$
$$H_0 : \mu_{.1} = \mu_{.2} = \mu_{.3} = \mu$$

- i.e., there is no significant difference in the performance of three detergents.
- i.e., there is no significant difference in the water temperature.

2. Alternative Hypothesis (H_1)

- not all $\mu_{i.}$'s equal
- not all $\mu_{.j}$'s equal

3. Level of Significance

Let $\alpha : 0.05$

The data are coded by subtracting 50 from each observation.

To carry out the analysis of variance we form following tables:

Water temperature	Detergents 1	2	3	Total	Squares
	+ 7	+ 5	+ 17	29	841
	– 1	+ 2	+ 18	19	361
	+ 4	– 4	+ 8	8	64
Total	**10**	**3**	**43**	**T = 56**	**1266**
Squares	**100**	**9**	**1849**	**1958**	

Individual Squares

Water Temperature	Detergents		
	1	2	3
	49	25	289
	01	04	324
	16	16	64
	Total = 788		

4. Test Statistic

Sum of all observation (T) = 56

(a) Correction Factor

$$(\text{C.F}) = \frac{T^2}{n} = \frac{(56)^2}{9} = \frac{3136}{9} = 348.44$$

(b) Total Sum of Squares (TSS)

This will be obtained by adding the squares of all the observation in the table and subtracting the correction factor. Thus,

$$\text{Total sum of squares (TSS)} = \Sigma\Sigma\, x_{ij}^2 - \text{C.F}$$

$$= 788 - 348.44 = 439.56 \qquad \text{[from squares table]}$$

(c) Sum of squares between water temperature (Rows)

This will be obtained by dividing the squares of the water temperature totals by the number of observation that make up each total adding all such figures and subtracting these from correction factor (C.F). Thus,

$$\text{Sum of squares between water temperature (SSR)} = \frac{\Sigma T_{i.}^2}{n_i} - \text{C.F}$$

$$= \left[\frac{(29)^2}{3} + \frac{(19)^2}{3} + \frac{(8)^2}{3}\right] - \text{C.F} = \frac{1266}{3} - 348.44 \quad \text{[see the first table]}$$

$$= 422 - 348.44 = 73.56$$

(d) Sum of squares between detergents (Columns)

This will be obtained by squaring the detergents totals, dividing each total by the number of observation included in it, adding these figures and then subtracting the correction factor. Thus,

$$\text{Sum of squares between detergents (SSC)} = \frac{\Sigma T_{.j}^2}{n_j} - \text{C.F}$$

$$= \left[\frac{(10)^2}{3} + \frac{(3)^2}{3} + \frac{(43)^2}{3}\right] - \text{C.F} = \frac{1958}{3} - 348.44 \quad \text{[see the first table]}$$

$$= 652.67 - 348.44 = 304.23$$

(e) Sum of squares for the residual (SSE)

$$\text{SSE} = \text{TSS} - (\text{SSC} + \text{SSR})$$

$$= 439.56 - (304.23 + 73.56)$$

$$= 439.56 - 377.79 = 61.77$$

5. Degrees of Freedom (d.f.)

- The degrees of freedom for sum of squares between treatments $(k - 1) = 2$
- The degree of freedom for sum of squares between varieties $(h - 1) = 2$
- The degrees of freedom for sum of squares $(k - 1)(h - 1) = (3 - 1)(3 - 1) = 4$

6. Mean Sum of Squares (MSS)

$$\text{MST} = \frac{\text{SSC}}{(k-1)} = \frac{304.23}{3-1} = \frac{304.23}{2} = 152.11$$

$$\text{MSV} = \frac{\text{SSR}}{(h-1)} = \frac{73.56}{3-1} = \frac{73.56}{2} = 36.78$$

$$\text{MSE} = \frac{\text{SSE}}{(k-1)(h-1)} = \frac{61.77}{4} = 15.44$$

7. ANOVA Table

The above information is presented in the following table:

ANOVA Table

Sources of Variation	Degrees of Freedom (d.f)	Sum of Squares (S.S)	Mean Squares (M.S.S)	*F*-values
Between detergents (columns)	3 – 1 = 2	304.22	152.11	$F_c = \frac{152.11}{15.44} = 9.58$
Between temperature (rows)	3 – 1 = 2	73.55	36.78	$F_r = \frac{36.78}{15.44} = 2.38$
Error	4	61.77	15.44	
Total	**8**	**439.56**		

Table Value: Table value of F_e for (2.4) d.f at 5% level of significance is 6.94.

8. Inference:

(a) Since calculated value of $F_c = 9.85$ at (2, 4) and $\alpha = 0.5$ is greater than its table value $F_e = 6.94$, the null hypothesis is rejected. Hence we conclude that there is significant difference between the performance of the three detergents.

(b) Since calculated value of $F_r = 2.38$ at (2, 4) and $\alpha = 0.5$ is less than its table value $F_e = 6.94$, the null hypothesis is accepted. Hence we conclude that the water temperature don not make a significant difference in the performance of the detergent.

EXAMPLE 18.4: A company appoints four salesman Anu, Arvind, Abhi and Anoop, and observe their sales in three seasons— summer, winter and monsoon. The figures (in lakhs) are given in the following table:

Season	Salesman			
	Any	Arvind	Abhi	Anoop
Summer	36	36	21	35
Winter	28	29	31	32
Monsoon	26	28	29	29

Carry out an analysis of variance. **[MBA, Madras Univ., 1999]**

Solution: Let us take the null hypothesis that there is no significant difference between the sales of salesman and that of seasons.

Let $\alpha = 0.05$. In order to simplify calculating, we code the data by subtracting 30 from each figure. To carry out the analysis of variance we form following tables:

Season	Salesman					
	Anu	Arvind	Abhi	Anoop	Total	Squares
	+ 6	+ 6	– 9	+ 5	+ 8	64
	– 2	– 1	+ 1	+ 2	0	0
	– 4	– 2	– 1	– 1	– 8	64
Total	0	+ 3	– 9	6	$T = 0$	128
Squares	0	9	81	36	126	

Individual Squares

Season	Salesman			
	Any	Arvind	Abhi	Annop
	36	36	81	25
	4	1	1	4
	16	4	1	1
	Total = 210			

Test Statistic

Sum of Observation (T) = 0

(a) Correction Factor (C.F) $= \dfrac{T^2}{n} = 0$

(b) Total Sum of Squares (TSS) $= \Sigma\Sigma x_{ij}^2 - \text{C.F}$

$= 210 - 0 = 210$

(c) Sum of squares between salesman (columns)

$$SSC = \frac{\Sigma T_{.j}^2}{n_j} - \text{C.F}$$

$$= \frac{126}{3} - 0 = 42$$

(d) Sum of squares between seasons (rows)

$$SSR = \frac{\Sigma T_{i.}^2}{n_i} - \text{C.F}$$

$$= \frac{128}{4} - 0 = 32$$

(e) Sum of squares for the residual error (SSE)

$$SSE = TSS - (SSC + SSR)$$

$$= 210 - (42 + 32)$$

$$= 210 - 74 = 136$$

Degrees of Freedom (d.f.)

- The degrees of freedom for sum of squares between treatments = (4 – 1) = 3
- The degree of freedom for sum of squares between varieties = (3 – 1) = 2
- The degrees of freedom for sum of squares = (4 – 1) (3 – 1) = 6

Mean Sum of Squares (MSS)

$$\text{MST} = \frac{\text{SSC}}{(k-1)} = \frac{42}{3} = 14$$

$$\text{MSV} = \frac{\text{SSR}}{(h-1)} = \frac{32}{2} = 16$$

$$\text{MSE} = \frac{\text{SSE}}{(k-1)(h-1)} = \frac{136}{6} = 22.67$$

ANOVA Table

The above information is presented in the following table:

ANOVA Table

Sources of Variation	Degrees of Freedom (d.f)	Sum of Squares (S.S)	Mean Squares (M.S.S)	*F*-values
Between salesman	3	42	14	$F_c = \frac{22.67}{14} = 1.62$
Between seasons	2	32	16	$F_r = \frac{22.67}{16} = 1.42$
Residual	6	136	22.67	
Total	**11**	**210**		

NOTE: If the value of MSE is greater than the value of MST and MSV. We use the value of MSE is in denominator.

Inference:

(a) Since calculated value $F_c = 1.62$ at (3, 6) and $\alpha = 0.5$ is less than the table value $F_e = 4.76$, we conclude that the sales of salesman do not differ significantly.

(b) Since calculated value of $F_r = 1.42$ at (2, 6) and $\alpha = 0.5$ is less than the table value $F_e = 5.14$. Hence there is no significant difference in the seasons as far as the sales are concerned.

Thus, the test shows that the salesman and the seasons are alike so far as the sales are concerned.

EXAMPLE 18.5: Three varieties of coal were analysed by four chemists and the ash-content in the varieties was found to be as under.

	Chemists			
Varieties	**1**	**2**	**3**	**4**
A	8	5	5	7
B	7	6	4	4
C	3	6	5	4

Carry out the analysis of variance.

Solution: To carry out the analysis of variance we form following tables

	Chemists					
Varieties	**1**	**2**	**3**	**4**	**Total**	**Squares**
A	8	5	5	7	**25**	**625**
B	7	6	4	4	**21**	**441**
C	3	6	5	4	**18**	**324**
Total	**18**	**17**	**14**	**15**	***T* = 64**	**1390**
Squares	**324**	**289**	**196**	**225**	**1034**	

Individual Squares

	Chemists			
Varieties	**1**	**2**	**3**	**4**
A	64	25	25	49
B	49	36	16	16
C	9	36	25	16
	Total = 366			

Null Hypothesis

$$H_0: \mu_{1.} = \mu_{2.} = \mu_{3.} = \mu$$
$$H_0: \mu_{\cdot 1} = \mu_{\cdot 2} = \mu_{\cdot 3} = \mu_{\cdot 4} = \mu$$

- i.e., there is no significant difference between varieties (rows)
- i.e., there is no significant difference between chemists (columns)

Test Statistic

$$\text{Correct factor (C.F)} = \frac{T^2}{n} = \frac{T^2}{h \times k}$$

$$= \frac{(64)^2}{3 \times 4} = \frac{(64)^2}{12} = \frac{4096}{12} = 341.33$$

$$\text{Total sum of squares (TSS)} = \sum_{i-1}^{k} \sum_{j-1}^{k} x_{ij}^2 - \text{C.F}$$

$$= 366 - 34133 = 24.67$$

$$\text{Sum of squares between varieties (Rows)} = \frac{\Sigma T_i^2}{n_i} - \text{C.F}$$

$$= \frac{1390}{4} - 341.33 = 347.5 - 341.33 = 6.17$$

$$\text{Sum of squares between chemists (Columns)} = \frac{\Sigma T_{.j}^2}{n_j} - \text{C.F}$$

$$= \frac{1034}{3} - 341.33 = 344.67 - 341.33 = 3.34$$

Sum of squares due to error (SSE) = TSS – SSR – SSC
= 24.67 – 6.17 – 3.34
= 24.67 – 9.51 = 15.16.

ANOVA Table

Sources of Variation	Degrees of Freedom (d.f)	Sum of Squares (S.S)	Mean Squares (M.S.S)	*F*-values
Between treatments	3 – 1 = 2	6.17	3.085	$F_c = \frac{3.085}{2.527} = 1.22$
Between varieties	4 – 1 = 3	3.34	1.113	$F_r = \frac{2.527}{1.113} = 2.27$
Error	6	15.16	2.527	
Total	**12 – 1 = 11**			

Table Value:

(i) Table value of F_e for (2,6) d.f at 5% level of significance is 5.14.

(ii) Table value of F_e for (6,3) d.f at 5% level of significance is 8.94.

Inference:

(i) Since calculated F_c is less than table value of F_e, we may accept our H_0 for between varieties and say that there is no significant difference between varieties.

(ii) Since calculated F_r is less than the table value of F_e for chemists, we may accept our H_0 and say that there is no significant difference between chemists.

SELF PRACTICE EXERCISES

I. CHOOSE THE BEST ANSWER

1. Equality of several normal population means can be tested by:
   (a) Bartlet's test (b) *F*-test
   (c) ÷2-test (d) *t*-test
2. Analysis of variance technique was developed by:
   (a) S. D. Poisson (b) Karl-Pearson
   (c) R.A. Fisher (d) W. S. Gosset
3. Analysis of variance technique originated in the field of:
   (a) Agriculture (b) Industry
   (c) Biology (d) Genetics
4. One of the assumption of analysis of variance is that the population from which the samples are drawn is:
   (a) Binomial (b) Poisson
   (c) Chi-square (d) Normal
5. In the case of one-way classification the total variation can be split into:
   (a) Two components (b) Three components
   (c) Four components (d) Only one component

6. In the case of one-way classification with n observations and t treatments, the error degrees of freedom is:
   (a) $n - 1$ (b) $t - 1$
   (c) $n - t$ (d) nt
7. In the case of one-way classification with t treatments, the mean sum of squares for treatment is:
   (a) SST/$n - 1$ (b) SST/ $t - 1$
   (c) SST/$n - t$ (d) SST/t
8. In the case of two-way classification with r rows and c columns, the degrees of freedom for error is:
   (a) $(rc) - 1$ (b) $(r - 1) \cdot c$
   (c) $(r - 1)(c - 1)$ (d) $(c - 1) \cdot r$
9. In the case of two-way classification, the total variation (TSS) equals:
   (a) SSR + SSC + SSE (b) SSR – SSC + SSE
   (c) SSR + SSC – SSE (d) SSR + SSC.
10. With 90, 35, 25 as TSS, SSR and SSC respectively in case of two way classification, SSE is:
   (a) 50 (b) 40
   (c) 30 (d) 20

II. FILL IN THE BLANKS

1. The technique of analysis of variance was developed by ....
2. One of the assumptions of Analysis of variance is: observations are ....
3. Total variation in two – way classification can be split into .... components.
4. In the case of one way classification with 30 observations and 5 treatments, the degrees freedom for SSE is ....
5. In the case of two-way classification with 120, 54, 45 respectively as TSS, SSC, SSE, the SSR is ....

III. SHORT ANSWER TYPE QUESTIONS

1. What is analysis of variance?
2. Distinguish between t-test for difference between means and ANOVA.
3. State all the assumptions involved in analysis of variance technique.
4. Explain the structure for one-way classification.
5. Write down the ANOVA table for one-way classification.
6. Distinguish between one-way classification and two-way classification.
7. Explain the structure of two-way classification data.
8. Explain the procedure of obtaining various sums of squares in one-way classification.
9. Write down ANOVA table for two-way classification.

IV. LONG ANSWER TYPE QUESTIONS

1. Explain the procedure of obtaining various sums of squares in two-way classification.

2. A test was given to a number of students taken at random from the eighth class from each of the 5 schools.

The Individual Scores of Schools				
I	II	III	IV	V
8	9	12	10	12
9	7	14	11	1
10	11	15	9	10
7	12	12	12	9
8	13	11	10	13

Carry out the analysis of variance and give your conclusions.

3. The following figures relate to production in kg of three varieties *A*, *B* and *C* of wheat shown in 12 plots.

A	20	18	19		
B	17	16	19	18	
C	20	21	20	19	18

Is there any significant difference in the production of the three Varieties

4. A special type of fertilizer was used in four agricultural fields *A*, *B*, *C* and *D* each field was divided into four beds and the fertilizer was applied over them. The respective yields of the beds of four fields are given below. Find whether the difference in mean yields of fields is significant or not?

Plot Yield			
A	*B*	*C*	*D*
8	9	3	3
12	4	8	7
1	7	2	8
9	1	5	2

5. The following table gives the retail prices of a commodity in (Rs Per Kg) in some shops selected at random in four cities.

A	22	24	20	21
B	20	19	21	22
C	19	17	21	18
D	20	22	21	22

Analysis the data to test the significance of the differences between the price of commodity in four cities.

6. For experiments determine the moisture content of sample of a powder, each man taking a sample from each of six consignments Their assessments are:

	Consignment					
Observer	**1**	**2**	**3**	**4**	**5**	**6**
1	9	10	9	10	11	11
2	12	11	9	11	10	10
3	11	10	10	12	11	10
4	12	13	11	14	12	10

Perform an analysis of variance of these data and discuss if there is any significant difference between consignments or between observers.

ANSWERS

I. CHOOSE THE BEST ANSWERS

1. (b) 2. (c) 3. (a) 4. (d) 5. (a)
6. (c) 7. (b) 8. (c) 9. (a) 10. (c)

II. FILL IN THE BLANKS

1. R.A. Fisher 2. Independent 3. Three 4. 25 5. 21

IV. LONG ANSWER TYPE QUESTIONS

2. Calculated F = 4.56, Table value of F (4,20) = 2.87
3. Calculated F = 9.11, Table value of F (9,2) = 19.39
4. Calculated F = 1.76, Table value of F (12,3) = 8.74
5. Calculated F = 3.29, Table value of F (3,12) = 3.49
6. Calculated FR = 5.03, Table value of F (3,15) = 3.29
   Calculated FC = 2.23, Table value of F (5,15) = 2.90

CHAPTER 19

Association of Attributes

19.1 INTRODUCTION

Association between variables was considered earlier under correlation analysis and in this chapter we discuss association between attributes.

The dictionary meaning of attribute is quality or characteristic. Some examples of attributes are beauty, honesty, gender (male or female), health, employment, smoking, drinking, blindness, etc. The theory of attributes deals with qualitative characteristics which cannot be measured quantitatively. Hence, the study of attributes requires special statistical treatment which is different from that of the study of variables and has been developed independently.

In the study of attributes, the objects (units of the population/sample) are classified according to the presence or absence of the attribute (quality) in them. For example, a person may be classified as smoker or non-smoker, blind or not blind, male or female, employed or un-employed, healthy or sick, literate or illiterate, and so on. This type of classification in which the units of the population are divided into two exhaustive, mutually exclusive classes viz., the one possessing the attribute and the other not possessing the attribute, with respect to one or more of the attributes is called dichotomous classification.

On the other hand, if the units of the population are divided into more than two classes with respect to an attribute, the classification may be termed as manifold classification.

For example, the population, may be divided *w.r.t.* the attribute 'intelligence' into the following classes: (*i*) Genius, (*ii*) Very intelligent, (*iii*) Average intelligent, (*iv*) Below average intelligent, (*v*) Dull.

The purpose of the study of association of attributes is to find out whether a given attribute shows association with the other.

19.2 CLASSIFICATION OF DATA

In the analysis of statistics relating to attribution the first thing is the classification of data. Here data are classified on the basis of presence or absence of particular attributes. If only one attribute, say, blindness, is being studied the population would be divided in two classes– One consisting of those people in whom this attribute is present and the other consisting of those in whom this attribute is not present. Thus one class would be at the 'blinds' and the other of 'non-blinds'.

If more than one attribute are taken into account, the number of classes would be more than two.

19.3 NOTATIONS

The presence of attributes in the units of the population is denoted by the capital letters of the english alphabet, say, *A*, *B*, *C*, *D*, etc., and their absence is denoted by the corresponding small letters of the Greek alphabet, say α, β, γ, δ respectively. For example,

(i) If '*A*' represents the attribute of literacy, then 'α' denotes absence of literacy.
(ii) If '*B*' represents the attribute of blindness then 'β' would represent the absence of blindness.
(iii) If '*C*' represents the attribute of criminality, then 'γ' would represent noncriminality.

NOTE: The number of units possessing a particular attribute represented by *A* would be termed as belonging to class *A*, and similarly those in whom this attribute is absent would be termed as belonging to class α.

The combinations of attributes are denoted by grouping together the corresponding letters. Thus, in the above example, the corresponding attribute *AB* denotes the simultaneous possession of both the attributes *A* and *B* viz. literacy blindness.

Similarly,

ABC represents literacy blindness criminality
βA represents non-blind literacy
AC represents literacy criminality

DO YOU KNOW?

The capital letters *A*, *B*, *C*, *D* etc. used to denote the presence of attributes, may be called positive attribute, while the corresponding Greek letter α, β, γ, δ etc. denote the absence of the attributes, called the negative attributes.

19.4 CLASS AND CLASS FREQUENCIES

Different attributes in themselves are called classes and the number of observations assigned to them are called class frequencies which are denoted by bracking the class symbols.

Thus (*A*) stands for the frequency of *A* and (*AB*) for the number of objects possessing the attributes *AB*.

NOTE:

- Class frequencies of the type (*A*), (*AB*), (*ABC*) etc. are known as frequencies of positive events.
- (α), (αβ), (αβγ) etc. are known as frequencies of negative events.
- (α*B*), (*A*β*C*), (αβ*C*) etc are called the frequency of mixed events.
- (α*A*), (β*B*), (γ*C*) are called the frequencies of complementary events.

19.5 ORDER OF CLASSES AND CLASS FREQUENCIES

A class represented by *n* attributes is called a class of nth order and the corresponding frequency as the frequency of the nth order. Thus (*A*), (*B*), (γ), etc., are class frequencies of order 1; (*AB*), (*A*γ), (α*C*), (βγ), etc., are class frequencies of second order; (*ABC*), (*A*βγ), (*A*βγ), (αβ*C*) etc., are frequencies of third order and so on. N, the total number of member of the population, without any specification of attributes, is known as frequency of zero-order.

If is not placed into braces. Thus,

Order	Frequencies			
0		N		
1.	(A)	(B)	(C)	
	(α)	(β)	(γ)	
2.	(AB)	$(A\beta)$	(αB)	$(\alpha\beta)$
	(AC)	$(A\gamma)$	(αC)	$(\alpha\gamma)$
	(BC)	$(B\gamma)$	(βC)	$(\beta\gamma)$
3.	(ABC)	$(AB\gamma)$	$(A\beta C)$	$(A\beta\gamma)$
	(αBC)	$(\alpha B\gamma)$	$(\alpha\beta C)$	$(\alpha\beta\gamma)$

19.6 TOTAL NUMBER OF CLASS-FREQUENCIES

A class frequency of order r will contain r attributes (symbols). In a dichotomous classification of the population *w.r.t.* n attributes, we can select r attributes out of n in ${}^nC_r$ ways. Further, since each of the r attributes contributes two symbols, [one representing the positive part, say, A and the other representing the negative part, say, α]

Total number of class frequencies of order $r = {}^nC_r \,.\, 2^r \quad ; \quad r = 0, 1, 2, ..., n$ ...(1)

Hence, in case of n attributes, the total number of class frequencies of all orders is:

$$\sum_{r=0}^{n} {}^nC_r 2_r = 1 + {}^nC_1 \,.\, 2 + {}^nC_2 \,.\, 2^2 + ... + {}^nC_n\, 2^n$$

$$= (1 + 2)^n \qquad \text{[By binomial expansion for positive integer index]}$$

$$= 3^n \qquad ...(2)$$

Remarks:

1. In particular, for n attributes, using (1), the total number of class frequencies of different orders are given in.

Order	0	1	2	...	r	...	n
No. of Frequencies	1	$2n$	${}^nC_2 2^2$	...	${}^nC_r 2^r$	...	2^n

2. In case of 3 attributes A, B and C [from (2)], the total number of class frequencies is 33 = 27, as given below:

   The number of positive frequencies in a class of order r is

   ${}^nC_r$; $r = 0, 1, 2, ..., n$. Hence, the total number of positive frequencies is:

$$\sum_{r=0}^{n} {}^nC_r = {}^nC_0 + {}^nC_1 + {}^nC_2 + ... + {}^nC_n$$

$$= (1 + 1)^n = 2^n \qquad ...(3)$$

In particular, for 3 attributes, the total number of positive frequencies is 23 – 8, as given below.

N, (A), (B), (C), (AB), (AC), (BC), (ABC)

19.6.1 Ultimate Class Frequencies

The classes specified by n attributes *i.e.*, those are the highest order are called ultimate class frequencies. Every class frequency can be expressed as the sum of the ultimate class frequencies.

In case of n attributes, the ultimate class frequencies will be the frequencies of the nth order *i.e.*, each of then will contain n symbols. Further, since each symbol can be written in two ways, positive or negative *e.g.*, A or α; B or β, etc.,

Total number of ultimate class frequencies = 2^n

In particular, for two attributes, say, A and B, there are $2^2 = 4$, ultimate class frequencies viz.,

$$(AB), \quad (A\beta), \quad (\alpha B) \text{ and } (\alpha\beta)$$

For three attributes, say, A, B, and C, there are $2^3 = 8$, ultimate class frequencies viz.,

$$(ABC), \ (A\beta C), \ (\alpha BC), \ (\alpha\beta C), \ (AB\gamma), \ (A\beta\gamma), \ (\alpha B\gamma) \text{ and } (\alpha\beta\gamma)$$

19.7 RELATIONSHIP BETWEEN CLASSES OF VARIOUS ORDER

In classifying statistical data according to attributes the following simple rule should be kept in mind. Any class frequency can always be expressed in terms of class frequencies of higher order.

Thus, the frequencies of first order can be expressed in terms of the frequencies of the order in turn can be expressed in terms of frequencies of the third order and so on.

On the basis of this rule, we can set up various types of relationships between the frequencies of different orders.

If there is one attribute only, represented by A, the frequency of universe or N can be divided into two classes (A) and (α) Thus,

$$\boxed{N = (A) + \alpha}$$

19.7.1 Two Attribute *A* and *B*

Now, If one more attribute B is taken into account the first order classes i.e., A and α can each be divided into two classes– one in which attribute B is present and the other in which it is not present.

$$(A) = (AB) + (A\beta) \qquad (B) = (AB) + (\alpha B)$$
$$(\alpha) = (\alpha B) + (\alpha\beta) \quad \text{and} \quad (\beta) = (A\beta) + (\alpha\beta)$$

The chart given below illustrate it clearly.

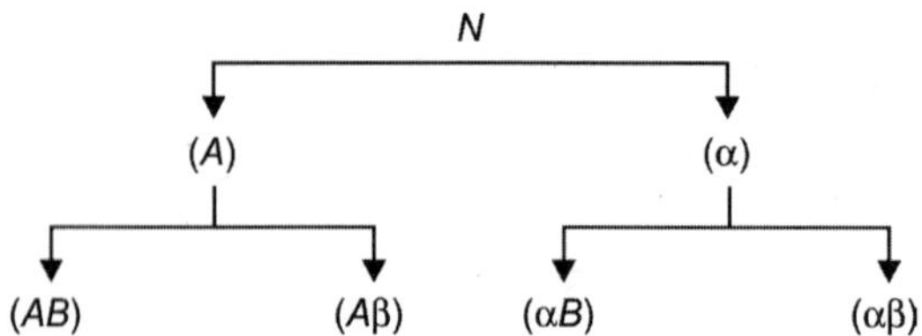

19.7.2 Two by Tow Table or Nine Square Table

It becomes easy to grasp the nature of the relations in case of two attributes if the frequencies are placed in a table with two rows and two columns known as 2×2 contingency table or nine square table, as follows:

Attributes	A	α	Total
B	(AB)	(αB)	(B)
β	(Aβ)	(αβ)	(β)
Total	(A)	(α)	N

If we are given some of the class frequencies we can obtain remaining class frequencies as follows:

$$(\alpha) = N - (A) \qquad (A\alpha) = (A) - (AB)$$
$$(\beta) = N - (B) \qquad (\alpha B) = (B) - (AB)$$
$$(\alpha\beta) = (\alpha) - (\alpha\beta) \quad = \quad N - (A) - (B) + (AB)$$

The above discussion leads to the following important result.

"Any class frequency can be expressed os the sum of some of the 2^n ultimate class frequencies."

DO YOU KNOW?

In dichotomous classification of attributes, the data can be specified completely by:

- The set of all ultimate class frequencies.
- The set of all positive frequencies.

NOTE: For n attributes $A_1, A_2, A_3 \ldots$, An. we can say that

$$(A_1, A_2, A_3 \ldots, An) \geq (A_1) + (A_2) + (A_3) + \ldots + (A_n) - (n-1)\,n$$

EXAMPLE 19.1: Given the following table, calculate the frequencies of the remaining classes:

$$(A) = 100, \quad (AB) = 60, \quad (B) = 80, \quad n = 200$$

Solution:

Nine Square Table

Attributes	*A*	α	Total
B	(AB) = 60	(αB) = 20	(B) = 80
β	(AB) = 40	(αβ) = 80	(β) = 120
Total	(A) = 100	(α) = 100	N = 200

$$(\alpha) = N - (A) = 200 - 100 = 100$$
$$(\beta) = N - (B) = 200 - 80 = 120$$
$$(A\beta) = (A) - (AB) = 100 - 60 = 40$$
$$(\alpha B) = (B) - (AB) = 80 - 60 = 20$$
$$(\alpha\beta) = (\alpha) - (\alpha B) = n - (A) - (B) + (AB)$$
$$= 200 - 100 - 80 + 60 = 80$$

EXAMPLE 19.2: In a very hotly fought battle, at least 80% of the combatants lost an eye, at least 70% lost an ear, at least 82% lost a leg and at least 78% lost an arm. At least how many lost all the four?

Solution: Let us denote by *A*, *B*, *C* and *D* the loss of an eye, an ear, a leg and an arm respectively by the combatants in the battle. If we assume that total number of combatants in the battle is 100, then in the usual notations, we are given:

$$N = 100, \quad (A) = 80, \quad (B) = 70, \quad (C) = 82, \quad (D) = 78$$

We know that,

$$(ABCD) \geq (A) + (B) + (C) + (D) - (4 - 1)\,N$$

$$\Rightarrow \quad (ABCD) \geq 80 + 70 + 82 + 78 - 3 \times 100 = 10$$

Hence, at least 10% of the combatants lost all the four organs.

EXAMPLE 19.3: Two different measurements are made on 1,000 husbands and their wives. If measurements of husbands exceed the measurements of wives in 800 cases for the first measure, in 700 cases for the second measure and in 660 cases for both measures, in how many cases will both measures on wives will exceed the measures on husbands?

Solution: Let us define the attributes:

A: Measurement of the husband exceeds the measurement of the wife for the first measure.

B: Measurement of the husband exceeds the measurement of the wife for the second measure.

Then α and β are the corresponding negative measures.

The given information can be summarised in the Table.

	A	α	Total
B	660	700 – 660 = 20	700
β	800 – 660 = 140	200 – 40 = 160	100 – 700 = 300
Total	**800**	1000 – 800 = 200	**1000**

We are given: $N = 1000, \quad (A) = 800, \quad (B) = 700, \quad (AB) = 660$ ...(1)

The number of cases in which both the measures on wives will exceed the measures on the husbands is given by:

$$(\alpha\beta) = 160$$

Hence, in 160 of the cases, both measures on wives will exceed the measures on husbands.

Aliter. Form (1) onwards. The number of cases in which both the measures on wives will exceed the measures on husbands in given by:

$$(\alpha\beta) = N - (A) - (B) + (AB)$$
$$= 1000 - 800 - 700 + 660 = 160$$

19.8 CONSISTENCY OF DATA

Any class frequencies which have been or might have been observed within one and the same universe, may be said to be consistent with one another. They conform with one another and do not conflict any way.

The necessary and sufficient condition for the consistence of data no ultimate class-frequencies be negative. Hence to test the consistency of the data, calculate ultimate class-frequencies. If any one of them is negative, the data is inconsistent, otherwise consistent.

Case I: If only one Attribute be noted.

The ultimate class-frequencies are (A) and (α),

The conditions of consistence are:

$$(A) \geq 0$$
$$(\alpha) \geq 0 \quad \text{or} \quad N - (A) \geq 0$$
$$(A) \leq N$$

Case II: Two Attribute are noted.

The ultimate class-frequencies:

$(AB) \geq 0$ ...(*a*)

$(A\beta) \geq 0$ or $(A) - (AB) \geq 0$ or $(AB) \leq (A)$ ...(*b*)

$(\alpha B) \geq 0$ or $(B) - (AB) \geq 0$ or $(AB) \leq (B)$ ...(*c*)

$(\alpha\beta) \geq 0$ or $N - (A) - (B) + (AB) \geq 0$ or $(AB) \geq (A) + (B) + N$ ...(d)

The conditions (*a*) and (*d*) give lower or minor limits to (*AB*), while (*b*) and (*c*) provide major limits or upper limits.

Case III: Three Attributes are noted.

The ultimate class frequencies are:

$(ABC) \geq 0$ $(ABC) \geq 0$ ...(*a*)

$(AB\gamma) \geq 0$ $(ABC) \leq (AB)$ ...(*b*)

$(A\beta C) \geq 0$ $(ABC) \leq (AC)$ ...(*c*)

$(A\beta\gamma) \geq 0$ or $(ABC) \geq (A) + (AC) - (A)$ ...(*d*)

$(\alpha B\gamma) \geq 0$ $(ABC) \geq (AB) + (BC) - (B)$ ...(*e*)

$(\alpha\beta C) \geq 0$ $(ABC) \geq (AC) + (BC) - (C)$ ...(*f*)

$(\alpha BC) \geq 0$ $(ABC) \leq (BC)$ ...(*g*)

$(\alpha\beta\gamma) \geq 0$ $(ABC) \leq (AB) + (AC) + (BC) - (A) - (B) - (C) + N$ ...(*h*)

The condition (*a*), (*d*), (*e*), (*f*) give minor limits, while (*b*), (*c*), (*g*), (*h*) major limits to (*ABC*).

These conditions are not of new form.

The major limits can not be less than the minor limits. Thus we get 16 comparisons. Out of these are new comparisons comparing (*b*) with (*a*), (*d*), (*e*) and (*f*), we have

$(AB) \geq 0$

$(AC) \leq (A)$

$(BC) \leq (B)$

$(AB) \geq (AC) + (BC) - (C)$ or $(AB) + (AC) + (BC) \leq (C)$

Out of thcsc, thc last onc is of the new type comparison. Similarly on comparing (*c*), (*g*), (*h*) with (*a*), (*d*), (*e*), (*f*), we have the following new comparisons.

$(AB) + (AC) + (BC) \geq (A) + (B) + (C) - N$

$(AB) + (AC) - (BC) \leq (A)$

$(AB) - (AC) + (BC) \leq (B)$

These are the conditions for the consistence of the second order frequencies with each other. The knowledge of certain class frequencies enable us to find the limits to other.

EXAMPLE 19.4: A labour welfare officer returns the following number of workers observed with certain classes of defects amongst a number of factory workers. *A* denotes development defects and *B*, low nutrition.

$$N = 1200, \quad (A) = 500, \quad (\alpha B) = 800, \quad (A\beta) = 400$$

Do you find the data Consistent?

Solution: From the given data, we have $N = 1200$, $(A) = 500$, $(\alpha B) = 800$, $(A\beta) = 400$

$$(AB) = (A) - (A\beta)$$
$$= 500 - 400 = 100$$
$$(B) = (AB) + (\alpha B)$$
$$= 100 + 800 = 900$$

Now, according to the conditions of consistence:

$$(AB) \nless (A) + (B) - N$$
$$(AB) \nless 500 + 900 - 1200$$
$$(AB) \nless 200$$

But the value of AB is 100 which is less than 200.

Hence the given data are inconsistent $(\alpha\beta)$ will be negative.

The same result can also be obtained by the nine square table after indicating the data given:

	A	(α)	Total
B	$(AB) = 600$	$(\alpha B) = 800$	**$(B) = 900$**
β	$(A\beta) = 400$	$(\alpha B) = -100$	**$(\beta) = 300$**
Total	**$(A) = 500$**	**$(\alpha\beta) = 700$**	**$N = 1200$**

Since in the above table (ab) is negative, the data are inconsistent.

EXAMPLE 19.5: Given that 50% of the inmates of a workhouse are men 60% are "aged" (over 60), 80% non-able-bodie, 35% aged men, 45% non-able-bodied men, and 42% non-able bodied and aged, find the greatest and least possible proportions of non-able-bodied aged men.

Solution: Let A denotes Men; B denotes aged (over 60); C denotes non-able-bodied.

We have $(A) = 50$, $n = 100$, $(BC) = 42$, $(B) = 60$, $(AB) = 35$, $(C) = 80$, $(AC) = 45$

We have to find the limits of (ABC).

Since
$$(ABC) \geq 0 \qquad ...(1)$$
$$(ABC) \geq (AB) + (AC) - A$$
$$\geq 35 + 45 - 50$$
$$\geq 30 \qquad ...(2)$$
$$(ABC) \geq (AB) + (AC) - B$$
$$\geq 35 + 42 - 60$$
$$\geq 7 \qquad ...(3)$$
$$(ABC) \geq (AC) + (BC) - C$$
$$\geq 45 + 42 - 80$$
$$\geq 7 \qquad ...(4)$$

Thus,
$$(ABC) \geq 30$$

Also for Major limit
$$(ABC) \leq (AB)$$
$$\leq 35 \qquad ...(5)$$
$$(ABC) \leq (AC)$$
$$\leq 45 \qquad ...(6)$$
$$(ABC) \leq (BC)$$
$$\leq 42 \qquad ...(7)$$

$$(ABC) \leq (AB) + (AC) + (BC) - (A) - (B) - (C) + N$$
$$\leq 35 + 45 + 42 - 50 - 60 - 80 + 100$$
$$\leq 32 \qquad ...(8)$$

$\therefore$ $(ABC) \leq 32$

Hence (ABC) lies between 30 and 32 percent.

EXAMPLE 19.6: If in a village actually involved by anthrax, 70% of the goats are attacked and 85% have been inoculated with vaccine, what is the lowest percentage of the inoculated that must have been attacked.

Solution: Denoting Attacked by A and Inoculated with vaccine by B. We have to find the lowest percentage of (AB).

$N = 100, \quad (A) = 70, \quad (B) = 85$

Since $(AB) \geq 0$

$$(AB) \geq (A) + (B) - N$$
$$(AB) \geq 70 + 85 - 100$$
$$(AB) \geq 55$$

Hence the percentage of Inoculated that must have attacked $= \frac{55}{85} \times 100 = 64.7\%$.

EXAMPLE 19.7: Among the adult population of a certain town 50% of the population are male; 60% are wage-earners, and 50% are 45 years of age of over. 10% of the males are not wage-earners and 40% of the males are under 45. Can we infer anything about the percentage of the population of 45 or over are wage-earners?

Solution: Let A stand for Male, B stands for wage-Earners, C stands for 45 years of age or over.

Given: $N = 100, \quad (A\beta) = \frac{10}{100} \times 50 = 5, \quad (A) = 50, \quad (B) = 60, \quad (A\gamma) = \frac{40}{100} \times 50 = 20$

We have to find the limits of (BC)

$$(A\beta) = (A) - (AB)$$

or
$$(AB) - (A) - (A\beta)$$
$$= 50 - 5 = 45$$
$$(A\gamma) = (A) - (AC)$$

or
$$(AC) = (A) - (A\gamma)$$
$$= 50 - 20 = 30$$

Using the comparisons

$$-(AB) + (AC) + (BC) \leq (C)$$
$$(AB) + (AC) + (BC) \leq (A)$$
$$(AB) - (AC) + (BC) \leq (B)$$
$$(AB) + (AC) + (BC) \geq (A) + (B) + (C) - N$$

Let $(BC) = x$

$$-45 + 30 + x \leq 50$$
$$x \leq 65$$

$$(AB) + (AC) + (BC) \geq (A) + (B) + (C) - N$$
$$45 + 30 + x \geq 50 + 60 + 50 = 100$$
$$x \geq -15$$
$$(AB) + (AC) - (BC) \leq A$$
$$45 + 30 - x \leq 50$$
$$25 \leq x \quad \text{or} \quad x \geq 25$$
$$(AB) - (AC) + (BC) \leq (B)$$
$$45 - 30 + x \leq 60$$
$$x \leq 45$$

Hence $\quad 25 \leq x \leq 45 \quad$ or $\quad 25 \leq (BC) \leq 45.$

Consequently the percentage of the population of 45 years old or more (C = 50% of total population), who are Wage-Earners lies between 50 and 90 percent.

EXAMPLE 19.8: Given: $N = 2000$, $(A) = 1500$, $(B) = 100$ and $(AB) = 350$, test the consistency of the data. **[B.Com., Punjab Univ., 1998]**

Solution: We are given: $N = 2000$; $(A) = 1500$; $(B) = 100$ and $(AB) = 350$.

To test the consistency of the data, we will find the ultimate class frequencies viz. (αB), $(A\beta)$ and $(\alpha\beta)$.

$$(\alpha\beta) = (B) - (AB)$$
$$= 100 - 350 = -250.$$

Since $(\alpha\beta) < 0$, i.e., negative, the given data are inconsistent.

EXAMPLE 19.9: Given that $(A) = (B) = (C) = \frac{N}{2}$, and 80% of A's are B's, 75% of A's are C's, find the limits of the percentage of B's that are C's.

Solution: We are given: $\quad (A) = (B) = (C) = \frac{N}{2}$ ...(i)

80% of A's are B's $\Rightarrow$ $(AB) = 80\%$ of (A)

$$= 0.8 \times \frac{N}{2} = 0.4\,N \quad \text{...(ii)}$$

and 75% of A's are C's $\Rightarrow$ $(AC) = 75\%$ of $(C) = \frac{0.75\,N}{2}$ ... (iii)

We have to find the limits for the percentage of $\frac{(BC)}{(B)} = \frac{2(BC)}{N}$

Note that $(BC) \leq (B)$ $\Rightarrow$ $0 \leq \frac{(BC)}{(B)} = \frac{2(BC)}{N} \leq 1$ ...(iv)

The conditions of consistency for three attributes A, B and C are:

$$(AB) + (AC) - (BC) \leq (A) \quad \text{...(v)}$$
$$(AB) + (BC) - (AC) \leq (B) \quad \text{...(vi)}$$
$$(AC) + (BC) - (AB) \leq (C) \quad \text{...(vii)}$$

and $(AB) + (AC) + (BC) - (A) - (B) - (C) + N \geq 0$ ...(viii)

On using (*i*), (*ii*) and (*iii*), we get from (*v*) and (*vi*) respectively:

$$0.4N + \frac{0.75}{2}N - (BC) \le \frac{N}{2}$$

$$\Rightarrow 0.80 + 0.75 - \frac{2(BC)}{N} \le 1$$

$$\Rightarrow 0.80 + 0.75 - 1 \le \frac{2(BC)}{N}$$

$$\Rightarrow \frac{2(BC)}{N} \ge 0.55 \quad \text{...(ix)}$$

$$0.4N + (BC) - \frac{0.75}{2}N \le \frac{N}{2}$$

$$\Rightarrow 0.80 + \frac{2(BC)}{N} - 0.75 \le 1$$

$$\Rightarrow \frac{2(BC)}{N} + 0.05 \le 1$$

$$\Rightarrow \frac{2(BC)}{N} \le 0.95 \quad \text{...(x)}$$

Similarly, from (vii) and (viii), we will get, on simplification:

$\frac{2(BC)}{N} \le 1.05$ and $\frac{2(BC)}{N} \ge -0.55$ respectively, both of which give inconsistent results [See (iv)]

Hence, from (ix) and (x), we get

$$\frac{(BC)}{(B)} \ge 0.55 \quad \text{and} \quad \frac{(BC)}{(B)} \le 0.95 \quad \Rightarrow \quad 0.55 \le \frac{(BC)}{(B)} \le 0.95$$

i.e., the percentage of *B*'s that are *C*'s lies between 55% and 95%.

EXAMPLE 19.10: A coin is tossed three times and the results, heads and tails, noted. The process is continued until there are 100 sets of threes. In 69 cases heads fell first, in 49 cases heads fell second, and in 53 cases heads fell third. In 33 cases heads fell both first and second, and in 21 cases heads fell both second and third. Show that there must have been at least 5 occasions on which heads fell three times, and that there could not have been more than 15 occasions on which tails fell three times, though there need not have been any.

Solution: Denoting $A \to$ Heads fell first; $B \to$ Heads fell second; $C \to$ Heads fell third.

$(A) = 69, \quad N = 100, \quad (B) = 49, \quad (AB) = 33, \quad (C) = 53, \quad (BC) = 21$

To show that $(ABC) \ge 5$ and $(\alpha\beta\gamma) \le 15$.

Since $(ABC) \ge 0$

$$(ABC) \ge (AB) + (BC) - (B)$$
$$> 33 + 21 - 49$$
$$\ge 5$$

Hence $(ABC) \ge 5$

Let $(\alpha\beta\gamma) = x$

Since $(\alpha\beta\gamma) = N - (A) - (B) - (C) + (AB) + (AC) + (BC) - (ABC)$

$$x = 100 - 69 - 49 - 53 + 33 + 21 + (AC) - (ABC)$$

or $(ABC) = (AC) - x - 17$

Applying the conditions of consistency, we have

$$(ABC) \ge 0$$
$$(AC) - x - 17 \ge 0$$

or $(AC) - 17 \ge 0$ ...(1)

$$(ABC) \ge (AB)$$

$$(AC) - x - 17 \leq 33$$

or $$x \geq (AC) - 50 \qquad \ldots(2)$$

$$(ABC) \leq (AC)$$

$$(AC) - x - 17 \leq (AC)$$

$$x \geq -17 \qquad \ldots(3)$$

$$(ABC) \leq (BC)$$

$$(AC) - x - 17 \leq 21$$

$$x \geq (AC) - 38 \qquad \ldots(4)$$

$$(ABC) \geq (AB) + (AC) - (A)$$

$$(AC) - x - 17 \geq 33 + (AC) - 69$$

$$69 - 17 - 33 \geq x$$

or $$x \leq 19 \qquad \ldots(5)$$

$$(ABC) \geq (AB) + (BC) - (B)$$

$$(AC) - x - 17 \geq 33 + 21 - 49$$

$$(AC) - 22 \geq x$$

or $$x \leq (AC) - 22 \qquad \ldots(6)$$

$$(ABC) \geq (AC) + (BC) - (C)$$

$$(AC) - x - 17 \geq (AC) + 21 - 53$$

$$32 - 17 \geq x$$

or $$x \leq 15 \qquad \ldots(7)$$

$$(ABC) \leq (AB) + (AC) + (BC) - (A) - (B) - (C) + N$$

$$(AC) - x - 17 \leq 33 + 21 + (AC) - 69 - 49 - 53 + 100$$

$$-x - 17 \leq -17$$

or $$-17 + 17 \leq x$$

or $$x \geq 0 \qquad \ldots(8)$$

Condition (1), (2), (4), (6) can not determine x as (AC) is not known, while only the conditions (5) and (7) provide the major limits. Hence $x \leq 15$ or $(\alpha\beta\gamma) \leq 15$.

19.9 INDEPENDENCE OF ATTRIBUTES

If there is no any kind of relationship between two attributes A and B, we expect the same proportion of A's amongst the B's as amongst B's

i.e., $$\boxed{\frac{(AB)}{(B)} = \frac{(A\beta)}{(\beta)}}$$

Under these circumstances the attributes are said to be independent.

The following criterion also holds for independence.

$$\frac{(\alpha B)}{(B)} = \frac{(\alpha\beta)}{(\beta)}$$

$$\frac{(AB)}{(A)} = \frac{(\alpha B)}{(\alpha)}$$

$$\frac{(A\beta)}{(A)} = \frac{(\alpha\beta)}{(\alpha)}$$

Other forms of the criterion of Independence.

Since $$\frac{(AB)}{(B)} = \frac{(A\beta)}{(\beta)} = \frac{(AB)+(A\beta)}{(\beta)+(B)} = \frac{(A)}{N}$$

$$\boxed{(AB) = \frac{(A)(B)}{N}}$$

and $$\boxed{A\beta = \frac{(A)(\beta)}{N}}$$

i.e., the proportion of A's amongst the B's is the same as in the universe at large.

The other criterion is obtained as follows:

$$(AB)(\alpha\beta) = \frac{(A)(B)}{N} \cdot \frac{(\alpha)(\beta)}{N}$$

$$= \frac{(A)(B)(\alpha)(\beta)}{N^2}$$

Which is equal to $$(A\beta)(\alpha B) = \frac{(A)(\beta)(\alpha)(B)}{N^2}$$

Hence, $$(AB)(\alpha\beta) = (A\beta)(\alpha B)$$

or $$\left.\begin{aligned}\frac{(AB)}{(\alpha B)} &= \frac{(A\beta)}{(\alpha\beta)}\\ \frac{(AB)}{(A\beta)} &= \frac{(\alpha B)}{(\alpha\beta)}\end{aligned}\right]$$

The 2 × 2 table in case of independence is given as below:

Attribute	*A*	(α)	Total
A	$\frac{(A)(B)}{N}$	$\frac{(A)(\beta)}{N}$	(*A*)
α	$\frac{(\alpha)(B)}{N}$	$\frac{(\alpha)(\beta)}{N}$	(α)
Total	**(*B*)**	**(β)**	***N***

EXAMPLE 19.11: If there are 144 A's and 384 B's in 1024 observations, how many AB's will be there, A and B being independent.

Solution: If A and B are independent, then

$$(AB) = \frac{(A)(B)}{N} = \frac{144 \times 384}{1024} = 54$$

$\therefore$ $$(AB) = 54$$

EXAMPLE 19.12: In a sample of 1000 individuals, 100 possess the attribute A and 300 possess attribute B. A and B are independent. How many individuals possess both A and B, and how many possess neither?

Solution: In the usual notations, we are given : $(A) = 100$; $(B) = 300$; $N = 1000$ ...(i)

$\therefore (\alpha) = N - (A) = 1000 - 100 = 900$; $(\beta) = N - (B) = 1000 - 300 = 700$ ...(ii)

Since A and B are independent, we have $(AB) = \dfrac{(A) \times (B)}{N} = \dfrac{100 \times 300}{1000} = 30$ [From (i)] ...(iii)

Hence, the number of persons who possess both the attributes A and B is 30.

Since A and B are independent, α and β are also independent.

$$\therefore \quad (\alpha\beta) = \frac{(\alpha) \times (\beta)}{N} = \frac{900 \times 700}{1000} = 630$$

Hence, the number of persons who possess neither of the attributes A and B is 630.

From (iii) onwards, for $(\alpha\beta) \cdot (\alpha\beta) = N - (A) - (B) + (AB)$

$$= 1000 - 100 - 300 + 30$$

$$= 630.$$

or Using (i), (ii) and (iii) the remaining class frequencies can be obtained as given in the 2 × 2 contingency.

	A	α	
B	30	300 – 30 = 270	(*B*) = 300
β	100 – 30 = 70	700 – 70 = 630	1000 – 300 = 700
	(*A*) = 100	**1000 – 100 = 900**	***N* = 1000**

$$\therefore \quad (\alpha\beta) = 630$$

Hence, the number of persons who possess none of the attributes A and B is 630.

19.10 ASSOCIATION

The word 'association' used in statistics is technically different from the general notation of association as used in our day-to-day life. Statistically two attributes are associated if they occur together in a greater number of cases than expected had they been independent if there is no association between two attributes A and B, we except to find the same proportion of A's amongst the B's as amongst the Non-B's.

DO YOU KNOW?

Association describes the relationship between two or more attributes. If the attributes A and B are not independent, they are said to be associated

i.e., if $(AB) \neq \dfrac{(A) \times (B)}{N}$,

the Attributes A and B are associated.

19.10.1 Type of Association

There can be three kinds of association between attributes:

Positive Association: Two attributes are said to be positively associated when they are present or are absent together in the data such association is found between vaccination and immunity from disease, illiteracy and poverty, etc.

Two attributes A and B are said to be:

Positively associated if $\frac{(AB)}{(B)} > \frac{(A\beta)}{(\beta)}$

or $\frac{(AB)}{(A)} > \frac{(\alpha B)}{(\alpha)}$

Negative Association: When the presence of an attribute is associated with the absence of the other attribute they are said to have negative association, say between vaccination and attack of a disease, education and ignorance.

Two attributes A and B are said to be:

Negatively associated if $\frac{(AB)}{(B)} < \frac{(A\beta)}{(\beta)}$

or $\frac{(AB)}{(A)} < \frac{(\alpha)(B)}{(\alpha)}$

Independence: Absence of association, as described above, shows independence. When two attribute do not have the tendency to be present together, or one's presence does not cause presence or absence of the other attribute, they are regarded as independence.

Two attributes A and B are said to be:

However, if $\frac{(AB)}{(B)} = \frac{(A\beta)}{(\beta)}$

or $\frac{(AB)}{(A)} = \frac{(\alpha B)}{(\alpha)}$

then A and B are independent.

Such relationships are given in the table below:

Proportion of	Independence	Positive Association	Negative Association
A in B and β	$\frac{(AB)}{(B)} = \frac{(A\beta)}{(\beta)}$	$\frac{(AB)}{(B)} > \frac{(A\beta)}{(\beta)}$	$\frac{(AB)}{(B)} < \frac{(A\beta)}{(\beta)}$
B in A and α	$\frac{(AB)}{(A)} = \frac{(\alpha B)}{(\beta)}$	$\frac{(AB)}{(A)} > \frac{(\alpha B)}{(\alpha)}$	$\frac{(AB)}{(A)} < \frac{(\alpha B)}{(\alpha)}$
α in B and β	$\frac{(\alpha B)}{(B)} = \frac{(\alpha\beta)}{(\beta)}$	$\frac{(\alpha B)}{(B)} > \frac{(\alpha\beta)}{(\beta)}$	$\frac{(\alpha B)}{(B)} < \frac{(\alpha\beta)}{(\beta)}$
β in A and α	$\frac{(A\beta)}{(A)} = \frac{(\alpha\beta)}{(\alpha)}$	$\frac{(A\beta)}{(A)} > \frac{(\alpha\beta)}{(\alpha)}$	$\frac{(A\beta)}{(A)} < \frac{(\alpha\beta)}{(\alpha)}$

EXAMPLE 19.13: Out of 3000 unskilled workers of a factory 2000 come from rural areas and out of 1200 skilled workers 300 come from rural areas. Determine the association between skill and residence in rural areas by the method of proportions.

Solution: Let 'A' denote skilled workers and 'B' residence in rural areas, then 'α' and 'β' would denote the unskilled workers and absence of residence in rural areas respectively.

We are given $(A) = 1200,\ (AB) = 300,\ (\alpha) = 3000$ and $(\alpha\beta) = 2000$.

The proportion of skilled rural workers amongst the skilled workers.

$$\frac{(AB)}{(A)} = \frac{300}{1200} = 0.25 \quad \text{or} \quad 25\%$$

The proportion of unskilled rural workers amongst the unskilled workers

$$\frac{(\alpha\beta)}{(\alpha)} = \frac{2000}{3000} = 0.667 \quad \text{or} \quad 66.7\%$$

since the proportion of skilled rural workers amongst the skilled workers is less than the proportion of unskilled rural workers amongst the unskilled workers, the skilled worker and residence in rural areas are negatively associated.

EXAMPLE 19.14: In an anti-malaria campaign in a certain area, quinine was administered to 812 persons of a total population of 3248. The number of fever cases is shown below:

Treatment	Fever	No Fever
quinine	20	792
No quinine	220	2216

Discuss the usefulness of quinine in checking malaria.

Solution: Denoting the attribute of quinine treatment by A, no quinine treatment by α and no attack of fever by B, attack of fever by β.

The given data are: $(AB) = 792,\ (\alpha B) = 2216,\ (A\beta) = 20$ and $(\alpha\beta) = 220$

$\therefore \quad (A) = (AB) + (A\beta) = 792 + 20 = 812$

and $\quad (\alpha) = (\alpha B) + (\alpha\beta) = 2216 + 220 = 2436$

Now, proportion of quinine treatment cases which were not attached is

$$\frac{(AB)}{(A)} = \frac{792}{812} = 0.975 \quad \text{or} \quad 75.5\%$$

and proportion of no-quinine treatment cases which were not attached is

$$\frac{(\alpha B)}{(\alpha)} = \frac{2216}{2436} = 0.910 \quad \text{or} \quad 91.0\%$$

since $\frac{(AB)}{(A)} > \frac{(\alpha B)}{(\alpha)}$, there is a positive association between the attributes A and B i.e., there is a positive association between quinine treatment and no attack of fever. Thus, it may be concluded that quinine is effective in checking malaria.

EXAMPLE 19.15: Out of 70,000 literates in a particular district at India, number of criminals was 500. Out of 9,30,000 illiterates in the same district the number of criminals was 15,000. On the basis of these figure do you and find any association between illiteracy and criminality?

Solution: Let A denote to attribute of illiteracy and B of criminality. Therefore a will denote literacy and β, non criminality. The nine-square table is as follows:

Nine Square Table:

Attribute	A	α	Total
B	$(AB) = 15$	$(\alpha B) = 0.5$	$(B) = 15.5$
β	$(A\beta) = 91.5$	$(\alpha\beta) = 69.5$	$(\beta) = 984.5$
Total	$(A) = 930$	$(\alpha) = 70$	$N = 1000$

Proportion of illiterate criminals to illiterates is

$$\frac{(AB)}{(A)} = \frac{15000}{930000} = 0.016 \quad \text{or} \quad 1.6\%$$

Proportion of literate criminals to literates is

$$\frac{(\alpha B)}{(\alpha)} = \frac{500}{70000} = 0.0071 \quad \text{or} \quad 0.71\%$$

Hence the proportion of criminals is more in illiterates than in the literates, therefore, criminality and illiteracy are positively associated.

19.11 METHODS OF MEASURING ASSOCIATION

Association can be measured by any one of the following methods:

1. Frequency Method.
2. Yule's Coefficient of Association Method.
3. Yule's Coefficient of Colligation Method.
4. Pearson's Coefficient of Contingency Method.

19.11.1 Frequency Method

Under this method the actual number of observations are required with the expected ones.

According to the theory of probability, the probability of a particular event is,

$$\frac{\text{Number of favourable cases}}{\text{Total number of cases}}$$

when two attributes A and B are studied in a universe N and the class frequencies of these attributes are (A) and (B), then

$$\text{Probability of } (A) = \frac{(A)}{N}, \qquad \text{Probability of } (B) = \frac{(B)}{N}$$

$$\text{The joint probability of } (A) \text{ and } (B) = \frac{(A)}{N} \times \frac{(B)}{N}$$

∴ The expectation of (A) and (B) jointly

$$= \frac{(A)}{N} \times \frac{(B)}{N} \times (N)$$

$$= \frac{(A) \times (B)}{N}$$

similarly, the expectation of $(\alpha\beta) = \dfrac{(\alpha) \times (\beta)}{N}$

In the same way the expected number can be found for other combinations too.

Attributes	Independence or Absence of Association	Positive Association	Negative Association
A and B	$(AB) = \dfrac{(A) \times (B)}{N}$	$(AB) > \dfrac{(A) \times (B)}{N}$	$(AB) < \dfrac{(A) \times (B)}{N}$
A and β	$(A\beta) = \dfrac{(A) \times (\beta)}{N}$	$(A\beta) > \dfrac{(A) \times (\beta)}{N}$	$(A\beta) < \dfrac{(A) \times (\beta)}{N}$
α and B	$(\alpha B) = \dfrac{(\alpha) \times (B)}{N}$	$(\alpha B) > \dfrac{(\alpha) \times (B)}{N}$	$(\alpha B) < \dfrac{(\alpha) \times (B)}{N}$
α and β	$(\alpha\beta) = \dfrac{(\alpha) \times (\beta)}{N}$	$(\alpha\beta) > \dfrac{(\alpha) \times (\beta)}{N}$	$(\alpha\beta) < \dfrac{(\alpha) \times (\beta)}{N}$

EXAMPLE 19.16: From the data given below, find out if the attributes A and B are independent, positively associated or negatively associated:

(i) $(A) = 60$, $(B) = 53$, $(AB) = 35$, $N = 80$

(ii) $(A) = 480$, $(AB) = 294$, $(\alpha) = 580$, $(\alpha B) = 380$

(iii) $(AB) = 256$, $(\alpha B) = 768$, $(A\beta) = 48$, $(\alpha\beta) = 144$

Solution:

(i) Here $\dfrac{(A) \times (B)}{N} = \dfrac{60 \times 35}{80} = 39.75 > (AB)$

Here A and B are negatively associated.

(ii) We have $N = (A) + (\alpha) = 480 + 580 = 1060$

$(B) = (AB) + (\alpha B) = 294 + 380 = 674$

$\therefore \quad \dfrac{(A) \times (B)}{N} = \dfrac{480 \times 674}{1060} = 305.21 > (AB)$

Hence, A and B are negatively associated.

(iii) $(A) = (AB) + (A\beta) = 256 + 48 = 304$

$(B) = (AB) + (\alpha B) = 256 + 768 = 1024$

$N = (AB) + (AB) + (\alpha B) + (\alpha\beta)$

$= 256 + 48 + 768 + 144$

$= 1216$

$\therefore \quad \dfrac{(A) \times (B)}{N} = \dfrac{304 \times 1024}{1216} = 256 = (AB)$

Hence, A and B are independent attributes.

19.11.2 Yule's Coefficient of Association

It measures the degree of relationship between two attributes. Yule has given the coefficient of association Q.

$$Q = \frac{(AB)(\alpha\beta) - (A\beta)(\alpha B)}{(AB)(\alpha\beta) + (A\beta)(\alpha B)}$$

The Yule's coefficient of association 'Q' varies between ± 1 and is interpreted like Pearson's Coefficient of correlation.

If $Q = 0$, it indicates the attributes are independent.
If $Q = +1$, it indicates the perfect positive association.
If $Q = -1$, It indicates the attributes have perfect negative association.

NOTE: The main limitation of proportion & frequency method is that each simply gives us an idea if the attributes are positively associated, negatively associated or independent. However, none of these methods gives us any idea about the extent of association between the two attributes.

EXAMPLE 19.17: In a sample of 500 children, 200 come from higher income group and the rest from lower income group. The number of delinquent children in these groups respectively was 25 and 100. Calculate the coefficient of association between delinquency and income group.

Solution: Let higher income be denoted by 'A', lower income by 'α' delinquency by 'B', and non-delinquency by 'B'.

In the usual notations we re given: $(A) = 200$, $(AB) = 25$, $(\alpha B) = 100$, $N = 500$

	A	**α**	**Total**
B	25	100	125
β	175	200	375
Total	**200**	**300**	**500**

The required Yule's coefficient of association q is

$$Q = \frac{(AB)(\alpha\beta) - (A\beta)(\alpha B)}{(AB)(\alpha\beta) + (A\beta)(\alpha B)}$$

$$= \frac{25 \times 200 - 175 \times 100}{25 \times 200 + 175 \times 100} = \frac{5000 - 17500}{5000 + 17500}$$

$$= -\frac{12500}{22500} = -0.56$$

Hence there is negative association between delinquency and income.

EXAMPLE 19.18: In a population of 1000 students, the number of married students is 400. Out of 300 students who failed, 120 belonged to the married group. Using Yule's coefficient of association, find out the extent of association between the attributes marriage and failure.

Solution: Let us define the following attributes:

A : Student is married.

B : Student failed in the test.

	A	α	Total
B	120	300 – 120 = 180	(B) = 300
β	400 – 120 = 280	600 – 180 = 420	1000 – 300 = 700
Total	**(A) = 400**	**1000 – 400 = 600**	**N = 1000**

Then, α represents the attribute that student is un-married and β represents the attribute that student passed the test.

In the usual notations, we are given: $N = 1000$, $(A) = 400$, $(B) = 300$, $(AB) = 120$.

Then the frequencies of various attributes are computed as given in the 2×2 table.

Yule's coefficient of association between the attributes A and B is given by:

$$Q = \frac{(AB)(\alpha\beta) - (A\beta)(\alpha B)}{(AB)(\alpha\beta) + (A\beta)(\alpha B)} = \frac{120 \times 420 - 280 \times 180}{120 \times 420 + 280 \times 180} = \frac{50,400 - 50,400}{50,400 + 50,400} = 0$$

Hence, the attributes A and B are not associated and we conclude that there is no association between the attributes A (marriage) and B (failure in the test).

EXAMPLE 19.19: A survey was conducted in respect of marital status and success in examination. Out of 2000 persons who appeared for an examination, 80% of them were boys, and the rest were girls, Among 300 married boys, 140 were successful. 1100 boys are successful among unmarried boys. In respect of 100 married girls, 40 were successful, 200 unmarried girls were successful. Construct two separate nine square tables, and find out the Yule's coefficient of association to discuss the association between marital status and success in examination.

Solution: Total number of persons who appeared in the examination = 2000

$$\text{Number of boys} = 80\% \text{ of } 2000 = \frac{80}{100} \times 2000 = 1600$$

$$\therefore \quad \text{Number of girls} = 2000 - 1600 = 400$$

Let us define the attributes :

A : Married person ; B : Success in the examination

α : Unmarried person ; β : Failure in the examination

Then, in the usual notation, we are given:

For Boys: $N = 1600$, $(A) = 300$, $(AB) = 140$, $(\alpha B) = 1100$

For Girls: $N = 400$, $(A) = 100$, $(AB) = 40$, $(\alpha B) = 200$

The above data can be expressed in two separate nine square tables for boys and girls, as given below.

Nine Square Tables For Boys

Attributes	A	α	Total
B	**140**	**1100**	140 + 1100 = 1240
β	300 – 140 = 160	360 – 100 = 200	1600 – 1240 = 360
Total	**300**	**1600 – 300 = 1300**	**1600**

Nine Square Tables For Girls

Attributes	A	α	Total
B	**40**	**200**	40 + 200 = 240
β	100 – 40 = 60	300 – 200 = 100	400 – 240 = 160
Total	**100**	**400 – 100 = 300**	**400**

In the above Tables, the frequencies in the bold type are the given values. The remaining frequencies can be obtained by appropriate additions or subtractions, as explained in the tables.

Yule's coefficient of association (Q) is given by :

$$Q = \frac{(AB)(\alpha\beta) - (A\beta)(\alpha B)}{(AB)(\alpha\beta) + (A\beta)(\alpha B)}$$

FOR BOYS:

$$Q = \frac{140 \times 200 - 1100 \times 160}{140 \times 200 + 1100 \times 160}$$

$$= \frac{28000 - 176000}{28000 + 176000} = -\frac{148000}{204000} - 0.725$$

FOR GIRLS:

$$Q = \frac{40 \times 100 - 200 \times 60}{40 \times 100 + 200 \times 60}$$

$$= \frac{4000 - 12000}{4000 + 12000} = -\frac{8000}{16000} - 0.5$$

Hence, in each case (for boys and for girls) there is a fairly good degree of negative association between marital status and success in the examination, and the degree of association is more in boys.

EXAMPLE 19.20: 1000 candidates appeared in a certain examination. Boys outnumbered girls by 20% of all candidates who appeared in the examination. Number of passed candidates exceeded the number of failed candidates by 166. Girls failing in the examination numbered 58. Construct the 2 × 2 table and then work out Yule's coefficient of association between male sex and success in the examination. Also interpret the said coefficient.

Solution: Let us define the attributes:

A : Boys, α : Girls; B: Passed in the examination, β : Failed in the examination

Then, we are given: $N = 1,000$ and $(\alpha\beta) = 58$

$$(A) - (\alpha) = 20\% \text{ of } N = \frac{20}{100} \times 1,000 = 200$$

Also $(A) + (\alpha) = N = 1000$

∴ Adding and subtracting, we get respectively:

$$2(A) = 1200 \Rightarrow (A) = \frac{1200}{2} = 600$$

$$2(\alpha) = 800 \Rightarrow (\alpha) = \frac{800}{2} = 400$$

$$(B) - (\beta) = 166$$

Also $(B) + (\beta) = N = 1000$

Adding and subtracting, we get respectively:

$$2(B) = 1166 \Rightarrow (B) = \frac{1166}{2} = 583$$

$$2(\beta) = 834 \Rightarrow (\beta) = \frac{834}{2} = 417$$

The above results can be expressed in 2 × 2 contingency table:

Attribute	A	α	Total
B	583 – 342 = 241	400 – 58 = 342	583
β	417 – 58 = 359	58	417
Total	**600**	**400**	**1,000**

From table, we have

$$(AB) = 241, \quad (\alpha\beta) = 58, \quad (A\beta) = 359, \quad (\alpha B) = 342$$

Yule's coefficient of association (Q) is given by:

$$Q = \frac{(AB)(\alpha\beta) - (A\beta)(\alpha B)}{(AB)(\alpha\beta) + (A\beta)(\alpha B)} = \frac{241 \times 58 - 359 \times 342}{241 \times 58 + 359 \times 342} = \frac{13978 - 122778}{13978 + 122778} = -\frac{108800}{136756} = -0.7956$$

Since $Q < -0.5$, there is a fairly high degree of negative association between the attribute A (boys) and B (success) in the examination.

EXAMPLE 19.21: In a co-education, out of 200 students, 150 were boys. In an examinations, 120 boys and 40 girls passed. Apply Yule's coefficient to determine the association between sex and success in the examination. Interpret your result.

Solution: Let us define the following attributes:

A : The student is a boy.
B : The student passed in the examination
Then α : The student is a girl.
and β : The student failed in the examination

In the usual notations, were are given:

$N = 200$; $(AB) = 120$, $(\alpha B) = 40$, $(A) = 150$

	A	α	*Total*
B	120	40	120 + 40 = 160
β	150 – 120 = 30	40 – 30 = 10	200 – 160 = 40
Total	**(*A*) = 150**	**200 – 150 = 50**	***N* = 200**

The remaining cell frequencies can be obtained as given in the 2 × 2 table

∴ $(AB) = 120$; $(\alpha\beta) = 10$; $(A\beta) = 30$; $(\alpha B) = 40$

Yule's coefficient of association is given by:

$$Q = \frac{(AB)(\alpha\beta) - (A\beta)(\alpha B)}{(AB)(\alpha\beta) + (A\beta)(\alpha B)} = \frac{120 \times 10 - 40 \times 30}{120 \times 10 + 40 \times 30} = \frac{1200 - 1200}{1200 + 1200} = 0 .$$

Hence, the attributes A and B are not associated and we conclude that there is no association between sex and success in the examination.

EXAMPLE 19.22: 200 candidates appeared for a competitive examination and 60 of them succeeded, 35 received special coaching and out of them 20 candidates succeeded.

Prepare contingency 2 × 2 table and using Yule's Coefficient discuss whether special coaching is effective or not.

Solution: Let A denote those who were successful and B denote those who received special coaching. Therefore, α and β would respectively denote unsuccessful candidate and candidates who did not receive the special training. The data given are:

	A	α	*Total*
B	20	—	35
β	—	—	—
Total	**60**	**—**	**200**

The complete data will be as follows:

2 × 2 Contingency Table

	A	α	*Total*
B	20	15	35
β	40	125	165
Total	**60**	**140**	***N* = 200**

The Yule's coefficient is given by:

$$Q = \frac{(AB)(\alpha\beta) - (A\beta)(\alpha B)}{(AB)(\alpha\beta) + (A\beta)(\alpha B)} = \frac{20 \times 125 - 40 \times 15}{20 \times 125 + 40 \times 15} = \frac{1900}{3100} = \frac{19}{31} = 0.61$$

EXAMPLE 19.23: Do you find any association between the tempers of brothers and sisters from the following data:

Good natured brothers and good natured sisters 1040
Good natured brothers and sullen sisters 160
Sullen brothers and good natured sisters 180
Sullen brothers and sullen sisters 120.

Solution: Let *A* denote the attribute of good natured brothers, and *B* that of good natured sisters. Hence, α will denote sullen brothers and β will denote sullen sisters.

The given data are:

$$(AB) = 1040, \quad (A\beta) = 160, \quad (\alpha B) = 180 \quad \text{and} \quad (\alpha\beta) = 120.$$

Yule's coefficient of association:

$$Q = \frac{(AB)(\alpha B) - (A\beta)(\alpha B)}{(AB)(\alpha\beta) + (A\beta)(\alpha B)} = \frac{1040 \times 120 - 160 \times 180}{1040 \times 120 + 160 \times 180} = \frac{124800 - 28800}{124800 + 28800} = 0.625$$

Thus, there is a positive association between tempers of brothers and sisters.

EXAMPLE 19.24: From the data given below, calculate Yule's coefficient of association between weight of children and their economic condition and interpret it.

	Poor children	**Rich children**
Below normal weight	75	23
Above normal weight	5	42

Solution: Let *A* denote poor children and *B* children below normal weight. Then α would denote rich children and β children above normal weight. The given data are:

$$(AB) = 75, \quad (A\beta) = 5, \quad (\alpha B) = 23 \quad \text{and} \quad (\alpha\beta) = 42.$$

Substituting the values in Yule's coefficient of association, we get.

$$Q = \frac{(75 \times 42) - (5 \times 23)}{(75 \times 42) + (5 \times 23)} = \frac{3035}{3265} = +0.93$$

Hence there is high degree of positive association between poor children and children below normal weight.

EXAMPLE 19.25: From the following data, prepare the 2 × 2 table and using Yule's coefficient discuss whether there is association between literacy and unemployment:

Illiterate unemployed	220 persons
Literate employed	20 persons
Illiterate employed	180 persons
Total number of persons	500

Solution: Let *A* denote the attribute literacy and *B* unemployment. Hence, α will denote illiteracy and β employment.

In the usual notation, we are given.

$(\alpha B) = 220$, $(A\beta) = 20$, $(\alpha\beta) = 180$ and $N = 500$

	A	α	*Total*
B	80	220	300
β	**20**	**180**	200
Total	100	400	***N* = 500**

Yule's Formula:

$$Q = \frac{(AB)(\alpha\beta) - (A\beta)(\alpha B)}{(AB)(\alpha\beta) + (A\beta)(\alpha B)}$$

$$= \frac{80 \times 180 - 220 \times 20}{80 \times 180 + 220 \times 20} = \frac{14400 - 4400}{14400 + 4400}$$

$$= \frac{10000}{18800} = +0.532$$

This shows that literacy and unemployment are moderately associated.

19.11.3 Yule's Coefficient of Colligation

This is another method for calculation of coefficient of association given by Yule. The two formulae used for the purpose are:

$$\text{Coefficient of Colligation } (Y) = \frac{1 - \sqrt{\dfrac{(A\beta) \times (\alpha B)}{(AB) \times (\alpha\beta)}}}{1 + \sqrt{\dfrac{(A\beta) \times (\alpha B)}{(AB) \times (\alpha\beta)}}}$$

$$\text{Coefficient of Association } (Q) = \frac{2Y}{1 + Y^2}$$

If

$Y = 0$, *A* and *B* are independent

$Y = +1$, *A* and B are completely positively associated

$Y = -1$, *A* and *B* completely disassociated.

EXAMPLE 19.26: Find coefficient of association between of a factory indicated below:

Attributes	Successful (B)	Unsuccessful (B)	Total
Trained (A)	(AB) = 58	(Aβ) = 42	100
Untrained (α)	(α B) = 49	(αβ) =51	100
Total	**107**	**93**	**200**

Solution: Substituting the values in the formula given above, we have

$$Y = \frac{1-\sqrt{\dfrac{42\times 49}{58\times 51}}}{1+\sqrt{\dfrac{42\times 49}{58\times 51}}} = \frac{1-\sqrt{.695}}{1-\sqrt{.695}} = \frac{1-\cdot 834}{1+\cdot 834} = .09$$

$$Q = \frac{2(\cdot 09)}{1+(\cdot 09)^2} = \frac{0.18}{1.008} = 0.179$$

19.11.4 Pearson's Coefficient of Contingency Method

If the attributes A and B are completely independent in the universe at large, then

$$(A_i)(B_i) = \frac{(A_i)(B_i)}{N} = (A_i\ B_i)_o$$

For all values of i and j.

If A and B are not completely independent, than $(A_i\ B_j)$ and $(A_i\ B_j)$, will not be identical we define the difference by

$$\delta_{ij} = (A_i\ B_j) - (A_i\ B_j)_o$$

If $\delta_{ij} \neq 0$, the attributes are associated some way. We define square contingency χ^2, (called also chi-square)

$$\chi^2 = \sum_{i=j} \frac{\delta_{ij}^2}{(A_i B_j)}$$

$$= \sum_{i=1}^{m}\sum_{j=1}^{n} \frac{[(A_i\ B_j) - (A_i\ B_j)_o]^2}{(A_i B_j)_o}$$

Karl Pearson proposed the coefficient of Mean Square contingency or coefficient of contingency, defined by

$$C = \sqrt{\frac{\chi^2}{\chi^2 + n}} = \sqrt{\frac{\phi^2}{\cdot 1 + \phi^2}}$$

where $$\phi^2 = \frac{\chi^2}{N}$$

In general, no sign is attached to the root. It indicates only whether two attributes are independent or not. If $C = 0$, the attributes are independent otherwise some way associated.

The value of C never reaches to 1. The maximum value of C depends upon the number of rows and number of columns (m and n) of the contingency table.

If $t \times t$ table, when there is a complete association the maximum value of C will be equal to

$$\boxed{C = \sqrt{\frac{t-1}{t}}}$$

in particular

If $t = 2$ C can not exceed .707

$t = 3$ C can not exceed .816

$t = 4$ C can not exceed .866

EXAMPLE 19.27: In a very hotly fought battle 70% at least of the combatants lost an eye, 75% at least lost an ear, 80% at least lost an arm and 85% at least lost a leg. How many at least must have lost all four?

Solution: Denoting A – Lost an Eye.

B – Lost an Ear

C – Lost an Arm

D – Lost a Leg.

Number of combatants at least must have lost all four

$$(ABCD) \geq (A) + (B) + (C) + (D) - 3N$$

Given: $N = 100$; $(A) = 70$; $(B) = 75$; $(C) = 80$; $(D) = 85$

$$(ABCD) \geq 70 + 75 + 80 + 85 - 300$$
$$\geq 310 - 30$$
$$\geq 10$$

Number of combatants at least must have lost all four = 10%.

EXAMPLE 19.289: Can vaccination be regarded as preventive measure for small-pox, from the data given below?

'Of 1, 482 persons in a locality exposed to small-pox, 368 in all were attacked.'

'Of 1,482 persons, 343 had been vaccinated and of these only 35 were attacked.'

Solution: Let A be the attribute of vaccination, α that of non-vaccination.

B, that of exemption from attack of small pox and β, that of attack of small-pox.

Then, the given data is: $N = 1482$; $(A) = 343$; $(\beta) = 368$; $(A\beta) = 35$

From the above $(A) = 343$

$$(AB) = (A) - (A\beta) = 343 - 35 = 308,$$
$$(\alpha) = N - (A) = 1482 - 343 = 1139,$$
$$(\alpha B) = (B) - (AB) = N - (\beta) - (AB)$$
$$= 1482 - 368 - 308 = 806$$

Now, percentage of vaccinated who were not attacked $= \dfrac{(AB)}{(A)} \times 100 = \dfrac{308}{343} \times 100 = 90\%$

and percentage of not vaccinated who were not attacked $= \dfrac{(\alpha B)}{(\alpha)} \times 100 = \dfrac{806}{1139} \times 100 = 71\%$

A comparison of the two percentages brings out the fact that vaccination and exemption from attack are positively associated. Here, vaccination may be regarded as preventive measure for small-pox.

EXAMPLE 19.29: 800 candidates of both sex appeared at an examination. The boys outnumbered the girls by 15% of the total. The number of candidates who passed exceed the number failed by 480. Equal number of boys and girls failed in the examination. Prepare a 2 × 2 table and find the coefficient of association. Comment.

Solution: Let the boys be denoted as A and pass candidates by B. Then the girls are denoted as α and failed candidates by β.

$$\text{Now number of girls } (\alpha) = \frac{1}{2}(800 - 120) = 340$$

$$\text{Number of boys } (A) = 800 - 340 = 460$$

$$\text{Total failed candidates } (\beta) = \frac{1}{2}(800 - 480) = 160$$

$$\text{Failed boys } (A\beta) = \frac{1}{2} \times 160 = 80$$

$$\text{Failed girls } (\alpha\beta) = 80$$

2 × 2 Contingency Table

	A	α	*Total*
B	380	260	640
β	80	80	160
Total	**460**	**340**	**800**

The coefficient of association Q is given by:

$$Q = \frac{(AB)(\alpha\beta) - (A\beta)(\alpha B)}{(AB)(\alpha\beta) + (A\beta)(\alpha B)}$$

$$= \frac{380 \times 80 - 80 \times 260}{380 \times 80 + 80 \times 260} = 0.19$$

EXAMPLE 19.30: "95% of the people who drink alcohol die before reaching the age of 85 years. Therefore, drinking alcohol is bad for longevity of life". Comment.

Solution: If we define the attributes:

A : Drinking alcohol and

B : Dying before reaching 85 years, then we are given: $\frac{(AB)}{(A)} = 95\% = 0.95$.

This information, is insufficient to arrive at any valid conclusion about any association between A and B. To arrive at any conclusion, we must be given the percentage of persons who do not drink alcohol and die before reaching the age 85 years i.e., we must be given $\frac{(\alpha B)}{(\alpha)}$

The given statement will be true only if $\frac{(AB)}{(A)} > \frac{(\alpha B)}{(\alpha)}$. Hence, as such the given statement is wrong.

NOTE: It might happen that the percentage of persons who do not drink alcohol but die before reaching 85 $\left[i.e., \frac{(\alpha B)}{(\alpha)} \times 100 \right]$ is, say, 98%. In that case, the given conclusion will be reversed i.e., then drinking alcohol will be regarded good for longevity of life.

EXAMPLE 19.31: A number of school-children were examined for the presence or absence of certain defects of which three chief descriptions were noted:

$A \rightarrow$ Development defects, $B \rightarrow$ Nerve Signs; $C \rightarrow$ Low Nutrition.

Given the following ultimate frequencies, find the frequencies of Positive classes, including N.

$(ABC) = 57$; $(\alpha BC) = 78$; $(AB\gamma) = 281$; $(\alpha B\gamma) = 670$

$(A\beta C) = 86$; $(\alpha\beta C) = 65$; $(A\beta\gamma) = 453$; $(\alpha\beta\gamma) = 8310$

Solution: We have to find N, (A), (B), (C), (AB), (AC), (BC) and (ABC).

$$(AB\gamma) = AB\gamma \cdot N = AB\,(1 - C) \cdot N$$

$$(AB\gamma) = (AB) - (ABC)$$

$$281 + 57 = (AB)$$

or $$(AB) = 338$$

$$(A\beta C) = (AC) - (ABC)$$

or $$(AC) = (A\beta C) + (ABC) = 86 + 57 = 143$$

$$(AB\gamma) = AB\gamma \cdot N = A\,(1 - B)\,(1 - C) \cdot N$$

$$= (A) - (AB) - (AC) + (ABC)$$

$\therefore$ $$(A) = (A\beta\gamma) + (AB) + (AC) - (ABC)$$

$$= 453 + 338 + 143 - 57 = 877$$

$$(\alpha BC) = \alpha BC \cdot N = (1 - A)\,BC \cdot N$$

$$= (BC) - (ABC)$$

or $$(BC) = (\alpha BC) + (ABC) = 78 + 57 = 135$$

$$(\alpha B\gamma) = \alpha B\gamma \cdot N = (1 - A)\,\mathrm{B}\,(1 - C) \cdot N$$

$$= (B) - (AB) - (BC) + (ABC)$$

$\therefore$ $$(B) = (\alpha B\gamma) + (AB) + (BC) - (ABC)$$

$$(B) = 670 + 338 + 135 - 57 = 1086$$

$$(\alpha\beta C) = \alpha\beta C \cdot N = (1 - A)\,.\,(1 - B)\,C \cdot N$$

$$= (C) - (AC) - (BC) + (ABC)$$

or $$(C) = (\alpha\beta C) + (AC) + (BC) - (ABC)$$

$$(C) = 65 + 143 + 135 - 57 = 286$$

$$(\alpha\beta\gamma) = \alpha\beta\gamma \cdot N = (1 - A)\,(1 - B)\,(1 - C) \cdot N$$

$$= N - (A) - (B) - (C) + (AB) + (AC) + (BC) - (ABC)$$

$$N = (\alpha\beta\gamma) + (A) + (B) + (C) - (AB) - (AC) - (BC) + (ABC)$$

$$N = 8310 + 877 + 1086 + 286 - 33833 - 143 - 135 + 57$$

$$N = 10000.$$

EXAMPLE 19.32: In a town of 1000,00 adult population, 52000 males and 48000 females were distributed according to Education and Employment as given below:

	Males (000's)	Females (000's)
Educated and Employed	38	6
Educated and Unemployed	2	4
Uneducated and Employed	4	18
Uneducated and Unemployed	8	20

Is there any association between Education and Employment in the two groups?

Solution:

(a) Let A denotes Education, B denotes Employment, C denotes Males.

$$Q_{AB\cdot C} = \frac{(ABC)(\alpha\beta C) - (A\beta C)(\alpha BC)}{(ABC)\cdot(\alpha\beta C) + (A\beta C)(\alpha BC)}$$

$$= \frac{38 \times 8 - 2 \times 4}{38 \times 8 + 2 \times 4} = \frac{304 - 8}{304 + 8} \simeq +\cdot 95$$

Thus the Education and Employment is positively associated in the sub-population of males.

(b) $$Q_{AB\cdot\gamma} = \frac{(AB\gamma)(\alpha\beta\gamma) - (A\beta\gamma)(\alpha B\gamma)}{(AB\gamma)(\alpha\beta\gamma) + (A\beta\gamma)\cdot(\alpha B\gamma)}$$

$$= \frac{6 \times 20 - 4 \times 18}{6 \times 20 + 4 \times 18} = \frac{120 - 72}{120 + 72} = -\frac{48}{192} = +.25..$$

Thus the education and employment is positively associated in the sub-population of Females.

EXAMPLE 19.33: In a free vote in the house of commons, 600 members voted. 300 government members representing English constituencies (including Welsh) voted in favour of the motion. 25 opposition members representing Scottish constituencies voted against the motion. The government majority among those who voted was 96. 135 of the members voting represented Scottish constituencies. 18 government members voted against the motion. 102 Scottish members voted in favour of the motion. The motion was carried by 310 votes. Analyse the voting according to the nationality of the constituencies and party.

Solution: Denoting $A \rightarrow$ Government Members.

$B \rightarrow$ Voting For .

$C \rightarrow$ English Members

Given:

$N = 600$ ...(1)

$(ABC) = 300$ ...(2)

$(\alpha\beta\gamma) = 25$ ...(3)

$(A) - (\alpha) = 96$ ...(4)

$(\gamma) = 135$ ...(5)

$(A\beta) = 18$ ...(6)

$(B\gamma) = 102$ ...(7)

$(B) - (\beta) = 310$ ...(8)

We have to find ultimate class frequencies

Since $N = (A) + (\alpha) = (B) + (\beta) = (C) + (\gamma)$

By (4) $(A) - (\alpha) = 96$

$(A) + (\alpha) = 600$

Solving $(A) = 348$

$(\alpha) = 252$

By (8) $(B) - (\beta) = 310$

$(B) + (\beta) = 600$

Solving $(B) = 455$

$(\beta) = 145$

Since $(C) + (\gamma) = 600$

$(C) + 135 = 600$

$(C) = 465$

By (6) we have $(A\beta) = A\beta \cdot N = A(1 - B) \cdot N$

$(A\beta) = (A) - (AB)$

$18 = 348 - (AB)$

$\therefore$ $(AB) = 348 - 18 = 330$

By (7) we have $(B\gamma) = (B) - (BC)$

$102 = 455 - (BC)$

$\therefore$ $(BC) = 353$

By (3) $(\alpha\beta\gamma) = \alpha\beta\gamma \cdot N = (1 - A)(1 - B)(1 - C) \cdot N$

$(\alpha\beta\gamma) = N - (A) - (B) - (C) + (AB) + (AC) + (BC) - (ABC)$

$25 = 600 - 348 - 455 - 455 - 465 + 330 + (AC) + 353 - 300$

$\therefore$ $(AC) = 310$

The ultimate frequencies are

$(ABC) = 300$

$(AB\gamma) = AB\gamma \cdot N = ABC(1 - C) \cdot N$

$= (AB) - (ABC) = 330 - 300 = 30$

$(AB\gamma) = 30$

$(ABC) = (AC) - (ABC) = 310 - 300$

$= 10$

$(A\beta\gamma) = (A) - (AB) - (AC) + (ABC)$

$= 348 - 330 - 310 + 300 = 8$

$(\alpha BC) = (BC) - (ABC) = 353 - 300 = 53$

$(\alpha B\gamma) = (B) - (AB) - (BC) + (ABC)$

$= 455 - 330 - 353 + 300$

$= 72$

$(\alpha\beta C) = (C) - (AC) - (BC) + (ABC)$

$= 465 - 310 - 353 + 300$

$= 102$

$(\alpha\beta\gamma) = 25.$

EXAMPLE 19.34: In a sample of 500 children, 200 came from higher income group and the rest from lower income group. The number of delinquent children in these groups respectively was 25 and 100.

Calculate the coefficient of association between delinquency and income group.

Solution: Let higher income be denoted by '*A*', lower income by 'α', delinquency by '*B*', and non-delinquency by 'β'.

In the usual notations we are given:

$$(A) = 200; \quad (AB) = 25; \quad (\alpha B) = 100; \quad n = 500$$

Nine Square Table

	A	α	*Total*
B	**25**	**100**	125
β	175	200	375
Total	200	300	500

The required Yule's coefficient of association, *Q* is

$$Q = \frac{(AB)(\alpha\beta) - (A\beta)(\alpha B)}{(AB)(\alpha\beta) + (A\beta)(\alpha B)} = \frac{25 \times 200 - 175 \times 100}{25 \times 200 + 175 \times 100}$$

$$= \frac{5000 - 17500}{5000 + 17500} = -\frac{12500}{22500} = -0.56$$

EXAMPLE 19.35: A survey was conducted in respect of marital status and success in examination. Out of 2,000 persons who appeared for an examination, 80% of them were boys and the rest were girls. Among 300 married boys, 140 were successful. 1100 boys were successful among unmarried boys. In respect of 100 married girls, 40 were successful. 200 unmarried girls were successful. Construct two separate nine-square tables, and find out the Yule's coefficient of association to discuss the association between marital status and success in examination.

Solution: Let the attribute *A* stand for married and *B* for success in the examination.

Nine Square Table

Boys

	A	α	*Total*
B	140	1100	1240
β	160	200	360
Total	**300**	**1300**	**1600**

Girls

	A	α	*Total*
B	40	200	240
β	60	100	160
Total	**100**	**300**	**400**

Using Yule's formula for coefficient of association, viz.,

$$Q = \frac{(AB)(\alpha\beta) - (\alpha\beta)(A\beta)}{(AB)(\alpha\beta) + (\alpha B)(A\beta)}$$

For Boys:

$$Q = \frac{140 \times 200 - 1100 \times 160}{140 \times 200 + 1100 \times 160} = \frac{28000 - 176000}{28000 + 176000} = 0.725$$

For Girls:

$$Q = \frac{40 \times 100 - 200 \times 60}{40 \times 100 + 200 \times 60} = \frac{4000 - 12000}{4000 + 12000} = -0.5$$

It shows that in each case, there is a negative association between marital status and passing of examination and the degree of association is more in boys.

SELF PRACTICE EXERCISES

I. CHOOSE THE BEST ANSWER

1. Measures of association in usually deal with:
   (a) Attributes (b) Quantitative factors
   (b) Variables (d) Numbers
2. The frequency of class can always be expressed as a sum of frequencies of:
   (a) Lower order classes (b) Higher order classes
   (c) Zero order classes (d) None of the above
3. With the two attributes the total number of class frequencies is:
   (a) Two (b) Four
   (c) Eight (d) Nine
4. If for two the attributes are A and B, $(AB) > (A)(B) / N$ the attributes are:
   (a) Independent (b) Positively associated
   (c) Negatively associated (d) No conclusion
5. In case of two attributes A and B the class frequency $(AB) = 0$ the value of Q is:
   (a) 1 (b) -1
   (c) 0 (d) $-1 \leq Q \leq 1$

II. FILL IN THE BLANKS

1. If an attribute has two classes it is said to be ....
2. In case of consistent data, no class frequency can be ....
3. If A and B are independent Yule's co-efficient is equal to ....
4. If A and B are negatively associated then ....
5. If $N = 500$, $(A) = 300$, $(B) = 250$ and $(AB) = 40$ the data are ....

III. SHORT ANSWER TYPE QUESTIONS

1. Give a brief idea of notations used in classification of attributes
2. How can the frequencies for various attributes be displayed in contingency table?
3. What do you understand by consistency of data?
4. Write briefly about association of attributes.
5. Give Yule's co-efficient of association.

IV. LONG ANSWER TYPE QUESTIONS

1. For two attributes A and B, we have $(AB) = 35$; $(A) = 55$; $N = 100$ and $(B) = 65$. Calculate the missing values.
2. From the following ultimate class frequencies, find the frequencies of positive and negative classes and the total number of observations. $(AB) = 9$; $(A\beta) = 14$; $(\alpha B) = 4$ and $(\alpha\beta) = 37$.
3. Verify whether the given data $N = 100$, $(A) = 75$, $(B) = 60$ and $(AB) = 15$ are consistent.
4. Find whether A and B are independent in the following data $(AB) = 256$; $(\alpha B) - 768$; $(A\,\beta) = 48$; $(\alpha\beta) = 144$.

5. In a report on consumer's preference it was given that out of 500 persons surveyed 410 preferred variety A 380 preferred variety B and 270 persons linked both. Are the data consistent?
6. For two attributes A and B, we have $(AB) = 35$, $N = 100$, $(\alpha\beta) = 20$. Calculate the Yule's co-efficient of association.
7. Given $N = 1500$; $(A) = 383$; $(B) = 360$ and $(AB) = 35$. Prepare 2×2 contingency table and compute Yule's coefficient of association and interpret the result.
8. In an experiment on immunization of cattle from tuberculosis the following results were obtained.

	Affected	Unaffected
Inoculated	12	26
Not inoculated	16	6

9. Calculate the co-efficient of association between the intelligence of fathers and sons from the following data:

   Intelligent fathers with intelligent sons = 300
   Intelligent fathers with dull sons = 100
   Dull fathers with intelligent sons = 50
   Dull fathers with dull sons = 500

10. Out of 3000 unskilled workers of a factory, 2000 come from rural area and out of 1200 skilled workers 300 come from rural area. Determine the association between skill and residence
11. In an anti-malarial campaign in a certain area, quinine was administrated to 812 persons out of a total population of 3428. The number of fever cases is shown below:

Treatment	Fever	No Fever
Quinine	20	792
No quinine	220	2216

   Examine the effect of quinine on controlling malaria.

12. 1500 candidates appeared for competitive examinations 425 were successful. 250 had attended a coaching class and of these 150 came out successful. Estimate the utility of the coaching class.
13. In an examination at which 600 candidates appeared of them 348 were boys. Number of passed candidates exceeded the number of failed candidates by 310. Boys failing in the examination numbered 88. Find the coefficient of association between male sex and success in examination.
14. Following data relate to literacy and unemployment in a group of 500 persons. Calculate Yule's co-efficient of association between literacy and unemployment and interpret it

   Literate unemployed = 220
   Literate employed = 20
   Illiterate Employed = 180

15. In a group of 400 students, the number of married is 160. Out of 120 students who failed 48 belonged to the married group. Find out whether the attributes of marriage and failure are independent.

ANSWERS

I. CHOOSE THE BEST ANSWERS

1. (a) 2. (b) 3. (d) 4. (b) 5. (b)

II. FILL IN THE BLANKS

1. Dichotomy 2. Negative 3. 0 4. $AB < (A) \cdot (B)/N$ 5. Inconsistent

IV. LONG ANSWER TYPE QUESTIONS

1.

2.

Total No. of observations = 64

3. Inconsistent
4. A and B are independent
5. Inconsistent
6. 0.167
7. –0.606, Negative association
8. –0.705, Vaccine is effective
9. + 0.935
10. Negative association between skill and residence
11. –0.59, Negative association quinine is effective.
12. + 0.68, coaching class are useful
13. –0.07
14. 0.92, Positive association between literacy and unemployment
15. $Q = 0$, Marriage and failure are independent.

CHAPTER 20

Statistical Decision Theory (SDT)

20.1 INTRODUCTION

Decision theory is primarily concerned with helping people and organizations in making decisions. It provides a meaningful conceptual frame work for important decision making. The decision making refers to the selection of an act from amongst various alternatives, the one which is judged to be the best under given circumstances.

The management has to consider phases like planning, organization, direction, command and control. While performing so many activities, the management has to face many situations from which the best choice is to be taken. This choice making is technically termed as ***"decision making"*** or decision taking. A decision is simply a selection from two or more courses of action. Decision making may be defined as - " a process of best selection from a set of alternative courses of action, that course of action which is supposed to meet objectives up to satisfaction of the decision maker.

The knowledge of statistical techniques helps to select the best action. The statistical decision theory refers to an optimal choice under condition of uncertainty. In this case probability theory has a vital role, as such, this probability theory will be used more frequently in the decision making theory under uncertainty and risk.

Theoretical Questions About Decisions

The following are examples of decisions and of theoretical problems that they give rise to.

Shall I bring the umbrella today? – The decision depends on something which I do not know, namely whether it will rain or not.

I am looking for a house to buy. Shall I buy this one? – This house looks fine, but perhaps I will find a still better house for the same price if I go on searching. When shall I stop the search procedure?

Am I going to smoke the next cigarette? – One single cigarette is no problem, but if I make the same decision sufficiently many times it may kill me.

The court has to decide whether the defendant is guilty or not. –There are two mistakes that the court can make, namely to convict an innocent person and to acquit a guilty person. What principles should the court apply if it considers the first of these mistakes to be more serious than the second?

A committee has to make a decision, but its member's have different opinions. – What rules should they use to ensure that they can reach a conclusion even if they are in disagreement? Almost everything that a human being does involves decisions. Therefore, to theorize about decisions is almost the same as to theorize about human activities. However, decision theory is not quite as all-embracing as that.

It focuses on only some aspects of human activity. In particular, it focuses on how we use our freedom. In the situations treated by decision theorists, there are options to choose between, and we choose in a non-random way. Our choices, in these situations, are goal-directed activities. Hence, decision theory is concerned with *goal-directed behaviour in the presence of options.*

20.2 MEANING AND SCOPE

Statistical decision theory consists of a large number of quantitative techniques which help in analysing a decision situation and enable us to arrive at a strategy which is the best under given circumstances of the case. We can say that decision analysis refers to logical and quantitative analysis of all factors that influence a decision. The theory tries to uncover the logical structure of the problem through proper analysis and classification of a decision problem into say the alternative course of action, the possible states of nature, the possible outcomes with each of the above and the likely pay off from each such outcome.

We do not decide continuously. In the history of almost any activity, there are periods in which most of the decision-making is made, and other periods in which most of the implementation takes place. Decision-theory tries to throw light, in various ways, on the former type of period.

The Decision Maker

The decision maker refers to individual or a group of individual responsible for making the choice of an appropriate course of action amongst the available courses of action.

Decision Matrices

The standard format for the evaluation-choice routine in (individual) decision theory is that of a *decision matrix*. In a decision matrix, the alternatives open to the decision-maker are tabulated against the possible states of nature. The alternatives are represented by the rows of the matrix, and the states of nature by the columns.

Let us use a decision whether to bring an umbrella or not as an example. The decision matrix is as follows:

	It rains	It does not rain
Umbrella	Dry clothes, heavy suitcase	Dry clothes, heavy suitcase
No umbrella	Soaked clothes, light suitcase	Dry clothes, light suitcase

For each alternative and each state of nature, the decision matrix assigns an outcome (such as "dry clothes, heavy suitcase" in our example).

For example, draw a decision matrix that illustrates the decision whether or not to buy a ticket in a lottery.

In order to use a matrix to analyze a decision, we need, in addition to the matrix itself, (1) information about how the outcomes are valued, and (2) information pertaining to which of the states of nature will be realized.

The most common way to represent the values of outcomes is to assign utilities to them. Verbal descriptions of outcomes can then be replaced by utility values in the matrix:

	It rains	It does not rain
Umbrella	15	15
No umbrella	0	18

Mainstream decision theory is almost exclusively devoted to problems that can be expressed in matrices of this type, *utility matrices*.

20.3 DECISION FRAMEWORK

The statistical decision theory tries to reveal the logical structure of the problem into alternative action, states of nature, possible outcomes and likely pay-offs from each such outcome. Let us explain the concepts associated with the decision theory approach to problem solving.

Acts (or courses of action): Decision making problems deals with the selection of a single act from a set of alternative acts. If two or more alternative courses of action occur in a problem, then decision making is necessary to select only one course of action.

Let the acts or action be $A_1, A_2, A_3,\ldots$ then the totality of all these actions is known as action space denoted by A. For three actions $A_1, A_2\, A_3$; A = action space = (A_1, A_2, A_3) or $A = (A_1, A_2, A_3)$. Acts may be also represented in the following matrix form i.e., either in row or column was

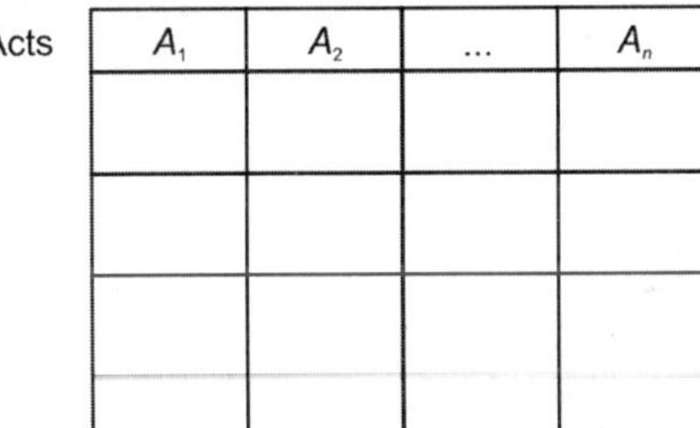

Fig. 20.1

In a tree diagram the acts or actions are shown as:

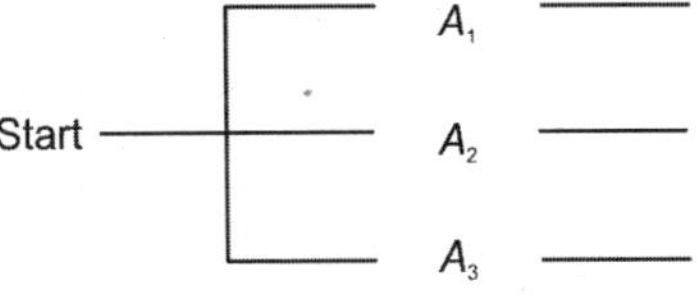

Fig. 20.2

Events (or States of nature): The events identify the occurrences, which are outside of the decision maker's control and which determine the level of success for a given act. These events are often called 'States of nature' or outcomes. An example of an event or states of nature is the level of market demand for a particular item during a stipulated time period.

A set of states of nature may be represented in any one of the following ways:

$S = \{S_1, S_2, ..., S_n\}$ or $E = \{E_1, E_2, ..., E_n\}$ or $\Omega = \{\theta_1, \theta_2, \theta_3\}$

For example, if a washing powder is marketed, it may be highly liked by outcomes (outcome θ_1) or it may not appeal at all (outcome θ_1) or it may satisfy only a small fraction, say 25% (outcome θ_1)

$$\Omega = \{\theta_1, \theta_2, \theta_3\}$$

In a tree diagram the places are next to acts. We may also get another act on the happening of events as follows:

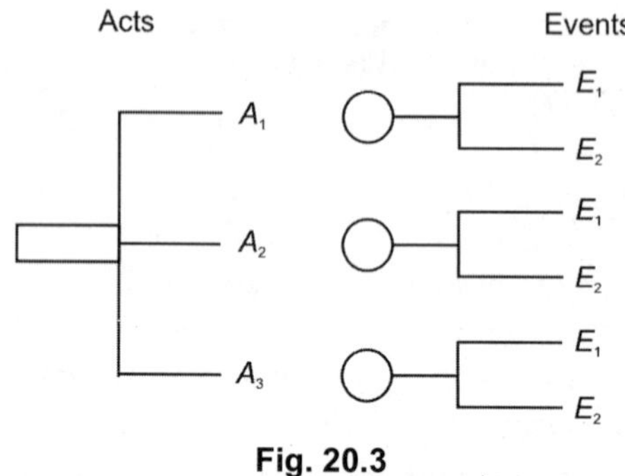

Fig. 20.3

In matrix form, they may be represented as either of the two ways:

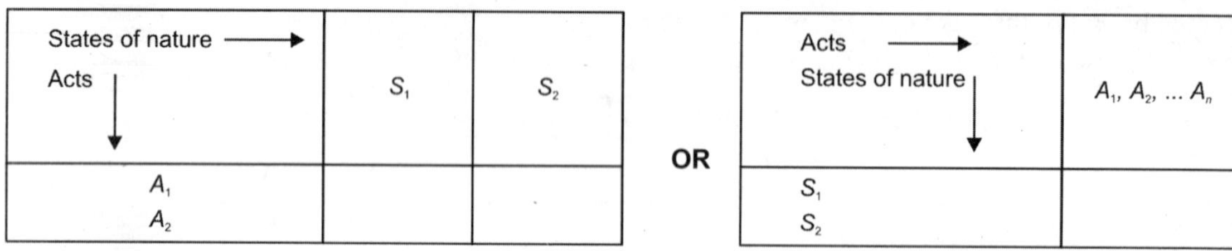

Fig. 20.4

Pay-off: The result of combinations of an act with each of the states of nature is the outcome and momentary gain or loss of each such outcome is the pay-off. This means that the expression pay-off should be in quantitative form.

Pay-off may be also in terms of cost saving or time saving. In general, if there are k alternatives and n states of nature, there will be $k \times n$ outcomes or pay-offs. These $k \times n$ pay-offs can be very conveniently represented in the form of a $k \times n$ pay-off table.

States of nature	Decision alternative			
	A_1	A_2	....	A_k
E_1	A_{11}	A_{12}	....	A_{1k}
E_2	A_{21}	A_{22}	....	A_{2k}
•	•	•	....	•
•	•	•	....	•
•	•	•	....	•
E_n	A_{n1}	A_{n2}	....	A_{nk}

Where a_{ij} = conditional outcome (pay-off) of the ith event when j^{th} alternative is chosen. The above pay-off table is called pay-off matrix.

For example: A farmer can raise any one of three crops on his field. The yields of each crop depend on weather conditions. We have to show pay –off in each case, if prices of the three products are as indicated in the last column of yield matrix.

		Weather			
		Dry (E_1)	Moderate (E_2)	Damp (E_3)	Price Rs per kg
Yield in kg per hectare	Paddy (A_1)	500	1700	4500	1.25
	Ground nut (A_2)	800	1200	1000	4.00
	Tobacco (A_3)	100	300	200	15.00

Pay-off Table			
	E_1	E_2	E_3
A_1	500 × 1.25 = 625	1700 × 1.25 = 2125	4500 × 1.25 = 5625
A_2	800 × 4 = 3200	1200 × 4 = 4800	1000 × 4 = 4000
A_3	100 × 15 = 1500	300 × 15 = 4500	200 × 15 = 3000

Regret (or Opportunity Loss): The difference between the highest possible profit for a state of nature and the actual profit obtained for the particular action taken is known as opportunity loss. That is an opportunity loss is the loss incurred due to failure of not adopting the best possible course of action. Opportunity losses are calculated separately for each state of nature. For a given state of nature the opportunity loss of possible course of action is the difference between the pay-off value for that course of action and the pay-off for the best possible course of action that could have been selected.

Let the pay-off of the outcomes in the 1st row be P_{11}, P_{12}, ... P_{1n} and similarly for the other rows.

Pay-off Table				
Acts	States of nature			
	S_1	S_2	....	S_n
A_1	P_{11}	P_{12}	....	P_{1k}
A_2	P_{21}	P_{22}	....	P_{2k}
•	•	•	....	•
•	•	•	....	•
•	•	•	....	•
A_m	P_{m1}	P_{m2}	....	P_{mn}

Consider a fixed state of nature S_i. The pay-off corresponding to the n strategies are given by P_{i1}, P_{i1},..., P_{in}. Suppose M_i is the maximum of these quantities. The P_{i1} if A_1 is used by the decision maker there is loss of opportunity of $M_1 - P_{1i}$, and so on Then a table showing opportunity loss can be computed as follows:

Regret (or opportunity loss table)				
Acts	**States of nature**			
	S_1	S_2	....	S_n
A_1	$M_1 - P_{11}$	$M_2 - P_{12}$	....	$M_n - P_{1n}$
A_2	$M_1 - P_{21}$	$M_2 - P_{22}$	....	$M_n - P_{2n}$
•	•	•	....	•
•	•	•	....	•
•	•	•	....	•
A_m	$M_1 - P_{m1}$	$M_2 - P_{m2}$	....	$M_n - P_{mn}$

20.4 TYPES OF DECISION MAKING

Decisions are made based upon the information data available about the occurrence of events as well as the decision situation. There are three types of decision making situations: certainty, uncertainty and risk.

20.5 DECISION MAKING UNDER CERTAINTY

In this case the decision maker has the complete knowledge of consequence of every decision choice with certainty. In this decision model, assumed certainty means that only one possible state of nature exists.

EXAMPLE 20.1: A canteen prepares a food at a total average cost of Rs. 4 per plate and sells it at a price of Rs 6. The food is prepared in the morning and is sold during the same day. Unsold food during the same day is spoiled and is to be thrown away. According to the past sale, number of plates prepared is not less than 50 or greater than 53. You are to formulate the

(i) action space (ii) states of nature space
(iii) pay-off table (iv) loss table

Solution:

(i) The canteen will not prepare less than 50 plates or more than 53 plates. Thus the acts or courses of action open to him are

a_1 = prepare 50 plates
a_2 = prepare 51 plates
a_3 = prepare 52 plates
a_4 = prepare 53 plates

Thus the action space is

$$A = \{ a_1, a_2 , a_3, a_4\}$$

(ii) The state of nature is daily demand for food plates. Then are four possible state of nature ie

S_1 = demand is 50 plates
S_2 = demand is 51 plates
S_3 = demand is 52 plates
S_4 = demand is 53 plates

Hence the state of nature space, $S = \{S_1, S_2, S_3, S_4\}$

(iii) The uncertainty element in the given problem is the daily demand. The profit of the canteen is subject to the daily demand.

Let n = quantity demanded

m = quantity produced

For $n \geq m$, profit = (Cost price – Selling price) × m

$= (6 - 4) \times m = 2m$

For $m > n$, profit = {(Cost price – Selling price) × n} – {Cost price × $(m - n)$}

$= 2n - 4(m - n) = 6n - 4m$

Pay-off Table

Supply (m)	**Demand (n)**			
	(S_1) 50	**(S_2) 51**	**(S_3) 52**	**(S_4) 53**
(a_1) 50	100	100	100	100
(a_2) 51	96	102	102	102
(a_3) 52	92	98	104	104
(a_4) 53	88	94	100	106

(iv) To calculate the opportunity loss we first determine the maximum pay-off in each state of nature. In this state

First maximum pay-off = 100
Second maximum pay-off = 102
Third maximum pay-off = 104
Fourth maximum pay-off = 106

Loss Table Corresponding to the Above Pay-off Table

Supply (m)	**Demand (n)**			
	(S_1) 50	**(S_2) 51**	**(S_3) 52**	**(S_4) 53**
(a_1) 50	100 – 100 = 0	102 – 100 = 2	104– 100 = 4	106 – 100 = 6
(a_2) 51	100 – 96 = 4	102 – 102 = 0	104 – 102 = 2	106 – 102 = 4
(a_3) 52	100 – 92 = 8	102 – 98 = 4	104 – 104 = 0	106 – 104 = 2
(a_4) 53	100 – 88 = 12	102 – 94 = 8	104 – 100 = 4	106 – 106 = 0

20.6 DECISION MAKING UNDER UNCERTAINTY (WITHOUT PROBABILITY)

Under conditions of uncertainty we do not have a set of probabilities for the states of nature.

Under conditions of uncertainty, only pay-offs are known and nothing is known about the likelihood of each state of nature.

Such situations arise when a new product is introduced in the criteria available under the condition of uncertainty is given below.

Certain of Optimism (Maximax)

The maximax criterion finds the course of action or alternative strategy that maximizes the maximum pay-off. Since this decision criterion locates the alternative with the highest possible gain, it has also been called an optimistic decision criterion. The working method is:

(i) Determine the best outcome for each alternative.
(ii) Select the alternative associated with the best of these.

Expected Monetary Value (EMV)

The expected monetary value is widely used to evaluate the alternative course of action (or act). The EMV for given course of action is just sum of possible pay-off of the alternative each weighted by the probability of that pay-off occurring.

Expected Opportunity Loss (EOL)

Expected opportunity loss or expected value of regards is calculated in the same manner as the expected value of an indicated earlier.

The EOL indicates the average opportunity loss for that act. According to EOL criterion, the act with minimum expected loss is selected or recommended. It is notable here that the optimal decision using EMV and EOL criteria will always be the same.

The Criteria of Pessimism or Maximin

This criterion is the decision to take the course of action which maximizes the minimum possible pay-off. Since this decision criterion locates the alternative strategy that has the least possible loss, it is also known as a pessimistic decision criterion. The working method is:

(1) Determine the lowest outcome for each alternative.
(2) Choose the alternative associated with the best of these.

Minimax Regret Criterion (Savage Criterion)

This criterion is also known as opportunity loss decision criterion because decision maker feels regret after adopting a wrong course of action (or alternative) resulting in an opportunity loss of pay-off. Thus he always intends to minimize this regret. The working method is

(a) Form the given pay-off matrix, develop an opportunity loss (or regret) matrix.
    (i) Find the best pay-off corresponding to each state of nature and
    (ii) Subtract all other entries (pay-off values) in that row from this value.
(b) Identify the maximum opportunity loss for each alternative.
(c) Select the alternative associated with the lowest of these.

Equally Likely Decision (Baye's or Laplace) Criterion

Since the probabilities of states of nature are not known, it is assumed that all states of nature will occur with equal probability. i e., each state of nature is assigned an equal probability.

As states of nature are mutually exclusive and collectively exhaustive, so the probability of each this must be 1 / (number of states of nature). The working method is

(a) Assign equal probability value to each state of nature by using the formula:

1/ (number of states of nature)

(b) Compute the expected (or average) value for each alternative by multiplying each outcome by its probability and then summing.

(c) Select the best expected pay-off value (maximum for profit and minimum for loss)

This criterion is also known as the criterion of insufficient reason because; expect in a few cases, some information of the likelihood of occurrence of states of nature is available.

Criterion of Realism (Hurwicz Criterion)

This criterion is a compromise between an optimistic and pessimistic decision criterion. To start with a co-efficient of optimism α $(0 \leq \alpha \leq 1)$ is selected.

When α is close to one, the decision maker is optimistic about the future and when α is close to zero, the decision maker is pessimistic about the future.

According to Hurwicz, select strategy which maximizes

$$H = \alpha \text{ (maximum pay-off in row)} + (1 - \alpha) \text{ minimum pay-off in row.}$$

EXAMPLE 20.2: Consider the following pay-off (profit) matrix:

Action	States			
	S_1	S_2	S_3	S_4
A_1	5	10	18	25
A_2	8	7	8	23
A_3	21	18	12	21
A_4	30	22	19	15

No Probabilities are known for the occurrence of the nature states. Compare the solutions obtained by each of the following criteria: (i) Maximin (ii) Laplace (iii) Hurwicz (assume that $\alpha = 0.5$)

Solution:

(i) Maximin Criterion:

A_1	5	10	18	25	**5 Minimum**
A_2	8	7	8	23	7
A_3	21	18	12	21	12
A_4	30	22	19	15	**15 Maximum**

Best action is A_4.

(ii) Leplace Criterion:

$$E(A_1) = 1/4\,[5 + 10 + 18 + 25] = 14.5$$
$$E(A_2) = 1/4\,[8 + 7 + 8 + 23] = 11.5$$
$$E(A_3) = 1/4\,[21 + 18 + 12 + 21] = 18.0$$
$$E(A_4) = 1/4\,[30 + 22 + 19 + 15] = 21.5 \quad \textbf{Maximum}$$

$E(A_4)$ is maximum. So the best action is A_4.

(iii) Hurwicz Criterion (with $\alpha = 0.5$)

	Minimum	Maximum	α(max) + (1 – α) min
A_1	5	25	0.5 (25) + 0.5 (5) = 15
A_2	7	23	0.5 (7) + 0.5 (23) = 15
A_3	12	21	0.5 (12) + 0.5 (21) = 16.5
A_4	15	30	0.5 (15) + 0.5 (30) = **22.5 Maximum**

EXAMPLE 20.3: Suppose that a decision maker faced with three decision alternatives and two states of nature. Apply (i) Maximin and (ii) Minimax regret approach to the following pay-off table to recommend the decisions.

Act	States of Nature	
	S_1	S_2
A_1	10	15
A_2	20	12
A_3	30	11

Solution:

(i) Maximin:

Act	Minimum
A_1	10
A_2	**12 maximum**
A_3	11

Act A_2 is recommended

(ii) Minimax regret:

Act	States of Nature		Maximum Regret
	S_1	S_2	
A_1	30 – 10 = 20	15 – 15 = 0	20
A_2	30 – 20 = 10	15 – 12 = 3	10
A_3	30 – 30 = 0	15 – 11 = 4	4

Minimum of the maximum regrets is 4 which correspond to the act A_3. So the act A_3 is recommended

EXAMPLE 20.4: A business man has to select three alternatives open to him each of which can be followed by any of the four possible events. The conditional pay-off (in Rs) for each action event combination is given below:

Alternative	Pay-offs conditional events			
	A	B	C	D
X	8	0	–10	6
Y	–4	12	18	–2
Z	14	6	0	8

Determine which alternative the businessman should choose, if he adopts the

(a) Maximin criterion (b) Maximax criterion

(c) Hurwicz criterion with degree of optimism is 0.7

(d) Minimax regret Criterion (e) Laplace criterion

Solution: For the given pay-off martrix, the maximum assured and minimum possible pay-off for each alternative are as given below.

Alternative	Maximum pay-off (Rs)	Minimum pay-off (Rs)	(α = 0.7) $H = \alpha$ (maximum pay-off) + (1 – α) (minimum pay-off)
X	8	–10	2.6
Y	18	– 4	11.4
Z	14	0	9.8

(a) Since *Z* yields the maximum of the minimum pay-off, under maximin criterion, alternative *Z* would be chosen.

(b) Under maximax criterion, the businessman would choose the alternative *Y*.

(c) It will be optimal to choose *Y* under Hurwicz Criterion.

(d) For the given pay-off matrix, we determine the regrets as shown below, when the regret payoffs amounts when event *A* occurs, are computed by the relation

Regret pay-off = maximum pay-offs from *A* – pay-off.

Similarly for the other events.

Alternative	Pay-off amount				Regret pay-off amount				Maximum Regret
	A	*B*	*C*	*D*	*A*	*B*	*C*	*D*	
X	8	0	–10	6	6	12	28	2	28
Y	– 4	12	18	– 2	18	0	0	10	18
Z	14	6	0	8	0	6	18	0	18
Maximum pay-off	**14**	**12**	**18**	**8**					

Since alternative *Y* and *Z* both corresponding to the minimal of the maximum possible regrets, the decision maker would choose either of these two

(e) Laplace Criterion:

In this method assigning equal probabilities to the pay-off of each strategy, results in the following expected pay-off.

Alternative	Pay-off value				Expected pay-off value
	A	*B*	*C*	*D*	
	p = 1/4	*P* = 1/4	*P* = 1/4	*P* = 1/4	
X	8	0	–10	6	¼ [8 + 0 – 10 + 6] = 1
Y	– 4	12	18	– 2	¼ [– 4 + 12 + 18 – 2] = 56
Z	14	6	0	8	¼ [14 + 6 + 0 + 8] = 7

Since the expected pay-off value for *Z* is the maximum the businessman would choose alternative *Z*

20.7 DECISION MAKING UNDER RISK (WITH PROBABILITY)

Here the decision maker faces many states of nature. As such, he is supposed to believe authentic information, knowledge, past experience or happenings to enable him to assign probability values to the likelihood of occurrence of each state of nature. Sometimes with reference to past records, experience or information, probabilities to future events could be allotted. On the basis of probability distribution of the states of nature, one may select the best course of action having the highest expected pay-off value.

EXAMPLE 20.5: The pay-off table for three courses of action (A) with three states of nature (E) (or events) with their respective probabilities (p) is given. Find the best course of action.

Events	E_1	E_2	E_3
Probability → Acts ↓	0.2	0.5	0.3
A_1	2	1	–1
A_2	3	2	0
A_3	4	2	1

The expected value for each act is:

$$A_1 : 2(0.2) + 1(0.5) - 1(0.3) = 0.6$$
$$A_2 : 3(0.2) + 2(0.5) + 0(0.3) = 1.6$$
$$A_3 : 4(0.2) + 2(0.5) + 1(0.3) = 2.1$$

The expected monetary value for the act 3 is maximum. Therefore the best course of action is A_3.

EXAMPLE 20.6: Given the following pay-off of 3 acts: A_1, A_2, A_3 and their events E_1, E_2, E_3.

States of Nature	Act		
	A_1	A_2	A_3
E_1	35	–10	–150
E_2	200	240	200
E_3	550	640	750

The probabilities of the states of nature are respectively 0.3, 0.4 and 0.3. Calculate and tabulate EMV and conclude which of the acts can be chosen as the best.

Solution:

Events	Prob.	A_1	A_2	A_3
E_1	0.3	35 × 0.3 = 10.5	–10 × 0.3 = – 3	–150 × 0.3 = –45
E_2	0.4	200 × 0.4 = 80.0	240 × 0.4 = 96	200 × 0.4 = 80
E_3	0.3	550 × 0.3 = 165.0	640 × 0.3 = 192	750 × 0.3 = 225
EMV		**= 255.5**	**= 285**	**= 260**

The EMV of A_2 is maximum, therefore to choose A_2.

EXAMPLE 20.7: A shop keeper has the facility to store a large number of perishable items. He buys them at a rate of Rs 3 per item and sells at the rate of Rs 5 per item. If an item is not sold at the end of the day then there is a loss of Rs 3 per item. The daily demand has the following probability distribution.

Number of items demanded	3	4	5	6
Probability	0.2	0.3	0.3	0.2

How many items should he stored so that his daily expected profit is maximum?

Solution:

Let m = number of items stocked daily

n = number of items demanded daily

Now, for $n \geq m$, profit $= 2m$

And for $m > n$, profit $= 2n - 3(m - n)$

$= 2n - 3m + 3n = 5n - 3m$

Pay-off table

Stock (m)	**Demand (n)**			
	3	**4**	**5**	**6**
3	6	6	6	6
4	3	8	8	8
5	0	5	10	10
6	–3	2	7	12
Probability	**0.2**	**0.3**	**0.3**	**0.2**

Stock (m)	**Expected gain**		
3	6 × 0.2 + 6 × 0.3 + 6 × 0.3 + 6 × 0.2	=	Rs 6.00
4	3 × 0.2 + 8 × 0.3 + 8 × 0.3 + 8 × 0.2	=	Rs 7.00
5	0 × 0.2 + 5 × 0.3 + 10 × 0.3 + 10 × 0.2	=	Rs 6.50
6	–3 × 0.2 + 2 × 0.3 + 7 × 0.3 + 12 × 0.2	=	Rs 4.50

Thus the highest expected gain is Rs 7.00 when 4 units stocked. So, he can store 4 items to get maximum expected profit daily.

EXAMPLE 20.8: A magazine distributor assigns probabilities to the demand for a magazine as follows:

Copies demanded	2	3	4	5
Probability	0.4	0.3	0.2	0.1

A copy of magazine which he sells at Rs 8 costs Rs 6. How many should he stock to get the maximum possible expected profit if the distributor can return back unsold copies for Rs 5 each?

Solution:

Let m = no. of magazines stocked daily

n = no. of magazines demanded

Now, for $n \geq m$, profit = Rs $2\,m$

and for $m > n$,

$$\begin{aligned} \text{profit} &= 8n - 6m + 5(m - n) \\ &= 8n - 6m + 5m - 5n \\ &= 3n - m \end{aligned}$$

Pay-off table				
Stock (*m*)	**Demand (*n*)**			
	2	**3**	**4**	**5**
2	4	4	4	4
3	3	6	6	6
4	2	5	8	8
5	1	4	7	10
Probability	**0.4**	**0.3**	**0.2**	**0.1**

Stock	**Expected Profit (in Rs)**		
2	4 × 0.4 + 4 × 0.3 + 4 × 0.2 + 4 × 0.1	=	Rs 4.0
3	3 × 0.4 + 6 × 0.3 + 6 × 0.2 + 6 × 0.1	=	Rs 4.8
4	2 × 0.4 + 5 × 0.3 + 8 × 0.2 + 8 × 0.1	=	Rs 4.7
5	1 × 0.4 + 4 × 0.3 + 7 × 0.2 + 10 × 0.1	=	Rs 4.0

Thus the highest expected profit is Rs 4.8, when 3 magazines stocked. So, the distributor can stock 3 magazines to get the maximum possible expected profit.

20.8 DECISION TREE ANALYSIS

A decision problem may also be represented with the help of a diagram. It shows all the possible courses of action, states of nature, and the probabilities associated with the states of nature.

The ***'decision diagram'*** looks very much like a drawing of a tree, therefore also called ***'decision tree'.***

A decision tree consists of nodes, branches, probability estimates and pay-offs. Nodes are of two types, decision node (designated as a square) and chance node (designated as a circle).

Alternative courses of action originate from decision node as the main branches (decision branches). Now at the terminal point of decision node, chance node exists from where chance nodes, emanate as sub-branches. The respective pay-offs and the probabilities associated with alternative courses, and the chance events are shown alongside the chance branches. At the terminal of the chance branches are shown the expected pay-off values of the outcome.

There are basically two types of decision trees-deterministic and probabilistic. These can further be divided into single stage and multistage trees. A single stage deterministic decision tree involves making only one decision under conditions of certainty (no chance events). In a multistage deterministic tree a sequence or chains of decisions are to be made, the optimal path (strategy) is one that corresponds to the maximum EMV.

In drawing a decision tree, one must follow certain basic rules and conventions as stated below:

- Identify all decisions (and their alternatives) to be made and the order in which they must be made.

- Identify the chance events or state of nature that might occur as a result of each decision alternative.
- Develop a tree diagram showing the sequence of decisions and chance events. The tree is constructed starting from left and moving towards right. The square box denotes a decision point at which the available courses of action are considered. The circle O represents the chance node or event, the various states of nature or outcomes emanate from this chance event.
- Estimate probabilities that possible events or states of nature will occur as a result of the decision alternatives.
- Obtain outcomes (usually expressed in economic terms) of the possible interactions among decision alternatives and events.
- Calculate the expected value of all possible decision alternatives.
- Select the decision alternative (or course of action) offering the most attractive expected value

20.8.1 Advantages of Decision Tree

- By drawing of decision tree, the decision maker will be in a position to visualise the entire complex of the problem.
- Enable the decision - maker to see the various elements of his problem in content and in a systematic way.
- Multi-dimensional decision sequences can be strung on a decision tree without conceptual difficulties.
- Decision tree model can be applied in various fields such as introduction of a new product, marketing strategy etc.

EXAMPLE 20.9: A manufacturing company has to select one of the two products A or B for manufacturing. Product A requires investment of Rs 20,000 and product B Rs 40,000. Market research survey shows high, medium and low demands with corresponding probabilities and returns from sales in Rs. Thousand for the two products in the following table.

Market demand	Probability		Return from sales	
	A	*B*	*A*	*B*
High	0.4	0.3	50	80
Medium	0.3	0.5	30	60
Low	0.3	0.2	10	50

Construct an appropriate decision tree. What decision the company should take?

Solution: See Figure 20.6 on next page.

Market demand		Probability			Return from sales	
	X('000)	*P*	*PX*	*X*('000)	*P*	*PX*
High	50	0.4	20	80	0.3	24
Medium	30	0.3	9	60	0.5	30
Low	10	0.3	3	50	0.2	10
Total			**32**			**64**

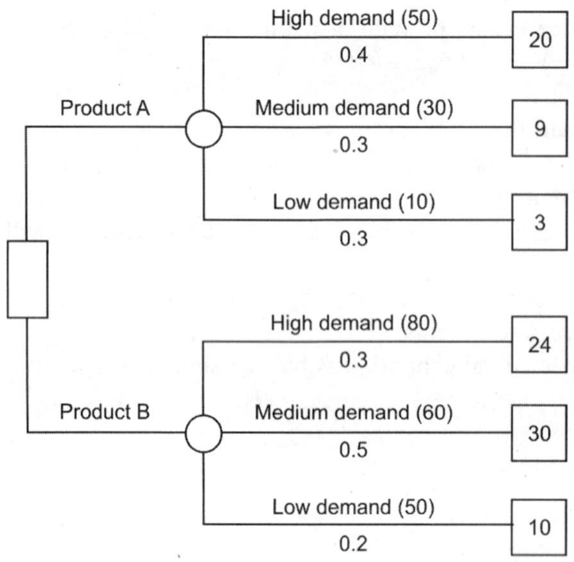

Fig. 20.6

Product	Return (Rs)	Investment (Rs)	Profit (Rs)
A	32,000	20,000	12,000
B	64,000	40,000	24,000

Since the profit is high in case of product B, so the company's decision in favour of B.

EXAMPLE 20.10: A farm owner is considering drilling a farm well. In the past, only 70% of wells drilled were successful at 20 metres of depth in that area. Moreover, on finding no water at 20 metres, some person drilled it further up to 25 metres but only 20% struck water at 25 metres. The prevailing cost of drilling is Rs 500 per metres. The farm owner has estimated that in case he does not get his own well, he will have to pay Rs 15000 over the next 10 years to buy water from the neighbour. Draw an appropriate decision tree and determine the farm owner's strategy under EMV approach.

Solution: The given data is represented by the following decision tree diagram.

Decision at point D_2				
Decision	**Event**	**Probability**	**Cash out flows**	**Expected cash out flow**
1. Drill upto 25 metres	Water struck	0.2	Rs 12500	Rs 2500
	No water struck	0.8	Rs 27500	Rs 22000
			EMV (out flows)	**Rs 24500**
2. Do not drill			**EMV (out flow)**	**Rs 25000**

The decision at D_2 is: Drill up to 25 metres

Decision at point D_1				
Decision	**Event**	**Probability**	**Cash out flows**	**Expected cash out flow**
1. Drill upto 20 metres	Water struck	0.7	Rs 10000	Rs 7000
	No water struck	0.3	Rs 24500	Rs 7350
			EMV (out flows)	**Rs 14350**
2. Do not drill			**EMV (out flow)**	**Rs 15000**

The decision at D_1 is: Drill up to 20 metres.
Thus the optimal strategy for the farm-owner is to drill the well up to 20 metres.

SELF PRACTICE EXERCISES

I. CHOOSE THE BEST ANSWER

1. Decision theory is concerned with:
   (a) The amount of information that is available
   (b) Criteria for measuring the 'goodness' of a decision
   (c) Selecting optimal decisions in sequential problems
   (d) All of the above
2. Which of the following criteria does not apply to decision-making under uncertainly:
   (a) Maximin return (b) Maximax return
   (c) Minimax return (d) Maximize expected return
3. Maximin return, maximax return and minimax regret are criteria that:
   (a) Lead to the same optimal decision (b) Cannot be used with probabilities
   (c) Both (a) and (b) (d) None of the above
4. Which of the following does not apply to a decision tree?
   (a) A square node is a point at which a decision must be made.
   (b) A circular node represents an encounter with uncertainty.
   (c) One chooses a sequence of decisions which have the greatest probability of success.
   (d) One attempts to maximize expected return.
5. The criterion which selects the action for which maximum pay-off is lowest is known as:
   (a) Max-min criterion (b) Min-max criterion
   (c) Max–max criterion (d) None of these

II. FILL IN THE BLANKS

1. Decision trees involve .... of decisions and random outcomes.
2. One way to deal with decision making in the 'uncertainty' context is to treat all states of nature as .... and maximize expected return.
3. Maximizing expected net rupee return always yields the same optimal policy as .... expected regret.
4. The different criteria for making decisions under risk always yield the same .... choice.
5. In decision under uncertainty, the Laplace criterion is the least conservative while the .... criterion is the most conservative.

III. SHORT ANSWER TYPE QUESTIONS

1. Explain the meaning of 'Statistical Decision Theory'
2. What techniques are used to solve decision making problems under uncertainty?
3. Write a note on decision tree.
4. What is a pay-off matrix?
5. Describe how you would determine the best decision using the EMV criterion with a decision tree.

IV. LONG ANSWER TYPE QUESTIONS

1. The pay-off table for three courses of action (A) with three states of nature (E) (or events) with their respective probabilities (P) are given. Find the best course of action.

Events → Acts ↓	E_1	E_2	E_3
A_1	2.5	2.0	–1
A_2	4.0	2.6	0
A_3	3.0	1.8	1
Probability	**0.2**	**0.6**	**0.2**

2. Calculate EMV and thus select the best act for the following pay-off table:

States of nature	Probability	Pay-off (Rs) by the player		
		A	*B*	*C*
X	0.3	–2	–5	20
Y	0.4	20	–10	–5
Z	0.3	40	60	30

3. Consider the pay-off matrix:

States of nature	Probability	Act A_1 do not expand	Act A_2 do not expand	Act A_3 do not expand
High demand	0.4	2500	3500	5000
Medium demand	0.4	2500	3500	2500
Low demand	0.2	2500	1500	1000

Using EMV criterion decide the best act.

4. Apply (i) maximin (ii) minimax regret to the following pay-off matrix to recommend the decisions without any knowledge of probability.

Act	States of Nature		
	S_1	S_2	S_3
A_1	14	8	10
A_2	11	10	7
A_3	9	12	13

5. A shop keeper of some highly perishable type of fruits sees that the daily demand X of this fruit in his area the following probability distribution.

Daily demand (in dozen)	6	7	8	9
Probability	0.1	0.3	0.4	0.2

He sells for Rs 10.00 a dozen while he buys each dozen at Rs 4.00. Unsold fruits in a day are traded on the next day at Rs 2.00 per dozen, assuming that the stocks the fruits in dozen, how many should he stock so that his expected profit will be maximum?

[**Hint:** profit = $6m$ for $n \geq m = 10n - 4m + 2(m - n) = 8n - 2m$ for $n < m$]

6. A florist, in order to satisfy the needs of a number of regular and sophisticated customers, stocks a highly perishable flowers. A dozen flowers cost Rs 3 and sell at Rs 10.00 Any flower not sold on the day are worthless. Demand distribution in dozen of flowers is as follows:

Demand	1	2	3	4
Probability	0.2	0.3	0.3	0.2

How many flowers should he stock daily in order to maximize his expected net profit?

7. A florist stock highly perishable flower. A dozen of flower costs Rs 3.00 and sells for Rs 10.00 Any flower not sold the day are worthless. Demand in dozen of flowers is as follows:

Demand (in dozen)	0	1	2	3	4
Probability	0.1	0.2	0.3	0.4	0.1

Assuming that failure to satisfy any one customer's request will result in future lost profit amounting to Rs 5.00, in addition to the lost profit on the immediate sale, how many flowers should the florist stock to expect maximum profit?

8. A newspaper agent's experience shows that the daily demand x of newspaper in his area has the following probability distribution:

Daily Demand (x)	300	400	500	600	700
Probability	0.1	0.3	0.4	0.1	0.1

He sales the newspapers for Rs 2.00 each while he buys each at Re 1.00. Unsold copies are treated as scrap and each such copy fetches 10 paisa. Assuming that he stocks the news papers in multiple of 100 only. How many should he stock so that his expected profit is maximum?

9. Suppose that a decision maker faced with three decision alternatives and four states of nature. Given the following profit pay-off table.

Act	States of Nature			
	S_1	S_2	S_3	S_4
A_1	16	10	12	7
A_2	13	12	9	9
A_3	11	14	15	14

Assuming that he has no knowledge of the probabilities of occurrence of the states of nature, find the decisions to be recommended under each of the following criteria.

(i) maximin (ii) maximax (iii) minimax Regret

10. Pay-off of three acts *A*, *B* and *C* and states of nature *X*, *Y* and *Z* are given below:

Pay-off (in Rs)			
States of Nature	Act		
	A	*B*	*C*
X	–20	–50	2000
Y	200	–100	–50
Z	400	600	300

The probabilities of the states of nature are 0.3, 0.4 and 0.3. Calculate the EMV for the above and select the best art.

ANSWERS

I. CHOOSE THE BEST ANSWERS

1. (d) 2. (d) 3. (b) 4. (c) 5. (a)

II. FILL IN THE BLANKS

1. Sequence 2. equally likely 3. minimizing 9. Optimal 5. Minimax

IV. LONG ANSWER TYPE QUESTIONS

1. A_2 is the best
2. Select A with the highest EMV Rs 194
3. EMV: 3200, decide, Act A_3, expand 400 units
4. (i) maximin : Act A_3 (ii) minimax regret Act a1
5. So the shop keeper should stock 8 dozen of fruits to get maximum expected profit.
6. He should stock 3 dozen of flowers to get maximum expected net profit.
7. He stocks 3 dozen of flowers to expect maximum profit Rs 9.50
8. To stock 405 copies so that his expected profit is maximum
9. (i) Act A_3 is recommended (ii) Act A_1 is recommended
   (iii) Act A_3 is recommended
10. EMA for *A* is highest. So the best act is *A* is selected

CHAPTER 21

Statistical Quality Control (SQC)

21.1 INTRODUCTION

Every product manufactured is required for a specific purpose. It means that if the product meets the specifications required for its rightful use, it is of good quality and if not, then the quality of the product is considered to be poor.

It is a well known fact that all repetitive process no matter how carefully arranged is not exactly identical and contains some variability. Even in the manufacture of commodities by highly specialised machines it is not unusual to come across differences between various units of production. For example, in the manufacture of corks, bottles, etc even though highly efficient machines are used some difference may be noticed in various units. If the differences are not much, it can be ignored and the product can be passed off as within specifications. But if it is beyond certain limits, the article has to be rejected and the cause of such variation has to be investigated.

DO YOU KNOW?

SQC is an effective system for co-ordinating the quality maintenance and quality improvement efforts of the various groups in an organization so as to enable production at the most economical levels which allow for full customer satisfaction.

21.2 CAUSES FOR VARIATION

The variation occurs due to two types of causes namely:

(i) Chance Causes (ii) Assignable Causes

(i) Chance Causes: If the variation occurs due to some inherent pattern of variation and no causes can be assigned to it, it is called **chance** or **random variation.** Chance Variation is tolerable, permissible inevitable and does not materially affect the quality of a product.

(ii) Assignable Causes: The causes due to faulty process and procedure are known as assignable causes is of non–random nature. These causes may creep in at any stage of the process, right from the arrival of the raw materials to the final delivery of goods. These causes can be identified and eliminated and are to be discovered in a production process before it goes wrong i.e., before the production becomes defective.

21.3 ROLE OF SQC

The role of statistical quality control is to collect and analyse relevant data for the purpose of detecting whether the process is under control or not. The value of quality control lies in the fact that assignable causes in a process can be quickly detected. In fact the variations are often discovered before the product becomes defective.

SQC is a well accepted and widespread process on the basis of which it is possible to understand the principles and techniques by which decisions are made based on variation. Statistical quality control is only diagnostic. It tells us whether the standard is being maintained or not. The remedial action rests with the technicians who employ techniques for the maintenance of uniform quality in a continuous flow of manufactured products.

The purpose for which SQC are used are two fold namely,

- Process Control
- Product Control

In process control an attempt is made to find out if a particular process is within control or not. Process control helps in studying the future performance.

21.4 PROCESS AND PRODUCT CONTROL

The main objective in any production process is to control and maintain quality of the manufactured product so that it confirms to specified quality standards. In other words, we want to ensure that the proportion of defective items in the manufactured product is not too large. This is called **process control** and is achieved through the technique of control charts.

On the other hand, by **product control** we mean controlling the quality of the product by critical examination at strategic points and this is achieved through sampling inspection plans pioneered by Dodge and Roming. Product control aims at guaranteeing a certain quality level to the consumer regardless of what quality level is being maintained by the producer. In other worlds, it attempts to ensure that the product marketed by the sale department does not contain a large number of defective items.

21.5 CONTROL CHARTS

The statistical tool applied in process control is the **control chart**. Control charts are the devices to describe the patterns of variation. The control charts were developed by the physicist, ***Walter A. Shewart*** of Bell Telephone Company in 1924. He suggested that the control chart may serve, first to define the goal or standard for the process that the management might strive to attain. Secondly, it may be used as an instrument to attain that goal and thirdly, it may serve as a means of judging whether the goal is being achieved. Thus, control chart is an instrument to be used in specification, production and inspection and is the core of statistical quality control.

A control chart is essentially a graphic device for presenting data so as to directly reveal the frequency and extent of variations from established standards or goals. Control charts are simple to construct and easy to interpret and they tell the manager at a glance whether or not the process is in control, i.e. within the tolerance limits.

In general a control chart consists of three horizontal lines

- A central line to indicate the desired standard or level of the process (C.L)

- Upper control limit (U.C.L) and
- Lower control limit (L.C.L)

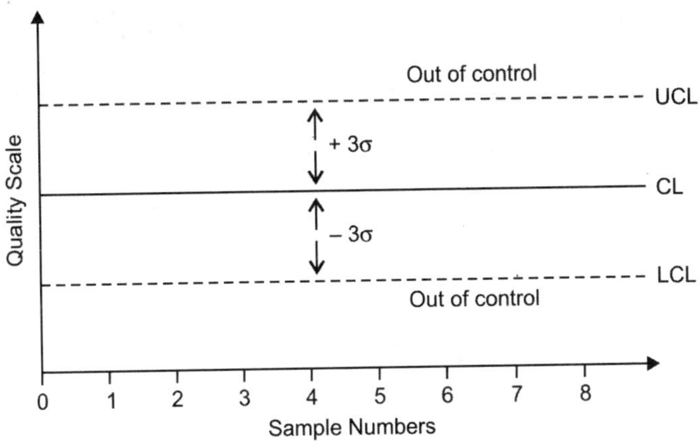

Fig. 21.1: Outline of a Control Chart.

From time to time a sample is taken and the data are plotted on the graph. If the entire sample points fall within the upper and lower control limits, it is assumed that the process is "in control" and only chance causes are present. When a sample point falls outside the control limits, it is assumed that variations are due to assignable causes.

21.6 CONTROL LIMITS

In the given figure, 21.1, the two control limits have been set at a distance of 3 σ each on either side of the mean. The 3 σ limits were proposed by ***Dr. Shewart*** for probabilistic considerations. If a variable *X* is normally distributed the probability that a random observation would lie $\mu \pm 3\sigma$ (where μ is the mean and σ is the standard deviation) is .9973. It means that the probability of an observation falling outside these limits is only .0027 which is very low. These limits are also known as Tolerance limits. Even for the non–normal distribution 3 – σ limits are almost universally used, as they have been found to be most suitable empirically in the sense that the 3 – σ control charts have been found to give excellent protection against both types of wrong actions.

21.7 TYPES OF CONTROL CHARTS

Broadly speaking control charts can be divided under two heads.

- Control charts for Variables
- Control charts for Attributes

Control Charts for Variables concern with measurable data on quality characteristics which are usually continuous in nature. Such type of data utilises $\bar{X}$, R chart and standard deviation (σ – chart)

Control Charts of Attributes, namely *c, np* and *p* charts concern with the data on quality characteristics, which are not amenable to measurement or attributes (product defective or non defective).

21.8 CONTROL CHARTS FOR VARIABLES

Control charts for variables are based on normal distribution and they are designed for sample means rather than individual measurements. These charts help to achieve and maintain a desired quality level for a process whose product is amenable to quantitative measurements. In case of variables the control charts are prepared for Mean ($\overline{X}$ – chart), for Range (R – chart) and for standard deviation (σ – chart).

21.8.1 Control Chart For Mean or $\overline{X}$ – Chart

In order to ascertain whether the process is in control or out of control, $\overline{X}$ – charts are constructed. The following steps are involved in the preparations of an $\overline{X}$ – chart:

(i) Take measurements of sample units which should be selected at random from process product.

(ii) Select a number of samples or sub–groups at random so that each unit in the lot has the same chance of selection.

(iii) Obtain the mean of each sample X_i ; $i = 1, 2, 3, \ldots\ldots n$.

(iv) Obtain the mean of the sample means i.e., $\overline{\overline{X}} = \dfrac{\overline{X}_1 + \overline{X}_2 + \ldots \overline{X}_n}{n}$

Where n is the total number of samples

(v) Set the upper and lower control limits as follows:

$$\text{U.C.L} = \overline{\overline{X}} + 3\sigma_{\overline{x}} = \overline{\overline{X}} + 3\frac{\sigma}{\sqrt{n}}$$

$$\text{L.C.L} = \overline{\overline{X}} - 3\sigma_{\overline{x}} = \overline{\overline{X}} - 3\frac{\sigma}{\sqrt{n}}$$

Hence to construct the control limits we need to estimate the standard deviation σ, of the process. If such estimation is not available, then the calculation of control limits is based on the average range values. It can be shown that an estimator of the process standard deviation σ is the average range $\overline{R}$ divided by d_2, a constant which depends on the sample size n. That is

$$\sigma = \frac{\overline{R}}{d_2}$$

If we substitute this value for σ, then the upper and lower control limits for the $\overline{X}$ – chart can be written as:

$$\text{U.C.L} = \overline{\overline{X}} + \frac{3\sigma}{\sqrt{n}} = \overline{X} + \frac{3}{\sqrt{n}} \cdot \frac{\overline{R}}{d_2} = \overline{\overline{X}} + A_2\overline{R}$$

and

$$\text{L.C.L} = \overline{\overline{X}} - A_2\overline{R}$$

Where $A_2 = \dfrac{3}{d_2\sqrt{n}}$ is a constant that depends on the sample size.

(vi) Construct the $\overline{X}$ – chart by taking the sample number on the horizontal scale (X – axis) and the quality level on the vertical scale (Y– axis). Sample points may be plotted by dots. Draw the central line prominently.

The U.C.L and L.C.L may be drawn by dots.

21.8.2 *R* – Chart (Range Chart)

The *R*– chart is used to show the variability or dispersion of the quality produced by a given process. *R*– chart is the companion chart to the $\overline{X}$ – chart and both are usually required for adequate analysis of the production process under study. The *R*– chart is generally presented along with the $\overline{X}$ – chart. The general procedure for constructing the *R*– chart is similar to that for the $\overline{X}$ – chart. The required values for constructing the range chart are:

(i) The Range of each sample, *R*.
(ii) The Mean of the sample ranges, *R*
(iii) The control limits are set at

$$\text{U.C.L}_R = D_2\,\sigma \quad \text{or} \quad \overline{R} + 3\,\sigma_R$$
$$\text{L.C.L}_R = D_1\,\sigma \quad \text{or} \quad \overline{R} - 3\,\sigma_R$$

Where the process standard deviation is known. If the process standard deviation is not known these limits are given by

$$\text{U.C.L}_R = D_4\,\overline{R}$$
$$\text{L.C.L}_R = D_3\,\overline{R}$$

Where D_1, D_2, D_3 and D_4 are constants depending on the sample size *n* and can be obtained from tables given in last of book.

Interpretation of $\overline{X}$ and R-Charts

In order to judge if a process is in control, $\overline{X}$ and *R* charts should be examined together and the process should be deemed in statistical control if both the charts show a state of control. i.e if all the sample points are scattered within the control limits, the process is under statistical control and is satisfactory.

If one or more points in any or both the charts go out of the tolerance limits, then the process is out of control. Such a situation indicates the presence of some assignable cause which must be identified and one should first eliminate the assignable cause in *R*–chart. In most of the cases this will automatically eliminate the assignable variations in $\overline{X}$ – chart. So if *R* chart show a state of out of control, $\overline{X}$ – chart should not be interpreted.

EXAMPLE 21.1: The following data relate to the life (in hours) of 10 samples of 6 electric bulbs each drawn at an interval of one hour from a production process. Draw the control chart for *X* and *R* and comment. **[UPTU, 2005, 2007]**

Sample No.	Life time (in hours)					
1	620	687	666	689	738	686
2	501	585	524	585	653	668
3	673	701	686	567	619	660
4	646	626	572	628	631	743
5	494	984	659	643	660	640
6	634	755	625	583	683	555
7	619	710	664	693	770	534
8	630	723	614	535	550	570
9	482	791	533	612	497	499
10	706	524	626	503	661	754

(Given for $n = 6$, $A_2 = 0.483$, $D_3 = 0$, $D_4 = 2.004$)

Solution:

Sample No.	Total	Sample Mean $\overline{X}$	Sample Range R
1	4086	681	118
2	3516	586	167
3	3906	651	134
4	3846	641	171
5	4080	680	490
6	3834	639	200
7	3990	665	236
8	3622	604	188
9	3414	569	309
10	3774	629	251
	Total	**6345**	**2264**

$$\text{Central line } \overline{\overline{X}} = \text{Mean of the sample means} = 634.5$$

$$\overline{R} = \text{Mean of the sample ranges} = 226.4$$

$$\text{U.C.L}_{\overline{X}} = \overline{\overline{X}} + A_2\,\overline{R}$$

$$= 634.5 + 0.483 \times 226.4$$

$$= 634.5 + 109.35 = 743.85$$

$$\text{L.C.L}_{\overline{X}} = \overline{\overline{X}} - A_2\overline{R}$$

$$= 634.5 - 0.483 \times 226.4$$

$$= 634.5 - 109.35 = 525.15$$

$$\text{Central } \overline{R} = 226.4$$

$$\text{U.C.L}_R = D_4\,\overline{R} = 2.004 \times 226.4$$

$$= 453.7056$$

$$\text{L.C.L}_R = D_3\,\overline{R} = 0 \times 226.4 = 0$$

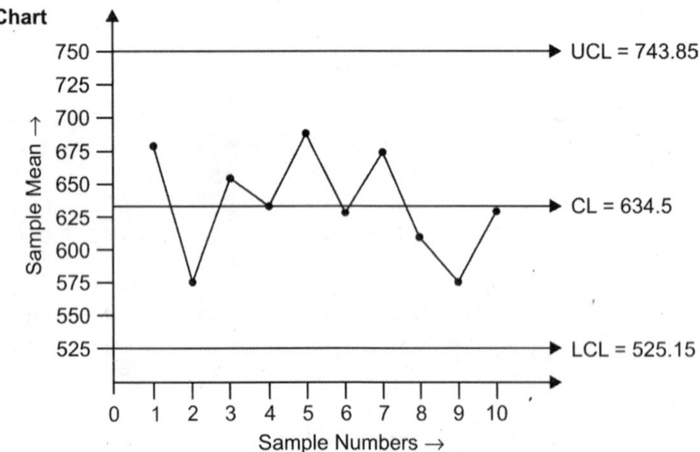

Fig. 21.2

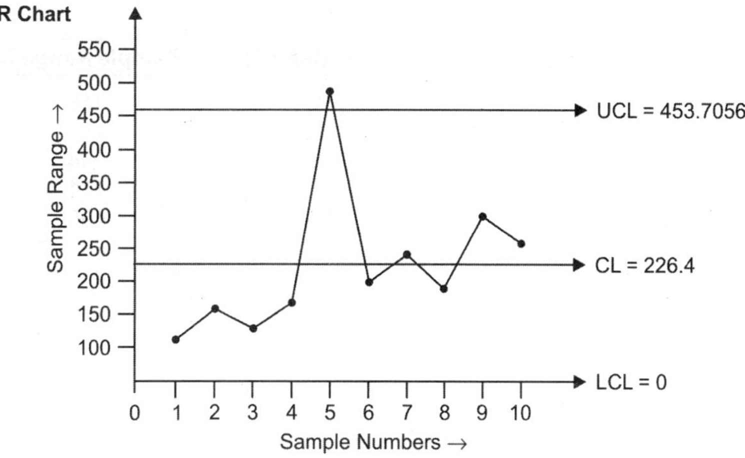

Fig. 21.3

Conclusion: Since one of the points of the sample range is outside the UCL of R chart, the process is not in control.

EXAMPLE 21.2: The following data shows the value of sample mean X and the range R for ten samples of size 5 each. Calculate the values for central line and control limits for mean chart and range chart and determine whether the process is in control. **[MBA, UPTU, (CO), 2005]**

Sample no.	1	2	3	4	5	6	7	8	9	10
Mean $\bar{X}$	11.2	11.8	10.6	11.6	11.0	9.6	10.4	9.6	10.6	10.0
Range (R)	7	4	8	5	7	4	8	4	7	9

(Given for $n = 5$; $A_2 = 0.577$; $D_3 = 0$; $D_4 = 2.115$)

Solution: Control limits for X chart

$$\bar{\bar{X}} = \frac{1}{n}\Sigma\bar{X} = \frac{1}{10}(11.2 + 11.8 + 10.8 + ... + 10.0) = 10.66$$

$$\bar{R} = \frac{1}{n}\Sigma R = \frac{1}{10}(63) = 6.3$$

$$\text{U.C.L}_{\bar{X}} = \bar{\bar{X}} + A_2\bar{R} = 10.66 + (0.577 \times 6.3) = 14.295$$

$$\text{L.C.L}_{\bar{X}} = \bar{\bar{X}} - A_2\bar{R} = 10.66 - (0.577 \times 6.3) = 7.025$$

$$\text{C.L}_X = \text{Central line} = \bar{\bar{X}} = 10.66$$

$$\text{U.C.L}_R = D_4\,\bar{R}$$
$$= 2.115 \times 6.3 = 13.324$$

$$\text{L.C.L}_R = D_3\,\bar{R} = 0$$
$$\text{C.L}_R = \bar{R} = 6.3$$

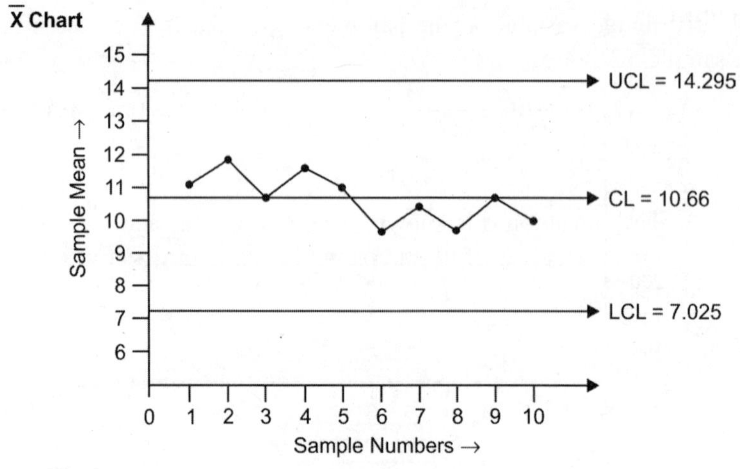

Fig. 21.4

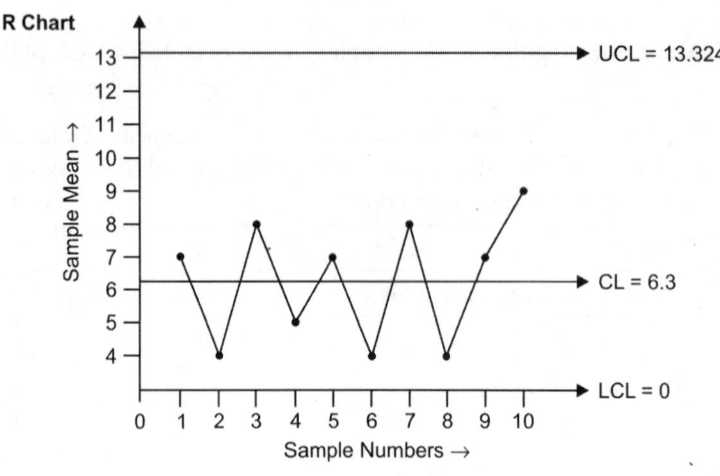

Fig. 21.5

Conclusion: Since all the points of sample mean and range are within the control limits, the process is in control.

21.8.3 S–CHART

As discussed earlier, that when the sample size n is moderately large, say $n \geq 10$, the estimates based on sample range loose in terms of statistical efficiency as compared to those based on sample *S.D.* In view of this, it is recommended that the variability in the quality characteristics be controlled by *S*–chart. Therefore, we calculate sample standard deviation, *S*, for each sample. for defining the statistical basis of *S*–chart, we consider $w = S$ as the sample statistic measuring the variability of the quality characteristics under consideration. Thus on using (2), the control limits for *S*–chart becomes:

$$\left.\begin{aligned} \textbf{U.C.L.} &= \mu_s + 3\sigma_s \\ \textbf{Central Line} &= \mu_s \\ \textbf{L.C.L.} &= \mu_s - 3\sigma_s \end{aligned}\right] \quad ...(1)$$

For a normally distributed variable *X*, the parameters μ_S and σ_S (i.e., the mean and *S.D* of the distribution of the sample *S.D.*) are

$$\left.\begin{aligned} \mu_s &= E(S) = c_2\sigma \\ \text{and} \qquad \sigma_s &= \sqrt{V(S)} = \sigma\sqrt{\frac{n-1}{n} - c_2^2} \end{aligned}\right] \qquad ...(2)$$

Now, when the standard deviation σ is known, the control limits and the central line for s –chart can be obtained by replacing the values of μ_S and σ_R in (2) by their respective values in (1). Thus, the control limits for *S*–chart are:

$$\left.\begin{aligned} \text{U.C.L} &= c_2\sigma + 3\sigma\sqrt{\frac{n-1}{n} c_2^2} = \left(c_2 + 3\sqrt{\frac{n-1}{n} - c_2^2}\right)\sigma = B_2\sigma \\ \text{C.L} &= c_2\sigma \\ \text{L.C.L} &= c_2\sigma - 3\sigma\sqrt{\frac{n-1}{n} - c_2^2} = \left(c_2 - 3\sqrt{\frac{n-1}{n} - c_2^2}\right)\sigma = B_1\sigma \end{aligned}\right] \qquad ...(3)$$

As usual, the values of c_2, B_1 and B_2 are given in Appendix for various values of *n*. Further, when σ, the standard is unknown, its estimate is obtained as:

$$\hat{\sigma} = \frac{\bar{S}}{C_2} \qquad ...(4)$$

Where, $\bar{S} = \frac{1}{k}\sum_{i=1}^{k} S_i$ and $S_i = \sqrt{\frac{1}{n}\Sigma\left(X_{ij} - \bar{X}_i\right)^2}$ is the standard deviation for the ith sample.

Using the estimate in (4) in (3), the control limits for *S*–chart become:

$$\text{U.C.L} = \frac{B_2\bar{S}}{c_2} = B_4\bar{S}$$

$$\text{C.L} = \frac{c_2\bar{S}}{c_2} = \bar{S}$$

$$\text{L.C.L} = \frac{B_1\bar{S}}{c_2} = B_3\bar{S}$$

Here, also the values of $B_3 = \frac{B_1}{c_2}$ and $B_4 = \frac{B_2}{c_2}$ can be obtained from Appendix table for various values of *n*.

21.9 CONTROL CHART FOR ATTRIBUTES

$\bar{X}$, *R* and *S*– charts have been discussed for controlling quality characteristic which is measurable along with a scale and thus expressible numerically. On the other hand, there are quality characteristics which are unmeasurable and can not be represented numerically. Such a characteristic is called an ***attribute***.

In control charts for attributes the sampled units are divided in two categories: defective and non–defective. Here a distinction should be made between the word 'defect' and 'defective'. If a unit does not confirm to specified quality standards it is defect in the unit. However, a defective unit is one which contains more than the permitted number of defects.

Control charts for attributes are:

(a) Control chart for number of defects per unit (*c*–chart)
(b) Control chart for proportion of defectives (*p*–chart)
(c) Control chart for total number of defectives (*np* – chart).

21.9.1 *C*–Chart: A Chart for Average Number of Defects per Unit

Sometimes the characteristics representing the quality of a product or service are discrete in nature and the data is obtained by counting such as if machine is idle or working, defects in automobiles, machine components. Service rendered by a restaurant or departmental store or bank, and so on. In such cases, it is more relevant to evaluate performance by keeping track of the number of undesirable occurrences (c), such as number of defects per unit or the number of complaints received, say per 100 customers served or per Rs 10,000 sales.

C–chart is used in situations where in opportunities for a defect in each production unit or a complaint from a customer are very large while the probability of their occurrence per unit tends to be very small and constant. The outcome of such a sampling process can be described by a poison distribution.

The steps for construction of control chart for number of defects where the sample size is constant are follows:

1. Count the defects individually in a sample
2. If C stands for the number of defects counted per unit, then the average (mean) rate with which such defects occur can be calculated as follows:

$$\text{Average defects } \bar{C} = \frac{\text{Number of defects in all samples}}{\text{Total number of samples}}$$

$$= \frac{C_1 + C_2 + ... + C_n}{N}$$

3. Placing control limits using the standard deviation of the Poison distribution which is equal to $\sqrt{C}$ as follows:

$$\text{C.L.} = \bar{C}, \text{ U.C.L.} = \bar{C} + 3\sqrt{\bar{C}} \text{ and L.C.L.} = \bar{C} - 3\sqrt{\bar{C}}$$

4. The sample points C_1, C_2, ..., C_n are plotted as points on a graph paper by taking the sample characteristic C along the y – axis and the sample number along the x – axis. The control lines are drawn in the same manner as discussed earlier.
5. With appropriate adjustments, ensure whether a process is under control or not.

EXAMPLE 21.3: Construct a control chart for C, that is, number of defectives, from the following data pertaining to the number of imperfections in 20 pieces of cloth of equal length in a certain make of polyster and infer whether the process is in a state of control: 2, 3, 5, 8, 12, 2, 3, 4, 6, 5, 6, 10, 4, 6,. 5, 7, 4, 9, 7, 3.

Solution: Let C denote the number of defects per price. Then

$$\Sigma C = 2 + 3 + 5 + 8 + 12 + 2 + 3 + 4 + 5 + 5 + 6 + 10 + 4 + 6 + 5 + 7 + 4 + 9 + 7 + 3$$
$$= 111$$

$$\therefore \text{ Average no. of defects per piece} = \frac{\Sigma C}{N} = \frac{111}{20} = 5.55$$

Hence, control limits are: $\bar{C} = 5.55$

$$\text{U.C.L} = \bar{C} + 3\sqrt{\bar{C}} = 5.55 + 3\sqrt{5.55} = 5.55 + 7.08 = 12.63$$

$$\text{L.C.L} = \bar{C} - 3\sqrt{\bar{C}} = 5.55 - 3\sqrt{5.55} = 5.55 - 7.08 = -1.53 \text{ or } 0$$

Conclusion: Since none of the points is falling outside the upper and lower control limits, the process is in control.

EXAMPLE 21.4: During an examination of equal length, the following number of defects were observed: 2, 3, 4, 0, 5, 6, 7, 4, 3, 2. Draw a control chart for the number of defects and comment whether the process is under control or not.

Solution: Let C denote the number of defects per piece. Then the average number of defects in 10 samples will be

$$\bar{C} = \frac{\Sigma C}{N} = \frac{36}{10} = 3.6$$

Hence, control limits are: $\bar{C} = 3.6$

$$\text{U.C.L} = \bar{C} + 3\sqrt{\bar{C}} = 3.6 + 3\sqrt{3.6} = 3.6 + 5.692 = 9.292$$

$$\text{L.C.L} = \bar{C} - 3\sqrt{\bar{C}} = 3.6 - 3\sqrt{3.6} = 3.6 - 5.692 = -2.092 \text{ or } 0$$

The control chart for C based on these limits is given in the figure below:

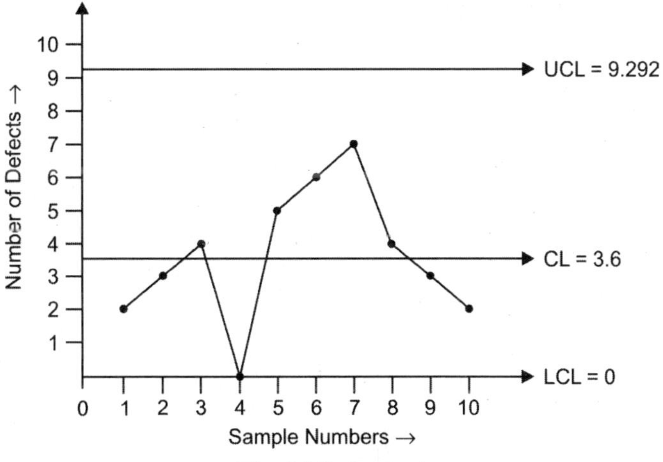

Fig. 21.6: C–chart

Conclusion: Since all the points are lying within control limits, the process is in control.

21.9.2 *p* – Chart: A Chart for Proportion of Defectives

The p – chart is designed to control the percentage or proportion of defectives per sample. This chart is based on the distribution of proportion or fraction defectives in each sample. The assumption that attributes that are classified as either good or bad follow the binomial distribution, implies that,

(a) There are only two possible outcomes (good or defective)
(b) The outcomes occur randomly, and
(c) The probability of either outcome remains unchanged for each trial.

Since the number of defectives (*C*) per unit can be converted into a fraction (proportion) defectives by dividing *C* by the sample size, therefore *p*–chart may be used in place of the C–chart. The *p*–chart has at least two advantages over the *C*–chart.

1. Expressing the defectives as a percentage or fraction of the given population is more meaningful and understood than the statement of the number of defectives.
2. Where the size of the sample varies from sample to sample, the *p*–chart permits a more meaningful and simple presentation.

When the sample size remains constant, the primary difference in *C*–chart and *np*–chart lies in the computation of the control limits.

1. Compute the fraction (proportion) defective for each of the samples by dividing the number of defectives in the sample of size n_i by the number of units inspected (sample size):

$$p_1 = \frac{x_1}{n_1},\ p_2 = \frac{x_2}{n_2},\ \ldots,\ p_i = \frac{x_i}{n_i}$$

In general, $$p = \frac{\text{Number of defectives in the sample of size } n}{\text{Total number of units inspected (sample size)}}$$

2. Obtain the mean and variance of *p* from all the samples combined, i.e.,
Average proportion defectives:

$$\bar{p} = \frac{\text{Total number of defectives in all the samples combined}}{\text{Total number of items in all the samples combined}}$$

$$= \frac{p_1 + p_2 + \ldots + p_n}{n}$$

and $$\sigma_{\bar{p}}^2 = \frac{\bar{p}(1-\bar{p})}{n}$$

3. Following the procedure outlined for variable control charts, the control limits are

$$\text{U.C.L} = \bar{p} + 3\sigma_{\bar{p}}$$

and $$\text{L.C.L} = \bar{p} - 3\sigma_{\bar{p}}$$

$$= \bar{p} + 3\sqrt{\frac{\bar{p}(1-\bar{p})}{n}}$$

$$= \bar{p} - 3\sqrt{\frac{\bar{p}(1-\bar{p})}{n}}$$

$$= \bar{p} + 3\sqrt{\frac{\overline{pq}}{n}}$$

$$= \bar{p} - 3\sqrt{\frac{\overline{pq}}{n}}$$

Where $\sigma_{\bar{p}}$ is the standard error (deviation) of proportion. While constructing the *p*–chart it is generally preferred to express results in terms of 'percent defective' rather than 'fraction defective'. The percent defective is 100 *p*. The sampling distribution of $\bar{p}$ can be approximated by a normal distribution whenever the sample size is large with mean $\bar{p}$ and standard deviation $\sigma_{\bar{p}}$.

EXAMPLE 21.5: Table below shows the number of defectives found in inspection of 4 lots of 25 items each.

Lot	*A*	*B*	*C*	*D*
No. of defectives	3	1	2	0

Plot *P* – chart.

Solution: Firstly, we find fraction defectives for each lot.

$$\text{Fraction defectives for lot } A = \frac{\text{No. of defectives}}{\text{No.of jobs inspected}} = \frac{3}{25} = 0.12$$

Similarly, $\text{Fraction defectives for lot } B = \frac{1}{25} = 0.04$

$$\text{Fraction defectives for lot } C = \frac{2}{25} = 0.08$$

and Fraction defectives for lot $D = 0$

Now, Average fraction defectives

$$\bar{p} = \frac{\text{Total no. of defective units}}{\text{Total no. of units inspected}} = \frac{3+1+2+0}{25+25+25+25} = \frac{6}{100} = 0.06$$

Hence, control limits of the *p*–chart are:

$$\text{U.C.L} = \bar{p} + 3\sqrt{\frac{\bar{p}(1-\bar{p})}{n}} = 0.06 + 3\sqrt{\frac{0.06(1-0.06)}{25}} = 0.2025$$

and

$$\text{L.C.L} = \bar{p} - 3\sqrt{\frac{\bar{p}(1-\bar{p})}{n}} = 0.06 - 3\sqrt{\frac{0.06(1-0.06)}{25}} = 0.0825 = 0$$

Now, we plot the graph for the above values

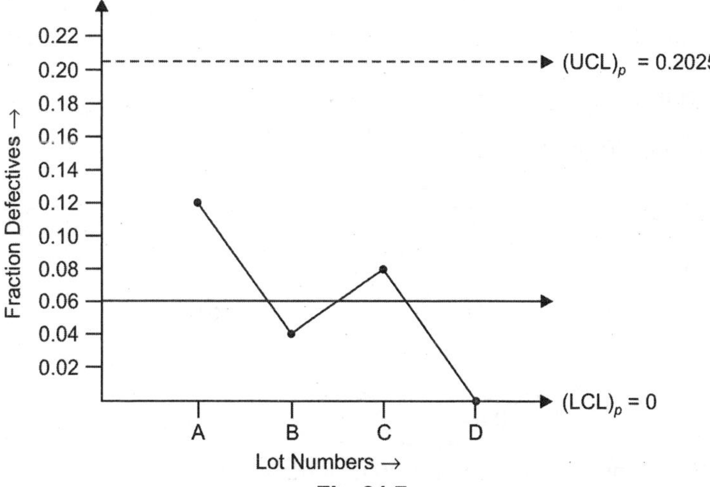

Fig. 21.7

Conclusion: Since all the points on the control chart are between the control limits hence the process is in state of control.

EXAMPLE 21.6: In a manufacturing process, the number of defectives found in the inspection of 20 lots of 100 samples is given below:

Lot no.	No. of defectives	Lot no.	No. of defectives
1	5	11	7
2	4	12	6
3	3	13	3
4	5	14	5
5	4	15	4
6	6	16	2
7	9	17	8
8	15	18	7
9	11	19	6
10	6	20	4

(i) Determine the control limits of p – chart and state whether the process is in control

(ii) Determine the new value of mean fraction defective if some points are out of control. Compute the corresponding control limits and state whether the process is still in control or not.

(iii) Determine the sample size when a quality limit not worse than 9% is desirable and a 10% bad product will not be permitted more than three times in thousand.

Solution:

(i)
$$\bar{p} = \frac{\text{Total number of defectives}}{\text{Total number of items inspected}} = \frac{120}{20 \times 100} = 0.06$$

$$\text{U.C.L}_{\bar{p}} = \bar{p} + 3\sqrt{\frac{\bar{p}(1-\bar{p})}{n}} = 0.06 + 3\sqrt{\frac{0.06(1-0.06)}{100}} = 0.13095$$

$$\text{L.C.L}_{\bar{p}} = \bar{p} - 3\sqrt{\frac{\bar{p}(1-\bar{p})}{n}} = 0.06 - 3\sqrt{\frac{0.06(1-0.06)}{100}} = -0.01095 \text{ or } 0$$

After observing the values of defectives in the given example, it is clear that only 8th lot having fraction defective $\frac{15}{100} = 0.15$ will go above $(\text{U.C.L})_{\bar{p}}$.

(ii) After eliminating the 8th lot,

$$\text{Revised value of } \bar{p} = \frac{120-15}{100 \times 19} = 0.056$$

Revised control limits will be

$$\text{U.C.L}_{\bar{p}} = 0.056 + 3\sqrt{\frac{0.056(1-0.056)}{100}} = 0.125$$

$$\text{L.C.L}_{\bar{p}} = 0.056 - 3\sqrt{\frac{0.056(1-0.056)}{100}} = 0.013 \text{ or } 0$$

It is clear that all the points are within control limits

$\therefore$ Revised quality level $\bar{p} = 0.056$

(iii) Since a probability that a defective worse than 9% defective quality will not be permitted is more than 3 times in thousand (0.3%) is corresponding 3 σ limits.

$$\therefore \quad \bar{p} + 3p = 0.09$$

$$0.056 + 3\sqrt{\frac{0.056 \times 0.944}{n}} = 0.09$$

$$\Rightarrow \quad \sqrt{\frac{0.056 \times 0.944}{n}} = \frac{0.034}{3}$$

Squaring both sides, we get

$$\frac{0.056 \times 0.944}{n} = \left(\frac{0.034}{3}\right)^2 = (0.01133)^2$$

or
$$n = \frac{0.056 \times 0.944}{0.01133 \times 0.01133} = 333$$

21.9.3 *np* – Chart: A Chart for Total Number of Defectives

When the sample size remains constant, the *np* –chart is used to control the actual number of defectives per sample. The construction and interpretation of a *np*–chart is similar to that of the *P*–chart because in this case we can directly plot the "number" rather than the fraction or percentage of defectives. In this case, the central control limit is drawn at *np* instead of *p*. The upper and lower control limits are given by:

$$\text{U.C.L} = np + 3\sqrt{\frac{\bar{p}(1-\bar{p})}{n}}$$

and
$$\text{L.C.L} = np - 3\sqrt{npq}$$

Where *p* is unknown, it can be estimated by sample values. The best estimate of *p* is $\bar{p}$. Then the control limits are written as:

$$\text{U.C.L} = n\bar{p} + 3\sqrt{n\bar{p}\bar{q}}$$

and
$$\text{L.C.L} = n\bar{p} - 3\sqrt{n\bar{p}\bar{q}}$$

Where $n\bar{p}$ = average no. of defectives per sample based on all possible samples of constant size from the process.

EXAMPLE 21.7: In a blade manufacturing factory, 1000 blades are examined daily. Draw the *np* chart for the following table and examine whether the process is under control?

Date	1	2	3	4	5	6	7	8	9	10	11	12	13	14	15
No. of defective blades	9	10	12	8	7	15	10	12	10	8	7	13	14	15	16

Solution: Here $n = 1000$

Total no. of defectives = $\Sigma np = 166$

Total no. of inspected = $\Sigma n = 1000 \times 15 = 15000$

$$\therefore \quad \bar{p} = \frac{\Sigma np}{\Sigma n} = \frac{166}{15000} = 0.011$$

$$\therefore \quad n\bar{p} = 1000 \times 0.011 = 11$$

Control limits are:

$$\text{C.L} = n\bar{p} = 11$$

$$\text{U.C.L}_{np} = n\bar{p} + 3\sqrt{n\bar{p}(1-\bar{p})} = 11 + 3\sqrt{11(1-0.011)} = 20.894$$

$$\text{L.C.L}_{np} = n\bar{p} - 3\sqrt{n\bar{p}(1-\bar{p})} = 11 - 3\sqrt{11(1-0.011)} = 1.106$$

Now we plot the graph for the *np*-chart as shown below:

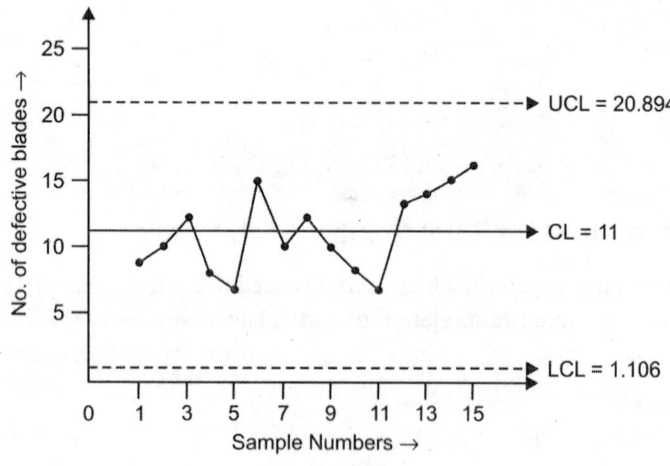

Fig. 21.8

Conclusion: Since all the points lie within the control limits, the process is under control.

EXAMPLE 21.8: If the average fraction defective of a large sample of a product is 0.1537, calculate the control limits given that sub– group size is 2000.

Solution: Average fraction defective $\bar{p} = 0.1537$

Sub–group size is 2000

$\therefore$ $n = 2000$

$$\text{Central line C.L} = n\bar{p} + 3\sigma_{np} = n\bar{p} + 3\sqrt{n\bar{p}(1-\bar{p})}$$

$$= 307.4 + 3\sqrt{307.4(1-0.1537)}$$

$$= 307.4 + 48.38774204 = 355.787742$$

and

$$\text{L.C.L}_{np} = n\bar{p} - 3\sigma_{np} = n\bar{p} - 3\sqrt{n\bar{p}(1-\bar{p})}$$

$$= 307.4 - 3\sqrt{307.4(1-0.1537)}$$

$$= 307.4 - 48.38774204 = 258.012258.$$

21.10 ADVANTAGES OF STATISTICAL QUALITY CONTROL

- **Efficiency:** The use of statistical quality control ensures rapid and efficient inspection at a minimum cost. It eliminate the need of 100% inspection of finished products because the acceptance sampling in SQC exerts more effective pressure for quality improvement than it.

- **Reduction of scrap:** It uncovers the cause of excessive variability in manufactured products forecasting trouble before rejections occur and reducing the amount of spoiled work.
- **Easy detection of faults:** In statistical quality control after plotting the control charts ($\bar{X}$, R, p, C, u) etc., when the points fall above the upper control limits or below the lower control limit, it gives an indication of deterioration in quality. Necessary corrective action may be then taken immediately.
- **Adherence to specifications:** So long as a statistical control continues, specifications can be accurately predicted for future by which it is possible to assess whether the production processes are capable of producing the products with the given set of specifications.
- Increases output and reduces wasted machine and man hours.
- Efficient utilization of personnel, machines and materials results in higher productivity.
- Creates quality awareness in employees. However it should be noted that statistical quality control is not a panacea for assuring product quality.
- Provides a common language that may be used by all three groups designers, production personnel and inspectors in arriving at a rational solution of mutual problems.
- Points out when and where 100% inspection, sorting or screening is required.
- Elimination of bottlenecks in the process of manufacturing.

It simply furnishes 'perspective facts' upon which intelligent management and engineering action can be based without such action, the method is ineffective.

Even the application of standard procedures is also very dangerous without adequate study of the process.

21.11 LIMITATIONS OF STATISTICAL QUALITY CONTROL

Despite the great significance of statistical quality control, it is believed that it is not a treatment for all quality evils. There are several highly complex problems where SQC may not be in a position to contribute much towards reduction of variability. The application of standard process without adequate study of the process is extremely dangerous, and has in the past led to statistical method being discredited. Statistical methods applied on a production process are only an information service, and as such must be conditioned by the process to which they are applied. Unless they are used as part of a general quality awareness, they may only lead to a false sense of security. The responsibility for quality and process decisions rests with the manager incharge of the process and not with the statistician. The charts do not reduce the manager's responsibility.

21.12 ACCEPTANCE SAMPLING

Acceptance sampling is a statistical method which enables us to make the decision of either accepting or rejecting a shipment of items in lots, based on the inspection of a sample of items from the lot. In most situations 100% inspection of all items is neither desirable nor economically feasible. There are some exceptions to this rule. For example, each parachute must be examined for its reliability. Each part going into the space shuttle must be examined, because failure of any one part could prove to be catastrophic. However, in most cases, a random sample of established size from a given lot of items is adequate for the purpose of inspection in providing the decision maker with a criterion as to whether to accept the lot or to reject it, based upon the results obtained from such a sample.

Since the judgement is based on a sample, there is always a risk of making an error of accepting a bad lot or rejecting a good lot. The general steps of acceptance sampling are shown in figure.

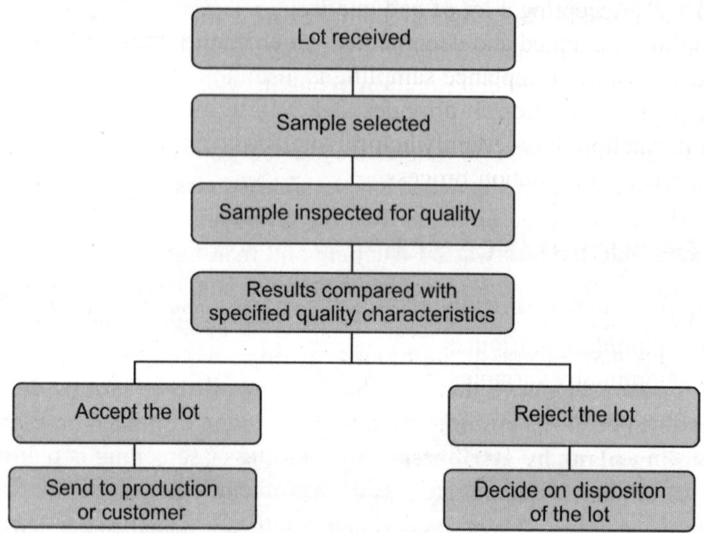

Fig. 21.9: Steps of Acceptance sampling procedure

DO YOU KNOW?

A major advantage of acceptance sampling is that it can motivate suppliers to improve the quality of their items.

21.13 ADVANTAGES OF ACCEPTANCE SAMPLING

As compared to 100% inspection, acceptance sampling has the following advantages:

1. It is less costly as the amount of inspection is less
2. It is the only possible procedure when testing is destructive
3. Less product damage occurs since it requires less handling of the product
4. Less manpower is required for quality inspection
5. It is usually more accurate than 100% inspection, since it allows less opportunity for inspection fatigue, which can be responsible for mistakes.

Since a decision is made to accept or reject a lot on the basis of a sample, there is a possibility of:

1. Rejecting the lot as unsatisfactory when it is of acceptable quality. This error is equivalent to the concept of type I error which is the probability of rejecting a lot of good quality and is denoted as α. It is also known as producer's risk. Thus, the producer's risk can be defined as the risk that the producer takes of having the lot rejected by the sampling plan, even though the product conforms to requirements and specifications.
2. Accepting the lot as satisfactory. When in fact its quality is relatively poor. This is a concept similar to type II error which is the probability of accepting a lot of bad quality and is denoted as β. It is also known as consumer's risk. Thus, the consumer's risk is the risk of accepting a lot which is of sub-standard quality.

Thus,

$$\alpha = P \text{ [Rejecting a lot of good quality]}$$
$$\beta = P \text{ [Accepting a lot of bad quality]}$$

Acceptance sampling is planned and documented which control these risks at a pre-assigned level on economic grounds. In short, acceptance sampling is a 'middle ground' between the two extremes of no inspection and 100% inspection. It provides us a way to move between these two extremes on the basis of sample information. It is certainly helpful to place economic and psychological pressure on the producer to improve the production process.

21.14 TYPES OF ACCEPTANCE SAMPLING PLANS

Acceptance sampling plans may be broadly classified into two categories:

1. Acceptance sampling by attributes
2. Acceptance sampling by variables

However, in this chapter, we will discuss some of the acceptance sampling plans by attributes only.

1. Acceptance sampling plans by attributes

The following three types of acceptance sampling plans are commonly used:

1. Single sampling plan 2. Double sampling plan 3. Multiple sampling plan

21.14.1 Single Sampling Plan

The procedure in which the decision to accept or reject the lot is based on the inspection of a single sample is known as single sampling plan.

In any systematic plan for single sampling, usually four things are specified. They are:

N = lot size
n = The sample size
c = The acceptance number i.e., maximum allowable number of defectives in the sample.
d = The actual number of defective in the sample.

The single sampling plan may be described as follows:

1. Select a random sample of size n from a lot of size N.
2. Inspect all the articles included in the sample and count the number of defectives d in the sample.
3. If $d \le c$, accept the lot, replacing defective pieces found in the sample by non–defective ones.
4. If $d > c$, reject the lot.

If a sample of 200 units from a lot of 2000 contains more than 65 defectives in it then the entire lot is rejected, otherwise the entire lot is accepted.

The action plan of a single sampling is shown in Fig. 21.10 also.

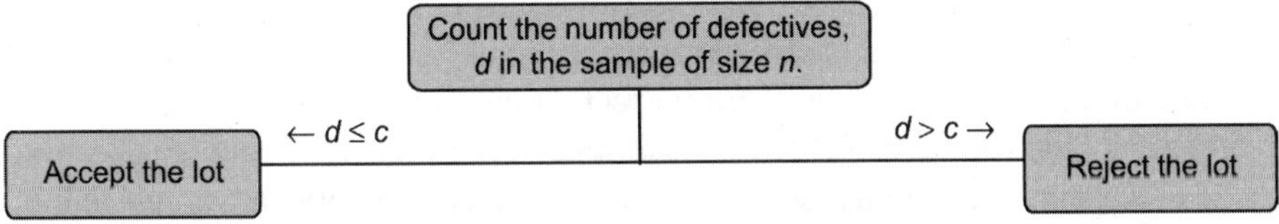

Fig. 21.10: Single sampling plan

21.14.2 Double Sampling Plan

In single sampling plan, the decision with regard to acceptance or rejection of a lot is based on only one sample from the lot whereas in double sampling a second sample is permitted if the first sample fails i.e., if the data from the first sample is not conclusive on either side (about accepting or rejecting the lot), then a definite decision is taken on the basis of the evidence from both the first and second samples.

A double sampling plan depends on the following specified numbers:

N = Lot size
n_1 = First sample size
c_1 = Acceptance number for first sample
n_2 = Second sample size
c_2 = Acceptance number for second sample
d_1 = Number of defective items in the first sample
d_2 = Number of defectives in the second sample.

The procedure of double sampling plan is as follows:

1. Take a sample of size n_1 from the lot of size N.
2. If $d_1 \le c_1$, accept the lot, replacing the defectives found in the sample by non–defectives
3. If $d_1 > c_2$, reject the lot. Have complete inspection and replace all bad items by good ones.
4. If $c_1 + 1 < d_1 \le c_2$, take a second sample of size n_2 from the remaining lot.
5. If $d_1 + d_2 \le c_2$, accept the lot replacing defective items by standard ones.
6. If $d_1 + d_2 > c_2$, reject the whole lot. Inspect the rejected lot 100%, replacing all the defective items by good ones.

DO YOU KNOW?

A plan of double sampling has been given by Dodge and Roming. It provides for minimum of inspection and in their plan the probability of acceptance on the basis of the first sample is the same as the probability of acceptance on the basis of the second sample.

The logic of a double sampling plan is shown in Fig. 21.11 on next page.

Single Sampling Vs Double Sampling Plans

1. Single sampling plans are simple, easy to design and administer, and since each sample can be plotted on a control chart, maximum information concerning the lot can be obtained.
2. A very important advantage of double sampling over single sampling seems to be psychological. To a layman, it seems unfair to reject a lot on the basis of one sample and appears more convincing to say that the lot was rejected after inspecting two samples. Double sampling permits the taking of two samples on which to make a decision.
3. A double sampling plan may reduce the total amount of inspection; for the first sample taken is less than that called for under a comparable single sampling plan, and, consequently, rejected on the basis of first sample, there may be considerable saving in total inspection. It is also possible to reject a lot without completely inspecting the entire second sample. Usually, double sampling requires 25% to 33% less, inspection on the average than single sampling.
4. The operating characteristics of double sampling scheme are generally steeper than those of corresponding single sampling procedure i.e. the discriminatory power of double sampling procedures is a bit higher than that of single sampling procedures

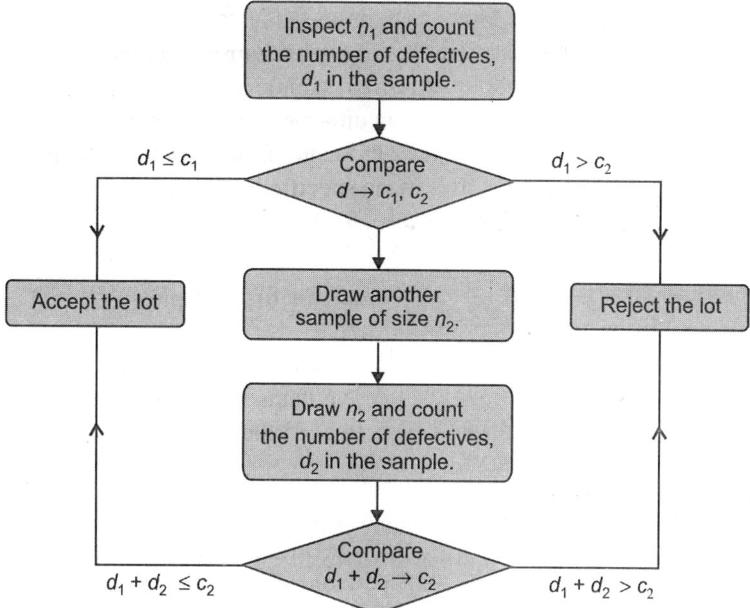

Fig. 21.11: Double sampling plan

21.14.3 Multiple or Sequential Sampling Plan

We have seen earlier that when a single –sampling plan is unable to give us a clear decision, we take recourse to the double – sampling plan. It may just be possible that even a double–sampling plan may not give us a clear decision. In such a case, we may go on to have another sample before we reach a decision. Thus, three or more sampling plans can be used. This is known as multiple or sequential sampling. Since such plans are extremely complicated, they are seldom used in practice.

21.15 THE OPERATING CHARACTERISTIC (OC) CURVE

All practical sampling plans have an OC curve. In judging various acceptance sampling plans, it is desirable to compare their performance over a range of possible quality levels of submitted product. An excellent picture of this performance is given by the operating characteristic curve or OC curve. The OC curve of an acceptance sampling plan shows how far a sampling plan is capable to differentiate between good and bad lots. For any given fraction of defective p in a lot under consideration, the OC curve brings out the probability p_a, that is, the lot will be accepted as per the given sampling plan.

Construction of an OC Curve

In drawing the OC curve, the following two terms are important:

(a) AQL (Acceptable Quality Level)
(b) LTPD (Lot Tolerance Percentage Defective)

In order to measure the producer's risk we define a minimum percentage of defective items in a lot below which the lot should be accepted. This is known as Acceptable Quality Level (AQL). Similarly to measure the consumer's risk, we must define maximum percentage of defective items in lots which the consumer wishes to accept. This is known as Lot Tolerance Percentage Defective (LTPD) or Rejection Quality Level (RQL).

It may be noted that both the producer and the consumer know that there is always some risk that lots would pass outside the range of AQL and LTPD. The chance that lots would be rejected while actually having lower percentage of defectives than the AQL is known as the producer's risk and is represented by α. As against this, the chance of a lot being accepted with a higher percentage of defectives than indicated by LTPD is known as the consumer's risk and is represented by β. These risks are usually taken as 5% and 10% respectively. The actual levels of these two types of risk are decided by negotiations between the consumer and the producer.

An OC curve can be constructed by using either the Poisson distribution of the Thorndike chart. The Poisson distribution can be used in all situations where p is less than 0.10 (or if the P_n is less than 5) and the lot size is at least 10 times the size of the sample. In situation in which these conditions are not met, the theoretically correct approach is to use the binomial or the hypergeometric distribution can be used without serious loss of accuracy.

The following would be the shape of an OC curve if it is assumed that the acceptable and rejectable qualities are measured as proportions of items that are defective, and these are p_a (Acceptance proportion) = 0.05 and p_r (Rejection proportion) = 0.15.

In this graph the points on the horizontal scale represent possible lot qualities and the height of the curve shows the probability that a lot of this quality will be accepted.

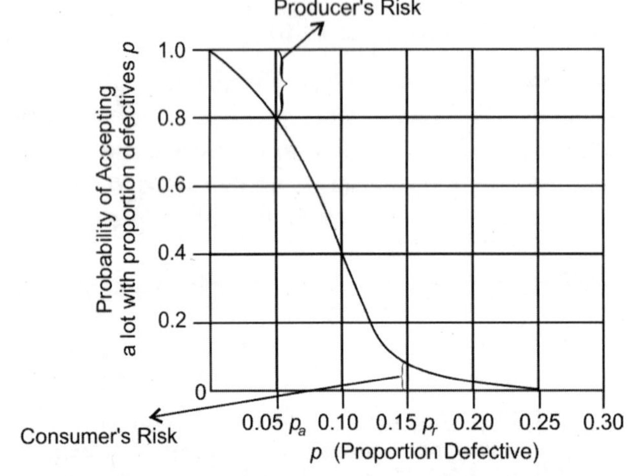

Fig. 21.12: OC Curve for a typical sampling plan

From the above figure, it is clear that the probability of acceptance of a lot with $p_a = 0.5$ is a little less than 0.9, so the chance of rejection is a little more than 0.1. This is the producer's risk. Similarly the probability of acceptance of a lot with $p_r = 0.15$ is little more than 0.1. This is consumer's risk. Thus the risk of both the producer and the consumer are more or less the same. In either case the risk is a little more than 0.1.

The steepness of the OC curve will vary on account of variation in sample size. The larger the sample size, the steeper will be the OC curve and vice versa. Also, as the steepness of the OC curve increases, the zone between the acceptable qualities and the rejectable qualities will shrink.

The location of the OC curve is determined by the maximum number of defective items allowable for acceptance, called the acceptance number. If the acceptance number is reduced, the curve is shifted to the left and if the acceptance number is increased, the curve is shifted to the right.

EXAMPLE 21.9: For the sampling plan $N = 1{,}200$, $n = 64$ and $C = 1$ determine the probability of acceptance of the following lots:

(i) 0.5% defective, (ii) 0.8% defective, (iii) 1% defective,
(iv) 2% defective, (v) 4% defective, (vi) 10% defective.

Also draw an OC curve.

Solution: If the lot contains 0.5% defective, the samples from it will also have an average of 0.5% defective. Hence in a sample of size 64, the average number of defective will be $\frac{64 \times 0.5}{100} = 0.32$. If the sample contains 1 or 0 defective, the lot is to be accepted under the sampling plan. We can obtain the cumulative probability on drawing a sample of 64 containing 0 or 1 defective by using the Poisson approximation to the binomial distribution. The calculation will be as follows:

S.No.	% defective in the lot	Average number of defectives	$P(0)$	$P(1)$	$P(0) + P(1)$ $P(a)$
(a)	0.5	$\frac{64 \times 0.5}{100} = 0.320$	0.73	0.23	0.96
(b)	0.8	$\frac{64 \times 0.8}{100} = 0.512$	0.60	0.31	0.91
(c)	1	$\frac{64 \times 1}{100} = 0.640$	0.53	0.35	0.88
(d)	2	$\frac{64 \times 2}{100} = 1.280$	0.28	0.36	0.64
(e)	4	$\frac{64 \times 4}{100} = 2.560$	0.08	0.21	0.29
(f)	10	$\frac{64 \times 10}{100} = 6{,}400$	0.002	0.01	0.01

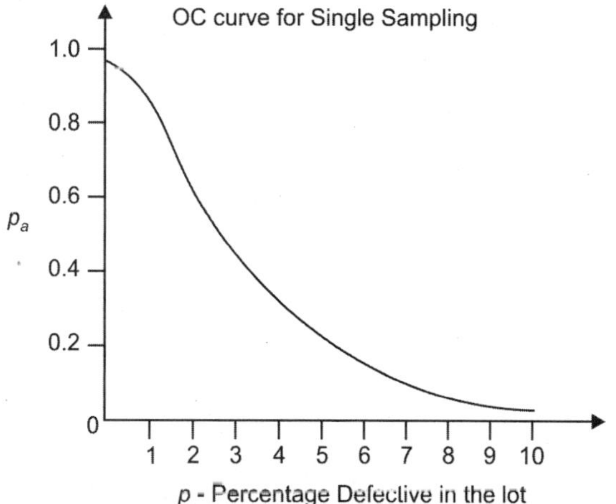

Fig. 21.13

The value 0.96 represents the probability of drawing a sample of 64 with 0 or 1 defective from a lot known to be 0.5% defective. Conversely, we can state that such a sample will enable acceptance of 96 per cent of lots containing 0.5 per cent defectives. In other words, if 1,000 such lots are submitted for inspection under the sampling plan, on an average 960 lots will be accepted and 40 will be rejected.

If we take the probabilities of acceptance (p_a) on the Y–axis with percentage defective in the lots submitted on the X–axis, and join the various points, the curve so formed is known as the operating characteristic (*OC*) curve of the sample plan. From the *OC* curve, we can easily obtain the probability of rejection of the lot, $(1 - p_a)$ will give the probability of rejection corresponding to any lot, having a specified proportion or percentage defective.

EXAMPLE 21.10: Draw the *OC* curve of the double sampling plan, given that $N = 1{,}000$, $n_1 = 50$, $c_1 = 1$, $n_2 = 25$, $c_2 = 5$.

Solution: This sampling plan means that a sample of size 50 is drawn, if it gives 0 or 1 defective it is accepted. If it gives 3 or more defective, it is rejected. But, if it gives 2 defectives, then a sample of 25 is drawn. If the total number of defectives is 2, the lot is accepted: if it is more than 2, the lot is rejected. For various values of percentage defective in lot x, the probability of acceptance shall be obtained as follows:

$$m = \frac{x \times n}{100}, \quad P(0) = e^{-m}, \quad P(1) = e^{-m} \times m, \text{etc.}$$

	1st sample n_1 = 50					2nd sample n_2 =25			Combined Sample
x	m	P(0)	P(1)	P(a)	P(2)	m	P(0)	P(a) P(2) × P(0)	P(a)
0	0	1.000	0.000	1,000	0.000	0.0	0.000	0.000	1,000
2	1	0.368	0.368	0.736	0.184	0.5	0.606	0.112	0.848
4	2	0.135	0.271	0.409	0.271	1.0	0.368	0.100	0.506
6	3	0.050	0.149	0.199	0.224	1.5	0.273	0.049	0.248
8	4	0.018	0.073	0.091	0.147	2.0	0.135	0.020	0.111
10	5	0.007	0.033	0.040	0.084	2.5	0.082	0.007	0.047
12	6	0.002	0.015	0.017	0.045	3.0	0.050	0.002	0.019

Let us plot these points on the graph paper to get the required OC curve.

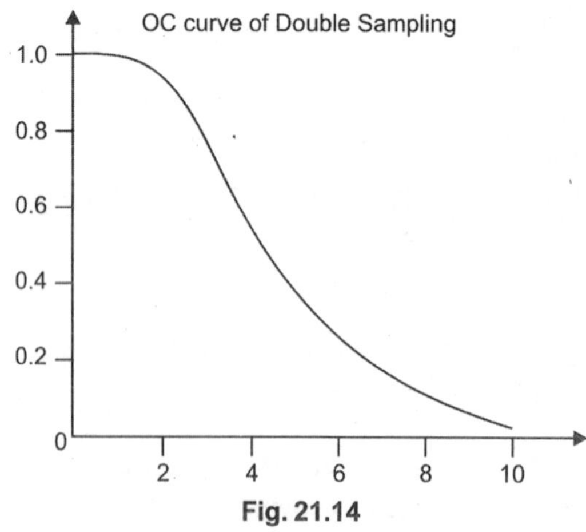

Fig. 21.14

MISCELLANEOUS SOLVED EXAMPLES

EXAMPLE 21.11: A machine is set to deliver packets of a given weight. 10 samples of size 5 each were recorded. Below are given relevant data:

Sample no.	1	2	3	4	5	6	7	8	9	10
Mean $\bar{X}$	15	17	15	18	17	14	18	15	17	16
Range (R)	7	7	4	9	8	7	12	4	11	5

Calculate the values for the central line and the control limits for mean chart and then comment on the state of control. (Conversion Factors for $n = 5$, are $A_2 = 0.58$, $D_3 = 0$, $D_4 = 2.11$).

Solution:

Calculation of Control Limits For $\bar{X}$ and R Chart

Sample No.	$\bar{X}$	R
1	15	7
2	17	7
3	15	4
4	18	9
5	17	8
6	14	7
7	18	12
8	15	4
9	17	11
10	16	5
$N = 10$	$\Sigma\bar{X} = 162$	$\Sigma R = 74$

Control limits for $\bar{X}$ chart

$$\text{U.C.L}_{\bar{X}} = \bar{\bar{X}} + A_2\bar{R}$$

$$\text{L.C.L}_{\bar{X}} = \bar{\bar{X}} - A_2\bar{R}$$

$$\text{Central line} = \bar{\bar{X}} = \frac{\Sigma\bar{X}}{N} = \frac{162}{10} = 16.2$$

$$\text{U.C.L}_{\bar{X}} = 16.2 + 0.58\ (7.4) = 16.2 + 4.292 = 20.492$$

$$\text{L.C.L}_{\bar{X}} = 16.2 - 0.58\ (7.4) = 16.2 - 4.292 = 11.908$$

Control limits for R chart

$$\text{Central line} = \bar{\bar{X}} = \frac{74}{10} = 7.4$$

$$\text{U.C.L}_R = D_4\bar{R}$$

$$\text{L.C.L}_R = D_3\bar{R}$$

$$\text{U.C.L}_R = 2.11\ (7.4) = 15.614$$

$$\text{L.C.L}_R = 0\ (7.4) = 0$$

Since all the points are lying within control limits, the process is in a state of control.

EXAMPLE 21.12: The following are the mean lengths and ranges of the lengths of a finished product from 10 samples each of size 5. The specification limits for length are 200 ± 5 cm. Construct $\overline{X}$ and R– chart and examine whether the process is under control and state your recommendations.

Sample no.	**1**	**2**	**3**	**4**	**5**	**6**	**7**	**8**	**9**	**10**
Mean $\overline{X}$	201	198	202	200	203	204	199	196	199	201
Range (R)	5	0	7	3	3	7	2	8	5	6

Solution:

(i) Let us suppose, for $n = 5$, $A_2 = 0.58$, $D_4 = 2.11$ and $D_3 = 0$

$$\text{U.C.L}_{\overline{X}} = \overline{\overline{X}} + A_2\,\overline{R} = \mu + A_2\,\overline{R}$$

$$\text{L.C.L}_{\overline{X}} = \overline{\overline{X}} - A_2\,\overline{R} = \mu - A_2\,\overline{R}$$

where $$\overline{R} = \frac{R_1 + R_2 + \ldots + R_{10}}{10} = \frac{46}{10} = 4.6$$

Then $$\text{U.C.L}_{\overline{X}} = 200 + (0.58 \times 4.6) = 202.668$$

$$\text{L.C.L}_{\overline{X}} = 200 - (0.58 \times 4.6) = 197.332$$

(ii) **Control limits for R Chart**

Central limit $$\text{C.L} = \overline{R} = 4.6$$

$$\text{U.C.L.}_R = D_4\overline{R} = 2.11 \times 4.6 = 9.706$$

$$\text{L.C.L.}_R = D_3\overline{R} = 0 \times 4.6 = 0$$

The $\overline{X}$ and R charts are drawn below:

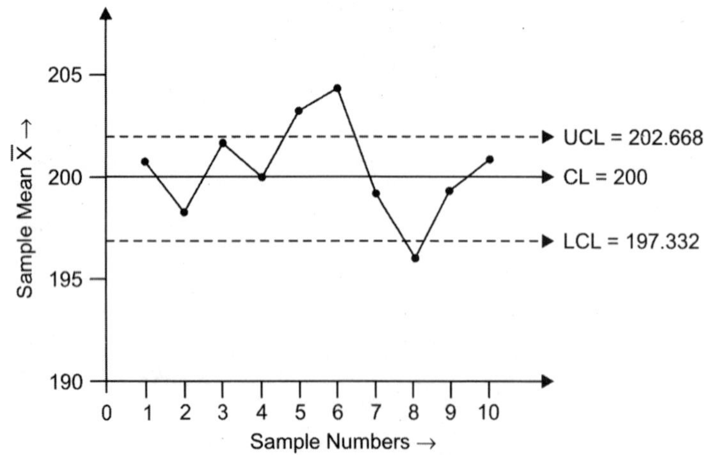

Fig. 21.15: X–Chart

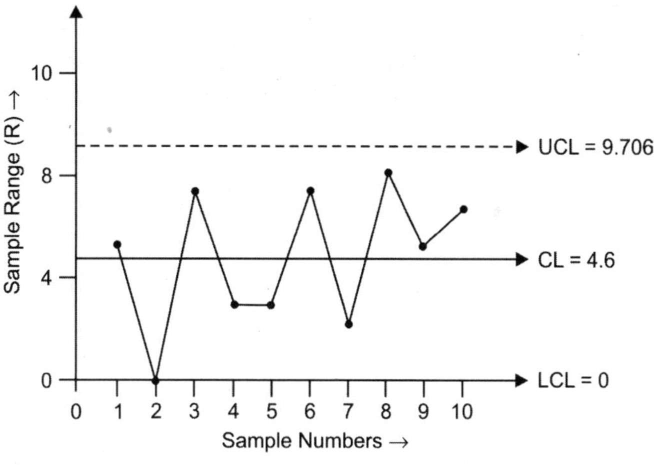

Fig. 21.16: R–Chart

Conclusion: It is noted that all points lie within the control limits on R chart. Hence the process variability is under control. But in $\overline{X}$ – chart, points corresponding to sample number 5, 6 and 8 lie outside the control limits. Therefore, the process is not in statistical control. The process should be halted and it is recommended to check for any assignable cause. Fluctuation will remain until these causes, if found, are removed.

EXAMPLE 21.13: A drilling machine bores holes with a mean diameter of 0.5230 cm and a standard deviation of 0.0032 cm. Calculate the 2- sigma and 3-sigma upper and lower control limits for means of sample of 4.

Solution:

$$\text{Mean diameter} = \overline{\overline{X}} = 0.5230 \text{ cm}$$

$$\text{S.D} = \sigma = 0.0032 \text{ cm}$$

$$n = 4.$$

(i) 2-sigma limits are as follows:

$$\text{C.L}_{\overline{X}} = \overline{\overline{X}} = 0.0032 \text{ cm.}$$

$$\text{U.C.L}_{\overline{X}} = \overline{\overline{X}} + 2\frac{\sigma}{\sqrt{n}} = 0.5230 + 2 \times \frac{0.0032}{\sqrt{4}} = 0.5262 \text{ cm}$$

$$\text{L.C.L}_{\overline{X}} = \overline{\overline{X}} - 2\frac{\sigma}{\sqrt{n}} = 0.5230 - 2 \times \frac{0.0032}{\sqrt{4}} = 0.5198 \text{ cm.}$$

(ii) 3-sigma limits are as follows:

$$\text{C.L.} = \overline{\overline{X}} = 0.5230 \text{ cm}$$

$$\text{U.C.L}_{\overline{X}} = \overline{\overline{X}} + 3\frac{\sigma}{\sqrt{n}} = 0.5230 + 3 \times \frac{0.0032}{\sqrt{4}} = 0.5278 \text{ cm}$$

$$\text{L.C.L}_{\overline{X}} = \overline{\overline{X}} - 3\frac{\sigma}{\sqrt{n}} = 0.5230 - 3 \times \frac{0.0032}{\sqrt{4}} = 0.5182 \text{ cm}$$

EXAMPLE 21.14: Determine the control limits for $\overline{X}$ and R charts if $\Sigma\overline{X} = 357.50$, $\Sigma R = 9.90$, number of subgroups = 20. It is given that $A_2 = 0.18$, $D_3 = 0.41$, $D_4 = 1.59$ and $d_2 = 3.735$. Also find the process capability.

Solution:

$$\overline{\overline{X}} = \frac{\Sigma\overline{X}}{n} = \frac{357.50}{20} = 17.875$$

$$\overline{R} = \frac{\Sigma R}{n} = \frac{9.90}{20} = 0.495$$

$$\begin{aligned} \text{U.C.L}_{\overline{X}} &= \overline{\overline{X}} + A_2\overline{R} \\ &= 17.875 + (0.18 \times 0.495) \\ &= 17.9641 \end{aligned}$$

$$\begin{aligned} \text{L.C.L}_{\overline{X}} &= \overline{\overline{X}} - A_2\overline{R} \\ &= 17.875 - (0.18 \times 0.495) \\ &= 17.7859 \end{aligned}$$

$$\begin{aligned} \text{U.C.L.}_R &= D_4\,\overline{R} \\ &= 1.59 \times 0.495 = 0.78705 \end{aligned}$$

$$\begin{aligned} \text{L.C.L.}_R &= D_3\,\overline{R} \\ &= 0.41 \times 0.495 = 0.20295 \end{aligned}$$

$$\sigma = \frac{\overline{R}}{d_2} = \frac{0.495}{3.735} = 0.13253$$

$$\begin{aligned} \therefore \quad \text{Process capability} &= 6\sigma \\ &= 6 \times 0.13253 = 0.79518 \end{aligned}$$

EXAMPLE 21.15: A random sample of 200 was taken from daily production of large output of pens and number of defective pens was noted. On the basis of information given below, prepare a control chart for fraction defective. What conclusion do you draw from the control chart?

Production each day	No. of defectives	Production each day	No. of defectives
1	10	13	8
2	5	14	14
3	10	15	4
4	12	16	10
5	11	17	12
6	9	18	11
7	22	19	26
8	4	20	13
9	12	21	16
10	24	22	9
11	21	23	11
12	15	24	12

Solution:

Production each day	No.of defectives	Fraction defectives	Production each day	No.of defectives	Fraction defectives
1	10	0.050	13	8	0.040
2	5	0.025	14	14	0.070
3	10	0.050	15	4	0.020
4	12	0.060	16	10	0.050
5	11	0.055	17	12	0.055
6	9	0.045	18	11	0.055
7	22	0.110	19	26	0.130
8	4	0.020	20	13	0.065
9	12	0.060	21	10	0.050
10	24	0.120	22	9	0.045
11	21	0.105	23	11	0.055
12	15	0.075	24	12	0.060

$$\bar{p} = \frac{\text{Total number of defectives}}{\text{Total production}} = \frac{294}{24 \times 200} = 0.061$$

$$\text{U.C.L} = \bar{p} + 3\sqrt{\frac{\bar{p}(1-\bar{p})}{n}} = 0.01 + 3\sqrt{\frac{0.061(1-0.061)}{200}}$$

$$= 0.061 + 3\,(0.0169) = 0.112$$

$$\text{L.C.L} = \bar{p} - 3\sqrt{\frac{\bar{p}(1-\bar{p})}{n}} = 0.061 - 3\,(0.0169) = 0.0103.$$

Since all the points don't fall within control limits, there seems to be something wrong with the production process.

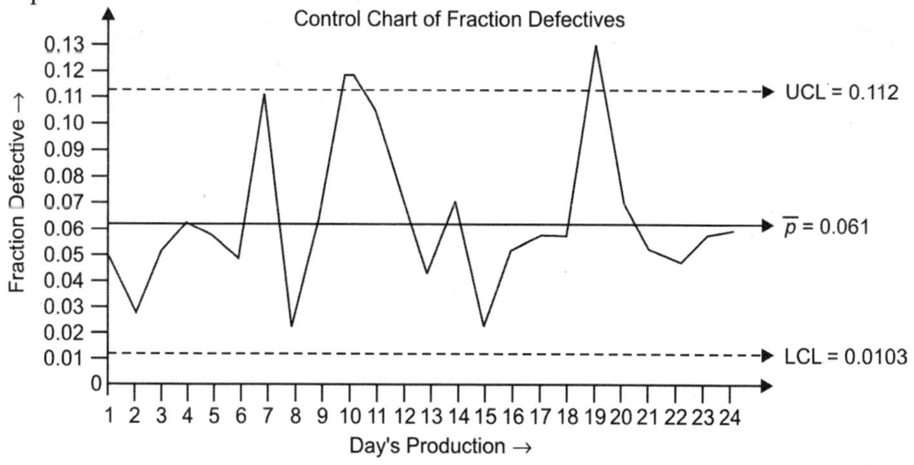

Fig. 21.17

EXAMPLE 21.16: Television sets were examined for quality control test. The number of defects for each television set are recorded below:

2, 4, 3, 1, 1, 2, 5, 3, 6, 7, 3, 1, 4, 2, 1, 3, 4, 6, 4, 1

Prepare a C–chart. What conclusion can you draw from it? [MBA, GND Univ. 1996]

Solution: Total number of defects = 60, Sample size = 20.

$$\bar{C} = \frac{60}{20} = 3$$

$$\text{U.C.L} = \bar{C} + 3 = 3 + 3\sqrt{3} = 3 + 5.196 = 8.196$$

$$\text{L.C.L} = \sqrt{C} - 3 = 3 - 3\sqrt{3} = 3 - 5.196 = -2.196 \text{ or } 0$$

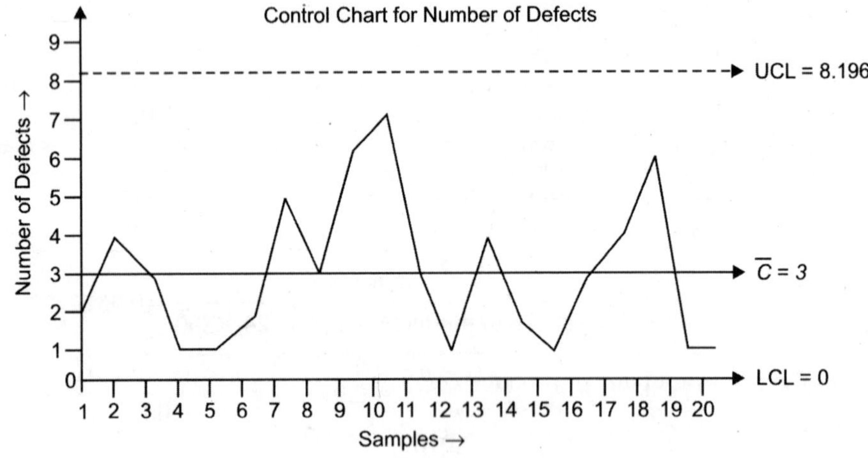

Fig. 21.18: Samples

Since all the points are lying within control limits, the process is in a state of control.

EXAMPLE 21.17: The number of defects on 20 items are given below:

Item no.	**1**	**2**	**3**	**4**	**5**	**6**	**7**	**8**	**9**	**10**
No. of defects	2	0	4	1	0	8	0	1	2	0
Item no.	**11**	**12**	**13**	**14**	**15**	**16**	**17**	**18**	**19**	**20**
No. of defects	6	0	2	1	0	3	2	1	0	2

Prepare a suitable control chart and draw your conclusion. **[MBA, Pune Univ. 1997]**

Solution: Let C denote the number of defects per item.

$$\bar{C} = \frac{\Sigma C}{n} = \frac{35}{20} = 1.75$$

$$\text{U.C.L} = \bar{C} + 3\sqrt{\bar{C}}$$

$$= 1.75 + 3\sqrt{1.75}$$

$$= 1.75 + 3 \times 1.323 = 5.719$$

$$\text{L.C.L} = \bar{C} - 3\sqrt{\bar{C}}$$

$$= 1.75 - 3\sqrt{1.75}$$

$$= 1.75 - 3 \times 1.323 = -2.219 \text{ or } 0$$

The control chart based on these limits is given below:

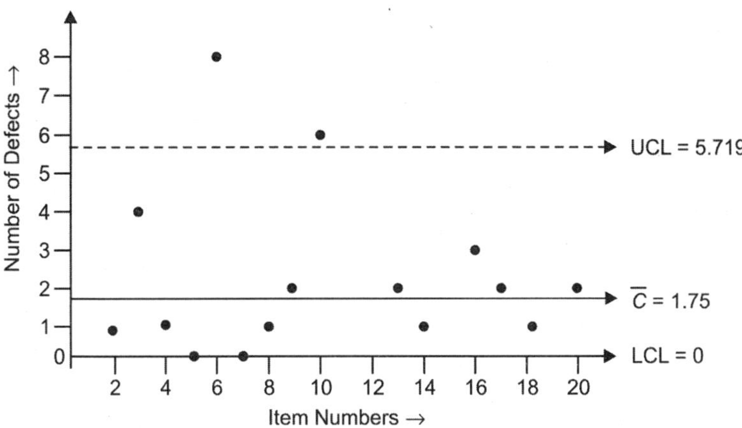

Fig. 21.19: Item Number

Since two of the points are lying outside the control limits, the process is not in a state of control.

EXAMPLE 21.18: The average percentage of defective in 27 samples of size 1500 each was found to be 13.7%. Construct a suitable control chart for this problem. Explain how the control chart can be used to control quality.

Solution: The P–chart is the suitable control chart for this problem. Here, we have

$$n = 1500; \quad k = 27; \quad \bar{p} = 0.137$$

The control limits are given by

$$\text{C.L} = \bar{p} = 0.137$$

$$\text{U.C.L} = \bar{p} + 3\sqrt{\frac{\bar{p}(1-\bar{p})}{n}}$$

$$= 0.137 + 3\sqrt{\frac{0.137(1-0.137)}{1500}}$$

$$= 0.137 + 3 \times 8.878 \times 10^{-3}$$

$$= 0.137 + 6.027$$

$$= 0.164$$

$$\text{L.C.L} = \bar{p} - 3\sqrt{\frac{\bar{p}(1-\bar{p})}{n}}$$

$$= 0.137 - 3\sqrt{\frac{0.137(1-0.137)}{1500}}$$

$$= 0.137 - 0.027$$

$$= 0.110$$

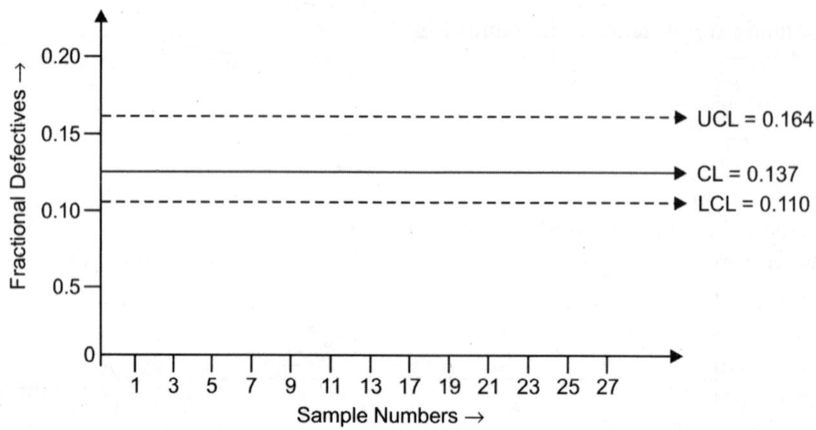

Fig. 21.20: P–chart

Conclusion: If all the defectives lie within the control limits, the process is under control. If some defectives fall outside these limits, are should look for assignable cause.

SELF PRACTICE EXERCISES

I. CHOOSE THE BEST ANSWER

1. Variation in product quality are due to:
   (a) chance causes (b) assignable causes
   (c) both (a) and (b) (d) None of there
2. Chance variations in the product quality are:
   (a) tolerable (b) untolerable
   (c) controllable (d) None
3. Variations due to assignable causes are due to:
   (a) faulty process (b) carelessness of operators
   (c) poor quality of raw material (d) all the above
4. $\overline{X}$ and R-charts are:
   (a) charts for attributes (b) charts for variables
   (c) charts for number of defects (d) None
5. When standards are known, the control limits for $\overline{X}$-chart are:
   (a) $\overline{\overline{X}} \pm A_2\sigma$ (b) $\mu \pm A\sigma$
   (c) $\overline{\overline{X}} + A_2\overline{R}$ (d) $\overline{\overline{X}} + A_1\overline{S}$
6. When standard σ is known, the control limits for R-chart are:
   (a) $D_1\sigma, D_2\sigma$ (b) $D_3\overline{R}, D_4\overline{R}$
   (c) $D_3\sigma, D_4\sigma$ (d) None

7. When standard p is known, the control limits for p-chart:

   (a) $p \pm 2\sqrt{\dfrac{pq}{n}}$ (b) $p \pm 3\sqrt{\dfrac{p(1-p)}{n}}$

   (c) $\bar{p} \pm 3\sqrt{\dfrac{\bar{p}(1-\bar{p})}{n}}$ (d) None

8. The statistical techniques used in statistical quality control are:

   (a) shewart control charts (b) acceptance sampling plans

   (c) both (a) and (b) (d) None

9. The process control is achieved through:

   (a) control charts (b) acceptance sampling plans

   (c) both (a) and (b) (d) None

10. The probability of rejecting a lot of good quality

    (a) producer's risk (b) consumer's risk

    (c) OC curve (d) None

II. FILL IN THE BLANKS

1. The causes due to faulty process are known as ....
2. The control charts were developed by ....
3. No. of defects per unit are controlled in ....
4. Proposition defectives are controlled in ....
5. .... is the basis of C-chart.
6. The probability of accepting a lot of bad quality is known as ....
7. The probability of rejecting a lot of good quality is known as ....
8. .... is the only solution in destructive testing.
9. Plans permitting more than two samples to reach a decision regarding the lot are called ....
10. .... displays the discriminatory power of sampling plan.

III. SHORT ANSWER TYPE QUESTIONS

1. What is SQC? Discuss the role of SQC in maintaining the quality of a product.
2. What do you understand by control charts.
3. Differentiate between process and product control.
4. What is $\overline{X}$-chart? How are the control limits determined while drawing the chart?
5. What is the difference between p and c-chart?
6. Define acceptance sampling with an example.
7. Explain the concepts of consumer's and producer's risk.
8. Distinguish between single sampling and double sampling plans.
9. Define OC curve and its utility.
10. Distinguish between defects and defectives.

IV. LONG ANSWER TYPE QUESTIONS

1. What do you mean by 'statistical quality control'? Discuss briefly its need and utility in industry. Discuss the causes of variation in quality.

2. Describe how a control chart for fraction defective is set? What modification is needed if varying numbers are inspected on different occasions?
3. What is an OC curve? Which OC curve would be called ideal ?
4. The data below give mean and range values for 20 samples of size $n = 6$ taken from a process producing bearings.

Sample No.	1	2	3	4	5	6	7	8	9	10
$\overline{X}$	35.4	34.0	37.2	34.9	33.5	31.7	34.0	35.1	33.7	32.8
R	8	6	5	7	4	3	8	4	2	1

Sample No.	11	12	13	14	15	16	17	18	19	20
$\overline{X}$	33.5	34.2	34.5	34.2	31.6	31.5	35.0	34.1	32.6	32.8
R	3	2	3	4	4	5	6	4	3	4

Draw $\overline{X}$ and *R*-charts. Does the process seem to be in statistical control ? If necessary, revise the trial control limits.

5. The following data refers to visual defect found during the inspection of the first 10 samples of size so each from a lot of Two-wheelless manufactured by an Automobile company:

Sample No.	1	2	3	4	5	6	7	8	9	10
No. of Defectives	4	3	2	3	4	4	4	1	3	2

Draw the '*p*' chart to show that the fraction defectives are under control.

6. When will you use a control chart for defects? Plot control chart for the following data pertaining plot control chart for the following data pertaining to number of defects in the T.V. sets manufactured by a company.

T.V. set No.	1	2	3	4	5	6	7	8	9	10	11	12	13	14	15
No. of Defects	5	1	0	7	3	6	0	10	2	11	5	8	6	4	1

ANSWERS

I. CHOOSE THE BEST ANSWERS

1. (c) 2. (a) 3. (d) 4. (b) 5. (b) 6. (a) 7. (b) 8. (c) 9. (a) 10. (a)

II. FILL IN THE BLANKS

1. assignable causes. 2. Walter *A.* Shewart 3. *C*– chart 4. *p*–chart
5. Poisson distribution 6. Consumer's risk 7. Producer's risk
8. Acceptance sampling 9. Multiple sampling plans 10. OC curve.

IV. LONG ANSWER TYPE QUESTIONS

4. $\overline{X}$-chart (31.71, 33.87, 36.01); *R*-chart (0, 4.45, 8.92); No.
5. UCL = 0.1608; LCL = 0

Appendix
Statistical Tables

T1. Areas under the Standard Normal Distribution

T2. Critical Value of χ^2

T3. Critical Value of t

T4. 1 % Points of F-Distribution

T5. 5 % Points of F-Distribution

T6. Binomial Coefficient

T7. Values of e^{-m}

T8. Central Chart Factors

Table T1: Areas under the standard distribution from 0 to *z*

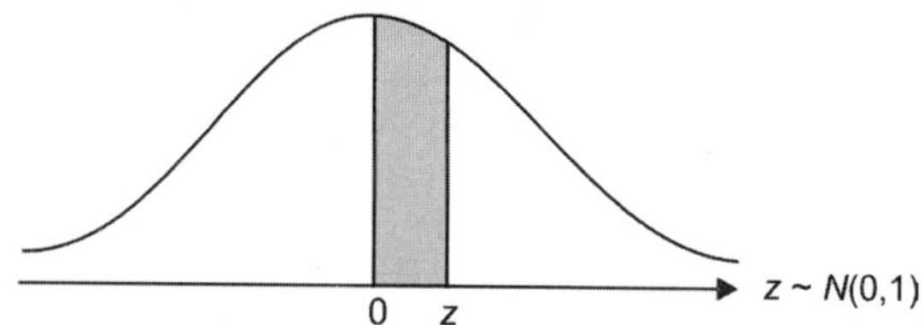

z	0	1	2	3	4	5	6	7	8	9
0.0	.0000	.0040	.0080	.0120	.0160	.0199	.0239	.0279	.0319	.0359
0.1	.0398	.0438	.0478	.0517	.0557	.0596	.0636	.0675	.0714	.0753
0.2	.0793	.0832	.0871	.0910	.0948	.0987	.1026	.1064	.1103	.1141
0.3	.1179	.1217	.1255	.1293	.1331	.1368	.1406	.1443	.1480	.1517
0.4	.1554	.1591	.1628	.1664	.1700	.1736	.1772	.1808	.1844	.1879
0.5	.1915	.1950	.1985	.2019	.2054	.2088	.2123	.2157	.2190	.2224
0.6	.2258	.2291	.2324	.2357	.2389	.2422	.2454	.2486	.2518	.2549
0.7	.2580	.2612	.2642	.2673	.2704	.2734	.2764	.2794	.2823	.2852
0.8	.2881	.2910	.2939	.2967	.2996	.3023	.3051	.3078	.3106	.3133
0.9	.3159	.3186	.3212	.3238	.3264	.3289	.3315	.3340	.3365	.3389
1.0	.3413	.3438	.3461	.3485	.3508	.3531	.3554	.3577	.3599	.3621
1.1	.3643	.3665	.3686	.3708	.3729	.3749	.3770	.3790	.3810	.3830
1.2	.3849	.3869	.3888	.3907	.3925	.3944	.3962	.3980	.3997	.4015
1.3	.4032	.4049	.4066	.4082	.4099	.4115	.4131	.4147	.4162	.4177
1.4	.4192	.4207	.4222	.4236	.4251	.4265	.4279	.4292	.4306	.4319
1.5	.4332	.4345	.4357	.4370	.4382	.4394	.4406	.4418	.4429	.4441
1.6	.4452	.4463	.4474	.4484	.4495	.4505	.4515	.4525	.4535	.4545
1.7	.4554	.4564	.4573	.4582	.4591	.4599	.4608	.4616	.4625	.4633
1.8	.4641	.4649	.4656	.4664	.4671	.4678	.4686	.4693	.4699	.4706
1.9	.4713	.4719	.4726	.4732	.4738	.4744	.4750	.4756	.4761	.4767
2.0	.4772	.4778	.4783	.4788	.4793	.4798	.4803	.4808	.4812	.4817
2.1	.4821	.4826	.4830	.4834	.4838	.4842	.4846	.4850	.4854	.4857
2.2	.4861	.4864	.4868	.4871	.4875	.4878	.4881	.4884	.4887	.4890
2.3	.4893	.4896	.4898	.4901	.4904	.4906	.4909	.4911	.4913	.4916
2.4	.4918	.4920	.4922	.4925	.4927	.4929	.4931	.4932	.4934	.4936
2.5	.4938	.4940	.4941	.4943	.4945	.4946	.4948	.4949	.4951	.4952
2.6	.4953	.4955	.4956	.4957	.4959	.4960	.4961	.4962	.4963	.4964
2.7	.4965	.4966	.4967	.4968	.4969	.4970	.4971	.4972	.4973	.4974
2.8	.4974	.4975	.4976	.4977	.4977	.4978	.4979	.4979	.4980	.4981
2.9	.4981	.4982	.4982	.4983	.4984	.4984	.4985	.4985	.4986	.4986
3.0	.4987	.4987	.4987	.4988	.4988	.4989	.4989	.4989	.4990	.4990
3.1	.4990	.4991	.4991	.4991	.4992	.4992	.4992	.4992	.4993	.4993
3.2	.4993	.4993	.4994	.4994	.4994	.4994	.4994	.4995	.4995	.4995
3.3	.4995	.4995	.4995	.4996	.4996	.4996	.4996	.4996	.4996	.4997
3.4	.4997	.4997	.4997	.4997	.4997	.4997	.4997	.4997	.4997	.4998
3.5	.4998	.4998	.4998	.4998	.4998	.4998	.4998	.4998	.4998	.4998
3.6	.4998	.4998	.4999	.4999	.4999	.4999	.4999	.4999	.4999	.4999
3.7	.4999	.4999	.4999	.4999	.4999	.4999	.4999	.4999	.4999	.4999
3.8	.4999	.4999	.4999	.4999	.4999	.4999	.4999	.4999	.4999	.4999
3.9	.5000	.5000	.5000	.5000	.5000	.5000	.5000	.5000	.5000	.5000

Table T2: Critical Values of Chi-Square (χ^2)

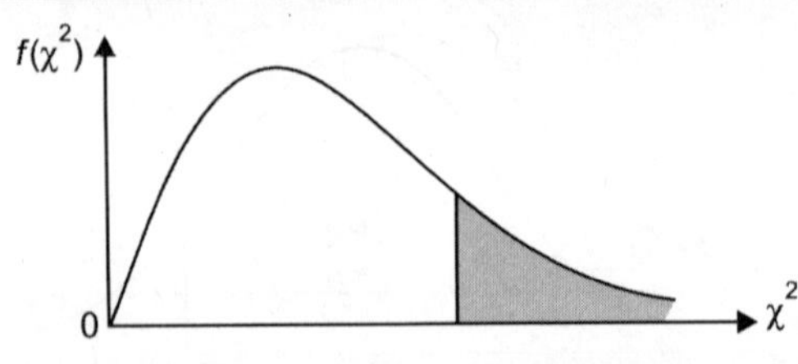

d.f. \ α	.100	.050	.025	.010	.005	.001
1	2.71	3.84	5.02	6.63	7.88	10.8
2	4.61	5.99	7.38	9.21	10.6	13.8
3	6.25	7.81	9.35	11.3	12.8	16.3
4	7.78	9.49	11.1	13.3	14.9	18.5
5	9.24	11.1	12.8	15.1	16.7	20.5
6	10.6	12.6	14.4	16.8	18.5	22.5
7	12.0	14.1	16.0	18.5	20.3	24.3
8	13.4	15.5	17.5	20.1	22.0	26.1
9	14.7	16.9	19.0	21.7	23.6	27.9
10	16.0	18.3	20.5	23.2	25.2	29.6
11	17.3	19.7	21.9	24.7	26.8	31.3
12	18.5	21.0	23.3	26.2	28.3	32.9
13	19.8	22.4	24.7	27.7	29.8	34.5
14	21.1	23.7	26.1	29.1	31.3	36.1
15	22.3	25.0	27.5	30.6	32.8	37.7
16	23.5	26.3	28.8	32.0	34.3	39.3
17	24.8	27.6	30.2	33.4	35.7	40.8
18	26.0	28.9	31.5	34.8	37.2	42.3
19	27.2	30.1	32.9	36.2	38.6	43.8
20	28.4	31.4	34.2	37.6	40.0	45.3
21	29.6	32.7	35.5	38.9	41.4	46.8
22	30.8	33.9	36.8	40.3	42.8	48.3
23	32.0	35.2	38.1	41.6	44.2	49.7
24	33.2	36.4	39.4	43.0	45.6	51.2
25	34.4	37.7	40.6	44.3	46.9	52.6
26	35.6	38.9	41.9	45.6	48.3	54.1
27	36.7	40.1	43.2	47.0	49.6	55.5
28	37.9	41.3	44.5	48.3	51.0	56.9
29	39.1	42.6	45.7	49.6	52.3	58.3
30	40.3	43.8	47.0	50.9	53.7	59.7
35	46.1	49.8	53.2	57.3	60.3	66.6
40	51.8	55.8	59.3	63.7	66.8	73.4
45	57.5	61.7	65.4	70.0	73.2	80.1
50	63.2	67.5	71.4	76.2	79.5	86.7
55	68.8	73.3	77.4	82.3	85.7	93.2
60	74.4	79.1	83.3	88.2	92.0	99.6
65	80.0	84.8	89.2	94.4	98.1	106.0
70	85.5	90.5	95.0	100.4	104.0	112.3
75	91.1	96.2	100.8	106.4	110.3	118.6
80	96.6	101.9	106.6	112.3	116.3	124.8
85	102.1	107.5	112.4	118.2	122.3	131.0
90	107.6	113.1	118.1	124.1	128.3	137.2
95	113.0	118.8	123.9	130.0	134.2	143.3
100	118.5	124.3	129.6	135.8	140.2	149.4

Table T3: Critical Values of *t*

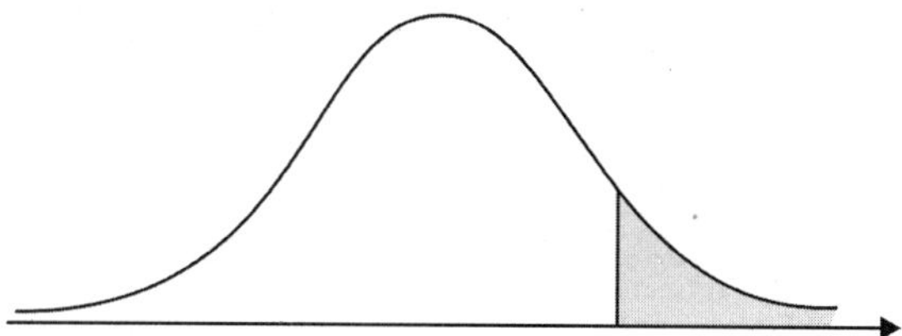

d.f.	$t_{.100}$	$t_{.050}$	$t_{.025}$	$t_{.010}$	$t_{.005}$
1	3.078	6.314	12.706	31.821	36.657
2	1.886	2.920	4.303	6.965	9.925
3	1.638	2.353	3.182	4.541	5.841
4	1.533	2.132	2.776	3.747	4.604
5	1.476	2.015	2.571	3.365	4.032
6	1.440	1.943	2.447	3.143	3.707
7	1.415	1.895	2.365	2.998	3.499
8	1.397	1.860	2.306	2.896	3.355
9	1.383	1.833	2.262	2.821	3.250
10	1.372	1.812	2.228	2.764	3.169
11	1.363	1.796	2.201	2.718	3.106
12	1.356	1.782	2.179	2.681	3.055
13	1.350	1.771	2.160	2.650	3.012
14	1.345	1.761	2.145	2.624	2.977
15	1.341	1.753	2.131	2.602	2.947
16	1.337	1.746	2.120	2.583	2.921
17	1.333	1.740	2.110	2.567	2.898
18	1.330	1.434	2.101	2.552	2.878
19	1.328	1.729	2.093	2.539	2.861
20	1.325	1.725	2.086	2.528	2.845
21	1.323	1.721	2.080	2.518	2.831
22	1.321	1.717	2.074	2.508	2.819
23	1.319	1.714	2.069	2.500	2.807
24	1.318	1.711	2.064	2.485	2.797
25	1.316	1.708	2.060	2.479	2.787
26	1.315	1.706	2.056	2.473	2.779
27	1.314	1.703	2.052	2.67	2.771
28	1.313	1.701	2.048	2.467	2.763
29	1.311	1.699	2.045	2.462	2.756
inf.	1.282	1.645	1.960	2.326	2.576

Table T4: '*F*'-Distribution-Values of '*F*'

Level of significance α = 0.01

n_1 = degrees of freedom for numerator

n_2 = degrees of freedom for denominator

n_1 \ n_2	1	2	3	4	5	6	7	8	9	10	12	15	20	24	30	40	60	120	α
1	161.4	199.5	215.7	224.6	230.2	234.2	236.8	238.9	240.5	241.9	243.9	245.9	248.0	249.1	250.1	251.1	252.2	253.3	254.3
2	18.51	19.00	19.16	19.25	19.30	19.33	19.35	19.37	19.38	19.40	19.41	19.43	19.45	19.45	19.46	19.47	19.48	19.49	19.50
3	10.13	9.55	9.28	9.12	9.01	8.94	8.89	8.85	8.81	8.79	8.74	8.70	8.66	8.64	8.62	8.59	8.57	8.55	8.53
4	7.71	6.94	6.59	6.39	6.26	6.16	6.09	6.04	6.00	5.96	5.91	5.86	5.80	5.77	5.75	5.72	5.69	5.66	5.63
5	6.61	5.79	5.41	5.19	5.05	4.95	4.88	4.82	4.77	4.74	4.68	4.62	4.56	4.53	4.50	4.46	4.43	4.40	4.36
6	5.99	5.14	4.76	4.53	4.39	4.28	4.21	4.15	4.10	4.06	4.00	3.94	3.87	3.84	3.81	3.77	3.74	3.70	3.67
7	5.59	4.74	4.35	4.12	3.97	3.87	3.79	3.73	3.68	3.64	3.57	3.51	3.44	3.41	3.38	3.34	3.30	3.27	3.23
8	5.32	4.46	4.07	3.84	3.69	3.58	3.50	3.44	3.39	3.35	3.28	3.22	3.15	3.12	3.08	3.04	3.01	2.97	2.93
9	5.12	4.26	3.86	3.63	3.48	3.37	3.29	3.23	3.18	2.14	2.07	3.01	2.94	2.90	2.86	2.83	2.79	2.75	2.71
10	4.96	4.10	3.71	3.48	3.33	3.22	3.14	3.07	3.02	2.98	2.91	2.85	2.77	2.74	2.70	2.66	2.62	2.58	2.54
11	4.84	3.98	3.59	3.36	3.20	3.09	3.01	2.95	2.90	2.85	2.79	2.72	2.65	2.61	2.57	2.53	2.49	2.45	2.40
12	4.75	3.89	3.49	3.26	3.11	3.00	2.91	2.85	2.80	2.75	2.69	2.62	2.54	2.51	2.47	2.43	2.38	2.34	2.30
13	4.67	3.81	3.41	3.18	3.03	2.92	2.83	2.77	2.71	2.67	2.60	2.53	2.46	2.42	2.38	2.34	2.30	2.25	2.21
14	4.60	3.74	3.34	3.11	2.96	2.85	2.76	2.70	2.65	2.60	2.53	2.46	2.39	2.35	2.31	2.27	2.22	2.18	2.13
15	4.54	3.68	3.29	3.06	2.90	2.79	2.71	2.64	2.59	2.54	2.48	2.40	2.33	2.29	2.25	2.20	2.16	2.11	2.07
16	4.49	3.63	2.24	3.01	2.85	2.74	2.66	2.59	2.54	2.49	2.42	2.35	2.28	2.24	2.19	2.15	2.11	2.06	2.01
17	4.45	3.59	3.20	2.96	2.81	2.70	2.61	2.55	2.49	2.45	2.38	2.31	2.23	2.19	2.15	2.10	2.06	2.01	1.96
18	4.41	3.55	3.16	2.93	2.77	2.66	2.58	2.51	2.46	2.41	2.34	2.27	2.19	2.15	2.11	2.06	2.02	1.97	1.92
19	4.38	3.52	3.13	2.90	2.74	2.63	2.54	2.48	2.42	2.38	2.31	2.23	2.16	2.11	2.07	2.03	1.98	1.93	1.88
20	4.35	3.49	3.10	2.87	2.71	2.60	2.51	2.45	2.39	2.35	2.28	2.20	2.12	2.08	2.04	1.99	1.95	1.90	1.84
21	4.32	3.47	3.07	2.84	2.68	2.57	2.49	2.42	2.37	2.32	2.25	2.18	2.10	2.05	2.01	1.96	1.92	1.87	1.81
22	4.30	3.44	3.05	2.82	2.66	2.55	2.46	2.40	2.34	2.30	2.23	2.15	2.07	2.03	1.98	1.94	1.89	1.84	1.78
23	4.28	3.42	3.03	2.80	2.64	2.53	2.44	2.37	2.32	2.27	2.20	2.13	2.05	2.01	1.96	1.91	1.86	1.81	1.76
24	4.26	3.40	3.01	2.78	2.62	2.51	2.42	2.36	2.30	2.25	2.18	2.11	2.03	1.98	1.94	1.89	1.84	1.79	1.73
25	4.24	3.39	2.99	2.76	2.60	2.49	2.40	2.34	2.28	2.24	2.16	2.09	2.01	1.96	1.92	1.87	1.82	1.77	1.71
26	4.23	3.37	2.98	2.74	2.59	2.47	2.39	2.32	2.27	2.22	2.15	2.07	1.99	1.95	1.90	1.85	1.80	1.75	1.69
27	4.21	3.35	2.96	2.73	2.57	2.46	2.37	2.31	2.25	2.20	2.13	2.06	1.97	1.93	1.88	1.84	1.79	1.73	1.67
28	4.20	3.34	2.95	2.71	2.56	2.45	2.36	2.29	2.24	2.19	2.12	2.04	1.96	1.91	1.87	1.82	1.77	1.71	1.65
29	4.18	3.33	2.93	2.70	2.55	2.43	2.35	2.28	2.22	2.18	2.10	2.03	1.94	1.90	1.85	1.81	1.75	1.70	1.64
30	4.17	3.32	2.92	2.69	2.53	2.42	2.33	2.27	2.21	2.16	2.09	2.01	1.93	1.89	1.84	1.79	1.74	1.68	1.62
40	4.08	3.23	3.84	2.61	2.45	2.34	2.25	2.18	2.12	2.08	2.00	1.92	1.84	1.79	1.74	1.69	1.64	1.58	1.51
60	4.00	3.15	2.76	2.53	2.37	2.25	2.17	2.10	2.04	1.99	1.92	1.84	1.75	1.70	1.65	1.59	1.53	1.47	1.39
120	3.92	3.07	2.68	2.43	2.29	2.17	2.09	2.02	1.96	1.91	1.83	1.75	1.66	1.61	1.55	1.50	1.43	1.35	1.25
α	3.84	3.00	2.60	2.37	2.21	2.10	2.01	1.94	1.88	1.83	1.75	1.67	1.57	1.52	1.46	1.39	1.32	1.22	1.00

Table T5: '*F*'-Distribution-Values of '*F*'

Level of significance $\alpha = 0.05$

n_1 = degrees of freedom for numerator

n_2 = degrees of freedom for denominator

n_1 \ n_2	1	2	3	4	5	6	7	8	9	10	12	15	20	24	30	40	60	120	α
1	4052	4999.5	5403	5625	5764	5859	5928	5982	6022	6056	6106	6157	6209	6235	6261	6287	6313	6339	6366
2	98.50	99.00	99.17	99.25	99.30	99.33	99.36	99.37	99.39	99.40	99.42	99.43	99.45	99.46	99.47	99.47	99.48	99.49	99.50
3	34.12	30.82	29.46	28.71	28.24	27.91	27.67	27.49	27.35	27.23	27.05	27.87	26.69	26.60	26.50	26.41	26.32	26.22	26.13
4	21.20	18.00	16.69	15.98	15.52	15.21	14.98	14.80	14.66	14.55	14.37	14.20	14.02	13.93	13.84	13.75	13.65	13.56	13.46
5	16.26	13.27	12.06	11.39	10.97	10.67	10.46	10.29	10.16	10.05	9.89	9.72	9.55	9.47	9.38	9.29	9.20	9.11	9.02
6	13.75	10.92	9.78	9.15	8.75	8.47	8.26	8.10	7.98	7.87	7.72	7.56	7.40	7.31	7.23	7.14	7.06	6.97	6.88
7	12.25	9.55	8.45	7.85	7.46	7.19	6.99	6.84	6.72	6.62	6.47	6.31	6.16	6.07	5.99	5.91	5.82	5.74	5.65
8	11.26	8.65	7.59	7.01	6.63	6.37	6.18	6.03	5.91	5.81	5.67	5.52	5.36	2.28	5.20	5.12	5.03	4.95	4.86
9	10.56	8.02	6.99	6.42	6.06	5.80	5.61	5.47	5.35	5.26	5.11	4.96	4.81	4.73	4.65	4.57	4.48	4.40	4.31
10	10.04	7.56	6.55	5.99	5.64	5.39	5.20	5.06	4.94	4.85	4.71	4.56	4.41	4.33	4.25	4.17	4.08	4.00	3.91
11	9.65	7.21	6.22	5.67	5.32	5.07	4.89	4.74	4.63	4.54	4.40	4.25	4.10	4.02	3.94	3.86	3.78	3.96	3.60
12	9.33	6.93	5.95	5.41	5.06	4.82	4.64	4.50	4.39	4.30	4.16	4.01	3.86	3.78	3.70	3.62	3.54	3.45	3.36
13	9.07	9.70	5.74	5.21	4.86	4.62	4.44	4.30	4.19	4.10	3.96	3.82	3.66	3.59	3.51	3.43	3.34	3.25	3.17
14	8.86	6.51	5.56	5.04	4.69	4.46	4.28	4.14	4.03	3.94	3.80	3.66	3.51	3.43	3.35	3.27	3.18	3.09	3.00
15	8.68	6.36	5.42	4.89	4.56	4.32	4.14	4.00	4.89	3.80	3.67	3.52	3.37	3.29	3.21	3.13	2.05	2.96	2.87
16	8.53	6.23	5.29	4.77	4.44	4.20	4.03	3.89	3.78	3.69	3.55	3.41	3.26	3.18	3.10	3.02	2.93	2.84	2.75
17	8.40	6.11	5.18	7.67	4.34	4.10	3.93	3.79	3.68	3.59	3.46	3.31	3.16	2.08	3.00	2.92	2.83	2.75	2.65
18	8.29	6.01	5.09	4.58	4.25	4.01	3.84	3.71	3.60	3.51	3.37	3.23	3.08	3.00	2.92	2.84	2.75	2.66	2.57
19	8.18	5.93	5.01	4.50	4.17	3.94	3.77	3.63	3.52	3.43	3.30	3.15	3.00	2.92	2.84	2.76	2.67	2.58	2.49
20	8.10	5.85	4.94	4.43	4.10	3.87	3.70	3.65	3.46	3.37	3.23	3.09	2.94	2.86	2.78	2.69	2.61	2.52	2.42
21	8.02	5.78	4.87	4.37	4.04	3.81	3.64	3.51	3.40	3.31	3.17	3.03	2.88	2.80	2.72	2.64	2.55	2.46	2.36
22	7.95	5.72	4.82	4.31	3.99	3.76	3.59	3.45	3.35	3.26	3.12	2.98	2.83	2.75	2.67	2.58	2.50	2.40	2.31
23	7.88	5.66	4.76	4.26	3.94	3.71	3.54	3.41	3.30	3.21	3.07	2.93	2.78	2.70	2.62	2.54	2.45	2.35	2.26
24	7.82	5.61	4.72	4.22	3.90	3.67	3.50	3.36	3.26	3.17	3.03	2.89	2.74	2.66	2.58	2.49	1.40	2.31	2.21
25	7.77	5.57	4.68	4.18	3.85	3.63	3.46	3.32	3.22	3.13	3.99	2.85	2.70	2.62	2.54	2.45	2.36	2.27	2.17
26	7.72	5.53	4.64	1.14	3.82	3.59	3.42	3.29	3.18	3.09	3.96	2.81	2.66	2.58	2.50	2.42	2.33	2.23	2.13
27	7.68	5.49	4.60	4.11	3.78	3.56	3.39	3.26	3.15	3.06	2.93	2.78	2.63	2.55	2.47	2.38	2.29	2.20	2.10
28	7.64	5.45	4.57	4.07	3.75	3.53	3.36	3.23	3.12	3.03	2.90	2.75	2.60	2.52	2.44	2.35	2.26	2.17	2.06
29	7.60	5.42	4.54	4.04	3.73	3.50	3.33	3.20	3.09	3.00	2.87	2.73	2.57	2.49	2.41	2.33	2.23	2.14	2.03
30	7.56	5.39	4.51	4.02	3.70	3.47	3.30	3.17	3.07	2.98	2.84	2.70	2.55	2.47	2.39	2.30	2.21	2.11	2.01
40	7.31	5.18	4.31	3.83	3.51	3.29	3.12	2.99	2.89	2.80	2.66	2.52	2.37	2.29	2.20	2.11	2.02	1.92	1.80
60	7.08	4.98	4.13	3.65	3.34	3.12	2.95	2.82	2.72	2.63	2.50	2.35	2.20	2.12	2.03	1.94	1.84	1.73	1.60
120	6.85	4.79	3.95	3.48	3.17	2.96	2.79	2.66	2.56	2.47	2.34	2.19	2.03	1.95	1.86	1.76	1.66	1.53	1.38
α	6.63	7.61	3.78	3.32	3.02	2.80	2.64	2.51	2.41	2.32	2.18	2.04	1.88	1.79	1.70	1.59	1.47	1.32	1.00

Table T6: Binomial Coefficients

n	$\binom{n}{0}$	$\binom{n}{1}$	$\binom{n}{2}$	$\binom{n}{3}$	$\binom{n}{4}$	$\binom{n}{5}$	$\binom{n}{6}$	$\binom{n}{7}$	$\binom{n}{8}$	$\binom{n}{9}$	$\binom{n}{10}$
0	1										
1	1	1									
2	1	2	1								
3	1	3	3	1							
4	1	4	6	4	1						
5	1	5	10	10	5	1					
6	1	6	15	20	15	6	1				
7	1	7	21	35	35	21	7	1			
8	1	8	28	56	70	56	28	8	1		
9	1	9	36	84	126	126	84	36	9	1	
10	1	10	45	120	210	252	210	120	45	10	1
11	1	11	55	165	330	462	462	330	165	55	11
12	1	12	66	220	495	792	924	792	495	220	66
13	1	13	78	286	715	1287	1716	1716	1287	715	286
14	1	14	91	364	1001	2002	3003	3432	3003	2002	1001
15	1	15	105	455	1365	3003	5005	6435	6435	3005	3003
16	1	16	120	560	1820	4368	8008	11440	12870	1440	8008
17	1	17	136	680	2380	6188	12376	19448	24310	24310	19448
18	1	18	153	816	3060	8568	18564	31824	43758	48620	43758
19	1	19	171	969	3876	11628	27132	50388	75582	92378	92378
20	1	20	190	1140	4845	15504	38760	77520	125970	167960	184756

Table T7: Values of e^{-m}
(For Computing Poisson Probabilities) (0 < m 1)

m	0	1	2	3	4	5	6	7	8	9
0.0	1.0000	.9900	.9802	.9704	.9608	.9512	.9418	.6324	.9231	.9139
0.1	0.9048	.8958	.8860	.8781	.8694	.8607	.8521	.8437	.8353	.8270
0.2	0.8187	.8106	.8025	.7945	.7866	.7788	.7711	.7634	.7558	.7483
0.3	0.7408	.7334	.7261	.7189	.7118	.7047	.6977	6907	6839	.6771
0.4	0.6703	.6636	.6570	.6505	.6440	.6376	.6313	.6250	.6188	.6126
0.5	0.6065	.6005	.5945	.5886	.5827	.5770	.5712	.5655	.5599	.5543
0.6	0.5488	.5434	.5379	.5326	.5278	.5220	.5160	.5117	.5066	5016
0.7	0.4966	.4916	.4868	.4810	.4771	.4724	.4670	.4630	.4584	.4538
0.8	0.4493	.4449	.4404	.4360	.4317	.4274	.4232	.4190	.4148	.4107
0.9	0.4066	.4025	.3985	.3946	.3906	.3867	.3829	.3791	.3753	.3716

(m = 1, 2, 3,..., 10)

m	1	2	3	4	5	6	7	8	9	10
e^{-m}	.36788	.13534	.04979	.01832	.006737	.002478	.00092	.000335	.000123	.000045

Table T8: Control Chart Factors

Number of observations in Sample	Chart for Averages					Chart for Ranges				
	Factor for Control Limits			Factor for Central Line		Factor for Control Limits				
n	A	A_1	A_2	d_2	$1/d_2$	d_3	D_1	D_1	D_3	D_4
2	2.121	3.760	1.880	1.128	0.8865	0.853	0	3.686	0	3.267
3	1.732	2.394	1.023	1.693	0.5907	0.888	0	4.358	0	2.575
4	1.500	1.880	0.729	2.059	0.4857	0.880	0	1.698	0	2.282
5	1.342	1.596	0.577	2.326	0.4299	0.864	0	4.918	0	2.115
6	1.225	1.410	0.483	0.534	0.3946	0.848	0	5.078	0	2.004
7	1.134	1.277	0.419	0.3698	0.833	0.205	5.203	0.076	1.924	
8	1.061	1.175	0.373	2.847	0.3512	0.820	0.387	5.307	0.136	1.864
9	1.000	1.094	0.337	2.970	0.3367	0.808	0.546	5.394	0.184	1.816
10	0.949	1.028	0.308	3.078	0.3249	0.797	0.687	5.469	0.223	1.777
11	0.905	0.973	0.285	3.173	0.3152	0.787	0.812	5.534	0.256	1.744
12	0.866	0.925	0.266	3.258	0.3069	0.778	0.924	5.592	0.284	1.716
13	0.832	0.884	0.249	3.336	0.2998	0.770	1.026	5.846	0.308	1.692
14	0.802	0.849	0.235	3.407	0.2935	0.762	1.121	5.693	0.329	1.671
15	0.775	0.816	0.223	3.472	0.2880	0.755	1.207	5.737	0.348	1.652
16	0.750	0.788	0.212	3.523	0.2831	0.749	1.285	5.779	0.364	1.636
17	0.728	0.762	0.203	3.588	0.2787	0.743	1.359	5.817	0.379	1.621
18	0.707	0.738	0.194	3.640	0.2747	0.738	1.426	5.854	0.392	1.608
19	0.688	0.717	0.187	3.689	0.2711	0.733	1.490	5.888	0.404	1.596
20	0.671	0.697	0.180	3.735	0.2677	0.729	1.548	5.992	0.414	1.586
21	0.655	0.679	0.173	3.778	0.2647	0.724	1.605	5.950	0.425	1.575
22	0.640	0.662	0.167	3.819	0.2618	0.720	1.659	5.979	0.434	1.566
23	0.26	0.647	0.162	3.858	0.2592	0.716	1.710	6.006	0.443	1.557
24	0.612	0.632	0.157	3.895	0.2567	0.712	1.759	0.031	0.452	1.548
25	0.600	0.619	0.153	3.931	0.2544	0.709	1.304	6.058	0.459	1.541

Index

D

E

F

G

H

I

J

K

V

W

X

Y